P9-CTB-549

Continued on back

HANDBOOK OF RESEARCH METHODS
IN CLINICAL PSYCHOLOGY

HANDBOOK OF
RESEARCH METHODS
IN CLINICAL PSYCHOLOGY

Edited by

PHILIP C. KENDALL
JAMES N. BUTCHER

University of Minnesota

1807 1982

175 YEARS OF PUBLISHING

A WILEY-INTERSCIENCE PUBLICATION

JOHN WILEY & SONS

New York   Chichester   Brisbane   Toronto   Singapore

This publication is designed to provide accurate and
authoritative information in regard to the subject
matter covered. It is sold with the understanding that
the publisher is not engaged in rendering legal, accounting,
or other professional service. If legal advice or other
expert assistance is required, the services of a competent
professional person should be sought. *From a Declaration
of Principles jointly adopted by a Committee of the
American Bar Association and a Committee of Publishers.*

Library of Congress Cataloging in Publication Data:

Main entry under title:

Handbook of research methods in clinical psychology.

  (Wiley series on personality processes, ISSN
0195-4008)
  ''A Wiley-Interscience publication.''
  Includes index.
  1. Clinical psychology—Research.   2. Clinical
psychology—Methodology.   3. Psychological research.
4. Psychiatric research.   I. Kendall, Philip C.
II. Butcher, James Neal, 1933-   . III. Series.

RC437.5.H36   616.89′0072   81-16290
ISBN 0-471-07980-4   AACR2

Printed in the United States of America

10   9   8   7   6   5   4   3   2   1

*We dedicate this volume as a tribute to the founder of
modern clinical psychology, David Shakow (1901–1981).
All clinical psychologists—present and future—
whether researchers, teachers, practitioners, or administrators,
will be forever indebted to him for the
breadth of his contributions to our discipline.*

Contributors

THOMAS M. ACHENBACH
Department of Psychiatry
University of Vermont College of
Medicine
Burlington, Vermont

LAURENCE A. BRADLEY
Department of Psychiatry and
Behavioral Medicine
Section on Medical Psychology
Bowman Gray School of Medicine
Winston-Salem, North Carolina

JAMES N. BUTCHER
Department of Psychology
University of Minnesota
Minneapolis, Minnesota

JOHN D. CONE
Department of Psychology
West Virginia University
Morgantown, West Virginia

PHILIP A. COWAN
Department of Psychology
University of California at Berkeley
Berkeley, California

SUSAN B. FILSKOV
Department of Psychology
University of South Florida
Tampa, Florida

SHARON L. FOSTER
Department of Psychology
West Virginia University
Morgantown, West Virginia

NORMAN GARMEZY
Department of Psychology
University of Minnesota
Minneapolis, Minnesota

ROBERT R. GOLDEN
Division of Biostatistics
School of Public Health
Columbia University
New York, New York

SAMUEL B. GREEN
Department of Psychology
Auburn University
Auburn, Alabama

MALCOLM D. GYNTHER
Department of Psychology
Auburn University
Auburn, Alabama

JANICE L. HASTRUP
Department of Psychology
State University of New York
at Binghamton
Binghamton, New York

ERASMUS L. HOCH
Professor Emeritus
University of Michigan
Ann Arbor, Michigan

L. ROWELL HUESMANN
Department of Psychology
University of Illinois at
Chicago Circle
Chicago, Illinois

EDWARD S. KATKIN
Department of Psychology
State University of New York
at Buffalo
Buffalo, New York

ALAN E. KAZDIN
Department of Psychiatry
Western Psychiatric Institute
and Clinic
University of Pittsburgh School
of Medicine
Pittsburgh, Pennsylvania

PHILIP C. KENDALL
Department of Psychology
University of Minnesota
Minneapolis, Minnesota

DONALD J. KIESLER
Department of Psychology
Virginia Commonwealth University
Richmond, Virginia

SHELDON J. KORCHIN
Department of Psychology
University of California at Berkeley
Berkeley, California

JEAN ANN LINNEY
Department of Psychology
University of Virginia
Charlottesville, Virginia

EILEEN LOCKLEAR
Department of Psychology
University of South Florida
Tampa, Florida

MICHAEL R. LOWE
Department of Psychology
Rutgers University
Camden, New Jersey

PAUL E. MEEHL
Department of Psychology
University of Minnesota
Minneapolis, Minnesota

MICHAEL MERBAUM
Department of Psychology
Washington University
St. Louis, Missouri

JIM MINTZ
Psychology Service
Brentwood Veterans Administration
Hospital
Los Angeles, California

JULIAN D. NORTON-FORD
Center for Health Enhancement
University of California
at Los Angeles
Los Angeles, California

CHARLES K. PROKOP
Department of Psychiatry
Texas Tech University Health
Sciences Center
School of Medicine
Lubbock, Texas

N. DICKON REPPUCCI
Department of Psychology
University of Virginia
Charlottesville, Virginia

DAVID SHAKOW
Department of Health, Education,
and Welfare
National Institute of Health
Bethesda, Maryland

STEPHEN J. SUOMI
Department of Psychology
University of Wisconsin
Madison, Wisconsin

JERRY S. WIGGINS
Department of Psychology
University of British Columbia
Vancouver, British Columbia

Series Preface

This series of books is addressed to behavioral scientists interested in the nature of human personality. Its scope should prove pertinent to personality theorists and researchers as well as to clinicians concerned with applying an understanding of personality processes to the amelioration of emotional difficulties in living. To this end, the series provides a scholarly integration of theoretical formulations, empirical data, and practical recommendations.

Six major aspects of studying and learning about human personality can be designated: personality theory, personality structure and dynamics, personality development, personality assessment, personality change, and personality adjustment. In exploring these aspects of personality, the books in the series discuss a number of distinct but related subject areas: their nature and implications of various theories of personality; personality characteristics that account for consistencies and variations in human behavior; the emergence of personality processes in children and adolescents; the use of interviewing and testing procedures to evaluate individual differences in personality; efforts to modify personality styles through psychotherapy, counseling, behavior therapy, and other methods of influence; and patterns of abnormal personality functioning that impair individual competence.

Irving B. Weiner

University of Denver
Denver, Colorado

Preface

Several factors influenced our decision to undertake the present volume. First, we are concerned that graduate education in clinical psychology has undergone an unfortunate shift, a turn away from the research training so critical to the research base of the profession and in a direction that could make its practitioners little different from other mental health professions such as psychiatry and social work. We view this shift as a reversion that weakens the very foundations of clinical psychology. We are convinced that, while clinical psychologists make substantial contributions in the professional application of psychological principles, the most outstanding contributions have been in, or rooted in, basic clinical research. One need not look far for examples: learning-based treatment procedures and standardized assessment devices are clear illustrations. It was to advance the science of clinical psychology, specifically the research skills of professionals and advanced preprofessionals, that this text was designed.

Second, we hope to stimulate the education of clinical psychologists with multiple perspectives on the research enterprise. Accordingly, we have intentionally not drawn theoretical boundaries. Our efforts have been directed toward the compilation of methodological chapters that dealt with each current area of research activity regardless of existing theoretical, philosophical, or methodological biases. We believe that the potential rewards of a broad-based methodological perspective clearly make such an undertaking worthwhile.

Third, we have each recognized a need, in our own graduate teaching, for a single text that would be appropriate for a course in research methodology. How often have blooming scientists been thwarted and overdosed by research course work in which fertilizers, corn yield, or mathematical formulae were central topics? Typically methodological topics are presented in separate courses, with each instructor addressing methodology in the context of other course material. This approach can produce redundancy, neglect of important topics, and contradiction—none of which benefit the student's education or advance the training of psychologists. This volume was designed to sample the wide range of clinical research topics and overcome the lack of a significant, relevant research text in the field.

Fourth, the *Handbook of Research Methods in Clinical Psychology* was designed to fill a gap in the existing standard handbooks for clinical psychologists. In general, the available handbooks deal with either multiple or single methods of assessment, procedures for therapy from a single or multiple theoretical perspective, procedures for treatment according to specific types of psychopathology, or detailed descriptions of the symptomatology of various types of psychopathology from specific vantage points. Nowhere to date have leading researchers in the field of clinical psychology collaborated on a text that addresses the specific methodological procedures and concerns in their respective areas of expertise.

Fifth, though not less influential, the editors have found themselves having frequent lunch conversations and free-time dialogues about the methodological issues of concern to clinical psychology. Our frustrations at not having an encyclopedic arbitrator for our own friendly disputes, and a reference guide for our own research endeavors, in part prompted this volume. We wanted a volume, not necessarily specific in content, but presenting the full regalia of clinical research methods, to give credence to the scientist side of the scientist–practitioner model.

The *Handbook* is intended to be a comprehensive collection of theoretical and methodological papers that span the major research domains in the field of clinical psychology. The contributions include chapters on general issues in clinical research as well as chapters that address basic methodological questions and problems in diverse clinical areas. The first section contains four chapters that provide an educational consideration of clinical research. Statements about the focus and training of researchers are presented by David Shakow; the contributions of experimental psychology are detailed by Erasmus Hoch; the necessary concerns of researchers dealing with human subjects are discussed by Sheldon Korchin and Philip Cowan; and Michael Merbaum and Michael Lowe comment on the role of serendipity in clinical psychology research.

The second section of the book contains a description and analysis of general research strategies. Taxometrics (Meehl and Golden), circumplex models (Wiggins), experimental methods (Huesmann), animal analogues (Suomi), and cross-cultural strategies (Butcher) are each carefully analyzed in relation to clinical research methods.

The third, fourth, and fifth sections of the *Handbook* deal in depth with the procedures and problems specific to distinct areas of clinical research: assessment techniques, intervention strategies, and special populations. Direct observation, self-report inventories, and psychophysiological methods are examined by Cone and Foster, Gynther and

Green, and Katkin and Hastrup, respectively. Four chapters focus on research methodologies associated with the evaluation of treatment procedures. Kendall and Norton-Ford cover therapy-outcome methodologies, Kazdin describes single-case designs, Mintz and Kiesler examine individualized measures of outcome, and Linney and Reppucci detail the methods for intervention evaluation in communities.

The special concerns of developmental psychopathologists (Achenbach), behavioral medicine researchers (Bradley and Prokop), and neuropsychologists (Filskov and Locklear) are the subjects of three separate chapters. The volume closes with an afterword by Norman Garmezy.

The *Handbook* reflects the current status of research methodologies employed in the study of human behavior and clinical services associated with the assessment and treatment of psychological dysfunctions. We consider the volume comprehensive, though we recognize that there are other areas that we might have included. Procedures of statistical analysis, including everything from analysis of variance to factor analysis and regression methods, could have been dealt with within our framework. Indeed we had planned to include coverage of certain statistical material in this text. As it turned out, the writing of a single chapter covering such a broad range of topics for a clinical audience was impossible. The chapter on statistics was not included in the present volume since it could not achieve the desired goal. According to the reactions of our readers, we will consider adding several chapters on separate portions of statistical analysis to any future editions.

The preparation of this volume was in some ways beyond our editorial expertise. We recognized our limitations with respect to serving as *the* reviewers of chapters as diverse and detailed as those included in this volume. Our policy was that each of us would serve as a separate reviewer for an individual chapter, with one of us having primary responsibility for it. In areas in which neither of us felt sufficiently competent to review decisively, we obtained the assistance of outside reviewers. Without their help we could not have dealt effectively with the technical aspects of some of the papers. In alphabetical order we express our sincere thanks to Roger Blashfield, Bernard Bloom, Robert Carson, Juris Draguns, Alfred Heilbrun, David Lykken, Joseph Matarazzo, James Moses, Alan Sroufe, Auke Tellegen, David Weiss, and Carolyn Williams.

We both contributed equally in editing this volume, and the order of authorship was arrived at through scientific means—a coin flip.

Portions of the present material were completed while Philip Kendall was a Fellow at the Center for Advanced Study in the Be-

havioral Sciences, Stanford, California. He is most grateful to the Center, and especially to its director, Gardner Lindzey, for making this most enjoyable and educational interlude possible. He is also grateful for financial support provided by the National Institute of Mental Health (#5-T32-MH14581-05), the John D. and Catherine T. MacArthur Foundation, and the Quarter Leave System of the University of Minnesota.

Philip C. Kendall
James N. Butcher

Minneapolis, Minnesota
February 1982

Contents

PART FOUR: AREAS OF CLINICAL RESEARCH: INTERVENTION
STRATEGIES

PART FIVE: AREAS OF CLINICAL RESEARCH: SPECIAL POPULATIONS

PART SIX: AFTERWORD

PART ONE

Perspectives on
Clinical Research

CHAPTER 1

Perspectives on Research in Clinical Psychology

DAVID SHAKOW

INTRODUCTION

Carrying out research, even with normal human beings, is, as Gardner Murphy has somewhere said, "fiendishly complex." Research with disturbed human beings is even more so, particularly with those in whom the impediments to communication are so formidable. The marked range of psychopathologies, the marked variance within the range and within the individual, the variety of shapes that psychological disorders take, and both the expressive and compensatory behavior that characterizes them, all reflect this special complexity. Recent years have seen even further complications because of the use of many therapeutic and other devices, such as drugs, that alter both the physiological and psychological nature of the organism. Research with psychological disorders therefore calls for awareness not only of the factors creating variance in normal human beings but

National Institute of Mental Health; Alcohol, Drug Abuse and Mental Health Administration; U.S. Department of Health, Education, and Welfare; Bethesda, Maryland, 20205. The preparation of this paper was in part aided by a grant from the Benevolent Foundation of Scottish Rite Freemasonry, Northern Jurisdiction, U.S.A.

David Shakow died on February 26, 1981. This chapter was his final publication. Although the ideas expressed are those of the author, the editors have been responsible for overseeing the manuscript from penultimate draft to final copy.

also of the many additional sources of variance that the disorder introduces.

The generalization that I am making about research with the disturbed—that it differs quantitatively from ordinary behavioral research—is obvious. I have at times even entertained the far-fetched notion that we may be dealing here with a difference that is more of the order of *quality* in the research relationship—a difference more like differences among species! Somebody has used the analogy of "Silly Putty" to illustrate the qualitative-quantitative paradox. Silly Putty can, when molded slowly, be worked into more or less the same kinds of shapes as ordinary putty. However, if Silly Putty is hit suddenly with a hammer, it shatters into myriad fragments. The minor quantitative difference from ordinary putty has now turned into a qualitative one. Whether this distinction holds for most of the ailments we are here concerned with will of course depend on the interpretations both of the problems encountered in investigative approaches and the results obtained from many studies. I do not really want to press this point, since it is still conjectural as far as I am concerned. I am merely presenting the idea for its heuristic value, so that caution is maintained in dealing with pathologies. It should be kept in mind as we review the problems of doing research with such subjects. For the present I am reasonably well satisfied that these disturbances represent extremes of normal distributions,

3

even though future research may lead to other conclusions.

The complexity I suggested seems to call for investigators who know the subtleties of the person they are working with; who, recognizing the many variables involved, are modest about their knowledge; who are as accurate as possible about making and reporting their observations; who check out these observations repeatedly for dependability; who have some appreciation of the meaning as well as the factual accuracy of the observations; but who are still willing to stick their necks out. A tall order for all of us!

To put the problem succinctly, I might say that a consideration of the explicit and implicit factors involved in doing research in psychopathology necessitates dealing successively with the full referents of each of the links of this deceptively simple chain of queries: *Why should who do what (how, when, where) to whom?* In the following pages, I shall suggest a few answers to each query in the chain.

PREPARATION FOR RESEARCH

With regard to training under the scientist-professional model[1] which this volume upholds (see also Kendall & Norton-Ford, 1982), let me start with the proposition that, as in other helping professions, two features are essential for the practice of clinical psychology. These are the acquisition of *knowledge* and the acquisition of *attitude* appropriate to the dispensing of that knowledge. Both require training, but of different kinds. From the first kind of training comes the limited security that grows with knowledge. From the second comes the humility that arises from self-knowledge.

[1]I prefer the designation "scientist-professional" to "research-practitioner," both for its greater specificity and for its emphasis on goals.

Attitude

(To take the second first.) Some people seem to be "god analyzed" and in need of little additional training in attitude, but fortunately we don't have to plan on such rare persons. The rest of us need to put ourselves through some form of self-evaluation under guidance, and to clarify our motivations, because goodwill alone, as we know, is not enough. If I had my way, I would emblazon at the entrance to all schools for clinical psychologists the quotation from Browning's "Light Woman":

> 'Tis an awkward thing to play with souls
> And matter enough to save one's own.

But knowing the human propensity for habituation, I would have it pop up in unexpected places and at unexpected moments so as to keep it fresh and attempt to foil this tendency.

What we want finally are persons with a distinct ethical code of their own who make no judgments about the ethical codes of their clients or patients. We want persons who do not use their prestige to practice beyond their competence, as Crothers (1932, p. 24) has put it. We want persons who recognize the responsibility that they take on in working with a human being, and who are aware of the danger of solving their own problems through the other person.

Recognition of how little is known in comparison to our knowledge would strengthen this trend toward humility. Even the most expert of us, with all the good will in the world, knows little more than the ignorant, and we must depend on this knowledge for our expertness. Humility is the sine qua non of practice at whatever level—the bachelor's, the master's, or the doctoral. Self-knowledge obtained under guidance is not a panacea, for the rationalizations of humans are insidious. But it is by far the best device we have for attaining this state of self-knowledge that is fundamental to the understanding of others.

The strength of the scientist-professional model lies in its basic appropriateness for a field such as psychology, which is at an interface between science and the humanities. The model's strength also lies in its remarkable flexibility, because the value systems on which it is based can tolerate great diversity within their legitimate limits. In some respects too it offers an ideal opportunity for combining the values of the scientist and the values of the humanist in actual practice. Such a combination is important for most branches of psychology. However, some specialties in psychology can achieve it by developing persons who only *in parallel* can be both good psychologists and good citizens. From this general level of preparation one can go on to practice as professional, as researcher, or any mixture of the two. And from the doctoral program one can go on to postdoctoral specialization.

Knowledge

As for *knowledge,* we can divide the fields into the substantive and the methodological. In the substantive area, I would include three kinds of training: in personality principles, in real-life situations, and in real clinical situations. In the methodological area I would include two kinds of training: in observation and in specific research methodology.

The programs on the nature and development of personality, given whenever possible in the context of actual life situations and concrete case material, would aim at producing an apperceptive mass in the student incorporating the five principles basic to the understanding of personality: the genetic, the cryptic, the dynamic, the psychobiological, and the psychosocial. The *genetic* principle acknowledges the role of continuity in the development of the individual's personality characteristics—the significance of earlier influences on present manifestations of one's personality. The *cryptic* principle recognizes that unconscious and preconscious factors act as crucial determiners of behavior, that behavior has, besides the obvious conscious motivations, further motivations that are not conscious. The *dynamic* principle states that behavior is drive-determined, that behind behavior lie certain innate or acquired impelling forces. The *psychobiological* principle holds that the personality is integral and indivisible, that there is a pervasive interrelationship between psyche and soma. This involves the acceptance of an organismic concept of total, rather than segmental, personality. The *psychosocial* principle recognizes the integration of the person and his or her social environment as a unit. It states that behavior is expressed as individual response within a social context, and that both the individual and his or her environment are important in the determination of personality and conduct.

The second substantive area would involve the student in as many normal settings, both adequate and deprived, as possible—home, community, school, playground, and so on— so that experience may be acquired with a broad range of normal individual and social behavior. The third substantive area would involve the student in experience with varieties of clinical situations, from the minor aberrations of personality through the most complex of the psychoses. I cannot emphasize strongly enough the importance of both of these kinds of field work for developing the psychologist we seek. Extensive "clinical" experience—experience with human beings in a diversity of human settings—is the very foundation of a sound program of education.

On the methodological side, two major areas of training are indicated. The first would provide varied experience with the different types of observation; the second, experience with more specific research methodology, in part based on training in observation, which is in turn based on training in diagnosis, psychological testing, therapy skills, and the like, all of which are the peculiar background of the psychologist. I will first consider the nature of the different kinds of observation, of which I distinguish four major types: objective, participant, subjective, and self.

Objective observation involves the careful description of the impact on the observed person of those impinging internal and external forces—physical, psychological, and social—that lead to certain behavior. Such observations are those of the naturalist; they are made from a point outside the subject and the situation. Here it is particularly important for the observer to become sensitive to the more transient, nonverbal aspects of behavior, such as body movement and facial expression. Objective observation plays a significant role as well in the process of building up the "computer" capability of the student. In the process of learning the clinical methods and tests, budding clinical students are sensitized to the complexities of the clinical situation and with experience learns to sharpen their inquisitions about it. (We must nevertheless keep in mind that objective observation is a misnomer, once one recognizes the Heisenberg Principle; cf. Wheeler, 1974. It is an ideal.)

The second kind of observation, *participant observation,* implies a distinctly more intimate relationship between the observer and the observed, for in this situation both are interacting within a group. To the observer falls the difficult task not only of making objective observations but also of determining how his or her role as a participant in the group modifies the situation. The observer needs also to evaluate, even more than in naturalistic observation, the effect of the very act of observing on the observed person and the observation itself.

The third kind of observation, *subjective observation,* is a particularly important one for psychologists. It involves the observer's attempt to empathize with disturbed persons, to try to understand how they feel about themselves, their family, and their illness. Whether these feelings be realistic or unrealistic, understanding them is essential in understanding the patient's difficulties.

The fourth kind of observation is *self-observation,* which comes about through a process of self-examination under guidance. It is the student's effort to understand personal feelings and attitudes. Here students ask why they behave the way they do—why, for instance, they are so anxious with one patient and so calm with another. This important quality in the person who undertakes clinical work has aleady been singled out for special consideration.

Clearly, in this discussion of observation methods, I am emphasizing techniques for learning by experiencing, as opposed to learning by listening. Real-life learning techniques, however, carry with them certain hazards. On the one hand, they may disturb the validity of the observations, and on the other, they may develop self-consciousness or exaggerated introspectiveness. Such hazards call for caution on the part of the preceptors and their students, and for careful consideration of ways of reducing these iatrogenic effects.

The second area of methodological training, though based fundamentally on the training in observation, is more directly related to research methodology in psychology. Obviously the range here is great. The general principles common to all researchers, such as accuracy and reliability of report, would presumably have been acquired largely through the training in observation. The specifics of the particular disciplinary techniques set up to yield dependable data, the experimental and statistical controls necessary to support them, and other substantive and methodological details remain the concrete problem of the educators in each of the disciplines, from the biological through the social.

Some points made by Cronbach (1957, 1975) about the two different kinds of methods in psychology, the correlational and manipulative, are relevant. In the first, "nature the old nurse" takes the investigator on its knee and unfolds the storybook, which Longfellow had conjectured Agassiz as experiencing. In this case *nature* determines the variances, and the correlator finds his or her data in the observations of already *existing* variations between individuals, between groups, and between species. In the manipulative or experimental, on the other hand, the *experimenter* is the manipulator. It is he or she who *changes* conditions in order to observe their consequences and variances. Clinical psychology has been substantially a correlational psychology from its beginnings. But in recent years there has been a distinct trend toward the experimental, and I now see a happy marriage of the two, if each recognizes its proper role. It is true that the clinician will tend to emphasize those aspects of "hierarchic transformations" that will permit adequate handling of field problems taken into the laboratory. But the experimental trend will grow, without interfering with the continuation of the correlational approach.

The *methods of investigation* used by the psychologist are in essence not different from those generally used in biology. The differences that do exist lie in the problems created by, and the advantages accruing from, work with subjects of greater complexity and having much more highly developed symbolic functions. We may roughly classify these methods into four groups, even though in actuality they shade off one into the other and are often not clearly distinguishable. These are: naturalistic observation, seminaturalistic observation, free laboratory, and controlled laboratory.

The first method, the *naturalistic,* provides for the study of the organism in a relatively free, natural habitat in which the widest range of stimuli and responses growing out of the particular setting are observed. These observations are made as completely and as accurately as possible, usually by an outside observer. Thus in a hospital setting it may be desirable to study group behavior as it naturally structures itself on the ward or to study the complex therapeutic situation with the free give and take of the patient-therapist dyad through the use of devices such as videotape.

The second method, the *seminaturalistic,* may be provided for either by a natural habitat or by a laboratory situation. In the former, the degree of freedom is somewhat limited as compared with the first group; in the latter, the degree of freedom as compared with the two following groups of laboratory approaches is greater. In either case the stimuli are varied, and the degrees of freedom of response permitted are considerable. Some controls and limitations on the situation are, however, set up in order to direct behavior along certain lines. In the field of test procedures, the analogous device is the projective technique. In the experimental area an investigation directed at studying the susceptibility of schizophrenic subjects to environmental stimulation might be cited as an example. In this situation various objects having different degrees of interest-demand character are left on a table in a room into which a patient is introduced. He or she is told that the examiner will return shortly after the latter has completed another piece of work. The patient is then observed through a one-way mirror for a stated period of time, and a detailed record made of the range and depth of his or her preoccupation with objects and with himself or herself.

With the third type of approach, the *free laboratory,* although some degree of variation in the stimuli and degree of freedom of response is still maintained, these are considerably reduced as compared with the former two methods. Here specific instructions are given the subject to respond in certain definite ways to the stimuli, and recordings may be made of various physiological functions accompanying the overt behavioral response. An example of this kind of situation is to be seen in a variation of the Luria (1932) experiment, in which the subject is required to respond orally to the stimulus words of a free association test. While so responding, the subject is required to press on a tambour with his or her preferred hand, with simultaneous recording of finger tremor from the other hand as well as respiration and/or galvanic skin response.

The fourth type, the *controlled laboratory* approach, carries the degree of control of the situation still further. Here both the stimulus and the response are quite fixed and limited. Studies of the latent time of patellar tendon reflex is an example of perhaps the lowest behavioral level, and reaction time or simple psychomotor learning, at a somewhat higher level, fall into this category. (The correlational-multivariate approach would fit anywhere among the four types.)

It is obvious that the methods of investigation described lend themselves to the collection of relevant data for methodological and descriptive as well as for theoretical purposes. It is likely that for some time into the future considerable effort will have to be expended by the psychologist in sharpening old tools and devising new ones. The problems in the field are so complex that considerable ingenuity will have to be devoted to this task. Psychologists do not of course limit themselves to the study of the disordered person. Depending upon the nature and needs of the problem, they use normal or even animal subjects, setting up, for greater control, experimental situations that nature provides reluctantly, or settings too complex for easy analysis.

One cannot of course end up merely with refined or new techniques; theory is essential and is consciously or unconsciously utilized while in the process of developing methodology. Otherwise it is nonproductive. The purpose of method is to obtain data that can be used for the establishment of theory.

Aside from the accurate descriptions of behavior that are the essential basis for any theoretical development, the psychologist can make a special contribution to some special problems of description. I refer here to objective studies in the evaluation of the effects of therapies or other observable modifications of behavior. Preferably, however, the activity of the psychologist should be

mainly directed to the exploration of the fundamental aspects of personality with a view toward developing comprehensive theories of personality. Hypotheses along these lines may be derived directly from experiment or from clinical experience and study, ideally from thoughtful integration of both. The great growth of hypothesis and theory, particularly that derived from psychoanalytic work based upon years of broad clinical experience and insight, now calls for a period of systematic experimental study in order to consolidate it into the body of psychological knowledge.

The important problems calling for study in the area centering around psychopathology and personality are numerous. They involve both structural and functional factors. Because of the manifold effects of need disturbance upon the ego structure, reflections of these disturbances are found in almost all aspects of the psyche. For this reason, apart from the immediate problems of motivation, the areas of receptive and perceptive processes, the mechanisms of response (psychophysiological and physiopsychological), learning and memory, thinking and imagination, intelligence, and social and group behavior call urgently for study, in both their cross-sectional and their longitudinal aspects.

In some of these areas experimental work may be carried out independently by the psychologists. But in most areas collaborative work with psychiatrists, neurologists, physiologists, internists, and other specialists is a necessity in order to obtain the most productive use of the material and to make the most meaningful advances (Shakow, 1949).

DEFINITION OF CLINICAL PSYCHOLOGY

The definition that is implied in my discussion of clinical psychology is that it is a branch of psychology, a body of knowledge growing out of both correlational and experimental techniques, which are based on genetic, cryptic, dynamic, psychobiological, and psychosocial principles. The skills of assessment and therapy that derive from this knowledge can be used to help persons with behavior disabilities or mental disorders to achieve better adjustment and self-expression. To practice these skills it is most often necessary to go through some course of personal self-evaluation under guidance. The acquired basis of clinical psychology is obtained through all of these means.

THE STATE OF THE FIELD
IN RESEARCH

As I review the studies of the disordered of the last several decades in the context of the research principles I have elaborated here, I believe that definite progress can be observed. My impression is that there has been increasing recognition of many of the factors I have mentioned, with a concomitant refinement in experimentation that has to a considerable extent taken them into account. We are far from Canopus, however, if that is our destination. Getting there is unavoidably slow, and we make progress haltingly. There are so many factors to deal with at once. And each investigator, and in some respects each discipline, tends to emphasize different ones. The complexity leads individual investigators and disciplines to make those compromises that we like to think of as the "few unavoidable and essentially important" ones even when they are not.

By such compromises I mean the substitution of minor and refined techniques of statistics and experimentation for basic principles of psychology and psychopathology, especially when the data are not at the time ready for these. There are steps in the development of a field in which rough approximations of differences are the major considerations. When these have been established, more refined techniques are gradually called for. It is the substitution of these niceties

when they are patently not relevant that has been one of the banes of psychological research—the retreat into refinement when brute coarseness is called for.

I do not believe, however, that equal progress has been made in acquiring sophisticated knowledge of patients—of knowing well with whom we are dealing. We may even have regressed in this respect. This neglect is reflected in the frequency of "single-shot" studies. Long-continued, deep involvement with patients is a luxury that few seem able to afford these days. I consider this most unfortunate, for I find it difficult to see how cross-sectional work with the disordered can in any way be as fundamentally productive as long-time studies.

I have always been somewhat resentful of some investigators—particularly those in biochemistry and physiology—who do research on schizophrenics using blood, urine, or other samples, feeling no need whatever to familiarize themselves with the sources of these samples. It is possible that this knowledge is not essential for what they are doing, but I wonder. The system seems to be highly unfair to the poor psychiatrists and psychologists who have to "waste" so much time in becoming acquainted with their patients.

RESEARCH GOALS

Earlier in this chapter I considered the problems of doing research in the field in the context of a chain of queries: *Why* should *who* do *what (how, when, where)* to whom? Here I might summarize the longer discussion in my paper "On doing research in schizophrenia," (1969) and apply it to the broader field of the disordered, which it fits as well.

Under *why,* I consider the motivations for doing research in this area: understanding disorders, the better to cure the individual patient; prevention of disorders; better understanding of the pathological process, particularly for its possible contribution to the understanding of normal process.

Under *who* I consider the range of disciplines relevant for research in the disorders, the types of interdisciplinary research and the concomitant problems each faces, and some of the special qualities needed by the individual investigator. My discussion of *what* is brief, since I consider this a problem fundamentally determined by the background and perspicacity of the investigator.

The *how* question requires the lengthiest discussion, since it encompasses so many of the difficulties of psychopathology research. These conditions include: *method of approach* (the naturalistic, seminaturalistic, free laboratory, and controlled laboratory); general *time scale* (cross-sectional or longitudinal); *modes* of approach within specific methods (choice of emphasis on the descriptive or theoretical, multisimple or single recondite, direct or inferential, emphasis on technique or subject, method or problem, qualitative or quantitative, molecular or molar, isolated or systematic, phenotypic or genotypic, nomothetic or idiographic, and contrived or spontaneous); *background status* of the subject—his or her disorder, and the less permanent modifiers, from drugs to psychosocial influences; *conditions of stimulation* seen against a background of the general conditions of stimulation (from impersonal stimulation to personal affective stimulation under stress) with varying preparatory "rest" states (from sensory deprivation through nonresting conditions); *contexts of presentation of stimuli* (rest intervals, knowledge about the experiment, warnings of approaching stimulation, concurrent stimulation, frequency of stimulation, and the setting in which it occurs); intrinsic *nature of the stimuli:* their quality (focal or peripheral, brief or expanded, simple or complex, discrete or continuous, novel or old, repetitive or varied, ambiguous or defined), their intensity, and their frequency; and the *instructions of the experimenter*. Besides the stimulus situation, I considered the problems inherent in the subject's response part of the paradigm, both the portion involving his or her reaction to the experimenter's instruc-

tions and that deriving from his or her cooperation.

In relation to the *when* of the query chain I point to the problems created by internal rhythms, and to the need for keeping in mind such extrinsic factors as temporary fatigue and indisposition. In relation to *where*, I consider the wide range of general environments in which the disordered person could be studied, not only the hospital ward but the many extra-hospital situations, such as the home, school, and job. Such a widening of the range calls for developing techniques to provide rigor of investigative conditions in these less-controlled environments.

The question of *whom*, the last link in the chain, necessitates a consideration of the problems of classification as they relate to the psychopathologies—the distinction between the *whom* and *not-whom*, and the various kinds of "whoms" involved, such as the chronic-acute and the premorbid good-premorbid bad. It also calls for a discussion of the problem of relevant control groups. I present several reasonable criticisms of classification schemes, yet conclude that classification in scientific activity is inevitable. However, I advocate active efforts to deal with these criticisms and suggest some steps that might be taken. I then examine the three phases of the diagnostic problem: accurate initial description of patient behavior and feelings, determination of syndromes, and assignment of patients to categories. I make some suggestions for dealing with each of these phases as objectively as possible, including the use of rating scales, clear-cut criteria for syndromes, and anonymity in the process of assignment. I then consider the problems raised by possible sources of contamination in the sampling, and suggest that we are not interested in obtaining *good* samples of the distribution of the psychoses but rather *pure* samples.

As to the nature of the control groups, I deal with the constitution of the particular pathological group as a whole and the details of matching with other groups, both pathological and normal. I consider particularly the problems created by the use of class membership criteria—the differences between the superficial symbols and the referents involved. I then touch on the problems raised by the use of dichotomies and subtypes.

Despite the length of the list I have presented, I am sure I have omitted some factors. But those presented should suffice. When the investigator has worked through such a roster of problems with at least some degree of definition and clarity, he or she comes to realize that the field of the disordered presents such an immense task that only the beginnings of a unified picture are likely to be attained in the near future. Tolerance for any critical and honest efforts, even when they are not ideally controlled, is vitally needed. Such efforts are especially valuable when carried out by investigators who have an understanding of the patients, have treated them as human beings, are sensitive to the richness of their explicit and implicit clinical characteristics, and have approached the task in their own ways as carefully and diligently as they know how. When this kind of investigator provides us with what are bound to be only partial results, we can combine those with the equally partial (and, one would hope, overlapping) results of other investigators to construct a composite picture that contains promise of sometime approximating the veridical one.

CONCLUSION

So here we are, finally confronted by this formidable inventory of the complexities and difficulties of doing research on the disordered. Where do we go from here? For me it immediately brings to mind an admonition that has stuck with me from adolescence and now seems peculiarly apt. It occurs in that delicious story "The Burglars" from *The Golden Age*, Kenneth Grahame's nostalgic stories of childhood as related by one of the adults originally involved as a child in the events. In "The Burglars" appears that memorable Olympian Aunt Maria—she was all of a venerable 26!—to the young curate one evening while they were out enjoying the night air on the garden bench. The curate had just nabbed the youngest nephew who was snooping around. The youngster was accounting for his presence outdoors, several hours beyond his usual bedtime, with a lurid story of being awakened by burglars he had seen approaching the house. (His story was classic, using phrases taken almost verbatim from the last penny-dreadful the brothers had been reading—you know the breed, terms like "nefarious comrades," "armed to the teeth," and "vanished silently with horrid implications.") In the midst of spinning his yarn, they were startled by a sudden noise from the bushes. The curate made as if to head in that direction. It was then that Aunt Maria emitted her immortal plea: "Oh, Mr. Hodgitts! You are brave! For my sake do not be rash!" Aunt Maria's sensitive distinction seems a notably appropriate guide for researchers on the disordered.

REFERENCES

Cronbach, L. J. (1957). The two disciplines of scientific psychology. *American Psychologist,* **12,** 671–684.

Cronbach, L. J. (1975). Beyond the two disciplines of scientific psychology. *American Psychologist,* **30,** 116–127.

Crothers, B. (1932). Psychology and psychiatry in pediatrics: The problem. Report of the Subcommittee on Psychology and Psychiatry. In *White House conference on child health and protection.* New York: Century.

Kendall, P. C., & Norton-Ford, J. D. (1982). *Clinical psychology: Scientific and professional dimensions.* New York: Wiley.

Luria, A. R. (1932). *The nature of human conflict.* New York: Liveright, p. 431.

Shakow, D. (1949). Psychology and psychiatry: A dialogue (Parts I and II). *American Journal of Orthopsychiatry,* **19,** 191–208, 381–396.

Shakow, D. (1969). On doing research in schizophrenia. *Archives of General Psychiatry,* **20,** 618–642.

Wheeler, J. A. (1974). The universe as home for man. *American Scientist,* **62,** 683–691.

CHAPTER 2

Perspective on Experimental Contributions to Clinical Research

ERASMUS L. HOCH

Some clinicians are more audacious than others—or perhaps more imaginative. At least one of them does not hesitate to proclaim the psychodynamic significance of what might otherwise seem a harmless pastime—rope-jumping. In a spritely article on "Girls Jumping Rope," Sonnenberg (1955) leaves little doubt as to what is really going on.

> The girl in jumping rope acts out the to and fro movement of the man during sex [sic] intercourse. Her own body takes the part of the active man, while the swinging rope imitates her own body adjusting to the movement of the man's. Thus, in this game, the girl acts both the role of the man and of the woman. (pp. 59–60)

Even the accompanying ditties, some of which are cited, are suspect: "In all these ditties love, marriage and babies appear, certainly not themes we would expect in the play of girls 7 to 11" (p. 62).

There are other similar fearless efforts. Though I have striven unavailingly to relocate one such reference, I still remember its frank title, "The Psychosexual Significance of Turning a Corner," and have been walking in circles ever since.

It is not my purpose to lampoon the foregoing, though in some quarters the somewhat peremptory tone of the article might invite such treatment. Rather Sonnenberg's article is cited in order to contrast it with an approach of quite different character, which I will here call "experimental." For present purposes, the term will be used broadly to connote such things as the following:

1. A willingness to cast clinical hunches in the form of testable hypotheses.
2. A systematic plan for pursuing their confirmation or disconfirmation.
3. A desire for data as "hard" as clinical problems will allow.
4. A readiness to modify theoretical positions if appropriate and to discard them if necessary.

Fortunately, there are such contributors—clinicians careful of their assertions, restrained in their claims, yet inventive in their conceptions. A short provocative piece by Brendan Maher (1974) qualifies nicely as a sharp contrast to the Sonnenberg brand of proclamation. Having authored a formidable text on psychopathology (Maher, 1966), Maher is entitled to speculate on such matters as the nature of delusional thinking. Many have done so. Freud, for example, viewed paranoid delusions as a device for projecting onto others certain feelings one cannot accept oneself, his Schreber case (1953) serving as a prime example. Less etiological in nature is the formulation of Von Domarus (1944), who described delusional thinking as an example of faulty syllogistic reasoning.

Maher (1974) suggests the converse—that paranoid individuals suffer not from impaired cognition but from a perceptual disorder.

Their problem lies "not in the manner of drawing inference from evidence but in the kinds of perceptual experience that provide the evidence from which the inference is to be drawn" (Maher, 1974, p. 99).

His article is cited here primarily as a contrast to Sonnenberg's piece. Where the latter offers flat assertions, Maher (1974) consistently uses phases on the order of "there is a rapidly increasing body of evidence to indicate that . . ." (p. 100); "there is a prima facie reason to suppose that . . ." (p. 101); "consideration of this *hypothesis* [emphasis added] may generate the criticism that . . ." (p. 108); and "for obvious reasons it is difficult to test this *hypothesis* [emphasis added] by direct experimentation" (p. 108). His summary closes with the sentence: "In brief, it is *suggested* [emphasis added] that . . ." (p. 112). As a creative scientist who has made experimental contributions in his own right, Maher (1974) offers a provocative hypothesis, one he feels is consistent with evidence accumulated to date, warrants appropriate testing, and, where findings point toward its confirmation, needs to be defended against alternative competing hypotheses.

In the classic sense, an experimental approach brings to mind the "operational definition" of terms, the prescribed manipulation of independent variables, and the careful measurement of dependent variables, all in the context of an acceptable experimental design and appropriate statistical treatment of the data. As used more broadly in the present chapter, however, the "experimental" contributions sampled include any systematic attempt to gather and evaluate reasonably objective evidence in the interest of putting one's data where one's mouth is. Correlational studies certainly qualify. So do other efforts in which the clinician, as observer and investigator, having defined terms as clearly as they permit, follows a predetermined plan for chasing down results that will serve to strengthen, weaken, or leave in abeyance convictions held.

As Spring and Zubin (1977) put it:

There are two aspects to scientific investigation: the conceptual framework or model, and testing the hypotheses emanating from it. In the conceptual framework we deal with abstractions in the form of concepts. In testing the hypotheses we deal with ostensible facts to determine the tenability of the hypotheses. (p. 256)

Fortunately, no one man, least of all the clinician, need be an island alone. When experimental psychologists (Brown, 1948; Miller, 1959) run rats in an approach-avoidance situation, the clinical relevance of the findings can hardly escape notice. When social psychologist Schachter (1971) studies avoidance learning in sociopaths, the outcome is of no less interest. And when a physiological psychologist (Brady et al., 1958) discovers that monkeys in decision-making roles are prone to ulcers, those treating people with psychosomatic symptoms do well to note the laboratory findings. For that matter, the mathematical psychologist working at optimal rules for decision-making may well have something to offer the working clinician struggling with whether to issue a weekend pass to a formerly suicidal patient who seems to be improving but still looks depressed.

Clinical psychology is not without friends; it simply may not recognize them. Or, having periodically suffered the slings and arrows of others, it sometimes feels that, with a hard-headed psychologist for a friend, who needs an enemy? Meehl (1954) has playfully portrayed conceptions and misconceptions colleagues may have of each other and themselves:

The clinical method . . . is labeled by its proponents as dynamic, global, meaningful, holistic, subtle, sympathetic, configural, patterned, organized, rich, deep, genuine, sensitive, sophisticated, real, living, concrete, natural, true to life, and understanding. The critics of the clinical method are likely to view it as mystical, transcendent, metaphysical, super-mundane, vague, hazy, subjective, unscientific, unreliable, crude, private, unverifiable, qualitative, primitive, prescientific, sloppy, uncontrolled, careless, verbalistic, intuitive, and muddleheaded. (p. 4)

Fortunately, this cold war has in most places yielded to détente and, where the real action is, to accord. A leading introductory text (Kimble, Garmezy, & Zigler, 1980) finds an experimental and a developmental psychologist joined with a clinician, thus having the best of several worlds.

There is something to be said for miscegenation. Where the Cabots speak only to the Lowells and they only to God, all must perforce raise themselves by their bootstraps. Where, however, there is a certain amount of piggy backing, log rolling, mutual back scratching (rather than stabbing), life is much easier.

Other voices in other rooms have been raised in this connection. More than a decade ago, Zubin (1969a) delivered himself of a homily to this effect. In another context, Cronbach (1957), and Bindra and Scheier (1954) before him, spoke of a related liaison that "two disciplines" can and should have with each other: "It is not enough for each discipline to borrow from the other. Correlational psychology studies only variance among organisms; experimental psychology studies only variance among treatments. A united discipline will study both of these." (Cronbach, 1957, p. 681).

Others (Edwards & Cronbach, 1952) have been generous with their suggestions as to how the clinical psychologist can go about his or her job as a behavioral scientist. Indeed whole books (e.g., Chassan, 1979) have been devoted to dealing with the not uncomplicated, and in some ways unique, problems faced in clinical research.

All in all, the stage is set.

PROSPECTUS

Succeeding chapters in this volume deal with specific areas of research in which their authors are expert. The present chapter is more

general in nature. It attempts to provide the flavor of some representative research, selects some as particularly illustrative for certain purposes, and tries to convey the panoramic character of experimental contributions to clinical psychology. To this end, some investigators will serve as prototypical and some approaches as paradigmatic. In short, the concern here is with what is being explored, how it is being done, why closure is hard to achieve, and where the field is moving.

PROTOTYPES

A very recent survey (Perlman, 1980) of authors most widely cited in psychology brings to light some strange bedfellows. With Sigmund Freud heading the list, there are names one would readily guess might make such a roster. Others come as a surprise. Evidently some very different kinds of contributions draw attention, at least as measured by such indexes as frequency of citation in the most widely used introductory texts.

Some clearly gain notice through consistently significant research over the years, others by evolving an elaborate theoretical network of impressive explanatory power. But there are those who venture into areas where strange things are to be discovered, things that upset the natural order and in confronting the collective wisdom cause ire to rise, if not blood to boil.

If, then, one were to select a few figures who either have made "experimental contributions" to clinical psychology themselves or have served as models for others, one would want a varied cast of characters. The following preamble accordingly centers around a handful of contributors who can serve as prototypes.

Dramatis Personae

Every field has its movers and shakers, some moving the enterprise ahead significantly through dramatic advances in knowledge, others periodically shaking it to its roots with irksome questions. David Shakow and Joseph Zubin exemplify the former, Paul Meehl the latter. Clinical psychology is different for their having contributed to it.

There are also those who, though reared in another school, seem unable to resist the urge to offer helpful suggestions. Although nonclinicians by training, one would sometimes hardly know it when a Neal Miller or other laboratory-bred psychologist undertakes research in an area that, if not outright clinical turf, certainly borders on it.

Meanwhile, almost as if standing above the whole business, there are those who, while not "treaters of the sick," certainly have some grand visions of what personality and behavior are all about. If they do not make a hands-on contribution as such, Albert Bandura and Walter Mischel have, each with his theoretical tour de force, provided a conceptual framework within which to view clinical practice. A few words about each of these representative figures make a fitting introduction.

Clinicians' Clinicians

Of David Shakow, Norman Garmezy has said:

David Shakow has never been guilty of simplistic thinking. Schizophrenia is a disorder of extraordinary complexity, one that places heavy demands on the investigator for conceptual clarity and precision of thought. These are Shakow's hallmarks as a researcher, and they provide a legacy for young investigators, irrespective of discipline, who seek to study a disorder that for centuries has resisted the efforts of those who have sought to discover its etiology. (Shakow, 1977, p. xii)

Shakow's concern has been less with comparing schizophrenic with normal performance or even schizophrenics with schizophrenics, and more with understanding his subjects in their own right.

Is the schizophrenic's reaction time woe-fully slower than that of normal persons? Yes—at first glance. But if one studies performances seriatim, as Shakow (1963) did, not only does the schizophrenic score improve, but in some cases it may equal and even exceed that of normal controls. Such, for example, were the results on a pursuit-meter task when subjects were tested not on a single occasion but over a 33-day period.

Or, if it seems that the schizophrenic's interpersonal relations are hopelessly impaired, this too deserves a closer look. When he did so (Shakow, 1963), Shakow's diligence once more paid off. On a simple card-sorting task, his schizophrenic subjects improved somewhat over trials when performing alone. But when placed in individual competition with one another, they were spurred to greater effort. And when—of all things—they competed against each other as groups, performance improved dramatically!

When an experimenter of Shakow's patience studies people rather than pathology, some rewarding things happen. He practices what he preaches—the need to study his subjects over time and across situations.

If anyone can serve as the antithesis of the previously cited rope-jumping interpreter (Sonnenberg, 1955) it is Joseph Zubin. Taking the large look at psychopathology in the company of colleagues wedded to a "biometric" approach, Zubin (1969b) had long espoused a multimodeled conceptualization of etiology embracing ecology, learning, development, genetics, internal environment, and neurophysiology.

The scope of the undertakings by Zubin's biometrics group is staggering. The responses they elicit from their subjects are enough to require a "Mendelejeff-like table" comprising physiological, sensory, perceptual, psychomotor, and conceptual areas, the stimuli consisting of an idling state as well as energy and signal variables.

An example of Zubin's current thinking, based on this lifetime of effort devoted to the objective measurement of behavior, is presented later in this chapter (Spring & Zubin, 1977). Suffice it to say, for the moment, that his concern with understanding the parameters of the ecological forces contributing to psychopathology is satisfied neither by unfounded speculation nor by simple good intentions. As he put it in an address (Zubin, 1968) in memory of Paul Hoch, his long-time collaborator:

It is not enough to speak of poverty, deprivation, low socio-economic status, migration, stress, etc. We must contrive methods for demonstrating how these factors impinge on the mental health of the person if we are not to merely join the ranks of the do-gooders and claim that elimination of these hazards will eliminate mental disorder. . . . Sheer intervention may produce improvement, but it will be short-lived or will soon exhaust its benefit if we do not analyze the essential components involved. (p. 308)

While Shakow and Zubin have spent the major part of their time in the laboratory, Meehl has spent his in thought—in reflections on the clinical process, the nature of schizophrenia, research design, methodological snares and delusions. Some have been tempted to call him Peck's bad boy, others a devil's advocate or even more telling sobriquets. But no one has ever called Paul Meehl's contributions dull. He keeps theoretical pots boiling.

A practicing clinician in his own right, Meehl is as hard on himself as on his colleagues. He feels a need to call a bluff, and a sense of guilt results whenever he hedges his bets. His pieces have gutsy titles: "Why I Do Not Attend Staff Conferences" (1973); or "When Shall We Use Our Heads Instead of the Formula?" (1957); even the enigmatic "Theoretical Risks and Tabular Asterisks: Sir Karl, Sir Ronald, and the Slow Progress of Soft Psychology" (1978). The latter is typical of what Meehl does best—speaking the language of the philosophy of science in a way comprehensible to clinicians, whether they are in the business of treating clients, formulating theory, or testing hypotheses. At the same time he can be counted on periodically to distill from the fruits of his own labors in the consulting room the kind of heady clinical treatise typified by his APA presidential address (1962). That is about all one has reason to expect of one man.

"Hard" and "Soft" Psychology

One might already have suspected 30 years ago that Neal Miller would be seduced by the implications his animal studies held for human behavior. He gave fair warning. His *Personality and Psychotherapy,* co-authored with Dollard (1950), set out frankly to "combine the vitality of psychoanalysis, the rigor of the natural-science laboratory, and the facts of culture" (p. 3). The task was ambitious, including as it did such jobs as substituting reinforcement for Freud's pleasure principle, explaining transference as a special case of generalization, and translating repression and suppression into the concepts of inhibition and restraint.

The Dollard-Miller episode was but the forerunner of Miller's continuing interest in various aspects of the clinical enterprise as seen in the titles of his studies: "Some Animal Experiments Pertinent to the Problem of Combining Psychotherapy with Drug Therapy" (1966) and "Experiments Relevant to Learning Theory and Psychopathology" (1969). In recent years his concern with clinical as well as physiological aspects of autonomic learning (1973) has obvious implications for the understanding and treatment of psychosomatic problems, especially when accompanied by his lively interest in the flourishing area of biofeedback. While his initial exuberance has been dampened a bit by exasperation over inability to replicate some dramatic results, as detailed later in this chapter, he remains indomitable. The clinical area stands to gain as a result.

Theoretical Substrata

Social learning theorists have in recent years been uttering some frank heresies, suggesting that psychodynamic clinicians have too long been worshiping false gods. Whether the indictments are valid can be debated, but not the harsh sound of these ex cathedra pronouncements, such as the statement that the psychodynamic model "has led to some tragic mistakes in clinical treatment and diagnosis for 50 years" (Mischel, 1971, p. 75).

Social behavior theory, as enunciated by Mischel (1971), has had a bracing effect. Remarking on the overweening emphasis on early experience as a broad explanatory mode he is forthright: "Psychodynamic theorizing assumes a set of basic personality motives and dispositions that endure, although their overt response forms may change. . . . This model is analogous to the closed hydraulic system in physics" (p. 75).

He draws some sharp contrasts:

Psychodynamic theories look for the motivational roots of personality in childhood. In contrast, social behavior analyses seek the current causes of the person's behavior. Social learning approaches to personality thus pay less attention to motivational and dispositional constructs and instead look more at the individual's behavior, and at the functional relations between what he does and the psychological conditions of his life. . . . Social behavior theorists suggest that it might be wiser to spend more time looking at what people are doing rather than try to infer the intrapsychic motives and traits propelling them. (Mischel, 1971, pp. 77–78)

If research and theory go hand in hand, this kind of theoretical charge and counter-charge may well determine the character of the problems on which clinical investigators will be working during the decade ahead.

Much the same kind of influence characterizes Bandura's contributions to the clinical enterprise. His present visibility might have been predicted from an early interest in the genesis and modification of human behavior (Bandura & Walters, 1963). For here social learning theory and its applications were clearly laid out. The theory in its present

form (Bandura, 1977a) has attracted wide attention. Meanwhile his theoretical interests have carried him into the general area of behavior modification, as is evident in what has become one of the authoritative sources (Bandura, 1969).

Like Mischel, Bandura finds theory, practice, and research inseparable. His recent "unifying theory of behavioral change" (1977b) represents "an integrative theoretical framework to explain and to predict psychological changes achieved by different modes of treatment" (p. 191). An ambitious attempt to formulate such processes in terms of the central concept of "self-efficacy," this treatise is a prime example of an effort to reconcile theory and practice in light of what seem divergent trends:

On the one hand, the mechanisms by which human behavior is acquired and regulated are increasingly formulated in terms of cognitive processes. On the other hand, it is performance-based procedures that are proving to be most powerful for effecting psychological changes. As a consequence, successful performance is replacing symbolically based experiences as the principle [sic] vehicle of change. . . . The apparent divergence of theory and practice can be reconciled by postulating that cognitive processes mediate change but that cognitive events are induced and altered most readily by experience of mastery arising from effective performance. (Bandura, 1977b, p. 191)

His exhaustive theoretical analysis is already giving clinicians, whether in practice or in research, the kind of inspirational jolt that is bound to influence the character of experimental work in clinical laboratories. If such contributors as Bandura and Mischel do not spend their time as clinicians per se, they will certainly have influenced those who do.

PARADIGMS

Kuhn's (1970) conception of paradigms aside, the fact remains that clinical problems can be, and have been, attacked in the most diverse ways. Anyone doubting the matter need only look at the incredible range of therapies that have been proposed to meet the straightforward proposition of how one helps another lead a more effective life. Unless one wants to end up with what Wertheimer called an and-summative list, it is necessary to impose some arbitrary order on the flurry of activity, especially in the area of clinical research, where in the study of psychopathology, for example, there is an embarrassment of riches.

In the interest of achieving some kind of conceptual unity, I have selected two high-volume research areas, schizophrenia and depression, for illustrative purposes. By way of contrast, they are discussed from two perspectives: schizophrenia in terms of representative "divergent" approaches, and depression in terms of converging studies.

Case A: Schizophrenia

The disorder called schizophrenia has evoked the widest ranging, most diverse attention in all of psychopathology. Hence it serves conveniently to illustrate the panorama of research efforts bearing on a problem of central interest.

The welter of studies can doubtless be catalogued in a dozen ways. Here the following simple structure will serve to outline a representative array of approaches, each of them offering an experimental contribution in its own right:

1. The molecular approach—chipping away at the larger problem.
2. The centripetal approach—homing in on a central process.
3. The biological-genetic approach—giving other-than-psychological aspects their due.
4. The molar approach—attempting to synthesize what is known.

The Molecular Approach. The procession of discrete studies of the schizophrenic

process seems endless. Schizophrenic subjects have been compared with normal controls on a limitless number of features—galvanic skin response, tachistoscopic threshold, anxiety level, reaction time, conditionability, ketosteroid production, language and syntax, conceptualization, and generalization curves, to name but a few of the dimensions. And schizophrenics have been compared with each other on just as many.

The disparate collection of studies has remained essentially a pool of ideas and a reservoir of findings into which others can dip further. With countless investigators sailing off in different directions, there remains a real need for the Columbuses who in their single-minded way have some grand destination in mind. A look at current issues of representative journals provides a convenient sample of illustrative studies of such discrete aspects as electrodermal response, dichotic shadowing, linguistic integration, and imagery, to name but a few.

If the term "molecular" seems inappropriate for characterizing such studies, some other will do, provided it carries the connotation of studies occupying a small but specific niche in the huge research structure that has been erected around the schizophrenic process.

There is, however, a second approach, one typified by such efforts as those of Heilbrun and of Cohen and his colleagues, as noted below.

The Centripetal Approach. Ever since their work drew attention in *Science* (Rosenberg & Cohen, 1964), Bertram Cohen and his collaborators have sought to zero in with increasing precision on one aspect of the schizophrenic process, communication, having evolved what he and his collaborators found a simple, yet effective, research tactic. The latter consists of an attempt by a speaker to convey to a listener a very simple message, using a prescribed procedure. Given a card on which two fairly synonymous words appear, for example, "lively" and "cheerful," the speaker must indicate to her listener, who also has a card listing the same two words, that "lively" (and not "cheerful") is the referent. This is accomplished by having the speaker say a word (in accordance with certain ground rules) that will tip off the listener. As it happens, this simple arrangement has proved very practicable in studying the dynamics of the communication process, using schizophrenic subjects and normal controls.

What is significant here is not the device as such but the persistence with which Cohen and his colleagues have sought to track down the nuances of the cognitive processes that must underlie the communication efforts of the schizophrenic. The investigators have explored successively a graded series of hypotheses (Rosenberg & Cohen, 1966; Cohen & Camhi, 1967; Cohen et al., 1974) that, it was hoped, would progressively delimit what is involved.

In a typical recent study (Kantorowitz & Cohen, 1977) the communication characteristics of process and reactive schizophrenics were compared with those of normal speakers on a task in which chips of various colors were to be described by speakers to listeners in accordance with the procedure noted above. What is significant in this chain of studies initiated by Cohen is not the serviceability of his simple technique but the progressive refinement of a thesis concerning what characterizes the efforts of schizophrenics to understand and respond in communication with others.

Thus an earlier two-stage model of this research group had posited a *sampling* stage in which the speaker sampled, but did not necessarily emit, a response from his repertoire of associations that was felt to convey the message to the listener. This, it was conjectured, was followed by a *comparison* stage, in which the respective response was subjectively evaluated in terms of its associative strength and communicational effectiveness. By the time the 1977 study was conducted, the model had become succes-

sively elaborated, Cohen et al. (1974) having found, for example, that, in comparison with normal subjects, their *acute* schizophrenic group had engaged in significantly more self-editing activity. The more recent study by Kantorowitz and Cohen (1977) found, interestingly enough, that such self-editing activity was diminished or even absent in a sample of chronic schizophrenics. How to account for the difference?

Kantorowitz and Cohen (1977) have some interesting reflections:

Acute patients, it would seem, persist in the struggle to find a fresh and more appropriate description to replace sampled but inappropriate responses and are unable to bring this off; chronic patients appear instead to have given up this attempt. It may be that after repeated futile efforts to self-edit, schizophrenics learn to abort the attempt altogether. A contributing factor may be that the behavioral contingencies prevalent in chronic patient wards are not geared to provide immediate selective reinforcement for referentially unambiguous speech. (p. 7)

Interesting as such conjecture is in its own right, what is particularly significant here is the fact that it was born of the sequential investigations that have preceded. It is the latest link in a chain. Whether the latter will eventually snap or prove long enough and strong enough to provide definitive insights into the schizophrenic communication process remains to be seen. But it is commendable that this group of investigators is systematically chasing down leads that grow progressively out of their studies in a systematically conceived series.

Equally illustrative of this "centripetal" approach in its own way is the "analogue study of disattentional processes" by Heilbrun (1977), in which a researcher sought to pursue the contrasting hypotheses of diverse investigators with respect to a common problem, the role of attention in the schizophrenic disorder. Thus, while a breakdown in the filtering mechanism has been held responsible for much of the difficulty experienced by schizophrenics, there exists a variety of competing hypotheses concerning the process of "disattention" presumed to be involved.

Broen (1973), for example, holds that the schizophrenic favors one sense modality at the expense of others, becoming a visual rather than auditory attender, for example, in the service of a defensive attentional style. Salzinger (1973), on the other hand, suggests that schizophrenics safeguard themselves by attending to the immediate stimulus at the expense of more remote stimuli that might also be present and relevant. Cromwell & Dokecki (1968) had been suggesting the opposite, namely, that schizophrenics find it so hard to disattend to a present stimulus once newer stimuli are at hand, that they are constantly continuing to respond to stimuli that are no longer relevant.

In contrast to the research strategy of Cohen and his colleagues, who were concerned with the internal consistency of their own model, Heilbrun (1977) is concerned with the contradictory hypotheses of others around a common problem. Hence, in a systematic effort to give each of the disparate hypotheses a chance, he conducted an analogue study using normal subjects in a double-experiment design intended to allow the contrasting views an opportunity to prove themselves. The hypotheses of Broen and of Cromwell and Dokecki fared better than that of Salzinger. Heilbrun focused on an alleged central process—disattention, in this case— by attempting to resolve differing or even contradictory conceptions of the dynamics at work.

Thus, while the Cohen group was fighting with itself, Heilbrun was refereeing the battles of others. In either case, spectators at ringside got their money's worth.

The Biological-Genetic Approach. While such studies as those on concordance rates in twins are certainly not new, and while other genetically oriented investigations have long existed in the literature on schizophre-

nia, large-scale, long-term projects remain the exception. The research program of Mednick and his colleagues (Mednick et al., 1974) is such an exception. With the unusually systematic record-keeping of the Danish government, it has proved possible for investigators based in Copenhagen to carry out longitudinal research. In contrast to the usual retrospective studies extant, the Mednick group has adopted a propective strategy. Their research on children-at-risk does what Albee and his colleagues advocate (Albee & Joffe, 1977). Prevention of disorder has top priority.

The Mednick team (Mednick et al., 1974) serves as a notable current example of interdisciplinary investigation of a huge problem over time. An advance look at the strategy was afforded by a paper (Mednick & McNeil, 1968) that presented the high-risk-group method as an alternative preferable to the research on etiology prevalent at the time. In particular, shortcomings were attributed to such practices as observation of individuals already schizophrenic, studies of families of schizophrenics, and analysis of childhood records. By contrast, significant advantages were claimed for the longitudinal study of high-risk individuals. The investigators offer a three-level design. They compare high-risk children (those of schizophrenic mothers) with low-risk children (those of "normal" mothers), using as controls for the high-risk children who become schizophrenic, those who either do not become schizophrenic or else succumb to other-than-schizophrenic deviancies.

The Mednick group has pursued its research along a variety of lines—longitudinal study of children at high risk, prevalence of mental illness in biological and adoptive families of adopted schizophrenics, perinatal conditions in children with schizophrenic parents, and such further aspects, among others, as the relation between social class, institutionalization, and schizophrenia. All in all, a large order.

Research and speculation of a qualitatively

different yet allied nature is exemplified by the scholarly efforts of E. Roy John. Though not a clinician, he has raised clinical issues in laboratory research on human subjects, including neurotic and schizophrenic individuals:

We can discern two classes of potential disorder: abnormal mental processes arising from malfunction of the machinery of a brain processing normal material, and abnormalities arising from proper functioning of the machinery of a brain processing abnormal material. [One is reminded here of the thesis advanced by Maher, 1974, and discussed earlier.] In either case, it would seem central to an understanding of these mental processes to understand the fundamental mechanisms by which sensory stimuli are coded in the brain, by which the *sequence* [emphasis in original] of stimuli that constitute an experience is represented and stored, and the mechanisms by which the representations of that experience can be released in an orderly sequence. (John, 1973, p. 321)

It is just such mechanisms and sequences with which John's research concerns itself, research of which clinicians may well take note. With neurotic and schizophrenic subjects among those studied, his laboratory provides some graphic data. For example, the synchronization of cortical biopotentials measured by electrodes on the head of a schizophrenic performing mental arithmetic differs strikingly from that of a normal person. For John (1973), in the case of the paranoid schizophrenic (and the obsessive neurotic):

These data . . . give indications of being involved in intense mental activity when we would expect them to be at rest, and that the schizophrenic does not integrate the activity of frontal regions of the cortex with more posterior regions under circumstances which normally accomplish this. (pp. 326–327)

The illustrations in John's (1973) report are striking. What makes these laboratory findings particularly significant, however, is the fact that he sees them as part of a broader and fundamental question for neuropsychology, "how mental phenomena arise" (p. 319). John finds little difficulty with the kind of disorder in which the properly functioning brain processes "abnormal" material: "Past traumatic experiences, stored by representational systems . . . , must be expected inevitably to arise in consciousness, to influence the content of thought, to be the subject of fantasy, to direct the imagination" (p. 338).

It is the second kind of disorder, one arising from "malfunction of the brain mechanisms necessary for processing, storing, and retrieving information and therefore essential to the processes of thinking, imagination, and fantasy" (p. 338), that prompts especially intriguing comments:

It might arise from changes in the metabolic characteristics of the system, resulting in an alteration of the signal-to-noise ratio, so that the coherence levels necessary for information to be stored and retrieved, reflecting the ease of access and the probability of access to memories, have been either drastically raised or lowered. There has been, as it were, *a change in the confidence level* [emphasis added] which the system requires to accept data. (John, 1973, p. 338)

This no-nonsense conceptualization of psychopathological processes is certainly qualitatively different from the terms in which clinicians usually cast their theories. As such, it provides the leavening influence clinical psychology can well use at this point in its history.

The Molar Approach.   The word "molar" is intended to designate two efforts, different in character but illustrative of attempts at encompassing the schizophrenic experience on a grand scale. One is armchair in nature, though born of years of clinical observation; the other grows out of a lifetime of research.

McReynolds' (1960) theoretical conception is an effort to speculate on how the schizophrenic experience comes about and what defenses are available to its victim, once caught in it. He invokes as few constructs as possible, proceeding largely on the basis of how percepts get processed.

Most of us, he suggests, are fortunate enough not to have too many "unassimilable" (hence anxiety-arousing) percepts. Either our life experiences are not all that traumatic or, where they are, we are adept at forcing them into "schemata" that make them less unassimilable. By contrast, the schizophrenia-prone individual, McReynolds speculates, either meets with more frequent misadventures, hence intolerable effects, as the result of an unfortunate social history, or else is less versatile (perhaps more guileless) in forcing incongruities into some acceptable mold. It is the accumulation of unassimilable percepts, he surmises, that ultimately spells schizophrenia.

Schizophrenics, according to this formulation, have one of two options. They can simply cut off further input, already having more than they can handle. Unfortunately, this self-enforced "sensory deprivation," like its laboratory counterpart, exacts hallucinations as its price. There is an alternative. They can instead place their own arbitrary interpretation on life events, turning what are otherwise intolerable realities into acceptable fictions. The artificial reconstruction of the world makes life more understandable (in the case of delusions of persecution), sometimes even downright enjoyable (in the case of delusions of grandeur). Unfortunately, this world is now a crazy one.

This brand of theorizing has a good deal of face validity. It invokes no special complexes, requires no mysterious "forces," and fabricates no new constructs. Whether it is basically "correct" remains to be seen. Meanwhile it serves as an example of a kind of parsimonious speculation attempting to integrate and make sense of a long series of clinical observations over the years.

McReynolds' view stands in contrast to a model of different character, one proposed by Spring and Zubin (1977). The latter review a collection of models, pulling out a thread running through all of them—hypotheses concerning the etiology of vulnerability—and weave a fabric of their own. The resulting conception, deceiving in its simplicity, represents again a plausible portrayal of what is clearly a complex process. The premise is straightforward: "that the person who has suffered one episode of schizophrenia will not always be schizophrenic. He will, however, always be *vulnerable to episodes* of schizophrenia [emphasis added]" (p. 255).

Elaborated, the position is equally straightforward:

Specifically, we suggest that schizophrenia, like other mental disorders, appears in time-limited episodes induced when life stressors surpass a threshold set by the patient's characteristic level of vulnerability. Once the episode has ended, a patient resumes functioning either at or close to his premorbid competence level. (p. 259)

Interestingly, Spring and Zubin (1977) are willing to grant that a chronic disease model may have been appropriate for the time when dementia praecox, as it was then called, was viewed as the progressively deteriorating affair commonly seen generations ago. Now, however, an "infectious disease model" distorts the situation far less. Indeed the Spring-Zubin model makes use of a careful distinction between what is trait and what is state.

We have contended that episodes of schizophrenia are psychopathological *states* [emphasis added] elicited when life event stressors surpass the threshold determined by the individual's characteristic level of vulnerability. Vulnerability, by contrast, is a stable *trait* [emphasis added] that characterizes the individual independently of the presence or absence of the episodes. To paraphrase, a schizophrenic is not a permanently sick individual, but a permanently vulnerable one. (Spring & Zubin, 1977, p. 277)

Deceptively simple, yet representing the distillation of years of research in schizophrenia, this formulation perhaps best illustrates how much laborious investigation is required before a disarmingly straightforward synthesis is possible.

Case B: Depression

When Seligman and his colleagues first tested their laboratory dogs, few—perhaps Seligman least of all—would have expected the results to find their way into clinical circles. But what began as animal research in the tradition of experimental psychology was to become the focus for vigorous debate concerning the genesis, even the treatment, of depression in people.

Had the Seligman group (Seligman & Maier, 1967; Overmier & Seligman, 1967) foregone the catchy phrase "learned helplessness" (Seligman et al., 1968), their research, interesting though it was, might have drawn the attention primarily of experimental psychologists, as a sequel to the earlier work of Solomon and his colleagues (Solomon et al., 1953). Where the latter had been astounded by the almost inextinguishable avoidance reactions of their dogs following removal of the aversive contingency that had initiated such reactions, the Seligman dogs showed virtually the opposite effect. Having been exposed initially to inescapable shock, unlike the Solomon animals, they subsequently *failed* to show avoidance behavior even when the latter would readily have removed them from further punishment.

This area, then, offers a paradigmatic moral of a sort, namely, that what begins as a fairly technical and circumscribed object of study in the animal laboratory may actually be almost imperceptibly transformed into an issue of deeply human concern. In the case of depression, the old argument about the noncomparability of animal and human behavior seems hardly to have surfaced. Instead a coterie of investigators has been drawn irresistibly into arguments over the clinical subject matter rather than the experimental subjects.

As it was, the dual notion that in the animal studies one was seeing "helplessness" in raw form and that such behavior, or the lack of behavior, brought to mind "depressed" subjects, could not help but capture others' imaginations. After all, like the Seligman dogs, depressed people look passive, immobile, energyless—"resigned," "helpless." The latter two adjectives represent inferences; the former, however, were clearly observable characteristics of the laboratory subjects.

It is understandable that the original work of Overmier and Seligman (1967) and Seligman and Maier (1967) should have led this group of experimenters to think increasingly in terms of human parallels. Their "helplessness model of depression" (Seligman et al., 1976) has in fact drawn active response from both clinical and social psychologists. Nor have experimental psychologists stopped seeking less "clinical" explanations for the findings in the animal laboratory. In two fairly recent studies, for example, Glazer and Weiss (1976a and b) have continued to experiment with various parameters of inescapable shock in the interest of evaluating the "helplessness" concept, only to conclude that the phenomenon is better explained in other terms, such as a "tendency to be inactive." Such assiduous experimentation to the contrary nonwithstanding, it is in social and clinical circles that the original research and its extrapolated implications continue to create the most notice.

Having translated their findings into human terms, that is, having frankly proposed a theoretical analysis of depression, Seligman and his collaborators (Seligman et al., 1976) offer their refurbished model for serious consideration. Certainly the challenge has been accepted, both by those bent on revising the latest version and by clinicians interested in the implications for treatment. Abramson et al. (1978), for example, have offered a reformulation of the helplessness model, claiming that with benefit of a revision of attribution theory the model's several inadequacies are corrected and it becomes a better model for it. Citing four classes of deficits as characterizing depression—motivational, cognitive, self-esteem, and affective—they profess to have resolved the model's shortcomings within an attributional framework. More significant from the clinical perspective is the set of specific strategies they feel follows from this reformulation.

Undertaking their own critique of the Abramson et al. critique, Wortman and Dintzer (1978) see the former as somewhat circular, yet grant that the reformulation by means of an attribution analysis is a step forward. Also interesting is the fact that they too cannot help offer some "suggestions for therapy and prevention" based on their own theoretical perspective. The situation, then, is one in which experimental psychologists working with animals have prompted the use of the theories of social psychologists to formulate practical suggestions for clinicians working with depressed people—a healthy kind of unplanned collaboration at a distance.

Meanwhile laboratories remain active, now with people instead of animals as subjects and with frankly applied as well as theoretical objectives. A typical example of the research is that on "immunization against learned helplessness in man," in which Jones et al. (1977) tested the premise that ". . . it should be possible to 'immunize' an organism or to prevent debilitation in responding *by a behavioral injection of the proper stimulus history* [emphasis added]" (p. 75). The organisms in this case were college students and the "history" one of having received either a 0, 50, or 100% success schedule on a series of discrimination problems. As expected, those having experienced a 50% success rate proved to have been more effectively immunized against the helplessness syndrome than the helplessness control and 0% groups. An interesting finding, however, was that the 100% group failed to show the immunization effect.

Significant for clinical work are both the theoretical explanation advanced for the lat-

ter and the practical suggestions accordingly offered. On the former count, Jones et al. (1977) explain:

Persistence occurs whenever an organism learns through counterconditioning to maintain responding under conditions that normally disrupt or interfere with behavior. One form of persistence is reflected in the partial reinforcement extinction effect . . . So, when partially reinforced subjects encounter future frustrative stimuli (i.e., in extinction), these stimuli elicit approach responses instead of the more usual competing responses that interfere with the goal-approach response. . . . Since continually reinforced subjects have never had frustration-related stimuli counterconditioned to approach, these subjects fail to show persistence effects and rapidly stop responding. (p. 81)

Now to the moral of the story as it concerns the practicing clinician:

From the limited basis of the present study, one would question the appropriateness of exclusively using schedules of complete success in the treatment of depressive clients. . . . It would seem that the use of total-success therapy would produce an unrealistic expectation of success and increase the chance of a relapse into the depressive state once the client was released from his therapy program. *The strategic use of failure* [emphasis added], properly interspersed with success in a therapy program, would, on the other hand, prepare the client for dealing realistically with his environment and handling failure in a competent manner. (Jones et al., 1977, p. 82)

Another pair of investigators (Garber & Hollon, 1980), comparing depressed and nondepressed college students, also intend their laboratory efforts to have implications for the clinic. The helplessness model is for them too sweeping in its implications. Doubting that depressed people harbor "a general belief in uncontrollability in the world," these investigators set up tasks that depressed and nondepressed persons could either attempt to perform themselves or observe another performing. They find, in effect, that while the depressed subjects may well experience a feeling of personal helplessness, that is, they view themselves as helpless actors in a test of skill, they do not see such helplessness as universal; that is, in observing others, they do not view the particular situation as uncontrollable. The helpless feeling is restricted to *their own* responses. Apart from some reflections on how such theories as that of Bandura (1977b) on self-efficacy apply here, these investigators too offer some interesting implications for treatment:

Role-playing strategies in which depressed clients are asked to generate predictions for themselves as if they were someone else provide an example of clinical use of the actor-observer manipulation. These strategies highlight distortions in thinking and are consistent with cognitively based treatments of depression. . . . Our results suggest that depressives are capable of generating nondepressive expectancies when they themselves are not part of the equation. (Garber & Hollon, 1980, p. 64)

That the healthy debate has been found worthy of a special forum is evident from the fact that the *Journal of Abnormal Psychology* has offered a whole issue for the purpose (Huesmann, 1978). In other journals and forums discussion also abounds, around apparent paradoxes—uncontrollability and self-blame (Abramson & Sackheim, 1977; Peterson, 1979)—the creation of integrative models (Eastman, 1976), or clinical and theoretical aspects (Lewinsohn, 1974). Lewinsohn (1974) concludes: "Our conceptualization of depression, our ways of dealing with it, are in a continuous state of flux. New possibilities suggest themselves continuously" (p. 116).

Clearly psychologists of various stripes can become "hooked" on such problems, be their typical subjects animal or human, their interests essentially theoretical or applied, and their identification with this area or that. This kind of intercourse simply has to feel good!

The foregoing deals essentially with substantive areas of knowledge (or ignorance), *content* areas around which much of current research is centered. Investigation of *process* is no less complex. The following section considers briefly two clinical functions illustrative of the latter, assessment and treatment, each of which has bred its own array of studies and counterstudies, claims, and refutations.

ASSESSMENT

Predicting how someone will behave, and making decisions that can crucially affect another, are not tasks for the modest. And daring to ask how effectively such functions are performed is not for the timid, as Meehl must soon have learned after the appearance of his "Clinical versus Statistical Prediction" (1954).

Predictions and Decisions

Meehl's (1954) presumably innocent search, revealing that clinical prediction usually came off second best in comparison with actuarial methods, raised hackles, suggesting he had touched some very sensitive spots. There was no mistaking the fact that Holt (1958) did not like what he heard: "Clinical students in particular complain of a vague feeling that a fast one has been put over on them, that under a great show of objectivity, or at least bipartisanship, Professor Meehl has actually sold the clinical approach up the river" (Holt, 1958, p. 1). Though in the next few years there appeared such peacemaking efforts as those of Sawyer (1966), who thought speaking of "Measurement *and* Prediction, Clinical *and* Statistical" might cause less blood to flow, Holt could not seem to forgive and forget. When in 1970 the latter took "Yet Another Look at Clinical and Statistical Prediction" (Holt, 1970), he had some pointed suggestions for future investigators.

In the same year Goldberg (1970) gave 29

clinical psychologists the task of differentiating psychotic from neurotic MMPI profiles in a large pool of cases. He constructed mathematical representations of the respective judgmental strategies. A new set of cases subsequently allowed comparison of the predictive efficiency of the mathematical models and the clinical judgments. The models outperformed their progenitors! As Goldberg puts it: "Within the generality restrictions obviously imposed by any one study, it has been demonstrated that linear regression models of clinical judges can be more accurate diagnostic predictors than are the humans who are modeled" (Goldberg, 1970, p. 430).

Dawes and Corrigan (1974) discerned ever more interesting facets of the clinical judgmental process. Not only can a linear model used to predict an expert's judgment—a "paramorphic representation," as Hoffman (1960) termed it—outpredict the expert, but even random linear models can outperform human judges (Dawes & Corrigan, 1974).

If we paid more than lip service to the notion of statistical regression, Kahneman and Tversky (1973) argue, we would all be better off. Even their bright graduate students did poorly in solving hypothetical situations, failing "to recognize an instance of regression when it was not couched in the familiar terms of the height of fathers and sons" (p. 251). For various reasons the concept of regression, though handled adequately on statistics exams, remains counterintuitive for most psychologists.

What makes these exchanges more than academic affairs is the fact that making clinical predictions can lead ineluctably to decisions influenced by them. The clinician testifying at a commitment hearing that a patient is not dangerous to others may well reassure the judge in the case that, if released, the man will not act on an earlier threat to kill his wife. The topic has in fact drawn the attention of a team of the professions involved (Livermore, Malmquist, & Meehl, 1968), attorney, psychiatrist, and psychologist respectively. Posing a series of hypothetical situations, the authors point up the fact that one's determinations in such cases rest on all kinds of estimates: the probability that some deviant behavior will take place, the social consequences of the behavior, and its treatability or untreatability, not to mention other elements that unwittingly influence the decision maker.

The situation is no less complicated in as ostensibly straightforward a proposition as arriving at a diagnosis, where by now computers have been enlisted to help translate clinical observations into diagnostic terms. As Spitzer and Endicott (1975) point out in their review of the area, both Bayesian classification (e.g., Birnbaum & Maxwell, 1960) as well as discriminant function approaches (e.g., Melrose, Stroebel, & Glueck, 1970) have been employed, with the decision-tree approach (e.g., Spitzer & Endicott, 1974) as an alternative to the statistical models. If most of the problems still cry for solution, at least it is not because people haven't been trying. Nonetheless, still other questions, for example, those dealing with validity, continue to hound the profession.

Validation

Ever since Forer (1949) had shown that people are incredibly gullible when it comes to accepting "clinical" jargon, the "Barnum effect," so termed by Meehl (1956), following Paterson, has given pause for thought. Clinicians have periodically returned to its study. A recent flurry of articles on the subject (Snyder et al., 1977; Greene, 1977; Collins et al., 1977) indicates that it is far from dead.

Forer's (1949) discovery that his class of introductory psychology students would not only accept, as applying to them individually, but even rate as very accurate a generalized set of high base-rate statements taken arbitrarily from an astrology book created some dismay, if not consternation. Despite efforts to rationalize the embarrassing discovery (e.g., Greene, 1977), it has not gone away, having been amply replicated (Sundberg, 1955; Stagner, 1958). Stagner (1958) found that the effect is hardly counteracted by sophistication; people in supervisory and managerial positions in industry prove as gullible as more naive subjects.

Clinicians are now beginning to define the parameters of the phenomenon. The review by Snyder et al. (1977) examines features that characterize the Barnum effect and increase the prospect of its occurrence. A bogus personality description, they assert, is more likely to be accepted "if the feedback is brief, ambiguous, and does not effectively identify ways in which the client is different from the majority of the human population" (p. 112). Even with personality descriptions presumably based on Art Buchwald's "North Dakota Null Hypothesis Brain Inventory," the Barnum effect appeared (Collins et al., 1977). When one considers the typical client, insecure as he or she is in the usual clinical situation, acceptance of such pronouncements from the high-status clinician is even more likely than in the case of the college students who served as the original Barnum study subjects.

For that matter, a string of studies has suggested that clinicians may themselves be a rather gullible lot. Kadushin (1963), for example, demonstrated that master's-level social work supervisors, a not unsophisticated group, could be taken in almost as readily as Forer's introductory psychology students. Having prepared a *single* Forer-like diagnostic report, presumably written by a supervisee, he gave each of three groups of supervisors a different case history on which the diagnostic report was allegedly based, asking that they rate the trainee's writeup. Although the latter, written in advance, bore no actual relationship to the respective case histories, almost three-quarters of the supervisors in two of the groups rated it either above average, excellent, or definitely superior. As in Forer's study, the "diagnostic report" was composed simply of what Ka-

dushin called "Aunt Fanny statements," that is, statements "designed to have universal validity."

Psychologists have fared no better in kindred studies, as Temerlin (1968) has found. Listening to a tape-recorded interview in which a professional actor portrayed a very normal person, clinicians were not misled into seeing psychopathology where there was none when the recording was presented as that of a person in such contexts as an employment interview or even a sanity hearing. When, however, the *same* taped interview was introduced by a "prestige suggestion," from a prestigious professional, "I know the man being interviewed today. . . . He looks neurotic but he actually is quite psychotic," 60% of the psychiatrists judged him as psychotic, 40% as neurotic. None of them judged him mentally healthy. Clinical psychologists did only slightly better; 28% regarded the subject as psychotic, 60% as neurotic, 12% as mentally healthy.

The situation clearly remains muddled. Weiss (1963) compared the accuracy scores of a group of clinical psychologists with those of physical scientists (nonclinicians), using Soskin's (1954) postdiction test—judging from information available as to how a person must have behaved in various situations. She found that physical scientists outperformed clinicians when more information was available; the roles were reversed when less information was at hand. Among the physical scientists those subgroups having more information did better than those having less; the clinicians showed the reverse, there being a trend (although not statistically significant) toward doing more poorly when given more information.

Aspects of the general problem continue to receive attention. More recently, Langer and Abelson (1974) have found that, while psychodynamically and behaviorally oriented clinicians offer similar assessments when presented with data on a person said to be a job applicant, they differ significantly from each other when told the same person is a patient. The latter characterization clearly influences the psychodynamically oriented to see significantly more psychopathology as being present. A recent reanalysis of the Langer and Abelson data (Snyder, 1977) amplifies the nature of the "bias" acquired in training and reflected in one's orientation.

Where all this leaves matters remains to be seen. In "ruminating" on the validation of clinical procedures some years ago, Meehl (1959) declared: "We must face honestly the disparity between current clinical practice and what the research evidence shows about the relatively feeble predictive power of present testing methods" (Meehl, 1959, p. 115). Even today, that may be telling it like it is.

TREATMENT

If clinical prediction and decision making leave much room for improvement, the process by which clinicians attempt to modify behavior is also far from a high art, let alone science. Certainly this is not because there has been a shortage of prescriptions. Edwards and Cronbach's (1952) paper on "Experimental Design for Research in Psychotherapy" laid out a blueprint for research in psychotherapy. More recently, Bergin and Strupp (1970) have issued some "new directions." Having surveyed the literature up to that point and consulted 35 psychologists and psychiatrists, clinicians and nonclinicians, they offered 21 recommendations on the conduct of collaborative research projects in psychotherapy. Their conclusions run the gamut from reluctant admission that large-scale multifactorial studies do not seem feasible to conviction that further process-outcome research on traditional therapy will not advance knowledge appreciably. Particularly pertinent for present purposes are their recommendations 13 and 14:

The fact is that to date research has exerted little influence on clinical practice, and the clinical work of therapists has generally not been informed, much less altered, by empirical research results. . . . The field urgently needs greater collaboration of a different sort. We need improved communication between clinicians and researchers, and between researchers of divergent theoretical orientations (Bergin & Strupp, 1970, pp. 22–23).

Almost a decade later Strupp and some other colleagues (Gomes-Schwartz, Hadley & Strupp, 1978) claim that further endless comparisons of treated and untreated groups with respect to degree of improvement will simply not get at the elements that matter. This conviction is now all the stronger in view of the attention that has meanwhile been accorded the "deterioration effect" sometimes associated with psychotherapy, an effect that gets washed out when group means are simply compared (Bergin, 1971).

Consequently, Gomes-Schwartz et al. (1978) see research as needing to take some new directions: (1) challenging some commonly held conclusions, for example, that lower-class clients are poor candidates for psychotherapy; (2) achieving experimental control without sacrificing the natural character of the therapy process; and (3) incorporating alternative methodologies and designs in future studies. Clearly the movement Carl Rogers launched some 40 years ago, empirical study of what is involved in psychotherapy, is alive, possibly well, but hardly complete.

Behavior therapists are taking stock in their own way, as a recent "overview" by Franks and Wilson (1978) indicates. For this school not only continues its tug of war with the psychodynamicists but at the same time needs to reckon with dissidents in its own ranks. These authors (Franks & Wilson, 1978) spot at least five classes of "malcontents": (1) those who, like Perry London, deny that behavior therapy is as firmly rooted in learning theory as it purports; (2) those advocating "psychodynamic fusionism," that is, the reconciliation of behavior modification and psychoanalytic procedures; (3) the "multi-modal eclecticists" à la Arnold Lazarus; (4) "cognitive exclusivists" in the tradition of Albert Ellis; and (5) the "one-way empiricists," as represented by Isaac Marks.

There are those who, like Bandura (1978), are willing, indeed eager, to give the devil his due, to grant that people are "capable of exercising some control over their own behavior" (p. 115). Among these self-regulatory possibilities, self-reinforcement occupies for him a prominent place, dealing as it does with "the self-administration of freely accessible reinforcers contingent upon requisite performances" (p. 117). Citing experimental evidence in support of his position, Bandura (1978) concludes unabashedly:

People who engage in contingent self-reward perform as well or better than do their counterparts whose behavior is reinforced by others. Although both procedures alter behavior, the practice of self-reinforcement can have the advantage of developing a generalizable skill in self-regulation that will be continually available. (p. 134)

Though Goldiamond (1978) is unhappy with the term "self-reinforcement," seeing it as a label that is both inadequate and misleading, he too is willing to grant that one has here "contingencies of considerable power" (p. 150).

Of greater moment in the behavior modification camp at this stage, however, is the battalion that marches under the banner of "cognitive behavior therapy" (Beck, 1976; Kendall & Hollon, 1979; Meichenbaum, 1977; Mahoney, 1974). With "central mediating processes" having acquired a progressively larger place in the explanatory systems of almost every area of psychology (Dember, 1974), cognitive influences have returned into clinical theory and practice as well. In fact "cognitive behavior therapy" has become a catchword.

As characterized by Mahoney (1977, pp. 7–8), this contemporary variant rests on a fourfold assumption that:

1. The human organism responds primarily to cognitive representations of its environments rather than to those environments per se.
2. These cognitive representations are functionally related to the processes and parameters of learning.
3. Most human learning is cognitively mediated.
4. Thoughts, feelings, and behaviors are causally interactive.

Though recognizing that accommodating this movement within the ranks may inject a revisionist emphasis into what had once been fairly straightforward doctrine, Franks and Wilson (1978) admit that the cognitive brand of behavior therapy is to be treated with respect. Others have their doubts. Ledwidge (1978) wonders frankly whether it might not be, as the subtitle of his article has it, "a step in the wrong direction," one that "could rob behavior therapy of its distinctiveness" (Ledwidge, 1978, p. 354). Hardly, Mahoney and Kazdin (1979) argue, for "persons labeled cognitive behavior modifiers are explicit in their emphasis on behavioral performance as a primary means of challenging maladaptive beliefs" (p. 1046). Evidently Ledwidge (1979) remains unconvinced, for in his reply to the Mahoney and Kazdin (1979) argument he urges that the term "behavior modification" not be adulterated by extending it to cognitive approaches, because "failure to distinguish the two kinds of therapy invites a conceptual confusion of cognition with behavior that could have unfortunate theoretical as well as practical consequences" (Ledwidge, 1979, p. 1053).

This transitional development is hardly without its price, having threatened to divide a house against itself. While some welcome, indeed champion, the new note (e.g., Meichenbaum, 1974; Mahoney, 1974; Beck, 1976), there are those who suggest that the cognitive element may prove a disruptive influence (e.g., Franks & Wilson, 1977). Mahoney (1977) nevertheless sees "the cognitive-learning trend in psychotherapy" as salutary: "It combines an appreciation for both internal (organismic) and environmental factors and addresses the challenge of untangling their relationships" (p. 12).

Like other issues in clinical psychology, this one is destined to be settled empirically rather than polemically. Efforts are already under way. In a study (Shaw, 1977) comparing the respective effectiveness of "cognitive therapy" as represented by Beck (1976) and "behavior therapy" as represented by Lewinsohn (1974) in the treatment of depression, the latter came off second best, though still as effective as nondirective procedures. The investigator himself (Shaw, 1977) hastens to point out limitations of the study: the subjects had positive attributes—youth, intelligence, middle-class status; they were in the main moderately rather than severely depressed; and a single therapist conducted all three treatment groups. The issue is far from settled.

HEALTHY FERMENT

Clinical psychology may actually relish its theoretical and methodological tugs of war. There really seem few dull moments. For that matter, the contretemps itself may best index where the enterprise stands, what constitute its current growing pains, and who is saying what the doctor ordered.

In this spirit it seems well to look at some representative brouhahas, for the matters at issue illustrate some of the sticky wickets in the minds of those researchers proclaiming what is cricket and what is not. Let Jones submit a "critique" of Smith's model, and the next issue of that journal is sure to carry Smith's "reply to Jones," who by then will have attracted enough followers to yield the floor to someone who will write the "rebuttal to Smith's reply to Jones." The following, intended as illustrative, are meant to convey the flavor of the give-and-take surrounding some representative issues.

Emotion

In 1962, for example, Schachter and Singer attracted wide attention with a study that seemed to show that emotions could be produced à la carte. With emotion defined as a function of arousal and cognition, the experimenters seemed to have been able to "manufacture" anger or euphoria by simply creating a state of arousal (with an injection of epinephrine), programming their subjects to expect various side effects (through instructions), and placing them in situations in which certain emotions were made to seem appropriate, as modeled by a presumed fellow subject, who was actually a confederate of the experimenters.

Though certain of the findings took a bit of explaining, the theoretical analysis of the results propounded by Schachter and Singer (1962) was compelling. Their research was subsequently cited extensively over the years and was taken seriously even in the face of some periodic critiques (e.g., Plutchik & Ax, 1967). Indeed one of its current critics admits that "The theoretical impact of this study cannot be overestimated" (Maslach, 1979, p. 954). Other critics put it even more strongly: "The theorizing and research on emotions by Schachter and Singer (1962) must be counted among the primary forces responsible for redirecting the field of social psychology toward a more cognitive orientation" (Marshall & Zimbardo, 1979, p. 970). Because emotion is one of the raw materials in which clinical psychology traffics, the Schachter-Singer study can hardly fail to have profound import for this field as well.

Where Schachter and Singer (1962) were wrong, Maslach (1979) insists, is in overlooking certain methodological flaws in their original design. In her modified replication of the experiment she had tried to introduce some procedural improvements, producing a state of arousal through hypnotic induction, for example, rather than by pharmacological means, thus, she felt, acquiring better control over the onset and maintenance of the arousal state. Further, several measures were added by way of allowing more precise evaluation of certain features. When all was said and done, the Schachter-Singer thesis did not exactly carry the day—indeed it lost out on at least two major counts:

The results [Maslach's] reveal a remarkably consistent and coherent pattern of emotional response . . . that is at variance with the interaction pattern predicted by Schachter and Singer. In all cases, subjects with unexplained arousal reported *negative* [emphasis added] emotions, irrespective of the confederate's mood. (Maslach, 1979, p. 963)

To complicate matters further:

Although subjects with unexplained arousal displayed sociable behaviors while in the presence of the happy confederate, their self-reported mood state was not positive. Their comments imply that their overt behavior was more influenced by social contingencies (i.e., norms of social appropriateness) than was their more private feeling state. (Maslach, 1979, pp. 964–965)

Although Maslach's (1979) study was not a true duplicate of the original experiment, Schachter and Singer fared no better when an actual replication of their work was attempted by Marshall and Zimbardo (1979), who concluded that:

There is no evidence in the data generated by this study to warrant acceptance of the Schachter and Singer (1962) reported demonstration of the interaction of cognitive and physiological determinants of emotion. In particular, there was no instance in which subjects with inadequately explained epinephrine-produced arousal were significantly more susceptible than placebo controls to the induction of affect by exposure to a confederate who modeled euphoric behavior. (p. 980)

If anything, Marshall and Zimbardo

(1979) found that "Whatever arousal treatment differences did exist were likely to suggest more positive affect in this situation for placebo subjects than for epinephrine subjects" (p. 980). And, like Maslach (1979), these experimenters discovered a "relatively negative affective bias, even given the presence of a euphoric confederate," whom the real subject perceived as a fellow subject (Marshall & Zimbardo, 1979, p. 981).

Schachter and Singer (1979) have risen to the challenge. Maslach's (1979) study, they contend, suffered a significant defect in the *timing* of its experimental conditions, so that her subjects experienced—not once but twice—various aspects of physiological arousal *prior to* the emotion-inducing manipulation. Further, the Marshall-Zimbardo (1979) experiment was felt to be anything but an exact replication, because these experimenters took it upon themselves "for no reason we [Schachter and Singer] can fathom" to change the original experimental instructions to subjects. Following additional counterarguments, one is not surprised to read that Schachter and Singer (1979) remain "unconvinced that either the Maslach or the Marshall-Zimbardo experiments demonstrate what is claimed for them" (p. 993).

With both Maslach (1979) and Marshall and Zimbardo (1979) having been afforded "Postscripts" for attempted rebuttal of the Schachter and Singer counterrebuttal of their earlier critiques, this central issue for clinicians—the nature and genesis of emotion—remains a battleground on which further skirmishes can be expected. Evidently these exchanges, while intellectual, can themselves take on an emotional tone, as Marshall and Zimbardo (1979) reveal (and for which, in sporting fashion, they later apologize in the same article): "Schachter and Singer sometimes use their considerable literary talent to misdirect the reader's attention toward inadequately justified conclusions such that what was 'never found' becomes one of the most cited findings in psychology textbooks" (p. 985).

If these arguments sometimes grow heated, well, as Harry Stack Sullivan once said, "above all else, we are all much more human than otherwise."

"Repression"

Investigation of the construct of "repression," another central concept in clinical theory and practice, offers a change of pace. Cast in purely laboratory terms, the debate is considerably more hard-headed and dispassionate—in short, *un*emotional.

The thoroughgoing review of "Investigations of Repression" by Holmes (1974) provides a fine example of the "piggy-back" strategy of research, one experimenter jumping on the next until a cascaded series of studies affords a nice evolution of increasingly refined conceptions of a problem of mutual interest. Interestingly, the story begins in the pages of the *Journal of Experimental Psychology,* a refreshingly ironic note in the study of what is a very clinical theme.

Zeller (1950a) set himself the task of taking a hardheaded look (Zeller, 1950b), at a theoretical concept that has long served as a convenient psychodynamic explanation. His was not only a search for an adequate test of the phenomenon of repression. The job would have been only half complete, he felt, without testing the notion that repression, if such there be, can also be "lifted."

Using nonsense syllables as his stimulus material, recall and relearning performance as the dependent variable, and an interpolated stressful procedure to which the experimental, but not control, groups were subjected as a repression-inducing experience, he found that: (1) such "ego threat" did indeed seem to produce repressionlike results, in that the performance of the stressed groups suffered; (2) the performance decrement subsequently disappeared on further testing when such stress was removed (by appropriate procedural manipulation); and (3) the deleterious effects of ego threat would not necessarily apply generally to performance

as a whole, but seemed to affect primarily the memory for material with which such threat had been associated (Zeller, 1950b, 1951). He was convinced: "Taken together, the results indicate that a phenomenon has been produced which is in most ways analogous to repression proper" (Zeller, 1951, p. 37).

Merrill (1954), however, remained unconvinced, even though he had replicated Zeller's work and obtained comparable results! For him, "The ease with which the task-anxiety effects were reduced raises serious questions as to the appropriateness of considering such experimentally induced effects as analogous to clinical repression" (p. 172).

Others followed in the wake of these efforts, their research confirming some but not all of Zeller's findings. Flavell (1955), for example, concurred that "repression" does take its toll on performance measures, and the decrement disappears when the repressive influence is "lifted" by experimental procedures. Unlike Zeller, however, he found that the effect of ego threat was not selective but generalized, a result obtained in later studies by others as well (Holmes & Schallow, 1969; Holmes, 1972). Nonetheless, the search initiated by Zeller (1950a and b) seemed to suggest that the construct of repression had a good deal of validity.

As Holmes (1974) was to make very clear in his subsequent review, however, there were alternative explanations for the foregoing series of results, as some had pointed out in relation to the Zeller paradigm. A more parsimonious explanation, suggested by Aborn (1953), was that in the case of subjects in the ego-threat condition one might be seeing primarily the effects of set on attentional processes; that is, poor recall on the part of subjects in the experimental group might simply reflect attenuated attention as a function of threat.

Pursuing this general line of research and focusing particularly on subjects' thoughts and feelings at various points during his study, D'Zurilla (1965) hit upon a different notion. He found in his interviews that subjects in his threatened group actually thought about the task *more* rather than less, as the repression hypothesis would have it. It seemed to him, then, that one might be dealing essentially with response competition or interference. As Holmes (1974) points out, having directed attention to similar possibilities earlier (Holmes & Schallow, 1969):

Whether or not it can be concluded that interference caused the performance deficit, it definitely can be concluded that the methodological approach used in previous research of this type on the relationship between ego threat and repression was inadequate because it did not rule out the possible effects of interference. (Holmes, 1974, p. 640)

Even another experiment (Holmes, 1972) intended to disentangle the possible results of interference and repression had not laid the matter completely to rest. Hence in his review Holmes (1974) devoted attention as well to the results of situations involving "naturally occurring ego threat," in contrast to the experimentally manipulated threat of the foregoing experiments. He said, "Overall . . . attentional processes seem to explain more adequately, more parsimoniously, and with more supporting data the clinical observations which generated the concept of repression and which seem to provide its only support" (Holmes, 1974, p. 650).

Eminently fair-minded to the end, he offers a very apt pronouncement on this collective effort by psychologists of various stripes and persuasions trying to untie this Gordian knot:

Notwithstanding the consistent failure of the research to provide support for the theory of repression, because it is impossible to prove the null hypothesis, we are unable to conclude that repression does not exist. Instead, at present we can only conclude that there is no evidence that repression does exist. (Holmes, 1974, p. 650)

This intricate progressive series of laboratory experiments can be seen as a genealogy of research attempts to ferret out and chase down a theoretical construct that clinicians have long invoked with impunity. What matters here is perhaps not so much how veridical the laboratory analogue is with respect to the clinical phenomenon. Even more significant, it seems, is the spectacle of conscientious investigators, each capitalizing on predecessors, painstakingly seeking to validate a construct widely used, if not overworked. The concatenated research effort shows a vigorous quest by clinicians, and nonclinicians as well, in search of clinical "truths."

Diagnosis

A reference previously cited (Perlman, 1980) contains a revealing tabulation of who and what gains attention, if not notoriety, in psychology. Not least among these highly visible people is D. L. Rosenhan, very likely in connection with his study "On Being Sane in Insane Places." Appearing originally in *Science* (Rosenhan, 1973), the article elicited heated pro and con reactions not only in that august journal but in a variety of other sources as well. The editor of the *Journal of Abnormal Psychology,* in fact, saw fit to devote space to five articles on the subject in one issue (Eron, 1975), one a reply by Rosenhan to his critics, after which the controversy continued (Davis, 1976).

Rosenhan had not been the first to study "pseudo-patients." Others before him (Deane, 1961; Goldman et al., 1970) had done so, except that these experimenters were concerned primarily with how it must feel to be a patient. They had, for the purpose, voluntarily assumed the role. Rosenhan's intent was quite different: to see whether normal persons posing as patients would find the ruse detected. The fact that it was not ruffled many professional feathers, the more so in view of his bluntly stated conclusion: "It is clear that we cannot distinguish the sane from the insane in psychiatric hospitals" (Rosenhan, 1973, p. 257).

The basis for this strong statement lay in the finding that his "pseudo-patient" collaborators, when presenting themselves to hospitals with the complaint of hearing voices (saying "empty," "hollow," "thud"), were not only admitted to the respective psychiatric units but diagnosed schizophrenic in 11 cases (and manic-depressive in the twelfth), even though, apart from the alleged presenting symptom, they behaved "normally" throughout their hospitalization. On discharge (following stays of from 7 to 52 days, with a mean of 19), each was labeled as being "in remission."

While Rosenhan's purpose had presumably been innocent, reaction was harsh. To call the Letters to the Editor (1973) a deluge would not be overstating the case. Rosenhan seemed to have found few friends. Or else the self-selected letter writers were not representative of the larger audience. In any case, feelings ran strong, judging from the blunt reactions to the study: "seriously flawed by methodological inadequacies" (p. 356); "the destructive potential of such pseudo-studies" (p. 358); "the conclusions and recommendations . . . miss the central issues" (p. 365). As for Rosenhan himself, he was described as one who "apparently lacks clinical knowledge" (p. 358) and "overlooks some obvious and important conclusions" (p. 362). Other critics charged Rosenhan with methodological flaws, incorrect inferences, or overstatement, even "pseudoscience" (Spitzer, 1975). Rosenhan himself replied with injured innocence, but the study had obviously touched raw nerves, suggesting that clinicians, whether psychiatrists or psychologists, react like normal people when duped. No one called the experiment a "scam," but the furor raised by professionals who felt they were stung could tempt some fearless analyst to interpret the ruckus in such terms.

Psychodynamics aside, this controversy around the general problem of clinical assessment has served the constructive purpose of bringing various issues into sharper focus. Whether informal (Letters to the Editor, 1973) or formal (Weiner, 1975; Spitzer, 1975; Millon, 1975; Crown, 1975; Farber, 1975; Davis, 1976), the critiques represent concerns that were once ground and are now figure in a continuing debate over just how sharp or dull clinical acumen is at this point. The responses are illustrative. Framing his reaction in the context of attribution theory, for example, Weiner (1975) finds the bulk of Rosenhan's criticisms unfounded, but does grant him some credit for having pointed up certain deficiencies in the diagnostic process as a result of which normal people were admitted to psychiatric units and given a corresponding diagnosis. If faking insanity were to become a widespread problem, however, Weiner (1975) is confident that appropriate clinical techniques for its detection would soon be devised.

Spitzer (1975) reacts a good bit more vigorously, feeling that Rosenhan has impugned psychiatric diagnosis with inadequate or misinterpreted evidence. Rosenhan, he insists, not only missed the real points concerning reliability and validity but even beclouded the issue:

I fail to see, and Rosenhan does not even attempt to show, how the reliability of psychiatric diagnoses applied to a population of individuals seeking help is at all relevant to the reliability of psychiatric diagnoses applied to a population of pseudo-patients . . . The two populations are just not the same. (Spitzer, 1975, p. 448)

Millon's (1975) tone is more subdued, though his charges are nonetheless direct. On the one hand, he faults some aspects of the Rosenhan design while indicating how it could have been improved. On the other, he feels some compassion for the diagnosticians who were taken in by the deception, suggesting Rosenhan has treated them too harshly. For Millon:

It would be a more accurate and charitable conclusion to recognize that their [the diagnosticians'] failures were wholly understandable given the situational context, their lack of guile concerning devious motives, and their naive willingness to accept as genuine the discomfort expressed by persons who volunteered hospitalization. (Millon, 1975, p. 458)

Rosenhan (1975) has replied. Taking his lead from the findings of research in perception, he argues that the results of his experiment suggest strongly that psychiatric diagnosis is very context-dependent. Set and setting apparently play a major role in what the diagnostician perceives. Further implicated in this particular experiment, he insists—even terms it the heart of the matter—was the "diagnostic leap" from a single symptom to a diagnosis. Responding to the specific criticisms of his detractors, he remains convinced that present diagnostic procedures and the system they employ not only fall short of the mark but are prey to the kind of faulty diagnosis that can spell significant harm for those mislabeled.

Rosenhan does not intend to throw out the baby with the bath. Indeed he offers some specific suggestions about new diagnostic systems prior to their publication and official acceptance:

First, we should ask that coefficients of agreements between diagnosticians in a variety of settings *commonly* [emphasis in original] reach or exceed .90. . . . Second, we should require that the proven utility of such a system exceed its liabilities for patients. . . . that the diagnoses lead to useful treatments that cannot be implemented without the diagnoses. (Rosenhan, 1975, p. 473)

To Farber (1975) has fallen the unenviable task of trying to render an impartial review of this particular go-around. In his comprehensive and broadly philosophical review, he has attempted to deal fairly with all concerned. On balance, he seems eventually to come down on the side of the critics:

There is ample basis for the view that psychodiagnostic criteria are unnecessarily vague, that clinicians are sometimes, perhaps even frequently, diagnostically unskilled and careless, and that hospital treatment can be dismal. But even bad practice and bad theoretical conceptualizations ought not to be discarded on illegitimate grounds, lest good practice and good theory be abandoned for those same reasons. (Farber, 1975, pp. 619–620)

Perhaps when the dust settles somewhat in such clinical storms, the house can be put in order more calmly. More dispassionate pieces, such as that by Davis (1976), seem intended to restore perspective. His interest is in the more frankly technical aspects of the diagnostic process. Casting his analysis in a Bayesian framework, he sees the base rate problem as a crucial one. His concern is with such matters as appropriate reference groups and probability estimates. He stresses one particularly significant element:

The willingness of a diagnostician to assign a diagnostic label ought to be a function not of simply picking the most probable category, but of utilities attached to the two types of error (or of correctness) . . . of either turning away a schizophrenic from the hospital or of admitting a sane person. It is likely that, as Rosenhan (1973, p. 252) suggests, the bias of hospital staff is toward Type II error, calling a sane person schizophrenic, while many who were shocked by the study would prefer to reduce such errors even at the cost of increased Type I error because they are convinced either of the nonexistence of schizophrenia or of the harmfulness of hospitals. (Davis, 1976, p. 421)

The whole topic is far from resolved and still manages to provoke further ire, but that is a hopeful sign, not a basis for regret. At the very least it promises to awaken dormant issues and clarify fuzzy ones. If a bit more blood gets spilled in the process, that presumably shows the clinical corpus is alive and well.

Replication

If there is one thing for which clinicians most envy their experimental colleagues, it may well be the seeming ease with which the work of the latter lends itself to replication. It seems nice to be able to specify that x volts were delivered to the grid, that a tachistoscopic slide was exposed for y milliseconds, or that the trough-to-peak amplitude of an average evoked response was z. Pity the poor clinician who so much as wants to describe, under the Procedure section of his or her journal article, how he or she treated multiple sclerosis patients therapeutically, so that others can attempt to replicate the study. It is especially noteworthy, then, when an animal psychologist conducting rigorous research on problems of clinical interest finds that dramatic results, once achieved, resist replication.

That has been Neal Miller's headache, and he has fought with himself to cure it. His painstaking quest for clues to the problem is in itself an object lesson for clinicians with respect to the diagnostic process. Fortunately, Miller has studiously chronicled his efforts (Miller & Dworkin, 1974) and generously shared them with the rest of us. His analysis of the dilemma posed by the inability to replicate initial success in instrumental learning of visceral responses is therefore instructive.

Working with DiCara and Banuazizi (DiCara & Miller, 1968; Miller & Banuazizi, 1968), Miller had been able not only to shape increases and decreases in the heart rates of rats through instrumental learning but even to show that such changes could be achieved independently of such other autonomic responses as intestinal contraction or relaxation. The significance of these accomplishments could hardly escape clinicians confronted with clients whose medical examinations had suggested that such symptoms as tachycardia or gastrointestinal disorders had a psychogenic basis. Yet several years later Miller and Dworkin were suffering unforeseen discouragement in trying to replicate these earlier efforts. In fact, when Dworkin (Miller & Dworkin, 1977) reviewed successive heart rate studies in their laboratory, he noted a progressive downward trend, so that, with the exception of two studies carried out successfully in other laboratories, difficulties in replication loomed large. How to account for these originally clinically promising, now discouraging, results?

The systematic effort to unravel the mystery can hearten clinicians whose once promising treatment methods turn out eventually to be less than effective. In successive order, Miller and Dworkin (1977) investigated the following possibilities, among others: (1) perhaps the inadvertent omission in later studies of a drug used originally to relieve possible pain at electrode implantation sites could have been responsible; (2) something might have changed over time in the strain of rat used in the series of experiments; (3) the method by which rats were respirated while curarized might have been the answer; (4) however unlikely it might seem, perhaps the fact that an epidemic of bedbugs, subsequently sprayed by coincidence in the laboratory at the time of the successful studies, could have been a factor; (5) indeed Miller and Dworkin even wondered whether those involved in the initial studies had been victims of mass hallucination! In doggedly methodical fashion Miller and his colleagues have explored yet other possibilities as they occurred to them, eliminating each in turn in a continuing search for ever newer leads, however outlandish any might appear. Their elaborate account is a model of exhaustive analysis, one that clinicians might emulate in their own perplexing study of a host of conundrums implicit in the behavior of their own subjects, whether in theory, in practice, or in research.

These indefatigable investigators say it well:

Although greatly puzzled and disappointed, we thought that in learning what was wrong and how to correct it we might discover something that would help us to improve human visceral learning and perhaps would even have therapeutic value. Thus, our difficulties could turn out to be a disguised opportunity if we only had the wit to comprehend what they were telling us. (Miller & Dworkin, 1974, p. 313)

Patience is indeed a virtue.

Conflict Resolution

Not too many psychodynamically oriented clinicians, it seems, make a habit of reading the literature in experimental psychology (and vice versa). Howard Shevrin obviously does. As much at home in the laboratory as in the clinic, it is understandable that his work has drawn attention at international symposia (Shevrin, 1978, 1979). Like Shakow, he has pursued a line of research exhaustively, in this case investigation of unconscious mental processes.

In a continuing series of interlocking studies on the evoked potential, Shevrin and his colleagues (e.g., Shevrin & Luborsky, 1961; Shevrin & Fritzler, 1968; Shevrin, Smith, & Fritzler, 1971) have used special laboratory techniques in the study of clinical phenomena and commonly accepted explanatory constructs. Their work provides an interface between clinical and experimental psychology in that "behavior cannot be understood without taking conscious experience into account and that conscious experience cannot be fully understood without taking unconscious psychological processes into account" (Shevrin & Dickman, 1980, p. 432).

Shevrin's modus operandi is to study evoked potentials under a variety of circumstances to shed additional light on unconscious mental processes. He and his colleagues have used electrophysiological evidence as their data base. They see no inevitable conflict between the concept of "unconscious mental processes" and the analysis of human behavior in the tradition of experimental psychology. If anything, a current

paper by members of this group (Shevrin & Dickman, 1980) suggests that these unconscious processes provide an interface between clinically and experimentally oriented conceptions of personality and behavior.

Shevrin and his collaborators are thoroughly cognizant of developments in the experimental camp, such as Broadbent's (1958) filter theory of attention, Treisman's (1964) model of perceptual processing, the theory of attention proposed by Deutsch and Deutsch (1963), Neisser's (1967) cognitively oriented conception, Posner's (1973) model, or Sternberg's (1975) research on memory in visual processing. Rather than regarding such multifaceted laboratory-based models as at odds with psychodynamic conceptions, Shevrin actually finds them quite congenial. All of them, for example, posit a phase of cognitive activity occurring outside awareness. Further, each of the theorists assumes that the processes involved "interact with and influence ongoing and subsequent conscious psychological processes, at the very least insofar as they determine what enters consciousness" (Shevrin & Dickman, 1980, pp. 425–426). Even more significantly, each conceives of the mental processes outside awareness as cognitively different from those occurring consciously.

Their review of research in the area of subliminal perception leaves Shevrin and Dickman (1980) no less hopeful. Some leading models are canvassed, those of Klein and Holt (1960), Spence (Spence, 1961; Spence & Smith, 1977), Fisher (1956), and Dixon (1971). And once more the reviewers conclude that, as with the theories of attention, the findings in the area of subliminal perception point to the conclusion that "A great deal of complex cognitive activity can go on without benefit of consciousness" (Shevrin & Dickman, 1980, p. 430), activity different in kind from that constituting conscious cognitive processes.

So too in the areas of retinal image stabilization, binocular rivalry, and backward masking—all mainstays among research paradigms in the experimentalist's laboratory—Shevrin and his colleagues find empirical support for their conviction that "The assumption of unconscious psychological processes appears to be a conceptual necessity in a variety of models . . ." (Shevrin & Dickman, 1980, p. 432). This is not to say that no differences remain. As they note, none of the foregoing theories countenances the notion of percepts stored in long-term memory acting on ongoing conscious processes without entering awareness, and long after the original perception. Such remaining differences aside, Shevrin and Dickman (1980) see the gap as much more bridgeable than commonly supposed: "The laboratory and the consulting room do seem to be sharing at least a common wall which may in fact turn out to have a door in it" (p. 432).

In short, the scenario, as Shevrin and his colleagues would have it, is not a divisive struggle between warring camps but, properly understood, a Camp David meeting of minds, so that while differences continue to be explored, the protagonists can live in amity.

FUTURE DIRECTIONS

Clinical psychology has begun to poke its nose under many a tent. Whether this inquisitive bent will fritter away energies that could be better concentrated can be argued; that clinicians are moving in all kinds of directions cannot. At this stage they find themselves tempted to investigate at least a dozen areas, each of which is increasingly attracting followers. Some may prove passing fancies, others blind alleys; all await the discerning analysis that systematic research can provide.

Some current representative areas will be noted briefly in turn, their characteristic research approaches serving to illustrate the range of problems and methods that must interest the clinician looking for new languages into which to translate questions and new approaches that might deliver answers.

Where more space is devoted to several of the areas, they are not selected as being more important but as illustrative of the struggle for new knowledge.

Sleep and Dreaming

On dream interpretation Freud (1938) had plenty to say. Lesser men have since parroted his thoughts without his keenly inquisitive mind and restless curiosity. Fortunately, in what seems a vast arena for further activity, new work is in progress. With Aserinsky and Kleitman (1953) having drawn particular attention to rapid eye movements during sleep, and with technological advances permitting delineation of sleep's several stages, the laboratory has proved an exciting bedroom. The data now become not the warmed-over vignettes patients bring their therapists of dreams experienced between visits but rather the material collected "live" in the laboratory. Sleep can be monitored precisely and dreams recorded moments after they end. With benefit of the electroencephalograph, the electrooculograph, and the electromyograph, the art of speculating, however creatively, about dream fragments is yielding to the scientist's urge to control conditions, manipulate variables, and collect cleaner and more complete data.

Altered States of Consciousness

Hypnosis has second cousins, several of them having recently emerged from relative obscurity to become active members of the research family. Conveniently classed under the now popular term "altered states of consciousness" (ASC) are several that have earned all manner of notice, meditative and hallucinogenic states among them. The laboratory research of Wallace and Benson (1972) had been instrumental in calling attention to the former; psychotomimetic drugs have illustrated the clinical relevance of the latter.

The area still retains an aura of quasi-scientific sorties "into the unknown." Yet some reputable investigators are demonstrating that research here can be not only sound but unique, offering access to varying levels of consciousness not as readily tapped by other modes of experimentation.

Nonverbal Communication, Kinesics, and Proxemics

Just as "altered states of consciousness" conveniently embrace a variety of conditions, so does "nonverbal communication" encompass a range of studies dealing with the capacity of organisms for sending pointed messages without benefit of words. Hall (1959) had titled his book well—"The Silent Language." One's grandmother would hasten to exclaim that she has always said "actions speak louder than words," but systematic research in this nonverbal domain has been long in coming. The recent wave should be sweeping the clinical field, which characteristically deals with many an unspoken message.

In his studies of kinesics, for example, Birdwhistell (1970) suggests that if clinicians feel the mother–child relationship is as crucial as they imply, they might well pay less attention to what mothers say to their children and more to what they *do* with them. As mundane a chore as diapering a baby, he points out, provides an unspoken, yet very telling, picture of this mother-child relationship when filmed and later subjected to a frame-by-frame analysis.

If exciting possibilities exist in the area of kinesics, the clinician is no less indebted to research in proxemics, systematic study of the use of space, where equally intriguing clinical aspects are being discovered by imaginative and inventive researchers. The work of Sommer (1969) is representative of thoughtful applications for the clinician. Indeed, taking account of these developments on a more comprehensive level, investigators in the relatively young field of "environmental psychology" are offering the working cli-

nician data that can at the very least challenge if not upset accepted notions.

Pupillometrics

A form of nonverbal communication in itself, this area, aptly termed "pupillometrics," entails something special in that its expression is based in autonomic rather than skeletomuscular processes. For, as Hess (1965) discovered, the size of one's pupil is a function not only of the amount of light falling on the eye but of other things as well—interest, apprehension, awe, cognitive processes, and others.

Of special appeal here is the objectively measurable dependent variable—pupil size—offered by the method that, under various laboratory procedures, permits equally good control of the independent variable. Interestingly, the findings that accrue to this relatively recent modus operandi can interest experimental psychologists and clinicians alike. Kahneman and his colleagues, for instance, find it a ready-made mode of indexing information-processing and cognitive operations (e.g., Kahneman & Beatty, 1966). Imaginative clinicians should be able to see equally fruitful possibilities in their own domain.

The research possibilities seem limitless. So that they do not appear to have been overlooked, since space does not permit discussing them, it is fitting to note in passing some very current areas deserving of clinical research, among them: (1) the psychology of women, by challenging some traditionally chauvinistic theoretical conceptions; (2) the singular clinical problems encountered as a result of surgical transplant operations; (3) the related issues found in such uniquely personal areas as gender identity and transsexualism; (4) the laboratory research (e.g., Ullman et al., 1973) on parapsychological phenomena; (5) the frankly clinical problems met in such areas as forensic psychology.

While the foregoing represent the widening horizons of clinical practitioners and theorists, other areas can be examined in more detail to convey the flavor of research in progress.

Hypnosis, Grist for Two Mills— Of Theories and Models

Whether hypnosis belongs properly in the realm of clinical psychology or not is, as players of sports would have it, a judgment call. At least one experimental psychologist is not about to give it up readily. For Hilgard (1977), hypnotic phenomena are not only relevant for abnormal psychology but indeed equally useful in understanding normal human behavior, and hence entitled to a place alongside perception, motivation, learning, and the other areas within the province of general psychology.

With all due respect to Hull's (1933) reservations on the subject, particularly with reference to the concept of dissociation, Hilgard (1977) has enunciated a "neodissociation" interpretation aimed at explicating how, under special circumstances, thought and action can be described as dissociated from conscious experience. Recognizing that consciousness has two modes, a receptive one and an active one, he views "divided consciousness" as reflecting both:

On one hand, memories may be split apart, so that reflection on experiences registered in the first mode [the receptive one] may be disrupted; on the other hand, the voluntary and involuntary controls systems may be reversed through dissociation, so that an activity that is usually involuntary may be brought under voluntary control. (Hilgard, 1977, p. 14)

Adopting the term "hidden observer" as a convenient label, not as a "homunculus lurking in the shadows of the conscious person" (p. 188), he uses the metaphor to describe some unique phenomena found in laboratory studies. In a cold pressor experiment, subjects in the normal waking state showed the typical curve of increasing pain report on immersion of the hand and forearm in ice water. Likewise, as shown in many previous studies, subjects reported verbally the reduced sense of pain in the hypnotic condition. An added feature brought to light a significant development. By means of a key-pressing device, the subject's other arm was to report without awareness (as in automatic writing) the degree of pain experienced covertly. The findings, on a scale of zero (no pain) to 10 (severe pain), proved revealing:

While she was overtly reporting "0," the hand out of awareness was simultaneously writing scale values for increasing pain—2, 5, 7, 8, 9. The "hidden observer" was reporting essentially normal pain while the hypnotized part of her was feeling no pain at all! (Hilgard, 1977, p. 189)

Hilgard would not go so far as to declare, as some practising hypnotists suggest, that it is thus feasible to "talk to the unconscious" directly by appropriate hypnotic devices. His systematic program of research on hypnotic phenomena does lead him, however, to conclude that findings in this area have both significant theoretical implications for cognitive psychology and treatment leads for clinicians. With respect to the former, for example, the disparity between the overt and covert reports of subjects in the foregoing type of experiment provides evidence for dissociation between two information-processing systems, suggesting parallel processing. One could speculate on the role of hemispheric laterality in this connection, though this is a point Hilgard hesitates to press too hard at this stage.

It is in its clinical implications that Hilgard sees dissociation as having a special significance. As he puts it:

In automatic writing or hypnosis, when a dissociated part of consciousness has been uncovered, the amnesic barrier is broken, and it is possible to converse *directly with the dissociated con-*

sciousness [emphasis in original]. . . . When a multiple personality surfaces and is engaged in conversation, or a hidden observer is uncovered in the laboratory, the dissociated parts talk normally, without either the distortions of primary process thinking or archaic symbols. (Hilgard, 1977, p. 249)

The fact that a respected experimental psychologist finds, in what is generally regarded a somewhat esoteric area, research opportunities for clinical psychology and for psychology in general can only be heartening for all concerned.

A clinical psychologist has found hypnosis equally fruitful for a somewhat different purpose.[1] For Blum it has long served as fertile soil on which to build a "model of the mind," by now more than 20 years in the making and remaking. His original construction, entitled just that (Blum, 1961), was already an impressive attempt at model building; his latest version, presented with Barbour (Blum & Barbour, 1979), is yet more elaborate. Throughout all of this, a systematic program of research in hypnosis has served for Blum and his collaborators as the medium for enlarging our understanding of perceptual, cognitive, affective, and behavioral processes.

The work of Blum and his group is especially significant in that it attempts to submit psychodynamic concepts to the kind of close scrutiny possible when analogues are subjected to experimental examination. Like Hilgard, these investigators see in hypnosis a special opportunity to study, under carefully controlled conditions, aspects of human thought, feeling, and action uniquely accessible through this medium. The result of their most recent work is particularly illuminating.

With "selective inattention" as the focus of three interrelated studies, the investigators use the term as subsuming "those phenomena whose *primary function* is the *active blocking or attenuation of partially processed contents en route to conscious expression* [emphasis in original]" (Blum & Barbour, 1979, p. 184). As they point out, it has been selective *attention* that has primarily concerned a variety of investigators—Broadbent (1958), Treisman (1969), Deutsch and Deutsch (1963)—though some are not unmindful of the aspect of inattention (Neisser, 1967; Bower, 1972; Bjork, 1972). The present trio of experiments was designed by Blum and Barbour (1979) to enlarge present knowledge of inhibitory action in relation to anxiety-linked stimuli. Experiments 1 and 2, in which hypnotic programming was used, employed projective test material and anagrams respectively as target stimuli; Experiment 3 served as a nonhypnotic replication of Experiment 2, again using the material of a projective test (Blum's Blacky Pictures, 1950).

The overall research strategy has, its proponents claim, marked advantages. It allows a distinctly clinical problem to be studied under rigorous laboratory conditions (presentation of stimuli being on the order of milliseconds). It permits control over such ordinarily intractable variables as anxiety, pleasure, and cognitive arousal. It disavows the influence of such confounding elements as experimental demand characteristics and fatigue (through posthypnotic relaxation instructions following sets of trials). And it gets around the possibility of response suppression that had hounded investigators as an alternative explanation in studies of perceptual defense. On the positive side, its use of response latency as a measure provides a reliable and sensitive index of inhibitory processes, permitting a more fine-grained analysis of the latter than has hitherto been possible, as study of the same subjects across a variety of conditions within a task has yielded intraindividual comparisons.

---

[1]While the work of Blum and his colleagues is cited here for illustrative purposes, a representative series of views on the applicability of hypnosis to the study of psychological problems is contained in a special issue of the *Journal of Abnormal Psychology,* 1979, **88,** No. 5.

One product of this intensive pursuit of inhibitory phenomena is the comprehensive latest version of the conceptual model Blum and Barbour (1979) offer as "a revised formulation of stages of amplification and attenuation of content signals en route to representation in consciousness" (p. 221). They are well aware of other possible explanations associated with the work of experimental psychologists—conditioned avoidance, for one, interference, for another—but find neither a compelling alternative to their own conception. Whatever the merits of this "long-term evolution of a model of the mind," this painstaking effort may well make its greatest contribution in that it "seeks to provide a conceptual framework for integrating psychodynamic and experimental approaches in psychology" (Blum & Barbour, 1979, p. 221). No small task, but one Blum has been working at long, hard, and effectively.

Simulation—in the Field, at the Laboratory, on the Computer

Clinical phenomena being as elusive as they are, it is fortunate that investigators can be found converging on them from all directions, setting up natural situations, conducting laboratory experiments, buying time on the computer. Some recent attempts serve as cases in point.

One has a double-barreled character, conducting initial tests of a hypothesis in the natural setting, and subsequently studying the same phenomenon in the laboratory, the sequence employed by Dutton and Aron (1974) in investigating the presumed relationship between heightened sexual attraction and strong emotion. Whereas earlier studies (Barclay & Haber, 1965; Barclay, 1969) had demonstrated a link between aggression and sexual arousal, something to which Freud (1938) had alluded long before, Dutton and Aron (1974) were interested in the relationship between sexual arousal and another strong emotion—fear. Specifically,

their study was intended "to test the notion that an attractive female is seen as more attractive by males who encounter her while they experience a strong emotion (fear) than by males not experiencing a strong emotion" (p. 511).

What makes their experimental approach intriguing is the inventiveness they bring to field studies. Creating a fear-arousing condition for their experimental group found Dutton and Aron (1974) running the experiment in the middle of a wooden bridge suspended from cables stretching across the Capilano River in British Columbia, a bridge with "a tendency to tilt, sway, and wobble . . . very low handrails . . . and a 230-foot drop to rocks and shallow rapids below" (p. 511). By contrast, the bridge for control group subjects was a solid affair of heavy cedar only 10 feet above "a small, shallow rivulet" (p. 511). Methodological details were handled with care. Interviewers remained unaware of the hypothesis being tested, suitable checks on arousal were employed, behavioral data supplemented projective material, and yet other precautions were built into the design. Even then the experimenters had second thoughts about accepting the results as confirming the hypothesis, and thus conducted a follow-up study in the natural setting by way of ruling out alternative explanations for the findings.

With this second study having borne out the results of the first, they resorted to yet a third experiment, this time in a laboratory setting employing an analogous situation, one intended to deal with any residual reservations. Only when this latter study likewise confirmed the hypothesis were they willing to rest their case, but not without trying to fit the findings into the array of relevant theories, some of which could accommodate the results, others of which could not. What matters here is less the nature of what was discovered and more the character of the search these two investigators conducted. Were more clinical research pursued with such relentless concern for touching all the bases, more hits would doubtless be scored.

Yet many paths lead to Rome. Granted, there is merit in trying to study phenomena in as "real" a form as possible. With a forthright hankering for simulation procedures, however, Colby (1976), for one, is not about to offer apologies on that account. If anything, he fully advocates an approach that is felt to have served other sciences well: "In sum, the general methodology of computer simulation of thought processes does not differ in principle from theory construction and testing in other sciences, and the approach is justified by its success in those sciences" (Colby, 1976, p. 855).

With his "shame-humiliation theory" of paranoid processes as a case in point, Colby (1976) argues that a computer simulation model offers significant leads to the clearer understanding and more effective management and treatment of a psychopathological process. Viewing such an experimental exploration as more than ad hoc in character, he would argue that it "potentially contributes new empirical content to existing knowledge" (Colby, 1976, p. 854). That he is actively committed to exploring the possibilities is evident in his book on "Artificial Paranoia" (1975).

The simulation technique, as summarized elsewhere (Blackmore, 1972, p. 230), is straightforward:

1. Formulate the problem and collect the necessary data.
2. Formulate the mathematical model.
3. Write and debug the computer code.
4. Check model results against real data under known conditions to validate the model. Modify the model as necessary to make calculated and observed results correspond.
5. Use the validated model to make predictions about the system's behavior in response to those inputs of interest.

But if programming machines to simulate people intrigues some, Blum is no less concerned with programming people to simulate machines. In a piece just so entitled (Blum, 1963) he confesses that, far from narrowing his outlook, an interest in simulation has actually broadened it:

In my own case, thinking of the human mind in systems terms has not only been a source of liberation from the value-laden language of psychoanalysis to which I had been accustomed, but also has opened my eyes to new kinds of experimental approaches. Even the rich, complicated psychodynamics of personality—defenses, primary process, and the rest—suddenly become susceptible to direct, controlled laboratory pursuit with the advent of a systematic conceptual framework, an impersonal language which cuts across areas of psychology, and a powerful technique like hypnosis to manipulate crucial variables in precise manner. (pp. 156–157)

That perhaps states the case as well as it can be stated.

Biofeedback

Anyone looking for contributions that are experimental in a dual sense—temporarily on trial, for one, and associated with laboratory settings, for another—will have found them in biofeedback. In simplest form, the term "refers to a group of experimental procedures in which an external sensor is used to provide the organism with an indication of the state of a bodily process, usually in an attempt to effect a change in the measured quantity" (Schwartz & Beatty, 1977, p. 1). The array of problems toward which the technique has been directed includes such diverse affairs as control of visceral functions, management of hypertension, cardiovascular control, temperature regulation, sexual functioning, selective brain wave production, and management of tension and migraine headaches.

Clinical in nature as these areas are, it is again an experimental psychologist who has done much of the pioneering work. Though his initial interest arises out of research on rats (Miller, 1969), Miller has taken progressively greater interest in the potentialities for treatment of various types of human dysfunction afforded by this new modality. Indeed his overview of the field, written with Dworkin (Miller & Dworkin, 1977), is directly concerned with the therapeutic applications of biofeedback.

The authors' caveats are as instructive as their enthusiasm is contagious. Attention is directed, for example, to the base rate problem. Since the human body has an exquisite capacity for self-repair, Miller and Dworkin (1977) argue, the success of biofeedback treatment must be evaluated against the rate of spontaneous recovery on the one hand, and alternative treatment possibilities on the other. Further, since many of the symptoms with which biofeedback is associated are themselves characterized by periodic fluctuations and remission, patients tend to come for treatment when feeling particularly bad and leave soon after feeling good. In terms of regression toward the mean, the double selection factor is biased in favor of improvement; hence the need for follow-up studies.

Miller and Dworkin (1977) have further cogent observations for clinical investigators. For one, placebo effects can be very strong in an area in which enthusiastic claims have been made and popularized accounts presented, the more so when the apparatus is impressive and the effects tangible. Nor is this treatment modality without its drawbacks. Its ultimate success rests not on laboratory results but on the generalization of these effects to the real life situations that may well have bred the symptoms in the first place. For that matter, Miller and Dworkin (1977) point out, the effects are not inevitably positive; one could wonder about whether preoccupation with techniques for managing a visceral or vascular response might not develop into a neurotic concern in itself.

Despite such precautions, it is obvious that Miller and Dworkin (1977) share the enthusiasm of those intrigued with the possibilities

for clinical research and treatment in an area where these investigators feel that "the evidence is strong enough to justify, but weak enough to require, the performance of more rigorously controlled studies" (p. 141).

It is only fitting to contrast the foregoing with the perspective of one who is not only not an animal psychologist but also emphasizes the cognitive factors in all of this. Lazarus' (1977) concern is less with the technicalities of instrumental learning and more with emotional processes and their role in human adaptation, a context in which mediating cognitive appraisals have a large part to play as people cope with events. For him, the encouraging prospect is that "the biofeedback laboratory seems to offer excellent opportunities to add to our knowledge of the mechanisms of self-regulation, especially the intrapsychic ones, and, indeed, this constitutes one of psychology's most important difficult issues" (Lazarus, 1977, p. 85).

Some of the principal proponents temper their enthusiasm with well-taken reservations. The comprehensive review by Shapiro and Surwit (1976), for example, contains as many words of caution as notes of optimism. Especially with respect to the technique's clinical applications, these authors see a variety of limitations—questions of economy, when the considerable investment of time and energy required in biofeedback must compete with the ease of taking a pill; motivational problems with types of patients known not to take even their medication regularly; questions of whether results obtained originally with intelligent, motivated, high socioeconomic status patients will be found with less favored patients as well.

Both Schwartz (1973) and Shapiro and Surwit (1976) point to technical issues needing clarification, the former referring to questions of mediation and specificity, the latter stressing the distinction between the instrumental model involved in reinforcement and the informational model of biofeedback. Of more directly clinical relevance, however, are their prescriptions. Schwartz (1973) urges a combined behavioral-biological approach with due respect for biological, cognitive, and environmental constraints. Shapiro and Surwit (1976) stress that "The need for medical participation in any biofeedback case is both an ethical and legal responsibility of the psychological practitioner" (p. 104).

This new field has drawn the attention of both laboratory scientists interested in the technical and theoretical implications for behavior change and clinicians sensing the arrival of a new modality for treating patients with certain problems. Whether it will eventually prove to satisfy one, both, or none of the above remains to be seen.

Cerebral Lateralization

Some topics burst upon the scene in grand style, being quickly embraced by researchers of many stripes in the belief that breakthroughs may be at hand. "Hemispheric laterality," as current parlance has it, is one. Interest in the area springs from several sources. One branch is eminently respectable in the orthodox sense; such investigators as Sperry (1967) and Gazzaniga (1970) have highlighted for the scientific community the pitiful struggles of "split-brain" patients when confronted with special laboratory tasks. At the same time, Ornstein (1977) has made the problem come alive for the less laboratory-oriented. If his writings have been essentially discursive, perhaps popularizing the subject, they have certainly attracted attention to an area that clearly warrants attention. Meanwhile, with his broadly philosophical treatise, Jaynes (1977) has brought the notion of a "bicameral mind" to an even wider audience.

The extent to which clinical investigators are attempting to mine this new field is significant, whether in terms of exploratory research, theoretical concepts, or practical applications. With split-brain patients, fortunately a fairly rare breed, given the unique difficulties found to follow cutting of the corpus callosum, attention has focused on lateralization of function in normal persons as well as in those with pathological conditions. On the one hand, investigators have sought, almost overzealously, to delineate processes associated with one hemisphere or the other, seeming impatient to arrive at a dichotomous list of attributes. Though some have cautioned that such neat partitioning is not only simplistic but actually misleading, the right-left assigners persist.

Meanwhile others are more concerned with formulating and testing hypotheses concerning the relationship between hemispheric laterality and psychopathology. Gur is one of them, her concern with cerebral activation and hemispheric dysfunction having recently centered on the investigations of such aspects in schizophrenia. A recent study (Gur, 1978) is illustrative, dealing as it does with investigation of functional brain asymmetry in schizophrenic subjects.

In a first experiment, tachistoscopically presented tasks served to measure verbal and spatial information processing in the two hemispheres; a second study used lateral movements to index contralateral hemispheric activation. Results of the combined studies implicated the left hemisphere in the schizophrenic subjects, suggesting not only dysfunction in this hemisphere but overactivation as well. Cautious in her interpretation, Gur (1978) suggested several possibilities. One might conclude that in schizophrenia the very hemisphere that is dysfunctional is the one that is overactivated. Alternatively, she suggests, it may be that the hemispheric dysfunction is actually the *result* of this overactivation.

Cautioning that more etiologically oriented studies are actually needed to determine the direction of causality, Gur (1978) offers some intriguing speculations about treatment implications:

The most reasonable course of psychological intervention should concentrate initially on ameliorating the left hemisphere dysfunction and then encouraging some measure of shift toward right hemsiphericity. Indeed, a number of psychoanalytically oriented treatment approaches that were found to be most effective in the treatment of schizophrenia (Karon & VandenBos, 1972) have recommended the approach of initial concentration on the thought disorder followed by a more insight-oriented stance. (Gur, 1978, p. 236)

With (1) a reasonably well controlled experimental investigation of (2) neuropsychological correlates in (3) a psychopathological disorder having led to (4) plausible speculations about treatment, this researcher seems to have tried to do it the honest way. Whether the now very trendy study of cerebral lateralization that is being launched in diverse quarters will lead to ever more promising clues for clinical theory and practice, or whether it will prove to have been a beguiling will-o-the-wisp, remains to be seen. At the moment there is grist for many a mill—experimental, physiological, clinical.

Clinical Technology

Though its subject matter is shot through with such protean stuff as "the unconscious," personality traits, and repressed wishes, one could not have expected even the clinical area to remain untouched by the technological age. It hasn't. If the analyst's couch still remains pretty much just that, it may simply be because no one has built a better one. Elsewhere, however, some changes have been made.

Experimental and physiological psychologists have long depended on their brass instruments. Since the introduction of Mowrer's (1938) pad-and-bell approach to the treatment of enuresis, at least some clinicians have adopted apparatus more complicated than their test kits. Now, largely under the impetus of the behavioral movement, clinical psychology has been inundated with gadgetry of a Rube Goldberg character. Value judgments aside, the equipment has come to include everything from devices to reinforce children for going to the "pottie" (Cheney, 1973) to electrifiable floors to encourage autistic youngsters to make contact with other human beings (Lovaas et al., 1965). The apparatus can be as simple as a rubber band for snapping one's wrist as punishment for obsessive thoughts, or as complex as electronic systems for telemmetering the wanderings of potentially explosive epileptics (Delgado, 1973). Fortunately, Schwitzgebel (1976) has conveniently supplied periodic inventories of the assortment of devices in current use, a surprising variety appearing in work of a clinical nature. If some—the so-called "cattle prod," for example—have earlier raised an Orwellian specter, the less controversial may have brought the possibility of getting a handle on what might otherwise have remained intractable problems.

Some of the current gadgetry has introduced an element of quantification previously lacking. Earlier cigarette smokers tried to kick the habit by achieving a clearer understanding of the origin and nature of their "oral dependent" needs. Today's addict may well find himself equipped by his research-oriented therapist with an unusual cigarette case that not only monitors his consumption but indeed regulates it, dispensing the next smoke only when its preprogrammed mechanism says it should (Azrin & Powell, 1973). Among other ills clinicians are asked to treat, stuttering, hyperactivity, sexual deviations, and test anxiety have also invited technological intervention.

It is not surprising that the area of assessment as well as that of treatment has been heir to gadgetry. As Klett and Pumroy (1971) point out in their review of automated procedures, such equipment as TAPAC (the Totally Automated Psychological Assessment Console) makes it possible to assess performance in areas ranging from short-term aural memory, through paired associates and reaction time, to general intelligence. Nor are projective tests excluded, several of them in turn having their automated counterparts. Even the interview has not escaped; the computer stands ready to conduct one in Rogerian fashion, if needed.

Recognizing fully the misgivings that have been expressed about some of these trends, Klett and Pumroy (1971) have nevertheless concluded:

In all fairness to those engaged in this work, it must be said that the demands of computer programming have probably forced psychologists to think harder and in more concrete terms about what they are doing in an assessment procedure than they ever had before. The programming process has great heuristic value. Every rule must be objective and unambiguous, and the logic must be flawless (Klett and Pumroy, 1971, p. 38).

If these products of technology make today's clinician seem as much engineer as psychologist, that, it seems, is one of today's facts of life.

CONTINUING DIALOGUE

Thesis, Antithesis, Synthesis

One might wish that clinical instrumentalities—concepts, constructs, theories—could be subjected to empirical test, found valid, invalid, or quasi-valid, and thus kept, discarded, or modified. As Meehl (1970) and Rapoport (1968) long since suggested in connection with psychoanalytic theory, the consummation remains devoutly to be wished. Some have tried, though not without some travail, as the following representative imbroglio attests.

The title of his article signals his position—"Psychoanalytic Theory: The Reports of My Death Are Greatly Exaggerated"—as Silverman (1976) reports with satisfaction the results of two independent research programs that leave him convinced that the widely accepted relationship between psychopathology and unconscious sexual and aggressive impulses is indeed a reality. Citing details of the two programs, one at New York University and the other at Michigan State, he stresses the fact that they came at the problem from different directions. Where

the former resorted to subliminal presentation of wish-related stimuli, the latter used hypnotic procedures. Yet the results in both cases substantiated the posited relationship between psychopathology and conflict on the one hand, and unconscious libidinal and aggressive wishes on the other. Thus Silverman (1976) takes special comfort from the fact that one has here "an instance of theory validation by convergent operations" (p. 634).

While the latter piece had not yet been available when a very skeptical Eysenck (1972) took issue with others of Silverman's persuasion, Eysenck made it very clear that an extensive treatise by Kline (1972) had left him quite unconvinced. Kline's survey of research on psychoanalytic theory purported to have marshaled a variety of experimental evidence on the side of Freud. Kline's allegedly partisan interpretation clearly rankled Eysenck, however. Not only had the latter's own research failed to replicate studies cited by Kline; in some cases it had actually yielded opposite results. Further, declared Eysenck, some of the findings offered by Kline in support of Freudian theory were much more accurately and parsimoniously explained by theories growing out of traditional research in general experimental psychology (Walker, 1958; Kleinsmith & Kaplan, 1963, 1964).

With characteristic bluntness, Eysenck concluded that in defense of Freudian theory Kline (1972) had made not only a bad case but in some respects an unconscionable one: "In other words, you make a prediction from Freudian theory, and use test X to verify the deductions made. If this works out, then you accept the test as valid; if it does not, you do not reject the theory—you reject the test!" (p. 266).

One suspects that Eysenck might even be more charitable toward Meehl's honest gut feeling that psychoanalytic theory has a lot going for it. For, when challenged by a colleague (Bouchard) for a seeming inconsistency between expressing the latter sentiment and yet at the same time insisting that a theory lend itself to falsifiability, Meehl (1978) replies with disarming candor:

I do have a soft spot in my heart (Minnesota colleagues would probably say in my head) for psychoanalysis. So, the most honest and straightforward way to deal with Bouchard's complaint might be simply to admit that the evidence on Freud is inadequate and that Bouchard and I are simply betting on different horses. (p. 829)

Anyone still doubting that Meehl means what he says can gasp once more: "I would take Freud's clinical observations over most people's *t* tests any time!" (Meehl, 1978, p. 817).

Heretical Speculation, Iconoclasm, and Sobering Thoughts

In this same brash but delightful essay, Meehl (1978) held forth at length on the perils and pleasures of research in "soft psychology." He said a mouthful, part of it probably blasphemous as far as traditional investigators are concerned. Having appeared in a special issue of the *Journal of Consulting and Clinical Psychology* on methodology in clinical research (1978, **46,** No. 4), his piece bears review.

Soft psychology (read clinical psychology, among others) cannot, he argues, hold a candle to the developed sciences, at least as things have gone up to now. Where the latter are cumulative in character, that is, theories either gain wide acceptance and are incorporated into the fabric of the science or else "flunk" in the face of hard facts and are scrapped, the situation in the softer areas of psychology is nebulous at best. For these theories "never die, they just slowly fade away" (Meehl, 1978, p. 807), usually as a function of simple loss of enthusiasm and flagging interest.

A weird situation, according to Meehl. And, trying to be fair about it, he offers at least 20 features of human psychology that make it so hard to "scientize." The heterogeneous off-the-top-of-the-head list includes everything from the pesky business of individual differences and the intrusion of nuisance variables to such things as polygenic heredity and cultural factors. Having warmed up by then, he comes down particularly hard on the deification by soft psychologists of their inevitable test of significance.

"Putting it crudely," he declares, "if you have enough cases and your measures are not totally unreliable, the null hypothesis will always be falsified, *regardless of the truth of the substantive theory* [emphasis in original]" (Meehl, 1978, p. 822). Too bad, as far as he's concerned: "Nothing is as stuffy and pretentious as the verbal 'pseudorigor' of the soft branches of social science" (p. 825). How different in the physical sciences, where "scientific power comes from two other sources, namely, the immense deductive fertility of the formalism and the accuracy of the measuring instruments" (p. 825).

Meehl (1978) offers a constructive solution in the form of "consistency tests." Nonetheless, he cannot help concluding on a somewhat melancholy note: "But I think we ought to acknowledge the possibility that there is never going to be a really impressive theory in personality or social psychology. I dislike to think that, but it might just be true" (p. 829).

There are others attempting to keep investigators, clinicians among them, honest. In a small paper, Tversky and Kahneman (1971) have made some big points. Psychologists in general have an exaggerated belief in the law of small numbers. As Tversky and Kahneman (1971) have discovered: (1) the believers gamble their hypotheses on small samples, apparently unmindful of the fact that they thereby have the odds considerably against them; (2) they seem to place unwarranted confidence on early trends in the data; (3) similarly, they have unduly high expectations that significant results are replicable; and (4) in a desire to find causal "explanations" for discrepant results, they overlook sampling variability as a factor. Hence the typical psychological investigator's belief in the law of small numbers seems quite resistant to extinction.

Looking at the prevalence and popularity of significance testing, as had Bolles (1962) and Meehl (1978), Tversky and Kahneman (1971) actually regret abandonment of the earlier convention of reporting a sample mean as $\overline{X} \pm PE$ (the Probable Error representing the 50% confidence interval around the mean). At least the latter practice had called sampling variability to one's attention, and thus could act as a hedge against its underestimation. In any case, they conclude: "The emphasis on significance levels tends to obscure a fundamental distinction between the size of an effect and its statistical significance. . . . the acceptance of the hypothesis-testing model has not been an unmixed blessing for psychology" (Tversky & Kahneman, 1971, p. 110).

In an equally short and equally significant piece, Bolles (1962) has spoken softly while carrying a big stick. His tone is gentle, his message unmistakable: scientists should remember that they are other than statisticians per se. The latter can act as though they are dealing with the properties of numbers; they are. Scientists cannot afford the same simple license; their concern is essentially with understanding one natural phenomenon or another. Bolles puts it succinctly: "When the statistician has rejected the null hypothesis, his job is virtually finished. The scientist, however, has only just begun" (p. 645).

Very simply, Bolles (1962) notes, in rejecting the null hypothesis at the .05 level, the statistician has pretty good assurance (p .95) that the alternative statistical hypothesis is correct. By contrast, under the same conditions, scientists have their remaining work cut out for them, namely, comparing their hypothesis with alternative hypotheses that might explain the data equally well or better. Even before, they must have assured themselves that the statistical model they assumed to be appropriate must indeed have been. Writing about "strong inference," Platt

(1964) adds a related injunction, namely, "that in every field and in every laboratory we need to try to formulate multiple alternative hypotheses sharp enough to be capable of disproof" (p. 5).

Given the abandon with which tests of significance are cited in psychological studies, Bolles' (1962) reminder remains a crucial one:

The fact that the null hypothesis can be rejected with a p of .99 does not give E an assurance of .99 that his particular hypothesis is true. . . . The final confidence he can have in his scientific hypothesis is not dependent upon statistical significance levels; it is ultimately determined by his ability to reject alternatives. (p. 642)

It is perhaps significant that in his preface to this special issue of the *Journal of Consulting and Clinical Psychology* (1978, **46,** No. 4) Editor Brendan Maher cannot help "inferring reluctantly that current doctoral training in research, as reflected by recent submissions to this journal, is deficient to the point of being disastrous" (Maher, 1978, p. 595). Such ominous declarations aside, the fact remains that the several contributors to this special journal issue leave no doubt that good clinical research is both challenging and tricky. With the respective authors covering both methodological issues in general as well as the special problems encountered in specific areas—the study of addictions, research with correctional populations, community program evaluation, and other aspects—this volume offers a panoramic view of the present state of the art (or science?).

POSTLUDE

Some thirty years ago, Edwards and Cronbach (1952) said something that is as true for clinical psychology in the 1980s as it was then:

Every research worker has to have two personalities if he is to get the most good from his data.

He must be the rigorous tester who believes nothing without conclusive evidence, when he is deciding what relations are to be admitted as proven facts. . . . after the tough-minded half of the investigator's personality has accepted what it will from the study, he must turn loose the inquiring, speculative, and tender-minded half which is willing to entertain doubtful ideas. If this tender-minded soul is gullible, *believing* [emphasis in original] in what has met no significance test, he will end with a science stuffed with superstitions. But if he holds these yet-unproven ideas in the air, as notions which may guide him in the next experiment or the treatment of the next patient, he is more likely to be correct than the man who casts the idea from his mind as soon as one experiment fails to provide significant confirmation. (p. 57)

Those may well be the most fitting sentiments with which to conclude a chapter purporting to present a perspective on experimental contributions to clinical psychology.

REFERENCES

Aborn, M. (1953) The influence of experimentally induced failure on the retention of material acquired through set and incidental learning. *Journal of Experimental Psychology, 45,* 225–231.

Abramson, L. Y., & Sackheim, H. A. (1977). A paradox in depression: Uncontrollability and self-blame. *Psychological Bulletin, 84,* 838–851.

Abramson, L. Y., Seligman, M. E. P., & Teasdale, J. D. (1978) Learned helplessness in humans: Critique and reformulation. *Journal of Abnormal Psychology, 87,* 49–74.

Albee, G. W., & Joffe, J. M. (Eds.) (1977) *Primary prevention of psychopathology.* Hanover, N.H.: University Press of New England.

Aserinsky, E., & Kleitman, N. (1953). Regularly occurring periods of eye motility and concomitant phenomena during sleep. *Science, 118,* 273–274.

Azrin, N. H., & Powell, J. (1968). Behavioral engineering: The reduction of smoking behavior by a conditioning apparatus and procedure. *Journal of Applied Behavior Analysis, 1,* 193–200.

Bandura, A. (1969). *Principles of behavior modification.* New York: Holt, Rinehart & Winston.

Bandura, A. (1977a). *Social learning theory.* Englewood Cliffs, N.J.: Prentice-Hall.

Bandura, A. (1977b). Self-efficacy: Toward a unifying theory of behavior change. *Psychological Review, 84,* 191–215.

Bandura, A. (1978). Self-reinforcement: Theoretical and methodological considerations. In C. M. Franks & G. T. Wilson (Eds.), *Annual review of behavior therapy: Theory and Practice.* New York: Brunner/Mazel, pp. 115–142.

Bandura, A., & Walters, R. H. (1963). *Social learning and personality development.* New York: Holt, Rinehart & Winston.

Barclay, A. M. (1969). The effect of hostility on physiological and fantasy responses. *Journal of Personality, 37,* 651–667.

Barclay, A. M., & Haber, R. N. (1965). The relation of aggressive to sexual motivation. *Journal of Personality, 33,* 462–475.

Beck, A. T. (1976). *Cognitive therapy and the emotional disorders.* New York: International Universities Press.

Bergin, A. E. (1971). The evaluation of therapeutic outcomes. In A. E. Bergin & S. L. Garfield (Eds.), *Handbook of psychotherapy and behavior change.* New York: Wiley, pp. 217–270.

Bergin, A. E., & Strupp, H. H. (1970). New directions in psychotherapy research. *Journal of Abnormal Psychology, 76,* 13–26.

Bindra, D., & Scheier, I. H. (1954). The relation between psychometric and experimental research in psychology. *American Psychologist, 9,* 69–71.

Birdwhistell, R. L. (1970) *Kinesics and context: Essays on body motion communication.* Philadelphia: University of Pennsylvania Press.

Birnbaum, A., & Maxwell, A. E. (1960). Classification procedures based on Bayes' formula. *Applied Statistics, 9,* 152–169.

Bjork, R. A. (1972) Theoretical implications of directed forgetting. In A. W. Melton & E. Martin (Eds.), *Coding processes in human memory.* Washington, D. C.: V. H. Winston.

Blackmore, W. R. (1972). Some comments on "Computer simulation of a model of neurotic defense processes." *Behavioral Science, 17,* 229–232.

Blum, G. S. (1963). Programming people to simulate machines. In S. S. Tomkins & S. Messick (Eds.), *Computer simulation of personality: Frontier of psychological theory.* New York: Wiley, pp. 127–157.

Blum, G. S. (1961). *A model of the mind.* New York: Wiley.

Blum, G. S. (1950). *The Blacky Pictures: A technique for the exploration of personality dynamics.* New York: Psychological Corporation.

Blum, G. S., & Barbour, J. S. (1979). Selective inattention to anxiety-linked stimuli. *Journal of Experimental Psychology: General, 108,* 182–224.

Bolles, R. C. (1962). The difference between statistical hypotheses and scientific hypotheses. *Psychological Reports, 11,* 639–645.

Bower, G. H. (1972). Stimulus-sampling theory of encoding variability. In A. W. Melton & E. Martin (Eds.), *Coding processes in human memory.* Washington, D. C.: V. H. Winston.

Brady, J. V., Porter, R. W., Conrad, D. G., & Mason, J. W. (1958). Avoidance behavior and the development of gastro-duodenal ulcers. *Journal of the Experimental Analysis of Behavior, 1,* 69–73.

Broadbent, D. (1958). *Perception and communication.* Oxford: Pergamon Press.

Broen, W. E., Jr. (1973). Limiting the flood of stimulation: A protective deficit in chronic schizophrenia. In R. L. Solso (Ed.), *Contemporary issues in cognitive psychology: The Loyola symposium.* Washington, D. C.: V. H. Winston.

Brown, J. S. (1948). Gradients of approach and avoidance responses and their relation to motivation. *Journal of Comparative and Physiological Psychology, 41,* 450–465.

Chassan, J. B. (1979). *Research design in clinical psychology and psychiatry.* New York: Halsted Press.

Cheney, Carl D. (1973). Mechanically augmented human toilet-training *or* the electric pottie chair. In R. L. Schwitzgebel & R. K. Schwitzgebel (Eds.), *Psychotechnology: Electronic control of mind and behavior.* New York: Holt, Rinehart & Winston, pp. 129–133.

Cohen, B. D., & Camhi, J. (1967). Schizophrenic performance in a word communication task. *Journal of Abnormal Psychology, 72,* 240–246.

Cohen, B. D., Nachmani, G., & Rosenberg, S. (1974). Referent communication disturbances in acute schizophrenia. *Journal of Abnormal Psychology, 83,* 1–13.

Colby, K. M. (1976). Clinical implications of a simulation model of paranoid processes. *Archives of General Psychiatry, 33,* 854–857.

Collins, R. W., Dmitruk, V. M., and Ranney, J. T. (1977). Personal validation: Some empirical and ethical considerations. *Journal of Consulting and Clinical Psychology, 45,* 70–77.

Cromwell, R. L., & Dokecki, P. R. (1968). Schizophrenic language: A disattention interpretation. In S. Rosenberg & J. H. Koplin (Eds.), *Developments in applied psycholinguistics research.* New York: Macmillan.

Cronbach, L. J. (1957). The two disciplines of scientific psychology. *American Psychologist, 12,* 671–684.

Crown, S. (1975). "On being sane in insane places": A comment from England. *Journal of Abnormal Psychology, 84,* 453–455.

Davis, D. A. (1976). On being detectably sane in insane places: Base rates and psychodiagnosis. *Journal of Abnormal Psychology, 85,* 416–422.

Dawes, R. M., & Corrigan, B. (1974). Linear models in decision making. *Psychological Bulletin, 81,* 95–106.

Deane, W. N. (1961). The reactions of a nonpatient to a stay on a mental hospital ward. *Psychiatry, 24,* 61–68.

Delgado, J. M. R. (1973). Intracerebral radio stimulation and recording in completely free patients. In R. L. Schwitzgebel & R. K. Schwitzgebel (Eds.), *Psychotechnology: Electronic control of mind and behavior.* New York: Holt, Rinehart & Winston, pp. 184–198.

Dember, W. N. (1974). Motivation and the cognitive revolution. *American Psychologist, 29,* 161–168.

Deutsch, J. A., & Deutsch, D. (1963). Attention: Some theoretical considerations. *Psychological Review, 70,* 80–90.

DiCara, L. V., & Miller, N. E. (1968). Changes in heart rate instrumentally learned by curarized rats as avoidance responses. *Journal of Comparative and Physiological Psychology, 65,* 8–12.

Dixon, N. F. (1971). *Subliminal perception: The nature of a controversy.* London: McGraw-Hill.

Dollard, J., & Miller, N. E. (1950). *Personality and psychotherapy: An analysis in terms of learning, thinking, and culture.* New York: McGraw-Hill.

Dutton, D. G., & Aron, A. P. (1974). Some evidence for heightened sexual attraction under conditions of high anxiety. *Journal of Personality and Social Psychology, 30,* 510–517.

D'Zurilla, T. (1965). Recall efficiency and mediating cognitive events in "experimental repression." *Journal of Personality and Social Psychology, 3,* 253–256.

Eastman, C. (1976). Behavioral formulations of depression. *Psychological Review, 83,* 277–291.

Edwards, A. L., & Cronbach, L. J. (1952). Experimental design for research in psychotherapy. *Journal of Clinical Psychology, 8,* 51–59.

Eron, L. D. (1975). Editor's note. *Journal of Abnormal Psychology, 84,* 433.

Eysenck, H. J. (1972). The experimental study of Freudian concepts. *Bulletin of the British Psychological Society, 25,* 261–267.

Farber, I. E. (1975). Sane and insane: Constructions and misconstructions. *Journal of Abnormal Psychology, 84,* 589–620.

Fisher, C. (1956). Dreams, images, and perception: A study of unconscious-preconscious relationships. *Journal of the American Psychoanalytic Association, 4,* 5–48.

Flavell, J. (1955). Repression and the "return of the repressed." *Journal of Consulting Psychology, 19,* 441–443.

Forer, B. R. (1949). The fallacy of personal validation: A classroom demonstration of gullibility. *Journal of Abnormal and Social Psychology, 44,* 118–123.

Franks, C. M., & Wilson, G. T. (1978). Behavior Therapy: An overview. In D. M. Franks & G. T. Wilson (Eds.), *Annual review of behavior therapy: Theory and practice.* New York: Brunner/Mazel, pp. 1–26.

Freud, S. (1938). The interpretation of dreams. In *The basic writings of Sigmund Freud* (trans. and ed. by A. A. Brill). New York: Modern Library, pp. 179–549.

Freud, S. (1958). Psycho-analytic notes on an autobiographical account of a case of paranoia (dementia paranoides). In *The complete psychological works of Sigmund Freud, Vol. 12.* London: Hogarth Press.

Garber, J., & Hollon, S. D. (1980). Universal versus personal helplessness in depression: Belief in uncontrollability or incompetence? *Journal of Abnormal Psychology, 89,* 56–66.

Gazzaniga, M. S. (1970). *The bisected brain.* New York: Appleton-Century-Crofts.

Glazer, H. I., & Weiss, J. M. (1976a). Long-term and transitory interference effects. *Journal of Experimental Psychology: Animal Behavior Processes, 2,* 191–201.

Glazer, H. I., & Weiss, J. M. (1976b). Long-term interference effect: An alternative to "learned helplessness." *Journal of Experimental Psychology: Animal Behavior Processes, 2,* 202–213.

Goldberg, L. R. (1970). Man versus model of man: A rationale, plus some evidence for a method of improving on clinical inferences. *Psychological Bulletin, 73,* 422–432.

Goldiamond, I. (1978). Self-reinforcement. In C. M. Franks & G. T. Wilson (Eds.), *Annual review of behavior therapy: Theory and practice.* New York: Brunner/Mazel, pp. 143–150.

Goldman, A. R., Bohr, R. H., & Steinberg, T. A. (1970). On posing as mental patients: Reminiscences and recommendations. *Professional Psychology, 1,* 427–434.

Gomes-Schwartz, B., Hadley, S. W., & Strupp, H. H. (1978). Individual psychotherapy and and behavior therapy. In M. R. Rosenzweig & L. W. Porter (Eds.), *Annual Review of Psychology,* Vol. 29.

Palo Alto, Calif.: Annual Reviews, Inc., pp. 435–471.

Greene, R. L. (1977). Student acceptance of generalized personality interpretations: A reexamination. *Journal of Consulting and Clinical Psychology, 45,* 965–966.

Gur, R. E. (1978). Left hemisphere dysfunction and left hemisphere overactivation in schizophrenia. *Journal of Abnormal Psychology, 87,* 226–238.

Hall, E. T. (1959). *The silent language.* New York: Doubleday.

Heilbrun, A. B., Jr. (1977). An analogue study of disattentional strategies in schizophrenia. *Journal of Abnormal Psychology, 86,* 135–144.

Hess, E. H. (1965). Attitude and pupil size. *Scientific American, 212,* 46–54.

Hilgard, E. R. (1977). *Divided consciousness: Multiple controls in human thought and action.* New York: Wiley.

Hoffman, P. J. (1960). The paramorphic representation of clinical judgment. *Psychological Bulletin, 57,* 116–131.

Holmes, D. (1972). Repression or interference: A further investigation. *Journal of Personality and Social Psychology, 22,* 163–170.

Holmes, D. S. (1974). Investigations of repression: Differential recall of material experimentally or naturally associated with ego threat. *Psychological Bulletin, 81,* 632–653.

Holmes, D. S., & Schallow, J. R. (1969). Reduced recall after ego threat: Repression or response competition? *Journal of Personality and Social Psychology, 13,* 145–152.

Holt, R. R. (1958). Clinical and statistical prediction: A reformulation and some new data. *Journal of Abnormal and Social Psychology, 56,* 1–12.

Holt, R. R. (1970). Yet another look at clinical and statistical prediction: Or, is clinical psychology worthwhile? *American Psychologist, 25,* 337–349.

Huesmann, L. R. (Ed.) (1978). Special issue: Learned helplessness as a model of depression. *Journal of Abnormal Psychology, 87,* 1–198.

Hull, C. L. (1933). *Hypnosis and suggestibility, an experimental approach.* New York: Appleton-Century.

Jaynes, J. (1977). *The origin of consciousness in the breakdown of the bicameral mind.* Boston: Houghton Mifflin.

John, E. R. (1973). Where is fancy bred? In M. Hammer, K. Salzinger, & S. Sutton (Eds.), *Psychopathology: Contributions from the social, behavioral, and biological sciences.* New York: Wiley, pp. 319–341.

Jones, S. L., Nation, J. R., & Massad, P. (1977). Immunization against learned helplessness in man. *Journal of Abnormal Psychology,* **86,** 75–83.

Kadushin, A. (1963). Diagnosis and evaluation for (almost) all occasions. *Social Work,* January, 12–19.

Kahneman, D., & Beatty, J. (1966). Pupil diameter and load on memory. *Science,* **154,** 1583–1585.

Kahneman, D., & Tversky, A. (1973). On the psychology of prediction. *Psychological Review,* **80,** 237–251.

Kantorowitz, D. A., & Cohen, B. D. (1977). Referent communication in chronic schizophrenia. *Journal of Abnormal Psychology,* **86,** 1–9.

Karon, B.P., & VandenBos, G.R. (1972). The consequences of psychotherapy for schizophrenics. *Psychotherapy: Theory, Research, and Practice.* **9,** 111–119.

Kendall, P. C. & Hollon, S. D. (Eds.) (1979). *Cognitive behavioral interventions: Theory, research, and procedures.* New York: Academic Press.

Kimble, G. A., Garmezy, N., & Zigler, E. (1980). *Principles of general psychology.* New York: Wiley.

Klein, G. A., & Holt, R. R. (1960). Problems and issues in current studies of subliminal activation. In J. G. Peatman & E. L. Hartley (Eds.), *Festschrift for Gardner Murphy.* New York: Harper & Row, pp. 75–93.

Kleinsmith, L. J., & Kaplan, S. (1963). Paired-associated learning as a function of arousal and interpolated interval. *Journal of Experimental Psychology,* **65,** 190–193.

Kleinsmith, L. J., and Kaplan, S. (1964). Interaction of arousal and recall interval in nonsense syllable paired-associate learning. *Journal of Experimental Psychology,* **67,** 124–126.

Klett, C. J., & Pumroy, D. K. (1971). Automated procedures in psychological assessment. In P. McReynolds (Ed.), *Advances in psychological assessment,* Vol. 2. Palo Alto, Calif.: Science and Behavior Books.

Kline, P. (1972). *Fact and fantasy in Freudian theory.* London: Methuen.

Kuhn, T. S. (1970). *The structure of scientific revolutions* (2nd ed.). Chicago: University of Chicago Press.

Langer, E. J., & Abelson, R. P. (1974). A patient by any other name . . . : Clinician group difference in labeling bias. *Journal of Consulting and Clinical Psychology,* **42,** 4–9.

Lazarus, R. S. (1977). A cognitive analysis of biofeedback control. In G. E. Schwartz & J. Beatty (Eds.), *Biofeedback: Theory and research.* New York: Academic Press, pp. 67–87.

Ledwidge, B. (1978). Cognitive behavior modification: A step in the wrong direction? *Psychological Modification,* **85,** 353–375.

Ledwidge, B. (1979). Cognitive behavior modification or new ways to change minds: Reply to Mahoney and Kazdin. *Psychological Bulletin,* **86,** 1050–1053.

Letters to the Editor (1973). *Science,* **180,** 356–365.

Lewinsohn, P. M. (1974). Clinical and theoretical aspects of depression. In K. S. Calhoun, H. E. Adams, & K. M. Mitchell (Eds.), *Innovative treatment methods in psychopathology.* New York: Wiley, pp. 63–120.

Livermore, J. M., Malmquist, C. P., & Meehl, P. E. (1968). On the justifications for civil commitment. *University of Pennsylvania Law Review,* **117,** 75–96.

Lovaas, O. I., Schaeffer, B., & Simmons, J. Q. (1965). Building social behavior in autistic children by use of electric shock. *Journal of Experimental Research in Personality.* **1,** 99–109.

Maher, B. A. (1966). *Principles of psychopathology: An experimental approach.* New York: McGraw-Hill.

Maher, B. A. (1974). Delusional thinking and perceptual disorder. *Journal of Individual Psychology,* **30,** 98–113.

Maher, B. A. (1978). A reader's, writer's, and reviewer's guide to assessing research reports in clinical psychology. *Journal of Consulting and Clinical Psychology,* **46,** 835–838.

Mahoney, M. J. (1974). *Cognition and behavior modification.* Cambridge, Mass.: Ballinger.

Mahoney, M. J. (1977). Reflections on the cognitive-learning trend in psychotherapy. *American Psychologist,* **32,** 5–13.

Mahoney, M. J., & Kazdin, A. E. (1979). Cognitive behavior modification: Misconceptions and premature evacuation. *Psychological Bulletin,* **86,** 1044–1049.

Marshall, G. D., & Zimbardo, P. G. (1979). Affective consequences of inadequately explained physiological arousal. *Journal of Personality and Social Psychology,* **37,** 970–988.

Maslach, C. (1979). Negative emotional biasing of unexplained arousal. *Journal of Personality and Social Psychology,* **37,** 953–969.

McReynolds, P. (1960). Anxiety, perception, and schizophrenia. In D. D. Jackson (Ed.), *The etiology of schizophrenia.* New York: Basic Books, pp. 248–292.

Mednick, S. A., & McNeil, T. F. (1968). Current methodology in research on the etiology of schizophrenia: Serious difficulties which suggest the use of the high-risk-group method. *Psychological Bulletin,* **70,** 681–693.

Mednick, S. A., Schulsinger, F., Higgins, J., & Bell, B. (1974). *Genetics, environment and psychopathology.* Amsterdam: North-Holland Publishing Company.

Meehl, P. E. (1954). *Clinical versus statistical prediction: A theoretical analysis and a review of the evidence.* Minneapolis: University of Minnesota Press.

Meehl, P. E. (1956). Wanted—A good cookbook. *American Psychologist,* **11,** 262–272.

Meehl, P. E. (1957). When shall we use our heads instead of the formula? *Journal of Counseling Psychology,* **4,** 268–273.

Meehl, P. E. (1962). Schizotaxia, schizotypy, schizophrenia. *American Psychologist,* **17,** 827–838.

Meehl, P. E. (1970). Some methodological reflections on the difficulties of psychoanalytic research. In M. Radner & S. Winokur (Eds.), *Minnesota studies in the philosophy of science, Vol. 4.* Minneapolis: University of Minnesota Press, pp. 403–416.

Meehl, P. E. (1959). Some ruminations on the validation of clinical procedures. *Canadian Journal of Psychology, 13, 102–128.*

Meehl, P. E. (1973). Why I do not attend staff conferences. In P. E. Meehl, *Psychodiagnosis: Selected papers.* Minneapolis: University of Minnesota Press, pp. 225–302.

Meehl, P. E. (1978). Theoretical risks and tabular asterisks: Sir Karl, Sir Ronald, and the slow progress of soft psychology. *Journal of Consulting and Clinical Psychology,* **4,** 806–834.

Meichenbaum, D. (1974). *Cognitive behavior modification.* Morristown, N. J.: General Learning Press.

Meichenbaum, D. (1977). *Cognitive behavior modification: An integrative approach.* New York: Plenum.

Melrose, J. P., Stroebel, C., & Glueck, B. (1970). Diagnosis of psychopathology using stepwise multiple discriminant analysis. *Comprehensive Psychiatry,* **11,** 43–50.

Merrill, R. (1954). The effect of pre-experimental and experimental anxiety on recall efficiency. *Journal of Experimental Psychology,* **48,** 167–172.

Miller, N. E. (1959). Liberalization of basic S-R concepts: Extensions to conflict behavior, motivation, and social learning. In S. Koch (Ed.), *Psychology: A study of a science,* Vol. 2. New York: McGraw-Hill, pp. 196–292.

Miller, N. E. (1966). Some animal experiments pertinent to the problem of combining psychotherapy with drug therapy. *Comprehensive Psychiatry,* **7,** 1–12.

Miller, N. E. (1969). Learning of visceral and glandular responses. *Science,* **163,** 434–445.

Miller, N. E. (1973). Autonomic learning: Clinical and physiological implications. In M. Hammer, K. Salzinger, & S. Sutton (Eds.), *Psychopathology: Contributions from the social, behavioral, and biological sciences.* New York: Wiley, pp. 127–145.

Miller, N. E., & Banuazizi, A. (1968). Instrumental learning by curarized rats of a specific visceral response, intestinal or cardiac. *Journal of Comparative and Physiological Psychology,* **65,** 1–7.

Miller, N. E., & Dworkin, B. R. (1974). Visceral learning: Recent difficulties with curarized rats and significant problems for human research. In P. A. Obrist, A. H. Black, J. Brener, & L. V. DiCara (Eds.), *Cardiovascular physiology: Current issues in response mechanisms, biofeedback, and methodology.* Chicago: Aldine, pp. 312–331.

Miller, N. E., & Dworkin, B. R. (1977). Critical issues in therapeutic applications of biofeedback. In G. E. Schwartz & J. Beatty (Eds.), *Biofeedback: Theory and research.* New York: Academic Press, pp. 129–161.

Millon, T. (1975). Reflections on Rosenhan's "On being sane in insane places." *Journal of Abnormal Psychology,* **84,** 456–461.

Mischel, W. (1971). *Introduction to personality.* New York: Holt, Rinehart & Winston.

Mowrer, O. H. (1938). Apparatus for the study and treatment of enuresis. *American Journal of Psychology,* **51,** 163–166.

Neisser, U. (1967). *Cognitive psychology.* New York: Appleton-Century-Crofts.

Ornstein, R. E. (1977). *The psychology of consciousness* (2nd ed.). New York: Harcourt Brace Jovanovich.

Overmier, J. B., & Seligman, M. E. P. (1967). Effects of inescapable shock upon subsequent escape and avoidance learning. *Journal of Comparative and Physiological Psychology,* **63,** 28–33.

Perlman, D. (1980). Who's who in psychology: Endler et al's SSCI scores versus a textbook definition. *American Psychologist,* **35,** 104–106.

Peterson, C. (1979). Uncontrollability and self-blame in depression: Investigation of the paradox in a college population. *Journal of Abnormal Psychology,* **88,** 620–624.

Platt, J. R. (1964). Strong inference. *Science,* **146,** 347–353.

Plutchik, R., & Ax, A. F. (1967). A critique of "Determinants of emotional state" by Schachter and Singer (1962). *Psychophysiology,* **4,** 79–82.

Posner, M. (1973). Coordination of internal codes. In W. Chase (Ed.), *Visual information processing.* New York: Academic Press.

Rapoport, A. (1968). Psychoanalysis as science. *Bulletin of the Menninger Clinic, 32,* 1–20.

Rogers, C. R. (1951). *Client-centered therapy.* Boston: Houghton Mifflin.

Rosenberg, S., & Cohen, B. D. (1964). Speakers' and listeners' processes in a word-communication task. *Science, 145,* 1201–1203.

Rosenberg, S., & Cohen, B. D. (1966). Referential processes of speakers and listeners. *Psychological Review, 73,* 208–231.

Rosenhan, D. L. (1973). On being sane in insane places. *Science, 179,* 250–258.

Rosenhan, D. L. (1975). The contextual nature of psychodiagnosis. *Journal of Abnormal Psychology, 84,* 462–474.

Salzinger, K. (1973). *Schizophrenia: Behavioral aspects.* New York: Wiley.

Sawyer, J. (1966). Measurement *and* prediction, clinical *and* statistical. *Psychological Bulletin, 66,* 178–200.

Schachter, S. (1971). *Emotion, obesity, and crime.* New York: Academic Press.

Schachter, S., & Singer, J. E. (1962). Cognitive, social, and physiological determinants of emotional state. *Psychological Review, 69,* 379–399.

Schachter, S., & Singer, J. E. (1979). Comments on the Maslach and Marshall-Zimbardo experiments. *Journal of Personality and Social Psychology, 37,* 989–995.

Schwartz, G. E. (1973). Biofeedback as therapy: Some theoretical and practical issues. *American Psychologist, 28,* 666–673.

Schwartz, G. E., & Beatty, J. (1977). *Biofeedback: Theory and research.* New York: Harcourt Brace Jovanovich.

Schwitzgebel, R. L. (1976). Behavioral technology. In H. Leitenberg (Ed.), *Handbook of behavior modification and behavior therapy.* Englewood Cliffs, N.J.: Prentice-Hall, pp. 604–626.

Seligman, M. E. P., Klein, D. C., & Miller, W. R. (1976). Depression. In H. Leitenberg (Ed.). *Handbook of behavior modification and behavior therapy.* Englewood Cliffs, N. J.: Prentice-Hall, pp. 168–210.

Seligman, M. E. P., & Maier, S. F. (1967). Failure to escape traumatic shock. *Journal of Experimental Psychology, 74,* 1–9.

Seligman, M. E. P., Maier, S. F., & Geer, J. (1968). The alleviation of learned helplessness in the dog. *Journal of Abnormal and Social Psychology, 73,* 256–262.

Shakow, D. (1963). Psychological deficit in schizophrenia. *Behavioral Science, 8,* 275–305.

Shakow, D. (1977). Schizophrenia: Selected papers. Psychological Issues, Vol. 10, Monograph 38. New York: International Universities Press.

Shapiro, D., & Surwit, R. S. (1976). Learned control of physiological function and disease. In H. Leitenberg (Ed.), *Handbook of behavior modification and behavior therapy.* Englewood Cliffs, N.J.: Prentice-Hall, pp. 74–123.

Shaw, B. F. (1977). Comparison of cognitive therapy and behavior therapy in the treatment of depression. *Journal of Consulting and Clinical Psychology, 45,* 543–551.

Shevrin, H. (1978). Evoked potential evidence for unconscious mental processes: A review of the literature. Paper presented at International Symposium on the Unconscious, Tbilisi, Georgia, USSR.

Shevrin, H. (1979). The psychological unconscious and correlated neurophysiological processes. Paper presented at International Symposium on the Unconscious, Tbilisi, Georgia, USSR.

Shevrin, H., and Dickman, S. (1980). The psychological unconscious: A necessary assumption for all psychological theory? *American Psychologist, 35,* 421–434.

Shevrin, H., & Fritzler, D. E. (1968). Visual evoked response correlates of unconscious mental processes. *Science, 161,* 295–298.

Shevrin, H., & Luborsky, L. (1961). The rebus technique: A method for studying primary-process transformations of briefly exposed pictures. *Journal of Nervous and Mental Disease, 133,* 479–488.

Shevrin, H., Smith, W. H., & Fritzler, D. E. (1971). Average evoked response and verbal correlates of unconscious mental processes. *Psychophysiology, 8,* 149–162.

Silverman, L. H. (1976). Psychoanalytic theory: "The reports of my death are greatly exaggerated." *American Psychologist, 31,* 621–637.

Snyder, C. R. (1977). "A patient by any other name" revisited: Maladjustment of attributional locus of problem? *Journal of Consulting and Clinical Psychology, 45,* 101–103.

Snyder, C. R., Shenkel, R. J., & Lowary, C. R. (1977). Acceptance of personality interpretations: The "Barnum Effect" and beyond. *Journal of Consulting and Clinical Psychology, 45,* 104–114.

Solomon, R. L., Kamin, L. J., & Wynne, L. C. (1953). Traumatic avoidance learning: The outcomes of several extinction procedures with dogs. *Journal of Abnormal and Social Psychology, 48,* 291–302.

Sommer, R. (1969). *Personal space.* Englewood Cliffs, N. J.: Prentice-Hall.

Sonnenberg, M. (1955). Girls jumping rope. *Psychoanalysis: Journal of Psychoanalytic Psychology,* **3,** 57–62.

Soskin, W. F. (1954). Bias in postdiction from projective tests. *Journal of Abnormal and Social Psychology,* **49,** 69–74.

Spence, D. P. (1961). The multiple effects of subliminal stimuli. *Journal of Personality,* **29,** 40–53.

Spence, D. P., & Smith, G. W. (1977). Experimenter bias against subliminal perception? Comments on a replication. *British Journal of Psychology,* **68,** 279–280.

Sperry, R. W. (1967). Split-brain approach to learning problems. In G. C. Quarton, T. Melnechuck, & F. O. Schmitt (Eds.), *The neurosciences: A study program.* New York: Rockefeller University Press.

Spitzer, R. L. (1975). On pseudoscience in science, logic in remission, and psychiatric diagnosis: A critique of Rosenhan's "On being sane in insane places." *Journal of Abnormal Psychology,* **84,** 442–452.

Spitzer, R. L., & Endicott, J. (1974). Can the computer assist clinicians in psychiatric diagnosis? *American Journal of Psychiatry,* **131,** 523–530.

Spitzer, R. L., & Endicott, J. (1975). Attempts to improve psychiatric diagnosis. In J. Zubin, K. Salzinger, J. L. Fleiss, B. Gurland, R. L. Spitzer, J. Endicott, & S. Sutton. Biometric approach to psychopathology: Abnormal and clinical psychology—statistical, epidemiological, and diagnostic approaches. *Annual Review of Psychology,* **26,** 643–648.

Spring, B., & Zubin, J. (1977). Vulnerability to schizophrenic episodes and their prevention in adults. In G. W. Albee & J. M. Joffe (Eds.), *Primary prevention of psychopathology,* Vol. 1: *The Issues.* Hanover, N. H.: University Press of New England, pp. 254–284.

Stagner, R. (1958). The gullibility of personnel managers. *Personnel Psychology,* **11,** 347–352.

Sternberg, S. (1975). Memory scanning: New findings and current controversies. *Quarterly Journal of Experimental Psychology,* **27,** 1–32.

Sundberg, N. D. (1955). The acceptability of "fake" versus "bona fide" personality test interpretations. *Journal of Abnormal and Social Psychology,* **50,** 145–147.

Temerlin, M. K. (1968). Suggestion effects in psychiatric diagnosis. *Journal of Nervous and Mental Disease,* **147,** 349–359.

Treisman, A. M. (1964). Selective attention in man. *British Medical Bulletin,* **20,** 12–16.

Treisman, A. M. (1969). Strategies and models of selective attention. *Psychological Review,* **76,** 282–299.

Tversky, A., & Kahneman, D. (1971). Belief in the law of small numbers. *Psychological Bulletin,* **76,** 105–110.

Ullman, M., & Krippner, S., with Vaughan, A. (1973). *Dream telepathy: Scientific experiments in the supernatural.* New York: Macmillan.

von Domarus, E. (1944). The specific laws of logic in schizophrenia. In J. Kasanin (Ed.), *Language and thought in schizophrenia.* Berkeley, Calif.: University of California Press.

Walker, E. L. (1958). Action decrement and its relation to learning. *Psychological Review,* **65,** 129–142.

Wallace, R. K., & Benson, H. (1972). The physiology of meditation. *Scientific American,* **226,** 85–90.

Weiner, B. (1975). "On being sane in insane places": A process (attributional) analysis and critique. *Journal of Abnormal Psychology,* **84,** 433–441.

Weiss, J. H. (1963). Effect of professional training and amount and accuracy of information on behavioral prediction. *Journal of Consulting Psychology,* **27,** 257–262.

Wortman, C. B., & Dintzer, L. (1978). Is an attributional analysis of the learned helplessness phenomenon viable?: A critique of the Abramson-Seligman-Teasdale reformulation. *Journal of Abnormal Psychology,* **87,** 75–90.

Zeller, A. (1950a). An experimental analogue of repression: I. Historical summary. *Psychological Bulletin,* **47,** 39–51.

Zeller, A. (1950b). An experimental analogue of repression: II. The effect of individual failure and success on memory measured by relearning. *Journal of Experimental Psychology,* **40,** 411–422.

Zeller, A. (1951). An experimental analogue of repression: III. The effect of induced failure and success on memory measured by recall. *Journal of Experimental Psychology,* **42,** 32–38.

Zubin, J. (1969a). Contributions of experimental and abnormal psychology to clinical psychology. *International Review of Applied Psychology,* **18,** 65–77.

Zubin, J. (1969b). The biometric approach to psychopathology—Revisited. In J. Zubin & C. Shagass (Eds.), *Neurobiological aspects of psychopathology.* New York: Grune & Stratton, pp. 281–309.

CHAPTER 3

Ethical Perspectives in Clinical Research

SHELDON J. KORCHIN AND PHILIP A. COWAN

THE GROWING CONCERN WITH RESEARCH ETHICS

Traditionally, discussions of the research process have centered largely on scholarly and scientific issues: What is already known, and what knowledge is needed? Is an experimental or correlational design preferable? What are the independent and dependent variables to be manipulated and measured? What controls are necessary? How can the reliability of the findings best be assessed? and so on. Dealing with the substance of these questions fills texts for the neophyte scientist and methods sections of journal articles published by established investigators; only incidentally, if at all, is attention given to issues of the scientist's ethical and social responsibility. Increasingly, however, scientists have become aware of the importance of ethical issues as a necessary part of the process of asking scientific questions and designing studies. In this chapter we will examine some of these ethical questions, particularly those having to do with the recruitment and treatment of human participants (informed consent), with the treatment of data obtained from these participants (privacy and confidentiality), and with the issues involved in deciding whether a particular study is to be done at all (risks and benefits to participants, to society, and to the profession). Although we will focus here specifically on issues raised by clinical research, most of these ethical problems and dilemmas are widely shared by investigators in all of the social and biomedical sciences.

Some contend that ethical considerations limit or slow the process of scientific discovery. We propose that respect for human dignity and well-being is sufficient justification for the time and attention paid to making certain that the basic human rights of individuals are protected. But we also believe that, in our field at least, humane concerns can facilitate gaining knowledge about psychological functioning and dysfunctioning. Participants who are treated as partners and not as subjects can provide us with better and more valid information about their thoughts, feelings, and behavior.

Science and Values

It is well to recognize at the outset that the entire scientific enterprise rests on a fundamental value of western society, at least since the Age of Enlightenment—the belief that gaining knowledge through scientific means contributes to the ultimate improvement of the human condition. In this ethic, scientific and humanistic values are fused; what is good for science is good for humanity, and vice versa. Nurturing scientific curiosity is of intrinsic merit in a civilized society. The accomplishments of science prolong and enrich life, contribute to its comforts, reduce its distresses, and, some even add, make it more meaningful. Psychologists share the powerful faith that through research-based knowledge we can improve the understanding and care of people in psychological distress, as this volume witnesses. Yet this very faith may contribute to some of the ethical dilemmas that concern us here.

A paradox in considerations of research ethics lies in the fact that we are as likely (perhaps, more) to sin because of the noblest of scientific motives than because of base human frailties. Gaining research knowledge is virtually a moral imperative to psychologists and other scientists. Mankind is bettered, we believe fervently, as our knowledge of man grows. Working toward such important ends, it is all too easy to justify less virtuous means. . . . It is far easier to rationalize shoddy treatment of people in the cause of science than in the pursuit of personal profit, yet no more right (Korchin, 1976, pp. 600–601).

Accepting the view of science as beneficent, we may still wonder whether there are any limits to be placed upon scientists who seek knowledge wherever it may lead. Is it legitimate to conduct *any* study as long as the results will help to resolve a scientific issue, regardless of the consequences to the participants? While concern with the rights and welfare of human participants in research goes back centuries (Katz, 1972), ethical questions about the limits of scientific investigation were rarely raised before the end of World War II, perhaps because most people accepted the view of science as value-free and automatically contributing to human well-being. But these beliefs were shaken by the atom bomb and the revelation of Nazi concentration camp experiments. Hiroshima forcibly brought back the question of "knowledge for what?" and raised serious doubts as to the value of unbridled scientific and technological advance; for many, Dr. Strangelove replaced Albert Einstein as the prototypical scientist. The medical experiments of the Nazi "doctors of infamy" (Mitscherlich & Mielke, 1949), which resulted in death or permanent mutilation of many concentration camp inmates, shook

people's faith in biomedical research. Physicians who were pledged to preserve life knowingly inoculated inmates with toxic substances, exposed them to virulent diseases, or to extreme stress, while meticulously recording symptoms and time to death. At their trials, some of the Nazi researchers protested that they were increasing scientific knowledge as well as serving their country. Even in the United States in more recent years, numerous if less flagrant abuses of patients in medical research have been discovered (Lear, 1966; Beecher, 1966a, 1966b, 1970). In one case, alien live cancer cells were inoculated into elderly cancer patients without their knowledge or consent. In another, institutionalized mentally retarded children were intentionally infected with hepatitis. Compared to biomedical research, psychological and behavioral science studies are far less likely to produce bodily harm, but there has been evidence of abuses in such fields as stress research and experimental social psychology, involving gross deception of unwitting subjects put into frightening, embarrassing, or degrading situations. While the vast majority of researchers in psychology as well as the biomedical sciences are entirely ethical, even a small minority of questionable instances points up the need for greater concern with the ethical and humane treatment of human participants in scientific research.

After the war years, the growth and increased visibility of science, the fact that people were more educated, and the increased media coverage of scientific events contributed to an intensified concern with the abuses as well as the uses of scientific investigation. All of this was happening as part of a *Zeitgeist*, a spirit of the times, in all parts of our society, in which a new consciousness arose concerning the life conditions and rights of traditionally powerless groups. Starting in the 1950s, peaking in the 1960s, and continuing into our time, the demands grew for more civil rights, increased opportunities, and social participation for ethnic minorities, students, women, gays, prisoners and mental patients, the disabled, and other groups; the call is for greater social justice and civil rights for the disadvantaged and for greater accountability for those with power. The trend has been toward more participatory democracy, whether for poor blacks or women, consumers or students, and toward including human participants in research. Another face of the same phenomenon has been a growing distrust of, or at least a distinct ambivalence toward, experts and greater reluctance to accept their views unquestioningly. This new populism contains potential threats to scientific freedom and growth, though on the whole it is a healthy expression of popular democracy. In any case, this is the social context within which ethical codes, regulations, and review boards are evolving.

Codes, Regulations, and Review Boards

From World War II until 1970, the ethics of human experimentation in the biomedical fields was formalized into at least 33 sets of guidelines and codes of ethics (Beecher, 1970). Among the more important were the Nuremberg Code (1946–1949), the Declaration of Helsinki (revised 1964), and the American Medical Association Code (1966). In 1974 a National Commission for the Protection of Human Subjects of Biomedical and Behavioral Research was founded to survey expert opinion in the field and report to the U.S. Department of Health, Education and Welfare. Ten volumes have appeared in recent years containing fascinating papers by philosophers, medical researchers, psychologists, and others and containing recommendations for public and professional policy (e.g., National Commission, 1978).

Similar efforts to produce codes of research ethics have been made in the behavioral sciences by the American Psychological Association (1973), the American Anthropological Association (1971), and the American Sociological Association (1971). All of these codes do in fact provide guidelines for both new and experienced researchers, but whether they can stop even the most flagrant

cases of unethical behavior is moot. For example, a psychologist can be dropped from membership in the American Psychological Association for flouting either the general professional code (APA, 1979) or the research code (APA, 1973). Some few memberships are rescinded, but it is our impression that this is invariably for unethical professional behavior rather than for dubious research practices. In any case, one can continue to work as a psychologist in any realm without ever becoming a member of the association.

By contrast, regulations adopted by the Department of Health, Education and Welfare (now the Department of Health and Human Services) have a real and immediate effect on the lives and work of researchers. In 1966 the Surgeon General of the U.S. Public Health Service issued the first official Policy and Procedure Order, which covered all PHS research and research training grants. PHS funding of each grant was contingent on an assurance that a committee of the institution from which the proposal is submitted has reviewed the grant and approved the plans for treatment of human participants. Within a short time, policy was revised so that institutions had to make a general assurance covering all projects forwarded to PHS, rather than approving each individually. In time, policy was extended from PHS grants to any research supported by DHEW, and more explicit guidelines were written, including specific rules for research with children, prisoners, and the mentally infirm, pregnant women and fetuses, and other vulnerable groups. Parallel activities went on in other government agencies, such as the Food and Drug Administration, and in Congress, which passed Senator Kennedy's National Research Act, setting up a National Commission for the Protection of Human Subjects of Biomedical and Behavioral Research. For an overview of this history and accounts of other congressional and executive actions relating to human research, see Gray (1975) and Bower and deGasperis (1978).

Under the present DHEW regulations on the protection of human subjects (45 CFR 46), all institutions seeking DHEW funding of research must give assurance of compliance with these rules. This must specify the nature of the review committee (Institutional Review Board), its procedures for initial examination and later review of studies in progress, the mechanisms for giving advice and for enforcing the regulations, and the university, hospital, or other research center that accepts responsibility for research involving human participants, including the care of any subject who might be hurt. DHEW regulations require that IRBs have at least five members, two of them licensed in the healing arts, two or more who are behavioral scientists, and one of whom must not be an employee of the university. Because of the wide variety of studies conducted at our university, the Berkeley committee consists of 16 people in varied fields, including those mandated by DHEW. In all or most research centers, as at the University of California, the IRB reviews all research done under the aegis of the institution, not only those studies supported by DHEW. In DHEW proposals, however, the institution is obliged to review and approve the project before funding can be made.[1]

Ethical codes and guidelines are not in themselves sufficient to prevent unethical behavior or enforce adherence to widely accepted ethical standards. DHEW regulation

[1]While this chapter was in press, a new set of regulations was issued by the Department of Health and Human Services (45 CFR Part 46, reported in the Federal Register, January 26, 1981). These "final rules" respond to the recommendations of the National Commission for the Protection of Human Subjects of Biomedical and Behavioral Research and apply only to research funded fully or in part by HHS. The major effort of these new rules is to exempt most social and behavioral research from IRB review. Studies using interviews, analyses of existing data and records, public observation, and various forms of testing, where subjects' behavior is not manipulated and subjects are not stressed, no longer need be reviewed by the IRbs. "Expedited reviews" by less than the full IRB panel are also recommended for research posing no more than minimal risk to participants.

and Institutional Review Boards also cannot prevent all research abuses and enforce minimal standards, but they do have certain power to make their guidelines a reality. The PHS can refuse to give financial support to research that exceeds the limits of accepted practice, and the IRB can refuse to approve proposals that place participants in unnecessary risk or treat participants unethically. These powers seem to some observers to create their own risks of stifling creative and innovative research; we will consider this issue at the end of this chapter. In our view, IRBs working under DHEW regulations do perform the desirable function of encouraging investigators to consider ethical issues whenever a new study is proposed.

This may not be sufficient, as some have argued, and there are real dangers in too much governmental regulation, as others have noted. More can be done within the professions themselves. Thus Beecher (1966b, 1970) has argued for some time that journal editors should refuse to publish studies involving dubious treatment of participants. Sieber (1979) has an interesting proposal that authors be asked to submit a copy of the research proposal as approved by the IRB along with the manuscript being submitted for publication. Should the two documents clearly differ, editors would have grounds for rejection. She also makes the appealing suggestion that journals encourage authors to describe ethical dilemmas faced and decisions reached, as we now describe methods and procedures, so that readers could understand and protest, if they wished, the author's ethical as well as scientific acts. These ideas all involve institutionalizing procedures within the profession itself for raising ethical consciousness of both the producers and consumers of research.

A Conception of Ethical Decision Making

Developing codes and regulations is a process fraught with controversy and disagreement. For example, in the late 1960s APA's

Ad Hoc Committee on Ethical Standards in Psychological Research, chaired by Stuart W. Cook, did a painstaking job which included: (1) inviting all APA members to suggest principles and to send in case examples; (2) surveying the accumulated wisdom of scientists, scholars, journal editors, and ethicists; and (3) circulating a draft copy of the principles in 1971 and inviting all members to respond. Many strong opinions were received, and a second draft was circulated, which received less criticism. A third draft was adopted by APA and published in 1973. As the committee recognized, and one of its members commented elsewhere (Smith, 1975), developing principles of general acceptability to American psychologists was necessarily a political process, balancing the values and interests of different groups and individuals.

While some may view such a political process with alarm, in our view it is a necessary outgrowth of the process of ethical decision making. We begin with the assumption that ethical *issues* arise in the first place only when there are honest disagreements about what is to be considered right behavior, or when dilemmas result from a conflict of values, each of which may be defensible in its own right. As long as everyone agrees that participants in experiments should not be seriously harmed, there is no ethical dilemma; only when someone seriously argues the contrary position do we need ethical principles as guidelines. In some studies there is a promise of therapeutic benefit that would help the participant and other people in the future; there may also be a risk that an unproven physical or psychological treatment could exacerbate the patient's problems. Given a conflict between promoting good and avoiding harm, what should the researcher do?

There are three levels at which conflicting viewpoints enter into the process of ethical decision making: (1) in defining the nature of ethical principles; (2) in deciding which specific principles to adopt; and (3) in determining whether specific cases are to be considered as instances of a given principles. First, there is no universal agreement on how to conceptualize an ethical principle or code. Is a principle to be absolute or is it relative? Should it affirm the ethically desirable or, more usually, does it define the ethically acceptable (Smith, 1967)? It is not generally agreed whether ethical principles should be stated as prescriptions ("Thou shalt") or proscriptions ("Thou shalt not"). In discussing the principles of research ethics we will make clear whether there is general agreement on unacceptable as well as permissible actions toward research participants, at the same time indicating what, at least in our view, are more desirable ways of behaving. But we must be clear that there is no agreement about which form is the "proper" way of defining what is right and wrong about research practice.

Strong disagreement about specific principles is commonplace. While Baumrind (e.g., 1978) decries the immorality of experiments involving deception (see below), Gergen (1973) replies, "I would judge the vast majority of instances in which these principles have been violated as inconsequential to subjects" (p. 908). Gergen would substitute empirical study of what harm is actually done in deception studies for prejudgments in terms of universal principles; "Absolute moral values corrupt absolutely" (p. 908). In this case, a disagreement about a specific principle also involves a dispute about the nature of ethical principles and the criteria for making ethical decisions. Even where principles are generally accepted—that no harm should be done to participants, or that the benefits should exceed the harm—there are predictable arguments in the specific case as to whether there are risks, whether there are any benefits, and whether, in the balance, one outweighs the other.

In the face of all this potential disagreement, are we to give up our search for ethical codes and guidelines? We think not. Rather the fact of disagreement means to us that no single investigator can function as the sole moral arbiter in connection with his or her own work. It is incumbent upon each of us to engage in some process of exchanging ideas, obtaining judgments from other scientists, and from research participants. This exchange will help us formulate general principles, define specific issues, and evaluate whether a single instance is an example of the general rule. Researchers may have some questions about whether a particular process (e.g., government regulation) is working well or fairly, but the very nature of ethical decision making requires at least some participation in a process of intellectual interchange that attempts to resolve differences in points of view and dilemmas in making choices among alternative courses of action.

Ethics and Methodology

Research projects always involve an intervention with each participant. Until the nineteenth and early twentieth centuries, the conceptual model of research in the physical sciences accepted the assumption that it was possible to investigate and measure a phenomenon without affecting it in some way. While this assumption has been largely abandoned in the physical sciences, it persists in many descriptions of the scientific method in psychology and psychiatry. But when we acknowledge that harm and benefit are potential outcomes of all research participation, we are accepting the view that researchers not only assess people, they may also change them.

This view obviously applies when people agree to participate in a psychotherapy research project. It may not be so obvious that people who "merely" push a lever or fill out a set of questionnaires may also be affected by their experience. One of us is involved in a study of couple relationship changes in the period from mid-pregnancy to after the birth of the first child; the study includes an evaluation of a couples' group experience as a preventive intervention. In pilot work (Cowan, Cowan, Coie, Coie, 1978) we found that "control" couples who filled out assessment instruments in mid-pregnancy but

had no group experience still felt that considering the issues raised by the instruments and discussing these issues with their partner had a marked impact on them as individuals and as a couple. The group session, then, was one intervention; the assessment itself was another. Research participants may thus be as affected by the specific research interventions as they are by their general treatment in the study. In either case their experiences can importantly influence how they perform and the information they give us.

Too often issues of research design and of research ethics are conceived as separate, with the former to be given first and greatest consideration and the latter to be considered only to the extent that changes must be made in the interests of humane treatment. Methodological and ethical issues, it seems to us, are inseparable, and indeed the ethically correct study may more likely be methodologically sound. Central to this view is the concept of the research participant as a partner or collaborator (a view shared with many others, e.g., Guttentag, 1968; Jonas, 1969; Engelhardt, 1978), rather than simply a cooperative subject or, at the extreme, a victim of the investigator. The term "participant" better conveys this meaning than does "subject." Particularly in research that depends on candid self-revelation, the collaborating participant is likely to give fuller and more dependable data, help call attention to shortcomings in measurements, and aid in the interpretation of the information provided. This does not of course guarantee that the ethical study will inevitably provide valid and useful findings.

The reverse proposition is, however, more defensible: the poorly designed study is unethical. We agree heartily with Rutstein (1969, p. 524):

It may be accepted as a maxim that a poorly or improperly designed study involving human subjects—one that could not possibly yield scientific fact (that is, reproducible observations) relevant to the question under study—is by definition unethical. Moreover, when a study is in itself scientifically invalid, all other ethical considerations become irrelevant. There is no point in obtaining "informed consent" to perform a useless study. A worthless study cannot possibly benefit anyone, least of all the experimental subject himself. Any risk to the patient, however small, cannot be justified. In essence, the scientific validity of a study on human beings is in itself an ethical principle.

Ethically responsible research, then, respects the dignity, rights, and welfare of those who participate in the study, and may affect the quality and quantity of the data that participants provide. In detailing and expanding on this general statement, we will consider more explicitly issues of informed and voluntary consent, privacy and confidentiality, and protecting participants from physical, psychological, and social harm, while maximizing benefits to participants themselves, to society, and to science.

INFORMED CONSENT

The Meaning of Informed Consent

Informed and voluntary consent is the cardinal principle of ethical research. Thus the Nuremberg Code states in its first principle: "The voluntary consent of the human subject is absolutely essential." It then goes on to detail the specific conditions required to assure such consent (see Katz, 1972, pp. 305–306 for the full statement). In a more modern version, the current DHEW regulations (45 CFR 46.3) enlarge on the principle and describe the conditions that must be met to ensure participants a free and rational choice:

"Informed consent" means the knowing consent of an individual or his legally authorized representative, so situated as to be able to exercise free power of choice without undue inducement or any element of force, fraud, deceit, duress, or any form of constraint or coercion. The basic elements of information necessary to such consent are:

1. A fair explanation of the procedures to be followed, and their purposes, including identification of any procedures which are experimental;
2. A description of any attendant discomforts and risks reasonably to be expected;
3. A description of any benefits reasonably to be expected;
4. A disclosure of any appropriate alternative procedures that might be advantageous for the subject;
5. An offer to answer any inquiries concerning the procedures; and
6. An instruction that the person is free to withdraw his consent and to discontinue participation in the project at any time without prejudice to the subject.

The "informed consent" requirement must be understood in the context of the potential conflict between societal and individual rights. In a utilitarian view of science implied in the risk-benefit formulation we shall shortly discuss, the good of society can be taken as justification for limiting individual freedoms. For example, it would justify using some people as subjects even unwillingly or at the cost of individual suffering if the social gains were sufficient. But the principle of informed consent rests on the recognition of the participant's right to self-determination (Veatch, 1975, 1978), a profoundly important principle of human rights that is increasingly being recognized in legislation and court decisions. Conceived as an instance of the right to self-determination, informed consent basically protects individuals from external control, although it may also protect them from harm by calling attention to potential risks or dangers. Even if risks could be minimized in other ways, the right to know and decide on one's own behalf is primary. Informed consent does therefore limit the freedom of scientists to seek new knowledge, even of demonstrable scientific or social importance; a fact deplored by some, accepted as necessary by most.

Wherever one stands on the philosophical issue, it is clear that there are many difficult and controversial issues in the application of the principle of informed consent. Of great importance and complexity are the cases arising in research, where subjects either do not know they are being studied or where the validity of the study is believed to depend on subjects being kept ignorant or misinformed about the true purposes, procedures, or measures. Before considering these cases, let us look at the somewhat simpler issues that arise when participants cannot fulfill the essential requirements of informed consent, which assume that the participant has sufficient information, is able to evaluate it, and is free to choose whether or not to participate in the proposed study.

Limitations on Informed Consent Related to Subject Characteristics

How Much of What Sort of Information Is Necessary? In any but the simplest studies, to tell everything about the study—its purpose(s), procedures, possible risks and benefits to the participants, expected findings and their interpretations, possible contribution—is manifestly impossible. Indeed, if all this were known in advance, it could be argued without undue cynicism that the study is not worth doing, for the outcome is already known. Intrinsic to the research process is uncertainty, which is shared by both investigator and subject. Purposes, procedures, and findings change and evolve as the study progresses. Moreover, the participant may not have sufficient background or the desire to understand the scientific points at issue. What matters basically is that participants know what is expected to them, how they will be treated in the study, what are its costs, and what they will get out of it. Each person needs to know enough to make a rational decision on his or her own behalf. To the extent that participants want more information, even of a technical or scientific sort, the investigator has to be ready to supply it. In fact, studies show that participants rarely want to know as much as is volunteered. In

one experiment it was found that the longer and more detailed the written statement (consent form) given to potential participants, the less likely were they to consent (Epstein & Lasagna, 1969). Many persons probably participate out of faith in the investigator, without clear understanding of what actually is involved, but all have the right to know if they wish.

Ability to Understand the Issues and to Give Consent. So far, our description of informed consent assumes that if individuals are given reasonable amounts of clear, pertinent information, they will be able to evaluate it. There are two very important categories of research participants where this assumption may not hold: children and adults with severe cognitive or emotional dysfunction, neither of whom are the "reasonable adults" defined by law as competent to make decisions in their own best interests. Even in these cases, however, prospective participants have the right to be told about a study and to decide whether or not they will take part.

Children. In an attempt by a new ad hoc committee of the American Psychological Association to revise the APA's ethical research guidelines once again, special attention is being given to work with children (e.g., Charlesworth, 1980). New DHEW regulations in this area are also forthcoming. There does not seem to be a consensus on the age at which children are autonomous enough to give their own consent to participation in a research project. One approach, especially in the area of clinical research, is to use the legal age at which they can consent to their own medical care. Before that time, parents must always be consulted before a child is approached.

At least one parent or guardian must be given a description of the proposed project, but in a technical sense cannot give consent for their child to participate. Rather, the parent is said to give *permission*. When the researcher approaches a child older than seven, that child may *assent,* once the project has been described and explained at the appropriate level. Children younger than seven must still be asked if they will participate even if the parents give permission. The child may *agree* or refuse; even the shy or sullen resistance of a child who prefers to go out and play must be honored. The use of the terms "permission," "assent," and "agreement" reserves the term "consent" for the case of an adult who is fully capable of making informed decisions about his or her own life.

The role of the parent or adult guardian is not limited to an initial "yes" or "no." As part of the informed consent procedure for infants and toddlers, and also as protection from risk, it has been argued that at least one of the parents should be present during the experiment itself. While this practice may inform the parent and protect the child, it would limit some research investigations. For example, in attachment research, part of the assessment of attachment depends on the child's reaction to the parent leaving the room for some limited period of time. When participants are older than infants, there is also the issue that at some as yet to be defined age of the child, the parent's presence begins to infringe on the child's right to privacy.

How does one determine the "appropriate level" at which to explain a project to a child? First, by knowing the particular children of the project well, and second, by appreciating developmental changes in children's thinking. Then the investigator can develop an explanation appropriate to the group(s) in the study. An analogy from cross-cultural research may be helpful. Instruments developed in one culture must usually be translated before being administered to people from another. A major test for the accuracy of a translation is to have a bilingual native translate back into the original language. Similarly, the researcher can explain a project to a child and have the child attempt to explain it in his or her own words. When the expla-

nations become reasonably accurate, the "appropriate level" has been reached; if children of widely different age levels are used in the study, the process of assessing the child's understanding should be repeated at each level.

Adults with Severe Cognitive or Emotional Dysfunction. Adults with severe impairments should not be used as research participants unless the purpose of the study specifically focuses on their condition. Thus investigtors studying mental retardation, neuropsychological impairment, or schizophrenia must of course seek persons so identified as participants, but they should not be sought for studies that could as well be done with others. While adults with severe dysfunction cannot be equated with children, their participation raises two similar issues. First, their legal, authorized representative or guardian must give permission. Second, there may be special problems in communicating the nature of the study and in eliciting an informed judgment about participation. For example, regulations and guidelines generally refer to written consent given in response to a written description of the study. Adults with dyslexia or perceptual-motor difficulties may be unable to read or to write their assent even when they understand the study; others may have particular difficulty in understanding, especially if information is presented in abstract form. In some cases the demands made on these participants in obtaining informed consent may be more stressful than the research procedures to which they would be subjected in the study proper.

Providing research information for a person recently hospitalized for psychosis also has its difficulties. It should be apparent that the task itself involves a high degree of clinical skill and sensitivity. These special difficulties dramatize a point that actually applies to all informed consent procedures. When a researcher describes a study to a potential participant, the two are engaged in an interpersonal interaction in which *how* information is conveyed, and how carefully the researcher listens and responds may affect the outcome as much as the information itself. Especially when the researcher is working with children or adults with impaired functioning, it is necessary to take time with each prospective participant, to establish rapport, to present the study, and to probe for the way in which the researcher's presentation is being understood.

Some General Problems with Written Consent Forms.   The difficulty of understanding written consent forms is not limited to children and dysfunctional adults. Morrow (1980) collected 60 typical consent forms from five national cancer research centers and analyzed them for readability using two standard scoring systems. Nearly three out of every four passages required college-level reading ability; in all, the consent forms were only slightly easier to read than the *New England Journal of Medicine!*

In a study of medical experiments, Gray (1975) found that although signed forms were obtained, the essential conditions of informed consent as laid out in HEW regulations were not met in many cases. In a study of voluntarily admitted psychiatric patients, Palmer and Wohl (1972) found that, within 10 days after entering the hospital, 60% of those questioned could not recall signing a form consenting to hospitalization. A full third of the group could not recall, at all or accurately, what the form said, and some even denied having signed one. Over one-quarter of the research patients in a VA Hospital study did not know that they were participating in an investigation (many of the others did not know what it was about) even though there was a careful explanation and all signed the proper forms (Committee on Biomedical Research in the Veterans Administration, 1977).

Another problem, perhaps more true with nonpatients, is that the consent form suggests an overly bureaucratic or legalistic way of dealing with an understanding that could better be sealed with a nod and a handshake. People are understandably suspicious of a formal-looking document that suggests a contract in which something is signed away, a document that might be more in the interests of the investigator than of the participant. Indeed it has been reported in one survey research study that *fewer* people were willing to serve as respondents when asked to sign a consent form than when the agreement was simply left verbal (Singer, 1977). Still, in most cases participants understand the need. For investigators and institutions, the file of consent forms is necessary both to show compliance with HEW regulations, if requested, and should controversy occur about whether or not the investigator overstepped the research understanding.

Research with People Less Free to Choose.   Even if information is available and the individual is able to evaluate it, the participant must be free to decide by his or her values whether to participate. As Kelman (1972) forcefully reminds us, there is usually a decided power imbalance between investigators and their subjects. Whether the investigator does in fact hold power over the participant, or whether the participant is simply in awe of the higher status of the investigator, the consequence may be the same; participants may feel obliged to agree as they might not if they held coequal status. Coercion might therefore exist, Kelman argues, in many more subtle ways than was originally intended in the Nuremberg statement about "force, fraud, deceit, duress . . ." This problem exists in many typical research situations. If a student is asked by a professor to participate in research, is the student fully free to refuse? Similar difficulties arise when employers recruit their employees or psychotherapists want to study their clients, and in research involving patients in public clinics, prisons, and indeed in any research in which the basic populations are poorer and less powerful than the researchers. Yet another form of the problem is raised by the issues we have discussed in connection with children and impaired adults. While the language of codes and guidelines makes clear that the parent or guardian gives permission and not consent, it may be difficult for the child or the patient to refuse once the guardian has agreed.

In the past, biomedical, behavioral, and social scientists have depended on groups of subjects less free to choose, precisely because of their availability and docility. These practices have not ended, but changes have been made, and new approaches are being considered. In fair measure the college sophomore has been the experimental animal of much human psychology. Recently the traditional practice of requiring undergraduates to participate in research has been dropped entirely in many universities, or the student may elect an alternative activity such as writing a paper in connection with a course. In another example, it has been recognized that clinic patients are asked to undergo procedures that would not be imposed on private patients. Veatch (1978) has proposed that ethical clinical research should not have clinic patients as more than half the participants in any single research project. In the context of biomedical research, it has been suggested that investigators not concerned with a specific disease should not impose on sick people but rather use the best and healthiest people available (Jonas, 1969); this population should even include the investigators themselves, who usually forego the privilege of serving science by subjecting themselves to their own research procedures. Drug companies might use prisoners for testing experimental drugs more sparingly if the financial incentive for the companies were reduced by requiring them to pay prisoners the same stipend usually given to outside volunteers; if prison regulations would not allow individuals to receive the entire amount, then the remainder could be placed in a general fund for activities benefiting all prisoners.

To argue categorically that investigators should be prevented from investigating less powerful subject populations is irresponsible and would effectively block much important research, especially studies directed precisely to the understanding of vulnerable populations. But honest recognition of the power imbalance between investigators and participants is needed, and possible excesses have to be guarded against. Even if it becomes more difficult and more expensive, using a broadly representative sample may increase the scientific validity and generalizability of the study.

Limitations on Informed Consent Related to Study Objectives and Design

We have been considering cases in which some quality of the participants limits their capacity to give informed consent. Another important set of problems derives from the fact that in many studies people may not know that they are being studied or, if aware, are misinformed about the purpose and procedures of the research.

Uninformed Participants. Two kinds of studies in which participants are unwittingly involved seem to us to raise few if any ethical objections. The first of these involves observation in public places. Children may be observed on playgrounds to note instances of pro- and antisocial behavior. Men and women are observed approaching a door; who opens the door for whom is treated as an index of changing social mores. In these cases the observer is visible, no individual is identified, and all measures are nonintrusive. The second area involves archival data, either clinical records or data of earlier studies. Here the matter is somewhat more complex, for the patients or participants never gave specific consent for this particular use of the data. As long as the data are treated with appropriate confidence and care, we see little difficulty in waiving the informed consent rule. Epidemiologists note the potentially disastrous effect on their science if clinical records could not be searched retrospectively out of overzealous concern with patients' rights (Gordis & Gold, 1979).

However, other types of studies involving unaware participants do pose moral questions. Hidden observers may note or record the behavior of patients in a waiting room or the actual deliberations of a jury, even with the judge's consent. In covert naturalistic experiments, lifelike situations have been contrived, such as having an apparently sick person fall down in a subway train in order to discover the conditions under which real passengers might volunteer help. A third type of example includes participant-observer studies in which subjects are never informed that they are part of a research project. A sociologist at a cocktail party observes and reports on this social custom; a psychologist gets himself admitted as a psychiatric patient by faking symptoms and then publishes a paper describing patient and staff behavior; a sociologist volunteers to serve as a lookout in a public toilet while men engage in homosexual activities, which he then describes in a research report. In all of these actual cases, there is an obvious disregard for informed consent, invasion of privacy, and in some cases deception. Investigators who do such research argue that it allows for the study of behavior as it actually occurs outside the laboratory, utilizing naturally occurring events or ones that, though contrived, could happen in everyday life, and—above all—that no one is harmed in the process. Others argue that such "snooping and duping" poses grave ethical issues for the social sciences (Mead, 1969; Baumrind, 1977, 1978; Jung, 1975, among others). Individual rights are violated and, in the jury case, a precious social institution may be endangered. The public may become more cynical about social scientists. Public behavior indeed may be altered; people may become more sensitized and, for example, less likely to offer help to people in real distress if they

come to believe that they might be "on candid camera." These are serious issues.

Misinformed Participants. In many other investigations, people know that they are participants, but they are not informed or are misinformed about the purposes and procedures. As noted earlier, it is virtually impossible and sometimes not entirely desirable to tell literally everything. It is commonplace in personality inventory research to label a procedure intended to assess neurotic trends a "personal information questionnaire," both out of consideration for participants feelings and to guard against response sets. Nor would most investigators believe it wrong to say that they are studying the relation between "social attitudes and child-rearing practices" when actually the study is concerned with a distinction between authoritative and authoritarian parenting. Similarly, the double-blind design, in which neither the participant nor the person administrating the procedure knows which of alternate drugs or other conditions this particular person is receiving, has been a powerful method for assuring valid findings, precisely because it limits both participant and experimenter expectancy effects. Though we will shortly suggest a more considerate alternative to the usual introduction to the double-blind experiment, in these examples the deceit is relatively minor, and the need for it could be readily understood by most participants.

More severe instances of misinformation and deception occur in laboratory study of topics such as stress, conformity, and obedience. The effort is made to create realistic situations (fictional environments), as in the subway study, but this time participants are deliberately misled in order to control the variables under study. For example, in an experimental stress study, individuals may be led to believe that they are intellectually inadequate or even that their lives are in danger.

Illustrative is Milgrim's (1974) much-discussed study of obedience, in which participants were nominally assistants in a learning experiment. Their task was to administer electric shocks of graduated intensity to "subjects" when they erred. In fact, these "subjects" were accomplices of the experimenter, and no shocks were actually delivered. The real subject was the nominal assistant, and the purpose was to discover to what extent he would obey authority and cause pain. Subjects obeyed to a surprising degree, causing what they believed to be intense pain, though themselves suffering anxiety and remorse in the process. At the end they were debriefed and told the truth.

The Issue of Deception

Deception studies are common. From the late 1940s through the early 1970s, the proportion of studies using deception published in major journals in personality and social psychology increased from near 20% to near 40% (Seeman, 1969; Menges, 1973). On specific topics such as cognitive dissonance and conformity, as many as 72% and 81% respectively of the published research involved deception (Stricker, 1967). Despite the cautions in the APA code of research ethics in 1973, Baumrind (1978) contends from a more limited and informal survey that deception studies continue to be carried out. In discussion of these issues, we find researchers on both sides of the fence and straddled on the top.

Arguments for Deception. The basic arguments supporting the use of deception is that it enables us to bring important phenomena into the laboratory for controlled observation. Instead of waiting until someone experiences a stressful situation in real life, it is possible to induce one in the laboratory. Laboratory research is regarded as more convenient, cheaper, and above all, more productive of trustworthy findings. At the heart of this argument is faith in the power of the experimental method, buttressed by the claim that in some cases it is necessary to have a "naive subject," unaware of the real reason for the study and unaware of the manipulation involved in setting it up.

A second justification for the use of deception is that it does little if any harm. Whatever negative effects do ensue can be dissipated by "debriefing" the participant in an interview after the experiment has been completed. Applying a cost-benefit logic, protagonists argue that when little harm is done on one hand, and scientific advance is possible on the other, then deception is ethically justifiable (e.g., Berkowitz, 1978, among others). Even in the contested Milgrim study, there is reasonable evidence from postexperimental and follow-up investigations that no subject was enduringly harmed (Milgrim, 1974).

Arguments against Deception. Critics have countered with two types of arguments. The first asserts that deception is by its nature unethical, and that it should simply not be done regardless of potential benefits or minimal harms. The second encompasses a range of views that challenge the belief that laboratory controls somehow yield better data, question the claim that little harm is done, and present evidence that debriefing may not in fact soften the impact of deception.

At the first level are matters of ethical principle, raised by critics such as Kelman (1966, 1967), Mead (1969), and Baumrind (1975, 1978, 1979). We are among the many who do not accept the cost-benefit analysis as providing a primary ethical criterion, and believe instead that the individual's right of voluntary consent must be given priority. Under the illusion that they have entered into a voluntary agreement and that investigators can be taken at their word, research participants may be led into self-revelations that they never intended to make. This raises the most profound ethical issues. "Fundamental moral principles of reciprocity and justice are violated when the behavioral scientists acts to deceive or diminish those whose extension of trust is based on the expectation that persons to whom trust is accorded will be trustworthy in return" (Baumrind, 1978, pp. 23–24). Kelman (1967) notes that most people do not, in ordinary human interactions, lie or mislead, make promises they do not intend to keep, or violate the respect due fellow human beings. Yet all of these are done in the name of scientific knowledge.

In response to the argument that deception is simply a device to bring phenomena into the laboratory for better investigative control, many psychologists are now questioning whether the experiment (with or without deception) is indeed the best scientific method for making valid inferences about behavior (Chein, 1972; Orne, 1962; Kelman, 1966). The laboratory environment is a particular one, with its unique demand characteristics; phenomena that can be reproduced there are at best analogs of behavior in the natural world; available subjects hardly represent humanity. For reasons such as these, generalizability of laboratory (and to a lesser extent naturalistic) experimental data has been questioned. Just as the study of white rats in mazes hardly yields a fair or complete picture of animal behavior, as ethologically minded colleagues insist, human laboratory experiments may similarly give a simplified or distorted view of human behavior. For scientific reasons, aside from ethical concerns, there has been a major move in many areas of psychology toward studies in natural environments that may be more ecologically representative (Gibbs, 1979). Bretano's caution, made early in the history of general psychology, that psychology would do better to be an empirical than an experimental science, is again meaningful.

Reviewing the deception literature, Seeman (1969) concludes: "It is an ironic fact that the use of deception, which is intended to control the experimental environment, may serve only to contaminate it." Participants in deception studies are made more

suspicious (Bonacich, 1970; Keisner, 1971, cited by Baumrind, 1978; Fillenbaum, 1966), even though, as Fillenbaum found, they may accept the necessity for deception and not act on their suspicions. As deception experiments are more common, both in the laboratory and in the field, it is reasonable to ask whether the primary justification will be lost as the pool of naive subjects decreases. When participants suspect the stated purposes of the experimenter, they act on their own interpretations and variability increases (Stricker, Messick, & Jackson, 1969). Instead of acting naturally, subjects may fake naiveté and role-play what they believe the experimenter expects (Orne, 1962). The cynical statement that there are no naive subjects, just naive experimenters, raises questions about the methodological value of deception research.

While there has been little evidence of direct physical or mental harm to participants in deception experiments (Berkowitz, 1978; Gergen, 1973; Reynolds, 1979; Bower & deGasperis, 1978), there may well be both more subtle and more pervasive dangers. We are deeply concerned with the general view of psychologists as tricksters. This point was brought poignantly home to the late David Krech on the morning that President Kennedy was assassinated. Before starting his class, Krech shared the news and his distress. After a moment of silence, there was laughter and someone called out "OK, Professor, so what's the experiment?" Might not this erosion of trust be harmful to those we teach? Might it not undermine public respect and support in the long run? More immediately, Jung (1975) calls attention to potential dangers as people become more cognizant of the existence of covert naturalistic experiments involving unwitting participants. People may be more self-conscious in public; mistrust and suspicion, already too common, increase; people may be desensitized to unusual events, suspecting them of being experiments. Such concerns, along with the possibility that some participants may be hurt or feel abused, all argue against deception research.

Debriefing. Debriefing is intended to undo the potential harm of deceiving a person involved in a research project. After the experiment the ruse is revealed, reasons given, and the experience discussed with the participants. But, despite debriefing, effects may linger. Thus Walster, et.al. (1967) gave false feedback to participants about personality test performance, telling them that they had either exceptional or poor social skills. Even after being debriefed, subjects given falsely positive information still tended to rate themselves higher than those given negative feedback. Other reports of continuing effects have been made, and elaborate debriefing procedures have been suggested to eliminate them (Ross, Lepper, & Hubbard, 1975).

A particular problem arises when debriefing itself might cause the participant greater pain than simply remaining ignorant. To be told the truth (worse, if told bluntly and unsympathetically) can reveal to participants their aggressiveness, cowardice, or other personal weaknesses, "insights" they hardly bargained for when enlisting in the research. Some years ago, one of us created an experimental situation intended to induce "disintegrative anxiety" (Korchin & Schwartz, 1960). College students were told that they were control subjects for the standardization of a test of psychopathology to be used with patients. The procedure was a perceptual test, for "As you know, psychiatric patients tend to distort reality in accord with unconscious needs, particularly if under pressure." Thus participants were shown a series of pictures for brief exposure; after describing each, it was shown for full exposure so that they could note any (minor) errors they might have made. In fact, the second picture in most cases differed from the first, depicting a more innocent scene. Thus participants described scenes suggestive of suicide, death, homosexuality, aggression, lust, and

so on only to discover that they had "projected" these themes. Participants were understandably disturbed, and dependent variables showed it.

In prospect, what was so acceptable about this procedure was that it seemed possible to reverse effects completely. Subjects did not have to take our word about the ruse. All we had to do is lay out the pairs of pictures and they could plainly see that, in actuality, they had not distorted at all. At the end, participants were visibly relieved, though not always without some residual resentment, for it had been a painful experience.

But one man put us in a moral predicament. Throughout the procedure, he seemed quite unperturbed. On "second viewing", he minimized, denied, or rationalized discrepancies from his original account. Whereas for all other participants, showing the picture pairs assured them of their sanity, for this man it would have exposed his pathology. Out of clinical concern, we simply thanked him and sent him home. To debrief honestly, in his case, would have been more brutal than to leave him in ignorance.

Thus deception experiments may pose for us the dilemma of choosing between *deceptive debriefing,* to protect the subject from the harm that might result from full disclosure, and *inflicted insight,* in which the subjects' flaws are painfully revealed to them in insights they never bargained for (Baumrind, 1978; 1979). In the choice, it is probably true that many investigators are not revealing fully their deceptive practices. Baumrind argues that this dilemma should not exist, and the only sure way is to stop designing studies that get us into this bind.

Some Alternatives to Deception Experiments

While we have presented a deliberately critical view of deception experiments, we do not agree with the absolute position that would ban any research that fails to provide full information to participants. We have presented examples of not informing participants that seem to us to protect privacy and avoid exposing participants to risk or harm. We also recognize the fact that deception is a loaded word; in daily life as in research, it is not always easy to draw the line between deception and tact or sensitivity. We are most concerned with examples in which participants are deliberately misinformed, and in which they might have chosen not to participate or not to reveal information if they were aware of the true purpose of the experiment.

In every case the investigator has a primary responsibility to consider every possible alternative to a deception design. Even if it is necessary for the participant to remain ignorant, the reason for this can be told and consent obtained to be uninformed. Thus, in the "blind" drug experiment, rather than telling participants nothing or an untruth, it would seem more appropriate to say something like: "We are comparing the effects of two drugs (perhaps naming both), one of which you will receive today. If you knew which one, your expectations might well color your reactions and we couldn't know about the drug effects themselves. If you can go along with this uncertainty, we will of course tell you everything at the end of the session." Then one should add whatever can be said about risks, benefits, side effects, duration of effects, and the like. In this way, it seems to us, the spirit if not the letter of the prinicple of informed consent is preserved, for participants are truthfully told that they cannot know everything, why that is so, and that they are free not to participate if they cannot accept the uncertainty. They are buying a pig in a poke, but at least they know that there is a pig, a poke, and a gimmick, and that they are necessary parts of the scientific game, which they can or cannot play in, as they choose.

It has also been suggested (Fost, 1975; Veatch, 1978; Jonas, 1969) that "surrogate subjects," people as much like the eventual participants as possible, should also be consulted in developing a research plan. The entire study including the deception and the necessity for it should be fully explained, and their judgement solicited as to whether they would participate in such a study if they knew the full story in advance, and whether they would feel mistreated if they had participated with less than full knowledge. Obviously the "consent" of such a group cannot substitute for that of the true subjects. Nor can it substitute for the judgment of professionals, colleagues, or members of the Institutional Review Board. But the contribution of surrogates can be great, for their values and concerns are closer to those of the actual participants. Surrogates and other professionals, each in their fashion, add objectivity to the investigator's decision, which may be colored by his or her eagerness to do the study as quickly and efficiently as possible. All such consultation, perhaps costly in money, time, or effort, reflects greater concern with the rights and dignity of research participants.

As another alternative to deception, Kelman (1967) has suggested the value of role-playing. Rather than trying to arouse experimentally actual attitudes or feelings, situations are described and participants asked how they would behave in them. Shortcomings in this procedure have been noted (Berkowitz, 1978). Though ethically appealing, role-playing seems to be a limited alternative to actual experiments (Miller, 1972).

A related idea involves simulating actual life situations, which amounts to a more dramatic form of role-playing. In Zimbardo's (1973) study, students at Stanford served as guards or prisoners. The simulation of prison life was so successful, bringing about feelings of helplessness and victimization in the "prisoners" and abuses of power in the "guards," that the study had to be terminated after six days.

There are obvious advantages and disadvantages of each research strategy, but one solution for the problems of laboratory deception may be found in moving from experimental to naturalistic models of research. Stress does not need to be produced in the laboratory; it exists in real life and in definable enough situations to allow systematic investigation, as has been shown in studies of paratroopers (Basowitz, Persky, Korchin, & Grinker, 1955; Epstein, 1962), surgical patients (Janis, 1958), or students during actual examinations (Mechanic, 1962). Observing and interviewing people during and following life experiences can provide perhaps more generalizable and in-depth data. The observations would be obtained under less controlled but also less limited conditions than those which can be created in experiments. In all, ethical concerns and scientific considerations converge to commend the search for alternatives to the experimental model.

PRIVACY AND CONFIDENTIALITY

The Right to Privacy

The right to personal privacy is on a par with, or indeed might even be considered a special instance of, the right of self-determination. Throughout our society, there has been growing concern with the rights of individuals to share or not to share, as they wish, information about themselves and, conversely, the need to constrain both private and public institutions in their instrusions into individual lives. Such concern has grown apace with technological advances that make it increasingly easy to record, store, and retrieve vast amounts of information. In behavioral and social research, similarly, there has been increased concern with potential invasions of personal privacy in the gathering and managing of information.

Although not constitutionally guaranteed, there has been a longstanding interest in privacy in U.S. law (see Bower & deGasparis, 1978, and Ruebenhausen & Brim, 1966, for discussion of legal and social science perspectives on privacy). An important starting point was an 1890 article by Warren and Brandeis, which propounded a right to be left alone and legal activities designed to protect this right. Over the years legal scholars came to see the right as protecting the individual from others (whether individuals or the government): (1) obtaining and using his or her ideas, writings, name, or other aspects of personal identity; (2) obtaining or revealing personal information; and (3) intruding physically or in more subtle ways into his or her life space. Social scientists have similarly defined privacy as "the right of the individual to decide for himself how much of his life—his thoughts, emotions and the facts that are personal to him—he will share with others" (Frankel, 1975), or the "selective control of access to the self or one's group" (Altman, 1975). Although more subtle and less anchored in the law than, for example, freedom of speech or religion or property rights, Reubenhausen and Brim (1966) see privacy as a growing moral imperative. In their view, it consists of two parts, the right to be let alone, the more usually emphasized, and its obverse, the right to share and communicate:

The essence of privacy is no more, and certainly no less, than the freedom of the individual to pick and choose for himself the time and the circumstances under which, and, most importantly, the extent to which, his attitudes, beliefs, behavior and opinions are to be shared with or withheld from others. The right to privacy is, therefore, a positive claim to a status of personal dignity—a claim for freedom, if you will, but freedom of a very special kind. (p. 426)

Like other individual freedoms, they point out, the right of privacy is not absolute, conflicting as it does with society's right to know. In attempting to define the limits of privacy, we see three major issues: (1) the degree of sensitivity of the information; (2) the manner in which the information is gathered (e.g., unobtrusive measures with unwitting participants); and (3) confidentiality, the treatment of the information after it has been received. There has been increased interest in this last issue as the courts have become involved in rulings about confidentiality of information sources; it is here that we see the clearest examples of conflict between individual privacy and the right of others to have access to important information.

Sensitivity of Information

The APA (1973) code states: "Religious preferences, sexual practices, income, racial prejudices, and other personal attributes such as intelligence, honesty and courage are more sensitive items than 'name, rank, and serial number.' " The investigator must judge how embarrassing the material might be and how much harm its revelation might cause. This is not always easy, for what might be personally embarrassing varies with groups, settings, and over time. Thus inquiring into sexual behavior at the time of the original Kinsey study seemed daring; today it is commonplace. Farr and Seaver (1975) report that college students did not consider as particularly sensitive questions about sex, drug use, or family income, nor did they think that nonanonymous intelligence or personality test data should be restricted in the context of psychological research. Undoubtedly other groups might find any or all of these areas offensive, and investigators would have to exert safeguards (notably anonymity and confidentiality, to be considered shortly), or at the extreme forego inquiry in some areas.

However, the risks to subjects may derive from more than just revealing personal data; participation in the study itself may expose them to social or legal dangers. As an instance, one of us was involved in an experimental therapeutic program for drug-abusing youth (Soskin, Ross, & Korchin, 1971). Originally these teenagers came to our Psychology Clinic, along with clients of diverse sorts, but as the project grew, it seemed better to establish a center with its own staff and facilities in a separate building. But now, we

were wisely reminded by the campus committee for the protection of human subjects, we might be exposing participants to a new danger. If only drug-abusing youth were subjects, then anyone entering the building regularly was instantly identifiable by any police officer who cared to watch the entrance. Consequently we extended the sample to include schoolmates, who might or might not be using drugs, not incidentally adding valuable control data at the same time.

Given recent concern about the effect of labeling and stigmatizing individuals, increased attention has been paid to both ethical and design issues in studies of children in school classrooms and other public settings. Garmezy (1975), for example, has studied children whose parents have been diagnosed as schizophrenic. These children themselves were in no way identified patients. Although they and their parents had completely agreed to the study, Garmezy was appropriately concerned with not revealing their status to schoolmates and teachers. Not only would this violate their confidentiality, but it could bias the observations of the teachers and the teachers' subsequent treatment of the children. Consequently he enlisted two other children, along with the critical subject, in each of the classrooms he studied. While reducing the possibility of labeling and stigmatizing the children of psychiatric patients, he also achieved a methodologically sound comparison group by recruiting these subject triads.

In the recent past there has been a considerable amount of ethical concern with personality tests, attitude scales, and other devices commonly used in psychological research, any of which can be viewed as invading privacy (Conrad, 1967). The items of such scales often touch on sensitive areas—sexual functions, bodily concerns, religious beliefs, racial attitudes, and the like—that may be offensive to individuals, even if the procedure is being taken anonymously and only group findings are to be reported. Research participants should have the right to ignore any items that offend, as well as to leave the study entirely.

However, the issue is made more complex by the fact that in many cases the purpose of the procedure or what is actually being measured is hidden. Thus inventories intended to measure pathology, aggessiveness, authoritarianism, Machiavellianism, as well as more desirable qualities, are given innocuous labels, and perhaps most of the items themselves seem harmless. In the case of projective and other indirect measures, the problem goes even further, for the participants can only guess what sense is made out of the stories they tell to TAT pictures or their responses to the Rorschach inkblots. Indeed the very purpose of personality assessment is to understand the subject's character, not as he or she would want us to know it but as it "truly is." Indirect methods are designed precisely to circumvent the subject's ability to withhold information of concern to us. How secure are the inferences that can be made from assessment techniques is an important but separate question; from the vantage of our present concern, do they invade the subject's privacy? In a classic text on clinical testing, Cronbach (1970, p. 459) says simply, "Any test is an invasion of privacy for the subject who does not wish to reveal himself to a psychologist."

After giving evidence for this assertion, however, Cronbach adds:

He (the subject) is willing to admit the psychologist into these private areas only if he sees the relevance of the questions to the attainment of his goals in working with the psychologist. The psychologist is not "invading privacy" where he was freely admitted and where he has a genuine need for the information obtained.

Therein, to our minds, lies the direction for resolving the dilemma. The limits of privacy can to some extent be defined by the participant. Privacy is not *invaded* when the individual has the right of informed consent and can make his or her own calculation of the potential risks and benefits to self and to society. To the extent that subjects understand the purpose and potential value of the study, and find their goals and ours congruent, the ethical danger is minimized. Perhaps they do not truly know that they are revealing, or how the test works, but they can have faith in the value of the inquiry. As researchers, our first task is to earn and maintain that faith.

Privacy Issues in Gathering Information

As we have indicated above, violations of informed consent also constitute potential invasions of privacy. Many studies using unobtrusive, nonreactive measures of social behavior do not intrude on individuals' right to privacy, as conceived here, such as studies measuring dust on library books to assess reading interests, counting broken windows to estimate pride in property, observing seating patterns in restaurants, and using photoelectric cells and recorders to study movement patterns in public places (Bouchard, 1976). More serious issues, as we have seen earlier, arise where the investigator may be violating an implicit social contract with the participants, as in the case of covert participant observer studies, or manipulating settings and people, as in covert naturalistic experiments. In fact, it is still not clear whether in some of these cases investigators might not be criminally as well as professionally unethical, although lawyers differ considerably in their judgments (Silverman, 1975; Nash, 1975).

Concern with invasion of privacy is more distinctly justified if there are intrusions into very private and important parts of our lives or where other basic values are threatened. Thus the jury-bugging studies mentioned earlier, even though done with the court's permission, understandably led to public anger, congressional hearings, and legislation forbidding such research in the future, for the integrity of our justice system seemed threatened. Observing people on the street or in the theater is permissible, but entering one's home under false pretenses to observe, say, furniture arrangement is reprehensible; sneaking into a bedroom at night to observe sexual behavior is even more so, and may be criminal as well.

But sometimes it is difficult to decide whether a setting is private or public and whether a person's privacy is or is not invaded. In one study Middlemist, Knowles, and Matter (1976) unobtrusively observed men urinating in a university toilet—a public place, but a private activity. They measured both delay in onset and time of urination as index of psychophysiological arousal when a confederate either used the adjacent urinal or one removed. Subjects took half again as long to start, but half the time to urinate, under "close" than under "distant" conditions. Koocher (1977) criticized the study for going beyond propriety and invading privacy. In reply, Middlemist, Knowles, and Matter (1977) noted that all they were doing was reconstructing an everyday event in a public place and that all data were collected and reported anonymously. Moreover, about half of the subjects were informed at the end and none expressed any objection. Still, people could be upset at learning about such research, and the public image of behavioral scientists as "snoopers and dupers" could be intensified.

Anonymity and Confidentiality

Anonymity is perhaps the best safeguard against the harmful effects of entering private life areas; where that is not possible, assuring the confidentiality of information obtained from identifiable people is the next best protection.

In many areas concern is only with the feelings, attitudes, or behavior of people in general rather than those of known individuals, and research can be conducted without

anyone knowing who has participated or what information any individual has given. Thus in personality assessment research involving self-administered procedures, instruments are commonly distributed to large groups by mail or handed out to an assembled group, then completed and returned unsigned or otherwise identified. Where the group is known to the investigator, as would be true in the classroom, it is a good procedure to have the questionnaires turned in at a different time or place, or to allow respondents to mark items "won't say," so that nonparticipants cannot even be identified. Anonymous data also protect participants should material be lost or even subpoenaed. Not least, it has been argued (e.g., Jourard, 1968) that people are less inhibited and more candid if their responses are unlabeled. Where subjects are identifiable but confidentiality has been assured, a number of studies have also shown that fuller and more accurate data emerge (Boruch, 1976). Thus there is scientific as well as ethical gain in anonymity and confidentiality.

It is a breach of research ethics to assure participants of anonymity when in fact this is not true. Thus in one incident reported by APA (1973) a psychologist was doing a job-satisfaction survey for a local company when he discovered that the employer was secretly marking the questionnaire to locate "troublemakers." We admire his straightforward solution: "I burned the questionnaire and told the sponsor where to place his money."

Where a study legitimately needs to link different bodies of data of the same individuals, simple techniques can be used without violating anonymity. Participants can provide personal codes (e.g., mother's maiden name, arbitrary letters or numbers). Or the need can be explained, personal identification requested, and confidentiality assured. Subterfuge is indefensible.

In many areas it is impossible to collect data anonymously; personal interviews, observation, or testing are necessarily involved. In such cases participants are normally assured that all material will be kept confidential and not disclosed to anyone without their explicit consent. To minimize the possibility of disclosure, such material is best kept in locked or inaccessible files after identifying information is deleted, protocols coded, and the code linking the information with the particular person kept well-guarded. In one study, accounts of participation in then-illegal activities by student activists were coded and the codes sent out of the country to make them unavailable to law-enforcement agencies. A number of ingenious methods have been developed by behavioral scientists for guaranteeing the anonymity or confidentiality of research data (e.g., Boruch, 1971a, 1971b, 1972, 1976; also see Diener & Candall, 1978, and Reynolds, 1979, for further discussion of proposed techniques).

Where participants' interests are served by disclosing research information to third parties, it can of course be shared with their consent. Thus material bearing on academic promise could be sent to school authorities or psychological assessment material to a treating clinician, if the participant wishes. However, requests from such people, without the participant's knowledge and consent, have to be resisted. In some cases this may be awkward, as for example in the study of children when parents wish to know individual findings, or from an organization, such as a school, that gave consent for a study to be done under its aegis. However, to the extent that a promise was made to individual participants, it must be kept. If this is not possible, and others have legitimate uses for information collected for research purposes, then this should be explained and consent obtained. In some situations of course research data can contribute to the education or treatment of participants; indeed it can constitute a proper reimbursement to the participant or to the setting for participating in the study. Additional test data may be valuable for the treatment of patients in a clinic; ability or achievement data can help a teacher

working with the individual child; these can legitimately be offered to the clinic or school, to the advantage of the participant and in gratitude for the organization's help with the study, but only with the participant's understanding and consent.

An ethical dilemma is posed if in the course of research testing important information emerges related to the subject's well-being or that of others. Suppose there are clear signs of pathology and the nonpatient-subject seems to need psychological help; suppose a crime is confessed or the subject shares the intent to do harm to someone; what are the limitations or obligations of the investigator? To stand firmly with the principle of confidentiality and deny any need to take actions beyond those literally contained in the research contract seems to us insufficient; we have obligations as psychologists and citizens that cannot be put aside lightly.

In one extreme case, though in the context of psychotherapy rather than research, a patient confessed the intent to kill his girl friend; the therapist, sufficiently concerned, told the police; the director of the university clinic, feeling that therapeutic ethics had been violated, overruled the clinician and asked the police not to act on the information. In fact the patient did kill the woman, and the family subsequently sued the university. At one level the courts held that psychotherapy required absolute confidentiality; at a higher level the decision was overthrown. This led subsequently to a change in the regulations governing privileged communication for psychotherapists in California. Today it is mandatory for a therapist to act if there is serious danger to the life of a third party, as revealed in the otherwise entirely private interaction of patient and therapist. So far these legal actions do not apply to investigators, but the moral issue is the same. In our judgment, the psychological researcher may have to step out of the limited research role (gathering information guaranteed to be kept confidential) and become more actively involved in counseling the subject or informing others as to dangers. When possible, such concerns should be shared first and primarily with the subject, but as outside intervention is required to avert dangers, investigators have to act on their consciences as pysychologists and citizens.

Moreover, it is well to realize that, as yet, confidentiality in the investigator-participant relation is not protected by law as it is in the case of many licensed professionals working with their clients. In one promising case, a court refused to force a professor to turn over his notes, stating that an academic researcher has the same right to protect confidential sources as a journalist and that forced disclosure would severely stifle research, thus damaging public interest in the long run (Culliton, 1976). On the other hand, Samuel Popkin of Harvard spent eight days in jail for refusing to divulge confidential research information. The fact is that research data and sources are not immune from the subpoena process, even when cooperating participants are promised anonymity and confidentiality (Reynolds, 1979). Wherever the threat of subpoena exits, investigators should take special precautions (as in the case of one group who sent their code out of the country), or apprise participants of their legal status.

HARMS AND BENEFITS

The Ethical Principle

That no harm should befall participants in research is perhaps the most commonly stated and the most widely accepted principle of research ethics. It was clearly articulated in the Nuremberg Code and in all subsequent biomedical and behavioral codes. The APA (1973) codes state in Principle 7:

The ethical investigator protects participants from physical and mental discomfort, harm, and danger. If the risk of such consequences exists, the investigator is requested to inform the participants of that fact, secure consent before proceeding, and

take all possible measures to minimize distress. A research procedure may not be used if it is likely to cause serious and lasting harm to participants.

The codes add in Principle 9:

Where research procedures may result in undesirable consequences for the participant, the investigator has the responsibility to detect and remove or correct these consequences, including, where relevant, long-term aftereffects.

It is probably true that psychological and social studies rarely put participants under great risk of physical or mental harm; certainly this proposition is true in the comparison with the field of biomedical research on human participants. It has been argued repeatedly that there have not been any documented cases of people seriously or permanently harmed as a result of research participation (Crandell & Diener, 1978; Bower & deGasparis, 1978; and Reynolds, 1979). Still there are risks, and the obligation to protect subjects from harm is uncontestable. Thus, in commenting on the APA (1973) ethical code, its authors remark:

The nearest that the principles in this document come to an immutable "thou shalt" or "thou shalt not" is in the insistence that the human participants emerge from their research experience unharmed—at least that the risks are minimal, understood by the participants, and accepted as reasonable. If possible, participants should enjoy an identifiable benefit. (p. 11)

Though mainly "low-risk research," psychological studies have involved potentially dangerous conditions (electric shock, intense sounds, or drugs) and can produce conceivable harms that are physical, psychological (painful affects, lowered self-esteem or exacerbated behavioral symptoms), social (loss of respect) or legal (exposing the participant to criminal charges). Nor are these dangers limited to the participants themselves; they may extend to members of their family, social groups with which they are identified, or even to society itself (Levine, 1978a).

A few illustrations can suffice. (1) In one study, subjects were shown pictures of concentration camp corpses in order to study the effects of the aroused anxiety on other psychophysiological and psychological functions in the laboratory. (2) Male students were attached to a psychogalvanometer and told that the needle would deflect if they were sexually aroused, indicating homosexual trends if the pictured person were male. Nude males were shown and false feedback given; at the end they were informed of the ruse. (3) To simulate a Watergatelike situation, a private detective contacted criminology students to enlist them in a burglary; in one condition, students were offered $2000 for their share. Many of the subjects agreed to participate, although of course the burglary never took place. (4) In lesser ways, many children have been tempted to cheat or steal in studies of moral development or resistance to temptation. In the most literal sense, none of these experiments resulted in discernible harm to the participants; even under the conditions of the military study, where subjects were grossly disturbed emotionally, there were no coronaries or other severe and lasting effects. The effects seemed to end at the conclusion of the experiment. One wonders, however, at more subtle dangers. Having discovered oneself ready to commit a crime or administer pain, as in the obedience study mentioned earlier, can leave lingering self-doubt, guilt, and anxiety; discovering the deceit in many of these experiments could result in continuing distrust and cynicism about the integrity of psychologists.

Precautions to Minimize the Possibility of Harm

If there is any discernible risk in the study, the investigator must do everything possible to minimize it. At the first level, of course, investigators must seriously consider whether the study can be done in alternate ways that do not intentionally put subjects at risk. Thus, for example, the field of stress research has benefited not only ethically but we believe scientifically as well by studying anxiety as it occurs naturally in clinical groups and in actual life situations, whether examinations or disasters. However, if investigators are convinced that a study involving some risk is necessary, then they should be attentive to the following issues.

1. Potentially dangerous equipment should be thoroughly checked; a shock generator can leak high voltage current. If drugs, alcohol, or other agents are used that might be medically harmful, participants should be fully informed about direct and side effects, dosage levels, and the like. If necessary, a physician should be in attendance.

2. Particularly vulnerable people should be screened out. Obviously a person with a known coronary history should not be taken as a participant in a study involving fairly intense stress, nor one with particularly fragile self-concept in a study involving an assault on self-esteem.

3. There should be every effort to discover potential harm in advance in pilot studies, involving particularly stalwart and knowledgeable subjects and perhaps the experimenter himself or herself, or using role-playing or surrogate groups.

4. One must be particularly alert, in the course of the research session, to any signs of undue discomfort, distress, or dysfunction, being prepared to stop the session immediately. Moreover, the participants' right to discontinue at any time should be made perfectly clear.

5. At points of distress, the psychological investigator must be prepared to shift to a more clinical role to deal with any emotional disturbance that may have appeared, putting aside the research role and the research procedures. It is true

of course that changing roles with people agreeing to be research participants (give information) rather than to be patients (be treated) might be looked on as morally questionable. However, in our judgment, if the study itself has either caused or triggered distress, then it is necessary. Shifting to a clinical orientation might be less awkward if, as sometimes happens, the participant reveals persistent psychological problems and asks the investigator (as psychologist) for assistance. Although less obligatory, it is more than appropriate to stand ready to help with suggestions as to counseling, therapy, or other psychological help.

6. Potential harm should be constantly monitored during the research session. If there is any possibility of any persistent or delayed effects, follow-up sessions over as long a period of time as necessary should be scheduled. In the planning of the research, every effort should be made to discover whether such problems might arise.

7. Should any harm be done to a participant, during or as a consequence of research, then the investigator or his or her institution must be prepared to make whatever amends are possible. Medical researchers, for example, have suggested that insurance coverage be provided to cover the costs of illness, lost work, or other damages resulting from research participation, even if all possible safeguards were taken prior and during the study. While such dire problems are highly unlikely in psychological research, the spirit of this suggestion is commendable.

Before concluding this section, we should realize that one of the major risks in psychological research, particularly in realms more relevant to clinical psychology, results not from the research procedures themselves, but from the possibility that the findings may be revealed in personally identifiable form to others. Thus the issue of anonymity and confidentiality are intertwined with the issue of risk.

Benefits to the Participant

Ideally participants themselves should derive some measurable benefit, as well as no harm, from aiding in the project. What kinds of benefits might an individual receive?

1. The tasks involved are intrinsically interesting. Rare as this possibility is, it is sometimes true.

2. There is financial recompense. Paid participation is common, particularly in funded research. The amount of course should be commensurate with the time and effort involved; if unduly large, it could be coercive and deprive the participants of necessary concern for their rights and welfare.

3. There may be potential clinical benefits. This is particularly true in therapeutic or quasi-therapeutic studies, such as analog studies, in which the participant, as patient, may gain from the application of some new diagnostic or therapeutic procedure. However, even in studies with nonclinical populations, there is the real possibility that the participant gains greater self-knowledge, personal or social skills, or even access to needed psychological help.

We have been impressed with how often in our own research and that of our students, we find that participants spontaneously volunteer the information that a research interview has helped them to clarify personal issues. They often report that it has validated their own thinking, and given them a rare opportunity to talk with a nonjudgmental person who is really interested in what they have to say. As we noted earlier, research is always an intervention, and often the results of this intervention are beneficial.

In a discussion of ethics mostly focusing on potenial dangers and abuses, it is important not to forget the other side of the coin.

4. Even if there is no direct clinical benefit, participants may have the satisfaction of feeling that they are contributing to new knowledge that will be of use to others. Participants find satisfaction in helping a researcher who is intensely involved and committed to something he or she feels is important. Participation is sometimes a genuinely altruistic act.

5. Participation may affirm the subject's sense of self-worth and social status. Not uncommonly, particularly in field students with relatively unsophisticated people, people feel honored that they were thought worthy enough to contribute; thus some respondents in survey research, who may demur at the outset ("Why should anyone want to know my opinions?"), end by thanking the interviewer for including them.

6. Finally, and one hopes increasingly often, the participant shares the investigator's concern with the particular problem or with contributing more generally to science and the welfare of humanity.

Risk-Benefit Analysis

A basic tenet of most codes is that the potential benefits from a study must clearly outweigh the risks for the study to be ethically justifiable. We would imagine that most contemporary researchers would agree heartily with a classic statement put forth by Claude Bernard, father of modern medical experimentation. In his famous *Introduction to the Study of Experimental Medicine* of 1865, Bernard asserts the limits and need for medical research in this simple proposition:

Christian morals forbid only one thing, doing ill to one's neighbor. So, along the experiments that may be tried on man, those that can only harm are forbidden, those that are innocent are permissible, and those that may be good are obligatory. (1957, p. 102; original, 1865)

All modern codes refer to a shifting point of balance between risk and benefit; greater risk is allowable when greater gains are likely. Where the risk is too great, however, a research study simply cannot be done. We believe strongly that not all research questions are equally deserving of an answer if their risks are very high in an absolute sense, or if they greatly exceed potential benefits. Below the point of denying permission to do a study, in so-called "high risk" studies, special precautions must be taken to protect the rights and welfare of the participants, including most centrally their right of informed consent. By contrast, in "low risk studies" it is argued that these precautions can be relaxed, though we believe that safeguards should never be eliminated. That there can be considerable difference in opinion as to the potential risks of a study and the potential benefits can be taken as a matter of fact. It is for this reason that the responsible investigator must engage in a process of exchange of viewpoints, as described earlier, in order to make the most ethical decisions.

In some cases both risks and benefits accrue to the participants themselves. For example, in tests of an innovative therapy, the risks to the patient of departing from "standard and accepted practice" may be more than offset by the potential gains. Clearly, if one were suffering from a terminal and untreatable disease, both patient and physician might be willing to experiment even if the risk were great and the promise of success small.

More commonly, however, risk to participants has to be weighed against potential benefits to science and society, and there the evaluation is more difficult. The risk-benefit ratio is a modern version of the old but morally questionable doctrine that the ends justify the means. It also reflects the enduring conflict between the common good and individual rights. There is ample precedent for the principle that society can and must constrain many individual rights in the interest of public welfare. Increasingly, however, the substantive rights of individuals, rather than utilitarian considerations, characterize philosophic and legal thinking (Wallwork, 1975), and may not be lightly ignored even if there are social advantages from so doing. In the larger society, such rights include freedom of speech and religion; in our present context, self-determination (informed consent) and privacy.

But in more pragmatic terms as well, the analysis of risks and benefits is difficult. A risk-benefit ratio suggests measurement and quantification that is rarely possible in the behavioral and social sciences. How harmful is it for a participant to suffer anxiety or lose self-esteem in a study? How much benefit results from these findings or this theoretical clarification? There simply is no way to measure and balance the costs and benefits of a study, as evidenced by the considerable disagreement among professionals about the potential harm to subjects and about the potential worth of many studies. Similarly, it is virtually impossible to predict in advance either the harm or the benefits of a specific study. What results will emerge can only be told at the end; that is why it is necessary to do the study. Dangers may emerge only as people actually become involved in the study. And finally, who should decide what are the risks and benefits? Obviously investigators must have a primary role, but they are not without competing motives. Because of their commitment to the study, investigators may overestimate its importance and underestimate potential hazards. In reformulating the risk-benefit ratio, Kimble (1978) gives the denominator as "risks as seen by reasonable people." Though these include participants and fellow professionals of the Institutional Review Board, foremost among these "reasonable people" are the investigators themselves, for they are the most informed of the three.

Despite all of these difficulties in assessing and evaluating harms and benefits, a risk-benefit analysis is still a necessary step in deciding the ethical appropriateness of research. In and of itself, it is not sufficient to justify a study, but it can give sufficient grounds for *abandoning* one. In our view, risk-benefit analysis should be subordinated to ethical concerns with individual human rights. Above all, we have to guard against the inherent danger of using a utilitarian formulation to rationalize the abuse of participants.

This statement of principle still leaves us with knotty ethical issues. For example, even with full knowledge and absolute clarity about the consequences, does an individual have the right to volunteer his or her life in an experiment that might produce a cure for cancer? Can a responsible investigator request or accept such consent, however informed and voluntary? Does the commitment to preserve life take precedence over the right of self-determination? Over scientific progress? Over social welfare? But these issues are beyond the scope of this chapter or the realities of research in psychology.

SOME ISSUES PARTICULAR TO CLINICAL RESEARCH

Thus far we have been considering issues of research ethics as they might arise in any area of the psychological and behavioral sciences, including but not limited to research in clinical psychology. Which ethical issues are particular to clinical research? Obviously any research that increases our understanding of human functioning is of relevance to the core concerns of clinical psychologists. But what is most distinctly clinical perhaps are studies involving patients, with the goal of understanding and treating psychological distress more effectively.

Most of the issues particular to clinical research involve an understanding of both similarities and differences between the process of therapy and the process of research. Patients have problems for which they seek help from clinicians who will do everything possible to alleviate their distress. Participants in studies are sought out by researchers to serve their interests in gaining knowledge. Clinician-patient and investigator-participant are thus pairs of complementary roles, each involving responsibilities and obligations, the critical difference between them being that the aim in one case is to improve psychological functioning and in the other to advance knowledge. Since the aims are different and may even be contradictory, some have argued that there is an inherent conflict of interest. They conclude that clinicians should not be allowed to use their own patients in their research, although other investigators might approach these patients who would be free to accept or reject the research role. On the other hand, one can be appropriately critical of clinicians who fail to study their own patients, at least to provide a systematic assessment of treatment outcome. We believe that there are important distinctions between clinical treatment and research investigation, but there are also very important areas of overlap.

Research in the Context of Treatment

The patient, biomedical authors note, should receive the "standard and accepted treatment" for his or her difficulties. However, in clinical psychology and in many realms of medicine, it is hard to distinguish between what is standard and accepted and what is innovative treatment requiring research evaluation (Levine, 1978b; Goldiamond, 1978; London & Klerman, 1978). In a real sense, therapy with each person or family is unique. A series of diagnostic assessments, formal or informal, is followed by an intervention, which in turn is followed by an evaluation

of the intervention's success in this particular case; this series may be repeated many times during each treatment session. The clinician is not just applying a standard procedure, but is in a continuous process of conceiving, testing, and reconceptualizing hypotheses in collaboration with the patient. The cognitive processes of the clinician are in all essential respects like those of the researcher.

Also like the researcher, the clinician uses many methods of investigation. Interviewing, psychometric testing, and even systematic experiments, such as assessing the impact of drug dosage, are part of the therapist's attempt to facilitate and evaluate patient improvement. Readers familiar only with the traditional model of hypotheticodeductive experimental science may be reluctant to label clinical work as research, but in fact the clinical method has a long-honored and productive scientific tradition with a firm epistemological foundation (Cowan, 1978). Drawing on Piaget and Freud as the prototypical developers of the clinical method, we can describe it briefly as a systematic but not necessarily standardized combination of tests, naturalistic observations, and single case experiments used to diagnose the underlying organization and meaning of observed behavior. Single case clinical research using the clinical method, then, is an important part of good treatment. In addition, the patient may become part of a larger research project, as clinicians attempt to apply the knowledge gained in one case to the well-being of other patients. It is clear that being a patient and being a research participant is not always an either-or proposition. Similarly, the roles of clinician and researcher cannot always be separated. The good clinician is investigating all the time, whether formally or informally; the responsible investigator has to be attentive to clinical problems as they might arise.

As we see it, no special issues of informed consent for research arise in these cases, because the research does not limit or interfere with the treatment. However, there are new and more complex ethical issues being raised about what patients should be told in their introduction to therapy (Everstine & Everstine et. al., 1980). When therapists are informing patients about the nature of therapy, it would be entirely appropriate to mention their intention to use the data in some future report or publication. Of course, in all instances in which case material is to be published, the patient must be consulted and must be able to refuse.

Although we have attempted to minimize the overly sharp distinctions sometimes made between the clinical and research roles and activities, we should not lose sight of some essential facts. Patients do come to the clinic to be treated, not to be the subjects of research; they do not want to be "guinea pigs," and this wish must be respected. As patients, they are apt to interpret all activities of the clinic as oriented to treatment. Despite efforts to distinguish a particular project as separate from clinical care, the patient may not appreciate the distinction. Even with careful explanations and signed consent forms, patients often assume that the research testing is part of their required treatment. Patients have faith in the clinic's staff and are likely to agree to whatever is requested of them. Unlike nonpatients, they less commonly examine with a "buyer beware" attitude the potential risks and benefits of participating. Finally, at the time they are seeking treatment, clients are more vulnerable people with more fragile self-esteem, and could be more readily hurt by seemingly innocuous procedures. For all of these reasons, special care must be taken not to exploit or abuse patients in clinical research.

Treatment in the Context of Research: The Study of Psychotherapy

Let us consider now the particular ethical issues intrinsic to therapy outcome research. In simplest form, the question might be, "Do patients in this clinic gain more from treat-

ment A than treatment B?" More appropriate, in the present state of the field, is a question of the sort: "Is treatment A or B more effective for different kinds of patients (e.g., age, sex, education, therapeutic expectations, nature and intensity of problems) as administered by therapists of differing characteristics (e.g., age, sex, theoretical orientation, experience), under varying social conditions (alone, in group, in relaxed atmosphere, etc.), and how do they compare with regard to differing outcome measures? But even the simplest experimental design points up some important ethical issues.

Contrast the methodological and ethical issues in human psychotherapy research with the scientifically analogous study of the relative effects of two drugs on the behavior of laboratory rats. In that case animals would be randomly assigned to treatments, the two drugs administered in identical fashion (even perhaps by a third party to minimize experimenter expectancy effects), and some measure taken before and after the drug to assess performance change. For baseline comparison, an untreated control group might be given a placebo and the same pre- and post-measures made. Here, by contrast, are some of the concerns of the therapy researcher, which simply do not exist in the animal-drug study: Is it ethically appropriate to assign subjects to treatments randomly? What should patients be told in advance? To what should they be asked to consent? Is it justified to withhold treatment or to attempt a "placebo" treatment? What about the patients' expectations? Suppose one treatment is found better than the other; what is our obligation to the other group? Might the research atmosphere and measurements inhibit the therapists and undermine the therapies?

Random Assignment to Treatments. Biomedical researchers have argued that random assignment is only justifiable if the experimenter thinks equally well (or is equally ignorant) of the two treatments being contrasted. If one or the other therapy is known to be better for particular patients, then it is our clinical obligation to use the most appropriate treatment (e.g., Walters, 1979). With psychological intervention we rarely have clear-cut prior information about which treatment is more effective, and so random assignment may often be quite appropriate. When there is an acknowledged difference in treatment effectiveness, or when clinical needs of the patient take precedence, there are two alternative strategies: (1) use clinical judgment to assign patients to groups and use pretest scores as baselines to evaluate later differences; or (2) after random assignment, make continuous assessments and shift the patient to an alternate treatment if he or she is doing poorly. This procedure has been called adaptive or sequential design in medical research. A related strategy would be to continue the prescribed course of treatment for all patients, assuming no crises and at the end offer them the treatment found to be most beneficial.

What Should Patient-Subjects Be Told at the Outset? As noted repeatedly, the participant in any study, therapy research included, has the right to know what is being done, why, and what consequences it might have. Along with the purpose of the study and the procedures involved, the investigator must convey in terms understandable to the patient what is already known about the value of the treatment. If it is new and largely untested, that too should be shared. Any possible dangers should be noted along with potential gains as they are known from available evidence. Why the participant was selected is an understandable question, and it should be answered honestly, even explaining if necessary the scientific value of random assignment. The alternate therapeutic approaches being compared in the study should be explained as well, if in less detail. Participants will probably want to know about their relative effectiveness and whether they are to be a "control." They may have a strong preference for another of the treatment approaches, and this must be respected. Similarly, the patient may simply not want to participate in any experiment, and he or she should be offered whatever alternatives exist. Above all, it has to be clear that participation in any study is not the price of clinical care.

But these considerations point up a paradox in therapy research. Full disclosure, honesty, and informed consent might limit the possibility of therapeutic gains. As Frank (1973) and others have argued persuasively, a major source of therapeutic gain lies in the patients' belief in the effectiveness of therapy, in their faith in the therapists' professional knowledge and skill, the status of the clinic, and other nonspecific expectations that may account for as much or more of the therapeutic effects than the specific acts of therapists. What happens then if the patient is told that this is an experiment, that untested techniques are being used, and that the investigator-clinician hopes for the best but is unsure of the results? It is of course true that honest psychotherapists avoid excessive promises and are modest in their claims, though they do convey hope and confidence. But the attitude in a therapeutic experiment is likely to be more removed than in normal clinical practice. Might we then be limiting the potential help we can give our clients by being honest? Might it not be justified to softpedal all this informing and consenting, in the interest of the clinical welfare of the patient?

The risks are not insignificant. We hold that if a study is being done, then the patient-subject has to know what is involved and agree to participate. Such issues, however, point up a number of additional considerations. Where possible, more fragile and disturbed people should be bypassed in setting up a research sample. People in great distress with urgent problems have to be seen immediately and given the best care the clinic offers. Indeed, on this logic, some have argued for the importance of analog studies, using people with more limited problems who have not sought out help, in lieu of real patients in a true clinical setting. This may reduce the ethical dilemma, but then one has to face the question of the extent to which such findings are applicable to real treatments, with real patients, in real clinical settings.

The therapists involved in an experiment should believe equally in the procedures they are practicing. It is fair to "run a horserace" between, say, behavior therapy and Gestalt therapy, if each condition is represented by equally trained and committed therapists. It is of dubious scientific value, and of potential clinical harm, however, to have a group of therapists of one of the persuasions also practicing in the other mode with, as it were, a text in the left hand and without true conviction. While it would seem methodologically neat to have the same people providing Treatment A and Treatment B, this may simply not be wise or possible, out of both scientific and clinical concerns.

Finally, gaining informed consent in a clinical study necessarily involves more consideration and tact than it might in a laboratory study of normal volunteers. There has to be continuous sensitivity to the patient's problems, expectations, and needs, and the consummate importance of maintaining faith in the clinical process.

Can Treatment Be Withheld? Treatment is sometimes denied a patient for a shorter or longer time in the interest of obtaining an untreated control group. Such a procedure raises ethical issues, though it may be scientifically desirable. Patients may be denied treatment they urgently need, or at least delayed in obtaining it, during which time their misery is prolonged and their clinical state may deteriorate.

Intentionally denying help that would otherwise be available to someone needing and seeking it is, to our minds, a simple breach of clinical ethics, and not justifiable under any circumstances. People who voluntarily avoid therapy or drop out after a brief ex- perience cannot serve as a proper comparison group, for they may differ in attitudes and motivation from those who seek psychological help. In many cases, testing the efficacy of a particular therapy can be done by comparing a group receiving an innovative therapy with one getting the treatment usually used in the setting. However, this cannot answer the question of what might have happened had there been no intervention at all over the same period of time.

One effort to circumvent the ethical dilemma is the waiting-list control group, commonly used in therapy research. In many clinics there are inevitable delays in being assigned to a therapist, since the setting has a limited staff and case load. During the period when the prospective clients would have to wait anyway, they can be asked if they would be willing to take the pre and post tests, perhaps spanning periods of time comparable to that of the treated group(s). Depending on the waxing and waning of the waiting list, participants could be drawn for the main treatment group(s). If there is always a waiting list and it is desirable to treat and test all participants at the same time, then randomly putting some patients directly into treatment does favor them, but those waiting are no more delayed than they would normally be. Such a procedure seems fair, though not as desirable as taking advantage of the normal fluctuations in case load. It might also be possible to take advantage of adventitious events (say, individuals who are waiting to move closer to the clinic, finish a job before coming into therapy, etc.) to provide comparison subjects. Waiting-list controls, since they will eventually go into treatment, also provide the considerable advantage of adding personolistic comparison data. Changes that take place in therapy can be compared to changes during the waiting period within the same persons; such comparison is simply impossible in a design that uses a different set of subjects as untreated controls from those in the treatment groups.

SOCIAL COSTS AND THE RISKS OF REGULATION

Throughout this chapter we have taken the position that ethical codes and guidelines serve a valuable function in protecting the individual from various potentially harmful effects of participating in research. In this final section we wish to consider two issues. First, in our emphasis on the potential costs of unethical behavior toward individual participants, we have slighted an important social arena; there are costs of unethical research to large social groups and to the profession itself. Second, we must acknowledge the fact that while codes, regulations, and review boards serve to reduce individual and social costs, they also carry some attendant risks in stifling the growth of science and the discovery of new knowledge.

The Issue of Social Costs

When the results of research are reported publicly, the ways in which they are publicized, and the social policy decision that may follow, may inflict distress or damage upon some identified groups in society. These issues pose ethical dilemmas for which no ready solutions are apparent (Reynolds, 1979).

Take as an instance a hypothetical study investigating the clinical sensitivity and ethical integrity of male and female psychologists. With our fully informed consent, we agree to complete a number of innocuous questionnaires, the responses to which are analyzed in ways that fully guarantee our individual confidentiality. Many other men and an equal number of women participate in the study, not one of whom feels that he or she was abused or mistreated in any way. Any one of us could have refused to participate if he or she believed that the study was pernicious or had any other reservation whatsoever.

Let us assume that the results show convincingly that women are more adequate clinicians and have more professional integrity. The findings are widely publicized in the popular press as well as professional literature. Many male colleagues are incensed, feeling that they are being held up to ridicule, that their clients are less likely to trust them, and that potential clients are less likely to engage them, and perhaps even that institutions may be less inclined to hire men in the future. We are being a bit dramatic to make the simple point that the well-being of a large number of people, at least as they perceive it, is affected by a study in which only a trivial fraction were actually participants. Levine (1978a) discusses a similar case. When research revealed that there was a higher incidence of suicide among female compared to male physicians, some women doctors found this to be perjorative and supportive of a "male chauvinist" position. Others, he notes, welcomed the information as beneficial and supportive of their efforts to achieve more constructive affirmative action plans. Minority people often actively distrust researchers because research designed by white investigators too often depicts them in stereotyped negative terms (see Jones & Korchin, in press, for a more extended discussion of minority attitudes toward research). One only need recall the current furor about IQ differences between black and white children to visualize the many issues involved.

In all of these cases there is no issue of ethical treatment of the research participants themselves. The problems arise in terms of the subsequent impact of the study findings. Questions might be raised as to whether considerations of social cost should figure in the initial review of research by institutional committees, as was considered by the human subjects committee at Berkeley (Irving, 1973; Reynolds, 1979). Some have suggested that where the well-being of a group is involved, then the principle of consent needs logically to be extended from individual participants to the group as a whole or its representatives. The most obvious difficulty in this suggestion is clear: whose consent should be sought for studies of sex differences or women doctors or black college students?

More important, there is a serious issue of prior constraint of scientific research and the censorship of unpopular ideas. In our view there must be two approaches to this problem. First, we deplore censorship of ideas and cannot accept the proposition that each group must have a say about how they are to be described and interpreted. Constraining controversial investigation may place us in the unhappy state in which ignorance rather than knowledge forms the basis of social policy. Second, we feel equally strongly that researchers should consider the uses to which their findings might be put before the study is done. If it is conceivable that studies can be used to further the stereotype of certain groups, perhaps the researcher can consider asking different or additional questions that will balance the picture; for example, in assessing children of lower socioeconomic status, rather than using a standard test, the investigator can create opportunities for the children to respond to items that reflect knowledge of their particular environment. Similarly, consideration of the potential uses of racial comparison studies might lead the researcher to decide to investigate individual and social differences within racial groups, and to give up plans for comparisons across racial lines if there were serious social costs involved in the originally planned study.

Further, the proposed project should be discussed with colleagues who have special knowledge of the affected groups or are themselves members. A white male undertaking a study of women or blacks is well-advised to discuss the proposed research with women or black psychologists, and possibly consider these colleagues as research collaborators. That more research of importance to the understanding of minority groups is being done by professionals of minority

background is a healthy development in and of itself, for it increases the likelihood of concern with the issues as seen from within (Korchin, 1980).

In reporting findings, more than usual caution should be used in interpreting and generalizing the results; any limitations due to sample size, representativeness, adequacy of measures, and the like should be reported. While these cautions are necessary in reporting any scientific research, they are especially critical for work in sensitive areas.

We should briefly mention another type of social cost incurred when unethical studies are carried out and reported. There is incalculable damage to the profession, not only in terms of image but also in terms of the willingness of people to participate in future research. Although conformity to ethical guidelines may limit some studies and may cause inconvenience in others, it can also help to repair the erosion of trust and increase the willingness of the public and the government to support psychological research.

The Risks of Regulation

The United States has moved further toward the codification and regulation of research ethics than any other country (Rosenzweig, 1979). We are not unambivalent about this trend. Aside from all else, regulation is a time-consuming process, using energies that might better be used in the work of science itself. IRBs can become bureaucratic in their operations, adhering slavishly to the letter of regulations. And they move ponderously, at least as seen by investigators eager to get on with testing their ideas. Further time is lost if the ongoing work suggests a change in procedure and one has to return to the IRB for reapproval. Colleagues from other disciplines, with less knowledge of the realities of research in the given field, may conjure up unreasonable dangers and block or delay the study further.

Administrative nuisances aside, there is the more profound question of whether this newfound concern with the rights and welfare of participants might not stifle scientific creativity. The more reviews for any purpose, the more constraints on the investigator from any source (slowness of the grant process, institutional timidity, etc.), and the more likely is research to suffer. When the freedom of science is limited, safe and pedestrian work results. True creativity requires the freedom to take risks; regulation of any sort limits it. Many years ago someone wrote a satiric piece on the research grant process; if Newton lived today, he would probably have spent the rest of his career doing research on "spoilage of fallen apples" under a Department of Agriculture grant, rather than discovering the law of gravity. And if, as many assert, the dangers to psychological research participants are actually so very small, then to risk the integrity of science is all the more unjustified.

Even if one agrees that there are important risks and distinct need for improvement in research ethics, the question still remains whether external regulation really accomplishes its purposes. In an ultimate sense, the answer must be "no," for no law can make humans moral, unless and until they accept a principle within their own consciences. Without minimizing the objections to regulation, we believe that codes and rules are necessary. There are ethical dilemmas in human research, and the development of guidelines and regulations can raise consciousness as to ways in which we may have slighted participants in our desire to get on with the obviously important work of science, and at the same time suggest alternate and more defensible ways of reaching our goals. The quest for principles, and efforts to test their applicability in particular cases, are necessary to keep us alert to the human as well as scientific issues in our field. Still it must be realized that issues are embedded in broad and longstanding value conflicts and will not be solved by simple formulations. We can best conclude with a statement by Ruebenhausen and Brim (1966, p. 428):

Absolute rules do not offer useful solutions to conflicts in values. What is needed is wisdom and restraint, compromise and tolerance, and as wholesome a respect for the dignity of the individual as the respect accorded the dignity of science.

REFERENCES

American Anthropological Association (1971). *Principles of professional responsibility.* Washington, D.C.: American Anthropological Association.

American Psychological Association (1973). *Ethical principles in the conduct of research with human subjects.* Washington, D.C.: American Psychological Association.

American Psychological Association (1979, revised). *Ethical standards of psychologists.* Washington, D.C.: American Psychological Association.

American Sociological Association (1971). *Code of ethics.* Washington, D.C.: American Sociological Association.

Altman, I. (1975). *The environment and social behavior: Privacy, personal space, territory, crowding.* Monterey, Calif.: Brooks/Cole.

Basowitz, H., Persky, H., Korchin, S. J., & Grinker, R. R. (1955). *Anxiety and stress.* New York: McGraw-Hill.

Baumrind, D. (1975). Metaethical and normative considerations covering treatment of human subjects in the behavioral sciences. In E. C. Kennedy (Ed.), *Human rights and psychological research.* New York: Crowell, pp. 37–68.

Baumrind, D. (1977). Snooping and duping: The application of the principle of informed consent to field research. Paper presented at Society for Applied Anthropology, San Diego, Calif.

Baumrind, D. (1978). Nature and definition of informed consent in research involving deception. In National Commission, *The Belmont Report, Appendix II.* DHEW Publication No. (OS) 78-0014. Washington, D.C.: U.S. Government Printing Office, Chapter 23, pp. 1–71.

Baumrind, D. (1979). IRBs and social science research: The cost of deception. *IRB: A Review of Human Subjects Research,* **1,** 1–4.

Beecher, H. K. (1966a). Documenting the abuses. *Saturday Review,* **49,** 45–46.

Beecher, H. K. (1966b). Ethics and clinical research. *New England Journal of Medicine,* **274,** 1354–1360.

Beecher, H. K. (1970). *Research and the individual: Human studies.* Boston: Little, Brown.

Berkowitz, L. (1978). Some complexities and uncertainties regarding the ethicality of deception in research with human subjects. In National Commission, *The Belmont Report: Appendix II.* DHEW Publication No. (OS) 78-0014. Washington, D.C.: U.S. Government Printing Office, Chapter 24, pp. 1–34.

Bernard, C. (1957, original 1865). *An introduction to the study of experimental medicine.* New York: Dover.

Bonacich, P. (1970). Deceiving subjects: The pollution of our environment. *American Sociologist,* **5,** 45–51.

Boruch, R. F. (1971a). Assuring confidentiality of responses in social research: A note on strategies. *American Sociologist,* **6,** 308–311.

Boruch, R. F. (1971b). Maintaining confidentiality of data in education research: A systematic analysis. *American Psychologist,* **26,** 413–430.

Boruch, R. F. (1972). Relations among statistical methods for assuring confidentiality of social research data. *Social Science Research,* **1,** 403–414.

Boruch, R. F. (1976). Strategies for eliciting and merging confidential social research data. In P. Nejelski (Ed.), *Social research in conflict with law and ethics.* Cambridge, Mass.: Ballinger.

Bouchard, T. J., Jr. (1976). Unobtrusive measures: An inventory of uses. *Journal of Sociological Methods and Research,* **4,** 267–300.

Bower, R. T. & de Gasparis, P. (1978). *Ethics in social research: Protecting the interests of human subjects.* New York: Praeger.

Charlesworth, W. R. (1980). Ethical issues in research with children. Paper read at the American Psychological Association, Montreal, September 1980.

Chein, I. (1972). *The science of behavior and the image of man* New York: Basic Books.

Committee on Biomedical Research in the Veterans Administration (1977). *Biomedical research in the veterans administration.* Washington, D.C.: National Academy of Sciences.

Conrad, H. S. (1967). Clearance of questionnaires with respect to invasion of privacy, public sensitivities, ethical standards, etc. *American Psychologist,* **22,** 356–359.

Cowan, P. A. (1978). *Piaget: with feeling.* New York: Holt, Rinehart & Winston.

Cowan, C. P., Cowan, P. A., Coie, L., & Coie, J. (1978). Becoming a family: The impact of a first child's birth on the couple's relationship. In W. Miller & L. Newman (Eds.), *The first child and family formation.* Chapel Hill: University of North Carolina Population Center, pp. 296–323.

Cronbach, L. J. (1970). *Essentials of psychological testing.* New York: Harper.

Culliton, B. J. (1976). Confidentiality: Court declares researcher can protect sources. *Science,* **193,** 467–469.

Department of Health, Education and Welfare (1975, Revised). *Protection of human subjects, code of federal regulations,* 45 CFR 46.

Diener, E., & Crandall, R. (1978). *Ethics in social and behavioral research.* Chicago: University of Chicago Press.

Engelhardt, H. T., Jr. (1978). Basic ethical principles in the conduct of biomedical and behavioral research involving human subjects. In National Commission, *The Belmont Report, Appendix I.* DHEW Publication No. (OS) 78-0013. Washington, D. C.: U. S. Government Printing Office, Chapter 8, pp. 1–45.

Epstein, S. (1962). The measurement of drive and conflict in humans: Theory and experiment. In M. R. Jones (Ed.), *Nebraska Symposium on Motivation,* Lincoln: University of Nebraska Press, pp. 127–209.

Epstein, L. C., & Lasagna, L. (1969). Obtaining informed consent: Form or substance. *Archives of Internal Medicine,* **123,** 682–688.

Everstine, L., Everstine, D. S., Heymann, G. M., True, R. H., Frey, D. H., Johnson, H. G., & Seiden, R. H. (1980). Privacy and confidentiality in psychotherapy. *American Psychologist,* **35,** 828–840.

Farr, J. L., & Seaver, W. B. (1975). Stress and discomfort in psychological research: Subject perceptions of experimental procedures. *American Psychologist,* **30,** 770–773.

Fillenbaum, S. (1966). Prior deception and subsequent experimental performance: The "faithful" subject. *Journal of Personality and Social Psychology,* **4,** 532–537.

Frank, J. D. (1973, rev. ed.). *Persuasion and Healing.* Baltimore, Md.: The Johns Hopkins University Press.

Frankel, M. S. (1975). The development of policy guidelines governing human experimentation in the United States: A case study of public policy making for science and technology. *Ethics in Science and Medicine,* **2,** 43–59.

Friedman, J. L. (1969). Role playing: Psychology by consensus. *Journal of Personality and Social Psychology,* **13,** 107–114.

Fost, N. C. (1975). A surrogate system for informed consent. *Journal of the American Medical Association,* **233,** 800–803.

Garmezy, N. (1975). The experimental study of children vulnerable to psychopathology. In A. Davids (Ed.).

Child personality and psychopathology: Current topics, Vol. 2. New York: Wiley.

Gergen, K. J. (1973). The codification of research ethics: Views of a Doubting Thomas. *American Psychologist,* **28,** 907–912.

Gibbs, J. C. (1979). The meaning of ecologically oriented inquiry in contemporary psychology. *American Psychologist,* **34,** 127–140.

Goldiamond, I. (1978). On the usefulness of intent for distinguishing between research and practice, and its replacement by social contingency. In National Commission, *The Belmont Report, Appendix II.* DHEW Publication NO. (OS) 78-0014. Washington, D.C.: U.S. Government Printing Office.

Gordis, L., & Gold, E. (1980). Privacy, confidentiality and the use of medical records in research. *Science,* **207,** 153–156.

Gray, B. H. (1975). *Human subjects in medical experimentation.* New York: Wiley.

Guttentag, O. E. (1968). Ethical problems in human experimentation. In E. G. Torrey (Ed.), *Ethical issues in medicine.* Boston: Little, Brown.

Irving, C. (August 19, 1973). Showdown on human subjects nears at UC. *San Francisco Sunday Examiner & Chronicle,* **1,** 24.

Janis, I. (1958). *Psychological stress.* New York: Wiley.

Jonas, H. (1969). Philosophical reflections on experimenting with human subjects. *Daedalus,* **98,** 219–247.

Jones, E. E., & Korchin, S. J. (Eds.), *Minority mental health.* New York: Praeger. in press.

Jourard, S. M. (1968). *Disclosing man to himself.* Princeton, N.J.: Van Nostrand.

Jung, J. (1975). Snoopology. *Human Behavior,* **4,** 56–59.

Katz, J. (1972). *Experimentation with human beings.* New York: Russell Sage Foundation.

Kelman, H. C. (1966). Deception in social research. *Trans-Action,* **3,** 20–24.

Kelman, H. C. (1967). The human use of human subjects: The problem of deception in social psychological experiments. *Psychological Bulletin,* **67,** 1–11.

Kelman, H. C. (1972). The rights of the subject in social research: An analysis in terms of relative power and legitimacy. *American Psychologist,* **27,** 989–1016.

Kennedy, E. C. (Ed.) (1975). *Human rights and psychological research.* New York: Crowell.

Kimble, G. (1978). The role of risk/benefit analysis in the conduct of psychological research. In National Commission: *The Belmont Report, Appendix II.*

DHEW Publication No. (OS) 78-0013. Washington, D.C.: U.S. Government Printing Office, Chapter 20, pp. 1–22.

Koocher, G. P. (1977). Bathroom behavior and human dignity. *Journal of Personality and Social Psychology,* **35,** 120–121.

Korchin, S. J. (1976). *Modern clinical psychology.* New York: Basic Books.

Korchin, S. J. (1980). Clinical psychology and minority problems. *American Psychologist,* **35,** 262–269.

Korchin, S. J., & Schwartz, M. (1960). Differential effects of "shame" and "disintegrative" threats on emotional and adrenocortical functioning. *Archives of General Psychiatry,* **2,** 640–651.

Lear, J. (1966). Experiments on people—the growing debate. *Saturday Review,* **49,** 41–43.

Levine, R. J. (1978a). The role of assessment of risk benefit criteria in the determination of the appropriateness of research involving human subjects. In National Commission, *The Belmont Report: Appendix I.* DHEW Publication No. (OS) 78-0013. Washington, D.C.: U.S. Government Printing Office, Chapter 2, pp. 1–59.

Levine, R. J. (1978b). The boundaries between biomedical or behavioral research and the accepted and routine practice of medicine. In National Commission, *The Belmont Report: Appendix I.* DHEW Publication No. (OS) 78-0013. Washington, D.C.: U.S. Government Printing Office, Chapter 1, pp. 1–44.

London, P., & Klerman, G. (1978). Boundaries between research and therapy, especially in mental health. In National Commission. *The Belmont report, Appendix II.* DHEW Publication No. (OS) 78-0014. Washington, D.C.: U.S. Government Printing Office, Chapter 15, pp. 1–17.

Mead, M. (1969). Research with human beings: A model derived from anthropological field practice. *Daedalus,* **98,** 361–386.

Mechanic, D. (1962). *Students under stress.* New York: The Free Press of Glencoe.

Milgrim, D. (1974). *Obedience to authority: An experimental view.* New York: Harper & Row.

Miller, A. G. (1972). Role-playing: An alternative to deception? A review of the evidence. *American Psychologist,* **27,** 623–636.

Mitscherlich, A., & Mielke, F. (1949). *Doctors of infamy: The story of the Nazi medical crimes.* New York: Henry Schuman.

Middlemist, D., Knowles, E. S., & Matter, C. F. (1976). Personal space invasions in the lavatory: Suggestive evidence for arousal. *Journal of Personality and Social Psychology* **33,** 541–546.

Middlemist, D., Knowles, E. S., & Matter, C. F. (1977). What to do and what to report: A reply to Koocher. *Journal of Personality and Social Psychology, 32,* 122–124.

Morrow, G. R. (1980). How readable are subject consent forms? *Journal of American Medical Association, 24,* 56–58.

Nash, M. (1975). Nonreactive methods and the law: Additional comments on legal liability in behavior research. *American Psychologist, 30,* 777–780.

National Commission for the Protection of Human Subjects of Biomedical and Behavioral Research (1978). *The Belmont report: Ethical principles and guidelines for the protection of human subjects of research.* DHEW Publication No. (OS) 78-0012. *Appendix I,* DHEW Publication No. (OS) 78-0013; *Appendix II,* (OS) 78-0014. Washington, D.C.: U.S. Government Printing Office.

Orne, M. T. (1962). On the social psychology of the psychology experiment: With particular reference to demand characteristics and their implications. *American Psychologist, 17,* 776–783.

Palmer, A. D., & Wohl, J. (1972). Voluntary-admission forms: Does the patient know what he's signing? *Hospital and Community Psychiatry, 23,* 250–252.

Reynolds, P. D. (1979). *Ethical dilemmas and social science research: An analysis of moral issues confronting investigators in research using human participants.* San Francisco: Jossey Bass.

Rosenzweig, M. R. (1979). Protecting rights of subjects in psychological research in the U.S.A. *International Journal of Psychology, 14,* 125–130.

Veatch, R. M. (1975). Ethical principles in medical experimentation. In A. M. Rivlin & P. M. Timpane (Eds.). *Ethical and legal issues of social experimentation.* Washington, D.C.: The Brookings Institution, pp. 21–59.

Ruebenhausen, O. M., & Brin, O. G., Jr. (1966). Privacy and behavioral research. *American Psychologist, 21,* 423–437.

Rutstein, D. D. (1969). The ethical design of human experiments. *Daedalus, 98,* 523–541.

Seeman, J. (1969). Deception in psychological research. *American Psychologist, 24,* 1025–1028.

Sieber, J. (1979). Working on ethics. *APA Monitor,* January 1979.

Silverman, I. (1975). Nonreactive methods and the law. *American Psychologist, 30,* 764–769.

Singer, E. (1978). Informed consent: Consequences for response rate and response quality in social surveys. Paper delivered at the American Sociological Association Meeting, Chicago. (Quoted by Bower and de Gasparis, !978, *Ethics in social research.* New York: Praeger.)

Smith, M. B. (1967). Conflicting values affecting behavioral research with children. *American Psychologist, 22,* 377–382.

Smith, M. B. (1975). Psychology and ethics. In E. C. Kennedy, *Human Rights and Psychological Research,* 1–22. New York: Crowell.

Smith, M. B. (1976). Some perspectives on ethical/political issues in social science research. *Personality and Social Psychology Bulletin, 2,* 445–453.

Soskin, W. F., Ross, N., & Korchin, S. J. (1971). The origin of Project Community: Innovating a social institution for adolescents. *Seminars in Psychiatry, 2,* 271–287.

Steiner, I. D. (1972). The evils of research: Or what my mother didn't tell me about the sins of academia. *American Psychologist, 27,* 755–768.

Stricker, L. (1967). The true deceiver. *Psychological Bulletin, 68,* 13–20.

Stricker, L. J., Messick, S., & Jackson, D. M. (1969). Evaluating deception in psychological research. *Psychological Bulletin, 71,* 343–351.

Sullivan, D. S., & Deiker, P. E. Subject-experimenter perceptions of ethical issues in human research. *American Psychologist, 28,* 587–591.

Veatch, R. M. (1975). Ethical principles in medical experimentation. In A. M. Rivlin & P. M. Timpane (Eds.). *Ethical and legal issues of social experimentation.* Washington, D.C.: The Brookings Institution, pp. 21–59.

Veatch, R. M. (1978). Three theories of informed consent: Philosophical foundations and policy implications. In National Commission, *The Belmont Report, Appendix II.* DHEW Publication No. (OS) 78-0014. Washington, D.C.: U.S. Government Printing Office, Chapter 26, pp. 1–66.

Wallwork, E. (1975). Ethical issues in research involving human subjects, and In defense of substantive rights: A reply to Baumrind. In E. C. Kennedy, *Human rights and psychological research.* New York: Crowell, pp. 69–82 and 103–125.

Walster, E., Berscheid, E., Abrahams, D., & Aronson, V. (1967). Effectiveness of debriefing following deception experiments. *Journal of Personality and Social Psychology, 6,* 371–380.

Walters, L. (1978). Some ethical issues in research involving human subjects. In National Commission, *The Belmont Report: Appendix I.* DHEW Publication No. (OS) 78-0013. Washington, D.C.: U.S. Government Printing Office, Chapter 11, pp. 1–30.

Zimbardo, P. G. (1973). On the ethics of intervention in human psychological research: With special reference to the Stanford Prison Experiment. *Cognition, 2,* 243–256.

CHAPTER 4

Serendipity in Research in Clinical Psychology

MICHAEL MERBAUM AND MICHAEL R. LOWE

If we could travel through time to a point a hundred years from now and look back upon the present developmental level of clinical psychology, we would undoubtedly be struck by how rudimentary our knowledge is. A century from now, currently popular theories of the development and remediation of psychopathology will be seen as only crude approximations to what will then be considered "the truth." We obviously have only begun to scratch the surface in understanding why some individuals develop behavioral (mental?) disorders, what approach is most helpful with what disorder, and so on. Given the incredible complexity of the subject matter and the relatively short history of clinical psychology, this state of affairs is understandable. In fact, even theories in the more fully developed physical sciences can only begin to explain the phenomena to which they address themselves. Taton (1957), writing about the role of reason and chance in scientific discovery, made this point when he stated that:

If we realize the apparent simplicity of numerous physical phenomena is nothing but a first approximation of a very much more complex reality, we shall understand that many laws could only have been discovered by means of oversimplified hypotheses and of observations, in which grossly approximate measurements minimize certain difficulties that otherwise might have prevented progress and thought. (p. 92)

Once such oversimplified hypotheses set the stage for systematic research, further insights into the nature of complex phenomena are often revealed by fortuitous events. Taton and others writing about the history of the physical sciences (Cannon, 1945; Selye, 1964) have pointed out that serendipitous discoveries have played a major role in wiping away areas of ignorance that had not succumbed to the systematic, determined efforts of research scientists. The purpose of this chapter is to consider the role of serendipity in psychology generally, and in clinical research in particular. Before doing so, however, consideration of the derivation and definition of this rather obscure term is warranted.

W. B. Cannon (1945), in a witty and charming book about the scientific enterprise, devotes one chapter to an intriguing phenomenon he labeled "serendipity." For those not familiar with the derivation of this word, it was first mentioned in a correspondence between Horace Walpole and his friend Horace Mann in the year 1754. In this letter Walpole proposed adding a new word to our lexicon to designate a faculty that some investigators had reported for happening upon or making fortunate discoveries when not actually in search for them. The origin of this word, Walpole disclosed to Mann, was based on a fairy tale entitled, "The Three Princes of Serendip." The heroes in this saga were from Ceylon, named Serendip at the time, and appeared to have had an uncanny knack for making fortunate yet accidental discoveries. Cannon was enormously impressed with the repeated instances in which "serendipity" set the occasion for novel scientific discovery, and in his chapter enumerated a number of outstanding examples of these creative efforts. Among the most noteworthy discoveries reported by Cannon were Columbus encountering a new world instead of a shorter route to the East Indies: Galvani adventitiously observing the twitches of frog legs hanging from copper wire in his home, which then led to experiments in electrical conduction; the life saving discovery of penicillin through the accidental contamination of a pus-producing bacteria; and other such episodes.

While obviously enamored by these tantalizingly lucky findings, Cannon was careful to point out that the conversion of an adventitious event into scientific discovery required not only good fortune but a "prepared mind" to profit from the harvest. A "prepared mind," according to Cannon, was the intellectual capacity to utilize an unexpected finding by integrating it into a meaningful scientific context. Thus if a mind were unprepared to receive chance conditions, these potentially serendipitous events in one context might either go unobserved, be viewed as an inconvenience, or be considered as an unimportant side effect in another. What appeared to facilitate the uniqueness of the experience was a proverbial "click" in the cognition of the scientist that captured the critical essence of the moment and translated it into a meaningful beginning. From this perspective it is perhaps an advantage for stimuli to be sufficiently dramatic to capture the attention of the scientific observer. For an event to be special, a major qualifying condition would seem to be that the event and the cognition of the observer be fortuitously intertwined.

A serendipitous observation is most usually only the first step in the discovery process. Once the suggestion of an interesting relationship takes hold, the next stage is likely to lead to a serious and systematic exploration of the phenomenon. Reliability, validity, and measurement issues must then be dealt with in order to establish the credibility of the serendipitous revelation to the scientific community. As we will eventually review in more detail, the serendipitous origins of a work are often not disclosed until later on when the phenomenon has been truly confirmed by repeated observations and integrated within a broader theoretical and empirical context. Certainly the rules of the science game favor logic, precision, and honest hard work in the pursuit of truth. Chance, luck, and messing around with ideas are not usually accorded the highest ranks. Nonetheless, as the career of the scientist matures and position, status, and recognition have been achieved, the homey and intimate stories of how it all began are often greeted with fascination and delight. These vignettes joyfully humanize the scientist and provide interesting bits of gossip (Skinner, 1968).

DEFINITIONS OF SERENDIPITY

Most formal definitions of serendipity are brief and lack descriptive elaboration. *The Webster New World Dictionary* refers to it as "an apparent aptitude for making fortunate discoveries accidentally." English and English in their *Comprehensive dictionary of psychological and psychoanalytical terms* view serendipity as "the process, art or fact of finding one thing while looking for another." In our opinion, however, these definitions are not inclusive enough to capture the intricate qualities of the serendipitous incident and thus highlight the important implications for scientific progress. In reviewing a wide range of scientific discoveries it seems likely that the term serendipity can be applied in at least three contexts, which can be heuristically differentiated.

The first prototype, which we label Type I, is most liable to appear in the course of actual research work itself. While systematically and scrupulously examining one problem, a new and startling finding may be suddenly revealed. If this unplanned variation is sufficiently interesting and novel, the researcher is galvanized to radically alter the direction of his or her original research program. Clearly some of the most tantalizing discoveries have been obtained in this manner. Usually the scientist is already carefully attuned to his or her project and thus powerfully sensitized to the quality of the emerging data. Unexpected variations that crop up may therefore be, in the long run, regarded as a failed experiment, a nuisance, or a godsend.

In the second prototype, which we will label Type II serendipity, the scientist inadvertently stumbles across an interesting natural event which whets his or her curiosity. This experience spontaneously evokes a compelling intellectual or emotional reaction, which motivates the observer to further monitor the progression of the phenomenon and its sequel. Given the urgency to confront the natural event as is, and denied the comfortable rigors of experimental manipulation and control, the scientist has no apparent influence over the process or the outcome. He or she is a passive bystander, unintentional victim, or natural participant. At this stage direct interference might actually contaminate the natural emergence of these data. Thus it is perhaps fortunate that passive observation is the rule rather than the exception. In all likelihood, however, the main reason for inactivity is that usually the scientist is taken unaware and is incapable of immediately manipulating the event. The laboratory for this sort of serendipity is the unplanned and unpredictable vicissitudes of life.

Finally, in Type III serendipity some surprising clinical treatment effects arouse the curiosity of the clinician. An original treatment plan accidentally yields additional treatment insights or unusual therapeutic correlates, which divert attention to a completely different disorder and its remediation. Usu-

ally controlled research is then conducted to verify the therapeutic action of the newly discovered treatment.

SERENDIPITY AND MODES OF SCIENTIFIC INQUIRY

Given the substantial evidence of the role of unplanned events in the advancement of scientific knowledge, it is important to consider how this fertile source of innovation and discovery may be capitalized upon. In the discussion that follows, we will consider factors that work against making discoveries through serendipity in psychological research and suggest how these hindrances may be overcome. We will then discuss how the research model employed by an investigator may partially determine his or her receptiveness to serendipitous observations.

Serendipity and Confirmatory Bias

For a variety of reasons, the deck is strongly stacked against the recognition and appreciation of unanticipated results in psychological research. Perhaps the major reason for this is that most researchers learn to take a strong confirmatory stance toward their work; the idea is to show that a hypothesis they've developed can be borne out by empirical data. In their commitment to the acquisition of "hard" data to support their theory or conviction, however, clinical researchers may pay a price in terms of the discovery of new phenomena by concentrating solely on the verification of their hypotheses.

Mahoney (1976), in his comprehensive critique of scientific behavior, describes a number of the characteristics of the researcher bent on acquiring supportive data for a particular theory or viewpoint. Mahoney admits that, taken as a whole, his description resembles a caricature more than a realistic portrait. However, many of us will recognize the existence of some of these characteristics in our own research behavior (and, undoubtedly, even more so in the behavior of our theoretical rivals.)

Mahoney divides the characteristics of the committed researcher (or the "true believer") into those pertaining to cognitive, emotional, and behavioral realms. The cognitive characteristics, which are most pertinent to the present discussion, may be paraphrased as follows:

1. *Selective attention and inattention.* The researcher perceives and attends to data congruent with his or her belief system and ignores or deemphasizes contradictory data.

2. *Data distortion and creation.* When research findings are vague or ambiguous, the researcher will tend to construe them as supportive of his or her belief system.

3. *Confirmatory set.* The researcher is likely to conceive of any set of belief-relevant data as supportive; this bias becomes more pronounced when the data are more equivocal.

4. *Discreditory defensiveness.* When confronted with anomalous data, the researcher is likely to minimize or deny the significance of the findings.

5. *Expedient reasoning.* The researcher will use relatively less stringent criteria for evaluating evidence supporting his or her belief system and for evaluating evidence contradicting competing systems; likewise he or she will use relatively more stringent criteria for contradictory evidence bearing on his or her beliefs or supportive criteria for competing beliefs.

6. *Certainty and closure.* The researcher becomes closed to examining the foundations of his or her belief system or to synthesizing new data into it.

7. *Memory dysfunction.* Supportive data tend to be remembered better than anomalous data.

8. *Pervasive exemplars and tacit submergence.* The researcher tends to "find" pervasive illustrations of the validity of his or her system (pervasive exemplars) and begins to view that system as axiomatic (tacit submergence).

9. *System saving.* The researcher will tend to "patch up" his or her system in the face of mounting contradictory data, rather than moving to a new belief system.

Mahoney's point is that because of the above-mentioned correlates of commitment to a belief system, all belief systems are costly. Of course no researcher could begin an investigation without making assumptions about the lawfulness of nature, the causal relation among the variables at hand, and so on. Mahoney (1976) notes that the costs of such necessary beliefs will be "related to the contents of the system, its flexibility, and the individual's degree of commitment of it" (p. 207).

Preparing the Mind

Mahoney discusses the costs of commitment primarily at the molar level of the maintenance and alteration of theoretical systems (after Kuhn, 1962). It is our contention, however, that a researcher's degree of commitment to a particular belief system will also influence his or her potential for discovering new phenomena at the more molecular level of his or her day-to-day research activities. The likelihood that researchers will be able to appreciate a potentially significant anomalous finding will largely depend on researchers' ability and willingness to examine not only the data they generate but also the data that is generated in spite of themselves.

An example of a serendipitous finding in the physical sciences illustrates this point nicely. In 1928 the English biologist Sir Alexander Fleming was growing colonies of staphylocci in order to study genetic mutations. As occurred frequently in biological laboratories of the day, one of the staphylocci cultures became contaminated by an airborne microorganism. Rather than disposing of the contaminated culture and dismissing the occurrence as an unfortunate accident, Fleming studied the culture more carefully. His observations suggested to him that the microorganism that infected his staphylocci colonies was having an antibacterial effect on it. Recognizing the potential significance of this effect, Fleming diverted his energies to exploring it systematically. His efforts led to the development of penicillin, one of the greatest discoveries in the history of medicine.

The skeptical reader might protest that Fleming had merely taken advantage of a fortunate turn of events that was of obvious significance. Yet Pasteur and his associates had made observations similar to those stumbled upon by Fleming more than 50 years earlier without appreciating their significance (Taton, 1957). Given the pervasive role of serendipitous findings in advancing various disciplines of scientific endeavor, the psychologically minded scientist may well wonder how a researcher might prepare himself or herself to reap the maximum harvest of discoveries from the numerous accidents and unanticipated results encountered in scientific research.

Walter Cannon, the famous medical researcher and philosopher of science, was intrigued by the pervasiveness of serendipitous discoveries in science. He became convinced, as Pasteur had before him, that "chance favors the prepared mind." To appreciate serendipitous events when they occur, the scientist's mind must be "prepared" in two senses. First, the scientist must be thoroughly familiar with the knowledge, data, and theories relevant to his or her field of investigation. An unexpected finding will captivate the attention of an investigator only if it runs counter to, or sheds new light on, information he or she already possesses.

A second aspect of a "prepared mind" is the maintenance of a type of subconscious

vigilance to counteract a researcher's natural tendency to overlook, downplay, or explain away unexpected and possibly counterattitudinal findings. Cannon (1948) has stated in reference to such findings:

The unusual is promptly dismissed because it does not fit into the established plan. To persons who live according to pattern, adventures in ideas are impossible . . . Consequently, wisdom counsels keeping our minds open and recipient, hospitable to new views and fresh advances. We err if we dismiss the extraordinary aspects of experience as unworthy of attention; they may be the little beginnings of trails leading to unexplored heights in human progress. (p. 77)

Of course they may also lead to dead ends. However, the fact that various prominent scientists have emphasized the central role that serendipitous findings played in the development of their work suggests that the researcher who is able to recognize the potential significance of unexpected results will be richly rewarded. Hans Seyle aptly described this ability to appreciate findings one was not looking for as "peripheral vision":

The ability not only to look straight at what you what to see, but also to watch continually, through the corner of your eye, for the unexpected. I believe this to be one of the greatest gifts a scientist can have. Usually, we concentrate so much upon what we intend to examine that other things cannot reach our consciousness, even if they are far more important. This is particularly true of things so different from the commonplace that they seem improbable. Yet, only the improbable is really worthy of attention! If the unexpected is nevertheless found to be true, the observation usually represents a great step forward. (p. 78)

While the ability to recognize the significance of lucky accidents is partly a "gift," this ability is certainly so influenced by the manner in which an investigator goes about doing research. The traditional approach to research utilizes the hypotheticodeductive method. Since the purpose of such research is to test the plausibility of specific hypotheses, a researcher is less apt to attend to or evaluate unexpected results that may be irrelevant to his or her hypotheses. This is not to say that research based on the hypotheticodeductive method has not produced serendipitous discoveries, only that it does little to facilitate such discoveries.

A second model of research activity, though one not always clearly distinguishable from its hypothesis-bound counterpart, is based on inductive logic. This approach places emphasis on establishing empirical relationships first and relating them theoretically second. Though this research strategy in practice may turn out more trivial, pedestrian data, it is also more likely to facilitate the recognition and pursuit of significant, though unexpected outcomes. Skinner, a great defender of the inductive approach to research, felt that unanticipated results played such an integral part in producing new knowledge that he argued for a "first principle not formally recognized by scientific methodologists: when you run onto something interesting, drop everything else and study it" (1968, p. 29). Recognizing that exclusive reliance on the hypotheticodeductive research methods could become a creative straitjacket that stifled new research directions, Skinner (1968) also argued that:

It is time to insist that science does not progress by carefully designed steps called "experiments" each of which has a well-defined beginning and end. Science is a continuous and often a disorderly and accidental process. We shall not do the young psychologist any favor if we agree to reconstruct our practices to fit the pattern demanded by current scientific methodology. (p. 38)

Serendipity in the Closet

As we read one after another testimony to the importance of fortuitous discoveries in scientific advances, we were struck by a curious fact. We could think of relatively few instances of serendipitous findings leading to important discoveries in psychology. We

also noted that the scientists who wrote about the importance of serendipity in their and others' discoveries (Cannon, 1945; Seyle, 1964; Skinner, 1968) did so in the middle to latter part of their careers, at a time when they could be considered to be attaining the noble position of "elder statesman" in their fields. We concluded that these two facts might share a common explanation. That is, while the dictionary defines serendipity as a "faculty," an investigator might assume that others would attribute *his* serendipitous discovery to *luck*. This explanation implies: (1) that the number of serendipitous discoveries reported is less than their actual frequency of occurrence; and (2) that only renowned "elder statesmen" feel secure enough about their place in history to openly discuss how serendipity helped advance their careers.

Anyone familiar with research related to clinical psychology might very well conclude that serendipity might be important in some fields of science, but not in clinical research. However, while introductions to our research articles make it sound as if hypotheses to be investigated were logically deduced before conducting tests of their credibility, there is no telling how often such hypotheses resulted from serendipitous discoveries that were later adorned with logical derivations. A case in point occurred in the serendipitous discovery of reward centers in the brain by Olds and Milner (1954). Olds (1955) acknowledged the fortuitous circumstances surrounding the discovery, but no mention is made of these circumstances in the original, now classic, report of the discovery (Olds & Milner, 1954).

Thus, while some psychologists have been willing to openly discuss the influence of serendipity on their research and thinking, many have not. This reluctance undoubtedly stems from the assumption that attributing a discovery to "serendipity" diminishes the credit and approbation due to the discoverer. An example of the derogatory light in which serendipity is often viewed comes from B. P. Babkin, one of Pavlov's biographers and a noted researcher himself. It is common knowledge that the production of conditioned salivary responses in Pavlov's laboratory was an unintended consequence of his in-depth physiological study of the digestive glands. Bablin (1949) argues, however, that:

Pavlov's abandonment of the physiology of the gastrointestinal tract for the study of conditioned reflexes must not be looked upon as "Serendipity" . . . the personal spiritual history of Pavlov made him the one who was destined to break this new path in science. Conditioned reflexes were not the result of Pavlov's "faculty of making happy and unexpected discoveries by accident" . . . The incident with Dr. Snarsky [Pavlov's collaborator] only threw a strong light on some conceptions and thoughts which were lying dormant in Pavlov's mind. (p. 280)

The role of serendipity in Pavlov's work is not being debated here. The point is that Babkin need not have been so vehement in his denial that serendipity palyed a role in Pavlov's dramatic career shift toward the study of conditioned reflexes. A man of lesser curiosity than Pavlov may not have taken note of the so-called "psychic secretions," or he might have noticed them but considered them unworthy of further study; or he may have noticed and studied them, but less productively than Pavlov did.

TYPE I: SERENDIPITY IN PSYCHOLOGICAL RESEARCH

Nearly all psychologists are familiar with at least one instance of serendipity in psychological research. For instance, most undergraduate psychology majors—even sophomores—learn somewhere along the lines that Pavlov started studying "psychic secretions" only after they occurred fortuitously while he was pursuing a different line of research. Most psychologists are also familiar with Skinner's (1968) "A Case History in Scientific Method" in which he details the ways in which serendipitous events shaped his research pursuits. However, as we noted ear-

lier, psychologists (and, undoubtedly, all scientists) are reluctant to publicize the fact that they benefited from accident or chance when making a discovery. They often will only do so long after they have received credit for their contributions. Thus it is likely that most psychologists underestimate the role that serendipity has played in furthering knowledge and pointing to new avenues of inquiry in many areas of psychological research.

Much of the research covered in the following review would be properly classified in specialty areas outside of clinical. However, while we may not agree with Skinner's (1968) observation that as the years go by it becomes easier and easier to imagine oneself as a clinical psychologist, it does seem that there has been an increasing transfusion in recent years of research findings from non-clinical areas (e.g., learning theory, physiological psychology) into clinical psychology itself. Of course some of the studies reviewed here have more obvious relevance to clinical psychology than others, so we have roughly ordered the review along a dimension of less to more obvious relevance to clinical psychology.

A Final Caveat. While our review of the literature on serendipity in psychological research was exhausting, it was not necessarily exhaustive. Unfortunately, one cannot look in the index of *Psychological Abstracts* nor at recent articles on serendipity to locate relevant sources. Instead we followed up on a few examples of serendipity we'd heard of, but mostly we thought of important research domains in clinical psychology and related areas and said to ourselves, "I wonder how that line of research got started?" Our digging sometimes produced surprising (one might say serendipitous) results. On a number of occassions, we found descriptions of the earliest work in a given area and discovered that the investigator did not relate how he or she became interested in the area or how his or her work follwed from that of previous researchers. For these reasons we in some cases could not determine if a lucky accident had played a role in generating the research being undertaken.

Examples of Research Serendipity

Our first example of serendipity in the research laboratory is most properly viewed as an instance of dumb luck, for like many other serendipitous discoveries, this one occurred as a result of human error. In the early 1950s it was known that electrical stimulation in certain areas of cats' brains produced an aversive emotional state. During the same period, James Olds and his colleagues learned that stimulation of the reticular formation in rats produced a hyperalert response (Valenstein, 1973). Reasoning that enhanced alertness would facilitate learning, Olds decided to do an experiment in which rats would receive electrical stimulation in the reticular formation at certain choice points in a maze. Peter Milner, a graudate student at McGill, had more experience in the surgical implanation of electrodes and carried out implantation for Olds.

A funny thing happened on the way to the reticular formation, however. A bent electrode resulted in Milner unwittingly implanting the device in the rat's hypothalamus, far from its intended location. Olds and Milner were aware that brain stimulation could potentially produce aversive reactions and decided—as good, thorough scientists—to make sure that their implantations were not placed so as to produce the aversive effect. They did this by placing the animal in a large, square, enclosed area and delivering a brief dose of stimulation each time the rat wandered into one corner of the enclosure. Olds and Milner need not have worried: rather than avoiding the targeted corner, the rat sought it out! Olds, in his astonishment, noted that "By the third time the electric stimulus had been applied the animal seemed indubitably to be coming back for more" (quoted in Valenstein, 1973, p. 37). Olds and Milner had stumbled across the now-famous "reward center" in the brain. They immediately dropped their original research plans on the facilitation of learning and launched a new research program into the reinforcing effects of hypothalamic stimulation on various tasks. It was not the first nor the last time that a faulty experimental technique or piece of apparatus would produce significant, though unexpected, contributions to the understanding of behavior.

Technology played an important role in our second example of serendipity as well, though in this case it served to clarify the surprising observations of a human observer (Dement, 1976; Snyder, 1973). The observer was a graduate student named Eugene Aserinsky. He was working in the laboratory of Dr. Nathaniel Kleitman, the famous sleep researcher. Kleitman and Aserinsky were investigating frequency of eyeblinks during sleep as a possible indicator of depth of sleep. Aserinsky was given the job of counting the blinks. He soon realized that he would have to count them himself, since there was no instrumentation available to do so. He then learned that he couldn't count "blinks" because he couldn't distinguish them from other eye movements. Rather than shelving the original research plan, however, he decided to count *all* eye movements and resigned himself to hour upon hour of monotonous recordings.

Aserinsky's perseverance paid off handsomely. It immediately became apparent to him that the infants' eye movements occurred in bunches and, even more interestingly, that the eye movements were accompanied by generalized body movements that were otherwise absent. Aserinsky and Kleitman wanted to find out if the same pattern of eye and body movements were characteristic of adult sleep, but by this time Aserinsky's own eyes were becoming fatigued. While the investigators had been unable to record eyeblinks electrically, they did devise a machine to record movements of the eyeball. The tracings of these movements revealed the remarkable discovery of synchronized, energetic rapid eye movements (REMs) reminiscent of eye movements recorded during the waking state. Aserinsky and Kleitman also thought to measure physiological responses along with the eye measurements and found, again to their great surprise, that the REM periods were associated with a clear state of physiological arousal. All of these observations suggested that the increases in physiological and motor activity may be associated with dreaming, and an experimental test proved this to be the case (Aserinsky & Kleitman, 1955). This discovery led to a torrent of research, which has vastly improved our understanding of sleep and dreaming. To think how much more Aserinsky and Kleitman learned than would have been learned if Aserinsky had doggedly pursued his goal of counting the eyeblinks of infants!

As suggested by the research that led to the discovery of REM sleep, serendipitous discoveries seem to "run" in the careers of certain behavioral scientists. A case in point is Harry Harlow. As he and his colleagues observed, "The endless effort required to solve any major problem frequently leads to other channels of thought and the creation of new areas of interest—often by chance or almost chance associations" (Harlow, Harlow, & Suomi, 1971, p. 74).

Harlow's early research interests lay in the effects of brain lesions on the learning ability of monkeys. Since they were interested in the ontogenetic development of learning capabilities, Harlow and his research team had to have readily available groups of monkeys of all ages from infancy to adulthood. Harlow instituted a program to breed monkeys in his laboratory to reduce the prevalence of contagious disease and uncontrolled environmental stimulation. Infant monkeys were separated from their mothers a few hours after birth and were cared for entirely by human hands. The infants were provided with cheesecloth diapers to serve as baby blankets. Not surprisingly, the blankets became soiled and had to be replaced period-

ically. What *was* surprising, especially because the work was done before Linus of *Peanuts* fame existed, was the rage the baby monkeys exhibited when their blankets were removed. This startling and somewhat disturbing reaction was filed away unexplained in Harlow's mind. The significance to the monkey of the cheesecloth blanket only dawned on him years later, whereupon he began his now famous research on surrogate mothers and the significance of contact comfort in the raising of infants.

Though he did not know it at the time, Harlow had not even milked his monkey-rearing practices of all their serendipitous potential. Long after the foregoing discovery, Harlow and his colleagues were in the process of developing methods of inducing psychopathological behavior syndromes in monkeys, a goal that had remained elusive for experimenters working with various animal species. Harlow began by exploring the potential of "surrogate mother rejection" (e.g., having the baby monkeys shot off their surrogate mothers with a blast of compressed air) with little success. In the middle of this project, he received help from a most unexpected source. The previously described monkeys, who had been raised away from their mothers and were now of breeding age, were housed together to produce the next generation of monkeys. However, no copulation was observed and no offspring were produced. An attempt to induce sexual behavior by grouping these monkeys with "normal" monkeys in a zoo also failed. Harlow realized that these same nonsexual animals showed other unusual behavior, such as self-clutching and rocking movements during their childhood, and a high degree of disinterest in the environment as adults. Harlow then saw that raising monkeys in partial isolation had produced more abnormal behavior than he had previously realized. At this point he launched a research program into the effects of total social isolation on monkey development and produced even more extreme behavioral abnormalities. Thus Harlow found what he was looking for—the experimental induction of psychopathology—though not where he was looking for it. Or, as he said, "By chance we had discovered what had been sought for years by design" (Harlow, Harlow, & Suomi, 1971, p. 79).

Our next example of serendipity is particularly intriguing because it involved researchers from different disciplines who were investigating different phenomena and stumbled upon something interesting that neither was looking for.[1] It all began with a group of physiologists at a state university. They were interested in determining if the effects of exposure to radiation were influenced by exercise. To investigate this question they exposed a group of rats to cobalt 60 radiation for prolonged periods and then had the rats exercise. A group of control rats were placed next to the experimental rats during the radiation period, but were shielded from the radiation by lead bricks.

In the department of psychology, meanwhile, John Garcia and Robert Koelling (a graduate student) were looking into the mechanism(s) by which radiation sickness produces its deleterious behavioral effects. Garcia and Koelling began to observe the work of their colleagues in physiology to learn more about the mechanics of inducing radiation sickness. The physiologists were experiencing an unexpected problem that was of interest to Garcia and Koelling. The experimental animals were eating and drinking less than the control animals while in the chamber where they received radiation, regardless of whether they were being radiated. However, the experimental animals' intake was not affected outside of the experimental chamber. To the physiologists, who were interested in the influence of exercise unconfounded by differences in food and water intake, this smelled like trouble. But to psychologists Garcia and Koelling, it smelled like learning (Garcia, Kimeldorf, & Koelling, 1955; Garcia, McGowan, & Green, 1972).

[1]Garcia, J. Personal communications, January 1980.

The question remained as to what cue or cues the animals were picking up that kept them from eating and drinking in the experimental chamber. Again, a chance event was behind it all. It turns out that there was insufficient room in this chamber for the usual water bottle that the animals drank from, so the experimenters substituted a smaller plastic centrifuge tube that happened to be handy. Garcia and Koelling suspected that the water in the plastic container tasted different from water held in the usual glass container, and that the pairing of radiation sickness (and nausea) with the "plasticized" water constituted the critical discriminative stimulus. Subsequent experiments using saccharine in place of "plastic flavor" confirmed that the animals developed a taste aversion by having a certain flavor associated with radiation-produced nausea. These chance observations altered Garcia's original plan of research, and culminated in the classic study demonstrating the existence of differential conditionality for different classes of stimuli and responses (Garcia & Koelling, 1966).

The fortuitous coming together of researchers with differing fields of expertise contributed to another major serendipitous discovery in psychology as well. Joseph Brady (1958) had been studying a number of conditioning procedures with monkeys when he was distressed to learn that many of his experimental subjects were dying prematurely. These unexplained deaths might have remained a mystery for some time had it not been for R. W. Porter, an ulcer researcher and military man who happened to be assigned to the same laboratories Brady was working in (Sidman, 1960). Porter heard about the deaths of the monkeys and asked Brady if he could do autopsies on the next few monkeys who died unexpectedly. Brady describes the outcome of Porter's investigations.

During the next few months, Porter would occasionally appear in my office bearing in his rubber-gloved hands a piece of freshly excised monkey gut. Somewhere in the tissue there would be a clean round hole which, as Porter carefully explained, was a perforated ulcer. "Too bad." I would murmur, and Porter would leave without saying anything more. Eventually, it began to get through to me that Porter was carrying a message in his hands. That message finally burst out in neon lights when he remarked that out of several hundred monkeys which he had occasion to examine in the past, not one had shown any sign of a normally occurring ulcer. (from Sidman, 1960, p. 11)

Brady noted that the conditioning procedure that seemed to be most closely related to the production of ulcers was one in which monkeys learned to avoid regularly scheduled shock by pressing a lever at least once during the period before a shock was to be delivered. By keeping one monkey on such a schedule and having a second monkey yoked to it so that it received the same number of shocks but had no opportunity to avoid them, Brady was able to demonstrate that it was being on the avoidance schedule, and not the shocks per se, that caused ulcers to develop.

Brady undoubtedly felt grateful for stumbling across this far-reaching discovery, but he had been even luckier than he first thought. When he initially decided to investigate the advoidance conditioning procedure as the source of ulcers, he found that he was short of laboratory space in which to house the experimental animals. It was decided to run the conditioning procedure in Porter's office. The conditioning protocol called for alternating shock avoidance and time out periods of equal duration. The investigators had little idea of how long the interval should be, but decided on six hours, since they could schedule six hours of down time during most of Porter's office hours and thereby avoid disturbing his work. Little did the researchers know what subsequent research demonstrated: that the six hours on, six hours off schedule was nearly optimal for the production of ulcers, and that time periods much shorter or longer than six hours produced no ulcers at all!

Serendipity has also made inroads in the fight against another occupational hazard of living in modern times, high cholesterol (*Science*, **80**, 1980). Researchers at Ohio State University were feeding rabbits high cholesterol diets to prepare them for an unrelated experiment. To their consternation they discovered that the arterial buildup of cholesterol they were trying to produce was much less than they had anticipated. A clue to this surprising finding came when one of the investigators mentioned that she had been regularly picking up and cuddling the rabbits several times a day during the period they were receiving the special diet.

It would probably have seemed preposterous to many to even consider a relationship between cuddling and reduced buildup of arterial plaque. What self-respecting, hard-nosed scientist would even entertain such a sentimental notion? Preposterous or not, principal investigator Robert Newton decided to see if cardiovascular health researchers hadn't overlooked the potential effects of the "cuddle factor." He and his colleagues did a controlled study in which two groups of rabbits were fed identical high cholesterol diets. The experimental group also received at least an hour of loving human handling, while the control received none. As expected, the cuddled group developed only one-third the amount of fatty deposits that the control group developed. Even though evidence has existed for some time that a supportive environment seems to reduce susceptibility to heart disease in humans, the discovery of a similar phenomenon in animals is significant, since it will permit a greater amount and variety of research to be conducted on the relationship between nurturance and cardiovascular health.

Perhaps the most candid account of the role serendipity played in the research career of a psychologist was written by B. F. Skinner (1968). We saw earlier how his inductive, atheoretical approach to conducting research left him open to pursuing interesting and even anomalous findings wherever they might be found. Though it is difficult to determined if Skinner's penchant for making discoveries he was not seeking was a cause or an effect of this philosophy, there can be little question of how often serendipitous events influenced the course and outcome of his research.

Cumulative recorders; operant extinction curves; intermittent reinforcement; fixed ratio schedules. Chance events played a role in each of these discoveries. Skinner (1968) attributes his development of the cumulative recorder to the "third unformalized principle of scientific practice: Some people are lucky" (p. 31). He had put together a runway that rats had to traverse to obtain pellets of food. The tilting motion of the oval runway as the rats moved around it deflected a recording pen up and down over a slowly moving kymograph, producing a flat record of the number or reinforcements obtained. Skinner realized that the tilting motion of the experimental apparatus itself could activate a food magazine, permitting the rat to produce its own reinforcement. It so happened that the wooden disk used as the food magazine, which Skinner found in a storeroom of discarded equipment, had a central spindle protruding from it. The round magazine and the spindle rotated with each reinforcement. The rotating spindle caught Skinner's attention; he realized in a flash that if he wound a string around the spindle and attached the string to the pen marking the kymograph, a *curve* would be produced. This new measurement method, which produced a cumulative record reflecting *rate* of response, has become standard in operant conditioning experiments.

It is not hard to guess how an extinction curve was first produced in an operant conditioning laboratory. As Skinner notes, he only had to wait for his "automatic" food magazine to jam to produce the first record of operant extinction. Interestingly, Skinner initially viewed these breakdowns as an annoyance to be quickly remedied. Eventually he disconnected the food magazine on purpose to produce complete extinction curves. Skinner acknowledges that he sooner or later would have investigated extinction, but also

notes that in his work "it still is no exaggeration to say that some of the most interesting and surprising results have turned up first because of similar accidents" (1968, p. 32).

Skinner's successes, won partly through sagacity and partly through serendipity, naturally increased the rate of his research behavior. This meant that he had more and more rats to feed. Skinner was producing his own food pellets, and one Saturday afternoon realized that he'd have to spend much of the remainder of the weekend making pellets to keep his lever-pressing rats continuously reinforced. This practical dilemma led Skinner to ask why *every* lever press had to be reinforced. As a result, interval (time-based) reinforcement schedules were born. Skinner's rats kept lever pressing even if only an occasional response was reinforced, and Skinner got the rest of the weekend off.

But serendipity was not finished working its wonders. Skinner was searching for a method of keeping a rat at a constant level of food deprivation. He reasoned that if he made reinforcement contingent on number of responses, then a rat would press a lever at a fairly constant rate around the clock. The animals would press faster when hungry, get reinforced more often, become less hungry and respond less often, until they became hungry again. He even envisioned being able to hold rats at any level of deprivation by adjusting the rate of reinforcement. He was completely wrong; this schedule did not keep the rats at a constant level of deprivation. However, the effects of the "fixed-ratio" schedule Skinner devised for this purpose— the same as a "piece-rate schedule"—were of considerable interest in their own right and became a subject of operant research for years to come. Yes, there can be little doubt that B. F. Skinner had a knack for serendipity. After all, the examples discussed here were drawn not from his entire career but from the research that culminated in *The Behavior of Organisms,* published in 1938.

It comes as no surprise that Skinner was so candid in describing how accidents and luck, rather than deduction and insight, influenced his research endeavors. After all, what psychologist would be more likely to look to the external environment for the causes of his behavior? As we suggested earlier, the same openness could not be said to characterize Ivan Pavlov, the man who probably influenced Skinner's early work the most. We have already discussed some of the controversy that surrounds the impetus for Pavlov's initial research on "psychic reflexes." Therefore we will only briefly review evidence that, despite claims to the contrary (Babkin, 1949), suggests to us that it was a serendipitous observation, made by an insightful observer, which initiated the study of conditioned reflexes.

Pavlov described his switch from the study of the purely physiological aspects of the digestive glands to their "psychic" aspects as follows:

More than twenty years ago [approximately 1901] I independently began these experiments passing to them from my former physiological work. I entered this field under the influence of a powerful laboratory impression. For many years previous, I had been working on the digestive glands. I had studied carefully and in detail all the conditions of their activity. *Naturally, I could not leave them without considering the so-called psychical stimulation of the salivary glands,* i.e., the flow of saliva in the hungry animal or person at the sight of food or during talk about it or even at the thought of it. (Pavlov, 1928, p. 37, italics added)

This passage makes it sound as if Pavlov decided—since he was finishing up his physiological study of the digestive glands anyway—to study psychic secretions for the sake of completeness. However, even Babkin, a staunch defender of Pavlov, described the transition from gastroenterology to classical conditioning in different terms.

It is interesting to note that as late as 1899 Pavlov had not as yet any intention of abandoning the filed of gastroenterology. From his address "The Experimental Method—an Indispensable Re-

quirement of Medical Research" (Pavlov, 1902) one may gather that he intended to begin a thorough study of the pathology of the gastrointestinal tract . . . This was never done, either by him or anybody else because Pavlov radically changed the course of his scientific work. (1949, p. 280)

Certainly Pavlov deserves no less credit for the 38-odd years of brilliant research he conducted in classical conditioning just because his initial interest in this area was caused by happenstance more than by design.

Next, we come to our first examples of serendipitous research findings obtained with human subjects. Two such results were achieved early in the development of what came to be called biofeedback. Though the concept of biofeedback was developed by several groups of researchers during a relatively short period of time, human applications of this procedure were strongly influenced by findings stumbled upon by Brown (1974) and by Sargent, Walters, and Green (1973).

Barbara Brown (1974) notes that her journey on the way to serendipity began in childhood. She recalls a traumatic incident as a child, during which she learned that her friends could imagine in colors whereas she saw only gray when she closed her eyes. In her laboratory many years later, she decided to study how the brain-wave patterns of "visualizers" and "nonvisualizers" might differ. She found that the brain-wave patterns of these two groups in response to flashes of colored light did differ, and even that a person's status as visualizer or nonvisualizer could be predicted from personality tests. Then, in a bold attempt to develop a measure of subjective states, she planned research into the brain-wave patterns and associated emotions evoked in response to various colors. This research was just beginning when Brown (1974) had a "most impossible, foolish thought and stumbled onto biofeedback" (p. 29). She asked herself why, instead of measuring subjects' brain-wave responses to colored lights, the paradigm couldn't be reversed to allow subjects to turn on variously colored lights by emitting particular brain wave patterns. To evaluate this idea, Brown started with a simple arrangement in which subjects could "see" the amount of alpha waves they were producing by watching a blue light that changed in brightness along with alpha wave production. Though this outcome alone was all Brown was looking for, she found much more. Subject after subject was able not only to turn the light on, but to keep it burning brightly for longer and longer periods. To Brown,

> The conclusion seemed obvious. If a person could see something of himself that up to now had been unknown and involuntary, he could identify with it and in some way learn to exert control over it. If a person could learn to do this with an obscure brain wave, couldn't he then learn to identify with almost any functioning part of himself, and also learn to control that too. (1974, p. 30)

When the second case of serendipity in biofeedback occurred, the biofeedback phenomenon had already been well established. However, it was the workings of chance that led to its human application in the treatment of migraine headaches. The discovery occurred in the middle of a research project (Sargent et al., 1973) that involved studying the physiological effects of Schultz and Luthe's autogenic training procedure. Sargent et al. were lucky enough to have solicited a research subject who not only suffered from migraines, but who recovered from one while the researchers were monitoring her hand temperature. As her migraine dissipated spontaneously, her hands became flushed and their temperature increased 10 degrees F in two minutes. Not surprisingly, "Knowledge of this event quickly spread throughout the laboratory and prompted two individuals with migraine to volunteer for training in hand temperature control" (Walters et al., 1973, p. 58). The success achieved with these individuals prompted these and other investigators into researching the use of bio-feedback to control peripheral blood flow as a treatment for migraine headaches.

The serendipitous research finding that has pervasively affected current thinking in psychopathology is the uncovering of the "learned helplessness" model of depression. Interest in learned helplessness was so keen that the *Journal of Abnormal Psychology* devoted an entire issue to the topic a few years back (1978, **87**, No. 1). Seligman (1975; Overmier & Seligman, 1967) didn't start out trying to produce learned helplessness in his laboratory dogs, but when he did the phenomenon was so striking that he made a career out of researching it.

The research leading up to the discovery of learned helplessness was designed to study the effect of a classically conditioned aversive stimulus (a tone) upon avoidance behavior. To endow the neutral stimulus of a tone with aversive properties, Seligman and his colleagues strapped a dog into a harness and delivered a series of moderately painful shocks, each of them preceded by the tone. After a dog had been through this conditioning regimen it was placed into a shuttle box made up of two compartments separated by a barrier. The animal could receive shock in either chamber. The dog's first task was to learn that it could escape from the shock by hurdling over the barrier, and eventually that it could avoid shock by jumping the barrier before the regularly scheduled shocks occurred. The plan was to train a number of dogs in the shuttle box until they became experts at avoiding shock and then to study the effects of introducing the classically conditioned tone on their avoidance behavior.

There was only one problem. "What my colleagues and I had forgotten about," Seligman later noted, "but were soon reminded of, was the defining feature of Pavlovian conditioning: the shock UCs were inescapable" (1975, p. 21). The preexperimental pairing of the tone with inescapable shock, while undoubtedly endowing the tone with aversive properties, had the unintended effect of informing the animal that it was powerless to escape shock. Therefore when the animals were tested in the shuttle box, most of them yelped and ran about initially, but quickly gave up on any escape attempts and simply laid down and took the punishment. Dogs who received no preexperimental conditioning involving inescapable shock proved quite efficient in learning to escape from and ultimately to avoid the shocks. The qualitative difference between the shuttle-box behavior of these two groups of animals was so striking that Seligman lost interest in studying variables affecting avoidance and instead concentrated entirely on learning more about the dramatic effects of helplessness.

Finally, we come to the only published example we located of a serendipitous outcome in research on a clinical problem using human subjects. The study was done by Lando and Davison (1975), who were attempting to make certain methodological improvements in the design used by Resnick (1968) in his smoking cessation study. In Lando and Davison's investigation, four groups of smokers who wanted to quit came to two treatment sessions. In the first, the smoker's operant rate of puffing was measured. The experimental manipulation was administered in the second session, during which each of three experimental groups received separate instructions via a tape recorded message to smoke either at their operant rate, at twice that rate, or at triple that rate. A fourth, control group simply engaged in normal, self-paced smoking.

Though the experimenters expected that the most rapid smoking rate would be most aversive and therefore most effective in reducing consumption, they were surprised to find that the self-paced "control" group had reduced their smoking more than the three experimental groups, which did not differ from each other. The self-paced groups also rated their cigarettes less favorably after the second session than did the three experimental groups.

Rather than ignoring or discounting their anomalous findings, Lando and Davison ventured an explanation. They knew that all four groups found smoking in the second treatment session aversive. However, while the three experimental groups could attribute their experiences to the artifical tape-recorded commands for them to smoke, self-paced smokers had no such explanation and were therefore more likely, à la cognitive dissonance, to devalue cigarettes themselves. This interpretation, which, as the authors note, is post hoc, is supported by the self-paced group's less favorable ratings of cigarettes. The important point illustrated by this example is that significant findings are significant regardless of whether they are sought after or stumbled upon. As such, they should be reported rather than rationalized away or reconstructed after the fact as if they were derived through rational analysis.

TYPE II: SERENDIPITY IN A NATURALISTIC CONTEXT

It is readily apparent that scientists operate in many different contexts. In the previous section the emphasis was on unexpected events arising out of rigorously planned laboratory experiments. The stage for Type II serendipity, however, is the natural environment, which cannot usually be controlled or regulated. It is free to wander unpredictably. The standard scientific preparations are simply not tenable in this context. What is crucial for discoveries here is the combination of scientific inspiration and effort to mobilize the necessary resources for a full-scale research investigation.

To take a well known example, Orson Welles and his talented Mercury Theater Company in 1938 presented a brilliantly conceived radio adaptation of H. G. Wells' "Invasion from Mars." In this program Orson Welles displayed his special genius for creating theatrical illusions. Despite warnings inserted throughout the broadcast explicitly reminding listeners that the program was purely fiction, large numbers of people were terrified by the implications of what they heard. The program appeared so authentic that panic gripped millions, many of whom literally abandoned their homes to escape the Martian invasion. Hadley Cantril (1940), the social scientist who studied the social hysteria generated by this incident, suggested in the following quote some of the elements of "preparedness" that are necessary to capitalize on events such as this:

Such real occurrences provide opportunities for the social scientist to study mass behavior. They must be exploited when they come. Although the social scientist, unfortunately, cannot predict such situations and have his tools of investigation ready to analyze the phenomenon while it is still on the wing, he can begin his work before the effects of the crisis are over and the memories are blurred. (p. 486)

An analysis of this example highlights some of the important qualities of Type II serendipity. As a social scientist, Cantril was programmed to be especially vigilant to unique social phenomena. Furthermore, he apparently had resources readily available to actualize a substantial research effort within a short period of time. Only a few weeks after the incident, he was able to obtain detailed interviews with 135 persons, most of whom were selected because they reported having been upset by the broadcast. Impressed by the emotional chaos generated by this splendid radio play, Cantril was struck by the profound emotional impact that radio was capable of stirring, and his interpretation of the panic is quite illuminating. At the same time, it is interesting to speculate as to why other psychologists were not so prepared to intervene with Cantril's vigor. Undoubtedly, immense curiosity was aroused on the part of many scientists. But the translation of the idea into a practical research reality was accomplished only in this one case. A cardinal feature of serendipity, therefore, is not the appearance of an idea alone, but the determination to pursue energetically the idea by converting it into a palpable quality, which can then be publicly shared.

Another example of Type II serendipity was reported by Merbaum and Hefez (1975). On the day of Yom Kippur on October I (M. M.) was sitting with my family on our terrace in Haifa, Israel, listening to the radio. Suddenly a voice broke in and calmly reported that Israel was being attacked by the Syrians to the north and the Egyptians to the south. Israel was under siege, and the destruction of the state was a serious possibility. Immediately after the attack was confirmed, large numbers of citizens who had not been called into the armed forces spontaneously and enthusiastically volunteered their service for the war effort. I also frantically wanted to do my bit and finally persuaded the director of psychiatry to give me work in the psychiatric ward treating soldiers who had broken down in combat. Already substantial numbers of soldiers had encountered enormous stress on the battlefield and were experiencing severe psychological repercussions. Upon entering the psychiatric ward I saw small, isolated groups of men dressed in military fatigues, trembling with fear and looking sorrowfully depressed. Surveying the ward, which I figured could handle about 50 civilian patients, I was suddenly struck by an incongruity. Where had the original patients disappeared? Had they been transferred to another hospital? What had happened to them during this crisis? I asked the chief psychiatrist about it, and he explained that each ward psychiatrist had briefly confronted his patients with the gravity of the situation and then arranged for their release back into the community. Finally, he recounted, within a few hours after the war emergency began, all psychiatric patients had been picked up by their relatives, or left the hospital alone by bus, train, or special transportation. Since my inquiry came only a day after their release, no one really knew what had happened to them. In fact, it seemed that no one was even particularly interested in view of the current turbulence that characterized the military situation.

I remember vividly tantalizing myself with what I thought to be the unique implications of this event. What might have happened to these people who were highly vulnerable to stress when they were unceremoniously discharged from relative safety into a stress-loaded environment with relatives or custodians who were also confronting a potentially catastrophic experience? What might be the psychological consequences to these individuals? At that moment, I had not the foggiest idea how to study the problem. There were obviously more pressing emergency therapeutic considerations to be dealt with. Furthermore, I had no idea of the whereabouts of the civilian patients or the ward psychiatrists, most of whom were currently on active duty at the front. However, the idea was so compelling that I was determined to follow it through. My biggest problem was to sell the chief psychiatrist on orchestrating a research project that I had quickly designed. Fortunately, in the midst of all the chaos, I was able to collect data and answer a few of the questions raised by an unexpected and intriguing social phenomena.

The major findings showed that most of the psychiatric inpatients who were unexpectedly released from the hospital did not display short-term (one month) or long-term (10 to 12 months) behavioral/emotional impairment. Our interpretation suggested that the war stress facilitated a powerful atmosphere of social support throughout the entire country. The former patients were beneficiaries of this reaction and after their discharge they were received into a positive though obviously stressful social context. Their personal reports vividly recalled an experience of genuine acceptance by their immediate family and a more general sense of relatedness to the rest of the population who were unavoidably sharing the hard times with them. The pervasive impact of social support seemed to be a major factor that assisted these individuals in more productively using their personal resources over an extended period of time.

Occasionally an unusual natural event may give rise to subsequent laboratory-based research. Such seems to be the case of what social psychologists have labeled the "bystander effect." In 1964 a woman was stabbed to death in a residential section of New York City. Investigation of the case revealed that at least 38 persons had witnessed the attack but none had even attempted to intervene. What was equally appalling was that no one even lifted the phone to call the police, even though the attacker took more than a half hour to kill the victim, Kitty Genovese. Not long after the incident, a book was written by A. M. Rosenthal, based partly on his interviews with many of the witnesses. Two social psychologists, Milgram and Hollander (1964), also wrote a brief piece on the murder.

Despite the arousal of public interest in this event, the first attempt to systematically examine some of the variables that might retard or initiate "bystander" intervention was planned somewhat later. Darley and Latane (1968) created a laboratory-type deception experiment in which subjects were confronted with what appeared to them to be a bona fide emergency. The number of subjects who responded with help, and the speed of their reaction, was related to the number of bystanders that the subject perceived to be present at the scene of the emergency. The authors found that the smaller the number of perceived bystanders the greater the probability of action to intervene in behalf of the victim. As the number of bystanders grew, the less likely help was forthcoming. Later studies (Latane & Darley, 1970; Piliavan & Piliavan, 1972; Piliavan, Rodin, & Piliavan, 1969) suggested that the chances of being helped in an emergency would be improved if, for example, the bystander were black rather than white, were a man rather than a woman, and the situation was viewed as a clear emergency. Would this area of research have evolved without the dramatic and serendipitous Genovese incident? There is of course no way to know. However, alert social scientists are continuing to use data based on real-life incidents to generate ideas for more highly controlled research.

Psychological theories are occasionally the beneficiaries of accidental and unexcepted tidbits of data. Originally working on the topic of rumor spreading, a study group lead by Festinger (1957) ran across an interesting report of an Indian earthquake that occurred in 1934. The details of this report raised a number of psychological incongruities, which stimulated the group to produce innovative theorizing in order to resolve certain provocative inconsistencies. In brief, rumors spread by earthquake victims that predicted even worse disaster were not apparently anxiety producing. Instead they had the unusual effect of justifying the anxiety the victims were already experiencing. The manner in which the information about this catastrophe was processed led to hypotheses concerning the concept of dissonance and the processes involved in dissonance reduction. Thus, from the initial stage of studying rumor reduction, a broad theory of cognitive behavior was conceived. Festinger (1957) points out that the theory of cognitive dissonance owed a major debt to the accidental stimulus provided by this Indian commentator's account of the earthquake and the intricacies of psychological responses to this event. Perhaps the group was already well along the way toward composing the theory of cognitive dissonance. However, the brief discussion by Festinger suggests that it was this bit of data that set the process of theorizing in motion.

Data Collection

Though the Type II serendipity research is by definition less controlled than laboratory research, an investigator doing field research will often have considerable leeway in the type and amount of data he or she can collect. At one end of the spectrum, the researcher may simply attempt to collect systematic data on the reactions of individuals affected by the event of interest. This type of investigation, of which Cantril's (1940) and Rosenthal's (1964) are examples, depend almost exclusively on self-reports of participants, often collected through interviews. Investigations such as these, though uncontrolled and based on self-report, nonetheless provide invaluable glimpses into the working of the human psyche when exposed to unique and often extreme natural events.

At the other end of the methodological spectrum is Type II research, which attempts both to comprehensively document participants' reactions to a natural event and to generate data that shed light on possible explanations for the observations made. Certain aspects of Merbaum's and Hefez's (1975) research on psychiatric patients' reactions to wartime stress exemplify this approach. In addition to collecting demographic and diagnostic information on the patients and interviewing them, psychiatrists and nurses interviewed the patients' relatives at one- and 10-month follow-ups. These authors also collected data on rehospitalization, medication use, and degree of involvement in the war effort shown by the discharged patients. These data permitted Merbaum and Hefez to speculate about the adjustment of the patients without having to rely solely on self-reports.

In some settings where Type II research is being undertaken, it is possible to conduct an even more rigorous investigation. Psychologists who report on the sequelae of some exceptional event usually speculate on the reasons for the reactions they observe. Rather than just idly speculating on causes, resourceful investigators will often have the opportunity to collect additional data to test the plausibility of their speculations. For instance, Merbaum and Hefez (1975) reasoned that the atmosphere of crisis after the outbreak of the Yom Kippur war may have enhanced familial support for patients who suddenly returned to their families. To evaluate this hypothesis, the authors might have correlated adjustment scores derived for the patients with the number of regular familial contacts the patients had in the community. Or, to test a more intrapsychic explanation for the patients' adjustment, they could have been given a measure of ego strength and these scores could then have been correlated with an index of adjustment.

Once an investigator posits a hypothesis to explain his or her observations, it would also be desirable to evaluate the plausibility of rival explanations. Thus he or she could collect data or retrieve data already available to test alternative hypotheses or to separate from an observed relationship any influence of a third variable that might account for the relationship. The point is that while the naturalistic researcher in the middle of a Type II serendipitous event has no control over unfolding circumstances, he or she may very well be able to retrieve existing data or generate new data that will greatly bolster confidence in the validity of his or her speculations and conclusions.

TYPE III: SERENDIPITY FROM MEDICAL TREATMENT

The search for useful treatments for physical and mental disorders has also been a fertile source of theoretical inspiration and technical innovation. While it is relatively rare to run across unequivocal documentation of serendipity, there are a sufficient number of cases to reveal some interesting facets to this phenomena. What occasionally complicates the accurate labeling of serendipity are the different accounts of the same episode reported by an investigator at separate points in time. Thus in some of the examples we reviewed we were impressed by the complex human motives that appeared to underlie the differing accounts of a single discovery. A striking example is posed by Valenstein (1973) in his discussion of insulin coma therapy, one of

several chemical and electrical psychiatric treatments that apparently arose out of a serendipitous discovery. Dr. Manfred Sakel, the originator of insulin coma therapy, initially created his method through the administration of insulin to morphine-addicted patients so as to hopefully achieve a more sedated and thus less agonizing withdrawal from the drug. Reviewing the background of his rather remarkable findings, Sakel (1938) offered a candid admission:

At this point, as so often happens in such matters I was helped by chance. By chance I produced deeper hypoglycemic reactions that I had intended. I was able then to observe that such reactions led to much quicker and more substantial alterations in mental states and could even cause psychotic symptoms to disappear. (from Valenstein, 1973, p. 153)

Some years later, following the sharp rise in the popularity of insulin coma therapy, Sakel (1958) reevaluated the genesis of his discovery and presented a somewhat more "respectable" version of the event.

I started my experiments with the idea that the key to combat mental disease lay in the discovery of a physiological approach to influence the center of the autonomic nervous system, the hypothalmus which appeared to be the bridge between physiological functions and mental manifestations.

Valenstein (1973) suggests that Sakel may have become overly sensitized to critics who challenged the "priority" of his discovery. Perhaps from Sakel's view, being at the right place at the right time was probably not the most enviable criterion for securing one's pivotal position in medical history. It is not our intention to dispute either of Sakel's statements. Nonetheless, as we suggested earlier in this paper, scientists are susceptible to the usual human frailties, and therefore one must assume that commitments to "consistency" and "truth" are understandably colored by the exigencies of the moment. This example stands out as a contrast to most tales of serendipity which are acknowledged in later rather than earlier accounts of the discovery.

The fate of insulin coma therapy as a viable treatment was relatively short-lived, partly due to the greater convenience of electroshock techniques. The story of how electroshock therapy evolved also seems to have some serendipitous aspects. It all started with an Italian psychiatrist named Ugo Cerletti, whose main target of study was epilepsy. He was struggling with the problem of creating an animal model of human epilepsy and reasoned that epileptic type seizures might be experimentally induced through electric shock. In the course of his studies he had routinely attached his electrodes to the mouth and rectum of his research animals. Either by design or chance he happened to visit a slaughterhouse and saw hogs "clamped at the temples with big metallic tongs which were hooked up to an electric current" (from Valenstein, 1973, p. 156). The electric current rendered the hogs unconscious and the butchers then stabbed and bled the animals to death. Cerletti was astonished to find that electric shock to the head was not the cause of death. This was an important revelation because it was commonly believed that animals were killed by electric current. On the basis of this experience at the slaughterhouse Cerletti applied electric shock at various intersites and durations to the heads of the animals, who survived the experience. Eventually he was convinced that his electroshock procedures were harmless and he was eager to try them out on a human subject. An opportunity arose when the Police Commisioner of Rome sent to him for referral a man who was in a seriously disordered mental state. Diagnosed as schizophrenic, this patient received the first electroshock treatment on record. The results were exciting and dramatic to Cerletti and his staff:

He rose to a sitting position and looked at us, calm and smiling, as though to inquire what we wanted of him. We asked "what happened to you?" He answered "I don't know, maybe I was asleep." Thus occurred the first electrically produced convulsion in man, which I at once named "electroshock." (from Valenstein, 1973, pp. 157–158)

Reading between the lines of this account, we may debate who was shocked more, Cerletti or his patient.

Outside of its direct therapeutic applications, another form of electrical stimulation of the brain has also led to important though unexpected breakthroughs in the understanding of brain functioning. While operating on an epileptic patient, the renowned neurologist Wilder Penfield applied a mild electric stimulus to an exposed portion of the right temporal cortex. The patient spontaneously relived an early emotional memory. Each stimulation produced extremely vivid recall. This remarkable response by his patient set Penfield on the trail of identifying the functions of what he later termed the "uncommitted cortex" or the nondominant hemisphere.

One day I stumbled on a clue. I applied the electrode to the right temporal cortex (non-dominant). The patient, a woman of middle-age, exclaimed suddenly, "I seem to be the way I was when I was giving birth to my baby girl!" *I did not recognize this as a clue.* I could not help feeling that the suddenness of her exclamation was strange, and so I made a note of it. (from Penfield, 1971, p. 192; italics added)

Several aspects of this account are intriguing. For one thing, the original event occurred around 1933, and the 1964 reminiscence reported above may be somewhat blurred in its details. Thus there is some question as to whether the stimulation of the right temporal lobe was truly accidental, a deliberate probe related to the surgical needs of his patient, or a semiplanned, nontherapeutic excursion into the unexplored quarters of the right hemisphere. Similarly, when Penfield remarks that he "made a note of it," was this a written note or simply a mental one filed away for later retrieval? It is likely that the full details of this early episode have disappeared. Nonetheless, the feelings of excitement, joy, and mystery that were poignantly felt at that moment of creative enlightenment were never destined to fade. In 1975, not long before his death, Penfield offered the following elaboration of his experience.

On the first occasion when these "flashbacks" were reported to me by a conscious patient (1933) I was incredulous. On each subsequent occasion I marvelled [p. 21]. . . . I was astonished each time my electrode brought forth such a response. How could it be? This had to do with the mind! I called such response "experiential" and waited for more evidence. (p. 27)

The psychopharmacological revolution in psychiatric treatment can also be traced to its serendipitous roots. Promethazine, an antihistamine drug, was being used by the French surgeon Henri Laboint to alleviate shock during surgical procedures. Highly attuned to his patients' behavior, he observed something even more interesting. The introduction of Promethazine produced drowsiness and appeared to lessen apprehensions about surgery without inducing any mental confusion. He therefore felt that the drug had great potential value as a preoperative medication, "for reasons we had not expected. Our patients are calm, somewhat somnolent, relaxed and look rested . . . even after major operations they are never excited, not complaining, and appear to suffer less" (from Snyder, 1974, p. 14).

Following the publication of Laboint's data, a French drug company synthesized a phenothiazine derivative that was given the name chlorapromazine. The new drug was submitted to Laboint for further testing. He found the drug to be extremely effective in rendering patients calm and tranquil but still alert. In the first clinical publication on chloropromazine, which cited his results with surgical patients, Laboint speculated that

"These facts let us foresee certain implications for this drug in psychiatry" (Snyder, 1974, p. 15).

Shortly after the synthesis of chloropromazine and its clinical applications with psychiatric patients, another serendipitous discovery occurred with the monoamine oxidase inhibitors. Tuberculosis patients being treated with iproniazid showed an unexpected euphoric reaction (Silverstone & Turner, 1974). The logical explanation was that if iproniazid had a mood elevating action, it might inhibit the enzyme monoamine oxidase and affect brain amine concentrations. It was then reasoned that these effects on brain chemistry might be of therapeutic benefit in cases of depression. As with the phenothiazines, a rash of other drugs of the same chemical class were produced to ameliorate depressive symptomology. These original chance observations have now resulted in the creation of at least 28 marketable phenothiazine derivatives and nine monoamine oxidase inhibitors (Silverstone & Turner, 1974).

The spectrum of drugs that may produce an ameliorative reaction of serious mental conditions is quite diversified. In prescribing a particular drug there is probably no sure way of knowing or even assuming without evidence that a predicted drug action might also influence the mental state of the patient. However, if the drug transcends its original goal, and other useful psychological consequences are identified, the investigators certainly have cause for excitement. Such was the case with the drug Propranolol in the treatment of schizophrenia.

The first inkling that Propranolol might reduce psychotic mental symptoms happened fortuitously in 1969 in Beilinson Hospital, Israel. Atsman and Blum (1978) administered Propanolol to a young woman who was suffering from severe abdominal pains, tachycardia, renal insufficiency, hypertension, and neurological symptoms. These symptoms were compatible with a disease labeled variegate prophyria. In addition, there were hysteria-like mental changes with possible acute organic psychosis. Based on the clinical literature Propranolol, a widely used beta-adrenergic blocking drug was introduced to reduce a dangerous increase in heart rate and blood pressure. Suffice it to say that Propanolol not only effectively depressed pulse rate, blood pressure, and improved renal function as expected but also produced a startling clearance of the mental symptoms. Quite fortuitously, a second patient, a relative of the first, was also hospitalized for suspected porphyria. She had developed an acutely severe psychosis shortly before her admission to the hospital. Spurred on by their earlier experience, Atsman and Blum administered Propronolol again; a rapid improvement of mental symptoms was noted during the first 16 hours, and complete recovery had taken place by the end of the third day. Crucial laboratory tests to detect the presence of porphyrin were negative. Thus Propranolol appeared to alleviate mental distrubances and, equally interesting, when the drug was withdrawn the same mental symptoms reappeared. The authors noted:

These remarkable and unexpected results and the wealth of information in the literature about the possible role of catecholamines in psychosis induced us to attempt further treatment of psychiatric patients with beta-adrenergic receptor blocking agents in high doses. (Atsman & Blum, 1975, p. 10)

Whether Propranolol will turn out to be a "wonder drug" for the treatment of schizophrenia is unknown at this juncture. However, this example highlights our rudimentary understanding of the multifaceted action of chemicals on complex behavior. Furthermore, as has been the case with many psychopharmacological treatments of schizophrenia and the psychoses, carefully controlled experimental trials are critical to establish the credibility of the many "cures" that have come and gone in the last two decades.

Another recent case study parallels the previously reported case. In this instance the patient was a 27-year-old female admitted to a medical service for ulcerative colitis. She had had a complicated delivery of her second child two weeks prior to admission. Upon arrival at the hospital she was "mute and immobile," was found to have enlarged ventricles, and was emaciated and hypertensive (Leigh, Callahan, & Einhorn, 1978). A psychiatrist diagnosed her as catatonic, but she was basically treated for advanced ulcerative colitis with colectomy and the tapering off of steroids she had previously received for colitis. After the colectomy all vital signs and laboratory findings returned to normal. By the end of five weeks she was completely oriented, and her judgment and affect were normal. She had no recollection of hallucinations or conversations with her psychiatrist during her psychotic episode. While the authors discuss the patient's recovery from severe psychosis with a kind of dispassionate curiosity, the fact that treatment for ulcerative colitis resulted in a corresponding disappearance of gross mental distress strikes us as quite remarkable. Their conclusion emphasizes the value of examining and treating all of the multifaceted factors in patients with catatonic syndrome, perhaps assuming that something might work even though we currently have no real idea what would. Since the treatment of mental disorders are still "wide open," it is incumbent upon the scientist to grasp at every lead and pursue as many associations as possible. One just might serendipitously turn out to be the real thing.

One final instance of suspected serendipity is the application of hemodialysis in chronic schizophrenia. In a 1977 paper entitled "The use of hemodialysis in chronic schizophrenia" published in the *American Journal of Psychiatry*, Wagemaker and Cade describe the following incident:

Several years ago one of us (R. C.) treated a hypertensive young woman with dialysis. The patient was also schizophrenic and had been in and out of the state hospital repeatedly because of this disorder. Repeated dialysis cleared up her hypertension: furthermore she lost the symptoms of schizophrenia. (p. 685)

Taking careful note of this "presumably" surprising finding, they then tested their dialysis procedures on four other schizophrenic patients. They were dialyzed from every two weeks to once every three months for at least one year. Three of the four patients who continued to be dialyzed continued functioning normally, while the one who dropped out rapidly decompensated. Currently six patients have undergone dialysis 16 times or more, and five have shown a complete remission of schizophrenia. The authors speculate that "a substance is removed from the blood during dialysis and that this substance builds up in the patient's system when he/she is not dialysed" (p. 685). The "substances," however, are unspecified and the procedure remains a biological enigma.

It is curious to note about this paper that previous case studies in which hemodialysis was attempted in schizophrenia were not mentioned. In 1960 Feer, Thoelen, Massini, and Staub in Basle, Switzerland, reported the dialysis treatment of five patients. Four were diagnosed as acute catatonic schizophrenia and one patient as having paranoid-catatonic schizophrenia. Unlike the extended series of dialysis treatments given by Wagermaker and Cade, four patients were dialyzed once and one, twice. Also arteriovenous shunts were not surgically placed in the arms of these patients. Nonetheless, after a single dialysis some mild improvements were noted, though the symptomatic remissions were relatively short term. The authors suggested that schizophrenia could be the product of hormones or amino acids that might be corrected by the infusion of foreign blood. This study was presented as fully planned and consistent with a literature on blood transfusion in schizophrenia, which suggested toxic factors in the blood of schizophrenics. On these

grounds they reasoned that a hemodialysis might yield better results. Wagermaker and Cade must have been at least dimly aware of previous work in this area. However, their paper, though a preliminary report, makes no mention of earlier studies.

TYPE III: SERENDIPITY IN PSYCHOTHERAPY

In the previous section we reviewed several instances in which treatments for medical problems fortuitously resulted in new treatments for psychological problems. In this section we consider how psychotherapy itself may lead to therapeutic improvements through accidental or chance occurences. Though the reader may wonder how this discussion fits into a chapter on *research,* we think it is reasonable to view psychotherapy as intensive research into individual cases. The therapist, regardless of his or her theoretical orientation, is involved in a continuous process of generating, testing, and reformulating hypotheses concerning diagnosis and treatment.

Before exploring this question, a definition of "serendipitious events" in the realm of clinical practice is needed. A serendipitous event in psychotherapy is one that occurs independently of (or despite) the therapist's intentions and generates new, unexpected information that furthers a client's diagnosis or treatment. Such events may occur within or outside of the therapeutic setting. In therapy, opportunities for serendipity will be greater the more often unplanned and unexpected occurrence disrupt the routine therapy format that has been established. Outside of therapy, serendipity could be said to have occurred when a patient unexpectedly derives therapeutic gain from some event occuring independently of therapy.

In a recent case report entitled "Serendipity in Psychotherapy," McCormick (1979) describes how the referral of a young girl experiencing distress at school led to the identification of the mother, rather than the child, as the source of trouble. Such "unexpected" redefinitions of who the patient is or what problems require treatment—a common occurrence in psychotherapy—would not qualify as serendipity in our use of the term. Missing in such instances is the occurrence of some unpredicted event that draws attention to useful information that may have remained obscured without the intervention of a lucky accident.

One of the most far-reaching instances of serendipity that had an impact on psychotherapy occurred not during clinical work but during the development of a diagnostic tool, the Rorschach inkblot cards. When Rorschach first attempted to publish his inkblots in book form, he planned on using 15 cards, all of which were uniform black or gray composition with no variation in shading. It seems that it was almost as difficult to get published then as now, and approximately seven publishers turned the book down before it was finally accepted for publication. However, when it finally was published, the quality of the printing was poor and the original uniform shading of the inkblots were replaced by various shades of gray. Rather than being upset by the shabby reproductions, Rorschach responded enthusiastically, recognizing that the shadings would give rise to a richer variety of percepts than would blots of uniform shadings (Ellenberger, 1954).

Despite its fortuitous beginnings, Rorschach and numerous other workers who followed him placed considerable emphasis on shading responses as a source of diagnostic impressions. Schachtel (1969) noted that the Rorschach literature has delineated a greater variety of shading responses than of any other determinant. The serendipitous origins of the shading determinant apparently escaped the knowledge of some Rorschach scholars long after the test was published (Beck, 1950; Bell, 1948). Beck (1950) noted that Rorschach himself wrote virtually nothing about shading, and that relatively little was known

about its significance even at the time of Beck's publication. He says: "The correlation of these two circumstances—Rorschach's silence, and our inadequate knowledge—can be no chance matter, the more so since our understanding is best in those aspects of his test that he does develop" (1950, pp. 126–127). Quite to the contrary, it appears that the lack of knowledge of the shading responses was precisely a chance matter.

Although our search was in no way exhaustive, we were able to locate relatively few published examples of serendipity occurring during psychotherapy itself. It is difficult to know how often serendipity actually rears its fortuitous head in clincial work. However, given the relatively infrequent publications of case reports, we think it likely that the number of published accounts of serendipity in psychotherapy represents an underestimate of its occurrence during treatment.

A couple of published examples of serendipity in therapy may help attune us to the potential of unplanned events and even "nuisances" for furthering our understanding and treatment of clinical cases. One such example was described by Levinson (1961) in a paper entitled "The Dog as Co-Therapist." During his treatment of a difficult problem child, Levinson's dog happened to be in the office with him. The child formed a strong attachment to the dog and refused to return for additional sessions unless the dog was present. Levinson then decided to include the dog in sessions with other children and found that the children's interactions with the dog gave rise to valuable clinical material that would have been difficult to evoke using other means. Without this happy accident, Levinson would have continued to pursue more customary but less successful means of gathering such material, leaving him, one might say, barking up the wrong tree.

A second example of serendipity, though the author did not describe it in this way, was contained in the book *Critical incidents in psychotherapy* (Standal & Corsini, 1959).

The therapist involved had seen a female college student diagnosed as a paranoid schizophrenic for 14 sessions. She then went away to college, but became so despondent during her first week there that she returned to see the therapist on a weekend. The therapist and patient agreed to leave the length of the session open, since she was acutely upset and because the clinic was inaccessible to her.

The session began at 5 p.m.; at 6:30 the therapist asked his patient how much more time she wanted. She did not answer, and they continued until 7 p.m., at which point the therapist indicated that he was weak from hunger and wasn't following her well. The patient took this as a rejection of her by the therapist. She became extremely upset and, standing up, began trembling, wringing her hands, and leaning to and fro. However, when the therapist indicated that the session could continue, the patient began to describe details of her relationship with her father (which included incest), trembling all the while. Though the therapist does not go on to describe her adjustment subsequent to this session, it does seem clear that a marked emotional reaction (possibly including hallucinations) and critical clinical material were evoked largely through fortuitous circumstances. The therapist's "rejection" of his patient, which sparked her intense catharsis, may never have occurred if they had continued to meet for sessions of uniform duration. The new information gleaned from this incident clearly would be of heuristic value in the treatment of similar therapy cases.

It is a curious fact about psychotherapy that therapists usually explore the circumstances surrounding unexpected difficulties but not unexpected gains experienced by their patients. When a patient's improvement catches the therapist by surprise, the therapist's first reaction might be to think, "Why didn't you show such improvement when I interpreted your anger at your wife?" or "Why didn't you become less fearful when we reached the top of your desensitization

hierarchy?" Rather than exploring the possible reasons for unanticipated improvement, we suspect that most therapists attribute such gains to unspecified curative factors operating in therapy and let the matter drop.

This sort of therapist attitude assumes both that therapeutic experiences occur only because of therapy, and that such experiences are always induced intentionally by the therapist. In regard to the unanticipated elimination of problems leading to therapy, Lazarus and Davison (1971) noted that:

> Unplanned or unexpected clinical improvements are often dismissed as "spontaneous remissions" but the clinical innovator is the one who carefully notes a variety of possible cause-effect sequences and thus discovers therapeutic levers that his less inquisitive colleagues are apt to overlook. (p. 198)

Thus, just as a wise researcher investigates the significance of anomalous results, so the wise clinician attempts to understand the factors responsible for therapeutic gain wherever they may lie.

A final way in which serendipity may influence psychotherapy is by aiding theorists in the development of models of psychopathology and psychotherapy. Though logical thinking is required to develop a theoretical system, discerning observers of human behavior are sometimes aided in their conceptualizing by attempting to account for surprising or puzzling behavior they happen to witness. In such instances, it is the interaction of the striking or unusual behavior pattern and a probing, insightful mind that results in a serendipitous discovery.

The lucky confluence of proper circumstances and a prepared mind is illustrated by Freud's derivation of the defense mechanism of sublimation. As told by Sachs (1944), the idea came to the master, of all places, while reading a cartoon.

> It happened while he was looking at a cartoon in a humerous periodical *(Fliegende Blatter)* which showed the career of a girl in two subsequent stages. In the first she was hearding a flock of

young geese with a stick, in the second she was shown as a governess directing a group of young ladies with her parasol. The girls in the second picture were arranged exactly in the same groups as the goslings in the first. (p. 100)

This example perhaps serves as a good reminder that new clues to the understanding of human behavior are occurring all around us, not just in research laboratories, waiting for prepared minds to appreciate their significance.

CONCLUSIONS

The conclusions we have come to from our fascinating though often frustrating search through the massive psychological literature are in many ways quite startling. Recalling our graduate student days, neither of us had ever been seriously led to believe that accidents, luck, adventitiousness, chance, or other close synonyms for serendipity had much impact on the scientific process or had heavily influenced current psychological knowledge. When examples of this sort did arise, they were cavalierly dismissed as curiosities that hardly represented the well-disciplined progress of scientific research. Scientists, it was implied, were duty bound to follow the carefully devised tenets of solid scientific research practice. Needless to say, the same researchers who were intellectually guiding us through the intricacies of good science were themselves flirting with peculiar notions and dabbling with insights that had suddenly sprung into their awareness without benefit of logical derivation. Yet the rather neat "prepackaged" view of scientific method taught in graudate school is advertised with a sense of certainty and profundity. We learned that it is somehow a bit less respectable to acknowledge accident than to attribute one's success to hard work and thorough dedication.

It is also noteworthy that the rather high occurrence of serendipity in scientific discovery is only meagerly disseminated within the scientific community. Exciting and dramatic events such as Fleming and penicillin are well known and are viewed as interesting curiosities. As we learned, however, many lesser known discoveries are deeply buried in the archives and rarely emerge until later, sometimes as little more than oblique admissions to signal their derivations. In our review we have tried to uncover representative occurrence of serendipity in psychology, some very significant and many not so ultimately significant, to dramatize this aspect of psychological research.

One of the questions we asked ourselves was why the field of clinical psychology is so noticeably barren of serendipitous acknowledgments. As we struggled through the major journals in clinical psychology and behavior therapy, we flirted with the conclusion that clinical psychology was immune from serendipitous discoveries. All of the studies seemed to be a product of exceptionally precise science, based upon sound theory and conscientious experimental methodology. This was especially the case in behavior therapy, in which the doctrine of ultimate scientific purity is carried to its highest level. It still remains a puzzle to us as to why a subject matter that is such prime territory for unexpected associations is so lacking in references to them. Probabilistically, we are well assured that serendipity is as prevalent in clinical psychology as it is in other areas of psychology. However, a number of factors may coalesce to blur the recognition of serendipity in clinical psychology.

Viewing the field of clinical psychology, we find it difficult to clearly guage the influence of serendipity in stimulating novel and exciting advances in psychotherapeutic techniques, in diagnostic assessment, or in conceptualizations of psychopathology. In important ways progress in these areas is somewhat less palpable or tangible than revelations in experimental psychology, perhaps because the experimental psychologist's findings are more often based on concrete, publicly verifiable data produced by mechanical and electromechanical appratus. Ironically, the experimental psychologist's greater reliance on mechanical apparatus results not only in more precision in his or her measurements, but also in more breakdowns of experimental equipment. These breakdowns often provide the basis for the serendipitous discoveries we reviewed. The social sciences, on the other hand, are confronted with enormous problems of verification largely because the events that characterize interpersonal behavior are composed of complex occurrences that are difficult to reliably measure and duplicate. In addition, use of human subjects tends to pose serious ethical constraints that are not usually present in working with infrahuman species. For example, it is unlikely that bystander research of the sort devised by Darley and Latane would now be allowable by most human subject committees.

Another formidable problem in relating serendipity to clinical psychology lies in the "intangibilities" of the discoveries that often underlie the field. Many of the innovations that might be considered as significant contributions to clinical work are of a conceptual nature. Though serendipitous events may have precipitated a conceptual revelation, such events lack dramatic impact because many conceptual insights by their very nature seem to flow from unexpected or chance associations. The conceptualizer intuitively recognizes this reality, and thus it is not perceived as unusual or special. Subjectively, it feels like a natural coming together of certain ideas and events.

There is a further reason why there have been so few reports of serendipity in clinical, as opposed to experimental, psychology. While experimental psychologists can almost always conduct experiments to investigate their subject matter, clinical researchers are more often limited to correlational studies. Since the researcher has more control over extraneous variables in experimental work, he or she will feel fairly confident that an anomalous outcome, if pursued, will be replicated under the same set of circumstances. The same confidence does not usually characterize a researcher's attitude toward anomalous results from a correlational study. Since it has been drilled into our heads that "correlation doesn't imply causation," it seems natural to rationalize the appearance of an unexpected relationship by attributing it to poor measurement, sampling error, and so on. Furthermore, our theories are so flexible that they can almost always be counted on to provide a "rational" explanation for a correlational finding, however surprising the finding may be.

The prevalence of correlational studies in clinical psychology, as compared to experimental, may minimize the opportunities for adventitious discoveries for another reason as well. Serendipitous results almost always result from an investigator *intervening* in something, although intervening to produce some other outcome. To produce truly surprising results it is necessary to try to produce *something* in the first place, and the correlational researcher is stuck studying facts that have already been produced.

Our excursion through the often perplexing but enlightening pathways of serendipity has in part reaffirmed the obvious. The context of science is clearly not wholly rational or even sensible. Part of the fun in research is in relishing the unexpected. Part of reality is also the recognition that great discoveries are rarely programmable. Or, as Liam Hudson, the philosopher of science, put it:

Human thought, before it is squeezed into its Sunday best for purposes of publication, is a nebulous and intuitive affair; in place of logic there brews a stew of hunch and partial insight, half submerged. (from Mahoney, 1976, p. 126)

REFERENCES

Aserinsky, E., & Kleitman, N. (1953). Regularly occurring periods of eye mobility and concomitant phenomena during sleep. *Science,* **118,** 272–274.

Atsmon, A., & Blum, I. (1978). The discovery. In E. Roberts & P. Amacher (Eds.), *Propranolol and schizophrenia*. New York: Alan R. Liss.

Babkin, B. P. (1949). *Pavlov: A biography*. Chicago: University of Chicago Press.

Beck, S. J., (1950). *Rorschach's test: 1. Basic processes*. New York: Grune & Stratton.

Bell, J. E. (1948). *Projective techniques*. New York: Longmans, Green.

Brady, J. V. (1958). Ulcers in "executive" monkeys. *Scientific American, 199*, 95–100.

Brown, B. B. (1974). *New mind, new body*. New York: Harper & Row,.

Cantril, H. (1940). *The invasion from Mars*. Princeton, N.J: Princeton University Press.

Cannon, W. B. (1945). *The way of an investigator*. New York: Norton.

Darley, J. M., & Latane, B. (1968). Bystander intervention in emergencies: Diffusion of responsibilities. *Journal of Personality and Social Psychology, 8*, 377–383.

Dement, W. C. (1976). *Some must watch while some must sleep*. New York: Norton.

Ellenberger, H. (1954). The life and work of Hermann Rorschach (1884–1922). *Bulletin of the Menninger Clinic, 18*, 173–219.

Festinger, L. (1957). *A theory of cognitive dissonance*. Stanford: Stanford University Press.

Garica, J., Kimeldorf, D. J., & Koelling, R. A. (1955). A conditioned aversion towards saccharin resulting from exposure to gamma radiation. *Science, 122*, 157–159.

Garcia, J., & Koelling, R. A. (1966). The relation of cue to consequence in avoidance learning. *Psychonomic Science, 4*, 123–124.

Garcia, J., McGowan, B. K., & Green, K. F. (1972). Biological constraints on conditioning. In A. H. Black & W. F. Prokasy (Eds.), *Classical conditioning II: Current research and theory*. New York: Appleton-Century-Crofts.

Kuhn, T. S. (1962). *The structure of scientific revolutions*. Chicago: University of Chicago Press.

Lando, H. A., & Davison, G. C. (1975). Cognitive dissonance as a modifier of chronic smoking behavior: A serendipitous finding. *Journal of Consulting and Clinical Psychology, 43*, 750.

Latane, B., & Darley, J. M. (1970). *The unresponsive bystander: Why doesn't he help?* New York: Appleton-Century-Crofts.

Lazarus, A. A., & Davison, G. C. (1971). Clinical innovation in research and practive. In A. E. Bergin & S. Garfield (Eds.), *Handbook of psychotherapy and behavior change*. New York: Wiley.

Leigh, H., Callahan, W. A., & Einhorn, D. (1978). Good outcome in a catatonic patient with enlarged ventricles. *Journal of Nervous and Mental Disease, 166*, 139–141.

Levinson, B. M. (1961). The dog as co-therapist. Paper presented to the American Psychological Association, September.

Mahoney, M. J. (1976). *Scientist as subject: The psychological imperative*. Cambridge, Mass.: Ballinger.

McCormick, C. G., (1979). Serendipity in psychotherapy. *Psychotherapy: Theory, research and practice, 16*, 98–99.

Merbaum, M., & Hefez, A. (1975). Emotional adjustment of psychiatric patients following their unexpected discharge due to war: Short- and long-term effects. *Journal of Abnormal Psychology, 84*, 709–714.

Milgram, S., & Hollander, P. (1964). Murder they heard. *Nation, 198*, 602–604.

Olds, J. (1955). Physiological mechanisms of reward. In M. R. Jones (Ed.), *Nebraska symposium on motivation*. Lincoln: University of Nebraska Press, 1955.

Olds, J., & Milner, P. (1954). Positive reinforcement produced by electrical stimulation of septal area and other regions of the rat brain. *Journal of Comparative and Physiological Psychology, 47*, 419–427.

Overmier, J. B., & Seligman, M. E. P. (1967). Effects of inescapable shock upon subsequent escape and avoidance learning. *Journal of Comparative and Physiological Psychology, 63*, 23–33.

Pavlov, I. P. (1962). *Lectures on the work of the digestive glands*. Trans. by W. H. Thompson. London: Charles Griffin & Co.

Penfield, W. (1971). The uncommitted cortex: The child's changing brain. In M. Merbaum & G. Stricker (Eds.), *Search for human understanding*. New York: Holt, Rinehart & Winston.

Penfield, W. (1975). *The mystery of the mind*. Princeton, N.J.: Princeton University Press.

Piliavan, J.A. & Piliavan, I. M. (1972). Effect of blood on reactions to a victim. *Journal of Personality and Social Psychology, 23*, 353–361.

Piliavan, I. M., Rodin, J., & Piliavan, J. A. (1969). Good samaritanism: An underground phenomenon? *Journal of Personality and Social Psychology, 13*, 289–300.

Resnick, J. H. (1968). Effects of stimulus satiation on overlearned maladaptive response of cigarette smoking. *Journal of Consulting and Clinical Psychology, 32*, 501–505.

Rosenthal, A. M. (1964). *Thirty eight witnesses*. New York: McGraw-Hill.

Sachs, H. (1944). *Freud, master and friend*. Boston. Mass.: Harvard University Press.

Sargent, J. D., Walters, E. D., & Green, E. E. (1973). Psychosomatic self-regulation of migraine headaches. In L. Birk (Ed.), *Biofeedback: Behavioral medicine*. New York: Grune & Stratton.

Schachtel, E. G. (1966). *Experimental foundations of Rorschach's test*. New York: Basic Books.

Seligman, M. E. P. (1975). *Helplessness: On depression, development and death*. San Francisco: W. H. Freeman.

Seyle, H. (1964). *From dream to discovery*. New York: McGraw-Hill.

Sidman, M. (1960). *Tactics of scientific research*. New York: Basic Books.

Silverstone, T., & Turner, P. (1974). *Drug treatment in psychiatry*. London: Routledge and Kegan Paul.

Skinner, B. F. (1968). A case history in scientific method. In A. C. Catania (Ed.), *Contemporary research in operant behavior*. Glenview, Ill.: Scott, Foresman.

Snyder, F. (1967). In quest of dreaming. In H. A. Witkin & H. B. Lewis (Eds.), *Experimental studies of dreaming*. New York: Random House.

Snyder, S. H. (1974). *Madness and the brain*. New York: McGraw-Hill.

Standal, S. W., & Corsini, R. J. (1959). *Critical incidents in psychotherapy*. Englewood Cliffs, N.J.: Prentice-Hall.

Taton, R. (1957). *Reason and chance in scientific discovery*. Tiptree, England: Anchor Press.

Try a little TLC. *Science 80,* 1980, **1,** 15.

Valenstein, E. S. (1973). *Brain control*. New York: Wiley.

Wagemaker, H., Jr., & Cade, R. (1977). The use of hemodialysis in chronic schizophrenia. *American Journal of Psychiatry,* **134,** 684–685.

PART TWO

General Strategies for
Clinical Research

CHAPTER 5

Taxometric Methods

PAUL E. MEEHL AND ROBERT R. GOLDEN

THE THREE KINDS OF TAXOMETRIC TASKS

"Taxometrics" may be roughly defined for present purposes as the branch of applied mathematics that treats of problems of classification. "Classification" in the broad sense includes both the process of constructing or inferring classes ("classification" in the narrow sense) and the sorting of individuals into such classes ("assignment," "identification," "diagnosis"). It is not of course confined to psychopathology or to the classification of persons, or even the classification of living organisms, whether by behavior or other attributes, since stars and stones are also the subject matter of numerical taxonomy (as one can learn by attending meetings of the Classification Society). Like any applied mathematics, the discipline includes metatheoretical concepts—not just a formalism, but an explanatory (interpretative and motivating) text.

The word "taxon" cannot be precisely defined without arbitrariness, as will become clear in the discussion that follows. But as in other fields of science—a point often not understood by social scientists—explicit and purportedly rigorous verbal definitions of a domain or a method are not necessary. The meaning of both theoretical and metatheo-

retical terms is best set forth contextually, that is, by the formalism and the interpretive text itself. As a first rough meaning-stipulation adequate to delimit our task in this chapter, we may say merely that a *taxon* in psychopathology is an entity, type, syndrome, species, disease, or more generally, a *nonarbitrary class*. The distinction aimed at by this crude definition is that between a taxonic situation and the mathematics appropriate to it, and a nontaxonic situation, such as a dimension. We think of schizoidia or Huntington's Disease as a taxon. We do not think of garden variety social introversion (such as measured by MMPI scale S_i) as a taxon or type, but rather as a dimension.

All taxa are classes, but not all classes are taxa. There are as many classes of individuals in psychopathology, or within normal populations of human beings, as there are cutting scores on dimensions, or conjunctions, disjunctions, and other logical functions of attributes. The purpose of taxometrics is to help the investigator identify and sort those categories of individuals that are in some sense "really in nature," that would be there whether or not clinical psychologists had bothered to take notice of them or were clever enough to detect them. In the famous phrase attributed to Plato, the aim of the taxometrician is to "carve nature at its joints." These crude meaning stipulations and metaphors will suffice for now, because the nature of taxonicity will be explicated in the rest of the chapter.

Initially, in contemplating a domain like

The senior author is indebted to the J. McKeen Cattell Foundation for support of research. We wish to express gratitude to Dr. Larry Krasnoff for his suggestions regarding the description of the taxometric models.

psychopathology where it occurs to an investigator to apply some statistical procedure to observations about the persons' behavior, dispositions, or inferred traits, to sort them into types or clusters or taxa (from here on we shall simply say "taxa"), we can notice three distinguishable states of antecedent information, states of the investigator's knowledge that will appropriately affect his or her strategy and tactics, and, in particular, help in selecting the mathematical formalism appropriate to a taxometric task. We do not here prejudge whether these three are basically different, that is, different *epistemologically, mathematically, causally,* or *pragmatically* (this latter in the context of decision making, what to do with an individual person taxometrically classified by the method chosen). Granting that these prior knowledge conditions may or may not be fundamentally (qualitatively) different, nothing hinges upon that question in our treatment. Perhaps the best way to see whether they are different in important ways is to consider that question *after* having concocted a research strategy associated with a substantive theory, or at the least a substantive metatheory, and *then* to distinguish the conditions contextually or implicitly. Putting it strongly, the character of the distinction between these three antecedent states of knowledge becomes clear only after the research task is well under way.

But at the extremes, despite borderline region cases, these states of knowledge seem usefully distinguishable as follows:

I. *Accepted criterion prediction.* Here the investigator knows with high confidence that there is a taxon, and he or she knows how to identify the individual persons who belong to it and who fall outside it. Here "accepted criterion" may designate something definitional, as a clinician literally *defining* schizophrenia as a psychosis involving a specified kind of thought disorder, so that the validity of the sign is, so to speak, stipulative. Alternatively, the investigator may have in mind a sufficiently good empirical causal connection, whether based upon a strong theory or previous research, so that he or she possesses a two-way pathognomonic sign, a trait or symptom serving almost perfectly both as an inclusion and an exclusion test. He or she does not quite want to call this sign definitional; but one can for most purposes treat it as almost so.

An investigator's willingness to consider a sign stipulative or definitional depends partly upon his or her long-term research program, and partly upon philosophy of science considerations that will be discussed below. Thus, in the case of schizophrenia, for some scholars it *is* a psychotic thought disorder of such and such quality and intensity. For others, thought disorder is a high weight indicator (for us it would be a nearly infallible inclusion test), but it is not definitional because a theory of schizotypy as a personality organization or as involving the specific etiology of a dominant schizogene would provide the explicit definition. Therefore the thought disorder, while a highly privileged indicator, is nevertheless not definitional for scholars holding those views. We should emphasize also that most philosophers of science today would question whether a clear distinction can be made here, in the light of current views concerning the implicit or contextual definition of theoretical entities in empirical science.

II. *Classical cluster analysis.* In this situation, the kind typically envisioned by investigators in the Classification Society, there is no known taxon having an accepted criterion as in Case 1, nor is there a conjectured taxon whose existence and indicators the investigator considers well enough corroborated so that he or she will allow it to play a major role in the taxometric search procedure. Instead the investigator has a kind of "metaconjecture" to the effect that taxa (usually plural in this knowledge state) do exist in the domain of entities under study, and hopes that he or she has succeeded in concocting a set of domain-relevant indicators for his or her initial list. In the extreme case of no theory or even theory-sketch, the provisional indicator list may have been made deliberately to include every attribute of the entities in the set on which there is any appreciable variation among individuals. If this has been done, and no initial differential weights are assigned on theoretical or clinical grounds, we have the extreme case of what some have complained of as "blind" numerical taxonomy. Such a list of unweighted indicators, in which we ask how many different ways one honeybee may observably differ from another, is that advocated by such eminent contributors as Sneath and Sokal (1973).

III. *Conjectured latent taxon.* Here the investigator has some degree of purported knowledge from his or her clinical experience, or statistical study of file data, and maybe the sketch of a theory, which leads him or her to conjecture the existence of a taxon. But the taxonic conjecture is highly problematic, and furthermore the investigator may have only moderate confidence in his or her list of admittedly fallible indicators, since their validity is conjectural even if one were to grant for the sake of argument the reality of the taxon itself. It is improbable that anyone would conjecture the existence of a latent taxon unless he or she had noticed clinically or detected statistically some kind of co-variation of behaviors.

In Case 1, accepted criterion of the taxon's membership, what is the motivation for a taxometric analysis? Why trouble ourselves to construct a linear discriminant function or some nonlinear function to discriminate the groups, or a Bayes Theorem inverse probability from symptom pattern, or a function-

free actuarial table such as advocated by Lykken (Lykken, 1956; Lykken & Rose, 1963)? It is initially puzzling, since we possess an accepted criterion, either definitionally or from previous causal knowledge, leading to an extremely high indicator weight so that there exists an indicator that is almost infallible, why we would concoct a function or table of fallible indicators. We already know that the taxon exists, and we already know "who is who," that is, which individuals belong to it and which fall outside it.

One reason we might want to do this is in cases of *concurrent validity* (Cronbach & Meehl, 1955), in which the accepted criterion used in identifying individuals as being within the taxon or outside it is too costly, painful, or dangerous to collect routinely on all patients or on all persons being screened, but in the investigator's research context this (normally unavailable) accepted criterion is available on all cases.

Another reason is in the *predictive validity* situation, in which the accepted criterion that defines taxon membership becomes available only at a later point in time. Ascertaining its presence is not costly, painful, or dangerous, but we may have good clinical or other reasons to try to make a decision in advance as to that person's taxon membership prior to the time when the defining sign appears. An example is forecasting who will develop Huntington's Disease among a group of individuals known to be at risk because of having a Huntington's afflicted parent, when the subject of genetic couseling must decide whether to marry and have children (see Lyle & Gottesman, 1977). Again, if one anticipated an epidemic of a disease in which only a minority of patients develop a certain dangerous or residual-producing complication, immunization against the disease might be strongly advised for persons especially prone to the complication. This sort of example is one that influenced Carnap in his classic paper on testability and meaning (Carnap, 1936, 1937) to distinguish *confirmability* and *testability* as positivist meaning criteria, and to advocate confirmability as the more "tolerant" criterion. If I can't produce the disease, I cannot (at will) *test* the dispositional hypothesis "Jones (presently not ill) is prone to complication C should he fall ill with disease D"; but I may yet *confirm* this hypothesis, because *if* he should fall ill with the disease, then we will discover whether he develops the complication or not. We do not wish to deny empirical significance to the statement "Jones is C-prone" prior to his falling ill, partly for clinical (prophylactic) reasons, but also because it is by attaching significance to the confirmable but untestable C-statement that we motivate a research strategy that includes search for antecedently available indicators of his complication proneness.

A third possibility, more common in economics and not there usually taxonic, but at least imaginable in psychopathology, is the case in which the qualitative nature of some of the fallible indicator variables put into the taxometric equation or actuarial table makes them plausible candidates to be *causative,* so that one may attach a causal weight or influence interpretation to the beta coefficients. An important variant of this one in psychopathology, as in schizophrenia research, is the possibility that one of the indicators of high weight, while not causative itself, is a pleiotropic indicator of the causal schizogene, for example, a soft neurological sign, or the alleged anomaly in nail-fold capillary bed in the nonpsychotic relatives of schizophrenic probands (Buchanan & Jones, 1969).

Why classify people at all? Arguably, part of the problem in taxometrics, such as the low yield of formal cluster algorithms in psychopathology research to date, lies in failure to put this initial rock bottom question before proceeding to invent interperson similarity measures and search procedures for clustering within such similarity matrices. One easy case to defend is that of purely administrative convenience. If we have a cutting score on an engineering aptitude test, we may sort people into "good risks," "probationary risks," and "poor risks—reject applicant." But nobody conjectures that these are taxonic, either in terms of the predictor variable or in terms of the ultimate criterion, since an administrative change in the honor point ratio required to remain in engineering school would reclassify individuals on the borderline. Despite its unavoidability, especially in legal contexts in which what the psychologist sees as dimensions are usually replaced by quality words (predicates, categories instead of continua), this situation has no theoretical importance and will not be discussed further.

A second consideration is convenience in communication, as when we summarize a great deal of our knowledge, including low probability or highly problematic conjectural knowledge about a patient, by saying "she is hysteroid" or "he is a borderline sociopath" or "so-and-so is a latent manic-depressive." It is doubtful that clinicians could talk with each other if they were strictly forbidden to employ such summarizing rubrics as this, although the dangers of reification when the entity has no existence, as well as premature diagnostic closure by one's adoption of the semantics, are well known.

Another case is somewhat more substantive, although related to the communication or summarizing function; that is, that *we don't have to gather all the research data on patients in one huge project.* Example: No one seriously imagines that there are fewer than, say, 100 test scores, traits, or life history facts that would be needed to characterize an individual adequately for most clinical purposes, including features such as the disposition to respond favorably to one drug rather than another, suicide risk, therapy stayability, job satisfaction, and the like. But even such a carefully pruned list of attributes means potentially 4950 pairwise correlations among them. Very few clinical research projects have sufficient staff and money to process a sizeable number of patients with respect to 100 variables. It would be wasteful if we lacked some way of allowing investigator X in Albuquerque to relate two drug responses to the amount of schizoid component in manic-depressive patients, and later make use of the fact, when we survey the research literature, that investigator Y in Minneapolis has discovered two new soft neurological signs of the schizoid component, although Y has not studied the therapeutic effects of psychotropic drugs on his cases. It is obvious that organic medicine would have progressed much more slowly had it not been possible for different clinicians (and pathologists, biochemists, epidemiologists, geneticists, physiologists, and bacteriologists) in different places, studying nonoverlapping groups of patients, to mediate the connection of their investigations via a diagnostic rubric. In terms of the difference between input and output variables, instead of having mn input-output correlations to investigate, we may substitute the stochastic relationship between the m indicators and the nosological entity on the input side, and the relationship between the nosological entity and the n indicators on the output side. There are then ($m + n$) relations to be studied instead of (mn) of them, a considerable economy in both communication and research costs.

Another consideration is a clumping in two kinds of spaces, say, as the space of job descriptions and the space of personal traits. Large-scale personnel contexts such as the military have found it useful to group jobs on the basis of a statistical study of the components in a job analysis, attempting to map, even though only probabilistically, clusters of enlisted men (in terms of their tested interests and abilities) against the job clusters. There is here an economy of transfer and retraining, and we note that might be the case even if there were no marked degree of "clumping" in the two phenotypic hyper-spaces, although the more clumping there is, the more saving is achieved. But even if there were homogeneity in the space, it might still be worthwhile to do it.

Finally, and of most interest to the present authors in connection with schizophrenia research, there is the purpose of theoretical

($=$ *causal*) understanding. A side aspect of this is file research, in which a statistical power function on some variable of interest may be greatly improved by homogenizing the patients, although failure to homogenize the patients would not constitute a vitiating error in most studies, contrary to what some clinicians have alleged. Nevertheless, if we are looking for a weak effect, or even an effect that is reversed in some categories, the fact that the patient is not available for assessment makes it desirable to find nosological discriminations recorded in the chart.

When we speak of a taxon as "latent," what meanings might this have? One meaning is environmental stimulation that has not yet been made explicit or discovered. This would be the only kind of latent taxon readily allowed by strong Skinnerians. Another meaning of "latent" in the psychopathology context is historical, a slight stretching of the meaning, but indicating that the factor is not presently visible in the patient's behavior or surround. It is an event in the past that may or may not be in the record, and in fact, even in extensive uncovering therapy as classical analysis, may or may not come to light as an alleged fact of memory. Examples are a battle-axe mother; Freud's early theory of prepubertal sexual seduction as the specific etiology of hysteria and the obsessional neurosis (which disorder, of the two, depends upon whether the future patient was mainly passive and experienced fear or disgust or mainly aggressive and experienced erotic pleasure); head injury; undiagnosed mumps encephalitis; and the like. These examples show that a latent taxon can be connected with a specific etiology that does not have to be a gene, or a germ, or a "disease" in any strong sense of that word. If Freud's theory had been factually correct, the specific life history event could have been taken as the stipulative definer of hysteria, or at least given such a high weight that a patient might be refused the diagnosis, even if he or she presented conversion phenomena when seen.

Another meaning of "latent" is a causal

factor within the person. This is perhaps the most natural meaning for the clinical psychologist. By "within" is meant literally *within,* that is to say a gene, a germ, a brain tumor, a psychological complex, an unconscious fantasy, a repressed memory, and the like.

CLINICAL DISCOVERY OF SYNDROMES

With these possible meanings in mind, let us reflect metatheoretically on a hypothetical example outside of psychopathology, namely, the discovery of a new organic disease. Dr. Fisbee is a practitioner with research interests (for a nice illustration in psychopathology, see Freud's classic paper on the anxiety neurosis and his reply to Loewenfeld's criticism of it, Freud, 1895, 1895). Dr. Fisbee is struck with the fact that in the last few months he has seen five patients who presented with complaints of headache and spots before the eyes, and on examination had a low-grade fever, a slightly purplish tongue, and pink ears. He hadn't really "noticed" this pattern until seeing the fourth patient, and the fifth patient seemed to corroborate that he was seeing something orderly that he hadn't studied in medical school. So he goes back to his charts and satisfies himself that he has in fact seen five patients with the combination. He then remembers a few others who had presented only a part of the combination; for instance, in several the purple tongue, the subjective complaints, and the elevated temperature were present, but the pink ears were not. He also reflects that he misdiagnosed some of these patients as having some other disease. On reading the chart notes for those who came back, as he asked, for follow-up, he finds that the subsequent course didn't fit the diagnosis that he had made of some entity already known to him. So he publishes a clinical note, and Fisbee's Syndrome gets into medical thinking, and then into the literature; and Dr. Fisbee is ultimately immortalized in Dorland's Medical Dictionary for this discovery. Although the particular syndrome is hypothetical, we are not here sketching out an improbable state of affairs, but on the contrary exemplifying the usual course of clinical investigation in organic medicine (see, e.g., Major, 1932).

How does Dr. Fisbee think about it, definitionally and in terms of causal understanding, and more importantly, how about the university's internal medicine professor who, having read the article, decides to research this entity? If one is a hard-line operationist, as some psychologists profess to be, although they are almost never consistently so when pressed, one wants first to arrive at a "clear operational definition" of Fisbee's Syndrome. Presumably this would mean specifying the list of defining symptoms. At this stage of our knowledge, we do not know what is the cause of the syndrome, and we may not even have any conjectures, although the fact that elevated temperature is part of it and that it runs a short self-limited course (nobody has died of it yet), makes us think it might be an infectious disease; but that's not totally clear. In any case, we do not know what kind of germ is involved, and we as yet do not have any tissue pathology. So one might say that the definition of Fisbee's Syndrome lay wholly in the symptom list. That's misleadingly simple, and it's wrong. Seeing why it's wrong will help the reader see why some of the statements made by psychologists about entities like schizophrenia that purport to be sophisticated are actually naive and based upon an undergraduate-level philosophy of science, and, it would seem, woeful ignorance of the history of developments in biology and medicine. We can't simply say that the "list of symptoms" operationally defines the entity. We have to say how that list is put together in the definition. We have symptoms S_1 (headache), S_2 (spots before eyes), S_3 (low-grade fever), S_4 (purple tongue), and S_5 (pink ears). First we think of a simple logical conjunction of the symptoms as defining Fisbee's Syndrome. Will that work? No, it will not. Try to write an explicit operational definition of disease D as $D = S_1 \cdot S_2 \cdot S_3 \cdot S_4 \cdot S_5$. This of course means that any patient lacking any one of the five symptoms is excluded. So the patient Dr. Fisbee remembered on reflection, who presented with the complaints of headache, spots before the eyes, purple tongue, and temperature elevation, but whose ears were not pink, cannot be "counted" as a case of Fisbee's Syndrome. Now admittedly this could be treated as a totally stipulative matter in the fashion of the old-line positivists, who thought that a definition simply "recorded one's decision to use a word in a certain way." (We are not here arguing about words, or about the correct view that definitions are *in some sense* ultimately stipulative.) Why does not the sensible physician or medical researcher consider doing it in this way? It's really very simple. In the history of medicine it has been repeatedly found upon thorough comprehension of a disease—in all of its important aspects, including its pathology and specific etiology, its course, the reasons why certain patients get well and others don't, and why certain therapies work in some patients and not others, all of them sharing the same disease when it is thoroughly understood— that *there are very few symptoms that are absolutely two-way pathognomonic*.

Our Dr. Fisbee, the research-oriented practitioner, may have no interest in philosophy of science. He may never have heard of Carnap's discussion of reduction sentences, or Pap's classic fundamental paper on open concepts (Pap, 1953; 1958, Chapter 11). But he is a sensible person, not having been brainwashed by some undergraduate social science course that delivered a simplistic view of "operationism," and he knows from common sense considerations that the color of somebody's ears is not likely to have a direct causal influence on the color of his tongue, and that neither one can produce a fever. Therefore, he reasons, if these various externally visible phenomena (together with

the subjective complaint of headache and spots before the eyes) have a tendency to go together—both in the sense that they are found in the same patients with a disproportionate frequency, and in the *P*-correlation sense that they covary over time in the same patient as he falls ill and recovers—*then there must be some common causal factor that produces all of them*. Unless that common causal factor is sun spots or witchcraft, which Dr. Fisbee rationally doesn't believe in, where does that common factor have to be? Well, if it's in the world of space and time and material entities, the only place for it to be is inside the patient. That "something or other," whatever it is, is the internal cause of the syndrome. In organic medicine it is the *pathology* of Fisbee's Syndrome. A further conjecture is that this pathology is in turn *caused* by something specific, and that something specific may be in the person (as a mutated gene or a toxin or a germ) or a historical event such as trauma. A combination of these commonsense considerations with his knowledge of the history of medicine leads a rational medical researcher to the conjecture (which he hardly treats as a conjecture but as a near certainty, despite his slight knowledge of the newly discovered entity) that a *specific etiology-cum-pathology* underlies the phenotypic syndrome that first called his attention to the disease. To such a sophisticated research-oriented doctor, the cliché remark of some psychologists that it is "tautologous" to refer a symptom to a disease entity called schizophrenia is not sophisticated but merely ignorant.

So the reason that a conjunction of symptoms won't do is that it's *too strong*. That is, it would result in too many false negatives, since every symptom must, on that view, be an infallible exclusion test. But the history of medicine, as well as our overall knowledge of how the innards of the body work makes it immediately comprehensible why the relations between the symptoms pairwise are only stochastic. The reason that the pairwise correlations of the five symptoms are stochastic, although some of them may be high (if the syndrome is "loose," it will be harder for Dr. Fisbee to notice it), is that they all have a merely stochastic connection with the specific pathology, and that fact results in their imperfect correlation among themselves.

Seeing that a conjunction of symptoms as the explicit operational definition of disease D is too strong, it then occurs to a philosophically oriented pathologist to substitute a *disjunction* of symptoms, that is, we try $D = S_1 V S_2 V S_3 V S_4 V S_5$. But a disjunction is just as bad as a conjunction, and in fact somewhat worse, because whereas a conjunction was somewhat too strong, a disjunction is grossly too weak. It suffers a vast excess of false positives, because it treats each of the separate elements of the syndrome as if it were a perfectly valid inclusion test. Notice how social science is unlike medicine in this respect. Most social scientists wouldn't like to pay much attention to a sign that is often present in a great variety of diseases. But no physician wants to drop a symptom like elevated temperature out of the list of symptoms of, say, an infectious disease, despite the fact that there are literally hundreds of conditions—and not all of them infectious diseases—that may produce fever. We don't want to leave elevated temperature out of our set of indicators for measles or malignancy or uremia, but obviously a disconjunctive definition of any of the diseases with elevated temperature as one of the disjuncts would result in a ratio of false positives to valid positives that would be an order of magnitude or two greater!

One important difference between the way organic medicine makes inferences and the way the psychologist or sociologist typically does is that a logical tree, with stepwise exclusion of possibilities, means that a sign may not be attended to at one stage in the diagnostic process but becomes critical at another stage because, while not powerful as an inclusion test, it is a powerful exclusion test. This is a different way of proceeding

from an assignment of beta weights, or the unit weighting of low validity test items in a personality inventory. An inclusion test is a sign that is almost never present unless the disease is present and whose manifestation therefore permits us to infer the disease with high confidence. An exclusion test rules out the disease, in that it is almost always present when the disease is present, so its absence makes the disease almost certainly absent. "Pathognomicity" in medicine, when not otherwise defined, more commonly seems to mean an inclusion test; but the strong meaning is two-way pathognomicity, that is, a sign whose presence rules the disease in and whose absence definitively rules it out. Some social scientists assume, quite wrongly, that two-way pathognomicity abounds in organic medicine, but we have yet to find any physician who claims to know of many literally pathognomonic signs for the various organic diseases.

Why is not the entity the same as the syndrome? Passing the inept objection about circularity, the reason that the entity is not the syndrome is that we have a conjectured latent cause, which we confidently anticipate will, given adequate research, some day be the explicit definition of the disease; but that pending that research outcome, the disease is an *open concept*. What we are saying, roughly, is in the form of a scientific "promissory note." We take it for granted that there exists a unitary underlying latent pathology-cum-etiology that gives rise to the correlation of the symptoms ($S_1, \ldots S_5$) but we don't yet know what that latent causal factor is. When we do know it, it will become definitive of the disease. At present, the disease D is not strictly defined. It's a fuzzy notion, an open concept (Pap 1953, 1958; Meehl 1972c, references cited p. 21). Its meaning is not empty because it is stipulated as partly *that which underlies the production of Fisbee's Syndrome,* as probabilistically linked to each of the phenotypic facets of the syndrome. But obviously it would be bad semantics to claim that we are *explicitly defin-*

ing "Fisbee's Disease" by Fisbee's Syndrome, or even that we're claiming that nobody can "have the syndrome" if any one of the elements is missing (conjunctive stipulation); or even worse, that anyone can be said to have the syndrome whenever any one of the elements is present (disjunctive stipulation).

There is an interesting and instructive oddity about symptom percentages in a medical book being presented for a disease whose specific pathology and etiology are not yet known. A hyperoperational critic might ask, what does it mean to say that a certain percentage of patients have each symptom of the disease when the entity consists of "nothing but" the symptoms? The answer, of course, is that the disease entity does *not* consist of "nothing but" the symptoms. The disease consists jointly of the (unknown, conjectured) latent pathology-cum-etiology taken together with the symptoms, this "taking together" being stochastically understood. If that Papian notion is too subtle or complicated for a psychologist, he or she should perhaps pursue some other area than psychopathology, since nature apparently is not simple enough for such a simplistic philosophy of science.

So we see that doctors were thinking about open concepts and promissory notes before a philosophy of science that treats of these notions came to be invented, and certainly long before any formal mathematical taxometrics was invented. It is worthwhile, however, to pursue the usual superoperationalist objection a bit further. While we are forced to grant that a conjunction is too strong and a disjunction too weak to make clinical or theoretical sense and to motivate meaningful research into the inner nature of Fisbee's Syndrome, it does seem a little strange to say that a person can have Fisbee's Disease without showing a single element of it. Now, of course, if the patient doesn't present any symptoms or complaints at all, he or she won't come to the doctor (or, if in a routine physical, no clinician will think anything's the matter with him or her.) Nevertheless, we do have to make some philosophical place for the accepted idea of a *silent disease*. In organic medicine it is taken for granted that diseases can be symptomatically silent. For instance, consider a person who has never gone to a physician complaining of any of the usual kidney symptoms, let alone the excruciating pain of a renal calculus. At post mortem, following being killed by a truck, it is discovered that the entire kidney lumen on one side is totally occluded by a huge mass of potassium phosphate and carbonates, the so-called "staghorn kidney." In an interesting study of his own diagnostic errors, a high-caliber Minneapolis internist (Peppard, 1949) showed that even being very hard on himself about the cause of his errors, the commonest single source of omission diagnostic error was literally *symptoms or signs not found,* meaning that he had carefully looked for them properly, with the best available techniques, and the patient simply did not show the sign. It is strange that psychologists would think that the mind is so much simpler than the innards in organic medicine that, whereas the idea of a neurologically silent brain tumor or a silent carcinoma of the liver or a silent staghorn kidney can exist, yet it couldn't be possible that there could be a silent schizoid component or a silent psychological complex or a silent temperamental disposition!

If we understand *why* each pairwise correlation is stochastic—because each sign is only probabilistically linked to the (unknown) causal factor that will ultimately become definitive of the entity—it is obvious that a certain probability attaches to each of the possible configurations, including having all five symptoms, four but not five, three but not the other two, and so on. Then it is quite arbitrary—given that causal model and our epistemic situation—to cut at having one symptom, at "symptom score" 0/1. Because the probability for each symptom S_i being $p(S_i/D) < 1$, *the joint probability for absence of all five S's is not zero,* excluding a very unlikely configural effect not disease-related. Consequently, a person can have Fisbee's disease ("silently") even if none of the symptoms is present. There is nothing complicated about this, once one understands the distinctions among epistemology, statistics, and causality.

Notice that the existence of degrees of a trait as an indicator of a latent taxon does not preclude taxonicity. One still hears the stupid objection that there can't be an "entity" schizophrenia because all degrees of thought disorder (or inappropriate affect, or withdrawal) exist. This is about as bright as saying that there can't be such a thing as meningitis since one of its exclusion tests is high fever, and all degrees of fever exist in sick people! We hope it is not necessary to treat further of that pseudo-sophisticated complaint.

CLINICAL TAXA AS OPEN CONCEPTS

This is not the place to develop a detailed philosophical analysis of open concepts, but readers are urged to look at the paper of Pap (1953; 1958), and, if the subject interests them sufficiently, the set of related articles cited in Meehl (1972c, p. 21). It is almost universally accepted among logicians and historians of science today that most theoretical concepts are not defined operationally in Bridgman's original sense, but are defined contextually or implicitly, that is, by their role in a network of nomological or statistical "laws." The possible exceptions to this statement are still in debate, and they are so rare, even in highly developed sciences like physics and chemistry, that it seems rather pointless to argue the question for psychopathology. Thus to say that intelligence is what an intelligence test measures, or that the intelligence factor g is adequately "defined" (in any strong, strict meaning of that term) by the subtests of an intelligence test, is an oversimplified and misleading account. But in a richer and subtler sense, it *is* contextually

"defined," although careful usage would say that the meaning is partially given or stipulated by the theoretical network, however tentative and as yet impoverished that network may be. The "meaning" thus contextually provided is an open concept meaning, a partially specified notion, so its denotation is a "fuzzy set." We hold with Sir Karl Popper (1962, pp. 18–21; 1974, pp. 12–23) that stipulating meanings is a trivial and unimportant exercise compared with testing theories, and that the scientifically valuable components of the former are normally achieved via the latter. Crudely put, you know what you mean by an entity to the extent that you have a set of concept-overlapping statements in the theoretical language, and a proper subset of those statements are linked to statements in the observational language. These statements are, in different ways, all about the entity—where it's found, what brings it about, what it does, what are its various properties (including "compositional properties," what it's made of and how). Only a few of these properties are directly tied to observables. A reader with philosophical interests should have a look at Carnap's classic paper on testability and meaning as a starter into the theory of open concepts, and then read Pap.

Three kinds of openness of concepts, which are not equivalent but which are related, are described in Meehl (1977, 1978). The first kind of openness is the kind expounded by Carnap, and further developed by Pap. It arises from the fact that even a *dispositional* concept (e.g., solubility, dominance, or, in psychopathology, depression proneness) is specified by a *list* of indicators or symptoms (whether testability or confirmability be imposed as a condition of scientific acceptability), and such a list is extensible. The extensibility of the list of indicators was one reason why Carnap introduced the idea of reduction pairs as a substitute for explicit definitions in his original classic paper. We find out that if a wire touching a frog's muscle makes it twitch, a compass needle brought near the wire will be deflected. So we now have two indicators of the latent mysterious "electric current" (long before we knew about electrons, let alone the Fermi mathematical theory of the electron gas). It then turns out that a wire that has these two properties will also, if snipped and immersed in a silver chloride solution, deposit silver at the cathode. If connected with a filament in an exhausted bulb, it will produce light; and so forth. As Carnap points out, although each of the reduction sentences added to the list might be looked upon as, in a sense, a definition (a convention, a meaning specifier), when we put two or more of them together, we are automatically committed to a synthetic claim about a question of fact, that is, that the indicators will agree. That is one of the earliest showings by a logician that the distinction between definitions and empirical statements is not a clean one in the theoretical sciences. In psychopathology we might originally give a tendency to striped muscle conversion reactions a privileged status in identifying the hysteroid disposition. But subsequent clinical experience and psychometric research leads us to consider a patient's preference for certain defense mechanisms (e.g., repression, denial) and various other attributes of the personality structure (impunitive reaction to frustration, a tendency to manipulate the environment by histrionic threats and gestures, a combination of hypersexual signaling with frigidity, etc.) as more privileged indicators than whether one uses a paralyzed arm to get out of washing the dishes.

A second kind of openness applies even to the single indicator, namely, that the connection between the latent entity (or even the open concept, without explicit reference to the promissory note of causality) is probabilistic rather than strict or nomological in character. This state of affairs is even true in the physical sciences, as Pap pointed out in his classic paper on why we can't have a strictly operational closed-concept definition of temperature. Nobody can stick a thermometer into the center of the sun, but we need to talk about the sun's temperature, and we don't wish to say or imply that this is a totally different concept from the temperature of a blast furnace or a bowl of soup. A fortiori, in the life sciences we have to rely on alternative epistemic paths. Any complicated organic system presents occasions for nuisance variables or random factors, usually both, to "get in the way" between the conjectured specific causal entity (germ, gene, complex, drive, memory, or whatever) and our fallible phenotypic indicators of the latter. They have to be fallible, because they are connected with the causal entity by a chain whose links always include stochastic rather than strictly nomological links. This is why one can give strictly operational definitions of most psychological attributes only by deceiving himself, or alternatively, by confining himself to the most trivial instances and insisting, by God, that the mind had better be simple because that's the way we want to think about it!

A third kind of openness in concepts Meehl has dubbed "Orphan Annie's Eyes." In the usual logician's diagram of the nomological network, the strands of the net are the conjectured laws connecting the conjectured entities between which the laws hold. The entities are the nodes of the network, and are implicitly defined by their role in the network. Those nodes of the net are drawn as little circles, and remind one of the vacuous eyes in the juvenile fascist "Orphan Annie," in a comic strip by that name during the Great Depression. The openness of these "Orphan Annie's Eyes" nodes in the nomological net corresponds to the fact that we don't know the inner nature, that is, the composition and structure, of the theoretical entities insofar as they are only contextually defined by their role in the net.

The gene provides a beautiful instance of "filling in Orphan Annie's Eyes." The gene begins as a Mendel *factor*, as a conjectural entity that is latent with respect to the observed statistics of fertilization in garden peas and the phenotypic traits of fruit flies. The discovery of linkage maps and the realization that the number of linkage groups corresponds to the number of chromosomes in a species makes it natural to conjecture that the "factors" are entities having a physical location at a certain position along the chromosome; hence we have the conjectured *gene*. Further evidence then shows us that cytological anomalies (e.g., translocation) are associated with pronounced aberrations in the linkage statistics of a fly strain. Finally, with the discovery of the giant chromosome in the salivary gland of *Drosophila* we are able to see that X-ray bombardment resulting in a recessive acting strangely like a dominant suggests that there ought to be a "hole" at a certain place on the giant chromosome. Sure enough, direct cytological study shows an "empty place" there in the predicted position!

Notice that every one of these operations, while it locks in the concept of a gene by a very nice and intellectually satisfying nomological network, nevertheless still has the gene as an Orphan Annie's Eye. Only with the solution of the DNA problem by Crick and Watson, where we now *explicitly define* the term "gene" as a cistron, and a cistron as a certain sequence of codons, and a codon as a certain sequence of the four bases, adenine, guanine, cytosine, and thymine, do we fill in Orphan Annie's Eyes. For the first time we can offer a truly explicit definition of the word "gene." It takes us over half a century to get there, and a very powerful and intellectually exciting science of genetics existed prior to Crick and Watson's solution of the double helix. Even that definition is not operational in the usual sense, because the term "gene" is itself defined reductively, that is, in terms of theoretical concepts from another science, namely, organic chemistry. We note, finally, that it is now conceptually detached, so that a gene made in the laboratory by human molecular biologists, and not put into a protoplasmic surround where

it is capable of controlling anything phenotypic as an indicator, would still be a gene in the full sense of the word.

It is foolish in psychopathology to pretend that there is any magical way, by either statistics or verbal definitions, to avoid these three kinds of openness. Part of the purpose of a taxometric formalism is to tighten up the open concept by refining the mathematical characteristics of the net. Putting that together with an embedding explanatory text tells us something about the entities that the abstract notation of the formalism denotes and quantifies.

We may have spent more time on general methodological considerations than necessary, but experience in attempting to explain our own new taxometric methods, and reading of the controversial literature on diagnostic categories (e.g., "labeling theory"), combine to convince us that a certain amount of Augean stable-cleaning is needed as propaedeutic to an intellectually respectable treatment of the taxometric problem in either its mathematical or epistemological aspects.

FORMS AND DEGREES OF TAXONICITY

We now approach the difficult question: what is *taxonicity* as a concept? After several years of philosophical and mathematical effort, plus surveying taxonic entities in several fields other than psychopathology, we have regretfully concluded that the reason it is so hard to give a good definition of "taxon" is that taxonicity itself is not taxonic but is a matter of degree. We use the word "taxonic" rather than "taxonomic" because taxonomy is the *metatheory of classification*. Strictly speaking, it is an abuse of language to speak of a taxonomy as being the taxonic entities themselves. The taxonomy is the taxonomist's science of taxonomizing; the taxa are entities that (if he or she is right in his or her conjectures) exist in the world. A fact-situation is not taxonomic; it is the investigator's approach that is taxonomic. When we refer to the state of nature that the scientist conjectures to exist when proceeding taxonomically in his or her research, that state of nature should be called "taxonic."

All efforts that we have made (and they will not be reported here) or that we have seen others present, whether in psychopathology or in the other life sciences, to give a purely phenotypic characterization of taxonicity are fuzzy at the edges and liable to misinterpretation. This holds true even for those "conventionalist" or "economical" taxonomies that avoid theory and causality and confine taxonic interpretation to densification in the phenotypic hyperspace. Such a clumping or clustering admittedly is what normally leads the clinician or researcher to notice a conjectured taxon in the first place. The initially unpleasant truth of the matter—it turns out to be pleasant, insofar as it relieves us of the burden of giving an explicitly operational definition of "taxonicity" that will satisfy everybody—is that there are several kinds of causal paths to generation of a clumping or clustering of phenotypic characteristics in the descriptive hyperspace, and some of them are not interesting theoretically or valuable pragmatically. Any factor, including arbitrary social selection factors that determine subpopulations to come before our eyes, that can densify the descriptive hyperspace in a certain region more than one might have anticipated by contemplating, say, the Pearson r's of the indicator variables taken pairwise (calculated over the whole realized space) can thereby produce a situation that one might legitimately call "taxonic" in one of the several senses presented above. Example: Most of us probably would think of "being a bridge player" as taxonic; witness the way the question is put: "Do you play bridge?" The person queried might answer, "Yes, but not very often," or "Not very well." But we do not expect him or her to say, "I don't know, it depends on your cutting score." It is an empirical fact that if a person knows the word "renege," he or she will ($p > .99$) know the words "vulnerable" and "slough." Those who know how to respond to a certain bid will almost certainly have a statistical tendency to avoid certain ways of dealing with the cards in the dummy if they are playing the hand. The taxonicity of some acquired skill patterns is so "tight" that industrial psychologists can make trade tests using as few as eight or 10 verbal items (e.g., "What is a chuck used for?", identifying lathe operators.) If one constructed an achievement test of terms from contract bridge playing without deliberately rigging it, employing a suitable kind of random choice from the words appearing in a bridge manual glossary, he would undoubtedly find a clearly bimodal distribution and would conclude that bridge playing was taxonic. It is nevertheless true that no matter how many such items we added in order to slice the pie finer, there would be an admittedly tiny (but not zero) number of scores in the valley between the two curves. They would be people who came to have these intermediate achievement scores in special and unusual ways. For example, a man goes hunting with his friends; they are snowed in; and his three friends insist on teaching him bridge. He doesn't want to learn, but he goes along to be cooperative. He isn't grabbed by the game, and he has never played it since. Such a person could have a score in the valley between the two modes.

A more distressing example of pseudo-taxonicity is what would happen if one foolishly threw together scores on the WAIS subtests for inmates of a state institution for the mentally retarded with a random sample of normals. There would be an appearance of a big taxon, but only some of the people in that low IQ group would represent truly taxonic entities, such as one of the Mendelizing mental deficiencies, or one of the developmental anomalies. Others would simply be the low end of the normal polygenic intelligence curve, appearing as a taxon because of the fact that an institutional population was thrown together with a general population of "normals." There is no point in multiplying examples. The simple fact is that there are various ways in which a phenotypic clumping or clustering in a descriptive hyperspace can be achieved. There are as many different defensible meanings of "taxonic" as there are causal origins of clumps or clusters.

Our own preference, which we have no desire to force upon others, is that if a strong meaning of the word "taxon" is to be adopted, it should be like that of medicine and genetics, namely, a *causal-theoretical meaning*. But even if this convention is accepted, it doesn't solve the problem. One may prefer to think of a true taxon—one that carves nature at its joints and is not merely administrative, or the demarcation of a region on a dimension for communicative ease, or because the courts understand category concepts better than metrical concepts—as causal, involving a *specific etiology*. We then have to ask the further metatheoretical question; what do we mean by the phrase "specific etiology"? Meehl (1977) has set out a series of meanings of "strong influence," only the strongest of which are specific etiologies as that term would be used in, say, medicine or genetics.

In a causal interpretation of strong taxonicity, we define the latent taxon in theoretical terms. That is true of our conceptualization and our research strategy, even if the theoretical terms themselves are only vaguely contextually understood at a given stage of the research enterprise. This means that we need not struggle to attain a definition of taxonicity by reference solely to the phenotypic distribution, that is, by the distribution properties of the fallible indicators. Furthermore, we know (see, e.g., Murphy, 1964, and the example above) that a latent taxon can exist, as theoretically comprehended with reference to its causality or inner nature, without generating a bimodality, although we

would hope that our indicators are powerful enough so that we can detect a latent taxon by means of *some* features of the distribution, when the multivariate distribution in the phenotypic hyperspace is analyzed by appropriate taxometric methods.

The strongest meaning of "taxonicity" in causal terms is that the disease entity or personality type has its causal origin in a *specific dichotomous etiological agent* such as a mutated gene, or a specific germ, or a particular life history event, for example, a head injury. In the ideal case, the specific causal agent C is nonarbitrarily dichotomous, that is, it is present or absent on the basis of a predicate or property that does not possess intermediate gray region degrees. (Perhaps it "could," conceptually, but in fact it does not.) The strongest meaning is exemplified when the dichotomous etiological agent C is both necessary and sufficient for the phenotypic disease syndrome to appear, as in Huntington's Disease, in which all those who carry the Huntington mutation will develop the symptoms provided they survive the morbidity risk period, although in some Huntington sibships this means that a person might have to live to be 70 years of age. A slightly weaker meaning, but one that we find readily accepted by everyone as inherently taxonic, is that of a sine qua non, a necessary but not sufficient condition for the syndrome (Meehl, 1972c). In medicine and genetics, *threshold effects* and *step functions* are also strong meanings of taxonicity. Thus one who receives less than a specified minimum intake of niacin for a sufficient time period will develop pellagra.

Once we pass beyond these forms—necessary and sufficient dichotomous etiology, necessary dichotomous etiology, and necessary threshold (or step-function) etiology—we are in a region of decreasing strengths of specific influence, in which it would be easy to find disagreement among reflective and informed persons as to whether they would consider them instances of specific etiology or not. For these other forms of strong influence mathematically defined, see Meehl (1977). The easiest way in this frame of reference to avoid semantic disputes about whether a situation should be called truly taxonic or not is simply to specify which of the kinds of strong influence the theoretician has in mind.

It is a puzzling historical fact (Meehl, 1979) that formal cluster algorithms, that is, taxometrics of the kind we have earlier called Type II, the classical cluster analytic problem, have not been responsible for discovering a single taxon in psychopathology or, so far as we are aware, in organic medicine. In fact, one cannot even make a clear case for saying that while informal clinical (or experimental) methods have initially revealed the entities, formal cluster algorithms have at least clarified subsequent taxonomic controversies. Should an entity be subdivided? Ought certain atypical clinical cases be subsumed under an entity as *formes fruste?* Is an entity genetically homogeneous? Should a taxon be extended, for example, is Hoch and Polatin's "pseudo-neurotic schizophrenia" concept useful (Hoch & Polalin, 1949), or is it an illegitimate and confusing extension of the concept schizophrenia?

Alas, even such a clarifying function as to entities provisionally conjectured from nonformal methods by clinical experience cannot be historically documented. Meehl (1979) has in the above cited article listed eight possible explanations of this somewhat surprising state of affairs, which, if left unexplained on the shelf, might reasonably discourage the psychoclinician from pursuing taxometrics, since it doesn't seem to have much payoff even if it's philosophically and mathematically amusing. We have no stake here in denigrating formal cluster algorithms, but content ourselves with that observation, referring the reader to Meehl's paper cited and moving now directly to that one of the three taxometric knowledge situations to

which we have devoted our efforts, namely, Type III, the conjectured latent taxon problem.

THE BOOTSTRAPS APPROACH

The first knowledge situation, that is, the case in which we have an accepted criterion and the investigator, knowing there is a taxon, wishes to do a better job identifying the persons who belong to it, is outside the scope of this chapter.

For Case I, where there is an accepted criterion variable telling us to which taxonomic class each individual actually belongs, there are well-known methods, such as linear discriminant function analysis first developed by R. A. Fisher (1936). For the handbook to be complete, it should include a chapter describing these methods, and we originally prepared this chapter with that understanding (see Preface). Here we refer the reader to only some of the textbooks and papers that the quantitative researcher in psychology will find useful. In order to be consistent with the usual terminology in this literature, we refer to the indicator variables (e.g., signs and symptoms) as the "independent" variables and the virtually infallible criterion variable as the "dependent" variable. The general mathematical-statistics problem is to find the function of the independent variables that gives the most accurate classification on (or, more generally, maximizes the statistical association with) the dependent variable. Probably the most commonly used solution to this problem is for *linear* functions of independent variables such as in the discriminant function and multiple regression methods. Several appropriate textbooks discuss different versions of these and related methods (e.g., Lindgren, 1962; Draper & Smith, 1966; Rozeboom, 1966; Cornfield, 1967; Tatsuoka, 1971; Overall & Klett, 1972; Kerlinger & Pedhagur, 1973; Finn, 1974; Lachenbruch, 1975; Morrison, 1976). The desirability of using differential rather than equal unit weights in the linear function should not be taken for granted, since the former are subject to sampling error so that the linear function sometimes lacks robustness when used in samples other than the one on which it was developed (e.g., see Guion, 1965; Nunnally, 1967; Darlington, 1968; Wainer, 1976; Dawes, 1979; Dawes & Corrigan, 1974). When using a weighted linear function, there are useful papers regarding missing data (Chan & Dunn, 1972), estimation of classification error rates in new samples (Lachenbruch & Mickey, 1967; Dunn & Varady, 1966; Dunn, 1971), and unreliability in the dependent variables (Gilbert, 1969; Goldstein, 1977).

Regarding the use of dichotomous independent variables, Lachenbruch and Mickey (1968) show that the "jackknife" method, where each individual is classified by a different discriminant function (that derived on the remaining $N - 1$ individuals in the sample) is superior to several other methods in that it yields (almost) unbiased estimates of error rates.

The advantages of using a function more complex than linear to capture interaction, configural, and nonadditive effects were suggested long ago (e.g., see Meehl, 1950) and studied (e.g., see Goldberg, 1969). The use of a function-free actuarial table was advocated by Lykken (1956) and Lykken and Rose (1963). When the independent variables are dichotomous (or categorical), Bayes' Theorem (e.g., see Hays, 1973) and applications of it (e.g., see Solomon, 1961; Bailey, 1965) are the most obvious nonlinear method.

The above references are in no sense complete and in part represent the result of our own selective sampling of the vast literature on Case I research methods.

We will briefly survey the formal cluster algorithm methods used for the classical cluster analytic problem and then devote the remainder of the mathematical discussion to

Case 3, the conjectured latent taxon problem, after saying something about bootstraps methods generally.

The term "bootstraps effect" was first introduced by Cronbach and Meehl (1955). Surprisingly, the terminology was criticized by some intelligent people on the grounds that it implied that you were lifting yourself by your bootstraps; whereas the reason Cronbach and Meehl chose that terminology was precisely to emphasize the counterintuitive finding that one can psychometrically "lift oneself by the bootstraps," if it is done right. The essential idea of the bootstraps effect as described by Cronbach and Meehl in 1955 was that one can construct an empirical scale such as an MMPI key by empirical keying against a rather poor, low-accuracy fallible criterion (such as unreliable diagnoses by unskilled psychiatrists) and, if one is lucky and clever and the item pool is rich enough, can nevertheless emerge with a scale that diagnoses more accurately than the clinical examiners did. It is incredible but true that there are still psychologists who don't understand this simple point. Bootstraps effects abound in the other sciences, and for that matter, in ordinary human artifacts. Thus, for instance, humankind began making tools with chipped flint, and it is paradoxical but true that we now can grind metal surfaces to a smoothness that involves a variation of only a few molecules' thickness.

A simple example of a bootstraps effect is a disease entity like general paresis. As late as the turn of the century, it was still argued whether or not lues was the specific etiology of "general paralysis of the insane," and the argument was not clinched until 1913 when Noguchi and Moore found the spirochete in the brains of paretics. But notice that in order to find the spirochete in the brains of paretics, one had to rely upon a fallible, although by then rather high accuracy, diagnosis of who is a paretic. Of course there was an intermediate finding of the characteristic cerebral *pathology* (without the etiology), so Noguchi and Moore did not have to rely solely upon phenotypic phenomena like the Argyll-Robertson pupil, or the patient spilling soup on his vest, showing poor judgment and irritability, having trouble saying "hard riding artillery brigade," and so forth. But suppose the biochemist or clinical neurologist had done as we sometimes are forced to do in psychometrics, that is, had tried a large number of *candidate* indicators on paretics versus patients suffering from various other kinds of neurological disorders also involving impairment of motor function and a dementing process. Suppose that the diagnosis of paresis at 1875 was only 75% accurate in the eyes of Omniscient Jones. If the neurologist had tried out a long list of tests, determining blood turpentine level and the Wasserman and the spinal fluid gold colloid test and the Schick test and the Mantoux, what would happen? Positive blood Wassermann and first zone gold colloid spinal fluid would each have an extremely high construct validity for paresis. An "item analysis" of a long list of candidate indicators would select these two items, (both in reality 95% or better two-way pathognomic for the disease entity) even though they had to be discovered on diagnoses that were only 75% accurate, and hence cannot *display* their true validity against formal clinical diagnosis as the available criterion.

Of course the problem is to know when you have successfully achieved a bootstraps effect of this sort; but it's obvious that medicine has done it repeatedly, as have other scientific disciplines. So there is nothing all that strange about the bootstraps effect in psychometrics, except that psychologists are so hooked on operationism that they have been reluctant to admit it. The best example of it in psychometrics is doubtless the intelligence test, which was originally seen to be valid, in contrast with previous efforts to measure general intelligence with Wundtian procedures like two-point touch threshold, because it showed a characteristic develop-

mental change with age, and it agreed well with the pooled judgments of schoolteachers as reflected in social facts like age-grade location.

Consider another example outside psychometrics. If three surveyors each come forward with new methods for estimating how far away a distant mountaintop is, and each of them offers a plausible, but not cogent, theoretical rationale for thinking his method works, then a discovery that the three methods converge in their estimates to a high numerical accuracy tends to corroborate the construct validity of all three of them. For this reason the common undergraduate principle, "Unreliability proves lack of validity, but reliability doesn't prove validity," is somewhat misleading because a nonchance agreement of anything, including a pair of test items or two forms of a test, does prove validity *for something or other*. If that kind of "convergent estimate" reasoning were not essentially valid, no science, including the physical sciences, could get off the ground.

The most dramatic example of bootstrapsing we know of in taxometrics is the "Super-Bootstraps Theorem" proved by Meehl in 1965 (pp. 37–48; cf. also Meehl 1973, pp. 216–217). Suppose that one has a set of fallible phenotypic indicators of a latent taxon that are substantially independent within the taxon and its complement, this being checkable by several nonredundant consistency tests (see below). Having estimated the taxon base rate P in a given population, we define subgroups of patients on the basis of the pattern of positive and negative indicators. Thus, if there are three fallible indicators, each cut at a certain point to maximize hits, we have $2^3 = 8$ cells of patients, within each of which a Bayes Theorem inverse probability of taxon membership is computable from the patient's indicator pattern. The Super-Bootstraps Theorem shows that if the latent structural model is satisfied and the sample is large enough to give stable estimates of the numerical values, then, if there exists an optimal cut on some new fallible indicator v, chosen so that the proportion of patients classified as within the taxon of interest matches the taxon membership probability of any one of the cells, in order for this cut to yield v^+ rates that match the Bayes Theorem probabilities in the remaining cells, it is *both necessary and sufficient that the v-cut be infallible* (two-way pathognomonic, functioning perfectly both as an inclusion and exclusion test.) This is such a remarkable theorem that we have been puzzled why, despite a generalization of it published by Dawes and Meehl (1966), it has come in for almost no attention in taxometrics.

MAXCOV-HITMAX METHOD

We illustrate our conception of bootstraps for taxometric Case 3, the conjectured latent taxon problem, with a simple crude form of one of our taxometric methods, MAXCOV-HITMAX (Meehl, 1973a, pp. 200–224). This is only for pedagogic illustrative purposes here, as a more general and rigorous formulation of the MAXCOV-HITMAX Method will be explained later on. Suppose we conjecture that in a population of psychiatric patients not formally diagnosed as schizophrenic, there exists a taxon, the *schizotype* (Rado, 1956; 1960; Rado & Daniels 1956; Meehl, 1962; 1972a, 1972c). Our theory sketch, based upon some combination of clinical experience, psychiatric genetics, and preliminary statistical analysis of file data, is that there are quite a few patients who have the schizotypal personality organization (and, on our dominant gene hypothesis of the disorder, are carriers of the specific schizogene) but who have not decompensated clinically to the extent of presenting the classical textbook picture of a "florid schizophrenia." These considerations from our antecedent state of knowledge are mentioned solely to motivate the research strategy. They are not going to be *relied on* in the traditional statistician's sense of "needful assumptions."

We do not treat any of the conjectures, main or auxiliary, as "assumptions" in that strong sense. Everything said, whether in the formalism or the interpretative text, is conjectural, although obviously at any given stage of scientific and clinical knowledge of a disease entity or personality type, some conjectures are more problematic than others. That a conjecture is highly problematic, in the sense of taking a big risk, going out on a limb far beyond the facts presently known, does not speak against it. From a neo-Popperian standpoint this is, on the contrary, a methodological plus. We are interested in trying to test this risky conjecture that a taxon "schizotype" really exists in our clinic population.

Note how much is conjectural and how little corroborated at this point. We conjecture that there is such a taxon, but we do not "know it." Philosophically, of course, one never knows anything empirical for certain, but in common sense and in most scientific usage, highly corroborated conjectures that also fit into a larger network of highly corroborated theoretical conceptions are said to be "known." If there is such a taxon, we do not know with what relative frequency it occurs in our population, that is, we are ignorant of its base rate P. We do not know whether the extra taxon class *(taxon complement)* is itself taxonically differentiated, although we think it likely, on general previous knowledge, that it is; but taxometric discrimination among the cases outside the conjectured schizotypal taxon is not of interest to us except as a dangerous source of error in identifying the schizotype. We have tentative notions about some indicators (interview, psychometric, neurological) of the taxon, but we lack numerical estimates of their validities and the optimal cut on those that are dimensional rather than a qualitative predicate. We do not know the valid and false positive rates achievable by the best cut. We do not know what the indicator distributions are shaped like, and we are unwilling to conjecture that they are normal or equal in variance. We do not know whether the candidate indicators are appreciably correlated within the schizotypal taxon, if it exists, or outside it. We are aware of the unpleasant possibility that a schizotypal discriminator may also have some validity for some unidentified extra-taxon groups, in which case the indicators will necessarily be correlated pairwise in the complement. In short, *we know essentially nothing,* and about some of these quantitative questions *we do not even have plausible conjectures.* Such a knowledge situation is evidently a classic case appropriate for bootstraps taxometrics. How can we get taxometric knowledge out of ignorance? We shall see.

Suppose we have three quantitative indicator variables conjectured to have some validity for the schizotypal taxon, namely, *x:* MMPI Scale 8 [$= S_c$], *y:* a Rorschach schizoid composite index, and *z:* quantified subclinical dysdiadochokinesia. The choice of indicators is motivated partly by previous experience suggesting validity, and partly by the desire to choose phenotypically "non-overlapping" behavior domains to minimize methods covariance, so that the conjectures of near-zero correlation within the taxon and within the complement have a good chance of being nearly correct. In addition, we may undertake a minimizing of undesired intra-taxon covariance by ordinary item analytic procedures (done on diagnosed groups) for those variables that are item composites, such as structured inventory scores, or in the case of nonitem measures, by a suitable nonlinear transformation of the metric.

If desired, a preliminary investigation of this intrataxon correlation question can be conducted, although the interlocking consistency tests discussed below should suffice to corroborate that auxiliary conjecture. The problem about direct testing of the near-zero correlation auxiliary conjecture is, obviously, that in a mixed psychiatric population, there is some unknown base rate *P* of schizotypy. *Therefore, cases categorized by formal diagnosis cannot be used to answer this question by direct empirical methods.* However, we can increase the prior probability of that auxiliary conjecture by testing not the mixed bag of psychiatric patients but a group of thoroughly studied patients diagnosed as clinically schizophrenic. Ideally, we would add some cases diagnosed "schizophrenia in remission" and, in some prospective studies, preschizophrenics (e.g., college students who took the MMPI as freshmen and subsequently are found in state hospitals with a diagnosis of schizophrenia). If the pairwise correlations of the three indicators *x, y, z* are close to zero in various diagnosed schizophrenic populations, we have some confidence that a semicompensated (e.g., pseudo-neurotic, borderline state) psychiatric population would also show low correlations, although that does not follow with necessity.

On the other side, consider a sample of nonpsychiatric presumed "normals." On our conjecture that the specific etiology is a dominant schizogene of low penetrance, the fact that the diagnosed schizophrenia rate in first-degree relatives of schizophrenic probands is in the neighborhood of 12%, instead of the theoretical 50% on a perfectly penetrant dominant gene hypothesis, means that the clinical penetrance is only about ¼. Since the general population lifetime risk for schizophrenia is in the neighborhood of 1%, this suggests that the frequency of persons in the general nonpsychiatric population carrying the schizogene is around 4%. This being a rather small proportion, we can safely assume that the statistical tail can't wag the normal population dog enough to generate a taxonically induced covariance of *x, y,* and *z* among normal persons via the presence of only $p = .04$ of schizotypes among them. Therefore, the auxiliary conjecture in the complement class of zero correlation is fairly directly testable by correlating *x, y,* and *z* pairwise in a normal population. We repeat, these preliminary investigations are worth pursuing from the standpoint of saving time by early discovery of indicators that are excessively correlated within the taxon or the complement, but they are not strictly necessary because the auxiliaries will be part of the network tested by the consistency tests.

We begin with a general formula for the covariance of a mixed population, where it is an algebraic truth (not dependent upon distribution assumptions) that the covariance of a mixed population is a simple sum of three terms. The schizotypes are represented by subscript t (= taxon), the nonschizotypes by subscripts c (= complement), and the base rate of schizotypy p. Then the (yz) covariance for a mixed population is given by

$$\text{cov}(yz) = p \, \text{cov}_t(yz) + q \, \text{cov}_c(yz)$$
$$+ \, p \, q \, (\bar{y}_t - \bar{y}_c) \, (\bar{z}_t - \bar{z}_c) \quad (1)$$

This expression is derived in Meehl (1965, pp. 12, 28–29; see also Meehl, 1968, pp. 4–5). It is intuitively obvious that the covariance of a mixed group should depend partly upon the two within group covariances, these components being weighted in proportion to the group rates; and the third term, a kind of "validity-mixture" term, reflects the influence of the crude validities expressed as differences of the latent means between the schizotypal and nonschizotypal subpopulation on the two indicators, weighted by the product term $p \, q$, which is a measure of taxonic "mix." One way to look at this third term intuitively is that patients high on indicator y will tend to be schizotypes, and therefore, if indicator z has validity, they will tend to be high on z. That is, *the covariance is generated by the fact of taxon mixture.* So this third term is the interesting one for taxometric purposes. We see that it tends to increase with increases in the true indicator validities, that is, the differences $(\bar{y}_t - \bar{y}_c)$ and $(\bar{z}_t - \bar{z}_c)$, and also with the degree of taxonic "mix," measured by the cross product of the schizoid taxon's rate p and its complement $q = 1 - p$. This accords with intuition, since if the indicators had zero validity for the taxon, or if they had taxonic validity but the taxon was unrepre-

sented in a population subjected to statistical study, this third term would vanish.

The greatest taxonic "mixture," that is, the opposite extreme from a "pure" population (consisting only of the schizoid taxon, or solely of individuals not belonging to it, where the cross product term $pq = 0$) is that of an even mix. For fixed crude indicator validities $\Delta\bar{y} = (\bar{y}_t - \bar{y}_c)$ and $\Delta\bar{z} = (\bar{z}_t - \bar{z}_c)$, the smallest values of the "validity-mixture" term of the general expression are those for $p = 0$, $q = 1$, or $p = 1$, $q = 0$; and the greatest value of this interesting term occurs for the even mix $p = q = \frac{1}{2}$, where the product is equal to $\frac{1}{4}$. That is, in a population in which half of the patients were members of the schizoid taxon and half were not, the expected value of the validity-mixture term would be $\frac{1}{4}$ the product of the latent mean differences, that is $\frac{1}{4} \Delta\bar{y}\Delta\bar{z}$.

Now making the simplifying approximate assumption (better, auxiliary conjecture) that the indicators have been chosen or constructed in one of the three ways indicated above, so that within the schizoid taxon each indicator correlates negligibly with each other one, and ditto for the complement class, then in our equation

$$\text{cov}(yz) = p \, \text{cov}_t(yz) + (1 - p) \, \text{cov}_c(yz)$$
$$+ \, pq \, \Delta\bar{y}\Delta\bar{z} \quad (2)$$

the first two terms vanish. Hence the total observed covariance $\text{cov}(yz)$ is simply the product of the schizoid and nonschizoid rates times the product of the crude latent validities. The observed covariance of such a mixed population is contributed solely by the indicator validities and the fact of taxonic mix.

In Figure 5.1 we have a diagram with the vertical axis being a measure of clerical ability, and the horizontal being a measure of *n Nurturance*. Assume that, for the female sex considered by itself, there is no correlation between clerical ability and *n Nurturance*. Then the bivariate frequency distribution for females can be drawn as a circle,

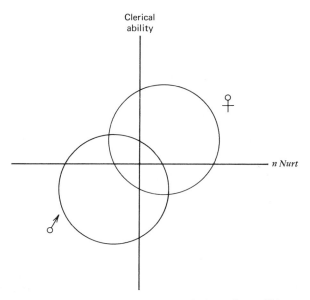

Figure 5.1.   Illustration of two indicator variables independent within two taxa.

and the regression line of y on z within that circle is flat, has slope $= 0$. Overlapping with that circle representing the females, but southwest of it on the graph, we see another circle representing the $(yz) -$ distribution for males, assuming that within the male sex also there is no correlation between clerical ability and *n Nurturance*. This situation is the idealized one for taxometric analysis, because the two indicator variables are completely independent within the two taxa. Now if we consider the mixed population of males and females, these two overlapping circles, the regression line within each of which is flat, are fused as an ellipse elongated in the northeast direction. The best fitting regression line for the mixed population does not have 0 slope but a positive slope, depending upon the size of the sex difference in clerical ability and *n Nurturance*.

If there were some way of arranging a sequence of clinical subpopulations in the order of their schizotypal rates, then, on the auxiliary conjecture that the covariances are zero within the taxon and its complement, the observed covariances cov(yz) of that or-

dered sequence of populations should commence at zero for the subpopulation that contains no representatives of the schizotypal taxon and should steadily increase to a maximum, achieved within the subpopulation with $p = q = \frac{1}{2}$, the maximum taxonic mix in which half the patients are schizotypal and half are not; and then should decline steadily to reach and remain at zero when we move into subpopulations in which all of the patients are schizotypal. This relationship between the observed covariance within a population of unknown but conjectured mix is already interesting and could be used for sign validation purposes, and to test the model, if we had before us any group of populations somehow identifiable as differing in the schizoid rate (see, e.g., Dawes & Meehl, 1966).

But we need not know how to identify such populations qualitatively, nor the successive increments in schizotypal base rate in moving from one to the other, in order to carry out a remarkably powerful bootstraps operation, as follows: We have conjectured that a third indicator x, not yet used, also has taxometric validity. Assuming that x is uncorrelated with y and z within the two classes, and that there is no significant moderator effect, so that with increasing values of x there is an increased correlation of y and z apart from the taxonicity, one way to proceed would be simply to arrange subpopulations as defined by their x-values. Imagining the picture of the latent distribution on x shown in Meehl (1973a, p. 209), we can simply compute the observed covariance of y and z for each x interval beginning at the extreme left of the manifest (mixed) distribution. With a sizeable sample, if the validities are such as to have less than complete overlap on the x-indicator, this means that the first few class intervals we study at the lower end of the x distribution will be schizotype-free. That is, for each of those intervals $p_i = 0$, and therefore the covariance of the two "output" indicators $\text{cov}_i(yz)$ will be at zero within all of those intervals. Then as we begin to pick up a few schizotypes in the low tail of the latent schizotypal frequency function so that $p > 0$ and increases steadily while q goes down from 1, the observed covariance of yz takes on nonzero values and begins to increase. The hitmax interval on x is the interval above the intersection of the latent frequency functions on x. Cutting there maximizes the hit rate, taking account of the base rate P, so that the functions we are dealing with here should be unrelativized frequency functions, their ordinates being not intrataxon density functions but frequency functions reflecting the base rates P, Q.

The hitmax interval h_i we do not observe directly, because we do not know the latent distributions including their base rates, and so on, and we have no accepted criterion. But h_i is nevertheless locatable by this boots-traps procedure. It will correspond to the class interval on the input variable x, which yields the maximum value of the output variable covariance $\text{cov}_i(yz)$, that being the interval for which $p = q = \frac{1}{2}$, that is, for which the taxon mixture term has its maximum ($= \frac{1}{4} \Delta \bar{y} \Delta \bar{z}$). As we pass through the hitmax interval on indicator x and move into

the higher region of the mixture distribution, where for each interval the proportion of schizotypes now exceeds one-half of the sub-population frequency, and for which—if each of the two distributions is separately unimodal—the schizotype proportion steadily declines, we find the covariance of y and z declining steadily. It reaches the value $\text{cov}(yz) = 0$ when we come to the end of the upper tail of the latent nonschizotype distribution, above which point all of the patients are schizotypes in all of the higher class intervals of x, so no further change in the observed covariance of y and z is to be expected on the independence assumptions of the model.

But we now have a very useful number, namely, the presumed constant product $K = (\Delta \bar{y} \Delta \bar{z})$ of the crude latent validity increments. We know that for cases lying in the hitmax interval, $\text{cov}(yz) = \frac{1}{4} \Delta \bar{y} \Delta \bar{z} = \frac{1}{4}K$, the constant K being the fixed product of the crude "validities" (latent mean differences), permitting us to solve for K. Further, the general expression for the covariance of a mixed group holds for each of the class intervals, not just for the hitmax interval. Now that we are able to estimate the latent constant K by means of the hitmax interval's observed (yz)-covariance, we can plug in that parameter K in the general expression $\text{cov}_i(yz) = p_i q_i K$ for each x-interval. So in each x-interval we have a quadratic in p,

$$Kp^2 - Kp + \text{cov}_i(yz) = 0 \qquad (3)$$

which we solve to obtain p_i in each x_i-interval. Of the two roots, which will of course be fractions, one less and one greater than $\frac{1}{2}$, we choose the smaller root for all the x-intervals below the hitmax cut, and the larger root for all the x-intervals above the hitmax cut.

Now we are in excellent shape, since by multiplying the observed crude frequency in each x_i-interval by the schizotypal rate p_i of that interval, we obtain the number N_i of schizotypes in each class interval of x. Adding these over the whole mixed population yields the total schizotype number for our sample $\Sigma N_i = N_s$, and dividing this by the grand N of our sample gives us the desired latent base rate P.

This bootstraps procedure is then repeated in the two other possible ways, which, while not totally independent, are largely nonredundant with respect to the first one. That is, we treat indicators x and z as output and plot their covariance against y as the abscissa variable, and similarly we treat z as the input variable and plot the covariance of x and y as output. In the course of these operations, the computer has, in effect, *drawn us the three latent frequency functions with their overlaps.* So we can calculate the valid and false positive rates achieved on each indicator taken separately when patients falling above the hitmax cut of that indicator are classified as schizotypal and those falling below the hitmax cut as nonschizotypal.

Finally, knowing the grand base rate P and the valid and false positive rates, p_{tx}, p_{ty}, p_{tz}, p_{cx}, p_{cy}, p_{cz}, we can plug these numerical values directly into Bayes' Formula for inverse probability. Thus, suppose we have a patient from this population who falls above the hitmax cut on indicators x and y, but below the hitmax cut on z. This pattern (x^+, y^+, z^-) of scores on the three indicators yields a Bayes' Theorem inverse probability that the patient is schizotypal as follows:

$$P(Sc/x^+y^+z^-)$$
$$= \frac{Pp_{tx}p_{ty}q_{tz}}{Pp_{tx}p_{ty}q_{tz} + Qp_{cx}p_{cy}q_{cz}} \quad (4)$$

We present here only one example of a consistency test, namely, the total covariance test. Since the general equation for observed covariance of a mixed population holds generally, it holds for the total population under study, as well as for any of the subpopulations, however identified. Consequently, the grand covariances of x and z, of y and z, and of x and y for the whole (mixed) population can be written in terms of the base rate P,

its complement $Q = 1 - P$, and the latent mean differences as follows:

$$\text{Cov}(xy) = PQ\,\Delta\bar{x}\Delta\bar{y}$$
$$\text{Cov}(xz) = PQ\,\Delta\bar{x}\Delta\bar{z} \quad (5)$$
$$\text{Cov}(yz) = PQ\,\Delta\bar{y}\Delta\bar{z}$$

CONSISTENCY TESTS AND AUXILIARY CONJECTURES

We must emphasize again that the auxiliary conjectures referred to, such as independence within the taxa and the absence of significant moderator effects, are made as assumptions to motivate the formalism but are not being empirically *relied upon* as trustworthy (or pious hope!) postulates. Rather they are jointly tested, together with all of the other auxiliary conjectures and the main assumptions of the model, by imposing numerical tolerance limits on departures from the theorems derived as consistency tests. The reader will totally misunderstand our bootstraps approach, and the neo-Popperian philosophy of science underlying it, and will consequently not know how seriously he or she should take the formalism, if he or she does not grasp our approach to this question. The satisfaction (within tolerances) of the several consistency tests, which are not equally responsive to departures from different aspects of the conjectural latent model, shows what? It corroborates the substantive theory that there is a taxon, and that these indicators have substantial validity for it, together with all of the other conjectural assumptions in the explanatory text that interpret the formalism or justify taking a given step within it. This means that we are testing the crude theory sketch of the schizoid taxon *and* the auxiliary conjectures; *and* we are also tightening up the network defining the loose concept, "schizotaxia," psychometrically; *and* we are also validating the indicators. All of these are done simultaneously. When we corroborate the consequences of the nomological network, we corroborate the network.

We do not dispute the desirability of being able to test substantive conjectures under circumstances in which the auxiliary conjectures are unproblematic. The difficulty is that in the life sciences, and certainly in the behavior sciences, this is an unusual state of knowledge for the investigator to be in when pursuing taxometric research. Example: In testing a dominant gene theory of schizotypy by studying the Rorschach responses of parent pairs of diagnosed decompensated schizotypal probands ("clinical schizophrenia"), we may rely upon psychometric extrapolation of Rorschach indicators from validation studies. But these studies are based not upon the compensated relatives of known schizophrenics but upon patients who themselves have been schizophrenic, or, very rarely, who were tested when normal and subsequently became schizophrenic. While this extrapolation has a certain plausibility, it is obviously not certain. An investigator who had immersed himself or herself in the genetics of schizophrenia might well surmise, at a given stage of knowledge, that the dominant schizogene theory is itself no more problematic than the Rorschach psychometric sign he or she plans to use in testing that theory. For a further discussion of this, see Meehl (1978) and a forthcoming book by Golden and Meehl. We must emphasize that *qualitatively* the situation in the life sciences is not different from that in the inorganic disciplines like astronomy and chemistry, in which breakthroughs have sometimes been achieved by challenging auxiliary assumptions that had been considered well corroborated. But there is a big *quantitative* difference, and it is foolish for the behavior taxometrist to pretend otherwise.

We do not wish to defend an orthodox Popperian position as to the inherent desirability of low probability substantive conjectures (Grünbaum, 1976). But we think it fairly clear from the history of the sciences that theories do get their best support in the

eyes of the scientific community by virtue of having made risky predictions. Our own view is that scientists usually prefer the theory *T* itself to be antecedently probable on the background knowledge, including other "accepted" theories. But they want its observational consequences to be antecedently improbable, *absent the theory*. This combination goes through nicely on a Bayes Theorem representation, but the logician then has to worry about how *T* can be antecedently probable and its observational consequence-class not. Be that as it may, as Salmon puts it (1966, p. 119):

A hypothesis risks falsification by yielding a prediction that is very improbable unless that hypothesis is true. It makes a daring prediction, for it is not likely to come out right unless we have hit upon the correct hypothesis. Confirming instances are not likely to be forthcoming by sheer chance.

Whether on a Bayesian or Popperian or commonsense approach, the scientist gains respect for a theory when it makes a numerical point prediction or any other kind of detailed specification of facts not foreseeable from some alternative theoretical construction. Put simply and without reference to technical philosophy of science controversies still current today, the general idea is that we are impressed when a theory makes detailed predictions that other competing theories don't, *because we think that for a theory to have no truth to it and yet make detailed predictions about facts would be a strange coincidence.*

Some such reasoning must underlie all empirical science, however the philosophers reconstruct it, because otherwise everyone could decide whimsically, apart from the strength or weakness of the empirical predictions theories make. Point predictions in which a narrow range of values of an observed variable is specified ("narrow" means with reference to background knowledge as to the order of magnitude of that observational measure's range of variability, theory aside) are the paradigm case. Other strong corroborators are predictions of rank orders, second order differences, function forms (when more complicated than a straight line and when the points to be fitted are considerably in excess of the number of parameters adjusted), and the like (see Meehl, 1978, pp. 824–825.)

One of the strongest kinds of support for any scientific concept is an inference to a numerical point value on the basis of a theoretical model in which the numerical value is independently arrived at through manipulations of the observational facts within a formalism that would have no rationale were it not for the conjectured latent causal or structural model of the theory. If we get the same answers when each numerical prediction took a risk, this provides very strong corroboration. Thus, for instance, physical chemists believe that we know the Avogadro constant N, the number of molecules in a gram molecular weight of a substance, with exactitude, because there are some 14 nonredundant ways of estimating it, ranging from the properties of soap films to purely theoretical considerations based upon quantum mechanics. Convergence of numerical point estimates is therefore to be sought wherever possible, and taxometric bootstraps operations are a good place to do this.

We have not found it possible to make a clear formal distinction between main estimators and consistency tests. A given expression into which numerical values can be plugged, or from which numerical values can be estimated when we have assigned all but one of the values in the expression, can evidently serve either as a main estimator of a latent parameter or as a consistency test. If we have more equations than unknowns, we have consistency tests. If we have fewer equations than unknowns, we have neither main estimators or a consistency test. If the number of equations equals the number of unknowns, then we have estimators but the system cannot be inconsistent, because empirically that will never happen. These mat-

ters are better discussed in the context of presenting the more detailed and generalized formalism below.

APPROXIMATIONS AND VERISIMILITUDE

It is important that the reader understand why we are not much interested in developing exact statistical significance tests for consistency formulas. We could say gently that it has low priority among the current research tasks of a taxometrist. But more honestly, we view it as largely a waste of time, springing from a misleading and counterproductive philosophy of science. An exact studentized significance test for a consistency test of the taxometric model would serve the purpose of refuting the theoretical latent model as taken literally. That is, if the consistency test is "failed," meaning that its numerical values have a low probability α of occurring on the theoretical hypothesis stated in the formalism, what this shows is that the functional relations stated in the formalism, such as complete independence, absence of moderator effects, continuity, and so on, are not literally true of the state of nature. *We do not understand why anyone would want to show that, since we already know that in advance.* Whether or not this α level is achieved will depend jointly, and in a complicated way (which nobody knows how to set out rigorously and analytically in the mathematics), upon the degree of departure of the state of nature from the idealized model as conceptualized in the embedding text that exposits and interprets the formalism, together with the inherent idealizations represented in any formalism, as for example, taking derivatives. In standard analysis differentiation involves assumptions of continuity about variables that must of course be discontinuous in the life sciences—certainly when we add finite numbers of test items in a psychometric score! The most important factor involved here other than the degree of distortion of the truth by the model is the power function of the significance test. Nobody could safely contradict the following assertion about taxometrics in the behavior sciences: Given a sufficiently large sample, all conceptualizations of latent taxa that cause certain indicators to covary in specified ways as stated in the language of differential calculus is literally false. Consequently whether or not an investigator succeeds in *showing* it to be literally false depends solely upon the power function, and therefore mainly on sample size (see Meehl, 1967; 1978, and more generally, Morrison & Henkel, 1970).

Of course this does not permit the taxometrist to be intellectually irresponsible. On the contrary, reflection on the uselessness of significance tests in these contexts leads to the desirability of constructing models of approximation theory, an important matter that has been insufficiently pursued in the social sciences. The problem is never one of literal truth of the conjectural model as stated in the formalism and the embedding text, since those are always false, taken literally. The problem is the setting up of tolerances in the light of robustness considerations, and as yet only limited inroads have been made into that problem.

Finally, we do not mistakenly suppose that the neo-Popperian concept "verisimilitude" is in satisfactory shape in contemporary philosophy of science. But we are convinced that *some such* metatheoretical concept is unavoidable, since all theories are false, being idealizations. A theory of schizotypy could have high verisimilitude, although it erred in regard to the absence of nuisance variables operating within the taxon to generate a certain correlation intrataxonically, violating the independence assumption in our derivation above. But that would be a small departure from the truth compared to the situation in which there is simply no such thing as the schizoid taxon at all, or one in which the indicators, while valid for the genetic schizoid taxon, also have high validity for a completely environmentally determined

phenocopy. Science cannot wait in the development of its instruments upon a completely satisfactory philosophical analysis of verisimilitude, any more than historically it has had to wait upon an adequate clarification of the notions of induction, proof, or even for that matter the core concept, truth, itself.

A TAXOMETRIC PROBLEM: TESTING A THEORY OF SCHIZOPHRENIA

Our work in taxometrics began with a desire to test a substantive theory of schizophrenia developed by Meehl. This theory conjectures that the genetic predisposition for schizophrenia is taxonic in nature. After briefly presenting the major features of this theory (for a complete description see Meehl, 1962), we will describe each of three taxometric methods we have developed for testing this theory. These taxometric methods are general in that they can be used for testing any theory regarding a conjectured taxon. After discussing the methods, we will report the results of applying them in a preliminary empirical test of the schizophrenia theory.

Twenty years ago Meehl (1962) proposed a theory of schizophrenia in which he hypothesized that only a certain class of people, those with a particular genetic constitution, have *any* liability for schizophrenia. This hypothetical class will be referred to here as the "schizoid taxon." While Meehl's theory has generated considerable interest, there has been little empirical evidence to either corroborate or refute it, probably because the taxonomic nature of the theory resulted in methodological and statistical problems that could not be adequately handled by methods that existed at that time.

A description of the general nature of methodological and statistical problems encountered in testing this theory was given by Meehl (1973a). If, as Meehl proposes, the specific etiology of the schizoid taxon (schizoidia) is a single dominant gene, and the only indicators available are highly fallible phenotypic ones, how can the probability that a person carries this gene be estimated? Currently there is no generally acceptable criterion variable and no definitive diagnostic touchstone, sign, symptom, or trait that can be measured reliably. Not all of the correlates of schizoidia are sufficiently pathological to be called "symptoms" or valid enough to be called "signs" (hence we will use the term "indicator"). Thought disorder or "cognitive slippage," which is viewed by Meehl (following Bleuler) as the primary indicator of schizoidia, is not sufficient by itself for taxonomic purposes. Some clinical manifestations of cognitive slippage can be noted during intensive psychotherapy of psychiatric patients, and can be used as *inclusion* tests for schizoidia, in that their presence is an almost infallible indication of the presence of this particular pathology.

Unfortunately, these manifestations are too rare to be used successfully as *exclusion* tests; their absence does not necessarily imply absence of schizoidia. No valid psychometric test of cognitive slippage is available—an especially serious problem for researchers who would like to study schizoidia as a hypothetical taxon that includes both schizophrenics and schizoids (who may never manifest diagnostically psychotic degrees of cognitive slippage). Therefore, we have a perfect example of a bootstraps problem (Cronbach & Meehl, 1955), in which we must start with a fallible set of indicators of unknown validities and hope to end up with accurate estimates of these validities on the basis of some internal statistical relationships among them.

CLUSTER ANALYSIS

The most popular taxometric methods are currently the cluster analytic ones. As discussed above, these methods are intended to solve taxometric problems where we do not have a conjectured taxon. According to

Blashfield (1976) six "agglomerative" cluster methods are the most commonly used. Before using these six methods to attempt to detect the schizoid taxon, we decided to subject each to an empirical trial where the underlying taxonomy is known. We will describe the empirical trials after giving a brief description of these agglomerative cluster methods.

Although cluster methods were first proposed in the social sciences by Zubin (1938) and Tryon (1939), general interest in their use paralleled the development of large computers. Now, according to Blashfield (1976), over 100 different cluster methods are found in Anderberg (1973), Bailey (1974), and Everitt (1974). Even though the cluster methods are most frequently used for generating clusters of related variables, they can also be used for generating clusters of similar individuals, as would be necessary in searching for a schizoid taxon.

The agglomerative methods are used in conjunction with a matrix of similarity-values for each pair of individuals' sets of indicator scores. The measure of similarity between the two individuals' indicator scores is usually some kind of correlation or distance in the indicator-hyperspace. From the similarity-values, clusters can be generated by assigning individuals with similar scores to the same cluster. A cluster method is iterative and generates a hierarchical tree, with each level of the tree representing a different clustering called a partition. If there are N individuals, then the first partition consists of N-1 clusters, the next of N-2 clusters, and so on until the last partition, which consists of two clusters.

Four of the most popular agglomerative methods are called by Blashfield the "single linkage," "complete linkage," "average linkage," and "minimum variance" methods. Two other cluster methods, mathematically related to the average linkage method, are the "centroid" and "median" methods. It has been shown by Lance and Williams (1967) and Wishart (1969) that all six methods can be described in terms of the same algorithm or iterative procedure.

Each of six clustering algorithms can be easily described to give a sense of how each works and how it differs from the others. For example, in the single linkage method, each member of a cluster is more similar to at least one member of that cluster than it is to any member of any other cluster. In the complete linkage method, each member of a cluster is more similar to the most dissimilar member of the same cluster than it is to the most dissimilar member of any other cluster. In the average linkage method, each member of a cluster has a greater average similarity with the other members of the same cluster than it does with the members of any other cluster. In the centroid method the members of a cluster have a greater similarity to the centroid of the cluster than they do to the centroid of any other cluster. The centroid of a cluster is the vector of indicator means calculated across the members of the cluster. The median method is similar to the centroid method except that the median of the cluster members is used in place of the centroid. In the minimum variance method, the clusters are formed so that the sum of the squared differences in the similarity-measures across pairs of individuals of the cluster is minimal.

Detection of the Biological Sexes: An Empirical Trial of a Taxometric Method

We have described a theory of schizoidia, taxonomic in nature, which requires an appropriate taxometric method in order to test it. Because cluster analysis is the best known taxometric method, we considered using it. However, before using a cluster method for our purpose, we need to be confident that it will usually produce "accurate" clusters, or that it will rarely produce totally inaccurate or "spurious" ones that would be mistaken for "real" clusters. For our purposes a set of clusters is "accurate" or has sufficient verisimilitude (Popper, 1962), if it corresponds

closely enough to an actual underlying taxonomy of real empirical classes; if the set of clusters does not have such a degree of verisimilitude, it will be said to be spurious. We can perform a simple empirical trial to obtain an idea of the accuracy of some of the cluster methods, and other taxometric methods we will describe, when used to detect real empirical classes such as those considered when testing a typical taxonomic theory in the social sciences.

In one study (Golden & Meehl, 1981) we evaluated six of the more popular cluster methods as to their accuracy in testing a pseudo-taxonomic theory, one that we knew in advance to be correct. In doing this, we attempted to determine which, if any, of these cluster methods are satisfactory for solving the pseudo-problem of detecting the taxonomic variable of biological sex when sex-discriminant Minnesota Multiphasic Personality Inventory (MMPI) items are used as indicators. Taxometric methods that can not pass this empirical trial are unlikely to be useful in detecting, as but one example, the schizoid taxon with (other) MMPI items. In this approach to evaluating cluster methods we determine how well each method detects a *known* taxon. General use of this approach is difficult in fields such as personality and psychopathology, since there are few known taxa. Fortunately, at least one physical taxon, biological sex, is virtually perfect on the criterion side. Also it is reassuring to note that a scale of MMPI masculine-feminine interest items produces bimodality for a larged mixed sample with equal numbers of males and females. We think it likely that many taxa in the social sciences have too much overlap to generate bimodality when psychometric indicators such as MMPI are used. If bimodality obtains, it is generally because the latent taxonic class distributions on the indicator-scale have very little overlap. For example, if the two taxonic class base rates are equal, and the two taxonic class distributions are normal in shape, then bimodality is only discernible when the two means are more than two within-taxon class sigma-units apart (Murphy, 1964).

The MMPI sex discriminant items are described in some detail here, since these items were also used to test each of our own taxometric models to be described below.

The MMPI item-indicators were chosen by comparing two samples of males and females on each of the 550 MMPI items. These two samples consisted of 430 male and 675 female adult psychiatric patients in the University of Minnesota Hospitals. The items were scored 1 for a "female" response and 0 for a "male" response, with "female" and "male" responses determined both by comparing the response proportions of these same male and female samples and by considering the item content (i.e., face validity). The two methods agree perfectly. It was found that 49 items discriminated between the two samples to the extent that the difference in the proportions that scored a 1 was .10 or more. This difference in proportions will be referred to as the "validity" of the item. Of these 49 items, 18 were found to have validities of .30 or more and will be referred to as the "highly discriminant" items. Examples of the highly discriminant items are given below. The letter in parenthesis indicates that a response of true (T) or a response of false (F) is scored as 1; otherwise the response is scored as 0. "I am not afraid of mice" (F), "I used to like hopscotch" (T), "I used to keep a diary" (T), "I very much like hunting" (F), "I like collecting flowers or growing houseplants" (T), "I would like to be a nurse" (T). The 12 items found to have validities between .20 and .30 are referred to as the "moderately discriminant" items. Examples of moderately discriminant items are: "I like poetry" (T), "I like to cook" (T), "I would like to be a soldier" (F), "If I were an artist, I would like to draw flowers" (T), "I have no fear of spiders" (F). The 21 items found to have validities between .10 and .20 are referred to as the "weakly discriminant"

items. Examples of weakly discriminant items are: "I gossip a little at times (T), "Sometimes when I am not feeling well I am cross" (T), "I would like to be a florist" (T), "At times I feel like swearing" (F), "I am certainly lacking in self-confidence" (T), "I am easily downed in an argument" (T), "I like science" (F). Finally, 26 items (scored arbitrarily with regard to sex direction) were selected at random from the remaining 501 items in the MMPI inventory with validity coefficients between −.10 and .10, and are referred to as "nondiscriminant" items. Examples of very weakly or, as we call them, nondiscriminant items are: "I have several times given up doing a thing because I thought too little of my ability" (T), "I have often met people who were supposed to be experts who were no better than I" (F), "At times I have worn myself out by undertaking too much" (F), "My plans have frequently seemed so full of difficulties that I have had to give them up" (T).

Objection has been made that this task is difficult or impossible, because MMPI items are too many steps removed from the sex-determining genome. One simply cannot expect, it is said, that verbal self-reports of interests, attitudes, feelings, and the like will possess sufficiently high construct validity vis-à-vis the XX genotype to permit a bootstraps taxometric identification of the biological taxon, let alone a highly accurate sorting of individual subjects into those taxa by the use of such fallible bootstrapped indicators.

The answer to this criticism is that we know as an empirical fact that it is possible to do so, as the authors of the MMPI did when they had available an external criterion available for empirical keying. Even the old MMPI M_f scale itself achieves between an 85 and 90% accuracy in identifying biological sex. This suffices to show that the net attenuated construct validity of these kinds of verbal items is *not* too poor for the sex identification task we set to it.

We will also present evidence that each

of our taxometric methods can be applied in a bootstraps fashion, without knowledge of the criterion membership of the individuals, to infer the biological sex taxonicity, estimate the taxa base rates accurately, and classify individuals with an accuracy of 85 to 90%. Thus we can bootstrap this taxonomy using MMPI items and get a true validity that compares favorably with that achieved by Hathaway and McKinley employing the objective sex membership dichotomy for criterion keying. For further analysis of the methodological fairness of the empirical trial, see Golden and Meehl (1981).

Our position on the fairness of this empirical trial is that the conjecture that a certain taxometric method will usually enable one to detect a taxon, to find the strong items, and to assign weights to them for classifying individuals into the detected taxon or out of it, is strongly discorroborated when the method fails at its task in a context in which the dichotomy is known to exist and the fallible indicators available to the taxometric method are known to be sufficiently valid so that when put together, even by a crude item analytic and unweighted procedure, they are highly accurate.

The Results of the Empirical Trial of the Cluster Methods

The accuracy with which each of six cluster methods detected the biological sex taxonomy was determined by observing how accurately a mixed-sex sample of individuals was classified according to biological sex. The last partition of two clusters was used; that with the most females was identified as the female cluster and the other as the male cluster.

For each trial, a mixed sample of size 200 consisting of 100 males and 100 females was analyzed. Two hundred is a common size for cluster analysis studies and was the maximum that the available computer program could accommodate. A second mixed sample of the same size and mixture was used for replication trials.

The six cluster methods were studied using four different sets of MMPI indicator-items for each of the two samples; Set I consisted of the 20 most highly discriminant items, Set II consisted of the 30 most highly discriminant items, Set III consisted of the 50 most highly discriminant items, and Set IV of those items in Set III plus 25 nondiscriminant or "garbage" items. Set IV provides the strongest test of the methods and is closest to the actual situation in much taxometric research.

Three of the methods (single linkage, centroid, and median) did not provide acceptable values for the female or male base rates or an adequate hit rate in classifying as to biological sex for any of the four sets of indicator items. In each case the absolute error in the estimate of the male or female base rate exceeded .15, and/or the overall correct classification rate was less than .65 where .50 is the chance rate. In contrast, the results of the other three methods (complete linkage, average linkage, and minimum variance) were much better. For the latter three methods the estimate of female or male base rate was between .40 and .60, and the correct classification rate exceeded .75 for 13 of a total of 24 trial samples.

Whether one views such results as encouraging or otherwise will depend on the research aim and (like it or not) one's philosophy of science. The "professional taxometrician," a typical member of the Classification Society, might be pleased to find three of the popular methods doing as well as they did here; or he or she might not care one way or the other, especially if he or she is philosophically a conventionalist or fictionist, for whom there are no "right answers" to a taxonomic problem.

A physician, psychopathologist, or behavior geneticist should, we think, be less than enthusiastic about findings such as these; and so such workers have been, almost uniformly. Only a tiny minority, surely less than

1%, of clinical psychologists or psychiatrists rely on formal cluster algorithms for help in solving their problems, whether theoretical or clinical. Should we expect them to? Suppose a psychoclinician employed by court services wants to find out whether there are different "types" of sex offenders; how could he or she rationally decide which of the six most popular cluster methods to use in answering such a general question? Three of them failed to achieve success, by very tolerant criteria, in such a simple, easy task as "telling the girls from the boys." They couldn't manage that on *any* of their eight trials (Golden & Meehl 1981, Table 3). Even the three most accurate were unimpressive as scientific detection instruments would normally be judged. Thus the very best method (average linkage) yielded tolerable results in six trials but failed in two. Would we want to trust such methods in taxonomizing criminals, psychotic patients, school behavior problems, or genetic mental deficiencies? Remember, this is not six out of eight "hits" in diagnosing *individuals*—a validity quite useful for some purposes. Rather the best among the six favorite cluster methods gave only six in eight accurate *nomothetic* (generic, conceptual) results, in detecting the taxon's existence and estimating its base rate.

No one even moderately familiar with the field will find these poor to mediocre results surprising. It is well known that: (1) different cluster algorithms do not tend, by and large, to agree very well with one another; (2) they sometimes detect the taxa generally recognized by competent scholars in a substantive field and sometimes do not; when not, (3) there are no objective (or even generally accepted) criteria telling us which classification to trust; and (4) there are no persuasive *theoretical* considerations for preferring one method over another.

As Meehl (1979, p. 567) points out, it is a striking historical fact that *not one single entity* in psychopathology, neurology, or medical genetics owes its initial discovery to formal cluster analytic methods. He con-

jectures eight reasons (pp. 571–572) why we might expect this to be so, for which the reader is referred to that paper. See also the critical discussion by the statistician Cormack (1971), and the excellent expositions by Blashfield (1976, 1978), Blashfield and Aldenderfer (1978), and Skinner (1981).

We have not wished to belabor the point that formal cluster algorithms, or at least the received ones in favorite use, have yet to prove their value for the psychoclinician's tasks. It is our own conjecture, which we venture to suggest is rather well corroborated by the evidence to date, that what we have labeled above the "Type 2" taxometric problem does not admit of a general solution. We think that there are strong epistemological, mathematical, and domain-substantive (structural, causal) reasons why this is so. That is our justification (other than personal interest and the *Handbook* editors' permission) for focusing this chapter mainly on methodological clarification of the taxometric problem, illustrating that by exposition of our own methods, these latter being *solutions*—strong and testable ones, as we believe—to taxometric problems of Type 3: conjectured latent taxon. It is our conviction that this third kind of problem is by far the commonest, despite its almost complete neglect by taxometricians. So we do not apologize for emphasizing strong Popperian methods in preference to methods of doubtful empirical utility and lacking in coherent theoretical rationale. Readers who remain optimistic about Type 2 cluster methods can readily find them explained in the excellent standard treatises by Hartigan (1975) and Sneath and Sokal (1973), or the brief summary exposition of Sokal (1974).

THE TAXOMETRIC MODELS

It is desirable to develop a taxometric method so that we know the conditions for which it will work perfectly. Then we can infer how much the actual latent situation departs from these ideal conditions or "assumptions" of the method and check that this departure is not so great that we are likely to be misled by the parameter estimates. If we do happen to conclude that the departure is too great, we can choose to disregard the particular results. The key assumption we used in each of the models described below is that indicators are uncorrelated within the taxon and within the complement of the taxon, referred to below as the "taxon complement" or simply the "complement."

We hypothesize that each individual is either a member of the taxon or a member of the taxon complement. In other literature on taxometric models the taxon and the taxon complement are referred to as "latent classes" (e.g., Clogg, 1977; Goodman, 1975; Green, 1952; Lazarsfeld & Henry, 1968; and Torgerson, 1958). We have emphasized that the taxonomic class should comprise an actual *empirical* taxon, that the classification "carves nature at its joints." Since our purpose is to detect a real, empirical taxonicity, it is not sufficient, for example, merely to produce classifications that optimize a statistical property such as a measure of intraclass homogeneity. We view such a procedure as desirable only to the extent that it helps in detecting real, empirical taxonomies (Meehl, 1979). Because of our emphasis on the empirical nature of the conjectured taxonomic classes, we refer to them as the "taxon" and the "taxon complement" or in general as "taxonomic classes" (for further discussion see Meehl, 1979).

We begin the description of the taxometric models by considering an ideal taxonomic latent situation. There exists a taxonomic class or taxon of individuals with the disease, disorder, or syndrome (denoted by subscript t) and a complementary taxonomic class or taxon complement of individuals without the disorder (denoted by subscript c). Let P be the base rate of the taxon and $Q = 1 - P$ be that of the complement. Suppose we have several dichotomous indicators that discriminate between these two taxonomic classes.

Let p_{tk} be the probability that an individual in the taxon has a positive response to the kth indicator (the "valid positive" rate) and p_{ck} be that for an individual in the complement (the "false positive" rate). Responses are scored as 1 if positive (i.e., deviant, pathological, indicative of the disorder), otherwise as 0. The direction of scoring is determined a priori by empirical or theoretical considerations, but checked empirically by the taxometric method.

Each of the taxometric models we have developed can be derived from the auxiliary conjecture that each pair of indicators (or in the case of the normal model, each pair of components of the indicator, such as items comprising an indicator-scale) are independent within the taxon and within the taxon complement. It is by elimination of the intrataxonomic class covariances (correlations between indicators) that each model becomes overdetermined so we can solve for unique values of the remaining latent parameters such as the taxonomic class base rates and the indicator valid and false positive rates. We trust these parameter estimates only if the auxiliary conjecture specifying independence between indicators within each taxometric class is inferred to be sufficiently close to the actual situation. How we make such inferences is discussed in detail below.

CLASSIFICATION OF INDIVIDUALS BY BAYES' THEOREM

When estimates of the latent parameters have been obtained taxometrically, one can then classify individuals, at least fallibly. We use Bayes' Theorem to obtain for each individual an estimate of the model-based probability that the individual is in the taxon. Suppose that a particular individual has a set of indicator scores $(\bar{x}) = (x_1, x_2, x_3, \ldots x_m)$. If each of these scores were $= 1$ (code for a positive response), then by Bayes' Theorem the probability of being in the taxon is

$$\frac{P \prod_{i=1}^{m} p_{ti}}{P \prod_{i=1}^{m} p_{ti} + Q \prod_{i=1}^{m} p_{ci}} \qquad (6)$$

We can use the model-based estimates of the parameters, P, p_{ti}, and p_{ci} in Bayes' Theorem to obtain an estimate of the probability of an individual being in the taxon. For any set of indicator values (a vector of ones and zeros) the probability of being in the taxon can be obtained from

$$p(t \mid \tilde{x}) = \frac{Pp (\tilde{x} \mid t)}{Pp (\tilde{x} \mid t) + Qp (\tilde{x} \mid c)} \qquad (7)$$

where

$$p (\tilde{x} \mid t) = \prod_{=1}^{m} P_{ti}{}^{x_i} q_{ti}{}^{1 - x_i},$$

$$p (\tilde{x} \mid c) = \prod_{=1}^{m} p_i{}^{x} q_{ci}{}^{1 - x_i}$$

$q_{ti} = 1 - p_{ti}$ and $q_{ci} = 1 - p_{ci}$ and we use estimated parameter values. For each individual we can calculate $p(t \mid \tilde{x})$ and then apply the following classification rule: If $p(t \mid \tilde{x}) \geq a$, classify as a taxon member; if $p(t \mid \tilde{x}) < a$, classify as a complement member. It can be shown that the cutting score a is set at .50 to maximize the total number of correct classifications. The use of Bayes' Theorem also requires the assumption that the indicators are independent within each taxonomic class. The error in this "probability score" caused by assumption departure depends on the robustness of the models, a matter that will be discussed below.

AN HEURISTIC METHOD

Indicators that discriminate between the two taxonomic classes and are approximately uncorrelated within each should also behave "consistently" with one another in various ways. For example, if different indicators can be used to obtain multiple estimates of some latent parameter, then these estimates should be sufficiently similar to one another. If the estimates are inconsistent, we know that (for sufficiently large samples) it is likely that one or more of the indicators do not conform to the assumptions underlying the model. Such internal consistency criteria, when used to check the assumptions of a model, can be regarded as statistical tests, christened "consistency tests" by Meehl (1965, 1968, 1973, 1978).

A series of these consistency tests can be used in a consecutive hurdle fashion; when an indicator fails a test, it is removed and not used in the remaining calculations. This series of tests comprises a taxometric method that we call the "consistency hurdles" method. The method is iterative, in that tests are repeatedly applied to the indicators, those failing a test being removed until none of the indicators remaining fail any of the tests. The computational procedures and derivations are partially described below. More mathematical details of the derivations are provided in Golden, Tyan, and Meehl (1974a), Golden and Meehl (1979), and in Meehl (1968). Here we describe in detail the first of four such tests comprising the consistency hurdles method.

Let y_i ($i = 1, 2, \ldots n$) denote a dichotomous indicator scored 1 (taxon direction) or 0 (taxon complement direction). Let x_i denote the scale or "key" formed by summing the scores from the $n - 1$ other indicators (all except indicator y_i).

$$x_i = \sum_{j \neq 1}^{n} y_j, \qquad (j \neq i) \qquad (8)$$

For each "output" indicator y_i and associated "input" scale x_i, we can create the function

$$d_i(c) = a_i(c) - b_i(c) \qquad (9)$$

where c is a score on x_i, $a_i(c)$ is the mean of the y_i scores for those individuals with scores *above* c on x_i, and $b_i(c)$ is the corresponding mean score for those individuals *below* c.

The maximum value of $d_i(c)$ over all of the c-values (the possible range is 0 to $n - 1$) tells us something about the underlying latent situation: If each pair of indicators in a set are correlated mainly because each indicator discriminates the two taxonomic classes, then a very poor choice of c should in general reduce ths statistical tendency of x_i and y_i to go together. For example, if a neurologist were dealing with the clinical diagnosis of meningitis versus nonmeningitis, and two indicators under consideration, temperature elevation and marked pain on anteroflexion of the neck, are clinical signs of meningitis, then the two signs should correlate significantly in a mixed sample of meningitic and nonmeningitic persons. But if the neurologist were so unwise as to have chosen a very low cutting point on these two indicators—such as temperature above 99.0° and any sign or complaint, however slight, of stiff neck or reluctance to flex the neck—then considerable numbers of patients without meningitis but with other milder infectious conditions, including the common cold, would show one or both of these "signs." Two untoward results would be expected; first, the correlation between the two clinical indicators would be reduced, and second, the identification of the taxonomic class of interest (meningitis) would be poorer.

Monte Carlo studies of the d_i functions for a wide variety of artificial data samples have indicated that its maximum value over all values of c must be at least .10 for the taxometric method to give sufficiently accurate results. Since in practice the estimate of this maximum value can be misleading due to sampling error, especially for samples of sizes less than 500, it is best to smooth the d_i curve by a method such as moving averages. Based upon these smoothed values, the first consistency test requires that max $[d_i(c)] \geq .10$. After the deletion of those k indicators

that fail this requirement, the x_i keys are then recalculated, using the remaining set of $n - k - 1$ indicators and the process is repeated until no items are deleted. The remaining hurdles of the method consist of checking that the indicators, when used in the output role, produce consistent estimates of the hitmax cut on the input scale, are sufficiently discriminating between the taxon and complement, and produce sufficiently consistent estimates of the taxonomic class base rates. The indicator positive rates for the taxon and the complement (i.e., the valid positive and valid negative rates, respectively) can be estimated by the use of the tails of the distribution on the input scale. That is, the method provides an estimate of the taxon base rate and the valid and false positive rates for each of the remaining indicators. The above description of the method is very brief; for a more complete description see Golden and Meehl (1979).

If the results of these consistency tests lead to acceptance of the latent model as an adequate approximation of the state of nature, then Bayes' Theorem can be used to calculate the probability of each individual's belonging to the taxon.

An empirical test in which the MMPI items previously described were used to identify the sexes suggests how well the method can work with real data. For example, the method was applied to the total 75 items (the toughest test used in testing the cluster methods) for a sample consisting of 100 males and 100 females. The estimates of the indicator taxonomic class positive rates and the male and female base rate estimates for the nine items selected by the method are presented in Table 5.1. As one can see, even with a sample of this small size the item positive rates were estimated quite accurately, as was the base rate (.54 vs. .50). The results of other such trials of this method are given in Golden and Meehl (1979) along with the results of applying this method to the schizoid taxon problem.

Table 5.1. The Estimates of the Male and Female Indicator Positive Rates and the Female Base Rate for 75-Item Male-Female Trial of the Consistency Hurdles Method ($N = 200$)

Item	Males			Females			Estimate of female base rate
	Estimate	True value	Error	Estimate	True value	Error	
1	.05	.08	−.03	.66	.64	.02	.53
2	.09	.10	−.01	.37	.30	.07	.57
3	.41	.50	−.09	.87	.90	−.03	.55
4	.42	.44	−.02	.84	.74	.10	.46
5	.46	.40	.06	.91	.84	.07	.48
6	.25	.36	−.11	.87	.78	.09	.54
7	.05	.14	−.09	.54	.52	.02	.56
8	.08	.08	.00	.47	.38	.09	.55
9	.30	.36	−.06	.80	.84	−.04	.57
Average							.54
True value							.50

THE MAXCOV-HITMAX MODEL

This model requires the use of three or more "graded" indicators rather than several dichotomous indicators. The indicators may be, for example, MMPI "keys" or scales formed by summing 20 or so MMPI items, each scored 1 and 0 as done previously.

We conjecture that we have a set of three or more indicator-scales, each of which has some validity for discriminating between the two taxonomic-classes, but which are uncorrelated with one another within each taxonomic-class. We need not make further assumptions that the frequency distribution for each indicator is unimodal within taxonomic-class, nor do we need further assumptions regarding the distributions, such as normality, symmetry, homogeneity of variance, or the like.

We will use the following notation.

W, X, Y: indicators and associated random variables

N: compound sample size

w_0: an arbitrary but fixed interval of indicator W

P: base rate of the taxon

$Q = 1 - P$: base rate of the complement

$p(w_0)$: proportion of those in the w_0 interval who are in the taxon

$\mu(X)$: compound population mean for indicator X

$\mu_t(X)$: taxon population mean for indicator X

$\mu_c(X)$: complement population mean for indicator X

$\sigma^2(X)$: compound population variance for indicator X

$\sigma_t^2(X)$: taxon population variance for indicator X

$\sigma_c^2(X)$: complement population variance for indicator X

$\sigma(X,Y)$: compound covariance for indicators X and Y

$\sigma_t(X,Y)$: taxon covariance for indicators X and Y

$\sigma_c(X,Y)$: complement covariance for indicators X and Y

$\sigma(X,Y/w_0)$: compound population covariance for indicators X and Y for subpopulation where $W = w_0$

$\sigma_t(X,Y/w_0)$: taxon population covariance for indicators X and Y for subpopulation where $W = w_0$

$\sigma_c(X,Y/w_0)$: complement population covariance for indicators X and Y for subpopulation where $W = w_0$

A carat above any of these parameters will be used to denote an estimate of the parameter.

Let W, X, and Y be three such indicator-scales, so that W is the "input" indicator and X and Y are the "output" indicators. The (latent) taxonomic class distributions on the input indicator are estimated by using manifest relationships between the two output variables.

As before, the input-output terminology is used merely to describe statistical procedures; nothing about causal relationships is implied. The taxon is the taxonic class with the higher scores on each of the input indicators and the complement class is that with the lower scores.

The covariance between X and Y for any interval w_o of indicator W is

$$\sigma(X,Y/w_o) = \\ p(w_o)\sigma_t(X,Y/w_o) + q(w_o)\sigma_c(X,Y/w_o) \quad (10) \\ + p(w_o)q(w_o)v(X/w_o)v(Y/w_o),$$

where $p(w_o)$ is the proportion of individuals in w_o interval that are members of the taxon, $q(w_o)$ is the corresponding complement proportion, so that $p(w_o) + q(w_o) = 1$, $\sigma_t(X,Y/w_o)$ is the latent covariance between X and Y for the taxon in interval w_o, $\sigma_c(X,Y/w_o)$ is the corresponding complement covariance, $v(X/w_o)$ is the mean on X for the taxon less that for the complement in interval w_o, and $v(Y/w_o)$ is the corresponding mean difference on Y. Letter v is chosen for "[crude] latent *validity*."

Earlier in this chapter we showed that a procedure for estimating the latent parameters can be derived from the following assumptions:

$$A_1: \sigma_t(X,Y/w_o) = \sigma_c(X,Y/w_o) = 0 \quad (11)$$

for each w_o interval

$$A_2: \sigma_t(X,Y) = \sigma_c(X,Y) = 0 \quad (12)$$

We studied by Monte Carlo method the robustness and accuracy of the MAXCOV-HITMAX model with respect to these assumptions. Artificial data were generated to produce multivariate normal distributions within each of the two taxonomic classes, because data of this kind are easily generated and can serve the purpose of an exploratory Monte Carlo study (for method see Golden et al. 1974c). Certain parameters of the latent situation were fixed because of constraints and cost. For each of the artificial data samples three indicators were used in the three different input-output role combinations. The values of the indicator taxonomic class means and standard deviations were assigned the same values for each of the three indicators, and each artificial number was rounded off to the nearest integer. For each set of latent parameter values (taxonic base rates, means, and sigmas on each indicator) 25 independent random samples were generated, and each was analyzed by the MAXCOV-HITMAX method.

To generate an artificial sample we specified: (1) the parameters of the multivariate normal distribution for the population taxon and complement; and (2) the taxonic base rates. The parameters of a multivariate normal distribution are the three indicator means and standard deviations and the $\binom{3}{2} = 3$ covariances or correlations between the indicators taken pairwise (Lindgren, 1962). The MAXCOV-HITMAX method is based on the assumption that these correlations are zero for each taxonomic class, and we can test the method for robustness with respect to this assumption by assigning nonzero values to these population correlations.

The various sets of parameter values are described in Table 5.2 (by columns labeled N, P, μ_c, μ_t, σ_c and σ_t). Twenty-five random samples were generated for each of the 24 latent conditions. In summarizing the results of applying the MAXCOV method to the 24 $\times$ 25 = 600 random samples, parameter estimates were regarded as accurate enough

Table 5.2. Population Parameter Values for the Monte Carlo Trials of the MAXCOV-HITMAX Method

Set	Variable	N	P	μ_c	μ_t	σ_c	σ_t	v	σ_t/σ_c	ρ		#F
1.1	N	1000	.5	8	12	2	2	2	1	0	*	0
1.2		800	.5	8	12	2	2	2	1	0	*	0
1.3		600	.5	8	12	2	2	2	1	0	*	0
1.4		400	.5	8	12	2	2	2	1	0	*	0
2.1	P	1000	.6	8	12	2	2	2	1	0	*	3
2.2		1000	.7	8	12	2	2	2	1	0	*	2
2.3		1000	.8	8	12	2	2	2	1	0	*	8
2.4		1000	.9	8	12	2	2	2	1	0		0
3.1	v	1000	.5	9	12	2	2	1.5	1	0	*	0
3.2		1000	.5	10	12	2	2	1	1	0	*	15
3.3		1000	.5	11	12	2	2	.5	1	0		0
3.4		1000	.5	12	12	2	2	0	1	0		0
4.1	σ_t/σ_c	1000	.5	8	12	1.9	2.1	2	1.1	0	*	0
4.2		1000	.5	8	12	1.7	2.3	2	1.3	0	*	0
4.3		1000	.5	8	12	1.5	2.5	2	1.7	0	*	0
4.4		1000	.5	8	12	1	3	2	3	0		0
5.1	p	1000	.5	8	12	2	2	2	1	.1	*	0
5.2		1000	.5	8	12	2	2	2	1	.3	*	0
5.3		1000	.5	8	12	2	2	2	1	.5	*	8
5.4		1000	.5	8	12	2	2	2	1	.8	*	0
										ρ_c/ρ_t		
6.1	N	1000	.8	8	12	2	2	2	1	.5/.125		0
6.2	$\rho_c/\rho_t = 4$	800	.8	8	12	2	2	2	1	.5/.125		0
6.3		600	.8	8	12	2	2	2	1	.5/.125		0
6.4		400	.8	8	12	2	2	2	1	.5/.125		0

KEY

N: sample size

P: base rate of the taxon

μ_t: mean of the taxon on each indicator

μ_c: mean of the taxon complement on each indicator

σ_t: standard deviation of the taxon on each indicator

σ_c: standard deviation of the complement on each indicator

v: $(\mu_t - \mu_c)/\sigma$ where $\sigma = (\sigma_t + \sigma_c)/2$

ρ: correlation between indicators within the taxon and the complement

*: parameter estimates are always or nearly always accurate

#F: number of failures of consistency tests in 25 samples

for our research purposes if the base rate and hit rate estimates were within .10 of the true (latent) values, and if the taxonomic class mean and sigma estimates were within one interval (usually about ½ of a taxonomic class standard deviation) of the true values.

We now describe the results. First, different sample sizes (N) of 1000, 800, 600, 400, for $\sigma_c^2 = \sigma_t^2 = \sigma^2$, a difference between the taxonomic class means of 2σ, $P = .5$, and zero taxonomic class correlations, each gave average errors of .01 (2%) in the estimation of P, and less than $\sigma/4$ (½ of an indicator interval) in the estimation of the taxonomic class means and standard deviations. Second, different base rates of .6, .7, .8, and .9 for $N = 1000$, $\sigma_t = \sigma_c$, taxonomic class mean separations of 2σ, and zero taxonomic class correlations, gave corresponding average errors of .03, .04, .02, and .60 in the estimation of the base rate and average errors of less than $3\,\sigma/8$, $\sigma/2$, σ, and $3\sigma/2$ in the estimation of the taxonomic class means and standard deviations. Third, different taxonomic class mean separations of $3\sigma/2$, σ, and $\sigma/2$, for $N = 1000$, $\sigma_t = \sigma_c$, $P = .5$ and zero taxonomic class correlations, gave average errors of .01 in the estimation of P and less than $\sigma/4$ in the estimation of the taxonomic class means and standard deviations. Fourth, different standard deviation ratios (σ_t/σ_c) of 11/10, 4/3, 5/3, and 3 for $N = 1000$, taxonomic class mean separations of $\tfrac{1}{2}(\sigma_t + \sigma_c)$, $P = .5$ and zero taxonomic class correlations, gave average errors of .02, .03, .08, and .14 in the estimation of P and average errors less than $\sigma/4$, $\sigma/4$, $\sigma/4$, $\sigma/2$ in the estimation of the taxonomic class means and standard deviations. Fifth, different taxonomic class correlations of .1, .3, .5, and .8 for $N = 1000$, taxonomic class mean separations of 2σ, $\sigma_t = \sigma_c = \sigma$, and $P = .5$ gave average errors of .01 in the estimation of P and $\sigma/4$, $\sigma/4$, $\sigma/2$, and σ, in the estimation of the taxonomic class means and standard deviations.

To summarize, the MAXCOV-HITMAX model requires the following conditions in order to provide base rates accurate to within .10 and taxonomic class means and standard deviations accurate to within $\sigma/2$ (an indicator interval):

1. Base rates not disproportionate more than (.2/.8).
2. Separation of means $\geq \sigma$.
3. Standard deviation ratio < 1.7.
4. Taxonomic class correlations $\leq .5$.
5. The difference between the two corresponding taxonomic class correlations $< .4$.

We developed four consistency tests for checking the auxiliary conjectures of the MAXCOV model. This is the analytical basis of one of these tests:

The covariance mixture formula when applied to the taxon and the complement is

$$\sigma(X,Y) = P\,\sigma_t(X,Y) + Q\sigma_c(X,Y) \\ + PQ\,v(X)\,v(Y) \quad (13)$$

where $\sigma(X,Y) =$ manifest covariance for the mixed or compound population

$\sigma_t(X,Y) =$ latent covariance for the taxon

$\sigma_c(X,Y) =$ latent covariance for the complement

$P,Q =$ base rates of taxon and complement

$v(X) =$ difference in means of taxon and complement on indicator x

$v(Y) =$ difference in means of taxon and complement on indicator y

If the assumptions of the model were perfectly met, then $\sigma_t(X,Y) = \sigma_c(X,Y) = 0$ and $\sigma(X,Y) - PQ\,v(X)\,v(Y) = 0$.

We next confront the question "What are the tolerance limits for the quantity $\hat{\sigma}(X,Y) - \hat{P}\,\hat{Q}\,\hat{v}(X)\,\hat{v}(Y)$?" The carat denotes a model-based parameter estimate. The parameter estimates are erroneous because of sampling error and departure from the model assumptions.

Consider the population parameter

$$T = \sigma(X,Y) - PQ\,v(X)\,v(Y) \quad (14)$$

which can be also written as

$$T = P\sigma_t(X,Y) + Q\sigma_c(X,Y) \quad (15)$$

Since the taxonomic class covariances are generally positive, T is generally positive. It will be useful to consider the differential of T, which is

$$dT = \frac{\partial T}{\partial \sigma(x,y)} d\sigma(x,y) + \frac{\partial T}{\partial P} dP$$

$$+ \frac{\partial T}{\partial v(x)} dv(x) + \frac{\partial T}{\partial v(y)} dv(y) \quad (16)$$

We can interpret this result by considering $d\sigma(X,Y)$ as the error in $\hat{\sigma}(X,Y)$ due to sampling, dP as the error in $\hat{P}$ due to sampling and assumption departure, and likewise for $d\,v(X)$ and $d\,v(Y)$. It follows then that $dT = \hat{T} - T$ is the resulting or propagated error in T caused by those errors in $\hat{\sigma}(X,Y)$, $\hat{P}$, $\hat{v}(X)$ and $\hat{v}(Y)$. The above equation for the differential of T is approximately true for small errors, the approximation being better the smaller the errors. The partial derivatives obtained by differentiation of the above covariance mixture equation are

$$\frac{\partial T}{\partial \sigma(X,Y)} = 1 \quad (17)$$

$$\frac{\partial T}{\partial P} = (2\,P - 1)\,v(X)\,v(Y) \quad (18)$$

$$\frac{\partial T}{\partial v(X)} = -PQ\,v(Y) \quad (19)$$

$$\frac{\delta T}{\partial v(Y)} = -PQ\,v(X) \quad (20)$$

Substituting parameter estimates into the expressions for these partial derivatives gives

$$\hat{T} \simeq \hat{\sigma}(X,Y) - \sigma(X,Y) +$$
$$(2\,\hat{P} - 1)\,\hat{v}(X)\hat{v}(Y)(\hat{P} - P) - \quad (21)$$
$$\hat{P}\hat{Q}\,\hat{v}(Y)(\hat{v}(X) - v(X)) -$$
$$\hat{P}\hat{Q}\hat{v}(X)(\hat{v}(Y) - v(Y))$$

We can proceed by specifying an upper limit for the absolute value of the difference in the estimate and actual value for each of

$$\sigma(X,Y),\ P,\ v(X),\ \text{and}\ v(Y).$$

Specifically, let us require that

(a) $|\hat{P} - P| \leq .10$

(b) $|\hat{v}(X) \quad - v(X)| \leq \frac{1}{2}\,\sigma_d(X) \quad (22)$

(c) $|\hat{v}(Y) \quad - v(Y)| \leq \frac{1}{2}\,\sigma_d(Y)$

(where $\sigma_a(X) = \frac{1}{2}(\sigma_t(X) + \sigma_c(X))$ and $\sigma_a(Y) = \frac{1}{2}(\sigma_t(Y) + \sigma_c(Y))$).

Finally, it is very likely that

(d) $|\hat{\sigma}(X,Y) - \sigma(X,Y)|$
$$\leq \frac{4\,\sigma(X)\,\sigma(Y)}{\sqrt{N}} \quad (23)$$

Since the MAXCOV-HITMAX method usually produces taxonomic class standard deviation estimates that tend to be too large, we have

$$|\hat{T}| \leq \frac{4\,\hat{\sigma}(X)\,\hat{\sigma}(Y)}{\sqrt{N}} + |\,2P$$
$$- 1\,|\,\hat{v}(X)\,\hat{v}(Y)\,(.10) \quad (24)$$
$$+ \hat{P}\hat{Q}\,\hat{v}(Y)(\frac{1}{2}\,\hat{\sigma}_d(X))$$
$$+ \hat{P}\hat{Q}\,\hat{v}(X)(\frac{1}{2}\,\hat{\sigma}_d(Y))$$

as our final result. The consistency test now is to compare the quantity

$$|\hat{T}| = |\hat{\sigma}(X,Y) - \hat{P}\hat{Q}\,\hat{v}(X)\,\hat{v}(Y)| \quad (25)$$

with the limit given in the above inequality. If the inequality is satisfied, the test is passed by our data set; if not, it is failed. This consistency test turns out to be a sensitive detector of situations in which the intrataxonomic class correlations are too large and result in inaccurate parameter estimates (sets 5 and 6 of Table 5.2). This sensitivity of the test is reasonable, since its derivation rests squarely on the assumption that these correlations are zero.

In a similar manner we developed three other tests designed to detect other kinds of assumption departure (Golden, Tyan, Meehl, 1974b).

The most significant result of the Monte

Table 5.3. Summary of Consistency Test Results for Monte Carlo Study of the MAXCOV-HITMAX Method

		Consistency test "advice"		
		Accept sample	Reject sample	
Sample's actual properties	Accurate	336	36	372
	Inaccurate	0	228	228
		336	264	600

Proportion of samples that were correctly accepted or rejected = .94

Carlo study was that every sample that produced inadequate parameter estimates failed at least one of the four consistency tests and was therefore detectable as untrustworthy (see Table 5.3). Only in set 3.2, where the separation between the taxonic means was small (σ), were the parameter estimates acceptable and incorrectly rejected. But these samples produced only marginally acceptable parameter estimates. So the consistency tests worked nearly perfectly for these artificial data samples. The few instances (6%) in which the consistency tests failed were "conservative" in that accurate results were needlessly rejected.

EMPIRICAL TRIAL OF THE MAXCOV-HITMAX MODEL

The MAXCOV-HITMAX method was also subjected to an empirical trial of detecting the biological sexes with MMPI keys (Golden et al., 1973). Three keys of 20 items each were constructed from the 60 most discriminating items (no "garbage" items were included) selected as described previously.

The actual and estimated male and female taxa indicator distributions and the corresponding descriptive statistics for each of the three arrangements of the indicators are given in Table 5.4. That the parameter estimates are accurate enough for most research in the

area of psychopathology measurement is clear simply by inspection. Usual tests of significance for comparing the actual and estimated frequency distributions are of no interest.

Inspection of Table 5.4 also shows the actual (sample) hitmax intervals for keys 1, 2, and 3 to be 12, 9, and 10 respectively. The corresponding maximum covariances occur in intervals 12, 9, and 10, which are in perfect agreement with the true sample values.

The predicted sex can be compared with the actual sex in terms of a hits-misses table. The proportion of "female" predictions that were correct was .90, the corresponding "male" hit rate was .81, and the overall hit rate was .86. Such a hit rate must surely be pushing the maximum theoretically possible with the MMPI item pool.

In order to evaluate the accuracy of the prediction of biological sex by the MAX-COV-HITMAX model, several methods of prediction of biological sex as a *dependent (criterion) variable* with the indicator variables as the independent variables were tried. None of these methods, including Fisher's linear discriminant function, did significantly better than the MAXCOV method in that the overall hit rate never exceeded .91.

THE NORMAL MODEL

We now develop a taxometric model based on the auxiliary conjecture that the indicator distributions are normal within each taxonomic class. When the MAXCOV-HITMAX and the normal models were first developed, little consideration was given to the relative merits of two basic assumptions, those of zero overall and conditional covariance within taxonomic class and of normality within taxonomic class. The different starting points were chosen mainly because of the resulting mathematical tractability. However, it turns out, as we shall see, that the two models can be developed from the same

Table 5.4. The Actual and MAXCOV Estimated Taxa Frequency Distributions for Each Key ($N = 1105$)

	Key 1				Key 2				Key 3			
	Male		Female		Male		Female		Male		Female	
Score	Actual	Estimated	Actual	Estimated	Actual	Estimated	Actual	Estimated	Actual	Estimated	Actual	Estimated
1	0	0	0	0	1	1	0	0	0	0	0	0
2	0	0	0	0	7	7	0	0	4	4	0	0
3	3	3	0	0	13	9	0	4	3	3	0	0
4	11	10	0	1	33	26	3	10	12	11	0	1
5	8	7	0	1	48	36	3	15	26	24	2	4
6	32	34	3	1	63	44	13	32	54	53	3	4
7	41	39	5	7	67	61	17	23	53	60	8	1
8	50	46	9	13	62	59	27	30	57	64	16	9
9	58	66	20	12	59	59	59	59	71	92	27	6
10	60	71	30	19	36	29	87	94	46	58	69	57
11	65	76	27	16	22	52	110	80	43	13	83	113
12	53	58	62	57	11	26	97	82	31	22	91	100
13	29	8	93	114	6	32	91	65	17	14	93	96
14	10	15	110	105	1	18	83	66	9	23	109	95
15	7	18	103	92	0	5	51	46	4	4	71	71
16	2	13	107	96	1	10	26	17	0	3	56	53
17	1	3	61	59	0	1	5	4	0	0	27	27
18	0	2	28	26	0	0	2	2	0	0	15	15
19	0	2	14	12	0	0	1	1	0	0	5	5
20	0	0	3	3	0	0	0	0	0	0	0	0
Base rate	.389	.426	.611	.574	.389	.430	.611	.570	.389	.405	.611	.595
Mean	9.57	9.94	14.10	14.12	7.31	8.66	11.68	10.97	8.60	8.61	12.84	12.95
SD	2.55	2.84	2.56	2.50	2.42	3.17	2.47	2.94	2.57	2.62	2.53	2.40

general assumption. When indicator keys consist of summed MMPI items, it is sometimes reasonable to assume normality within taxonomic class because of the generalized version of the central limit theorem (Von Mises, 1964, p. 302). This theorem states that the distribution of the sum of many different independent Bernoulli variables with virtually any set of values for their means approximates a normal distribution. It follows then that independence between the items or any kind of dichotomous components of the indicator scales within each of the taxonomic classes is a sufficient assumption for both the normal and MAXCOV-HITMAX models.

Whereas the MAXCOV-HITMAX model discussed in the last section requires that there be only two taxonomic classes, the normal model is easily generalized to any number of taxonomic classes. The model was developed first for use with just one indicator (Meehl, 1968) but it was later generalized for any number of indicators (Golden, Tyan, & Meehl, 1974).

One method of solving for the parameter estimates is by trial and error. The procedure for this kind of numerical solution for the single indicator dichotomous taxonomy case is extremely simple. Considering the three taxonomic class distribution parameters required on the normality assumption (i.e., the base rate, mean and standard deviation), we choose a triplet of these values (P, μ_t, σ_t) for the taxon. If we have a sufficiently large sample, then the manifest sample values determine the corresponding parameters (Q, μ_c, σ_c) for the complement. The procedure therefore consists of assigning arbitrary (sliding) values to the base rates $P, Q, (Q = 1 - P)$, then to the latent means, μ_t, μ_c, and finally to the latent standard deviations σ_t, σ_c. This logical tree terminates in predicted resultant values for the observed (mixed) frequency distribution. We then compute a chi-square on the discrepancy between the predicted and observed frequencies. It serves first as a significance test (testing departure

from the postulated latent model-cum-parameter values) but also, more importantly, as a rough measure of the poorness of our approximation. See Meehl et al. (1969) and Golden and Meehl (1973a) for empirical trials of this numerical method. Suffice it to say here that the method generally provided estimates comparable in accuracy to those of the MAXCOV-HITMAX model in the detection of the biological sex taxonomy with MMPI indicator scales.

It has been shown that the maximum-likelihood method and the minimum chi-square method produce the same results for large enough samples (Cramér, 1946). However, the maximum-likelihood method requires much less calculation. An outline of the calculations for the maximum likelihood solution is given below; the interested reader is referred to the original article by Hasselblad (1966) for further analytical development.

Suppose that there are n taxonomic classes denoted by the subscript j with distributions on an indicator X and the taxonomic class means, variances, and base rates denoted by $\mu_j, \sigma_j,$ and p_j ($\sum_{j=1}^{n} p_j = 1$). Let X be divided into N intervals denoted by the subscript i so that the interval width is small compared to each σ_j. We assume that the density of the jth taxonomic class in the ith interval, represented by q_{ij}, is approximated by

$$q_{ij} = \frac{1}{\sqrt{2\pi}\,\sigma_j} \exp\left[\frac{-(x_i - \mu_j)^2}{2\sigma_j^2}\right] \quad (26)$$

Let Q_i be the compound density for the ith interval so that

$$Q_i = \sum_{j=1}^{n} q_{ij}p_j \quad (27)$$

Hasselblad (1966) has shown that the maximum-likelihood estimates of the unknown latent parameters can be found by the steepest descent iterative procedure. The only required manifest parameter values are the compound sample distribution interval frequencies f_i, $i = 1,2,3, \ldots , N$. The procedure results in the following equations:

$$\mu_j = [\sum_{i=1}^{N} (f_i/Q_i)q_{ij}x_i]/d_j \quad (28)$$

$$\sigma_j^2 = [\sum_{i=1}^{N} (f_i/Q_i)(x_i - \mu_j)^2]/d_j \quad (29)$$

$$p_j = [\sum_{i=1}^{N} (f_iq_{ij}p_j/Q_i)]/N \quad (30)$$

where

$$d_j = \sum_{i=1}^{N} (f_i/Q_i)q_{ij}$$

The iterative procedure begins with initial guesses of μ_j, σ_j, and P_j. It has not been analytically determined how accurate the initial guesses must be, or whether convergence to the true values will necessarily obtain. However, several empirical trials have been encouraging with regard to both matters. The initial guesses can be obtained by a method that makes use of probability paper (Harding, 1949), but subsequent study has indicated that reasonable estimates will suffice for most detectable taxonic situations. Each of the three MMPI keys used for the trial of the MAXCOV model was analyzed. The results are given in Tables 5.5 and 5.6. It is seen that the single indicator normal method gave accurate parameter estimates on the second and third keys after just 100 iterations, and it was about at this point that the series of estimates showed convergence. However, for the first key, the base rate estimate is only marginally acceptable, especially after the process had been continued until convergence was apparent. The exact significance of the larger number of iterations required for apparent convergence is not known; however, the result is illustrative of a general finding from trials of the method that when several hundred iterations are re-

quired for convergence, it is an indication the results may not be accurate. We see from Table 5.6 that the chi-square poorness-of-fit values (comparing the estimated and the observed compound sample frequency distributions) do not approach significance for the three keys.

An obvious consistency test for the normal model compares the estimated compound distribution with the observed. The chi-square measures discrepancies between frequencies and is a statistic providing a significance test. But here we do not ask whether the chi-square exceeds a critical value for statistical significance. Rather we ask whether it exceeds some "practical" value that casts doubt that accurate parameter estimation and nonspurious taxon detection obtain. We have found that such a critical value for the chi-square parameter does not seem to exist.

Many of the consistency tests suggested for the MAXCOV-HITMAX model can be used with the normal model. Several other tests flowing directly from the normality assumption are possible.

One such test rests on the fact that the sum of two or more normally distributed variables is also normally distributed. Suppose we have two indicators X and Y and use the method with each and with a third indicator formed from the sum of the indicators. The base rate estimates should be the same when the indicators are used singly as when used as a sum. The mean and variance of the sum of indicators within each taxonomic class are given by

$$\mu_t(X + Y) = \mu_t(X) + \mu_t(Y) \quad (31)$$

$$\mu_c(X + Y) = \mu_c(X) + \mu_c(Y) \quad (32)$$

$$\sigma_t^2(X + Y) = \sigma_t^2(X) + \sigma_t^2(Y) + 2\sigma_t(X,Y) \quad (33)$$

and

$$\sigma_c^2(X + Y) = \sigma_c^2(X) + \sigma_c^2(Y) + 2\sigma_c(X,Y) \quad (34)$$

Table 5.5. The Actual and the Normal Model* Estimated Frequency Distributions for Each Key for Male and Female (N = 1105)

	Key 1				Key 2				Key 3			
	Male		Female		Male		Female		Male		Female	
Score	Actual	Estimated	Actual	Estimated	Actual	Estimated	Actual	Estimated	Actual	Estimated	Actual	Estimated
1	0	0	0	0	1	3	0	0	0	0	0	0
2	0	0	0	0	7	7	0	0	4	4	0	0
3	3	4	0	0	13	17	0	0	3	7	0	0
4	11	7	0	0	33	32	3	1	12	16	0	0
5	8	16	0	0	48	52	3	4	26	29	2	1
6	32	29	3	1	63	70	13	11	54	44	3	2
7	41	45	5	5	67	78	17	25	53	59	8	6
8	50	57	9	13	62	72	27	48	57	66	16	15
9	58	61	20	29	59	56	59	77	71	64	27	31
10	60	54	30	56	36	35	87	102	46	53	69	53
11	65	39	27	89	22	19	110	112	43	37	83	79
12	53	24	62	118	11	8	97	102	31	22	91	100
13	29	12	93	129	6	3	91	77	17	12	93	100
14	10	5	110	118	1	1	83	48	9	5	109	100
15	7	2	103	89	0	0	51	25	4	2	71	79
16	2	1	107	56	1	0	26	11	0	1	56	53
17	1	0	61	29	0	0	5	4	0	0	27	31
18	0	0	28	13	0	0	2	1	0	0	15	15
19	0	0	14	5	0	0	1	0	0	0	5	6
20	0	0	3		0	0	0	0	0	0	0	0
Base rate	.389	.322	.611	.679	.389	.410	.611	.586	.389	.381	.611	.614
Mean	9.57	8.83	14.10	13.99	7.31	7.09	11.68	11.90	8.60	8.24	12.84	12.97
SD	2.55	2.33	2.56	2.29	2.42	2.30	2.47	2.41	2.57	2.48	2.53	2.48

*Minimum chi-square solution used.

Table 5.6. Examples of Empirical Trials of the Normal Model* Using MMPI Keys to Identify the Sexes

	$\hat{P}_m$	$\hat{\mu}_m$	$\hat{\sigma}_m$	$\hat{P}_f$	$\hat{\mu}_f$	$\hat{\sigma}_f$	X''
First Key (N = 1105)							
Initial guess	.500	6.00	3.00	.500	13.00	3.00	
No. of iterations							
50	.417	9.45	2.50	.582	14.40	2.16	14.89
100	.449	9.66	2.58	.551	14.51	2.12	14.58
200	.483	9.88	2.67	.516	14.64	2.07	14.37
300	.499	9.98	2.71	.501	14.69	2.05	14.33
True sample value	.389	9.57	2.55	.611	14.10	2.56	
Error	.110	.41	.16	−.110	.59	−.51	
Second Key (N = 1105)							
Initial guess	.500	6.00	3.00	.500	13.00	3.00	
No. of iterations							
10	.428	7.33	2.36	.572	11.95	2.27	13.34
50	.411	7.24	2.32	.589	11.89	2.29	13.28
100	.368	6.98	2.23	.632	11.72	2.35	13.18
True sample value	.389	7.31	2.42	.611	11.68	2.47	
Error	.021	−.33	−.19	.021	.04	−.12	
Third Key (N = 1105)							
Initial guess	.500	6.00	3.00	.500	13.00	3.00	
No. of iterations							
10	.418	8.64	2.54	.582	13.02	2.42	15.25
50	.418	8.59	2.48	.582	13.06	2.38	14.92
100	.416	8.58	2.48	.584	13.06	2.38	14.92
200	.409	8.54	2.46	.591	13.03	2.40	14.91
True sample value	.389	8.60	2.57	.611	12.84	2.53	
Error	.020	−.06	−.11	−.020	.19	−.13	

*Maximum-likelihood solution used.

where $\sigma(X,Y)$ is the intrataxonic covariance for the pair of indicator keys. We see then that when two indicators are summed, the single intrataxonic-class covariance between the two indicators can be estimated from the above equation. If both indicators are made up of, for example, MMPI items randomly assigned to each, then this covariance estimate should be sufficiently close to zero.

THE BOOTSTRAP PROCESS

We have repeatedly urged that successively improving the agreement of the model to the data should be one of the fundamental aims of taxometrics. If many bootstrap steps or iterations are required, care must be taken that excessive "psychometric drift" (Loevinger, 1957) does not occur. Through many iterations, the shared content of the set of indicators may change substantially, especially if only a few are found to fit the assumptions of the model. Consistency tests cannot ensure against "convergence" in a *pseudo*-bootstrap sequence resulting in erroneous inferences. It may seem that one has successfully used a bootstraps procedure when in fact there is decreased verisimilitude due to psychometric drift. The convergence is to the wrong latent situation, or at least to one further from the correct latent situation than obtained at an earlier stage of the process. Since this conceptual danger exists in taxometric bootstrapsing, as in *all* empirical inference to latent causal entities, we look for ways to corroborate the desired increase in verisimilitude. We have used the following multiple criteria:

1. Select indicators with clinical or face validity.
2. Further select those that are positively correlated in the mixed sample.
3. Delete or combine indicators that are inferred to be highly correlated within a taxonomic class. If a pair of indicators is highly correlated in this way, then one of the indicators should be deleted, or possibly, if it is substantively desirable, the two indicators should be combined to form a single indicator.
4. Delete the indicators that do not discriminate sufficiently between the taxonomic classes.
5. Check the parameters for reasonableness with regard to considerations such as the following:
   a. Rank order of indicators in terms of validity.
   b. Size of P compared to previous research and to clinical experience.
   c. Indicators with a low false positive rate.
   d. Indicators with a high valid positive rate.
6. Repeat the analysis with the modified indicator set if criteria (3), (4), or (5) are not met.

DETECTION OF THE SCHIZOID TAXON

In a pilot study (Golden & Meehl, 1979) MMPI items were selected as candidate indicators of schizoidia. Items were required to discriminate between schizophrenics and normals, the hypothesis being that such items have better average potential to discriminate between schizoids and nonschizoids than items nonvalid against formal diagnosis. Fifty-three items discriminated between 96

diagnosed schizophrenics and the Minnesota normal sample by a difference of at least .20.

Next we required that the item not be highly correlated with decompensation-related variables, such as severity of illness. This requirement should reduce selection of items highly correlated with each other within the schizoid group mainly through underlying decompensation-related variables. We also wanted items that do not discriminate appreciably among other diagnostic classes (e.g., psychotics vs. neurotics), but were able only to require that an item not discriminate highly among diagnosed subtypes of schizophrenia, or among those other psychoses for which we had samples of sufficient size. These "negative" requirements, aimed to minimize nuisance covariance (Meehl 1972b, pp. 160–174), were failed by 20 of the 53 previously selected items, leaving 33 items for further analysis.

The sample used consisted of 211 male inpatients at the University of Minnesota Hospital who had been diagnosed as having a neurosis, personality disorder, or transient situational disorder. No diagnosed schizophrenics, patients with other psychotic diagnoses, or brain syndromes were included in this sample, so as to reduce the probability of detecting taxonomic classes other than the one of interest.

When the consistency hurdles method was applied to this sample, using the 33 selected MMPI items, it deleted all but seven items. The taxon base rate was estimated to be .37. Applying Bayes' Theorem to the estimated valid and false positive rates and base rate, individuals were classified as either schizoid or not. The Bayes' probabilities tended to be close to zero or one, a result that previous Monte Carlo analyses have shown to indicate a real taxonomy.

If one method correctly classifies a proportion p_1 (a quantity we don't know in practice) of the total mixed sample, while a second method does so with a proportion p_2, and if the two methods make *independent* errors of classification, then the proportion of classifications for which the two methods agree is $p_1 p_2 + (1 - p_1)(1 - p_2)$. For example, if $p_1 = p_2 = .80$, then the agreement rate would be .68. An estimate of the correct classification rate, p, for a single set of indicators can be obtained by a method developed in Golden and Meehl (1974, 1979). For each individual, we use Bayes' Theorem to calculate the probability of being schizoid and that of being nonschizoid, and select the larger of these two values. It can be shown that an estimate of the overall correct classification is the average of the larger of these two probability values across all individuals. The model-based, estimated correct classification rate for each of the two sets of items was found to be about .85, which is quite high. The estimated agreement rate between the two classifications should then be about $(.85 \times .85) + (.15 \times .15) = .75$, close to the observed value of .70; so the concordance shows satisfactory agreement with what the separate classification estimates would have predicted.

The MMPI item data were also analyzed by the MAXCOV-HITMAX and normal methods (described earlier). Each of these taxometric methods was used to detect the schizoid taxon, but with different sets of MMPI items than the above.

Three scales were constructed from the 113 items that discriminated between the detected taxonomic classes of "schizoids" and "nonschizoids" by a difference of .20 or more. Factor analysis (Varimax rotation) of the 113 items in the total mixed sample (N = 211) suggested three factors; the 20 highest loading items for each factor were selected to form the three scales. When these three keys were used with the MAXCOV method, the taxon detected had a base rate estimate of .40, which agrees well with that of the first method. The MAXCOV method also includes consistency tests that help avoid being misled by inaccurate parameter estimates, and Monte Carlo study indicates that these work quite well (Golden & Meehl, 1973b). The passage of these tests provides

additional support that the detected taxon is not spurious.

Factor analysis of the 13 standard MMPI scale scores in the total sample ($N = 211$) produced a Varimax factor that accounted for 41% of the common variance and correlated highly with the Psychasthenia (.69), Schizophrenia (.53), Depression (.61), and Social Introversion (.79) scales; all other loadings were below .30, except for K ($-.43$). The items in these four scales were combined to make a long scale that was used as the single indicator. The schizoid taxon base rate was estimated by the Normal method to be .41, again in excellent agreement with previous estimates. The chi-square value of 2.3 was nonsignificant and below even the value expected if the assumptions of the method were perfectly satisfied. The difference between the two taxonomic class means on this indicator was estimated to be about two class standard deviations. Since this is about the same degree of separation obtained for the sexes in the previous analysis using MMPI items, we have additional evidence that the schizoid taxonomy appears to be detectable with MMPI items as indicators. Recent unpublished research indicates that the seven items described above lack validity in other samples; we advise other researchers to use the indicator consisting of the above four MMPI scales in future work.

All three of the taxonomic methods classified individuals as either "in" or "out" of the schizoid taxon, with agreement rates between pairs of methods near to that expectable from estimates of their misclassification rates. This result obtained even though the three methods are based on loosely related assumptions, and were used with different MMPI indicators. Also the three base rate estimates were close to each other and to a personal clinical estimate of .40 to .45 by Meehl; the latter was a prerecorded "impressionistic guess" based on some 30 years of outpatient private practice and the use of the Checklist of Schizotypal Signs (Meehl, 1964).

Each individual whose probability of being

a member of the schizoid taxon exceeded .50 was classified as "probable schizoid" and others as "probable nonschizoid," thereby forming two subsamples that could be compared on other variables. The mean MMPI profile for the individuals classified as members of the schizoid taxon, presented in Figure 5.2, was nearly identical to the "2-7-8" code type. The mean MMPI profile for those individuals classified as *not* members of the schizoid taxon was considerably lower, and not similar to any standard code type. This subsample is presumably quite heterogeneous, as one would expect.

The most impressive evidence of construct validity was that the mean MMPI profile of the schizoid taxon was very similar to that of a sample of preschizophrenics studied by Peterson (1963). A search of Lanyon's (1968) *Handbook of Group MMPI Profiles* revealed few nonschizoid diagnostic groups that also have the 2-7-8 mean profile pattern exhibited by both the present schizoid taxon and the Peterson preschizophrenic sample.

There probably are neurological and physiological variables more powerful as indicators of schizoidia than MMPI responses. However, MMPI responses, even though far removed causally from any genetic etiological source, may still suffice, in samples of a thousand or more, to provide a convincing test of the existence or nonexistence of the schizoid taxon. The results of the present preliminary trial, even though the sample size is quite small, indicate that such a taxon is likely to exist. These results are sufficiently encouraging to justify an attempted replication of the present study with a much larger sample. The substantive results presented here are not regarded as confirmation of a theory, but are offered in the "context of discovery" (Reichenbach, 1938).

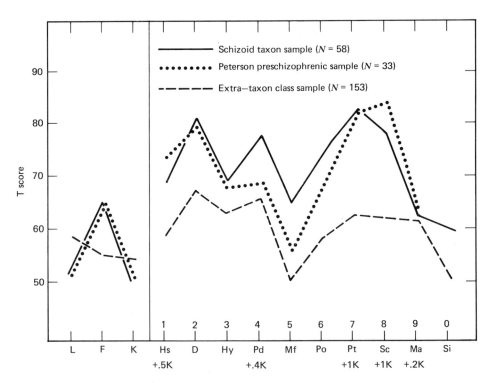

Figure 5.2.   Mean NMPI profiles for taxometrically identified schizoids and nonschizoids and for clinically identified preschizophrenics.

TESTING THE SINGLE DOMINANT GENE HYPOTHESIS

Meehl (1962) hypothesized that schizotaxics are born with a neurological predisposition to acquire a personality organization with four cardinal personality traits: cognitive slippage, ambivalence, anhedonia, and social aversiveness, the inheritance mechanism conjectured to underly schizotaxia being a dominant gene. This genetic hypothesis is related to the taxonicity aspect of Meehl's theory. A theory taxonic at the genetic level permits stronger refutation tests than does one at the levels of personality or psychopathology.

We have developed an interrelated set of tests that require the use of indicators on the *parents of* schizophrenic probands, who, according to the theory, must carry the schizogene because of their observable phenotypic condition. Suppose each member of the parent-pairs responds (+) or (−) to several dichotomous fallible indicators of the schizogene, such as a personality questionnaire item, a "soft" neurological sign, or whatever. Since the indicator is fallible, the dichotomy on the indicator is imperfectly correlated with the genetic dichotomy. We assume nonassociative mating so that (nearly) always one and only one parent of each pair of parents, under the single dominant gene model, is a schizotype. We assume that in the population of such parents the base rate of schizotypy is exactly one-half.

To make the model mathematically tractable, we make the following auxiliary conjectures. These assumptions are made, for the moment, in the context of discovery, but later will be subjected to indirect empirical testing.

A₁ Each pair of indicators is independent within the schizotypic and within the nonschizotypic populations and

A₂ The response to an indicator by the schizotypic parent is independent of that of the nonschizotypic mate.

Let us use the following notation:

p_s: the proportion of schizotypic parents that respond in + (schizotypic) direction on a given indicator

p_n: the same for the nonschizotypic parents

A: one of the parents determined by an indexing procedure either dependent or independent of schizotypy (as specified; A will also be used for the class of such parents)

B: the parent (or class of parents) that is not A

C: the (compound) class of all parents (the union of A and B)

p_c: the proportion of the parents that responded in (+) direction

p_{AB}: the proportion of the parent pairs where both parents responded in the (+) direction

σ_{AB}: the covariance between the responses of the A parents with those of B parents for a given indicator

Thus p_s and p_n are latent and unknown, and we first wish to express them as functions of manifest parameters. We have shown that:

Under the assumption A_2 and the single dominant gene hypothesis,

$$p_s = p_c + (p_c^2 - p_{AB})^{1/2} \quad (35)$$

$$p_n = p_c - (p_c^2 - p_{AB})^{1/2} \quad (36)$$

for any indicator. Derivations of this and the following results are given in Golden and Meehl (1978).

Next we shall propose a set of consistency tests that follow from A_1, A_2, and the single dominant gene hypothesis. If these tests are grossly unsatisfied by the observational facts, a strong suspicion arises that the model represents a poor approximation to the state of nature. Either the estimates of the latent quantities are untrustworthy, or, more importantly, the dominant gene hypothesis is discorroborated. First we have shown that:

The covariance between the responses of the A parents with that of the B parents for any such valid indicator must be negative and is equal to the quantity $-\frac{1}{4}(p_s - p_n)^2$ when the indexing is independent of schizotypy.

If we have three indicators X, Y, Z, then under the assumption A_1 we have for indicator X

$$p_s = p_c + 2\left[\frac{\sigma_{xy}\,\sigma_{xz}}{\sigma_{yz}}\right]^{1/2} \quad (37)$$

and

$$p_n = p_c - 2\left[\frac{\sigma_{xy}\,\sigma_{xz}}{\sigma_{yz}}\right]^{1/2} \quad (38)$$

where the three covariances refer to those of manifest-compound parent population.

For any indexing independent of schizotypy, we have

$$\sigma_{AB}(X) = \frac{-\,\sigma(X,Y)\,\sigma(X,Z)}{\sigma(Y,Z)} \quad (39)$$

for indicator X. It should be noted that $\sigma_{AB}(X)$ is the covariance between parent pairs indexed independently of schizotypy, whereas $\sigma(X,Y)$, $\sigma(X,Z)$, and $\sigma(Y,Z)$ refer to the compound parent population between two different indicators.

Further, we have derived the following result: Under the independence assumption A_2 and the single dominant gene hypothesis and for any indexing of the parent pairs, the base rates of schizotypes among the A and B parents are given by

$$P = \frac{1}{2} \pm \frac{1}{2}K \quad (40)$$

where

$$K = \frac{p_A - p_B}{[(p_A - p_B)^2 - 4\,\sigma_{AB}]^{1/2}} \quad (41)$$

$$(P \neq \frac{1}{2})$$

Any indicator that satisfies A_1, A_2, and the single dominant gene hypothesis will produce the same value of P; in other words,

the above expression of manifest parameters for K is invariant across such indicators and thus provides another means of indicator selection.

Once we have determined P and Q as above, we can use the Dawes-Meehl equations (Dawes & Meehl, 1966) to obtain p_s and p_n.

If P is determined as in Equation (40), then

$$p_s = \frac{Pp_A - QP_B}{P - Q} \quad (42)$$

and

$$p_n = \frac{Qp_B - Pp_A}{P - Q} \quad (43)$$

The two kinds of covariances, those between the two responses of parent pairs to the same indicator X, denoted by $\sigma_{AB}(X)$, and those between two indicators X and Y within either the A or the B parents, denoted by $\sigma_{XY}(W)$, are related according to the next result.

Under the above independence assumptions and the single dominant gene hypothesis,

$$\sigma_{AB}(X)\,\sigma_{AB}(Y) = \sigma_{XY}(W) \quad (44)$$

for any two such indicators X and Y for any indexing of the parents.

SUMMARY

We view taxometrics as the application of formal (mathematical) methods to the problem of detecting nonarbitrary classes (types, species, disease entities, *real syndromes* that exist in the external world—"carving nature at its joints"), with a derivative formal procedure for sorting individuals in or out of such inferred taxa. There are three broad classes of taxometric problems, set by the investigator's state of knowledge and his or her theoretical or clinical aims: In Type I, Accepted Criterion Prediction, the taxon is known to exist and a defining (or quasi-infallible "proxy") indicator is available in the research context. The aim is to devise, relying on the accepted criterion, a taxometric function of the (more usually available) fallible indicators that will classify future individuals where the accepted criterion is unavailable, at least at the time of classification. In Type II, Classical Cluster Analysis, the existence, number, and nature of taxa in a domain are highly problematic, so the investigator has no accepted criterion and, typically, does not wish to rely on substantive theoretical conjectures even for identifying privileged ("high-validity") indicators. Instead he or she proceeds by constructing a matrix of interindividual similarity measures on a (usually large) number of indicators of unknown relative weight, hoping that by applying a suitable cluster algorithm to this data-summarizing matrix he or she will be able to discern the taxometric structure underlying the observed pattern. In Type III, which we have labeled the Conjectured Latent Taxon Problem, our knowledge situation lies somewhere between that of Type I and Type II, and the taxometric methods we advocate are tailor-made for that intermediate case. From prior knowledge of the domain (experimental studies, statistical analysis of file data, clinical experience, theory, common sense, intuition, or sheer guesswork) we conjecture the existence of a hypothetical taxon.

Our own interest being theoretical, and our philosophy of science being realist rather than instrumentalist or fictionist, we think mainly of "true taxon" as designating an objective entity whose nature will ultimately be understood in some strong *theoretical* (structural, compositional, historical, or causal) sense. The clearest and most interesting examples in psychopathology (and the clinical sciences generally) are those in which the phenotypic taxon arises from a quasi-dichotomous specific etiology (ideally a germ, a major gene, or a traumatic event, but including polygenic or environmental threshold effects, step-functions, Cattell's "environmental molds," etc.). However, while these methodological preferences inform our

own thinking and have guided our research, a weaker view of latent taxonicity is compatible with the conjectured latent taxon strategy, since our "taxonicity" concept is pretty well specified implicitly by the formalism and the data.

We think Type III is by far the commonest knowledge/aim situation presented in psychopathology. But whether that is true or not, Type II seems on present evidence, some offered by us here, to have no persuasive general solution, either theoretically or empirically. (See Skinner, 1981 for an illuminating discussion.) Focusing therefore on Type III, the conjectured latent taxon problem, we sketch out the usual mode of informal, nonmathematical discernment of a taxon by clinicians, with special attention to logical and methodological clarification of open concepts, contextual (implicit) definition, alleged circularity of causal explanation via inferred entities, the bootstraps effect, and the role of auxiliary conjectures in empirical testing. We emphasize the necessity for numerical point-estimation or other "risk-taking" predictions, capable of yielding strong Popperian tests of a taxonomic model. We downplay traditional significance testing as a feeble, low-risk way to do science, and we advocate use of multiple joint consistency tests. But strict falsificationism is rejected in favor of specifying numerical tolerances and approximations, recognizing that all mathematical models in the life sciences have imperfect verisimilitude.[1]

---

[1]The senior author, while still skeptical about the atheoretical cluster approach, has recently attempted to generalize our conjectured latent taxon methods to permit a "blind inductive scanning" of miscellaneous indicators for the multiple taxa case (Meehl, 1982). As of this writing, the method has not been tested and a computer program does not yet exist. In the second half of this chapter we briefly describe the analytical and empirical research in taxometrics by the present authors. Recently, Golden has developed an improved bootstraps model (Golden, in press) and applied it to the detection of conjectured taxonomic classes of dementia and other disorders in older individuals (Golden et al., in press), schizotypy in children (Golden et al., in press), and kidney disease in children.

Three new taxometric methods of our devising are explained, the MAXCOV-HIT-MAX, the consistency hurdles, and the normal. Monte Carlo runs and a biological sex pseudo-problem with real data are offered (although the mathematical derivations in *this* kind of taxometrics "speak for themselves") as evidence of their usefulness. A preliminary study of the nondiagnosed schizoid taxon, identified by MMPI items, is presented. Finally, we derive equations for a theoretical extension of our taxometrics to the problem of testing a dominant gene theory using fallible phenotypic indicators.

REFERENCES

Anderberg, M. R. (1973). *Cluster analysis for applications*. New York: Academic Press.

Bailey, K. D. (1974). Cluster analysis. In D. Heise (Ed.), *Sociological methodology*. San Francisco: Jossey-Bass.

Bailey, N. T. J. (1965). Probability methods of diagnosis based on small samples. *Mathematics and Computer Science in Biology and Medicine*. HMSA.

Blashfield, R. K. (1976). Mixture model tests of cluster analysis: Accuracy of four agglomerative hierarchical methods. *Psychological Bulletin, 83,* 377–388.

Blashfield, R. K. (1978). Failure of cluster analysis in psychiatric research. Paper presented at the meeting of the American Psychological Association, Toronto, Canada, August 30.

Blashfield, R. K., & Aldenderfer, M. S. (1978). The literature on cluster analysis. *Multivariate Behavioral Research, 13,* 271–295.

Buchanan, C. E., & Jones, M. B. (1969). A within family study of schizophrenia and a visible subpapillary plexus in the nailfold. *Schizophrenia, 1,* 61–75.

Carnap, R. (1936, 1937; 1950). Testability and meaning. *Philosophy of Science, 3,* 420; **4,** 2. Reprinted with corrigenda and additional bibliography. New Haven: Yale University Graduate Philosophy Club.

Chan, L. S., & Dunn, O. J. (1972). The treatment of missing values in discriminant analysis, I: The sampling experiment. *Journal of the American Statistical Association, 67,* 473–477.

Clogg, C. C. (1977). *Unrestricted and restricted maximum likelihood latent structure analysis: A manual for users.* (Population Issues Research Office Working paper 1977–04), University Park, Pa.

Cormack, R. M. (1971). A review of classification. *Journal of Royal Statistical Society,* Series A, **134,** 321–367.

Cornfield, J. (1967). Discriminant functions. *Reviews of the International Statistical Institute, 35,* 142–153.

Cramér, H. (1946). *Mathematical methods of statistics.* Princeton, N.J.: Princeton University Press.

Cronbach, L. J., & Meehl, P. E. (1955). Construct validity in psychological tests. *Psychological Bulletin, 52,* 281–302.

Darlington, R. B. (1968). Multiple regression in research and practice. *Psychological Bulletin, 69,* 166–168.

Dawes, R. M. (1979). The robust beauty of improper linear models in decision making. *American Psychologist, 34,* 571–582.

Dawes, R. M., & Corrigan, B. (1974). Linear models in decision making. *Psychological Bulletin, 81,* 95–106.

Dawes, R. M., & Meehl, P. E. (1966). Mixed group validation: A method for determining the validity of diagnostic signs without using criterion groups. *Psychological Bulletin, 66,* 63–67.

Draper, N. R., & Smith, H. (1966). *Applied regression analysis.* New York, Wiley.

Dunn, O. J. (1971). Some expected values for probabilities of correct classification in discriminant analysis. *Technometrics, 13,* 345–353.

Dunn, O. J., & Varady, P. D. (1966). Probabilities of correct classification in discriminant analysis. *Biometrics, 22,* 908–924.

Everitt, B. S. (1974). *Cluster analysis.* London: Halsted Press.

Finn, J. D. (1974). *A general model for multivariate analysis.* New York: Holt, Rinehart & Winston.

Fisher, R. A. (1936). The use of multiple measurements in taxonomic problems. *Annals of Eugenics, 7,* 179–188.

Freud, S. (1895; 1962). A reply to criticisms of my paper on the anxiety neurosis. In J. Strachey (Ed.), *Standard edition of the complete psychological works of Sigmund Freud,* Vol. 3. London: Hogarth Press, pp. 119–139.

Freud, S. (1895; 1962). On the grounds for detaching a particular syndrome from neurasthenia under the description "anxiety neurosis." In J. Strachey (Ed.), *Standard edition of the complete psychological works of Sigmund Freud,* Vol. 3. London: Hogarth Press, pp. 85–115.

Gilbert, E. S. (1969). The effect of unequal variance-covariance matrices on Fisher's linear discriminant function. *Biometrics, 25,* 505–515.

Goldberg, L. R. (1969). The search for configural relationships in personality assessments: The diagnosis of psychosis vs. neurosis from the MMPI. *Multivariate Behavioral Research,* **4,** 523–536.

Golden, R. R. (in press). A taxometric model for detection of a conjectured latent taxon. *Multivariate Behavioral Research.*

Golden, R. R., & Meehl, P. E. (1973). *Detecting latent clinical taxa, IV: Empirical study of the maximum covariance method and normal minimum chi-square method, using three MMPI keys to identify the sexes* (Rep. PR–73–2). Minneapolis: University of Minnesota, Reports from the Research Laboratories of the Department of Psychiatry.

Golden, R. R., & Meehl, P. E. (1973). *Detecting latent clinical taxa, V: A Monte Carlo study of the maximum covariance method and associated consistency tests* (Rep. PR–73–3). Minneapolis: University of Minnesota, Reports from the Research Laboratories of the Department of Psychiatry.

Golden, R. R., & Meehl, P. E. (1978). Testing a dominant gene theory without an accepted criterion variable. *Annals of Human Genetics* (London), **41,** 507–514.

Golden, R. R., & Meehl, P. E. (1979). Detection of the schizoid taxon with MMPI indicators. *Journal of Abnormal Psychology,* **88,** 217–233.

Golden, R. R., & Meehl, P. E. (1981). Detection of biological sex: An empirical test of cluster methods. *Multivariate Behavioral Research,* **15,** 475–496.

Golden, R. R., & Meehl, P. E. (in preparation). *Taxometric analysis of causal entities: Detection of the schizoid taxon.* New York: Academic Press.

Golden, R. R., Tyan, S. H., & Meehl, P. E. (1974a). *Detecting latent clinical taxa, VI: Analytical development and empirical trials of the consistency hurdles theory* (Rep. PR–74–4). Minneapolis: University of Minnesota, Reports from the Research Laboratories of the Department of Psychiatry.

Golden, R. R., Tyan, S. H., & Meehl, P. E. (1974b). *Detecting latent clinical taxa, VII: Analytical development and empirical and artificial data trials of the multi-indicator, multi-taxonomic class maximum likelihood normal theory* (Rep. PR–74–5). Minneapolis: University of Minnesota, Reports from the Research Laboratories of the Department of Psychiatry.

Golden, R. R., Tyan, S., & Meehl, P. E. (1974c). *Detecting latent clinical taxa, IX: A Monte Carlo method for testing taxometric theories* (Rep. PR–74–7). Minneapolis: University of Minnesota, Reports from the Research Laboratories of the Department of Psychiatry.

Golden, R. R., Teresi, J. A., & Gurland, B. J. (in press). Detection of taxonomic classes of health and social problems using the Comprehensive Assessment Evaluation and Referral interview schedule. *Journal of Gerontology.*

Golden, R. R., Erlenmeyer-Kimling, L., & Cornblatt, B. (in press). *Taxometric detection of schizotypy in children using a battery of attention, motor and cognitive indicator-tests.* New York: Columbia University, Columbia University Statistical Reports, Division of Biostatistics.

Goldstein, M. (1977). A two group classification procedure for multivariate dichotomous responses. *Journal of Multivariate Behavioral Research,* **12,** 335–346.

Goodman, L. A. (1975). A new model for scaling response patterns: An application of the quasi-independence concept. *Journal of the American Statistical Association,* **70,** 755–768.

Green, B. F. (1952). Latent structure analysis and its relation to factor analysis. *Journal of the American Statistical Association,* **47,** 71–76.

Grünbaum, A. (1976). Is the method of bold conjectures and attempted refutations *justifiably* the method of science? *The British Journal for the Philosophy of Science,* **27,** 105–136.

Guion, R. M. (1965). *Personnel testing.* New York: McGraw-Hill.

Harding, J. P. (1949). The use of probability paper for the graphical analysis of polymodal frequency distributions. *Journal of the Marine Biological Association,* **28,** No. 1, 141–153.

Hartigan, J. A. (1975). *Clustering algorithms.* New York: Wiley.

Hasselblad, V. (1968). Estimation of parameters for a mixture of normal distributions. *Technometrics,* **8,** 431–444.

Hays, W. L. (1973). *Statistics for the social sciences.* 2nd ed. New York: Holt, Rinehart & Winston.

Hoch, P., & Polatin, P. (1949). Pseudoneurotic forms of schizophrenia. *Psychiatric Quarterly,* **3,** 248–276.

Kerlinger, F. N., & Pedhazuer, E. J. (1973). *Multiple regression in behavioral research.* New York: Holt, Rinehart & Winston.

Lachenbruch, P. A. (1968). On expected probabilities of misclassification in discriminant analysis, necessary sample size, and a relation with the multiple correlations coefficient. *Biometrics,* **24,** 323–334.

Lachenbruch, P. A. (1975). *Discriminant analysis.* New York: Hafner Press.

Lance, G. N., & William, W. T. (1967). A general theory of classificatory sorting strategies. I. Hierarchical system. *The Computer Journal,* **9,** 373–380.

Lanyon, R. I. (1968). *A handbook of MMPI group profiles*. Minneapolis: University of Minnesota Press.

Lazarsfeld, P. F., & Henry, N. W. (1968). *Latent structure analysis*. Boston: Houghton Mifflin.

Lindgren, B. (1962). *Statistical theory*. New York: Macmillan.

Loevinger, J. (1957). Objective tests as instruments of psychological theory. *Psychological Reports, 3,* 635–694.

Lykken, D. T. (1956). A method of actuarial pattern analysis. *Psychological Bulletin, 53,* 102–107.

Lykken, D. T., & Rose, R. (1963). Psychological prediction from actuarial tables. *Journal of Clinical Psychology, 19,* 139–151.

Lyle, O. E., & Gottesman, I. I. (1977). Premorbid psychometric indicators of the gene for Huntington's Disease. *Journal of Consulting and Clinical Psychology, 45,* 1011–1022.

Major, R. H. (1932). *Classic descriptions of disease*. Springfield, Ill.: Charles C. Thomas.

Meehl, P. E. (1950). Configural scoring. *Journal of Consulting Psychology, 14,* 165–171.

Meehl, P. E. (1962) Schizotaxia, schizotypy, schizophrenia. *American Psychologist, 17,* 827–838.

Meehl, P. E. (1964). *Manual for use with checklist of schizotypic signs*. Minneapolis: University of Minnesota, Medical School, Psychiatric Research Unit.

Meehl, P. E. (1965). *Detecting latent clinical taxa by fallible quantitative indicators lacking an accepted criterion* (Rep. PR–65–2). Minneapolis: University of Minnesota, Reports from the Research Laboratories of the Department of Psychiatry.

Meehl, P. E. (1968). *Detecting latent clinical taxa, II: A simplified procedure, some additional hitmax cut locators, a single-indicator method, and miscellaneous theorems* (Rep. PR–68–4). Minneapolis: University of Minnesota, Reports from the Research Laboratories of the Department of Psychiatry.

Meehl, P. E. (1970). Theory-testing in psychology and physics: A methodological paradox. In D. E. Morrison & R. E. Henkel (Eds.), *The significance test controversy*. Chicago: Aldine.

Meehl, P. E. (1972a). A critical afterword. In I. I. Gottesman & J. Shields, *Schizophrenia and genetics*. New York: Academic Press.

Meehl, P. E. (1972b). Reactions, reflections, projections. In J. N. Butcher (Ed.), *Objective personality assessment*. New York: Academic Press.

Meehl, P. E. (1972c). Specific genetic etiology, psychodynamics, and therapeutic nihilism. *International Journal of Mental Health, 1,* 10–27.

Meehl, P. E. (1973a). MAXCOV-HITMAX: A taxonomic search method for loose genetic syndromes.

In P. E. Meehl, *Psychodiagnosis: Selected papers*. Minneapolis: University of Minnesota Press.

Meehl, P. E. (1973b). *Psychodiagnosis: Selected papers*. Minneapolis: University of Minnesota Press.

Meehl, P. E. (1977). Specific etiology and other forms of strong influence: Some quantitative meanings. *Journal of Medicine and Philosophy, 2,* 33–53.

Meehl, P. E. (1978). Theoretical risks and tabular asterisks: Sir Karl, Sir Ronald, and the slow progress of soft psychology. *Journal of Consulting and Clinical Psychology, 46,* 806–834.

Meehl, P. E. (1979). A funny thing happened to us on the way to the latent entities. *Journal of Personality Assessment, 43,* 563–581.

Meehl, P. E. (1982). *Detecting latent clinical taxa, X: Extension of methods to problem of inductive scanning for multiple taxa*. Reports from the Research Laboratories of the Department of Psychiatry, University of Minnesota, (Report No. PR–82–1) Minneapolis: University of Minnesota.

Meehl, P. E., Lykken, D. T., Burdick, M. R., & Schoener, G. R. (1969). *Identifying latent clinical taxa, III: An empirical trial of the normal single-indicator method, using MMPI scale 5 to identify the sexes* (Rep. PR–69–1). Minneapolis: University of Minnesota, Reports from the Research Laboratories of the Department of Psychiatry.

Morrison, D. F. (1976). *Multivariate statistical methods*. 2nd ed. New York: McGraw-Hill.

Morrison, D. E., & Henkel, R. E. (Eds.) (1970). *The significance test controversy*. Chicago: Aldine.

Murphy, E. A. (1964). One cause? Many causes? The argument from a bimodal distribution. *Journal of Chronic Diseases, 17,* 301.

Nunnally, J. C. (1967). *Psychometric theory*. New York: McGraw-Hill.

Overall, J. E. & Klett, C. J. (1972). *Applied multivariate analyses*. New York: McGraw-Hill.

Pap, A. (1953). Reduction-sentences and open concepts. *Methodos, 5,* 3–30.

Pap, A. (1958). *Semantics and necessary truth*. New Haven, Conn.: Yale University Press.

Peppard, T. A. (1949). Mistakes in diagnosis. *Minnesota Medicine, 32,* 510–511.

Peterson, D. R. (1963). The diagnosis of subclinical schizophrenia. In G. S. Welsh & W. G. Dahlstrom (Eds.), *Basic readings on the MMPI in psychology and medicine*. Minneapolis: University of Minnesota Press.

Popper, K. R. (1962). *Conjectures and refutations*. New York: Basic Books.

Popper, K. R. (1974). Autobiography. In P. A. Schilpp (Ed.), *The philosophy of Karl Popper*. LaSalle, Ill.: Open Court.

Rado, S. (1956). *Psychoanalysis of behavior*. New York: Grune & Stratton.

Rado, S. (1960). Theory and therapy: The theory of schizotypal organization and its application to the treatment of decompensate schizotypal behavior. In S. C. Scher & H. R. Davis (Eds.), *The outpatient treatment of schizophrenia*. New York: Grune & Stratton, pp. 87–101.

Rado, S., & Daniels, G. (1956). *Changing concepts of psychoanalytic medicine*. New York: Grune & Stratton.

Reichenbach, H. (1938). *Experience and prediction*. Chicago: University of Chicago Press.

Rozeboom, W. W. (1966). *Foundations of the theory of prediction*. Homewood, Ill.: Dorsey Press.

Salmon, W. C. (1967). *The foundations of scientific inference*. Pittsburgh: University of Pittsburgh Press.

Skinner, H. A. (1981). Toward the integration of classification theory and methods. *Journal of Abnormal Psychology*, **90**, (1), 68–87.

Sneath, P. H. A., & Sokal, R. R. (1973). *Numerical taxonomy*. San Francisco: Freeman.

Sokal, R. R. (1974). Classification: Purposes, principles, progress, prospects. *Science*, **185**, 1115–1123.

Solomon, H. (Ed.) (1961). *Studies in item analysis and prediction*. Stanford, Calif.: Stanford University Press.

Tatsuoka, M. M. (1971). *Multivariate analysis: Techniques for educational and psychological research*. New York: Wiley.

Torgerson, W. S. (1958). *Theory and methods of scaling*. New York: Wiley.

Tryon, R. C. (1939). *Cluster analysis*. Ann Arbor, Mich.: Edwards Brothers.

Von Mises, R. (1964). *Mathematical theory of probability and statistics*. New York: Academic Press.

Wainer, H. (1976). Estimating coefficients in linear models: It don't make no nevermind. *Psychological Bulletin*, **83**, 213–217.

Wainer, H. (1978). On the sensitivity of regression and regressors. *Psychological Bulletin*, **85**, 267–273.

Zubin, J. (1938). A technique for measuring like-mindedness. *Journal of Abnormal and Social Psychology*, **33**, 508–516.

CHAPTER 6

Circumplex Models
of Interpersonal Behavior
in Clinical Psychology

JERRY S. WIGGINS

Interpersonal conceptions of disordered behavior have figured prominently in the history of clinical psychology since the seminal
writings of Harry Stack Sullivan. Of particular import have been the attempts by Leary
(1957) and others (see especially Carson,
1969, 1971, 1979) to provide a systematic
language for the description of interpersonal
transactions and to demonstrate that this language permits the specification of a set of
variables that are common to the enterprises
of assessment, diagnosis, and treatment. In
this chapter I will review, from an historical
perspective, the major systems that have been
proposed for the measurement of interpersonal behavior, and I will indicate the manner
in which these systems have been applied to
clinical practice and research. Because space
limitations preclude a detailed review of
these systems, I will provide only selected
examples of their application.

Readers familiar with the topic at hand will
be aware that impassioned pleas for the utility
of this approach for clinical practice have
been issued approximately every five years
over the last three decades (e.g., Freedman

This work was supported by Social Sciences and Humanities Research Council of Canada Grant
410–79–0148. I am grateful to Robert C. Carson, Lisa
Gaelick, and James A. Russell for their helpful suggestions and comments on an earlier version of this chapter.

et al., 1951; Leary, 1957; Foa, 1961; Adams,
1964; Carson, 1969; Benjamin, 1974;
McLemore & Benjamin, 1979), suggesting
that the approach has not been accorded as
prominent a place in tbe mainstream of clinical thought as its proponents would desire.
Although I too will celebrate the past accomplishments of interpersonal systems, I will
also stress the essential compatibility of this
line of thought with recent developments
outside the field of clinical psychology, and
I will argue that this compatibility justifies
the conclusion that models of this type are
every bit as viable today as they were 30
years ago. To make this point, I will focus
on the topic of psychiatric diagnosis, but in
so doing I will bring to bear concepts from
fields as diverse as cognitive psychology and
psychometrics. Although the argument is
wide ranging, its focus throughout is on the
utility of a particular kind of model for representing descriptions of interpersonal behavior.

Figure 6.1 presents a two-dimensional representation of interpersonal behavior in
which the variables are arrayed in a circular
fashion. There are actually 16 variables represented here: ambitious (P), dominant (A),
arrogant (B), calculating (C), and so on, although for convenience they have been "collapsed" into eight categories: ambitious-
dominant (PA), arrogant-calculating (BC),

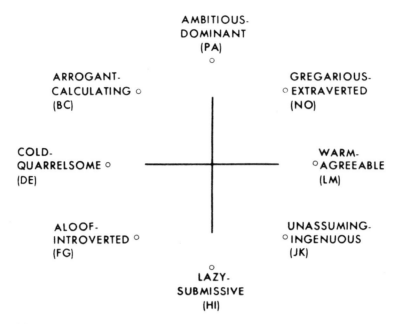

Figure 6.1.   A two-dimensional representation of interpersonal behavior (after Wiggins, 1979).

and so on. The circular arrangement of variables is meant to imply that, in some sense, variables that are close to one another on the circle are more "similar" than are variables that are more widely separated from one another.

The least restrictive assumption concerning the circular array of variables in Figure 6.1 is that the relationship among variables reflects an *ordering*. The particular ordinal relationship displayed is a circular one; an order without beginning or end. This non-metric model for representing a circular ordering among variables is called a circumplex (Guttman, 1954). Alternatively, one could assume that the variables of Figure 6.1 are located in a two-dimensional Euclidean space, and that their distance from the origin of the coordinates represents an "intensity" metric. In this interpretation, variables that are located opposite to each other on the circle are bipolar contrasts (lazy-submissive is the opposite of ambitious-dominant). In either interpretation, one can postulate latent variables or facets that give rise to the observed circular ordering. Most commonly,

theorists speak of *affiliation* and *dominance* as the two components responsible for the circular ordering. From this perspective, each of the interpersonal variables in Figure 6.1 may be thought of as representing a particular blend of affiliation and dominance.

PRINCIPAL ASSESSMENT SYSTEMS

Historical Background

The first published reference to an interpersonal system of personality diagnosis appeared in a classic paper by Mervin Freedman, Timothy Leary, Abel Ossorio, and Hubert Coffey (1951).[1] In that paper the authors presented a circular conception of operationally defined interpersonal variables that was meant to apply to both normal and maladaptive behavior. The authors also emphasized that the same set of interpersonal

[1]Freedman et al. acknowledge the similarity of their variables to those developed independently by Bales (1950).

variables could be measured from different perspectives or "levels," such as behavior ratings, self-reports, and Thematic Apperception Test (TAT) protocols. In the second of what was apparently intended to be an extended series of papers, LaForge, Leary, Naboisek, Coffey, and Freedman (1954) explored the implications of interlevel discrepancy scores. For example, a discrepancy between a person's self-reported hostility and the hostility he or she attributes to central characters in his or her TAT stories may serve as an objective index of repression. In the third and final paper in this series, Rolfe LaForge and Robert Suczek (1955) described the construction of the Interpersonal Check List (ICL). This instrument was, and to a large extent still is, the standard psychometric device for measuring the dimensions of the interpersonal system.

Although it is difficult to assess the impact that these three pioneering papers had on the conceptualization and practice of clinical psychology in ensuing decades, it is no exaggeration to say that Leary's (1957) *Interpersonal diagnosis of personality* had a major impact. This extraordinary book continues to inspire successive generations of psychodiagnosticians. It summarizes the results of the extensive investigations of the original research group and provides detailed descriptions of clinical syndromes and personality types identified through the multilevel assessment of interpersonal variables. Despite the appeal and suggestiveness of the empirical data summarized by Leary, this book is more a sketch of what an interpersonal system of diagnosis might be, rather than a description of a wholly validated and psychometrically sound set of existing procedures (Wiggins, 1965).

The period immediately following the publication of Leary's (1957) book was characterized by a proliferation of two-dimensional models of interpersonal behavior, most of them having been developed independently of each other. As can be seen from Table 6.1, Leary's model was but one of a

number of models that shared a striking similarity of conceptualization. The list of studies provided in Table 6.1 is not meant to be exhaustive, nor are the particular studies cited meant to be the most significant of the particular author or authors. Instead this list provides a representative sampling of studies arranged in the chronological order of a given author or authors' first publication on the topic.

From Table 6.1 it can be seen that the zeitgeist of the mid- and late 1950s was particularly ripe for two-dimensional representations of interpersonal behavior. Of these, the systems of Leary (1957), Schaefer (1957), Schutz (1958), and Stern (1958) were destined to become widely used and well developed systems of assessment. The 1960s was a period of integration and theoretical elaboration. Foa's (1961) seminal article on "Convergences in the analysis of the structure of interpersonal behavior" called attention to the strong convergence of thinking and results in some of the models developed in the 1950s. Despite differences in populations studied, in measures employed, and in theoretical rationales, these studies appeared to be converging on a common paradigm. Foa (1961) formalized this paradigm in terms of Guttman's (1958) facet analysis, and incorporated the notion of social exchange of interpersonal resources within the paradigm. Other notable integrative efforts of the sixties included Lorr and McNair's (1963) system that provided an integration of earlier work, Becker and Krug's (1964) integration of the literature on ratings of children, Rinn's (1965) extension of the circumplex model to domains other than interpersonal, and Carson's (1969) theoretical integration that defined interpersonal behavior as a broad field of inquiry rather than as a specialized assessment model. The seventies was a period of refinement and elaboration, during which many of the authors listed in earlier periods continued to pursue the implications of their models. In addition, that decade was the occasion for a number of methodological re-

Table 6.1. Milestones in the History of Two-Dimensional Models of Interpersonal Behavior

Author(s)	Subjects	Dimension I	Dimension II
Freedman et al. (1951)	Psychiatric patients	Dominance vs. submission	Affiliation vs. hostility
Carter (1954)	Small groups	Individual prominence	Sociability
Leary (1957)	Psychiatric patients	Dominance vs. submission	Love vs. hate
Schaefer (1957)	Mothers	Control	Hostility
Roe (1957)	Literature review	Overdemanding vs. casual	Loving vs. rejecting
Schutz (1958)	College students	Control	Affection
Stern (1958)	College students	Achievement orientation	Emotional expression
Borgatta et al. (1958)	Small groups	Individual assertiveness	Sociability
Chance (1959)	Families in treatment	Active vs. passive	Positive vs. negative
Foa (1961)	Literature review	Dominance vs. submission	Love vs. hostility
Slater (1962)	Reported parental behavior	Discipline	Warmth
Lorr & McNair (1963)	Therapists' ratings of patients	Control	Sociability
Becker & Krug (1964)	Ratings of children	Emotional stability	Extraversion
Rinn (1965)	Counselors	Dominant vs. submissive	Affectionate vs. critical
Baumrind & Black (1967)	Ratings of children	Stable vs. unstable	Conforming vs. nonconforming
Bayley (1968)	Interviews of adults	Outward vs. inward orientation	Accepting vs. hostile
Carson (1969)	Literature review	Dominance vs. submission	Love vs. hate
Benjamin (1973)	Psychiatric patients	Interdependence	Affiliation
Conte (1975)	Judges' similarity ratings	—	—
Wiggins (1979a)	College students	Dominance vs. submission	Love vs. hate
Kiesler (1979b)	College students	Dominance vs. submission	Love vs. hate

186

finements such as Benjamin's (1973) elaborate structural analysis of social behavior system, Conte's (1975) multidimensional scaling studies, Wiggins' (1979a) efforts to taxonomize interpersonal behavior in relation to other domains of human characteristics, and Kiesler's (1979b) procedures for measuring the impact of interpersonal messages.

The Leary System

As indicated in our historical review, the interpersonal system of personality diagnosis was the collective product of a number of individuals who were associated with the Kaiser Foundation Hospital in Oakland during the early 1950s. Because of the sustained impact of Leary's (1957) book, the system is now most generally known as the "Leary System," although that designation represents an historical oversimplification. In addition, there are sufficient differences of opinion between Leary and other members of the original group (e.g., LaForge, 1977) to suggest that the label "Leary System" represents an intellectual oversimplification. To avoid unproductive nitpicking, I will follow the common practice of referring to this system as the Leary System and indicate, when appropriate, significant differences in conceptualization between Leary and some of his former colleagues.

The Kaiser Foundation Group was concerned with interpersonal interactions in small groups, both inside and outside of a psychiatric setting. Their basic concern was to develop a descriptive language by which subjects' interpersonal behavior in such settings could be summarized. Interactions of subjects in small groups were observed by psychologists who attempted to use ordinary language to describe both the *activity* and *content* of interpersonal transactions. Transitive *verbs* were most frequently employed in describing interpersonal activity, and *adjectives* were used most frequently for describing the content or attributes of the actors. Thus, what individuals actually *do* in

a social situation is described by a verb (help) and can be related to their description of themselves (helpful) and to descriptions of them given by others (helpful) (Leary, 1957, p. 63).

Categories of action verbs and their corresponding attributive adjectives were developed in such a way as to include intense (statistically rare) terms as well as more moderate (statistically frequent) categories. Thus, for example, under "hostile activities" transitive verbs might range from "insult" through "attack" to "murder." Sixteen categories were finally selected to represent "generic interpersonal motivations." In what now appears to be a particularly prescient decision, the Kaiser Group decided that the structural arrangement of these 16 variables was best represented as a circular ordering around the orthogonal axes of power and affiliation. Although this decision was made without knowledge of Guttman's (1954) circumplex model or of course of Foa's (1961) facet approach, the reasoning seems quite similar. However, LaForge (1977) recalls: "A close-fought battle with empirical fact, not lofty considerations of logical symmetry, produced the sixteen categories. In the closing stages, the circle emerged" (p. 8).

The 16 generic interpersonal motivations of the Leary System are listed in the first column of Table 6.2. As just indicated, the circular ordering was based on empirical considerations, as well as considerations of the extent to which each sixteenth represented a blend of the primary axes of power and affiliation. Consequently some of the implied bipolarities are intuitively obvious (e.g., power vs. weakness) while others are not (e.g., success vs. masochism). Although the original diagnostic system employed 16 diagnostic categories (Freedman et al., 1951), Leary (1957) felt that the most efficient system for clinical use was one in which octants were formed by collapsing adjacent categories (PA. Success/Power), a practice with which LaForge (1977) disagrees.

In the identification and development of

Table 6.2.   Sixteen-Variable Systems of Interpersonal Behavior

	Leary (1957)	Chance (1959)	Lorr & McNair (1965)	Benjamin (1979)	Wiggins (1979a)
P.	Success	Teach	—	Remind	Success
A.	Power	Lead	Dominance	Enforce conformity	Power
B.	Narcissism	Boss-rebel	Recognition	Act superior	Narcissism
C.	Exploitation	Compete	Aggression	Delude	Exploitation
D.	Punishment	Punish	Mistrust	Approach menacingly	Punishment
E.	Hostility	Hate	(Autonomy)[a]	Angry dismiss	Hostility
F.	Rebellion	Resent-complain	Detachment	Feel alone[b]	Disaffiliation
G.	Distrust	Distrust	Inhibition	Wall-off[b]	Withdrawal
H.	Masochism	Retreat	Abasement	Overconform[b]	Failure
I.	Weakness	Submit	Submissiveness	Apathetic compliance[b]	Weakness
J.	Conformity	Conform-admire	Succorance	Act put upon[b]	Modesty
K.	Trust	Trust	Deference	Appease[b]	Trust
L.	Collaboration	Cooperate	Agreeableness	Warmly welcome	Love
M.	Love	Appreciate-love	Nurturance	Nurture	Collaboration
N.	Tenderness	Support	Affiliation	Protect	Affiliation
O.	Generosity	Give	Sociability-exhibition	Pamper	Extraversion

KEY

[a]: expected location

[b]: second surface reactions

interpersonal variables, the Kaiser Group employed a circumplex model in which a circular ordering was held to hold among variables according to the principle that the correlations between adjacent categories would be higher than the correlations between nonadjacent categories. In subsequent diagnostic applications of the system, the circular arrangement among variables was given a metric interpretation, within conventional Euclidean space, to which conventional trigonometric formulas were held to apply (LaForge et al., 1954, p. 139). Thus the interpersonal circle was interpreted as a set of eight vectors in a two-dimensional space. Within this metric interpretation of the circle, the length of a given vector (interpersonal variable) may be expressed with reference to the magnitude of two orthogonal components, in this case dominance (PA) and love (LM). The origin of the circle may be interpreted as the mean standard score of a normative population, and a given patient's score on any vector (variable) may be interpreted as a deviation from that mean. Note that variables opposite to each other on the interpersonal circle are now interpreted as

end points on a bipolar continuum. If a patient's dominance score (PA) falls below that of the mean of the normative group, the score would be represented as falling within the submissive octant (HI).

The assumption of variable bipolarity is not important when a patient's test results are considered as simply a profile of scores on eight (or 16) interpersonal variables. This assumption is important, however, when a patient is diagnosed with reference to the geometric typology introduced by LaForge et al. (1954). In this latter procedure, direct estimates of the contributions of the dominance and love components of the sum of vectors are made by means of trigonometric functions. Estimates of the contributions of dominance and love, based on interpersonal variable scores, provide the coordinate values for locating the central tendency of a patient's profile as a single point in space. Thus the patient's total profile can be summarized as falling within one of eight or 16 categories. It is on this basis that a patient is diagnosed in terms of an eight- or 16-variable typology.

In addition to specifying the octant or sixteenth in which a given patient's profile may be classified, the computation of a mean of vectors also permits classification of the intensity or extremeness of the single point diagnosis with reference to the distance of the vector mean from the center of the circle. Single point scores that differ from a normative population by more than one standard deviation are classified as maladaptive. For example, a single point score that falls close to the center of the circle within the PA octant is classified as a "managerial personality," while a score that falls close to the perimeter of the circle within the same octant is classified as an "autocratic personality" (Leary, 1957, pp. 216–221).

In the original formulation of the interpersonal system, three "levels" of measurement of the same system of variables were distinguished: I. Public level; II. Conscious level; and III. Private level (Freedman et al., 1951). To these Leary (1957) added: IV. Level of the unexpressed; and V. Level of values. For Leary, a complete multilevel diagnosis of personality would include a single point diagnosis of personality type (adaptive or maladaptive) at each of these "levels" of personality. Moreover, Leary placed a heavy emphasis on the calculation of interlevel *discrepancies* that were interpreted as reflecting such diverse phenomena as preconscious idealization, displacement, and repression (1957, p. 85). There are two rather serious reasons for concern with this procedure, one of them empirical and the other conceptual.

Calculation of the discrepancies among the "same" variables measured by different methods requires, at the very least, empirical justification of the assumption that the same set of variables is being measured by different methods. In the case of the Leary System this would require a demonstration that (1) the system of eight variables conforms to a circumplex structure under all methods of measurement, and (2) the metric assumptions involved in the calculation of mean vector scores are appropriate under all methods of measurement. To put it another way, the criteria of convergent and discriminant validity that must be met here are more stringent than those suggested by Campbell and Fiske (1959), and since there are no existing data sets that meet all of Campbell and Fiske's requirements, one might be justifiably skeptical of this aspect of the interpersonal system. In investigating the structure of interpersonal variables measured by the TAT (Level III), Terrill (1960) found no evidence supporting a circumplex model. More recently, Truckenmiller and Schaie (1979) claimed "modest" support for a circumplex model in TAT (level III) data, although their method of analysis may not have provided a rigorous test of circumplexity (Wiggins, Steiger, & Gaelick, 1981). Although there is no reason, in principle, why a five-level circumplex of interpersonal behavior (i.e., a radex) could not be constructed, the available evidence on Leary's (1957) system does not justify the calculation of interlevel discrepancy indices in clinical practice.

The conceptual issues involved in the multilevel measurement of interpersonal behavior have been stated with clarity by LaForge (1963, 1977). LaForge noted that although Freedman et al. (1951) spoke of "levels" of measurement, and hence were influenced to some extent by the topographic viewpoint of psychoanalysis, they provided operational definitions of these levels by reference to *methods* of measurement rather than levels of awareness. In contrast, Leary (1957) explicitly emphasized the psychoanalytic connotations of "levels," and in fact added the "unconscious" to the system (Level IV). As a consequence the interpersonal system has come to be regarded as one in which the "same" variables are viewed from different levels of conscious awareness.

LaForge (1977) argues that the first three levels of the interpersonal system represent different domains of measurement, each of which involves different laws. Thus a given instrument would be classified as a Level II instrument if its relationships with other variables obeyed the laws that are unique to self-report data. Such classification does not require consideration of the level of awareness involved in assessment with a given instrument. More generally, LaForge notes the correspondence between the three domains of interpersonal behavior and the three media of measurement distinguished by Cattell (1957): Level I. Peer ratings (life-data); Level II. Self-report (questionnaire data); and Level III. Projective techniques (objective test data). The different laws that appear to characterize these three domains have been considered in detail by Cattell (1961, 1968; Cattell & Digman, 1964). In this sense, then, the measurement and conceptual problems associated with the "multilevel" measurement of interpersonal behavior are no different than those associated with any comprehensive system of personality measurement.

The Chance System

One of the earliest extensions and clinical applications of the Leary system is found in the work of Erika Chance (1959, 1966). Chance's work is noteworthy for its eclectic theoretical orientation and for the ingenuity displayed in applying an interpersonal system to clinical phenomena. The context of her work required a system for the content analysis of interpersonal experience in psychotherapy (1959). Although interpersonal experiences were felt to constitute the basic units of psychotherapy, Chance (1966) emphasized that such units could be construed from a variety of theoretical perspectives, as Kelly (1955) has so often reminded us. Thus, if one can define a system of sufficiently small units, alternative theoretical perspectives can be viewed as alternative ways of combining these units into sets of molar variables.

The system of interpersonal units chosen by Chance was that of Freedman et al. (1951) and, as can be seen from the second column of Table 6.2, her "extension" of that system was relatively minor. Chance's (1959) ex-

tended system involved 20 instead of 16 categories that were postulated to have a circular ordering. The definition of the coordinates that underlies this system, and further groupings into specific octants or quadrants, would depend on the research context and the theoretical orientation of the investigator. Thus for orthodox psychoanalysts, the polarities of activity–passivity and friendliness–hostility would provide meaningful coordinates for clinical ratings (Chance & Arnold, 1960). For Adlerians, the coordinates might be striving for superiority and social interest. Followers of Horney might divide the circle into unequal parts to represent moving toward, against, and away from people. Similarly, Fromm's receptive, exploitative, hoarding, and marketing orientations may be represented by a somewhat different grouping. Thus it is Chance's (1966) conviction that this system contains the units that serve as the common denominator of a variety of theories, and that it can be employed, in differing ways, by clinicians of different theoretical persuasions.

A relatively complete account of interpersonal experience must include, as a minimum: (1) classification of the *content* of the experience; (2) an indication of its *intensity* for the experiencing individual; and (3) an appraisal of the *quality* of the experience in terms of its acceptability to the individual in himself or herself and in others (Chance, 1966). The content of interpersonal experience is represented by the 20 categories in Table 6.2, and the intensity of that experience can be rated on a three-place scale ranging from minimal or understatement ("1") to maximal or extreme intensity ("3"). Within the context of a therapy transcript, the quality of a given category of interpersonal experience is rated as entailing either self-acceptance (+) or self-rejection (−). Statements about significant others can be similarly rated as entailing acceptance (e.g., spouse acceptance) or rejection (e.g., child rejection).

In an example from a coded psychotherapy transcript, Chance (1966, pp. 135–136) provides the following statements by a patient: "I used to repress my feelings about this. In fact it used to be a thing." These statements are coded as falling within the retreat category (H), assigned an intensity value of "3," and judged to be an instance of self-rejection ($-$), since the patient's attitude toward his previous suppression of feelings appears to be negative. Combination of the last two categories of rating yields a weighted rejection score that provides an additional perspective for interpreting traditional content categories. Statements that involve self-rejection may be taken as indicative of conflict. The number of categories in which self-rejection occurs may be interpreted as an index of the pervasiveness of conflict. The proportion of total statements involving self-rejection may serve as an index of the intensity of conflict (Chance, 1966).

Chance's (1959) intensive study of families in psychotherapy provides an excellent example of the usefulness of a structured interpersonal system for describing personality change. Thirty-four families were followed through a year of family therapy, and were systematically interviewed and tested at the third, sixteenth, and thirtieth treatment sessions. Statements elicited in the interviews were coded for content, intensity, and acceptance-rejection within the 20-variable interpersonal system. Following each of the interviews, the patients rated themselves and their therapists on a 60-item Q-sort version of the interpersonal system. At the same time, therapists rated the current status of their patients on the interpersonal Q-sort and predicted their patients' future self-reports during later sessions. The structured interpersonal system employed by Chance provided a frame of reference for generating and testing specific hypotheses and for evaluating outcomes in a meaningful fashion.

The Lorr-McNair System

On the basis of the empirical and theoretical work of others, Lorr and McNair (1963) hy-

pothesized 13 categories of interpersonal behavior that should form a circular order. Building on the earlier work of Leary (1957), Schutz (1958), Stern (1958), Schaefer (1959), and Foa (1961), they provided 10 psychologists with descriptions of interpersonal categories and asked them to generate statements describing manifest behaviors within each category. After revisions and editing, a set of 171 behavioral statements in Yes-No format was selected to form the first version of the Interpersonal Behavior Inventory (IBI_1). The medium of observation chosen for the development of the IBI was that of behavioral ratings; in Leary's (1957) terminology, measurement took place at Level I (public communication). A group of 163 psychotherapists was asked to describe the behavior of 346 patients with respect to each of the 171 statements. From the intercorrelations of the 171 behavioral statements, 14 group factors were extracted, eight of which were judged to be those originally hypothesized. When intercorrelations were computed among 11 scales derived from the oblique factor structure, nine were judged to exhibit the postulated circular ordering.

In a subsequent investigation, Lorr and McNair (1965) attempted to expand their nine-variable circumplex to include the full set of 16 variables hypothesized by Leary and others. New items were added to those that were included in the earlier nine categories, and a sample of 265 therapists rated 523 outpatients on the 144 items of IBI_2. Fourteen group factors were extracted from the intercorrelations among items, and factor loadings were used as a basis for constructing 12 scales. Correlations among these scales confirmed the order of most of the original scales and enabled the identification of three new categories.

In a third effort to map the full spectrum of interpersonal behaviors, Lorr and McNair (1965) generated new items to represent five additional categories of interpersonal behavior and requested a nationwide sample of 115 therapists to rate 525 outpatients on the 160 items of IBI₃. At this point the rating format was modified from "Yes-No" to a five-place scale ranging from "not at all" to "quite often." Fourteen scales were developed in this study and an additional scale was later confirmed (Lorr & McNair, 1966).

The 15 dimensions of the most recent version of the Interpersonal Behavior Inventory are listed in the third column of Table 6.2, where they may be compared with those obtained by Leary and by later investigators. The most notable modification of Leary's circumplex occurs in the N and O vectors, where affiliation and sociability-exhibition replace Leary's tenderness and generosity. Conceptually, tenderness and generosity are too weak and loving to be classified as falling in the upper-right quadrant of the system. Psychometrically, batteries that employ tenderness and generosity to mark this segment of the circle will reveal a noticeable gap (Wiggins, 1979). In fact tenderness and generosity (NO) are weaker than Leary's collaboration and love (LM). Note also that Lorr and McNair (1965) were the first to emphasize the suspicious and mistrusting nature of the D category. This is compatible with the more recent notion that the DSM-III diagnosis of paranoid personality disorder is closely related to this octant. Lorr and McNair were unable to develop an autonomy scale that fit the hypothesized circular ordering. Perhaps a better fit would have been obtained with a scale emphasizing irritability and quarrelsomeness.

On both substantive and psychometric grounds, the Interpersonal Behavior Inventory appears to be a useful clinical device for assessment of patient characteristics and evaluation of therapeutic outcome. Although developed from professional ratings of patient samples, a similar structure was obtained when college students were asked to rate acquaintances (Lorr & McNair, 1965). In principle, the inventory could be employed in a self-report format, although the structure of self-reports has not yet been investigated. A possible advantage of the professional rater

format of the IBI is the minimization of social desirability in ratings. The correlation between therapists's item endorsements and independently rated item social desirability values of only .37 (Lorr & McNair, 1963) is dramatically less than the correlation between self-report and rated social desirability value typically obtained among college students (Edwards, 1957). Lorr and McNair conclude that: "Therapists are relatively unbiased in their descriptions of patients by the social desirability of the statement" (1963, p. 70).

As was true of earlier investigators (Leary, 1957; Schutz, 1958), Lorr and McNair were intrigued by the possibility of employing interpersonal variables in a classification scheme that would permit the identification of distinct interpersonal "types" representing homogeneous subgroups of individuals. To investigate this possibility, Lorr, Bishop, and McNair (1965) requested 116 experienced psychotherapists to rate a sample of 525 male and female psychiatric outpatients on IBI₃. A profile of standard scores on 15 interpersonal variables was obtained for each patient. Correlations among profiles across patients were used to form clusters of profiles whose members were maximally correlated with each other and minimally correlated with members of other clusters.

Four profile types were identified that classified somewhat less than half of all patients' profiles. The four interpersonal types were described in terms of the interpersonal variables within each type whose mean values were at least one standard deviation above those for the entire sample. Under these criteria, the four types that emerged each clustered around one of the four nodal points defining the interpersonal system: (1) Type I (inhibited-abasive-submissive) included patients whose profiles were elevated on variables surrounding the *submission* node of the system; (2) Type II (agreeable-nurturant-sociable) included patients whose profiles were elevated on variables surrounding the *love* node of the system; (3) Type III (hostile-mistrustful-detached) included patients whose profiles were elevated on variables surrounding the *hate* node of the system; and (4) Type IV (competitive-dominant-exhibitionistic) included patients whose profiles were elevated on variables surrounding the *dominance* node of the system.

With the exception of the fact that Type II patients tended to be older than patients in other groups, the background variables of age, marital status, and education were not systematically related to type membership. However, interesting trends were noted with respect to occupation and psychiatric diagnosis when the four profile types were compared. Type I patients were predominantly housewives, Type II were predominantly white collar workers, Type III were predominantly unskilled and semiskilled workers, and Type IV patients were predominantly from management and professional occupations. Although sharp diagnostic distinctions among types would not be expected in this relatively homogeneous group of neurotic outpatients, some interesting trends nevertheless emerged. Patients in the first three types tended to be diagnosed as psychoneurotic as contrasted with Type IV patients, who tended to be diagnosed as personality trait disturbance (DSM-II). The diagnosis of personality pattern disorder was more frequent for Type I and III than it was for Type II and IV.

The four profile types of Lorr and McNair represent distinct and meaningful categories within the general logic of the interpersonal circumplex in that they are organized around the four nodal (Freedman et al., 1951) or basic (Benjamin, 1974) points of the system. In contrast, the fourfold typology employed by Leary (1957), Carson (1969), and others is based on a quadrant interpretation of the circumplex that emphasizes the *off-quadrant* vectors of friendly-dominance, hostile-dominance, hostile-submission, and friendly-submission. Thus the Lorr-McNair typology and the Leary-Carson typology appear to be related to each other through a 45° rotation.

Considered together, the two typologies comprise the basic octant variables of the interpersonal circumplex.

The Benjamin System

The recent circumplex model of interpersonal behavior presented by Benjamin (1973, 1974, 1977, 1979; McLemore & Benjamin, 1979) is the most detailed, clinically rich, ambitious, and conceptually demanding of all contemporary models. In addition to attempting a more fine-grained specification of points around the circle, the Benjamin model attempts to reconcile the different interpretations placed upon the *power* dimension by such writers as Leary (1957) on the one hand and Schaefer (1965) on the other. This reconcilation is accomplished by incorporating the logical and relational distinctions among opposite, complementary, and antithetical behavior within a model that includes three planes or perspectives corresponding to actions, reactions, and self-actions.

The discrepancy between Leary's (1957) and Schaefer's (1965) conceptualizations of the power dimension stems in part from the fact that Schaefer's model was meant to apply to parental behavior that is by definition active in nature. Whereas Leary (and most other writers) view the poles of the power dimension in terms of dominance and submission, Schaefer views it in terms of control and autonomy. Benjamin (1974, 1979) considers autonomy to be the *opposite* of control and submission to be the *complement* of dominance. The distinction Benjamin makes between "opposites" and "complements" is not lexicographically precise (see Webster, 1976, pp. 12a–14a), but it seems to be based on a distinction between initiated actions and complementary reactions to these actions. Thus controlling and granting autonomy are opposite actions, while submitting is a complementary reaction to dominating. In this sense, the original Leary system is a mixture of opposites (love vs. hostility), complements (dominance vs. submission), and contrasts that do not make a great deal of intuitive sense (success vs. masochism). To avoid these and other inconsistencies, Benjamin proposed that the interpersonal circumplex be represented as two separate planes, one of which is composed of actions and their opposites, and the other of which is composed of reactions and their opposites.

A highly simplified version of Benjamin's (1979) two planes of interpersonal behavior is presented in Figure 6.2. The first plane is composed of primarily *active* behavior, and it is similar in conception to the descriptions of parents' behavior offered by Schaefer (1965). Such behavior may be thought of as actions of another directed toward self. The second plane describes reactions to these actions and, for consistency, may be thought of as childlike. The designations "parent" and "child" are not meant to restrict these actions and reactions to parents and their children, nor do they imply that one member of the interacting dyad has more responsibility for the interaction pattern than does the other. In her presentations of these two planes, Benjamin displays the vertical axis of the first plane in a 180° rotation so that reactions on the second plane correspond directly (i.e., are complementary) to the corresponding geometric location of actions on the first plane. In the present exposition, the dominant pole of the first plane is placed on top to maintain consistency with other expositions in this chapter.

The complete interpersonal circumplex presented by Benjamin consists of 36 finely distinguished points around a circle for each of two planes. The poles or nodal points (Freedman et al., 1951) of the axes that define the circular system are held to represent primitive or "basic" behavior; sexuality and murder in the case of the affiliation axis, and power and autonomy (separate territory) in the case of the vertical axis called "interdependence" by Benjamin. The other 32 points around each circle are held to be more balanced and "genteel" expressions of this basic behavior (Benjamin, 1974, p. 397).

With a little effort, the reader can readily see the patterns of actions and complementary reactions between these two planes illustrated in Figure 6.2. Thus managing and controlling on the first plane stand in a complementary relationship to yielding and submitting on the second plane. Annihilating attack on the first plane is reacted to by desperate protest on the second plane, and so on. In addition to opposite behavior (behavior appearing at 180° on each plane) and complementary behavior (systematically related *between* planes), Benjamin also distinguishes antithetical or antidotal responses. Antidotal responses are strategies for eliciting from the other person a response that is the *opposite* of his or her initial action. They are defined as the complement of an opposite. Thus to

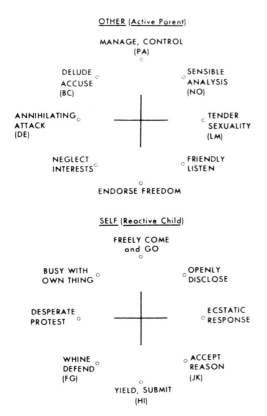

Figure 6.2. Simplified representation of Benjamin's (1979) two-plane model of interpersonal behavior.

find the antidote to managing and controlling behavior on the first axis, one finds its opposite (endorse freedom) and then behaves in a complementary fashion toward that opposite (freely come and go). This algorithm generates a number of fascinating hypotheses concerning the dynamics of impression management (Goffman, 1959), and the strategy implied by this approach is reminiscent of Potter's (1970) notion of "stopping the flow" as a lifemanship gambit.

Returning to the simplified version of the interpersonal system presented in Figure 6.2, we find that it is evident, from the capital letters in parentheses, that the system described in Benjamin's first plane differs from Leary's primarily in the conceptualization of the withdrawn (FG), submissive (HI), and dependent (JK) octants. It should also be clear from an examination of the second plane that the Benjamin system includes five categories of reaction that are not formally indexed within systems such as Leary's. The questions immediately arise, therefore, whether the two planes do in fact form separate circumplexes, and whether the complementary relations between these two planes are as specified. Despite the large amounts of evidence presented as relevant to these issues (Benjamin, 1974), it is difficult to answer these questions with any degree of certainty. This difficulty stems in large part from the fact that Benjamin tends to analyze all 36 variables on each plane rather than reducing items to a smaller set of octant or sixteenth scales. As a consequence, the reader is somewhat overwhelmed by tables of intercorrelations (Benjamin, 1974, pp. 406–407) and factor plots (Benjamin, 1974, pp. 410–411). Nevertheless, inspection of one of these plots (1974, p. 410) suggests that on the plane of active behavior, the poles of emancipation and control form an interdependency coordinate that is orthogonal to one defined by murderous attack and tender sexuality. As in the original Leary (1957) system, the NO dimension (sensible analysis) tends to fall slightly below

the warmth pole (LM), and consequently there is a noticeable gap in the upper-right quadrant of this system (Lorr & McNair, 1965; Stern, 1970; Wiggins, 1979a).

The plane for reactive or childlike behavior also appears to form a circumplex ordered around the coordinates of individualism versus submission and desperate protest versus ecstatic response. In contrast with the active circumplex of plane one, the reactive circumplex of plane two is not clearly defined in the upper-left quadrant, which should include such behavior as noncontingent reaction, busy with own thing, wall-off, and nondisclose (Benjamin, 1974, p. 412). Instead these distancing patterns of reaction tend to cluster around the desperate protest pole of the horizontal axis.

In addition to the two interpersonal planes just described, the Benjamin system also attempts to specify an intrapsychic plane in accord with the psychoanalytic notion of "introject." This third plane attempts to portray what happens when behavior represented on the top or active plane is "turned inward." Thus, for example, it is assumed that if others attempt to manage and control a person, and if the person turns these reactions upon his or her "self," the result is self-control. Similarly, if others attempt to endorse freedom with respect to a person, and the person turns this action inward, the result is a happy-go-lucky self that drifts with the moment. The basic idea is that attitudes toward self are determined by the way one is treated by others. This third plane may or may not be a useful psychoanalytic appendage to an otherwise interpersonal system. In early versions of this instrument, the hypothesized circular structure of the introject plane rather consistently failed to appear, particularly with reference to the power dimension (Benjamin, 1974, pp. 411–414).

It should be noted that the items of the instrument just described have undergone continuous revision in the light of new empirical findings. Five different versions of the instrument have been employed since its inception, although the characteristics of the newer versions have not as yet been published. Benjamin (personal communication, June 27, 1980) reports that a 1980 version provides a much closer fit to a circumplex model, for all three planes, than does the 1974 version described here. Of equal interest is the fact that a cluster version of the system has been developed in which scores are expressed as octants and for which a clear circumplex structure obtains, as one would expect from more reliable octant categories. This cluster version forms the basis of a commercially available automated clinical report that provides information related to interpersonal diagnosis, interpersonal treatment planning, and measurement of progress.[2]

The outstanding feature of the Benjamin system is the degree of specificity attempted in the identification of subtle and complex patterns of interaction from three perspectives. Despite this complexity, Benjamin has made an effort to present the results of structural analyses in language that is intelligible to both clinicians and their patients. Nevertheless, those who are contemplating using this system in clinical work have no alternatives to mastering the details of an unusually rich and complex theory of interpersonal behavior. Required reading would include both an overview of the theoretical orientation (Benjamin, 1973; 1974) and of the model itself and its psychometric characteristics (Benjamin, 1974). The clinical utility of the system is well illustrated by a structural analysis of a family in therapy (Benjamin, 1977), in which the model is used to describe family dynamics, develop a treatment plan, describe changes in therapy, analyze resistance, and measure movement toward a therapeutic goal. Additional clinical applications are described elsewhere (Benjamin, 1979), as are the formal diagnostic implications of the system (McLemore & Benjamin, 1979). Although the Benjamin

system is too recent to have been absorbed into the mainstream of interpersonal diagnosis, it clearly deserves the careful scrutiny of both clinicians and psychometricians.

A Taxonomy of Interpersonal Adjectives

In the course of an ambitious project whose eventual aim is the development of a taxonomy of trait-descriptive terms in the English language, a set of semantic marker scales was developed that may prove useful in comparing one interpersonal assessment system with another (Wiggins, 1979a). This research was predicated on the assumption that the universe of content of significant human tendencies (traits) is contained within the covers of an unabridged dictionary, and it capitalized on the previous taxonomic work of Allport and Odbert (1936), Norman (1967), and especially Goldberg (1977). The painstaking lexicographic work of these earlier investigators defined a universe of content of trait-descriptive words in the English language that embraced approximately 27,000 entries. By a variety of rating procedures, this potential universe was reduced to a list of 4063 terms that were relatively familiar and representative of the total universe.

Allport and Odbert (1936) distinguished between "stable biophysical traits" on the one hand and temporary states, moods, social roles, and physical characteristics on the other. Our own taxonomic efforts made finer distinctions within the realm of stable biophysical traits, many of which were first made by Allport (1937) in his classic text, but were not implemented in his taxonomy. Thus we attempted to distinguish between different *domains* of traits on the basis of the different kinds of descriptive jobs performed by words within these domains. For example, within the domain of stable biophysical traits we distinguished temperament traits (excitable, tense), character traits (moral, principled), material traits (miserly, stingy), attitudes (prejudiced, devout), mental predicates

[2]INTREX Interpersonal Institute, Inc., 2581 University Avenue, Madison, Wisconsin, 53705.

(intelligent, perceptive), and social roles (devilish, masculine). On both conceptual and empirical grounds, we developed preliminary categories within each of these broad domains to serve as a frame of reference for the development of a taxonomy of interpersonal traits.

Our working definition of interpersonal traits had reference to *dyadic interactions that have relatively clear-cut social (status) and emotional (love) consequences for both participants (self and other)*. On this basis we attempted to distinguish interpersonal traits from other categories such as temperament, moods, and cognitive traits. Starting with a pool of 1710 stable biophysical traits (Goldberg, 1977), we identified approximately 800 terms as meeting our working definition of interpersonal trait. Working as a team, three judges were able to distribute 567 of these terms across the 16 categories of interpersonal behavior described by Leary (1957), with unanimous agreement among raters. With reference to empirical self-report data, we were able to form 16 clusters of interpersonal adjectives that corresponded to those in the Leary system. When these adjectives were subsequently administered in eight-place, self-report format, the circular arrangement among octant scores corresponded to that previously reported for the ICL. This correspondence with the Leary system was considered to be of limited value, however, since it included the shortcomings of the system as well; namely, a noticeable gap between PA and NO, as well as a reversal of NO and LM. Consequently we attempted to devise a revised system that would incorporate the psychometric properties assumed by the circumplex model.

The principal shortcoming of the original Leary system, from a psychometric point of view, was seen to be the lack of bipolarity between variables opposite to each other on the circle. Thus we revised our definition of the basic 16 interpersonal variables in such a way that they would represent genuine semantic contrasts. Hence, for example,

Leary's contrast of success versus masochism was reconstrued as ambitious versus lazy; his contrast of narcissism versus conformity was reconstrued as arrogant versus unassuming, and so on. In addition, the empty upper-right quadrant of the Leary system was defined as gregarious-extraverted versus aloof-introverted (lower-left quadrant). In developing these revised clusters, an attempt was made to identify items that were highly negatively correlated with their opposite cluster and that had zero correlations with their theoretically orthogonal clusters. Once tentative markers of these bipolar semantic clusters had been identified, the entire taxonomy was revised and interpersonal adjectives were distinguished from those in other domains.

By a variety of psychometric procedures, we identified those eight items in each of 16 interpersonal categories that had optimal circumplex properties. When these 128 adjectives are scored as octant scales, they provide the best circumplex structure recorded in the literature to date (Wiggins, Steiger, & Gaelick, 1981). It is not surprising that they do, since they were derived with this in mind. Having clearly identified the vectors of interpersonal behavior, it was then possible to classify 817 interpersonal adjectives into 16 categories with reference to their location in circumplex space (Wiggins, 1979b). This taxonomy may prove useful to those concerned with the more formal, itemmetric aspects of trait measurement.

The 16 variables of the interpersonal adjective scales are listed in the final column of Table 6.2. The variables have been labeled in such a way as to permit comparison with the generic interpersonal themes of the Leary system listed in the first column. Although the two systems correspond with respect to the first six variables (P, A, B, C, D, E) and with respect to the weakness variable (I), they differ with respect to conceptualization or placement on the remaining nine variables. These differences reflect redefinitions of variables as bipolar opposites and a reconstruing of the upper-right quadrant in terms of strong affiliation. Evidence for the superior structural properties of the interpersonal adjective scales is based primarily on *octant* scales (Wiggins, 1979a), and hence the utility of the fine distinctions made among sixteenths is still an open question.

Despite their admirable psychometric properties, the interpersonal adjective scales were not devised for the purpose of routine clinical assessment. Instead they were meant to serve as semantic markers of interpersonal space for purposes of comparison with other assessment systems, and for identifying dimensions of interpersonal behavior measured by scales employed in experimental personality research (Wiggins, 1980). Within each octant of the interpersonal system, the interpersonal scales measure narrow semantic dimensions with a high degree of fidelity. Hence they may serve as structural reference points for scales and inventories that are more substantively rich.

The interpersonal adjective scales are currently being employed in a series of studies designed to identify circumplex dimensions in existing personality scales and inventories, such as Jackson's (1974) Personality Research Form, Edwards' (1959) Personal Preference Schedule, Campbell's (1959) need scales, Stern's (1970) Activities Index, and Gough and Heilbrun's (1965) Adjective Check List. The scales have recently been revised for clinical administration by replacing a number of awkward and difficult adjectives with more familiar terms.

The Impact Message Inventory

The instruments for assessing interpersonal behavior considered thus far focus on the characteristic behaviors of "actors" in their transactions with significant "others." Who is the actor and who is the other depends on one's perspective, of course, but the emphasis is placed upon what persons *do* to one another rather than upon what immediate effects such actions may have. The impact of an actor's actions upon another may be distinguished conceptually from subsequent actions that other may take toward the original actor. For example, A's behavior toward B may make B *feel* a certain way about A; and B's feeling, together with a variety of other factors, will influence B's subsequent behavior toward A. The Impact Message Inventory (IMI) developed by Kiesler and his associates (Kiesler, 1979b; Perkins et al., 1979) is directed at the measurement of this intermediate impact link in the chain of interpersonal actions and reactions.

The construct of impact message is central to Kiesler's (1979a) analysis of dyadic relationships from the perspective of interpersonal communication theory. In this formulation, the actor transmits an "evoking message" (Beier, 1966) to the other through both verbal and nonverbal channels, and this message is meant to impose a particular encoder-decoder relationship. The other receives (decodes) an "impact message" (Kiesler, 1979a) that elicits covert affective and cognitive reactions in him or her (decoder-to-encoder meanings) and influences the relationship message that he or she countercommunicates to the original actor. Although decoders are not ordinarily aware of their affective and cognitive reactions to impact messages, these reactions are potentially available to awareness, and indeed this type of introspection is felt by Kiesler (1979a) to provide an invaluable source of information about the interpersonal style of an actor, namely, the *impact* that actor has on significant others.

According to Kiesler, the emotional problems experienced by disordered persons stem from the aversive countercommunications they unknowingly elicit from others. Thus the two major tasks of the interpersonal psychotherapist are seen as: (1) identifying the covert thoughts and feelings the client elicits from the therapist (and presumably from other significant persons); and (2) "metacommunicating" with the client about the self-defeating consequences of the client's evoking style (Kiesler, 1979a, p. 307). The Impact Message Inventory was developed with this and other practical applications in mind.

The overall strategy of scale construction for the IMI was one in which descriptions of the overt interpersonal behavior of an actor were employed as stimuli to elicit subjective reactions to that actor. These subjective reactions (items) were then scaled in such a way as to align them with their corresponding evoking behavior from the interpersonal circumplex. The end result was a standardized inventory that permits the systematic assessment of a subject's covert affective and cognitive reactions to a specified significant other.

Items from the 15 scales of Lorr and McNair's (1967) Interpersonal Behavior Inventory were used to generate paragraph descriptions of the overt interpersonal behavior typical of each of 15 pure interpersonal types. These interpersonal vignettes were then presented to six members of Kiesler's research team with instructions to imagine being in the company of the persons described and to record their reactions in response to the stem: "He makes me feel . . ." Content analysis of the 784 impact message items thus generated suggested that they could be classified inclusively under the four categories of: (1) *direct feelings* (e.g., irritated); (2) *action tendencies* (e.g., I want to take care of him or her); (3) *perceived evoking message* (e.g., he or she wants me to put him or her on a pedestal); and (4) *reciprocal impact message* (e.g., I make him or her uncomfortable). The fourth category was later abandoned when too few items survived a multistage item-selection strategy.

Each of the 784 impact message items was rated independently by six judges on a four-place scale indicating its descriptiveness of their reaction to the vignette to which the item was originally keyed. Items were eliminated on the grounds of low descriptiveness ratings, redundancy in meaning, and complex wording. An attempt was also made to achieve a broad range of messages distributed equally across the four categories of reaction. The result of these item selection procedures was a pool of 259 items classified as descriptive reactions to one or another of the 15 categories of interpersonal behavior proposed by Lorr and McNair. The generalizability of these classifications was assessed in a group of 451 introductory psychology students, who were each required to rate the descriptiveness of all 259 impact messages for *one* of the 15 interpersonal vignettes originally employed for item generation. Students were assigned randomly to one of 15 groups, each of which received a different vignette as a stimulus.

Data from the student sample were used to select items for inclusion in the most recent version of the Impact Message Inventory (IMI-Form II). The goal of item analysis was the selection of the six best items for each of the 15 interpersonal scales, with two items each coming from the reaction categories of direct feelings, action tendencies, and perceived evoking message. On the assumption that the structure of the final version of the IMI should be isomorphic to that of Lorr and McNair's (1967) IBI, the major emphasis in item analysis was upon identifying item sets that would yield a circular ordering in two-dimensional space. A second, and when possible equally important, consideration was the selection of items whose mean rated applicability was highest for their own categories.

The most recent version of the IMI (Kiesler, 1979b) consists of three sets of 30 items grouped under the headings of: (1) When I am with this person he or she makes me feel . . . (direct feelings); (2) When I am with this person he or she makes me feel that . . . (action tendencies); and (3) When I am with this person it appears to me that . . . (perceived evoking messages). Within each section, the respondent is required to rate the applicability of each of 30 items to the target person. The 15 impact message scales are each composed of two items from each of the three categories of reaction. The interpersonal impact of a given target person can thus be represented as a profile of 15 scale scores.

The 15 scales of IMI-Form II did not exhibit a clear circumplex structure in the sample of students on which the scales were derived (Perkins et al., 1979). A lack of distinctiveness among several scales is suggested by the fact that 12 of the scale intercorrelations exceeded .80, and six of these were .90 or greater. Principal component analysis of the intercorrelations among scales revealed that three approximately equal-sized components accounted for 85% of the variance. In part because the submissiveness pole of the dominance axis appeared as a separate third component, the configuration of scales around the first two circumplex components was far from circular. This rather substantial deviation from the hypothesized circumplex structure may not pose significant problems for many applications of the IMI. However, interpretations of IMI profiles in terms of the purportedly corresponding variables of Lorr and McNair's system should be qualified with this in mind. Similarly, the high degree of redundancy that exists among several of the scales suggests that a number of them could be combined into more reliable and more distinctive variables.

Although the 15 IMI scales are each composed of only six items, they appear to be internally consistent, in terms of mean item-total correlations (Perkins et al., 1979). Nevertheless, the scales are substantively heterogeneous in that they each contain items from the conceptually distinct domains of direct feelings, action tendencies, and perceived evoking messages. A more precise understanding of the links of interpersonal action-reaction sequences might be achieved by developing separate and larger item pools for each of these domains. The domain of perceived evoking messages, for example, would seem to be closely related to, if not redundant with, the Lorr and McNair scales, which measure the perceived interpersonal behavior of others. The domain of self-reported action tendencies might be found to

be correlated with the subsequent overt reactions of the other toward the stimulus person. The domain of direct feelings would seem to be a highly distinctive feature of the IMI, and it may provide a bridge to a body of work concerned with affective reactions to interpersonal stimuli (e.g., Plutchik, 1980). If nothing else, the availability of such separate item pools might contribute to the development of a future version of the IMI that provided separate profiles of subscales for direct feelings, action tendencies, and perceived evoked messages.

The Impact Message Inventory is a much needed and welcome addition to the clinician's collection of methods for measuring dimensions of interpersonal behavior. The focus of the instrument upon the covert impact of a patient upon significant others provides a valuable source of clinical information that could not be derived from previous assessment devices. Moreover, the theoretical framework within which the IMI is embedded (Kiesler, 1979a) represents a significant extension of the efforts of Leary (1957), Carson (1969), and others to provide a systematic framework for measuring the central concepts of Sullivan's theory of interpersonal psychiatry.

CLINICAL APPLICATIONS

As one might expect from its original focus of convenience (Freedman et al., 1951), the circumplex model of interpersonal behavior lends itself well to analysis of the dyadic transactions that occur between therapist and client in the course of psychotherapy, as well as to the evaluation of therapeutic outcome. Most of the major clinical assessment systems just described have been utilized in psychotherapy research (Benjamin, 1977; Chance, 1959; Leary & Coffey, 1955; Leary & Harvey, 1956; Lorr & McNair, 1966). In addition, the formulations of Leary (1957) and of Carson (1969, 1979) have provided a general set of expectations with respect to specific patterns of action and reaction that are likely to occur between therapist and client in the course of psychotherapy. In general, at least for early interaction sequences, interpersonal actions tend to "pull" responses that are complementary with respect to affection and symmetric with respect to dominance (Carson, 1969; Leary, 1957). These expectations have received some confirmation in the relatively small empirical literature dealing with this topic (Celani, 1974; Heller, Meyers, & Kline, 1963; Mueller, 1969; Mueller & Dilling, 1968; Shannon & Guerney, 1973).

Although there would appear to be norms or conventions governing the appropriate reactions to specific interpersonal actions, the client seeking treatment is likely to be characterized by a behavioral rigidity that violates these conventions (Carson, 1969). Recent thinking on this matter has focused on the proposition that inappropriate reactions to interpersonal actions reflect, at least in part, distortions in the *interpersonal construal style* of disordered persons (Carson, 1979; Golding, 1977, 1978, in press). That is: "There may be substantial and mutually supportive relationships between a person's more characteristic social behavior and the manner in which the person construes the social environment" (Carson, 1979, p. 264). This proposition in turn leads to a set of specific predictions of clients' misperceptions of others that are based on their own salient interpersonal tendencies. It is this type of fine-grained, substantively rich research that highlights the utility of employing circumplex models of interpersonal behavior in clinical research.

The circumplex model also provides a useful frame of reference from which to view the behavior of the psychotherapist (Swensen, 1967). As Bierman (1969) has shown, the extensive and at times inconsistent literature of the influence of therapists' behavior on clients' responses and outcomes becomes more comprehensible when viewed from the perspective of Leary's circumplex model. In Bierman's view, optimal therapeutic effects appear to be associated with the therapist's active engagement with and positive regard for the client as expressed in behavior falling in the upper-right quadrant of the circumplex. Perhaps more generally, the effective therapist is one who is flexible enough to adopt stances complementary to those the client needs to experience (Carson, 1969, p. 288).

Although the focus of treatment in psychotherapy is frequently upon interpersonal problems, outcome research often focuses upon symptoms (e.g., depression, anxiety). Horowitz (1979) has recently pointed out that the internal structure of symptoms has failed to reveal any compelling conceptual scheme, and he has focused instead on the structure of *interpersonal problems* as presented by patients entering psychotherapy. Ratings of videotaped interviews revealed that 76% of the problems presented by patients were interpersonal in nature. When these problems were subjected to multidimensional scaling analysis, the familiar dimensions of friendly versus hostile and dominance versus submission emerged. Horowitz is currently exploring the possibility of developing a standardized method for assessing interpersonal problems within this structural model. The availability of such a method would facilitate a shift of focus in outcome research from symptoms to interpersonal problems.

It is tempting to explore the application of circumplex models to psychotherapy in detail, but that would only detract from the principal focus of the present section, which is on psychiatric diagnosis. Although the decision to emphasize psychiatric diagnosis as an area to which circumplex models may be applied is in part a reflection of my own interests, it is also based on the conviction that the topic of psychiatric diagnosis provides a particularly apt illustration of the compatibility of circumplex formulations with very recent ideas from related areas of psychology.

Psychiatric Diagnosis

McLemore and Benjamin (1979) have recently observed that the time may now be ripe for an interpersonal taxonomy of disordered behavior as a viable alternative to traditional intrapsychic and disease entity classification systems. This observation is supported by several converging lines of thought that suggest a renewed interest in interpersonal categories of disordered behavior. First, the view that mental illness is a metaphor for problems of living (Szasz, 1961; Sarbin, 1969) and particularly problems of interpersonal relationships (Adams, 1964; Carson, 1969, 1971; Leary, 1957; McLemore & Benjamin, 1979) has its historical roots in Sullivanian psychiatry, and in its modern form is compatible with theories of social exchange and person perception (Carson, 1979). Second, within the area of cognitive psychology, there has been a renewed interest in the nature of human categorization, due in large part to Rosch's radical reformulation of the manner in which cognitive categories are organized (Rosch, 1978). Third, the recognition that Rosch's analysis may be applied to person perception (Cantor & Mischel, 1979a) and specifically to categories of interpersonal behavior (Wiggins, 1980) has provided a new paradigm for investigating an old problem. Fourth, the specific extension of the preceding line of reasoning to the categories of descriptive psychiatry (Cantor et al., 1980) brings together the diverse threads of a variety of disciplines. I will not review the arguments of the first view, as they are likely to be familiar to most readers and are well discussed elsewhere. I will summarize the second and third, and then discuss their conceptual implications within the hopefully neutral context of the concept of intelligence (Neisser, 1979) before extending the argument to categories of psychiatric diagnosis.

Prototypes within Fuzzy Sets. The traditional view of the nature of cognitive cat-

egories is that elements within a category must possess *all* of a small set of critical criterial features. Elements that exhibit only some of these features are by definition not in the category of interest, and hence the categories are mutually exclusive, with clearly defined boundaries. This is the manner in which categories were defined in early studies of concept formation (red *and* tall *and* rectangular). It is also the basis for the syndrome definition of disease (cough *and* fever *and* rash), and within the area of psychometrics this conception has been called a class model (Loevinger, 1957). By contrast, the Roschian categories of human thought are not based on sets of critical defining features. They contain elements whose features are distributed somewhat as follows: AB, BC, CD, DE, and so on. Each element has a feature or features in common with one or several of the other elements, but there are no features common to all elements in this set. Such categories will tend to have "fuzzy" boundaries, and class membership is more continuous than discrete (Rosch & Mervis, 1975).

Despite the loosely defined nature of Roschian categories, there is a principle of organization within categories that facilitates our use of them. Within each category there is a *prototype* or exemplar of that category, which serves as a cognitive reference point for all members of that category (Rosch, 1975). Thus within the natural language category of *bird*, we would tend to identify a robin as being more birdlike (prototypical) than, for example, a penguin. In this sense, then, elements within a category can be said to be clustered around a prototype, with less prototypic elements merging into the fuzzy boundaries of related categories. One can view a prototype as a hypothetical element within a category, which has the highest multiple correlation with all other members of that category and the lowest multiple correlations with members of other categories. In this context it is important to note that the concept of prototype is a "convenient grammatical fiction" (Rosch, 1978). It is not assumed that prototypes exist in nature; it is only assumed that people can make judgments of prototypicality.

In addition to exhibiting an internal structure, Roschian categories are also organized in relationship to each other within a two-dimensional structure. The vertical dimension of categorization is one of inclusiveness or abstractness, as would be found in the ordered categories of dining room chair, chair, furniture, and inanimate object. The horizontal dimension of Roschian categories divides categories of different content that are at the same level of inclusiveness, as in the categories of chair, dog, and bus. The different levels of abstraction along the hierarchy of inclusiveness are not equally useful as categories of thought. In fact, for any hierarchical structure of concepts, there is a *basic level* that is optimally useful (Rosch, Mervis, Gray, Johnson, & Boyes-Braem, 1976). At this optimal or basic level, categories are both information rich and maximally differentiated from one another. Superordinate (more abstract) categories are highly differentiated, but less rich in information. Subordinate (more concrete) categories are highly rich in detail, but poorly differentiated from other categories at their level.

Person Perception from a Roschian Perspective. In an important series of papers, Cantor and Mischel (1977, 1979a, 1979b) have demonstrated that Rosch's analysis of categories of natural objects and events, such as fruit, furniture, and game, may also hold for categories of persons, such as extraverted person, cultured person, and emotionally unstable person. They hypothesized that categories of persons, such as those listed in Figure 6.3, are organized along a vertical dimension of inclusiveness ranging from subordinate level categories (door-to-door salesman) through basic level categories ("P.R. type") to superordinate categories (extraverted person). This hypothesized hierarchy

was verified by hierarchical cluster analysis of judges' sortings of 36 categories, some of which are listed in Figure 6.3 (Canter & Mischel, 1979a). The authors also demonstrated that categories at different levels of the hierarchy differ from one another in the richness and distinctiveness of attributes associated with them, as would be expected of Roschian categories.

When subjects were asked to list those attributes they associated with each of the category names under investigation, the lists for superordinate categories (extraverted person, cultured person) contained relatively few attributes; but these attributes were distinctive in the sense that they tended not to be listed in other superordinate categories. In contrast, the lists for subordinate categories (door-to-door salesman, campaign manager) included many more attributes, but these attributes frequently appeared in more than one subordinate category. These results, together with other results illustrating the operation of prototypes within person categories (Cantor & Mischel, 1977, 1979a, 1979b), suggest that the categories we employ to encode aspects of persons may indeed be organized in the manner specified by Rosch for categories of objects in the natural environment.

The illustrative hierarchy of person concepts displayed in Figure 6.3 was used by Cantor and Mischel to demonstrate a point about the Roschian nature of person categories, rather than to suggest a particular theoretical taxonomy. In contrast, the circumplex model of interpersonal behavior is meant to be a substantive taxonomy, and its categories are hypothesized to be employed by both ordinary persons and interpersonal theorists. In this connection it is important to note the structural similarities between Rosch's two-dimensional framework of category organization and Guttman's (1954) two-dimensional framework for representing the interrelationships among test scores (Wiggins, 1980). The first dimension of Guttman's framework is a vertical dimension

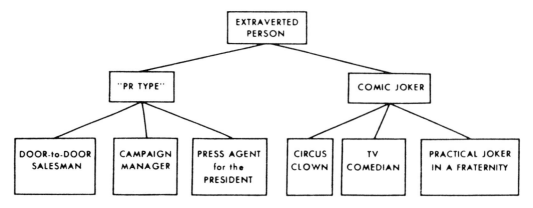

Figure 6.3.   Illustrative hierarchy of person categories (after Cantor & Mischel, 1979a).

of complexity, called a *simplex,* on which tests of similar content can be ordered, for example, tests of addition, subtraction, multiplication, and division. The second dimension of Guttman's framework is a *circumplex,* which describes the ordering that exists among tests of different content at the same level of complexity, such as reasoning, verbal ability, and numerical ability. Thus the complete Guttman model, called the *radex,* is isomorphic with the Roschian model of categories, with the exception that the Guttman model is more explicit concerning the nature of relationships to be expected among categories at a given level of complexity. This greater specificity is seen as an advantage, in that more precise specifications can be made regarding the relative distinctiveness of attributes between categories that are adjacent, orthogonal, or opposite to each other along the circumplex.

Guttman's (1954) horizontal dimension of circumplexity provides a geometric representation of a relationship among fuzzy sets in which membership is probabilistic and continuous rather than determinate and discrete. Categories may be represented as wedge-shaped segments of a circle, in which elements of a category are organized with reference to a prototype that falls near the center of the perimeter of a given wedge. Guttman's dimension of complexity is similar to Rosch's dimension of inclusiveness,

which, in terms of interpersonal behavior, translates into the *number* of categories employed for analysis. Thus, for example, the fourfold taxonomy of interpersonal behavior employed by Carson (1969) is based on relatively superordinate categories, and the 36 category system employed by Benjamin (1974) utilizes relatively subordinate categories. In sum, the circumplex representation of categories of interpersonal behavior is highly compatible with Rosch's principles of category organization, and it provides a highly explicit model for testing the organization among and within categories in the interpersonal domain.

Conceptual Implications of the Roschian Perspective   A recent conceptual analysis of the concept of intelligence from a Roschian perspective has been provided in a provocative theoretical paper by Neisser (1979). Neisser begins by noting that agreement as to the nature of intelligence, that is, what intelligence *is,* is not much greater today than it was during the time that Boring (1923) offered the rather unsatisfactory proposition that intelligence is what intelligence tests measure. Nevertheless, there has always been a reasonable consensus as to who *has* intelligence (e.g., Einstein), irrespective of what intelligence *is.* From a Roschian perspective, the concept of *intelligent person* is a category whose members have, collectively, a large number of attributes, no single set of which is definitive in the sense that all members possess that set of attributes. Nevertheless, Neisser explains, some attributes are typical in that, on the average, many members have them; and it is this profile of average or representative characteristics that provides us with the *prototype* of an intelligent person. Thus when we characterize a person as intelligent, bright, or clever, we do so not with respect to a small set of necessary and sufficient attributes, but rather by comparison with a prototype of the intelligent person.

The conceptual implications of Neisser's analysis become more evident when he returns to the issue of what intelligence is.

There are no definitive criteria of intelligence, just as there are none for chairness; it is a fuzzy-edged concept to which many features are relevant. Two people may both be quite intelligent and yet have very few traits in common—they resemble the prototype along different dimensions. Thus, there is no such quality as *intelligence,* any more than there is such a thing as *chairness*—resemblance is an external fact and not an internal essence. There can be no process-based definition of intelligence, because it is not a unitary quality. It is a resemblance between two individuals, one real and the other prototypical. (1979, p. 223)

It is within the above context that Neisser raises the issue of how one might *measure* intelligence. The answer is that one might attempt to quantify all relevant prototypical features of the category of intelligent person, but any such effort would necessarily fall short of complete measurement, since indexes of many of the features cannot be easily or practically obtained. Nevertheless, one can approximate such an ideal by measuring some of the relevant dimensions of the prototype, thereby adopting what is essentially a "psychometric prototype."

Perhaps the most intriguing aspect of Neisser's analysis is its apparent *generality* of application. The same set of considerations that were brought to bear on the question of

what intelligence *is* would apply to the question of what extroversion *is,* and, as will become evident in the next section, to the question of what schizophrenia *is.*

Psychiatric Diagnoses as Prototype Categorizations. Cantor, Smith, French, and Mezzich (1980) have extended the Roschian analysis to categories of psychiatric diagnosis. They develop their argument with respect to the hierarchy of categories implicit in the section on functional psychosis of DSM-II, as illustrated in Figure 6.4. At a superordinate level, this system identifies such broad and inclusive categories as functional psychosis, psychoneurosis, and organic brain disorders. At this level of inclusiveness, the expectation would be that category prototypes would be relatively "impoverished," since there would be few features that were representative of all members of such categories. At the next and perhaps "basic" level, the categories of schizophrenia and affective disorder would be expected to have relatively rich and distinctive prototypes, although borderline cases would be anticipated between these two fuzzy sets. At the subordinate level, where finer distinctions are made between, for example, schizoaffective and chronic undifferentiated schizophrenia, one would expect somewhat richer prototypes with fewer distinctive features and many more borderline cases. On the basis of the previous empirical work of Rosch and of Cantor and Mischel, one would also expect "imperfect nesting" to occur within this total system (Cantor et al., 1980). Thus, for example, although the feature of "hallucinations" might be expected to be part of the prototype for functional psychosis, this feature might not occur in prototypes of all eight of the categories that are subordinate to functional psychosis.

Cantor et al. (1980) asked 13 experienced psychiatrists to list the clinical features characterizing prototypical patients in each of the nine diagnostic categories displayed in Figure 6.4. The resulting lists of features for the

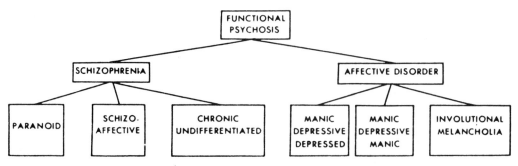

Figure 6.4. DSM–II hierarchy of diagnostic categories (after Cantor et al., 1980).

nine categories exhibited the pattern one would expect of Roschian categories: many unique features, listed by only one psychiatrist, very few features listed by most of the psychiatrists; and a substantial number of features listed by 15 to 30% of the psychiatrists. Although there was a tendency for features to be nested at different levels within the hierarchy, the nesting was imperfect, as expected. Examination of the richness and distinctiveness of category attributes at different levels of the hierarchy led Cantor et al. to suggest that the categories of schizophrenia and affective disorder comprise a basic level of psychiatric diagnosis. The superordinate category of functional psychosis had fewer attributes associated with it, and the subordinate categories (e.g., manic-depressive: manic), although richer on the average, were considerably less distinctive in terms of overlapping attributes.

Cantor and her collaborators (1980) reasoned that if psychiatric diagnostic categories are in fact Roschian, then the ease, accuracy, and reliability with which clinicians can diagnose a single case should be a function of the prototypicality of the presenting features of that case with reference to its diagnostic category. To test this prediction, they assembled case histories, from the files of a Veterans Administration Hospital, of patients who had been previously diagnosed as falling within one of four subordinate categories listed in Figure 6.4. These case histories were in turn classified in terms of their prototyp-

icality with reference to the features of each diagnostic category established in the study just described. Highly prototypical case records contained between eight and 13 features of the prototype for their category, records of medium prototypicality contained between five and eight features of the prototype, and atypical case histories contained only four features of their associated prototype. Nine psychiatrists were asked to read the case histories and to decide on an appropriate diagnostic category, as well as to indicate on a seven-place scale how well the patient fit the chosen category ("confidence"). In general, it was found that both accuracy and confidence increased with the prototypicality of the case history being rated. However, the results were not entirely in accord with the hypothesis, and this important study needs to be replicated. Nevertheless, the overall results of both studies provide support for the notion that categories of formal psychiatric diagnosis are Roschian in nature.

Although conceived within the context of a disease entity or class model, the categories of psychiatric diagnosis may now be viewed as being organized according to the same principles as are categories of natural objects, events, and persons. The difference of course is that the categories of psychiatric diagnosis are specialized categories developed in the context of psychiatric practice, and consequently they are less generally employed. Thus, for example, Bleuler (1911 and 1950) coined the term "schizophrenia" to describe the prototypic features of a rather heterogeneous group of psychiatric patients. Some, although certainly not all, of the features associated with this prototype may be associated with genetically determined predispositions; and some, although again not all, of the features associated with the prototype may be associated with dysfunctions of neural transmission. But it should be clear that such issues have to do with what schizophrenia *is,* rather than with the diagnostic issue of who *has* schizophrenia, which is a judged resemblance between two individuals, one real and the other prototypical (Neisser, 1979). If the concept of "mental illness" is indeed a metaphor for describing problems of living, then one would expect a relationship to exist between prototypes of psychiatric illness and categories of interpersonal behavior (Carson, 1971).

Psychiatric Diagnoses as Interpersonal Prototypes. A promising method for evaluating the interpersonal implications of categories of psychiatric diagnosis has been employed by Plutchik and his associates (Plutchik, 1967; 1980; Plutchik & Platman, 1977; Schaefer & Plutchik, 1966). In this method clinicians are provided with diagnostic labels (e.g., schizoid, paranoid) and are requested to rate the applicability of interpersonal traits (e.g., obedient, quarrelsome) to these diagnostic labels. Clinicians' ratings of each trait are pooled, and the results for each diagnostic category are displayed as a profile of interpersonal traits. These profiles may be viewed as interpersonal prototypes of diagnostic categories. Multivariate analysis of the intercorrelations among profiles reveals the structure of diagnostic categories with reference to interpersonal traits.

One such study (Plutchik & Platman, 1977) focused on seven nonpsychotic personality disorders described in DSM-II: compulsive, cyclothymic, hysterical, paranoid, passive-aggressive, schizoid, and sociopathic. The category of "well-adjusted" was

also included. Each diagnostic category was rated by four psychiatrists, with a total of 20 psychiatrists participating in the study. Twelve interpersonal trait terms were selected so as to be representative of an interpersonal circumplex (Schaefer, 1961). The interjudge reliability in the assignment of traits to diagnostic categories was generally high; the average correlation among the four judges rating each category ranged from .79 (cyclothymic) to .96 (hysterical personality).

The pooled judges' ratings for each diagnostic category provided an interpersonal profile of the prototype of that category. For example, the schizoid personality was most frequently described as shy, self-conscious, and brooding, and least frequently described as affectionate, sociable, and adventurous. The mean interpersonal profile of each diagnostic category was correlated with the mean interpersonal profile of all other diagnostic categories, and two principal components were extracted from the matrix of intercorrelations. These two components accounted for 91% of the variance, and they serve as coordinates for the factor plot given in Figure 6.5. It is clear from this figure that the implicitly assumed similarity among diagnostic categories results in a circumplex that is organized around the familiar coordinates of dominance-submission and love-hate.

A similar set of findings was obtained when clinicians were asked to indicate the applicability of emotion terms (e.g., fearful, angry, sad) to categories of psychiatric diagnosis (Plutchik, 1967). This result might have been expected from the structural similarities between circumplexes of interpersonal trait terms and circumplexes of interpersonal affect terms (Plutchik, 1980). More generally, it has been demonstrated that interpersonal trait terms, emotion terms, and diagnostic labels are closely related to each other within a circumplex model whose coordinates are dominance-submission and love-hate (Schaefer & Plutchik, 1966). All of these results are of course compatible with

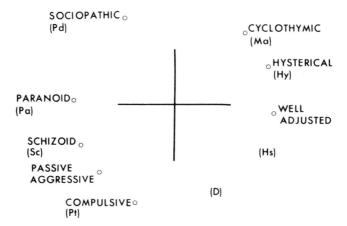

Figure 6.5. The structure of rated diagnostic categories (Plutchik & Platman, 1977) and the hypothetical location of MMPI scales (Schaefer, 1961).

the idea that the prototypes around which categories of psychiatric diagnosis are organized contain features that are interpersonal in nature. Although this is not a novel idea, it is one that deserves more attention than it has received (McLemore & Benjamin, 1979).

Schaefer (1961) has suggested that the MMPI clinical scales, that were developed with reference to categories of psychiatric diagnosis, may also be ordered according to a circumplex. It is well known that most of the variance among MMPI clinical scales can be accounted for in terms of two orthogonal factors. This fact prompted Kassebaum, Couch, and Slater (1959) to suggest a two-dimensional circular model for MMPI clinical scales that bears some resemblance to the interpersonal circumplex. Schaefer's (1961) argument is developed with reference to the apparent circular ordering that exists among eight MMPI clinical scales *(Ma, Pd, Pa, Sc, Pt, D, Hs, Hy)* in the table of intercorrelations reported by Williams and Lawrence (1954). Extrapolating from Schaefer's argument, these MMPI clinical scales have been superimposed upon the Plutchik and Platman data illustrated in Figure 6.5. The placement of these MMPI clinical scales is hypothetical rather than empirical.

If the MMPI clinical scales reflect conventional diagnostic labeling, they too would be expected to exhibit a circular ordering (Wiggins, 1979a). Although this is an appealing argument, it is unfortunately not supported by the data at issue. The intercorrelations among the eight MMPI clinical scales reported by Williams and Lawrence (1954), in fact, form a *simplex* of variables that are ordered with respect to psychopathology, the highest loading occurring on *Sc* and the lowest loading occurring on *Ma* (Wiggins, Steiger, & Gaelick, 1981). In retrospect, this is quite evident from an examination of the correlation matrix at issue (Schaefer, 1961, p. 155). Whether this simplex is interpreted as psychopathology (Block, 1965) or as social desirability (Jackson & Messick, 1961), it is clear that it precludes the possibility of finding the hypothesized circular ordering of MMPI clinical scales. In principle, however, one might expect a circular ordering among scales designed to measure the prototypic features of categories of psychiatric diagnosis. The problems of measurement here are psychometric in nature, rather than conceptual.

Millon's System of Psychiatric Diagnosis. Although cast within a different theoretical perspective, the diagnostic system of Millon (1969) shares features in common with the interpersonal systems considered in this chapter. Millon characterizes his system as:

Merely an interpretive synthesis, a set of "armchair" prototypes drawn from diverse sources such as hospital psychiatry, multivariate cluster studies, learning research and psychoanalytic theory. It is not a typology documented by systematic empirical research; rather, it is like a theory, a provisional tool which hopefully will aid us in organizing our subject more clearly and with greater understanding, a convenient but essentially fictional format designed to focus and systematize our thinking about psychopathology (p. 219).

Despite this overly modest assessment, Millon's (1969) *Modern psychopathology* is a remarkable summary and integration of what was known and of what was suspected about psychopathology in the late sixties. As an alternative to DSM–II, Millon devised a system in which the major clinical syndromes are coordinated within a theoretical framework that specifies their interrelationships. The major distinction of this system is between *pathological symptom disorders* of moderate (neurotic, psychophysiologic) and marked (psychotic) severity and *pathological personality patterns* of mild (e.g., asocial), moderate (e.g., schizoid), marked (e.g., schizophrenic), and profound (terminal) degree. The most distinctive feature of this system is the emphasis it places upon mild pathological patterns of personality and the manner in which these patterns are related to more severe forms of disturbance. Millon (1969) feels that interpersonal dimensions of personality are especially relevant for the classification of mild pathological patterns, since the persons characterized by these patterns are functioning in a normal social milieu in which their interpersonal style will determine the future course of their impairments (p. 223).

The mild pathological patterns are classi-

fied within a scheme based on two underlying dimensions, which from our point of view might be considered "facets." The facet of *source of reinforcement* specifies the primary source from which persons derive their emotional satisfactions (self or others). The elements differentiated by this facet are dependent, independent, detached, and ambivalent, referring respectively to relying on others, relying on self, relying on neither, and being conflicted about whom to rely upon. The facet of *coping behavior* specifies the pattern of instrumental behavior employed to gain reinforcement (active or passive). Active persons initiate activity and energetically manipulate their environment to secure satisfactions. Passive persons are apathetic and resigned to accepting whatever satisfactions may come their way. In combination, the four elements of source of reinforcement and the two elements of coping behavior generate the eight diagnostic types listed in the first column of Table 6.3. Because the dimensions of active-passive and self-other bear a superficial resemblance to Leary's dimensions of dominance-submission and affiliation-disaffiliation, it should be emphasized that these are not at all the same dimensions. Similarly, although the facet elements of Millon's system may be represented in a circular fashion (Millon, 1969, p. 106), this representation is not meant to correspond to Leary's (1957) circumplex.

Although Millon's eight mild pathological types were derived from different theoretical considerations than those of Leary's interpersonal types, there are many similarities between the resultant types of the two systems. Millon (1969, p. 301) has noted the correspondences between the two systems, and his suggestions are listed in the fifth column of Table 6.3. To facilitate comparison, the Millon personality types are listed in the order of the Leary system, to which they purportedly correspond, rather than in the order of the Millon system. Table 6.3 also provides, for each Millon type, the characteristic view of self, attitude toward others,

Table 6.3.   Millon's (1969) Diagnostic Typology of Mild Pathological Personality Patterns

Coping strategy	Self-image	Attitude	Interpersonal behavior style	Leary (1957) type	DSM–II
Passive-ambivalent	Conscientious	Respectful	Conforming	NO. Hypernormal PA. Autocratic	Obsessive-compulsive
Passive-independent	Admirable	Exploitative	Narcissistic	BC. Narcissistic	—
Active-independent	Assertive	Vindictive	Aggressive	DE. Sadistic	Antisocial
Active-detached	Alienated	Distrustful	Avoidant	FG. Distrustful	Schizoid
Passive-detached	Complacent	Indifferent	Asocial	—	Asthenic
Active-ambivalent	Discontented	Vacillating	Negativistic	HI. Masochistic	Explosive Passive-aggressive
Passive-dependent	Inadequate	Compliant	Submissive	JK. Dependent	Inadequate
Active-dependent	Sociable	Seductive	Gregarious	LM. Overconventional	Hysterical

manifest interpersonal behavior, and most likely DSM–II diagnosis (personality disorders). Thus, for example, the passive-ambivalent personality type views himself or herself as conscientious, views others respectfully, is conforming in relations with others, bears some resemblances to both the hypernormal (NO) and autocratic (PA) types of Leary's system, and corresponds most closely to the obsessive-compulsive personality disorder category of DSM-II.

Millon (1969, pp. 220–301) provides a detailed description of each of the eight mild pathological types in terms of the clinical picture, the etiology and development (biogenic and psychogenic factors), coping strategies, the manner in which the pattern is self-perpetrated, and appropriate treatment procedures. It is instructive to compare these descriptions with those provided by Leary (1957, pp. 269–350) for presumably comparable types, although that cannot be done here. For one who is theoretically committed to the Leary System and its variants, the Millon types occasionally appear out of focus or not quite "right." Yet the same would be true of the Leary types viewed from a Millonian perspective.

The recently published Millon Multiaxial Clinical Inventory (MMCI) provides operational measures of 20 clinical syndromes from the author's theory of psychopathology (Millon, 1977). In accord with the theoretical system on which it is based, the MMCI provides separate scales to distinguish enduring personality characteristics from acute clinical states. Eight scales assess the personality styles listed in Table 6.3, three scales measure pathological personality syndromes (e.g., schizoid-schizophrenic), and nine scales measure symptom disorders (e.g., anxiety). Hand scoring templates are not currently available for the 20 scales of the MMCI because the instrument is meant to be used in conjunction with a commercially available automated clinical interpretive report devised by the author.[3] In addition to a narrative clinical description, the interpretive report provides a multiaxial diagnosis with respect to (1) clinical symptom picture, (2) personality pattern, (3) course, (4) psychosocial stressors, (5) severity of disturbance, and (6) therapeutic implications. Although the basis for the interpretive report is described as a "mixed actuarial-theoretical system," it appears to be much more the latter than the former.

The construction of the MMCI was guided by the substantive, structural, and external considerations of construct validity formulated by Loevinger (1957). It was also influ-

[3]National Computer Systems, 4401 West 76th Street, Minneapolis, Minnesota, 55435.

enced by recent thought on a number of issues relating to the Minnesota Multiphasic Personality Inventory and its possible revision (Butcher, 1972). The MMCI is strong on substantive grounds, stemming as it does from a systematic and detailed theory of psychopathology (Millon, 1969). Item generation and classification procedures relied heavily on informed clinical judgments obtained in innovative and quite sensible rating tasks.

The MMCI is less strong on structural grounds, and therein may lie its major weaknesses. The type of measurement model underlying the instrument is quite clear and in accord with recent thinking on person categories:

No personality type or psychopathological state consists of entirely homogeneous and discrete psychological properties. Rather, they are comprised of diffuse and complex characteristics, which share many traits, as well as contain certain more distinctive features. (Millon, 1977, p. 37)

But instead of representing these categories by intercorrelated and hierarchically ordered scales, Millon chose to represent them by scales with *overlapping items*. When 20 scales averaging 37 items per scale are scored from a common pool of only 171 items, the psychometric consequences of such a high degree of scale redundancy will almost certainly be unfavorable.

The eight scales listed in Table 6.3 that measure "basic personality styles" (column 4 of Table 6.3) appear to be the pivotal focus of the diagnostic system, and consequently their structure is of critical importance. The test manual provides the intercorrelations among these scales in a large sample of patients (p. 49); we extracted principal components from these intercorrelations to examine the structure among scales. Two components accounted for 72.5% of the covariance among scales. The effects of item overlap are evident in this solution in which the first bipolar factor is defined at one pole

by the cluster of gregarious, narcissistic, and aggressive, and at the opposite pole by the cluster of asocial, avoidant, and submissive. The second bipolar factor is marked by conforming at one pole and negativistic at the other. There is potential for a circumplex in these data, but the circular order is not that which would be expected from the correspondences with the Leary system indicated in Table 6.3. Thus regardless of its diagnostic utility—and this is not yet clear from available evidence—the MMCI does not provide measures of the categories of interpersonal behavior considered elsewhere in this chapter.

DSM–III and Interpersonal Behavior. The revised version of the American Psychiatric Association's (1980) Diagnostic and Statistical Manual (DSM–III) requires the clinician to make an evaluation on five separate axes. Of particular interest is Axis II, Personality Disorders, which is concerned with configurations of long-term personality traits not limited to the episodes of "illness" coded on Axis I. At least seven of these categories of personality disorder emphasize interpersonal behavior rather than symptoms or social evaluations, and these categories bear a close resemblance to the octants of the interpersonal circumplex. This correspondence is largely due to the fact that the initial drafts of the personality disorders section were written by Theodore Millon. The detailed relations between Millon's theoretical system and the categories of Axis II are given elsewhere (Millon, in press). The expected structure among categories within the interpersonal circumplex model is shown in Figure 6.6.

The diagnostic criteria listed in DSM-III for each of the categories of Figure 6.6 stress the rigid and inflexible reliance upon one type of interpersonal response at the expense of others. The reaction types are thus extremes or caricatures of normal interpersonal types. *The compulsive personality disorder* is an exaggeration of ambitious-dominant behav-

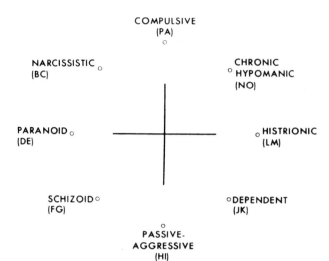

Figure 6.6. Hypothesized correspondences between DSM–III categories and an interpersonal circumplex.

ior (PA) involving excessive formality and "stiffness," preoccupation with rules and trivial details, insistence that others submit to one's way of doing things, and excessive devotion to work and productivity. The inclusion of "indecisiveness" among the DSM–III diagnostic criteria for compulsive personality disorder serves to protract the longstanding disagreement between interpersonal theory and descriptive psychiatry (see Leary, 1957, pp. 288–289) concerning the interpersonal implications of obsessive (weak, indecisive) and compulsive (strong, overdecisive) symptoms. Otherwise the match with PA is quite close.

The *narcissistic personality disorder* is an exaggeration of arrogant-calculating behavior (BC) involving a grandiose sense of self-importance, preoccupation with fantasies of unlimited success, exhibitionism and lack of empathy for others, feelings of special entitlement and interpersonal exploitativeness. The *paranoid personality disorder* is an exaggeration of cold-quarrelsome behavior (DE) involving pervasive and unwarranted suspiciousness (hypervigilance, guardedness), hypersensitivity (easily slighted and quick to take offense, readiness to counter-

attack), and restricted affectivity (cold, unemotional, absence of tender feelings). As previously noted, Lorr and McNair were the first to emphasize the mistrust component of DE, and Benjamin has explicitly identified this octant as the predominant one in paranoid personality disorders.

The *schizoid personality disorder,* called "introverted personality disorder" in earlier versions of DSM–III, is an exaggeration of aloof-introverted behavior (FG) involving emotional coldness and aloofness, indifference to others, and few if any close friends. Such individuals show little desire for social involvement and are described as reserved, withdrawn, and seclusive. The *passive-aggressive personality disorder* is an exaggeration of lazy-submissive behavior (HI) involving resistance to demands for adequate social and emotional performance, as manifest in procrastination, dawdling, stubbornness, intentional inefficiency, and "forgetfulness." This diagnostic category helps to clarify the significance of lazy, inefficient, and incompetent behavior in the realm of normal behavior (H). The "aggression" associated with this category is of a different kind than that associated with the orthogonal octant of DE. It is perhaps best detected in our own feelings of anger at the frustration imposed by calculated incompetence. Whereas earlier interpersonal diagnostic categories emphasized the masochistic component of this octant (I), the passive-aggressive category stresses the incompetence component (H).

The *dependent personality disorder* is an exaggeration of unassuming-ingenuous behavior (JK) involving the passive allowing of others to assume responsibility for major areas of one's life, the subordination of one's own needs to those on whom one is dependent, and a lack of self-confidence (seeing oneself as helpless). The *histrionic personality disorder* (formerly "hysterical personality") is an exaggeration of warm-agreeable behavior (LM) involving overly dramatic, reactive, and intensely expressed emotions, irrational outbursts of anger, egocentricity, and demandingness. Although superficially warm and charming, such persons are perceived as shallow and lacking genuineness. In identifying hysteria as an exaggeration of LM behavior, Leary emphasized interpersonal characteristics rather than the colorful symptoms traditionally associated with this disorder (1957, pp. 310–311). The DSM–III category of histrionic personality disorder is compatible with this emphasis.

The most recent version of DSM–III does not include a diagnostic category that represents an exaggeration of gregarious-extraverted behavior (NO). In the penultimate version of DSM–III (American Psychiatric Association, 1978), the Axis I category of *chronic hypomanic disorder* (hypomanic personality) seemed to provide a close fit. This disorder is characterized by extreme gregariousness (uninhibited people-seeking), talkativeness, extreme optimism, hypersexuality, inappropriate laughing and joking, high energy level, and an elevated, expansive mood. In the current version of DSM–III: "The existence of such a syndrome has not been well enough established to warrant in-

clusion as a distinct disorder" (APA, 1980, p. 206).

Although it is tempting to speculate further on the apparent correspondence between the categories of personality disturbance of DSM–III and the octants of the interpersonal system, these speculations have not yet been empirically demonstrated. Moreover, since categories of psychiatric diagnosis are thought to be fuzzy sets organized around prototypes derived from clinical experience, there is no reason to expect a one-to-one correspondence between such categories and the octants of a more formal interpersonal system. Instead it is more reasonable to expect that there will be a characteristic or prototypic *profile* of interpersonal variables associated with each diagnostic category. The same expectation would be held for the more complex psychiatric syndromes coded on Axis I of DSM–III (schizophrenic disorder, affective disorder, etc.). To the extent that Axis II is used to record prominent trait disturbances (e.g., compulsive traits) in addition to formal diagnoses on Axis I, a wealth of information will be obtained concerning the interpersonal implications of psychiatric syndromes. This issue is being explored directly in an extensive research program, currently being conducted by Lorna Benjamin at the University of Wisconsin. Carefully diagnosed psychiatric inpatients and outpatients are being assessed with the structural analysis of social behavior model to explore the possibility of either incorporating interpersonal behavior into traditional psychiatric nosology or of developing a new classification system based on interpersonal nomenclature. Needless to say, the results of this program will be of great interest to clinical psychologists.

Theoretical Considerations

It should now be evident that circumplex models of interpersonal behavior have been employed in a variety of contexts for a multitude of purposes. The extent to which theoretical considerations guided these applications has also varied widely, as have the theoretical orientations of different investigators. For some investigators, the circumplex model provides a convenient representation of the empirical relationships that have been found to exist among the major variables of interpersonal behavior for a given population of subjects (e.g., Becker & Krug, 1964). For others the model is interpreted in the light of theoretical constructs from one or another formal theory of personality (e.g., Benjamin, 1973, 1974; Carson, 1969, 1979; Foa & Foa, 1974; Leary, 1957; Schutz, 1958). In its clinical application the model has most frequently been interpreted within the context of neo-Freudian theories of personality, particularly that of Harry Stack Sullivan (e.g., Leary, 1957; Carson, 1969, 1979; Kiesler, 1979a). Traditional psychoanalytic concepts have also been employed (Chance, 1959), as have perspectives as diverse as structuralism (Foa & Foa, 1974), biopsychology (Benjamin, 1973), and social exchange theory (Carson, 1979). Thus it cannot be concluded that the use of a circumplex model commits a clinician to a particular theoretical position with respect to interpersonal behavior. Nor can it be conclusively demonstrated, at our present state of knowledge, that the structural regularities found among interpersonal variables should be taken as evidence for the propositions of one theoretical perspective rather than another.

It is a well-established empirical generalization that interpersonal variables have a circular structure, and this fact alone can contribute to systematic assessment and prediction in the absence of any theoretical speculations about the nature of interpersonal behavior. Similarly, the circumplex model can be viewed as simply a convenient geometric representation of empirical fact. However, it should also be recognized that the formality and specificity of the circumplex model make it a potentially useful vehicle for the generation of theoretical propositions. To illustrate the manner in which theoretical considerations can lead to an increased understanding of the phenomena represented by a circumplex model, I will discuss a line of reasoning that has been successively refined by Leary (1957), Foa (1961, 1965, 1966; Foa & Foa, 1974), Rinn (1965), and Carson (1969, 1979).

Foa (1961) was the first to suggest that the nature of the interpersonal variables proposed by Leary (1957) could be illuminated through the application of Guttman's (1958) procedures for facet design and analysis. It should be emphasized at the outset that facet analysis is no more and no less than a logical framework within which a set of variables is given systematic definition in terms of more basic sets or "facets." Once the theorist has provided substantive definitions, the analytic tools of facet anlaysis may be employed, but facet analysis itself is a content-free method. Foa and Foa (1974) maintain that the interpersonal variables described by Leary are best thought of as a set of cognitive categories for processing social information. The origins of this schema are to be found in the cognitive development of the child's conception of social events. Foa and Foa speculate that cognitive categories of social perception are based on a progressive differentiation of structure organized around the facets of *directionality, object,* and *resource*. The discrimination of the directionality of social events is the first to develop, and it involves concepts such as giving versus taking and accepting versus rejecting. Once social objects are discriminated (self vs. other), the facets of directionality and object permit the discrimination of four categories of social meaning (giving to self, taking from self, giving to other, taking from other).

The facets of directionality and object are included in one form or another in most theories of social development (Foa & Foa, 1974). The facet of *resource* is a more theoretically critical one, because it essentially provides the content of the cognitive categories. Foa and Foa (1974) present a cognitive-developmental account of the manner in which the resource classes of *love* and *status* become differentiated as the significant elements in interpersonal exchange. Once acquired, the discrimination between social (status) and emotional (love) resources results in a differentiated cognitive schema that distinguishes eight classes of social meaning (giving love to oneself, giving status to oneself, taking status from another, taking love from another, etc.). Social information is thus assumed to be encoded, stored, and retrieved in terms of the eight categories of social meaning inherent in this schema.

One of many possible ways of representing the cognitive categories of social perception described by Foa and Foa is illustrated in Table 6.4. The basic facet of directionality is represented there by the two values of $+1$ and -1, which may be thought of as granting and denying, respectively. The facets of object (self vs. other) and resource (status vs. love) are represented at the top of the table. The rows of Table 6.4 represent interpersonal variables. Any given interpersonal variable may be reduced to its underlying facet elements with reference to its profile coding on these elements. The specific pattern of positive and negative values in Table 6.4 is based on intuition, rather than on any properties of facet analysis. Again there are many possible arrangements of patterns for Table 6.4 that might be postulated.

In fact, the particular patterns given in the table (Wiggins, 1979a) are different from those suggested by other theorists (Foa, 1961; Rinn, 1965).

The values in the rows of Table 6.4 stem from hypotheses concerning the interpersonal significance or "meaning" of different categories of behavior. The import of each category is specified in terms of the social and emotional implications of an action for *both* participants. For example, ambitious-dominant behavior is hypothesized to involve the granting of status and love to oneself, the granting of love to the other, and the denial of status to the other. The implication here is that the variety of topographically dissimilar behaviors subsumed under the heading of ambitious-dominant behavior have these semantic features in common. Notice that a different profile of facet elements is postulated for each category of interpersonal behavior, since the eight categories are thought to be distinct from one another in meaning.

Although it is difficult to justify a particular set of hypothesized facet elements on an a priori basis, it is possible in principle to test predictions generated from a given arrangement of facet elements. This may be illustrated with reference to the notion of *complementarity* in dyadic transactions, which has been a longstanding concern of interpersonal theorists (Carson, 1969; Foa & Foa, 1974; Kiesler, 1979a; Leary, 1957;

Table 6.4.   Facet Composition of Interpersonal Variables

	Self		Other	
	Status	*Love*	*Love*	*Status*
PA (ambitious-dominant)	$+1$	$+1$	$+1$	-1
BC (arrogant-calculating)	$+1$	$+1$	-1	-1
DE (cold-quarrelsome)	$+1$	-1	-1	-1
FG (aloof-introverted)	-1	-1	-1	-1
HI (lazy-submissive)	-1	-1	-1	$+1$
JK (unassuming-ingenuous)	-1	-1	$+1$	$+1$
LM (warm-agreeable)	-1	$+1$	$+1$	$+1$
NO (gregarious-extraverted)	$+1$	$+1$	$+1$	$+1$

KEY

$+$:   grants

$-$:   denies

Sullivan, 1953; Watzlawick, Beavin, & Jackson, 1967). According to Leary (1957, pp. 122–123), interpersonal actions tend to initiate or "invite" reciprocal interpersonal reactions that serve to sustain or reinforce the original actions. Although Leary did not specify the exact basis of this reciprocity, he predicted characteristic reactions to actions in all octants of his system (e.g., ambitious-dominant behavior pulls submissive-unassuming behavior). Carson (1979) construes the initial behavior of an actor as involving a subtle metacommunication designed to influence the definition of the interpersonal situation in terms of love and status (see also Goffman, 1959, and Watzlawick et al., 1967). According to Carson (1969, p. 112), such initial behavior is typically responded to with complementary behavior that tends to reinforce the initial definition of the situation.

Although the notions of reciprocity and complementarity in interpersonal transactions are intuitively appealing, they have not been given precise or uniform definitions. Most would agree that a complementary relationship is one in which the "needs" of both participants are fully met or, alternatively, one in which the participants are in agreement as to the definition of the situation in terms of love and status. In this context the facet profiles given in Table 6.4 may be thought of as implied definitions of interpersonal situations associated with different categories of behavior. For example, ambitious-dominant behavior (PA) defines a situation in which status and love are granted to the actor and love, but not status, is granted to the other. A complementary response to ambitious-dominant behavior would be one that completely and literally accepted such a definition of the situation.

Table 6.5 lists the kinds of dyads formed when an initial definition of an interpersonal situation is accepted by the other participant. In the first pair listed, the complementary response to ambitious-dominant behavior is one in which the other (now the self) grants love but not status to himself or herself, while granting both love and status to the actor (now the other) as requested. This profile of facet elements is coded as warm-agreeable (LM) in the system given in Table 6.4, and it suggests that warm-agreeable behavior is what is implicitly requested by ambitious-dominant behavior. This of course runs counter to the intuition that the ambitious-dominant person is asking for a lazy-submissive response (HI). But it follows directly from the hypothesized facets of Table 6.4 and the assumption that complementary behavior involves an acceptance of an initial definition of a situation with respect to status and love for both participants.

The remaining pairs of Table 6.5 represent additional hypotheses concerning complementarity in social exchange. In pair 2, cold-quarrelsome behavior is seen as a request for

Table 6.5.   Dyadic Relations in Which the Other Accepts the Actor's Initial Definition of the Situation

			Self		Other	
			Status	*Love*	*Love*	*Status*
Pair 1	PA	Ambitious-dominant	+1	+1	+1	−1
	LM	Warm-agreeable	−1	+1	+1	+1
Pair 2	DE	Cold-quarrelsome	+1	−1	−1	−1
	HI	Lazy-submissive	−1	−1	−1	+1
Pair 3	BC	Arrogant-calculating	+1	+1	−1	−1
	JK	Unassuming-ingenuous	−1	−1	+1	+1
Pair 4	NO	Gregarious-extraverted	+1	+1	+1	+1
	NO	Gregarious-extraverted	+1	+1	+1	+1
Pair 5	FG	Aloof-introverted	−1	−1	−1	−1
	FG	Aloof-introverted	−1	−1	−1	−1

lazy-submissive behavior. In pair 3, unassuming-ingenuous behavior is the complementary response to arrogant-calculating behavior. In pairs 4 and 5, the complementary behavior is the same behavior exhibited by the initiating actor. Similar predictions may be easily generated for "noncomplementary" dyadic relationships, in which the actor's initial definition of the situation is completely rejected by the other participant (e.g., a cold-quarrelsome reaction to ambitious-dominant behavior). Such relationships would be expected to be both unsatisfactory and unstable.

Whether or not the reactions predicted in Table 6.5 are indeed the most likely to occur is still largely an empirical question. The small body of literature on this topic, cited earlier in this chapter, cannot be considered conclusive in this regard. The construct of complementarity itself appears to be defined differently by different investigators. Although Leary (1957) provided a wealth of anecdotal clinical material on this topic, he did not specify the facets involved in interpersonal exchange. Carson (1969) identified love and status as elements involved in exchange, but his formulations are restricted to four quadrants, and they do not specify implications for both self and other. At this time the postulated facet structure of Table 6.4 cannot be said to be any better or any worse than alternative conceptualizations. The point I wish to make, however, is that this and other hypothesized facet structures are potentially falsifiable by empirical findings. The resolution of this and many other issues in the study of interpersonal behavior may eventually be achieved by more explicit theorizing of the kind encouraged by facet analysis.

Overview

This chapter has asserted that explicit circumplex models of interpersonal behavior are of both practical and theoretical value in the field of clinical psychology. The history of two-dimensional representations of interpersonal behavior over the last thirty years was reviewed to illustrate the remarkable convergences of conceptualization among different investigators that have occurred and the diversity of populations and topics to which such models have been applied. The principal clinical applications of circumplex models have occurred in the areas of assessment and psychotherapy. A detailed consideration of the topic of psychiatric diagnosis suggested that circumplex models are highly compatible with the recent thinking on this topic that has evolved from other areas of psychology. Finally, it was argued that formal efforts to specify the facet elements underlying interpersonal variables can bring both substantive and psychometric clarity to the study of interpersonal behavior.

The review of methods employed to assess attributes of interpersonal transactions was not meant to be exhaustive, but rather was meant to call attention to the *variety* of procedures that have been employed to assess the same and different aspects of interpersonal behavior. From the time of the earliest system (Freedman et al., 1951) until the present (e.g., Kiesler, 1979a), it has been recognized that interpersonal behavior should be assessed from multiple perspectives, and that these different perspectives require different measurement operations, each of which presents somewhat different methodological challenges to the investigator (LaForge, 1977). Although the problems of "multilevel" or multiple-perspective assessment are not unique to the domain of interpersonal behavior, they appear to be especially well informed by explicit theoretical considerations within this domain (e.g., Carson, 1969; Foa & Foa, 1974; Kiesler, 1979a; Leary, 1957).

As circumplex models of interpersonal behavior become more refined and explicit, it is hoped that greater consensus will be achieved regarding both the variables themselves and the appropriate methods for measuring them. Although there are a number of promising instruments in current use, none are "standard," and agreement on a standard set of measuring procedures would greatly facilitate communication among investigators. Agreement as to a standard set of measures would also bring continuity and cumulative knowledge to important areas of current research on such topics as interaction sequences in dyadic relationships, affective reactions to interpersonal communications, individual differences in interpersonal construal styles, and interpersonal implications of psychiatric diagnoses.

REFERENCES

Adams, H. B. (1964). "Mental illness" or interpersonal behavior? *American Psychologist,* **19,** 191–197.

Allport, G. W. (1937). *Personality: A psychological interpretation.* New York: Holt.

Allport, G. W., & Odbert, H. S. (1936). Trait names: A psycho-lexical study. *Psychological Monographs,* **47** (1, Whole No. 211).

American Psychiatric Association. (1978). Diagnostic and statistical manual of mental disorders. Draft version. Washington, D.C.: American Psychiatric Association.

American Psychiatric Association. (1980). *Diagnostic and statistical manual of mental disorders.* 3rd ed. Washington, D.C.: American Psychiatric Association.

Bales, R. F. (1950). *Interaction process analysis: A method for the study of small groups.* Cambridge, Mass.: Addison-Wesley.

Baumrind, D., & Black, A. E. (1967). Socialization practices associated with dimensions of competence in pre-school boys and girls. *Child Development,* **38,** 291–328.

Bayley, N. (1968). Behavioral correlates of mental growth: Birth to thirty-six years. *American Psychologist,* **23,** 1–17.

Becker, W. C., & Krug, R. S. (1964). A circumplex model for social behavior in children. *Child Development,* **35,** 371–396.

Benjamin, L. S. (1973). A biological model for understanding the behavior of individuals. In J. Westman (Ed.), *Individual differences in children.* New York: Wiley.

Benjamin, L. S. (1974). Structural analysis of social behavior. *Psychological Review,* **81,** 392–425.

Benjamin, L. S. (1977). Structural analysis of a family in therapy. *Journal of Consulting and Clinical Psychology,* **45,** 391–406.

Benjamin, L. S. (1979). Structural analysis of differentiation failure. *Psychiatry,* **42,** 1–23.

Bierman, R. (1969). Dimensions of interpersonal facilitation in psychotherapy and child development. *Psychological Bulletin,* **72,** 338–352.

Bleuler, E. P. (1911, 1950). *Dementia praecox or the group of schizophrenias.* New York: International Universities Press.

Block, J. (1965). *The challenge of response sets.* New York: Appleton-Century-Crofts.

Borgatta, E. F., Cottrell, L. S., Jr., & Mann, J. M. (1958) The spectrum of individual interaction characteristics: An interdimensional analysis. *Psychological Reports,* **4,** 279–319.

Boring E. G. (1923). Intelligence as the tests test it. *The New Republic,* June 5, 35–37.

Butcher, J. N. (Ed.) (1972). *Objective personality assessment.* New York: Academic Press.

Campbell, D. T., & Fiske, D. W. (1959). Convergent and discriminant validation by the multitrait-multimethod matrix. *Psychological Bulletin,* **56,** 81–105.

Campbell, M. M. (1959). The primary dimensions of item ratings on scales designed to measure 24 of Murray's manifest needs. Unpublished manuscript, University of Washington, Seattle.

Cantor, N., & Mischel, W. (1977). Traits as prototypes: Effects on recognition memory. *Journal of Personality and Social Psychology,* **35,** 38–48.

Cantor, N., & Mischel, W. (1979a). Prototypes in person perception. In L. Berkowitz (Ed.), *Advances in experimental social psychology,* Vol. 12 New York: Academic Press.

Cantor, N., & Mischel, W. (1979b). Prototypicality and personality: Effects on free recall and personality impressions. *Journal of Research in Personality,* **13,** 187–205.

Cantor, N., Smith, E. E., French, R. deS., & Mezzich, J. (1980). Psychiatric diagnosis as prototype categorization. *Journal of Abnormal Psychology,* **89,** 181–193.

Carson, R. C. (1969). *Interaction concepts of personality.* Chicago: Aldine.

Carson, R. C. (1971). Disordered interpersonal behavior. In W. A. Hunt (Ed.), *Human behavior and its control.* Cambridge, Mass.: Schenkman.

Carson, R. C. (1979). Personality and exchange in developing relationships. In R. L. Burgess & T. L. Houston (Eds.), *Social exchange in developing relationships.* New York: Academic Press.

Carter, L. F. (1954). Evaluating the performance of individuals as members of small groups. *Personnel Psychology, 7,* 477–484.

Cattell, R. B. (1957). *Personality and motivation structure and measurement.* Yonkers-on-Hudson, N. Y.: World Book.

Cattell, R. B. (1961). Theory of situational, instrument, second-order and refraction factors in personality structure research. *Psychological Bulletin, 58,* 160–174.

Cattell, R. B. (1968). Trait-view theory of perturbations in ratings and self-ratings (L-, BR- and Q-data): Its application to obtaining pure trait score estimates in questionnaires. *Psychological Review, 75,* 96–113.

Cattell, R. B., & Digman, J. M. (1964). A theory of the structure of perturbations in observer ratings and questionnaire data in personality research. *Behavioral Science, 9,* 341–358.

Celani, D. P. (1974). The complementarity hypothesis: An exploratory study (Ph.D. dissertation, University of Vermont, 1974.) *Dissertation Abstracts International.*

Chance, E. (1959). *Families in treatment; from the viewpoint of the patient, the clinician and the researcher.* New York: Basic Books.

Chance, E. (1966). Content analysis of verbalizations about interpersonal experience. In L. A. Gottschalk & A. H. Auerbach (Eds.), *Methods of research in psychotherapy.* New York: Appleton-Century-Crofts.

Chance, E., & Arnold, J. (1960). The effect of professional training, experience, and preference for a theoretical system upon clinical case description. *Human Relations, 13,* 195–213.

Conte, H. R. (1975). A circumplex model for personality traits. (Ph.D. dissertation, New York University, 1975.) *Dissertation Abstracts International* (University Microfilms, No. 7601731).

Edwards, A. L. (1957). Social desirability and probability of endorsement of items in the Interpersonal Check List. *Journal of Abnormal and Social Psychology, 55,* 394–396.

Edwards, A. L. (1959). *Edwards Personal Preference Schedule.* New York: Psychological Corporation.

Foa, U. G. (1958). The contiguity principle in the structure of interpersonal relations. *Human Relations, 11, 229–238.*

Foa, U. G. (1961). Convergences in the analysis of the structure of interpersonal behavior. *Psychological Review, 68,* 341–353.

Foa, U. G. (1965). New developments in facet design and analysis. *Psychological Review, 72,* 262–274.

Foa, U. G. (1966). Perception of behavior in reciprocal roles: The ringex model. *Psychological Monographs, 80* (15, whole no. 623).

Foa, U. G., and Foa, E. B. (1974) *Societal structures of the mind.* Springfield, Ill.: Charles C Thomas.

Freedman, M. B., Leary, T. F., Ossorio, A. G., & Coffey, H. S. (1951). The interpersonal dimension of personality. *Journal of Personality, 20,* 143–161.

Goffman, E. (1959) *The presentation of self in everyday life.* (1959). Garden City, N.Y.: Doubleday Anchor Books.

Goldberg, L. R. (1977). Language and personality: Developing a taxonomy of trait-descriptive terms. Invited address to the Division of Evaluation and Measurement at the 86th Annual Convention of the American Psychological Association, San Francisco.

Golding, S. L. (1977). Individual differences in the construal of interpersonal interactions. In D. Magnusson & N. Endler (Eds.), *Personality at the crossroads: Current issues in interactional psychology.* New York: Wiley.

Golding, S. L. (1978). Toward a more adequate theory of personality: Psychological organizing principles. In H. London & N. Hirschberg (Eds.), *Personality: A new look at metatheories.* Washington D.C.: Hemisphere Press.

Golding, S. L., Valone, K., & Foster, S. W. (in press). Interpersonal construal: An individual differences framework. In N. Hirschberg (Ed.), *Multivariate methods in the social sciences: Applications.* Hillsdale, N.J.: Erlbaum.

Gough, H. G., & Heilbrun, A. B. (1965). *The adjective check list manual.* Palo Alto, Calif.: Consulting Psychologists Press.

Guttman, L. (1958). Introduction to facet design and analysis. In *Proceedings of the 15th International Congress of Psychology,* Brussels, 1957. Amsterdam: North Holland.

Guttman, L. (1954). A new approach to factor analysis: The radex. In P. R. Lazarsfeld (Ed.), *Mathematical thinking in the social sciences.* Glencoe, Ill.: Free Press.

Heller, K., Myers, R. A., & Kline, L. V. (1963). Interviewer behavior as a function of standardized client roles *Journal of Consulting Psychology, 27,* 117–122.

Horowitz, L. M. (1979). On the cognitive structure of interpersonal problems treated in psychotherapy. *Journal of Consulting and Clinical Psychology, 47,* 5–15.

Jackson, D. N. (1974). *Personality research form manual.* Goshen, N.Y.: Research Psychologists Press.

Jackson, D. N., & Messick, S. J. (1961). Acquiescence and desirability as response determinants on the MMPI. *Educational and Psychological Measurement,* **21,** 771–792.

Kassebaum, G. G., Couch, A. S., and Slater, P. E. (1959). The factorial dimensions of the MMPI. *Journal of Consulting Psychology,* **23,** 226–236.

Kelly, G. A. (1955). *The psychology of personal constructs,* Vols. 1 & 2. New York: Norton.

Kiesler, D. J. (1979a). An interpersonal communication analysis of relationship in psychotherapy. *Psychiatry,* **42,** 299–311.

Kiesler, D. J. (1979b). *Manual for the impact message inventory.* Richmond: Virginia Commonwealth University.

LaForge, R. (1977). Using the ICL: 1976. Unpublished manuscript, Mill Valley, Calif.

LaForge, R. Interpersonal domains or interpersonal levels? A validation study of Leary's MMPI Level I indices. Paper read at the Western Psychological Association Meetings in Santa Monica, Calif. 1963.

LaForge, R., Leary, T. F., Naboisek, H., Coffey, H. S., & Freedman, M. B. (1954). The interpersonal dimension of personality: II. An objective study of repression. *Journal of Personality,* **23,** 129–153.

LaForge, R., & Suczek, R. F. (1955). The interpersonal dimension of personality: III. An interpersonal check list. *Journal of Personality,* **24,** 94–112.

Leary, T. (1957). *Interpersonal diagnosis of personality.* New York: Ronald Press.

Leary, T. F., & Coffey, H. S. (1955). The prediction of interpersonal behavior in group psychotherapy. *Psychodrama and group psychotherapy monographs,* No. 28.

Leary, T. F., & Harvey, J. S. (1956). A methodology for measuring personality changes in psychotherapy. *Journal of Clinical Psychology,* **12,** 123–132.

Loevinger, J. (1957). Objective tests as instruments of psychological theory. *Psychological Reports,* **3,** 635–694 (Monograph No. 9).

Lorr, M., & McNair, D. M. (1963). An interpersonal behavior circle. *Journal of Abnormal and Social Psychology,* **67,** 68–75.

Lorr, M., and McNair, D. M. (1965). Expansion of the interpersonal behavior circle. *Journal of Personality and Social Psychology,* **2,** 823–830.

Lorr, M., & McNair, D. M. (1966). Methods relating to evaluation of therapeutic outcome. In L. A. Gottschalk & A. H. Auerbach (Eds.), *Methods of research in psychotherapy.* New York: Appleton-Century-Crofts.

Lorr, M., Bishop, P. F., & McNair, D. M. (1965). Interpersonal types among psychiatric patients. *Journal of Abnormal Psychology,* **70,** 468–472.

McDonald, R. P. (1975). Testing pattern hypotheses for correlation matrices. *Psychometrika,* **40,** 253–255.

McLemore, C. W., & Benjamin, L. S. (1979). Whatever happened to interpersonal diagnosis? A psychosocial alternative to DSM–III. *American Psychologist,* **34,** 17–34.

Millon, T. (1969). *Modern psychopathology.* Philadelphia: W. B. Saunders.

Millon, T. (1977) *Millon multiaxial clinical inventory manual.* Minneapolis: National Computer Systems.

Millon, T. (in press). *Disorders of personality: DSM III, Axis II.* New York: Wiley-Interscience.

Mueller, W. J. (1969). Patterns of behavior and their reciprocal impact in the family and in psychotherapy. *Journal of Counseling Psychology Monograph,* **16** (No. 2, Part 2).

Mueller, W. J., & Dilling, C. A. (1968). Therapist-client interview behavior and personality characteristics of therapists. *Journal of Projective Techniques and Personality Assessment,* **32,** 281–288.

Neisser, U. (1979). The concept of intelligence. *Intelligence,* **3,** 217–227.

Norman, W. T. (1967) 2800 personality trait descriptors: Normative operating characteristics for a university population. Unpublished manuscript, University of Michigan.

Perkins, M. J., Kiesler, D. J., Anchin, J. C., Chirico, B. M., Kyle, E. M., & Federman, E. J. (1979). The Impact Message Inventory: A new measure of relationship in counseling/psychotherapy and other dyads. *Journal of Counseling Psychology,* **26,** 363–367.

Plutchik, R. (1967). The affective differential: Emotion profiles implied by diagnostic concepts. *Psychological Reports,* **20,** 19–25.

Plutchik, R. (1980). *Emotion: A psychoevolutionary synthesis.* New York: Harper & Row.

Plutchik, R., & Platman, S. R. (1977). Personality connotations of psychiatric diagnoses: Implications for a similarity model. *Journal of Nervous and Mental Disease,* **165,** 418–422.

Potter, S. (1970). *The complete upmanship.* New York: New American Library.

Rinn, J. L. (1965). Structure of phenomenal domains. *Psychological Review,* **72,** 445–466.

Roe, A. (1957). Early determinants of vocational choice. *Journal of Counseling Psychology,* **4,** 212–217.

Rosch, E. (1975). Cognitive reference points. *Cognitive Psychology,* **7,** 532–547.

Rosch, E. (1978) Principles of categorization. In E. Rosch and D. B. Lloyd (Eds.), *Cognition and categorization*. Hillsdale, N.J.: Erlbaum.

Rosch, E., & Mervis, C. B. (1975). Family resemblances: Studies in the internal structure of categories. *Cognitive Psychology, 7,* 573–605.

Rosch, E., Mervis, C. B., Gray, W. D., Johnson, D. M., & Boyes-Braem, P. (1976). Basic objects in natural categories. *Cognitive Psychology,* **8,** 382–439.

Sarbin, T. R. (1969). The scientific status of the mental illness metaphor. In S. C. Plog & R. B. Edgerton (Eds.), *Changing perspectives in mental illness*. New York: Holt, Rinehart & Winston.

Schaefer, E. S. (1957). Organization of maternal behavior and attitudes within a two dimensional space: An application of Guttman's radex theory. *American Psychologist,* **12,** 401 (abstract).

Schaefer, E. S. (1959). A circumplex model for maternal behavior. *Journal of Abnormal and Social Psychology, 59,* 226–235.

Schaefer, E. S. (1961). Converging conceptual models for maternal behavior and child behavior. In J. C. Glidewell (Ed.), *Parental attitudes and child behavior*. Springfield, Ill.: Charles C Thomas.

Schaefer, E. S. (1965). A configurational analysis of children's reports of parent behavior. *Journal of Consulting Psychology,* **29,** 552–557.

Schaefer, E. S., and Plutchik, R. (1966). Interrelationships of emotions, traits, and diagnostic constructs. *Psychological Reports,* **18,** 399–410.

Schutz, W. C. (1958). *FIRO: A three-dimensional theory of interpersonal behavior*. New York: Rinehart.

Shannon, J., & Guerney, B., Jr. (1973). Interpersonal effects of interpersonal behavior. *Journal of Personality and Social Psychology,* **26,** 142–150.

Slater, P. E. (1962). Parent behavior and the personality of the child. *Journal of Genetic Psychology,* **101,** 53–68.

Steiger, J. H. (1980). Tests for comparing elements of a correlation matrix. *Psychological Bulletin,* **87,** 195–201.

Stern, G. G. (1958). *Preliminary manual: Activities Index-College Characteristics Index*. Syracuse, N.Y.: Syracuse University Psychological Research Center.

Stern, G. G. (1970). *People in context: Measuring person-environment congruence in education and industry*. New York: Wiley.

Sullivan, H. S. (1953). *The interpersonal theory of psychiatry*. New York: Norton.

Swensen, C. H. (1967). Psychotherapy as a special case of dyadic interaction: Some suggestions for theory and research. *Psychotherapy: Theory, Research and Practice,* **4,** 7–13.

Szasz, T. S. (1961). *The myth of mental illness*. New York: Hoeber-Harper.

Terrill, J. M. (1960). *The relationships between Level II and Level III in the interpersonal system of personality diagnosis*. Ph.D. dissertation, Stanford University.

Truckenmiller, J. L., & Schaie, K. W. (1979). Multilevel structural validation of Leary's interpersonal diagnosis system. *Journal of Consulting and Clinical Psychology,* **47,** 1030–1045.

Watzlawick, P., Beavin, J. H., & Jackson, D. D. (1967). *Pragmatics of human communication*. New York: Norton.

Webster's new dictionary of synonyms (1976). Springfield, Mass.: Merriam.

Wiggins, J. S. (1965). Interpersonal diagnosis of personality. In O. K. Buros (Ed.), *The sixth mental measurements yearbook*. Highland Park, N.J.: Gryphon Press.

Wiggins, J. S. (1979a). A psychological taxonomy of trait-descriptive terms: The interpersonal domain. *Journal of Personality and Social Psychology,* **37,** 395–412.

Wiggins, J. S. (1979b). *Taxonomy of interpersonal trait-descriptive terms*. Unpublished manuscript, University of British Columbia.

Wiggins, J. S. (1980). Circumplex models of interpersonal behavior. In L. Wheeler (Ed.), *Review of personality and social psychology,* Vol. 1. Beverly Hills: Sage Publications.

Wiggins, J. S., Steiger, J. H., & Gaelick, L. (1981). Evaluating circumplexity in personality data. *Multivariate Behavioral Research.* **16,** 263–289.

Williams, H. L., & Lawrence, J. F. (1954). Comparison of the Rorschach and MMPI by means of factor analysis. *Journal of Consulting Psychology,* **18,** 193–197.

CHAPTER 7

Experimental Methods in Research in Psychopathology

L. ROWELL HUESMANN

The legitimate approaches to empirical research practiced by clinical psychologists fall into three major groupings: true experiments, quasi-experiments, and observational studies. Each type has advantages and disadvantages for the clinical researcher, and each presents different technical problems. The failure of researchers to master these technical considerations can result in deficient studies from which valid conclusions cannot be drawn.

Investigators conducting empirical research on psychopathology aim to infer population characteristics from sample characteristics. Sometimes an investigator may wish to estimate a population parameter. More commonly, though, the researcher wants to test an hypothesis about the relations among variables. In some cases he or she may be satisfied with determining whether or not two variables are *stochastically independent,* but more frequently he or she would like to determine much more precisely the functional relation between the variables. In particular the researcher may want to test the hypothesis that a certain *causal model* of the relationship between the variables is true. Most of the inferences psychologists made about populations fall into these three classes: (1) simple parameter estimation, for example, what proportion of the population has schizophrenia? (2) testing dependency hypotheses about the relation between two variables, for example, do schizophrenics have slower reaction times than normal persons? (3) testing causal hypotheses about the relation between variables, for example, is a defect in attention a cause of slower reaction times in schizophrenics? Similarly, the statistical procedures used in such studies can be divided into two broad classes defined by the primary sample statistic used: tests on means or tests on correlations. Tests on means are generally most appropriate for true experiments, somewhat less appropriate for quasi-experiments, and least appropriate for observational studies. Tests on correlations are used most frequently in observational studies, less frequently in quasi-experiments, and least frequently in true experiments. Yet either class of analyses may be appropriate in many situations. A common misconception is that correlational analyses cannot be used to test causal models. Most scientists are taught very early in their careers that a correlation (i.e., stochastic dependency) between variables does not imply causation. However, this does not mean that correlational analyses can never be used to test causal models. In fact, with certain types of data, that is, longitudinal observational data, special types of correlational analyses provide good tests of causal hypotheses.

It is common to hear methodologists talk about the *validity* of a particular study. Validity, as used in such a context, means something slightly different than when one talks about the validity of a variable. Methodologists are talking about the truth of the conclusions of a study when they refer to the validity of a study. Campbell and Stanley (1963) have distinguished between two types of validity for the conclusions of studies: internal validity and external validity. *Internal validity* is the degree to which the conclusions of the study are justified within the narrow context in which the study was performed. *External validity* is the degree to which the conclusions are generalizable to other contexts. Internal validity is necessary but not sufficient for external validity. Consider the case of a scientist who measures the concept learning ability of a sample of schizophrenics, administers a drug, remeasures their concept learning ability, and finds it greatly enhanced. Such a study would have low internal validity. Even the narrow conclusion that the drug facilitated concept learning in schizophrenics would be unjustified, since the improvement could have been due to many factors including retesting, maturation, or an unknown factor intervening in time. Suppose, however, the experimenter had tested a comparable *control group,* administered a placebo to them, retested the control group, and found that their concept learning ability was enhanced significantly less. Now the experimenter has a much more internally valid study, since he or she has eliminated many alternative explanations for the result by adding a control group. The conclusion that the drug enhances concept learning is more justifiable. However, the external validity of the study is limited. One cannot really say whether the drug would enhance learning in subjects suffering from other disorders or enhance learning on other tasks.

This chapter focuses on the methodology for conducting "experimental" studies of psychopathology. By an "experimental" study we mean a study in which one or more variables are *manipulated* (the independent variables), and the effects on other variables (the dependent variables) are observed. Such manipulative studies can be subdivided along

a dimension of increasing validity for causal inferences into preexperimental, quasi-experimental, and true experimental designs. Preexperimental designs have virtually no potential for testing causal hypotheses. Probably the most widely used paradigm of this type has been the pretest-manipulation-posttest design without any control group. A great deal of psychotherapy research has been of this type, with a client's improvement from pretest to posttest being accredited to the therapy manipulation. The threats to the validity of such a causal conclusion (alternative causal explanations) include the uncontrolled between-test history of the subject, improvement due to retesting, motivation, subject mortality, statistical regression upward (spontaneous recovery), the interaction of subject selection with the treatment, and other factors. Fortunately, journal editors no longer smile on such research, and it is being seen less often.

True experiments, on the other hand, possess the greatest validity for causal inferences. The sine qua non of a true experiment is a control group that is functionally equivalent to the treatment groups on all relevant dimensions except the one being manipulated. While perfect equivalence is an impossible ideal, some procedures for achieving equivalence are much better than others. Without exception the most acceptable procedures all involve a *random* assignment of observations to treatments. There is *no* completely adequate substitute for randomization. Unfortunately, randomization is not always possible because of ethical considerations, institutional policies, subject limitations, or other reasons. Furthermore, even perfect randomization cannot counteract the effect of confounding factors introduced with the manipulation.

A quasi-experiment is defined here as a manipulative study that does not meet the rigid standards required of true experiments, but whose design permits some causal inferences to be drawn, though with less validity than in true experiments. In the canonical case the experimental and control group are nonequivalent, perhaps because of limitations on who is acceptable for the experimental group, for example, requirements of skill, volunteering, pathology, or other characteristics. As a result, the manipulation is confounded with preexisting subject attributes. However, also included in the quasi-experimental category are the differential studies in which groups differing on one or more attributes such as psychopathology are exposed to a common experimental manipulation. While the group differences are orthogonal to the manipulation, the problems encountered are similar to those of other quasi-experiments. Probably the most frequently employed experimental design in clinical research is the quasi-experiment in which one performs the same manipulation on a pathological sample and a control sample presumed to be equivalent except for the lack of pathology. But there is no guarantee that the two samples are equivalent except for the pathology. Even when there are no obvious confounding factors such as medication, age, hospitalization, or socioeconomic status, there is no guarantee of equivalence. Furthermore, the manipulation may interact with subject selection within each population to cause confounding within as well as across the samples. For example, certain segments of a pathological population may be systematically eliminated from an experimental group because they cannot function sufficiently well, while they are accepted in a control group (Kisz & Parsons, 1979). In such differential studies one must remember that the distinction between the pathological and normal group is an *observed* not manipulated distinction. As a result, the validity of any conclusion about the pathology's effect on the manipulation can never be strong and depends critically on the elimination of alternative correlated group differences.

One of the best ways to understand the relative merits of a particular experimental or quasi-experimental design is by examining three components of each design: how the subjects were selected, what manipulation was performed, and how the data were analyzed. While the components are obviously interrelated, the advantages and disadvantages of the possible alternatives within each design component can be discussed relatively independently.

SUBJECT SELECTION AND ASSIGNMENT

The procedure used in selecting the samples is one of the most critical determinants of both the external and internal validity of a study. The extent to which experimental and control groups can be considered equivalent depends upon how they are selected, and the generality of any conclusion depends upon how representative the samples are of the population. Yet surprisingly many researchers neglect to specify exactly *how* the sample was chosen, especially in quasi-experimental studies. It is not sufficient to state every characteristic of the sample with great precision; one needs to designate exactly *how* the sample was selected from the population of interest. It may be interesting to know that the college-student subjects in a drug experiment were all seniors with no history of mental illness and a mean IQ of 120; but it is more important to know whether they were chosen randomly from the senior class, randomly from volunteers who responded to an advertisement, were the first students to reply to an advertisement, or were chosen in some other way.

Random Assignment from a Single Population

The most powerful approach for testing causal hypotheses requires the researcher to randomly select subjects from a single population and then randomly assign them to the different experimental conditions. Unfortunately, such a technique is often impractical for the researcher of psychopathology. Nevertheless, when possible, random selection and assignment allow the strongest causal conclusions to be drawn. Experiments of this type using only abnormal subjects are rare, since one generally wishes to compare abnormals with normals. Nonetheless, a few studies of schizophrenic cognition (Chapman & Knowles, 1964), many experiments on hypnosis (e.g., Spanos & Bodorik, 1977; Spanos, Ansari, & Stam, 1979), and a few other experiments have employed randomly assigned abnormal subjects. More commonly, random assignment has been used with normal populations to select subjects for treatments in which abnormal states would be induced. The abnormal states might be induced physically with alcohol (Abrams & Wilson, 1979; Polivy, Schueneman, & Carson, 1976; Wilson & Lawson, 1978), drugs (Pihl & Sigal, 1978), or food (Ruderman & Wilson, 1979); or they might be induced through behavioral manipulations as in studies of mood states (Velten, 1968; Polivy & Doyle, 1980), hypnosis (Banyai & Hilgard, 1976; Coe, Basden, Basden, & Graham, 1976), learned helplessness (Hiroto & Seligman, 1975), anxiety (Glad & Adesso, 1976) and schizophrenic associations (Meiselman, 1978).

Random assignment of subjects to conditions can be accomplished in at least three different ways. First, each subject selected from the population may be assigned at random to one experimental condition independently of the assignment of any other subject (*independent groups design*). Second, subjects may be paired (or grouped into triplets, quadruplets, etc.) on the basis of possessing similar attributes (e.g., IQ and SES). Then one member of each matched k-tuple would be assigned at random to one of the experimental conditions. Such *randomized block designs* have the advantage that much of the between-subject variance is removed from the error variance. One particular type of randomized block design deserves special mention. The *yoked control* design increases the equivalence of the paired subjects by assuring that they receive exactly the same exposure to irrelevant characteristics of the stimuli. For example, in many learned helplessness studies each experimental subject is paired with a control subject and is given the same number of reinforcements as the control subject earns (Cole & Coyne, 1977; Seligman & Maier, 1967). Yoking each experimental subject's reinforcements to a control subject's usually eliminates reinforcements as a confounding variable (for some potential problems with yoking, see Church, 1964, and Costello 1978).

The third approach to random assignment involves letting each subject appear in each experimental condition with the order of presentation randomized and counterbalanced (Chapman & Knowles, 1964; Teasdale & Fogarty, 1979). These *repeated measures designs* allows between-subject variance to be removed from the error variance. Unfortunately, other error variance may be introduced because of "testing" effects. Repeated measures designs are probably overused in research on psychopathology.

While random assignment is the one technique that assures equivalence of subject groups, it has not been utilized as frequently in clinical research as have other less demanding procedures. Random assignment is not possible in many settings, and where possible, often is not used because the experimental conditions of interest are existing subject attributes such as existing pathologies. Thus quasi-experiments appear more frequently than true experiments in clinical research.

Selection from Different Populations

By far the most common procedure for subject selection in experimental studies of psychopathology has involved drawing some subjects from a pathological population and others from a control population. Over 75% of the experimental articles published in the *Journal of Abnormal Psychology* between

1976 and 1979 were of this type. In most studies of schizophrenic cognition, the effect of a variety of manipulations on schizophrenics' memory processes, reaction times, and perceptual processes has been compared with the manipulation's effect on control groups consisting of normal subjects or subjects with another pathology (Koh & Peterson, 1978; Knight, Sherer, Putchat, & Carter, 1978; Bellissimo & Steffy, 1972). Similarly, the differences between the effects of various manipulations on pathological subjects and their effects on control subjects have been measured to investigate social and cognitive processes in depression (Smolen 1978; Sacco & Hokanson, 1978; Miller & Lewis, 1977) psychopaths (Hare, 1978; Steinberg & Schwartz, 1976), alcoholics (Brown & Cutler, 1977; Tucker, Vuchinich, & Sobel, 1979), and those suffering appetitive disorders (Elman, Schroeder, & Schwartz, 1977; Spencer & Fremouw, 1979). These studies are quasi-experimental because the major "independent" variable, pathology, is a subject attribute, and other subject differences may be confounded with it (see Chapman & Chapman, 1977, for good examples). The manipulation is sometimes also confounded with populations, but more often is performed within both subject groups. For example, in studies comparing reaction time in schizophrenics with reaction time in normals, the preparatory interval is manipulated over a range of values (Bellissimo & Steffy, 1972); so the interaction of preparatory interval with pathology can be examined.

Often researchers comparing a pathological and normal population attempt to increase the equivalence of their samples by *forming matched pairs* across the different populations (e.g., schizophrenic and normal) and eliminating unmatched subjects from the experiment. This procedure should not be confused with the matching of subjects in randomized blocks experiments. There, subjects are assigned randomly to conditions after matching. Here, their population determines their treatment condition. As a result, the

matching may introduce more problems than it remedies. Matching subjects' observed scores may seem to increase the equivalence of the groups, but the subject's underlying "true" scores may be quite different if the matching variable is less than perfectly reliable. If the two populations have substantially different means on the matching variable (as is often the case), the matching procedure selects subjects unrepresentative of the populations, because most of those who match will fall between the means. Further, regression effects are likely to operate in opposite directions and make the groups seem to move apart on the matching variable and on any correlated variable (e.g., the dependent variable). Generally the statistical corrections discussed later in the chapter are preferable to such matching.

Selection from Population Extremes

Another mode of subject assignment frequently employed in clinical research requires the selection of the extreme scorers on a particular test. For example, in much of the learned helplessness research on humans, two groups of subjects are selected and contrasted: those who score high and those who score low on a depression inventory (Miller & Seligman, 1975; Rizley, 1978). While such an approach may seem very similar to the comparison of the analogous clinically differentiated groups, the similarity is based on an assumption that psychopathology falls on a continuum. Many question this presumption (Depue & Monroe, 1978). Are college students who score above the median on a depression inventory similar in essential characteristics to clinically depressed patients? Certainly the external validity of the conclusions drawn from such studies is weaker than for those drawn from studies employing clinical populations. One must also be careful in this kind of quasi-experiment to avoid the matching errors discussed earlier with regard to clinically differentiated populations. While one may be tempted to match the subjects selected from the two extremes on such variables as IQ and SES, it is likely to harm more than it helps for the reasons discussed above.

One type of selection from the "extremes" that is particularly prevalent is the *volunteer* experiment. It is common for the subjects in one experimental condition to represent a population that volunteered for a therapy, treatment, or procedure for which the subjects in the other condition did not volunteer. For example, one might compare women who come to a clinic, ask for, and receive assertiveness training with control women selected from a class in introductory psychology. Why are such volunteers considered to be from an extreme? It is assumed that the volunteers selected themselves for the treatment on the basis of their true assertiveness scores, which were probably below average for the population. While it would be possible to measure, estimate, and statistically correct for the volunteers' initial assertiveness level, it would be preferable to divide the volunteers into an early treatment and late treatment group randomly. The late treatment group could then serve as a control (waiting list control) for the early treatment group. In experimental studies of psychopathology, one should be suspicious of any design in which one group consists of volunteers and the other does not.

MANIPULATIONS

The manipulations commonly performed in experimental studies of psychopathology are diverse enough to defy easy classification. Nevertheless, a few general categories stand out.

Induction of Abnormal States

One broad category of manipulations are those clearly designed to induce special psychological states or modes of behavior. These states may be of interest because they occur often among the population (e.g., inebriation), because they are analogous to certain pathological states (e.g., learned helplessness), or because they provide insight into certain psychological processes (e.g., hypnotic trance). The states may be induced with physiological or behavioral procedures.

Among the most common of such experiments are those employing drugs, food, or alcohol. Alochol–no-alcohol manipulations have been used to investigate alcohol's effects on social behavior such as aggression (Lang, Goeckner, Adisso, & Marlatt, 1975; Zeichner & Pihl, 1979) and sexual behavior (Wilson & Lawson, 1978), to investigate its influence on certain cognitive processes such as memory (Rosen & Lee, 1976), and pain (Brown & Cutler, 1977) and to investigate the etiology of alcoholism (Brown & Williams, 1975; Marlatt, Demming, & Reed, 1973; Tucker, Vuchinich, & Sobell, 1979). Similarly, drug manipulations have been used to simulate abnormal behavior such as hallucinations (Heaton & Victor, 1976; Klee, Bertino, Weintraub, & Calaway, 1961; Metzner, Litwin, & Weil, 1965). In experiments using such physiological manipulations, it is particularly critical to control subject expectations. The best manipulations appear to be those that vary actual substance dose and expected substance dose orthogonally. The control group receives a placebo that is indistinguishable from the "real thing," and instructions are carefully designed to manipulate what the subject expects to receive. For example, in most alcohol studies the drinks are made bitter enough that alcohol cannot be detected. Half the subjects in each group are thus told they are getting alcohol and half told they are not. The need for such an expectancy manipulation has been amply demonstrated by the numerous experiments finding significant expectancy effects (e.g., Abrams & Wilson, 1979; Polivy, Schueneman, & Carlson, 1976). Of course the physiological effects of a substance administered in a large dose may be detected by the subject; so posttest measurements of subjects' attributions are a necessity.

A more difficult problem associated with using substances to induce psychological states concerns the equivalency of the states across subjects. The same dose may have quite different effects on different subjects. While varying dose as a function of body weight may reduce the differences, it may not eliminate them. Probably the best solution is to employ more than two dose levels so the effect of dose on behavior can be estimated. Still another problem is presented in these studies by the ethical necessities of substance research. All subjects must be informed ahead of time of what substances they may receive, and must be given a chance to withdraw. This introduces two potential threats to the validity of an experiment: (1) certain classes of subjects may be less likely to agree to participate; and (2) subject expectancies may predispose them to certain behavior. For example, in Ruderman and Wilson's (1979) experiment on eating behavior, it appears that the ethical warning that subjects would be asked to consume a high caloric drink predisposed subjects to behave as if they already had received the drink.

Abnormal psychological states may be induced by other than physiological means. The subject may be exposed to certain environmental situations or contingencies designed to elicit behavior analogous to that observed in certain pathologies. The learned helplessness induction procedure is perhaps the best recent example of such a manipulation. Be exposing a subject to a situation in which his or her reinforcements are noncontingent on behavior, a state of helplessness can be induced that is putatively analogous to depression (Blaney, 1977; Abramson, Seligman, & Teasdale, 1978; Hiroto & Seligman, 1975). Mild mood staes may be induced by even simpler procedures such as reading lists of affectively toned words (Teasdale & Fogarty, 1979), while states of heightened aggressiveness may be induced by frustration paradigms (Buss, 1966). Sensory and sleep deprivation have been used to engender psychological states in which hallucinations, anxiety, or disconnected thoughts are displayed (Cohen, 1979; Dement, 1960; Heaton & Victor, 1976).

For anyone using either physiological or nonphysiological induction techniques to investigate a pathology, a major concern should be how similar the induced state is to the real state. Too often analog states are treated as if they are real states when general conclusions are enumerated. A nonalcoholic who has been given alcohol may behave quite differently than an alcoholic; a helpless subject may behave quite differently than a depressed subject; and the hallucinations experienced in states of sensory deprivation may be quite different from those experienced by schizophrenics. But what if they do appear to be the same? That does not prove the analog either. The analog and real subject may behave similarly for quite different reasons. This is not to say that analog research is not valuable. It is valuable because it is the only experimental research on psychopathology allowing the manipulation of psychological states and hence random assignment of subjects. Still the conclusions of analog experiments must be supported by the results of other kinds of research on pathological subjects before they gain substantial credibility.

One other widely used induction technique deserves special mention: hypnosis. Experimental studies utilizing hypnotic induction have focused most often on characteristics of the hypnotic state itself rather than on its similarity to any psychopathology. The exact technique used to hypnotize a subject has varied greatly, but most frequently subjects selected for their suggestibility are exposed to tape recorded instructions for entering a trancelike state and engaging in certain behavior. The susceptibility of such subjects to obeying instructions has provided unusual opportunities to gather data on a number of kinds of behavior and processes including memory (Coe, Basdin, Basdin, & Graham, 1976; Kihlstrom, 1980), tolerance for pain (Spanos, Radike-Bodorek, Ferguson, & Jones, 1979), perception (Miller & Leibowitz, 1976) and logical thought (Sheehan, Obstoj, & McConkey, 1976). However, a major difficulty in interpreting the results of hypnosis experiments arises because it is unclear whether the behavior observed is more a function of the induction or simply of the subjects selected. The best design would seem to be one in which subjects are randomly assigned to the hypnosis and no hypnosis group either from the general population or the "hypnotically susceptible" population. However, this procedure is not commonly used, because many researchers believe that "susceptible" subjects will be hypnotized no matter what the procedure. Unfortunately, these researchers do not seem to realize that a valid experiment is impossible under such an assumption.

While most experiments in which special psychological states are induced are aimed at understanding specific states or psychopathologies, one type is aimed more at understanding variations in cognitive processes across states. These are the state-dependent learning studies. In such experiments, the subject learns certain responses while in the special state (e.g., inebriated). Then the subject's performance is measured in the same state and the normal state (i.e., sober). The evidence from these experiments suggests that the reimposition of the state active during learning enhances performance (Eich, Weingartner, Stillman, & Gellin, 1975; Weingartner, Miller, & Murphy, 1977). This general approach of comparing the cognitive processes of the same subject in different states appears to have substantial potential for the understanding of cognitive processes in psychopathology.

Mitigation of Pathological Behavior

The methodology for research on therapy techniques is discussed elsewhere in this book. Therefore only a few general comments about the experimental paradigms most often employed will be made here. First, one must be careful about generalizing the power of a manipulation. A technique that inoculates college students against the effect of a learned helplessness induction (Jones, Nation, & Massad, 1977; Teasdale, 1978) may be ineffective in preventing clinical depression. Second, natural improvement over time and subject attrition must always be carefully considered as alternative explanations for any improvements. Usually a random assignment to treatment and control group is impossible, but control must be accomplished in some way. A waiting group control is often the best solution. In any case, control groups in such studies should always receive placebo treatments with demand characteristics equivalent to those found in the experimental group. With small numbers of subjects the best approach may be a time series design with repeated introductions of the manipulation and measurements of the behavior. If enough observations are made, even the data from a single subject can be statistically significant. What suffers is the external validity (generalizability) of the results. Time series designs are discussed in more detail in the section on data analysis.

Interaction of Pathology with Cognitive or Social Processes

As mentioned earlier, it is very common for researchers of psychopathology to compare the responses of normal and abnormal subjects to a particular manipulation. Most often the manipulation is directed at a particular cognitive or social process believed to be of relevance to a psychopathology. The objective of such an experiment is usually twofold: to learn more about the pathology by examining how the abnormal subjects perform compared to normals, and to learn more about the cognitive or social process by examining how it is affected by the pathology. In these experiments the manipulation is performed on both the normal and abnormal groups, so the outcome of interest is the interaction between group and manipulation. With schizophrenics, for example, one popular paradigm has been to study reaction times as a function of the interval between a warning signal and the stimulus signal. The duration and regularity of the preparatory interval are manipulated factorally within the schizophrenic and normal groups, and the interaction of these manipulations with the group (schizophrenic-normal) are examined. These experiments led to the discovery of the "reaction time corss-over effect" for regular and irregular intervals in schizophrenics (Bellissimo & Steffy, 1972). Numerous other paradigms from experimental psychology have been employed to investigate cognitive processes of schizophrenics and depressives in much the same way. Among these have been experiments on recall, (Koh & Peterson, 1978; Raulin & Chapman, 1976), recognition (Miller & Lewis, 1977), memory scanning (Koh, Szoc, & Peterson, 1977), organization of memory (Russel & Beekhuis, 1976), visual search (Russel & Knight, 1977), iconic memory (Knight, Sherer, & Shapiro, 1977), sentence verification (Neufeld, 1977), interference in short-term memory (Bauman & Kolisnyk, 1976), attention (Chapman, 1956; Straube & Germer, 1979; Oltmans, 1978), and concept formation (Payne, Mattusek, & George, 1959). Many of these manipulations were originally motivated more by a general interest in schizophrenic cognition than by particular theoretical expectations.

The manipulations employed in investigation of depression have had a firmer theoretical grounding, probably because of the existence of theories suggesting effects of certain social and cognitive processes. Many manipulations have been stimulated by the learned helplessness paradigm described earlier. One popular approach has been to induce learned helplessness in groups differing on level of depression (Miller & Seligman, 1975; Price, Tryon, & Raps, 1978). Unfortunately, the importance of these experiments has been overemphasized. A comparison of learned helplessness effects in depressed and normal populations is not a strong test of the learned helplessness model of depression. A causal variable may have a quite different effect on a pathological population after the pathology emerges than before it emerges.

Recently some researchers studying depression have attempted to manipulate and measure attributions about success and failure among depressed and normal subjects (Dweck, 1975; Rizley, 1978; Krantz & Hammen, 1979; Seligman, Abramson, Semmel, & von Baeyer, 1979). Attributions are generally manipulated by giving a subject false information about himself or herself and the task he or she is performing, for example, "this task clearly relates to intelligence." Because one cannot directly observe attributions, most of the evidence regarding the success of such manipulations has been inferential. However, a few psychologists have also either asked subjects to report what attributions they made (retrospective verbalizations) or asked subjects to think aloud while they are making attributions (concurrent verbalizations). Nisbett & Wilson (1977) have pointed out the weakness of retrospective verbalization as data, but concurrent verbalizations can be valid and useful (Ericsson & Simon, 1980). Unfortunately, the distinction between retrospective and concurrent is often missed.

While the above classification of manipulations is by no means exaustive, it does provide a framework in which most experiments and quasi-experiments on psychopathology can be placed. Let us now turn to the types of analyses most commonly employed in psychopathology research and to a more formal classification of experimental designs. Table 7.1 summarizes this classification.

ANALYSIS OF DATA FROM EXPERIMENTAL AND QUASIEXPERIMENTAL DESIGNS

The analysis of data from experimental studies of psychopathology differs from the analysis of other experimental data only in that

Table 7.1. Summary of Commonly Used Experimental Designs for Research on Psychopathology

Design	Subject selection and assignment	Manipulation	Recommended analyses	Some recent examples
True Experiments				
Independent groups	Randomly select subjects from a single population. Assign subjects randomly to treatments.	Treatments differ only in value of independent variable.	Posttest only: ANOVA or MANOVA Pre–post test: ANOVA or MANOVA on difference scores or with test of time by treatment interaction. Intergroup comparison of regressions.	Polivy et al., 1976 Meiselman, 1978 Abrams & Wilson, 1979 Sacco & Hokanson, 1978 Bachrach et al., 1977
Randomized blocks	Randomly select subjects from a single population. (a) Match subjects into blocks of *k* subjects and randomly assign one from each block to each of the *k* treatment groups. (b) Or randomly pair subjects and randomly assign one of each pair to the experimental and "yoked" control group.	Treatments differ only in value of independent variable. In "yoked" control design, each subject's manipulation is matched to his or her controls except for value of independent variable.	Same as for independent groups except that *randomized blocks* ANOVA or MANOVA is used.	Knox & Shum, 1977 Cole & Coyne, 1977 Hiroto & Seligman, 1975 Seligman & Maier, 1967
Counterbalanced repeated measures	Randomly select subjects from a single population.	Each subject receives each treatment but in a different order; so order can be removed as a potential explanation for treatment effects	MANOVA with the subjects score under each treatment as a separate dependent variable (or, if assumptions are not violated, a repeated measures ANOVA)	Chapman & Knowles, 1964 Teasdale & Fogarty, 1979

Quasi-Experiments				
Nonequivalent independent groups	Subjects are selected randomly from different populations, or from the extremes of one population, or in some other way so groups differ in essential characteristics.	Confounded: The manipulation is confounded with the group differences. Factorial: The manipulation is orthogonal to the group differences. Within groups, treatments differ only in value of independent variable.	Post test only: None Pre-posttest: ANCOVA, or ANCOVA with reliability correction in which pretest is covariate, or ANCOVA on standardized change scores without pretest as covariate. Same as independent groups under true experiments except measured group differences should be used as covariates in ANCOVA, if assumptions are not violated.	Kenny, 1965 Bellissimo & Steffy, 1972 Koh & Peterson, 1978 Chapman, 1976
Matched groups	Subjects are selected from two different populations or from the extremes of one population so they *match* on one or more variables believed to correlate with the dependent variable.	Confounded: Same as nonequivalent independent groups. Factorial: Same as nonequivalent independent groups.	It is recommended that these designs be avoided because the effect of matching on observed scores is uncertain. If used, analyses would be similar to randomized blocks design.	Miller et al., 1979 Straube & Germer, 1979
Time series	Randomly select subjects from a single population.	Each subject receives the treatment one or more times and is measured on the dependent variable many times before and after each treatment	Autoregressive time-series analysis or, as a first approximation, a comparison of before and after regression of the dependent variable on time.	Kazdin & Wilson, 1978 Ayllon & Axrin, 1967

the preponderance of studies are quasi-experiments rather than true experiments. Nevertheless, the starting point for any discussion of analysis issues must be the true experiment.

Independent Randomized Groups Design

Posttest Only. While not the most commonly occurring design in clinical research, the independent groups posttest-only design serves as a good starting point for a discussion of analysis issues. Subjects from a single population are assigned at random to treatment cells and measured after the treatments are performed. If p independent variables are manipulated and each has r treatment levels, such a design will require $p \times r$ groups of subjects (cells). For maximizing the power of the analysis, one would like to have an equal number of subjects in each cell, but this may not always be possible. Recent examples of this approach include Polivy, Schueneman, & Carson (1976), and Meiselman (1978). Discussion of the numerous variations of this basic design is beyond the scope of this chapter; rather I will deal with only a few specific issues that have sometimes arisen when the independent groups design is used in experimental studies of psychopathology.

Usually the principal hypothesis tested in an independent groups design is that the population means for the different levels of the independent variables are equal, and the principal technique applied is analysis of variance. Frequently the experimenter has measured a number of dependent variables in each cell. Unfortunately, a common approach for this situation has been to compute separate analyses of variance for each of the dependent variables. Such a method is deficient on two grounds: (1) it raises the probability of at least one Type I error (rejecting the null hypothesis when it's really true) from α to about about $1 - (1 - \alpha)^v$ where v is the number of dependent variables;[1] and (2) the probability of a Type II error (not rejecting the null hypothesis when it's really false) is higher than for alternative techniques if the dependent variables are correlated. The appropriate procedure with multiple dependent variables is a multivariate analysis of variance (MANOVA) followed by tests of the individual variables.

A second common error concerns the appropriate model for the ANOVA or MANOVA. A fixed-effects model is legitimate for an independent variable whose levels represent exaustively the range of levels of the variable (e.g., hospitalized or not hospitalized), while a random-effects model is appropriate for an independent variable whose levels represent a few arbitrary or randomly selected values from a range of values (e.g., Hospital A or Hospital B). The choice of a fixed-effects model, which most computer programs use as a default, when random effects are appropriate, can lead to an inflated Type I error rate (Clark, 1973; Martindale, 1978).

A third type of error may be observed when the experimenter utilizes a design requiring tests of the interactive effect of the independent variables on the dependent variables. Too often only the F-statistics for the interaction and main effects are examined in these experiments. But *if an interaction is significant,* tests of the main effects for the variables involved in the interaction are misleading. Instead one should test the *simple effects* of each variable within each level of the other variables in the interaction. Care must be taken with such procedures so that the probability of a Type I error is not inflated unacceptably because too large a number of

---

[1]Alpha (α) is the significance level chosen for each test by the experimenter. If, for example, the experimenter decides to reject a hypothesis whenever the probability of his or her being wrong is less than .05, then Alpha is .05. But the probability of *at least* one error in 10 such tests (i.e., on 10 dependent variables) will be much higher than .05. In fact, according to the formula, it will be about .40.

F-statisitcs have been tested. A similar problem occurs when one attempts to determine which levels of a manipulated variable produced any significant main effect. While a discussion of the various techniques for overcoming the multiple comparison problem is beyond the scope of this chapter (see Morrison, 1976; Miller, 1966), even a cursory survey of clinical experimentation reveals that researchers need to be more cognizant of the problem.

Pretest–Posttest Designs. In deciding whether to measure the dependent variable before and after the treatment or only after, two factors must be balanced. The main advantage of the pre–post design is that the within-subject error variance can be estimated separately from the between-subject variance. As a result, the statistical tests generally are more powerful (i.e., have lower probability of a Type II error) when both pretreatment and posttreatment measurements are made. The effect of the treatment can be measured by comparing the change from pretest to posttest in the experimental groups with the change in the control groups relative to the within-subject variance (Abrams & Wilson, 1979; Sacco & Hokanson, 1978). One can perform a one-way analysis of variance directly on the difference scores of the groups, or one can test the treatment by time interaction with a two-factor repeated measures analysis of variance model. The procedures generate identical results.

One should remember that the advantage of the difference score analysis stems from the fact that posttest and pretest scores are substantially correlated. If they are not highly correlated (e.g., $r^2 > .25$) for some reason, then the difference score analysis may be less powerful than a posttest-only analysis. Usually, however, the scores are highly correlated.

While the greater statistical power of pre–post designs is desirable, it must be balanced against a potential deficit—the pretest may substantially affect the posttest. Such a testing artifact is particularly serious if it raises the dependent variable's mean close to a ceiling, or if the magnitude of the testing effect depends upon the treatment the subject receives (treatment by testing interaction). For example, in experimental studies of memory, a pretreatment recall test may both enhance posttreatment recall for all subjects and sensitize experimental subjects to an objective of the study (recall changes) before the subjects receive the treatment. The effect of such a treatment might be quite different if a posttest-only design were used.

One other quite different type of analysis is also appropriate for pre–post independent groups designs in which the researcher is primarily interested in the effect of a manipulation on the relation between two psychological variables, for example, the effect of setting on the relation between mood and performance. If both variables of interest are measured before and after the manipulation, one can examine how the manipulation affected their relation by comparing the multiple regression equations predicting post-manipulation scores from premanipulation scores in the experimental group with the corresponding equations in the control group. One of the variables may be the manipulated variable, or they may both be unmanipulated. The advantage of this approach is that it can reveal both how the manipulation affected the relation between the variables and how the variables influenced the power of the manipulation. While this technique has been used widely by economists (see Johnston, 1972, for details), it has only been employed infrequently by psychologists (Bachrach, Huesmann, & Peterson, 1977).

Randomized Blocks Designs

In a randomized blocks design with k treatment levels, subjects are formed into sets of k people (blocks) on the basis of similarities (matching). Then the k subjects in each block are randomly distributed among the k treatment groups. Thus every subject in treatment condition *i* can be paired with a subject in any other condition *j* during the data analysis (Cohen, 1979; Cole & Coyne, 1977; Hiroto & Seligman, 1975; Knox & Shum, 1977). The value of this procedure depends upon the extent to which blocking reduces error variance in the analysis of the results. Error variance is partitioned into "between block" variance and "within block" variance. If the blocking accounts for a substantial portion of variance, the error term in an analysis of variance will be reduced, and the test of the null hypothesis will be more powerful than for the corresponding independent groups design. While the "yoked control" version of the randomized blocks design is often used in clinical research (Seligman & Maier, 1967; Cole & Coyne, 1977), other types of randomized blocks designs are less frequently seen (although they are recommended in therapy outcome research, Kendall & Norton-Ford, this volume). It is worth reemphasizing that a randomized blocks design is a valid true experimental design and is quite different from the experiments that use matched subjects from two different populations. When the subject's characteristics determine the subject's treatment, matching is not very valuable; but when matching can be followed by random assignment (as with a randomized blocks design), it can be a powerful tool.

With a randomized blocks design, one can use a posttest-only procedure or a pretest-posttest procedure. The same arguments apply for the advantages and disadvantages of pretesting as with independent groups designs. Similarly, the analysis of variance procedures are not greatly different, and the cautionary statements outlined above apply here as well.

Counterbalanced Repeated Measures Designs

In these designs every subject receives every treatment but in a different order (Chapman & Knowles, 1964; Teasdale & Fogarty, 1979). The ordering of the treatments must be carefully counterbalanced to eliminate order as a potential explanation. The repeated measures design looks similar to a pre–post design, but differs in that every subject receives every treatment; so there are no separate experimental and control groups. With pre–post designs the important analysis of variance effect is the time by treatment interaction (i.e., differences in change scores between groups). In repeated measures designs it is the main effect for treatment level. The traditional linear model for conducting an analysis of variance of a repeated measures design requires one to assume that the correlations between the repeated measurements on the dependent variable are the same for every pair of measurements, for example, placebo versus dose 1 is the same placebo versus dose 2 is the same as dose 1 versus dose 2, and so on. Since this assumption is often seriously violated, it is preferable to treat each measurement as a separate dependent variable in a multivariate analysis of variance (MANOVA). With such an analysis one examines the hypothesis of equal means for all pairs of treatment levels simultaneously (Morrison, 1976).

Quasi-Experimental Nonequivalent Independent Groups Design

By far the most common type of design in experimental studies of psychopathology is the nonequivalent independent groups design. In this design samples are selected from different populations for the same or different treatments. For example, clustering in free recall might be compared between hypnotically susceptible subjects and normal control subjects. If the only question were whether the populations differed in their scores on the dependent variable, the statistical test could be a simple one-factor analysis of variance. But such a design is not really even a quasi-experiment, since no variables were manipulated. The designs of more interest occur when another independent variable is either manipulated identically within each group (*factorial manipulation*), or manipulated across groups so its levels are confounded with population (*confounded manipulation*). An example of the first kind would be experiments on schizophrenic cognition in which a sample of schizophrenics and normals receive the same manipulation (Bellissimo & Steffy, 1972; Chapman, 1956; Koh & Peterson, 1978). The hypothesis to be tested is whether the pathology (schizophrenia vs. normal) caused the manipulation to have a different effect, that is, is there a group by treatment interaction? Examples of the second kind of experiment would be studies of hypnosis in which the hypnotized and control group differed on susceptibility (Stevenson, 1976), studies of therapist effectiveness in which therapist-patient pairs are not randomly assigned (Gomes-Schwartz, 1978), studies of cognitive processes in which subject pathology is confounded with drugs received (Russel & Beekhuis, 1976), or studies in which the experimenter does not control who gets the treatment (Dennis, 1960; Feldman-Summers et al., 1979). The question of interest in these experiments would be whether the manipulations caused a difference between the groups, that is, is there a main effect for therapy? Of course, both factorial and confounded designs can be generalized to have several grouping variables (e.g., psychopathology, sex, hospitalized status) and to have several manipulated variables. In all cases, however, these designs cannot be called true experiments because the difference between groups is due to a preexisting condition that might be correlated with many other variables. As a result, one can never answer the causal questions posed with as much confidence as when differences are produced by an experimental manipulation across equivalent groups (i.e., randomly selected).

As with randomized independent group experiments, an important decision for nonequivalent group quasi-experiments is whether one uses both a *pretest and a posttest* or *only a posttest*. The arguments are similar and clearly favor the pretest-posttest approach for quasi-experiments in which population is *confounded* with treatment. If one does not measure preexisting differences in these designs, it is almost impossible to know whether to attribute a postmanipulation difference to preexisting conditions or the manipulation.

Factorial Manipulations. The analysis of data from nonequivalent independent group designs with factorial manipulations proceeds very similarly to analysis of data from randomized independent group designs. The analysis of variance model appropriate for the exact design is applied and the group by manipulation interaction is tested. One cannot, however, state a strong causal conclusion even if a significant group by manipulation interaction is found. For example, a difference in the effect of preparatory intervals on the reaction times of schizophrenics and normals might be "caused" by the pathology, but it might also be "caused" by some other factors correlated with the pathology in the same studied. One technique that may aid in clarifying such relations is *analysis of covariance*. With it the effect of any variable that correlates similarly with the dependent variable within all groups can be removed as a potential explanation for the group by manipulation interaction. For example, if the ages of schizophrenics and normal persons were significantly different, covarying out age could eliminate it as a potential confounding factor. Analysis of covariance is discussed in more detail in the next section.

Confounded Manipulations. When the treatment condition is confounded with preexisting differences in the subjects, analysis of the data is more difficult. Yet often researchers are forced to use designs in which pathological subjects are assigned to experimental and control groups by other than random means, for example, on the basis of volunteering, hours of availability, severity of psychopathology, or ethical considerations (who needs a potentially valuable treatment the most?). Abnormal subjects almost inevitably differ on other factors than diagnosis, for example, drug maintenance. In some cases the manipulation itself may be a naturally occurring event out of the experimenter's control, for example, changes in hospitalized patients' diets, changes in psychotherapy programs, changes in drug administration. Pretests are almost always given in such cases, but a simple analysis of variance of the pre–post change scores to test for a difference between groups (or equivalently a test for a group by time interaction in a repeated measures analysis) would not be adequate because of the confounding. One common alternative is to use the pretest as a covariate along with any other measured variables that discriminate between the groups. In the resulting analysis of covariance the main effect for groups (instead of a group by time interaction) would be of greatest interest. Of course, if a number of dependent variables need to be examined, a multivariate analysis of covariance would be used.

The appropriateness of any analysis of covariance depends upon a number of assumptions. First, the covariates must correlate about the same with the dependent variable within each treatment group (homogeneity of regression). For example, if age related to performance quite differently within a sample of schizophrenics and a sample of normal persons, then analysis of covariance with age as a covariate should not be used. Second, an analysis of covariance assumes that everyone is regressing toward the same mean. If subjects were selected by pretest for the manipulation they would receive (e.g., as they might be for a remedial or therapy treatment), then the samples might represent different ends of the distribution. If the dependent variable were only moderately reliable, there would be substantial regression effects on the posttest. An analysis of covariance would correct for the assumed pre-post regression appropriately. But if the groups represent two qualitatively different populations with different mean true scores,

this assumption would be incorrect. The analysis would be based on an overestimate of regression toward the grand mean, and would have an increased chance of Type I or Type II errors. For groups that appear to be from distinctly different populations with substantially different mean true scores on the dependent variable, Kenny (1975) advocates deleting the pretest as a covariate because of this difficulty. Instead one can use the change in standardized score for each subject as the dependent variable in the analysis of covariance. The scores are standardized at each time using the entire sample of subjects; so the change in standardized score for a subject represents his or her change corrected for changes in the overall mean or standard deviation. On the other hand, if the groups come from one population and have different pretest means because the subjects *volunteered* for the treatments they received, the pretest can be used as a covariate as long as one corrects for its unreliability. The reasoning is that volunteering is based on a true score; but the covariance analysis is based on the less reliable observed pretest score. Therefore, the covariance analysis predicts too much regression, and is inaccurate. The solution is to divide the regression coefficient for the pretest by its reliability. In other cases in which the subjects can be considered to come from one population but differ in pretest scores, an uncorrected analysis of covariance can be used.

Quasi-Experimental Matched Groups Design

Sometimes researchers attempt to remedy the problem of nonequivalent groups by discarding the subjects in each group who cannot be matched with any subject in the other groups (Miller, Saccuzzo, & Braf, 1979; Straube & Germer, 1979). Such a technique is quite different from the randomized blocks technique because the matched subjects come from distinctly different populations and are not randomly assigned to a treatment condition after being matched. The population determines the treatment condition. On the whole, this design probably should be avoided. The problem is that one can only match subjects on observed scores not on true scores. If the populations from which the samples are drawn have different mean true scores, matching biases both samples away from their own means and exacerbates the likelihood of regression effects masking or being mistaken for real effects. For example, if a schizophrenic and normal sample were matched for pretest performance on a cognitive task, but the population mean were really lower for schizophrenics, one would have selected above-average schizophrenics and below-average normal persons. The best prediction for posttest performance would be an increase for normals (toward their mean) and a decrease for schizophrenics (toward their mean). Of course, if the matching variable were uncorrelated with the dependent variable, matching could not hurt; but then why match? The only situation in which a case might be made for matching subjects from two different populations would be when the *population* means on the matching variable were equal and the matching variable was correlated with the dependent variable. If the available subjects were unrepresentative of their populations, then simple random sampling would yield biased samples. In this case matching might produce a more representative sample and would allow a paired observation statistical test with reduced error variance and greater power. Unfortunately, this is not the situation in wh1ch matching is most often used.

Not everyone agrees with this viewpoint on matching. For example, Chapman and Chapman (1977) have recently argued in favor of matching in studies of schizophrenic cognition. They argue that there are many differences between the normal and schizophrenic populations that are correlated with cognitive processes, and these differences somehow must be controlled. There is merit to this argument. The problem is that when

control is accomplished by matching, one ends up with samples unrepresentative of the populations and perhaps unmatched on true scores. Still this can be an acceptable situation if one is more interested in differences between certain subgroups of the populations than in drawing inferences about the populations, for example, one may be interested in comparing young schizophrenics with young normals. The danger is that the generalizations made from such research may go beyond the subgroups studied. For example, if one found a difference in the cognitive processes of schizophrenics and normal persons matched for IQ, one would certainly be tempted to conclude it was a difference between schizophrenics and normal persons in general. Yet it may only be a difference in high IQ schizophrenics. The generality of the conclusion must depend upon the matching variable, its distribution in the two populations, and its theoretical relevance to the pathology. Certainly, in some cases, if used with care, matching can be beneficial as long as judicious conclusions are drawn. However, more often an appropriate use of covariates with an independent groups design can accomplish the desired result with greater safety.

Quasi-Experimental Time Series Design

In time series designs control is achieved by repeating the measurement of the dependent variable a large number of times before and after each of a series of interventions. Then one tests whether the intervention produced a change in the relation between time and the dependent variable. A time series design is a special kind of repeated measures experiment in which a trend over time (perhaps due to maturation, testing, or spontaneous remission) is expected and corrected for. In a typical repeated measures experiment a subject is observed only once in each treatment condition, and the order of treatments is counterbalanced across subjects. In a time series quasi-experiment a subject may be observed hundreds of times in each condition, and no attempt is made to counterbalance order of treatments. The internal validity of the quasi-experiment does not depend so much on the number of subjects studied as on the number of observations made. The sample size for the statistical tests is the number of observations not the number of subjects. Even a single-subject time series design can be internally valid, though the external validity (generality) of such single-subject experiments may be very limited. While time series designs have been widely used in therapy outcome research (Kazdin & Wilson, 1978) and in behavior modification experiments with abnormal subjects (Ayllon & Azrin, 1965), most researchers have not employed an appropriate statistical analysis.

For a complete description of the methods for analyzing time series data, one must consult other texts (Cook & Campbell, 1979; Box & Jenkins, 1976). The simplistic approach is to derive three linear equations for predicting the dependent variable as a function of time. One equation is computed for all observed data; one is computed for the data collected before each intervention; and one is computed for the data collected after each intervention. The researcher then tests the null hypothesis that the slopes and intercepts of the three lines are identical.

There are several problems with this approach. First, the particular theoretical model being tested may predict a different pattern of results than a simple change in slope or intercept after the intervention. For example some intervention procedures might have delayed, temporary, nonlinear, or cyclical effects. As a result, the exact prediction equation to be used and the range of times from which data are used must depend upon the theoretical model being tested. Second, the use of an ordinary least-squares regression analysis to estimate and compare the prediction equations is of questionable validity. The slopes and intercepts of the three lines would be valid unbiased estimates, but the statistical tests for comparing such regression lines would be faulty. These tests assume independence of observations, while in fact each observation in a time series is almost inevitably correlated with the previous observations (autocorrelated). In other words, a score observed at time t is correlated not only with time itself but with the score observed at time $t - 1$, time $t - 2$, and so on. The procedures developed to cure this difficulty allow the specification of a variety of models and remove the autoregressive effect before testing the intervention effect (Box & Jenkins, 1976). Yet like many multivariate techniques, the analysis is only feasible with specialized computer programs and requires statistical sophistication. As a result, many researchers use ordinary regression analysis as a first approximation (see Johnston, 1972, for details).

THREE EXPERIMENTAL STUDIES OF PSYCHOPATHOLOGY

Having examined systematically the gamut of designs and analyses frequently used in experimental studies of psychopathology, let us look at three specific experiments in greater detail in order to see how well theory and practice coincide. These three are specimens of some of the better published experiments, and if flawed in places, they are near the top overall. Each also represents a popular area of experimental research on psychopathology.

Cognitive Processes in Schizophrenics

Bellissimo and Steffy's (1972) experiment on attention in schizophrenics is representative of the large body of experiments performed to understand cognitive processes in schizophrenics. The authors selected their schizophrenic and nonschizophrenic patients in a manner typical of many similar experiments. Essentially all the female patients in two wards who met the diagnostic criteria and agreed to participate were used. However, as usual a few patients refused to participate, and a few had some characteristics the experimenters considered inappropriate (e.g., excessive hospitalization) and were excluded. Another normal control group consisted of volunteers from the hospital staff. Obviously this study must be considered a *quasi-experiment with nonequivalent groups*.

The dependent variable was reaction time to a 300 Hz, 70db tone, and the manipulated independent variables were the duration and regularity of the time between when the experimenter said "ready" and when the tone was sounded (preparatory interval). Within each group a Latin square repeated measures design was used for manipulating the preparatory interval along two dimensions: duration, and regular versus irregular. A particular preparatory interval would be called regular if the preceding three intervals had been the same length. Since the manipulations were combined factorially with groups, the major statistics of interest would be the groups by manipulation (duration and regularity) interactions.

After some preliminary tests, Bellissimo and Steffy appropriately examined the group by duration by regularity interaction, which was found to be highly significant. They then proceeded with tests of the two-way duration by regularity interations within each group to determine the cause of the three-way interaction. This is equivalent to testing for simple effects after a significant two-way interaction is found. The only group for which the two-way interaction was significant was the process schizophrenics, indicating the reason for the three-way interaction. The process schizophrenics respond more rapidly to regularly spaced warning signals when the interval is short and to irregularly spaced warning signals when the interval is long (reaction time crossover). All other subjects always respond more rapidly to regularly spaced warnings. Other analyses were performed, but these are the critical ones.

Overall, the Bellissimo and Steffy experiment provides a reasonably good model for experiments comparing cognitive processes in schizophrenics and normals. It has flaws, for example, pathology is confounded with

other factors, but not many flaws compared to most experiments of this type.

Learned Helplessness

Cole and Coyne's (1977) experiment on learned helplessness is a good example of the use of *yoked* controls in experiments on psychopathology. It was an analog study in that the manipulation was intended to *induce* a state analogous to depression in human subjects. The dependent variables were the subject's performance (latency, failures, and trials to criterion) on an anagram task and the subject's change in affective mood. Each subject was assigned *randomly* to either "escapable noise" pretraining or "inescapable noise" pretraining and to posttesting in either the "same" room or a "different" room. These two independent variables were combined factorially in a posttest only design for the anagram task and a pre–post design for the mood measure. Although the groups were independently selected and randomly assigned, each subject in the "inescapable" group was yoked to a subject in the "escapable" group for the pretraining. During pretraining, subjects in the escapable noise group would learn to turn off an aversive tone by pressing the appropriate pattern of buttons. Since the tone might terminate anyway, a green light would appear when the subject caused it to turn off. The yoked control subject's tone would be terminated at the same instant, but a red light would always be shown to him or her denoting failure. Thus the escapable subject and yoked control inescapable subject received the same amount and pattern of aversive stimulation, but the escapable subject could learn to control the aversive stimulation, and the inescapable subject could not. This procedure was intended to induce learned helplessness in the inescapable noise subjects, which would be revealed by lowered performance on the anagram task and depressed mood.

Cole and Coyne believed this effect might not generalize to a different setting (room); so their major statistic of interest should have been the interaction of escapability and room on the dependent variables. Since there were three performance measures and one mood measure, a multivariate analysis of variance would seem to be appropriate. Cole and Coyne recognized this fact, unlike most learned helplessness researchers, and executed a MANOVA. Unfortunately, the application of the MANOVA and ordering of tests were not the most appropriate. First, Cole and Coyne treated the escapable variable as an independent groups variable when it could have been analyzed with a randomized blocks model (because yoking was used). Second, instead of including all the dependent variables in the MANOVA, they only included the three performance measures. Third, univariate tests were reported before the MANOVA was discussed for hypotheses made irrelevant by the MANOVA's results. The most appropriate procedure would have been to examine the escapability by room interaction first with the MANOVA. Since it was insignificant, the authors could then look at the two main effects, of which only the room effect was significant. An inspection of which dependent variables contributed to the effect was then proper and revealed high canonical loadings for anagram failures and latency but a low loading for trials to criterion. However, since the three dependent variables are very highly intercorrelated, not much should be made of this difference. When multicolinearity is high among dependent variables, regression and canonical coefficients will fluctuate wildly over replications.

While Cole and Coyne's analysis of their data did not proceed in the most efficient manner, they reached the correct conclusions, and the experiment is a well-executed example of the type of study widely seen in learned helplessness research.

The Effect of Alcohol on Normal Persons

The study of alcohol's effects on normal persons is one of the topics in clinical psychol-
ogy that is most amenable to investigation with true experiments. Abrams and Wilson's (1979) experiment on alcohol and social anxiety in women serves as a good specimen of this genre. The subjects were paid female undergraduates selected from volunteers who reported only moderate drinking. Two independent variables, alcohol dose and expectancy, were manipulated by randomly assigning subjects to one of four groups— expect alcohol and receive alcohol, expect alcohol and receive placebo, expect placebo and receive alcohol, or expect placebo and receive placebo. This design is typical of a large number of studies, and procedures have been devised that seem to assure its integrity. The manipulation was double blind—neither the subject nor the person running the subject knew the subject's actual treatment condition, that is, what the subject was drinking. Each subject was told that both alcohol and nonalcohol groups must be tested in the study and that he or she had been randomly assigned to the alcohol (or tonic only) group. The subjects gargled with a mouthwash that reduced their taste sensitivity, under the guise of preparing for a breathalyzer test. The drinks were mixed from labeled bottles in full view of the subject, and the glasses in the "receive placebo" group were surreptitiously smeared with vodka. Finally, the breathalyzer was altered to give false feedback. Manipulation checks based on self-reports of alcohol consumed clearly indicated the manipulations were highly successful. In experiments involving alcohol consumption expectancy checks are just as necessary as breathalyzer tests and should always be included.

After the drink manipulation and breathalyzer test, the subjects were placed in a controlled social interaction with a male confederate. The dependent variables included physiological measures of anxiety (heart rate and skin conductance) taken before, during, and after the interaction, self-report measures of anxiety taken before and after the interaction, and observer ratings of the subject's anxiety during the interaction. Thus the design was an independent randomized groups design with pre–post data on the physiological and self-report measures.

Abrams and Wilson's major analysis was a neatly done multivariate analysis of variance of change scores including all the dependent variables. After finding no significant interaction, the authors reported a significant main effect for "expectancy". Those subjects who expected alcohol were significantly more anxious than those who did not expect alcohol regardless of what they actually received. Examination of the canonical coefficients and appropriate post-hoc univariate analyses of variance of each dependent variable showed that expectancy had its greatest effect on the physiological measures and observer ratings. The effect on self-reported anxiety appears minimal, but when change in self-reported anxiety was used as a dependent variable, a significant effect was found. This is a good illustration of a situation in which a pre–post design produced greater statistical power. All in all, Abrams and Wilson's analyses serve as one of the best published examples of the proper way to deal with data from experiments of this type.

SOME GENERAL THREATS TO THE VALIDITY OF CAUSAL CONCLUSIONS

Experimental studies of psychopathology are no different from any other experiments in their susceptibility to sampling errors, manipulation mistakes, and analysis failures. Each of the specific designs discussed above has its own pitfalls for the unwary researcher. Some of the common errors discussed earlier have been *biased sampling, matching across populations, testing main effects before interactions,* and *using a large number of univariate tests* when one multivariate test is appropriate. Nevertheless, a few threats to the validity of causal conclusions have not

been discussed sufficiently because they are not specific to any particular design.

Differential Mortality Among Subjects

When one selects pathological subjects for an experiment, it is almost inevitable that certain subjects will be dropped from the sample before the experiment is completed or even before it is begun. The seriously pathological subjects may be too incapacitated to perform the experimental task, biasing the sample in the direction of the less pathological. Worse, subject mortality may interact with the treatment conditions, so that the subjects drop out at different rates from the experimental and control groups. Klisz and Parsons (1979) have demonstrated the importance of this factor for investigations of cognition in alcoholics, but it is no less serious a problem for other pathologies. For example, when one discards subjects from a hypnotic treatment because they could not be hypnotized, one has committed the same error. One cannot know whether differences between the hypnotic group and other subjects are due to the treatment or subject selection. The most satisfactory solution for the mortality problem is to impose strong enough motivational conditions that mortality is minimized. Unfortunately, this is sometimes not possible, for example, in hypnosis experiments. In such cases the experimenter can resort to using additional control groups to measure the effect of mortality, that is, compare the dropouts with an unhypnotized group of hypnotizable subjects.

Attention and Demand Effects

In many experiments the procedures are designed so that the researcher must spend a great deal of time with the experimental subjects and only a little with the control subjects. Among hospitalized subjects such attention may be highly rewarding, and the subjects may be particularly complaint in order to maintain the attention. Thus differential attention is always an alternative explanation for a difference between an experimental and control group of pathological subjects. The solution is to be sure that the control group receives equal attention through a placebo treatment with similar demand characteristics.

Stimulus Specificity

Cognitive and social processes in abnormal subjects may be particularly sensitive to stimulus characteristics to which the experimenter is unattentive, for example, affective tone, remote associations, experimenter attractiveness, sex of experimenter. Too often there has been a tendency to conclude that one particular characteristic of a stimulus caused an effect when other characteristics could just as easily have produced it (Maher, 1978). If a sex of therapist by treatment interaction is found, was it really due to sex of therapist or to another characteristic correlated with sex in the particular therapists used? If a noncontingent aversive noise produces a helplessness effect, does one conclude that "noncontingency" is necessary? In order to generalize one's conclusions beyond the narrow context of the stimuli used, one should employ a sample of stimuli in each experimental treatment. If sex of experimenter is an independent variable, then use several different male and female experimenters. If the critical stimulus has several attributes besides the ones manipulated, then use a random sample of stimuli of each type (for example, see Elman, Schroeder, & Schwartz, 1977, and Hammen & Peters, 1978).

Fallacious Causal Reasoning in Normal–Abnormal Comparisons

Often in experimental studies comparing normal and abnormal populations, one discovers that a particular cognitive or social process operates differently in pathological than in normal populations. This difference may coincide perfectly with the researcher's model

for the etiology of the pathology. Nevertheless, a conclusion that the difference causes the pathology is unjustifiable. These studies are only quasi-experiments. Any difference between the normal and abnormal subjects may be a cause of the pathology, may be caused by the pathology, may be caused by another characteristic of the pathological sample, or may be caused by some variable correlated with the pathology. Furthermore, the lack of a difference between the groups on a cognitive or social process does not imply that the process is irrelevant to the etiology of the pathology. A causal process critical to the development of a disorder may be masked by the emergence of the full symtomatology of the disorder. In general the results of any quasi-experiment comparing normal and pathological subjects cannot provide definitive evidence about the etiology of the pathology.

SUMMARY

In reading over this chapter one might be tempted to become very pessimistic about the utility of experimental research for answering important questions about the development of psychopathologies. Clearly researchers are handicapped by the fact that psychopathological states cannot be manipulated very well, and analog states differ from true pathological states in important respects. Nevertheless, if one evaluates the contributions of experimental research relative to other types of empirical research, one can be optimistic. Recent experimental and quasi-experimental studies have yielded major contributions to our understanding of schizophrenic cognition (Chapman, 1956; Bellissimo & Steffy, 1972; Knight et al., 1977; Koh et al., 1977; Payne et al. 1959), depression (Cole & Coyne, 1977; Hammen & Peters, 1978; Hiroto & Seligman, 1975; Price et al. 1978; Rizley, 1978; Seligman & Maier, 1967; Smolen, 1978), appetitive disorders (Brown & Wiliams, 1975; Glad & Adesso, 1976; Marlatt et al., 1973; Polivy et al., 1976; Ruderman & Wilson, 1979), state-dependent learning (Eich et al., 1975; Weingartner et al., 1977), and hypnotism (Banyai & Hilgard, 1976; Coe et al., 1976; Kihlstrom, 1980; Spanos & Brodorik, 1977), as well as other disorders. The goal for future researchers should be to take advantage of recent advances in design and analysis techniques to expand the experimental study of these and other psychopathologies.

REFERENCES

Abrams, D. B., & Wilson, G. T. (1979). Effects of alcohol on social anxiety in women: cognitive versus physiological processes. *Journal of Abnormal Psychology,* **88,** 161–173.

Abramson, L. Y., Seligam, M. E. P., & Teasdale, J. (1978). Learned helplessness in humans: critique and reformulation. *Journal of Abnormal Psychology,* **87,** 49–74.

Aylon, T., & Azrin, N. H. (1967). The measurement and reinforcement of behavior of psychotics. *Journal of Experimental Analysis of Behavior,* **8,** 357–383.

Bachrach, R. S., Huesmann, L. R., & Peterson, R. (1977). The relation between locus of control and the development of moral judgment. *Child Development,* **48,** December, 1340–1352.

Banyai, E., & Hilgard, E. R. (1976). A comparison of active-alert hypnotic induction with traditional relaxation induction. *Journal of Abnormal Psychology,* **85,** 218–224.

Bauman, E., & Kolisnyk, E. (1976). Interference effects in schizophrenic short-term memory. *Journal of Abnormal Psychology,* **85,** 303–308.

Belissimo, A., & Steffy, R. A. (1972). Redundancy associated deficit in schizophrenics reaction time performance. *Journal of Abnormal Psychology,* **80,** 229–307.

Blaney, P. H. (1977). Contemporary theories of depression: critique and comparison. *Journal of Abnormal Psychology,* **86,** 203–223.

Box, G. E. P., & Jenkins, G. M. (1976). *Time series analysis: Forcasting and control.* San Francisco: Holden-Day.

Brown, R. A., & Williams, R. J. (1975). Internal and external cues relating food intake in obese and alcoholic persons. *Journal of Abnormal Psychology,* **84,** 660–665.

Brown, R. A., & Cutler, H. S. (1977). Alcohol, customary drinking behavior and pain. *Journal of Abnormal Psychology,* **86,** 179–188.

Buss, A. H. (1966). Instrumentality of aggression, feedback, and frustration as determinants of physical aggression. *Journal of Personality and Social Psychology,* **3,** 153–162.

Chapman, L. J. (1956). Distractibility in the conceptual performance of schizophrenics. *Journal of Abnormal and Social Psychology,* **53,** 286–291.

Chapman, L. J., & Knowles, R. R. (1964). The effects of phenothiazine on disordered thought in schizophrenia. *Journal of Consulting Psychology,* **28,** 165–169.

Chapman, L. J., & Chapman, J. P. (1977). Selection of subjects in studies of schizophrenic cognition. *Journal of Abnormal Psychology,* **86,** 10–15.

Clark, H. H. (1973). The language-as-fixed-effect fallacy: A critique of language statistics in psychological research. *Journal of Verbal Learning and Verbal Behavior,* **12,** 335–359.

Coe, W. C., Basden, G., Basden, D., & Graham, C. (1976). Posthypnotic amnesia: Suggestions of an active process in dissociative phenomena. *Journal of Abnormal Psychology,* **85,** 455–458.

Cohen, D. B. (1979). Dysphoric affect and REM sleep. *Journal of Abnormal Psychology,* **88,** 73–77.

Cole, C. S., & Coyne, J. C. (1977). Situational specificity of laboratory induced learned helplessness. *Journal of Abnormal Psychology,* **86,** 615–623.

Cook, T. D., & Campbell, D. T. (1979). *Quasi-experimentation: Design and analysis issues for field settings.* Chicago: Rand McNally.

Costello, C. G. (1978). Learned helplessness and depression in humans. *Journal of Abnormal Psychology,* **87,** 21–31.

Dement, W. (1960). The effect of dream deprivation. *Science,* **131,** 1705–1707.

Dennis, W. (1960). Causes of retardation among institutional children. *Journal of Genetic Psychology,* **96,** 47–59.

Dweck, C. S. (1975). The role of expectations and attributions in the alleviation of learned helplessness. *Journal of Personality and Social Psychology,* **31,** 674–685.

Eich, J. E., Weingartner, H., Stillman, R., & Gillin, J. C. (1975). State-dependent accessibility of retrieval cues in the retention of a categorized list. *Journal of Verbal Learning and Verbal Behavior,* **14,** 408–417.

Elman, D., Schroeder, H. E., & Schwartz, M. J. (1977). Reciprocal social influence of obese and normal weight persons. *Journal of Abnormal Psychology,* **86,** 408–413.

Ericson, K. A., & Simon, H. A. (1980). Verbal reports as data. *Psychological Review,* **87,** 215–251.

Feldman-Summers, S., Gordon, P. E., & Meagher, J. R. (1979). The impact of rape on sexual satisfaction. *Journal of Abnormal Psychology,* **88,** 101–105.

Gald, W., & Adesso, V. J. (1976). The relative importance of socially induced tension and behavioral contagion for smoking behavior. *Journal of Abnormal Psychology,* **85,** 119–121.

Gomes-Schwartz, B. (1978). Effective ingredients in psychotherapy: Predictors of outcome from process variables. *Journal of Consulting and Clinical Psychology,* **46,** 1023–1035.

Hammen, C. L., & Peters, S. D. (1978). Interpersonal consequences of depression: Responses to men and women enacting a depressed role. *Journal of Abnormal Psychology,* **87,** 322–332.

Hare, R. D. (1979). Psychopathy and literality of cerebral function. *Journal of Abnormal Psychology,* **88,** 605–610.

Heaton, R. K., & Victor, R. G. (1976). Personality characteristics associated with psychedelic flashbacks in natural and experimental settings. *Journal of Abnormal Psychology,* **85,** 83–90.

Hiroto, D. S., & Seligman, M. E. P. (1975). Generality of learned helplessness in man. *Journal of Personality and Social Psychology,* **31,** 311–327.

Johnston, J. (1972). *Econometric methods.* New York: McGraw-Hill.

Jones, S. L., Nation, J. R., & Massad, P. (1977). Immunization against learned helplessness in man. *Journal of Abnormal Psychology,* **86,** 75–83.

Kazdin, A. L., & Wilson, G. T. (1978). *Evaluation of behavior therapy: Issues, evidence, and research strategies.* Cambridge, Mass.: Ballinger.

Kihlstrom, J. F. (1980). Posthypnotic amnesia for recently learned material: Interactions with episodic and semantic memory. *Cognitive Psychology.* **12,** 227–251.

Klee, G. D., Bertino, J., Weintraub, W., & Calaway, E. (1961). The influence of varying dosage on the effects of lysergic acid diethylamide. *Journal of Nervous and Mental Disease,* **132,** 404–409.

Kenny, D. A. (1975). A quasi-experimental approach to assessing treatment effects in the nonequivalent control group design. *Psychological Bulletin.* **82,** 345–362.

Klisz, D. K., & Parsons, O. A. (1979). Cognitive functioning in alcoholics: The role of subject attrition. *Journal of Abnormal Psychology,* **88,** 268–276.

Knight, R., Shirer, M., & Shapiro, J. (1977). Iconic imagery in overinclusive and nonoverinclusive schizophrenics. *Journal of Abnormal Psychology,* **86,** 242–255.

Knight, R., Shirer, M., Putchat, C., & Carter, G. (1978). A picture integration task for measuring iconic memory in schizophrenics. *Journal of Abnormal Psychology,* **87,** 314–321.

Knox, V. J., & Shum, K. (1977). Reductions of cold-pressor pain with acupuncture analgesia in high and low hypnotic subjects. *Journal of Abnormal Psychology,* **86,** 639–643.

Koh, S. D., Szoc, R., & Peterson, R. A. (1977). Short-term memory scanning in schizophrenic young adults. *Journal of Abnormal Psychology,* **86,** 451–460.

Koh, S. D., & Peterson, R. A. (1978). Encoding orientation and the remembering of schizophrenic young adults. *Journal of Abnormal Psychology,* **87** 303–313.

Krantz, S., & Hammen, C. (1979). Assessment of cognitive bias in depression. *Journal of Abnormal Psychology,* **88,** 611–619.

Lang, A. R., Goecker, D. J., Adesso, V. J., & Marlatt, G. A. (1975). Effects of alcohol on aggression in male social drinkers. *Journal of Abnormal Psychology,* **84,** 508–518.

Maher, B. A. Stimulus sampling in clinical research: Representative design reviewed. *Journal of Consulting and Clinical Psychology,* 1978, **46,** 643–647.

Marlatt, G. A., Demming, B., & Reid, J. B. (1973). Loss of control drinking in alcoholics: An experimental analogue. *Journal of Abnormal Psychology,* **81,** 233–241.

Martindale, C. (1978). The therapist-as-fixed effect fallacy in psychotherapy research. *Journal of Consulting and Clinical Psychology,* **46,** 1526–1530.

Meiselman, K. C. (1978). Inducing "Schizophrenic" associations in normal subjects. *Journal of Abnormal Psychology,* **87,** 291–293.

Metzner, R., Litwin, G., & Weil, G. W. (1965). The relation of expectations and mood to psilocybin reactions. *Psychedelic Review,* **5,** 3–39.

Miller, E. & Lewis, P. (1977). Recognition memory in elderly patients with depression and dementia: A signal detection analysis. *Journal of Abnormal Psychology,* **86,** 84–86.

Miller, R. G. (1966). *Simultaneous statistical inference.* New York: McGraw-Hill.

Miller, R. J., & Leibowitz, H. W. (1976). A signal detection analysis of hypnotically induced narrowing of the peripheral visual field. *Journal of Abnormal Psychology,* **85,** 446–454.

Miller, S., Saccuzzo, D., & Braf, D. (1979). Information processing deficits in remitted schizophrenics. *Journal of Abnormal Psychology,* **88,** 446–449.

Miller, W. R., and Seligman, M. E. P. (1975). Depression and learned helplessness in man. *Journal of Abnormal Psychology,* **84,** 228–238.

Maher, B. A. (1978). Stimulus sampling in clinical research: Representative design reviewed. *Journal of Consulting and Clinical Psychology,* **46,** 643–647.

Morrison, D. F. (1976). *Multivariate statistical methods.* New York: McGraw-Hill.

Neufeld, R. W. J. (1977). Components of processing deficit among paranoid and nonparanoid schizophrenics. *Journal of Abnormal Psychology,* **86,** 60–64.

Nisbett, R. F., & Wilson, T. D. (1977). Telling more than we can know: Verbal reports on mental processes. *Psychological Review,* **84,** 231–259.

Oltmans, T. (1978). Selective attention in schizophrenia and manic psychoses: The effect of distraction on information processing. *Journal of Abnormal Psychology,* **87,** 212–225.

Payne, R. W., Mattusek, P., & George, E. I. (1959). An experimental study of schizophrenic thought disorder. *Journal of Medical Sciences,* **105,** 627–652.

Pihl, R. O., & Sigal, H. (1978). Motivation levels and the marihuana high. *Journal of Abnormal Psychology,* **87,** 280–295.

Polivy, J., Schueneman, A. L., & Carson, K. (1976). Alcohol and tension reduction: Cognitive and Physiological effects. *Journal of Abnormal Psychology,* **85,** 595–600.

Polivy, J., & Doyle, C. (1980). Laboratory induction of mood states through the reading of self-referent mood statements: Affective change or demand characteristics? *Journal of Abnormal Psychology,* **89,** 286–290.

Price, K. P., Tryon, W. W., & Raps, C. S. (1978). Learned helplessness and depression in a clinical population: A test of two behavioral hypotheses. *Journal of Abnormal Psychology,* **87,** 113–121.

Rizley, R. (1978). Depression and distortion in the attribution of causality. *Journal of Abnormal Psychology,* **87,** 32–48.

Rosen, L. J., & Lee, C. L. (1976). Acute and chronic effects of alcohol on organizational processes in memory. *Journal of Abnormal Psychology,* **85,** 309–317.

Ruderman, A. J., & Wilson, G. T. (1979). Weight, restraint, cognitions, and counterregulation. *Behavior Research and Therapy,* **17,** 581–590.

Russel, P. N., & Beekhuis, M. E. (1976). Organization in memory: A comparison of psychotics and normals. *Journal of Abnormal Psychology,* **85,** 527–534.

Russel, P. N., & Knight, R. G. (1977). Performance of process schizophrenics on tasks involving visual search. *Journal of Abnormal Psychology,* **86,** 16–26.

Raulin, M. L., & Chapman, L. J. (1976). Schizophrenic recall and contextual constraint. *Journal of Abnormal Psychology,* **85,** 151–154.

Sacco, W. P., & Hokanson, J. E. (1978). Expectations of success and anagram performance of depressives in a public and private setting. *Journal of Abnormal Psychology,* **87,** 122–130.

Seligman, M. E. P., & Maier, S. F. (1967). Failure to escape traumatic shock. *Journal of Experimental Psychology,* **74,** 1–9.

Seligman, M. E. P., Abramson, L., Semmel, A., & von Baeyer, C. (1979). Depressive attributional style. *Journal of Abnormal Psychology,* **88,** 242–247.

Shakow, D. (1963). Psychological deficit in schizophrenia. *Behavioral Science,* **8,** 275–305.

Sheehan, P. W., Obstoj, I., & McConkey, K. (1976). Trans logic and cue structure as supplied by the hypnotist. *Journal of Abnormal Psychology,* **85,** 459–472.

Smolin, R. C. (1978). Expectancies, mood, and performance of depressed and non-depressed psychiatric inpatients on chance and skill tasks. *Journal of Abnormal Psychology,* **87,** 91–101.

Spanos, N. P., & Bodorik, H. L. (1977). Suggested amnesia and disorganized recall in hypnotic and task-motivated subjects. *Journal of Abnormal Psychology,* **86,** 295–305.

Spanos, N. P., Ansari, F., & Stain, H. (1979). Hypnotic age regression: A failure to replicate. *Journal of Abnormal Psychology,* **88,** 88–91.

Spanos, N. P., Radtke-Bodorik, H. L., Ferguson, J. D., & Jones, B. (1979). The effects of hypnotic susceptibility, suggestions for analysis, and the utilization of cognitive strategies on the reduction of pain. *Journal of Abnormal Psychology,* **88,** 282–292.

Spencer, J. A., & Fremouw, W. J. (1979). Binge eating as a function of restraint and weight classification. *Journal of Abnormal Psychology,* **88,** 262–267.

Steinberg, E. P., & Schwartz, G. E. (1976). Biofeedback and electrodermal self-regulation in psychopathy. *Journal of Abnormal Psychology,* **85,** 408–413.

Stevenson, J. H. (1976). Effect of post-hypnotic dissociation on the performance of interfering tasks. *Journal of Abnormal Psychology,* **85,** 398–407.

Straube, E. R., & Germer, C. K. (1979). Dichotic shadowing and selective attention to word meaning in schizophrenia. *Journal of Abnormal Psychology,* **88,** 346–353.

Teasdale, J. D. (1978). Effects of real and recalled success on learned helplessness and depression. *Journal of Abnormal Psychology, 87,* 155–164.

Teasdale, J. D., & Fogarty, S. J. (1979). Differential effects of induced mood on retrieval of pleasant and unpleasant events from episodic memory. *Journal of Abnormal Psychology, 88,* 248–257.

Tucker, J. A., Vuchinich, R. E., & Sobeil, M. B. (1979). Differential discriminative stimulus control of nonalcoholic beverage consumption in alcoholics and in normal drinkers. *Journal of Abnormal Psychology, 88,* 145–160.

Velten, E. (1968). A laboratory task for induction of mood states. *Behavior Research and Therapy, 6,* 473–482.

Weingartner, H., Miller, H., & Murphey, D. L. (1977). Mood-state-dependent retrieval of verbal associations. *Journal of Abnormal Psychology, 86,* 276–284.

Wilson, G. T., & Lawson, D. M. (1978). Expectancies, alcohol, and sexual arousal in women. *Journal of Abnormal Psychology, 87,* 358–367.

Zeichner, A., & Pihl, R. O. (1979). Effects of alcohol and behavior contingencies on human aggression. *Journal of Abnormal Psychology, 88,* 153–160.

CHAPTER 8

Relevance of Animal Models for Clinical Psychology

STEPHEN J. SUOMI

Animal models of psychopathology have not traditionally been found in the mainstream of clinical theory and practice. Although some major approaches to therapy historically were based upon principles orginally established through experimentation with laboratory animals, most clinicians over the years have paid little attention to the animal literature and have shown even less inclination to apply its findings directly to their everyday practice. Indeed, until the last decade those animal researchers who claimed that their subjects' behavior could be made to mimic specific forms of human psychopathology were generally greeted with considerable skepticism, if not outright ridicule (Kubie, 1953). Yet despite their rather shaky history in the clinical field, animal models of human psychopathology in recent years have been gaining increasing respectability. This rise in respectability has been the result of not only changing views among many clinicians regarding possible biological factors in the etiologies of various psychopathologies, but also an increasing sophistication in the animal models themselves.

In this chapter, I will present an overview

and analysis of animal models of human psychopathology. I will begin by considering what animal models are, and what they are not. Next I will examine why animal models of human disorders are created, as well as how they might be used. I will then describe different ways in which these animal models can be generated and, of perhaps greater importance, how they can be evaluated. I will finish by considering different ways to apply the fruits of animal modeling research to clinical theory and practice.

WHAT ARE ANIMAL MODELS?

Animal models of psychopathology can be broadly defined as experimental attempts to reproduce the essential features of various human disorders in nonhuman subjects. Being models, they are basically empirical expressions of theories about human psychopathology. In other words, an animal model reflects a particular theoretical viewpoint concerning the psychopathological disorder in question; the model's basic elements are derived from the theory's assumptions, postulates, and parameters. Just as any theory represents a simplified version of reality, with certain elements emphasized and others ignored, an animal model represents a simplified version of the human phenomenon, as it is expressed in a nonhuman organism. As McKinney (1977, p. 117), among others,

Some of the research described in this chapter was supported by USPHS Grants MH-11894 and MH-28485 from the National Institute of Mental Health and Grant BNS77-06802 from the National Science Foundation. Final preparation of the manuscript was done by Judy Markgraf.

has stated, "A model is a model is a model"; it is not the disorder itself.

If an animal model of human psychopathology is not the disorder itself, how close does it come to embodying the "real thing"? That, of course, all depends on the particular model under scrutiny. For one thing, an animal model will be only as true a representation of a given psychopathological disorder as the theory upon which it has been based is able to capture the essential features of that disorder. For another, the animal model will only be as faithful a replica of the human disorder as the extent to which the phenomenon generalizes between animal subjects and human patients.

Now, not all human phenomena are uniquely human, although some aspects of some phenomena clearly are. Human beings share certain elements of their evolutionary history with members of other species, as reflected in the biochemistry of their genes. Indeed, it has been estimated that over 98% of the genes of any one human are shared by every normal chimpanzee (Lovejoy, 1981), although obviously the percentages of genetic overlap with humans are much lower for most other species. On the other hand, the cognitive capabilities of most humans greatly surpass those of any animal, while many human experiences and feelings clearly can be shared only by other humans. The extent to which the form of psychopathology being modeled reflects the former characteristics, rather than the latter ones, in the species studied determines in large part the degree to which the animal model will be able to provide a valid representation of the human psychopathology. As will be detailed in a later section on the use of animal models, there are several different levels at which such species generality can be assessed.

However, in virtually no case is an animal model a perfect and exact replica of the human disorder under study. Rather, it is usually a highly simplified, theoretically biased, and incompletely generalized version, expressed in members of a nonhuman species.

An animal model is almost never the "real thing"; it is, instead, only a model of the real thing.

WHY ARE ANIMAL MODELS OF PSYCHOPATHOLOGY DEVELOPED?

Given the fact that animal models can at best provide an imperfect representation of any given human psychopathology, why should anyone bother to develop and/or utilize them? Why should attempts be made to study a human disorder in an alien species when there are, in all likelihood, more than enough cases at the human level to fill up any laboratory? The answer is relatively simple: the primary rationale for creating most animal models lies not so much in any obvious and impressive strengths of such models as it lies in the problems inherent in conducting research with humans as subjects.

Very few experienced clinical investigators would ever claim that vigorously controlled, scientifically acceptable research involving human subjects is easy to carry out. It is instead fraught with severe (but proper) ethical constraints and considerable practical obstacles. Perhaps the biggest problem from a purely scientific standpoint is the virtual impossibility of carrying out *prospective* studies of human psychopathology. Deliberate induction of psychopathology in human subjects is always repugnant and never acceptable from either an ethical or a moral standpoint. Nonobtrusive monitoring of appropriate numbers of high-risk individuals in the "hope" that some will develop psychopathology before the investigator's very eyes is usually highly impractical; moreover, the clinical investigator who fails to intervene, even in the interest of science, if and when psychopathology does appear is most likely neglecting his or her professional responsibility as a clinician. Thus, the one most powerful research methodology that we know of, the prospective experiment, is all but prohibited from use in studies of psychopathology in humans. Investigators instead must invariably depend on retrospective data to address questions about etiology, and the problems inherent in establishing causality from retrospective data are considerable (Agnew & Pike, 1969).

It is possible of course to develop *human* models of various psychopathologies and to use such models to conduct prospective tests of competing hypotheses regarding etiologies. Such a strategy has recently been employed for the learned helplessness model of depression (Miller, Rosellini, & Seligman, 1977). However, such models face a fundamental dilemma: experimental manipulations that produce more than trivial effects in any human model are ethically impermissible, while models involving only trivial consequences are unlikely to provide convincing analogs to severe psychopathologies, except perhaps in a strictly heuristic sense. Thus, human models of human psychopathology can provide at best an incomplete substitute for prospective studies of the psychopathology itself.

Another area of difficulty for clinical research concerns limitations on the types of data that can be collected from human patients. Most human clinical data are derived from questionnaires, interviews, and various retrospective sources. Detailed and precise behavioral records can be obtained in theory, but in actual practice such data are rarely collected for more than brief periods, and then typically in highly structured situations not always representative of the subject's everyday experiences. It is usually impractical and often unethical to observe any individual over a major portion of his or her total living environment, unless that environment happens to be an institution. Physiological measures that can be gathered from human subjects usually only reflect indirect assessment of actual brain mechanisms. For example, one can obtain estimates of levels and turnover rates of brain neurotransmitter substances via their metabolites in blood, urine, or cerebrospinal fluid, but such esti-

mates often provide only crude approximations that are at best inaccurate and at worst grossly misleading (Kraemer et al., 1977). Ethical considerations usually prohibit direct assessment of brain neurochemistry or neuroanatomy, no matter how valuable such data might be for diagnosing, understanding, or treating a psychopathological disorder.

Finally, research interests are often overruled by therapeutic necessities when developing or assessing new treatment procedures for human psychopathologies. A rigorous experimental design for evaluation of treatment efficacy ideally should involve before-, during-, and after-treatment assessment with double-blind techniques. Individuals receiving treatment ideally should be compared with matched controls who initially display comparable psychopathology but who subsequently receive no treatment or an appropriate placebo. Specificity of treatment effects ideally should be determined by examining the reactions of control subjects lacking psychopathology (or exhibiting a different form of psychopathology of comparable severity) to exactly the same treatment protocol.

While such assessment procedures might well be found in textbooks, they are rarely found in actual practice. It is not often that a therapist has the luxury of obtaining a useful pretreatment baseline from a client; more often, that individual needs help as soon as possible. On the other hand, not all clients remain readily available for vigorous followup data collection once treatment has been completed, especially those for whom the treatment has been most successful. Double-blind assessment invariably involves additional staff and elaborate procedures to keep them truly "blind." Random assignment of some clients to placebo treatment conditions may be unethical to the extent that they are denied access to "real" therapy for the duration of the study. Finally, exposure of "normal" controls or those displaying other forms of psychopathology to a treatment regimen that for them is either unnecessary or potentially inappropriate presents additional practical and ethical problems. Effective therapy and scientifically acceptable assessment do not, unfortunately, always go hand in hand.

The above discussion highlights some of the reasons why meaningful human research is often exceedingly difficult to carry out in clinical settings. Ethical and practical considerations clearly limit the extent to which human patients and clients can be used as "guinea pigs" for experimental research (Korchin & Cowan, this volume). Our society justifiably demands that this be the case. Given these considerations, it is perhaps not so surprising that some clinical investigators have resorted to using *real* guinea pigs—or members of other nonhuman species—in their research on psychopathology.

Research with animals is not subject to the same limitations and restrictions that clearly characterize human clinical research. Although there presently exist numerous regulations and ethical standards governing animal research—and they recently have become far more restrictive than they were only a decade ago—such regulations and standards nevertheless permit manipulations and measurements with animals that simply are not ethically permissible or practically possible with human subjects. For example, animals can be placed in prospective studies specifically designed to induce pathology. They can be reared, maintained, and observed in well-controlled laboratory environments literally every day of their lives. A variety of measures of behavioral and physiological functioning too obtrusive to be gathered from humans can routinely be collected in animal subjects, including those requiring subject sacrifice. Various therapeutic treatments can be administered to animal subjects, and their effects can be determined with certainty via comparison with scientifically appropriate controls. Finally, because most laboratory animals develop more rapidly and have shorter natural lifespans, long-

term consequences of pathology or effectiveness of treatment can be assessed in a fraction of the time it would take to obtain comparable longitudinal data from humans.

Given these advantages of conducting research with animals, it should be obvious why animal models have enjoyed widespread usage throughout the biomedical sciences for some time. Actually, one would be hard-put to name any major medical breakthrough over the past century that was *not* preceded by research or practice with animal subjects. Indeed, in areas like pharmacology extensive testing with animals by law must now precede any clinical trials with humans. Thus, animal models have been developed in large part because they make it possible to address experimental questions that may be crucial for understanding and treatment of human pathology but that cannot be asked directly with human subjects. That is the primary rationale for using animal models in biomedical research, and the very same rationale underlies attempts to produce animal models of human psychopathology.

HOW CAN ANIMAL MODELS BE UTILIZED?

The potential ways in which animal models of any human disorder can be utilized are numerous, but the actual ways in which any one model can be employed depend on the model itself and on the nature of the human disorder upon which it is based. Many possible uses for animal models accrue from the previously discussed fact that much more rigorous experimentation, using more powerful independent variables and more extensive dependent variables, can usually be carried out on animals than is ethically permissible or practically possible with human subjects. On the other hand, most of the limitations on the degree to which animal models can contribute to our understanding and treatment of human psychopathology can be directly traced to problems of generalization between the animal data and the human disorder.

An appreciation for the vast number of potential uses for animal models can perhaps be best gained by looking beyond the psychopathology literature per se, where use of animal models historically has been limited, to those areas of the biomedical sciences in which animal models have enjoyed extensive use over the years. Consider, for example, how animal models have contributed to our understanding of *causal* factors in various human pathologies. To begin, one can run prospective studies in which the goal is to produce the pathology in question in at least some animal subjects. Not only can such experiments permit direct empirical tests of competing hypotheses regarding the etiology of the pathology under study, but also sufficient and/or necessary conditions for inducing the disorder can be clearly established. Sometimes this type of research uncovers multiple causes that are distinct from one another but nevertheless share some common final pathway, as appears to be the case for pathologically high blood pressure (Schwartz, 1977). In other cases, etiologically oriented animal models have demonstrated that several factors can interact synergistically to dramatically increase a subject's risk for developing pathology, as has been shown for various heart diseases. Animal models have also been extensively employed to determine "dose-response" relationships between levels of specific toxins and degree of tissue, organ or organism pathology (e.g., Bushnell & Bowman, 1979). Finally, they have been used to screen substances with respect to likelihood of increasing risk of pathology for a large population, even though the incidence rate in that population may be very low. A well-known example of this latter use can be found in the tests for potential carcinogens that by law must be administered to animals before any new foodstuff or additive is approved for

general use by the Food and Drug Administration.

The broad potential of animal models for furthering our knowledge of *symptoms* characterizing a particular human disorder is also apparent from many examples throughout the biomedical literature. As mentioned previously, animal models permit direct and "uncontaminated" assessment of an induced pathology at multiple levels of analysis. Thus, any aspect of behavior, any characteristic or component of the central or peripheral nervous system, as well as the whole or any part of other organ systems is potentially available for detailed scrutiny by the animal investigator. Not only can any of these types of measures be obtained (at least in theory) at any point in the animal subject's lifetime, or during prenatal periods, but also *rates* of symptom development can often be determined as well. Furthermore, this range of measures can be obtained on subjects matched with respect to genetic factors, age, sex, and previous and current environmental histories to a far greater degree than is almost ever possible with human subjects. It is an axiom of science that increased breadth, control, and precision of measurement improves one's capacity to determine the effects of independent variables. Additionally, having multiple and precise measures of the modeled disorder can often shed light on underlying mechanisms, as well as provide an empirical basis for identifying the most "sensitive" index of the syndrome, a finding not without potential practical import for clinicians interested in optimizing diagnostic techniques.

Perhaps most relevant for most clinical practitioners are the potential uses of animal models with respect to *treatment* or *prevention*. Consider pharmacological approaches to treatment. Development and assessment of pharmacological treatments is predicated on animal models; as previously noted, use of some form of animal model is mandated by law in the United States for the preclinical development and testing of any drug before it can be legally administered to human patients. Surgical treatment and prevention of pathology is equally dependent on animal models. Here animal models are employed not only to determine the therapeutic efficacy of new or competing surgical techniques but also to practice existing techniques—and to teach them to others. Indeed, practice on laboratory animals is as much (or more) a part of a current surgical student's training as is the traditional human cadaver. In contrast, animal models would appear to be of no use for studying therapies based on verbal exchanges (Kendall & Norton-Ford, this volume).

Without listing any further examples (there are many), it should be obvious that animal models enjoy widespread usage throughout most of the biomedical sciences, especially with respect to treatment and preventive practices. Why then have animal models traditionally been ignored or even discredited by most clinical psychologists? The answer most likely lies in the issue of cross-species generalization, more specifically in generalization between humans and nonhumans.

Cross-species generalization means that phenomena or characteristics that appear in members of one species also appear *in like form* in members of the comparison species. Thus, generalization between humans and a nonhuman species implies that the characteristic or phenomenon under analysis has an exact counterpart in the animal species and vice versa. For example, there is almost perfect generality between humans and apes with respect to teeth: both species have the same number and the same type of teeth— molars, premolars, canines, and incisors. On the other hand, vertebrae number does not generalize between humans and apes, because humans possess five lumbar vertebrae, while great apes possess only three lumbar vertebrae.

There exist different *degrees* of cross-species generality. Briefly, one can differentiate between cases of cross-species *homology,*

analogy or *convergence,* and mere *similarity.* Homologies occur when the phenomena or characteristics are identical in the two species, as are their underlying causes or mechanisms. An example of a homology is the visual system in humans and chimpanzees. Here the basic components (cornea, iris, lens, rods, cones, optic nerve) are essentially identical in the two species, as is the mode of operation of the system, its neural connections to the brain, its development, and even types of visual disorders (myopia, astigmatism, glaucoma, etc.) that can develop.

Cross-species *analogies* refer to cases in which the phenomena in question are highly similar but have different underlying causes or, conversely, where the mechanisms are identical but the resulting phenomena take a somewhat different form in the two species. The first type of analogy is also referred to as "convergence" by biologists. A typical example can be seen in snowshoe hares, Arctic foxes, and ptarmigans (an Arctic bird species), all of whose coats are brown or grey during the summer months but turn to white during the long, snow-filled winters that characterize their natural habitats. Here the annual change in coat color is highly similar in timing and appearance in these species, although the physiological mechanisms involved are different. An example of the second type of analogy can be seen in the effects of amphetamine on activity in nonstressful environments in rats and monkeys. At low doses, amphetamine "speeds up" rats but "slows down" monkeys, even though the effects of the drug on brain neurotransmitters are virtually identical in the two species (Randrup & Munkvad, 1967; Segal, 1975).

Finally, there is the case of cross-species *similarities.* Here the phenomena clearly appear to be guided by similar general principles in the species being compared, although the phenomena are definitely not identical and most likely are under the control of different mechanisms in the two species. An example of such a similarity can be found in filial imprinting to mother occurring in newly hatched ducklings and the development of attachment to mother by human infants. In both cases the ducklings and the human infants must be exposed to their mothers during "sensitive phases" early in life in order for species-typical social relationships with their mothers to emerge and be maintained later in life (Lorenz, 1935; Bowlby, 1969; Immelmann & Suomi, 1981). However, the characteristics of the sensitive phases, as well as the actual mechanisms involved in forming and maintaining the relationships, are obviously different in ducklings and human infants (Harlow, Gluck, & Suomi, 1972).

It is often the case when comparing two species that different degrees of generalization exist for a particular characteristic or phenomenon, depending on the *level of analysis* under consideration. For example, members of two species who are subjected to the same stressful stimulus may display homologous reactions within their respective autonomic nervous systems but only share analogous or similar central nervous system reactions. For some species a particular drug may have an identical biochemical effect on brain neurotransmitters but very different behavioral consequences, as in the amphetamine example cited above. Thus, discovery of a homologous characteristic between two species at one level of analysis does not guarantee that a homology will necessarily exist at any other level of analysis. Furthermore, at least among mammals, it appears that homologies are far more common at anatomical, physiological, and biochemical levels of analysis than they are at behavioral levels, at least as expressed in the literature to date.

It should be apparent that the degree of generality between an animal model and its human counterpart represents a very important limiting factor with respect to how that animal model can be utilized. For animal models based on clear-cut homologies, there are few if any limitations—animal subjects can essentially be used as full-blown substitutes for human patients or clients in developing, practicing, and assessing diagnostic and treatment procedures. In contrast, the ways in which animal models can be utilized if they are based only on analogies between the human condition and the animal model are considerably more limited. In these cases investigators should probably be especially cautious when drawing inferences involving different levels of analysis in the respective human and animal data. Finally, the usefulness of animal models based only on similarities is probably restricted to providing heuristic insight in viewing the human disorder (Kornetsky, 1977).

This line of reasoning is not meant to denigrate the potential value of heuristic advances, as has been elegantly pointed out by McKinney and Bunney (1969), or to overlook the useful information that can be provided by discovery of differences between human disorder and animal model (Hinde, 1976). Nevertheless, it is the case that the greater the degree of generality, the wider the range of appropriate uses for a given animal model. Considering that most animal models in the biomedical sciences have tended to be anatomically, physiologically, or biochemically based, whereas most early animal models of psychopathology were based on generalizations about behavior, it is little wonder that historically the former models have been more widely employed than the latter. However, as knowledge concerning physiological and biochemical characteristics of human psychopathology have accumulated and as more ecological and ethological interpretations of human behavior have become fashionable over the past decade, the actual use of animal models of human psychopathology has expanded as well (Serban & Kling, 1976; Maser & Seligman, 1977; Hanin & Usdin, 1977). In view of the practical and ethical advantages that animal models clearly bring to an investigator, such a development should not seem surprising at all.

HOW ARE ANIMAL MODELS DEVELOPED?

Given that animal models can provide an investigator with experimentally rigorous research tools with which ethically delicate and practically difficult questions about pathology can be addressed, how does one go about creating an animal model for a particular human disorder? How do animal models originate?

In actual practice, most animal models of human psychopathology have been generated in one of two basic ways. Historically the first animal models were formulated initially on the basis of an apparent similarity between behavior displayed by animal subjects and some symptoms of human psychopathology. In the first years of the twentieth century Ivan Pavlov noticed that during the course of learning difficult conditioned discriminations, some of his experimental dogs began to develop bizarre, maladaptive patterns of behavior that appeared to be quite out of proportion to the demands of their experimental tasks. To Pavlov, this pattern of behavior resembled the symptoms of human neurosis, and so he labelled the dogs' reactions "experimental neurosis" (Pavlov, 1927).

More than half a century later M. E. P. Seligman, B. Overmier, and S. Maier, graduate students working in Richard Solomon's laboratory at the University of Pennsylvania, discovered that dogs subjected to treatment with inescapable shock showed severe deficits in performance of subsequent learning tasks in which shock served as a punishment for incorrect responses. In addition, such dogs appeared to have reduced motivation and affect. Noting that similar deficits in cognitive functioning, motivation, and affect were symptomatic of human patients displaying severe depression, these researchers proposed that "learned helplessness," as they

termed the dogs' reaction to inescapable shock, provided a convincing model of reactive depression (Overmeier & Seligman, 1967; Seligman & Maier, 1967; Seligman, 1975).

In both of these examples of well-known animal models of human psychopathology the model was initially based on the apparent similarity between common symptoms of specific forms of psychopathology in humans and the behavior of animal subjects in certain experimental settings. The investigators did not originally set out to develop models of specific disorders; instead, in the process of carrying out animal research for other purposes, they serendipitously induced quite unexpected behavioral reactions in their subjects that seemed to resemble characteristic symptoms of common human psychopathologies. Thus, the creation of these animal models was marked both by good fortune and by good observation and insight on the part of the investigators. Similar serendipity often occurs in human research (Merbaum & Lowe, this volume).

In contrast, other animal models have been generated out of *deliberate* attempts by some researchers to reproduce postulated etiologies of specific human disorders in nonhuman subjects. For example, in the early 1960s Harry Harlow sought to model in young rhesus monkeys the human child syndrome of anaclitic depression. From the observations of Spitz (1946) and Bowlby (1960) it had been concluded that the immediate cause of the human condition was long-term separation from parents. Accordingly, Harlow and his students reared rhesus monkey infants with their mothers for their first six months of life and then separated the mother-infant pairs for a three-week period, after which time the pairs were reunited. The infant monkeys' behavior during the period of maternal separation bore a striking resemblance to symptoms characteristic of human anaclitic depression—a relatively brief period of extreme behavioral agitation ("protest") followed by extreme hypoactivity and social withdrawal ("despair") (Seay, Hansen, & Harlow, 1962). This work provided the prototype for current monkey separation models of depression.

Another classic example of a model designed to reproduce in animals a postulated etiology for a specific human psychopathology is provided by the "reserpinized rat" model of depression. This model was originally based on the hypothesis that a deficit in the synthesis of brain amines was responsible for the appearance of clinical symptoms of depression in humans. Evidence for this hypothesis came from reports that many human patients treated for hypertension with reserpine, a drug that inhibits synthesis of both catecholamines and serotonin, soon became severely depressed (Freis, 1954; Limieux, Davignon, & Genst, 1956). Accordingly, investigators began to administer reserpine to laboratory rats in order to study the effects of the drug treatment. They were not particularly interested in the behavioral reactions of the rats (after all, how would a "depressed" rat be expected to behave?), but they were exceedingly interested in the changes in levels of brain amines associated with reserpine treatment (Bunney & Davis, 1965; Schildkraut, 1965; Schildkraut & Kety, 1965). Many pharmaceutical firms still use the "reserpinized rat" model as a screening device for potential antidepressant drugs. Drugs that are found to reverse the pharmacological effects of reserpine in rodent subjects are thus deemed to be potential antidepressant compounds, worthy of additional testing leading to actual clinical trials with depressed human patients.

Perhaps the most extreme cases of animal models being developed on the basis of postulated etiology are the so-called "models of models" (Kornetsky, 1977). Here the animal model is *not* specifically designed to reproduce as many aspects of the human psychopathology as is possible. The animal model is instead based on an existing *human* model of the human disorder, in which the induction procedure used for the human model is re-

produced as faithfully as possible for animal subjects. The classic example of this type of model is amphetamine psychosis. Several investigators have noticed that individuals who are chronic amphetamine users or abusers frequently display reactions that are clinically indistinguishable from characteristic symptoms of paranoid schizophrenia (e.g., Argrist & Gershon, 1970; Bell, 1973; Griffith et al., 1970). Viewing human amphetamine psychosis as a model of human schizophrenia, other investigators have used these data to infer a dopamine-based etiology for schizophrenia, and they have subsequently produced amphetamine "psychosis" in animal subjects for the purpose of analyzing brain mechanisms associated with chronic administration of high doses of amphetamine (e.g., Ellinwood, 1971; Haber et al., 1977; Paul, 1977). Of course, this animal model at best is only as valid a model for schizophrenia as is the human amphetamine psychoses model, from which it essentially has been copied.

Thus, animal models can originate on the basis of apparent similarity of some animals' behavior to human psychopathological symptomology, they can be created initially for the purpose of reproducing a postulated etiology for the human disorder being modeled, or they can even be based on human models of the human disorder. There is no single "best" way to create a given animal model; any one of several approaches is possible, each with its own relative advantages and potential disadvantages. For example, symptom-based animal models may provide compelling parallels to characteristic disorders displayed by human patients, but if the factors that produce the animal model bear no resemblance to postulated etiologies of the human syndrome, the animal model is unlikely to be convincing. On the other hand, if an animal model has been designed to reproduce in animals the factors thought to cause the human disorder but the actual reactions of animals so treated are very different from characteristic symptoms of the human disorder, the model will lack face validity. Thus, no matter how an animal model is initially created, if it does not satisfy other criteria it is unlikely to have much appeal to many clinicians. In the next section we will examine some of the criteria by which any given animal model can be evaluated.

HOW ARE ANIMAL MODELS EVALUATED?

Once generated, an animal model is supposed to help investigators and practitioners better understand, diagnose, treat, and/or prevent the disorder being modeled. Good, appropriate animal models can indeed serve such purposes, but poor, inappropriate models cannot. At best such models may turn out to be inconsequential. At worst they might be dangerous, erroneously leading investigators to conclusions and practices that actually worsen rather than improve the plight of human patients and clients. Clearly it is in everyone's best interest to be able to evaluate effectively the merits of any given animal model of any particular psychopathology. But what criteria should such an evaluation be based upon?

In the early days of animal modeling there were no established criteria, no set of standards by which to judge any given model. It was perhaps because of this lack of clear-cut ground rules for developing animal models that they generally lacked much credence in clinical circles, except in the Soviet Union, where Pavlov's previously described model of "experimental neuroses" dominated psychiatric thinking for almost half a century (Abramson & Seligman, 1977). In recent years, however, numerous investigators have put forward several criteria by which animal models of psychopathology might be judged. These criteria tend to fall into three general categories: those dealing with the *validity* of the animal model being evaluated, those

dealing with the *specificity* or clarity of the model, and those dealing with its *practicality*.

Validity of the Animal Model

Foremost among evaluative criteria for animal models in most investigators' eyes are those concerning the *validity* of the model under consideration. These criteria address the degree to which the model accurately reflects the essential features of the human disorder. Several such criteria have been put forward. For example, McKinney and Bunney (1969) argued that to be valid, animal models should possess at least the following three characteristics: (1) the objectively definable symptoms of the disorder in humans should be mirrored in the animals under study; (2) known predisposers and direct causes of the dysfunction in humans should effectively and consistently produce the parallel dysfunction in the animal species; (3) finally, procedures that reverse the disorder in humans should be therapeutic to the species in which the model has been produced. Abramson and Seligman (1977) have added a criterion of similarity of preventive techniques for the disorder in both humans and nonhuman species under study, while McKinney (1974) and Harlow & Suomi (1974) have included similarity of underlying physiological or biochemical mechanisms in the two species. These various authors all agree that the more of these criteria a given animal model is able to satisfy, the more valid that model will be.

All of these validity criteria are directly related to the issue of cross-species generality discussed earlier. The extent to which an animal model faithfully reproduces the essential features of a human disorder depends on the degree to which that animal model generalizes to the human case. And as we now know, there are different degrees of generality; homologies are not the same as "mere" similarities, and they each carry their own credentials with respect to validity. In terms of evaluating the validity of an animal model, homologies should be judged superior to analogies and analogies superior to similarities, all other factors being equal. An additional point concerns levels of analysis. The more levels of analysis in which generality between human and animal data are found with respect to etiology, symptomology, therapy, or prevention, the greater should be the validity of the animal model.

It should be obvious that these validity criteria are among the most basic and important determinants of an animal model's worth. After all, a model that lacks validity, like any other source of invalid data, is scientifically worthless and, in the case of data that might influence clinical decisions, potentially dangerous. Assessment of validity clearly represents a crucial aspect of the evaluation process. Unfortunately, assessment of the validity of each component of an animal model most often is neither easy nor straightforward. These assessments must be made with respect to what we currently know about the *human* disorder being modeled—and often that knowledge is sorely lacking.

For example, consider the problems one encounters in trying to determine the etiological validity of an animal model of schizophrenia. At present there is no consensus among researchers as to what causes schizophrenia in humans, although there are plenty of competing hypotheses. It is not even known if schizophrenia is a single disorder with a single cause, a single disorder with many possible causes, a "family" of disorders with similar etiologies, a collection of superficially similar but etiologically very different disorders, or some combination of those. Under these circumstances it would seem fruitless if not foolish to try to determine the etiological validity of any animal model of schizophrenia. Instead, validity would have to be determined on the basis of other aspects of the model, for example, symptomology. Thus, our ability to deter-

mine the validity of any part of any animal model will be only as complete as our current knowledge of the human disorder being modeled.

Specificity of the Animal Model

A second set of criteria for evaluating animal models has to do with the *specificity* or the "clarity" of the animal model, in terms of what it can tell us about the human disorder. Seligman (1975) and Abramson and Seligman (1977) have outlined such criteria:

(a) Is the experimental analysis of the laboratory phenomena thorough enough to describe the essential features of its causes as well as its prevention and cures? . . . (b) Does the laboratory model describe in all instances a naturally occurring psychopathology or only a subgroup? Is the laboratory phenomenon a model of a specific psychopathology, or does it model general features of all psychopathologies? (Abramson & Seligman, 1977, p. 5)

A related criterion concerns the parsimony of the model in accounting for the human disorder (Seligman, 1975).

These criteria certainly appear worthwhile and consistent with a good, rigorous experimental analysis of any phenomenon. However, there is some potential danger in attempting to refine the animal model, as well as one's view of the human disorder, so as to incorporate only most basic "essential features" possible, i.e., to oversimplify in the name of parsimony. As Hinde (1976) has aptly warned, our animal models at best represent simplistic translations of what are almost always complex phenomena at the human level. In taking too simplistic a view of such phenomena we may be inadvertently overlooking contributing factors that have crucial implications for diagnosis, treatment, or prevention.

Evidence for such a tendency to occur can be found in the development of two of the most "popular" current animal models of depression, learned helplessness and social separation models, respectively. In its early years learned helplessness theory was highly touted for its elegant parsimony in accounting for cognitive, motivational, and affective components of depression in simple terms of loss (or lack) of control of important life events (Seligman, 1975). Accumulating evidence that lack of control per se was not always sufficient to induce learned helplessness, and that learned helplessness did not always result in depression, has necessitated a substantial reformulation of the original theory. In similar fashion, early accounts of depression in infant monkeys being "caused" by separation from mother (e.g., Kaufman & Rosenblum, 1967; McKinney et al., 1971) now appear too simplistic, as considerable subsequent research has demonstrated that maternal separation "by itself" is often not sufficient to precipitate depression in young monkeys, just as it is not always sufficient in human children (Lewis et al., 1976; Mineka & Suomi, 1978).

One must therefore be careful not to overlook possible contributing factors in trying to satisfy specificity-clarity-parsimony criteria. Nevertheless, models that are able to specify testable features of a human disorder are almost always preferable to those in which the features of the model are as ambiguous as they appear to be at the corresponding human level.

Practicality of the Animal Model

A final set of criteria concerns the *practicality* of the animal model for diagnosing, understanding, and ultimately curing the corresponding human disorder. A model may be totally valid for a particular human disease, yet useless in the practical sense. For example, suppose that a certain disease could be modeled perfectly in a macaque species, such that all physiological symptoms were identical in both man and monkey. Further suppose that there existed an infallible diagnostic test for this disorder in monkeys, one that would enable an investigator to determine long in advance whether the disorder would disable a given individual. However, what if such a test had to be conducted through chemical assay of the entire frontal lobe, which necessitated its surgical removal. Such an animal model would then be valid, but it would have definite practical limitations, inasmuch as few humans would be willing to give up their frontal lobes for a mere diagnosis. Similarly, a rehabilitative procedure that was totally effective for monkey subjects, but that required several years of solitary incarceration in a padded room, would probably generate little enthusiasm among either human therapists or patients. Thus, when considering the practicality of any animal model for human disorders, one must weight not only the empirical validity of the model but also the practical consequences of its adaptation for a human population.

To summarize, in recent years various criteria concerning the validity, specificity, and practicality of animal models of psychopathology have been developed in order to provide a basis for objective evaluation of such models. Although each set of criteria can clearly be justified (all have proven to be useful in assessing the relative merit of many animal models in other fields), their application to any particular model of psychopathology is not always simple and straightforward. Inadequate information about the human disorder being modeled may limit the extent to which validity criteria can be utilized, while too-strict adherence to criteria involving relative clarity or parsimony of the model can prematurely restrict one's search for explanatory principles. Nevertheless, these criteria do provide some guidelines for model assessment that have been badly needed in the psychopathology field for some time.

However, I know of no animal model of human psychopathology that currently can satisfy all of the various criteria outlined above to the point that further improvement is unnecessary. Indeed, few if any animal models in other fields presently can satisfy all these criteria either, no matter how insightful they have proven to be or how widespread their practical applications have become. This is largely because animal models are only models of their "parent" human disorders; they are not the disorders themselves. In a way, the various criteria outlined above serve as idealized standards to be striven for in developing or modifying a model, but also ones that realistically are unlikely ever to be achieved in an absolute sense.

Even though most animal models may never be able to fulfill perfectly all the criteria that have been suggested, this does not mean that the criteria should be ignored or the models necessarily abandoned. Rather, such criteria can be used to point out areas in which a given animal model can be improved, as well as identifying its relative strengths. Most investigators currently working with animal models of psychopathology are only too aware of the problems inherent in their particular models, and usually they are constantly looking for ways to make them more realistic, parsimonious, and practical. Additionally, objective use of these criteria can facilitate decisions regarding feasible applications of the animal data to diagnosis, treatment, or prevention of the human disorder.

HOW CAN FINDINGS FROM ANIMAL MODELS BE APPLIED TO CURRENT CLINICAL PRACTICES?

In this chapter we have explored the various forms animal models can take, the different ways in which they can be generated, the standards by which they can be judged, and the ways in which they have been and can be utilized. But how relevant is such information for most clinical psychologists, since after all, this is a handbook on research methods in clinical psychology? How can data

from animal models actually be applied to everyday clinical settings?

In the final section of this chapter I will discuss some ways in which findings from animal models can be applied more or less directly to clinical research and practice. I will do so by way of example, using each of three specific animal models to illustrate how such clinical applications might be derived from animal data. The three examples come from recent research at the University of Wisconsin Primate Laboratory. It should be pointed out that these three examples are *not* meant to provide a representative cross-section of the entire animal modeling field, nor were they necessarily chosen as the very best that animal modeling has to offer to clinical psychologists. They were instead chosen largely on the basis of my first-hand knowledge of their origin, their theoretical and empirical basis, and their current and potential applications to the clinical field. These examples include a symptom-based model of anxiety, a model of depression involving biochemical-situational interactions, and an example of a therapeutic strategy originally designed to rehabilitate a specific monkey psychopathology, rather than a human one.

A Monkey Model of Anxiety

I am currently working with a model of anxiety in rhesus monkey subjects that is essentially based on symptomology. The model has identified certain behavior patterns exhibited by some monkeys that appear to correspond in several ways to what in humans would be diagnosed as characteristic displays of anxiety. In rhesus monkeys such behavior patterns very closely resemble obvious fear reactions, except that they occur in the clear absence of any apparent fear stimulus or precipitating event; a similar operational definition for anxiety has been utilized in some human studies (Zuckerman & Spielberger, 1975). In rhesus monkeys this "anxious" behavior is almost always accompanied by autonomic arousal, it is typically regressive (i.e., behavior patterns displayed much earlier in life reappear in the subjects' repertoires), and it is amenable to treatment by at least some human antianxiety drugs (Suomi et al., 1981); in these respects it closely resembles human displays of anxiety (Klein, 1981).

Just as rhesus monkeys of different ages and rearing backgrounds have different ways of expressing fear, so do they have different characteristic ways of displaying anxiety. Some examples of these displays are illustrated in Figures 8.1 to 8.4. We have been using these characterizations of "monkey anxiety" to identify those situations in which such reacions are most likely to appear. We have also been looking for factors that seem to predispose some subjects to exhibit anxious behavior under circumstances in which most other monkeys appear to be unaffected and unconcerned.

To date, findings from such research have

Figure 8.2. Anxious behavior displayed by monkeys reared without mothers but in the presence of peers.

indicated that exposure to some social situations that in a monkey's natural habitat would be potentially life-threatening is probably the most reliable way to increase the incidence of subsequent anxious behavior in any subject. The "potentially life-threaten-

Figure 8.1. Anxious behavior displayed by mother-reared infant.

Figure 8.3. Anxious behavior displayed by monkeys reared and maintained in tactile isolation from conspecifics.

Figure 8.4. Infantile clinging by anxious juvenile rhesus monkeys: an example of a regressive behavior pattern.

ing" social manipulations we have employed are forcible separation from cagemates or involuntary introduction into a group of strangers. During such exposure subjects typically display intense fear reactions that one could readily describe as panic, although such behavior quickly disappears when the monkeys are returned to their familiar group and surroundings. However, in the days, weeks, and even months after such manipulations subjects display much higher levels of the behavior shown in the above figures than they did prior to the manipulations; they appear to be "jumpy" and on edge. Stimuli that immediately preceded a given subject's separation or stranger group introduction thereafter may be able to trigger an extreme "anxiety attack" in that subject by themselves. Such powerful conditioning effects

do *not* occur when more "traditional" laboratory manipulations, such as exposure to electric shock, are employed instead of separation or stranger group introduction (Suomi et al., 1981).

Evidence to date also suggests that there exists a variety of experiential factors that can not only increase a monkey's likelihood of displaying anxious behavior later in life but also affect the relative severity of such reactions when they are displayed. These factors include early or frequent separation from mother, rearing by a neglectful or abusive mother, frequent changes in the subject's social group composition, and lack of stability in that group's dominance hierarchy (Suomi et al., 1981). Compelling parallels to virtually all of these monkey data can be found in the human anxiety literature (e.g., Klein & Rabkin, 1981).

Yet despite the fact that our monkey subjects can be raised in rigorously controlled social rearing environments and exposed to precisely administered anxiety-inducing manipulations on carefully predetermined schedules, we still have found substantial individual differences among like-reared and similarly stressed subjects in both the frequency and the severity of their displays of anxiety. In an effort to account for and to predict these individual differences, we have recently begun to search for inborn or constitutional factors that might affect individual monkeys in terms of their "thresholds" for display of anxious behavior. Numerous sources in the human literature (e.g., James, 1890; Spence, 1964) have suggested that relative anxiety has strong autonomic components, and thus we have set out to measure autonomic "reactivity" in rhesus monkey infants. One index that to date appears to be highly promising is the *magnitude of heart rate change* displayed by infants in response to a conditioned tonal stimulus.

In two independent prospective studies (Suomi et al., 1981) we have found that individual differences on this heart rate change index obtained during the subjects' first month of life are highly predictive of individual differences in anxious behavior displayed during the rest of infancy, throughout childhood, and even into adolescence (at present these subjects have not yet grown to adulthood). Monkey infants in the first study were raised in socially sterile but exceedingly stable environments. The correlation between these subjects' heart rate change scores at one month and their mean levels of anxious behavior calculated over the rest of year 1 (based on daily observations) was $+.93$, accounting for over 85% of all intersubject variance in behavioral anxiety! In contrast, the heart rate change scores failed to correlate significantly with levels of behavior not associated with anxiety. At 2 1/2 years of age these monkeys' levels of anxious behavior still correlated with their one-month heart rate change scores at $+.84$.

Infants in the second study were reared in peer groups after heart rate change scores had been obtained during their first month of life. In contrast to the first group, they were periodically separated for brief periods several times during their first year. Once again, heart rate change scores were correlated with levels of anxiety displayed during year 1. Correlations with anxious behavior were highly significant during and immediately after separations, but during nonstressful periods they remained at chance levels. Other behavior failed to correlate significantly with the heart rate change scores at any time. These results suggest that among more socially sophisticated subjects growing up in changing environments, early autonomic reactivity is highly predictive of later displays of anxiety, but only during and shortly after periods of stress. During nonstressful periods these differences disappear.

There is also suggestive evidence that differences between monkeys in autonomic reactivity and/or levels of anxiety exhibited are at least in part genetically determined. Several of the subjects in both studies were paternal half-sibs (same father, different mother) to each other, and it was found that the heart rate scores of half-sibs were significantly closer to one another then they were to unrelated subjects; the same was found for levels of anxious behavior. Because all subjects had different biological mothers and all were separated from their mothers at birth and reared in the same nursery under identical conditions, such results cannot be attributed to prenatal or experiential factors. A genetic basis seems far more plausible, and we are now investigating this hypothesis with some selective breeding experiments in which we are essentially breeding for "high risk" and "low risk" infants with respect to predisposition for anxiety reactions.

What possible applications might these monkey data have for diagnosis, treatment, or prevention of anxiety at the human level? To date, the findings that behavioral manifestations of anxiety in rhesus monkeys are often regressive in nature, are usually accompanied by autonomic arousal, are readily precipitated by certain specific stimuli, are influenced by adverse social rearing experiences, and appear to have some genetic component, essentially have merely replicated what is already generally known about anxiety in humans. While perhaps validating the notion that anxiety in monkeys has clear-cut parallels to anxiety in humans, these results do not add measurably to our knowledge about human anxiety.

On the other hand, if the apparent relationship between infant autonomic reactivity and predisposition to display anxiety later in life continues to hold up in ongoing and proposed monkey studies, and if it further generalizes to humans, then the potential practical applications of this monkey model to diagnosis, treatment, and even prevention at the human level are likely to be considerable. For example, if clinicians were able to tell ahead of time which individuals were at high risk for severe reactions to stressful situations, prophylactic treatment could be administered to such individuals, and/or they could be encouraged to avoid such situations.

Inasmuch as the monkey heart rate measures have been obtained in paradigms that were originally developed for human infants, there should be little difficulty in gathering comparable heart rate measures from human subjects or patients of all ages. Thus direct application of this model to clinical practice is clearly possible in the future.

Potential of Separation Reactions by Catecholamine Depletion: An Interactive Model of Depression

As discussed earlier, catecholamine depletion models of depression (e.g., the "reserpinized rat") have been relatively popular ever since it was discovered that reserpine treatment precipitated depressive reactions in some patients being treated for hypertension. However, in recent years these models have begun to lose some of their luster as more data have been accumulated. One problem is that there is no direct evidence that depressed humans have *any* catecholamine deficits relative to normal controls; numerous studies of levels of catecholamine metabolites in the urine, blood, and cerebrospinal fluid of depressed patients and normal controls have produced equivocal findings. Indeed, a reexamination of the original human reserpine data has shown that only individuals with a prior history of depression actually exhibited depressive symptoms following reserpine treatment (Mendels & Fraizier, 1974). A second problem is that monkey subjects given biogenic amine-depleting drugs like reserpine or alpha-methylparatyrosine (AMPT) do not behave as if they were depressed, even when brain levels of catecholamines are depleted by 80 to 90%. Instead, they only appear to be sedated.

Taken together, these data suggest that massive catecholamine depletion is neither sufficient to precipitate depressive reactions (in monkeys) nor necessary to do so (in humans). Nevertheless, there is an enormous amount of circumstantial evidence to the effect that *some* sort of alteration of brain cate-

cholamines is associated with depressive symptomology. Recently Kraemer and McKinney (1979) have performed a series of studies with rhesus monkeys that provide considerable insight on this issue.

These investigators chose to manipulate their monkey subjects' social environment *at the same time* they were administering amine-depleting drugs to these subjects. The environmental manipulation that they used was *social separation*. Social separation in primates has been studied intensely by many researchers working at several different laboratories since Harlow's pioneering work in the early 1960s, and as mentioned earlier, it represents a very stressful manipulation for most young primates, nonhuman or human. Many investigators have documented frequent cases of severe depression in subjects following separation from mothers, peers, or other social companions. Such depression is characterized by extreme social withdrawal, retardation of movement, lack of responsiveness to previous reinforcers, loss of appetite, and disruption of sleep cycles. A typical example of a "depressed" monkey is illustrated in Figure 8.5; the hunched-over posture and facial expression shown in the figure are highly characteristic of subjects who become depressed following separation manipulations. However, not all monkeys subjected to social separations become de-

Figure 8.5. Depressed (left) and normal (right) rhesus monkey infants in playroom setting.

pressed; some only display transient agitation and then rapidly return to their preseparation patterns of activity. At present it is not fully understood why some subjects become depressed following separation while others do not, but it is clear that numerous factors can influence primate separation reactions (for a recent comprehensive review of this complex literature, see Mineka & Suomi, 1978).

At any rate, Kraemer and McKinney (1979) subjected juvenile-aged rhesus monkeys to repetitive, short-term separations from their peers. The subjects' reactions to these separations were relatively mild, consistent with findings from previous studies of peer separation in juvenile macaques (Mineka & Suomi, 1978). The investigators then began to administer AMPT at very low dosages to these juveniles, both during periods of separation and during the times when the subjects were reunited with their social group. The results were dramatic.

When administered AMPT concomitant with social separation, the juvenile monkeys reacted with severe depression, in sharp contrast to their mild separation reactions when not on AMPT. However, the effect of AMPT on these monkeys' behavior during reunion periods was nil; subjects administered AMPT displayed the same levels of behavior during reunion as they did when they were only given placebo. Thus, the effect of AMPT treatment was to greatly exaggerate the separation reactions of these juvenile monkeys but to leave their reunion behavior intact.

It is to be emphasized that these effects were obtained with remarkably low dosages of AMPT. Clear potentiation of separation-induced depression occurred at dosages one to two *orders of magnitude less* than that required to produce any behavioral effects during reunion periods. These low levels of AMPT stand in stark contrast to the huge dosages employed in the previously described studies, in which the degree of catecholamine depletion was massive (80 to 90% of baseline) but the behavioral effects other than sedation were trivial. Indeed, the degree

of brain catecholamine depletion resulting from the low doses of AMPT utilized in this study probably would be beneath the detection threshold for measures utilized in previous human studies. Thus, AMPT administration and social separation can interact in a highly synergistic fashion for juvenile monkeys, yielding depressive symptomology that definitely is not produced when either manipulation is performed by itself.

Kraemer and McKinney (1979) also discovered substantial differences between these juvenile rhesus monkeys in the threshold dose of AMPT needed to precipitate or exaggerate depressive reactions to repetitive peer separation. These differences in threshold were related to the previous social histories of the subjects. Specifically, mother-reared, peer-grouped monkeys required four to eight times the dose of AMPT that peer-reared monkeys needed to produce comparable effects on separation reactions, while peer-reared monkeys with many previous separations were more susceptible to the effects of AMPT than peer-reared monkeys with few previous separations by a dose factor of two.

Taken as a whole, Kraemer and Mc-Kinney's (1979) primate data strongly suggest that substantial modification of the original biogenic amine metabolism models of depression is in order. Alteration of brain biogenic amine metabolism is not sufficient in and of itself to precipitate depressive reactions in nonhuman primate subjects. However, such biochemical treatments interact with at least one type of social stressor to produce or exaggerate depressive reactions. There are individual differences in the magnitude of amine metabolism alteration required for precipitation of depression following separation, and it appears that such individual differences in susceptibility can be in part attributed to differences in the social rearing backgrounds or previous separation histories of the subjects.

If these findings generalize to cases of human depression, then the practical implications of the monkey model for diagnosis and treatment at the human level could well be considerable. From the standpoint of diagnosis, it would seem to make little sense to continue searches in human patients for relatively large changes in catecholamine metabolites concomitant with depressive episodes, because such changes, if they exist, are probably much smaller in magnitude and may even be beneath our current thresholds for detection. Along parallel lines of reasoning, it might be well for those engaged in developing more effective pharmacological treatments for depression to search for substances whose catecholamine-enhancing effects are more subtle and refined than can be detected with current "reserpinized rat" screening paradigms. Finally, if Kraemer and McKinney's (1979) findings regarding the effects of previous experiences on threshold levels of catecholamine depletion for potentiation of depressive symptomology are indicative of a common pathway for multiple stressors that can be synergistic in their cummulative effects (Akiskal & McKinney, 1975) then it might be prudent for clinicians to try to identify specific sources of stress for individual clients and work to eliminate or at least reduce their exposure to such sources.

Monkey Therapists: Generalization of a Rehabilitative Strategy

My final example of animal data that can hold considerable relevance for clinicians working with human patients and clients comes from a study I performed with Harry Harlow (Suomi & Harlow, 1972) that was designed to reverse the social deficits displayed by rhesus monkeys reared in social isolation from conspecific peers or parents. For many years there had been general agreement among developmental researchers, educators, pediatricians, and child psychologists and psychiatrists that the adverse consequences of early social deprivation were basically permanent and that any resulting social deficits were essentially irre-

versible. These views were strongly reinforced by the results of classic studies of rhesus monkeys reared from birth in social isolation from conspecific peers or parents. Those studies had shown that subjects reared for at least the first six months of life in isolation subsequently displayed gross deficits in virtually every aspect of their social behavior. Moreover, they typically displayed bizarre patterns of idiosyncratic, stereotypic, self-directed behavior almost never seen in well-socialized rhesus monkeys. Early attempts to rehabilitate these isolates were summarily unsuccessful, suggesting that isolation-induced deficits might be permanent (Harlow & Harlow, 1971).

However, Suomi and Harlow (1972) reasoned that isolates could be rehabilitated if they were exposed to monkey "therapists" who would promote physical contact without threatening the isolates with aggression or overly complex play interactions. To fill such a therapeutic role, we chose socially normal monkeys who were only three months old, an age at which they still exhibited considerable infantile clinging to social partners but were too young to exhibit aggression or to have developed complex repertoires of social play. Monkeys who had been reared in total social isolation for the first six months of life were exposed to these "therapists" for five two-hour periods per week for a total of six months.

The isolates' initial reaction to the younger therapists was to withdraw and to roll into a ball, and the therapists' response was to approach and cling to the isolates, as is illustrated in Figure 8.6. Within two weeks the isolates were reciprocating the social contact, and correspondingly their incidence of abnormal self-directed behavior, which was incompatible with contact-maintaining activity, began to decline significantly. The therapists themselves continued the normal development of their own social repertoires, and as a result their clinging diminished and their play activity increased steadily in frequency, intensity, and sophistication as they

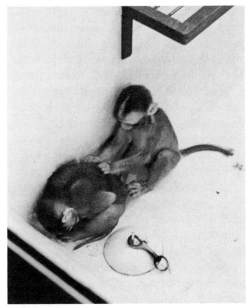

Figure 8.6. Younger "therapist" monkey clinging to socially withdrawn isolate.

matured. Some of the play was directed toward the isolates, and during succeeding months the isolates began to reciprocate such behavior with increasing frequency. By the end of the six-month therapy session they were actively initiating play bouts with both the therapists and each other. Moreover, during the therapy sessions most of the isolates' self-directed behavior had disappeared, and so it was difficult to distinguish isolates from therapists in levels of most behaviors. Significant rehabilitation had obviously occurred.

It should be explicitly pointed out that the rehabilitative strategy we employed for these isolate-reared monkeys was *not* designed to model any particular human therapeutic approach. Rather, it was chosen in order to provide the specific social stimulation that we thought was necessary to enable the isolates to gradually develop appropriate social behavior repertoires while minimizing their own idiosyncratic self-directed activities. In-

deed, we have consistently maintained that the form of psychopathology displayed by isolate-reared monkeys prior to therapy has no exact counterpart at the human level, except possibly for those few historical cases of "wild" children apparently reared by animals, such as Romulus and Remus or Itard's "wild boy." In other words, we do not believe that total social isolation-rearing in monkeys is a valid model of any "standard" human psychopathology, the above exceptions notwithstanding.

Nevertheless, the implications of these research findings of isolate monkey rehabilitation have turned out to be substantial, even at the human level. They directly contradict the once-conventional wisdom that social deficiencies developed in impoverished early rearing environments are necessarily permanent and irreversible. It is true that spontaneous recovery rarely if ever occurs in a rhesus monkey isolate. However, these monkey data have demonstrated that significant social rehabilitation is possible, if the proper social agents can be discovered. Subsequent research of human children raised under conditions of social deprivation but later exposed to "therapeutic" environments has revealed parallel results. Indeed the very techniques used to rehabilitate the isolate monkeys, that is, the use of younger, socially normal "therapists," have been applied successfully to treatment of socially retarded and withdrawn children (Furman, Rahe, & Hartup, 1979), as well as those at high risk for schizophrenia (Schulsinger, 1975). Thus, these monkey data have proven to have considerable practical applications for human therapeutic approaches even though they did not originate from an animal model of any particular human psychopathology per se.

The three examples in this section provide evidence that research directed toward study of psychopathology in animal subjects can be relevant to human clinical concerns. In some cases the relevance derives from deliberate attempts to reproduce a specific human psychopathology in animals in order to address questions about etiology, symptomology, therapy, or prevention that cannot be studied directly in humans for ethical or practical reasons. In other cases the relevance derives from heuristic insights the animal data can provide in terms of general principles, even though such data may not have come from an animal model created for any specific human disorder. These examples demonstrate that practical applications can be realized from animal data in a variety of different ways.

However, the extent to which animal data prove to be useful in advancing our current knowledge of or treatment for human psychopathology will always be dependent on several factors. One factor, as expressed throughout this chapter, is the degree to which any given set of animal findings generalizes to the human disorder under consideration. Compelling as any of the previous examples may have seemed, it is wise to keep in mind that the subjects in those studies were not furry little humans with tails, but rather members of a different species. True homologies, especially with respect to behavior, are relatively rare in nature. Animal models of human psychopathology are only animal models—they are not the real thing.

On the other hand, the potential usefulness of any animal model is in part a function of the willingness of human clinical investigators and practitioners to look beyond their own particular subjects for sources of potential insight, understanding, and inspiration. The best animal model in the world will not add to clinical knowledge if clinicians are unaware of its contents or are unwilling to consider its implications as a matter of principle (e.g., Kubie, 1953). Thus, any future benefits to be realized from animal modeling ultimately will depend not only on the sophistication, creativity, and rigor of the animal researchers but also on careful and objective judgment from the clinical community as well.

REFERENCES

Abramson, L. Y., & Seligman, M. E. P. Modeling psychopathology in the laboratory: History and rationale. In J. D. Maser and M. E. P. Seligman (Eds.) *Psychopathology: Experimental models.* San Francisco: Freeman, 1977.

Agnew, N. M., & Pike, S. W. (1969). *The science game.* Englewood Cliffs, N.J.: Prentice-Hall.

Akiskal, H. S., & McKinney, W. T. (1975). Overview of recent research in depression. *Archives of General Psychiatry,* **32,** 285–305.

Argrist, B., & Gershon, S. (1970). The phenomenology of experimentally induced amphetamine psychosis—Preliminary observations. *Biological Psychiatry,* **2,** 95–107.

Bell, D. S. (1973). The experimental reproduction of amphetamine psychosis. *Archives of General Psychiatry,* **29,** 35–40.

Bowlby, J. (1960). Grief and mourning in infancy and early childhood. *Psychoanalytic Study of the Child,* **15,** 9–52.

Bowlby, J. (1969). *Attachment and loss.* New York: Basic Books.

Bunney, W. E., & Davis, J. M. (1965). Norepinephrine in depressive reactions. *Archives of General Psychiatry,* **13,** 483–494.

Bushnell, P. J., & Bowman, R. E. (1979). Effects of chronic lead ingestion on social development in infant rhesus monkeys. *Neurobehavioral Toxicology,* **1,** 207–219.

Ellinwood, E. H. (1971). Effect of chronic methamphetamine intoxication in rhesus monkeys. *Biological Psychiatry,* **3,** 25–32.

Freis, E. D. (1954). Mental depression in hypertensive patients treated for long periods with large doses of reserpine. *New England Journal of Medicine,* **251,** 1006–1015.

Furman, R., Rahe, D. F., & Hartup, W. W. (1979). Rehabilitation of socially-withdrawn children through mixed-age and same-age socialization. *Child Development,* **50,** 915–922.

Griffith, J. D. (1970). Experimental psychosis induced by the administration of d-amphetamine. In Costa & Garantinni (Eds.), *Amphetamines and related compounds.* New York: Raven Press.

Haber, S., Barchas, P. R., & Barchas, J. D. (1977). Effects of amphetamine on social behaviors of rhesus macaques: An animal model of paranoia. In I. Hanin & E. Usdin (Eds.), *Animal models in psychiatry and neurology.* New York: Pergamon Press.

Hanin, I., & Usdin, E. (1977). *Animal models in psychiatry and neurology.* New York: Pergamon Press.

Harlow, H. F., Gluck, J. P., & Suomi, S. J. (1972). Generalization of behavioral data between nonhuman and human animals. *American Psychologist,* **27,** 709–716.

Harlow, H. F., & Harlow, M. K. (1971). Psychopathology in monkeys. In H. D. Kimmel (Ed.), *Experimental psychopathology.* New York: Academic Press.

Harlow, H. F., & Suomi, S. J. (1974). Induced depression in monkeys. *Behavioral Biology,* **12,** 273–296.

Hinde, R. A. (1976). The use of similarities and differences in comparative psychopathology. In G. Serban & A. Kling (Eds.), *Animal models in human psychobiology.* New York: Plenum Press.

Immelmann, K., & Suomi, S. J. (1981). Sensitive phases in development. In K. Immelmann, G. Barlow, L. Petrinovich, & M. Main (Eds.), *Behavioral development: The Bielefeld interdisciplinary project.* New York: Cambridge University Press, in press.

James, W. (1890). *The principles of psychology,* Vol. 2. New York: Holt.

Kaufman, I. C., & Rosenblum, L. A. (1967). The reaction to separation in infant monkeys: Anaclitic depression and conservation-withdrawal. *Psychosomatic Medicine,* **29,** 648–675.

Kline, D. F. (1981). Anxiety revisited. In D. Klein & J. Rabkin (Eds.), *Anxiety: New research and changing concepts.* New York: Raven Press.

Kline, D. F., & Rabkin, J. (Eds.) (1981). *Anxiety: New research and changing concepts.* New York: Raven Press.

Kornetsky, C. (1977). Animal models: Promises and problems. In I. Hanin & E. Usdin (Eds.), *Animal models in psychiatry and neurology.* New York: Pergamon Press.

Kraemer, G. W., & McKinney, W. T. (1979). Interactions of pharmacological agents which alter biogenic amine metabolism and depression. *Journal of Affective Disorders,* **1,** 33–54.

Kraemer, G. W., McKinney, W. T., Breese, G. R., & Prange, A. J. (1977). Behavioral and biochemical effects of microinjections of 6-hydroxydopamine into the substantia nigra of the rhesus monkey. *Neurosciences Abstracts,* **2,** 494.

Kubie, L. S. (1953). The concept of normality and neurosis. In M. Heiman (Eds.), *Psychoanalysis and social work.* New York: International Universities Press.

Lewis, J. K., Young, L. D., McKinney, W. T., & Kraemer, G. W. (1976). Mother-infant separation as a model of human depression: A reconsideration. *Archives of General Psychiatry,* **33,** 699–705.

Limieux, G., Davidson, A., & Genest, J. (1956). Depressive states during rauwolfia therapy for arterial hypertension—A report of 30 cases. *Canadian Medical Association Journal,* **74,** 522.

Lorenz, K. Der Kumpan in der Umwelt des Vogels. (1935) *Journal für Ornithologie,* **83,** 137–213.

Lovejoy, C. O. (1981). The origin of man. *Science,* **211,** 341–350.

Maser, J. D., & Seligman, M. E. P. (1977). *Psychopathology: Experimental models.* San Francisco: W. H. Freeman.

McKinney, W. T. (1974). Animal models in psychiatry. *Perspectives in Biology and Medicine,* **17,** 529–541.

McKinney, W. T. (1977). Biobehavioral models of depression in monkeys. In I. Hanin & E. Usdin (Eds.), *Animal models in psychiatry and neurology.* New York: Pergamon Press.

McKinney, W. T., & Bunney, W. E. (1969). Animal model of depression. *Archives of General Psychiatry,* **21,** 240–248.

McKinney, W. T., Suomi, S. J., & Harlow, H. F. (1971). Depression in primates. *American Journal of Psychiatry,* **127,** 1313–1320.

Mendels, J., & Fraizier, A. (1974). Brain biogenic amine depletion and mood. *Archives of General Psychiatry,* **30,** 447–451.

Miller, W. R., Rosellini, R. A., & Seligman, M. E. P. (1977). Learned helplessness and depression. In J. Maser & M. E. P. Seligman (Eds.), *Psychopathology: Experimental models.* San Francisco: W. H. Freeman.

Mineka, S., & Suomi, S. J. (1978). Social separation in monkeys. *Psychological Bulletin,* **85,** 1376–1400.

Overmier, J. B., & Seligman, M. E. P. (1967). Effects of inescapable shock on subsequent escape and avoidance learning. *Journal of Comparative and Physiological Psychology,* **63,** 23–33.

Paul, S. M. (1977). Movement, mood, and madness: A biological model of schizophrenia. In J. Maser & M. E. P. Seligman (Eds.), *Psychopathology: Experimental models.* San Francisco: W. H. Freeman.

Pavlov, I. P. (1927). *Conditioned reflexes* (G. V. Arrep., Trans.). London: Oxford University Press.

Randrup, A., & Munkvau, I. (1967). Stereotyped activities produced by d-amphetamine in several animal species and man. *Psychopharmacologia,* **11,** 300–310.

Schildkraut, J. J. (1978). Current status of the catecholamine hypothesis of affective disorders. In M. A. Lipton, A. DiMascio, & K. Killam (Eds.), *Psychopharmacology: A generation of progress.* New York: Raven Press, pp. 1223–1234.

Schildkraut, J. J., & Kety, S. S. (1967). Biogenic amines and emotion. *Science,* **156,** 21–30.

Schulsinger, F. (1975). The early detection and prevention of mental illness. In *Proceedings of the Working Group on Primary Prevention of Schizophrenia in High-Risk Groups.* Copenhagen: World Health Organization.

Schwartz, G. A. (1977). Psychosomatic disorders and biofeedback: A psychobiological model of disregulation. In J. Maser & M. E. P. Seligman (Eds.), *Psychopathology: Experimental models.* San Francisco: W. H. Freeman.

Seay, B. M., Hansen, E. W., & Harlow, H. F. (1962). Mother-infant separation in monkeys. *Journal of Child Psychology and Psychiatry,* **3,** 123–132.

Segal, D. S. (1975). Behavioral characterization of *d-* and *l-* amphetamine: Neurochemical implications. *Science,* **190,** 475–477.

Seligman, M. E. P. (1975). *Helplessness: On depression, development, and death.* San Francisco: W. H. Freeman.

Seligman, M. E. P., & Maier, S. F. (1967). Failure to escape traumatic shock. *Journal of Experimental Psychology,* **74,** 1–9.

Serban, G., & Kling, A. (Eds.) (1976). *Animal models in human psychobiology.* New York: Plenum Press.

Spence, K. (1964). Anxiety (drive) level and performance in eyelid conditioning. *Psychological Bulletin,* **61,** 129–139.

Spitz, R. A. (1946). Anaclitic depression. *Psychoanalytic Study of the Child,* **2,** 313–347.

Suomi, S. J., & Harlow, H. F. (1972). Social rehabilitation of isolate-reared monkeys. *Developmental Psychology,* **6,** 487–496.

Suomi, S. J., & Harlow, H. F. (1976). The facts and function of fear. In M. Zuckerman & C. Spielberger (Eds.), *Emotions and anxiety: New concepts, methods, and applications.* New York: Halsted Press.

Suomi, S. J., Kraemer, G. W., Baysinger, C. M., & DeLizio, R. D. (1981). Inherited and experiential factors associated with individual differences in anxious behavior displayed by rhesus monkeys. In D. Klein & J. Rabkin (Eds.), *Anxiety: New research and changing concepts.* New York: Raven Press.

Zuckerman, M., & Spielberger, C. (Eds.) (1976). *Emotions and anxiety: New concepts, methods, and applications.* New York: Halsted Press.

CHAPTER 9

Cross-Cultural Research Methods In Clinical Psychology

JAMES N. BUTCHER

Clinical psychology can be viewed as an essentially Western discipline that developed from academic psychology in response to the needs of society to understand and ameliorate individual maladjustment. The models of clinical psychology that emerged, largely in English-speaking Western nations, have recently begun to be adapted to other settings throughout the world, as many Eastern nations open their borders to outside influence, and Third World nations develop similar scientist-practitioner professions. Clinical psychology, although always a lender, borrower, and adapter of ideas and methods, presently finds itself bumping into the boundaries of highly different cultural forces as concepts and procedures are transplanted into new societies or multiethnic populations. Clinical psychology, with its traditional focus on practical problems and its concern with its own methodological and theoretical base, is finding itself in the forefront of an active and expanding cross-cultural psychology.

Perhaps even practicing clinicians, who are generally content to remain within their clinic or laboratory, are finding it difficult to avoid the complexities of multicultural or multiethnic practice or research. Stay-at-home clinicians and researchers, who are reluctant to venture into cross-cultural psychology, preferring the "certainty" of their concepts and procedures in their own society, are becoming aware that their own daily practice is in fact multicultural, that it includes clients or subjects from different socioeconomic strata and different religious backgrounds; from Asian, Black, Chicano, or Native American minority groups; from ethnic neighborhoods with "old country" ways; or from the growing number of refugees from Asian countries. Attempting to assess and treat clinically or do psychological research with individuals from these groups may represent just as much a cross-cultural experience as one that attempts a similar project across geographic boundaries.

Newly arrived clinical psychologists on the cross-cultural scene will find many well-trodden paths leading to partially explored jungles. They may be amazed at first that so much has been done in cross-cultural psychology. Areas such as learning, genetics, perception, cognition, psychometrics, abnormal behavior, and personality development are some of the domains receiving wide attention. Most often, the newcomer to cross-cultural study will be perplexed by the old-timer's obsession with rigorous methodology and skepticism about the generality and credibility of findings that emerge from cross-cultural comparisons.

Cross-cultural research has focused upon many psychological processes relevant to clinical psychology, for example, motivation (Gough, 1964; McClelland, 1961), anxiety (Sharma, 1977; Spielberger & Diaz-Guerra, 1976), child-rearing practices (Whiting &

Whiting, 1975), developmental psychology (Dasen, 1972), group process (Triandis, 1977), learning (Cole, Gay, Glick, & Sharp, 1971; Guthrie, 1975), infant development (Leiderman, Tulkin, & Rosenfeld, 1977), perceptual processes (Campbell, 1969; Segall, Campbell, & Herskovits, 1966), personality process (Holtzman, 1973; Guthrie & Bennett, 1971), and social change (Inkeles, 1971). Research has involved many traditional problems of clinical psychology, such as abnormal behavior (Marsella, 1979; Draguns, 1980; Yap, 1969); diagnosis (Butcher & Pancheri, 1976; Cooper, Kendall, Gurland, Sharpe, & Simon, 1976), and psychotherapy (Draguns, 1975; Henderson, 1979; Torrey, 1972; Pederson, 1980).

This chapter will survey cross-cultural research methods and the pertinent issues related to conducting clinical investigations across cultural boundaries. The goals of this presentation will include: sensitizing clinical researchers and practitioners to the importance of cross-cultural generalization for our concepts and procedures; exploring some of the most persistent methodological problems in cross-cultural and multiethnic research; and surveying and evaluating the adequacy of the most widely used methods for conducting cross-cultural research.

VALUE OF CROSS-CULTURAL RESEARCH IN PSYCHOLOGY

A growing number of psychologists in recent years have been turning to cross-cultural research to study a wide variety of psychological phenomena. Reasons for the widening use of cross-cultural research strategies are many. This section will highlight some of the factors that might influence an investigator's wish to extend his or her research beyond the bounds of a single culture.

One of the most important reasons for the use of a cross-cultural research strategy is that it provides *a wider range or broader distribution of the variable(s)* under study than is available in monocultural research. As Devereux, Bronfenbrenner, and Suci (1962) noted, cross-cultural studies are good for "catching strategic variables in new ranges." Cross-cultural studies enable researchers to sample a range or extreme of variables not found in a single culture. One assumption made here is that the variable(s) under study have been significantly influenced by cultural considerations in some perhaps unknown way, for example, that some sociogeographic environments may have allowed fuller expression of a particular variable, while others have restrained their expression. Thus an investigator, by selecting a range of cultures for inclusion in the study, may greatly increase the generality of the resulting research findings. A study, following up the observation that rates of symptomatic depression differ cross-culturally, might include in the study a broad range of cultures in an effort to determine possible causes of the differing rates.

A related issue is that certain factors that are known to vary in some cultures, such as child-rearing practices, may in turn influence psychological variables. The researcher may study weaning practices, which vary considerably across cultures, to determine their relationship with psychological attributes such as conservatism, dominance-passivity, optimism, and so on. Frijda and Jahoda (1966) noted that cross-cultural research enables investigators to uncover causal relationships that may not be evident in the more limited variance of monocultural research.

Another reason for the importance of cross-cultural studies is that they force, in Strodtbeck's (1964) words, a "revision of the investigator's culturally given taxonomy of human experience" (p. 226) or as Devereux, Bronfenbrenner, and Suci (1962) pointed out, that cross-cultural studies are good at shaking hypotheses free from particular sets of cultural entanglements. The awareness that the conceptual framework of our research is culturally limited and inappropriate for use in other cultures *enables us to gain perspective on our conceptualization of the problem under study*. If our research is only appropriate for a single culture, and will not generalize beyond River City, the Big Apple, or to the Midwest at most, we may question whether there is any ultimate value in doing the research. It may well be that our "limited" study would still be worth conducting, but the limited generality of the research would nevertheless have a sobering effect on the long-range implications of the study, since cultures, even River City, change over time.

Cross-cultural research enables an investigator to test the generality of hypotheses, observations, or theories to demonstrate the effect of culture, or to demonstrate that cultural influences make no difference on a given psychological variable. Whiting (1954) considered cross-cultural research to be important for *testing hypotheses developed in one culture across groups that are culturally diverse* in order to determine the universality of psychological variables.

The inclusion of cross-cultural conditions in psychological research or the replication of research findings across cultural groups helps to *assure that research results are robust* and do not simply result from artifacts tied to particular cultural situations.

A socially significant value of cross-cultural research in psychology is that it might serve to *enhance broader intercultural* understanding and international professional relationships and would stimulate further the development of the field. In clinical psychology this may be seen as broadening the methodological and practical base underlying the field. It has been noted that most of the intervention methods currently in practice in the United States are known and employed by professionals in other cultures; however, there are a large number of alternative viewpoints available in other cultures that are relatively unknown to North American psychology (Torrey, 1975). Thus even highly developed and industrialized nations like the United States, with a long history of professional development, may stand to be enriched from intercultural exchange.

MULTIETHNIC RESEARCH

In many modern societies people are not homogeneous with respect to language, custom, and cultural backgrounds. Large groups of religiously, politically, or racially "different" people live in relative isolation, unassimilated into the majority culture. Some ethnic groups remain separate by choice, in an effort to maintain their religious or old-world cultural ties, while others may not be fully assimilated because the majority culture has not fully accepted them.

Nonassimilation or nonacceptance into the mainstream of society can have numerous adverse influences upon personality development, educational and occupational opportunity, psychological health, and social well-being of the individuals in these culturally encapsulated groups. Being a member of an ethnic minority group such as Native American, Mexican-American, Black, or Asian refugee may, for a number of reasons, make one vulnerable to adjustment problems in adapting to broader societal demands and expectations. Consequently adjustment problems of ethnic minorities have become a central concern to many applied psychologists in recent years.

Psychological research in subcultural influence on personality development and adjustment has actually had a rather long history in clinical psychology. A large body of literature has grown up around the issues of relative intellectual capabilities, personality adjustment, rates of mental disorder, and so on, of the various ethnic populations in the United States. Many of the empirical studies on various subcultural groups have been approached as monocultural research, using research strategies that are appropriate to comparison of groups with similar cultural background. A more appropriate strategy for research with ethnic minority groups would be to approach the study as though it were a cross-cultural research investigation (Berry, 1979).

Multiethnic research or the study of subcultural group influences on psychological factors is a complicated process. The scientific validity of subcultural comparisons shares most of the problems of cross-cultural research, the focus of this chapter, as well as some special problems arising out of relationships between the minority groups and the dominant society. One of the most salient factors that potentially limits subcultural research, which has been recognized for some time, is referred to as "Galton's problem." This refers to the lack of independence between two cultural groups as a result of cultural borrowing or cultural diffusion inherent in the groups being geographically adjacent to each other. Thus subcultural groups cannot be considered as independent units, thereby weakening or violating assumptions underlying most statistical procedures (Naroll, 1970). The problem of interdependence of groups is difficult to resolve in many subcultural comparisons. Berry (1979) recommended a refinement of Naroll's procedure of analyzing groups according to their relative interdependence upon other groups. Groups would be selected for study according to known characteristics and according to explicit specification of the "cultunits." The high degree of specification of each cultunit would enable the researcher to evaluate the degree of independence of each unit.

Other problems involved in multiethnic research need to be carefully considered before launching into any subcultural research investigation. These include: the suspicion of many subcultural group members that social scientists have made negative comparisons of them in the past; the linguistic problem resulting from isolation (e.g., Black language) or from keeping the native tongue (e.g., some Latinos or Asian immigrants);

and the powerful influence that social class factors play in ethnic group research.

Multicultural research, an important and socially relevant activity, appears to be increasing in importance in contemporary clinical psychology. The methodological problems inherent in these endeavors loom as a large and ominous shadow over efforts to study these critical problems. Perhaps the sharp conceptual distinctions and the rigorous methodological concerns, so long a part of cross-cultural research, may now be applied to monocultural, multiethnic research investigations.

IMPORTANCE OF THE CROSS-CULTURAL RESEARCH PARADIGM TO CLINICAL PSYCHOLOGY

Although the disciplines of clinical psychology and psychiatry are relatively modern, many of their roles and functions as helping professions have been in existence for centuries and can be found in most known cultures (Fichter & Wittchen, 1980). The functions of psychological healer or helper have been fulfilled by physicians, priests, teachers, witch doctors, and others (Torrey, 1975). Some present-day clinical psychological practices, though we may like to view them as modern and sophisticated, often bear a striking resemblance to early "primitive" healing practices or to those relatively simple and superstitious ceremonies of isolated or nonindustrialized societies. Even the psychological testing movement, so much a part of twentieth century clinical psychology, had its early precursors in ancient China (DuBois, 1970).

Modern clinical psychology is characterized by: highly refined conceptualizations about human processes and development; the distinctive nosological systems we employ to gain an overview of patients' problems; the standardized and highly studied assessment methods; and the specific treatment strategies we employ—psychopharmacotherapy, behavior modification, rational-emotive and cognitive restructuring therapy, and so on. Thus, although present day clinical psychology appears to be complex and highly technical, its origins are varied, multicultural, and often direct descendants or cousins of primitive ideas and practices.

The field of clinical psychology, unlike some professions, specializes in both empirical research into the procedures and techniques underlying its operations and the practical application of that research. Thus an important function of the clinical psychologist is appraisal of its conceptualizations, scrutiny of its procedures, and evaluation of the basic concepts of the discipline.

Next we shall look at several areas that are central to present day clinical psychology and explore their multicultural scope.

Understanding Personality

The basic disciplines of personality and human development underlie clinical psychology. Advances in those fields can stimulate and the lack of development can delay progress in clinical practice. For example, in recent years, when social learning principles emerging from learning-based research were applied to problems of personality, great strides were also made in behavior intervention techniques. Similarly, the seeming lack of progress in systematizing personality has deterred the development of personality assessment in many ways, for example, by not providing acceptable criteria for empirical research (Hathaway, 1972). Critical to the advancement of personality has been the robustness with which its constructs can be applied to understanding personality development over diverse environments. A personality theory or explanatory model that only applies to a limited population or an isolated part of the world would have little generalization or applicability. For example, a personality psychology that takes the "self" as a central concept may not be relevant to

Oriental countries, where the ideal of self, as we view it, is nonexistent.

Psychological theorists interested in personality processes have long been interested in comparative research, to test the generality of a theory, to determine the range of the operation for a variable, or to discover alternative explanations or conceptualizations of a problem. Psychological researchers interested in determining the generality of their research often find themselves exploring situations or environments that are quite different from their own.

Clinical Assessment and Diagnosis

Clinical practice and psychopathology research often require the professional to use a classification schema to provide an overview perspective of an individual case or a descriptive categorization of individuals under study. The use of standard diagnostic criteria to provide a framework of classification can serve a valuable function in psychopathology research. A number of systems are in use: the International Classification of Diseases (ICD-9), Diagnostic and Statistical Manual of the American Psychiatric Association (DSM III), or the Research Diagnostic Criteria (Feighner et al., 1972).

How well these systems apply when they are employed with individuals from mixed ethnic or national backgrounds has not been sufficiently studied. Some related questions arise:

1. Are some diagnostic entities or "disorders" universal? Do the same disorders, such as depression or schizophrenia, exist in the same form and with the same relative frequency in each culture? Do some groups, such as Black Americans, have a greater or less preponderance of some problems than other groups?
2. Are there culture-specific disorders? Do some disorders appear in isolated form and bear little resemblance to disorders in other cultural contexts? Many ex-

amples of "culture specific" disorders have been reported in the literature—Amok, Koro, Kitsunetsuki, etc. (Yap, 1969). However, the resemblance of these conditions to other disordered states, such as anxiety disorder or hysteria, is high.

3. Do the presently available diagnostic criteria, which by no means are widely accepted in any single culture, apply in cross-ethnic or cross-national situations? Can a standardized classification schema be developed and employed in national groups that have quite different histories, traditions, beliefs, and politicoeconomic systems? There is some indication that diagnostic classification systems developed in Western countries apply quite well in other groups: Cooper, Kendall, Gurland, Sharpe, Copeland, and Simon (1972); Philips and Draguns (1971); Dohrenwend and Dohrenwend (1974); and Gottesman and Shields (1972). However, some research has suggested that the fit between Western diagnostic schema and problems in other cultures is not snug, and that different diagnostic procedures result in different rates of disorders (Leighton, Lambo, Hughes, Leighton, Murphy, & Macklin, 1963; and Seifert, Draguns, & Caudill, 1971). There is strong indication that some disorders, such as depression, may have different manifestations, patterns, or course in different cultures (Marsella, 1979).

Comparative studies in psychopathology, cross-national and multiethnic research in heterogeneous cultures, can broaden our understanding of psychopathology. Determining the limits of our conceptualizations and procedures by applying them in a broader range of conditions can help sharpen our diagnostic schema. The limitations or inapplicability we encounter may result in finer and more accurate conceptualizations by forcing us to account for a broader range of variables.

Test Adaptations in New or Different Cultures

One of the earliest cross-cultural clinical ventures involved the use of psychological tests developed in one culture to understand the cognitive behavior or personality of individuals in a different context. Adaptations of the Binet intelligence measures and the Rorschach inkblot tests from their settings in Western Europe to the United States early in the twentieth century were two of the most successful intercultural test adaptations. The main reason for this successful adaptation in the United States was the pragmatic one—the assessment methods demonstrated clinical utility and validity. Work on these test adaptation projects in time far excelled the original scope of the test in terms of theoretical development, empirical applications, and widespread clinical use. The actual origins of these instruments at times may become obscure in our minds, and we may even forget that these techniques were actually imports from other cultures.

The development of anthropology as an empirical science in the twentieth century stimulated the use of psychological procedures, like the Rorschach or versions of the Thematic Apperception Test, for understanding the differences in personality development in different cultures. Early psychologically oriented researchers used the Rorschach to define "national character structure" or the modal personality appearing as a result of living under different environmental conditions. This application of projective techniques was filled with numerous problems and added little reliable information to the field of personality development (Lindzey, 1961).

Contemporary cross-cultural test applications are directed more by the pragmatic test adaptation approach than the desire to typify national character types or other cultural constructs. Most present-day test translation and adaptation studies are aimed at providing a workable, valid alternate form of the test for use in the new culture and the application of the test's constructs and interpretations for individual personality description and clinical prediction in the new culture. For example, the MMPI has been widely translated and adapted for clinical use in over 45 countries (Butcher & Pancheri, 1976; Butcher & Clark, 1979). In most instances the translation and adaptations have been done by psychologists and psychiatrists in the target culture as a diagnostic aid in clinical work. The early MMPI translations tended to be simply translated with little concern for maintaining psychological equivalence and very little developmental or test adaptation work on the translation was done. More recently the test translations are following carefully specified procedures, including team or committee translation (back translation of items by independent translators and bilingual equivalence studies; see Butcher & Gur, 1973). Determining the adequacy of the MMPI as a clinical instrument has been approached in a number of ways. One important requirement for test equivalence is that tests used in cultural contexts that are different from their original environment show a similar or equivalent factor structure in the target culture. Butcher and Pancheri (1976) demonstrated that the factor structure of the MMPI is quite consistent across several diverse cultural groups. Another important consideration in addition to internal validity is whether or not the instrument has predictive validity in the new culture. The MMPI has been shown to operate clinically in much the same way as in the United States in a number of different cultures, for example, Mexico (Nunez, 1968; Lopez-Ortiz, 1979); Italy (Pancheri, 1971; Butcher & Pancheri, 1976); Israel (Merbaum & Hefez, 1977), Pakistan (Mirza, 1976); Chile (Butcher & Clark, 1979; Rissetti et al., 1979); Japan (Kosugi, Tsujimoto, Tanaka, & Masumoto, 1979; Yasuno, Hashimoto, & Makai, 1979); Korea (Kim, 1979); Kuwait (Torki, 1979).

The cross-national adaptation of psychological tests is a growing field of importance in clinical psychology. The development of clinical psychological specialties in many countries and the absence or lack of a developed psychotechnology make test adaptations from other, perhaps more psychologically developed nations, an attractive enterprise. Although many technical problems are encountered in such test adaptations and some alterations are frequently required, especially in countries with wide cultural differences, many of the transplanted methods and instruments thrive in the new cultures.

Cross-Cultural Psychotherapy and Counseling

Widening cultural contact between different national and subcultural groups is paralleled by increasing professional contacts between psychotherapists and clients of highly diverse backgrounds. Psychotherapists reared and trained in Western thought and psychological theory may inappropriately employ systems of personality and behavior change techniques that originate in modern Western culture with minority patients, such as migrant workers, Asian refugees, deaf mutes, or foreign students. Mixed cultural professional situations are shrouded in unknowns that require consideration if the therapeutic situation is to be given a chance of success (Draguns, 1975; Henderson, 1979; Torrey, 1972; Pedersen, 1980). Many factors in the therapists' attitudes and expectations about the client may operate as negative bias in the treatment process. The therapist is likely to have particular views of personality, causation, or values that may differ drastically from the cognitive and personality factors that actually dominate the client. The client's expectations, wishes, views of the "helper," and life goals may be both alien to the therapist and difficult to conceptualize from the vantage point of differing cultural origin.

Theories of psychological intervention and the procedures employed may, when adapted to a different culture, not apply or work effectively in a new context. Some behavioral or life change viewpoints successful in some cultures may have little relevance to other environments, for example, psychoanalysis in rural China or Morita therapy in middle-class America. However, their successful explanatory power or application in one context may warrant giving them sufficient trial in other cultures.

Indeed many such intervention procedures have been established in cross-cultural contexts. In many instances this has involved the transplantation of a technique or an approximation of it into Western or United States psychology, for example, Zen, Yoga, or meditation techniques, without critical appraisal or evaluation of the technique.

These cross-cultural aspects of clinical psychology highlight the importance for clinical practitioners and researchers of being cognizant of the issues and problems inherent in cross-cultural applications. The comparative method in personality and clinical psychology is becoming an essential element of graduate preparation in clinical psychology and a continuing concern for clinical researchers who are studying real life clinical problems. It is virtually impossible for researchers to study a relevant and generalizable problem without including multicultural conditions. The inclusion of these factors in research design necessitates explicit concern for comparative or cross-cultural research issues, to which we now turn.

ISSUES IN PLANNING MULTICULTURAL PSYCHOLOGICAL RESEARCH

Multicultural psychological research poses some general problems that require careful planning in the early stages of research design. Many of these issues are haunting problems that are difficult if not impossible to resolve sufficiently and pose serious threats to the validity of the study; others are issues that produce constraints on the research and,

if left unattended, can result in ambiguous results. All of the problems to be discussed are inherent in multicultural research and require serious consideration.

The Emic-Etic Distinction and Implications for Psychological Research

These terms may be new to the psychological researcher's vocabulary, but the distinctions underlying them are nearly as old as personality research itself. Allport's (1937) conceptualization of *nomothetic* versus *idiographic* personality research represents, on the level of the individual personality, the same basic issue as the emic-etic problem. The focus is on the individual, and all the personal uniqueness represented by the idiographic approach to personality was compared with the more normative, common characteristic involved with comparison between individuals—the nomothetic approach to personality. The concepts "emic" and "etic" refer to different approaches to understanding culture. Emic studies involve monocultural approaches, or those involved with studying the culture on its own terms and employing culture-based constructs. Etic research, on the other hand, seeks to understand or to compare cultures using a common framework for each. Standard concepts and procedures are employed to compare each cultural group, as nomothetic research compares individuals across standard measures. The importance of the emic-etic distinction in cross-cultural clinical research is shown in the study of clinical diagnosis. If one assumes a purely emic approach in viewing abnormal behavior in a given culture, one may arrive at highly specific diagnostic entities (often referred to as "exotic" mental disorders) such as Koro (a fear reaction in which the person fears that his penis will withdraw into his abdomen and he will die) or Kitsunitsu (a disorder in which victims believe that they are possessed by foxes and are said to change facial expressions to resemble foxes) which have low cross-cultural generality. Taking an etic approach to diagnosis, on the other hand, requires that each diagnostic category be found relevant to each culture. This requirement may make the resulting diagnostic system superficial and "blind" to important abnormal conditions in some cultures under study.

Cross-cultural researchers are quite sensitive to the influence of cultural context on behavior and may be concerned that behavior or group processes may be highly unique and incomparable to other behavior or group processes in differing cultures. There has been concern that researchers may distort their data or in some way fail to capture the true variables by imposing an *etic* design or sets of procedures upon emic data. This concern, referred to as a *pseudoetic* approach, involves, for example, applying a procedure or a test developed in a Western culture to another group that is highly different in tradition, language, cultures, or background.

The emic-etic distinction should be carefully considered by the cross-cultural researcher in assuring that procedures and methods are applicable in all cultures to be studied. However, giving consideration to the emic-etic question should not be equated with a suggestion to avoid conducting etic studies or with postponing comparative research until this philosophical concern is resolved. Comparative research involves etic studies. Behavioral science and comparative clinical studies must of necessity involve comparing cultural groups on standard variables. The emic-etic controversy serves as a warning to the researcher—a conscience that constantly reminds us that cross-cultural research is a precarious matter, filled with problems that require conceptual attention, suitable controls, prudent interpretation, and careful generalization from our findings.

The Need for Multicultural Research

Early research in cross-cultural psychology focused upon finding and describing differences between diverse cross-cultural groups.

These studies were done without regard for the relevance of the constructs, behavior, and tasks for the different groups and without a general accounting of the range of possible interpretation for the findings. Research studies conducted with the limited goal of finding differences between two groups or cultures have contributed little of substance to accumulated knowledge in the cross-cultural field. Likewise contemporary one-shot investigations without a grand scheme or sequence of related studies generally add very little to knowledge in the field. Campbell (1964) pointed out that comparisons with only two cultures are limited since "no two naturally occurring things are comparable." Lonner (1980, p. 153) noted that built-in biases are likely to occur in unicultural, single research studies:

And when two, and only two, cultures are studied (as in methodologically indefensible "one-shot" studies), neither complete universality nor its complete absence can be established, for here only a bimodal "sameness-difference" dimension can be used. On any behavioral variable, culture A would be either the same or different from culture B. Since there cannot be any intermediate position in a binary system, there are no alternatives. . . . Behavioral phenomena can be clustered, categorized, or otherwise found to co-vary in some theoretically valid way in multicultural studies.

Of course the recommendation for the inclusion of several comparison groups refers particularly to naturalistic studies (that is, naturally occurring) in which there are a number of possible groups distributed on the dimensions or characteristics under investigation.

Two culture research may be appropriate for some controlled experimentation studies in which, for example, several treatment conditions are included with the variable of culture. In such studies the limitations of the design, imposed by the narrow range of cultures included in the design, should be noted in evaluating the generalization validity of the research.

The Role of Theory in Cross-Cultural Research

The meaning and eventual contribution of research findings cannot be fully understood in the limited context of the isolated experiment. Rather the fit or the lack of congruence between the research results and the broader context of findings, both previous and future research, is required if the research is to be cumulative. Jahoda (1980, p. 71) pointed out:

However, perhaps the main objection to be raised against much of the earlier work is that, with some important exceptions, it remained innocent of theory. The prevailing tendency was pursuing a topic that appeared interesting, without much concern as to how it would fit in the broader scheme. The result has been largely a patchwork—often fascinating and sometimes insightful, but not as a *cumulative* science.

Triandis (1980) pointed out that research programs in cross-cultural psychology often are isolated from and do not relate other findings into their own research. Research without rationale, without a broader theoretical purpose, or without consideration of the fit with other research contributions adds little to the advance of science.

An important distinction should be made here between theory per se and accumulated knowledge. We are not arguing for the necessity of a "grand theory"—such as the theory of relativity, psychoanalysis, or dissonance theory—for research in cross-cultural psychology to be meaningful. On the contrary, there are no available general theories of human behavior or even "specific theories" that explain much human behavior sufficiently and parsimoniously. Thus a cross-cultural empirical science would need to be delayed or postponed indefinitely if the requirement of a theory were rigidly maintained. Not only are general theories of be-

havior lacking in contemporary psychology but some of the more lasting and valuable bodies of knowledge in clinical psychology have actually grown in an atheoretical and simply empirical fashion, for example, operant learning techniques and MMPI-based assessment research.

We are, however, recommending that comparative research not be done in isolation, that research investigations be launched only with a clear understanding of successes and failures of other efforts at studying the problems in the past. All too often psychological research is initiated without sufficient preparation and planning, many times because the researcher finds himself or herself in a foreign culture with a ready sample, referred to as a "sample of convenience" by Butcher and Tellegen (1978).

Problems of Equivalence in Cross-Cultural Research

The most pervasive problems facing researchers who enter into the multiculture research domain are those referred to as problems of *equivalence*. The basic issue is that researchers need to assure that the experimental conditions employed in each cultural group are comparable, if not identical, in all important respects. Throughout all phases of a multicultural study, from the early planning to choosing appropriate research designs and stimulus materials, to selecting samples, to the data collection, interpretation, and analysis phases of the research, problems of equivalence are paramount considerations. In order for comparative research to be unambiguously interpretable, the interexperimental conditions must be assured. Problems of equivalence provide an abundance of alternative hypotheses that will plague generalizations from the research.

Some of the most important sources of nonequivalence in comparative research are given in Table 9.1. Research designs that are ethnocentric or culture bound as a result of not assuring method equivalence are not

Table 9.1.   Some Sources of Nonequivalence in Cross-Cultural Research

Conceptual Equivalence

The constructs underlying the study and the concepts employed in the problem definition and interpretation of the findings may not have the same phychological meaning in all cultures under investigation. For example, the construct of introversion-extroversion may have quite different meanings, values, and distributions in Oriental versus Western nations.

Experimental Condition Equivalence

The experimental procedures or even the idea of research inquiry may be alien and unacceptable to some cultural groups.

Behavioral Equivalence

The psychological phenomena under investigation may not have the same meaning in all cultures. For example, "shy" behavior may have different meanings in different cultures. Certain psychological characteristics may have different frequencies in different cultural groups.

Contextual Equivalence

The behavioral context may be different in different cultural groups. Some variables such as peer influence operate differently in different cultures (Bronfenbrenner, 1967).

Linguistic Equivalence

The accurate translation of instructions, questionnaires, and other material is an important task. Materials must communicate the appropriate psychological meanings as well as being linguistically accurate.

Sampling Equivalence

Assuring that samples of subjects or patients used in the research are comparable across groups is one of the most difficult problems. In addition to the problems with matching research subjects generally (Meehl, 1969) in cross-cultural research, it is difficult to assure that the rules for subject selection, availability of appropriate people (Manaster & Havighurst, 1972), and appropriate subject "attitudes" such as cooperativeness (Hudson, Barakat, & Laforge, 1959) are the same for all groups.

Psychometric Equivalence

The psychometric characteristics of the measures should be equivalent across cultural groups. For example, the internal relationships of scores should have the same factor structure in each cultural comparison (Brislin, Lonner, & Thorndike, 1973; Buss & Royce, 1975).

---

likely to be comparable. Fiske (1974) pointed out that a conventional science of personality is limited, partly through its dependence upon words and the lack of agreement about data and higher-level conceptualizations. He noted that the problem is even more complex since most of the data, the conceptualizations, and the "words" are English ones, generated from a single culture. Method variance resulting from using nonequivalent procedures may generate a large number of alternative hypotheses to explain the experimental findings.

Importance of Indigenous Collaboration

Much of the earlier research in cross-cultural psychology involved researchers from one culture, usually Western scholars, initiating the study, collecting the data, interpreting the results, and publishing the conclusions with little or no input from individuals living in the culture under investigation. This type of comparative study, often referred to as "safari research," was conducted without indigenous collaboration because there often were no professionals in the target country who had the training, the time, or the professional inclination to become involved in comparative research. As a result, many of the earlier attempts to study psychological constructs across cultural boundaries suffered from biased designs and resulted in ethnocentric conclusions.

Research studies of the "carpetbagger" variety should be discouraged. In many countries, particularly in the Third World, people are highly sensitive to Western "imperialism" and resent the perceived imposition and domination that has been so characteristic in many areas of life in the past. Within multicultural societies, such as the

United States and Canada, this problem is also reflected in the resentment by minority groups of the research dominance and control of the majority cultural group.

The scientific merit of "imperialistic" or monoculturally dominated studies is low; they are generally fraught with equivalency problems, and at best are ethnocentric distortions of the real world. In order for comparative research to avoid subjective bias, research projects should be based upon equal participation and full collaboration from psychologists who are identified with, live and work in, and thoroughly understand the cultural groups under study. Fortunately, in many countries and different cultural groups, even in "underdeveloped" nations, there is a growing number of psychological professionals who have interest in collaborative research. In many developing countries the psychologically oriented professionals are generally more concerned with practical issues and questions related to the problems of personal and national development, such as how to improve psychological services or how to adapt successful clinical procedures from other countries to apply in their own context. Thus, rather than being perceived as an imperialistic imposition, psychological research, especially the more applied varieties, may actually be welcomed by professionals from other cultures. This was recently illustrated by the expressed interests of psychologists from mainland China, when the cultural interchange with Western nations resumed after more than 30 years in relative isolation. The greatest interest appeared to be in learning about Western developments in clinical and developmental and social psychology, with the aim of solving individual problems of adjustment and of altering some deviant social patterns, such as the lack of personal motivation and incentive, that often accompany communistic or collective economies.

There are still many psychological research problems that are perhaps less "socially relevant" or may need to focus upon less well developed populations in areas where no indigenous professionals reside. In these instances, investigators would be well advised to avail themselves of "acceptable" collaborators and broad counsel about the suitability of their measures, lest their well-meaning project be misconstrued by the target population and considered to be unacceptable.

Problems of Intercultural Collaboration

The success of a cross-cultural research project is dependent upon obtaining intercultural collaboration. However, having collaborators in other cultural groups does not necessarily insure a project's success. It is much easier to write about cross-cultural collaboration than it is to assure its effective operation. Many things can go awry in intercultural cooperative efforts. I suspect that about as many such projects falter or fail as actually succeed. A truly equal collaboration in cross-cultural research may be an ideal that is seldom realized. There are many possible sources of problems in cross-cultural work apart from those typically occurring in collaborative research efforts generally, for example, failed communication, different priorities among collaborators, differences in work output, presence of unproductive personality styles such as procrastination or lack of organization, and so on.

In cross-cultural collaboration there may be quite differing views of science, for example, there may be quite different assumptions underlying cause-effect relationships, the nature and processes of human development, or differing values placed upon objectivity in research among the collaborators. Researchers from different cultural backgrounds may have divergent views on the focus, the scope, and the timetable of the project. Even how or whether the research will conclude in a published form may be a point of difference. For example, on one project, researchers from a certain cultural group never completed the write-up of a key part of a collaborative study. In their view the publication of the results was a very low priority, since "publishing" was not considered very important in their country, even for academics.

Projects have a way of diminishing in importance when the collaborators are temporally or geographically separated, across the expanse of an ocean or even the length of a college campus or the hegemonies of different administrative units. Problems of communication can become compounded with delays and misunderstandings that result in unilateral changes in project design and threaten the equivalence of the cross-cultural components of the project.

Economic factors may produce difficulties in research collaboration. In some countries, particularly those less well developed professionally, research may be a luxury that cannot be afforded. Some researchers, being unable to receive financial support for research, fund their own projects through private means. However, in most countries research grant support is not available except through Western, particularly United States, funded projects. The situation in which a powerful, dominant nation underwrites research in "underdeveloped" countries can produce serious problems. An excellent discussion of the sponsorship issue, which is a must reading for cross-cultural researchers, can be found in a paper by Warwick (1980).

National and international political problems can adversely influence research programs. Psychological research is always done with a political backdrop, no matter how value free or politically void the researchers attempt to make themselves and their research. Even well-formulated collaborative studies are subject to political influence or problems; thus it behooves the researchers to determine, in advance, possible sources of political problems. Many national or cultural environments do not lend themselves well to psychological research, for example, antiscientific religious dictatorships, fascistic military regimes, and those

with severe political-revolutionary chaos. However, these often openly hostile environments are not the only political contexts that are destructive to well-intended research. More subtle forms of antiscientific attitudes may be found in government or public attitudes referred to as "Proxmireism" (official ridicule of pure research) or in highly bureaucraticized, inefficient governmental situations that can frustrate a project to its death by unending paper work, permissions, requirements, and so on, which never receive approval.

Researchers who are fortunate enough to find environments that are relatively free of national or international political upset may find that the local academic political scene can be just as disrupting to planned research. Cultural factors, differing training or academic expectations, different administrative structures, and many other personal situations that result in conflict may lead to difficulties in collaborative relationships. Projects may be begun with high degree of cooperative spirit, only to run into delays or divisiveness due to internal competition or factionalism within cooperative groups. It is difficult to know with certainty whether one's collaborators, within a particular nation or cultural group, are the ones most appropriate for the project.

Cross-cultural researchers may thus find themselves in the unpleasant situation of needing indigenous collaboration if research is to succeed and yet not being able to count on full, wholehearted participation on the part of indigenous colleagues. It is of course desirable to assure oneself, funding agencies, sponsors, and collaborators in other countries that the project will proceed, as structured, to its successful completion. It is better for the sake of the science of cross-cultural psychology, as well as for one's mental health, to consider, in fact plan for, the "unlikely event" of project failure in some cultural groups. Having had projects terminated abruptly due to factors such as political upheaval, academic politics, and partially committed collaborators, I cannot overemphasize the importance of being aware of the range of potential problems that can turn a scientific work into a disappointment.

Problems in Communication and Translation

Communication problems are frequently encountered in intercultural research. Difficulties can result from factors inherent in cultural group interaction produced by different ideologies, lifestyles, politicoeconomic systems, and so on. Intercultural communication failures can result from people making assumptions about or having certain expectations of their collaborators or subjects that are unwarranted. Some of the problems resulting from this claim of differing values or cultural systems were discussed in the previous section.

Another source of communication problems enters into much cross-cultural research—matters of failed communication due to translation inadequacies. The problems poor translations can cause are illustrated in the following excerpt from an article released by the Associated Press in 1976 following an incident in the United Nations:

"In the garden there's a mulberry tree, but my uncle's in Kiev," the Soviet representative solemnly pronounced in Russian before the parliament of the world. (The proverb literally means "It is neither here nor there.")

The English interpreter had never heard the Russian word for mulberry tree; he hadn't the foggiest notion what the proverb meant, and the speaker was already on his next sentence.

So he gambled, and the people at the United Nations whose earpieces were tuned to the English translation heard: "Something is rotten in the state of Denmark."

This brought the Danish ambassador to his feet. In mock indignation, he objected to the slur on his nation and declared: "We don't deserve this kind of treatment."

The Soviet delegate sat dumbfounded. He had never mentioned Denmark. The incident ended there, but it illustrated the occupational hazards of the United Nations interpretation services.

Accurate communication in research is just as important, though perhaps not as dramatic as in international politics. Assuring translation adequacy and equivalence of verbal materials is an important aspect of many cross-cultural projects, even those involving linguistically close national languages such as the United States and Australia. Some of the MMPI item content, developed for the United States in the early 1940s, appears quite quaint or inappropriate in other countries, for example, feeling "blue" or liking to play "drop the handkerchief." Proper attention to linguistic equivalence in the early stages of research will lead to a clearer interpretation of results when the study is completed, since translation problems provide an important source of alternative hypotheses to results in multilanguage projects.

Recommended procedures for assuring translation adequacy are given in Table 9.2. The recommended steps for preparing a translation involve: using more than one translator, working independently or in committees to prepare an initial translation of the material; using a back translation procedure to detect any difficulties or failed communication; field testing translated material—assuring readability, style, and accuracy of content communication; conducting bilingual studies in the case of translated tests; and determining the psychometric adequacy or translanguage equivalence of the test in all the target languages. Table 9.2 provides some guidelines on preparing translations that aim to communicate clearly both the linguistic and psychological meaning of the material.

METHODS OF CROSS-CULTURAL RESEARCH

A wide array of research methods and data gathering techniques await the cross-cultural researcher. Techniques for obtaining data on

Table 9.2.   Guide to Translation of Psychological Material

1. Translators should have a high degree of familiarity with *both* languages, preferably having lived for extended periods in both cultures. Most psychological materials to be translated require more sensitive translation than just dictionary consultation.
2. Use of more than one translator in the initial translation phase is recommended. Independently translated material can later be combined, eliminating weak or inaccurate renderings.
3. After the material has been translated into the target language, it is desirable to employ a *back translation* procedure to detect items or concepts that are poorly translated. Discrepancies between the original and the back translated version provides a means of checking the equivalence of the translation. The back translation should be done by different bilingual persons than those involved in the translation.
4. A field pretest of the translated material is recommended after the translation and back translation are completed.
5. The field pretest may incorporate inquiries with subjects to determine if any problems emerge with the translated materials. It is desirable to conduct the field test on samples from the full range of subjects to be included in the study.
6. Study of the translation itself is desirable before the translated material is accepted. This is particularly true in the case of translated tests. Several methods of evaluation have been developed to determine the adequacy of translated tests, including: giving bilingual persons both language versions and comparing their responses; determining and comparing endorsement percentages of subjects from normative populations in each language; determining whether the factor structures of the various language versions are comparable.
7. In the case of translated tests validity and reliability should be demonstrated for the target language version.
8. It may be desirable to provide a translator's guide for the material, especially for a psychological test translation. The translation problems encountered, the alterations required, and the philosophy underlying content changes could be appended to the test manual so that other researchers using the materials would be aware of the original translator's decision processes.

Specific Recommendations

1. The translated material should be grammatically correct—an important requirement, though often difficult to assure. Native speakers of the target language should be used, since they tend to produce more readable translations.
2. The translation should read naturally in the target language. Problems of syntax and awkward wording are frequent problems of translated psychological materials.
3. Translate passage or items so that the translated version accurately conveys the meaning of the original. Interchange of item content may be necessary to assure equivalence.
4. Use concrete rather than abstract expressions.
5. In translating figurative expressions an explanation may be added to the item, in parentheses, to add clarity.
6. Idiomatic expressions may produce translation problems in the target culture. They may have to be translated by nonidiomatic expressions. It may be best, for clarity, to use both the idiom and the literal translation in parentheses.
7. In some languages verb tenses and gender are employed with more precision than other languages. Tense changes may be required to convey the original text. It may be necessary to repeat nouns to avoid using the passive tense, the subjunctive mood, or hypothetical phrasing.
8. The use of double negatives, such as in personality test items, may cause problems in translation. The item may need to be changed from negative to the positive in words added to clarify the item meaning. If item meaning direction is changed, the scoring direction should reflect this change.
9. Some psychological materials or items may not mean the same thing, that is, may have different behavioral implications, in the target culture. Such items may need to be substituted for material that is psychologically more meaningful though linguistically different.
10. The meaning of the translation may be improved by the process of *decentering*. This procedure involves changing the original text in instances where the material is not translatable. The final two versions are made more equivalent. This procedure cannot be used in instances where the original material cannot be altered, such as an established personality questionnaire.

Sources: Brislin, 1970; Brislin, Lonner, & Thorndike, 1973; Butcher & Clark, 1979; Butcher & Garcia, 1978; Butcher & Pancheri, 1976; Rosen, 1958; Sechrest, Fay, & Zaidi, 1970; Werner & Campbell, 1970.

different national and ethnic populations range from ethnographic, descriptive studies done by trained observers to oral and questionnaire survey methods to approaches that attempt to control or manipulate variables simultaneously in the different comparison groups. The methods employed in cross-cultural studies vary along a number of dimensions; for example, in their rigorous application of controls versus naturalistic data collection, their exploratory versus confirmatory thrust, their reliance on indigenous research collaborators versus "safari" research, their use of available written materials versus the acquisition of novel information, as well as many other research design characteristics. In this section we shall explore a large number of possible research methods for cross-cultural studies. The merits of each approach, the overall goal of the research method, along with some of the more salient limiting factors will be surveyed for each of the methods. A detailed outline of the relevant characteristics of these research approaches is presented in Table 9.3 for comparative purposes. A selection of pertinent references is provided for each method for readers who wish to pursue their examination in greater detail.

A clinical researcher has many possible methods of investigation to select from depending upon the questions to be asked, the support for the project, and the amenability of the population at hand for data collection. It may be desirable for researchers to avail themselves of the existing data on the cultures under study, for example, through the Human Relations Area files, before proceeding to other approaches. A researcher may choose, if the problem lends itself to it, an extensive documentary study of available printed materials from each culture. Demographic and epidemiological data may be available to test broad hypotheses and help the researcher to narrow down questions of interest. Data collection on selected samples may proceed from a number of angles depending upon the researcher's orientation and

hypotheses to be tested. Some approaches, such as interviewing and naturalistic observation, may require a great deal of training of researchers in different cultures, but may provide more extensive information than some of the other approaches such as survey methods or self-report measures.

The psychological researcher who ventures into the cross-cultural domain might well consider the wide array of research strategies open to him or her before settling on a given approach or set of methods to be employed in the study. All too often in the cross-cultural field, and in the field of psychology generally, investigators have allowed the availability of a sample, or their acquaintance with a particular method to determine the scope and nature of the research. Quite often the nature or limitations inherent in the problem itself are not given sufficient weight in the design of the study. It is easy for investigators to lose sight of the research question and follow the dictates of a particular methodological approach or a technique in spite of its possible inappropriateness and the availability of attractive alternatives. Although the selection of methods and the modes of data collection, analysis, and interpretation are exceedingly important considerations, they should not be the first destination in a cross-cultural study trek. Rather the important consideration centering around specifying and elaborating the research question is of primary concern. What phenomena or questions are we seeking to study? Are the phenomena, as we have outlined and defined them, amenable to empirical research? How have other investigators approached this matter? What limitations or troublesome problems have previous investigators encountered? What have been the major findings that emerged from the previous research? Are there alternative methodological approaches to answering the questions of interest?

Before the methods of investigation are selected, the researcher should examine critically a number of limiting considerations in

Table 9.3. Outline of Cross-Cultural Research Methods

Data sources and processes	Goals of research	Potential methodological problems

Cultural Description: Ethnography

Observation; systematic recording; classification of observed events and activities; use of informants.	Goodenough (1980); Honigmann (1970); Pelto & Pelto (1973) Description of culture; delineation of activities, institutions, family and social relationships, economic and political system.	1. Built-in observer biases from being a member of a particular culture. 2. Subjectivity of analyses. 3. Reliance upon cooperation from informants. 4. Necessity of categorization of observations. 5. Linguistic problems. 6. May uncover "demeaning" information, which if published could produce more harm than good. 7. Questions and observations may be looked upon as exploitative.

Cultural Description: Human Relations Area Files (HRAF)

A vast source of descriptive data is contained in the HRAF. Over 1000 societies are described in over 500,000 pages of information. The information is coded for a number of cultural attributes and can be readily accessed for comparative research. The files are available in more than 20 sites in the U.S. and four locations abroad (Paris, Kyoto, Osaka & Seoul).	Murdock (1975); Murdock (1967); Lagace (1974); Barry (1980) To provide extensive descriptive data on many cultural attributes of world societies for comparative analyses.	1. There are problems in defining the cultural unit(s) to be studied. 2. Inconsistent or confusing information can be generated when ethnographic sources are mismatched. For example, using data collected at different points in time. 3. Important categories, as defined, may not be readily found in the information. 4. The files provide only a limited amount of data for psychological analyses. 5. Hypotheses to be studied must conform to the available data; thus the scope of studies may be restricted.

Hologeistic or "Allcultures" Research

The hologeistic method employs currently available data sources such as the HRAF. Information is coded in a quantifiable form for computer analysis.	Murdock (1975); Jahoda (1979); Naroll, Michik & Naroll (1974a); Naroll, Michik & Naroll (1980b) A method of analysis of existing ethnographic or survey data to evaluate comparative hypotheses. A method used to test theories (using correlational analysis) with data on representative samples from all known cultures.	1. Sampling bias resident in available sources. Investigation samples should be widely obtained from known extensive data pools. 2. The definition of "cultural unit" may be arbitrary and result in overlapping groups. 3. It is important to define groups clearly according to both geographic characteristics and temporal considerations. Some cultural descriptions may have been made earlier than others.

Table 9.3. *Continued*

Data sources and processes	*Goals of research*	*Potential methodological problems*

Hologeistic or "Allcultures" Research (Continued)

		4. Holocultural analyses are only as good as the data on which they are based. Conclusions should consider that data sources, such as field observations and information reports, may contain considerable inaccuracies.
		5. The process of coding and quantification of the data may result in vaguely summarized and invalid categories.
		6. Data from some cultures may be scarce or absent, thus limiting comparability of samples.
		7. The use of "proxy" variables in holocultural research (i.e., using one variable to stand in for a weak or missing variable) may be inappropriate unless the relationship between the original and proxy variables is clearly established.
		8. The overlap of characteristics between "adjacent" cultures resulting from clinical diffusion may result in an independence of cultures to such a degree as to violate assumption of statistical independence (often referred to as Galton's problem).

Documentary Studies or Analysis of Content

Folktales, newspapers, textbooks.	Frijda & Jahoda (1966); Brislin (1980); Colby & Peacock (1973); McClelland (1964); Holsti (1968) Description and analysis of cultures, institutions, social traditions and histories, psychological variables, etc. through analysis of verbal products or communications.	1. Analysis is dependent upon available sources. Sample of materials may not be representative of phenomena or of the society.
		2. Comparable source material may not be available in other cultures, thus limiting etic comparisons (e.g., an analysis of editorials in newspapers).
		3. Data from different cultures may not be comparable. Equivalence of content or processes must be demonstrated.
		4. Coding system or categorization system may result in a loss of information and distortion of the data.
		5. Emergent classification system or categories need to have a demonstrated construct validity.

Table 9.3. *Continued*

Data sources and processes	Goals of research	Potential methodological problems

Documentary Studies or Analysis of Content (Continued)

6. Content analyses need to have more than internal consistency. External validation of components or categories must be demonstrated.
7. Difficulties of tying content analyses to theoretical viewpoints.

Demographic and Epidemiological Strategy

Uses national statistics on demographic and epidemiological phenomena such as rates of suicide, alcoholism, accidents, cigarette and caffeine consumption, psychosis, heart disease, caloric intake, divorce, illegitimacy, murder, and crime. These phenomena are theoretically linked to psychological variables such as neuroticism, anxiety, and extraversion.	Lynn (1971); Lynn & Hampson (1975) To determine or measure national differences in personality by examining differential rates on variables that are highly related to the psychological dimensions, e.g., anxiety, neuroticism, extraversion.	1. Indexes used are only crude measures of the phenomena. 2. Indexes used may not be valid. For example, the index "alcoholism" was not believed related to extraversion. 3. The "rates" employed in the study are often suspect and not the only ways of assessing variables, e.g., in determining rates of alcoholism. 4. The index variables may be more influenced by factors such as geography, economic and other variables rather than personality considerations. Thus the psychological meaningfulness of these variables may be questioned. 5. The model employed assumed independence of national groups. However, Galton's problem of cultural borrowing was not taken into account. 6. Much of the existing work employs a simplistic 2-factor model of personality. 7. Referring to nations as more anxious or neurotic, etc., may be too vague to be heuristic. For example, does it mean that all Irish people are less neurotic than the Austrians? 8. The characterizations, though invalid, may lend themselves to misinterpretations and premature invidious comparisons.

Naturalistic or Behavioral Observation

Behavioral observations in the natural environment. Systematic recording of behavior in clinical settings.	Cone & Foster (this volume); Charlesworth & Spiker (1975); Ekman (1973); Kazdin (1980); Longabaugh (1980); Whiting, Child, & Lambert (1966);	1. Theoretical view should be clearly defined to guide observation. Vaguely defined research or "theoryless" observations are apt to lead to meaningless data.

291

Table 9.3. *Continued*

Data sources and processes	Goals of research	Potential methodological problems
	Naturalistic or Behavioral Observation (Continued)	
	Willems (1964) Observe, classify, and systematize behavior in the naturalistic setting. Analyze complex behavioral processes into components. Describe, formulate hypotheses, and test hypotheses using verbal content and observed behavioral activities.	2. The high cost of behavior observation data may lead investigators to take short cuts or use less well trained observers in data collection. 3. Behavior under study must be shown to be equivalent in each cultural unit under study. For example, hand clapping may mean different things in different cultures. 4. Behavioral context equivalence needs to be ascertained. 5. Adequate translation of recorded verbal behavior must be assured. Translation of instructions to observers, coders, etc., should follow rigorous, careful procedures. 6. Problems in coding behavior result when "purely descriptive" vs. "inference involved" coding criteria are followed. Unreliability may creep into the data when highly general categories (requiring inferences on the part of coders) are used. Yet the vast amount of data collected may require refined classification. 7. Equivalence of coding systems across cultural units needs to be assured. 8. A careful training program for behavioral analysts or coders in each culture needs to be done to assure that the criteria and coding rules are uniformly applied. 9. Cross-validation of observation studies needs to be employed to assure the reliability and generality of the findings. 10. The dependent measure should actually reflect the construct being assessed. 11. Global ratings of behavior provide a convenient format for summarizing diverse problems; however, criteria for rating should be clearly specified.

Table 9.3. *Continued*

Data sources and processes	*Goals of research*	*Potential methodological problems*
	Naturalistic or Behavioral Observation (Continued)	
		12. Direct measures of behavior, e.g., behavior samples, may be used, but some behavior in the interest of the study, e.g., sexual behavior, may not readily appear in the natural environment or may appear differentially in different cultures.
		13. Validity and representativeness of behavior studied needs to be assured.
		14. Behavioral measurement may be reactive.
		15. Behavior is usually complex and multifaceted, thus multimethods are preferred.
	Unobtrusive Research: Naturalistic Observation	
Observations of subjects in a naturalistic setting in which they are unaware that they are being studied. The data may be naturally occurring, in response to a contrived situation, archival or "traces" of previous behavior.	Bochner (1971); Bochner (1980); Kazdin (1980); Webb, Campbell, Schwartz, & Sechrest (1966); Tapp, Kelman, Triandis, Wrightsman, & Coelho (1974) Observation of subjects who are unaware of being studied, thus eliminating a major source of experimental bias. This method, often used as a supplementary research strategy, may add to the credibility of other research data. The naturalistic basis of unobtrusive research may lend further credibility to generalizations and conclusions.	1. The equivalence of the behavior observed and the meaning of the experimental situation needs to be assured.
		2. The frequency of the observed behavior is frequently unknown and may vary across cultural groups.
		3. Internal validity of the study may be difficult to establish, e.g., the contrived situation may have different meanings across cultures. The constancy of the desired stimulus needs to be assured.
		4. It is difficult to standardize measurement in unobtrusive studies.
		5. The type of information revealed in unobtrusive research is descriptive (the "what" of behavior), not directly reflecting causes (the "why" of behavior). Causation is often difficult to infer.
		6. A series of studies of specific hypotheses is usually required rather than single-shot research. The studies need to be tied to a theoretical view to be meaningful.
		7. Some unobtrusive methods, e.g., trace method, may have limited applicability for clinical research problems.

Table 9.3. *Continued*

Data sources and processes	*Goals of research*	*Potential methodological problems*

Unobtrusive Research: Naturalistic Observation (Continued)

| | | 8. External validity of unobtrusive research is difficult to establish; thus this facet of the research should be given serious consideration. |
| | | 9. Research on human subjects without their consent may present numerous ethical problems. |

Survey Methods

Samples of respondents are determined according to some specified criteria and given questionnaires. The questionnaire responses are scored or analyzed and interpreted by comparing responses across cultural units.	Brislin, Lonner, & Thorndike (1973); Frey (1970); Kish (1965); Pareek & Rao (1980); Warwick & Lininger (1975) To obtain respondent views about psychological variables from generally large samples. The data are used to test hypotheses and establish generality of theories across cultural groups.	1. Assuring survey topic relevance in all cultural groups.
		2. Assuring comparable meanings for psychological characteristics studied.
		3. Assuring adequate translation of items; both linguistic and psychological adequacy should be ascertained.
		4. Clarity of research goals is required for the design of explicit questionnaires.
		5. Questionnaire format may limit types of content included with study, e.g., sensitive and highly personal information are probably not appropriate.
		6. Pretesting of materials is extremely important to assure relevance, adequacy, appropriateness, and acceptability of the questions.
		7. Indigeneous and equally credible sources (sponsorship) of the survey are required in each culture.
		8. Sampling design is extremely critical to the conclusion of the study. Comparable cross-cultural samples need to be assured.
		9. Questionnaire research may have problem in cross-cultural research, since some cultural groups may have low reading level, or may be unaccustomed to questionnaire tasks.
		10. Mailed questionnaires tend to have low response rates. Methods of determining the comparability of samples need to be developed to assure that comparable samples are obtained.

Table 9.3. *Continued*

Data sources and processes	Goals of research	Potential methodological problems
	Interview	
Self-reported verbal information is obtained through the process of personal interaction. Respondents are asked to provide information about themselves or their environmental context in a series of questions. Interviewers record code and interpret their responses.	Brislin, Lonner, & Thorndike (1973); Kahn & Cannel (1961); Matarazzo & Wiens (1972); Pareek & Rao (1980); Wiens (1976) To obtain personal information on individuals for purposes of comparison with responses of individuals in other situations. Interview data can be used to provide descriptive accounts, to formulate hypotheses, and to serve as a basis for comparing theoretical views cross-culturally.	1. Interviewers need to employ rapport-gaining techniques that maximize self-disclosure. Self-disclosure behavior may differ extremely across cultures. 2. Interview content needs to be carefully selected, since some topics are taboo in some cultures. 3. Status and affiliation of interviewers will influence respondent cooperation; thus program sponsorship needs to be carefully weighed. 4. Authenticity or accuracy of respondents' responses needs to be assured. Response sets in interviews may be particularly problematic in some cultural settings. 5. Rapport-gaining techniques differ across cultures. Thus culturally appropriate and maximally effective approaches need to be developed. 6. Interview settings and arrangements may need to be varied in different cultural contexts. For example, in some cultures home-based interviews may be more appropriate, while in others a different setting may be required. How respondents are contacted and who conducts the interview (e.g., male or female) may determine the quality, quantity, and accuracy of the responses. 7. The selection and training of interviewers are important considerations. Use of indigeneous personnel who are familiar with the culture is a necessity. Since rapport-gaining techniques differ cross-culturally, different types or personalities of interviewers are important variables.

Table 9.3. *Continued*

Data sources and processes	*Goals of research*	*Potential methodological problems*
	Interview (Continued)	
		8. Type of interview is an important consideration. Free, open-ended interviews do not provide uniform and consistent data for rigorous cross-cultural research. Structured interviews, in which questions are structured according to content and sequence, are more readily quantified and compared. However, structured interviews may be cumbersome and too rigid for use in some cultural contexts and thus produce reduced cooperation.
		9. Adequacy and reliability of interview data depends to a great extent upon objectivity and skill of interviewers. Interviewer bias may be even more problematic in studies employing interviewers from diverse cultural backgrounds. Interviewer bias and the comparability of the interview data across research groups needs to be assured.
		10. Relative unreliability of interview research may be ameliorated by using a reinterviewing procedure as a reliability check.
	Achievement, Cognitive, and Intellectual Assessment	
Responses to standard stimuli purported to reflect psychological attributes involved in achievement, intelligence, or cognitive behavior.	Brislin, Lonner, & Thorndike (1973); Cronbach & Drenth (1972); Irvine & Carroll (1980); Kendall & Hollon (1981) The use of standardized tests to measure, to compare, or to test performance differences between diverse cultural groups.	1. Response differences to standard stimuli in different cultural groups may be subject to numerous alternative hypotheses.
		2. Differing educational systems or experiences with instruments of advanced technology (e.g., television) might influence cultural group variation.
		3. Some cultural groups may not be familiar with testing "tasks."
		4. Motivation to perform well or poorly may vary, thus resulting in obtained performance deficits.
		5. The presence of "foreigners" or the use of foreign tests may adversely influence test performances in some groups.
		6. Translation of instructions and test materials need to be carefully studied and assured.

Table 9.3. *Continued*

Data sources and processes	Goals of research	Potential methodological problems

Achievement, Cognitive, and Intellectual Assessment (Continued)

		7. Stimulus materials must be shown to be equivalent in all cultures under investigation.
		8. Guiding constructs (intelligence, cognitive complexity, conservation, achievement motivation, etc.) must be shown to have relevance and similar structural makeup in the cultures under investigation.
		9. If standardized measures or tests are used, new norms should be developed for target populations. In cases where multination norms are available, it should be assured that the test parameters for the target population are equivalent.
		10. Factor analysis should be employed to ascertain the factorial validities cross-culturally.
		11. Multimethod, multiculture research is preferable to single-variable, two-culture studies.
		12. An adequate sampling of behavior that has been "overlearned" in each culture should be represented in the measures.

Personality Assessment: Projective Techniques

Projective techniques are indirect measures of personality. Subjects respond to or associate with ambiguous stimuli such as inkblots, pictures, sentence stems, etc. The responses are scored, coded, or organized in some way. Interpretation may be based on: (a) the structure of the subjects' performance, e.g., number, quality or type of response, whether they respond to whole or part of stimulus, use of color, etc; or (b) the content of the response. Content analysis may follow a particular personality theory such as psychoanalysis.	Holtzman (1980); Lindzey (1961) To compare inferred personality characteristics of subjects or group performances across cultures.	1. Low reliability characterizes the scoring and interpretation procedures. 2. Often projective research is contaminated in that interpretations need to be based upon external factors. Responses are not interpreted at face value. 3. Situational factors and context greatly influences projective test responses. 4. Interpretation systems and practices are too subjective to be employed in research. 5. Number of responses generally differ between *S*s, thus limiting psychometric treatment of data. 6. Equivalence between scores, scoring categories, meanings of responses cannot be assured between cultural groups.

Table 9.3. *Continued*

Data sources and processes	*Goals of research*	*Potential methodological problems*
	Personality Assessment: Projective Technique (Continued)	
		7. Too much time is required for administration, scoring, and interpretation.
		8. Training of personnel to administer, score, and interpret responses is quite expensive and may overly tax the resources of other national research teams.
		9. The cost of projective techniques is generally too high for extensive cross-cultural research.
	Personality Assessment: Questionnaires	
Responses of individuals to verbal written items are scored to provide summary profiles of personality. Responses and scale scores are compared both with subjects from the same culture and with test norms derived in other cultures.	Brislin, Lonner, & Thorndike (1973); Butcher & Pancheri (1976) To compare individual and group personality characteristics on standardized objective measures.	1. Literacy is required of subjects.
		2. Translation problems include the necessity to get translations that are both linguistically and psychologically equivalent versions of the original.
		3. Conceptual equivalence must be shown: do the test scores measure the same constructs in the target culture?
		4. The test score interrelationships, e.g., factor structure should be demonstrated to be equivalent.
		5. Response bias may occur in some cultures.
		6. Some cultures may be unaccustomed to personality questionnaire formats.
		7. New test norms may need to be developed in the target cultures.
		8. Construct and predictive validities of instruments need to be assured.
	Clinical Diagnosis	
Clinical interview, informant report, personal history, clinical observations, and possibly psychological tests are employed to place an individual's behavior and problems into a diagnostic classification. The system employed may be one of the standard nosological systems widely used in western cultures (1CD–9, DSM–III, Reseach Diagnostic Criteria, etc.) or may be specially developed for the national groups being studied.	Butcher & Pancheri (1976); Dohrenwend & Dohrenwend (1969); Draguns (1980); Marsella (1979); Murphy & Leighton (1965); Sartorius, Jablensky, & Shapiro (1978); Wittkower & Dubreil (1973) To classify individuals or groups of patients into homogeneous problem types in order to compare psychological disturbance cross-culturally.	1. Available nosological systems (DSM–III, 1CD–9, etc.) are rigid systems that do not include the behavior problems, symptoms, etc., manifest in some cultures.
		2. Available nosological systems suffer from problems of reliability and validity, even in Western nations where they were developed. Cross-national applications may result in more serious reliability and validity problems.
		3. Ethnocentricity of Western concepts of psychopathology may limit their application to other groups.

298

Table 9.3. *Continued*

Data sources and processes	Goals of research	Potential methodological problems
	Clinical Diagnosis (Continued)	
		4. Different cultural groups may define "abnormality" differently. There is no unambiguous standard index of disturbance that applies cross-culturally.
		5. Symptoms may be differently expressed in different cultures.
		6. A particular symptom crucial to the classification of a disorder may have different frequencies in different cultures.
		7. Rates of various disorders may differ across cultures.
		8. Underlying causes of psychological disorder may differ in different cultures. Cultures differ in the amount and type of stressors they present.
		9. Some cultural groups employ different personality "defenses," e.g., projection, internalization, thus influencing the form and expression of disorder.
		10. Although similarities in diagnostic picture may be seen for some disorders, the prognosis and course of the disorder may differ considerably.
		11. Psychodiagnostic practices differ in different cultures partly due to training of clinician, reliance on different systems, and the forms of disorder the clinician is accustomed to seeing. Thus studies using clinical diagnosis across cultural groups need to employ standard classification system, cross-cultural reliability checks, and a standard training program.
	Controlled Experiments	
Comparison of psychological responses given to standard stimuli in experimental conditions vs. responses in untreated control groups across two or more cultural settings.	Brislin, Lonner, & Thorndike (1973); Brown & Sechrest (1980); Cole, Gay, Glick, & Sharp (1971); Werner & Campbell (1970); Price-Williams (1972); Sechrest (1977)	1. The meaning of experimental research can best be interpreted in the context of theory. Research conducted in the absence of a clear explanatory view is noncumulative.
		2. One-shot cross-cultural experiments are weak. Research should be in the context of a series of studies testing related hypotheses.

Table 9.3.   *Continued*

Data sources and processes	Goals of research	Potential methodological problems
	Controlled Experiments (Continued)	
	Determining causal relationships of variables in cross-cultural research by manipulating or controlling the efforts of some variables and observing the influences upon others.	3. Cross-cultural experimental research should not be evaluated in isolation but should be interpreted in the context of other research, e.g., ethnographic data.
		4. Equivalence of experimental conditions between cultures needs to be determined, e.g., that the variables appear and are identical in all cultures studied.
		5. Translation problems may account for experimental results; thus careful attention needs to be paid to what is being communicated.
		6. Pretesting of all variables and manipulations is required, with a careful assessment of the experimental manipulation.
		7. The experimental conditions may need to be altered for some cultural groups—"experimenting with experiments."
		8. Internal validity of the experiment needs to be carefully assessed, assuring random assignment to groups and the provision of at least one untreated control group in each culture.
		9. Construct validity of the research should be maximized by multiple operations to eliminate confounding elements.
		10. Statistical conclusion validity should be carefully assured. Assuring the appropriateness of statistical procedures used, determining a critical effect size, selecting the most appropriate sample size, etc.

the study. What are the psychological attributes to be studied, and are these variables sufficiently and equivalently represented in all populations? How available are the data, or how easy or difficult will it be to collect this information from available samples?

What constraints will be placed on the study by such sample characteristics as: size of sample, heterogeneity within cultures, poor reading ability of subjects, lack of sophistication about research, suspiciousness about "strangers," and so on. What is the level of cooperation that can be expected of indigenous research collaborations? Will extensive training programs need to be carried out? How can collaborators be supervised in the field or, as it frequently occurs in cross-cultural research, from a great geographic distance?

Relative Efficiencies or Power of Cross-Cultural Study Methods

Choice of research methods is influenced by a number of general and practical considerations. Among the factors that dictate the scope and conduct of the research are the *cost* elements. What are the financial bases of the research? Financial matters enter into such considerations as funds for the purchase of material, travel for investigators, salaries for field workers, and clerical and data computation resources that are essential to the study; and indirect costs also need consideration, for example, subjects' time and the *time* required of indigenous research collaborators. Cross-cultural study is one of the most expensive research endeavors and also one of the most difficult areas to obtain research support. Researchers in the cross-cultural area usually must ask themselves "what research is possible on a limited research budget?" rather than "which methods will provide me with the most and most useful information?"

Often related to the question of financial resources is the issue of *sponsorship* for the research. Certain research questions and perhaps the research strategies to be used will depend upon who or what organization sponsors the research. An excellent discussion of sponsorship issues and how this factor might determine the shape of research is provided in Warwick (1980). Whether a project is financially supported by government agencies, church organizations, international health organizations, or other institutions can have a direct influence upon the "acceptability" of the research topic, and the means for collecting data. Sponsorship may also determine

whether the research is acceptable to the various cultural groups to be studied. Even when sponsorship does not involve a financial commitment to the research, the status (or lack thereof) and image of the sponsoring group determines to a significant degree whether the research can be conducted and whether research subjects will cooperate fully.

Ethical considerations about the conduct and use of psychological procedures has become a central concern for cross-cultural researchers in recent years (Tapp et al., 1974; Warwick, 1980). The employment of certain research strategies, such as deception research or unobtrusive designs, may be unacceptable for cross-cultural studies. Varying ethical standards about psychological research in different cultures may present difficult questions for the researchers to resolve before research is initiated.

Acceptability of the research topic is an important and sensitive question for cross-cultural investigators to explore. Are there issues that might not be researchable because the content of research questions or the directness with which they are asked might be offensive? It could be that some methods of collecting data, such as asking informants about a subject's behavior, may not be acceptable. It has even been found that comparative research generally may be unacceptable in some cultures in which officials and even research psychologists are concerned that their country might suffer from invidious comparison with other nations.

The environmental impact of the research needs to be considered. What immediate problems might result with the use of particular research methods? Will some research methods result in less serious or better yet *no* problems while the data are being collected? The investigator should also consider the consequences of the completed research project. How will the information be used? Will there be negative reactions to the findings of the study? A related consideration is whether the research has any intrinsic, heuristic, or practical value to the people in the different countries involved. The question of what the payoff will be for the countries participating in the study is an important one (Jahoda, 1974). Will the results of the study be more beneficial to the countries involved if certain research questions are asked or if different strategies are taken?

The research designs and data collection methods will be determined in large part, in cross-cultural studies, by the particular make-up of the available samples of subjects. Sampling problems are among the most difficult constraints that cross-cultural researchers face (see Manaster & Havighurst, 1972, for a thorough discussion). Whether or not subjects are literate, are cooperative to research tasks, have the necessary time available, or are capable of responding objectively will determine, for example, whether one chooses a questionnaire method versus an interview or observational approach. The size of the available sample may limit the types of analyses and statistical procedures used in the study.

The research design will also be influenced by the general purposes of the study and the level of generalization the investigator hopes to achieve. Some of the designs employed in cross-cultural research are more exploratory, that is, provide a broad range of information that may vary in accuracy, veridicality, and reliability, yet may be sufficient for preliminary scientific aims or for generating further hypotheses. Other research designs may aim to test more specific hypotheses or theories and provide quite accurate information over a narrow range of behavior. The researcher's goals and desires regarding the generalizability of the proposed research should have a bearing on the types of research strategies that are chosen.

Multimethod Approaches

In order to avoid the tunnel vision that frequently accompanies the use of a single methodological approach, many research theorists recommend the use of multimethod

research strategies for cross-cultural studies (Tapp, 1980). It is clear that our view of a phenomenon or the results of an investigation is highly influenced by the constructs, observations, and methods by which we approach our topic. This is at the same time both the strength and weakness of empirical science. The reliance on a given method dictates what we ignore as well as what we see. It determines whether we look at the whole or the component parts, whether we count varieties of behavior or seek to define relationships. Our method is both our eyesight and our blindness.

Research programs that can accommodate the use of several research strategies will be strengthened in that the known limitations of one approach might be offset or strengthened by data provided through an alternate method. For example, the studies that employ the generally unreliable clinical approach, clinical diagnosis, might be strengthened by the use of a more reliable, objective personality questionnaire or stringently defined behavioral observation criteria. Or a quite narrow experiment aimed at exploring cognitive styles that uses a standard cognitive testing situation would be strengthened by employing an ethnographic study to explore obtained differences (Cole et al., 1971).

The multimethod multidisciplinary approach to cross-cultural research has been considered to be the most sound research strategy. Tapp (1980) recommended what she called an Elephant Research Strategy (ERS) (taken from the story of the three blind men who were asked to describe an elephant, an animal they had never seen, by sampling different features of its anatomy; one held the tail, another the trunk, and another the foot). This strategy's central underlying assumption is that a single approach is not sufficient to provide a veridical view of cross-cultural phenomena. She recommends a multidisciplinary strategy that includes elements of ecological, ethnographic, ethnocentric, ethological, ethical, and experimental approaches to knowledge. The various views of human behavior that can be obtained through using a multimethod approach will more accurately reflect the complexities of human personality. However, the multimethod approach to cross-cultural psychology is not without its problems. The summation of negative findings, even from different methods, remains insignificant. If the research methods employed do not rule out plausible alternative hypotheses through following rigorous procedures, the total research product will still add up to zero.

Another problem that needs to be weighed, preferably in advance of the research, is: what does one do with inconsistent and incompatible findings resulting from the use of different methods? How are disagreements in conclusions resolved? Other factors that are critical to the employment of multimethod research strategies involve matters of cost of the project and the necessity of providing for training in the clear and competent application of all methods in every culture involved. Once these problems are resolved in a satisfactory manner, the multimethod approach to cross-cultural problems promises to resolve significant problems generated by monomethod limitations. The use of a multitrait-multimethod strategy, in which both discriminant and convergent validity are examined, should enable cross-cultural researchers to evaluate, to some extent, the results of multimethod investigations.

SUMMARY

The discipline of clinical psychology has, in the past few years, expanded its horizons beyond the clinics and laboratories of Western middle class society. Clinical methods and procedures have been increasingly employed in international programs of application and research, as well as being more extensively applied with heterogeneous multiethnic groups in the United States and Canada. Both the extensive international "exchange" of clinical methods and techniques and the greater application of clinical methods to minority, ethnic, and refugee populations in modern Western societies has made many clinical researchers aware of the growing field of cross-cultural psychology and acutely concerned about potential limitations of our basic techniques when adapted to new cultural contexts.

Rigorous research designs that are based on a cross-cultural perspective are becoming central elements in much clinical psychological research. Several areas of extensive multicultural research in clinical psychology were highlighted: efforts to understand personality development from a cross-cultural perspective; examination of the "universality" of clinical diagnosis and assessment; the expanding adaptation of psychological tests in different cultures; and the increased need for the therapists from one culture to treat patients from different national, ethnic, or social backgrounds. Work in these areas has demonstrated the importance of the cross-cultural perspective in clinical psychology and the necessity of employing cross-cultural research strategies.

Several important issues in cross-cultural psychological research were discussed to sensitize the reader to the complex nature of cross-cultural research. It is extremely difficult to conduct rigorous cross-national research. Several factors that bear on the validity of the research and the ultimate generalizability of the findings were considered. The important issue of whether to study a culture in and of itself as opposed to comparing it with other cultures (the emic-etic controversy) requires consideration. Although cross-cultural research necessarily involves examining or comparing several cultures, it is important to be aware that such comparative evaluations require some "standardization" and force fitting. The researcher who is aware of the trade-offs required in etic research, that is, aware of the loss of emic (culture specific) information, may be appropriately more conservative in generalization from the findings. I also noted the limitations inherent in two-culture comparisons and recommended, when possible, the inclusion of a broad range of cultures in the research. I considered the often held viewpoint that research, if it is to be cumulative, must be in the service of theory. Although this view was discarded in terms of adhering strictly to "general" theories of behavior, the conclusion was that research in the framework of existing accumulated knowledge was indeed important. Research done in isolation or simply playing around with a sample of convenience is not likely to contribute much to the field.

Some of the most serious threats to the validity of cross-cultural research, the problems of equivalence, were discussed, and suggestions for alleviating these problems were made. The importance of indigenous collaboration and some problems that go along with cross-cultural research collaboration were noted. It is clear that, while necessary, cross-cultural research collaboration is often more an ideal than a practical reality. Problems of research collaboration and political forces present some of the most challenging threats to successful research. Investigators should attempt to become aware of potential problems well in advance of their emergence—and always expect the unexpected. Problems of communication, particularly those involving translation of materials, were considered in some detail. An extensive guide to adequate translation was presented along with some problems that can result from weak translations.

In the final section of the paper I surveyed the most widely used cross-cultural research methods. These methods were presented in tabular form (Table 9.3) for handy reference. The goal of the method, selected references, and some potential problems with each approach were presented. Some rationale for using the various approaches, along with some criteria for their inclusion in projects, were presented. The recommendation for employing a multimethod research strategy was discussed.

It is likely that the cross-cultural perspective in clinical psychology will gain in importance over the coming years. The world indeed appears to be growing smaller and more intertwined; events in previously remote parts of the world now have immediate and profound impact on our very existence. Clinical psychology has traditionally and actively spilled over into new and broadened areas of application as environmental needs arise. We may see the day when psychology sheds its ethnocentric mantle and becomes truly the science of human behavior. Clinical psychology, with its emphasis upon real life problems, has an invitation to become multicultural and international in its scope. Time will tell if its methods and procedures are robust enough to survive the cross-culture shock.

REFERENCES

Allport, G. W. (1937). *Personality, a psychological interpretation*. New York: Holt.

Barry, H., III (1980). Description and uses of the Human Relations Area files. In H. C. Triandis & J. W. Berry (Eds.), *Handbook of cross-cultural psychology*, Vol. 2. Boston: Allyn & Bacon.

Berry, J. W. (1979). Research in multicultural societies: Implications of cross-cultural methods. *Journal of Cross-Cultural Psychology*, **10** (4), 415–434.

Bochner, S. (1980). Unobtrusive methods of cross cultural research. In H. C. Triandis and J. W. Berry (Eds.), *Handbook of cross-cultural psychology*, Vol. 2. Boston: Allyn & Bacon.

Bochner, S. (1971). The use of unobtrusive measures in cross-cultural research. In R. M. Berndt (Ed.), *A question of choice: An Australian Aboriginal dilemma*. Nedlands, W. A.: University of Western Australia Press.

Brislin, R. W. (1980). Analysis of oral and written materials. In H. C. Triandis & J. W. Berry (Eds.), *Handbook of Cross Cultural Psychology*, Vol. 2. Boston: Allyn & Bacon.

Brislin, R. (1970). Back translation for cross cultural research. *Journal of Cross-Cultural Psychology*, **1**, 185–216.

Brislin, R. W., Lonner, W. J., & Thorndike, R. M. (1973). *Cross-cultural research methods*. New York: Wiley.

Brown, E. D., & Sechrest, L. (1980). Experiments in cross cultural research. In H. C. Triandis & J. W. Berry (Eds.), *Handbook of cross-cultural psychology*, Vol. 2. Boston: Allyn & Bacon.

Buss, A. R., & Royce, J. R. (1975). Detecting cross-cultural communalities and differences: Intergroup factor analysis. *Psychological Bulletin, 82*, 128–136.

Butcher, J. N., & Clarke, L. A. (1979). Recent trends in cross-cultural MMPI research and application. In J. N. Butcher (Ed.), *New developments in the use of the MMPI*. Minneapolis: University of Minnesota Press.

Butcher, J. N., & Garcia, R. (1978). Cross-national application of psychological tests. *Personnel and Guidance, 56*, 472–475.

Butcher, J. N., & Gur, R. (1974). A Hebrew translation of the MMPI: An assessment of translation adequacy and preliminary validation. *Journal of Cross-Cultural Psychology, 5*, 220–227.

Butcher, J. N., & Pancheri, P. (1976). *Handbook of cross-national MMPI research*. Minneapolis: University of Minnesota Press.

Butcher, J. N., & Tellegen, A. (1978). Common methodological problems in MMPI research, *Journal of Consulting and Clinical Psychology, 46*, 620–628.

Campbell, D. T. (1964). Distinguishing differences of perception from failures in communication in cross-cultural studies. In F. S. C. Northrop & H. H. Livingston, *Cross-cultural understanding: Epistemology in anthropology*. New York: Harper & Row.

Charlesworth, W. P., & Spiker, D. (1975). An ethological approach to observation in learning settings. In R. A. Weinberg & F. H. Woods (Eds.) *Observation of pupils and teachers in mainstream and special education settings*. Minnesota: Leadership Training Institute Special Edition.

Colby, B., & Peacock, J. (1973). Narrative. In J. Honigmann (Ed.), *Handbook of social and cultural anthropology*. Chicago: Rand McNally.

Cole, M., Gay, J., Glick, J, & Sharp, D. (1971). *The cultural context of learning and thinking*. New York: Basic Books.

Cooper, J. E., Kendall, R. E., Gurland, B. J., Sharpe, L., Copeland, J. R. M., & Simon, R. (1972). *Psychiatric diagnosis in New York and London*. New York: Oxford University Press.

Cronbach, L. J., & Drenth, P. J. D. (Eds.) (1972). *Mental tests and cultural adaptation*. The Hague: Mouton.

Dasen, P. (1972). Cross-cultural Piagetian research: A summary. *Journal of Cross-Cultural Psychology, 3*, 23–40.

Devereux, E., Bronfenbrenner, U., & Suci, G. (1962). Patterns of parent behavior in the United States of America and the Federal Republic of Germany: A Cross-national comparison. *International Social Science Journal, 14*, 488–506.

Dohrenwend, B., & Dohrenwend, B. (1969). *Social status and psychological disorder: A causal inquiry*. New York: Wiley.

Dohrenwend, B. P., & Dohrenwend, B. S. (1974). Social and cultural influences on psychopathology. *Annual Review of Psychology, 25*, 417–423.

Draguns, J. G. (1975). Resocialization into culture: The complexities of taking a worldwide view of psychotherapy. In R. W. Brislin, S. Bochner, & W. J. Lonner (Eds.), *Cross-cultural perspectives on learning*. New York: Wiley.

Draguns, J. G. (1979). Culture and personality. In A. J. Marsella, R. Tharp, & T. Cibrowski (Eds.), *Perspectives on cross-cultural psychology*. New York: Academic Press.

Draguns, J. G. (1977). Advances in the methodology of cross-cultural psychiatric assessment. *Transcultural Psychiatric Research Review, 14*, 125–143.

Draguns, J. G. (1980). Psychological disorders in clinical severity. In H. C. Triandis & J. Draguns (Eds.), *Handbook of Cross-cultural Psychology*, Vol. 5. Boston: Allyn & Bacon.

DuBois, P. H. (1970). *A history of psychological testing*. Boston: Allyn & Bacon.

Ekman, P. (1973). Cross-cultural studies of facial expression. In P. Ekman (Ed.), *Darwin and facial expressions: A century of research in review*. New York: Academic Press.

Feighner, J. P., Robins, E., Guze, S. B., Woodruff, R. A., Winoker, G., & Munoz, R. (1972). Diagnostic criteria for use in psychiatric research. *Archives of General Psychiatry, 26*, 57–63.

Fiske, D. W. (1974). The limits for the conventional sciences of personality. *Journal of Personality, 42*, 1–10.

Frey, F. (1970). Cross-cultural survey research in political science. In R. Holt & J. Turner (Eds.), *The methodology of comparative research*. New York: Free Press.

Frijda, N., & Jahoda, G. (1966). On the scope and methods of cross-cultural research. *International Journal of Psychology, 1*, 109–127.

Goodenough, W. H. (1980). Ethnographic field techniques. In H. C. Triandis & J. W. Berry (Eds.), *Handbook of cross-cultural psychology*, Vol. 2. Boston: Allyn & Bacon.

Gottesman, I. I., & Schields, J. (1972). Schizophrenia and genetics: A twin study vantage point. New York: Academic Press.

Gough, H. G. (1964). A cross-cultural study of achievement motivation. *Journal of Applied Psychology*, **48**, 191–196.

Guthrie, G. M. (1975). A behavioral analysis of culture learning. In R. W. Brislin, S. Bochner, & W. Lonner (Eds.), *Cross-cultural perspectives on learning*. New York: Wiley.

Guthrie, G. M., & Bennett, A. B., Jr. (1971). Cultural differences in implicit personality theory. *International Journal of Psychology*, **6**, 305–312.

Hathaway, S. R. (1972). Where have we gone wrong: The mystery of missing progress. In J. N. Butcher (Ed.), *Objective personality assessment: Changing perspectives*. New York: Academic Press.

Henderson, G. (Ed.) (1979). *Understanding and counseling ethnic minorities*. Springfield, Ill.: Charles C. Thomas.

Holsti, O. (1968). Content analysis. In G. Lindzey & E. Aronson (Eds.), *Handbook of social psychology* (2nd ed.), Vol. 2. Reading, Mass.: Addison-Wesley.

Holtzman, W. H. (1973). Cross-cultural and longitudinal comparisons of cognitive, perceptual and personality measures in Mexico and the United States. Paper presented at the American Educational Research Association Meeting, New Orleans.

Holtzman, W. H. (1980). Projective techniques. In H. C. Triandis & J. Berry (Eds.), *Handbook of Cross-cultural psychology*, Vol. 2. Boston: Allyn & Bacon.

Honigmann, J. J. (1970). Sampling in ethnographic field work. In R. R. Narroll & R. Cohen (Eds.), *A handbook of method in cultural anthropology*. New York: Natural History Press.

Hudson, B., Barakat, B., & Laforge, R. (1959). Problems and methods of cross-cultural research. *Journal of Social Issues*, **15**, 5–19.

Inkeles, A. (1971). Continuity and change in the interaction of the personal and the sociocultural systems. In B. Barber & A. Inkeles (Eds.), *Stability and social change*. Boston: Little, Brown.

Irvine, S. H., & Carroll, W. K. (1980). Testing and assessment across cultures. In H. C. Triandis & J. W. Berry (Eds.), *Handbook of Cross-cultural Psychology: Methodology*, Vol. 2. Boston: Allyn & Bacon.

Jahoda, G. (1974). Is cross-cultural psychology in a crisis? Symposium given at the Second International Conference of the International Association for Cross-Cultural Psychology, Kingston, Ontario.

Jahoda, G. (1980). Theoretical and systematic approaches in cross-cultural psychology. In H. C. Triandis & W. W. Lambert (Eds.), *Handbook of cross-cultural psychology*. Vol. 1. Boston: Allyn & Bacon.

Kahn, R. L., & Cannel, C. F. (1961). *The dynamics of interviewing: Theory, techniques and cases*. New York: Wiley.

Kazdin, A. E. (1980). *Research design in clinical psychology*. New York: Harper & Row.

Kendall, P. C., & Mollon, S. D. (Eds.). (1981). *Assessment strategies for cognitive-behavioral interventions*. New York: Academic Press.

Kim, K. S. (1979). Use of the MMPI in Korea. In J. Butcher, H. Hama, & Y. Matsuyama, (Eds.), *Proceedings of the 6th International Conference on Personality Assessment*. Kyoto: Doshisha University.

Kish, L. (1965). *Survey sampling*. New York: Wiley.

Kosugi, Y., Tsujimoto, S., Tanaka, M., & Masumoto, Y. (1979). Personality of alcoholics. In J. Butcher, H. Hama, & Y. Matsuyama (Eds.), *Proceedings of the 6th International Conference on Personality Assessment*. Kyoto: Doshisha.

Lagace, R. O. (1974). Nature and use of the HRAF files; a research and teaching guide. New Haven: Human Relations Area Files, Inc.

Leiderman, P. H., Tulkin, S. R., & Rosenfeld, A. (1977). *Culture and infancy: Variations in the human experience*. New York: Academic Press.

Leighton, A. H., Lambo, T. A., Hughes, C. C., Leighton, D. C., Murphy, J. M., & Macklin, D. B. (1963). *Psychiatric disorders among the Yoruba*. Ithaca: Cornell University Press.

Lindzey, G. (1961). *Projective techniques in cross-cultural research*. New York: Appleton-Century-Crofts.

Longabaugh, R. (1980). The systematic observation of behavior in naturalistic settings. In H. C. Triandis & J. W. Berry (Eds.), *Handbook of cross-cultural psychology*, Vol. 2. Boston: Allyn & Bacon.

Lonner, W. (1980). The search for psychological universals. In H. C. Triandis & W. W. Lambert (Eds.), *Handbook of cross-cultural psychology*, Vol. 1. Boston: Allyn & Bacon.

Lopez-Ortiz, A. (1979). MMPI responses of schizophrenics and normals in Mexico. In J. Butcher, H. Hama, & Y. Matsuyama (Eds.), Proceedings of the *6th International Conference on Personality Assessment*. Kyoto: Doshisha University.

Lynn, R. (1971). *Personality and national character*. Oxford: Pergamon Press.

Lynn, R., & Hampson, S. L. (1975). National differences in extraversion and neuroticism. *British Journal of Social and Clinical Psychology*, **14**, 223–240.

Lynn, R., & Hampson, S. L. (1977). Fluctuations in

national levels of neuroticism and extraversion. *British Journal of Social and Clinical Psychology,* **16,** 131–137.

Manaster, G. J., & Havighurst, R. J. (1972). *Cross-national research: Social psychological methods and problems.* New York: Houghton Mifflin.

Marsella, A. J. (1979). Cross cultural studies of mental disorders. In A. J. Marsella, R. Tharp, & T. Cibrowski (Eds.), *Perspectives in cross-cultural psychology.* New York: Academic Press.

Matarazzo, J. D., & Wiens, A. N. (1972). *The interview: Research on its anatomy and structure.* Chicago: Aldine-Atherton.

McClelland, D. (1961). *The achieving society.* Princeton, N.J.: Van Nostrand.

Meehl, P. E. (1969). Nuisance variables and the ex post facto design. *Reports from the Research Laboratories of the Department of Psychiatry, University of Minnesota, Report No. PR 6904.* Minneapolis: University of Minnesota.

Merbaum, M., & Hefez, A. (1977). Some personality characteristics of soldiers exposed to extreme war stress. *Journal of Consulting and Clinical Psychology,* **33,** 558–562.

Mirza, L. (1976). Translation and standardization of the MMPI for Pakistan. In J. N. Butcher & P. Pancheri (Eds.), *Handbook of cross-national MMPI research.* Minneapolis: University of Minnesota Press.

Murdock, G. P. (1975). *Outline of world cultures* (5th ed., revised). New Haven: Human Relations Area files.

Murdock, G. P. (1967). *Ethnographic atlas.* Pittsburgh: University of Pittsburgh Press.

Murphy, J., & Leighton, A. (Eds.), (1965). *Approaches to cross-cultural psychiatry.* Ithaca, N.Y.: Cornell University Press.

Naroll, R. (1970). "Galton's problem," in R. Naroll & R. Cohen (Eds.), *Handbook of method in cultural anthropology.* New York: Natural History Press.

Naroll, R., Michik, G., & Naroll, F. (1980b). Holocultural research methods. In H. C. Triandis & J. W. Berry (Eds.), *Handbook of cross-cultural psychology,* Vol. 2. Boston: Allyn & Bacon.

Naroll, R., Michik, G., & Naroll, F. (1974a). Hologeistic theory testing. In J. G. Jorgensen (Ed.), *Comparative studies by H. E. Driver and essays in his honor.* New Haven: Human Relations Area files Press.

Nunez, R. (1968). *Aplicacion del Inventario multifasico de la personalidad (MMPI) a la psicopathologia* (Application of the MMPI to psychopathology). Mexico: El Manual Moderno, S. A.

Pancheri, P. (1971). Metodo per la valutazione quantitativa della sintomatologia schizofrenica attraverso l'impiego del MMPI (A method for the quantitative evaluation of schizophrenic symptoms by means of the MMPI). *Rivesta di Psichiatria,* **6,** 64–84.

Pareek, U., & Rao, T. V. (1980). Cross-cultural surveys and interviewing. In H. C. Triandis & J. W. Berry (Eds.), *Handbook of cross-cultural psychology,* Vol. 2. Boston: Allyn & Bacon.

Phillips, L., & Draguns, J. (1971). Classification of behavior disorders. *Annual Review of Psychology,* **22,** 447–482.

Pedersen, P. (1980). The cultural inclusiveness of counseling. In P. Pedersen, J. Draguns, W. Lonner, & J. Trimble (Eds.), *Counseling across cultures* (revised ed.). Honolulu: University of Hawaii.

Pelto, P. J., & Pelto, G. H. (1973). Ethnography: The fieldwork enterprise. In J. J. Honigmann (Ed.), *Handbook of social and cultural anthropology.* Chicago: Rand McNally.

Price-Williams, D. (1974). Psychological experiment and anthropology: The problem of categories. *Ethos,* **2,** 95–114.

Rissetti, F., Butcher, J. N., et al. (1979). Translation and adaptation of the MMPI in Chile. Paper given at the *14th Annual Conference on Recent Developments in the Use of the MMPI.* St. Petersburg.

Rosen, E. (1958). Translation and adaptation of personality tests for use in other cultures. Unpublished paper, University of Minnesota.

Sartorius, N., Jablensky, A., & Shapiro, R. (1978). Cross-cultural differences in short-term prognosis of schizophrenic psychoses. *Schizophrenia Bulletin,* **4,** 102–113.

Sechrest, L. (1977). On the need for experimentation in cross-cultural research. In L. L. Adler (Ed.), Issues in cross-cultural research. *Annals of the New York Academy of Science,* **285,** 104–118.

Sechrest, L., Fay, T., & Zaidi, S. (1972). Problems of translation in cross-cultural research. *Journal of Cross-cultural Psychology,* **1,** 41–56.

Segall, M., Campbell, D., & Herskovits, M. (1966). *The influence of culture on visual perception.* Indianapolis: Bobbs-Merrill.

Seifert, J., Draguns, J., & Caudill, W. (1971). Role orientation, sphere dominance, and social competence as bases of psychiatric diagnosis in Japan: A replication and extension of American findings. *Journal of Abnormal Psychology,* **78,** 101–106.

Sharma, S. (1977). Cross-cultural comparisons of anxiety: Methodological problems. *Topics in Culture Learning,* **5,** 166–173.

Spielberger, C. D., & Diaz-Guerro, R. (1976). *Cross-cultural anxiety.* New York: Wiley.

Strodtbeck, F. (1964). Considerations of meta-method in cross-cultural studies. *American Anthropologist,* **66**, 223–229.

Tapp, J. L. (1980). Studying personality development cross-culturally. In H. C. Triandis & A. Heron (Eds.), *Handbook of cross-cultural psychology,* Vol. 4. Boston: Allyn & Bacon.

Tapp, J. L., Kelman, H. C., Triandis, H. C., Wrightsman, L. S., & Coelho, G. V. (1974). Continuing concerns in cross-cultural ethics: A report. *International Journal of Psychology,* **9**, 231–249.

Torki, M. (1979). Validation of the Mf scale in Kuwait. In J. Butcher, H. Hama, & Y. Matsuyama (Eds.), *Proceedings of the 6th International Conference on Personality Assessment.* Kyoto: Doshisha University.

Torrey, E. F. (1972). *The mind game: Witchdoctors and psychiatrists.* New York: Emerson Hall.

Triandis, H. C. (1977). Cross-cultural social and personality psychology. *Personality and Social Psychology Bulletin,* **3**, 143–158.

Triandis, H. C. (1980). Introduction to Handbook of cross-cultural psychology. In H. C. Triandis & W. W. Lambert (Eds.), *Handbook of cross-cultural psychology,* Vol. 1. Boston: Allyn & Bacon.

Warwick, D. P. (1980). The politics and ethics of cross-cultural research. In H. C. Triandis & W. W. Lambert (Eds.), *Handbook of cross-cultural psychology,* Vol. I. Boston: Allyn & Bacon.

Warwick, D. P., & Lininger, C. (1975). *The sample survey: Theory and practice.* New York: McGraw-Hill.

Webb, E. J., Campbell, D. T., Schwartz, R. D., & Sechrest, L. (1966). *Unobtrusive measures: Nonreactive research in the social sciences.* Chicago: Rand McNally.

Werner, O., & Campbell, D. (1970). Translating, working through interpreters, and the problem of decentering. In R. Naroll & R. Cohen (Eds.), *A handbook of method in cultural anthropology.* New York: American Museum of Natural History.

Whiting, J. (1954). The cross-cultural method. In G. Lindzey (Ed.), *Handbook of social psychology,* Vol. 1. Reading, Mass.: Addison-Wesley.

Whiting, J. W. M., & Whiting, B. B. (1975). *Children of six cultures: A psychocultural analysis.* Cambridge, Mass.: Harvard University Press.

Whiting, J. W. M., Child, I. L., & Lambert, W. W. (1966). *Field guide for the study of socialization: Six cultures series,* Vol. 1. New York: Wiley.

Wiens, A. N. (1976). The assessment interview. In I. Weiner (Ed.), *Clinical methods in psychology.* New York: Wiley-Interscience.

Willems, E. P. (1969). Planning a rationale for naturalistic research. In E. P. Willems & H. L. Raush (Eds.), *Naturalistic viewpoints in psychological research.* New York: Holt, Rinehart & Winston.

Wittkower, E., & Dubreil, G. (1973). Psychocultural stress in relation to mental illness. *Social Science and Medicine,* **7**, 691–704.

Yap, P. M. (1969). The culture-bound reactive syndromes. In W. Caudill & T. Lin (Eds.), *Mental health research in Asia and the Pacific.* Honolulu: East-West Center Press.

Yasuno, T., Hashimoto, E., & Nakai, E. (1979). A study of the personality of speech disordered individuals with the MMPI. In J. Butcher, H. Hama, & Y. Matsuyama (Eds.), *Proceedings of the 6th International Conference on Personality Assessment.* Kyoto: Doshisha University.

PART THREE

Areas of
Clinical Research

Techniques in Assessment

CHAPTER 10

Direct Observation
in Clinical Psychology

JOHN D. CONE AND SHARON L. FOSTER

> All of the social sciences but psychology owe most of their empirical accomplishments
> to direct recording of conditions and events in society . . . Psychology appears to stand
> alone as a science without a substantial descriptive, naturalistic, ecological side.
>
> (WRIGHT, 1967, p. 3)

With these words Wright introduced his ecological approach to psychology in 1967, an approach that was to rely heavily on the direct observation of human behavior. While observation had been a tool of developmental psychologists for decades previously (e.g., Chittenden, 1942), clinical psychology as a field saw few reports relying on direct observational data prior to the early days of applied behavior analysis. With this came a growing recognition that behavior was a relevant dependent variable in its own right, no longer requiring relegation to the role of an incomplete index of a trait or personality characteristic. As psychologists legitimized the study of behavior, a literature related to the methodology of direct observation in clinical research germinated and grew. This chapter reflects the fruits of that literature, and attests to the growth of psychology's reliance on behavioral observation procedures since Wright's (1967) quote.

The term "behavioral observation," as used in this chapter, refers to the recording of observable activities of persons. Observable behavior is a response that is discernable "by detectable displacement in space through time of some part of the organism" (Johnston & Pennypacker, 1980). Thus thoughts and feelings are not behavior; they represent no displacement of part of the organism. Physiological responses, as detected by the human eye or by the human eye augmented with equipment, are classed as behavior. Psychophysiological sensing and recording equipment, strictly speaking, provides behavioral observations regarding physical responses such as heart rate and GSR. Most observation of other types of behavior, however, is conducted by human observers using a coding system that they have been trained to employ. Because human observers differ substantially from their mechanical counterparts, this chapter will focus specifically on issues related to the design and implementation of observation systems for human observers. Further, we will assume that the investigators employing such systems are interested in observing behavior for the purpose of describing clinical phenomena and monitoring behavior change, and not as an indirect representation of superordinate global constructs.

Following the indirect-direct distinction of Cone and Hawkins (1977, pp. xx–xxii) we refer to the methods to be described in this chapter as "direct" because they assess the behavior of clinical interest per se rather than a surrogate of it. Moreover, the behavior is observed or recorded, as with audio- or videotaping procedures, at the time and place of its occurrence. Thus direct observation assessment methods differ from interviews and self-reports in that the latter rely on verbal representations of clinically relevant behavior occurring at some other time and in some other place.

Direct observations may be performed by anyone having the appropriate physiology and being in contact with the behavior as it occurs. In addition to observation by others, we may observe and record our own responding. A body of literature dealing with self-observation exists, but has grown up somewhat independently of the direct observation literature (for reviews see Kazdin, 1974; Nelson, 1977). In this chapter our primary focus is direct observation procedures. We will discuss self-observation only as it relates to direct observation, acknowledging that the voluminous and currently separate literatures in the two areas may certainly benefit from increased rapprochement in the future.

A direct observation system will only produce reliable and valid data if it is appropriate to the behavior of interest, carefully designed, and correctly implemented. The purpose of this chapter is to explore each of these criteria in detail, highlighting critical questions and issues that face the researcher interested in collecting high quality observational data. The initial section focuses on factors to consider in choosing or creating a system. We then turn to design considerations, including characteristics of behavior, types of recording methods, and issues in response definition. Next we discuss a number of issues relating to generalizability in direct observation from both conceptual and data-based perspectives. We end with some recommendations for the use and evaluation of direct observation assessment systems.

SELECTING THE APPROPRIATE OBSERVATION RECORDING SYSTEM

A bewildering variety of approaches can be taken to developing a direct observation coding system. By considering the factors to be described in this section, the sometimes difficult task of selecting or developing the appropriate system should be made a great deal easier.

General Considerations

One critical factor in designing or selecting an observation system is the *accessibility* of the behavior to the observer. Is the response something that is readily observable, such as lighting a cigarette? Or is it more difficult to detect, such as the positive verbal interchanges between children as they interact quietly in class? One of the authors (SLF) recently had the unsettling experience of meticulously defining molecular categories of children's verbal communication, only to discover that observers in the classroom could not get close enough to hear the children. She therefore created a more molar category, "verbal initiations," whose dimensions were accessible to the observers. A related characteristic is the *frequency* of occurrence of the behavior of interest. Low frequency behavior is not efficiently observed and recorded in infrequent, short-duration observation periods. High frequency responses, in contrast, may be readily sampled during short periods, but may require the sustained attention of trained nonparticipant observers to discriminate their presence accurately.

Another important characteristic to consider is the critical *response property* of the behavior in question. All behavior can be characterized by frequency, duration, and quality, and the importance of each of these properties will vary with the behavior and the research question(s) being asked. A researcher interested in changing a student's total study time would find the number of study episodes (frequency) a meaningless dependent variable, for example. This issue is particularly important for multibehavior coding systems in which several kinds of behavior are observed and recorded simultaneously. Frequency may be the most relevant response property of some of the behavior, whereas latency or duration might be the more relevant for others. For example, in assessing sexual interaction the frequency of verbal categories such as vocal guidance (e.g., "touch me there") will be important, while duration of intromission or the latency of ejaculation might be their most important response properties. The use of a uniform recording system that ignored these differences would lead to potentially meaningless data for some of the responses.

In addition to accessibility and response properties, the *purpose* for which the data are being collected should be considered. Observational data can be used for description, determining functional relationships, intervention monitoring, and program evaluation. If the primary interest is in collecting information for general descriptions of the behavior of a particular client or group of clients, a fine-grained analysis of any one response is probably unnecessary and would give way to less precise focus on a variety of behavior in the client's repertoire. If data are being collected to plan an appropriate intervention, a finer-grained analysis of one or a few kinds of behavior will be necessary. If a primary reason for collecting the data is to determine functional relationships between some characteristic of the behavior and its environmental determinants, a multidimensional system that reflects relevant antecedents or consequences will be required. For such uses the system must be sensitive enough to reflect differences in behavior produced by variations in the environment.

When direct observation data are to be used for program evaluation, the system should be designed after considering both the nature of the program and the quality to be required of the data. Large-scale programs where relatively infrequent observations are collected for many participants might require the use of interval or momentary time-sampling systems and restrict assessment to high-frequency behavior that is applicable to all the individuals in the program. Such a system would have limited potential for assessment focused on specific individuals in the program.

Related to these issues is the *breadth* of data desired by the investigator. This includes the number of different kinds of behavior assessed and the number of individuals observed. Momentary time sampling is easier to use than event recording for more complex systems, as the observer must simply note whether the behavior occurs at all during the given interval.

A consideration in determining the breadth of a system is the amount of *resources* available to the researcher. A large number of personnel and extensive training time are required for more complex multiresponse and interactional coding systems. Participant observers, in contrast, can only use systems simple enough to be practical in light of their ongoing roles in the environment. A related resource issue is the availability of technological support for data storage and processing. For example, making videotapes or audiotapes of behavior provides relatively permanent records that can be observed repeatedly and from which large amounts of data can be extracted (Gottman, 1979). Similarly, if solid state, hand-held data entry devices with keyboards are available (e.g., a Datamyte), response properties of numerous responses can be recorded. With a Datamyte, for example, frequency, duration, and location in real time can easily be recorded for much behavior. At a later time the data can be automatically transmitted to a computer file for storage and subsequent analysis. The availability of such technological support increases the complexity of data manageable by direct observation coding systems, but can be costly in both personnel and equipment.

The *availability of already developed coding systems* is another important factor to consider in choosing a direct observation system. A measure that has already been used and reported in the literature should have information concerning its adequacy as a measuring device, detail that would have to be generated *de nouveau* for any new system. The amount and kind of information provided will be widely variant and may not be enough to make a reasonable decision. At the very least the investigator will need information as to the system's characteristics as a measuring device. Thus, in traditional terms, it must be possible to ascertain its reliability and validity. The specifics of establishing these characteristics are discussed later in this chapter. Here it is enough to note that any assessment procedure must be able to be evaluated as such. If the nature of the device precludes determining the quality of the data it generates, then it is impossible to have any confidence that the measure is appropriate for its assessment purposes.

A final consideration in designing a system lies, ironically, in the possibility that direct observation may not be the most appropriate or efficient assessment strategy for a particular purpose. For example, direct observation will be inappropriate when the variable of interest is not behavior. Response products are often not behavior. As defined in this chapter, private events such as thoughts are not behavior until they are verbalized. Yet many clinical problems involve private events such as hallucinations, deprecatory self-statements, and sensations subjectively labeled as hopelessness or anxiety, which may be better assessed by self-report inventories or self-recording methods. In other cases data regarding perceptions, evaluations, and expectations may be desirable for the purposes of description or functional analyses related to directly observable responses. Gottman (1979), for example, reported the use of a "talk table" to assess couples' evaluation of their interaction. After each verbal statement, the spouse who makes the statement presses a button to indicate the intended impact of the comment (choices range from "superpositive" to "supernegative"). The other spouse indicates the actual impact, using the same scale. Using this method, Gottman and his colleagues have discriminated differences between stated intent and subjective impact of the verbal communication of distressed and nondistressed couples.

In the situations described above, the investigator is interested in variables other than observed behavior. Under other conditions, a researcher may wish to assess behavior per se, but may find that direct observation is impractical, impossible, or unethical. Very low frequency responses and behavior that occur only in the absence of other people (e.g., masturbation) might best be monitored by self-report or self-monitoring. Other responses might be discernible to the person performing them but not to an external observer (e.g., whispered threats, mild hand tremors). Direct observation of some behavior, such as the sexual responding of a dysfunctional couple, may be distasteful to the client and professionally controversial. Further, direct observation will be contraindicated when the observer's presence in the client's environment could lead to undesirable side effects. For example, placing an observer in a work setting to monitor an ex-mental patient's appropriate behavior could lead the individual to be identified, labeled, and socially ostracized.

In the preceding sentences, we have assumed that alternatives to direct observation are available and produce both reliable and valid data. If the researcher wishes to use an alternative measure as an indirect indicator of behavior, validity requires empirical demonstration that responses on the indirect measure in fact covary with the actual behavior to which the investigator wishes to generalize. This in turn requires that the indirect measure be developed in conjunction with direct observation, so that at some point the generalizability of data collected by direct and indirect methods can be assessed. The generalizability of direct observation data will be discussed in a later section.

If, after considering the general issues included in this section, an investigator has selected direct observation as the assessment method of choice, the concept of what is to be assessed must then be translated into a measurement system. Three major classes of decision involved at this point are: (1) choice of the appropriate characteristic or property of the behavior of interest; (2) the level of analysis with which response categories are to be formed; and (3) the type of observation system best suited to the purposes of the assessment. These will now be discussed.

Properties of the Response

Frequency. Frequency refers to the number of times a response occurs within a given period of time. For example, a clinician interested in decreasing a child's tantrums may record the number of times the child screams or cries each day. When data are collected over nonequivalent periods of time, frequencies may be transformed into rates of behavior per unit of time to make them comparable. Tantrum frequency collected daily during baseline (two weeks) and treatment (six weeks) could thus be expressed as frequency per day, hour, or minute.

Because frequency measures ignore other properties of behavior such as duration and latency, they are most appropriate when these properties are equivalent across responses or are irrelevant to the investigation. For example, if one is targeting snacking behavior

for weight reduction, frequency of snacking would be an appropriate measure if the investigator did not care about the nutritional or caloric value of snacks, or if the individual only consumed a single type of food (e.g., chocolate) during snack times.

Duration. Duration is a temporal characteristic of responding that can be looked at in three different ways: (1) the interval between the initiation of the response and its cessation; (2) the interval between the onset of a stimulus and the initiation of the response; and (3) the interval between successive responses. The first of these has most often been regarded as response duration; the second, as latency of response; the third, as interresponse interval.

Examples of response duration include how long a student sits at a desk, the amount of time spent engaging in social interaction, and length of eye contact. As with frequency, duration is sometimes assessed over unequal time periods, and equilibration is necessary. For example, a student may study for two 15-minute periods during a one-hour observation session on Day 1. On Day 3, six five-minute studying periods are observed in three hours. Total duration of studying for both days is 30 minutes, but the response patterns are clearly different.

Two kinds of data reduction have been used to make these differences more salient. With the first, a percentage is computed by dividing the total time spent responding by the total observation time. In the present example, this would yield 50% for Day 1 and 16.7% for Day 2. The second method computes average duration per response: 15 minutes for Day 1 and 5 minutes for Day 2. The first method masks duration per response. The second ignores the length of the time interval over which data are collected. Obviously the former method is preferable when the clinician or researcher is interested in how much time an individual spends in a particular activity relative to other activities and cares less about the durations of individual instances of the target response. This might be the case for a couple in marital therapy who wish to increase the total time they spend interacting. Conversely, in some cases average duration per response is important, as when a gradual increase in the average duration of attentional responses is used to assess treatment success with a hyperactive child.

The use of latency and interresponse interval variants of latency is appropriate when the duration of the response itself is not as important as the temporal relationship between an external stimulus, that is, an antecedent event or the previous response, and the target response.

Since frequency data can be derived from duration measures and their variants, duration measures offer the advantage of yielding data that can be expressed in varying ways. However, they require that an observer discriminate not only whether behavior falls within the defined response class, but also when that behavior or antecedent event begin and end. Thus duration recording is easiest when beginning and end points are readily able to be discriminated. Furthermore, the observer must have some kind of equipment to measure the passage of time. When a single behavior is assessed, a watch can be used, but when more than one kind of behavior is observed, more cumbersome and expensive equipment such as multiple channel event recorders may be required. Less expensive time-sampling interval recording procedures can be used if approximate durations will suffice. These will be discussed later.

Quality. Often an investigator is concerned not with frequency, duration, or latency of a target response, but rather with qualitative aspects of the behavior. A teacher may complain that "Susie turns in all her assignments, but just doesn't try." A woman may complain about her spouse's sarcasm when he makes appropriately phrased requests for behavior change. In this case the

assessment procedure must assess not only whether the behavior occurs, but *how* it occurs as well, and this requires topographic discrimination of the different forms responses can take.

Three types of qualitative response properties predominate in the literature. *Intensity* or *magnitude* refers to the degree or force with which a response is performed. GSR assesses the magnitude of skin conductance evidenced by the subject; decibel level indicators measure noise intensity. *Accuracy* refers to how well the behavior corresponds to a preselected criterion. The percentage of correct responding on an examination is an example. *Acceptability* refers to a judgment made along a good/bad dimension, such as "appropriate" assertiveness or "positive" initiation to peers.

All three quality dimensions require definition of a continuum of behavior, specified so that one response can be judged as having "more" or "less" of the measured aspect than another response. In addition, accuracy and acceptability incorporate a standard against which the target response can be evaluated. Thus the relevant dimensions of the continuum or the standard should be as clearly specified as the response itself. This is equivalent to defining subcategories of the response, differentiated by critical topographic features that can be expressed in terms of frequency, duration, or latency. Susie's "trying," for example, might be subdivided into three different subtypes: (1) hands in assignment on time with no complaints; (2) hands in assignment late with no complaints; (3) hands in assignment late and complains.

Unfortunately, many observational systems that attempt to assess the acceptability of the response rely on subjective observer judgments rather than anchoring qualitative judgments in response topography. This is particularly true of verbal behavior content codes, in which topography is less easily specified than with codes based on motor behavior. To the extent that these judgments are idiosyncratic, agreement between observers will be lowered (Curran, 1979).[1] In addition, subjective global ratings of behavior appear to be more readily influenced by expectancy biases of various sorts than are observations of clearly defined discrete responses (Kent, O'Leary, Diament, & Deitz, 1974; Shuller & McNamara, 1976). Unfortunately, the relative contributions of "global" and "subjective" aspects of the rating scales to biased data are not clear. However, given these considerations, the investigator is safest translating subjective elements of response evaluation into more objective topographic description.

By-Products of Behavior. The results of behavior are not, strictly speaking, properties of behavior per se. We include them in this section because, as mentioned earlier, there are times when they may be more appropriate than direct observation of particular target responses themselves. For example, a clinician may be interested in achieving a particular outcome and have little interest in or available resources for assessing the behavior that led to it. If a parent cared only that a child's room was clean and not how this happy result was effected, she or he might count the number of clothing and toy items on the floor as an index of neatness. The number of missed days of work might be monitored as an indication of the effects of a program to reduce alcoholic drinking. Webb, Campbell, Schwartz, and Sechrest (1966) detailed a variety of creative methods that could be adapted to assess the physical products of clinical intervention.

Product measures are quite useful if the target response is relatively inaccessible to observation. However, they do not indicate the methods by which results were obtained. Johnston and Pennypacker (1980) discuss two additional potential problems with use of a response product. One is knowing the responsible producer. In the example above, if two children shared a messy room and the target child were to be rewarded for cleanliness, a parent might inappropriately reward the child when in actuality the child has coerced his or her neat sibling into straightening up the mess. The second difficulty occurs when the investigator wants to assume "a one-to-one correspondence between response products and actual movements" (Johnston & Pennypacker, 1980, p. 111). This underscores the point made above: assessing the product alone tells us nothing about process.

Level of Analysis

Independent of the properties of behavior the investigator chooses to observe are questions related to the level of analysis of the observational system. These questions concern the ways in which target responses or response classes are specified. A second and related concern involves deciding whether to assess single response classes in isolation or to assess interdependent behavior. Both issues raise conceptual as well as practical considerations.

Definitional Concerns. An initial step in the design of an observational system is the precise definition of each response or response class to be observed. The first question of definition lies in the molecularity of the response description. At its most molecular, any behavior can be described as a series of transient sequential subcomponents; at its most molar, any behavior can be described with a summary label which, by inference, includes relevant subcomponents. "Hitting," for example, could be defined on

---

[1]Prinz and Kent (1978) developed an alternative to coding qualitative aspects of family verbal interaction defined via response topography, which to some extent addresses this concern. Their observational system relies on consensus among observers to rate subjective dimensions such as sarcasm and friendliness. Each interaction sample is rated by four observers, whose ratings are averaged. Reliability of this average is computed using the Spearman-Brown prophecy formula. If this coefficient is high, the average can be said to represent a stable consensus of a set of judges regarding the quality of a response.

a molar level as "forcibly striking another," whereas a more molecular definition might read "contact between the subject's hand or extension of the hand (e.g., a stick) and a body part or piece of clothing of another individual with such force that the contact could inflict physical injury." Obviously the molecular definition provides greater detail. In some cases this may be unnecessary, as, for example, when a molar response definition is less cumbersome and implicitly connotes predictable molecular elements.

The molecular-molar distinction is also relevant when grouping behavior into response classes. There are two ways to form these classes. The first groups responses that are *topographically* similar, that is, have similar shape or form (Sulzer-Azaroff & Mayer, 1977). Defining responses grouped by topography involves enumerating the relevant visible aspects of the behavior so that relevant exemplars will be included, and similar but irrelevant behavior excluded. For example, an investigator assessing a child's verbal aggression may wish to include angry name-calling but exclude playful bravado or joking. To distinguish angry verbal behavior from enjoyable teasing, the investigator might choose the absence of smiling as a relevant topographic dimension that must occur to score a behavior as "verbal aggression." A good definition of a response class of topographically similar behavior thus specifies critical response parameters so that false positives and false negatives are minimized in observations of behavior.

The second major way of defining a response class is by the *functional* similarity of its members (Wahler, 1975). If an investigator were interested in "pleasurable marital behavior" (a category that might include affectionate behavior, empathic responses, giving gifts, etc.), functionally similar responses that might be topographically dissimilar would be included. This type of classification involves the definitional considerations just described plus several potential concerns as a result of combining different behavior in a single index. Investigators who form such classes typically *assume* functional similarity among behavior, that is, that they are cued by the same antecedent stimuli, or have similar consequences. For example, Charlesworth and Hartup (1967) defined "positive reinforcement" to include behavior ranging from making a request to imitation (Boyer, Simon, & Karafin, 1973). However, dissimilar behavior cannot be assumed to have similar functions on an a priori basis (Kent & Foster, 1977). Rather such similarity must be demonstrated empirically. Johnston and Pennypacker (1980) point out that failure to do so may lead investigators to misrepresent treatment effectiveness, as, for example, if an intervention increased one response in a class comprised of dissimilar behavior but decreased another response that was included in the same class as a "spillover effect" (Strain, Shores, & Kerr, 1976).

Coding Response Interdependencies. When creating an observation system, investigators often assess solely the target behavior of interest. Sometimes, however, data on other responses temporally related to the target may enhance significantly the information obtained. Such responses may be of three types: those that precede or are antecedent to the target behavior, those that are concurrent with the target, and those that follow it. This type of antecedent, behavior, consequence coding ("ABC," Bijou, Peterson, Harris, Allen, & Johnston, 1969) is useful under several conditions. First, when the behavior of interest occurs only after readily definable antecedents, coding the antecedents as well as the response allows for analyses of the occurrence of alternative as well as target responding. For example, noncompliance can only occur after a command has been issued. Percentage of noncompliant responses to commands may be a more meaningful dependent variable than mere frequency of compliance, which can fluctuate as a function of the number of commands a subject receives. In addition, A-B or B-C coding may be essential if a sequence of behavior is the unit of analysis employed to evaluate outcome. For example, Patterson and Fleischman (1979) have suggested that behavioral treatments with families will be most successful if escalating negative "bursts" are altered. To assess this, conditional probabilities (e.g., B-C chains) would be required as dependent variables.

Antecedent-behavior-consequence coding can also be helpful in determining functional relationships between behavior and environmental events contiguous to them. Such relationships are crucial for planning interventions based on restructuring the environmental determinants of behavior. For example, Madsen, Becker, Thomas, Koser, and Plager (1968) observed "sit down" commands and children's in-seat behavior. Examining the covariation between these events showed that the teachers' commands actually reinforced out-of-seat behavior. The children in turn negatively reinforced the teachers' behavior by sitting down following the command.

Data from interactional systems can also be used to build theory and to describe reliable interdependencies in behavioral chains. From their use of a complex interactional coding system with families of deviant boys, Patterson and his colleagues have derived the concepts of reciprocity and coercion as critical aspects of family dynamics (Patterson & Reid, 1970). Gottman (1979) presents data on verbal marital interaction of distressed and nondistressed couples, which both describe the nature of sequential verbal statements and contribute to a more conceptual understanding of the functional relationships among complex communication patterns.

Interactional observational systems can provide more complete and fine-grained information than response-in-isolation systems. However, with this additional information come potential difficulties. First, when employing a sequence of behavior as

a dependent variable, the reliability of the observations of the target sequence must be evaluated rather than simply computing reliabilities for the single categories of behavior that comprise the sequence(s) (Kent & Foster, 1977). Second, highly complex sequential systems have only recently been employed in clinical research. Statistical analyses, computer technology, and special methodological issues in handling sequential data therefore have not yet fully evolved (see Lamb, Suomi, & Stephenson, 1979; and Sackett, 1978, for edited volumes with chapters related to these issues). Finally, the conceptual considerations involved in defining single response classes of topographically different behavior expand geometrically when an investigator is interested in demonstrating functional relationships among *multiple* response classes, each of which requires validation.

Some of these potential difficulties can be reduced when an investigator is less interested in fine-grained exhaustive analysis of multiple behavior and wishes to use an interactional (sequential) coding system for limited sequences that are relatively circumscribed. Parental attention following a child's aggression toward a sibling and compliance with teacher requests are two examples of such sequences (see Reid, 1978a, for excellent examples of these kinds of alternatives to the complex interactional codes).

Types of Observational Systems

There are several major types of observational recording that can be adapted to assess most or all of the properties of behavior described earlier. These fall into three generic classes: narrative recording, event recording, and interval recording.

Narrative Recording. An observer's written or spoken description of behavior is a narrative recording. Ethologists have long used written narratives in attempts to derive inductively the organization of an organism's responses (Blurton Jones & Woodson, 1978; Burghardt, 1973). In its purest form narrative recording includes no preestablished response definitions for the observer to use. However, because of the obvious difficulties in longhand recording of high-frequency behavior, investigators sometimes develop abbreviated codes to represent frequently ocurring responses (e.g., Blurton Jones & Woodson, 1978; McGrew, 1972), or observers make tape-recorded rather than handwritten recordings of their observations.

Narrative recording methods are flexible, as observations can enumerate many different response topographies. Frequency measures can also be derived from narratives. However, narratives inherently contain two sources of unreliability: (1) observers may fail to record the same event, or may represent the same event with different verbal descriptors; and (2) in quantifying the narratives, different coders may disagree in cataloguing the same protocol.

Investigators have attempted to reduce the potential unreliability of the original observation either by providing exhaustive behavior codes (e.g., McGrew, 1972) or by supplying observers with a list of rules constraining the type of descriptor they might use in their narratives (e.g., avoiding inferential adjectives, Wright, 1967). While constraints may improve reliability, they also make the systems increasingly like the more structured observation methods discussed below, thereby reducing their flexibility.

Narrative records are also limited by the amount of time involved in data reduction from written or tape-recorded protocols. Holm (1978) estimates that transcribing a vocal narrative, coding the transcript, and summarizing the data can take as long as 15 hours for each hour of actual observation! Nonetheless, observationally oriented researchers have increasingly suggested the use of narrative recordings prior to designing a less cumbersome behavioral observation code (Kent & Foster, 1977; Rosenblum, 1979), particularly if the investigator is un-

familiar with the behavior or population being assessed. Such records can provide preliminary information on the frequency and topographic parameters of behavior of interest, and can be used as guides in forming clear definitions and in grouping behavior into response classes.

Narrative recordings can also be useful for low-frequency but highly salient behavior that is recorded by participant observers. An episode log (Wood, Callahan, Alevizos, & Teigen, 1979), for example, can be used by psychiatric ward staff or by teachers to record specific instances of low-frequency problem behaviors. Antecedent and consequent events can also be recorded if relevant to the researcher's assessment. If only limited behavior is recorded, data reduction time is considerably reduced. Unfortunately, the methodological adequacy of this procedure as a research tool has not been thoroughly explored, although different forms of episode logs may yield significantly different behavior frequencies (Wood et al., 1979). Certainly the use of narrative recording as a research tool warrants further systematic study.

Event Recording. The simplest type of recording system involves recording the appropriate response property of every codable behavior that occurs within the observation period. Unlike the narrative method, the observer records selected response properties for one or more kinds of operationally defined behavior selected in advance by the investigator. When the response property recorded is frequency, this method is often called frequency recording.[2] Event recording is relatively straightforward and can be used by participant observers. It has been chosen repeatedly by clinical researchers who use summary statistics to indicate pre–post change, or for ongoing monitoring of treat-

[2]The term "event recording" has been used synonymously with "frequency recording" (Sulzer-Azaroff & Mayer, 1977). We use "event recording" here to refer to a generic method that can be used to assess any response property.

ment effects with $N = 1$ experimental strategies.

Event recording methods have several limitations, however. Ordinarily observers record only the defined dimensions of target responses and not the time at which they occur. Therefore, unless recording procedures are modified, sequences or temporal patterns often cannot easily be discriminated from observer records. Instead the investigator obtains relatively gross indexes of behavior. Also Reid (1978a) anecdotally commented that observers tend to "nod off" when target responses are relatively infrequent. For behavior where the onset and offset are difficult to discriminate, event recording will be less reliable than other types of recording (Sulzer-Azaroff & Mayer, 1977). Finally, when two observers' data show poor correspondence, it is often difficult to ascertain the particular instances on which they disagreed. Conversely, it is possible for observers to generate identical total response frequencies or durations based on very different behavior during the observation period.

Interval Recording. Some of these difficulties are offset by using interval recording systems that divide the observation period into intervals (ordinarily of equal duration), then record categories of behavior as they occur within each interval. Like event recording, categories of behavior are operationally defined. Unlike event recording, however, a temporal dimension is indicated on the observer's protocol. Observers carry a signaling device such as a stop-watch or portable tape recorder with an earphone to provide a visual or auditory indication of the onset of a new interval.

In its simplest form, interval recording involves breaking up the recording into time blocks, during which observers record the relevant response property whenever the target response occurs. A parent, for example, might tally the frequency of his or her child's complaints for three 15-minute intervals per evening. Three more complex forms of interval recording are also used, typically with intervals of short duration (e.g., 5 seconds). In *whole-interval* sampling, behavior is recorded if and only if it occurs throughout the entire interval. If behavior need only occur for a fraction of the interval to be recorded, a *partial-interval* sampling system is being used. When the behavior must occur at some specific moment within the interval (e.g., beginning or end) to be recorded, a *momentary sampling* system is in effect (Powell, Martindale, & Kulp, 1975; Sulzer-Azaroff & Mayer, 1977). Each of these three systems can be employed to estimate either frequency or duration of a behavior.

Because temporal patterns of responses are indicated, interval recording with short-duration intervals eliminates several of the problems with event recording. Specifically, sequences of behavior are more readily discriminated and sources of unreliability more easily located. Because observers must attend to transitions between intervals as well as to the subject's behavior, the probability of sustained inattention is reduced. In addition, several kinds of behavior can be recorded simultaneously. Thus interval systems have the potential for greater data yield than does event recording, and are better suited to theoretical or practical research questions that require analyses of fine-grained data.

Interval systems are not without their limitations, however. Because they ordinarily require more observer effort than event recording, they are rarely suitable for participant observers, particularly when target behavior is very high in frequency or difficult to discriminate. A teacher, for example, would find it virtually impossible to record the duration of a child's on-task behavior using a whole-interval system while simultaneously overseeing 20 additional students. And because of the increased complexity of the observation system, observers cannot record behavior for long periods of time without becoming fatigued. Thus interval systems are not efficient for collecting data on low-frequency behavior (Sulzer-Azaroff & Mayer, 1977).

Whole interval, partial interval, and momentary sampling systems also provide only estimates of frequency or of duration of responding. Several investigations have recently explored the validity of these estimates by comparing interval and event recording of frequency and durational response properties. Powell, Martindale, Kulp, Martindale, & Bauman (1977) compared data from each type of interval recording with continuously recorded durations of a subject's in-seat behavior. Observers scored groups of videotapes in which an experimental confederate stayed in his seat either 20%, 50%, or 80% of the time. Interval durations varied from 5 seconds to 300 seconds for whole- and partial-interval sampling, and from 5 to 1800 seconds for momentary sampling. Results revealed that all three interval sampling methods produced increasingly biased data as the measurement interval increased in duration. When biases occurred, whole-interval methods consistently underestimated the actual percentage of in-seat behavior, partial-interval methods provided overestimates, and momentary samples led to both over- and underestimates. At 5-second interval durations, all estimates were relatively accurate. As the interval duration increased, whole-interval sampling became increasingly inaccurate. Partial-interval sampling became inaccurate after 10-second durations, while momentary sampling was generally accurate through interval durations as long as one minute. Other investigators have found similar results (Green & Alverson, 1978; Powell et al., 1975). In fact, the degree of bias for partial and whole interval measures appears to be related not only to interval length but also to the actual rate and duration of the target response and the time between behavior (Green & Alverson, 1978; Repp, Roberts, Slack, Repp, & Berkler, 1976).

These results highlight the potential invalidity of interval sampling systems. However, the minimal bias with short-duration intervals in the Powell et al. (1975, 1977) studies indicates that the problem can be avoided with a carefully designed system, and that investigators must attend to variations in the duration of the target behavior in selecting the interval length to be used, both for frequency and for duration estimates.

Summary

In discussing the selection of an appropriate observation recording system, we have mentioned the need to consider the accessibility and frequency of behavior of interest as well as certain critical response properties. In addition to frequency, we noted the importance of response duration and quality, and the value of attending to the products of the behavior in question. The level of analysis to be undertaken (molar vs. molecular) and the coding of response interdependencies were also discussed. Finally, the different types of direct observation coding systems most frequently used were described, and preliminary research comparing them was mentioned.

Regardless of which system is selected to assess which critical response property of which behavior, it is necessary to evaluate the resulting system in terms of its adequacy as a measuring device. This evaluation will deal primarily with different ways in which the data from the measure can be generalized, a subject to which we now turn.

EVALUATING THE GENERALIZABILITY OF DIRECT OBSERVATION DATA

Most clinical psychologists cut their professional eyeteeth on the concepts of reliability and validity and need not be reminded of the definitions of these terms, their various forms, or their importance as properties of measuring devices. Over the years, partialing reliability and validity into subcategories (e.g., temporal consistency, internal consistency, construct) became cumbersome, and in 1972 Cronbach and his colleagues published a landmark text that introduced a new level of conceptual order into the field (Cronbach, Gleser, Nanda, & Rajaratnam, 1972). By noting that most questions of reliability and validity resolve to ways in which scores from a measuring instrument may be generalized, Cronbach et al. collapsed these concepts parsimoniously into the single notion of generalizability. In examing interscorer reliability, for example, what is really investigated is the extent to which the score obtained depends on the person doing the scoring. If independent scorers agree with one another, it does not matter which scorer we use. Similarly, if alternate forms of a test are highly correlated, the scores we obtain using one form are generalizable to the correlated alternate forms.

Other forms of reliability and validity can be similarly reinterpreted in terms of generalizability theory, since each is merely another way in which scores can be generalized. More detailed discussions of generalizability theory can be found elsewhere (Cronbach et al., 1972; Jones, Reid, & Patterson, 1975; Wiggins, 1973). The following discussion addresses generalizability issues related to the quality of direct observation measurement systems. Before considering the more familiar forms of generalizability, a few words will be said about *accuracy,* a concept that has been reserved almost exclusively for direct observation assessment.

Determining the Accuracy of Directly Observed Data

Direct observation coding systems are designed to assess certain verifiable facts about behavior. The five facts of most concern are: (1) the occurrence of the behavior; (2) its repeated occurrence; (3) its occurrence in more than one setting; (4) its occurrence in comparison with other behavior; and (5) its

occurrence as measured by alternative methods (Cone, 1978). A coding system will be said to be accurate if it is sensitive to each of these facts, that is, if it correctly reflects what is true about the behavior of interest.

The need to attend to the accuracy of direct observation systems has been appreciated for some time (Gewirtz & Gewirtz, 1969; Johnson & Bolstad, 1973; Kazdin, 1977a). The methodology for doing so has not been well-developed, however. Many researchers appear to assume that agreement between observers is tantamount to demonstrating accuracy, but as Johnston and Pennypacker (1980) have noted, such a view involves a serious error in logic. The fact that observers agree carries no logical implication that either is accurate. As will be shown in the next section, pairs of observers can maintain high levels of agreement without agreeing with other pairs of observers using the same coding system or with a criterion protocol (Romanczyk, Kent, Diament, & O'Leary, 1973; Taplin & Reid, 1973).

A methodology for assessing a system's accuracy must start with an incontrovertible criterion or index of the facts about the behavior of interest. Other sciences that rely heavily on equipment have established methods for doing this. In biology, for example, when new microscopes are checked for accuracy, they are used to observe phenomena the characteristics of which are already known. Moreover, they are used according to established rules. If they are sensitive (within stated limits) to the known characteristics of the phenomenon being viewed when used as prescribed, they are said to be accurate. Thus there are two requirements for ascertaining accuracy: (1) a measurement device must be correctly used, that is, according to its rules for usage; and (2) the data from such usage must correspond with the preestablished criterion.

In direct observation assessment various procedures can be followed to establish an incontrovertible criterion. A mechanical device can be programmed to "behave" in certain ways. For example, Repp et al. (1976) used computer-generated protocols to examine the accuracy of various recording methods. Alternatively, behavior can be measured mechanically and those measurements compared with data from a direct observation coding system. A pressure-sensitive device can be employed to assess "in-seat" behavior for comparison with observational data. As another possibility, actors can be "programmed" by a script, and video-audiotape records of events can be used to generate criterion protocols against which the data of an observation system can be compared (e.g., Powell et al., 1977).

There are problems with each of these approaches, and space does not permit their elaboration here. However, the use of criterion protocols will not usually suffice, since they are typically generated using the very observation system the investigator is trying to calibrate. Obviously the accuracy criterion must be independent of the newly developed measure of it. Criterion protocols are more appropriately used as a basis for checking consistency of use once the basic accuracy of a system has been demonstrated (e.g., DeMaster, Reid, & Twentyman, 1977).

When a criterion has been established and an observation system has been shown to produce data of high fidelity regarding the criterion, it is said to be accurate. This accuracy can only be assured if subsequent uses of the system do not vary greatly from the original calibration conditions. To minimize such variability the rules, instructions, or procedures for using the system must be set down explicitly. Rules include definitions of the behavior. Further, procedures necessary to effect consistent adherence to the rules, such as training and data collection methods, should be specified. Once this information is assembled, its adequacy can be evaluated by training novices to use the system and determining the accuracy of the data they produce. If the instrument is well-calibrated, that is, has sound rules and training procedures, subsequent applications will yield accurate information, and observers will require relatively little continued training.

Unfortunately, such calibration efforts have yet to be systematically implemented. Methods used in observer training are virtually never specified in the literature, although variations in training procedures can substantially affect subsequent data (Wildman, Erickson, & Kent, 1975). Indeed, even following highly specific rules and procedures for systematic training of observers using a family interaction code, Foster et al. (1980) found that replication of the same code in two settings yielded lower cross-laboratory than within-laboratory agreement for several categories. Certainly this implies that cross-laboratory replication is not guaranteed by specified category definitions and training procedures, and indicates that further research should attempt to establish how best to design and describe a system that will produce equivalent data when used properly in different settings and by different experimenters.

In the sections that follow we will discuss various ways in which the data from direct observation coding systems may be generalized. It is important to note that studies of data generalizability frequently confound two different issues. On the one hand, the instrument is being evaluated. On the other, information is being obtained on the behavior assessed by the instrument. Thus if a measure produces scores that do not generalize across settings, either the measure is not sensitive to cross-setting consistencies in the behavior, or no consistencies exist. Unless it has previously been shown that the measure accurately reflects cross-setting consistency, at least in its original derivation or calibrating conditions, the implications of such negative evidence are uncertain.

It is important to separate questions about the measure from those about the behavior being assessed. In the following sections we will in general *assume* the measure was originally accurate and focus largely on issues related to generalizability independent of the original instrument calibration.

Generalizability over Observers

When a measure has demonstrated accuracy in observing and recording behavior under specified conditions of use, it can be applied to particular assessment questions. During the routine application of the measure, periodic recalibration checks are necessary to determine whether its use is sufficiently like the original calibration conditions to permit continued faith in its accuracy. Deterioration in the quality of most measuring devices over time is assumed and has been referred to as instrument decay (Campbell & Stanley, 1963).

Investigators frequently examine the consistency with which direct observation coding systems are used by calculating the agreement between independent observers. In generalizability theory terms, then, interobserver agreement checks indicate the extent to which data about particular behavior depend on the person doing the observing. A high level of agreement implies that the information from the measure is not biased by peculiarities of individual observers. However, as mentioned earlier, agreement between observers does not imply that either is accurate (Bijou, Peterson, & Ault, 1968; Gewirtz & Gewirtz, 1969; Johnson & Bolstad, 1973). It is merely an index of the extent to which the same data are obtained by two or more persons functioning independently of one another.

Agreement between observers, sometimes referred to as interobserver reliability, can be compared with the concepts of interscorer and interrater reliability often associated with less direct forms of assessment. Wiggins (1973) has referred to interobserver agreement as "specific true score reliability" and noted that it "represents the lowest order of generalizability" (p. 323). Berk (1979) has

recently pointed out that the term "reliability" as it is commonly used in reference to interobserver agreement is "really a misnomer," since the usual psychometric notion of reliability as a ratio of true to observed score variance is "neither assumed nor considered in the measurement of interobserver reliability" (p. 460). In a different vein Johnston and Pennypacker (1980) have restricted reliability to the consistency with which a single observer obtains the same information from repeated observations of the same event. Others have similarly noted different ways in which reliability can be conceptualized when using direct observation assessment procedures (Dunnette, 1966; Medley & Mitzel, 1963; Weick, 1968).

Calculating Interobserver Agreement. Despite differences in conceptualization, various ways of calculating and representing agreement have been published over the past 15 years. Indeed Berk (1979) reported 22 different measures! At least one additional approach has been suggested since that review (e.g., Birkimer & Brown, 1979).

Berk divided the measures he found into those dealing with interobserver agreement on the one hand, and those providing estimates of coefficients of interobserver reliability on the other. The distinction roughly separates percentage agreement and nonparametric approaches from correlational ones, and continues an argument voiced previously in the literature (Baer, 1977a; Hartmann, 1977). After noting serious limitations of the first category for representing the traditional psychometric concept of reliability (i.e., the ratio of true score to error variance), Berk argues the superiority of the second. However, he concludes that "only the intraclass correlation-generalizability theory approach seemed to offer the precision, comprehensiveness, and flexibility required to deal with the complexity of reliability assessment" (p. 460). Interested readers should consult Berk (1979) for the specifics of his argument.

In spite of such pleas, users of direct observation coding systems are not likely to switch quickly from simple percentage agreement measures. As Kelly (1977) observed, such measures have been characteristic of the vast majority of at least the applied uses of direct observation assessment. Which particular agreement measure is used depends greatly on the type of observation system employed. With frequency recording systems, the most common approach is to divide the data from the observer with the smaller frequency by those from the observer with the larger. Similarly, with duration recording, the smaller amount of time collected by one observer is divided by the larger amount collected by the other. Often referred to as "total reliability," these measures have certain difficulties, not the least of which is their possible insensitivity to the occurrence of specific events (cf. Kelly, 1977; Sulzer-Azaroff & Mayer, 1977).

When interval recording procedures are used, interobserver agreement is frequently computed using a formula that divides the number of intervals in which observers agree by the total number of intervals reflecting either agreement or disagreement. Here the investigator must decide exactly what constitutes an agreement. With an *overall agreement* method, an agreement is scored if both observers record either occurrence or nonoccurrence in an interval. Total agreements are divided by the total number of intervals observed. With the second method, agreement is defined more restrictively, requiring both observers to agree on occurrences or nonoccurrences only. Agreement on occurrence is referred to as *scored interval* or *occurrence agreement,* and it divides the number of intervals in which both observers noted an occurrence by the sum of the intervals in which either did so. *Unscored interval* or *nonoccurrence agreement* is simply the reverse. That is, the number of intervals in which neither observer scored the behavior is divided by the sum of the intervals in which either failed to score it.

Advocates of scored or unscored interval agreement base their arguments on the U-shaped relationship between agreement due merely to chance and the frequency of the behavior being observed. That is, the overall agreement method will yield relatively high levels of chance agreement for behavior occurring at very low or very high frequencies (Bijou et al., 1968; Hawkins & Dotson, 1975). Therefore, a more conservative test of observer agreement includes only unscored intervals for high frequency behavior and only scored intervals for low frequency responses. However, when rates of behavior vary widely across subjects or experimental conditions, this rule of thumb would require the investigator to use different computational methods at different points in the study, a conceptually inelegant and pragmatically inconvenient approach.

Other approaches eliminate this problem and simultaneously address the issue of chance agreement. Yelton, Wildman, and Erickson (1977) proposed a probability-based formula for calculating agreement that shows the exact probability that the number of agreements reached could be due to chance. An investigator can compare this probability to conventional standards of significance to ascertain the acceptability of the level of agreement reached. Thus if two observers obtain an overall agreement of 80% over 10 intervals with each noting six occurrences, the probability of obtaining such a value by chance is .12. Unlike percentage agreement, Yelton et al.'s formula is sensitive to the number of observation intervals. Thus the same 80% agreement over 20 intervals would be associated with a chance probability of .01.

More recently, procedures have been suggested that combine numerous features of earlier approaches. Harris and Lahey (1978) proposed a modification of a formula suggested by Clement (1976), which combines occurrence and nonoccurrence agreement and weights their relative contribution. The result is a weighted index that minimizes chance agreement since both types (i.e., occurrence and nonoccurrence) have been included. In addition, Kappa and its variants (Cohen, 1960, 1968; Fleiss, Cohen, & Everitt, 1969) utilize formulas that adjust interobserver agreement values for chance levels of occurrence or nonoccurrence (Hartmann, 1977; Kent & Foster, 1977).

A comprehensive and face valid approach to representing generalizability over observers has been proposed by Birkimer and Brown (1979). Their strategy involves calculating percentage of *disagreement* between two observers and plotting this as a range around the midpoint of their separate values on the dependent variable. Thus the data of both observers would be shown on a graph along with the disagreement range. The distance between the top of the range and 100% would be the percentage of agreement on nonoccurrence; that between the bottom of the range and zero would be the percentage of agreement on occurrences. The range for chance disagreement can also be calculated and represented on the same graph. The Birkimer and Brown approach combines the information of several previous suggestions and represents them graphically, a feature that is especially useful in judging the effects of an independent variable when moving from one phase to another in a time series design. However, such graphic representation also requires decision rules for translating visual patterns into judgments of satisfactory or unsatisfactory levels of agreement, a controversy found in single-subject research (Baer, 1977a; Hersen & Barlow, 1976). Nonetheless, because Birkimer and Brown's (1979) suggestions are simple, straightforward, and face valid, they warrant consideration by researchers and clinicians alike.

Variables Influencing Agreement Between Observers. A naive optimism that agreement between independent observers allows some confidence in their accuracy has often characterized observation-based studies. Nonetheless, the phenomenon being observed is only one of several variables that can influence agreement scores. Among these variables are the explicitness of the definitions of behavior in the system, the number of different kinds of behavior included, the training given observers, their subsequent supervision, the very act of conducting agreement checks themselves, and repeated use of the system with another observer without periodic recalibration against a standard.

The first of these, definitional explicitness, has received less than adequate attention to date. Hawkins and Dobes (1977) compared intra- and interpair agreement for definitions found in the literature versus definitions they generated themselves. Their definitions were designed to be clearer, more specific, more objective than the published definitions, and were found to produce consistently higher levels of agreement. Unfortunately, the behavior defined by Hawkins and Dobes was not the same as the behavior defined in the literature. Because content and specificity were confounded, therefore, these differences cannot be unambiguously attributed to increased specificity.

A recent study by Wyatt, Callahan, and Michael (in press) eliminated this confound. Eight undergraduate observers viewed videotaped subjects and recorded "not eating" after reading just the category name. They were then given a specific definition to use in recording "studying" behavior from additional videotapes. Eight other observers reversed the category order and the level of definition specificity. Agreement coefficients were computed three ways (event-by-event, percentage, and correlational). Specific definitions consistently improved agreement levels for all three computation methods, with mean improvements ranging from 20 to 34%. While this study demonstrated that providing an explicit definition enhances interobserver agreement, it did not examine the specific components of a definition that could contribute to this effect. Topographic distinctions, degree of inference, and presence of examples that do and do not fit a particular category are all definitional characteristics that could contribute to observer accuracy, agreement, and susceptibility to other forms of bias.

Experimenters have also explored the relationship between the number of categories in an observation system, termed "code complexity" or "observer load," and interobserver agreement. Mash and McElwee (1974) developed two exhaustive codes to score audiotapes. One code contained eight categories. The second collapsed pairs of categories to form four definitions. Comparisons with a criterion protocol yielded better agreement with the four-category than with the eight-category code. In contrast, Frame (1979) required observers to record between one and 14 categories, and found no differences in interobserver agreement. Several differences between the two studies may have contributed to the discrepant results, however. Frame used experienced observers and 10 to 12 hours of training, while Mash and McElwee's naive observers received only 10 minutes of training. In addition, Mash and McElwee's eight-category code required finer topographic discriminations of categories employed in the simpler code, whereas Frame added distinct categories as he increased the number of kinds of behavior the observers had to record. Finally, Mash and McElwee's coding systems were exhaustive, Frame's were not.

Prior to actual data collection, observers must be trained to use the observational system they will later employ. Both the method and the materials used in training could potentially influence levels of interobserver agreement. Wildman, Erickson, and Kent (1975) compared two training methods. Two groups of undergraduate observers met for seven one-hour sessions to learn a nine-category classroom behavior code designed by O'Leary and his associates (O'Leary, Kaufman, Kass, & Drabman, 1970). One of these, a self-trained group, viewed video-

tapes and discussed their recordings among themselves. The second group discussed and compared their ratings with an experimenter who served as a trainer. Following training, agreement scores computed within each group showed no differences between the two procedures.

Mash and McElwee (1974) and Mash and Makohoniuk (1975) explored a different aspect of observer training, the materials with which observers learn an observational system. Mash and McElwee (1974) trained paid observers to record audiotaped verbal interaction using either the four- or eight-category exhaustive coding system previously mentioned. Half the observers using each coding system were trained with an audiotape where the sequence of verbal interaction was unpredictable, that is, each category had an equal probability of being followed by any of the other categories. The other half were trained with a tape in which behavior was reliably followed by other specific categories. After each group had viewed and coded the training tape five times, a second tape was coded, again five times. For half the subjects, the new tape was similar to the one they had seen in training (i.e., a "predictable" training tape was followed by a "predictable" second tape, etc.), and for half it was different. Observer protocols were then compared with a criterion protocol to compute agreements. The groups trained with predictable and unpredictable materials showed no difference in agreement during training. However, when a novel tape was introduced, the groups trained with predictable sequences showed a slight mean decrement in agreement (approximately 3%), whereas the groups trained with unpredictable sequences showed virtually no mean decrease. Furthermore, the eight-category code seemed more sensitive to the effects of prior training than did the four-category system: "predictably" trained observers showed an average performance decrement of 3.5% after training; the "unpredictably" trained observers showed a 1 to 2% improvement.

In contrast, agreement levels on the four-category code remained stable from the first to the second tape, and did not differ as a function of prior training.

In a replication and extension of these findings, Mash and Makohoniuk (1975) used the eight-category scoring system. Procedures for observer training with a predictable or unpredictable tape and subsequent ratings of another tape (either predictable or unpredictable) were identical to those used by Mash and McElwee (1974). They also added an information variable: half the observers in each group were told to expect the interaction to be either redundant (predictable) or nonredundant; the remaining observers were told nothing. Information affected agreement during training, but not later performance. During training, the informed group who viewed predictable tapes showed significantly poorer agreement scores than did either the informed group who trained on nonredundant tapes or the uninformed group whose training was with predictable sequences. Similar to the Mash and McElwee study, training with unpredictable sequences appeared to enhance interobserver agreement on the second tape by approximately 7%.

It should be noted that the training procedures employed in both of these studies differ substantially from those typically used in clinical research. Mash and McElwee (1974) and Mash and Makohoniuk (1975) used a single tape repeated five times for training observers; most experimenters employ many different behavior samples before training is completed. It is possible that if high levels of agreement were consistently demonstrated for several tapes, changes from predictable to unpredictable sequences would have minimal effects. Nonetheless, reliable differences did emerge despite minimal training with the different sequences. Thus, until other research can establish the generalizability of these findings, it would be wise to structure training materials so that code categories are not predictably sequenced.

Once behavior has been defined, the number of behavioral acts to include has been determined, and observers have been trained in the use of the system, it may be a good idea to supervise the consistency of this use. There is preliminary evidence suggesting that agreement between observers is related to the general supervision they receive. Several researchers have obtained higher agreement levels when the experimenter did not supervise data collection than under supervised conditions (Kent, Kanowitz, O'Leary, & Cheiken, 1977; O'Leary & Kent, 1973). Kent et al. (1977) in fact documented that lack of supervision inflated interobserver agreement scores an average of six percentage points. Therefore, whenever possible, data collection should probably be supervised.

Related to the effects of general supervision are studies examining the influence of agreement checks themselves. There is now good evidence that interobserver agreement calculation can be a reactive process, producing different levels of agreement than exist in its absence. Thus far it has been shown that agreement scores vary when observers: (1) are informed of the specific sessions in which agreement will be assessed; (2) are familiar with the agreement assessor; and (3) compute their own coefficients of agreement.

Taplin and Reid (1973) examined the first of these conditions, the amount of information provided to the observer regarding when agreement will be assessed. They trained 18 undergraduate observers to record videotaped mother-child interaction, then divided the observers into three groups. One group was told that their observations would not be checked for agreement. A second group was informed that occasional agreement checks would occur and would be announced. A third group was told that agreement would be checked by the experimenter on a random, unannounced basis. In actuality, all subsequent data were continuously evaluated via comparison with criterion protocols. The group with announced agreement checks demonstrated the lowest levels of correspondence with the criterion during "unchecked" sessions. Agreement soared during obtrusive checks. The highest and most consistent agreement scores were obtained by the group that expected random spot checking. The group told that no checks would be performed demonstrated intermediate agreement scores.

Thus information regarding when an agreement check will occur appears to function as a cue for improved observation. However, when agreement assessment is obtrusive, the observer is ordinarily aware of a second piece of information: the identity of the person who will serve as the assessor. Romanczyk, Kent, Diament, & O'Leary (1973) explored the possibility that observers may actually alter their own use of a coding system to match the idiosyncracies of familiar agreement assessors.

Undergraduate observers experienced in the use of the O'Leary classroom behavior code practiced recording behavior with two agreement assessors who were actually experimental confederates. One of the confederates employed very stringent definitions of two of the nine categories and very lenient definitions of two others. The second assessor also applied stringent and lenient criteria, but reversed the categories to which the criteria were applied. After approximately four practice sessions with each assessor, each observer conducted eight live observations in a classroom for disruptive children. Observers were told when agreement would be assessed and which confederate would act as an assessor during each session. In actuality, both confederates collected data continuously, thus permitting comparison of overt and covert agreement checks as well as an examination of the assessor variable. As in the Taplin and Reid (1973) study, agreements from overt assessments substantially exceeded those computed for covert assessment sessions. The differences ranged from approximately 10 to 70%. In addition, knowledge of assessor led to enhanced agreement with the identified assessor on the modified categories. Kent et al. (1977), using a different design, later replicated these findings, demonstrating that knowledge of assessment produced drops in interobserver agreement scores and that further drops occurred when the identity of the specific assessor was also provided.

Exactly how increased agreement is achieved under overt agreement checking conditions is unclear at this point. However, a reduced level of complexity in the behavior recorded by observers has been associated with such conditions. Defining complexity as the proportion of different categories in a code actually used during an observation session, Jones et al. (1975) showed negative correlations (ranging from -.52 to -.75) between complexity and agreement, findings recently replicated by House and House (1979). Jones et al. also reported reduced levels of complexity under overt agreement check conditions. It is therefore possible that observers record behavior more conservatively during overt than during covert checks, thus making fewer errors of commission.

Thus typical overt assessment procedures employed in observational data collection may lead investigators to overestimate the quality of their data. Some precautions can be taken to minimize these problems. When data are collected on video- or audiotape, random checks such as those employed by Taplin and Reid (1973) can be used. When data collection occurs in vivo in laboratory settings, agreement checks can be made unobtrusively through a one-way mirror. When this is not available, observations can be conducted in pairs, with occasional randomly determined overlapping observations. For example, observers in the classroom could occasionally observe the same child (for agreement purposes) and at other times collect information on different children. While this would not conceal the identity of the assessor (an impossibility with overt assessment unless three or more observers are present simultaneously), it would eliminate knowledge of exactly when an agreement check was occurring. Finally, agreement can be continuously assessed so that observation conditions are at least uniform throughout the study.

There is a potential difficulty with the last suggestion, however. Considerable evidence documents that observers working together may shift their definitions of behavior in concert and away from those on which they were originally trained. This phenomenon, a type of instrument decay, has been termed "observer drift" (Johnson & Bolstad, 1973). The research of Romanczyk et al. (1973) demonstrated that observers can learn to match the definitions of the observer with whom they are paired. Kent et al. (1974) also documented the occurrence of observer drift. Twenty observers were trained as a group to record children's behavior using the O'Leary code until their recordings matched those of the experimenter. They were then divided into pairs. Each pair observed and discussed subsequent videotapes together. Interobserver agreement scores were computed within and between observer pairs; the former averaged a significant nine points higher than the latter. DeMaster, Reid, and Twentyman (1977) later corroborated these effects using a family interaction coding system, undergraduate observers, and videotapes of mothers and their children.

These findings underscore the fact that high observer agreement scores may be unrelated to consistent, accurate use of an observation code, and indicate that data collected by different groups of observers may not be comparable. This would be a particular problem when a change in observer pairs coincided and thus was confounded with a change in experimental conditions. Even when a single pair of observers records behavior throughout an experiment, data recorded at the beginning and end of the experiment might not be comparable, due to shifts in the ways category definitions are applied.

Several procedures have been suggested to control potential biases that could result from observer drift. Behavior samples that are video- or audiotaped can be scored in random order (Kazdin, 1977a; Kent & Foster, 1977). While this would not eliminate observer drift, it would guarantee that error attributable to drift was randomly distributed across experimental conditions. When taping behavior for later scoring is impractical, different observer groups can be assigned, so that each observes an equal number of times during each experimental condition (Kent & Foster, 1977). However, this is not a guaranteed solution: If different groups "drift" in a similar fashion, data from later observations would still not be directly comparable to data from earlier recordings.

Alternatively, the experimenter can take steps to evaluate the presence of observer drift. Occasionally videotaping in vivo behavior, having all observers rate the tapes, and computing agreement among all possible pairs of observers could indicate which observers, if any, were "drifting," relative to the others. Of course, lowered pair reliabilities would only occur if individuals were changing their application of the code, and not if the entire group were shifting consensually. Alternatively, observer pairs could be frequently reassigned. In this case interobserver agreement figures would better reflect generalizability across observers, but drift would not be prevented or controlled. The periodic use of calibration observers (cf. Patterson, Cobb, & Ray, 1973) is another way of checking on observer drift.

A final solution has frequently been offered as a preventive strategy. An experimenter can establish several videotapes with criterion scoring protocols prior to training observers. Observers are trained using some of these videotapes, and continue to "recalibrate" by practicing with other criterion videotapes throughout the data collection period. Because the criterion protocols are established at the same point in time, they presumably reflect stable, standardized application of category definitions (Johnson

& Bolstad, 1973; Kazdin, 1977a; Kent & Foster, 1977; DeMaster et al., 1977).

DeMaster et al. (1977) examined this strategy with 14 undergraduate observer pairs trained to code videotaped mother-child interaction. All pairs were trained individually for seven sessions. The pairs were then divided into three groups. The first group received warm-up sessions with feedback and discussion on both intrapair and criterion agreement for a warm-up tape. The second group also participated in a warm-up, but computed and discussed only intrapair agreement scores. The third group rated the warm-up tapes but received no feedback. Results indicated that, regardless of group, intrapair agreement consistently and significantly overestimated agreement with the criterion tapes. Levels of agreement (both intrapair and with the criteria) were highest for the first (total feedback) group, followed by the second (feedback on pair agreement), with the no-feedback group the lowest. Furthermore, intrapair and criterion reliabilities of the total feedback group improved (gaining 11 and 17%, respectively, over seven sessions), whereas the no-feedback agreement scores deteriorated (losing 8 and 2%). Thus both intrapair agreement and agreement with a criterion are best maintained and can even be enhanced by recalibration with both kinds of feedback.

A potential problem with the use of videotape protocols is that the observers may have practically memorized the training tapes and *know* how the behavior on them is supposed to be recorded. They may easily shift back to the original definitions while watching the tapes and yet continue with their own idiosyncratic definitions when observing otherwise (Romanczyk et al., 1973). This problem is perhaps best solved by an ample supply of novel training tapes.

Variables Influencing What Is Reported by Observers.   In the previous section we dealt with research that used interobserver agreement as its primary dependent variable.

A related body of literature has dealt with variations in actual levels of behavior reported by observers. Some of the same independent variables have appeared in this literature, and indeed some studies have examined both agreement and levels of behavior at the same time. Among the influences on levels of behavior that have been investigated are the characteristics of the observers themselves, their training and prior history with observational procedures, the behavior of the experimenter, and the process of calculating interobserver agreement.

In direct observation research, observers may be of two different sorts: *nonparticipant observers* who do not participate in the ongoing activities of a setting while they are collecting data, and *participant observers* who do. Participant observers have the advantage of being part of the natural environment and thus, once trained, can collect data over long periods of time. Nonparticipant observers, in contrast, must be scheduled, must observe for short periods of time, and sometimes must be paid. Participant observers are preferable when behavior occurs with relative infrequency, and nonparticipant observers are unlikely to see it without very long observation periods. However, participant observers are of limited value when the observation of target behavior and the performance of their regular daily routine are incompatible. This is the case with extremely high frequency behavior and with responses that are difficult to detect without continuously watching the subject.

Although comparisons of data collected from participant and nonparticipant observers are rare, there is some evidence of less than complete isomorphism. For example, Hay, Nelson, and Hay (1977) examined the reactivity of teacher and student responses when teachers began to record the behavior of some of their students. Nonparticipant observers collected data for one hour each day during a five-day baseline and a five-day participant observation period. Data included records of teachers' and observed students' behavior as well as observations of control children who were not observed by the teachers. Results indicated that introduction of the participant observation task was associated with a change in one of three kinds of teacher behavior. Observed children's behavior changed as well, relative to the controls.

More studies of this type are needed, as is research on the importance of characteristics of observers other than their participatory status. For example, do paid research assistants make better observers than volunteer college sophomores? Without such research it is difficult to know the extent to which the data collected depend on the collector.

The type of training observers receive can also affect what they subsequently record. In the Wildman et al. (1975) study described previously, experimenter-trained observers recorded significantly less disruptive behavior than did self-trained observers. Also the data of the self-trained observers showed greater variability. Number of training sessions (Arrington, 1932; Thomas, Loomis, & Arrington, 1933) has also been explored.

In addition to training, the observer's prior experience with the subject may affect what is recorded. Redfield and Paul (1976) developed two series of videotapes of ex-mental patients. The second series of tapes showed higher frequencies of appropriate behavior than the first. Tapes were scored by highly trained, professional observers who had extensive previous experience collecting observational data on half of the subjects in the videotapes. Previous contact with the subject had no influence on absolute frequencies of behavior recorded by the observers for either series of videotapes.

Examining a different type of prior experience with the observed individual, Robinson and Price (1980) obtained somewhat different results. They compared married couples' observations with naturalistic observations by trained observers. Eight volunteer couples recruited from a university class were placed into either a well-adjusted

or poorly adjusted group, based on their scores on the Locke-Wallace Marital Adjustment Test. Couples and trained observers recorded the frequencies of the same set of nine pleasurable kinds of behavior during four one-hour observation periods conducted in each couple's home. Although trained observers recorded equivalent exchanges of positive behavior for high-adjustment and low-adjustment couples, the low-adjustment sample recorded significantly fewer pleasurable exchanges than did the nondistressed sample. Thus the low-adjustment sample was less accurate in their recordings than their better-adjusted counterparts. The study unfortunately was limited in generalizability by the small sample size and subject selection procedures. Moreover, because procedures used to train the couples were not specified, the possibility that better adjusted couples responded better to training—possibly having a better understanding of behavioral definitions—might account for the results. Nonetheless, the findings imply that individuals with poor marital histories provide different types of data on their interactions and can be less accurate participant observers than individuals who report higher levels of satisfaction. If this finding were to hold, the differential accuracy would confound comparisons of participant observations of distressed and nondistressed couples, and of pre- and posttreatment comparisons of data from couples in therapy.

The contrast in history effects in the Redfield and Paul (1976) and Robinson and Price (1980) studies is marked. Several features distinguish the two investigations. Redfield and Paul (1976) used experienced professional observers, an observation device that required minimal inference, and they required 100% levels of interobserver agreement prior to beginning data collection. Robinson and Price (1980) used naive participant observers and did not specify category definitions or training procedures. In addition, the observers in the Redfield and Paul study had only observed and presumably not interacted with the familiar subjects, whereas Robinson and Price's observers differed in the presumed quality of their prior interaction with their subjects, that is, each other. Any of these features, either alone or in combination, might account for differences between the studies.

In addition to the type of training he or she provides, the behavior of an experimenter may influence the data collected by research assistants in other ways. Rosenthal and his colleagues (Rosenthal, 1966, 1969) have demonstrated that providing data collectors with knowledge of experimenters' expectations could substantially alter the data reported. Though dependent measures in these studies were less clearly specified than most behavioral observation code categories, the possibility that more objective observational recordings could be biased in a similar fashion has led to several studies to investigate this question.

Early studies did in fact document expectation bias in observational recording (Kass & O'Leary, 1970; Scott, Burton, & Yarrow, 1967). However, these studies contained confounding elements that rendered their findings tenuous. Later, better-designed studies failed to replicate early findings. In one of these, Kent, O'Leary, Diament, and Dietz (1974) randomly divided trained undergraduate observer pairs into two groups. Each group viewed the same series of videotapes that the experimenter told them had been filmed during the baseline and treatment phases of an intervention with disruptive children. One group of observers was informed that disruptive behavior should decrease from baseline to treatment; the other group was told to expect no change. The children in the videotapes in fact exhibited equivalent rates of behavior in both so-called experimental phases. Observers recorded disruptive behavior using the O'Leary classroom code. After all observations were collected, observers were asked to indicate whether they had seen changes in the children's behavior.

Results revealed that none of the nine categories was influenced by the expectation manipulation, nor was a composite linear sum of the nine codes. Furthermore, this lack of bias held across treatment conditions, across observer pairs, and when different children were observed. The observers' subjective estimates of change, in contrast, showed significant bias in the direction of the expectation manipulations.

Shuller and McNamara (1976) replicated these findings using a slightly different methodology. Undergraduate observers were briefly trained, then viewed a five-minute videotape in which they recorded six categories of behavior of a child engaged in a play activity. Two of the categories represented aggressive behavior (hit-throw and take); two, hyperactivity (run, jump); and two were characterized as normal (give, touch). Prior to recording observations of the tape, each observer was either told simply to record the child's behavior (a no-expectation control group) or verbally presented with one of three expectation sets, disguised as nursery school reports. One report described the child as hyperactive; a second, as aggressive; the third, as normal. After observing the videotape, observers completed a checklist containing adjectives reflecting these three dimensions.

As in the Kent et al. (1974) study, data from none of the six behavioral categories were significantly influenced by the expectation manipulations. Groups of observers given descriptions labeling the child as deviant, either hyperactive or aggressive, rated the child as significantly higher on both dimensions than did either the normalcy expectation or the no-expectation groups. Conversely, the latter two groups rated the child as more normal than either of the other observer groups. Taken together, these two studies imply that behavioral observations done by undergraduate observers viewing videotapes of children are unlikely to be biased by knowledge of experimental hypotheses alone. Global evaluations, in contrast, can reflect substantial bias. Whether these effects would hold with participant or paid observers, using in vivo observations, and with adult subjects, is an empirical question.

Providing knowledge of expected experimental results is not the only way an experimenter can influence observers. O'Leary, Kent, and Kanowitz (1975) speculated that when data collection occurs throughout a treatment study, an experimenter's remarks about changes in a client's behavior as reflected in the data could inadvertently "shape" observer inaccuracy. To examine this possibility, four female undergraduate observers were trained to use four observation categories from the O'Leary code. They were then shown videotapes ostensibly from baseline and treatment phases of a token program intervention, and told to expect changes in two kinds of behavior. The other two categories, they were told, should not change. In actuality, none of the behaviors changed. Observers recorded behavior from four baseline videotapes without experimenter intervention. After each "treatment" videotape, however, the experimenter examined the observer's data with her, praising her if her data showed the expected decrease in either of the two experimental categories, expressing disappointment if the decreases did not appear. Frequencies of all categories were compared with those recorded by criterion observers. Recorded frequencies of behavior were consistent across phases for the two kinds of control behavior, but showed decreases of 27% and 38% from "baseline" to "treatment" for the two "shaped" categories. These differences are even more striking given that only four 12½-minute videotapes were viewed during the "treatment" phase, indicating rapid shaping of biased data.

It is not likely that an experimenter would be as systematic in providing feedback to observers as was the experimenter in the O'Leary et al. (1975) study. Nonetheless, the fact experimenter feedback coupled with knowledge of experimental hypothesis produced changes in observational recording indicates that researchers could inadvertently direct "observer drift" in a way that would misrepresent treatment effects as more powerful than they actually are. Thus enthusiasm or disappointment with reported data should not be expressed to observers responsible for ongoing data collection.

Unfortunately, further exploration of these findings with participant and paid observers has not been done. Participant observation seems particularly vulnerable to possible data inaccuracy exaggerating treatment effects. Participant observers such as parents and teachers often also implement treatment procedures, and presumably are pleased when data reflect treatment effectiveness. Furthermore, the fact that time-consuming observation procedures will probably be discontinued when treatment effects are documented adds an additional contingency that could shape inaccurate data.

While studies showing direct attempts by the experimenter to bias results by conveying expectations have not demonstrated clear and consistent bias, there are other ways in which observers may be biased more subtly. In a recent study, for example, Harris and Ciminero (1978) examined the effects of cues presumably correlated with the target behavior. In a series of single-subject designs, observers recorded face touching and eye contact of a videotaped subject engaged in a mock interview. In some of the videotapes, the interviewer praised the subject for eye contact, sometimes after eye contact had actually occurred and at times unrelated to the subject's behavior. Face touching was never mentioned by the interviewer. When ratings of face touching were compared with criterion protocols, all observers were accurate across conditions. Half the observers, however, showed highly inaccurate recordings of eye contact when the videotapes with inaccurate praise were introduced. Ratings of eye contact were accurate when the praise was eliminated. These effects, however, tended not to replicate with a second introduction of the praise condition. Unfortunately, these findings are limited by their inconsistency and by the limited number of subjects in the study. Nonetheless, the possibility that salient environmental cues can bias recordings of behavior finds further support in the previously mentioned findings of Mash and Makohoniuk (1975) that observers trained with predictable sequences of behavior continued to record those sequences, even when the predicted pattern was no longer actually present.

Finally, the very act of checking agreement, previously shown to affect levels of agreement, has also been related to the amount of behavior reported by observers. In the Romanczyk et al. (1973) study, observers recorded only 75% as much behavior during covert agreement checks as they did when they knew agreement was being assessed. The proportion of different categories used by the observers (i.e., "complexity") also appears to vary with presence or absence of agreement checking, as was mentioned earlier. As Jones et al. pointed out, it is unclear whether reduced complexity is the result of changes in the observers' recording behavior, or whether the persons being observed actually reduce their behavioral variability in the presence of more than one observer. Future research using complexity as a dependent variable could clarify this issue.

Summary. Once shown to be adequately sensitive to certain facts about behavior in their original derivation or calibration conditions, direct observation coding systems are ready for use. In their various applications it is important that they be used in accord with the rules specified by their developers, in order that the accuracy originally established can be assumed for the applications as well. As a check on consistency of use it has been popular to compare the data of independent observers in order to determine their generalizability over different users of the system. It has been shown that interobserver agreement does not nec-

essarily reflect accuracy and that agreement can be influenced by numerous variables in addition to the behavior being observed. It has also been shown that the overall amount of behavior reported by observers can be influenced by a variety of factors.

It appears that much of the foregoing literature reflects an interest in generalizability over observers that is disproportionate to the importance of its demonstration. This interest seems predicated on the view that characteristics of an observer can contribute significantly to the nature of the data obtained. To the extent that an observer accurately reflects the dimensional quantity of the event of interest, the data do not depend on the person collecting them. But accuracy can only be established by comparing an observer against an unimpeachable source of information about the phenomenon of interest, for example, automatic mechanical recording, products of the performance, and records such as audio- and video-tapes.

Despite a nodding appreciation of the logic of this argument, we continue to "find the data from a variety of multiple observer procedures to be convincing estimates of true values" (Johnston & Pennypacker, 1980, p. 166). We have discussed generalizability over observers because it is a time-honored concern in the use of direct observation assessment methodology. However, we agree with Johnston and Pennypacker that the limited information provided relative to the costs of such tactics argues for redirecting our assessment resources in other areas, most notably toward questions related to other forms of generalizability.

Generalizability over Time

The major issue with respect to generalizability over time deals with the extent to which it matters when we perform our direct observations. If the data collected at any time are comparable to those we would have collected at any other time, we can generalize our results to periods not actually observed.

Few available data specifically address this issue. Johnson, Christensen, and Bellamy (1976) did find differences in parent and child behavior when observed at "picked" versus random times, but behavior and recording procedures (aware vs. unaware) were also different, so the effect of time alone is indeterminant.

Johnson and Bolstad (1973) and Patterson (1974) have examined the consistency of data collected under standard conditions but at different time periods (e.g., odd vs. even days of baseline). In the Johnson and Bolstad study, an odd-even split-half reliability of .72 was obtained for a set of behavior comprising a "total deviant behavior score." Data were collected on 33 normal children over five days of observations and divided into halves by taking data from the first, third, and first half of the fifth day and comparing them with data from the second, fourth, and second half of the fifth day. Application of the Spearman-Brown prophecy formula resulted in a stepped-up correlation of .83. Johnson and Bolstad reported comparable correlations for other scores from their coding system. Cobb (1972) and Patterson (1974) have likewise examined the temporal stability of response classes from similar direct observation coding systems. From a Spearman-Brown corrected value of .61, Patterson concluded that "five or six baseline sessions provided minimally stable estimates" of the behavior being assessed (p. 475).

The use of classical internal consistency measures in this way gives us some information about the consistency of the behavior studied. It should be noted, however, that failure to find such consistency might mean either that the behavior is not stable or that the measure is inadequate to detect it. This question can be resolved to some extent by demonstrating that the system is accurate in reflecting repeated occurrences during the original calibration conditions, and periodically corroborating this accuracy through recalibration.

While the type of generalizability information provided by the use of split-half reliability procedures is of some interest, it may not be directly relevant to the concerns typically expressed by researchers using direct observation procedures. At least in clinical psychology research and application, investigators generally ask whether data observed at a particular time are representative of those observable at other times not selected. Alternatively, one wishes to know how accurately projections can be made from data collected over one period of time or set of measurements to other periods not yet measured (e.g., White, 1977). One form of the latter question deals with examining the stability of baseline data, that is, the likelihood that behavior will continue at its present level in the absence of treatment.

The use of internal consistency measures as described above deals directly with neither of these questions. These measures simply reflect the consistency of subjects' behavior *relative to one another* from one set of measurement occasions to the next. All subjects' behavior could be increasing, decreasing, or staying the same, and we could still get high split-half reliability values. The use of such values to estimate the representativeness of data collected over some period of time is similarly limited to the relative positions of the subjects in the distributions of observed behavior frequencies. That is, the corrected reliability value of .61 reported by Patterson (1974) provides "minimally stable estimates" only of these positions. Actually it allows us merely to say that, in general, the ordering of children with respect to this behavior is about the same whether we look at one half of the data or the other, and will be about the same if we look at data from twice as many occasions of measurement. It is hard to see how this information will be of value if the research concern is in intervening to produce changes in absolute levels of behavior, not relative ones.

The bulk of the evidence for the temporal generalizability of direct observation data comes from studies concerned less with assessing behavior than with changing it. Thus baseline frequencies will be collected over long periods of time and an independent variable then introduced. The data are usually graphically portrayed, but specific attention is not called to their stability over time. An implicit examination of two forms of temporal generalizability is usually conducted by consumers of such graphs, however, as they note the comparability of data from different observation occasions (e.g., Sessions 1 vs. 3 vs. 7) and over different intervals of time (e.g., early sessions vs. later ones).

To be sure, this is not a very systematic examination of the generalizability of direct observation data over time. It is likely that the development of both assessment and intervention technology would benefit from specific investigations of the temporal generalizability of such data. Until these studies are conducted it will be advisable to restrict the generalizations we make about behavior to those relatively narrow time frames in which it is observed.

Generalizability over Settings

Are data collected in one observational context representative of those obtainable in others? If we observe ad lib drinking in laboratory bars (Nathan, Titler, Lowenstein, Solomon, & Rossi, 1970), for example, do we obtain data representative of drinking in a more natural context? Is deviant children's behavior observed in school comparable to what goes on at home (Wahler, 1975)?

Certain minimal accuracy requirements would have to be met before the generalizability of behavior across settings could be studied with a particular direct observation recording system. First, the system would have to be shown to be accurate with regard to the behavior in question. Second, the system would have to produce data that accurately reflected generalizability of the behavior over time, using time intervals comparable to the time lapse between observations

in the different settings. And third, the system would have to be capable of detecting behavioral occurrence in multiple settings, ideally ones comparable to those in which the behavior would be observed.

Before examining the literature in this area, we should clearly define the meaning of levels of "setting." Any change in the stimulus environment is, in effect, a change in setting. In a sense, therefore, one is never in the same setting twice. For our purposes, however, we shall refer to settings as relatively gross stimulus complexes such as "school," "home," "clinic," and "office." Variations within these will be referred to as changes in circumstances (e.g., structured vs. unstructured recess at school).

The use of direct observation assessment procedures to examine the occurrence of the same behavior in different settings has been rare. In one such effort, Wahler (1975) compared the behavior of two boys in home and school settings over a period of nearly three years. Using an interval recording system (Wahler, House, & Stambaugh, 1976), covariation in behavior categories over observation sessions was examined in each setting separately and in combination. Perhaps because he was primarily interested in interrelationships among the different categories, Wahler did not report intrabehavior-intersetting correlations. He was able to identify stable clusters of behavior categories, but found these to be "specific to the children's two general environments" (p. 41).

Using data collected at home and in the clinic, G. K. Lobitz and Johnson (1975) compared families with a child referred for behavior problems with families with a nonreferred child. Observational data were recorded using a modified version of the Family Interaction Coding System (Reid, 1978b). In the clinic, parents were given a series of structured tasks to perform with their children. In the home, families were instructed to behave as they usually would, but to stay in a two-room area with the television off. Of the six summary observational categories for which data were presented, four discriminated the two groups in the home setting, while only two did so in the clinic. Four of the categories correlated significantly (.41 to .56) across settings with the referred group; only one category was significantly related for the nonreferred group, and this was in a direction opposite expectations.

Unfortunately, this study confounded experimental tasks with changes in setting, making it impossible to determine whether task structure or setting differences accounted for the different behavior patterns observed in the clinic versus the home. However, the results imply that cross-setting and crosstask stability of responding cannot be assumed. Furthermore, certain individuals or groups of individuals may show greater cross-setting behavior generality than others. Finally, some responses may be generalizable across settings while others may not.

Before adding these findings to the accumulation of studies (e.g., Hartshorne & May, 1928) that have found behavior to be situation-specific, one or two cautions should be noted. The situation specificity of behavior issue should be tested by examining the occurrence of the same identical response in different environmental contexts. The use of well-defined but relatively *molar* behavior categories leaves unanswered the question of situation specificity of molecular responses. For example, one of Wahler's categories was "social interaction child," which was scored for "any interaction between peers and the target child" (p. 29). Numerous topographically and functionally different responses could comprise such a class. It is conceivable that one or two relatively low frequency members could occur consistently in several settings but not be noticed in analyses based on larger aggregates.

With respect to variations within the same setting, considerable research has shown effects on directly observed behavior. For example, Boulter (1979) found the specific classroom behavior that discriminated popular children from their rejected and ignored peers depended on whether observations occurred during an unstructured activity, an activity led by the teacher, or a semistructured activity in which the children worked on assigned tasks. It appears that when direct observations are performed in the same setting under different circumstances, salient differences could cancel each other when data are combined. Of greater concern is the possibility that an investigator sampling across different circumstances within a setting will inadvertently confound changes in these circumstances with changes in experimental conditions.

Generalizability of Data Collected in Analogue Settings. Additional evidence on the cross-setting generalizability of directly observed behavior comes from the use of analogue assessment procedures conducted in laboratory or controlled naturalistic conditions. Typically used to set the occasion for behavior that may be low-frequency or inaccessible in the natural environment, role-play analogue assessments of assertiveness and social skills have come under particular methodological scrutiny recently. Numerous investigators have found cross-task consistencies to be variable, sometimes showing significant differences, sometimes not, depending on the behavior assessed and the task per se. Different tasks (e.g., role play vs. interview) have been associated with variations in subject responses (Bellack, Hersen, & Lamparski, 1979; Bellack, Hersen, & Turner, 1979; Martin, Johnson, Johansson, & Wahl, 1976). Even within the same task, behavior has been shown to be influenced by: (1) the sex of the person with whom the subject interacts (Eisler, Hersen, Miller, & Blanchard, 1975); (2) whether single or multiple responses are required (Galassi & Galassi, 1976); (3) the information provided to subjects about such factors as their hypothetical past histories with the confederate (Eisler et al., 1975) and the elaboration of situational descriptors (Bellack, 1979); and (4) whether the subject responds to a live confederate or to a tape-recorded presentation of a confederate (Taskey & Rich, 1979). In the Bellack, Hersen, and Turner (1979) study, responses to programmed naturalistic incidents on a psychiatric unit were compared with responses to identical situations presented in role plays. Correlations showed only modest relationships for three of the six observational variables compared. Thus responses observed in laboratory analogues are generalizable to in vivo situations only under restricted sets of conditions, the specific parameters of which have yet to be established.

Effects of Varying Demand Characteristics. Other research has investigated generalizability across minor variations in setting characteristics. Some of these have involved altered levels of demand characteristics; others have examined variations in the obtrusiveness of the observation procedures themselves. In an investigation of variations in demand characteristics, W. C. Lobitz and Johnson (1975) instructed the parents of deviant and nondeviant boys to attempt to make their children appear well-behaved, disturbed, and normal over consecutive two-day periods. Children showed the most deviant behavior under the "fake bad" condition. Moreover, parents were less positive and more negative, and gave more commands than they did in the normal or "fake good" conditions. Frequency of parent commands and a global parent negative category were the only responses to differentiate the "fake good" from the "normal" instructions, and these differences were found for the nondistressed sample only.

Using a similar design, Vincent, Friedman, Nugent, and Messerly (1979) explored the effects of "fake good" or "fake bad" versus neutral instructions on the verbal problem-solving interaction of distressed and nondistressed couples. While all four verbal response summary categories observed showed changes in predicted directions from the neutral to both faking conditions, the two

nonverbal categories remained stable. Unlike the Lobitz and Johnson results, distressed and nondistressed couples showed similar patterns of response to both "fake good" and "fake bad" instructions.

These results indicate that variations in experimental instructions can significantly affect behavior. Studies of demand characteristics often use highly salient instructional differences, however, and it is difficult to know to what extent these results are applicable to other more subtle variations in experimenter instructions (e.g., "Discuss this problem" vs. "Try to solve this problem"). In addition, the possibility that instructional set will interact differentially with treatment conditions and bias treatment results should not be overlooked. Instructing marital therapy subjects to "negotiate and problem solve on issue X" might elicit highly generalizable behavior samples from treatment and control couples prior to therapy. At posttreatment assessment, the same instructions could yield equally generalizable results for the controls, but highly situation-specific discussions from the treated couples who learned to respond to the words "negotiate" and "problem solve" during therapy.

Setting Changes Produced by Observation Itself: Reactivity. The final setting variable we shall consider is the effect of observation itself. As Weick (1968) has noted, "There is little argument that the observer, in the process of watching an event, affects its course" (p. 369). This process has been termed "reactivity." There is a rather extensive literature documenting the reactive effects of direct observation on the persons being assessed. Even observers themselves have been shown to behave differently when observed (Romanczyk et al., 1973), a type of reactivity mentioned earlier in relation to generalizability over observers. Recent reviews of reactivity (e.g., Baum, Forehand, & Zegiob, 1979; Kent & Foster, 1977) make it unnecessary to repeat the evidence for reactivity here. Instead we will summarize the major findings and offer some comments aimed at placing the phenomenon in proper perspective.

Johnson and Bolstad (1973) identified two major paradigms for studying reactivity: habituation, and varying the level of observer conspicuousness. A subcategory of the second involves manipulating the subject's awareness of being observed (Baum et al., 1979). In the first paradigm, levels of behavior are observed to change over time in the absence of specific intervention. Reactivity is assumed at the outset, and the subsequent change is attributed to the observed persons habituating to the observational process. Of course, simply seeing changes in behavior over time does not prove that reactivity initially was present. Unmeasured and unrelated environmental changes coincidental with the observer's presence could also be responsible for the presumed "habituation."

In the second reactivity paradigm, data are compared under varying levels of observer conspicuousness or obtrusiveness. For example, the observer might be visible to the subjects in one condition and behind a one-way mirror in another. As noted by Baum et al. (1979), a third paradigm is an elaboration of the second, and involves manipulating the observed person's awareness of being observed. Mercatoris and Craighead (1974) provided an example of the awareness manipulation paradigm when they observed a teacher's behavior directly in the classroom in one condition, and led her to believe no data were being collected in a second condition in which the observer was absent. Actually observations were continuously recorded throughout all phases of the study using a videotape camera that the teacher was told operated only when the observer was present.

Another variation on this strategy recently employed by Cone, Hanson, and Gruber (1980) involved systematically increasing the obtrusiveness of the direct observation procedures. Teacher volunteers were told some of their classes would be videotaped, but that because of equipment and personnel scheduling complexities it would be impossible to tell them ahead of time just when observations would occur. This covert videotaping phase was followed by a condition in which teachers were told they were to be taped immediately prior to the observation of that class. Next, teachers were told when they would be videotaped as well as what specific behavior would be observed and scored from the tapes. Finally, a live observer entered the classroom and collected data on the behavior of interest. None of these four conditions was associated with systematic changes in teacher behavior. However, it was possible that all of the conditions simply produced equivalently high levels of reactivity. To evaluate this, a simple auditory cueing procedure (Van Houten & Sullivan, 1975) was introduced on the assumption that if behavior increased easily, significant reactivity had probably not been produced. Two- to three-fold increases in teacher behavior accompanying the audio cueing suggested the prior observation phases were nonreactive.

Evidence for reactivity is not entirely consistent. In their review of the literature on reactivity in adult–child interactions, Baum et al. (1979) found adults to be reactive in 12 of 15 studies examining the issue. Reactivity for children was found in 10 of 15 studies. Other reviews have found similarly mixed results (Johnson & Bolstad, 1973; Kent & Foster, 1977; Wildman & Erickson, 1977). Generally it appears that more studies demonstrate reactive effects than do not. It is possible, though, that a publication bias could inflate these figures if studies that failed to document reactivity were more often rejected by journals than studies that documented it.

A number of variables have been related to reactivity. Among those identified and analyzed by Baum et al. were age of the person observed (adult vs. child), research paradigm, observation setting, status of the person observed (clinical vs. nonclinical), and type of behavior observed. Adults appeared somewhat more susceptible to observer influence than children (75% vs. 66%). Examining research paradigm factors, reactivity has been reported consistently less often in studies manipulating variations in observer obtrusiveness (50%) than in studies using the habituation and manipulation of awareness paradigms (75% and 83%, respectively). The child's referral status was not associated with systematic differences in reactivity. With adults, positive and neutral verbal interactions and physical performance showed greater evidence of reactivity than negative categories of behavior. Laboratory settings tended to have a higher probability of reactive effects than naturalistic settings, but, as Baum et al. noted, this increased reactivity may result because the majority of studies conducted in laboratory settings have used the awareness paradigm. Classroom studies, which show the least reactivity, more typically employ the variations in obtrusiveness approach.

In addition to the variables isolated in the excellent review by Baum et al., several others have been suggested in the literature. Among these are the length of time over which reactivity is assessed (Mash & Hedley, 1975), identity of the observer (Callahan & Allevizos, 1973; Johnson & Bolstad, 1973; Martin, Gelfand, & Hartmann, 1971), prior interactional history with observers (Mash & Hedley, 1975), and the behavior of the observers during observation sessions (Grimm, Parsons, & Bijou, 1972).

Direct observation recording procedures are often used in time series designs. When the independent variable is sometimes present, sometimes not (as in ABAB designs), it is possible that reactivity to observational procedures interacts with the experimental manipulations. Thus observer effects may be noted during baseline but not experimental phases, or vice versa, confounding the effects of the independent variable. Recently researchers have begun to examine the seriousness of this potential confounding influ-

ence. Dubey, Kent, O'Leary, Broderick, and O'Leary (1977) reported two studies involving observations of eight first-grade children during a baseline and a subsequent token reinforcement intervention. During each phase both observer present and observer absent conditions were in effect. Of the 10 child behavior categories recorded, only one showed a significant phase by observation condition interaction in the first of the studies. There was less "time off task" during intervention as compared with baseline when observers were present. In fact, time off task *increased* from baseline to intervention in observer absent conditions. However, this interactive effect was not replicated in the subsequent study.

Weinrott, Garrett, and Todd (1978) also examined the observer effect by treatment interaction question and obtained similar results. They analyzed the data separately for each of six elementary-age boys during baseline and token reinforcement conditions of an ABAB design in two different classroom contexts (math and language) and found no evidence of reactivity or of an observer effect by treatment phase interaction. As Weinrott et al. noted, however, their subjects were relatively "observer-sophisticated," a condition that could limit the generalizability of their results.

To summarize, as Weinrott et al. noted, "observee reactivity is neither ubiquitous nor well understood. The presence or absence of the phenomenon is probably controlled by a number of variables" (pp. 902–903). We have delineated many of these, and Baum et al. (1980) summarized the evidence concerning some of them. Considerably more research is needed before the effects of observation procedures on persons observed are fully understood.

Utility of Reactive and Nonreactive Assessment Procedures. Before pursuing studies of reactivity further, it is important to clarify the reasons for using a particular direct observation assessment procedure in the first place. It may be that reactivity poses problems for some research and clinical objectives and not for others. The important issue seems to be not whether observed individuals react differently under conditions of known observation but rather whether data collected under such conditions are less useful than those collected surreptitiously. As Medley and Mitzel (1963) noted some years ago, people probably behave differently when taking an intelligence test than they do normally. Yet intelligence tests have been shown to predict behavior in a variety of circumstances. While behavior is occasionally directly observed for purely descriptive purposes, it is more likely that it is being related to other behavior, just as intelligence test performance is. For example, in most applied research on deviant child behavior in schools, direct observation of problem behavior comprises the dependent variable of immediate interest. Changes in behavior are related to manipulations of one's independent variables and effects are determined. Unless these changes are related to changes in others' (e.g., parents, teachers, administrators) evaluations of the problem behavior, the data will have limited utility, regardless of the extent to which they are free of observer influence. Wolf (1978) and Kazdin (1977b) have discussed this issue under the rubric of "social validation."

In this vein it is conceivable that reactive data may have even greater utility or social validity than nonreactive data in some circumstances. This could occur when the experimenter wishes to generalize to situations involving similar levels of obtrusive observation. For example, in assessing the adequacy of vocal presentations before audiences, it is probably the case that data obtained from conditions in which the client is aware of being observed will correlate more highly with subsequent real-life presentations. Similarly, it may be the case that relatively reactive heterosocial skills assessment will evidence greater utility than less reactive assessment, given that most heterosocial interactions contain an evaluative component. Removing a significant portion of this component from the assessment process could lead to lower correlations with relevant criteria. As Barker and Wright (1955) pointed out long ago, interaction between an observer and a person observed is important in its own right, not just as a potential confounding element to be uniformly eliminated or controlled.

Thus explorations are needed of what if any differences reactivity makes in terms of the validity of the assessment process. Since our research and clinical resources are limited, it makes sense to study the differential validity of data collected under varying degrees of observer obtrusiveness. Moreover, logic suggests looking at the differential validity question first. If data collected under different conditions are in fact differentially valid, *then* it would make sense to begin exploring the relative contributions of the various components (stimulus elements) of the conditions. To do this first may in actuality beg the question.

Generalizability over Behavior

Most forms of what has typically been referred to as validity deal with relationships between different kinds of behavior. Traditionally, concern with behavior-behavior relationships has been to establish either the criterion-related validity of a measure or its construct validity. Both concerns have been addressed by users of direct observation methodology. Many uses of direct observation procedures with common clinical problems specifically address the criterion-related validity issue. Thus the observation that obese and nonobese persons differ in their rates of eating (Stunkard & Kaplan, 1977) validates direct observations of eating speed against weight. Similar concerns are evident in direct observations of other consuming behavior (e.g., smoking, drinking) as well as of interactions between parents and children and between husbands and wives.

The direct observation of interrelationships among behavior for purposes of validating or clarifying a construct has also been relatively common. In his studies of dependency, for example, Sears (1963) examined the interrelatedness of five different forms of dependent behavior in preschool children. Similarly, Gewirtz (1956) provided early evidence of the relationships among various measures of one form of dependency, attention seeking. He was able to identify two relatively independent types of attention seeking, that is, active and passive efforts to maintain adult attention. More recently Jones, Reid, and Patterson (1975) explored the construct validity of categories in the Family Interaction Coding System. And as mentioned in the previous section, Wahler (1975) examined the relationship among various behavior categories in his system.

Other investigators have recently addressed the question of the interrelationships among specific kinds of behavior making up a particular category of responses in systems such as Patterson's, Wahler's (Wahler et al., 1976), and O'Leary's (Kent & O'Leary, 1976). For example, what is the nature of the relationship among the different behavior comprising a category labeled "disruptive"? What is the best way to combine scores on the individual components of such a category in order to predict other behavior? In one study, Kent, O'Leary, Coletti, and Drabman (cited in Kent & Foster, 1977) compared unweighted and differentially weighted sums of nine categories of a code for disruptive behavior in school-aged children. The criteria were the judgments of teachers who were asked to give global ratings of the level of disruptiveness of students viewed on videotape. The unweighted sum of the nine categories correlated .65 with teacher ratings. Weighted sums produced from multiple regression analyses correlated .95 and .85 with teacher ratings in derivation and cross-validation samples, respectively.

In an alternative approach to the same issue, Gottman (1979) described the initial development of a 28-category code to assess marital interaction. Because the system was cumbersome, he and his colleagues wanted to develop more global yet meaningful categories. To do this, they computed conditional probabilities for the relationships among behavior in the large code, and combined behavior that produced similar consequences, as determined by those conditional probabilities. Thus the constituents of molar categories were kinds of behavior that the investigators had empirically determined to function similarly. While Gottman did not detail the mechanics of these procedures, the methodology provides a framework for grouping behavior empirically rather than intuitively as has heretofore been common practice.

As was true for research on the generalizability of directly observed behavior over settings, it is important to pay careful attention to the way in which the interrelatedness of different behavior is studied. With very few exceptions (e.g., Wahler, 1975), this issue has been approached from an interindividual differences perspective. Thus we may know that "total child deviance" is positively correlated with "parent negatives" across a number of different child-parent combinations analyzed together. But a fine-grained analysis of the probabilistic relationships among either these molar categories or their molecular constituents for individual child-parent dyads is missing. Even the correlation of different categories over time and the inductive compilation of covarying clusters (e.g., Wahler, 1975) for individual children could be subjected to alternative, finer-grained analyses as suggested in the previous section. Fortunately, some work in this area has begun, with the calculation of conditional probabilities among mother and child behavior in mother-infant interaction studies (Bakeman, 1978), and in examining single-subject parent-child patterns in the interaction of distressed families (Patterson & Moore, 1979).

Generalizability over Methods

In this final section on the generalizability of directly observed behavioral data we will concern ourselves with the extent to which data thus obtained relate to those collected by alternative methods of assessment. There are practical as well as scientific reasons for concern with this issue. On the practical side, direct observation data are typically very resource-intensive to collect. Therefore it is useful to know just how these data compare with those of less time-consuming methods such as interviews, self-reports, or ratings by others.

From a research-scientific perspective, there is very little choice but to examine the correspondence of data from different assessment methods. In the personality assessment and research arena, Campbell and Fiske (1959) long ago noted the inevitable intrusion of method variance into measurement of any behavior. That is, scores on a measure are jointly determined by "true" differences between individuals and by characteristics of the measure itself. Campbell and Fiske (1959) articulated the need to separate variability in scores due to real differences on the characteristic being measured from variability due to characteristics of the measure. In so doing, the response in question would thus be shown to be more than simply the measure of it, and relationships between different responses could be assumed to be more than the fortuitous use of a common assessment device. Campbell and Fiske proposed the multitrait-multimethod matrix for separating method and trait variance. Such a matrix is produced from all possible correlations of two or more characteristics measured in two or more ways. When different ways of measuring a single characteristic are more highly correlated than different characteristics measured by a single method, the

methods are said to have convergent validity. The necessity to show convergent validity when studying interresponse relationships is the basis for cross-method comparisons from a research-scientific perspective.

Space does not permit extensive review of research on the issue of generalizability across methods of data produced with direct observation recording systems. We shall cite some typical studies, however, and follow them with a few suggestions about directions for future research in this area.

While direct observation assessment data can be compared with those obtained from any other method of assessment, most frequently they have been compared with self-reports, ratings by others, and self-monitoring. A study by Blunden, Spring, and Greenberg (1974) compared teacher ratings of behavior associated with hyperactivity with direct observation measures of the same behaviors. The 40-item Classroom Behavior Inventory (CBI; Greenberg, Deem, & McMahon, 1972) was used to obtain teacher ratings. Ratings on specific items such as "looks around" and "twists and turns" were summed to get scores for 10 general categories such as distractibility and restlessness.

Blunden et al. developed direct observation coding procedures for seven of the 10 CBI categories and trained observers to collect data in three 15-minute observation sessions for each of 40 kindergarten boys. Correlation coefficients in the convergent validity diagonal of the resulting multitrait-multimethod matrix ranged from −.01 to .50, with only one of the seven categories ("impulsiveness") showing convergence across the two measures. Each of the seven rating scale and direct observation categories was also examined to see how well it distinguished 13 boys who were nominated by their teachers as having behavior problems from 22 boys who were not. Five of the seven rated categories discriminated the groups at a statistically significant level, while only one ("impulsiveness") of the direct observation categories did so. The authors discussed their lack of convergence in terms of low interrater reliabilities and possible instability of behavior samples based on only 45 minutes of observation.

The correspondence between self-reported and directly observed behavior has been investigated in children and adults (e.g., Fixsen, Phillips, & Wolf, 1972; McReynolds & Stegman, 1976; Peacock, Lyman, & Richard, 1978; Robinson & Price, 1980). In one such study, Risley and Hart (1968) found very little relationship between four- and five-year-olds' statements about what they had played with and what observers noted until self-report accuracy was reinforced. Thus, whereas nearly all of the children said they played with certain objects, very few actually did so. Similarly, in a study of the accuracy of cabin-cleaning reports among emotionally disturbed boys between 12 and 14 years of age, Peacock et al. (1978) found significant overreporting of cleaning for both easy and difficult items. A close correspondence between campers' self-reports and direct observations of cabin cleanliness was produced when access to breakfast was made contingent upon accurate reporting.

Finally, in the study of the correspondence between self-reports and direct observation of marital interactions mentioned previously, Robinson and Price (1980) found rates of specific pleasurable behavior were not accurately reported by the couples, though the self-reported rates of overall pleasurable behavior more closely matched those of the observers.

With respect to self-monitoring-direct observation correspondence, Nelson's (1977) recent review of the self-monitoring literature identified nine different factors that have been associated with correspondence. Overall the results were mixed, with some studies finding correspondence and others not.

It should be pointed out that research related to the generalizability of directly observed data to other methods of assessment has not generally been conducted to address this specific question. Rather, direct observation data have been used as criteria against which to validate other assessment procedures (Nelson, 1977) or as a means of comparing one type of behavior (e.g., motoric) with another (e.g., physiological). Thus clear conclusions about the correspondence between direct observation and other methods of assessing the *same* behavior cannot be offered at this time.

Importance of Response Equivalence in Cross-Method Comparisons.   As has been discussed in another context (Cone, 1979), careful attention must be given the equivalence of responses being assessed when measurement procedures are being compared. It is common, for example, to examine the adequacy of self-report data by comparing them with direct observation data in the interest of showing correspondence between different modes of responding (Lang, 1968; 1971). Such comparisons are not, strictly speaking, dealing with the generalizability of behavior over methods, since they usually confound method and behavior. Thus self-reports of fear of parachute jumping might be compared with success in a course of parachuting (Walk, 1956), or self-reports of spider fear might be correlated with direct observations of motor behavior in the presence of spiders (Fazio, 1969). To conclude anything about the correspondence between self-report and direct observation as methods of assessing behavior, it would be necessary to compare them on identical behavior.

A study that approximated this requirement showed closer correspondence between the methods as the comparability of the behavior assessed by the investigators increased. In comparing self-reports against direct observations of actual behavior, McReynolds and Stegman (1976) found 95% accuracy for measures asking subjects what they *would do* in certain fear-provoking contexts, but only 61% accuracy for measures of *how fearful* they were. More recently,

Zuckerman (1979) compared self-report measures of varying degrees of specificity against observers' ratings and direct observation of performance in snake, height, and darkness avoidance situations. The broad trait measures (e.g., manifest anxiety, neuroticism) showed no correlation with directly observed behavior. The specific trait measures (e.g., fear survey schedule) were somewhat predictive ($r = .40$), but the state measures (e.g., measures of fear in the "actual situations after the tasks were described to the subjects but before they actually began to attempt to perform the tasks," p. 49) were most predictive of all ($r = .47$). The McReynolds and Stegman data suggest that asking subjects what they would probably do rather than simply asking them about their fear might have led to even higher predictabilities.

Direct Observation and Ratings by Others. The convergence of data from direct observation methods and ratings by others is probably the next most important type of generalizability across methods to be studied. It is not unusual for comparisons of both types of data against a relevant criterion to come out favoring the ratings (Eyberg & Johnson, 1974; Rosenshine & Furst, 1973). Rosenshine and Furst found that studies using both methods to predict student achievement consistently supported the superiority of ratings.

Speculation as to the reasons for this superiority might be instructive. The appropriate assessment method must be largely determined by the criterion being predicted. Ratings typically measure the rater's subjective *experience* of the phenomenon of interest. Indeed they may be more sensitive to this than to the objective characteristics of the phenomenon itself. To the extent that the criteria against which the different methods are being compared similarly reflect the rater's experience, the scales are tipped in favor of the ratings. This contamination is not avoided by comparing ratings by one set of judges against criterion ratings of a second set of judges, as it is likely that the predictor and criterion will be contaminated by the shared experience of the raters. For example, predictor teachers are likely to have many things in common with criterion teachers. These commonalities are likely to be associated with similar experiences of the behavior being assessed. Direct observation procedures cannot share in this experience and hence may be less predictive of it.

Thus it may be that comparisons of ratings and direct observation methods will almost always favor ratings to the extent that ratings or other measures of human experience comprise all or a significant portion of the criteria. In predicting such criteria it makes sense to emphasize ratings over direct observations. This is especially true in the applied arena such as with social skills assessment. However, if a more objective topographic focus is taken by the cross-method matching, ratings will approximate direct observation as the degree of inference is lowered and the rater's experience of the behavior is minimized or eliminated altogether (Curran, 1979). As this happens, of course, there is less and less reason to prefer one method over the other. A more extensive theoretical discussion of the relationship between direct observation and ratings has recently been provided by Cairns and Green (1979).

Direct Observation and Interviews and Self-Reports. The comparison of self-reports and interviews with direct observations invokes many of the same issues discussed for ratings by others. However, with self-reports, the method taps the *subject's* experience of the behavior of interest rather than the experience of the rater. Since there are relatively few meaningful criteria that also tap a significant portion of the subject's experience of the behavior, there is less predictor-criterion overlap with interviews and self-reports than with ratings by others. As a result, direct observations are not as likely to be automatically inferior. As a more topographic emphasis is taken, the data from self-report and interview forms of assessment become less subjective and potentially more reflective of the objective features of the behavior of interest. By minimizing the person's experience of his or her behavior, these forms of assessment will approximate direct observation or self-monitoring.

It could be useful to have studies involving cross-method matching of direct observation and self-report and interview data in which degree of subjectivity was systematically manipulated. Comparisons against criteria similarly varied in terms of subjectivity would yield a wealth of data about behavioral assessment generally, and about the relative utility of direct observation and other methods specifically.

A complete catalogue of the relationships between direct observation and other assessment methods would require listing of assessment purposes, topographies of the responses to be assessed, relationships between these responses to be assessed, relationships between these responses and relevant criteria, and costs of obtaining the assessment data using each type of method. To date only the barest beginnings have been made toward assembling the kinds of information that would make such a cross-referencing possible. Indeed the problem is one of such enormous complexity that it is unlikely we will ever have even a marginally adequate system for matching different assessment methods. Research in this area should accelerate, however, if only to document the complexity just mentioned and perhaps to develop ways of simplifying the entire process. In sum, the generalizability of direct observation data over other methods of assessment must be studied because a science based on interrelationships among kinds of behavior requires it. There are practical reasons for studying this type of generalizability as well. Nonetheless very little research has focused specifically on this correspondence. Future studies should address this issue directly, and should be careful to assure that the same behavior is assessed by the multiple methods in order to avoid ambiguities associated with confusions between method and behavior.

SUMMARY

This chapter has integrated three major issues related to direct observation assessment methodology. Practical, how-to-do-it topics have threaded their way through liberal discussions of research findings on the one hand, and conceptual-theoretical discourse on the other.

After starting with some general considerations and practical suggestions for the design of direct observation recording systems, the need to determine the specific response properties to be observed was discussed. In addition to frequency and duration, we noted the importance of attention to qualitative features of behavior as well. Expressing these features in terms of topographic aspects of a response minimizes the need for subjective judgments. Products can also be used as indirect measures of behavior and have associated advantages and limitations.

Issues in establishing the appropriate level of analysis were also considered. In particular, behavior categories included in direct observation systems may be ordered along a continuum from gross, general, molar analysis at one end, to narrow, specific, and molecular at the other. While researchers have typically assumed the equivalence of the specific responses lumped into molar categories, recent research challenges this assumption. Combining responses on the basis of similar response functions, and differentially weighting responses within categories, are two practices that address this issue and are likely to be pursued in the future.

Following the discussion of level of analysis, different types of systems were presented. Three major types of direct observation coding systems include narrative, event, and interval recording. Narratives are useful in reflecting "streams of behavior" and as preliminary pilot operations for later code definition and development. Problems in establishing the objectivity of narratives has often led to the selection of particular behavior or events for more specific assessment. The partitioning of observation periods into smaller segments or intervals was discussed as a way of further objectifying the recording process and increasing the probability that independent observers would see the same behavior at the same time.

The sensitivity of measuring device to the occurrence of target behavior surfaced in different forms throughout the ensuing discussion of the quality of data produced by direct observation recording systems. It is critical to separate quality of measurement issues from questions about the behavior being measured. Most quality concerns have to do with the accuracy with which the system reflects certain information about behavior. The "facts" at issue are typically the occurrence of a response, its repeatability, its repeatability over time and setting, and its measurability by more than one means. The accuracy with which a system detects these facts can be established in initial derivation or calibration conditions, much as one would calibrate a microscope.

While the accuracy of direct observation recording systems has generally not received the attention it merits, some evidence has developed with respect to temporal, setting, and method generalizability. Some problems in the conduct of research in this area were noted. In studying the generalizability of direct observation data on one behavior to data on other behavior it was stressed that behavior-behavior relationships should be studied with more than one assessment method, and care should be taken to avoid method-behavior confusion.

Unlike the conclusion drawn by Wright (1967) and quoted at the beginning of this chapter, direct observation has assumed increasing importance in clinical assessment over the past two decades. Its continued prominence as an assessment method will depend upon the integration and resolution of current practical and psychometric considerations in direct observation methodology. Thus we hope that the liberal intertwining of practical, research, and conceptual-theoretical threads throughout this chapter produced something more than a state-of-the-art review, and that evidence for its heuristic potential will have a short latency and a long duration.

REFERENCES

Arrington, R. E. (1932). Some technical aspects of observer reliability as indicated in studies of the "Talkies." *American Journal of Sociology,* **38,** 409–417.

Baer, D. M. (1977a). Reviewer's comment: Just because it's reliable doesn't mean that you can use it. *Journal of Applied Behavior Analysis,* **10,** 117–119.

Baer, D. M. (1977b). "Perhaps it would be better not to know everything." *Journal of Applied Behavior Analysis,* **10,** 167–172.

Bakeman, R. (1978). Untangling streams of behavior: Sequential analyses of observational data. In G. P. Sackett (Ed.), *Observing behavior, Vol. 2: Data collection and analysis methods.* Baltimore: University Park Press.

Barker, R. G., & Wright, H. F. (1955). *Midwest and its children: The psychological ecology of an American town.* New York: Harper & Row.

Baum, C. G., Forehand, R., & Zegiob, L. E. (1979). A review of observer reactivity in adult-child interactions. *Journal of Behavioral Assessment,* **1,** 167–178.

Bellack, A. S. (1979). Behavioral assessment of social skills. In A. S. Bellack & M. Hersen (Eds.), *Research and practice in social skills training.* New York: Plenum Press.

Bellack, A. S., Hersen, M., & Lamparski, D. (1979). Role-play tests for assessing social skills: Are they valid? Are they useful? *Journal of Consulting and Clinical Psychology,* **47,** 335–342.

Bellack, A. S., Hersen, M. & Turner, S. M. (1979). Relationship of role playing and knowledge of appropriate behavior to assertion in the natural environment. *Journal of Consulting and Clinical Psychology,* **47,** 670–678.

Berk, R. (1979). Generalizability of behavior observations: A clarification of interobserver agreement and interobserver reliability. *American Journal of Mental Deficiency,* **83,** 460–472.

Bijou, S. W., Peterson, R. F., & Ault, M. H. (1968). A method to integrate descriptive and experimental field studies at the level of data and empirical concepts. *Journal of Applied Behavior Analysis,* **1,** 175–191.

Bijou, S. W., Peterson, R. F., Harris, F. R., Allen, K. E., & Johnston, M. S. (1969). Methodology for experimental studies of young children in natural settings. *The Psychological Record,* **19,** 177–210.

Birkimer, J. C., & Brown, J. H. (1979). A graphical judgmental aid which summarizes obtained and chance reliability data and helps assess the believability of experimental effects. *Journal of Applied Behavior Analysis,* **12,** 523–533.

Blunden, D., Spring, C., & Greenberg, L. M. (1974). Validation of the classroom behavior inventory. *Journal of Consulting and Clinical Psychology,* **42,** 84–88.

Blurton Jones, N. G., & Woodson, R. H. (1979). Describing behavior: The ethologist's perspective. In M. E. Lamb, S. J. Soumi, & G. R. Stephenson (Eds.), *Social interaction analysis.* Madison: University of Wisconsin Press.

Boulter, L. T. (1979). The identification of socially competent behaviors in preschool and first-grade children. Ph.D. dissertation, West Virginia University.

Boyer, E. G., Simon, A., & Karafin, G. R. (Eds.) (1973). *Measures of maturation: An anthology of early childhood observation instruments,* Vol. 2. Philadelphia: Research for Better Schools, Inc.

Burghardt, G. M. (1973). Instinct and innate behavior: Toward an ethological psychology. In J. A. Nevin & G. S. Reynolds (Eds.), *The study of human behavior.* Glenview, Ill.: Scott, Foresman, & Co.

Cairns, R. B., & Green, J. A. (1979). How to assess personality and social patterns: Observations or ratings. Appendix A in R. B. Cairns (Ed.), *The analysis of social interactions: Methods, issues, and illustrations.* Hillsdale, N.J.: Lawrence Erlbaum Associates.

Callahan, E. J., & Alevizos, P. N. (1973). Reactive effects of direct observation of patient behaviors. Paper presented at the meeting of the American Psychological Association, Montreal.

Campbell, D. T., & Fiske, D. W. (1979). Convergent and discriminant validation by the multitrait-multimethod matrix. *Psychological Bulletin,* **56,** 81–105.

Campbell, D. T., & Stanley, J. C. (1963). *Experimental and quasi-experimental designs for research.* Chicago: Rand McNally.

Charlesworth, R., & Hartup, W. W. (1967). Positive social reinforcement in the nursery school peer group. *Child Development,* **38,** 993–1002.

Chittenden, G. F. (1942). An experimental study in measuring and modifying assertive behavior in young children. *Monograph of the Society for Research in Child Development,* **7,** 1–87.

Clement, P. G. (1976). A formula for computing interobserver agreement. *Psychological Reports,* **39,** 257–258.

Cobb, J. A. (1972). The relationship of discrete classroom behaviors to fourth-grade academic achievement. *Journal of Educational Psychology,* **63,** 74–80.

Cohen, D. C. (1977). Comparison of self-report and overt-behavioral procedures for assessing acrophobia. *Behavior Therapy,* **8,** 17–23.

Cohen, J. (1960). A coefficient of agreement for nominal scales. *Educational and Psychological Measurement,* **20,** 37–46.

Cohen, J. (1968). Weighted Kappa: Nominal scale agreement with provision for scaled disagreement or partial credit. *Psychological Bulletin,* **70,** 213–220.

Cone, J. D. (1978). Truth and sensitivity in behavioral assessment. Paper presented at the meeting of the Association for the Advancement of Behavior Therapy, Chicago.

Cone, J. D. (1979). Confounded comparisons in triple response mode assessment research. *Behavioral Assessment,* **1,** 85–95.

Cone, J. D., Hanson, C. R., & Gruber, B. (1980). Systematically varying obtrusiveness to determine effects of direct observation on teacher behavior. Unpublished manuscript, West Virginia University.

Cone, J. D., & Hawkins, R. P. (1977). Introduction. In J. D. Cone & R. P. Hawkins (Eds.), *Behavioral assessment: New directions in clinical psychology.* New York: Brunner/Mazel.

Cronbach, L. J., Gleser, G. C., Nanda, H., & Rajaratnam, N. (1972). *The dependability of behavioral measures.* New York: Wiley.

Curran, J. P. (1979). Pandora's box reopened? The assessment of social skills. *Journal of Behavioral Assessment,* **1,** 55–72.

DeMaster, B., Reid, J., & Twentyman, C. (1977). The effects of different amounts of feedback on observer's reliability. *Behavior Therapy,* **8,** 317–329.

Dubey, D. R., Kent, R. N., O'Leary, S. G., Broderick, J. E., & O'Leary, K. D. (1977). Reactions of children and teachers to classroom observers: A series of controlled investigations. *Behavior Therapy,* **8,** 887–897.

Dunnette, M. D. (1966). *Personnel selection and placement*. Belmont, Calif.: Wadsworth.

Eisler, R. M., Hersen, M., Miller, P. M., & Blanchard, E. B. (1975). Situational determinants of assertive behaviors. *Journal of Consulting and Clinical Psychology, 43,* 330–340.

Eyberg, S. M., & Johnson, S. M. (1974). Multiple assessment of behavior modification with families: Effects of contingency contracting and order of treated problems. *Journal of Consulting and Clinical Psychology, 42,* 594–606.

Fazio, A. (1969). Verbal and overt behavioral assessment of a specific fear. *Journal of Consulting and Clinical Psychology, 33,* 705–709.

Fixsen, D. L., Phillips, E. L., & Wolf, M. M. (1972). Achievement Place: The reliability of self-reporting and peer reporting and their effects on behavior. *Journal of Applied Behavior Analysis, 5,* 19–30.

Fleiss, J. L., Cohen, J., & Everitt, B. S. (1969). Large sample standard errors of Kappa and weighted Kappa. *Psychological Bulletin, 72,* 323–327.

Foster, S. L., Fabry, B. D., Steinfeld, B. I., Robin, A., & Fox, M. (1980). Replicating behavioral observation codes in different settings: An exploratory investigation. Paper presented at the meeting of the Association for Behavior Analysis, Dearborn, Michigan

Frame, R. (1979). Interobserver agreement as a function of the number of behaviors recorded simultaneously. *The Psychological Record, 29,* 287–296.

Galassi, M. D., & Galassi, J. P. (1976). The effects of role-playing variations on the assessment of assertive behavior. *Behavior Therapy, 7,* 343–347.

Gewirtz, J. L. (1956). A factor analysis of some attention-seeking behaviors of young children. *Child Development, 27,* 17–36.

Gewirtz, H. B., & Gewirtz, J. L. (1969). Caretaking settings, background events and child-rearing environments: Some preliminary trends. In B. M. Foss (Ed.), *Determinants of infant behaviour*, Vol. 4. London: Methuen.

Green, S. B., & Alverson, L. G. (1978). A comparison of indirect measures for long duration behaviors. *Journal of Applied Behavior Analysis, 11,* 530.

Gottman, J. M. (1979). *Marital interaction: Experimental investigations*. New York: Academic Press.

Greenberg, L. M., Deem, M. A., & McMahon, S. (1972). Effects of dextroamphetamine chlorpromazine, and hydroxyzine on behavior and performance in hyperactive children. *American Journal of Psychiatry, 129,* 532–539.

Grimm, J. A., Parsons, J. A., & Bijou, S. W. (1972). A technique for minimizing subject-observer looking interactions in field settings. *Journal of Experimental Child Psychology, 14,* 500–505.

Harris, F. C., & Ciminero, A. R. (1978). The effect of witnessing consequences on the behavioral recordings of experimental observers. *Journal of Applied Behavior Analysis, 11,* 513–522.

Harris, F. C., & Lahey, B. B. (1978). A method for combining occurrence and nonoccurrence interobserver agreement scores. *Journal of Applied Behavior Analysis, 11,* 523–527.

Hartmann, D. P. (1977). Considerations in the use of interobserver reliability estimates. *Journal of Applied Behavior Analysis, 10,* 103–116.

Hartshorne, H., & May, M. A. (1978). *Studies in the nature of character*, Vol. 1: *Studies in deceit*. New York: Macmillan.

Hawkins, R. P., & Dobes, R. W. (1977). Behavioral definitions in applied behavior analysis: Explicit or implicit. In B. C. Etzel, J. M. LeBlanc, and D. M. Baer (Eds.), *New developments in behavioral research: Theory, methods, and application. In honor of Sydney W. Bijou*. Hillsdale, N.J.: Lawrence Erlbaum Associates.

Hawkins, R. P., & Dotson, V. A. (1975). Reliability scores that delude: An Alice-in-Wonderland trip through the misleading characteristics of interobserver agreement scores in interval recording. In E. Ramp & G. Semb (Eds.), *Behavior analysis: Areas of research and application*. Englewood Cliffs, N.J.: Prentice-Hall.

Hay, L. R., Nelson, R. O., & Hay, W. M. (1977). The use of teachers as behavioral observers. *Journal of Applied Behavior Analysis, 10,* 345–349.

Hersen, M., & Barlow, D. H. (1976). *Single case experimental designs: Strategies for studying behavior change*. New York: Pergamon Press.

Holm, R. A. (1978). Techniques of recording observational data. In G. P. Sackett (Ed.), *Observing Behavior*, Vol. 2: *Data collection and analysis methods*. Baltimore: University Park Press.

House, B. J., & House, A. E. (1979). Frequency, complexity, and clarity as covariates of observer reliability. *Journal of Behavioral Assessment, 1,* 149–166.

Johnson, S. M., & Bolstad, O. D. (1973). Methodological issues in naturalistic observation: Some problems and solutions for field research. In L. A. Hamerlynck, L. C. Handy, & E. J. Mash (Eds.), *Behavior change: Methodology, concepts, and practice*. Champaign, Ill.: Research Press.

Johnson, S. M., Christensen, A., & Bellamy, G. T. (1976). Evaluation of family intervention through unobtrusive audio recordings: Experiences in "bugging" children. *Journal of Applied Behavior Analysis, 9,* 213–219.

Johnston, J. M., & Pennypacker, H. S. (1980). *Strategies and tactics of human behavioral research.* Hillsdale, N.J.: Lawrence Erlbaum Associates.

Jones, R. R., Reid, J. B., & Patterson, G. R. (1975). Naturalistic observation in clinical assessment. In P. McReynolds (Ed.), *Advances in psychological assessment,* Vol. 3. San Francisco: Jossey-Bass.

Kass, R. E., & O'Leary, K. D. (1970). The effects of observer bias in field-experimental settings. Paper presented at the symposium *Behavior analysis in education,* University of Kansas.

Kazdin, A. E. (1977a). Artifact, bias, and complexity of assessment: The ABCs of reliability. *Journal of Applied Behavior Analysis,* **10,** 141–150.

Kazdin, A. E. (1977b) Assessing the clinical or applied importance of behavior change through social validation. *Behavior Modification,* **1,** 427–451.

Kazdin, A. E. (1974). Reactive self-monitoring: The effects of response desirability, goal setting and feedback. *Journal of Consulting and Clinical Psychology,* **42,** 704–716.

Kelly, M. B. (1977). A review of the observational data-collection and reliability procedures reported in the *Journal of Applied Behavior Analysis. Journal of Applied Behavior Analysis,* **10,** 97–101.

Kent, R. N., & Foster, S. L. (1977). Direct observational procedures: Methodological issues in applied settings. In A. Ciminero, K. S. Calhoun, & H. E. Adams (Eds.), *Handbook of behavioral assessment.* New York: Wiley.

Kent, R. N., Kanowitz, J., O'Leary, K. D., & Cheiken, M. (1977). Observer reliability as a function of circumstances of assessment. *Journal of Applied Behavior Analysis,* **10,** 317–324.

Kent, R. N., O'Leary, K. D., Diament, C., & Dietz, A. (1974). Expectation biases in observational evaluation of therapeutic change. *Journal of Consulting and Clinical Psychology,* **42,** 774–780.

Lamb, M. E., Suomi, S. J., & Stephenson, G. R. (Eds.) (1979). *Social interaction analysis.* Madison: University of Wisconsin Press.

Lang, P. J. (1971). The application of psychophysiological methods to the study of psychotherapy and behavior modification. In A. E. Bergin and S. L. Garfield (Eds.), *Handbook of psychotherapy and behavior change.* New York: Wiley.

Lang, P. J. (1968). Fear reduction and fear behavior: Problems in treating a construct. In J. M. Shlien (Ed.), *Research in psychotherapy,* Vol. 3. Washington, D. C.: American Psychological Association.

Lobitz, G. K., & Johnson, S. M. (1975). Normal versus deviant children: A multimethod comparison. *Journal of Abnormal Child Psychology,* **3,** 353–374.

Lobitz, W. C., & Johnson, S. M. (1975). Parental manipulation of the behavior of normal and deviant children. *Child Development,* **46,** 719–726.

McGrew, W. C. (1972). *An ethological study of children's behavior.* New York: Academic Press.

McReynolds, W. T., & Stegman, R. (1976). Sayer versus sign. *Behavior Therapy,* **7,** 704–705.

Madsen, C. H., Jr., Becker, W. C., Thomas, D. R., Koser, L., & Plager, E. (1968). An analysis of the reinforcing function of "sit down" commands. In R. K. Parker (Ed.), *Readings in educational psychology.* Boston: Allyn & Bacon.

Martin, M. F., Gelfand, D. M., & Hartmann, D. D. (1971). Effects of adult and peer observers on boys' and girls' responses to an aggressive model. *Child Development.* **42,** 1271–1275.

Martin, S., Johnson, S. M., Johansson, S., & Wahl, G. (1976). The comparability of behavioral data in laboratory and natural settings. In E. J. Mash, L. A. Hamerlynck, & L. C. Handy (Eds.), *Behavior modification and families.* New York: Brunner/Mazel.

Mash, E. J., & Hedley, J. (1975). Effect of observer as a function of prior history of social interaction. *Perceptual and Motor Skills,* **40,** 659–669.

Mash, E. J., & McElwee, J. D. (1974). Situational effects on observer accuracy: Behavioral predictability, prior experience, complexity of coding categories. *Child Development,* **45,** 367–377.

Mash, E. J., & Makohoniuk, G. (1975). The effects of prior information and behavioral predictability on observer accuracy. *Child Development,* **46,** 513–519.

Medley, D. M., & Mitzel, H. E. (1963). Measuring classroom behavior by systematic observation. In N. L. Gage (Ed.), *Handbook of research on teaching.* Chicago: Rand McNally.

Mercatoris, M., & Craighead, W. E. (1974). The effects of non-participant observation on teacher and pupil classroom behavior. *Journal of Educational Psychology,* **66,** 512–519.

Nathan, P. E., Titler, N. A., Lowenstein, L. M., Solomon, P., & Rossi, A. M. (1970). Behavioral analysis of chronic alcoholism. *Archives of General Psychiatry,* **22,** 419–430.

Nelson, R. O. (1977). Methodological issues in assessment via self-monitoring. In J. D. Cone and R. P. Hawkins (Eds.), *Behavioral assessment: New directions in clinical psychology.* New York: Brunner/Mazel.

O'Leary, K. D., Kaufman, K. F., Kass, R. E., & Drabman, R. S. (1970). The effects of loud and soft reprimands on the behavior of disruptive students. *Exceptional Children,* **37,** 145–155.

O'Leary, K. D., & Kent, R. (1973). Behavior modification for social action: Research tactics and problems. In L. A. Hamerlynck, L. C. Handy, & E. J. Mash (Eds.), *Behavior change: Methodology, concepts, and practice*. Champaign, Ill.: Research Press.

O'Leary, K. D., Kent, R. N., & Kanowitz, J. (1975). Shaping data collection congruent with experimental hypotheses. *Journal of Applied Behavior Analysis,* **8,** 48–51.

Patterson, G. R. (1974). Interventions for boys with conduct problems: Multiple settings, treatments, and criteria. *Journal of Consulting and Clinical Psychology,* **42,** 471–481.

Patterson, G. R., Cobb, J. A., & Ray, R. S. (1973). A social engineering technology for retraining the families of aggressive boys. In H. E. Adams & I. P. Unikel (Eds.), *Issues and trends in behavior therapy*. Springfield, Ill.: Charles C. Thomas.

Patterson, G. R., & Fleischman, M. J. (1979). Maintenance of treatment effects: Some considerations concerning family systems and follow-up data. *Behavior Therapy,* **10,** 168–185.

Patterson, G. R., & Moore, D. (1979). Interactive patterns as units of behavior. In M. E. Lamb, S. J. Suomi, & G. R. Stephenson (Eds.), *Social interaction analysis*. Madison: University of Wisconsin Press.

Patterson, G. R., & Reid, J. B. (1970). Reciprocity and coercion: Two facets of social systems. In C. Neuringer & J. Michael (Eds.), *Behavior modification in clinical psychology*. New York: Appleton-Century-Crofts.

Peacock, R., Lyman, R. D., & Rickard, H. C. (1978). Correspondence between self-report and observer-report as a function of task difficulty. *Behavior Therapy,* **9.** 578–583.

Powell, J., Martindale, A., & Kulp, S. (1975). An evaluation of time-sample measures of behavior. *Journal of Applied Behavior Analysis,* **8,** 463–469.

Powell, J., Martindale, B., Kulp, S., Martindale, A., & Bauman, R. (1977). Taking a closer look: Time sampling and measurement error. *Journal of Applied Behavior Analysis,* **10,** 325–332.

Powell, J., & Rockinson, R. (1978). On the inability of interval time sampling to reflect frequency of occurrence data. *Journal of Applied Behavior Analysis,* **11,** 531–532.

Prinz, R. J., & Kent, R. N. (1978). Recording parent-adolescent interactions without the use of frequency or interval-by-interval coding. *Behavior Therapy,* **9,** 602–604.

Redfield, J., & Paul, G. L. (1976). Bias in behavioral observation as a function of observer familiarity with subjects and typicality of behavior. *Journal of Consulting and Clinical Psychology,* **44,** 156.

Reid, J. B. (1970). Reliability assessment of observation data: A possible methodological problem. *Child Development,* **41,** 1143–1150.

Reid, J. B. (1978a). The development of specialized observation systems. In J. B. Reid (Ed.), *A social learning approach to family intervention,* Vol. 2: *Observation in home settings*. Eugene, Ore.: Castalia Publishing Co.

Reid, J. B. (Ed.) (1978b). *A social learning approach to family intervention,* Vol. 2: *Observation in home settings*. Eugene, Ore.: Castalia Publishing Co.

Repp, A. C., Roberts, D. M., Slack, D. J., Repp, C. F., & Berkler, M. S. (1976). A comparison of frequency, interval, and time-sampling methods for data collection. *Journal of Applied Behavior Analysis,* **9,** 501–508.

Risley, T. R., & Hart, B. (1968). Developing correspondence between the non-verbal and verbal behavior of preschool children. *Journal of Applied Behavior Analysis,* **1,** 267–281.

Robinson, E. A., & Price, M. G. (1980). Pleasurable behavior in marital interaction: An observational study. *Journal of Consulting and Clinical Psychology,* **48,** 117–118.

Romanczyk, R. G., Kent, R. N., Diament, C., & O'Leary, K. D. (1973). Measuring the reliability of observational data: A reactive process. *Journal of Applied Behavior Analysis,* **6,** 175–186.

Rosenblum, L. A. (1978). The creation of a behavioral taxonomy. In G. P. Sackett (Ed.), *Observing behavior,* Vol. 2: *Data collection and analysis methods*. Baltimore: University Park Press.

Rosenshine, B., & Furst, N. F. (1973). The use of direct observation to study teaching. In N. L. Gage (Ed.), *Handbook of research on teaching* (2nd ed.). Chicago: Rand McNally.

Rosenthal, R. (1966). *Experimenter effects in behavioral research*. New York: Appleton-Century-Crofts.

Rosenthal, R. (1979). Interpersonal expectations: Effect of the experimenter's hypothesis. In R. Rosenthal & R. L. Rosnow (Eds.), *Artifact in behavioral research*. New York: Academic Press.

Sackett, G. P. (Ed.) (1978). *Observing behavior,* Vol. 2: *Data collection and analysis methods*. Baltimore: University Park Press.

Scott, P. M., Burton, R. V., & Yarrow, M. R. (1967). Social reinforcement under natural conditions. *Child Development,* **38,** 53–63.

Sears, R. R. (1963). Dependency motivation. In M. R. Jones (Ed.), *Nebraska symposium on motivation*. Lincoln: University of Nebraska Press.

Shuller, D. Y., & McNamara, J. R. (1976). Expectancy factors in behavioral observation. *Behavior Therapy, 7,* 519–527.

Strain, P. S., Shores, R. E., & Timm, M. A. (1977). Effects of peer social initiations on the behavior of withdrawn preschool children. *Journal of Applied Behavior Analysis, 10,* 289–298.

Stunkard, A., & Kaplan, D. (1977). Eating in public places: A review of reports of the direct observation of eating behavior. *International Journal of Obesity, 1,* 89–101.

Sulzer-Azaroff, B., & Mayer, G. R. (1977). *Applying behavior analysis procedures with children and youth.* New York: Holt, Rinehart & Winston.

Taplin, P. S., & Reid, J. B. (1973). Effects of instructional set and experimenter influence on observer reliability. *Child Development, 44,* 547–554.

Taskey, J. J., & Rich, A. R. (1979). Effects of demand characteristics and format variations in role-playing assessment. Paper presented at the meeting of the American Psychological Association, New York.

Thomas, D. S., Loomis, A. M., & Arrington, R. E. (1933). *Observational studies of social behavior,* Vol. 1. New Haven: Yale University, Institute of Human Relations.

Van Houten, R., & Sullivan, K. (1975). Effects of an audio cueing system on the rate of teacher praise. *Journal of Applied Behavior Analysis, 8,* 197–201.

Vincent, J. P., Friedman, L. C., Nugent, J., & Messerly, L. (1979). Demand characteristics in observations of marital interaction. *Journal of Consulting and Clinical Psychology, 47,* 557–566.

Wahler, R. G. (1975). Some structural aspects of deviant child behavior. *Journal of Applied Behavior Analysis, 8,* 27–42.

Wahler, R. G., House, A. E., & Stambaugh, E. E. (1976). *Ecological assessment of child problem behavior: A clinical package for home, school, and institutional settings.* New York: Pergamon Press.

Walk, R. D. (1956). Self ratings of fear in a fear-invoking situation. *Journal of Abnormal and Social Psychology, 22,* 171–178.

Webb, E. J., Campbell, D. T., Schwartz, R. D., & Sechrest, L. (1966). *Unobtrusive measures: Nonreactive research in the social sciences.* Chicago: Rand McNally.

Weick, K. E. (1968). Systematic observational methods. In G. Lindzey and E. Aronson (Eds.), *The handbook of social psychology* (2nd ed.), Vol. 2. Reading, Mass.: Addison-Wesley.

Weinrott, M. R., Garrett, B., & Todd, N. (1978). The influence of observer presence on classroom behavior. *Behavior Therapy, 9,* 900–911.

White, O. R. (1977). Data-based instruction: Evaluating educational progress. In J. D. Cone & R. P. Hawkins (Eds.), *Behavioral assessment: New directions in clinical psychology.* New York: Brunner/Mazel.

Wiggins, J. S. (1973). *Personality and prediction: Principles of personality assessment.* Reading, Mass.: Addison-Wesley.

Wildman, B. G., & Erickson, M. T. (1977). Methodological problems in behavioral observation. In J. D. Cone & R. P. Hawkins (Eds.), *Behavioral assessment: New directions in clinical psychology.* New York: Brunner/Mazel.

Wildman, B. G., Erickson, M. T., & Kent, R. N. (1975). The effect of two training procedures on observer agreement and variability of behavior ratings. *Child Development, 46,* 520–524.

Wood, D. D., Callahan, E. J., Alevizos, P. N., & Teigen, J. R. (1979). Inpatient behavioral assessment with a problem-oriented psychiatric logbook. *Journal of Behavior Therapy and Experimental Psychiatry, 10,* 229–235.

Wolf, M. M. (1978). Social validity: The case for subjective measurement or how applied behavior analysis is finding its heart. *Journal of Applied Behavior Analysis, 11,* 203–214.

Wright, H. F. (1967). *Recording and analyzing child behavior.* New York: Harper & Row.

Wyatt, W. J., Callahan, E. J., & Michael, J. (in press). Variations in methods of calculating reliability of duration data. *Journal of Behavioral Assessment.*

Yelton, A. R., Wildman, B. G., & Erickson, M. T. (1977). A probability-based formula for calculating interobserver agreement. *Journal of Applied Behavior Analysis, 10,* 127–132.

Zuckerman, M. (1979). Traits, states, situations, and uncertainty. *Journal of Behavioral Assessment, 1,* 43–54.

CHAPTER 11

Methodological Problems in Research with Self-Report Inventories

MALCOLM D. GYNTHER AND SAMUEL B. GREEN

The purpose of this chapter is to delineate the problems that have interfered with understanding the relations between personality as measured by self-report inventories and various other criteria. Butcher and Tellegen (1978), in a more circumscribed treatment of methodological problems in MMPI research, elected to analyze the data in terms of categories such as MMPI short forms, scale proliferation, and assessment of profile change. Typical treatments of methodological problems usually focus on reliability and validity. Although these issues are treated when appropriate, we decided to use an approach that parallels the steps involved in performing an empirical investigation. Thus we examined: (1) how one chooses research ideas, that is, problems with conceptualization; (2) how one goes about doing the study, that is, problems with execution; (3) how one decides what the results mean, that is, problems with interpretation; and (4) what steps to take after a study is completed to determine the generalizability of its results, that is, problems with verification. To provide a context for this evaluation of research problems with self-report inventories, an historical overview and an examination of the strengths and weaknesses of the instruments themselves precede the other sections. As a lead-in to the brief history of self-report inventories, the question arises, are we confronted

with novel problems in 1980, or are we still struggling with problems first recognized many years ago?

HISTORICAL INTRODUCTION

Woodworth's (1920) Personal Data Sheet is usually thought of as the prototype of the personality assessment device. Apparently the items on this questionnaire were taken from or stimulated by early sources such as Heymans and Wiersma (1906), Hoch and Amsden (1913), and Wells (1914). Although Woodworth's product is almost the only one now remembered from this period, others were equally well known then. Allport (1921), for example, stated that "the completest lists of questions are Watson's and Woodworth's." The Watson in question is not Goodwin Watson, who was well known in the personality measurement area in the 1920s and 1930s, but John B. Watson himself, the founder of behaviorism. Although many of us have seen examples taken from Woodworth's Personal Data Sheet (e.g., "Are you happy most of the time?" and "Does the sight of blood make you sick or dizzy?"), Watson's questions, which are found in *Psychology from the Standpoint of a Behaviorist* (1919), are less familiar and in some cases could be described as quaint. One wonders what today's experts in item writing would make of the following item given by Watson: "Has his early home, school or religious training implanted fixed modes of reacting which are not in line with his present environment—that is, is he easily shocked, for example, at seeing a woman smoke, drink a cocktail or flirt with a man; at card playing; at the fact that many of his associates do not go to church?"

Another major figure of the period was S.L. Pressey, who developed the X-O tests. Directions required the subjects to cross out unpleasant words, words describing activities considered to be wrong (e.g., spitting), and words describing sources of worry (e.g., money). In what sounds like a recent comment on behalf of inventories currently in use, Pressey (1921) stated that "a 600 item examination can thus (1) be given by an examiner without any special training or preparation whatever, can (2) be taken by the average adult in about thirty minutes, can (3) be scored by any clerk in three minutes" (p. 60).

Inventories were thus available and in use 60 years ago. Much energy went into their creation, especially toward modifying Woodworth's set of items for use with other subgroups of people. Yet critics could be found. Allport (1921) said, "However highly this method may be developed, as an instrument for accurate study of the personality it will always face the weakness of permitting falsification or rationalization on the part of the subject" (p. 452). Allport and Allport (1921) offered a possible solution to these problems of response distortions:

To ask the subject whether he is honest, moral, thoughtful, literary in tastes, etc., or to analyze himself by inward searching, is only to encounter the obstacles of carelessness, rationalization, and defense reactions. The questions asked should be in terms of what the subject actually does in his daily life; let the subject judge himself as another person might—by his habitual behavior. (p. 11)

This perspective is similar to that held by some researchers today (e.g., Owens & Schoenfeldt, 1979), who believe that biographical questionnaires are optimal for the description of personality.

But the possibilities of examining groups of people in the "cost-effective" manner described by Pressey led to further proliferation of self-report inventories. Travis (1924), for example, developed a new diagnostic test to measure fundamental character traits. There were 10 groups of items with 10 items in each group. The subject was to rank order statements in terms of the one liked best, the one liked next best, and so on. Laird (1925) constructed a questionnaire to detect abnormal behavior. Questions were arranged in diagnostic groupings, corresponding to the generally accepted classical entities (i.e., hysteroid, schizoid, etc.). Hartshorne and May's tests of honesty, which were developed in school situations, were described by Watson (1927) as "the most thoroughgoing character tests that have been developed." A few years later Bernreuter (1931) developed his very popular test to measure neurotic tendencies, introversion-extroversion, ascendance-submission, and self-sufficiency. This inventory was greeted with such enthusiasm that Super's (1942) review devoted entirely to it contained 147 references.

However, people wanted something better. Watson (1933) said, "There is need for a symptom questionnaire, which will not be a potpourri of items of much or little or no or unknown significance like the Woodworth-Thurstone-Bernreuter series, but which will be built around some worthy hypothesis of adjustment and maladjustment" (pp. 71–72). Perhaps one reason for the feeling of disenchantment was that researchers were beginning to find out that questions that seemed related to the criterion were not necessarily so. Landis and Katz (1934), for example, showed that more normal persons than abnormal reported a tendency to daydream, to cross streets to avoid meeting people, to have ideas run through their heads. Also other problems began to be recognized: the influence of the desire to do well and the desire for social approval (Rundquist & Sletto, 1936), test sophistication, and signing one's name or not. All these complications led some psychologists to give up on inventories and eagerly board the projective technique bandwagon that was just beginning to get underway. Even the most enthusiastic proponents of objective test methods never promised that their procedures would yield an X-ray of the personality, as Frank (1939) said the Rorschach would.

Yet others stubbornly forged ahead. The Humm-Wadsworth Temperament Schedule (1935) was followed in short order by the Minnesota Multiphasic Personality Inventory (MMPI) (Hathaway & McKinley, 1940) and An Inventory of Factors STDCR (Guilford, 1940), and somewhat later by the Sixteen Personality Factor Questionnaire (Cattell, 1949), the Edwards Personal Preference Schedule (Edwards, 1954), the California Psychological Inventory (CPI) (Gough, 1957), and the Maudsley Personality Inventory (Eysenck, 1959). We do not intend to describe or evaluate these inventories, nor indeed have we done anything more than indicate the tip of the iceberg, as estimates of the number of objective personality tests range into the hundreds; our point is simply that despite the problems and shortcomings clearly recognized in the 1920s and 1930s, the self-report inventory has flourished and today is probably the dominant form of personality assessment. However, the inability of personality test constructors to go beyond the tests of the 1940s and 1950s is demonstrated by the continued use of tests such as the MMPI and the CPI in the 1980s.

Perhaps the stagnancy is due to the inability of test constructors to go further within a trait-oriented framework. In 1924 Allport lamented the analysis of personality into traits, and pointed out that this approach "results in the loss of the crucial factor of individual personality itself." In 1928 Hartshorne and May offered a conclusion that sounds like those from articles of the 1970s dealing with situation-trait interactionism:

Our contention, however, is that this common factor is not an inner entity operating independently of the situations in which the individuals are placed but is a function of the situation in the sense that an individual behaves similarly in different situations in proportion as these situations are alike. (p. 385)

Situations were not brought systematically into self-report personality tests until the 1960s, and even then not in a fashion that is useful to the clinical psychologist. It is apparent that the challenge of the 1920s is still present in the 1980s.

One of the best reviews of the strengths and weaknesses of personality inventories was conducted by Albert Ellis (1946), now better known as the originator and promoter of rational emotive therapy. He cited 360 studies covering the period from the late 1920s to 1946 and concluded that, "The older, more conventional, and more widely used forms of these tests seem to be, for practical diagnostic purposes, hardly worth the paper on which they were printed" (p. 425). He conceded that the tests, which included the Bell Adjustment Inventory, the Bernreuter Personality Inventory, the Thurstone Personality Schedule, and the Woodworth Personal Data Sheet, are likely to validly discriminate between groups of adjusted and maladjusted individuals about half the time, but felt the evidence gave little credence to the belief that they might be used to diagnose individual cases. Ellis reviewed MMPI studies separately. He evaluated this instrument as "the most promising one—perhaps because it gets away from group administration which has hitherto been almost synonymous with personality test-giving" (p. 425).

His prediction was an accurate one, since, at least in terms of popularity, the MMPI has been a successful test. However, future inventories must take into account the criticisms that have accompanied, but seldom affected, the development and utilization of the instruments. From 1921 on, psychologists have pointed out that inventories fail to: (1) take situational variation into account; (2) control distortion of responses; (3) capitalize on a personality theory in the development of the item pool; and (4) make accurate predictions or descriptions of individual clients.

PROBLEMS WITH INSTRUMENTS

In the last decade, personality theorists and researchers have argued among themselves about the degree of consistency displayed by individuals across response modes, situations, and time. Although this debate continues, one conclusion is evident: most individuals do not behave as consistently as they believe they do. Unfortunately, constructors of self-report personality inventories have explicitly or implicitly assumed consistency across the dimensions being measured. This overly simplistic postulate about behavior has led to self-report personality tests with built-in limitations, and to disappointing results when such tests are used for predictive purposes. Within this perspective we will attempt in this section to highlight some of the problems with these inventories.

Test constructors have always included items on personality inventories that refer to situations and behavior. It is difficult to develop a set of items for a scale otherwise. However, they have not used any well-defined procedure to ensure an adequate sample of response modes and situations. An inspection of popular self-report personality tests such as the MMPI and the CPI shows no systematic selection of items for the individual scales to represent the complete domain of the respective traits. Of course, this judgment may be viewed as unfair, since both of these instruments were developed through empirical keying rather than through a rational selection of items. However, even rationally developed scales, such as Jackson's (1967) Personality Research Form, seem to neglect important aspects of the potential trait domain. Many items are stated in such a general fashion that test takers can only respond on the basis of their implicit personality theories rather than how they actually behave and feel in specific situations. How might test constructors better sample the trait domain?

One response to this question was made by Endler, Hunt, and Rosenstein (1962), who created the S-R Inventory of Anxiousness. This questionnaire consists of a series of possibly disturbing situations ("making a speech before a large audience") paired with various types of anxious responses ("can't concentrate," "heart beats faster"). Subjects were asked to report how strongly each response occurs in each situation. Endler and Hunt's (1969) analyses of the results revealed that by far the most potent effects were attributable to the interaction between person, situation, and response mode. Taken alone, neither individual differences nor situations accounted for more than a trivial fraction of the test results.

Interpretation of these findings is problematic. Buss (1977) and Alker (1977) have discussed a number of limitations of the analysis of variance approach to the elucidation of the trait-situation controversy. Moreover, Jackson and Paunonen (1980) stated:

It is evident that differences in mean level of responding to questionnaires do not directly confront the issue of cross-situational consistency as it might be revealed, for example, in an examination of correlations between responses to different anxiety situations, which usually yields a large general factor. Mean effects and effects due to response covariation are distinctly different ways of treating data. (p. 523)

Regardless of the merits of the analysis of variance approach to solving this long-standing controversy, many personality theoreticians would criticize this type of inventory as overly simplistic. Bowers (1973), for example, has argued that individuals tend to place themselves in situations that are congruent with their personality. Consequently, although a person might become very anxious making a speech in front of a large audience, he or she might be able to successfully avoid these situations. On the other hand, other individuals may not be able to avoid the situations. The items on the S-R Inventory of Anxiousness make no attempt to differentiate these individuals, and consequently the two types of individuals would not be distinguishable.

A second criticism of this type of instrument is that its content deals only with overt or covert behavior. Beliefs and feelings should not be excluded from self-report personality tests, even though scores from the cognitive and affective domains are often relatively highly correlated with scores from the behavioral domain. Since the trait that is being measured is viewed as a latent disposition, these other domains should not be neglected. Consequently a measure must, at least initially, consist of a very large number of items in order to be truly representative of a trait domain.

As an alternative to this approach, the psychometrician might choose to develop tests for more specific criteria. Criterion referenced testing, for example, emphasizes content validity and the assessment of narrowly defined areas of achievement (Popham, 1978). The current emphasis within this approach is on the development of algorithms to select test items. Of course personality test constructors cannot define domains as neatly as achievement test constructors, and consequently one cannot realistically anticipate algorithms for personality tests in the immediate future. However, if Jackson (1971) is correct that self-report personality tests are relatively simple to develop *if* it is clear what

is to be measured, then it should be possible to develop very specific scales for specific purposes. These types of scales would enable the constructor to include items that do range over a variety of situations.

How might one best do this? One answer was provided by Burisch (1978) who replicated Hase and Goldberg's (1967) study showing that different test construction methods yield measures with comparable validity. However, he concluded that the deductive, rational approach is preferable on efficiency grounds. He recommended that test constructors investigate methods to develop tests deductively. Epstein (1979) showed that tests developed rationally to predict specific sets of behavior yielded higher validities (in the .60 range) than standard personality inventories (.40 range). Of course empirical item analytic methods could be used to further refine the item domain once a rationally developed pool of items is available.

If the responses to such items were made on a Likert type scale from highly likely to highly unlikely, not only could a total score be computed, but also a variance measure could be derived to indicate the degree of consistency in responding. Velicer and Stevensen (1978) compared the standard two-choice version of the Eysenck Personality Inventory with a seven-point Likert version of the same inventory. The latter format yielded a superior factorial structure. These results are consistent with the findings of Lissitz and Green (1975), who showed that the Likert format produces scales with higher reliabilities. The use of a variance index as a measure of consistency across Likert type items may, however, lead to results that are difficult to interpret. A larger variance may not mean that a person shows a lack of consistency across situations and response modes, but rather a tendency to respond to items on the extremes of scales. Research is necessary to determine the usefulness of this suggestion as a means to assess situational consistency.

Another alternative to traditional trait

measures are state measures, which take into consideration the lack of consistency over time. Thorne (1967) has defined a psychological state as "the momentary condition of Being occurring at any longitudinal cross-section of the stream of life of a person" (p. 75). How might one measure such an apparently elusive bit of behavior? Thorne (1967) offered the following suggestions: "The simplest method simply is to ask the person what his state is, using introspective reporting to describe subjective contents as completely as possible" (p. 82), and "Psychological states also may be studied by any of the standard psychometric and personality testing methods providing that a post-test inquiry is used to discover why the person made clinically significant responses" (p. 82). Thorne (1965) has published the Integration Level Test Series to measure various aspects of the psychological state. These seven 200-item objective questionnaires include The Ideological Survey, The Life Style Analysis, and The Existential Analysis. Although empirical predictor-criterion relationships have not been established for all of these scales, some interesting results (e.g., Thorne & Pishkin, 1977) have been obtained.

Spielberger (1966) has also emphasized the importance of making a distinction between trait and state constructs. For example, anxiety as a trait would suggest a continuing, generalized condition of the individual, while anxiety as a state would suggest a more transitory or momentary condition. He and his associates (Spielberger, Gorsuch, & Lushene, 1970) have developed the State-Trait Anxiety Inventory (STAI) to investigate the interrelations between these two "types" of anxiety, situational stress, and behavior. This instrument has been widely used by researchers as attested by the 300+ references in the *Eighth mental measurement yearbook* (Buros, 1978).

A somewhat different approach to the assessment of state-trait variables has been taken by Zuckerman and Lubin (1965). Their *Multiple Affect Adjective Check List*

(MAACL) yields scores on three dimensions, anxiety, depression, and hostility, and may be given under either "how you generally feel" (trait) or "how you feel now-today" (state) instructions. Nearly 250 studies are cited in the *Eighth mental measurements yearbook* (Buros, 1978). Reviews are somewhat unclear as to the usefulness of this instrument. Kelly (1972), for example, stated that "In spite of the very high interscale correlations noted above, the three scales of the MAACL appear to have sufficient differential validity to reflect meaningful changes in affect for *groups* of Ss subjected to different types of stresses and stress-reducing manipulations" (p. 272). Cronbach (1970), on the other hand, stated: "The research on 'state' scales is somewhat bewildering as it now stands." As evidence of the confused state of this field, he cited some research that compared Taylor Anxiety Scale scores with MAACL scores obtained under "general" and "today" sets and found correlations "far from expectations."

Whatever one may make of these state instruments we have briefly described, it is clear that they have been used almost entirely for research purposes, except perhaps by behavioral therapists. Examination of the battery of tests used to evaluate patients in traditional clinical settings is highly unlikely to include the Existential Survey, the STAI, or the MAACL. Yet these theoreticians and test developers all seem to make a valid point, that is, behavior is influenced not only by "permanent" dispositions but also by momentary states. If people believe in the existence of states and traits, why are both not included on multiphasic personality inventories? Some have argued that MMPI Depression and Psychasthenia scales reflect states, while Psychopathic Deviate, Masculinity-Femininity, and Social Introversion scales tap traits; however, examination of the sets of retest coefficients given in Dahlstrom, Welsh, and Dahlstrom (1975) reveals little evidence to support this position.

These instruments also seem to have some

characteristics in common with measures that incorporate situations such as the S-R Inventory of Anxiousness. For example, the state measure of the STAI asks the test taker to report how he or she is behaving "now" in terms of a variety of response modes. Therefore, the responder states how he or she is responding in a specific situation. The major difference between the two approaches is that the state measure assesses behavior in one specific situation; whereas the S-R Inventory attempts to measure response modes in a variety of situations. Also the state measure is ascertained in the actual situation as defined by the test taker, while the S-R inventory includes situations defined by the test constructor.

Regardless of whether test constructors choose to develop tests that are trait or state oriented, they should approach cautiously the measurement of private dimensions, which may be viewed by test takers as too revealing. It is unreasonable to expect that test takers who enjoy lying will respond True to the item, "I enjoy lying" or that most applicants for a salesman position would not respond True to the item "I like to meet new people." Yet if content saturated items are the most appropriate ones to include on personality scales, as Jackson (1971) asserts, then the above items are clearly suitable for the assessment of honesty or the selection of salesmen. Psychometric methods such as correction scales (e.g., K scale of the MMPI), forced choice item format, the inclusion of items that are not face valid, and other options cannot make individuals divulge what they do not wish others to know. Unobtrusive measurement of these private dimensions appears to be a more fruitful alternative to self-report instruments, although ethical issues must be considered in determining if this approach is an appropriate one.

Whatever form the self-report personality measure takes, one must determine its reliability and validity. Classical test theory defines reliability as the ratio of true variability to true plus error variability. The various methods used to estimate this ratio yield different results because they each define true and error variability somewhat differently and, as applied, arbitrarily. On the other hand, generalizability theory (Cronbach, Gleser, Nanda, & Rajaratam, 1972) explicitly defines what is to be considered true and error variability by linking the design of the generalizability (reliability) study to the situational parameter that varies within the decision study (how the instrument will be used). For example, if the test is to be administered individually and in groups and comparisons are to be made across individuals in both settings, the generalizability study should incorporate both types of administrations within its design to determine the comparability of the results. From a more clinically relevant perspective, an anxiety scale might be administered at nonstandardized times upon entry to an institution. Under these conditions not all test takers will have been treated similarly. Some will have received medication; others will have discussed their problems with a clinician; still others will have just been admitted. However, diagnostic and treatment decisions might be made ignoring these time factors. A generalizability study would be appropriate to evaluate the consistency of scores obtained at various times of testing. Clients would be randomly assigned to groups who are tested with different amounts of time between entry to the institution and the administration of the anxiety measure to determine if scores vary systematically with time.

Traditionally, validity studies with self-report instruments have also addressed the generality of an instrument: do the results from one measure generalize to other measures? One of the major difficulties with establishing the validity of self-report personality inventories is the selection of a criterion. Although most of our measures are supposed to be trait measures, we tend to ignore the implications involved in the trait definition in the selection of a criterion. For example, many researchers choose a single criterion to assess the validity of a personality scale. Yet Cronbach (1970) made very clear that the consistency postulate means that a person shows the habitual reaction *over a range of similar situations.* If the criterion used does not reflect this range, the poor showing of trait measures as predictors may well be due to the inappropriateness of the criterion rather than the inadequacies of the predictors. Fishbein and Ajzen (1974), in the context of attitude-behavior relationships, have shown that dispositional measures do poorly in predicting single acts, but much better in predicting multiple acts. Jaccard (1974) examined this proposition in the personality area by correlating various measures of dominance with criterion behaviors of dominance likely to be performed in a variety of circumstances. He found that, on the average, traits correlated .20 with individual dominant behaviors. This value is not only predictively worthless but also statistically insignificant. When trait measures were correlated with the sum of the multiple acts, however, the coefficient was approximately .60, which is significant and perhaps high enough to be useful in decision making.

Since many of the items from personality inventories ask the test taker to respond true or false as to whether they engage in some behavior *on a regular or irregular basis,* a reasonable extension of the multiple act criterion would include multiple assessments of the same individuals in similar situations, differing only in time of testing. Perhaps the argument could be made that by assessing over situations, the regularity of a set of a behaviors is being obtained. However, we believe this argument is only reasonable if a large set of behaviors in situations is actually measured. If the state concept is ignored, the researcher is likely to include too few measurements.

Once the test has been constructed and evaluated in terms of reliability and validity, it may be used to make practical decisions or as a substantive variable within a research study. However, the goodness of the instrument from a psychometric perspective does

not seem to be related to its popularity. To illustrate this point, one might ask: "Why has the MMPI not been replaced by a better, more effective instrument?" Here is an instrument that was "invented" 40 years ago and "finalized" (by the addition of the *Si* scale) in 1951. Is it that everyone thinks it's wonderful? Hardly. Norman (1972), for example, said:

From a strictly diagnostic viewpoint, the Multiphasic is a mess! Its original clinical criteria are anachronistic; its basic clinical scales are inefficient, redundant, and largely irrelevant for their present purposes; its administrative format and the repertoire of responses elicited are, respectively, inflexible and improverished; and its methods for combining scale scores and for profile interpretation are unconscionably cumbersome and obtuse. (p. 64)

This statement is from an article in Butcher's (1972) *Objective personality assessment: Changing perspectives,* which was devoted to the question of whether the MMPI needed to be revised, and if so, how.

Although Norman's (1972) statement may be the most negative in the book, all of the other contributors—Butcher, Hathaway, Loevinger, Dahlstrom, Campbell, and Meehl—felt that the MMPI, or at least the way the MMPI is used, could be improved. Two comments may be of particular interest. Loevinger (1972) said, "If a diagnostic decision is the aim, why devise a series of quantitative scales? If a series of quantitative measures is the aim, why take diagnostic groups as the basis for scoring keys? If a truly radical revision is attempted, this is one place to start" (p. 46). Dahlstrom (1972) suggested that since assessment with the MMPI is attempting to get at personality structure *and* current emotional status, a revised version should include three profile plots: validation scales; typifying scales, which would include defenses such as denial, projection, and repression; and syndromic scales, which would focus on depression, hostility, anxiety, and excitement.

What features would a psychometric purist like Norman want a multiphasic inventory to contain? He recommended the following: (1) "linear composites of items which are to be used as the component scales of a profile . . . must each be statistically homogeneous"; (2) "it would also be desirable . . . for the separate scales to be relatively uncorrelated with each other"; and (3) "it would be nice if some interpretation of each component scale based on the content of its items could be given" (1972, p. 66). (It is interesting to note that this brief summary includes no mention of predictive validity or utility, but then those objectives are not usually high on the list of purists.)

Two inventories designed to assess psychopathology have been developed in recent years: Jackson and Messick's Differential Personality Inventory (DPI) (Hoffman & Jackson, 1976; Jackson & Carlson, 1973; Trott & Morf, 1972) and the Clinical Analysis Questionnaire (CAQ), which was developed by Cattell and his associates (Cattell & Bolton, 1969; Delhees & Cattell, 1971a; Delhees & Cattell, 1971b). The DPI was hailed by Goldberg (1974) as "the MMPI's successor . . . if it can be lured out of hiding," but to our knowledge it has not as yet been published. Since it contains "28 scales spanning the content domain of psychopathology, based on rational and statistical procedures designed to foster scale independence, internal consistency, and freedom from desirability bias" (Hoffman & Jackson, 1976), one hopes that it will emerge soon. The CAQ, unlike the DPI, appears in the *Eighth mental measurements yearbook* (Buros, 1978), but the Pathology Supplement, which includes 12 factors dealing with psychopathology, was not treated kindly by McNair (1978) in his review. Actually this inventory does not meet Norman's criteria. Cattell does not consider the production of uncorrelated scales a desideratum of test construction, nor does he believe that items on a scale must necessarily be significantly correlated with each other (Cattell, Eber, &

Tatsuoka, 1970). Two other multiscale inventories might also be mentioned as possible competitors with the MMPI: the Psychological Screening Inventory (PSI) (Lanyon, 1970) and the Experiential World Inventory (EWI) (El-Meligi & Osmond, 1970). Goldberg (1974) praised the former and made fun of the latter. No research past 1974 is reported for the EWI in the *Eighth mental measurements yearbook* (and only three references altogether), but the PSI with 39 references appears to be attracting research interest.

These three or four tests, then, are the answer of the 1970s to the plea for an improved device to assess psychopathology. There is no evidence as yet that any will supersede the MMPI, which had almost 1200 citations during the same time period. The answer to the question of why the MMPI with all its faults hasn't been replaced appears to be that nothing better, at least in the view of users, has come down the pike.

Of course, based upon what we have stated about the manner in which a test might be constructed and evaluated, it is clear that nobody has taken on the burdensome task of establishing a better test. We do not believe the MMPI will be replaced until a test constructor can incorporate the situational, time, and response variables within a self-report personality inventory format. The user of self-report personality tests may be telling the constructor that he or she does not believe that other tests can outperform the MMPI and CPI unless these new tests are radically different from the "tried and true." Until those improvements occur, why should the user leave the friendly confines of the MMPI for an .02 change in the multiple correlation squared?

PROBLEMS WITH CONCEPTUALIZATION

How does one come up with ideas for research with inventories? Perhaps some have solved problems in a dream, as Kekule is said to have done with the chemical structure of benzene. Possibly others have had flashes of insight due to long previous periods of immersion in the topic. However, if one looks at lists of articles on inventories (e.g., Dahlstrom, Welsh & Dahlstrom, 1975 or the *Mental measurement yearbooks*), creativity of an exciting or dramatic type does not seem to play much of a role. Not only are new insights in short supply, but it is clear that not much thought of a theoretical nature has gone into the question. Rather we find study after study devoted to the momentous issue of comparing this group with that. Examples taken from citations concerning the Edwards Personal Preference Schedule (any other questionnaire would yield similar results) in the *Eighth mental measurements year book* (Buros, 1978) include: effective versus ineffective teachers of the trainable mentally retarded, counseling seekers versus non-counseling seekers, acceptors versus rejectors of newer educational media, career women versus homemakers, two year versus four year college commuters, college student smokers versus nonsmokers, empathic versus nonempathic counselor education students, open versus traditional teachers of the poor, and so on. If comparisons are not made, personality characteristics of a special group are focused on. From the same source we find the following being studied: religious professionals, students at the Air Force Academy, female youthful suicide attempters, medical students, honor students, student nurses, credit union members, professional police personnel, obese persons, pathological gamblers, and so on. What hypotheses are being tested in both these types of studies? If any are explicitly being examined, they are probably based on folklore rather than theory. Where a theory is used to frame a hypothesis, it is likely that it was developed after the data were examined, and its testing adds little to the credence of either the instrument or the theory. Why then do

people do these studies? One might say to get Master's and Doctor's degrees and be right in a fair number of cases. But in all cases the subjects are investigated for the same reason Mallory attempted to climb Mt. Everest—because it was there. We are referring here to what has recently been called the sample of convenience, which seems to be a classic example of putting the cart before the horse. In other words, availability of the subjects determines the study to be done. Yet one might well ask: are these studies worth doing?

No doubt most psychologists, if asked to do so, could rank studies on a dimension of importance or "worthwhileness." Consulting editors of journals make such judgments about every manuscript sent to them for review. Sometimes laypeople get into the act, such as Senator Proxmire with his Golden Fleece awards. What criteria are the editors and the Senator using? Personal values, which pervade every stage of the research enterprise from choice of problem to analysis and interpretation of the data. Some years ago science used to be described as a totally objective, value-free activity, but no one believes that anymore.

How does one select a problem for investigation? Graduate students typically become involved in the kind of research done by their mentors. Faculty usually say they don't give students problems, but it is not difficult for the student to discern what his or her major professor is interested in or the general trend of his or her publications. Sometimes Ph.D. candidates make the error of assuming that the "original research" referred to in the catalog means that they have to come up with something no one has ever thought of before. If they emerge from the library weeks later shouting "Eureka!," the most probable explanations are that all that concentrated reading has distorted their view of reality, or they missed the relevant articles in their review of the literature. Some kind person usually points out, before it is too late, that "original" is usually taken to mean "different." Therefore, it is perfectly acceptable to do what someone has done before, provided one uses a different class of subjects (e.g., males instead of females), a different measure of the dependent variable, more sophisticated designs, and so on. This orientation opens up a whole new world to the doctoral candidate and makes obvious that the number of potential studies approaches infinity.

If given some flexibility, novice researchers frequently choose an area of investigation that appears from their literature review to be important. However, sometimes it is difficult to disentangle what is important from what is popular. Two very popular recent topics involving self-report questionnaires have been androgyny (Bem, 1974) and internal-external locus of control (Rotter, 1966). Whether these are important only time will tell. Meehl (1978) remarked that when he was a graduate student in the late 1930s and early 1940s, level of aspiration was being investigated as vigorously as these two areas are now. Yet recent textbooks of general psychology do not even have the phrase in their index. What happened? "It just kind of dried up and blew away" (Meehl, 1978, p. 807). If anyone wants to follow the rise or decline and fall of interest in a given topic, scanning the Social Science Citation Index volumes will give a good picture.

If a prospective research project cannot be adequately judged on the basis of its popularity, what other criteria are available in order to evaluate it? One means to enhance the meaningfulness of a research project is to enmesh it within a theoretical framework. Eysenck (1976) asserted that "It is the absence of such a theory in all too many cases which is responsible for the failure of personality variables to make as large a contribution in empirical studies as they might" (p. 3). However, some researchers might reject this criterion, given the state of theories within the personality realm. In this regard Meehl (1978) said that "Most so-called 'the-

ories' in the soft areas of psychology . . . are scientifically unimpressive and technologically worthless" (p. 806). Elsewhere in the same article Meehl asserted:

It is simply a sad fact that in soft psychology theories rise and decline, come and go, more as a function of baffled boredom than anything else; and the enterprise shows a disturbing absence of that *cumulative* character that is so impressive in disciplines like astronomy, molecular biology, and genetics. (p. 807)

One might conclude, at least for now, that theories will not be available to guide research with inventories toward the promised land (i.e., prediction, or at least accurate postdiction, of behavior). Cronbach (1975) offered what may be a viable alternative:

Though enduring systematic theories about man in society are not likely to be achieved, systematic inquiry can realistically hope to make two contributions. One reasonable aspiration is to assess local events accurately, to improve short-run control . . . The other reasonable aspiration is to develop explanatory concepts, concepts that will help people use their heads. (p. 126)

Cronbach's conclusions imply that full-blown theories similar to the physical sciences are not attainable in the near future, but on the other hand, we should not be satisfied with folklore; low-level abstractions, close to behavior, are reasonable alternatives. Also it is appropriate to suggest linkage among these concepts, even though established relations are likely to change over time. Research should be embedded within this type of framework.

Assuming that a researcher has chosen a set of concepts to investigate, is there some strategy that he or she might take to maximize the importance of the research? One that has paid off for many people is concentration on a very specific area. This does not mean, for example, to do research with the MMPI. This is a specific instrument, true, but over 7000 studies using it have been done, and these cover dozens or perhaps hundreds of subareas. In this case concentration might mean examination of alcoholism, drug addiction, schizophrenia, or whatever via this instrument in a series of interrelated investigations. Better yet, focus on a subarea within alcoholism or drug addiction. Perhaps it is possible to design a crucial experiment in physics or chemistry, but that is not the case in psychology. To solve a problem requires repeated attacks, variations on a theme. Even when the investigator is satisfied, he or she is likely to find critics who do not agree with his or her conclusions. People have poohpoohed this approach as leading to knowing more and more about less and less, but reflection will show that the well-known people in a discipline have usually achieved what status they have by taking this route.

But we have still not answered the question as to what subarea might be concentrated on. Although formal approaches to research design tend to conceal rather than reveal a solution concerning this point, we could suggest that persons look at problems they have a personal investment in, that is, marital stability, ability and competency in aging individuals, racial prejudice, differential response to various psychological treatments, and so on. The self-report inventory is a tool that, notwithstanding its limitations, can be applied to most any problem involving the measurement of emotional, motivational, interpersonal, and attitudinal characteristics. If, then, one has a burning desire to find out what kinds of persons are most apt to fail to adjust to the stresses and strains accompanying marriage, pursuit of answers via a research program could well be recommended.

The best areas for investigation, if one does not have a personal commitment to a specific topic, are problems that have already attracted some interest. One might almost say that a bibliography of 20 to 40 items is ideal. Let us first consider the extremes. Zero or one reference is the obverse side of the "original idea" notion. This may appear attractive, but further consideration with the

help of colleagues usually shows the hypothesis hasn't been investigated, not because others haven't thought of it, but because they have and rejected it as a waste of time. (Some arrogance may be helpful here, because what could have been unproductive in 1935 or 1955 might be worthwhile in the different context of 1980.) The other end of the distribution, when hundreds of articles exist, is usually not attractive because the researcher can find no angle that hasn't already been explored. The notion of discovery, even if illusory, is an important motivator. However, even here there are possibilities, especially if summaries take the form that "Everyone knows that such and such a relationship has been established."

Why should one investigate the topic that has attracted a moderate amount of research? The most important reason is that it is possible to master the area. That is, if one will take the trouble to make up a table with columns indicating type of subjects, major findings, and shortcomings, it is possible to see at a glance the status of the field. Almost invariably close analysis will show consistencies and inconsistencies. And it may very well be possible to pinpoint the source of the inconsistencies. For example, X is strongly related to Y across the board, except for the subcategory schizophrenics with IQs below 90. This provides the entree that one has been looking for and a study can be designed to attempt to explain this anomaly.

Where does that leave the person who wants to do something more creative than giving tests to sheepherders from a western state or comparing men who wear English Leather with men who don't? Parenthetically, either of these notions, which were put forward in a spirit of fun, could be investigated. In the latter case, one might speculate that the English Leather wearer is more narcissistic, or more suggestible, or more concerned with making a good impression than the non-English Leather wearer. Measures of these three constructs could probably be found, and then one is off to the races. In the former case one could hypothesize that sheepherders are inclined to be social isolates, or persons who have an affinity for nature, or individuals who hate to wear suits and ties, and check these ideas out in the usual way. Although these proposed studies may sound a bit farfetched, and our previous remarks with regard to lists taken from the *Eighth mental measurements yearbook* were less than enthusiastic, we are not suggesting that there is no utility associated with the method of contrasted groups. Such studies might be undertaken when first attempting to establish the validity of some personality scale because they are relatively easy to execute. They can offer some preliminary information about the criterion validity of an instrument. However, if a relationship is found, the researcher cannot feel confident that there is a scale-behavior relationship. The best approach to ascertain if a personality scale is related to some set of behaviors is to obtain actual measures on all relevant behaviors and to correlate these with the personality scale.

If scale-behavior relationships have been established, a potentially fruitful avenue of attack is to explore personality-by-treatment interactions from either a theoretical or applied viewpoint. For example, Wener and Rehm (1977) hypothesized that initial level of depression as measured by the MMPI *D* scale and locus of control using Rotter's scale might interact with a rate of reinforcement factor in terms of performance on a pseudosocial intelligence measure. They derived this prediction from Lewinsohn's (1974) theory suggesting that depression is a function of the rate of reinforcement. Exploring social facilitation, Kohfeld and Weitzel (1969) found that susceptibility to peer group status was greater for subjects who scored relatively low on five scales of the CPI than for those scoring relatively high on these scales. That is, people who work equally hard for both high and low status observers possess certain positive personality attributes to a greater degree than individuals who are more sensitive to the social status of their audience. The importance of these studies is that they integrate the self-report personality measures within a conceptual framework.

From a more clinical perspective, studies need to be done to tie personality scales to treatment. Some studies of this type have been executed. For example, therapists have been differentiated into A and B types, based on a set of items from the Strong Vocational Interest Blank. Whitehorn and Betz (1960) suggested that A therapists were more successful with psychotic patients than B therapists. Based on a study by McNair, Callahan, and Lorr (1962), this hypothesis was extended to suggest that B therapists were better with neurotic patients. Although a long series of studies offers little support for these hypotheses, they have served to draw attention to interactional considerations. Investigators have also attempted to determine if the degree of similarity of MMPI profiles between therapists and clients affects outcome measures in psychotherapy (Parloff, Waskow, & Wolfe, 1978). It would be quite useful if, on the basis of personality measures, a clinician could rule out uses of certain therapeutic techniques. Cronbach (1975), in discussing aptitude-by-treatment interactions, raised a number of problems with this type of research. Those interested in using this strategy should familarize themselves with this perspective.

Dreams, ah-hah experiences, and dogged perseverance are the routes to research ideas, with the latter far more common than the former. Whatever the source, the idea does not usually appear in splendid isolation. Rather the hypothesis and the means to explore the hypothesis often appear at the same time. On the other hand, rarely do theories accompany hypotheses unless the researcher actively pursues this orientation in the development of the idea. Although strictly empirical work has a place in early stages of exploration, meaningful advances require theoretical underpinnings. New tests continue to pour out of test constructors' laboratories, but where are the persons with new or integrative concepts?

PROBLEMS WITH EXECUTION

Suppose one has developed what appears to be a reasonable research idea including some workable hypotheses. The next step in the process is to determine the most appropriate methods to evaluate these hypotheses. This step includes selecting subjects, measurement instruments, procedures, and statistics. These interrelated decisions should be determined by one underlying principle: the ability of the method to accurately test the hypothesis. However, practical limitations frequently disrupt this decision-making process.

Selection of subjects illustrates the conflict between theoretical and practical considerations. If one examines subject sections in psychology journals, it is obvious that nearly all samples are what might be called "captive audiences." That is, one finds the ubiquitous college sophomore from introductory psychology classes, psychiatric patients, prisoners, or more recently, drug abusers. On rare occasions, samples of people in general, that is, community residents, are reported. Stratified sampling at the national level seems to be the exclusive prerogative of the Survey Research Institute at the University of Michigan or polls connected with politicians or political issues or Nielsen ratings of TV programs.

Now there is absolutely nothing wrong with testing college sophomores if that is the population one wants to make assertions about on the basis of the results obtained. This seems to be *the* sample of choice if one is interested in the kinds of people who join fraternities or sororities, the extent of marijuana smoking or dating behavior among middle-class youth aged 18 to 22, the relations between ability and academic achievement, and similar questions. However, research questions are often not restricted to these kinds of issues.

One solution to the apparent conflict of obtaining either a diverse sample for generalization purposes or a narrow sample for efficiency reasons is to choose the latter approach initially. If the hypotheses are confirmed within the more restricted sample, other homogeneous samples can be obtained to see if the results replicate. Consistency of findings should yield comparable conclusions from a generalization perspective, and in fact this strategy offers some advantages over the one-shot, heterogeneous sample study. For example, with a more homogeneous sample, the power of the statistical analyses should in general be greater with a comparable number of subjects by reducing the error term. In addition, each study should give investigators some insights into the difficulties associated with their line of research, and consequently permit them to alter their methods in future studies to obtain a more sensitive design to test their hypotheses.

Another perspective has been offered by Webb (1976). He has described what he refers to as "natural outcroppings of a phenomenon" among occupations, already formed social and interest groups, or people who have common experiences. For example, if one were interested in superior depth perception, one might use as subjects magnetic core threaders, jugglers, or grand prix automobile drivers. If one were interested in high risk-taking, one might study not only race drivers but also sport and military parachute jumpers. If altruism is the issue, one might enlist volunteer blood donors, or contributors to charitable causes as subjects. To see how persons are affected by isolation, one might obtain data from interstate truck drivers, orthopedic patients in iron lungs, or prisoners who have spent time in solitary confinement. Megargee (1979) has recently stated that, "One reason I devoted much of my early career to validating scales of hostility and aggressiveness using samples of murderers was that editors generally accepted homicide as *prima facie* evidence of aggressive tendencies" (p. 6).

Most of this type of research has sought to contrast a group with one set of characteristics with another group having a different set of characteristics. As suggested in the conceptualization section, we advocate this line of research only when first exploring a personality instrument. The chosen groups typically demonstrate only a limited repertoire of behaviors of the domain that most personality instruments attempt to measure. Certainly murderers have been aggressive at least once in their lives, but they are probably not aggressive across all situations, modes, and times. Researchers that wish to use the contrasted groups approach will frequently be faced with a paradoxical decision. They will want subjects that clearly exemplify some personality dimension. However, the selection is almost inevitably based on one or a few single act criteria from the multi-faceted domain. Only studies that include multiple act criteria can reflect our current views of traits.

With the contrasted groups approach, normative data are often used to draw conclusions about a personality measure. This has the built-in advantage of getting a very large comparison group with no effort other than that involved in looking up means, standard deviations, ranges, and so on in published tables. However, it is unlikely that this approach is justified unless the norms are of very recent vintage. In the case of the MMPI, it would not make sense to use the norms in this manner, even though such analyses are very tempting. The senior author is involved in a project that addresses the problem of special norms. MMPIs have been obtained from nearly 900 normal blacks. When you have item endorsement rates for blacks and can get item endorsement rates for whites simply by looking at Appendix A of Dahlstrom, Welsh, and Dahlstrom (1975), it is difficult to resist doing statistical tests to see which items blacks and whites respond significantly differently to. But what should significant differences be attributed to: race, the passage of time, or an interaction between

these variables? Since these effects cannot be disentangled, one must resist the temptation. No one knows what the half-life of norms is. No doubt the duration of applicability is in part a function of the rapidity with which the culture as a whole is changing (contrast the 1950s in the United States with the 1960s).

Another sampling procedure used by investigators is the extreme group approach; that is, individuals are prescreened on some personality dimension, and only those who score in the upper or lower extremes (e.g., 10%) on the variable are included in the study. This strategy is more likely to be used when a personality-by-treatment interaction is being explored than with a correlational study. With the experimental study, the experimenter may not be able to run all subjects through one or more treatments; whereas with a correlational study, the collection of data on the middle group is more likely to be relatively inexpensive. An example of such an experimental study is that by Domino (1971), who investigated the relationship between achievement orientation and performance under teacher press consistent or inconsistent with the orientation. Eighty percent of the potential subjects were eliminated through prescreening. His results were impressive, but one wonders just how the interactive principle he demonstrated applies to college students who do not obtain extreme scores on CPI scales Achievement via Conformance or Achievement via Independence. Is the relationship linear, curvilinear, or nonexistent for the majority? This is an important question because his results suggested that treatments could be tailored to aptitudes so as to produce optimum performance.

The extreme group approach can of course be used to explore the relationship between some personality measure and potential correlates. If multiple act criteria are employed in future studies, this method offers some advantages. A study that compared a scale with multiple act criteria would require a large expenditure of time per subject and, if a linear relationship could be assumed, choosing extreme scores on a personality scale would be a reasonable alternative to running subjects who span the entire range of scores on the personality dimension. Assuming the same number of subjects were used in an extreme group study as in a study that included individuals who had not been preselected, the former study would generally have greater power in finding significant relationships. Myers (1979) offers an excellent summary of the statistical considerations of these designs. It should be noted that he not only recommends that the standard *t*-test not be used to determine if a relationship exists between variables with this design, but also gives a more powerful alternative, which involves calculating a modified correlation coefficient and testing its significance.

A somewhat different issue associated with sampling is the degree to which experimenters should restrict their samples in terms of demographic variables such as age, race, gender, socioeconomic status, and so on. When this is done, generalization to other segments of the population cannot be taken for granted. Many were puzzled when the MMPI code types, which Marks and Seeman (1963) found accounted for 80% of their population, fit only 15 to 25% of populations in other clinical settings. Furthermore, when profiles were classifiable, correlates often did not match up with patients' actual behavior. The fact that Marks and Seeman's final code types were based on white women who typically had one year of college, above average intelligence, and were voluntary admissions or outpatients considered likely to benefit from short-term treatment undoubtedly had something to do with these problems. In other words, these characteristics are very different from the usual VA or state hospital patient. As the senior author has stated elsewhere, an elevated MMPI profile obtained from a 16-year-old black male in trouble with the law may have to be interpreted very differently from a similar profile obtained from a 35-year-old white woman who has been admitted to a mental hospital with complaints

that people are following her, poisoning her food, and making obscene remarks about her.

Whatever the sampling procedure being utilized, one question that always needs addressing is the number of subjects to be included in the investigation. It seems as if this decision is frequently based on folklore rather than statistical concerns. The folklore "rules" probably vary from location to location, but here is an illustrative set. If researchers are simply correlating a personality measure with criteria, then 100 subjects may be thought to be necessary, unless multivariate procedures are used, in which case 200 subjects may be the minimum recommended. Sometimes these rules become more sophisticated by suggesting a subject to variable ratio, such as 10 subjects for each variable included in the analysis. When an analysis of variance design is used, 15 or 20 subjects per cell may be "required" because of the weak nature of personality variables. These types of guidelines are extremely questionable. Only by inspecting power tables such as those supplied by Cohen (1977) and by invoking some rational thought can the researcher reach a reasonable decision. To use power tables, the investigator must decide on at least three values: (1) the probability of rejecting a true null hypothesis (traditionally set at .05); (2) the desired power, that is, the probability of rejecting a false null hypothesis (a reasonable value for many experiments would be .80); and (3) the minimal level of relationship between variables (e.g., r^2 of .20) that would be interpreted as clinically important. The choice of this latter value is highly judgmental and may explain why many researchers do not resort to power tables. However, Cohen does give some guidelines on how one might select appropriate values.

There are numerous other problems associated with sampling, but let us now consider another prestudy problem, namely, selection of the instruments. For illustrative purposes, let us say that a relationship between sociability and sex role has been posited, that is, subjects who identify themselves as having masculine values are more outgoing than those who identify with feminine values. What measure of sociability should we choose? Jackson's (1967) Personality Research Form includes a scale named Affiliation, as does Edwards' (1954) Personal Preference Schedule. Both of the scales are said to measure one's tendency to be outgoing and participative. Moreover, Gough's (1957) California Psychological Inventory has a Sociability scale, and the first and most important of the 16 factors on Cattell's (1949) Sixteen Personality Factor Questionnarie is named Affectothymia, which translates into the same trait. Even the MMPI, with its heavy emphasis on psychopathology, has had Extraversion (Giedt and Downing, 1961) and Love of Others (MacDougald, 1970) scales derived from its 550 items. No doubt other familiar and less familiar inventories include a measure of this well-known trait. Since all versions cannot be used, what principles does one follow to select the best measure? Reliability and validity coefficients deserve considerable weight. It would take us too far afield to get into a lengthy discussion of these matters, but answers can be found by looking at the test's manuals or handbooks. Typically, the evidence for validity, especially external validity, will be less compelling than the evidence for reliability. Let us suppose, however, that one is able to select a measure of sociability that has satisfactory reliability and at least some evidence of external validity.

A question that is often raised at this point is: can the scale be administered by itself or does the entire inventory have to be given? This is an important pragmatic question, since the time a subject has available for testing is usually restricted. Without meaning the following to be the only possible answer to this issue, it is instructive to consider Megargee's (1979) observations on this subject:

I once extracted the O-H (overcontrolled hostility) scale and administered each O-H item using as buffers the items which immediately preceded and followed it. The correlation between the scores obtained on the extracted version and O-H scores obtained from the full MMPI administered the same day was only .55. (p. 8)

Perkins and Goldberg (1964), on the other hand, found no differences in mean scale scores between an MMPI scale administered singly and the same scale embedded in the MMPI item matrix. Dahlstrom, Welsh, and Dahlstrom (1972) indicated that the separate scale sometimes produces a lower mean than when the items are encountered in the context of other MMPI items, but added that these effects have not been definitely established.

The other variable we mentioned in our hypothetical study was masculinity/femininity. This construct can also be found in numerous inventories, of which the MMPI and CPI are probably best known. However, both these versions contain a deficit that Bem's (1974) scale was designed to correct. That is, these older inventories consider masculinity/femininity to be a unidimensional trait. One could characterize himself or herself as masculine or feminine in terms of the norms, but not both. Bem (1974) hypothesized that these traits were independent, so that one could be high on both, low on both, high on masculinity and low on femininity, or vice versa. Those in the latter two categories are said to be sex-typed, while those in the first category are said to be androgynous and those in the second category undifferentiated (Bem, 1977). Although androgyny has been an extremely popular research topic, recent work (e.g. Helmreich, Spence, & Holahan, 1979) suggests that instruments used to tap this construct are largely measures of masculine and feminine traits and only minimally related to sex role behaviors. Also Pedhazur and Tetenbaum (1979) have demonstrated that just two items on the Bem Sex Role Inventory, masculine and feminine, accounted for nearly 80% of the variance. Furthermore, despite Bem's contention that masculinity and femininity are independent trait dimensions, females who rate themselves high on "feminine" tend to rate themselves low on "masculine," and vice versa for males.

In any case, the measures have been selected and we are almost ready to roll on data collection. But wait, hasn't something been omitted? Yes; as it stands, the investigator is simply correlating one paper-and-pencil measure with another. Before carrying out the study, it is extremely important to determine item overlap between paper-and-pencil measures. As Goldberg (1972) has pointed out, the widespread practice of item borrowing has created item overlap between inventories, which may result in spuriously high convergent validity coefficients. Also, correlations between scales supposedly measuring different constructs might be achieved because of item overlap or near overlap. For example, the dominance scale of the CPI includes the following two items: "I am embarassed with people I do not know well," and "I am a better talker than listener." Are not these items parallel forms of items from the social extroversion scale of the Omnibus Personality Inventory (Heist & Yonge, 1968): "I find it difficult to carry on a light conversation with strangers" and "I am a better listener than conversationalist"? Certainly the lack of discriminant validity of many self-report personality instruments might be due to overlap in item content. When researchers are relating scales together, they would be wise to correlate the measures with and without the overlapping items to understand better the relationship among constructs.

Also it would be almost mandatory, especially within the realm of self-report research, to obtain data at a different level. As Meehl (1959) stated, a study that shows that a scale predicts behavior is more impressive than one that demonstrates concurrent validity, especially if the criterion data are easily obtained. Ratings by friends of the subjects' sociability and masculinity/femininity involve different operations and would, if the data cooperate, help establish a relationship less open to criticism. One might question,

however, whether these data could be *easily* obtained. If the subjects of this study were high school seniors, counting the lines devoted to activities adjacent to their pictures could yield an unobtrusive measure of sociability (see Meehl, 1971, for a critical discussion of this procedure). A compromise solution, which the writers have used, is to ask for face-sheet information tailored to the hypothesis being investigated. Although this is also self-report, if one asks for answers to factual questions and guarantees anonymity, the data are apt to reflect reality quite accurately and could be construed as life history rather than questionnaire data. In the case of sociability, questions involving number of close friends, number of acquaintances, frequency of attending parties or other social events, number of organizations one belongs to, and the like would be appropriate. An interesting unobtrusive measure would be the number of telephone numbers entered in one's "little black book."

Clearly we have not discussed all issues involved with the execution of a study dealing with a self-report personality instrument. The researcher also has to decide how to order the administration of the measures, whether to run the subjects in groups or individually, and so on. Also a large number of statistical decisions must be made, for example, the choice between univariate and multivariate statistics. However, we hoped only to illustrate some of the difficulties with the execution of a study, and attempted to show that once the idea is formulated the researcher cannot simply start collecting data with no thought for sampling, inventory or scale selection, and similar matters.

PROBLEMS WITH INTERPRETATION

The study has been conducted and the data have been obtained. Now the investigator is faced with the problem of deciding what the results signify. This would appear to be relatively simple if the hypotheses were clearly stated and the study well designed. However, as illustrated in the beginning of the conceptualization section, rarely do studies dealing with self-report personality instruments meet these criteria. Consequently some researchers view the presentation of the conclusions from a study as an art form: to create a silk purse from a sow's ear (i.e., the data). Other investigators hoodwink themselves into believing that the study they conducted was important and present it as such in the conclusion section. However, most researchers arrive at conclusions that are consistent with their results and their theoretical frameworks, but neglect equally valid interpretations. Through a series of illustrations, we want to show how easy it is for a investigator to develop tunnel vision, but how other researchers frequently broaden the perspective. We will begin by presenting some of the findings in the area of black-white differences on the MMPI.

Such studies got off to a slow start. Between 1939 and 1960 only four were reported. Three were of prisoners in state institutions and one was of tuberculosis patients in a veterans administration hospital. All showed that blacks obtained higher scores than whites on scales *Sc* or *Ma*. How did the various authors interpret these results? Caldwell (1954) obtained a mean score of 68 on scale *Sc* for his sample of youthful black "rural-farm offenders" and said that this finding "discloses specific tendencies toward schizophrenia" (p. 297). Panton (1959) stated that "negroes, irrespective of age, are more inclined toward bizarreness and externalization in their behavior, especially when subject to frustration and stress" (p. 35). Hokanson and Calden (1960) concluded that "Negroes . . . manifest more of what are considered to be bizarre or unusual thoughts and behavior" (p. 33). Although these quotations all seem to imply that the differences reflect more psychopathology in the black subjects, Hokanson and Calden (1960) felt that "a more careful consideration of an in-

dividual's sociocultural background may be necessary for an adequate evaluation of his MMPI record" (p. 33). How did Dahlstrom and Welsh (1960) summarize these data? They stated that these findings are "the sort that would be expected from known effects of socioeconomic inequities" (p. 273).

So higher scores by blacks on MMPI scales *Sc* or *Ma* were seen as a function of differences in psychopathology, sociocultural background, or socioeconomic class. Approximately 30 additional studies have addressed this issue in the past 20 years, but the problem has not been completely resolved. There are additional explanations for the differences—intelligence (Rosenblatt, 1976) and education (Davis, 1975; Marks, Bertelson, & May, 1977)—and even those who argue that there are no differences (Pritchard & Rosenblatt, 1980). The senior author's views of this matter have been expressed elsewhere (Gynther, 1972; Gynther, 1979). This is not the place to put in another plug for any given explanation. Rather the point is how many interpretations can be offered for what amount to esentially the same phenomena. On the plus side, this says something for psychologists' intelligence and creativity; on the negative side, one gets the feeling that certain problems are resistant to solution by mere data. Perhaps values play a part in this particular case. Edwards (1974) is quite specific on this point. He argued that:

Race is not a relevant variable for the study of personality but is a relevant variable for understanding the theorizing and conclusions emphasized by researchers. This hypothesis maintains that there is a process of selective perception caused mainly by racist cultural biases which prevent investigators from seeing and emphasizing results which contradict the Negro stereotype. (p. 47)

The ethnicity research with the MMPI illustrates well the difficulties involved with contrasting a priori groups on self-report personality instruments. The research idea is chosen because of the ease of data collection and its apparent relevance to sociocultural issues. If differences are found, researchers may conclude that they were due to differences between races in prevalence of psychopathology. However, other investigators with a different orientation choose not to believe these conclusions and seek to rectify the "misinterpretation" by controlling for a series of demographic variables. Of course these new studies are done without postulating in a meaningful fashion the relationships among these controlling variables, the groups factor, and the personality dimensions. Certainly socioeconomic status does not influence the race of an individual, although the reverse may be true. Therefore, we are controlling with a variable that potentially is influenced by one that might be conceived of as an independent variable. Also the personality variable is not without fault. For one thing, the influence of response distortions such as social desirability may explain the results. Furthermore, the ability to comprehend the items might differ by group. Also, in the case of the MMPI, what may be defined as a reasonable cutoff for abnormality in one group may differ for another group. Simply put, researchers conclude something from their initial data that they really should not until many, many studies are performed. Even after an extensive program of research, we are often better able to state what is irrelevant rather than what are the important variables. These studies share in common with contrasted groups studies a naive philosophy that the ways people behave can be explained simply rather than through a complex, multivariate interface.

As a second example of difficulties of interpreting what may appear to be fairly simple results, MMPI differences associated with age will be considered. Typically an older group is compared to a younger group; any differences obtained are said to indicate personality changes associated with aging. Aaronson (1958) analyzed peak scores of a large sample of psychiatric patients. He found that peaks on scales *Hs* and *D* are

comparatively uncommon in early life, but become much more common as the individuals become older. The reverse was true of scales *Pd* and *Sc*. He interpreted these findings as indicating that younger psychiatric patients seem characterized by behavior patterns maladaptive to societal demands, while older patients seem characterized by problems centering around their own physical and mental functioning. Swenson (1961) tested 95 normal persons whose average age was 71. He interpreted his findings—the highest mean T-scores were 59 and 58 on scales *D* and *Hs*, respectively—as follows: "The typical or median profile for this group is a neurotic one with an absence of evidence of psychotic or behavior disorder tendencies . . ." (p. 304). Postema and Schell (1967) found that older psychiatric patients scored significantly higher on scales *Hs, D* and *Hy* than on scales *Pa, Pt, Sc* and *Ma* and concluded that "Aged adults appear to respond in a more neurotic fashion than younger adults" (p. 143).

Good agreement concerning the interpretation of personality changes associated with aging is found in the studies cited above: younger subjects have problems with impulse control, while older subjects display "neurotic" concerns with their physical and mental functioning. However, all of these studies are cross-sectional and do not answer the questions of whether differences are truly developmental or simply cohort (generational) effects. The only longitudinal MMPI study that could clarify this issue was recently published by Leon, Gillum, Gillum, and Gouze (1979). These investigators obtained data from 1947, 1953, 1960, and 1977 on the same 71 "psychologically healthy" men recruited for the Cardiovascular Disease Project at the University of Minnesota. Systematic increases in scores over time occurred on a number of scales. The largest increase was on Scale *D*, which would appear to confirm the results of the cross-sectional studies. Although the mean T-scores shifted from 51.64 to 61.63, the latter score would not suggest much depressive affect. Indeed Leon et al. (1979) stated that "the increase in mean score on scale 2 may reflect somatic concerns and a preference for a more tranquil life existence rather than being reflective of the emotional and cognitive concomitants of depression" (p. 523).

Longitudinal studies are valuable in tracing the relative stability or changes in individuals, but do not necessarily lead to correct generalizations about the aging process. Data collection in this area involves three factors: age of subject, time of testing, and time of birth. Cross-sectional and longitudinal methods each deal with only two of the three components, and consequently they are not only likely to yield partially correct answers but also results in disagreement with each other. For a number of years Schaie (1965) has recommended the use of designs involving the replication of cross-sectional or longitudinal procedures to tease out the variance due to chronological age from that attributable to cohort differences or non-age-related environmental factors. No MMPI studies using these designs have been carried out. However, Douglas and Arenberg (1978) did such an investigation, using Guilford-Zimmerman Temperament Survey data collected from participants in the Baltimore Longitudinal Study. Cross-sequential and time-sequential analyses were performed. They found that maturational change alone (i.e., aging) could account for declines on General Activity and Masculinity with increasing age. With regard to generational differences, later-born cohorts were lower in Restraint and higher in Ascendance than early-born cohorts. Time of testing differences involved Thoughtfulness and Personal Relations; both decreased during the time frame of the study. Sociability, Emotional Stability, and Objectivity were not affected by maturation, generation, or time of testing.

It is obviously difficult to translate these dimensions into those typically discussed in MMPI studies. That is, how the above findings bear on Depression and Hypochon-

driasis is not clear. What is obvious, however, is that the simplified designs used in MMPI studies cannot give complete answers to the question of personality changes associated with aging. Are older people more neurotic, depressed, and concerned with bodily functioning than younger people? Do younger people have more energy, problems with impulse control, and clashes with authority than older people? These interpretations sound reasonable because they fit our stereotypes of young and old, but as far as MMPI studies are concerned the conclusion would have to be: not yet demonstrated. In fact the conclusion might be: never to be demonstrated. Even the soundest design to investigate developmental processes cannot overcome difficulties associated with scales that are heterogeneous with respect to content. Although investigating at the item level might be more fruitful, the reliability of these items would certainly attentuate results. Perhaps the Wiggins' (1966) MMPI content scales would be an improvement over individual items. However, alternative procedures to derive MMPI psychopathology scales are unlikely to yield more definitive conclusions due to the lack of content considerations in the original development of the item pool.

A third example of difficulties in interpretation will be taken from recent work with scale *Ma* of the MMPI, and illustrates the difficulties addressed above in terms of the heterogeneous content of some personality scales. This scale was originally created to identify psychiatric patients manifesting symptoms such as "elevated mood, accelerated speech and motor activity, instability, flight of ideas, and brief periods of depression" (Graham, 1977, p. 57). High scorers, whether patients or normal persons, are said to be energetic and talkative, creative, enterprising, and ingenious, and have a wide range of interests, but little interest in routine or details. Graham (1977) gives many additional descriptors of individuals who obtain high or low scores on this scale. There is a high degree of agreement between this source and other well-known references (e.g., Dahlstrom, Welsh, & Dahlstrom, 1972).

How certain can we be of these authoritative interpretations of the *Ma* scale? Graham (1977) stated that "Scores on scale 9 clearly are related to age and race" (p.58); blacks obtain higher scores than whites and young people obtain higher scores than older people. Obviously these variables may present interpretive problems. But what about one's score on the *Ma* scale? How is it achieved? By responding to obvious or to subtle items? Or by endorsing items measuring imperturbability but not ego inflation, amorality but not psychomotor acceleration (Harris & Lingoes, 1968)? The *Ma* scale is heterogeneous and, as Graham (1977) puts it, "No single dimension accounts for much of the variance in scores" (p.58). A recent study (Hovanitz & Gynther, 1980) has shown that if one endorses subtle *Ma* scale items, the trait of imperturbability is implied; on the other hand, psychomotor acceleration and ego inflation can be expected if the *Ma* scale score is made up primarily of endorsement of obvious *Ma* scale items. Experience Seeking and Thrill and Adventure Seeking (Zuckerman, 1977) were significantly related to endorsement of *Ma*-Obvious and *Ma*-Subtle items, respectively. Life history data (e.g., "How many different jobs have you held?", "How many men or women have you dated?", "How many times have you run out of gas?", "How long do you spend eating breakfast?") were significantly correlated with *Ma*-S items, but not with *Ma*-O items. Time spent on the Porteus Mazes, as well as total error score, was positively associated with *Ma*-O, but not with *Ma*-S. This brief summary clearly indicates that obvious items predict some *Ma* scale criteria, while subtle items are predictive of other *Ma* scale criteria. Since the usual *Ma* or *Ma* + .2*K* score offers no enlightenment as to how it was obtained, interpretation is not as simple as the manuals and handbook might lead one to believe.

The preceding examples have tended to stress negative findings as much as positive results. Many journal articles emphasize only positive findings, those that are in agreement with some theory and statistically significant. However, as Mahoney (1978) and others have recently pointed out, no hypothesis can ever be empirically confirmed. This error is known as affirming the consequent (Popper, 1959), which takes the form of believing that a predicted conclusion confirms the premise from which it is drawn. Clearly this is illogical, since any of a number of premises could underlie the so-called positive result. However, negative results do have important logical implications. As Megargee (1979) said:

It would not be particularly exciting to learn that college students with T-scores over 70 on Scale 0 (Social Introversion) had fewer dates or were less likely to join social organizations than students with T-scores of 30 or lower; however, *failure* to find a significant difference between two such extreme groups would cast serious doubt on the validity of the scale. (p. 7)

Interpretation of results should therefore put more weight on predictive failures than on predictive successes. This frequently runs counter to our cherished beliefs and also to the apparent acceptance patterns of journals. Many of us have jokingly discussed the need for a *Journal of Negative Results*. Had we been more familiar with Popper, we would have made serious recommendations to that effect. Positive results at best corroborate an hypothesis. This simply means that the hypothesis has survived falsification on this occasion.

The heavy reliance on significance level has also created a problem for the psychological researcher. As Meehl (1978) has stated:

I suggest to you that Sir Ronald has befuddled us, mesmerized us, and led us down the primrose path. I believe that the almost universal reliance on merely refuting the null hypothesis as the standard method for corroborating substantive theories in the soft areas is a terrible mistake, is basically unsound, poor scientific strategy, and one of the worst things that ever happened in the history of psychology. (p. 817)

Why is this an unacceptable approach? According to Meehl (1978): "If you have enough cases and your measures are not totally unreliable, the null hypothesis will always be falsified, *regardless of the truth of the substantive theory*" (p. 822). What sort of approach would give evidence that the relationships in question are valid? The senior author is reminded of a conversation he had with a physiological psychologist on the issue of accepting or rejecting hypothesized relationships via statistical tests. He said he never performed statistical analyses on his data; he simply repeated the experiment 10 times. If it came out the same every time, he accepted the relationship as established.

If these comments about interpretation have made the reader uneasy, our purpose has been accomplished. Psychologists apparently cannot restrain themselves from making inferential statements at the drop of a *t*-test. It might be desirable for them to spend more time coming up with interesting questions and systematic research programs that have some promise of yielding clear-cut empirical relations than the current practice of telling it *as it is* on the basis of a single study whose results can be interpreted in many different ways.

PROBLEMS WITH VERIFICATION

What occurs after a research project has been completed? All researchers know the "proper" answer to this question: the results are replicated. However, viewing the behavior of many self-report personality researchers suggests a different conclusion: find another topic that has potential in terms of publication. Why do they choose not to replicate their results? One reason is that they have learned that many journal editors allow

publication of research without some type of replication included. We might guess that some editors have chosen to take this stand because self-report personality research normally requires a large number of subjects, and consequently the sheer magnitude of the work involved in doing a nonreplicated study dictates this policy. This type of research differs quite dramatically, for example, from information processing research where, for the most part, a very small number of subjects is required and the conclusions are warranted from within-subject manipulations. It is much easier for the editor of an information processing journal to suggest additional research must be included before the manuscript is in publishable form. Nevertheless, the willingness of some editors to publish nonreplicated studies with self-report personality measures does not mean that the same or related research hypotheses should not be explored by researchers and that they instead choose an unrelated area to explore. To some extent these investigators must not realize what the results of the current study imply for the next study. Because self-report personality research has had a strong emphasis on empiricism to the partial or total exclusion of theory, the researcher tends to see each project as a separate entity rather than attacking some larger issue. Without a theory, programmatic research is nearly impossible.

Assuming that investigators do seek to explore their findings further, how should they do it? They might choose among a number of alternatives. If they have used a statistical procedure that through capitalization on chance yields an unsatisfactory estimate of some parameter, cross-validation is mandatory. For example, in a first study, items might have been chosen to be included on a scale on the basis of item-scale correlations. An internal consistency estimate of reliability such as coefficient alpha would yield an overestimate of the reliability (Cureton, 1950) for this subset of items. Consequently a second sample, similar to the first sample in characteristics, should be used to calculate an unbiased estimate of coefficient alpha.

A slight variation of this procedure might be called partial cross-validation or cross-validation generalization. For example, a multiple regression equation might be derived that yields optimal weights to predict some criterion for a particular sample. Theoretical estimates are available to determine what the multiple correlation would be with this equation when applied to other similar samples. However, the sample might not represent all populations that the equation might be applicable to. Therefore, the weights derived in the first sample might be used on the same measures to predict the same criterion in a second sample, which differs in terms of certain demographic variables. Alternatively, the predictors might be the same and the sample drawn from the same population, but the researcher might be interested in how well the weighted combination of predictors relates to a slightly different criterion. In other words, partial cross-validation is the application of results from a study in which chance factors have influenced the findings to a second sample in which some systematic change in the sample, predictors, or criterion has taken place.

Similar distinctions can be made when no capitalization on chance has taken place. The researcher may choose between directly replicating the results of the first study and partially replicating them. With direct replication, a second sample would be drawn from the same population, but every other aspect of the first study would remain the same. Partial replication implies that some other facet or facets of the study have changed.

A programmatic research program always incorporates partial cross-validation or replication. If generalization is found when certain dimensions of a study are varied, the results from both studies are strengthened. Of course, if generalization is not found, the investigator might be forced to vary fewer dimensions until consistency in results occurs. Inconsistent findings might eventually

force direct replication to determine if the positive results of the first study were due to sampling error. From this perspective the choice between direct or partial cross-validation or replication depends on the knowledge of the investigator and his or her willingness to risk generalizing across the various facets of the first study.

We will now examine some research from the literature to see how researchers have in the past made decisions to verify their results. We will first examine research in which, initially, investigators did not attempt to cross-validate their results, but more recently have done so.

A number of MMPI code type interpretations have been developed by various investigators. The correlates available from Marks and Seeman (1963) and Gilberstadt and Duker (1965) obviously entailed a great deal of work. Yet the senior author can vividly recall how surprised he was to discover that virtually no one was doing any cross-validation studies. True, there were studies of fit rates (i.e., percent of profiles classifiable according to the rules), but what verification of the original correlates were being carried out? The most extensive investigation was an unpublished dissertation (Palmer, 1970), which, naturally, had little influence on system usage. Since the original developers of the code types did not cross-validate their results when their systems were created, and system users did not publish cross-validation generalization studies, how can one know which relationships are universally valid, if any, which ones hold under certain circumstances, and which ones have no relevance to any but the derivation group? More recent actuarial systems (Gynther, Altman, & Sletten, 1973; Lewandowski & Graham, 1972; Marks, Seeman, & Haller, 1974) have used cross-validational procedures by splitting their original samples in two halves and performing separate analyses in each half sample. More faith should probably be placed in the 20 to 30% of correlates that survived this winnowing process, although it is interesting to note that very few tests of the validity of *these* systems to other populations have been reported in the literature. As a postscript, one might point out that the code type approach is methodologically primitive. A more sophisticated way to study clinical correlates of the MMPI would involve multivariate procedures such as discriminant analysis with all scale scores used as predictors (Butcher & Pancheri, 1975).

Sometimes the verification studies are carried out so long after the original study that it is difficult to interpret the results. In 1968 Gough published correlates of each of the California Psychological Inventory scales. These had been obtained by having five peers describe each subject on the Adjective Check List (Gough & Heilbrun, 1965). Patterns of relationships were specified by correlating the ACL scores with scores on the CPI scales for males and females separately. Thus for the Dominance *(Do)* scale, high-scoring males were characterized as ambitious, dominant, and forceful (only the first three correlates are given) and high-scoring females as aggressive, bossy, and conceited. Low-scoring subjects on the same scale were described as apathetic, indifferent, interests narrow, if male, and cautious, gentle, inhibited, if female. These correlates, as well as those for the remaining scales, obviously have played an important role in the clinical interpretation of the CPI. However, it should be noted that these relationships were not corroborated by cross-validation samples by Gough or his collaborators at Berkeley, and further that the data were actually gathered in the mid-1960s (Gough, 1979).

Gregory and Morris (1978) recently replicated that part of Gough's study dealing with females: They stated: "A comparison of Gough's findings and those of the current study revealed dramatic changes in the qualitative nature of the positively correlated adjectives" (p. 260). With regard to the *Do* scale in particular, they pointed out that while Gough's results characterized high *Do* women in unfavorable terms, their results

lend no support to a stereotypic negative conception of high dominance in women. These changes were interpreted as reflecting the differences in the way women were viewed by society and their peers in the 1960s and the 1970s or, as Cronbach (1975) might say, a treatment by decade interaction. Although this conclusion is understandable, it can be questioned. Mean feminity *(Fe)* scale scores were no different (49.3 vs. 50) for the current group of subjects and the 192 women for whom correlates were reported in the Interpreter's Syllabus (Gough, 1968). According to Gough (1979), there have been no significant changes on *Fe* scale scores for female graduate students in psychology at Berkeley during the period 1950 to 1972 inclusive. However, the culture-change hypothesis put forth by Gregory and Morris (1978) would have predicted changes on the *Fe* scale. Next, how do we know that there have been changes in the correlates associated with high and low scale scores? Certainly Gregory and Morris found different significantly correlated adjectives than those reported in the Syllabus, but then Gough would have also *if* he had cross-validated his results. Third, because the results from the original study and the partial cross-validation study disagreed, it is difficult if not impossible to tease out differences due to cultural changes from those attributable to differences in social class, intelligence, rural-urban residence, and other factors that may affect results.

It is curious that Gough used only an original sample to derive the correlates for the CPI scales, since he and his co-workers have been exemplary in their use of cross-validational procedures. In a typical study, Gough, Fox, and Hall (1972) divided their subjects into odd-numbered and even-numbered subsamples and then stepwise regression analyses were conducted within each subgroup limiting the number of predictors to five to minimize chance factors. The equation developed on the odd-numbered subjects was then cross-validated on those that are even-numbered and vice-versa. The mean of these two cross-validations was taken as the estimate of the degree to which criterion ratings can be predicted from a linear combination of scales on the inventory. (The procedure we have just described is known as double cross-validation. An alternative to this approach is to derive a regression equation for the total sample and then to estimate the population cross-validated correlation coefficient with a shrinkage formula. Theoretical estimates are preferable to empirical ones unless the researcher is interested in determining the applicability of a regression equation to a different population from the one on which that equation was derived).

Another tactic that Gough used that is highly desirable is to conduct repeated investigations of scales or indices with many different samples. Thus the CPI Socialization scale's ability to discriminate between delinquent and nondelinquent groups has been studied on numerous occasions in this country and also in other countries (Gough, 1965; Gough, 1975, pp. 22–23; Gough & Sandhu, 1964). More recently, a social maturity index based on six scales of the CPI has been used extensively (Gough, 1971; Gough, DeVos, & Mizushima, 1968; Gough & Quintard, 1974) to differentiate delinquents from nondelinquents. Hit rates typically ranged from 82 to 92% for American and foreign subjects. These may all be considered as validity generalization studies. Consistent results give one much more confidence in the scale or index than is the case with the many scales that are introduced with a single study, but not followed up.

The research that has related conformity to the Marlowe-Crowne Social Desirability Scale (SD) indicates the benefits that accrue by performing a series of studies on a single topic (Strickland, 1977). Strickland and Crowne (1962) had females listen to a tape that had 18 series of "knocks" presented at a rate that could be accurately perceived. The subjects heard an accurate response by three confederates for six of the trials, but an inaccurate report for the remaining 12 trials. Females who scored high on SD conformed

significantly more often than low SD females to the inaccurate responses of the accomplices. Marlowe and Crowne (1961) attempted to verify these results, but changed the actual experiment quite dramatically. Subjects were exposed to a visual perception discrimination task, and the confederates actually interacted with the subjects. The high SD subjects again conformed more often with the inaccurate responses of the confederates. Miller, Doob, Butler, and Marlowe (1965) researched the relationship between SD and the changing of initial responses to personality statements to conform to experts' judgments. In their first study, they found no differences between high and low SD subjects with all subjects conforming to a significant degree. The feedback in this investigation was purported to be by four Harvard psychology professors. In a second study, the degree of expertise and several additional dimensions were varied. These results indicated that high SD subjects did conform more when the judges were experts, whereas no differences were found for the low SD subjects. Although additional attempts to replicate the above results have not always been successful (e.g., Breger, 1966; Wiesenthal, 1974), the interrelated research projects presented above do appear to indicate that social desirability is related to conformity, given appropriate conditions.

Replication and cross-validation may not always be necessary in order to reach proper conclusions. We have heard a champion of single subject research state: it takes only a single elephant to demonstrate that elephants can fly. However, most psychologists are interested in general principles underlying behavior. Consequently the more interesting issue is the ability of elephants in general to fly. To demonstrate this relationship requires replication.

SUMMARY AND CONCLUSIONS

As soon as self-report inventories were published, critics pointed out their inadequacies.

However, these instruments yielded numerical data and were clearly cost-effective, so their development continued and flourished.

Although some recently constructed self-report measures may be considered to be technically superior to those created many years ago, they are still open to criticism. The mystical aura surrounding many of the personality scales is at least partially responsible for this vulnerability. Just the names given these scales, for example, existentiality and personal integration, suggest higher-order, complex abstractions. The fact that these scales are enmeshed within trait theory only enhances the mirage of scientific and theoretical sophistication. Faced with the momentous task of constructing scales measuring broad-based traits, most test developers have selected items without clearly defining the boundaries of the item-population.

Constructors of trait measures should define a priori what situations and response modes are to be included and excluded on their tests. These judgments should be based not only on theoretical concerns, but also on empirical findings such as correlations of responses averaged over time between situations. Once the test has been properly defined, researchers are likely to do better criterion validity studies. From this perspective a multiple act criterion is necessary to validate such a measure. Also users of the measure should be able to interpret the result directly as the self-perception that the individual is willing to make public to others. With these types of instruments available, the researchers may then attend to developing a project without as much ambiguity in the measuring process.

Current and past studies in this area have, unfortunately, typically been undertaken on the basis of popularity of topic and easy availability of subjects. Guidance by means of theory would be preferable, but it now appears that full-blown theories are unlikely to become available in the "soft" areas of psychology. However, accurate assessment of local events and development of explanatory concepts should be possible. A good strategy would involve focusing on an area that has attracted a moderate amount of research. A recommended topic is personality by treatment interactions, which is important both theoretically and clinically.

Homogeneous samples are useful when first investigating a problem. The "natural outcroppings of a phenomenon" approach is also worth considering. The extreme group analysis can lead to illuminating results, especially with experimental as opposed to correlational studies. One should always attend to the possible limitations in generality associated with restrictions of distribution of demographic variables. One should also be aware of the dangers of using norms as comparison samples. The number of subjects needed can be determined better from power tables than by appealing to experts. It is important to collect data at behavioral as well as self-report levels; sometimes biographical data might be substituted for the behavioral data.

Most investigators interpret the results of a single study as having this particular meaning or supporting that certain theory, even when alternative explanations are equally plausible. One could make a cogent case that explanation should await the findings from an extensive program of interrelated studies. Despite the reinforcement given from many sources for positive results, it is clear that they should be given less weight than negative results, especially for hypothesis-testing.

Psychologists seem to take great pleasure in developing new scales (e.g., the nearly 500 MMPI scales), but little interest in determining what scores on them mean. Partial cross-validation or direct replication is strongly recommended to evaluate the generality of any finding. If this procedure is not carried out by the original investigator, it is difficult if not impossible for later investigators to do it adequately due to inability to disentangle effects of the variable of interest from others involved.

When first encountered, trait theory has a disarming simplicity compared to other personality theories. This has led many to believe that relatively simple instruments and designs could provide answers to what in actuality are complex problems. Although some encouraging findings have recently been reported (Epstein, 1979; Hogan, De-Soto, & Solano, 1977; Jackson & Paunonen, 1980), past results have often been so disappointing that many people have become thoroughly disenchanted with this approach. Yet one might argue that this old warhorse has still not had a fair trial. If one were to use properly constructed tests, design studies more carefully, and utilize adequate criteria, who knows what predictive validities might be obtained? We hope that there are investigators with enough resources, creativity, analytic ability, and perseverance to attempt this rocky road.

REFERENCES

Aaronson, B. S. (1958). Age and sex influence on MMPI profile peak distribution in an abnormal population. *Journal of Consulting Psychology, 22,* 203–206.

Alker, H. A. (1977). Beyond ANOVA psychology in the study of person-situation interactions. In D. Magnusson & N. S. Endler (Eds.), *Personality at the crossroads: Current issues in interactional psychology.* New York: Lawrence Erlbaum.

Allport, F. H., & Allport, G. W. (1921). Personality traits: Their classification and measurement. *Journal of Abnormal and Social Psychology, 16,* 6–40.

Allport, G. W. (1921). Personality and character. *Psychological Bulletin, 18,* 441–455.

Allport, G. W. (1924). The study of the undivided personality. *Journal of Abnormal and Social Psychology, 19,* 132–141.

Bem, S. L. (1974). The measurement of psychological androgyny. *Journal of Consulting and Clinical Psychology, 42,* 155–162.

Bem, S. L. (1977). On the utility of alternative procedures for assessing psychological androgyny. *Journal of Consulting and Clinical Psychology, 45,* 196–205.

Bernreuter, R. G. (1931). *The personality inventory.* Palo Alto, Calif.: Consulting Psychologists Press.

Bowers, K. (1973). Situationism in psychology: An analysis and a critique. *Psychological Review, 80,* 307–336.

Breger, L. (1966). Further studies of the social desirability scale. *Journal of Consulting Psychology, 30,* 281.

Burisch, M. (1978). Construction strategies for multiscale personality inventories. *Applied Psychological Measurement, 2,* 97–111.

Buros, O. K. (Ed.) (1978). *The eighth mental measurements yearbook.* Highland Park, N.J.: Gryphon Press.

Buss, A. R. (1977). The trait-situation controversy and the concept of interaction. *Personality and Social Psychology Bulletin, 3,* 196–201.

Butcher, J. N. (Ed.) (1972). *Objective personality assessment: Changing perspectives.* New York: Academic Press.

Butcher, J. N., & Pancheri, P. (1975). *A handbook of cross-national MMPI research.* Minneapolis: University of Minnesota Press.

Butcher, J. N., & Tellegen, A. (1978). Common methodological problems in MMPI research. *Journal of Consulting and Clinical Psychology, 46,* 620–628.

Caldwell, M. G. (1954). Case analysis method for the personality study of offenders. *Journal of Criminal Law, Criminology, and Police Science, 45,* 291–298.

Cattell, R. B. (1949). *Manual for forms A and B: Sixteen Personality Factor Questionnaire.* Champaign, Ill.: Institute for Personality and Ability Testing.

Cattell, R. B., & Bolton, L. S. (1969). What pathological dimensions lie beyond the normal dimensions of the 16PF? A comparison of MMPI and 16PF factor domains. *Journal of Consulting and Clinical Psychology, 33,* 18–29.

Cattell, R. B., Eber, H. W., & Tatsuoka, M. M. (1970). *Handbook for the Sixteen Personality Factor Questionnaire (16 PF).* Champaign, Ill.: Institute for Personality and Ability Testing.

Cohen, J. (1977). *Statistical power analysis for the behavioral sciences* (rev. ed.). New York: Academic Press.

Cronbach, L. J. (1970) *Essentials of psychological testing* (3rd ed.). New York: Harper & Row.

Cronbach, L. J. (1975). Beyond the two disciplines of scientific psychology. *American Psychologist, 30,* 116–127.

Cronbach, L. J., Gleser, G. C., Nanda, H., & Rajaratam, N. (1972) *The dependability of behavioral measurements: Theory of generalizability for scores and profiles.* New York: Wiley.

Cureton, E. E. (1950). Reliability, validity, and baloney. *Educational and Psychological Measurement,* **10,** 94–96.

Dahlstrom, W. G. (1972) Whither the MMPI? In J. N. Butcher (Ed.), *Objective personality assessment: Changing perspectives.* New York: Academic Press.

Dahlstrom, W. G., & Welsh, G. S. (1960). *An MMPI handbook.* Minneapolis: University of Minnesota Press.

Dahlstrom, W. G., Welsh, G. S., & Dahlstrom. L. E. (1972). *An MMPI handbook,* Vol. I: *Clinical interpretation.* Minneapolis: University of Minnesota Press.

Dahlstrom, W. G., Welsh, G. S., & Dahlstrom, L. E. (1975). *An MMPI handbook,* Vol. II: *Research applications.* Minneapolis: University of Minnesota Press.

Davis, W. E. (1975). Race and the differential "power" of the MMPI. *Journal of Personality Assessment,* **39,** 138–140.

Delhees, K. H., & Cattell, R. B. (1971a). The dimensions of pathology: Proof of their projection beyond the normal 16PF source traits. *Personality,* **2,** 149–173.

Delhees, K. H., & Cattell, R. B. (1971b). *Manual for the Clinical Analysis Questionnaire (CAQ).* Champaign, Ill.: Institute for Personality and Ability Testing.

Domino, G. (1971). Interactive effects of achievement orientation and teaching style on academic achievement. *Journal of Educational Psychology,* **62,** 427–431.

Douglas, K. & Arenberg, D. (1978). Age changes, cohort differences, and cultural change on the Guilford-Zimmerman Temperament Survey. *Journal of Gerontology,* **33,** 737–747.

Edwards, A. L. (1954). *Manual for the Edwards Personal Preference Schedule.* New York: Psychological Corporation.

Edwards, D. W. (1974). Blacks versus whites: When is race a relevant variable? *Journal of Personality and Social Psychology,* **29,** 39–49.

Ellis, A. (1946). The validity of personality questionnaires. *Psychological Bulletin,* **43,** 385–440.

El-Meligi, A. M., & Osmond, H. (1970). *Manual for the clinical use of the experiential world inventory.* New York: Mens Sana.

Endler, N. S., & Hunt, J. McV. (1969). Generalizability of contributions from sources of variance in the S-R inventories of anxiousness. *Journal of Personality,* **37,** 1–24.

Endler, N. S., Hunt, J. McV., & Rosenstein, A. G. (1962). An S-R inventory of anxiousness. *Psychological Monographs,* **76,** (17, whole No. 536).

Epstein, S. (1979). The stability of behavior: I. On predicting most of the people much of the time. *Journal of Personality and Social Psychology,* **37,** 1097–1126.

Eysenck, H. J. (1959). *Maudsley Personality Inventory.* London: University of London Press.

Eysenck, H. J. (1976) *The measurement of personality.* Baltimore: University Park Press.

Fishbein, M., & Ajzen, I. (1974). Attitudes toward objects as predictors of single and multiple behavioral criteria. *Psychological Review,* **81,** 59–74.

Frank, L. K. (1939). Projective methods for the study of personality. *Journal of Psychology,* **8,** 389–413.

Giedt, F. H., & Downing, L. (1961). An extraversion scale for the MMPI. *Journal of Clinical Psychology,* **17,** 156–159.

Gilberstadt, H., & Duker, J. (1965). *A handbook for clinical and actuarial MMPI interpretation.* Philadelphia: W. B. Saunders.

Goldberg, L. R. (1972). Some recent trends in personality assessment. *Journal of Personality Assessment,* **36,** 547–560.

Goldberg, L. R. (1974). Objective diagnostic tests and measures. *Annual Review of Psychology,* **25,** 343–366.

Gough, H. G. (1957). *California Psychological Inventory manual.* Palo Alto, Calif.: Consulting Psychologists Press.

Gough, H. G. (1965). Cross-cultural validation of a measure of asocial behavior. *Psychological Reports,* **17,** 379–387.

Gough, H. G. (1968). An interpreter's syllabus for the California Psychological Inventory. In P. McReynolds (Ed.). *Advances in psychological assessment,* Vol. 1. Palo Alto, Calif.: Science and Behavior Books.

Gough, H. G. (1971). Scoring high on an index of social maturity. *Journal of Abnormal Psychology,* **77,** 236–241.

Gough, H. G. (1975). *California Psychological Inventory* (revised manual). Palo Alto, Calif.: Consulting Psychologists Press.

Gough, H. G. (1979). Personal communication, December.

Gough, H. G., DeVos, G., & Mizushima, K. (1968). Japanese validation of the CPI social maturity index. *Psychological Reports,* **22,** 143–146.

Gough, H. G., Fox, R. E., & Hall, W. B. (1972). Personality inventory assessment of psychiatric residents. *Journal of Counseling Psychology,* **19,** 269–274.

Gough, H. G., & Heilbrun, A. B. (1965). *The Adjective Checklist manual.* Palo Alto, Calif.: Consulting Psychologists Press.

Gough, H. G., & Quintard, G. (1974). A French application of the CPI social maturity index. *Journal of Cross-Cultural Psychology, 5,* 247–252.

Gough, H. G., & Sandhu, H. S. (1964). Validation of the CPI socialization scale in India. *Journal of Abnormal and Social Psychology, 68,* 544–547.

Graham, J. R. (1977). *The MMPI: A practical guide.* New York: Oxford University Press.

Gregory, R. J., & Morris, L. M. (1978). Adjective correlates for women on the CPI scales: A replication. *Journal of Personality Assessment, 42,* 258–264.

Guilford, J. P. (1940). *An inventory of factors STDCR.* Beverly Hills, Calif.: Sheridan Supply.

Gynther, M. D. (1972). White norms and black MMPIs: A prescription for discrimination? *Psychological Bulletin, 78,* 386–402.

Gynther, M. D. (1979). Ethnicity and personality: An update. In J. N. Butcher (Ed.), *New developments in the use of the MMPI.* Minneapolis: University of Minnesota Press.

Gynther, M. D., Altman, H., & Sletten, I. W. (1973). Replicated correlates of MMPI two-point code types: The Missouri actuarial system. *Journal of Clinical Psychology, 29,* 263–289.

Harris, R. E., & Lingoes, J. C. (1955). Subscales for the MMPI: An aid to profile interpretation. Mimeographed materials. Department of Psychiatry, University of California (San Francisco), (Corrected version, 1968).

Hartshorne, H., & May, M. A. (1928). *Studies in deceit.* New York: Macmillan,

Hase, H. D., & Goldberg, L. R. (1967). Comparative validity of different strategies of constructing personality inventory scales. *Psychological Bulletin, 67,* 231–248.

Hathaway, S. R., & McKinley, J. C. (1940). A multiphasic personality schedule (Minnesota): I. Construction of the schedule. *Journal of Psychology, 10,* 249–254.

Heist, P., & Yonge, G. (1968). *Omnibus Personality Inventory manual.* New York: Psychological Corporation.

Helmreich, R. L., Spence, J. T., & Holahan, C. K. (1979). Psychological androgyny and sex role flexibility: A test of two hypotheses. *Journal of Personality and Social Psychology, 37,* 1631–1644.

Heymans, G. & Wiersma, E. (1906). Beitrage zur speziellen Psychologie auf Grund einer Massenuntersuchung. *Zeitschrift für Psychologie, 43,* 81–127, 258–301.

Hoch, A., & Amsden, G. S. (1913). A guide to the descriptive study of personality. *Review of Neurology and Psychiatry, 11,* 577–587.

Hoffmann, H., & Jackson, D. N. (1976). Substantive dimensions of psychopathology derived from MMPI content scales and the Differential Personality Inventory. *Journal of Consulting and Clinical Psychology, 44,* 862.

Hogan, R., DeSoto, C. B., & Solano, C. (1977). Traits, tests, and personality research. *American Psychologist, 32,* 255–264.

Hokanson, J. E., & Calden, G. (1960). Negro-white differences on the MMPI. *Journal of Clinical Psychology, 16,* 32–33.

Hovanitz, C. A., & Gynther, M. D. (1980). The prediction of impulsive behavior: Comparative validities of obvious versus subtle MMPI Hypomania *(Ma)* items. *Journal of Clinical Psychology, 36,* 422–427.

Humm, D. G., & Wadsworth, G. W. (1935). The Humm-Wadsworth Temperament Scale. *American Journal of Psychiatry, 92,* 163–200.

Jaccard, J. J. (1974). Predicting social behavior from personality traits. *Journal of Research in Personality, 7,* 358–367.

Jackson, D. N. (1967). *Personality Research Form manual.* Goshen, N. Y.: Research Psychologists Press.

Jackson, D. N. (1971) The dynamics of structured personality tests: 1971. *Psychological Review, 78,* 229–248.

Jackson, D. N., & Carlson, K. A. (1973). Convergent and discriminant validation of the Differential Personality Inventory. *Journal of Clinical Psychology, 29,* 214–219.

Jackson, D. N., & Paunonen, S. V. (1980). Personality structure and assessment. *Annual Review of Psychology, 31,* 503–551.

Kelly, E. L. (1972). Multiple Affect Adjective Check List. In O. K. Buros (Ed.) *The seventh mental measurements yearbook.* Highland Park, N. J.: Gryphon Press, pp. 271–272.

Kohfeld, D. L., & Weitzel, W. (1969). Some relations between personality factors and social facilitation. *Journal of Experimental Research in Personality, 3,* 287–292.

Laird, D. A. (1925). Detecting abnormal behavior. *Journal of Abnormal and Social Psychology, 20,* 128–141.

Landis, C., & Katz, S. E. (1934). The validity of certain questions which purport to measure neurotic tendencies. *Journal of Applied Psychology, 18,* 343–356.

Lanyon, R. I. (1970). Development and validation of a Psychological Screening Inventory. *Journal of Consulting and Clinical Psychology Monograph, 35,* (1, Pt. 2).

Leon, G. R., Gillum, B., Gillum, R., & Gouze, M. (1979). Personality stability and change over a 30 year period—middle age to old age. *Journal of Consulting and Clinical Psychology,* **47,** 517–524.

Lewandowski, D., & Graham, J. R. (1972). Empirical correlates of frequently occurring two-point MMPI code types: A replicated study. *Journal of Consulting and clinical Psychology,* **39,** 467–472.

Lewinsohn, P. M. (1974). A behavioral approach to depression. In R. J. Friedmann & M. M. Katz (Eds), *The psychology of depression: Contemporary theory and research.* New York: Halstead Press.

Lissitz, R. W., & Green, S. B. (1975). Effect of the number of scale points on reliability: A Monte Carlo approach. *Journal of Applied Psychology,* **60,** 10–13.

Loevinger, J. (1972). Some limitations of objective personality tests. In J. N. Butcher (Ed.), *Objective personality assessment: Changing perspectives.* New York: Academic Press.

MacDougald, D. (1970). *Emotional Maturity Development Profile: Tables for scales.* Decatur, Ga.: Emotional Maturity Instruction Center.

Mahoney, M. J. (1978). Experimental methods and outcome evaluation. *Journal of Consulting and Clinical Psychology,* **46,** 660–672.

Marks, P. A., Bertelson, A. D., & May, G. D. (1977) Race and MMPI: Some new findings and considerations. Paper presented at the meeting of the American Psychological Association, San Francisco, August.

Marks, P. A., & Seeman, W. (1963). *Actuarial description of abnormal personality.* Baltimore: Williams & Wilkins.

Marks, P. A., Seeman, W., & Haller, D. L. (1974). *The actuarial use of the MMPI with adolescents and adults.* Baltimore: Williams & Wilkins.

Marlowe, D., & Crowne, D. P. (1961). Social desirability and response to perceived situational demands. *Journal of Consulting Psychology,* **25,** 109–115.

McNair, D. M. (1978). Clinical Analysis Questionnaire, Research Edition. In O. K. Buros (Ed.), *The eighth mental measurements yearbook.* Highland Park, N. J.: Gryphon Press, pp. 745–747.

McNair, D. M., Callahan, D. M., & Lorr, M. (1962). Therapist "type" and patient response to psychotherapy. *Journal of Consulting Psychology,* **26,** 425–429.

Meehl, P. E. (1959). Some ruminations on the validation of clinical procedures. *Canadian Journal of Psychology,* **13,** 102–128.

Meehl, P. E. (1971). High school yearbooks: A reply to Schwarz. *Journal of Abnormal Psychology,* **77,** 143–148.

Meehl, P. E. (1978). Theoretical risks and tabular asterisks: Sir Karl, Sir Ronald, and the slow progress of soft psychology. *Journal of Consulting and Clinical Psychology,* **46,** 806–834.

Megargee, E. I. (1979). How to do publishable research with the MMPI. In J. Butcher, G. Dahlstrom, M. Gynther, & W. Schofield (Eds.), *Clinical notes on the MMPI* (No. 2). Nutley, N. J.: Roche Psychiatric Service Institute.

Miller, N., Doob, A. N., Butler, D. C., & Marlowe, D. (1965). The tendency to agree: Situational determinants and social desirability. *Journal of Experimental Research in Personality,* **1,** 78–83.

Myers, J. L. (1979). *Fundamentals of experimental design* (3rd ed.). Boston: Allyn and Bacon.

Norman, W. T. (1972). Psychometric considerations for a revision of the MMPI. In J. N. Butcher (Ed.), *Objective personality assessment: Changing perspectives.* New York: Academic Press.

Owens, W. A., & Schoenfeldt, L. F. (1979). Toward a classification of persons. *Journal of Applied Psychology,* **65,** 569–607.

Palmer, W. H. (1971). Actuarial MMPI interpretation: A replication and extension. (Ph.D. thesis, University of Alabama, 1970.) *Dissertation Abstracts International,* **31,** 6265–B.

Panton, J. H. (1959). Inmate personality differences related to recidivism, age and race as measured by the MMPI. *Journal of Correctional Psychology,* **4,** 28–35.

Parloff, M. B., Waskow, I. E., & Wolfe, B. E. (1978). Research on therapist variables in relation to process and outcome. In S. Garfield and A. E. Bergin (Eds.), *Handbook of psychotherapy and behavior change* (2nd ed.). New York: Wiley.

Pedhazur, E. J., & Tetenbaum, T. J. (1979). Bem Sex Role Inventory: A theoretical and methodological critique. *Journal of Personality and Social Psychology,* **37,** 996–1016.

Perkins, J. E., & Goldberg, L. R. (1964). Contextual effects on the MMPI. *Journal of Consulting Psychology,* **28,** 133–140.

Popham, W. J. (1978). *Criterion-referenced measurement.* Englewood Cliffs, N. J.: Prentice-Hall.

Popper, K. R. (1959). *The logic of scientific discovery.* New York: Basic Books.

Postema, L. J., & Schell, R. E. (1967). Aging and psychopathology: Some MMPI evidence for seemingly greater neurotic behavior among older people. *Journal of Clinical Psychology,* **23,** 140–143.

Pressey, S. L. (1921). A group scale for investigating the emotions. *Journal of Abnormal and Social Psychology,* **16,** 55–64.

Pritchard, D. A. & Rosenblatt, A. (1980). Racial bias in the MMPI: A methodological review. *Journal of Consulting and Clinical Psychology,* **48,** 263–267.

Rosenblatt, A. I. (1976). A multivariate analysis of racial differences on the MMPI. M.A. thesis, University of Mississippi.

Rotter, J. B. (1966). Generalized expectancies for internal *versus* external control of reinforcement. *Psychological Monographs,* **80,** (1, whole No. 609).

Rundquist, E. A., & Sletto, R. F. (1936). *Personality in the depression.* Minneapolis: University of Minnesota Press.

Schaie, K. W. (1965). A general model for the study of developmental problems. *Psychological Bulletin,* **64,** 92–107.

Spielberger, C. D. (1966). Theory and research on anxiety. In C. D. Spielberger (ed.) *Anxiety and behavior.* New York: Academic Press, pp. 3–20.

Spielberger, C. D., Gorsuch, R. L., & Lushene, R. E. (1970). *Manual for the State-Trait Anxiety Inventory.* Palo Alto, Calif.: Consulting Psychologists Press.

Strickland, B. R. (1977). Approval motivation. In T. Blass (Ed.), *Personality variables in social behavior.* Hillsdale, N. J.: Lawrence Erlbaum Associates.

Strickland, B. R., & Crowne, D. P. (1962). Conformity under conditions of simulated group pressure as a function of the need for social approval. *Journal of Social Psychology,* **58,** 171–181.

Super, D. E. (1942). The Bernreuter Personality Inventory. *Psychological Bulletin,* **39,** 94–125.

Swenson, W. M. (1961). Structured personality testing in the aged: An MMPI study of the gerontic population. *Journal of Clinical Psychology,* **17,** 302–304.

Thorne, F. C. (1965). *The Integration Level Test Series,* Information Sheet #1. Brandon, Vt.: Psychological Research Associates.

Thorne, F. C. (1967). *Integrative psychology: A systematic clinical viewpoint.* Brandon, Vt.: Clinical Psychology Publishing Co.

Thorne, F. C., & Pishkin, V. (1977). The objective measurement of femininity. *Journal of Clinical Psychology,* **33,** 5–23.

Travis, R. C. (1924). The measurement of fundamental character traits by a new diagnostic test. *Journal of Abnormal and Social Psychology,* **19,** 400–420.

Trott, D. M., & Morf, M. E. (1972). A multimethod factor analysis of the Differential Personality Inventory, Personality Research Form, and Minnesota Multiphasic Personality Inventory. *Journal of Counseling Psychology,* **19,** 94–103.

Velicer, W. F., & Stevensen, J. F. (1978). The relation between item format and the structure of the Eysenck Personality Inventory. *Applied Psychological Measurement,* **2,** 293–304.

Watson, G. B. (1927). A supplementary review of measures of personality traits. *Journal of Educational Psychology,* **18,** 73–87.

Watson, G. B. (1933). Next steps in personality measurement. *Character and Personality,* **2,** 66–73.

Watson, J. B. (1919). *Psychology from the standpoint of a behaviorist.* Philadelphia: Lippincott.

Webb, E. J. (1976). Unconventionality, triangulation and inference. In W. L. Barnette, Jr. (Ed.), *Readings in psychological tests and measurements* (3rd ed.). Baltimore: Williams & Wilkins.

Wells, F. L. (1914). The systematic observation of the personality—in its relation to the hygiene of mind. *Psychological Review,* **21,** 295–333.

Wener, A. E., & Rehm, L. P. (1977). Depressive affect: A test of behavioral hypothesis. *Journal of Abnormal Psychology,* **84,** 221–227.

Whitehorn, J. C., & Betz, B. J. (1960). Further studies of the doctor as a crucial variable in the outcome of treatment with schizophrenic patients. *American Journal of Psychiatry,* **117,** 215–223.

Wiesenthal, D. L. (1974). Some effects of the confirmation and disconfirmation of an expected monetary reward on compliance. *Journal of Social Psychology,* **92,** 39–52.

Wiggins, J. S. (1966). Substantive dimensions of self-report in the MMPI item pool. *Psychological Monographs,* **80,** (22, whole No. 630).

Woodworth, R. S., (1920). *Personal data sheet.* Chicago: Stoelting.

Zuckerman, M. (1977). Preliminary manual with scoring keys and norms for Form V of the Sensation Seeking Scale. Unpublished manuscript, University of Delaware.

Zuckerman, M., & Lubin, B. (1965). *Manual for the Multiple Affect Adjective Check List.* San Diego, Calif.: Educational and Industrial Testing Service.

CHAPTER 12

Psychophysiological Methods In Clinical Research

EDWARD S. KATKIN AND JANICE L. HASTRUP

BASIC DEFINITIONS

Psychophysiology is a relatively new sub-discipline of psychology, created in part by the interests of clinical psychologists, physiological psychologists, psychiatrists, and biomedical engineers, all of whom share a common interest in the integration of physiological and behavioral data using a defined set of bioelectric responses and sophisticated electronic techniques. Although the discipline is heterogeneous, and the areas of interest include the evaluation of physiological responses at all levels of the nervous system from cerebral to adrenal cortex, there are nevertheless some constant factors that unite these interests and define "psychophysiology."

Psychophysiology is a discipline somewhat distinct from, and yet closely linked to, physiological psychology; both disciplines study the central nervous system, especially the brain. Physiological psychologists, however, tend to study brain functions using invasive procedures such as surgery or electrical stimulation, whereas psychophysiologists tend to study the brain by recording its electrical activity, but not intervening in its structure or function. Also, throughout its history psychophysiology has paid considerably more attention to peripheral autonomic functions than has physiological psychology. Stern has addressed these distinctions and suggested that physiological

psychology may be described as "the manipulation of physiological variables and the recording of behavioral events," while psychophysiology may be described as "the manipulation of behavioral events and the recording of physiological variables" (1964, p. 90).

There are other distinctions between these two disciplines. Physiological psychology has tended to emphasize controlled animal research rather than research on human subjects. Perhaps because many of the theoretical issues to which psychophysiologists have addressed themselves have been derived from uniquely human phenomena (e. g., the role of physiological activity in the experience of emotion and physiological responses in mental disorder) psychophysiological research has been addressed primarily to human subjects.

Although the historical roots of psychophysiology may be traced to the discoveries of electrical properties of the skin in the nineteenth century by Féré (1888) and Tarchanoff (1890), it is clear that the discipline as we know it today is also a product of the recent revolution in medical electronics. The founding of the Society for Psychophysiological Research in 1961 and the establishment of that society's journal, *Psychophysiology,* in 1964 closely paralleled the emergence of the startling technological developments that have characterized the past two decades. We do not wish to imply, however, that psychophysiological research was waiting for a technology to get started. Quite to the contrary, long before the transistor and the integrated circuit made their appearance, psychophysiologists were making their research presence known with the instrument that has come to be the symbol of their society—the polygraph. After a brief review of the structure of the nervous system, and a description of the primary response measures employed in psychophysiological research, we will return to the polygraph and describe its uses.

Brief Review of Central and Peripheral Nervous Systems

Although it is common to talk of "central" and "peripheral" nervous systems, or "somatic" and "autonomic" nervous systems, it is important to bear in mind that behavior is the result of the integrated action of a single nervous system. The variety of subdivisions of this nervous system, of course, reflect relative specificity of functions, and also provide a convenient taxonomic scheme that facilitates communication. Yet, one clear conceptual risk of describing subdivisions of the nervous system is that one can be lulled into false assumptions concerning their independence.

By convention, the central nervous system consists of the brain, the brain stem, and the spinal cord. All other nerves that originate outside of the central nervous system, and outside of the hard, bony, skull and spine that contain it, are designated the peripheral nervous system, which in turn is subdivided into somatic and autonomic systems.

The somatic nervous system is said to consist of those nerves going to and coming from peripheral striate muscles. It is the action of peripheral somatic nerves that enables walking, running, sitting, standing, and playing games such as tennis. Obviously the integration of the variety of nerves and muscles required for complex behavior like tennis requires coordination by the central nervous system. It is an oversimplification therefore

to assert that any specific activity is "under the control" of only one division of the nervous system.

The autonomic nervous system consists of those peripheral nerves that serve the smooth muscles of the visceral organs, the heart, and the endocrine glands. These nerves are referred to as autonomic because of their seeming autonomy from voluntary control or consciousness. They control the visceral organs and glands during various states of consciousness including sleep. Without their autonomous function, obviously, survival would be in doubt. Even so, the action of the autonomic nervous system is inextricably tied to action at "higher" central nervous system levels, and it is misleading to assume that it functions autonomously. Rather it is so named because the end organs to which it is connected function apparently independently of conscious wishes.

The autonomic nervous system is also usually subdivided into two divisions: the sympathetic division and the parasympathetic division. The sympathetic division of the nervous system is so named because the many nerves contained in it tend to respond en masse when any one of them is stimulated. Hence they are said to respond *in sympathy* with each other. The ganglia of the sympathetic nervous system are located in two neat columns, bilaterally symmetrical, alongside the spinal cord at the thoracic and lumbar levels of the spine. Thus the sympathetic system is sometimes referred to as the thoracicolumbar system. The anatomy of the sympathetic system is such that there are very short (presynaptic) fibers emanating from the spine and synapsing right there with longer (postsynaptic) fibers that travel to the end organ. There are also many connections among the postsynaptic fibers, so that if only one or two presynaptic fibers are activated, it can result in "mass action" among the postsynaptic fibers. The neurotransmitter substances found in the sympathetic division are generally adrenergic; thus the end result of sympathetic activation is generally a heightened state of activation of the end organ, for example, faster heart rate, vasoconstriction, increased secretion of epinephrine.

The parasympathetic division of the autonomic nervous system receives its name from its anatomical location "around" the sympathetic system. The presynaptic fibers of the parasympathetic system emanate from the central nervous system at the cranial and sacral regions, above and below the sympathetic system. The parasympathetic nerves are quite different from those of the sympathetic division both in structure and in function. Presynaptic nerves of the parasympathetic system are very long, reaching from their central point of emanation out to the end organ, where they link up with short postsynaptic fibers that terminate at the target organ. The parasympathetic innervation of visceral organs is therefore specific, as opposed to the mass action of the sympathetic division. Furthermore, the primary transmitter substance of the parasympathetic system is acetylcholine, and consequently the end result of parasympathetic innervation (e.g., heart rate slowing, vasodilation) is opposite in effect to that of sympathetic innervation. Whereas sympathetic arousal is associated with states of emergency and emotional distress, parasympathetic arousal is related to normal vegetative functions, including digestion, and is often correlated with relaxation. Some visceral organs are innervated by both sympathetic and parasympathetic fibers, while others, notably the sweat glands and the blood vessels, are either exclusively or predominantly innervated by the sympathetic division.

This brief review of the divisions of the nervous system has emphasized the autonomic nervous system (ANS) more than either the central nervous system (CNS) or the somatic nervous system. This reflects the fact that, until recently, psychophysiology placed more of its research emphasis on the ANS than on the CNS. The psychophysiologist interested in the function of any aspect of the nervous system, whether it be central

or autonomic, has to choose appropriate response indexes.

Responses of Interest

With respect to the assessment of CNS function, we will discuss only the measurement of electrical activity of the brain as it is reflected in the electroencephalogram, or EEG. The EEG is the major methodological tool of the psychophysiologist interested in CNS, and especially cortical, functioning.

Similarly, the assessment of somatic nervous system activity has focused on one technique, the electromyogram, or EMG, a measure of the voltage generated by contraction of striate muscles.

Assessment of autonomic functions has generated a great many more techniques. However, most studies of ANS function have focused on cardiovascular and electrodermal activity. Therefore, the methods to be discussed in this chapter will include techniques for the assessment of heart rate, blood pressure, and blood volume, three indexes of cardiovascular activity, as well as a variety of techniques for assessing electrodermal activity (EDA), more commonly referred to as the "GSR."

INSTRUMENTATION, DEVICES, AND PROCEDURES

The Polygraph

All six of the response measures described above are assessed with the use of a polygraph and associated preamplification circuits. Polygraphy is a three-stage operation including detection, amplification, and display (Hassett, 1978). A set of electrodes or other devices such as a blood pressure cuff or a photocell are applied to the surface of the body in order to detect the presence of physiological activity. In some cases an electrical voltage is detected; in other cases a sound or a mechanical movement may be detected. If the signal of interest is electrical, then the detection device will be electrodes, which serve to pick up the signal and send it to the polygraph's amplifiers; if the signal is not electrical, then the detection device must not only pick it up, but transduce it into an electrical signal to be sent to the polygraph.

The second stage of polygraphy is the amplification and shaping stage, during which the electrical signal is filtered and modified as required. For instance, if a pair of electrodes are placed on the body to pick up signals generated by the heart, as is the case for the electrocardiogram (EKG), it would be distracting to have the EKG "contaminated" by electrical signals from muscles and sweat glands. Since each of these responses possesses unique amplitude and frequency characteristics, amplifiers can be designed to filter out the "unwanted" elements of the signal and allow only the desired ones to pass. Thus commercially available polygraphs are offered with a variety of special-purpose plug-in amplifiers to suit the needs of virtually any research requirement.

The third stage of polygraphy is display. Traditionally the amplified electrical signal is forwarded to a very sensitive voltmeter, which is fitted with an ink-writing pen instead of a typical meter needle. This pen is placed in contact with paper, which can be set to move at a desirable speed, and the polygraph then makes a permanent record of the fluctuations in the detected signal in "real-time." It should be pointed out that the use of the ink-writing polygraph, while still very popular, is probably already obsolete. The advent of low cost, on-line computers has made it possible to bypass the ink-written display in favor of the simultaneous "temporary" display on an oscilloscope and the permanent storage of the signals, in digital form, in computer storage. Traditions die hard, however, and while most psychophysiologists recognize the advantages of such new techniques, few, at least few over the age of 35, have felt comfortable abandoning the ink record.

In the following sections we will describe more specific procedures for the recording of each of the six response indexes, and discuss the behavioral and neurological phenomena to which they relate.

Electroencephalography (EEG)

Electroencephalography refers to the measurement of small (20 to 50 microvolts) amplitude potentials generated by the brain. Although it is possible to implant needle electrodes or microelectrodes in the brain tissue directly, measurement of the human EEG relies upon surface recordings obtained from the scalp. Hans Berger (1929) was the first to report successful measurement of "brain waves" from human subjects. He reported that when his subjects were quiescent but awake, they emitted brain waves with a frequency of approximately 10 Hz, and amplitude of about 50 microvolts; Berger designated these waves "alpha." When his subjects were more alert, Berger reported, the alpha pattern disintegrated and was replaced with faster frequency, smaller amplitude activity, which he dubbed "beta." Berger's nomenclature has remained fairly standard, along with later discoveries of theta waves (4 to 8 Hz), associated with drowsiness, and delta waves (less than 4 Hz), associated with sleep. In current EEG research alpha refers to large amplitude waves between 8 and 12 Hz, and beta refers to lower amplitude activity faster than 13 Hz.

The popular description of alpha, beta, delta, and theta waves represents a rather gross oversimplification of the actual state of electrical activity within the brain. Actually, at most times the brain is generating a complex combination of all of the available frequencies. The categories described above are convenient classifications, and represent the result of very careful data reduction techniques. In practice, the EEG record is subjected to a Fourier analysis, and a measure of the dominance of all available frequencies is determined. A simpler approach is to express the percentage of time that a given frequency is present. This is most usually assessed for alpha, and scores of "percent alpha" are commonly seen in the literature.

Evoked Potentials. In addition to assessing the relative dominance of total brain wave activity, it is possible to assess the degree to which the brain, or at least certain areas of the brain, show discrete changes in electrical activity to a specific stimulus. This change in activity that is elicited by stimuli is called an "evoked response" or "event-related potential" (ERP). It is usually the case that a stimulus will elicit an ERP that is so small compared to the background activity that it is not discernible. However, it is apparent that if the same stimulus is presented repeatedly, the background activity will not be the same on each presentation. If the stimulus lawfully evokes a specific small response, and that small response is superimposed on different backgrounds, then averaging over a number of trials should reveal the response. That is, if the EEG traces present after the presentation of the stimuli are averaged, the background activity, being random, will cancel out; but the ERP, being stimulus specific, will remain. This technique of averaging is generally used to measure the ERP, and thus these evoked responses are more commonly referred to as "average evoked potentials" or AEPs. If the AEP is evoked by visual stimulation, it is referred to as the visual evoked potential (VEP) or visual evoked response (VER). The EEG literature is filled with acronyms that are simple, but take some time to get used to. The most familiar ones, in addition to those already mentioned, are the auditory evoked response (AER) or potential (AEP), the somatosensory evoked response (SER) or potential (SEP), and the general synonym for the ERP, "cortical evoked response" (CER).

Evoked potentials may be either negative waves or positive waves, and the response to a stimulus may be a complex series of both negative and positive responses. One standard way of referring to these is to number them sequentially so that the first positive wave is P1, and the first negative wave is N1, and so on. A second mode of description is to define the waves according to the time (msec) that passes between stimulus presentation and the evoked potential; hence a positive wave that occurs 300 msec after the stimulus is referred to as P300. This system has the advantage of being more precise and allowing for clearer communication between laboratories. For example, the designation P3 merely refers to the third positive going wave in a response. For some traces it might occur 200 msec after stimulation, and in others 400 msec after stimulation. The designation P300, however, specifies a time relationship between the stimulus and response and thus communicates more information.

The "contingent negative variation" (CNV) is a specific subtype of an evoked response, which is elicited by specific situations. If a subject is presented with two stimuli that are contingent upon each other, such as a ready signal followed by an imperative signal in a reaction time task, a slow negative drift in the EEG occurs between the first and the second stimulus (Tecce, 1972). This is referred to as the CNV, and it is presumed to be related to the cognitive state of expectancy.

Technical Considerations. It is unlikely that EEG techniques will be employed by casual investigators, because the technology is complex. The assessment of EEG responses requires fairly sophisticated computer programming, and a substantial amount of technical training. Comprehensive descriptions can be obtained in an edited volume by Thompson and Patterson (1974), and in an earlier presentation by Margerison, St. John-Loe, and Binnie (1967). As compared with other areas of psychophysiological measurement, assessment of EEG patterns has been well standardized; the International Federation of Societies for Electroencephalography and Clinical Neurophysiology has adopted an official electrode placement configuration known as the "10-20" system, which is depicted in Figure 12.1. This system is based upon exact measurement of the distance from the depression at the bridge of the nose (nasion) to the hard bone at the back of the head (inion), and also the distance from the slight depressions that exist just in front and above the earlobes. Each of the standard electrode placements has a letter and number designation, to facilitate communication among workers. The letter designations are derived from the area of cortex over which they lie; O for occipital, P for parietal, T for temporal, and F for frontal. In addition, electrodes along the central fissure are designated C. Electrodes placed along the longitudinal fissure running from nasion to inion are designated z. Using this system, an electrode 20% in front of the vertex on the longitudinal fissure is designated Fz; the vertex

electrode is Cz; and an electrode over the frontal area, just off the longitudinal fissure, is designated F3 or F4 (the left side is assigned odd numbers and the right side even numbers). A complete description of this system may be found in Jasper (1958). This standardized system allows for great ease of communication among workers in different laboratories, and is universally adopted as a standard.

Finally, a neutral, or ground, electrode is placed at an inactive site such as an earlobe, and the EEG voltages are then read with reference to that site. In *monopolar* recording, the voltage is read between one active electrode and ground; in *bipolar* recording, a potential difference between two active scalp electrodes is measured. The monopolar method may appear to have more face validity, but there is considerable evidence to suggest that bipolar recording may have superior

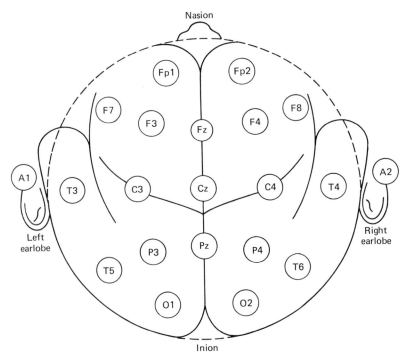

Figure 12.1. A schematic top view of EEG electrode placement in the "10–20" system. A1 and A2 are earlobe ground placements.

value in localizing brain function (Thompson & Patterson, 1974).

The development of technical standards for measurement resolves only a minor part of the difficulty inherent in interpreting EEG records, for the precise physiological basis of the EEG is still unknown. There is considerable debate over the origin of brain waves, with some investigators concluding that the characteristic rhythm of the EEG is actually generated by the thalamus, which acts as a sort of pacemaker for the cortex (Andersen & Andersson, 1968). Although the underlying mechanisms are not clearly understood, a voluminous empirical literature on the relationship between EEG activity and various behavioral phenomena has been generated.

Areas of Application. The areas to which EEG technology has been applied are widespread, ranging from the attempt to localize cerebral function to studies of schizophrenia, sleep disturbances, personality traits and states, and intelligence. EEG measurements of monozygotic and dizygotic twins have even been employed to evaluate the heritability of EEG patterns (Lykken, Tellegen, & Thorkelson, 1974). During the recent past there was a great amount of interest devoted to the analysis of the use of biofeedback training for increases in alpha activity as a means of achieving altered states of consciousness (Kamiya, 1969); however, recent critical experiments have cast some doubt upon the legitimacy of the EEG contribution to the "alpha experience" (Plotkin, 1976, 1980; Plotkin & Cohen, 1976).

The literature on clinical phenomena that are associated with EEG phenomena is so great that it would take a volume to cover it. Some important source materials for the interested novice would be Lykken's (1975) paper on psychometric applications of EEG, Callaway's (1975) book on individual differences, and Shagass' (1972) chapter in the *Handbook of psychophysiology*.

Electromyography (EMG)

Electromyography is the measurement of the electrical activity of muscles. The EMG provides information about the relative state of contraction of a muscle, its frequency and pattern of firing. Although the term refers technically to the recording of the electrical activity of *any* muscle, in practice it is restricted to the recording of electrical activity of skeletal muscle. Single muscle fibers are composed of filaments of contractile protein, which form the characteristic striations of skeletal muscle. Electromyographic techniques have been developed to record the activity of small numbers of these fibers that are innervated by a single neuron (the single motor unit) as well as larger groupings of muscle fibers that may be innervated by more than one neuron.

The electrical activity recorded as an EMG results from changes in the electrical potential of the muscle fiber when it is fired. As is true for nerve cells, there is a resting potential between the inside and outside of the muscle fiber, caused by an excess of sodium ions outside the fiber and an excess of potassium ions within. When the muscle fiber is stimulated by the release of acetylcholine from an adjacent motor neuron, there is a resultant wave of excitation and contraction of the fiber; the EMG is a record of this change in electrical potential (see Geddes & Baker, 1975, for more details).

EMG as an Index of Tension. Although the EMG can be used for identifying the functions of specific muscle fibers, this is a minor aspect of its use. Generally the most common use of the EMG has been for the measurement of physical tension, often presumed to be associated with psychological tension. More than 40 years ago Jacobson (1938) developed a method of "progressive relaxation" to enhance a tranquil state for patients suffering from insomnia, essential hypertension, and other disorders. Although Jacobson initially measured the strength of the knee-jerk reflex as an index of relaxation, he later came to rely upon the EMG as the primary index of relaxation (Hassett, 1978).

Research has shown that EMG levels are associated with many variables, including effort, motivation, thinking, and a variety of other aspects of personality (Goldstein, 1972). Most recently Schwartz and his colleagues (Schwartz, Brown, & Ahern, 1980; Schwartz, Fair, Salt, Mandel, & Klerman, 1976) have studied patterns of facial expression using EMG records from a variety of facial muscles. These investigators have found that many different emotions are associated with characteristic EMG patterns, as one might expect from research on communication of emotion through facial expression. Schwartz et al. (1976) found also that the ability of depressed patients to generate EMG patterns associated with happy imagery was related to their clinical improvement. Such specific findings should warn against a simple interpretation of EMG activity as an anxiety equivalent.

Nevertheless, there has been a tendency in studies of anxiety to interpret enhanced EMG activity as a measure of "tension," and reduced activity as a measure of relaxation. In such studies it is typical to record the EMG from the arms, or legs, or forehead. However, when EMGs are recorded simultaneously from multiple sites, it becomes obvious that different sites yield a varied picture of "muscle tension." Part of the reason for this lack of concordance may be because at different skin surface sites, the electrodes are at different distances from the underlying muscle tissue, but it is likely that the variation also represents true variation in the tension at the different sites. Considerable research has been devoted to trying to find a single muscle group that would be most representative of general muscle tension, but evidence even for the existence of a single muscle tension factor is equivocal (Goldstein, 1972).

Biofeedback. A second area in which the EMG has enjoyed widespread use is biofeedback. Generally EMG biofeedback has been addressed to two areas: the rehabilitation of patients who have lost specific motor control subsequent to lesion (Brudny, Korein, Grynbaum, Friedmann, Weinstein, Sachs-Frankel, & Belandres, 1976); and the use of feedback for altering general muscle tension (Budzynski & Stoyva, 1969). Although the common practice in EMG biofeedback for tension reduction is to use the muscles of the frontal (forehead) area, there is some doubt concerning its efficacy as a general treatment. For instance, Fridlund, Fowler, and Pritchard (1980) provided subjects with biofeedback of frontal EMG, and recorded muscle tension from seven other areas of the body. They found little evidence of generalization and suggested that EMG training is like other motor skills; with training subjects show greater discrimination, not greater generalization. As a further cautionary note, Gatchel, Korman, Weis, Smith, and Clarke (1978) found that although frontal area EMG training could effectively reduce muscle tension during stress, the EMG biofeedback had no effect on heart rate, skin conductance, or self-reported anxiety.

Technical Considerations. There are two basic types of EMG recording: surface electrodes and intramuscular electrodes. For most applications typically employed by psychologists, surface electrodes are preferred, even though a major concern associated with their use is artifact. To avoid contamination of surface EMG readings by high levels of skin resistance, it is common to rub the electrode sites with acetone and then to abrade them with an abrasive conducting jelly. Next, care must be taken to place the electrodes carefully over the desired muscle. The placement of surface electrodes is much less accurate than the insertion of intramuscular needle electrodes. Despite the possible problems of placement, the use of surface recording is generally preferred in psychological studies because it eliminates the discomfort and pain associated with intramuscular electrodes.

EMG surface electrodes are most efficient if they are quite small; this enables greater precision of placement. Further, the closer they are placed to each other, the smaller the number of muscles being recorded. The general procedure is to place two electrodes lengthwise along a muscle; some knowledge of the anatomy of the muscle is required for proper technique. One common error that is found frequently in the biofeedback literature concerns the measurement of the frontalis muscle. Davis, Brickett, Stern, and Kimball (1978) noted that many researchers place a single electrode above each eye in order to measure "frontalis EMG." However, the frontalis muscle runs vertically above the eye, and there are frontalis muscles over both eyes. The horizontal electrode placement on the forehead does not measure the activity of either muscle, but rather measures the potential difference between them, actually subtracting out the activity in both.

The second major method of assessing electrical activity of muscle fibers is by single motor unit recording used for studies of muscle function and neuromuscular rehabilitation. Case studies have described persons with spasticity or paralysis learning to decrease, increase, or fine-tune muscle function. For example, a stroke victim or spine-injured accident victim may retain some intact motor nerve fibers to a muscle, but be unaware of their action. Initial efforts to move a muscle may result in contractions too small to be visible to the eye, but clearly measurable on an EMG record. Thus EMG feedback to the patient may potentially speed rehabilitative progress. Basmajian (1978) has reported that most people can learn to control single muscle fibers, even to the extent of learning to control their rate of firing.

To achieve such fine control an electrode had to be designed to provide information on the electrical activity of an individual fiber; surface electrodes yield too much gross information, sometimes including crosstalk from other major muscle groups. Basmajian (1978) has described the design of such fine needle and wire electrodes. Still, they are unlikely to replace surface electrodes for more routine muscle tension assessments in much psychological research.

After the proper electrodes are in place, some additional measurement issues still must be addressed. First, EMG records are notoriously subject to interference by other voltages, including electrocardiogram signals; therefore, special-purpose amplifiers must be used that will effectively filter out unwanted signals. Second, the frequency of EMG signals may go as high as 1000 Hz; mechanically driven pens on an ink-writing polygraph are not capable of tracking such frequencies. For these reasons, it is common to use integrating amplifiers for EMG recording. These amplifiers integrate the total amount of voltage detected in a short time unit and write out a signal that is proportional to the integrated value. This technique obliterates the "raw signal," but it provides a much simpler way of assessing large muscle contractions, and makes the quantification of such changes feasible. If a true "raw signal" is desired, it is necessary to record it on a cathode ray oscilloscope because of the high frequencies involved. Unless films of the oscilloscope are made, the record is only temporary.

Electrodermal Activity (EDA)

The electrodermal response (EDR), sometimes referred to as the galvanic skin response (GSR) or the psychogalvanic response or reflex (PGR), has been among the most widely used indexes of psychological responsivity, probably because it is simple to use and quantify, and it is relatively inexpensive to set up. Although there is still considerable controversy concerning the precise psychological phenomena reflected by electrodermal activity (see Prokasy & Raskin, 1973, for an exhaustive review of electrodermal research), it is widely accepted that there is a lawful relationship between conscious experience and changes in the electrical activity of the palmar surface of the skin. Some have suggested that EDA reflects attention (Katkin, 1975); others have concluded that some aspects of EDA are excellent indexes of anxiety (Spziler & Epstein, 1976); and some have theorized that individual differences in electrodermal response habituation rate may be used to define a personality construct (Crider & Lunn, 1971).

There is little doubt that the measurement of electrical changes in the skin has been the most widely employed tool of psychophysiologists in this century. There are many reasons for its widespread use. First, it is uncannily lawful; virtually any form of stimulation results in contingent, easily observed changes in electrical activity of the skin. Second, the measurement of EDA is inexpensive and relatively easy to implement. Third, a mystique about its validity as an index of emotion has emerged. This mystique has been fostered to some extent by the reliance upon its use by professional lie detection experts.

Interest in electrodermal responsivity can be traced back to the discoveries of Féré (1888) and Tarchanoff (1890), who demonstrated that the electrical properties of the skin appeared to covary with certain behavioral events. Féré discovered that if a small current was passed through the surface of the skin it would encounter apparent resistance, and that the resistance would vary with the presentation of different stimuli. Tarchanoff discovered that the imposition of a current was unnecessary; if a pair of electrodes were placed on the skin surface, a resting potential could be observed between them. Further,

Tarchanoff observed, the skin potential varied with the mental activity of his subjects. After 100 years of continuing refinement and research these two techniques remain the basic approaches to electrodermal measurement. Féré's technique of measuring the skin's apparent resistance to an imposed current is used to assess skin resistance or its reciprocal, skin conductance. Tarchanoff's technique of measuring the resting potential of the skin surface is used to assess skin potential.

Measurement Conventions and Definitions. In general, the palmar and plantar sweat glands are responsive primarily to psychological experience and not to temperature changes. These sweat glands, as noted earlier, are under the exclusive innervation of the sympathetic nervous system, although, paradoxically, their neurotransmitter substance is cholinergic. Furthermore, it is now understood that almost all of the variance in electrodermal measurement can be attributed to the activity of the sweat glands. Thus it is likely that electrodermal activity reflects relative activation of the sympathetic division of the ANS. For a more elaborate analysis of the neurophysiological and biophysical basis of electrodermal activity, the interested reader should see Edelberg (1972), Fowles (1973), or Venables and Christie (1973).

Although there are no official standards for electrodermal measurement, there is an informal set of definitions that are widely accepted (Prokasy & Raskin, 1973). First, one must decide if skin resistance, skin conductance, or skin potential will be measured. Regardless of choice, three aspects of EDA can be defined: *electrodermal level, elicited electrodermal response,* and *spontaneous electrodermal response.* "Level" refers to the average amount of resistance (ohms), or conductance (mhos), or potential (millivolts) observed during some predetermined time period. Note that ohms and mhos are mathematical reciprocals, so it is possible to ob-

Table 12.1. Common Abbreviations Used in Electrodermal Research

SCL = Skin Conductance Level
SCR = Skin Conductance Response
SSCR = Spontaneous Skin Conductance Response

SRL = Skin Resistance Level
SRR = Skin Resistance Response
SSRR = Spontaneous Skin Resistance Response

SPL = Skin Potential Level
SPR = Skin Potential Response
SSPR = Spontaneous Skin Potential Response

tain a measure of conductance even if resistance is being measured, and vice versa. An "elicited electrodermal response" is a transitory change in level that is elicited by a specific stimulus, and a "spontaneous electrodermal response" is a transitory change in level that occurs in the absence of any known or specific elicitor. Traditionally an elicited EDR is assessed with respect to its amplitude. When assessing spontaneous electrodermal responses, however, the amplitude is considered less important than the frequency of occurrence. In order to eliminate ambiguity and to enable researchers to communicate easily about the various possible indexes of electrodermal activity being employed, a few conventions concerning terms for describing various aspects of electrodermal activity have been agreed upon. They are summarized in Table 12.1.

Electronics and Assorted Paraphernalia. There are no agreed-upon standard procedures for measuring electrodermal activity. Arguments over the relative advantages of measuring resistance, conductance, or skin potential have been going on for almost 50 years. Yet during the last decade there has been an increasing acceptance of the technique recommended by Lykken and Venables (1971), who argued for the measurement of skin conductance using a constant voltage source of 0.5V applied to homologous sites of the palmar surface. Using their circuitry and a standard polygraph, direct

measurement of SCL and SCRs can be obtained. Using this circuit, the SCL is read directly from the polygraph in units of millionths of mhos, or micromhos.

Some researchers report the magnitude of elicited SCRs as changes in the log SCL. Specifically, the SCL at response onset is converted to log SCL; the SCL at the point of maximum response amplitude is similarly converted to log SCL; then a simple difference is taken between them. It may be seen readily that the difference score between log values is equivalent to a log of the ratio of the two levels ($\log X - \log Y = \log [X/Y]$). The use of the log convention therefore avoids the problem of interpreting identical absolute changes as equivalent when they are superimposed on widely different baselines (Montagu & Coles, 1966). For instance, a two-micromho response from a SCL of one micromho to one of three micromhos should not be interpreted the same as a two micromho change from 21 to 23 micromhos. The use of the "change in log conductance" measure resolves the problem to some extent, and has become conventional.

Finally, it is most important to use proper electrodes and electrode technique in electrodermal measurement. Direct current passing through the junction of a metal in contact with an ionic conductor such as a salt-solution electrode paste will tend to polarize either the junction or the electrode, thereby increasing resistance and decreasing conductance. Since the measurement of either SC or SR requires the passage of direct current across two electrode junctions, it is important to use nonpolarizing electrodes. The simplest and most efficient electrode preparation is a compound of silver and silver-chloride, embedded in a plastic cup. These are commercially available; they are nonpolarizing, and have a long life. It is also necessary for an electrode paste to be employed as a contact medium between the skin and the metal. Proper standards for electrolytes have been published by the Society for

Psycophysiological Research. The new researcher should consult these standards before proceeding (Fowles, Christie, Edelberg, Grings, Lykken, & Venables, 1981). Many commercially available pastes for EKG and EEG recording are *totally inappropriate* for electrodermal recording and should not be used.

Electrocardiography (EKG)

The electrocardiogram (EKG) is actually a special form of the electromyogram (EMG), for it is a measure of electrical activity associated with the contraction of cardiac muscle. Unlike the electrodermal system, the heart is innervated by fibers from both divisions of the ANS. Activation of sympathetic fibers generally results in faster beating, and activation of parasympathetic fibers generally results in slower beating of the heart, although a variety of complex, interacting feedback mechanisms also have some

influence on cardiac rate (Obrist, Langer, Grignolo, Sutterer, Light, & McCubbin, 1979). For example, *withdrawal* of vagus nerve (parasympathetic) stimulation will result in increased heart rate. Although it is well known that psychological events such as intense emotion or vigilance are associated with cardiovascular changes, it is important to recognize that the primary function of the heart is to pump blood through the vascular system, providing oxygen to the body. Therefore, although cardiac changes may accompany behavioral phenomena, these changes must be interpreted in the context of the primary homeostatic function of the cardiovascular system. Figure 12.2 depicts a normal EKG for one complete cardiac cycle from the initiating neural impulse, through the ejection of the blood into the aorta, to the postejection quiescent period.

The Cardiac Cycle.   The cardiac cycle is initiated by neural innervation at the si-

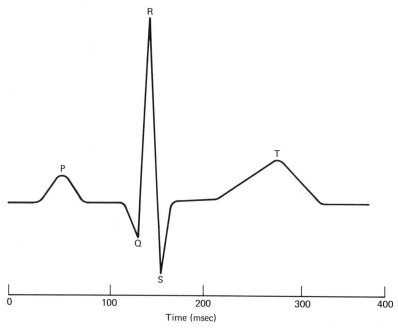

Figure 12.2.   An idealized representation of one cardiac cycle. Cycle is initiated (0 point on time line) by neural innervation at the sinoatrial node.

noatrial node in the right atrium (time 0 in Fig. 12.2). The impulse is then conducted throughout the atria, which contract about 60 msec after sinoatrial innervation; this atrial contraction is reflected in the P-wave of the EKG. The impulse is then conducted throughout the heart muscle by a combination of neural cells and specialized cardiac conduction cells, arriving at the atrioventricular (AV) node about 125 msec after sinoatrial innervation, the Q-wave. After the impulse reaches the AV node and the bundle of His, a large voltage spike appears in the EKG. This spike, the R-wave, represents the innervation of the ventricles, and actually precedes ventricular contraction by about 50 msec. When the ventricles contract, blood is ejected into the aorta, reaching peak pressure at the point of the T-wave. The time between the T-wave and the next P-wave is the quiescent period, known as the diastole. This cycle is repeated approximately once per second throughout the entire lifespan, although there is definite variation with age (children have fast rates) and physical condition (physical fitness results in slower heart rate, presumably reflecting increased cardiac efficiency.)

Measurement Issues. Technically the EKG can be detected by placing electrodes on any two points of the body; however, clinical cardiologists have devised a standard set of electrode points that include various areas of the chest and the limbs. By developing a set of actuarial norms concerning the "normal" wave form recorded from each of these points, cardiologists have achieved great success using the EKG as a noninvasive aid in the diagnosis of cardiac lesions.

Behavioral scientists, however, have usually focused their attention on the relationship between stimulus events and changes in the heart rate. In its simplest form, the heart rate is merely the number of cardiac cycles that occur in a unit of time, expressed as beats per minute (bpm). The simplest technique for counting cardiac cycles is to count the oc-

currence of R-waves, the most prominent feature of the cycle. No fancy equipment is required to feel someone's pulse at the wrist (radial artery), and indeed, a clinician who wants a patient to monitor his or her own heart rate can probably use self-observed measures of radial pulse frequency with confidence in their reliability and validity (Bell & Schwartz, 1975).

For detailed study of heart rate changes during an experimental session, however, the use of a polygraph is necessary, and the fundamental technique is usually to measure the time interval between successive R-waves and divide that interval (in sec.) into 60 to express it as bpm. This procedure is tedious and subject to measurement error. A *cardiotachometer* is often employed to eliminate the tedium, although it too is subject to measurement error of about 5%. A cardiotachometer "reads" the time between successive R-waves and produces a signal that is proportional to the corresponding rate (in bpm) for the interval. Thus, by simply reading the polygraph chart, the researcher can obtain a direct measurement of heart rate on each beat of the heart. The advent of low cost microcomputer systems has enabled much more precise reading of interbeat intervals, and is rapidly replacing "stand alone" cardiotachometers. In addition to the greater precision of computerized measurement, an additional feature of such instrumentation is that it allows the investigator to record easily the raw interbeat interval, as well as the rate. It is obvious that the rate and the interbeat interval are reciprocally related. Hence they are not distributed equally, and statistical tests carried out on one may not lead to similar results when carried out on the other. Heslegrave, Ogilvie, and Furedy (1979) have suggested that cardiac rate is probably best scored in interbeat intervals rather than in bpm units.

Some of the most serious issues in cardiac rate assessment concern the proper interpretation of the heart rate, and sophisticated measurement techniques are of no help in resolving these issues. First, there is the question of what a "heart rate response" is. To be sure, the heart is an organ capable of responding to homeostatic demands of the system in such ways that its rate may vary. There is some doubt, however, whether the heart rate change can be interpreted as a behavioral entity in itself, or whether it must be interpreted in the context of the underlying response mechanisms it represents (Obrist, 1976).

Interest in heart rate measurement was fostered by proponents of general arousal theory (Duffy, 1962; Malmo, 1958), who argued that heart rate levels could be used to assess levels of arousal. "Arousal" was postulated to be a unidimensional motivational construct, similar in some ways to Hull's (1943) concept of general drive (Malmo, 1959). The use of heart rate measures to index arousal, and the general utility of a unidimensional ubiquitous arousal construct, were both dealt a serious blow by Lacey's (1959) demonstration of "directional fractionation." Lacey found that under conditions in which subjects were required to attend to the environment, their heart rates decreased, even though skin conductance and behavioral observation indicated high "arousal" levels; under conditions in which subjects had to do difficult mental work, turning their attention away from the environment, their heart rates increased, along with skin conductance and behavioral signs of arousal. Thus, in two different situations that should be associated with equal levels of arousal, the heart rate responses were "directionally fractionated." Lacey derived a complex theory in which the directionality of the heart rate response was thought to have a causal effect on the level of cortical activity, based upon subtle interactions between heart rate, blood pressure, and the baroreceptor cells of the carotid arteries. In the Lacey theory, which has enjoyed widespread popularity and attention (see Graham & Clifton, 1966), tasks that require environmental rejection are associated with heart rate increases, and tasks that re-

quire environmental intake are associated with heart rate decreases.

Obrist (1976) and his colleagues (Obrist, Webb, Sutterer, & Howard, 1970) describe a view of heart rate responses quite different from the directional fractionation hypothesis. Obrist's view may be of particular interest to clinical psychologists because of observations of the effects of different kinds of stressful experiences on heart rate. In certain situations, such as classical aversive conditioning, in which the subject has a passive role, heart rate changes are under vagal control. According to Obrist, these changes are small and biologically trivial from a pathophysiological point of view. On the other hand, in situations in which the subject can cope actively, such as a shock-avoidance reaction-time task, heart rate is under sympathetic control, and large increases may be observed even though attention is directed toward the environment, and the subject is "receptive." Thus, according to this view, the particular type of stress and the nature of the coping required influence the neural control of cardiovascular functions and determine changes in heart rate.

Blood Pressure

The rhythmic contraction of the heart forces blood into the arteries with each beat rather than as a continuous stream. Consequently the pressure within the arteries varies during each cardiac cycle, from a high level during contraction (systolic pressure) to a lower level when the heart relaxes (diastolic pressure). The labels systolic and diastolic are derived from the cardiac systole, which lasts from the QRS complex to the T-wave of the EKG, and from the diastole, or relaxation phase between the T-wave and the subsequent P-wave of the EKG (see Fig. 12.2). The arterial walls are elastic and recoil during the diastolic phase, continuing to force blood through the capillaries (Berne & Levy, 1977). The blood pressure varies among different blood vessels, with a reduction in force as the blood travels further from the heart; thus the pressure in the major arteries is substantially higher than in the smaller ones, and venous pressures are very low (Guyton, 1979).

Normal resting blood pressure in the arteries of the upper arm can vary greatly with age, physical condition, sex, and race. For example, 20-year-old males may have systolic pressures 10 to 20 mm Hg higher than females of the same age. Criteria for deciding that a person's blood pressure is too high vary as well; Hassett (1978) notes that readings of 140 mm Hg systolic and 90 mm Hg diastolic blood pressure are commonly accepted norms for the upper limit of "normal" blood pressure; yet in an important epidemiological survey (Kannel & Sorlie, 1975) a person was described as hypertensive if his or her blood pressure exceeded 160 systolic and 95 diastolic (commonly stated as 160/95, and read as "160 over 95"). Some physicians prefer to use an even higher diastolic reading such as 110 mm Hg as the limit for beginning drug treatment, because the efficacy of drugs has been demonstrated more clearly above that level; but blood pressure is a continuous variable, and resting elevated pressures are indications of higher risk of mortality, even when systolic and diastolic levels stay below traditional dividing lines for "high blood pressure."

The blood must carry oxygen and nutrients to the tissues that require them, and also remove metabolic wastes. Pressure must be maintained for the blood to flow adequately, but too high a pressure within the system may cause damage by breaking through a vessel wall, as in a stroke, or by loosening a clot that can then block a narrower vessel and impede passage of the blood. For these important homeostatic functions the blood pressure is automatically regulated and is not generally under voluntary control; however, indirect regulation is readily demonstrated, either through imagining stressful events or

through physical exercise. Although there has been considerable attention to techniques for training patients to learn to modify their blood pressure voluntarily, the results to date have been quite discouraging (Blanchard & Epstein, 1978; Katkin, Fitzgerald, & Shapiro, 1978; Shapiro & Surwit, 1976).

Blood pressure is determined by two major factors: the output of the heart (cardiac output, or CO) and the resistance of the blood vessels (total peripheral resistance or TPR). In turn, CO is the product of heart rate × stroke volume (the volume of blood pumped on a given beat). Any change in any one of these factors will alter blood pressure; for example, a blood pressure increase may result from increased heart rate, increased stroke volume, or increased resistance of the peripheral blood vessels. One of the major mechanisms behind these changes is the ANS; sympathetic activation may increase the heart rate, increase CO, and constrict peripheral blood vessels. Parasympathetic influences such as vagal excitation and withdrawal, which slow and speed the heart respectively, will also have consequences for blood pressure; thus a change in blood pressure associated with a change in heart rate cannot simply be ascribed either to sympathetic or parasympathetic influences without further investigation.

When the physiological basis of sustained high blood pressure is unknown, as is true in perhaps 90% of the cases, the condition is referred to as primary or essential hypertension. There have been ample demonstrations that certain kinds of psychological stress elevate blood pressure, particularly in individuals who have familial tendencies toward the development of hypertension (Falkner, Onesti, Angelakos, Fernandes, & Langman, 1979; Shapiro, 1961). Many psychophysiologists are actively engaged in evaluating the role of stress in producing essential hypertension (Obrist, 1976); for example, a study by Friedman and Iwai (1976) found that repeated stress elicited pronounced and prolonged blood pressure increases in a strain of rats bred for susceptibility to hypertension upon ingestion of excess salt.

Blood Pressure Measurement. Direct measurement of blood pressure can be accomplished by inserting a catheter into an artery and connecting it to a pressure transducer, which converts the blood pressure to an electrical signal for polygraph recording. This procedure is both risky and painful, so it is not routinely used. For most purposes, blood pressure is measured indirectly with a sphygmomanometer, a cuff containing an inflatable pouch wrapped around the upper arm. Forcing air into the pouch until the pressure is well above the systolic blood pressure occludes the brachial artery; if a microphone is then placed over the brachial artery below the cuff, there will be no distinct "Korotkoff" or high-frequency pulse sound. If pressure in the cuff is released slowly, a Korotkoff sound will be heard at the point where the pressure in the cuff is equal to the systolic pressure in the artery. As the pressure is continuously decreased from that point, the Korotkoff sounds continue to be heard until the pressure in the cuff falls below the diastolic pressure in the artery. Thus, if the cuff is connected to a pressure meter, the meter reading at the first Korotkoff sound is the systolic pressure, and the meter reading at the last Korotkoff sound is the diastolic pressure (Rushmer, 1976). The proper rate of deflation of the cuff is about 2 to 3 mm Hg per heartbeat. Too slow a deflation rate may alter the pressure in the artery or cause numbness in the subject's lower arm; too rapid a deflation introduces error in estimating blood pressure. Excellent technical descriptions of blood pressure assessment procedures are available in Berne and Levy (1977), Geddes (1970), and Rushmer (1976).

Recently electronic Korotkoff sound detectors have been devised to allow for automatic blood pressure recording. These devices promise to facilitate blood pressure measurement by standardizing the method of detection and reducing random error variance due to the listener's fatigue or variations in auditory sensitivity or training of different listeners. These instruments may, however, introduce systematic error if the Korotkoff sound detector is inaccurate. Frequent validating of automatic equipment against direct readings or against polygraphic tracings of the sound recordings is an important procedure. Figure 12.3 shows simultaneous direct and indirect recordings.

Indirect blood pressure recording requires very slow sampling; a complete cycle of inflation and deflation of the cuff can take as long as 60 seconds. Therefore research applications that require continuous or frequent assessments of the blood pressure traditionally have relied upon the more painful and invasive direct method. Tursky, Shapiro, and Schwartz (1972), however, have developed a noninvasive automatic system that is capable of "tracking" the Korotkoff sound at either the systolic or the diastolic level, depending on the choice of the investigator. This device allows for approximate determinations of the systolic or diastolic pressure on each heart beat, and it is particularly valuable for biofeedback applications in which the patient must be receiving continuous information about the blood pressure level.

Another relatively new noninvasive measure of blood pressure is the pulse transit time (PTT), which is the time interval between the R-wave of the EKG (which signals imminent ejection of the blood from the ventricle) and the arrival of the pulse wave at the distal radial artery (the common pulse point at the wrist). This measure, pioneered by Steptoe and his colleagues (see Steptoe, Smulyan, & Gribbin, 1976), has been used effectively in providing biofeedback information about blood pressure, on the assumption that the time interval between R-wave and radial pulse is inversely correlated with mean arterial blood pressure. In fact Obrist, Light, McCubbin, Hutcheson, and Hoffer (1979) have demonstrated that the

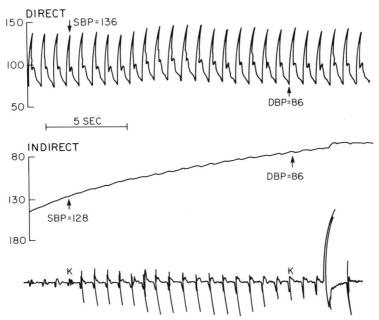

Figure 12.3.   Examples of direct and indirect measurement of arterial blood pressure. Top channel represents recording from catheter in left uppermost point representing sysradial artery. Note how wave form reflects each beat of the heart, with uppermost point representing systole and lowermost point representing diastole on each beat. Middle channel represents pressure recorded from air chamber of external cuff. Notice there is no direct reading of pressure on each beat; pressure is estimated from reading middle channel at point where Korotkoff sounds are first detected, and then lost. These points are identified on bottom channel, and were detected by a piezoelectric microphone placed over the right brachial artery. (Redrawn from polygraph records provided by Drs. M. Pollak and P. A. Obrist.)

PTT is a relatively robust indicator of systolic blood pressure, but a less useful index of diastolic pressure. Further, Obrist et al. (1979) found that the strong inverse correlations between systolic pressure and PTT were substantially reduced by the administration of beta-adrenergic blocking agents, implying that the relation between PTT and blood pressure is mediated by common beta-adrenergic influences. Although the PTT measure is still not understood fully, it promises to be a simple, noninvasive technique for assessing systolic blood pressure continuously.

Blood Volume

In addition to measuring the rate and pressure with which blood is pumped through the system, psychophysiologists have also developed a technology for measuring changes in the volume of blood that is present in a local area. The total amount of blood flowing through the system at any time is constant. As a result of a variety of sympathetic and parasympathetic influences, however, different organs receive differing proportions of the total blood volume. This is especially evident in sexual arousal, during which the blood volume in the penis or clitoris increases as a result of vasocongestion. It is also obvious in embarrassed blushing, in which the blood volume in the face increases dramatically. The most popular techniques for assessing blood volume are both indirect: plethysmographs and thermometers.

Plethysmography.   "Plethysmograph" is the hundred-dollar word that describes an instrument used for the measurement of the volume in a container; in psychophysiology it usually refers to a device used for the assessment of peripheral blood volume (see Cook, 1974, for an excellent discussion of peripheral vascular activity). The most widely used plethysmographs rely upon light transmission through or light reflectance off body tissue; this technique is known as photoplethysmography. If a light source is focused on an earlobe or a fingertip, the amount of light that will pass through the tissue is inversely related to the density of blood contained therein. If a photocell is placed on the opposite side of the ear or finger, therefore, it is possible to get fairly accurate readings of momentary changes in blood volume. Exact calibration of photoplethysmographs is not possible, however, and they are used only for the assessment of relative change. Reflectance plethysmographs work on the same principle, except that the photocell is on the same surface as the light source, and the reflected light is measured. The reflectance plethysmograph is used for measuring blood volume in areas where light cannot be transmitted through the organ, such as forehead and temple blood flow, or vaginal blood flow. Since photoplethysmographs measure the transitory flow of blood through an organ, the signals they produce show a marked similarity to EKG signals, with a characteristic spike representing the systole.

Although the application of plethysmography to research questions in clinical psychology has not been as widespread as other indexes of cardiovascular activity, it has been applied extensively to the assessment of sexual arousal, particularly in women. The use of vaginal reflectance plethysmography has shown substantial promise as a technique for the assessment of psychophysiological sexual response in women (Geer, 1975; Hoon, Wincze, & Hoon, 1976; Sintchak & Geer, 1975). While male sexual arousal could also be assessed with a reflectance plethysmogram, it is more usual to use a strain gauge wrapped around the penis (see Abel & Blanchard, 1976, for details).

Thermometers. Skin temperature is a reasonably valid index of peripheral vascular blood volume. As vessels dilate, the temperature of the skin around them is increased. Most of the variance in peripheral dilation and constriction is homeostatically determined, in response to external temperature; however, it is also clear that within normal limits of external temperature, vascular changes reflect emotional responses. Thus the measurement of peripheral skin temperature is thought to be a rough index of blood volume. Typically, skin temperature is measured by placing a thermistor over the skin surface and passing small electrical currents through it. A thermistor has the property of changing its electrical resistance systematically as its temperature varies, so that a simple reading of resistance can yield a calibrated measure of skin temperature (Hassett, 1978).

Skin temperature measurement has been applied widely in biofeedback treatments for migraine and Raynaud's disease, both of which are disorders of vascular activity. The use of skin temperature feedback to train people to counteract pathological vascular activity has achieved varying degrees of success (see Katkin, Fitzgerald, & Shapiro, 1978). The primary advantages of skin temperature measures rather than plethysmographic measures in biofeedback appear to be ease of implementation and comparatively low cost.

EXAMPLES OF AREAS OF APPLICATION

It would be impossible, in the space of one chapter, to survey all the areas of clinical psychology to which psychophysiological methods have been applied. Prokasy and Raskin (1973), for instance, filled a large volume just detailing the applications of electrodermal activity in psychological research, and Fowles (1975) produced an entire volume covering just six areas of psychophysiological applications to clinical psychology. It is our intention in this section to describe briefly some clinical areas that have been continuing foci of applied psychophysiological methods. These areas are not meant to be exhaustive, nor are they necessarily the areas likely to be the most fruitful for future research. Rather they represent a sample of research approaches to clinical phenomena that have used psychophysiological methodology as a primary tool.

Anxiety and Desensitization

There are few if any theories of anxiety that do not postulate a psychophysiological component of the phenomenon. Furthermore, most such theories focus on the role of peripheral rather than central responses, with particular emphasis on the role of the ANS. For these and other reasons, it has become quite common for investigators to employ psychophysiological measures when investigating anxiety. Lang (1968, 1969) has commented on the difficulty of defining anxiety operationally; he suggests that anxiety is a tripartite construct, which can be indexed by motor behavior, physiological response, and self-report. It is not necessary for all three indexes to be observable in order to infer a state of anxiety, but it is also clear that the use of any one index (including the physiological) by itself does not do full justice to the concept.

Spielberger (1966) has popularized the distinction between trait and state anxiety. In this dichotomy, trait anxiety is defined as an individual's predisposition to respond to certain perceived threats with a constellation of responses which are, collectively, the anxiety state. This model gives little reason to predict differences in physiological activity among subjects who differ in trait anxiety, unless they are exposed to conditions that will elicit different states of anxiety. A number of empirical investigations have supported this view. Rappaport and Katkin (1972) demonstrated that subjects who were

selected from extreme ends of the distribution of a trait anxiety inventory (the Taylor Anxiety Scale) did not show any differential electrodermal activity during rest; however, when placed in an ego-threatening situation, those subjects high on the trait scale showed significantly greater increases in SSRRs than those who scored low on the scale. Earlier studies from the same laboratory had shown that when a severe threat to the body (threat of painful electric shock) was employed, subjects who were high and low in trait anxiety (Katkin, 1965) or prethreat state anxiety (Katkin, 1966) showed similar increases in SSRR rate. These findings are an important reminder that while trait anxious people may be predisposed to respond with state anxiety, under severe circumstances anybody may be induced into an anxious state. It is quite unlikely that psychophysiological assessment is useful in assessing trait anxiety, but it may be of considerable significance in aiding the precise identification of state anxiety.

The studies of Katkin (1965, 1966) and Rappaport and Katkin (1972) indicate the importance of a subject's *cognitive appraisal* of the threat value of a situation in eliciting physiological responses associated with the anxiety state. This point has been emphasized by Lazarus (1966), who has demonstrated that individual differences in cognitive coping style modify significantly the physiological response to threatening stimuli. Similar views have been expressed by Fenz and Epstein (1967), who found that novice parachutists reported the greatest experience of fear just before jumping, whereas experienced parachutists reported the greatest fear at the beginning of the day, leveling off as they approached the jump. Measurements of heart rate, skin conductance, and breathing rate obtained from the parachutists up until the moment of the jump showed consistency between self-reports and bodily responses. The novice parachutists showed continuing increases in their physiological responses, peaking at the moment before the jump; the experienced parachutists showed a constant and low level of physiological response throughout the experience. Fenz and Epstein suggest that the cognitive coping skills acquired with experience modulate the fear experience, thereby reducing autonomic arousal.

In the Lazarus and the Fenz and Epstein models cognitive coping style is considered central to the experience of fear. This view is quite distinct from the view that underlies systematic desensitization, in which the fear response is defined as an autonomic response. Wolpe (1971) has defined anxiety "as an individual organism's characteristic constellation of autonomic responses to noxious stimulation (p. 341)." Wolpe has also suggested that the mechanism by which systematic desensitization succeeds is the "reciprocal inhibition" of these conditioned autonomic responses. Specific tests of this theoretical view have been carried out using psychophysiological measures.

The conclusions of two reviews of this literature (Katkin & Deitz, 1973; Mathews, 1971) are quite similar: Psychophysiological research on desensitization leaves no doubt that "the EDR to phobic and nonphobic stimulus objects provides an accurate index of a subject's fear state" (Katkin & Deitz, 1973, p. 369). This is true for real stimulus objects (Barlow, Agras, Leitenberg, & Wincze, 1970), pictures of stimulus objects (Geer, 1966; Wilson, 1967) and imagined stimulus objects (Lang, Melamed, & Hart, 1970). Further, on the basis of the evidence it appears unlikely that progressive relaxation serves as a counterconditioning agent. More likely, progressive relaxation reduces autonomic arousal, thereby facilitating the habituation or extinction of conditioned fear responses. This is supported by much evidence, including Katkin & McCubbin's (1969) demonstration that electrodermal orienting responses habituate more rapidly in low states of arousal. The data also indicate that there is no special advantage to the specific relaxation ritual employed in systematic desensitization; the preponderance of evidence indicates that any type of instruction to relax works as well as the specific progressive relaxation instructions preferred by Wolpe (Katkin & Deitz, 1973).

In summary, the applications of psychophysiological methods to the study of anxiety and systematic desensitization are numerous. In the case of desensitization, certain tests of theoretical postulates have been made that might not have been possible without psychophysiological methods. Obviously there are myriad unresolved questions for future research, but this is one area in which psychophysiology has made a substantial contribution.

Schizophrenia

Psychophysiological research on schizophrenia has been extensive, and the focus has been primarily upon electrodermal and electroencephalographic responses, although there have been studies of schizophrenics using virtually every psychophysiological index that can be recorded (and some that cannot). Most of the early psychophysiological research on schizophrenia was derived from arousal theory and attempted to test the theory that schizophrenics were either over- or underaroused (Lang & Buss, 1965). Most of that early research focused on ANS rather than CNS measures, partly because of technical ease, and partly because of an overriding theoretical assumption that schizophrenia was at least partially caused by limbic system (amygdala, hippocampus, and septum) dysfunction, which is reflected in the ANS (Venables, 1975). A major rationale for the application of psychophysiological methods to research on schizophrenia was that autonomic responses would be relatively free of the error variance contributed by motivational and attentional deficits common to schizophrenic subjects. Later research, especially in the last decade, has been addressed to CNS function, with increasing attention being paid to evoked responses (Buchsbaum, 1977; Itil, 1977; Roth, 1977;

Shagass, 1977). In addition, there has been a recent surge of interest in the recording of smooth pursuit eye movements (Holzman & Levy, 1977), using a special form of EMG recording known as the electrooculogram (EOG).

Electrodermal Activity. The rationale for most of the electrodermal research on schizophrenia has been summarized elegantly by Venables (1975), who states

that several not entirely similar approaches have produced the idea that what may be at least a partial feature of schizophrenic pathology is a disturbance of limbic system function, and that if this is so, then certain disturbances of autonomic function can be predicted and investigated by psychophysiological techniques. (p. 107)

Venables identified three "not entirely similar" lines of evidence that suggest limbic system involvement in schizophrenia. First, obstetric and perinatal complications lead to a greater incidence of manifest schizophrenic symptoms among the offspring of a schizophrenic parent (Mednick, 1970); a major result of perinatal complications is anoxia, and it has been demonstrated that the hippocampus is particularly vulnerable to anoxia (Freides, 1966; Spector, 1965). Second, lesions of the dominant temporal lobe, which is implicated in limbic system function, result in schizophreniform symptoms. Third, one of the main features of schizophrenic disorders is attentional deficit (McGhie & Chapman, 1961). Douglas (1967), Douglas and Pribram (1966), and Kimble (1968) have demonstrated that the limbic system is involved in the attentional process.

Direct recording from human limbic structures with indwelling electrodes is, in Venables' words, "in general ethically undesirable" (1975, p. 112). Therefore, an appropriate noninvasive index of limbic system activity was sought. Venables and many other investigators, spurred on primarily by the theorizing of Bagshaw (Bagshaw & Benzies, 1968; Bagshaw, Kimble, & Pribram, 1965) chose the electrodermal component of the orienting response (OR) as their measure of choice. The OR, according to Pavlov, is a generalized response to any change in the environment, irrespective of its significance. According to Sokolov's (1963) elaborate model of the OR, any novel stimulus will elicit unconditional central, motor, and autonomic responses, including phasic changes in SC. With repeated presentations of the same stimulus, a "neuronal model" of that stimulus is generated; as the neuronal model becomes strengthened by repeated exposures, the central, motor, and autonomic response to stimulus presentation habituates. When the "neuronal model" is complete, and there is thus no mismatch between it and the stimulus, the OR disappears. Bagshaw and her colleagues, working with primates, found that ablation of the amygdala produced a marked diminution of the skin conductance component of the OR, and that ablation of the hippocampus led to greater resistance to habituation of the SC OR. Venables and his co-workers postulated, therefore, that close examination of the SC OR and its habituation would be a methodologically sound approach to studying the role of the limbic system in schizophrenia.

At the time that Venables began his research program he was confronted with two conflicting sets of data from other laboratories. Zahn and his colleagues (Zahn, Rosenthal, & Lawlor, 1968) had found that schizophrenics showed larger SCRs and habituated less than normals; Bernstein (1964, 1970) found smaller responding and more habituation for schizophrenics than normals. Substantial data from Venables' laboratory indicated that both sets of data might be right. Approximately 50% of the schizophrenics in Venables' sample failed to respond at all. Among the remaining 50%, schizophrenics tended to be large responders and slow habituators. This led to the dichotomous classification of schizophrenics as "responders" and "nonresponders"; much subsequent research has been devoted to the delineation of behavioral factors to which the "responder-nonresponder" variable may be related. Unfortunately, some of the subsequent studies from Venables' own laboratory and others have failed to confirm the findings of differential habituation (Patterson & Venables, 1978; Zahn, 1976); thus the current status of the "responder-nonresponder" dimension, like so much in schizophrenia research, remains unclear. Nevertheless, this program of research on the SC OR represents one rather productive way in which electrodermal responses have been employed to test current clinical theory.

Electroencephalography. The earliest research on EEG correlates of schizophrenia was addressed to the identification of resting differences in patterns of brain wave activity. The field has been plagued with a number of interpretive difficulties. For instance, are differences in resting EEG predictive of differences in EEG during alert, active states? Are differences between schizophrenic and normal patterns antecedents or consequents of the disorder? The most carefully controlled studies, taking into account the effects of medication and other important extraneous variables, suggest that schizophrenics manifest reduced levels of alpha and increased levels of fast beta (24 to 33 Hz) waves (Itil, 1977). According to Itil (1977) these are also the patterns that can be induced by psychotomimetic drugs such as LSD–25. Itil also notes that these patterns, along with significant increases in early delta (3 to 4 Hz) are observed in some nonpsychotic children who have been identified as being at high risk for schizophrenia. Longitudinal studies of such children to see if the "reduced alpha-increased beta-increased delta" pattern predicts morbidity among high risk children are in process. These studies should provide important evidence concerning the utility of brain wave analysis as a diagnostic predictor of schizophrenic morbidity.

A second line of EEG research, on event-related potentials, has emerged during the past decade. This research has been divided roughly into three areas: analysis of "early" ERPs (occurring within 50 msec of stimulation); "middle" ERPs (occurring between 100 to 200 msec after stimulation); and "late" ERPs (occurring at least 300 msec after stimulation).

The current literature on early ERPs is rather inconclusive (see Spohn & Patterson, 1979), although the rationale for continuing studies is that early ERPs are thought to represent stimulus registration in the cortex, and by implication, intactness of the reticular formation.

Middle ERPs have been the subject of intense investigation, with particular emphasis on a complex consisting of P100, N140, and P200 from auditory, visual, or somatosensory cortex. Buchsbaum (1977) has noted that the middle potentials all seem reduced in the ORs of schizophrenic subjects. Since N140 is presumed to reflect "stimulus selection" and P200 is presumed to reflect response to novelty, it is inferred that the reduced middle potentials in schizophrenia reflects the well known attentional deficits associated with the disorder. Of course, as always, data such as these only tell us that there are brain activity correlates of schizophrenia; they do not address seriously the issues of etiology or causality.

Whereas early components of the ERP are believed to reflect the neurological integrity of the cortical system, late components are widely believed to represent the functional, or psychological integrity of the cortex. Roth (1977) has provided an excellent review of the literature on both the CNV and late ERPs such as P300. The data in this realm are clouded by severe methodological problems, but there is some reason to believe that schizophrenics show reduced CNV amplitude, although it is not clear to what extent this is typical of all patients, or merely a subgroup. With respect to late evoked potentials, which are generally presumed to reflect expectancy or readiness, there is some evidence that schizophrenics show delayed responding.

This is not a solid finding, however, and may be an artifact of the inability of the laboratory task to engage the patient's attention.

Roth (1977) has raised profound questions concerning not only the current status of EEG research with schizophrenia, but also the conceptual basis for its future:

In general, the quality of research in the area of EPs and psychopathology is poorer than in experiments designed to answer questions of theoretical interest to psychology. . . . It is not surprising that event-related potentials most influenced by behavior should be sensitive to psychopathology. A more pertinent question is whether they have anything to add to behavioral assessment. For this reason, the trend in the pure psychological study of event-related potentials to assess behavior concomitantly with EEG recording is recommended to investigators of the CNV and other late waves in patient populations. (Roth, 1977, p. 116)

Smooth Pursuit Eye Movements. As early as 1908 Diefendorf and Dodge noted that schizophrenics were not as able as normals or other mental patients to track visually the movement of a swinging pendulum. More than 60 years later, using modern electrooculogram (EOG) techniques, Holzman and his associates (Holzman & Levy, 1977; Holzman, Proctor, & Hughes, 1973; Holzman, Proctor, Levy, Yasillo, Meltzer, & Hurt, 1974) reported similar findings. Holzman's group, however, also reported that *non*psychotic first-degree relatives of schizophrenic patients showed similar deviant patterns of smooth pursuit eye tracking. Although Holzman found that nonschizophrenic functional psychotics manifested high rates of deviant eyetracking, the incidence of deviance in first-degree relatives of nonschizophrenic patients was only about 10%, whereas for relatives of schizophrenics it was between 40% and 50%.

A variety of theoretical statements have come forth to deal with these striking data. One popular view is that the deviant eye tracking may represent a genetic marker; this view is strengthened somewhat by the report of Holzman, Kringlen, Levy, Proctor, Haberman, & Yasillo (1977) that deviant eye tracking is more concordant within monozygotic twins than within dizygotic twins. Unfortunately, the twin samples were not perfectly matched, and the data must be accepted as merely suggestive. There have also been a number of questions raised concerning the possible confounding effects of medication, differences in attentiveness, and EOG artifacts. Despite the relative lack of closure about the true significance of smooth pursuit eye tracking, it remains an exciting area of psychophysiological investigation and promises to occupy research attention for some time. The methodological issues involved in proper quantification of the EOG for such assessment are very complicated. The interested reader should see papers by Lindsey, Holzman, Haberman, and Yasillo (1978) and Iacono and Lykken (1979a and b).

Psychopathy

Although it is sometimes assumed that prison populations are synonymous with psychopathic populations, Hare (1978) has suggested that psychopaths are a distinct subgroup among other criminals, and that prison inmates who are not diagnosed psychopaths constitute a good control group. Conversely, Widom (1977) has developed methods for identifying nonprisoners who are psychopaths, a long neglected research population. Despite these concerns for proper identification of psychopaths for careful research, one of the most critical problems facing researchers in this area is the development of a reliable and valid definition of psychopathy. Having issued this disclaimer, we will now review research on electroencephalographic, cardiovascular, and electrodermal approaches to psychopathy.

Electroencephalography. Most of the research on the EEG in psychopaths has been disappointing. Although there have been some reports of "abnormal" EEGs obtained from psychopaths (Hare & Cox, 1978), Syndulko (1978) has described four studies that find no differences in EEG between psychopaths and controls. Furthermore, Syndulko argues, although excessive slow wave activity in psychopaths is often reported to reflect cortical immaturity, it may actually reflect drowsiness, drug status, or boredom, to which psychopaths are especially prone. Studies of evoked potentials have also yielded inconsistent results. While some studies have suggested low levels of cortical arousability for psychopaths, it is likely that these results are not generalizable, and may reflect the responses of only certain subgroups of psychopaths (Syndulko, 1978).

Cardiovascular Measures. Data on cardiovascular changes among psychopaths have been uninformative; there are no observed differences in resting heart rate or blood pressure between psychopaths and control subjects (Hare, 1978). Psychopaths, like normal persons, show heart rate acceleration following a strong shock; however, they show greater acceleration than normal persons in *anticipation* of a shock (Hare & Quinn, 1971). Hare (1978) has suggested, in terms of Lacey's "directional fractionation" hypothesis (Lacey & Lacey, 1974), that this enhanced cardiac acceleration in anticipation of pain may reflect a tendency to reject the forthcoming stimulation. According to Hare, this reduced sensory input may reduce the psychopath's likelihood of experiencing fear of punishment, resulting in a greater likelihood of deviant behavior. This line of reasoning is supported by some of the evidence from studies of electrodermal activity in psychopaths.

Electrodermal Activity. A programmatic series of studies by Hare and his colleagues (Hare, 1965; 1968; 1972; 1975; Hare & Craigen, 1974; Hare & Quinn, 1971) has indicated that psychopaths generally tend to show lower levels of skin conductance and fewer SSCRs than control subjects. Taken together with the observation of accelerated heart rate in anticipation of shock, these data have been interpreted by Hare (1978) as evidence that the psychopath effectively rejects threatening sensory input, and experiences lower levels of sympathetic arousal (fear) in anticipation of punishment.

There is also some evidence that the recovery rate of the SCR is slower for psychopaths than for normals. There is considerable uncertainty about the precise mechanisms underlying the recovery rate of SCRs (Bundy & Fitzgerald, 1975), so it is not known whether the differential rate of SCR recovery in psychopaths reflects a unique process or an artifact of correlated electrodermal events. Nevertheless, Mednick (1977) and Mednick and Hutchings (1978) have postulated that the slow recovery rate observed in psychopaths may represent a slow rate of fear dissipation. Mednick (1977) has suggested that in nonpsychopaths a learned fear of punishment results in the inhibition of potentially aggressive responses. For acquisition of fear to occur, according to this model, one requires a punishing agent (e.g., family), and a fear response (e.g., SCR); in order for the acquisition of the inhibition of aggressive responses to occur, *fast* dissipation of the fear is required as a reinforcer. In this model the psychopath is doubly handicapped because he has a minimal anticipatory fear response, and it dissipates slowly.

While there are some data to support this rather complicated psychophysiologically based learning theory of psychopathic behavior, there are sufficient null results to warrant extreme caution about conclusions (Siddle & Trasler, in press). It is likely that there is considerable error in the selection of subject samples; failures to confirm any hypothesis may reflect nonuniform samples rather than the absence of a true relationship. Future research combining psychophysiological results with objectively agreed-upon behavioral criteria are very much needed.

Psychophysiological (Psychosomatic) Disorders

It is only natural that psychophysiological methods have been applied with some regularity to the study of psychophysiological disorders, for these disorders are usually defined as physical symptoms that are caused by emotional factors involving organs that are usually under the control of the ANS. Although much of the research on psychosomatic disorders has been grounded in psychoanalytic theory, there has been a strong behavioral and psychophysiological influence emerging through the discipline of "Behavioral Medicine." Shapiro and Katkin (1980) have suggested that psychophysiology may be considered a basic science for the field of behavioral or psychosomatic medicine, although obviously not the only one.

Instrumental Learning. Among the clearest lines of development in the behavioral approach to psychosomatic disorders has been the operant biofeedback strategy. Basically the operant view of psychosomatic disorders states that a symptom may be reinforced if its expression consistently is instrumental in obtaining reinforcement. Historically, an operant conceptualization such as this was ignored because of the widely held belief that autonomically mediated responses could not be conditioned in an operant manner (Skinner, 1938). During the 1960s, however, a number of laboratories began to demonstrate that autonomically mediated responses could be conditioned instrumentally (Miller, 1969). Despite the continuing controversy about the underlying mechanisms involved in the operant control of autonomic responses (Crider, Schwartz, & Shnidman, 1969; Katkin & Murray, 1968; Katkin, Murray, & Lachman, 1969) there was general agreement that subjects can somehow gain some degree of voluntary control over autonomically mediated responses. This belief led to the development of bio-

feedback, a technique that uses instrumentation to provide a person with immediate and continuing signals concerning bodily functions of which that person would not otherwise be aware.

Miller (1975) pointed out that learning to control visceral responses may be likened to learning to shoot a basketball. Whereas muscles used to shoot baskets provide the learner with immediate and usable feedback, the smooth muscles, glands, and blood vessels that are the typical target organs for psychophysiological disorders do not provide readily usable feedback. With electronic interfaces, such feedback can be obtained, and the learner can use it to modify previously uncontrollable functions, according to the same principles used to increase one's field goal percentage. These principles were applied first to the regulation of autonomic functions in normal subjects, and later to the regulation of pathological autonomic functions in patients suffering from psychophysiological disorders.

From the numerous studies demonstrating that autonomic functions could be modified instrumentally, there emerged a growing interest in the idea that psychophysiological symptoms may be developed through a process of instrumental learning. In a series of investigations carried out on primates, Harris and his colleagues (Harris & Brady, 1977; Harris, Findley, & Brady, 1971; Harris, Goldstein, & Brady, 1977) have demonstrated that baboons can learn to elevate their blood pressure in order to avoid shocks or receive food:

Large magnitude elevations in diastolic blood pressure, 50 to 60 mm Hg above resting levels, could be generated under conditions which made shock-avoidance and food-acquisition contingent upon the required pressure elevations. Furthermore, these experiments confirmed that such instrumentally-conditioned circulatory changes could be brought under explicit exteroceptive environmental stimulus control and that they could be produced on a relatively acute basis (i. e., intervals up to 5 minutes in duration) seventy or more times each day over the extended course of these initial studies. (Harris, Goldstein, & Brady, 1977, p. 206)

Such studies form the empirical basis for a growing interest in the idea that psychophysiological symptoms may be instrumentally learned patterns of autonomic response. If such a model is to be fruitful in the future, careful research will be required to discover the nature of effective reinforcers and the extent to which there are response-reinforcement specificities that can be identified and then interrupted by preventive intervention.

Psychophysiological Models. Several basic concepts have been proposed in psychophysiology that involve the phenomena of psychophysiological disorders. First, there is the concept of *stimulus-response specificity,* which means that "a given stimulus consistently evokes the same pattern or hierarchy of physiological responses (sometimes referred to as 'stereotypy') among most subjects" (Roessler & Engel, 1977, p. 51). An example of such stimulus-response specificity is the inevitable increase in blood pressure that follows immersion of the hand in ice water.

A second type of specificity is called *individual response specificity.* Engel (1972) gives this example of the phenomenon: A group of hypertensive patients showed more blood pressure reactions to *all* stimuli than did patients with rheumatoid arthritis; the arthritic patients showed more reactions in muscles surrounding symptomatic joints. This type of specificity is also referred to as "symptom specificity." Both stimulus-response specificity and individual response specificity are involved in psychophysiological disorders, although it is obvious that individual response specificities are critical. To the extent that susceptibility to a particular disease may be related to the tendency to overreact in one given physiological modality related to that disease, then we can explain the adverse consequences of environmental pressure and stress for the development of specific disorders (Ader, 1977).

Miller and Dworkin (1977) have advanced a psychophysiological hypothesis about the reinforcement of increases in blood pressure in essential hypertension. Their theory is based on two pieces of psychophysiological evidence. First, vascular baroreceptor stimulation has an inhibitory effect on the reticular formation and therefore on cortical arousal. Second, baboons have shown large increases in blood pressure that were learned by instrumental conditioning. Taking these two facts together, Miller and Dworkin hypothesized:

in a situation in which a person is suffering from aversive stimulation, an increase in blood pressure will stimulate the carotid sinus and produce an inhibition of the reticular formation which, in turn, should decrease the strength of the aversiveness. Then this decrease in aversiveness should serve as a reward to reinforce the learning of the increase in blood pressure. (p. 139)

This hypothesis has not been tested, although it has the virtue of being testable, particularly in animals. The proponents of this hypothesis point out that other ingredients in the individual need to be considered in relation to the hypothesized process: unusual sensitivity to aversive stimulation, unusually strong inhibition of the reticular formation from a given increase in blood pressure, and unusual ability to learn increases in blood pressure. They believe that the vulnerability to this process would be increased to the degree that the environment has subjected the individual to levels of aversive stimulation that can be reduced via inhibition of the reticular formation but not by other means. Whether or not this particular hypothesis is confirmed, the thinking behind it is unique in that it embodies a multiplicity of interacting physiological and psychological properties, each of which is relevant. This model may stimulate further hypotheses about possible psychophysiological bases of other psychosomatic disorders.

Another example of a psychophysiologically based approach to psychosomatic disorders comes from activation theory. For example, there is evidence that the ANS is involved specifically in some patients with borderline essential hypertension, although it is unclear, as usual, whether the ANS activation is primary or secondary to the disease (Julius & Esler, 1975; Julius & Schork, 1971). Some abnormality of the ANS may predispose certain individuals who are otherwise susceptible to increases in blood pressure to develop hypertension on a chronic basis. Increased sympathetic nervous system activity has been thought to be implicated in other disorders as well. By delineating the role of physiological activation of this sort in particular subgroups of patients, it may be possible to fashion behavioral therapies directed toward decreasing sympathetic nervous system tone through such techniques as relaxation, biofeedback, or meditation.

UNRESOLVED METHODOLOGICAL PROBLEMS

It is quite common for a review of the psychophysiological literature on a particular topic to end with a statement such as the following: "Undoubtedly, much of the discrepancy among results from various laboratories lies in the fact that widely disparate measurement systems, stimulus paradigms, and subject samples have been used" (Bell, Mednick, Gottesman, & Sergeant, 1977, p. 218). Psychophysiological responses may be quite fragile; the difference between a "soft" and a "moderately loud" tone may be crucial in predicting electrodermal habituation rate (Katkin & McCubbin, 1969). In addition to simple problems created by variability in stimulus parameters, there are a number of other methodological problems specific to

psychophysiology. Some of these are described below.

Measurement Artifact

There are two varieties of measurement artifact: those that are specific to one response measure, for example, proper salt concentration in the electrode paste is crucial for electrodermal measurement, but irrelevant for the EKG; and those that may alter several responses simultaneously, for example, gross body movement, which will affect most response parameters. Dealing with both of these classes of artifact requires detailed understanding of the nature of the response being recorded, and familiarity with techniques. Although a number of handbooks and technical articles are available (we have referred to most of them at various points throughout this chapter), there is no substitute for long hours of hands-on experience. Proper technique for recording and reducing psychophysiological data requires a substantial artistic talent; practice may not make perfect, but it will surely sensitize the researcher to sources of artifact.

Among other sources of artifact are sex differences among experimenters, subjects, and experimenter-subject interactions. Bell, Christie, and Venables (1975) have noted that many experimental reports do not even mention the sex of the experimenter despite frequent reports of effects of this variable on electrodermal activity. Age and sex of subject present a more complex source of error; while many experimenters randomly assign males and females to treatment groups, disproportions among small experimental cells may substantially alter experimental results. With respect to female subjects, practically no researchers in psychophysiology control for menstrual cycle phase, despite observations of central and autonomic changes related to the cycle (Bell et al., 1975).

Oral contraceptives, caffeine, nicotine, and various forms of medication constitute other sources of potential measurement artifact. The most popular solution to these problems is random subject assignment and faith in the distribution of error variance. Clearly, more research is required to determine the specific effects of these variables, so that their contribution to the error variance can be subtracted.

Even ambient changes in the environment itself may have profound if unexpected systematic effects on responsiveness. Venables (1978) reported that when he used subjects from tropical climates in a European lab kept at 21 degrees C, the subjects showed an absence of "normal" electrodermal responsiveness; when he raised the temperature 10 degrees C they showed "normal" responsiveness.

Response Habituation and Long-Term Assessment. In psychophysiological research, the phenomenon of response habituation presents difficulties on two levels: physiological and psychological. On the physiological level, even an aversive stimulus such as an electric shock may elicit smaller responses after several trials. A related problem is the effect of previous responses on subsequent ones. The magnitude and recovery of electrodermal responses, for instance, is known to be affected by the frequency of prior responses (Bundy & Fitzgerald, 1975). At the psychological level, habituation is perhaps even more difficult to handle. Surwit, Shapiro, and Good (1978) have reported that blood pressure during "baseline" resting sessions is substantially lower than that measured by a physician. Thus failure to obtain true resting measurements prior to treatment may result in attribution of change to a particular treatment when psychological habituation to the laboratory or clinic is the real source of the change. Change scores obtained shortly before an anticipated stressor may actually attenuate observed group differences between fearful and nonfearful subjects, or reactive and nonreactive ones, since the anticipation

of the stress already may have increased "resting" autonomic response levels. Optimal conditions for obtaining a baseline measurement vary with the situation. For example, in research with insomniacs the "first night effect" (decreased REM sleep and increased time awake) is well-known. Scharf, Kales, and Bixler (1975) found that even for experienced laboratory sleepers, as little as a week of sleeping at home required another period of adapting to the sleep laboratory to eliminate the reinvoked "first night effect."

Individual Response Stereotypy and Patterning. Lacey (1956) and his co-workers (Lacey, Bateman, & Van Lehn, 1953; Lacey & Lacey, 1958) have defined an important methodological issue in psychophysiological research: individual response stereotypy. This refers to the tendency for subjects to show maximum responsivity to stimuli in only one particular response modality. One subject, for instance, might be a heart rate responder, and another a blood pressure reactor; another subject might show minimal reactivity in all cardiovascular modes but show maximum responsivity in the skin conductance channel. Lacey and Lacey (1958) reported that some individuals were inconsistent in their patterns of responding, but most showed a degree of consistency across stress situations that differed both in physiological and psychological demands. Individual response stereotypy makes it difficult to assess "the" psychophysiological response in clinical research. At the least, it suggests the need for recording multiple channels of ANS response data if one is interested in assessing the responsivity of a given individual.

Several solutions for comparing data from different autonomic responses have been proposed, including percent-change scores, standard scores, and range-corrected scores. Yet there does not appear to be one best way of treating all data. For example, Lykken (1972) found that his range correction technique was useful for skin conductance measures, but not for heart rate responses. More recently, Sersen, Clausen, and Lidsky (1978) have pointed out that the amount of stereotypy of autonomic responses depends in part upon the method chosen for standardization of scores and in part upon the stimuli used. Other investigators have suggested that pragmatic considerations such as reliability and validity should determine the method of response analysis for each new situation (Johnson & Lubin, 1972).

One may not always wish to minimize the effects of individual response stereotypy. For example, as we discussed earlier, individual response stereotypy may contribute to an understanding of why some individuals develop a particular psychosomatic disorder. Research on such individual difference characteristics, therefore, might choose to maximize the effects of individual response stereotypy. For example, Engel and Bickford (1961) found that essential hypertensives showed maximal blood pressure responses to several kinds of stress, whereas they did not show such responses in other autonomic channels.

A different approach to the problem of response patterning emphasizes the role of interindividual consistency in complex patterning of responses. For instance, Schwartz (1974) has described a series of studies in which reinforcement for a particular "natural" pattern of responses (decreases or increases in both heart rate and systolic blood pressure) was more effective than reinforcement for some other less "natural" pattern, for example, heart rate increase and blood pressure decrease. The implication of Schwartz's finding is that there may be some underlying integrated patterning of cardiovascular mechanisms that is constant across individuals.

Finally, mention must be made of the so-called "Law of Initial Values" described by Wilder (1950). According to this "law," a subject who has a high resting level of autonomic activity will show reduced response amplitude to stimulation. This "law" has been used in various arguments alternately to justify both negative and positive findings in psychophysiological research. It has considerable status as a methodological caveat, but its virtues are unclear. Depending on whose data are cited, there either is or is not evidence that the law is correct, and there is much reason to suspect that it is not generally applicable to all physiological response measures, but only to some (Venables & Christie, 1973). Further, to the extent that there is a statistical law of initial values, it remains unclear whether it is determined by homeostatic mechanisms, measurement artifact, or ceiling effects.

RESEARCH QUESTIONS OF CURRENT CONCERN

It is difficult for any individual to identify the few research issues that are of major concern in a field as diverse as clinical psychophysiology. A glance through a few current issues of journals such as *Psychophysiology, Psychosomatic Medicine,* or the *Journal of Behavioral Medicine* might provide some guidance about the issues that are currently taking up a great deal of time and energy. There are a few issues, however, that strike us as having substantial significance for clinical research, and in which there are already some promising empirical gains. These issues are described very briefly below, with the warning that any or all of them may soon be obsolete.

Is Biofeedback an Active Treatment Technique?

Few techniques of psychotherapeutic intervention have achieved as much simultaneous attention from both professional and lay communities as biofeedback; yet there are still no definitive studies that attest to its specific effectiveness. Shapiro and Surwit (1976) once concluded that "there is *not one* well controlled scientific study of the effectiveness of biofeedback and operant conditioning in treating a particular physiological disorder" (p. 113). Five years after they came to that conclusion, there is still little reason to disagree with it. Biofeedback is a promising therapeutic tool; many clinicians are routinely incorporating it into their practice, not only in psychology but in rehabilitation medicine and physical therapy. Yet there is little evidence of its specific effectiveness, and there is little understanding of the mechanism by which it works, if it works.

Psychophysiological research on these questions is particularly important, especially with respect to process. Even if it can be demonstrated that biofeedback has specific therapeutic value as compared to a control condition, the issue of placebo effects cannot be addressed without psychophysiological assessment. This point has been discussed by Katkin and Goldband (1979), who point out that a treatment is not classified as a placebo because its mechanism is not understood, but rather because its mechanism is well understood and there is no valid reason for it to work. There is some controversy about the presumed underlying mechanism of biofeedback. Some investigators (Shapiro & Surwit, 1976) maintain that biofeedback is a special form of operant conditioning; others (Lang, 1975) believe that biofeedback is akin to motor-skills learning. Either of these views leads to specific predictions about the effects of training on the regulation of bodily responses; experimental tests of these views will require psychophysiological methodology, since a clear understanding of the process requires data on the relationships among training procedures, physiological responses, and symptom reduction.

Early Identification of Candidates for Psychopathological Risk

Psychophysiological methods have been employed with increasing frequency to try to identify early signs of individual differences in responsivity that might be predictive of future pathological syndromes. Although there have been such research attempts in a broad variety of areas, the two that have received the most systematic attention are in schizophrenia and psychopathy.

Schizophrenia

Based upon Venables' (1975) pioneering research on electrodermal correlates of schizophrenia, and the reports of Mednick (1970) and Mednick and Schulsinger (1968) on prenatal and perinatal factors increasing risk for schizophrenia (presumably via selective anoxia adversely affecting limbic system structures) a large, cross-cultural, longitudinal study of children at risk for schizophrenia has been initiated on the island of Mauritius (see Venables, 1977). From an initial pool of 1800 three-year-old children, a final longitudinal sample of 200 has been selected. These children have all been screened on family history, health, obstetric history, behavioral observation of play and parent–child interaction, and finally, electrodermal and EEG patterns.

The children were placed in three categories of electrodermal responsiveness: a normal category, and both hyperresponsive and hyporesponsive categories, as defined earlier by Venables' research on adult schizophrenic populations. The 200 children were then subdivided, with half entering nursery schools and half remaining in the community. A follow-up study about three years later showed that the nursery school experience had little positive social effect upon hyper- and hyporesponsive children, but that it led to substantial improvement in constructive play among the normally responsive children, as compared to the nonnursery school control group. Furthermore, although the nursery school experience did not affect the "abnormal" responders as compared to controls, it was noted that hyperresponders showed considerably more constructive play than hyporesponders.

This very preliminary description of some of the research for this study is presented here to suggest that even in very young children the abnormal hyperresponsive-hyporesponsive dichotomy does appear to be a viable distinction. It is perhaps remarkable in this instance that children selected in a very brief psychophysiological testing procedure at the age of 3 showed distinctive patterns of behavior 3 years later as a result of their experience in the intervening period. It is also not unreasonable to suggest that the sorts of behavior shown are in accord with the patterns that might be expected to be associated with the psychophysiological types of behavior measured. (Venables, 1977, p. 44)

Psychopathy. Most studies of psychopathy are carried out on convicted criminals. Few researchers have addressed the problem of identifying potential psychopaths prior to lawbreaking. Any attempts to do so are likely to be faced with some serious confounding problems, for Kirkegaard-Sorensen and Mednick (1977a) have noted that the offspring of schizophrenics also demonstrate elevated risk for criminal activity. In fact, Kirkegaard-Sorensen and Mednick note, schizophrenic mothers themselves have a higher than normal crime rate. Thus research on predictors of risk for psychopathic criminal behavior must be careful to eliminate schizophrenics and potential schizophrenics from their sample. With this in mind, Loeb and Mednick (1977) examined 104 teen-age children of nonschizophrenic families, who had no history of criminal offenses. A psychophysiological examination was administered, and an eight-year follow-up study was conducted to determine if the electrodermal signs present in known psychopaths (low conductance, nonresponsiveness, and slow response recovery time) would be predictive of criminal behavior. After eight years, seven of the original sample had been convicted of at least two legal offenses. These seven were then matched for sex, age, and social class with another sample of the original population who had not committed offenses; the electrodermal data obtained eight years ear-

lier discriminated the two groups. Most importantly, the offender group had shown the typical pattern of electrodermal activity associated with adult known psychopaths.

According to Loeb and Mednick (1977) these results show that psychophysiological differences antedate criminal behavior, and thus cannot be attributed to the consequences of the behavior, such as imprisonment. Nevertheless, it is important to treat these findings with some tentativeness until they can be replicated or at least demonstrated in a larger sample. A number of interpretive problems are raised by this study. It would be most important to try to obtain psychophysiological data from children at a much earlier age, for by the time teen-age years arrive, the subjects have been socialized to a large extent. Kirkegaard-Sorensen and Mednick (1977b) themselves have pointed out that the subjects in Loeb and Mednick's study who became criminals already had shown some school behavior difficulties before the original testing.

Heritability of Psychophysiological Responsivity

The question of genetic transmission of psychophysiological response tendencies is in some respects related to the research on high-risk groups. As discussed above, some theories of psychopathy presume that ANS deficits characterize psychopaths and cause their inability to show anticipatory anxiety. Inheritance of such ANS patterns would increase the likelihood of familial trends in psychopathy; however, it is not a prerequisite, since common environments might also account for the familial patterns. More likely, one would expect some genetic-environmental interaction for which psychophysiological reactivity might contribute to etiology in a high-risk population. A complete description of current research on heritability of autonomic responses would require a chapter of its own; we will only note some of the trends.

With the importance that electrodermal

activity plays in theories about genetic contributions to psychopathy and to schizophrenia, it is not surprising that some attention has been paid to the problem of determining the genetic component of individual differences in electrodermal responding. Bell, Mednick, Gottesman, and Sergeant (1977) have shown higher correlations for monozygotic than dizygotic twins on electrodermal recovery rate, although their findings were limited only to responses from the left hand. The laterality interaction is as yet baffling. Zahn (1977) has presented evidence from 68 pairs of twins for greater monozygotic than dizygotic correlations on five different indexes of electrodermal responsivity.

Animal studies have implicated genetic factors in psychophysiological parameters such as blood pressure response to dietary salt (Dahl, 1977) and catecholamine synthesis (Barchas, Ciaranello, Kessler, & Hamburg, 1975). Of course the interaction of genetic variables and environmental factors in human populations may not be accurately estimated by animal research; such work represents possibilities rather than definite conclusions about mechanisms. Even in human research, some methods of estimating genetic factors have come under sharp criticism recently (Elston & Boklage, 1978; Kamin, 1975). It is clear that different methods of genetic estimation, dependent upon a variety of both reasonable and unreasonable assumptions, may arrive at quite varied estimates of heritability. For example, Miall and Oldham (1963) measured systolic blood pressure in first degree relatives of hypertensives and estimated 20 to 30% of the variance to be genetically determined. Using the same data, but a different method of analysis and assumptions, Cavalli-Sforza and Bodmer (1971) found 84% of the variance to be accounted for by genetic factors.

In addition to questions raised about particular methods for assessing genetic components of psychophysiological responding, one must also estimate the expression of a given trait. In constructing pedigrees of dom-

inant traits, it occasionally occurs that a person who must have had a particular genotype does not manifest the phenotype, or does so only to a limited extent (incomplete penetrance). In psychophysiological research this is a particular problem because a "trait" may appear only under a limited set of conditions. For example, Falkner, Onesti, Angelakos, Fernandes, and Langman (1979) found that under the stress of a mental arithmetic task offspring of hypertensive parents showed higher blood pressure and pulse rate than offspring of normotensives; however, during rest, there were minimal differences between the groups. Psychophysiological phenotypes may change over the course of development as well. Hennekens, Jesse, Klein, Gourley, and Blumenthal (1976) found some degree of familial concordance for blood pressure as early as one month of age, but not among neonates. Clarification of the parameters that elicit distinctive psychophysiological changes in individuals may aid in the identification of high-risk groups and in the elucidation of etiological processes.

SUMMING UP

Our summary is brief. Psychophysiological methods have been employed in clinical research, and more recently in clinical practice, with mixed results. We *know* that the future will be marked by enormous technological changes and therefore by opportunities to conduct research on problems that are currently unapproachable. We *believe* that psychophysiological methods have a unique contribution to make to the understanding of clinical phenomena. We *hope* that the level of conceptualization in the field will improve even at a fraction of the pace that the technical developments unfold, for in the final analysis, no method is any better than the clarity of the theory under investigation. The future of clinical psychophysiology rests on the ability of researchers to move from the demonstration of correlations among behavioral and psychophysiological variables to the demonstration of causal chains in which behavioral, phenomenological, and psychophysiological variables affect each other.

REFERENCES

Abel, G. G., & Blanchard, E. B. (1976). The measurement and generation of sexual arousal in male sexual deviates. In M. Hersen, R. M. Eisler, & P. M. Miller (Eds.), *Progress in behavior modification*. New York: Academic Press.

Ader, R. (1977). The role of developmental factors in susceptibility to disease. In Z. J. Lipowski, D. R. Lipsitt, & P. C. Whybrow (Eds.), *Psychosomatic medicine: Current trends and clinical applications*. New York: Oxford University Press.

Andersen, P., & Andersson, S. A. (1968). *Physiological basis of the alpha rhythm*. New York: Appleton-Century-Crofts.

Bagshaw, M. H., & Benzies, S., (1968). Multiple measures of the orienting reaction and their association after amygdalectomy in monkeys. *Experimental Neurology, 20,* 175–187.

Bagshaw, M. H., Kimble, D. P., & Pribram, K. H. (1965). The GSR of monkeys during orienting and habituation and after ablation of the amygdala, hippocampus, and inferotemporal cortex. *Neuropsychologia, 3,* 111–119.

Barchas, J. D., Ciaranello, R. D. Kessler, S., & Hamburg, D. A. (1975). Genetic aspects of catecholamine synthesis. In R. R. Fieve, D. Rosenthal, & H. Brill (Eds.), *Genetic research in psychiatry*. Baltimore: Johns Hopkins University Press, pp. 27–62.

Barlow, D. H., Agras, W. S., Leitenberg, H., & Wincze, J. P. (1970). An experimental analysis of the effectiveness of "shaping" in reducing maladaptive avoidance behavior: An analogue study. *Behaviour Research and Therapy, 8,* 165–173.

Basmajian, J. V. (1978). *Muscles alive: Their functions revealed by electromyography*. Baltimore: Williams & Wilkins.

Bell, B., Christie, M. J., & Venables, P. H. (1975). Psychophysiology of the menstrual cycle. In P. H. Venables & M. J. Christie (Eds.), *Research in psychophysiology*. New York: Wiley, pp. 183–207.

Bell, B., Mednick, S. A., Gottesman, I. I., & Sergeant, J. (1977). Electrodermal parameters in male twins. In S. A. Mednick and K. O. Christiansen (Eds.), *Biosocial bases of criminal behavior*. New York: Gardner Press, pp. 217–225.

Bell, I. R., & Schwartz, G. E. (1975). Voluntary control and reactivity of human heart rate. *Psychophysiology, 12,* 339–348.

Berger, H. (1929). Über das elektrenkephalogramm des menschen. *Archiv für Psychiatrie und Nervenkrankheiten, 87,* 527–570.

Berne, R. M., & Levy, M. N. (1977). *Cardiovascular physiology*. St. Louis: C. V. Mosby.

Bernstein, A. S. (1964). The galvanic skin response orienting reflex in chronic schizophrenics. *Psychonomic Science, 1,* 391–392.

Bernstein, A. S. The phasic electrodermal orienting response in chronic schizophrenics. II: Response to auditory signals of varying intensity. *Journal of Abnormal Psychology, 75,* 146–156.

Blanchard, E. B., & Epstein, L. H. (1978). *A biofeedback primer*. Reading, Mass.: Addison-Wesley.

Brudny, J., Korein, J., Grynbaum, B. B., Friedmann, L. W., Weinstein, S., Sachs-Frankel, G., & Belandres, P. V. (1976). EMG feedback therapy: Review of treatment of 114 patients. *Archives of Physical Medicine and Rehabilitation, 57,* 55–61.

Buchsbaum, M. S. (1977). The middle evoked response components and schizophrenia. *Schizophrenia Bulletin, 3,* 93–104.

Bundy, R., & Fitzgerald, H. (1975). Stimulus specificity of electrodermal recovery time: An examination and reinterpretation of the evidence. *Psychophysiology, 12,* 406–411.

Callaway, E. (1975). *Brain electrical potentials and individual differences*. New York: Grune & Stratton.

Cavalli-Sforza, L. L., and Bodmer, W. F. (1971). *The genetics of human populations*. San Francisco: W. H. Freeman.

Cook, M. R. (1974). Psychophysiology of peripheral vascular change. In P. A. Obrist, A. H. Black, J. Brener, & L. V. DiCara (Eds.), *Cardiovascular psychophysiology*. Chicago: Aldine Press.

Crider, A., & Lunn, R. (1971). Electrodermal lability as a personality dimension. *Journal of Experimental Research in Personality, 2,* 145–150.

Crider, A., Schwartz, G. E., & Shnidman, S. (1969). On the criteria for instrumental autonomic conditioning: A reply to Katkin and Murray. *Psychological Bulletin, 71,* 455–461.

Dahl, L. K. (1977). Salt intake and hypertension. In J. Genest, E. Koiw, & O. Kuchel (Eds.) *Hypertension: Physiopathology and treatment*. New York: McGraw-Hill.

Davis, C. M., Brickett, P., Stern, R. M., & Kimball, W. H. (1978). Tension in the two frontales: Electrode placement and artifact in the recording of forehead EMG. *Psychophysiology, 15,* 591–593.

Diefendorf, A. R., & Dodge, R. (1908). An experimental study of the ocular reactions of the insane from photographic records, *Brain,* **31,** 451–489.

Douglas, R. J. (1967). The hippocampus and behavior. *Psychological Bulletin,* **67,** 416–442.

Douglas, R. J., & Pribram, K. H. (1966). Learning and limbic lesions. *Neuropsychologia,* **4,** 197–220.

Duffy, E. (1962). *Activation and behavior.* New York: Wiley.

Edelberg, R. (1972). Electrical activity of the skin: Its measurement and uses in psychophysiology. In N. S. Greenfield and R. A. Sternbach (Eds.), *Handbook of psychophysiology.* Holt, Rinehart & Winston.

Elston, R. C., & Boklage, C. E. (1978). An examination of fundamental assumptions of the twin method. In W. E. Nance, G. Allen, & P. Parisi (Eds.), *Twin research: Psychology and methodology.* New York: Alan R. Liss, pp. 189–199.

Engel, B. T. (1972). Response specificity. In N. S. Greenfield and R. Sternbach (Eds.), *Handbook of psychophysiology.* New York: Holt, Rinehart & Winston.

Engel, B. T., & Bickford, A. F. (1961). Response specificity: Stimulus-response and individual response specificity in essential hypertensives. *Archives of General Psychiatry,* **5,** 478–489.

Falkner, B., Onesti, G., Angelakos, E. T., Fernandes, M., & Langman, C. (1979). Cardiovascular response to mental stress in normal adolescents with hypertensive parents. *Hypertension,* **1,** 23–30.

Fenz, W. D., and Epstein, S. (1967). Ratings of physiological arousal in parachutists as a function of an approaching jump. *Psychosomatic Medicine,* **29,** 33–51.

Féré, C. (1888). Note sur des modifications de la résistance électrique sous l'influence des excitations sensorielles et des émotions. *Comptes Rendus des Séances de la Société de Biologie,* **5,** 217–219.

Fowles, D. C. (1973). Mechanisms of electrodermal activity. In R. F. Thompson & M. M. Patterson (Eds.), *Methods in physiological psychology.* New York: Academic Press.

Fowles, D. C. (Ed.) (1975). *Clinical applications of psychophysiology.* New York: Columbia University Press.

Fowles, D. C., Christie, M. J., Edelberg, R., Grings, W. W., Lykken, D. T., & Venables, P. H. (1981). Publication recommendations for electrodermal measurements. *Psychophysiology,* **18,** 232–239.

Freides, R. (1966). The histochemical architecture of Ammon's Horn as related to its selective vulnerability. *Acta Neuropathologica,* **6,** 1–13.

Fridlund, A. J., Fowler, S. C., & Pritchard, D. A. (1980). Striate muscle tensional patterning in frontalis EMG biofeedback. *Psychophysiology,* **17,** 47–55.

Friedman, R., & Iwai, J. (1976). Genetic predisposition and stress-induced hypertension. *Science,* **193,** 161–162.

Gatchel, R. J., Korman, M., Weis, C. B., Smith, D., & Clarke, L. (1978). A multiple-response evaluation of EMG biofeedback performance during training and stress-induction conditions. *Psychophysiology,* **15,** 253–258.

Geddes, L. A. (1970). *The direct and indirect measurement of blood pressure.* Chicago: Year Book Medical Publishers.

Geddes, L. A., & Baker, L. E. (1975). *Principles of applied biomedical instrumentation.* New York: Wiley.

Geer, J. H. (1966). Fear and autonomic arousal. *Journal of Abnormal Psychology,* **71,** 253–255.

Geer, J. H. (1975). Direct measurement of genital responding. *American Psychologist,* **30,** 415–418.

Goldstein, I. B. (1972). Electromyography. In N. S. Greenfield & R. A. Sternbach (Eds.), *Handbook of psychophysiology.* New York: Holt, Rinehart & Winston.

Graham, F. K., & Clifton, R. K. (1966). Heart rate change as a component of the orienting response. *Psychological Bulletin,* **65,** 305–320.

Guyton, A. C. (1979). *Physiology of the human body.* Philadelphia: W. B. Saunders.

Hare, R. D. (1965). Temporal gradient of fear arousal in psychopaths. *Journal of Abnormal Psychology,* **70,** 442–445.

Hare, R. D. (1968). Psychopathy, autonomic functioning and orienting response. *Journal of Abnormal Psychology. Monograph Supplement,* **73,** 1–24.

Hare, R. D. (1972). Psychopathy and physiological responses to adrenalin. *Journal of Abnormal Psychology,* **79,** 138–147.

Hare, R. D. (1975). Psychophysiological studies of psychopathy. In D. C. Fowles (Ed.), *Clinical applications of psychophysiology.* New York: Columbia University Press.

Hare, R. D. (1978). Electrodermal and cardiovascular correlates of psychopathy. In R. D. Hare & D. Schalling (Eds.), *Psychopathic behaviour: Approaches to research.* New York: Wiley.

Hare, R. D., & Cox, D. N. (1978). Psychophysiological research on psychopathy. In W. H. Reid (Ed.), *The psychopath: A comprehensive study of antisocial disorders and behavior.* New York: Brunner/Mazel.

Hare, R. D., & Craigen, D. (1974). Psychopathy and physiological activity in a mixed motive game situation. *Psychophysiology,* **11,** 197–206.

Hare, R. D., & Quinn, M. J. (1971). Psychopathy and autonomic conditioning. *Journal of Abnormal Psychology, 77,* 223–235.

Harris, A. H., & Brady, J. V. (1977). Long term studies of cardiovascular control in primates. In G. E. Schwartz & J. Beatty (Eds.), *Biofeedback: Theory & research,* New York: Academic Press.

Harris, A. H., Findley, J. D., & Brady, J. V. (1971). Instrumental conditioning of blood pressure elevations in the baboon. *Conditional Reflex, 6,* 215–226.

Harris, A. H., Goldstein, D. S., & Brady, J. V. (1977). Visceral learning: Cardiovascular conditioning in primates. In J. Beatty & H. Legewie (Eds.), *Biofeedback and behavior.* New York: Plenum.

Hassett, J. (1978). *A Primer of psychophysiology.* San Francisco: W. H. Freeman.

Hennekens, C. H., Jesse, M. J., Klein, B. E., Gourley, J. E., & Blumenthal, S. (1976). Aggregation of blood pressure in infants and their siblings. *American Journal of Epidemiology, 103,* 457–463.

Heslegrave, R. D., Ogilvie, J. C., & Furedy, J. J. (1979). Measuring baseline-treatment differences in heart rate variability: Variance versus successive difference mean square and beats per minute versus interbeat interval. *Psychophysiology, 16,* 151–157.

Holzman, P. S., Kringlen, E., Levy, D. L., Proctor, L. R., Haberman, S. J., & Yasillo, N. J. (1977). Abnormal pursuit eye movements in schizophrenia: Evidence for a genetic indicator. *Archives of General Psychiatry, 34,* 802–805.

Holzman, P. S., & Levy, D. L. (1977). Smooth pursuit eye movements and functional psychosis: A review. *Schizophrenia Bulletin, 3,* 15–27.

Holzman, P. S., Proctor, L. R., & Hughes, D. W. (1973). Eye tracking patterns in schizophrenia. *Science, 181,* 179–181.

Holzman, P. S., Proctor, L. R., Levy, D. L., Yasillo, N. J., Meltzer, H. Y., & Hurt, S. W. (1974). Eye tracking dysfunctions in schizophrenic patients and their relatives. *Archives of General Psychiatry, 31,* 143–151.

Hoon, B. W., Wincze, J. P., & Hoon, E. F. (1976). Physiological assessment of sexual arousal in women. *Psychophysiology, 13,* 196–204.

Hull, C. L. (1943). *Principles of behavior.* New York: Appleton-Century-Crofts.

Iacono, W. G., & Lykken, D. T. (1979a). Electrooculographic recording and scoring of smooth pursuit and saccadic eye tracking: A parametric study using monozygotic twins. *Psychophysiology, 16,* 94–107.

Iacono, W. G., & Lykken, D. T. (1979b). Comments on "smooth pursuit eye movements: A comparison of two measurement techniques", by Lindsey,

Holzman, Haberman, and Yasillo. *Journal of Abnormal Psychology, 88,* 678–680.

Itil, T. M. (1977). Qualitative and quantitative EEG findings in schizophrenia. *Schizophrenia Bulletin, 3,* 61–79.

Jacobson, E. (1938). *Progressive relaxation.* Chicago: University of Chicago Press.

Jasper, H. H. (1958). Report of committee on methods of clinical examination in EEG: Appendix: The ten-twenty electrode system of the international federation. *Electroencephalography and Clinical Neurophysiology, 10,* 371–375.

Johnson, L. C., & Lubin, A. (1972). On planning psychophysiological experiments: Design, measurement and analysis. In N. S. Greenfield & R. A. Sternbach (Eds.), *Handbook of psychophysiology.* New York: Holt, Rinehart & Winston, pp. 125–158.

Julius, S., & Esler, M. (1975). Autonomic nervous cardiovascular regulation in borderline hypertension. *American Journal of Cardiology, 36,* 685–696.

Julius, S., & Schork, M. A. (1971). Borderline hypertension—a critical review. *Journal of Chronic Diseases, 23,* 723–754.

Kamin, L. J. (1975). *The science and politics of IQ.* New York: Wiley.

Kamiya, J. (1969). Operant control of the EEG alpha rhythm and some of its reported effects on consciousness. In C. Tart (Ed.), *Altered states of consciousness.* New York: Wiley.

Kannel, W. B., & Sorlie, P. (1975). Hypertension in Framingham. In O. Paul (Ed.), *Epidemiology and control of hypertension.* New York: Stratton Intercontinental Medical Book Corporation.

Katkin, E. S. (1965). Relationship between manifest anxiety and two indices of autonomic response to stress. *Journal of Personality and Social Psychology, 2,* 324–333.

Katkin, E. S. (1966). The relationship between a measure of transitory anxiety and spontaneous autonomic activity. *Journal of Abnormal Psychology, 71,* 142–146.

Katkin, E. S. (1975). Electrodermal lability: A psychophysiological analysis of individual differences in response to stress. In I. G. Sarason & C. D. Spielberger (Eds.), *Stress and anxiety,* Vol. 2. Washington, D.C.: Hemisphere Publishing Co.

Katkin, E. S., & Deitz, S. R. (1973). Systematic desensitization. In W. F. Prokasy & D. C. Raskin (Eds.), *Electrodermal activity in psychological research.* New York: Academic Press.

Katkin, E. S., Fitzgerald, C. R., & Shapiro, D. (1978). Clinical applications of biofeedback: Current status and future prospects. In H. L. Pick, H. W. Leibowitz, J. E. Singer, A. Steinschneider, & H. W.

Stevenson (Eds.), *Psychology: From research to practice*. New York: Plenum Press.

Katkin, E. S., and Goldband, S. (1979). The placebo effect and biofeedback. In R. Gatchel & K. Price (Eds.), *Clinical applications of biofeedback: Appraisal and status*. New York: Pergamon Press.

Katkin, E. S., & McCubbin, R. J. (1969). Habituation of the orienting response as a function of individual differences in anxiety and autonomic lability. *Journal of Abnormal Psychology,* **74,** 54–60.

Katkin, E. S., & Murray, E. N. (1968). Instrumental conditioning of autonomically mediated behavior: Theoretical and methodological issues. *Psychological Bulletin,* **70,** 52–68.

Katkin, E. S., Murray, E. N., & Lachman, R. (1969). Concerning instrumental autonomic conditioning: A rejoinder. *Psychological Bulletin,* **71,** 462–466.

Kimble, D. P. (1968). Hippocampus and internal inhibition. *Psychological Bulletin,* **70,** 285–295.

Kirkegaard-Sorensen, L., & Mednick, S. A. (1977a). A prospective study of predictors of criminality: A description of registered criminality in the high-risk and low-risk families. In S. A. Mednick & K. O. Christiansen (Eds.), *Biological bases of criminal behavior*. New York: Gardner Press.

Kirkegaard-Sorensen, L., & Mednick, S. A. (1977b). A prospective study of predictors of criminality: 4. School behavior. In S. A. Mednick & K. O. Christiansen (Eds.), *Biological bases of criminal behavior*. New York: Gardner Press.

Lacey, B. C., & Lacey, J. I. (1974). Studies of heart rate and other bodily processes in sensorimotor behavior. In P. Obrist, A. Black, J. Brener, & L. V. DiCara (Eds.), *Cardiovascular psychophysiology*. Chicago: Aldine.

Lacey, J. I. (1956). The evaluation of autonomic responses: Toward a general solution. *Annals of the New York Academy of Sciences,* **67,** 123–164.

Lacey, J. I. (1959). Psychophysiological approaches to the evaluation of psychotherapeutic process and outcome. In E. A. Rubenstein & M. B. Parloff (Eds.), *Research in psychotherapy*. Washington, D.C.: American Psychological Association.

Lacey, J. I., Bateman, D. E., & VanLehn, R. (1953). Autonomic response specificity: An experimental study. *Psychosomatic Medicine,* **15,** 8–21.

Lacey, J. I., & Lacey, B. C. (1958). Verification and extension of the principle of autonomic response stereotypy. *American Journal of Psychology,* **71,** 50–73.

Lang, P. J. (1968). Fear reduction and fear behavior: Problems in treating a construct. In J. M. Schlien (Ed.), *Research in psychotherapy*, Vol. III. Washington, D.C.: American Psychological Association.

Lang, P. J. (1969). The mechanics of desensitization and laboratory studies of human fear. In C. M. Franks (Ed.), *Assessment and status of the behavioral therapies and associated developments*. New York: McGraw-Hill.

Lang, P. J. (1975). Acquisition of heart rate control: Method, theory, and clinical implications. In D. C. Fowles (Ed.), *Clinical applications of psychophysiology*. New York: Columbia University Press.

Lang, P. J., & Buss, A. (1965). Psychological deficit in schizophrenia. II. Interference and activation. *Journal of Abnormal Psychology,* **70,** 77–106.

Lang, P. J., Melamed, B. G., & Hart, J. (1970). A psychophysiological analysis of fear modification using an automated desensitization procedure. *Journal of Abnormal Psychology,* **76,** 220–234.

Lazarus, R. S. (1966). *Psychological stress and coping process*. New York: McGraw-Hill.

Lindsey, D. T., Holzman, P. S., Haberman, S., & Yasillo, N. J. (1978). Smooth pursuit eye movements: A comparison of two measurement techniques for studying schizophrenia. *Journal of Abnormal Psychology,* **87,** 491–496.

Loeb, J., & Mednick, S. A. (1977). A prospective study of predictors of criminality: 3. Electrodermal response patterns. In S. A. Mednick & K. O. Christiansen (Eds.), *Biological bases of criminal behavior*. New York: Gardner Press.

Lykken, D. T. (1972). Range correction applied to heart rate and GSR data. *Psychophysiology,* **9,** 373–379.

Lykken, D. T. (1975). Psychometric applications of the EEG. In D. C. Fowles (Ed.), *Clinical applications of psychophysiology*. New York: Columbia University Press.

Lykken, D. T., Tellegen, A., & Thorkelson, K. (1974). Genetic determination of EEG frequency spectra. *Biological Psychology,* **1,** 245–259.

Lykken, D. T., & Venables, P. H. (1971). Direct measurement of skin conductance: A proposal for standardization. *Psychophysiology,* **8,** 656–672.

Malmo, R. B. (1958). Measurement of drive. In M. R. Jones (Ed.), *Nebraska symposium on motivation*. Lincoln: University of Nebraska Press.

Malmo, R. B. (1959). Activation: A neuropsychological dimension. *Psychological Review,* **66,** 367–386.

Margerison, J. H., St. John-Loe, P., & Binnie, C. D. (1967). Electroencephalography. In P. H. Venables & I. Martin (Eds.). *A manual of psychophysiological methods*. New York: Wiley.

Mathews, A. M. (1971). Psychophysiological approaches to the investigation of desensitization and related procedures. *Psychological Bulletin,* **76,** 73–91.

McGhie, A., & Chapman, J. S. (1961). Disorders of attention and perception in early schizophrenia.

British Journal of Medical Psychology, **34,** 103–116.

Mednick, S. A. (1970). Breakdown in individuals at high risk for schizophrenia: Possible predispositional perinatal factors. *Mental Hygiene,* **54,** 50–63.

Mednick, S. A. (1977). A biological theory of the learning of law-abiding behavior. In S. A. Mednick & K. O. Christiansen (Eds.), *Biosocial bases of criminal behavior.* New York: Gardner Press.

Mednick, S. A., & Hutchings, B. (1978). Genetic and psychophysiological factors in asocial behavior. In R. D. Hare & D. Schalling (Eds.), *Psychopathic behaviour: Approaches to research.* New York: Wiley.

Mednick, S. A., & Schulsinger, F. (1968). Some premorbid characteristics related to breakdown in children with schizophrenic mothers. In D. Rosenthal & S. Kety (Eds.), *Transmission of Schizophrenia.* London: Pergamon.

Miall, W. E., & Oldham, P. D. (1963). The hereditary factor in arterial blood pressure. *British Medical Journal,* **1,** 75–80.

Miller, N. E. (1969). Learning of visceral and glandular responses. *Science,* **163,** 434–445.

Miller, N. E. (1975). Clinical applications of biofeedback: Voluntary control of heartrate, rhythm, blood pressure. In H. I. Russek (Ed.), *New horizons in cardiovascular practice.* Baltimore: University Park Press.

Miller, N. E., & Dworkin, B. R. (1977). Clinical issues in therapeutic applications of biofeedback. In G. E. Schwartz & J. Beatty (Eds.), *Biofeedback: Theory and research.* New York: Academic Press.

Montagu, J. D., & Coles, E. M. (1966). Mechanism and measurement of the galvanic skin response. *Psychological Bulletin,* **65,** 261–279.

Obrist, P. A. (1976). The cardiovascular-behavioral interaction—As it appears today. *Psychophysiology,* **13,** 95–107.

Obrist, P. A., Langer, A. W., Grignolo, A., Sutterer, J. R., Light, K. C., & McCubbin, J. A. (1979). Blood pressure control mechanisms and stress: Implications for the etiology of hypertension. In G. Onesti & C. R. Klimt (Eds.), *Hypertension: Determinants, complications, and interventions.* New York: Grune & Stratton.

Obrist, P. A., Light, K. C., McCubbin, J. A., Hutcheson, J. S., & Hoffer, J. L. (1979). Pulse transit time: Relationship to blood pressure and myocardial performance. *Psychophysiology,* **16,** 292–301.

Obrist, P. A., Webb, R. A. Sutterer, J. R., & Howard, J. L. (1970). Cardiac deceleration and reaction time. An evaluation of two hypotheses. *Psychophysiology,* **6,** 695–706.

Patterson, T. T., & Venables, P. H. (1978). Bilateral skin conductance and skin potential in schizophrenic and normal subjects: The identification of the fast habituator group of schizophrenics. *Psychophysiology,* **15,** 556–560.

Plotkin, W. B. (1976). On the self regulation of the occipital alpha rhythm: Control strategies, states of consciousness, and the role of physiological feedback. *Journal of Experimental Psychology: General,* **105,** 66–99.

Plotkin, W. B. (1980). The role of attributions of responsibility in the facilitation of unusual experiential states during alpha training: An analysis of the biofeedback placebo effect. *Journal of Abnormal Psychology,* **89,** 67–78.

Plotkin, W. B., & Cohen, R. (1976). Occipital alpha and the attributes of the "alpha experience." *Psychophysiology,* **13,** 16–21.

Prokasy, W. F., & Raskin, D. C. (Eds.) (1973). *Electrodermal activity in psychological research.* New York: Academic Press.

Rappaport, H., & Katkin, E. S. (1972). Relationships among manifest anxiety, response to stress, and the perception of autonomic activity. *Journal of Consulting and Clinical Psychology,* **38,** 219–224.

Roessler, R., & Engel, B. T. (1977). The current status of the concepts of physiological response specificity and activation. In Z. P. Lipowski, D. R. Lipsitt, & P. C. Whybrow (Eds.), *Psychosomatic medicine: Current trends and clinical applications.* New York: Oxford University Press.

Roth, W. T. (1977). Late event-related potentials and psychopathology. *Schizophrenia Bulletin,* **3,** 105–120.

Rushmer, R. F. (1976). *Cardiovascular dynamics.* Philadelphia: W. B. Saunders.

Scharf, M. B., Kales, A., & Bixler, E. O. (1975). Readaptation to the sleep laboratory in insomniac subjects. *Psychophysiology,* **12,** 412–415.

Schwartz, G. E. (1974). Toward a theory of voluntary control of response patterns in the cardiovascular system. In P. A. Obrist, A. H. Black, J. Brener, & L. V. DiCara, *Cardiovascular psychophysiology.* Chicago: Aldine.

Schwartz, G. E., Brown, S. L., & Ahern, G. L. (1980). Facial muscle patterning and subjective experience during affective imagery: Sex differences. *Psychophysiology,* **17,** 75–82.

Schwartz, G. E., Fair, P. L., Salt, P., Mandel, M. R., & Klerman, G. L. (1976). Facial muscle patterning to affective imagery in depressed and nondepressed subjects. *Science,* **192,** 489–491.

Sersen, E. A., Clausen, J., & Lidsky, A. (1978). Autonomic specificity and stereotypy revisited. *Psychophysiology,* **15,** 60–67.

Shagass, C. (1972). Electrical activity of the brain. In N. S. Greenfield & R. A. Sternbach (Eds.), *Handbook of psychophysiology*. New York: Holt, Rinehart & Winston.

Shagass, C. (1977). Early evoked potentials. *Schizophrenia Bulletin*, **3**, 80–92.

Shapiro, A. P. (1961). An experimental study of comparative responses of blood pressure to different noxious stimuli. *Journal of Chronic Diseases*, **13**, 293–311.

Shapiro, D., & Katkin, E. S. (1980). Psychophysiological disorders. In A. S. Bellack & M. Hersen (Eds.), *New perspectives in abnormal psychology*. New York: Oxford University Press.

Shapiro, D., & Surwit, R. S. (1976). Learned control of physiological function and disease. In H. Leitenberg (Ed.), *Handbook of behavior modification and behavior therapy*. Englewood Cliffs, N.J.: Prentice-Hall.

Siddle, D. A. T., & Trasler, G. B. (in press). The psychophysiology of psychopathic behaviour. In M. J. Christie & D. G. Mellett (Eds.), *Psychosomatic approaches to medicine*, Vol. 1. *Behavioural Science Foundations*. London: Wiley.

Sintchak, G., & Geer, J. H. (1975). A vaginal plethysmograph system. *Psychophysiology*, **12**, 113–115.

Skinner, B. F. (1938). *The behavior of organisms: An experimental analysis*. New York: Appleton Century.

Sokolov, E. N. (1963). *Perception and the conditioned reflex*. New York: Macmillan.

Spector, R. T. (1965). Enzyme chemistry of anoxic brain injury. In C. W. N. Adams (Ed.), *Neurohistochemistry*. New York: Elsevier.

Spielberger, C. D. (Ed.) (1966). *Anxiety and behavior*. New York: Academic Press.

Spohn, H. E., & Patterson, T. (1979). Recent studies of psychophysiology in schizophrenia. *Schizophrenia Bulletin*, **5**, 581–611.

Spziler, J. A., & Epstein, S. (1976). Availability of an avoidance response as related to autonomic arousal. *Journal of Abnormal Psychology*, **85**, 73–82.

Steptoe, A., Smulyan, H., & Gribbin, B. (1976). Pulse wave velocity and blood pressure change: Calibration and applications. *Psychophysiology*, **13**, 488–493.

Stern, J. A. (1964). Toward a definition of psychophysiology. *Psychophysiology*, **1**, 90–91.

Stoyva, J. M. (1979). Musculoskeletal and stress-related disorders. In O. F. Pomerleau & J. P. Brady (Eds.), *Behavioral medicine: Theory and practice*. Baltimore: Williams & Wilkins.

Surwit, R. S., Shapiro, D., & Good, M. I. (1978).

Comparison of cardiovascular biofeedback, neuromuscular biofeedback, and meditation in the treatment of borderline essential hypertension. *Journal of Consulting and Clinical Psychology*, **46**, 252–263.

Syndulko, K. (1978). Electrocortical investigations of sociopathy. In R. D. Hare & D. Schalling (Eds.), *Psychopathic behaviour: Approaches to research*. New York: Wiley.

Tarchanoff, J. (1890). Über die galvanischen Erscheinungen an der Haut des Menschen bei reizung der Sinnesorgane und bei verschiedenen Formen der psychischen Tatigkeit. *Pflüger's Archiv Psycholischen*, **46**, 46–55.

Tecce, J. J. (1972). Contingent negative variation (CNV) and psychological processes in man. *Psychological Bulletin*, **77**, 73–108.

Thompson, R. F., & Patterson, M. M. (Eds.) (1974). *Bioelectric recording techniques* (Parts B & C). New York: Academic Press.

Tursky, B., Shapiro, D., & Schwartz, G. E. (1972). Automated constant cuff pressure system to measure average systolic and diastolic pressure in man. *IEEE Transactions on Biomedical Engineering*, **19**, 271–275.

Venables, P. H. (1975). A psychophysiological approach to research in schizophrenia. In D. C. Fowles (Ed.), *Clinical applications of psychophysiology*. New York: Columbia University Press.

Venables, P. H. (1977). The electrodermal psychophysiology of schizophrenics and children at risk for schizophrenia: Current controversies and developments. *Schizophrenia Bulletin*, **3**, 23–48.

Venables, P. H. (1978). Psychophysiology and psychometrics. *Psychophysiology*, **15**, 302–315.

Venables, P. H., & Christie, M. J. (1973). Mechanisms, instrumentation, recording techniques, and quantification of responses. In W. F. Prokasy & D. C. Raskin (Eds.), *Electrodermal activity in psychological research*. New York: Academic Press.

Widom, C. S. (1977). A methodology for studying noninstitutionalized psychopaths. *Journal of Consulting and Clinical Psychology*, **45**, 674–683.

Wilder, J. (1950). The law of initial values. *Psychosomatic Medicine*, **12**, 392.

Wilson, G. D. (1967). GSR responses to fear related stimuli. *Perceptual and Motor Skills*, **24**, 401–402.

Wolpe, J. (1971). The behavioristic conception of neurosis: A reply to two critics. *Psychological Review*, **78**, 341–343.

Zahn, T. P. (1976). On the bimodality of the distribution of electrodermal orienting responses in schizophrenic patients. *Journal of Nervous and Mental Disease*, **162**, 195–199.

Zahn, T. P. (1977). Autonomic nervous system characteristics possibly related to a genetic predisposition to schizophrenia. *Schizophrenia Bulletin,* **3,** 49–60.

Zahn, T. P., Rosenthal, D., & Lawlor, W. G. (1968). Electrodermal and heart rate orienting reactions in chronic schizophrenia. *Journal of Psychiatric Research,* **6,** 117–134.

PART FOUR

Areas of
Clinical Research

Intervention Strategies

CHAPTER 13

Therapy Outcome Research Methods

PHILIP C. KENDALL AND JULIAN D. NORTON-FORD

Clinical psychologists have conducted research to evaluate the outcome of therapeutic intervention for several decades, with controlled (although quasi-experimental) studies appearing in print as early as 1948 (Hamlin & Albee, 1948). In order to provide for the continuous improvement of the clinical services offered to their thousands of clients, clinical psychologists have adopted and refined the methods and guidelines of science. Although initial formulation of effective therapeutic strategies may often result from activities other than rigorous clinical research, such as careful clinical observation or theoretical extrapolations, empirical validation of the effects of therapy intervention is considered necessary before widespread utilization can be sanctioned. As a result, clinical psychologists have evolved a sophisticated array of research methods for the evaluation of the outcome of therapeutic intervention.

The development of therapy outcome research methods within clinical psychology has stemmed largely from the fundamental commitment of clinical psychologists to a scientist-practitioner model for training and professional practice (Shakow, 1976, this volume; Albee, 1970; Thorne, 1947). Therefore, we begin with a brief discussion of this model, its implications for research evaluations of therapy, and the empirical-clinical model of clinical practice and research that has developed as an operationalization of this guiding philosophy. In the second section, we define the issues that are addressed by therapy outcome research, and discuss questions concerning the therapy intervention, the therapist, the client, and the optimal matching of intervention, therapists, and clients. Specific methods for scientifically addressing these issues are described in the third section. A fourth section analyzes the methodological problems that make definitive clinical outcome research difficult, and discusses the tactics evolved by clinical researchers to handle these challenges. Finally, the recently initiated methods for cumulative analyses of therapy outcome studies are overviewed.

Portions of this chapter were completed while the first author was a Fellow at the Center for Advanced Study in the Behavioral Sciences, Stanford, California. I am grateful for the financial support provided by the John D. and Catherine T. MacArthur Foundation, the National Institute of Mental Health (Grant 5-T32-MH14581-05), and the Quarter Leave System of the University of Minnesota. I am also grateful to the Graduate School of the University of Minnesota and the National Institute of Mental Health (Grant 1-RO–MH34623-01) for their financial support of my research, some of which is discussed in this chapter.

SCIENTIST-PRACTITIONER MODEL OF CLINICAL RESEARCH AND INTERVENTION

Clinical psychologists are trained to fill the dual role of scientist/researcher and practitioner/clinician. Though the feasibility of such an ambitious role has been questioned, a succession of national conferences has reaffirmed the position first stated by the

429

American Psychological Association Committee on Training in Clinical Psychology (1947): clinical psychologists are scientists who evaluate their work and their theories with rigor *and* practitioners who utilize a research-based understanding of human behavior in social contexts to aid people in resolving psychological dysfunctions and enhancing their lives (Raimy, 1950; Strother, 1957; Hoch, Ross, & Winder, 1966; Korman, 1974). In practice, the scientist-practitioner model is not intended to create professional split personalities but rather to train clinical psychologists to be both service providers who validate their intervention scientifically and researchers who study applied questions and interpret their findings with an understanding of the richness and complexity of human experience (Kendall & Norton-Ford, 1982). Two clinical psychologists whose careers exemplify such a scientist-practitioner integration offer these observations:

The scientist-professional (is) a person who, on the basis of systematic knowledge about persons obtained primarily in real-life situations, has integrated this knowledge with psychological theory, and has then consistently regarded it with the questioning attitude of the scientist. . . . Thus, what defines the "scientist/professional" is the combination of the skilled acquisition of reality-based psychological understanding and the attitude of constant inquiry toward this knowledge. (Shakow, 1976, p. 554)

One of the unique beauties of being a psychotherapist in the 20th century is the opportunity for oscillation between observation and participation, between taking part and standing back, between feeling and thinking, between (controlled) abandonment and study. It is this process of *oscillation,* the unique human ability to resonate, identify, and therapeutically respond to the *themes* in the patient's experience (that is essential). . . . It should be possible to encourage research that is both rigorous and relevant to clinical and social issues; it should be possible for the therapist to become immersed in the patient's emotional experience *and* to reflect critically on the nature of

the problem, that is, how, as a therapist, he or she might best proceed to alleviate the problem; it should be possible to be open to one's own humanity and range of emotional experience *and* as a psychological scientist to bring the methods of science to bear on understanding them. (Strupp, 1976, p. 570; p. 563)

An immediate implication for clinical research on the outcome of therapy is that it must reflect both the guidelines of science and an understanding of the subtleties of human experience and behavior change, if results are to be meaningful. Finely controlled investigations that are arid or distant from the realities of human living and the therapeutic experience may offer only limited conclusions. Studies of intriguing therapeutic results that fail to pinpoint the effects that can be accurately attributed to the therapy provide at most speculative knowledge. For these reasons, clinical psychologists have developed a variety of methods for studying meaningful therapeutic interventions and outcomes in a scientific fashion.

At the heart of these methods is an *empirical-clinical* principle. This principle is a methodology, a set of guidelines, designed to enable practicing clinicians to achieve scientific rigor and clinical researchers to achieve ecological validity. In the former case, each client is handled as a participant in what Thorne (1947) described more than 30 years ago as

a single well-controlled experiment. The treatment may be carefully controlled by utilizing single therapeutic factors, observing and recording results systematically, and checking through the use of appropriate quantitative laboratory studies. . . . Individual clinicians are encouraged to apply experimental and statistical methods in the analysis of case results, and larger scale analyses are made of the experience of a whole clinic over a period of years. (pp. 159, 166)

Although behavior therapists have provided the major impetus for the development of single-subject methods for clinical practitioners (Baer, Wolf, & Risley, 1968; Gold-fried & Davison, 1976; Hersen & Barlow, 1976; Kazdin, this volume; Mintz & Kiesler, this volume), the empirical-clinical methodology that spawned these methods is shared by many clinical psychologists of diverse theoretical orientations. As Thorne's statement suggests, clinical researchers also have an integral role in operationalizing the empirical-clinical methodology. This operationalization can take place in at least two ways: (1) research projects involving groups of clients and experimental control of the therapeutic intervention provided to each participant may be designed to scientifically validate hypotheses generated by practitioners' single-subject case evaluations; or (2) program evaluation studies in which the results achieved by one or more clinicians (or an entire clinic) with many clients can be assessed and experimentally compared to appropriate control groups.

Thus the scientist-practitioner model and the empirical-clinical methodology have established an overriding orientation that guides clinical psychologists in their research on therapeutic outcome. Therapy conducted by trained and experienced therapists with clients who are referred for aid with significant psychological dysfunctions offers a "context of discovery," that is, a source of hypotheses concerning the effects and effectiveness of therapeutic intervention strategies. Controlled large-scale clinical research that involves scientific precautions necessary to attain conclusive and generalizable results (for example, multiple clients and therapists to control for the effects of special personal characteristics) offers a "context of verification," that is, a source of confirmation of hypotheses. Although individual therapeutic efforts contribute more reliable information when the precautions of the single-subject experimental designs are used, and research studies provide more definitive evaluations when true-to-life clinical interventions are provided, neither approach to the investigation of the results of therapy alone is sufficient.

cient. Only through a continuous dialectic of science and practice can meaningful research on the effects of therapy evolve.

This chapter focuses on the issues to be considered and the methods to be employed when undertaking group comparisons in the study of the effects of therapy. Researchers may also wish to consult other sources that consider additional and related methodologies (Campbell & Stanley, 1963; Cook & Campbell, 1979; Fiske, Hunt, Lubosky, Orne, Parloff, Reiser, & Tuma, 1970; Goldstein, Heller, & Sechrest, 1966; Gottman & Markman, 1978; Kazdin, 1980; Kazdin & Wilson, 1978; Kiesler, 1971; Mahoney, 1978; Paul, 1967).

ISSUES ADDRESSED BY THERAPY OUTCOME RESEARCH

Research on the results of therapeutic intervention focuses on one or more of four basic issues: (1) What are the effects, effectiveness, and efficiency of different types of therapeutic *intervention?* (2) What professional and personal characteristics of *therapists* exert an impact on therapy outcome? (3) What personal, experiential, and behavioral characteristics of *clients* exert an impact on therapy outcome? (4) What are the *optimal matches* of intervention, therapists, and clients?

Intervention: Effects, Effectiveness, and Efficiency

Clinical researchers have addressed increasingly sophisticated questions concerning the results of different kinds of therapeutic intervention (Bergin, 1971, Bergin & Lambert, 1978). Nevertheless, the basic question "Do clients change for the better during and after engaging in therapy?" is the single most important problem (Strupp, 1978) and must be answered before more complex concerns are tackled. The demonstration of significant change as a result of a therapeutic intervention is a prerequisite for any further research. This fact is at times forgotten in the whirl of complex experimental comparisons of several different therapies; however, it matters little if one therapy produces more positive changes at a statistically significant level than other therapies, if the clients involved in the therapies have not changed meaningfully (this is addressed in detail in a later section on clinical vs. statistical change).

Just as meaningful pre–post improvements are the key initial criterion for "successful" therapeutic intervention, two corollary issues must also be considered. First, do some clients change for the *worse* during or after participating in therapy? Here again, statistical findings summarizing the impact of therapeutic intervention on several clients may obscure the fact that a minority of clients actually deteriorated! If clients deteriorate, the therapy must be considered potentially dangerous. It then remains to be determined if such "casualties" were chance occurrences, by-products of phenomena separate from the therapy, or unintended products of the therapy itself. It is also important to discover whether certain limited types of clients are "at risk" for deterioration in the therapy, so that the therapy may be contraindicated in the future for similar persons.

Second, the longevity of the outcome must be assessed. When gains in psychosocial functioning are attained by clients during or immediately after involvement in a therapy, it is sometimes erroneously assumed that these improvements represent a permanent cure. The durability of therapeutic outcome is an empirical question; it must be measured through follow-up assessments of clients months and years after therapy has been terminated. Until recently, therapeutic intervention rarely provided systematic mechanisms to ensure that clients maintained their gains after therapy terminated. Even with contemporary interventions that "program maintenance" (Stokes & Baer, 1977), long-lasting positive results can be very difficult to produce, let alone to demonstrate empirically.

Demonstrating that clients involved in therapy do in fact change for the better is not equivalent to showing that the therapy, as opposed to other potentially influential factors such as advice from friends or clergy, was the *cause* of the improvement. Experimental controls must be instituted (Campbell & Stanley, 1963) in order to eliminate the possibility that forces other than therapy have caused a change. Once done, there still remains the question of what component(s) of the therapeutic intervention were actually responsible for causing client improvement. Thus a fundamental issue in therapy outcome research is whether or not a therapy can be definitively shown to produce positive changes, and what part or combination of parts of the therapeutic intervention are the primary causal agents. The latter concern is essentially a search for the "active ingredients" in therapies, and "dismantling strategies" (Kazdin & Wilson, 1978) are designed with this goal in mind. For the sake of economy and of impact, the delineation of the specific causal forces in a therapy is a valuable endeavor.

In view of the literally dozens of contemporary therapeutic methods (Belkin, 1980; Corsini, 1979; Prochaska, 1978), and because therapy can be a costly venture, research also deals with the issue of the comparative effectiveness and efficiency of alternative therapies. The question is posed, "Is one of several potentially valuable therapies superior to other approaches?" Several criteria must be considered when contrasting alternative therapeutic interventions: (1) cost—in dollars, professional and client time, and equipment, for example, biofeedback apparatus, or other necessary resources; (2) client improvements; (3) client deterioration; (4) durability of client gains; (5) relative importance to the client, and persons significant to the client, of the areas of functioning where improvement versus deterioration or no change occur. There is as yet no single equation for computing the efficiency of various therapies, but each of these criteria should be addressed when comparisons are conducted.

Therapists: Personal and Professional Factors

Who the therapist is, both as a person and as a trained expert, can affect any interpersonal interaction and the outcome of therapy (Gurman & Razin, 1977). An abbreviated list of the characteristics of therapists that may influence the outcome of therapeutic intervention includes: personality type; interpersonal style; beliefs, values, and prejudices; gender; power; physical attractiveness; socioeconomic status (current and family of origin); length and types of professional experience as a clinician; length and types of training and supervision; profession. Interestingly, some potentially potent therapist parameters have *not* been found to consistently affect therapy outcome (e.g., race or theoretical orientation), and it is often likely that varying *combinations* of these factors will have effects that could not be predicted from a knowledge of the general influence of any one of the factors in isolation. As a result, it appears that the outcomes of therapy may not be attributed solely to the therapy techniques, because not only the intervention itself but also the kind of person and professional who conducts it can determine the outcome.

The medium through which therapists' individual characteristics are communicated to the client includes the therapist's appearance and verbal and nonverbal behavior in therapy interviews. Dozens of clinical researchers have investigated the impact of this aspect of the therapy process, the therapist's observable communications to the client, to search for links between therapist characteristics and client results (Marsden, 1971; Kiesler, 1973; Orlinsky & Howard, 1978;

Truax & Mitchell, 1971; Parloff, Waskow, & Wolfe, 1978). In some cases therapists who view themselves as conducting very different therapies (e.g., behavior therapy vs. client-centered therapy) tend to be more similar in their interactions with clients (e.g., degree of empathy communicated) than would be expected on the basis of differences in kind of intervention (Ford, 1978; Sloane, Staples, Cristol, Yorkston, & Whipple, 1975). The hypothesis that therapists with different personal and professional characteristics may communicate differently in therapy, and thereby have differing impacts on clients, is thus an important avenue for research.

Clients: Personal, Experiential, and Behavioral Factors

Clients with differing characteristics may benefit (or deteriorate) differently in therapy as well. Just as therapist variables merit research as potential determinants of therapeutic outcome, so too have client variables received research attention (Garfield, 1971, 1978). In addition to investigations of the relationship between clients' personal characteristics (e.g., age, gender, personality profile) and behavioral characteristics (e.g., agreements with therapist, defensive statements, verbal productivity) and therapeutic results, studies have also been conducted to search for a connection between clients' phenomenological experiencing of therapy and their gains. For example, the client's perception of the therapist's degree of empathy, warmth, and genuineness has been found to predict therapeutic success or failure in a variety of therapeutic situations (Gurman, 1977), even though measurement of the behavior that is typically considered to reflect these facilitative conditions has not consistently shown a link with therapeutic outcome (Mitchell, Bozarth, & Krauft, 1977). Thus a hypothesis warranting further clinical research is that the client's interpretation of therapy interaction may be more important in determining positive results than the therapist's specific actions or type of intervention.

Matching Clients with Optimal Therapists and Intervention

Fifteen years ago, clinical researchers first began to enunciate what has now become a guiding principle for therapy outcome research: *What* intervention, conducted by *what* therapist with *what* client to resolve *what* psychosocial dysfunctions, produces *what* effects (Kiesler, 1966; Paul, 1967; Strupp & Bergin, 1969; Vale & Vale, 1969)? Given the impact of differences in the type of therapeutic intervention, the characteristics of therapists, and the characteristics of clients on therapy results, it stands to reason that outcome research might best be focused on identifying the optimal matches of intervention and therapist with client, rather than attempting to delineate the "best" intervention, or the "best" therapist, or the "best" client.

To assert that one therapeutic kind of intervention is better than another is to make several implicit assumptions that appear untenable:

1. That a certain therapy is "better" for all clients and all therapists. It is equally plausible that each kind of therapy might be highly beneficial, but for different kinds of clients or different types of therapists.

2. That it is sufficient to globally label the effects of therapy as "good" or "bad" in order to determine if one kind of therapy produces more good effects and fewer bad effects, and so can be considered better than another therapy. It is equally plausible that each type of therapy will produce some effects that, *in some circumstances,* would be desirable for some clients. Hence each type may be beneficial depending on the goals and problems of the specific client.

3. That the clients who do *not* benefit from the "best" intervention must be in some way deficient; after all, these clients have failed to profit from the "best" therapy. It is equally plausible that these clients might simply be better served by a different therapy or by a different therapist through no fault of their own.

Since almost every therapeutic intervention will likely produce distinctive effects in different domains of clients' lives, the search for a "holy grail" has been abandoned in favor of attempts to identify the therapeutic intervention and type of therapist that will be most likely to produce the results that are most important in the case of each different type of client. In this way therapy can be individualized for each client, and intervention and therapists can be selected on the basis of a match-up between their special capabilities and the needs of that client. Though there have been prescriptive efforts (e.g., Goldstein & Stein, 1976), this objective has not yet been totally attained in the field of therapy outcome research. Nevertheless, the search for optimal matching of client and therapist provides a sophisticated and humanistic direction for the application of research methodologies that is congruent with the ethical standards of clinical psychology (American Psychological Association, 1973) and the requirements of logical and systematic scientific research.

METHODS FOR CLINICAL RESEARCH ON THERAPY OUTCOMES

A variety of methodological innovations has been developed to address each of the four basic issues and their component questions. Both correlational and experimental research strategies have been adapted to this task, as well as a variety of tactics for dealing with the many practical barriers to meaningful yet precise therapy outcome research.

Methods to Address Issues Concerning the Intervention

Research evaluations of the effects and effectiveness of therapeutic intervention have evolved from simple tallies of the percentage of clients who were judged by the therapist to have improved, to multimethod experimental investigations of carefully defined components of therapies. While the ideals to be described in this section are only sometimes achieved in full by any single study, clinical researchers have increasingly taken care to follow the guidelines exemplified by these ideals.

Multiple Assessments of Therapy Outcomes. No single measure of the outcome of therapeutic intervention possesses either the reliability or the comprehensiveness to serve as the sole indicator of clients' gains (or setbacks). For example, although a therapist's estimate of the degree of improvement shown by a client offers one valuable perspective (Mintz, 1977), such a criterion for therapeutic outcome is subject to many potential biases (for example, social desirability or demand characteristics) and is not equivalent to other equally important viewpoints, such as the client's own subjective self-appraisal.

It has become almost standard in contemporary research on therapy outcome to utilize a variety of measures of outcome that tap *multiple sources.* The list of sources for therapy outcome data include assessments of client self-report, client test (or task) performance, therapist judgments and ratings, observations by trained, unbiased, blind observers, ratings by significant people in the client's life, and independent judgments by professionals.

In addition to the multiple sources available for gathering outcome data, *multiple tar-gets* of assessment must be considered. For instance, one can measure overall psychological/psychosocial adjustment, specific interpersonal skills, self-reported mood, cognition, or dimensions of personality, life environment, vocational status, or quality of interpersonal relationships.

Strupp and Hadley (1977) presented a tripartite conceptualization to facilitate the evaluation of the outcome of psychotherapy. According to their model, outcome should be viewed and simultaneously assessed from the vantage point of *society,* the *individual,* and the *mental health professional.* The societal concerns reflect the need to evaluate therapeutic improvements in deviant, undesirable, or potentially dangerous behavior. The client as an individual should be evaluated to assess the happiness, sense of relief, or sense of well-being brought forth by therapy. Theoretical analyses of the effective aspects of therapy and the understanding of healthy human adjustment are provided by the mental health professionals' perspective.

The evaluation of treatment is also facilitated by a recognition of different *levels of assessment.* Assessment can be designed to help the clinician determine exactly what did or did not change—the *specifying level*—and to help determine whether or not treatment had noticeable effects outside of therapy— the general *impact level.*

Specifying level assessments are intended to determine the exact skills or behaviors that changed due to treatment. Assessments should focus on discrete behaviors or skills using assessment methods such as naturalistic observation or specific-skills tests. General impact level assessments seek answers to questions such as, Does the client's spouse notice change? Do professional judgments or friends' opinions recognize that the client is less disturbed? The concern here is with the overall impact of therapy; and ratings by persons significant to the client, sociometrics, and perhaps archival data such as work records can be used to estimate therapeutic impact.

When there are changes at the general impact level, the specifying level assessments help to identify what exactly changed that caused the improvements noticed by others. For instance, blind professional judgments and spouse ratings indicate that a client's depression has been treated successfully. This outcome is clearly desirable, and one can feel confident that the treatment produced improvement. But one would be left wondering what exactly was it that changed to produce the noticeable improvement? Specifying level assessments are needed to determine the specific changes that led to the raters' judgments. Did the client's thinking change? Are sleep disturbances absent? Does the client engage in more pleasant events? That is, what specific behaviors or skills were changed? On the other hand, when changes at the general impact level are not seen, any changes in specific behavior or specific tests must be interpreted cautiously.

It is also recommended that specifying level assessments of outcome include both the behavioral change measures (Ciminero, Calhoun, & Adams, 1977) so common within behavioral therapies, and measures of client cognitive and affective states, as is often the case in more traditional therapies. The measurement of both cognitive and behavioral change (Kendall & Hollon, 1981; Kendall & Korgeski, 1979) has been emphasized for the evaluation of cognitive-behavioral intervention, but is equally relevant to the study of psychotherapy of diverse theoretical persuasions.

The simplistic approach of classifying clients as globally "better," "worse," or "not changed" is replaced with a more precise and meaningful analysis of the specific changes that occur during and after therapy. Important but perhaps less obvious effects of therapy are thus less likely to be overlooked, and a clearer picture is provided of the outcome of therapy on the many facets of the "whole person." When alternative therapies are compared, the use of multiple measures of outcome permits researchers to pinpoint the strengths and weaknesses of each modality.

Assessment of Change over Time. In order to examine empirically the durability of therapeutic outcomes, researchers increasingly require the use of follow-up assessments at specific times following the termination of therapist-client contact. The exact length of time necessary for a meaningful follow-up assessment varies depending on the specific therapy, client population, and therapy goals involved. For example, intervention designed to assist clients in losing weight often shows excellent success immediately after the program and often after a three-month interval. However, in the minority of studies that have reevaluated clients' weight loss at 12-month or longer intervals, the apparent gains frequently have diminished greatly or dissipated entirely (Stunkard & Mahoney, 1976). This finding suggests that innovative procedures for enhancing the likelihood of long-term client gains are necessary in addition to the strategies already utilized. This conclusion, and the "maintenance" tactics that have evolved as a result (e.g., booster sessions; gradually phasing out, rather than abruptly discontinuing, therapist-client contact; focusing on cognitive as well as behavioral change) might not have occurred except for the emphasis on assessment of long-term client changes.

An important methodological precaution in the areas of follow-up assessment is that of assuring comparability between the measurements obtained immediately after therapy and at the follow-up intervals. If multiple reliable instruments are used to evaluate clients before and immediately after therapeutic intervention, the results from these assessments could not be compared with a single questionnaire or phone call at follow-up. Although it may be difficult to obtain clients' cooperation in completing batteries of assessment measures several months after therapy has ended, the quality and comprehensiveness of follow-up assessments determine the meaningfulness of the conclusions that can be drawn about the intervention's long-term effects.

One of the earliest experimental studies of

the results of a psychosocial-like intervention illustrates the importance of follow-up assessment. In 1951, Powers and Witmer reported an evaluation of the effects of a multicomponent intervention on the subsequent criminal behavior, health, socioeconomic status, and family adjustment of 506 five to 13-year-old boys who had been selected by schools, welfare agencies, churches, and police as either "average" (control group) or "difficult" (treatment group). This "Cambridge-Somerville Youth Study" actually began in 1939 and offered several forms of aid, such as informal counseling from a supportive adult, to the treatment group youths over several years in an attempt to prevent or reduce delinquency. Both three (Powers & Witmer, 1951) and 30 (McCord, 1978) years after the program's termination, the 253 untreated subjects fared no worse and in some cases (for instance, their health as adults) better than the 253 subjects who had received aid for an average of five years. Although participants gave very positive ratings of the program at the 30-year follow-up, its benefits on the principal assessment criteria were minimal. Despite the unfortunate lack of demonstrated positive impact, this study has contributed important knowledge by challenging clinical researchers to develop alternative intervention with greater durability and efficacy, and by providing an example of long-term follow-up.

A second important methodological point related to follow-up assessment concerns the comparability of subjects in the different groups. Has there been differential attrition? Have some clients sought assistance outside the therapy outcome study during the follow-up interval? Examinations of therapeutic change over time must check that comparison groups have not become sufficiently dissimilar to undermine follow-up comparison.

Experimental Controls for Between-Groups Studies. Control procedures derived from experimental science have been adapted by clinical researchers to evaluate the *causal* impact of therapeutic intervention.

The objective is to separate the effects of the therapy per se from the changes that result from other factors. These other influences, often called "extraneous" variables, are "controlled," since they are built into the experiences provided to members of the control group. Comparable persons are then placed into either the control group or the group that receives the therapeutic intervention. By contrasting the changes evidenced by the persons in the control versus therapy group, the effects of therapy over and above the outcome produced by the extraneous factors may be determined.

Scholars have described a host of factors for which researchers should ideally control in order to produce unconfounded results (Campbell & Stanley, 1963). These "sources of internal invalidity" are the factors that, if not controlled in the experimental design, might result in treatment effects that are confounded by the unwanted effects of the uncontrolled factor. Sources of *internal* invalidity (see Table 13.1) include: history, maturation, testing, instrumentation, regression, mortality, and selection. Control groups are designed to eliminate the potential confounding effect of each of these factors.

In addition, there are several threats to *external* validity (see Table 13.2), factors that may prevent the study's results from being generalizable to the real-life people and situations that it is intended to evaluate. These threats to external validity include interactions of the intervention and testing, interactions of selection and intervention, reactive arrangements, and multiple-intervention interference. A variety of control procedures has been developed to study the effects of therapeutic intervention in which the outcome attributable to therapy per se is clearly separated from the influences of these extraneous factors.

When clients assigned to different conditions, such as treatment versus nontreatment, are compared, *random assignment* of participants to the therapy or control group is essential to achieve comparability between the two groups. For instance, random assign-

Table 13.1. Sources of Internal Invalidity as Related to Therapy Outcome Research

Source	Definition	Examples	
		General	*Specific instance*
History	Events other than therapy that occur during the time period when therapy is provided; simultaneous occurence of extratherapy events	Informal counseling by peers; important lifestyle change	A long phone call from a former roommate relieves a client's depression and gives a new meaning to his life. The phone call comes about the time that the therapist begins an important part of treatment. The depression is relieved.
Maturation	Psychological or biological changes that appear to occur naturally with the passage of time	Children's development of the capacity for abstract thought; menopausal effects	The normal cognitive development of a child may result in an increased ability to take another person's perspective, and therefore behave in a more sensitive and empathic manner. The child displays less aggression.
Testing	The impact of repeated exposure to the assessment measures	Increased skill due simply to the practice provided by repeated testing; reduced anxiety due to repeated exposure to the feared stimulus; increased self-disclosure due to multiple instances of asking personal questions	A client becomes more interpersonally skilled in social situations as a result of the researcher's role-play tests. Performing the role-play tests over and over has beneficial effects. The client more comfortably interacts with members of the opposite sex.
Instrumentation	Decay in the sensitivity-accuracy of the assessment instruments	Fatigue of the part of observers; decreased sensitivity of psychophysiological equipment due to usage	Children's attentiveness in the classroom appears to show less off-task behavior due to the observers paying less attention after having been an observer for several weeks. The observers are not seeing or recording the off-task behavior. The child appears to be paying more attention, but only because the off-task behavior is not being noticed.
Statistical regression	The tendency for persons whose initial scores on assessment measures are extreme (high or low) to have later scores that drifted toward the mean	Extreme depression (bottom of the scale) is more likely to rise, since it cannot drop further; hyperactive children are more likely to show less activity	A client who scores particularly high on a measure of anxiety before therapy is statistically more likely to score nearer the mean on a second testing than to score even higher.

438

Table 13.1.   (Continued)

Source	Definition	Examples	
		General	Specific instance
Mortality	Attrition of participants-clients	Clients who drop out from therapy and for whom posttherapy assessments are not available	Clients in a study of the treatment of depression terminate prematurely. Their data is lost, even though they may have terminated because of a sense of already achieved relief. The client has not returned to complete the assessments.
Selection	Utilization of participants-clients who might appear to change simply because of personal factors that predispose them to do so rather than due to the intervention	Clients who volunteer for a therapy program advertised in a local newspaper may be on the verge of changing due to a high level of personal motivation.	Using adolescents in studies of peer pressure or persuasion. The characteristics of adolescent subjects tends to make them especially susceptible to peer pressure and persuasive maneuvers.

ment of clients would likely eliminate the unwanted effects of age or socioeconomic status, since in most cases random assignment would not result in one group being older or more wealthy and educated than another group.

Randomization may be accomplished by any procedure that gives every participant an equal chance of being assigned to either the control or therapy groups, for example, assignment by coin toss. There are problems when the desired outcome of random assignment is not achieved, and only approximated, for instance, when the first 30 clients are assigned to therapy while the next 30 clients are placed on the wait list. Such quasi-random assignment may hide subtle selection biases. Perhaps the first 30 clients sought therapy more quickly due to stronger motivation than the next 30. Perhaps the first 30 clients were exposed to a temporary environmental stress that was no longer a factor when the next 30 clients applied for aid.

Random assignment does not absolutely assure comparability of the control and therapy groups on all measures, although it does maximize the likelihood that this will obtain.

An alternative procedure, randomized blocks assignment, or assignment by stratified blocks, involves matching prospective clients in subgroups that (1) each contain clients that are highly comparable on key dimensions such as initial severity, and (2) contain the same number of clients as the number of experimental groups. For example, if the study requires a control group and one therapy group, clients could be paired off so that each pair is highly comparable. The members in each subgroup are then randomly assigned to either the therapy or control condition, thus increasing the likelihood that each group will contain mirror-image participants while retaining the randomization factor. Randomized blocks assignment of clients to groups (e.g., Kendall & Wilcox, 1980), often using initial severity as the blocking factor, is a highly recommended research methodology.

In order to control for sources of internal invalidity such as history, maturation, or testing, researchers employ no-treatment control groups. Clients who are assigned to a no-treatment control group are administered the assessments on repeated occasions, separated

Table 13.2. Threats to External Validity as Related to Therapy Outcome Research

		Examples	
Threat	Definition	General	Specific instance
Interactions of the environment and testing	Preintervention assessments may sensitize clients to the intervention, thus potentiating the intervention's influence.	When clients who are to receive a therapy for fear are asked to role play the feared situation, this action may increase their motivations to change.	An otherwise ineffective treatment may appear to alleviate fear, but the fear reduction is due to increased motivation from some aspect of the study. This increased motivation would not be present when the treatment is provided outside of the context of a study and would then be ineffective.
Interaction of selection and intervention	If all clients selected are a special subgroup who are particularly amenable to participation, these clients cannot be considered comparable to the rest of the population.	If only two of the four clinics that are asked to be involved in a therapy outcome study agree to do so, the results cannot be generalized to all clinics. The two that refused might be significantly different from the two that agreed.	A project designed to compare psychological therapy, medications, and a control condition for the treatment of hyperactivity requires parents to give their informed consent. Many parents refuse to participate, not wanting their child assigned to the control condition. This selection problem reduces the researcher's ability to generalize the results to all hyperactive children.
Reactive arrangements	Clients may change due to a reaction to the fact of participating in a novel experience, rather than due to the therapy interaction.	Clients may change due to an expectancy on their parts or on the part of their therapist. Therapy must, or should, cause change, and clients change simply because they expect they ought to.	A father's physical abuse of family members is reduced by therapy: not as a result of the therapist's actions, but a function of the father's belief that going to therapy will make him stop being abusive.
Multiple intervention interference	When several kinds of intervention are combined in one experience, the total effect may be very different than the outcome of any one of them in isolation.	Clients involved in multicomponent therapies may fail to change because the plethora of intervention obscures the positive impacts of each separate component.	A child's acting-out, aggressive behavior pattern elicits aggression from his father, rewarding attention from his mother and his peers, and attempts at rational discussion by school authorities. A single consistent approach designed to reduce the aggression would be more effective when not interfered with by other efforts.

by an interval of time equal to the length of the therapy provided for the treatment group. Any changes seen in the treated clients are compared to the changes seen in the no-treatment clients. When treated clients evidence significantly superior improvements over nontreated clients, the treatment is credited with producing the changes. This control procedure is desirable and eliminates several rival hypotheses, but does not control for such factors as anticipation of change due to therapy, expectancy of change, and seeing a therapist—independent of what the therapist actually does.

An alternate no-treatment control procedure, the wait-list control, provides for additional control. For example, clients in a wait-list control group also anticipate change due to therapy. Wait-list control groups involve participants who do not receive therapy until after posttherapy assessments have been conducted on those subjects who have received the treatment; sometimes they receive none until after the follow-up assessment. Wait-listed clients' changes are evaluated exactly as are the changes undergone by clients who receive therapy. If the clients in the wait-list and the therapy groups are comparable in terms of variables such as sex, severity of presenting problem, and motivation, then the researcher can infer that any changes evidenced by the therapy group clients over and above those manifested by wait-list control clients must be due to the intervention rather than to several of the sources of internal invalidity. There is no guarantee that the therapy group clients did not "by chance" experience a different history or maturation than the control clients, but the odds are that when the entire group of therapy clients is compared to the entire group of wait-list clients, the people are sufficiently comparable to rule out such unexpected influences. Data on the important factors should be gathered so that statistical comparisons can be conducted to determine group comparability.

A potential problem with wait-list controls is that a wait-list client might experience life crises that require immediate aid. It is recommended that each control client's status frequently be monitored informally. If such an emergency occurs, it is the researcher's responsibility to provide swift therapeutic help, even though this will somewhat confound the study's results (Stuart, 1973). Wait-list clients should be offered the therapy, or an equally acceptable and effective substitute, as soon as possible after the study is complete.

Several variations of the no-treatment control group procedure may be employed. The standard experimental design involves assessing both control and therapy groups both before and after intervention and again at follow-up. Such a procedure, though it controls for the effects of pretesting (both groups are pretested), does not allow for an examination of the potentially sensitizing effects of pretesting, that is, what were the effects from pretesting alone. Two alternative designs have been developed to address this question: the Solomon Four-Groups procedure involves adding a second control group and a second therapy group, both of which are assessed only *after* therapy has terminated; the Posttest Only procedure simply eliminates the pretherapy assessment for both control and therapy groups. Although the Solomon design requires two additional groups, it enables the researcher to conclude that: (1) the therapy group did in fact change significantly, which is not demonstrated by the Posttest Only design because no pretest is conducted; and (2) that the change was not due to sensitization effects from pretest assessment.

When a control group cannot be arranged, such as at a clinic that never has a sufficiently large wait-list to hold people the full time period of therapy, a quasi-experimental alternative is offered by either using a group of similar but not exactly comparable people in place of a completely comparable control group, or contrasting the therapy group's scores on the assessment measures with normative standards for "normal" or "dysfunctional" persons comparable to the participating clients. In the latter instance, the researcher might demonstrate that the therapy group scored in the normal range on assessment measures by the end of therapy, after having scored in the dysfunctional range prior to therapy. Both quasi-experimental alternatives offer only a very tentative approximation of the control provided by true control groups, but they do bolster somewhat a clinician's otherwise anecdotal evaluation of the treatment.

Attention-placebo control groups are an alternative to the wait-list control that not only rules out threats to internal validity but also controls for reactivity effects. Participants in attention-placebo groups receive *contact* with and *attention* from a therapist as well as a therapy rationale, that is, a statement of the purpose and likely positive results given to clients at the beginning of the intervention. The rationale provided to attention-placebo clients is intended to mobilize an *expectancy* of positive gains. Although the research is equivocal (Berman, 1979; Wilkins, 1977; Shapiro, 1971), these three "nonspecific" elements in the therapy process may account for client change, just as placebos have been found effective in some medical situations (Rosenthal & Frank, 1956). Attention-placebo groups enable clinical researchers to identify the changes produced by specific therapeutic intervention over and above the effects of nonspecific factors (Paul, 1967).

Several potential problems are posed by attention-placebo controls (O'Leary & Borkovec, 1978). When long-term therapy is being evaluated, it is questionable from an ethical viewpoint to offer some clients a therapist contact (placebo) that does not deal directly with their goals and problems. Attention-placebo controls must be "theoretically inert" while nevertheless providing professional contact and attention and instilling positive expectancies in clients. To offer such an intervention in the guise of effective therapy is not acceptable in light of the American Psychological Association's (1973) code of ethics, *unless* clients are fully

informed in advance and sign an informed consent form acknowledging their willingness to take a chance on receiving either a placebo or a therapy intervention (O'Leary & Borkovec, 1978). Although clinical researchers take it as ethically mandated that they conduct scientifically rigorous evaluations to validate practiced therapies as effective and safe—and controls for "nonspecific" effects are essential to an accurate understanding of the true efficacy of specific interventions—many nevertheless have qualms about providing seriously dysfunctional clients with a nonspecific therapy *even if* informed consent is assured. Clients with grave and pressing needs may feel impelled by the severity of their crises to consent to the possibility of placebo treatment because they feel they must receive some kind of help immediately. This is an indirectly coercive situation, and it diminishes the validity of the client's consent. In less severe cases, however, attention-placebo control groups are less problematic.

Methodologically, it is difficult to ensure that the therapists who conduct attention-placebo groups have the same degree of positive expectancy for client gains as do therapists conducting specific interventions (O'Leary & Borkovec, 1978). Research on therapist expectancies suggest that when therapists predict a favorable outcome, clients tend to improve accordingly (Berman, 1979; Wilkins, 1977). Thus therapist expectancies may not be equated in therapy versus placebo groups, and this produces a confounding factor. Similarly, even if clients in an attention-placebo condition have high expectations at the start, they are likely to grow disenchanted when no specific intervention is offered over the course of their participation, particularly if long-term therapy is being evaluated.

Conceptually, a treatment rationale used in therapy outcome research as an attention-placebo control tends to have a short life span because

If one finds placebo effects, the determinants of the effects should soon be isolated and documented. As determinants of the placebo become known, conceptualizations of the control procedure are relabeled. What was originally labeled a placebo procedure might be relabeled as demand stimuli for improved posttest behavior, implicit or explicit instructional sets to establish the espectation of benefit from the particular treatment procedures, confidence in the therapist, response to societal or community expectations of benefit from a treatment, or desire to please the therapist who spends many hours with the patient (O'Leary & Borkovec, 1978, p. 823).

Thus nonspecific effects tend to be specified and redefined as components of effective therapy when they show a consistent robust effect. The factors that cause client change in attention-placebo groups merit delineation and inclusion in therapeutic intervention, rather than being left vague and mysterious.

Best alternative intervention controls (O'Leary & Borkovec, 1978) involve replacing attention-placebo intervention with the intervention that is currently best validated or most widely used for treatment of the problems and clients involved in the therapy being evaluated. If it is demonstrated that the best alternative intervention and the therapy under investigation are equated for all "nonspecific" factors, for example, duration of treatment, client and therapist expectancies, then this approach enables the researcher not only to control for attention and placebo effects but also to test the relative efficacy of one type of intervention against its major contemporary competitor.

Dismantling is a procedure that can be applied to creating substitutes for attention-placebo controls. Dismantling requires that the primary components of one kind of intervention be identified, with each component translated into an independent kind of intervention (equivalent to the total therapy on all nonspecific factors), and then used as a comparison condition with what would otherwise be a control group. For example, psychoanalytic therapies involve several components that, with ingenuity, could be isolated and converted into separate types of intervention: free association; analysis of the

transference; dream analysis; provision of corrective emotional experiences; interpretations designed to enhance client insight into unconscious conflicts, their symptoms, and their origins; and so on. When one type of intervention is directly contrasted with one or more components, the researcher can begin to determine the relative power and importance of each of the components. Components can also be combined in different arrangements and orders for example, first dream analysis, then transference analysis versus first transference analysis, then dream analysis, in an effort to determine the optimal combination and ordering. Again assuming that "nonspecific" factors are equated in all intervention conditions—and this may be difficult when only one or a few components are used instead of the total intervention—the dismantling strategy also provides a test of the intervention's impact over and above placebo effects. However, unless a variety of combinations of components are eventually created as control conditions, the true value of each component will not be known. In some cases a component may appear worthless on its own, but it may have significant therapeutic impact when combined with certain other components.

The identification and confirmation of the active components of a particular psychotherapeutic treatment remains an important function for therapy-outcome researchers. However, depending in the dismantling strategy that is employed, a thorny control problem can emerge. The problem concerns the number of treatment components provided to different client groups and the need to control for length of therapy. The following example, though not an ideal study, illustrates the dilemma. Suppose the clinical researcher was conducting a dismantling investigation of systematic desensitization (Wolpe, 1969), in which it was decided that one group would receive relaxation training, a second group would receive training in the imagining of increasingly fearful scenes, a third group would receive both treatment components, and a fourth group would receive neither (control). Controlling for the amount of therapist contact would result in the decision to provide 10 one-hour sessions to all groups.

If the effects of this study were to indicate that each component and the combined treatment were equally effective, does this necessarily indicate that the combined approach is no better than its components? Perhaps not; since the amount of therapy time was held constant across conditions, there was insufficient time to provide the combined treatment in an adequate fashion. Though one is likely to consider designing the study with 20 one-hour sessions to guarantee sufficient time for the combined treatment, this effort would leave greater lengths of potentially empty time in the separate component conditions. Researchers must strike a balance between therapist contact time and number of components in order to conduct meaningful dismantling studies.

Neutral or *counterdemand expectancy* controls involve, respectively, providing clients with no basis for expecting therapeutic improvement, and inducing clients to actually expect to *not* change for a stated length of time (O'Leary & Borkovec, 1978). Neutral expectancy control groups would be expected to show change only if the specific therapy intervention has an impact over and above placebo effects. However, several problems appear inescapable in this method: (1) while expectancy effects may be controlled, other placebo factors such as therapist attention are not ruled out; (2) once clients begin to receive the intervention, it is doubtful that they would fail to generate positive expectancies simply because they can see that help is being provided; and (3) ethically, it is a violation of informed consent to involve a client in therapy without forewarning him or her of the therapy's possible and likely effects (see also Korchin & Cowan, this volume).

The counterdemand procedure suffers from these limitations as well. In addition, it requires that the researcher have a solid

basis for predicting the time interval required before change will occur due to the intervention. If change does begin to occur during the time that clients are instructed to not expect it, a host of positive and negative expectancies may be engendered, thus confounding the control procedure. Furthermore, the counterdemand instructions are remarkably similar to an intervention widely used by systems-oriented family therapists—"paradox" or "prescribing the symptom" (Haley, 1976). Although experimental validation is lacking for this intervention, an extensive theoretical rationale (Watzlawick, Weakland, & Fisch, 1974) and clinical case literature (Watzlawick, 1978) offer support for paradoxical intervention. Thus, rather than providing an expectancy-minimizing and inert control condition, the counterdemand procedure may in fact be a type of therapeutic intervention meriting evaluation in its own right!

Experimental Comparison of Kinds of Intervention. The methods described thus far are employed in the evaluation of the effects of a treatment. In order to determine the comparative efficiency and effectiveness of therapeutic intervention, between-groups experimental controls must be applied to a direct comparison of that intervention and one or more alternative kinds (akin to the best-alternative-intervention comparison). Several precautions are necessary in such investigations.

As in all between-groups comparisons, each client must be assigned to receive one and only one kind of therapy. The assignment of clients to conditions should be conducted in a fashion that results in the comparability of the clients receiving each intervention. As mentioned earlier, a randomized blocks procedure, with subjects blocked on an important variable (e.g., initial severity), is a highly desirable design characteristic. It is also wise to check the comparability of the clients in the different treatment conditions on other important variables (e.g., age, SES, prior therapy experiences) before undertaking the intervention. If all subjects are not available at the outset of treatment, such as when subjects come from successive clients entering a clinic, then the comparability of groups should be checked at several intervals as the therapy outcome study progresses toward completion.

It is important for the comparison of treatments that the therapists conducting each type must be equated for such potentially influential factors as: (1) training background; (2) length and type of professional and clinical experience; (3) expertise in conducting the particular intervention; and (4) expectancy that the intervention is effective. To control for, and if possible also rigorously delineate, these therapist effects, researchers have either required each therapist to conduct each type of intervention with at least one client per intervention, or utilized a stratified blocking procedure to assure that each intervention is conducted by several comparable therapists. The first method enables an experimental examination of the effects of differing therapists, but this evaluation is valid only if therapists are equally expert and positively oriented toward each intervention.

For example, it would be an invalid test to ask a group of behaviorally oriented therapists to conduct both a behavioral therapy (in which their expertise is high) and an existial therapy (in which their expertise, and probably their expectations, are lower). The second method enables the researcher to examine the effect of a variety of therapists in one intervention with the effect of a variety of therapists in an alternative intervention. For example, in a large-scale comparison of psychotherapy versus behavior therapy, Sloane et al. (1975) used six white male therapists; three were behavior therapists and three were psychoanalysts. Assuming that these samples of therapists represent the larger population of therapists, then one can generalize to other behavior therapists and psychoanalysts. Because all therapists were white males, however, one could not generalize across therapist gender and racial/cultural background.

Treatment comparisons also require that the intervention procedures be equated for salient variables such as: (1) duration; (2) length, intensity, and frequency of therapist contacts with client; (3) believability and impact of the rationale; (4) setting; and (5) involvement of persons significant to the client. In some cases these factors may be the basis for two alternative therapies (e.g., conjoint vs. individual marital therapy), in which case the variable becomes part of the experimental contrast rather than a matter for control.

The assessment measures used for evaluation when different kinds of intervention are compared must: (1) cover the range of psychosocial functioning that is a target for therapeutic change; (2) include measures that tap the costs and possible negative side effects of the intervention as well; and (3) be unbiased with respect to the alternative kinds of intervention. The latter precaution is necessary because the outcome of a comparison of therapies can be determined before it ever starts if the assessment measures are not equally sensitive to the type of changes that are most likely caused by one kind of intervention and not the other. The Sloane et al. comparison of psychoanalysis and behavior therapy might be criticized as biased against behavior therapy, since it did not gather situation-specific behavioral assessments that might have indicated the effectiveness of behavior therapy. In comparisons of different therapies, the dependent variables must not be preferential to one treatment over another.

An important issue often ignored in comparative therapy studies pertains to the level of effectiveness of each individual therapeutic approach in relation to the "expected effectivenss" of each therapy based on prior studies. For example, two treatments are compared, and therapy A is found superior to therapy B. The question arises, was therapy A superior, or did therapy B fail to be effective in this instance? It would be desirable in demonstrating the effectiveness of therapy A if the results due to therapy B reflected the level of effectiveness found in earlier demonstrations of therapy B's effectiveness. Interpretations of the results of comparative studies are dependent upon the level of effectiveness of each of the therapies in relation to their "expected" (or standard) effectiveness.

Methods to Address Issues Concerning the Client and the Therapist

Unlike the experimental methods described thus far, in which the researcher directly manipulates the independent variable, characteristics of clients and therapists cannot always be manipulated for the experiment. Rather client and therapist characteristics are often manipulated by selection. For example, if the researcher is interested in evaluating treatment effects for clients with varying levels of presenting symptom severity, the researcher does not directly manipulate client symptom severity but evaluates the variable by comparing subjects who are selected as high or low on level of initial severity. Correlational/regression methods can be applied to test the predictive relationship between certain client or therapist characteristics or in-session actions and measures of outcome. For example, Ford (1978) assessed the correlation between client perceptions of therapist empathy, warmth, and genuineness and a variety of behavioral outcome measures, such as observations of behavior indicative of anxiety in a role play simulation requiring assertive behavior, as well as self-reports, for example, questionnaires measuring the client's self-esteem and general assertiveness. All clients received eight sessions of one-to-one therapy designed to help them overcome low self-esteem and unassertiveness. With sufficient numbers of clients, it was possible to compute correlations between the client perception variable and each of the outcome measures. While caution was necessary due to the large number of separate correlations calculated, an interesting pattern

emerged: the client perception measure was consistently not correlated with clients' degree of therapeutic change when this perception was assessed in an early (i.e., third) and final session; however, a consistent positive relationship was found between the perception measure and the full range of outcome measures when client perception was assessed in a midtherapy session (i.e., sixth). Thus, while it cannot be concluded that positive client perceptions played a causal role, the results indicate an important relationship meriting further exploration. Further, the fact that this client variable was measured several times across the course of therapy enabled the researcher to identify the time point during intervention at which this client variable appeared most influential.

In some cases, though the client or therapist variable remains manipulated by selection, the researcher may wish to create an experimental evaluation. This strategy is employed when one wishes to examine the possibility of significant interactions.[1] An interaction exists when the relationship between an independent variable and a dependent variable is different for different levels of a second independent variable. For instance, the relationship between an intervention procedure and changes in clients' level of functioning may interact with clients' level of self-awareness. The effect of the treatment differs for clients who differ in self-awareness.

A study by Abramowitz, Abramowitz, Roback, and Jackson (1974) illustrates an interaction. Clients who are high versus low scorers on a locus of control measure were divided into two groups, and half of the members of each group were given a structured encounter group experience, while the other half received an encounter group experience that was comparable in all respects except that a lesser degree of structure was provided. Thus not only was a client characteristic ex-

[1]Some researchers might prefer to use regression analyses (see Cohen & Cohen, 1975).

amined, but it was crossed with an intervention factor (degree of structure) to create a factorial (2 x 2) design. This design enabled the researchers to determine not only that clients' locus of control had an impact on their gains in therapy, but also that an interaction of this characteristic and the type of intervention was a crucial factor. Specifically, clients with high internal locus of control fared best in an unstructured group, while low internal locus of control clients were best served by a structured group.

Despite the availability of feasible methods for studying the impact of (1) client characteristics, (2) therapist characteristics, (3) variations in clients' in-session behavior and perceptions, and (4) variations in therapists' in-session behavior and perceptions, limited conclusions have emerged from research in these areas (Garfield & Bergin, 1978). While future research may identify new and more promising directions, many outcome researchers have turned their attention to investigations of the optimal matchings of ther-

apists, clients, and kinds of intervention (Berzins, 1977).

Methods to Delineate Optimal Matching

In order to identify the optimal matching of different clients with different therapists and different kinds of intervention, a conceptual scheme is necessary. Among the thousands of possible ways that clients, therapists, and therapies differ from one another, researchers must identify the fundamental differences that will be sufficiently influential to affect the outcome of therapy. Kiesler (1966, 1971) provides a conceptual overview for this challenging endeavor through his "grid model" for the study of therapy outcomes (Figure 13.1).

Based on Kiesler's analysis of the "myths" of psychotherapy research, he suggested that every outcome study systematically vary: (1) at least one client characteristic, to overcome the "patient uniformity myth" by experimentally examining the impact of client differ-

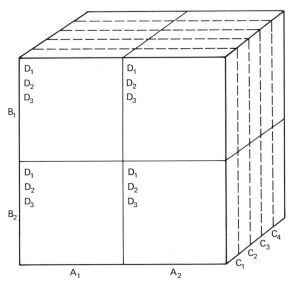

Figure 13.1 Kiesler's grid model for the use of factorial designs to evaluate psychotherapy. A = different homogeneous groups of subjects (clients); B = different homogeneous groups of therapists or types of therapy; C = different times of assessment; D = different behavior that is being monitored to assess change (dependent variable). Adapted from D. J. Kiesler, Experimental designs in psychotherapy research. In A. E. Bergin & S. L. Garfield (Eds.) *Handbook of psychotherapy and behavior change.* New York: Wiley, 1971.

ences; (2) at least one therapist characteristic, to deal with the "therapist uniformity myth" by experimentally examining the impact of therapist differences; (3) at least two distinct outcome measures, to avoid the "outcome uniformity myth" by assessing a range of possible therapy effects; and (4) the time point at which outcome is assessed, to determine when different types of change occur for different clients or therapists, rather than assuming that all change occurs at a particular stage. Kiesler called for the use of factorial experimental designs in therapy outcome studies. This methodological directive has been largely accepted by current therapy outcome researchers.

Dougherty (1976) addressed the question of optimal matching from a different perspective. He applied a correlational methodology, with an additional twist, to delineate empirically optimal therapist-client matching in a university-sponsored clinic. All clients *and* therapists completed a battery of personality instruments prior to therapy. Based on multiple measures of client outcome, Dougherty classified clients as "improved," "no change," or "deteriorated." The clients were separated into clusters based on statistical analyses of their personality profiles, with each cluster representing a distinctive profile. Similarly, therapists were clustered based on their personality profiles. Next, the overall success achieved by therapists in each cluster with clients in each cluster was assessed, and predictions were made as to the types of therapists who were most and least effective with each type of client.

The extra twist is added by a repetition of this process. However, rather than randomly pairing therapists and clients, as was done in the first phase, Dougherty (1976) used the derived predictions to create client-therapist matching that should be "optimal," producing the greatest benefits for the client, versus "minimal," producing the fewest benefits and greatest risk of deterioration for the client. The second phase of the study thus repre-

sented an experimental manipulation of client-therapist matching. As predicted, the optimally matched clients accrued significantly greater gains than minimally matched clients. Perhaps the greatest importance of Dougherty's study is not the specific matching but rather the methodological paradigm. Although a number of therapists and clients are required, and the statistical operations are somewhat complex, this process can be replicated in other clinics. In fact, given the possible impact of geographical, cultural, and other differences between clinics in different areas of the country or the world, it might be unwise to assume that matches derived from one setting would be generalizable to other clinics. Further, the matches identified today might change even for the same clinic over time due to changes in societal ethos or the kinds of persons who are involved as clients and therapists. It is possible that up-do-date and effective matching of clients and therapists can be defined through the continued application of such a process.

Both Kiesler's and Dougherty's approaches suggest that meaningful therapy outcome research requires a large, carefully planned, and ongoing scientific-professional effort. It is simply impossible to conduct *one* study that will examine all the relevant factors. Consider the following: if one were to design a study to evaluate therapist characteristics, client characteristics, therapist in-session behavior, client in-session behavior, therapist subjective experiencing, client subjective experiencing, type of therapeutic intervention, time point within the therapeutic intervention, time point within each therapy session, primary and secondary client goals, and treatment setting, it would require, at a minimum, a $2 \times 2 \times 2 \times 2 \times 2 \times 2 \times 2 \times 2 \times 2 \times 2 \times 2$ factorial design (11-way, with 2048 possible separate effects)! To expand the design to include several variables from each domain would create an even more unthinkable challenge. To further complicate matters by evaluating the effects of these factors on not one but a comprehensive array of outcome measures is still another addition to an overwhelming undertaking.

Although each domain is potentially important to the outcome of therapeutic intervention, it is clear that researchers must narrow the scope of the task, unless they are prepared to spend a lifetime on a single massive study, only to find themselves faced with virtually uninterpretable eight and nine and 10-way interactions, and then to confront the fact that their findings are 25 years outdated. The generally accepted strategy is one in which the researcher addresses certain circumscribed factors within the grid model, varying different independent variables in successive studies, while replicating other aspects of the study. Factorial designs that address portions of the grid can then be accumulated and evaluated together.

CONTINUING CONCERNS

The experienced therapy-outcome researcher understands and can successfully describe the essential features of an ideal therapy outcome study. The ideal study is, however, more easily understood and described than conducted, and the experienced researcher constantly struggles to overcome the numerous problems that can mangle the methodology and render the results less than clearly interpretable.[2] For instance, a study designed to test a specific therapy may produce valuable evidence to demonstrate treatment effectiveness, but due to an extreme attrition rate, waiting-list subjects acquiring therapy elsewhere, or control subjects failing to return for posttesting, the results have to be intrepreted cautiously. The following discussion isolates certain problems in therapy outcome research, and in some cases offers suggestions for their resolution.

---

[2]Limiting factors exist in all studies. Authors should state in their publications the limitations of the study that might affect the interpretation of the results.

Clinical versus Statistical Significance

The data produced by research projects designed to demonstrate the effectiveness of therapy are submitted to statistical tests of significance. Group means are compared, the within-group and between-group variability is considered, and the analysis produces a numerical figure, which is then checked against critical values. An outcome achieves statistical significance if the magnitude of the mean difference is beyond that which could have resulted by chance alone. Statistical anlyses and statistical significance are essential for therapy evaluation, but they alone do not provide evidence of *clinical significance*.

Generally speaking, clinical significance refers to the meaningfulness of the magnitude of change, the remediation of the presenting problem to the point that it is no longer troublesome. In an anxiety disorder, for example, changes in anxiety would have to be of the magnitude that, after therapy, the person no longer suffers from debilitating anxiety. Specifically, this can be made operational as changes on a measure of the presenting problem (e.g. anxiety) that result in the client's being within normal limits on that measure. Statistically significant change requires that the change is beyond that which could have resulted by chance alone, but this "beyond-chance" variation may nonetheless result in a patient who is still more anxious than normal and still greatly troubled by it. Statistically significant improvements are not equivalent to "cures," and clinical significance is an additional, not a substitute, evaluative strategy.

In order to examine clinical significance, it is necessary to provide appropriate information within research reports. *Normative comparisons,* a method for operationalizing clinical significance testing, essentially requires that normative data be presented along with the data for the clients in the treated and control groups. Though examples have appeared in various literatures (Braud, 1978; Kazdin, 1979; Kendall & Wilcox, 1980;

Kendall & Zupan, 1981; Meichenbaum, Gilmore, & Fedoravicious, 1971), two examples from the child-clinical treatment literature will be used for illustration. One example uses a rating scale, and another uses behavioral observations.

In a recent evaluation of a cognitive-behavioral treatment for teaching children self-control (Kendall & Wilcox, 1980), teachers referred behavior-problem children for treatment, children lacking self-control as indicated by high scores on the Self-Control Rating Scale, SCRS (Kendall & Wilcox, 1979). Referred children's pretreatment scores averaged in the 170's, higher SCRS scores indicating a greater *lack* of self-control. Statistical tests of significance performed on the SCRS data indicated, among other findings,[3] that there was a significant interaction between types of treatment (experimental conditions) and changes in teacher's blind ratings over time (see left-hand portion of Figure 13.2). Additional statistical analyses indicated that, unlike the control subjects, who did not show statistically significant changes, the children receiving cognitive-behavorial training showed a significant increase in self-control. Statistically speaking, the cognitive-behavioral treatment produced significant behavioral changes.

A return look at the left-hand portion of Figure 13.2 provides a slightly different perspective. The wavy line across the figure at an SCRS score of 100 is the average score for 110 randomly selected normal children. The shorter wavy line at approximately 145 is one standard deviation above the mean. Were the statistically significant changes clinically significant? Judgments of clinical significance can be made by means of the normative comparisons provided by the inclusion of normative data. In this case the changes produced by the conceptual cognitive-behavioral training brought the average nonself-controlled classroom problem chil-

dren to within one standard deviation above the mean. It remains possible, however, that teachers could still identify the treated children as somewhat lacking in self-control. Since the length of treatment in this study was minimal, greater improvement might be anticipated when a lengthier version of the intervention is provided. Indeed, more favorable evidence of the clinical significance of this treatment procedure was provided by Kendall and Zupan (1981) in their comparison of individual and group cognitive-behavioral training. As seen in the right-hand portion of Figure 13.2, the treatment (provided over more sessions than in the Kendall and Wilcox study) brought the children well within the one standard deviation limits. In both studies, normative comparisons provided a clinically meaningful perspective on the outcome of therapy.

The work of Patterson (1974) illustrates how normative comparisons can be conducted using behavioral observations. As part of Patterson's evaluation of behavioral treatments for conduct problem boys, he collected observations of specific behavior in specific settings. In addition to a time-series examination of the changes in the data for the treated children, Patterson included data on matched nondeviant subjects (see Figure 13.3). By so doing, one can make some statement about the degree to which clinically meaningful changes—returning deviant behavior to within a nondeviant rate—have been accomplished.

In addition, the normative comparison procedure provides an indication of how severely disturbed the treated subjects were prior to treatment in relation to the range of scores of nondisturbed subjects. It should be noted, however, that a *mean change* to within one standard deviation of the normative *mean* does not indicate that all individual subjects showed similar improvements. The distribution of treated subjects' scores about their mean should be examined to identify whether or not the mean change is representative of the majority of cases. Reporting the per-

---

[3]The reader is referred to the published reports of these studies for detailed statements of their findings.

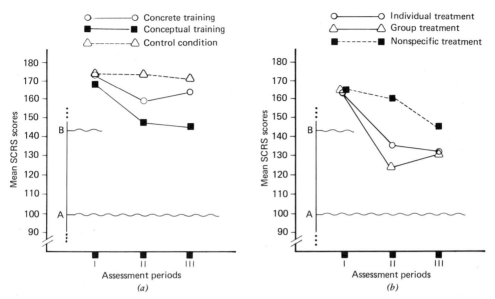

Figure 13.2. Mean Self-Control Rating Scale (SCRS) ratings: (a) for the concrete training, conceptual training, and control groups across the assessment periods; (b) for the individual treatment, group treatment, and nonspecific treatment groups across the assessment periods. The A represents the mean for over 100 randomly selected children; the B indicates one standard deviation from the mean. (a) Adapted from P. C. Kendall & L. E. Wilcox, A cognitive-behavioral treatment for impulsivity: Concrete versus conceptual training with non-self-controlled problem children. *Journal of Consulting and Clinical Psychology*, 1980, *48*, 80–91. Reprinted by permission of the American Psychological Association. (b) Adapted from P. C. Kendall & B. A. Zupan, Individual versus group application of cognitive-behavioral self-control procedures with children. *Behavior Therapy*, 1981, *12*, 344–359. Reprinted by permission of the Association for the Advancement of Behavior Therapy.

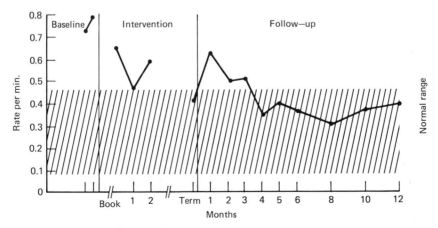

Figure 13.3. Total deviant behavior in the home. The area delineated by the grid lines constitutes the "normal range." Adapted from G. Patterson, Interventions for boys with conduct problems: Multiple settings, treatments, and criteria. *Journal of Consulting and Clinical Psychology*, 1974, *42*, 471–481. Reprinted by permission of the American Psychological Association.

centage of clients reaching the criteria of clinical significance would be highly desirable. This aspect of the methodology is important, since as one points to the distribution of normal scores, one must also examine the distribution of the treated groups' scores. Moreover, statistical tests can be employed to determine whether the treated group is significantly different from the normative group. In such cases it would be desirable to discover that the differences were nonsignificant (e.g., Kendall, 1982). A nonsignificant difference between treated and normative samples would support the effectiveness of the treatment since treated subjects were no longer deviant.

Attrition

Reductions over time in the number of subjects in a research project can occur as a result of any of a long list of possibilities: relocation, disenchantment, external pressures, or new personal relationships, to mention only a few. The upshot is that all research participants may not complete their assignments. While attrition is problematic in all research involving repeated measurements, attrition in therapy outcome studies can pose serious problems.

The attrition of clients can occur at any time during the course of the study, although the effects of attrition depend largely on whether or not clients left therapy before or after assignment to treatment conditions. For example, if one is studying the effects of a treatment in an outpatient clinic where 50% of the clients refused to participate, then one is left with a restricted sample, a sample that has reduced representativeness and is not generalizable to all outpatients. As a result, external validity is jeopardized. On the other hand, if clients agree to participate, but discontinue treatment after they have been assigned to treatment conditions, then internal validity is jeopardized, especially where the attrition rate is different for the different treatment conditions. Thus, attrition can det-

rimentally affect both the internal and external validity of the study.

Beyond the problematic nature of differential attrition rates, these data may contain important information that should not be overlooked. What is it about therapy A as opposed to therapy B that results in an 80% attrition rate as opposed to 5%? Differential attrition after treatment assignment may provide valuable information. These data are especially curious when psychological therapies and medications are being compared (Hollon & Beck, 1978).

Having to make decisions as to whether or not a client remains part of a study is another methodologically menacing aspect of attrition. At what point in the course of a study can a client discontinue treatment and yet be considered a part of the study? How does one define treatment completes (remainers) and incompletes (defectors)? Baekeland and Lundwall (1975) suggested that the number of visits be used to determine "completes," but no specific cut-off was provided. Apparently no established guidelines exist and according to Riecken and Borush (1974), there are no purely statistical methods for precise correction of differential attrition. Nevertheless, attrition rates should be reported, differential attrition should be analyzed and reported, and generalizations should be properly restricted to the sample that participated. In instances where attrition occurs after treatment but before the follow-up assessments, the remainers should be compared to the original sample to determine if these subjects are representative of the complete original sample (compare remainers and defectors). Defectors can also be examined in an effort to isolate characteristics that may be predictive of their dropping out of therapy.

Manipulation Checks

In controlled outcome evaluations, the manipulated independent variable is typically a characteristic of the treatment. The researcher designs the study so that dissimilar treatments will be provided for clients in the different conditions. By design, all clients are not treated the same. However, simply because the study has been so designed does not guarantee that the independent variable has been manipulated as intended.

The clinician-researcher works to assure that the independent variable is properly manipulated by requiring a treatment plan to be followed, careful therapist training, employing therapy manuals, and supervision and monitoring of progress. The researcher must nevertheless provide an independent check of the manipulation. For example, requiring that tape recordings be made of the therapy sessions allows for such a manipulation check by an independent rater. Quantifiable judgments regarding characteristics of the independent variable provide the necessary manipulation check. In addition, tape recordings are inexpensive, can be used for subsequent training, and can be analyzed for other research purposes.

Tape recordings of therapy sessions in outcome studies not only provide a check on the treatment manipulation within each separate study but also can allow for a check on the comparability of treatments provided across studies. That is, the therapy provided as cognitive-behavior therapy in one clinician's study, for example, could be checked to determine its comparability to other clinician-researchers' cognitive-behavior therapy. Moreover, the *quality* of the therapy that was studied and reported can be calibrated and subsequently examined. It may be the case that the cognitive-behavioral therapy in one study was provided in a less-than-optimal fashion, whereas it was maximally provided in another. If the outcome data were more supportive in the second report, then quality of the treatment can be identified as an influential factor in outcome. Treatment manuals that describe the therapy procedures in detail are essential for different researchers to conduct comparable types of intervention,

but independent checks alone can show the comparability and examine quality.

METHODS FOR CUMULATIVE ANALYSES OF OUTCOME RESEARCH

Beginning with Eysenck's (1952) provocative review of therapy outcome research, several major cummulative analyses have been reported (e.g., Meltzoff & Kornreich, 1970; Bergin & Garfield, 1971; Leitenberg, 1976; Gurman & Razin, 1977; Garfield & Bergin, 1978; Kazdin & Wilson, 1978). However, only recently have clinical researchers attempted to apply formal techniques to derive "meta-analyses" of the research literature. Some approaches have employed simple tabulations of the number of studies favoring one type of intervention versus competitors (Luborsky, Singer, & Luborsky, 1975; Beutler, 1979), while others have developed multidimensional multivariate analyses of the impact of potential causal factors on therapy outcome (Smith & Glass, 1977). Several difficult choices confront the would-be meta-analyzer of a body of research as diverse in quality, methodology, theoretical orientation, target issues and variables, and number of studies as that for the evaluation of therapy results.

First, should studies of inferior methodological quality be omitted? Some researchers argue that the truism, "garbage in, garbage out," holds true (Eysenck, 1978; Luborsky et al., 1975). However, others take the position that the vagaries of individual studies will cancel out in favor of truly meaningful trends and conclusions, if a substantial body of research is tapped, much as individual differences in clients are presumed to be unimportant if a large enough sample is utilized (Smith & Glass, 1977). The "quality selection" approach provides a meta-analyzer with studies in which unexpected extraneous variables have the least chance of distorting results. Yet in so doing, the number of available investigations is often sufficiently reduced that it becomes difficult to assess whether or not the findings are replicated (Smith, 1970). However, additional "quality" research will resolve this problem. It can also be argued that the most methodologically rigorous studies also run a serious risk of trivializing their own conclusions (Gelder, 1976). On the other hand, the analysis of unselected studies avoids the confounding factor of narrow selection, but not without assuming a gamble that hundreds of sows's ears can be statistically processed into a silk purse. Some form of selection appears warranted to guarantee that the results of cumulative analyses are based on valid individual studies.

Once a sample of studies is obtained, the next issue concerns the method by which the findings are combined and analyzed. At one end of the continuum, meta-analyzers have simply tallied or eyeballed the separate analyses from each study to produce a "box score" (Luborsky et al., 1975; Beutler, 1979). In contrast, other meta-analyzers use each study's correlation (e.g., Berman, 1979) or analysis of variance (e.g., Smith & Glass, 1977) data to calculate "effect sizes" in terms of either *standard deviation scores* or *percentages of variance*. Effect sizes in terms of standard deviation scores entails subtracting the means score for one therapy group from that from a competing therapy group, and dividing the difference by either or both groups' standard deviations. The percentage of variance method involves calculating expected mean squares from the analyses of variance effect data.

Although the box score method can be criticized as an oversimplification, the more sophisticated analytic techniques have been said to be capable of producing almost contradictory conclusions depending upon the type of effect size calculated (Gallo, 1978). To date, however, authors of cumulative analyses have drawn similar conclusions: essentially, it appears that most therapies help most clients to improve the average level

of adjustment of wait-list control clients, and that no therapeutic intervention has emerged as consistently and dramatically superior to all its competitors.[4]

However, these meta-analyses have not until recently gone beyond a general comparison of intervention modalities to search for optimal matching of clients, therapists, and interventions. Smith and Glass (1977) incorporated several client variables, such as diagnosis and intelligence, and therapist variables, such as experience, into regression equations to attempt to predict the effect of these factors on outcome in psychodynamic versus behavioral therapies. While few specific conclusions are reported, and the reader is cautioned to interpret these as directions for research verification rather than as solid conclusions, this approach offers a direct method for meta-analytic study of potential client-therapist-intervention matches.

Alternatively, theoretical predictions concerning optimal matching can be made and then tested by individual and cumulative analysis. For example, Beutler (1979) formulated three bipolar dimensions of clients: situational versus intrapsychic dysfunction; internal versus external defensive style; high versus low reactance to external threats. In addition, five types of therapeutic intervention were formulated: cognitive modification; cognitive insight; behavior therapy; behavior modification; and affective insight. From this foundation, Beutler derived a series of hypotheses concerning the results of the 30 (6 client types × 5 therapy types) possible client-intervention matches. For example, behavioral therapies will be superior to insight therapies with clients with situational dysfunctions. Unfortunately, the number of studies that provided sufficient information to permit a classification of their clients was limited. For this reason, very few of the hypotheses could be fairly tested. Of

---

[4]A recent meta-analysis employing only a select sample of quality studies resulted in a similar conclusion (Dawes, 1981).

those for which more than two or three studies were available, the findings only rarely provided unequivocal support for any hypothesis. Nevertheless, as Beutler points out, the development of an integrative theoretical conceptualization is necessary *now* if researchers are to avoid the pitfall of producing thousands of studies that fail to investigate comparable (and therefore meta-analyzable) therapy outcome determinants and measures. Beutler's model is only one of many possible schemas, and it has shortcomings, but a unifying set of guidelines and foci are prerequisite to systematic advancement in this field.

This recommendation echoes that of several prominent therapy outcome researchers who have called for a collaborative effort among clinical researchers of all theoretical orientations and from all geographic-cultural-professional settings (e.g., Goldfried 1980; Kiesler, 1971; Parloff, 1979). One straightforward, though by no means easy, approach would be to bring such an array of outcome researchers together with the express purpose of developing a consensus on the major variables from each of the domains of potential determinants of therapy outcome. Clinicians and researchers of different theoretical or pragmatic orientations could agree to disagree, but to nevertheless delimit the range of possible variables to a limited number. This limited number of variables might be those that receive substantial endorsement based on their prior research validation, including studies from other areas than outcome research, or their theoretical omnipresence. Even if certain variables were considered trivial by many researchers, their inclusion, based on strong support from other researchers, would permit an empirical test by proponents as well as by skeptics.

Cautionary Comments

While the merits of integration and summation of the results of related outcome studies are recognized, some cautions must be

exercised in any meta-analysis. First, as noted briefly earlier, one must check on the quality of studies, eliminating those that cannot contribute meaningful findings due to basic inadequacies. Consider the following: Would you accept the recommendation that one treatment approach is superior to another if the recommendation were based on *inadequate* research? Probably not. Would you accept this same evidence in support of the refutation of the recommendation? Probably not. If the research is sufficiently inadequate as to be insufficient evidence for a recommendation, it remains inadequate as evidence against a recommendation. Simply stated, if a study is methodologically unsound, then its findings are not useful in the support or refutation of a treatment recommendation, and should therefore not be included in cumulative analyses. If a study is methodologically sound, then regardless of the outcome, it must be included.

Second, the manner in which studies are assembled into groups for drawing specific conclusions must be guided by the necessity that these studies be comparable. Assembling groups of studies in which clients were diagnosed by different procedures, where therapists were markedly diverse, and where the length of treatment varied enormously will not clear the picture. Initial groupings must be homogeneous. Subsequently the generality of the conclusions can be assessed with more heterogeneous groups of studies.

Caution is paramount in meta-analyses in which various studies are said to provide evidence that treatment is superior to "controls." The exact nature of the control group in each specific treatment outcome study must be examined, especially in the case of attention/placebo control groups. This caution arises from the indefinite definition of control groups such as attention/placebo. Consider, for example, the control group employed by one of the authors of this chapter in an evaluation of cognitive-behavioral and patient-education procedures for reducing the stress of invasive medical procedures (Kendall,

Williams, Pechacek, Graham, Shisslak, & Herzoff, 1979). Two control groups were included in the study: a current-conditions control, in which patients completed the assessment measures but otherwise received only standard hospital practices; and an attention/placebo control, in which patients participated in individual, nondirective discussions. One might choose to argue that the attention/placebo control condition resembles strongly a Rogerian client-centered treatment. In fact it is not uncommon for one researcher's attention control group to resemble another's treatment condition! Meta-analyzers cannot tabulate the number of studies in which treatment was found to be efficacious in relation to controls without examining the nature of the control conditions.

CONCLUDING COMMENTS

With the variety of available methods for experimental and correlational analyses and meta-analyses of the effects of therapy and the factors contributing to therapy results, the key challenge is now one of developing focused and integrative research. Political as well as scientific concerns dictate this conclusion (Parloff, 1979). With the potential for national health insurance and the increasing public pressure for accountability in governmental fiscal policies, the effects and effectiveness of therapeutic intervention may become a survival issue for psychotherapists.[5]

Clinicians and government officials are experiencing mounting pressures from such not easily disregarded sources as the courts, insurance companies, and national health insurance planners. Third-party payers—ultimately the public—are demanding crisp and informative answers to questions regarding the quality, quantity, durability, safety, and efficiency of psychosocial treatments

[5]A recent News and Comment article in *Science* (Marshall, 1980) has placed this issue before the greater scientific community.

provided to an ever-widening range of consumers and potential consumers. (Parloff, 1979, p. 297)

At present we can be comfortable with the methodological advances that have been made thus far, but we are puzzled by the fragmentation and lack of any consensual guidelines or metaconceptualizations in the field of therapy outcome research. This void tends to obscure any but the most tentative and general answers to the question, what therapy, conducted by what therapist with what clients, produces what effects? Indeed many conclude that therapy works pretty well for some of the people on some of their problems, some of the time. This conclusion is imprecise, yet it summarizes the conclusions of both clinical researchers and political analysts (see Parloff, 1979, for an informative review of the recent report of the President's Commission on Mental Health). In an era of growing recognition of the value of positive mental health and of the pervasiveness of psychological dysfunctions, it is ironic that the once revered psychotherapist is now being challenged for evidence of accountability.

However, the growing uncertainty and discontent can be a positive, mobilizing force for outcome researchers. The role of clients' value judgments about the relative importance of different kinds of life changes can be examined both clinically and scientifically to provide systematic bases for assessing the social meaning of different therapeutic results. The central foci for outcome research can be consensually evolved from a multidisciplinary and multitheoretical perspective. The quality of services delivered in community clinics and in private practitioners' offices can become a target issue for outcome researchers and program evaluators jointly. Therapy outcome research can grow, as a field, from a scattered and sheltered adolescence to a mature, integrated, and principled adulthood. That scientific inquiry will assist in the discovery of the optimal procedures for therapy is a necessary assumption. If it is not assumed, the possibility of true discovery dissolves.

REFERENCES

Abramowitz, C.V., Abramowitz, S.I., Roback, H.B., & Jackson C. (1974) Differential effectiveness of directive and nondirective therapies as a function of client internal-external control. *Journal of Consulting and Clinical Psychology,* **42,** 849–853.

Albee, G. (1970). The uncertain future of clinical psychology. *American Psychologist,* **25,** 1071–1080.

American Psychological Association (1973). *Ethical standards of psychologists.* Washington, D.C.: American Psychological Association.

American Psychological Association Committee on Training in Clinical Psychology (1947). Recommended graduate training program in clinical psychology. *American Psychologist,* **2,** 539–558.

Baekeland, F., & Lundwall, L. (1975). Dropping out of treatment: A critical review. *Psychological Bulletin,* **82,** 738–783.

Baer, D.M., Wolf, M.M., & Risley, T.R. (1968). Some current dimensions of applied behavior analysis. *Journal of Applied Behavior Analysis,* **1,** 91–97.

Belkin, G.S. (1980). *Contemporary psychotherapies.* Chicago: Rand McNally.

Bergin, A.E. (1971). The evaluation of therapeutic outcome. In A.E. Bergin & S. L. Garfield (Eds.), *Handbook of psychotherapy and behavior change.* New York: Wiley.

Bergin, A.E., & Lambert, M.J. (1978). The evaluation of therapeutic outcomes. In S.L. Garfield & A.E. Bergin (Eds.), *Handbook of psychotherapy and behavior change* (2nd ed.). New York: Wiley.

Bergin, A.E. & Garfield, S.L. (Eds.) (1971). *Handbook of psychotherapy and behavior change.* New York: Wiley.

Berman, J. (1979). Therapeutic expectancies and treatment outcome: A quantitative review. Paper presented at the American Psychological Association Annual Convention, New York.

Berzins, J. (1977). Therapist-patient matching. In A. Gurman & A. Razin (Eds.), *Effective psychotherapy: A handbook of research.* New York: Pergamon Press.

Beutler, L.E. (1979). Toward specific psychological therapies for specific conditions. *Journal of Consulting and Clinical Psychology,* **47,** 882–897.

Braud, L.W. (1978). The effects of frontal EMG biofeedback and progressive relaxation upon hyperactivity and its behavioral concomitants. *Biofeedback and Self-Regulation,* **3,** 69–89.

Campbell, D.T., & Stanley, J.C. (1963). *Experimental and quasi-experimental designs for research.* Chicago: Rand McNally.

Ciminero, A., Calhoun, K., & Adams, H. (Eds.) (1977). *Handbook of behavioral assessment.* New York: Wiley.

Cohen, J., & Cohen, P. (1975). *Applied multiple regression/correlation analyses for the behavioral sciences.* Hillsdale, N.J.: Erlbaum.

Cook, T.D., & Campbell, D.T. (1979) *Quasi-experimentation: Design and analysis issues for field settings.* Chicago: Rand McNally.

Corsini, R. (Ed.) (1979) *Contemporary psychotherapies* (2nd ed.). Itasca, Ill.: Peacock.

Dawes, R. (1981). Personal communication. Center for Advanced Study in the Behavioral Sciences, Stanford, California, May.

Dougherty, F. (1976). Patient-therapist matching for optimal and minimal therapeutic outcome. *Journal of Consulting and Clinical Psychology,* **44,** 889–897.

Eysenck, H.J. (1952). The effects of psychotherapy: An evaluation. *Journal of Consulting Psychology,* **16,** 319–324.

Eysenck, H.J. (1978). An exercise in mega-silliness. *American Psychologist,* **33,** 517.

Fiske, D.W., Hunt, H.F., Luborsky, L., Orne, M.T., Parloff, M.B., Reiser, M.F., & Tuma, A.H. (1970). Planning of research on effectiveness of psychotherapy. *Archives of General Psychiatry,* **22,** 22–32.

Ford, J.D. (1978). The therapeutic relationship in behavior therapy. *Journal of Consulting and Clinical Psychology,* **46,** 1302–1314.

Gallo, P.S., Jr. (1978). Meta-analysis—A mixed metaphor? *American Psychologist,* **33,** 515–517.

Garfield, S.L. (1971). Research on client variables in psychotherapy. In A.E. Bergin & S.L. Garfield (Eds.), *Handbook of psychotherapy and behavior change.* New York: Wiley.

Garfield, S.L. (1978). Research on client variables in psychotherapy. In S.L. Garfield & A.E. Bergin (Eds.), *Handbook of psychotherapy and behavior change* (2nd ed.). New York: Wiley.

Garfield, S.L. & Bergin, A.E. (Eds.) (1978) *Handbook of psychotherapy and behavior change* (2nd ed.). New York: Wiley.

Gelder, N.G. (1976). Research methodology in psychotherapy—Why bother? *Proceedings of the Royal Society of Medicine,* **69,** 505–508.

Goldfried, M.R. (1980). Toward the delineation of therapeutic change principles. *American Psychologist,* **35,** 991–999.

Goldfried, M.R. & Davison, G.C. (1976). *Clinical be-*

havior therapy. New York: Holt, Rinehart & Winston.

Goldstein, A.P., Heller, K., & Sechrest, L.B. (1966). *Psychotherapy and the psychology of behavior change*. New York: Wiley.

Goldstein, A.P., & Stein, N. (1976). *Prescriptive psychotherapies*. New York: Pergamon Press.

Gottman, J., & Markman, H.J. (1978). Experimental designs in psychotherapy research. In S.L. Garfield & A.E. Bergin (Eds.), *Handbook of psychotherapy and behavior change* (2nd ed.). New York: Wiley.

Gurman, A. (1977). The patient's perception of the therapeutic relationship. In A. Gurman & A. Razin (Eds.), *Effective psychotherapy: A handbook of research*. New York: Pergamon Press.

Gurman, A., & Razin, A. (Eds.) (1977). *Effective psychotherapy: A handbook of research*. New York: Pergamon Press.

Haley, J. (1976). *Problem solving therapy*. San Francisco: Jossey-Bass.

Hamlin, R.M., & Albee, G.W. (1948). Muench's tests before and after nondirective therapy: A control group for his subjects. *Journal of Consulting Psychology*, **12**, 412–416.

Hersen, M., & Barlow, D. (1976). *Single case experimental designs*. New York: Pergamon Press.

Hoch, E.L., Ross, A.O., & Winder, C.L. (Eds.) (1966). *Professional preparation of clinical psychologists*. Washington, D.C.: American Psychological Association.

Hollon, S.D., & Beck, A.T. (1978). Psychotherapy and drug therapy: Comparison and combinations. In S.L. Garfield & A.E. Bergin (Eds.), *Handbook of psychotherapy and behavior change* (2nd ed.) New York: Wiley.

Kazdin, A.E. (1979). Imagery elaboration and self-efficacy in the covert modeling treatment of unassertive behavior. *Journal of Consulting and Clinical Psychology*, **47**, 725–733.

Kazdin, A.E. *Research design in clinical psychology*. New York: Harper & Row. 1980.

Kazdin, A.E., & Wilson, G.T. (1978) *Evaluation of behavior therapy: Issues, evidence, and research strategies*. Cambridge, Mass.: Ballinger.

Kendall, P.C. (1982). Individual versus group cognitive-behavioral self-control training: One-year follow-up. *Behavior Therapy*, in press.

Kendall, P.C., & Hollon, S.D. (Eds.) (1981). *Assessment strategies for cognitive-behavioral interventions*. New York: Academic Press.

Kendall, P.C., & Korgeski, G.P. (1979). Assessment and cognitive-behavioral interventions. *Cognitive Therapy and Research*, **3**, 1–21.

Kendall, P.C., & Norton-Ford, J.D. (1982). *Clinical psychology: Scientific and professional dimensions*. New York: Wiley.

Kendall, P.C., Williams, L., Pechacek, T.F., Graham, L., Shisslak, C., & Herzoff, N. (1979). Cognitive-behavioral and patient education interventions in cardiac catheterization procedures: The Palo Alto medical psychology project. *Journal of Consulting and Clinical Psychology*, **47**, 49–58.

Kendall, P.C., & Wilcox, L.E. (1980). A cognitive-behavioral treatment for impulsivity: Concrete versus conceptual training with non-self-controlled problem children. *Journal of Consulting and Clinical Psychology*, **48**, 80–91.

Kendall, P.C., & Wilcox, L.E. (1979). Self-control in children: Development of a rating scale. *Journal of Consulting and Clinical Psychology*, **47**, 1020–1030.

Kendall, P.C., & Zupan, B.A. (1981). Individual versus group application of cognitive-behavioral self-control procedures with children. *Behavior Therapy*, **12**, 344–359.

Kiesler, D.J. (1966). Some myths of psychotherapy research and the search for a paradigm. *Psychological Bulletin*, **65**, 110–136.

Kiesler, D.J. (1971). Experimental design in psychotherapy research. In A.E. Bergin & S.L. Garfield (Eds.), *Handbook of psychotherapy and behavior change*. New York: Wiley.

Kiesler, D.J. (1973). *The process of psychotherapy*. Chicago: Aldine.

Korman, M. (1974). National conference on levels and patterns of professional training in psychology: The major themes. *American Psychologist*, **29**, 441–449.

Leitenberg, H. (Ed.) (1976). *Handbook of behavior modification and behavior therapy*. New York: Appleton-Century-Crofts.

Luborsky, L., Singer, B., & Luborsky, L. (1975). Comparative studies of psychotherapies. *Archives of General Psychiatry*, **32**, 995–1008.

Mahoney, M.J. (1978). Experimental methods and outcome evaluation. *Journal of Consulting and Clinical Psychology*, **46**, 660–672.

Marsden, G. (1971). Content analysis studies of psychotherapy: 1954–1968. In A.E. Bergin & S.L. Garfield (Eds.), *Handbook of psychotherapy and behavior change*. New York: Wiley.

Marshall, E. (1980). Psychotherapy faces test of worth. *Science*, **207**, January, 35–36.

McCord, J. (1978). A thirty-year follow-up of treatment effects. *American Psychologist*, **33**, 284–289.

Meichenbaum, D.H., Gilmore, J.B., & Fedoravicious, A. (1971). Group insight versus group desensitization in treating speech anxiety. *Journal of Consulting and Clinical Psychology*. **36,** 410–421.

Meltzoff, J., & Kornreich, M. (1971). *Research in psychotherapy*. New York: Atherton.

Mintz, J. (1977). The therapist's evaluation of outcome. In A. Gurman & A. Razin (Eds.), *Effective psychotherapy: A handbook of research*. New York: Pergamon Press.

Mitchell, K., Bozarth, J., & Krauft, C. (1977). A reappraisal of the therapeutic effectiveness of empathy, nonpossessive warmth, and genuineness. In A. Gurman & A. Razin (Eds.), *Effective psychotherapy: A handbook of research*. New York: Pergamon Press.

O'Leary, K.D., & Borkovec, T.D. (1978). Conceptual, methodological, and ethical problems of placebo groups in psychotherapy research. *American Psychologist*, **33,** 821–830.

Orlinsky, D.E., & Howard, K.I. (1978) The relation of process to outcome in psychotherapy. In S.L. Garfield & A.E. Bergin (Eds.), *Handbook of psychotherapy and behavior change* (2nd ed.). New York: Wiley.

Parloff, M.B. (1979). Can psychotherapy research guide the policymaker? A little knowledge may be a dangerous thing. *American Psychologist*, **34,** 296–306.

Parloff, M.B., Waskow, I.E., & Wolfe, B.E. (1978) Research on therapist variables in relation to process and outcome. In S.L. Garfield & A.E. Bergin (Eds.), *Handbook of psychotherapy and behavior change* (2nd ed.). New York: Wiley.

Patterson, G.R. (1974). Interventions for boys with conduct problems: Multiple settings, treatments, and criteria. *Journal of Consulting and Clinical Psychology*, **42,** 471–481.

Paul, G. (1967). Strategy of outcome research in psychotherapy. *Journal of Consulting Psychology*, **31,** 109–119.

Powers, E., & Witmer, H. (1951). *An experiment in the prevention of deliquency*. New York: Columbia University Press.

Prochaska, J. (1979). *Systems of psychotherapy: A transtheoretical analyses*. Homewood, Ill.: Dorsey.

Raimy, V.C. (Ed.) (1950) *Training in clinical psychology*. New York: Prentice-Hall.

Riecken, H.W. & Boruch, R.F. (1974). *Social experimentation: A method for planning and evaluating social intervention*. New York: Academic Press.

Rosenthal, R., & Frank, J.D. (1956). Psychotherapy and the placebo effect. *Psychological Bulletin*, **53,** 294–302.

ꓤhakow, D. (1976). What is clinical psychology? *American Psychologist*, **31,** 553–560.

Shapiro, A.K. (1971). Placebo effects in medicine, psychotherapy, and psychoanalysis. In A.E. Bergin & S.L. Garfield (Eds.) *Handbook of psychotherapy and behavior change*. New York: Wiley.

Sloane, R.B., Staples, F.R., Cristol, A.H., Yorkston, N.J., & Whipple, K. (1976). Patient characteristics and outcome in psychotherapy and behavior therapy. *Journal of Consulting and Clinical Psychology*, **44,** 330–339.

Smith, M.L., & Glass, G.V. (1977). Meta-analysis of psychotherapy outcome studies. *American Psychologist*, **32,** 752–760.

Smith, N.C., Jr. (1970). Replication studies: A neglected aspect of psychological research. *American Psychologist*, **25,** 970–975.

Stokes, T.E., & Baer, D. M. (1977). An implicit technology of generalization. *Journal of Applied Behavior Analysis*, **10,** 349–367.

Strother, C.R. (Ed.) (1957). *Psychology and mental health*. Washington, D.C.: American Psychological Association.

Strupp, H.H. (1976) Clinical psychology, irrationalism, and the erosion of excellence. *American Psychologist*, **31,** 561–571.

Strupp, H.H. (1978). Psychotherapy research and practice: An overview. In S.L. Garfield & A.E. Bergin (Eds.) *Handbook of psychotherapy and behavior change* (2nd ed.). New York: Wiley.

Strupp, H.H., & Bergin, A.E. (1969). Some empirical and conceptual bases for coordinated research in psychotherapy. *International Journal of Psychiatry*, **7,** 18–90.

Strupp, H.H., & Hadley, S.W. (1977). A tripartite mode of mental health and therapeutic outcomes: With special reference to the negative effects of psychotherapy. *American Psychologist*, **32,** 187–196.

Stuart, R.B. (1973). Notes on the ethics of behavior research and interventions. In L.A. Hamerlynck, L.C. Handy, & E.J. Nash (Eds.), *Behavior change: Methodology, concepts, and practice*. Champaign, Ill: Research Press.

Stunkard, A.J., & Mahoney, M.J. (1976). Behavioral treatment of the eating disorders. In H. Leitenberg (ed.), *Handbook of behavior modification and behavior therapy*. Englewood Cliffs, N.J.: Prentice-Hall.

Thorne, F.C. (1974). The clinical method in science. *American Psychologist*, **2,** 159–166.

Truax, C.B., & Mitchell, K.M. (1971) Research on certain therapist interpersonal skills in relation to process and outcome. In A.E. Bergin & S.L. Garfield (Eds.), *Handbook of psychotherapy and behavior change*. New York: Wiley.

Vale, J.R., & Vale, C.A. (1969). Individual differences and general laws in psychology: A reconciliation. *American Psychologist,* **24,** 1093–1108.

Watzlawick, P. (1978). *The language of change.* New York: Norton.

Watzlawick, P., Weakland, J., & Fisch, R. (1974) *Change.* New York: Norton.

Wilkins, W. (1977). Expectancies in applied settings. In A. Gurman & A. Razin (Eds.), *Effective psychotherapy: A handbook of research.* New York: Pergamon Press.

Wolpe, J. (1969). *The practice of behavior therapy.* Elmsford, N.Y.: Pergamon Press.

CHAPTER 14

Single-Case Experimental Designs

ALAN E. KAZDIN

Single-case experimental designs have been employed extensively with a variety of clinical populations and in a wide range of inpatient and outpatient settings (Hersen & Barlow, 1976; Kazdin, 1978a, in press). The designs are not necessarily restricted to the single case, and for that reason other names, such as "intrasubject-replication designs," have been used. Even though the designs can evaluate interventions for groups of individuals, their unique methodological contribution to experimentation is examination of the individual case. From the standpoint of clinical psychology, an experimental methodology to study the individual case is highly significant. Single-case research offers an alternative to the uncontrolled case study that has been heavily relied upon to make conclusions about the individual case.

Use of single-case experimentation in clinical psychology has been largely restricted to behavior modification. Although this can be explained historically (Kazdin, 1978b), it is unfortunate to view the methodology as uniquely applicable to one conceptual approach over another. Single-case methodology provides a variety of options for combining clinical treatment and empirical evaluation. The methodology can be extended beyond a particular set of techniques, problems, and clients to provide a broad basis for validating clinical techniques.

The purpose of the present chapter is to describe the basic approach of single-case experimental methodology. The basic logic of single-case research, specific designs, and methods of data evaluation will be described. Problems and special data requirements that arise in single-case experiments and the advantages that various designs offer for clinical work will be discussed.

LOGIC OF SINGLE-CASE DESIGNS

In all experimental research, the underlying rationale for drawing inferences is based upon making comparisons of performance under different conditions. In between-group research, the different conditions are provided to separate groups. For example, in the most rudimentary case, the effects of treatment are evaluated by comparing performance of a group of persons who receive treatment with another group of persons who do not. In single-case research, the different conditions are compared within a subject or several subjects. The comparison usually is achieved by presenting alternative conditions to the subject at different points in time. For example, treatment might be evaluated by alternating periods of treatment and no treatment over time. Performance of the subject is assessed repeatedly under these conditions to make the comparison of interest.

Single-case designs depend upon continuous assessment of behavior to provide the basis for comparing different conditions. Continuous assessment refers to observations that are obtained often (e.g., daily) for extended periods (e.g., several weeks). The assessment of behavior for extended periods is crucial to the designs, because the inferences made about treatment are based upon patterns of the data across different treatment conditions.

Usually single-case designs begin with observations of a client's behavior for several days prior to treatment. This period of observation, referred to as the *baseline* phase, has two purposes. First, the data obtained during baseline provide a description of the extent of the client's problem. An accurate description is useful for deciding the extent and type of changes needed in treatment. Second, the information serves as a basis for predicting the level of performance in the immediate future if treatment is not provided. Thus the initial baseline observations serve a descriptive and predictive function. The logic of the designs depends heavily upon the predictive function because single-case research, as between-group research, is fundamentally based upon testing predictions about performance.

The baseline data predict what behavior will be like in the future if treatment is not implemented. A projection of baseline performance into the future is the implicit criterion against which treatment is eventually evaluated. Hypothetical baseline data are plotted in the first phase of Figure 14.1. Observation of baseline performance (solid line) can be used to predict performance into the future (dashed line). If the observations are continued into the future under the same conditions, the projected line would be the expected result. If the baseline data are relatively stable and do not show systematic changes over time, the prediction is relatively straightforward. After baseline is stable and performance can be extrapolated into the future with some degree of confidence, treatment is implemented.

Assessment of behavior continues during treatment to determine if the level of performance during this phase (solid line) departs from the level previously predicted by baseline (dashed line). If treatment is effective, as it is portrayed in Figure 14.1, the actual level of behavior should deviate considerably from the projected level of behavior

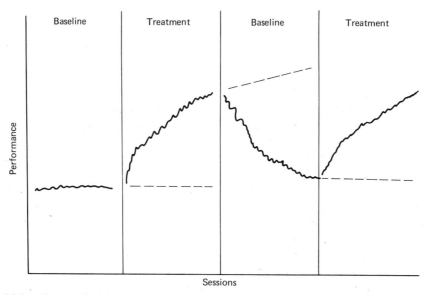

Figure 14.1.   Hypothetical data for the frequency of behavior across baseline and treatment phases. A solid (wavy) line reflects actual performance during each of the particular phases. A dashed line reflects the projected level of performance predicted from the previous phase.

from baseline. Thus the data obtained during the treatment phase are tested against the predicted data from the previous phase. The data during the treatment phase in Figure 14.1 suggest that changes are occurring that would not be predicted by the original baseline. The change may well have resulted from the intervention, but it is premature to make this claim with confidence.

The data from the treatment phase not only are compared with the projected level from baseline but also predict how the client will perform in the future. Treatment data are used to project future performance in the same way that baseline data were used. Perhaps performance during the treatment phase is not really the result of treatment but some extraneous event that will continue to account for the level of performance after treatment is withdrawn. To test this, treatment is withdrawn and the new level of behavior during this (third) phase is compared with the projected level from the treatment phase. In addition, by withdrawing treatment, the investigator reinstates the conditions of the original baseline. In the original baseline, a projection was made of what performance would be like in the future if baseline conditions were continued. By withdrawing treatment, a direct test is made to determine whether the original prediction was accurate. Without treatment, would behavior have continued at this original level? A return to baseline conditions after treatment is a direct test of this.

Single-case designs proceed in the fashion highlighted here by gathering data over time under one set of conditions (baseline) and making predictions of what performance would be like in the future if such conditions were continued. Then changes are made in the conditions (treatment) to test whether behavior departs from the predicted performance levels. New levels of behavior are predicted, and these predictions in turn are tested in subsequent phases. Each phase makes a prediction about future performance and tests whether the prediction made in a previous

phase is accurate. If performance changes in response to alterations of the experimental conditions, the changes can be accounted for more parsimoniously by experimental conditions rather than by other events that would explain the repeated departures from predicted levels of performance.

The method of making predictions and testing them within a subject illustrates the general rationale for single-case research. The precise manner in which the predictions are made and tested depart slightly from the description as a function of the specific experimental design. Descriptions and illustrations of several basic designs can convey the logic and utility of the single-case approach for clinical research.

SPECIFIC DESIGNS: AN OVERVIEW

Several single-case designs are available, and each of these includes multiple variations (Hersen & Barlow, 1976; Kazdin, 1978a, in press; Kratochwill, 1978; Leitenberg, 1973). Four basic designs are considered below, along with examples to illustrate the methodology and how it is applied.

ABAB Design

The ABAB design is the basic design of single-case research, because it follows and illustrates the logic of the approach in the clearest fashion. Indeed Figure 14.1 illustrates the design in which the effects of treatment are evaluated by alternately presenting and withdrawing treatment at different points in time. The design usually begins with a baseline (or A) phase in which behavior is observed without treatment. After a stable rate of behavior is evident, the treatment (or B) phase is implemented. When behavior during the treatment phase departs from the projected level of baseline performance and stabilizes, treatment is withdrawn.

The baseline phase usually is reinstated. This phase, often referred to as a "reversal phase," is designed to return behavior to or near its original baseline level. Several procedures can achieve this goal, but usually treatment is simply withdrawn (Kazdin, 1980a). After behavior reverts to baseline levels, treatment is again reinstated so that the final phase of the ABAB design is implemented. If behavior approaches the level achieved in the previous treatment phase and departs from the immediately prior baseline phase, the effect of the intervention is quite clear.

An interesting illustration of treatment evaluated in an ABAB design was provided by Neisworth and Moore (1972), who reduced the asthmatic attacks of a seven-year-old boy. The child's asthmatic attacks consisted of prolonged wheezing, coughing, and gasping, at bedtime. This behavior usually was associated with verbal and physical attention on the part of the child's parents immediately before he went to bed. The inves-

tigators believed that these attacks might be maintained by the excessive attention they received. An extinction procedure (cessation of reinforcement for asthmatic attacks) was tried to test this relationship directly. After baseline observations of the duration of asthmatic attacks, an extinction procedure was used by the parents. The child did not receive attention after he was put to bed, and asthmatic attacks that occurred at this time were ignored. When the asthmatic attacks were of a shorter duration than on the previous night, the child was rewarded in the morning with lunch money so he could buy his lunch at school rather than take his lunch from home.

The results of the program are provided in Figure 14.2. As evident in the figure, the duration of asthmatic attacks increased at the beginning of the program. An increase (or burst) of the undesired behavior often occurs at the beginning of extinction, but usually drops out quickly (see Kazdin, 1980a). After

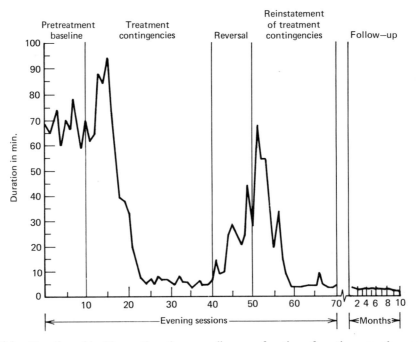

Figure 14.2. Duration of bedtime asthmatic responding as a function of contingency changes in an ABAB design. From J. T. Neisworth and F. Moore, Operant treatment of asthmatic responding with the parent as therapist, *Behavior Therapy,* 1972, *3,* 95–99. Reprinted by permission of the Association for Advancement of Behavior Therapy.

several days of treatment the duration of the attacks systematically declined. To assess whether the intervention accounted for change, a reversal phase was implemented in which parents responded as they normally had on the occurrence of an attack. And the duration of the attacks increased. Finally, the program was reinstated and the attacks, after another brief burst of responses, quickly declined to their previously low level. The program was eventually terminated and attacks remained low (a few minutes per day) up to the 11-month follow-up assessment. Overall, the pattern of data is relatively clear and shows that implementation and withdrawal of the program were associated with the predicted changes in performance.

The most frequently reported version of the ABAB design probably is the four-phase version illustrated in the above example. However, the ABAB design refers to a family of designs in which treatment and nontreatment phases are alternated. In some variations, the treatment is begun immediately without gathering baseline data, and essentially the order of phases is reversed (BABA). On other occasions, more than one treatment may be implemented in the design, for example, in cases in which the initial treatment has not been effective or sufficiently effective. So the design variation may be represented as $AB_1B_2AB_2$. The method of demonstrating a functional relationship between the intervention and performance is not altered.

Special Considerations. The ABAB design and its variations depend upon showing improvements in performance with the implementation of treatment and decrements upon withdrawal or alteration of the treatment. This latter characteristic of course raises serious problems when considering the design for clinical work. Withdrawing treatment to demonstrate a relationship between intervention and behavior raises obvious ethical issues. Once behavior is improved, it is difficult to justify withdrawing treatment to

make performance worse. And indeed for many problems where clinically important behavior is treated, it may be impractical and undesirable to suspend the intervention temporarily if the possibility exists that performance will become worse. Even if ethical and clinical concerns did not preclude withdrawing treatment temporarily to demonstrate a relationship between the intervention and performance, other problems may arise as well. In many instances withdrawal of treatment does not result in changes in behavior t025oward baseline levels (Baer, Rowbury, & Goetz, 1976; Thompson, Fraser, & McDougall, 1974). In such cases the intervention may have caused therapeutic change. However, without a reversal of performance it is not clear that the intervention was responsible for change.

In general the ABAB design and its variations provide a compelling experimental demonstration of the effects of treatment on performance. Unfortunately, the problems raised by the use of a reversal phase often make the designs inapplicable to the clinical situation. Several other single-case designs are available that do not require temporarily suspending treatment.

Multiple-Baseline Design

The multiple-baseline design also consists of a family of designs rather than a single design. The defining characteristic is demonstration of an experimental effect by showing that behavior change occurs whenever treatment is introduced at different points in time. Once the intervention is presented it need not be withdrawn or altered, so that the clinically objectionable feature of the ABAB design does not apply to the multiple-baseline design.

In a multiple-baseline design, treatment is examined by first collecting data concurrently on two or more baselines. The variations of the design are distinguished on the basis of the specific baselines that are observed. The baselines can consist of different responses for a particular individual, the same response across different persons, or the same response for a given individual across different situations. For example, in the multiple-baseline across behavior, several kinds of behavior for an individual (or group) are observed each day. Each kind of behavior is one that will eventually be subjected to treatment. After baseline data stabilize for each behavior, treatment is applied to one of the responses. Baseline conditions remain in effect for the other responses, although data continue to be collected for all of the responses. The initial behavior to which treatment was applied is expected to change, while the other responses remain at baseline levels. When the treated behavior stabilizes, the intervention is applied to the next behavior, and observations continue to be taken. Eventually each response is exposed to treatment but at different points in time. A causal relationship is evident if each response changes when and only when the intervention is introduced and not before.

An especially interesting clinical application of the multiple-baseline design was reported by Hayes, Brownell, and Barlow (1978), who treated multiple sexual deviations of a hospitalized adult male. The patient's history included attempted rape, multiple fantasies involving sadistic sexual acts (forced acts with bound women, use of pins and whips during intercourse), and exhibitionism. The patient had been arrested both for attempted rape and exhibitionism.

Treatment was designed to alter the patient's attraction toward socially censured stimuli and deviant sexual acts. An imagery-based procedure, referred to as *covert sensitization,* was used in which the patient imagined aversive consequences associated with situations in which exhibitionistic and sadistic acts were performed. For example, the patient was instructed to imagine engaging in a sexually deviant act that was followed by being pursued and arrested by the police.

Treatment was conducted in several ses-

sions and evaluated in a multiple-baseline design across responses. Initially the patient imagined aversive consequences associated with exhibitionistic situations. After several days, aversive consequences were imagined for sadistic acts. Over the course of treatment, the patient's level of sexual arousal was measured directly by the degree of erec-

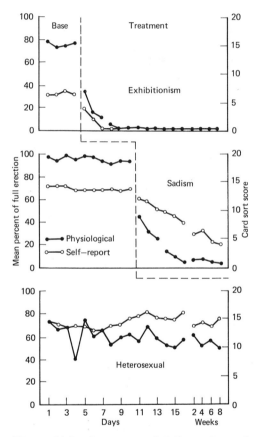

Figure 14.3. Percentage of full erection and self-reported arousal to exhibitionistic, sadistic, and heterosexual stimuli during baseline treatment, and follow-up phases in a multiple-baseline design. Card sort data are daily averages in the baseline and treatment phases and weekly averages in the follow-up phase. From S. C. Hayes, K. D. Brownell, and D. B. Barlow, The use of self-administered covert sensitization in the treatment of exhibitionism and sadism. *Behavior Therapy,* 1978, *9,* 283–289. Reprinted by permission of the Association for Advancement of Behavior Therapy.

tion (penile blood volume) as he viewed slides of exhibitionistic, sadistic, and heterosexual (socially appropriate) scenes. Also, the patient reported his degree of arousal to cards describing various sexual situations.

The effects of treatment are illustrated in Figure 14.3, which provides data on three different responses. As evident from the figure, physiological and self-reported sexual arousal decreased to exhibitionistic and sadistic scenes at each point that treatment was introduced and not before. On the other hand, arousal to heterosexual scenes, which was not associated with aversive consequences, remained relatively high. This case nicely illustrates the application and evaluation of treatment in a multiple-baseline design.

Special Considerations. The multiple-baseline design can demonstrate the effect of the intervention without a return to baseline conditions and a temporary loss in the gains that have been achieved with treatment. The clarity of the relationship is a function of the magnitude of treatment effects and the number of baselines across which this effect is demonstrated. Two baselines are a minimum in any particular demonstration. In the example provided in Figure 14.3, the intervention was applied to two different baselines, and the results were clear because of the abruptness of the changes, the stability of the baselines prior to the intervention, and the absence of changes on the final baseline that never received treatment. In most applications, three or more baselines are used. Thus if one of the baselines changes even before treatment is implemented, unambiguous inferences can be derived from the pattern of data for all of the other baselines.

One of the problems that may arise in the design is that alteration of one of the baselines may be associated with changes in the other baselines as well. The behavior that is observed may be interdependent, so that anything that affects one might affect the others as well (Wahler, 1975). For example, in the multiple-baseline design across behavior, it

is possible that changes in one behavior will be associated with changes in other behavior as well (Hersen & Bellack, 1976). Also, when the design examines behavior across several persons, application of the intervention to one person may alter the behavior of other persons as well (Kazdin, 1979). Finally, when the design examines the behavior of one or more persons across several situations, it is possible that application of the intervention to performance in one situation may alter performance in other situations too (Bennett & Maley, 1973).

With each version of the multiple-baseline design, generalized treatment effects may occur in which the intervention, when applied initially, extends to more than one baseline. In such cases the results would not show that behavior changed when and only when the intervention was applied to a particular baseline. Fortunately, generalized effects across different baselines appear to be the exception rather than the rule, at least in reported applications of the design. And when generalized effects are evident, other features from single-case research designs have been added, such as a brief reversal phase for one or more of the baselines to demonstrate a causal relation between treatment and behavior (Kazdin & Kopel, 1975).

Changing-Criterion Design

With the changing-criterion design, the effect of the intervention is demonstrated by showing that behavior changes in increments to match a performance criterion. A functional relationship is demonstrated if behavior matches a constantly changing criterion over the course of treatment (Hartmann & Hall, 1976). After initial baseline observations, the intervention phase is introduced. The intervention includes specification of a criterion for performance for the client. The criterion indicates the number of responses that need to be performed to achieve a particular response consequence. For example, a certain number of cigarettes, calories, minutes of exercise, or social activities might serve as the basis for setting a performance criterion, after negotiation with the client. Consequences such as monetary incentives or prizes are provided on a daily basis only if performance meets the criterion. Essentially the client receives reinforcement for performing as well as, or better than, the criterion level. After performance stabilizes at or better than the criterion level, the criterion is altered so that a slightly more stringent demand is made to earn the reinforcer. The criterion is repeatedly changed throughout the intervention phase until the terminal goal of the program is achieved. The effect of the intervention is demonstrated if behavior matches the criterion as that criterion is changed. If behavior matches each criterion, it is likely that the intervention and criterion change rather than extraneous influences accounted for behavior change.

As an illustration of the changing-criterion design, Foxx and Rubinoff (1979) developed a treatment program for persons who consumed excessive amounts of caffeine in their daily diets. Caffeine consumed in large quantities is considered potentially harmful and is associated with a variety of symptoms including irritability, palpitations, and gastrointestinal disturbances; it has been linked to serious cardiovascular disorders as well. Treatment consisted of having the subjects deposit a sum of money ($20), which would be returned in small portions if they fell below the criterion for maximum level of caffeine that could be consumed on a given day. Bonuses were provided for consistently meeting the criteria. The subjects signed a contract that specified how the money they initially provided would be earned back or lost based upon their daily consumption of caffeine. Each day, subjects recorded their

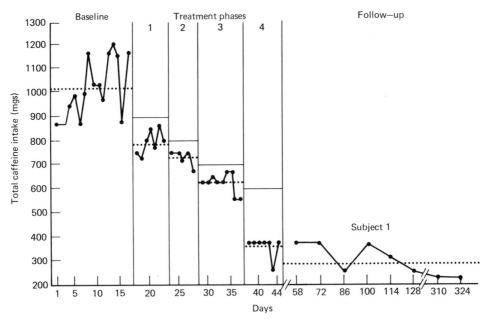

Figure 14.4.   Subject's daily caffeine intake during baseline, treatment, and follow-up as evaluated in a changing-criterion design. The criterion of caffeine intake in each phase is indicated by the solid horizontal line. Broken horizontal lines indicate the mean caffeine intake in each condition. From R. M. Foxx and A. Rubinoff, Behavioral treatment of caffeinism: Reducing excessive coffee drinking. *Journal of Applied Behavior Analysis*, 1979, *12,* 335–344. Copyright 1979 by the Society for the Experimental Analysis of Behavior. Reproduced by permission.

total caffeine consumption on the basis of a list of beverages that provided caffeine values (in milligrams).

The program was implemented and evaluated separately for three subjects in individual changing-criterion designs. The effects of the program for one subject, who was a female school teacher, are illustrated in Figure 14.4. As evident from the figure, her average daily consumption of caffeine was at about 1000 mg, a relatively high rate that is equivalent to approximately eight cups of brewed coffee (at approximately 125 mg each). When treatment was initiated, the subject was required to reduce her daily consumption by about 100 mg less than baseline. Over four treatment phases, the criterion (solid line) was reduced by approximately 100 mg each phase. To earn the reinforcer (money), daily caffeine consumption had to fall below the criterion. The figure shows that performance consistently fell below the criterion. And the subject's performance shows a steplike function in which caffeine consumption systematically decreased in each treatment phase. At the end of the fourth treatment phase, the program was terminated. Assessment over a 10-month follow-up period indicated that treatment effects were maintained.

Special Considerations. The design relies upon repeatedly altering the performance criterion and evaluating whether behavior matches the new standard. The gradual approach toward a terminal goal is especially well suited to many clinical problems in which the skills that are needed on the part of the client are practiced and achieved gradually. If performance is likely to change abruptly and completely, the small incremental steps required by the design may not be evident.

A possible ambiguity of the changingcriterion design is that it usually looks for unidirectional changes, that is, increases or decreases, in performance during the intervention phase. If performance does not

closely follow changes in the criterion, it may be difficult to discern a clear effect of treatment, as opposed to a general trend toward an increase (or decrease) in performance. If there is ambiguity about whether a general improvement in performance accounts for changes during the intervention phase, the design can be strengthened by making bidirectional changes in the criterion. Rather than making the criterion increasingly stringent, the criterion can be made more stringent at some points and less stringent at others. The less stringent criterion shifts amount to "mini-reversal" phases and can assess whether the performance follows the criteria set by the investigator.

Simultaneous-Treatment Design

The previous designs are well suited to evaluating the effects of a particular kind of intervention. However, the designs are difficult to use for comparing alternative kinds of intervention. If two or more kinds are applied to an individual client, one will be administered before the other, and their relative effectiveness may be influenced by the sequence or order in which they are presented.

The simultaneous-treatment design permits comparison of different treatments within single-case experiments (Barlow & Hayes, 1979; Kazdin & Hartmann, 1978). The unique characteristic of the design is administration of different treatments concurrently in the intervention phase. Because of the manner in which the alternative treatments are administered, their relative effectiveness can be assessed.

The design begins with baseline observations of performance for a given client. The behavior must be observed under different circumstances or at different times during the day, so that there are at least two observation periods. If this requirement cannot be met for practical reasons, a single period can be divided in half so that "separate" periods can be discerned. After baseline observations, two or more kinds of treatment are implemented to alter behavior. The treatments are implemented concurrently, for example, on the same day, but during the different observation periods. The treatments are varied daily so that they are *balanced* across the separate observation periods, and so that their effects can be separated from these periods. The intervention phase is continued until the response stabilizes under each of the separate treatments. If one of them emerges as su-

perior to the others, it can be implemented across each period in the final phase.

The simultaneous-treatment design has only recently received attention, and hence few examples are available in the context of treatment. The use of the design to compare alternative treatment variations can be illustrated in a program in a special education classroom (Kazdin & Geesey, 1980). In this program, mentally retarded elementary

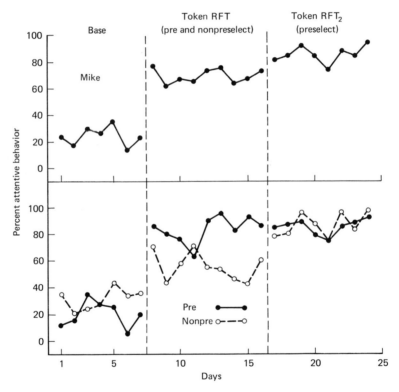

Figure 14.5.   Attentive behavior for Mike across experimental conditions. Baseline—no experimental intervention. Token reinforcement—implementation of the token program where Mike selected the back-up reinforcer for which he would use his tokens in advance (preselect), or selected the reinforcer only after he had earned sufficient tokens to purchase the event (postselect). These separate methods of selecting and exchanging back-up events were administered across different time periods each day. Token reinforcement₂—implementation of the preselect method of identifying the back-up reinforcer across both daily time periods. The *upper* panel presents the overall data collapsed across time periods and interventions. The *lower* panel presents the data according to the time periods across which the interventions were balanced, although both interventions were presented only in the second phase. From A. E. Kazdin and S. Geesey, Enhancing classroom attentiveness by preselection of back-up reinforcers in a token economy. *Behavior Modification*, 1980, *4*, 98–114. Reprinted by permission.

school children participated in a token economy in which they earned tokens (marks on a card) for appropriate classroom performance, such as completing their assignments and attending to their work. The marks could be exchanged for privileges and prizes within the classroom.

A simultaneous-treatment design was used to compare the alternative ways of providing the reinforcers to the children. Baseline data were obtained during two observation periods each day in which children worked on academic tasks. After baseline an intervention phase was implemented, which consisted of two variations of token reinforcement. The two treatments consisted of having children select in advance various prizes and rewards that they would work for or decide after they earned what they would purchase. The difference between the two treatments was only whether the children would select in advance the rewards they would work for or would wait until they earned the requisite number of points before making that decision. The exact rewards available, for example, extra recess, free time, tangible prizes, were the same for both treatments. Each program variation was implemented on a daily basis. The children included in the program had separate cards that kept track of point earnings under the different conditions. The treatments were alternated daily between the two time periods.

Figure 14.5 presents the data for a six-year-old boy named Mike, who was included in the program. As evident in the figure, during the token reinforcement phase Mike was more attentive to his assignments when he worked for the preselected reinforcer than when he worked without having selected the reinforcer in advance. Hence, in the final phase of the program, Mike was instructed to preselect the reinforcer he would purchase for both observation periods. Performance achieved the high levels for both observation periods when the preselection condition was extended to these periods.

Special Considerations. The simultaneous-treatment design is useful for identifying the more (or most) effective intervention among likely alternatives for a particular client. If the different treatments have different effects on behavior, the pattern of results is not likely to be explained by extraneous events that coincided with the onset of treatment. Also, because the interventions are balanced across different observation periods, it is unlikely that unique events during these periods would favor one intervention over another.

The design depends upon balancing the kinds of intervention across time periods. If more than two are compared, the task of balancing them may become formidable, because a very large number of occasions may be needed to ensure that each is administered equally across each occasion. Also, in some variations of the design, the treatments are balanced across time periods and staff members who administer treatment (Kazdin, 1977b). In such cases the number of occasions required for balancing alternative treatments becomes prohibitive if more than two kinds of intervention are compared. In most applications, however, two treatments alternated across time periods is not difficult and allows use of the design.

An obvious practical issue is to ensure that the kinds of intervention are kept distinct so that the client and staff know which intervention is applied during a particular observation period. The balancing of different intervention strategies across different observation periods is a more complex treatment arrangement than usually applied in most programs. Also the design depends upon having intervention strategies with few or no carryover effects from one treatment to another. For example, administering drugs usually would be inappropriate as one of the treatments if it is possible that drug effects continue throughout the day and influence performance during a period in which the other treatment is to be administered. If the separate effects of the treatments are of interest, the types of intervention employed should have no carryover effects.

One type of carryover effect may be difficult to predict or detect. It is possible that administering two or more treatments concurrently will dictate the effects that each of them exerts on performance. The effect of a given treatment may be determined in part by the other treatment with which it is juxtaposed. This influence, referred to as multiple-treatment interference, may lead to conclusions about the alternative treatments that would not be reached had the treatments been evaluated separately in another design.

General Comments

The ABAB, multiple-baseline, changing criterion, and simultaneous-treatment designs illustrate the approach of single-case experimental research, but do not exhaust the design variations and combinations reported in the research. The majority of applications have used variations of ABAB designs (Kazdin, 1975). It is likely that the prevalence of this particular version of the designs has decreased for several reasons. First, other design options have since been elucidated in the literature (Barlow & Hayes, 1979; Hartmann & Hall, 1976; Kazdin, in press; Kazdin & Hartmann, 1978). Hence a larger number of design options is available that can be suited to clinical and other applied settings. Second, the ABAB design demonstrates the effect of the intervention by showing how performance improves and declines when the treatment is applied and withdrawn. The design, by its very nature, seeks transient, that is, reversible, effects (Hartmann & Atkinson, 1974). However, as many intervention techniques have been shown to alter behavior, the attention in research has begun to shift more toward maintenance of behavior. The ABAB design is not especially well suited to investigation of maintenance because of the need to reverse behavior. Several design options, such as the multiple-baseline design,

are better suited to showing changes in behavior that are maintained.

ASSESSMENT AND DESIGN REQUIREMENTS

Application of the single-case experimental designs depends upon several assessment and design considerations. Major considerations pertain to whether there are trends in the data, the extent of variability, and the criteria for shifting from one phase to another within a design.

Trends in the Data

Evaluation of intervention effects is greatly facilitated when baseline data show little or no trend prior to implementing the intervention. Occasionally data may show a trend that behavior is changing in the direction opposite of that anticipated when treatment is implemented. For example, oppositional behavior of a child observed in the home may become progressively worse during the baseline phase. Because the direction of change during the baseline phase is opposite from the anticipated direction when treatment is invoked, this trend will not greatly interfere with evaluating the intervention. Indeed, in the general case as applied to any phase, trends in one phase opposite from what the anticipated data will show in the next phase should not interfere with drawing conclusions about treatment.

Trend in the data is a problem when behavior during baseline observation is changing in the same direction that the intervention technique is likely to produce. During baseline observation behavior may be improving, even though the rate of improvement may not be sufficient for therapeutic purposes. For example, crime rate in a community may be on the decline. However, intervention may be of considerable use in increasing the slope and decreasing the overall level of crime. Hence it may be necessary to intervene in situations in which a trend in the baseline phase is in a therapeutic direction. However, if a trend is present in a therapeutic direction, it may be especially difficult to evaluate intervention effects in single-case designs.

Essentially the investigator needs to evaluate whether the existing trend is improved upon by adding the intervention. Judgments of this sort tend to be more difficult to make than those based upon stable data without initial trend. Without baseline trends, changes in performance during the intervention phase can be judged on the basis of emergence of a trend that was not previously evident.

Several recommendations have been provided regarding the presence of trends in the data. The usual recommendation, of course, is to wait until the baseline stabilizes so that no trend is present before intervening (Baer, Wolf, & Risley, 1968). For obvious practical reasons, this often cannot be achieved in clinical situations in which intervention may be needed quickly.

Depending upon the specific design, other recommendations can be made. For example, the trends in the data of an ABAB design often can be reversed as needed to demonstrate the functional control of the intervention over behavior. Intervention phases might show increases in behavior, and these trends conceivably might be evident in baseline or return to baseline phases as well. Occasionally specific schedules of reinforcement can be used, such as differential reinforcement of other behavior, which are likely to result in trends opposite from those achieved during the intervention phase (Goetz, Holmberg, & LeBlanc, 1975; Lindsay & Stoffelmayr, 1976). Altering the contingencies from baseline to intervention phases so that alternative behavior is reinforced in these phases can dramatically illustrate the effects of the program and can eliminate the problem of existing trends in the data. The option of altering reinforcement contingenices to handle the problems of trends may satisfy experimental demands, but is clinically untenable

because the contingencies operate to make performance worse.

Another recommendation is to select designs in which trends in the data provide minimal ambiguity for interpreting the results. For example, multiple-baseline designs are likely to provide minimal ambiguity when trends exist in baseline, because several baselines are used. If one or two baselines show initial trends, several other baselines may not. The effects of the intervention can be inferred from the data pattern across all baselines. Similarly, in a simultaneous-treatment design, trends in the data need not interfere with conclusions about treatment. Different treatments are implemented and their relative impact on performance is evaluated. Differences in performance among the treatments, where they exist, presumably can be detected even if superimposed upon an overall trend pervading the baseline and treatment phases.

A final recommendation to handle trends is the application of statistical techniques. Time-series analysis in particular provides a statistical tool for identifying whether change occurs at the point when the intervention is implemented, and whether a change in trend occurs between phases (Glass, Wilson, Gottman, 1975; Jones, Vaught, & Weinrott, 1977; Kazdin, 1976). The analysis can determine whether the changes in the data surpass those that might have occurred as a function of preexisting trends.

Variability

Trends in the data in the direction of therapeutic change is only one of the obstacles that can compete with drawing unambiguous inferences about intervention effects. Excessive variability in the data is likely to be a more common problem, which can obscure the effects of treatment. Variability here refers to the fluctuations of performance of the client over time within a particular phase. Whether the variability is "excessive" depends upon the initial level of behavior and the amount of change when the intervention is implemented. As a general rule, the greater the variability in the data, the more difficult it is to infer a treatment effect. If the client's performance fluctuates from the most extreme points on the continuum of the measure (e.g., 0 to 100%), demonstrating clear changes in performance across phases may be difficult. A highly variable baseline does not provide a clear basis for predicting a particular level of performance against which intervention effects are evaluated. Occasionally high variability in the data may be of interest in its own right because it reflects inconsistency in performance. In this case the variability itself is the focus of treatment, and the intervention can be evaluated by showing a reduction in variability. However, in most applications the interest is in altering the mean level of performance rather than changes in fluctuations. And highly variable baselines present obstacles for evaluating subsequent phases.

Evaluation of interventions sometimes is facilitated by reducing the *appearance* of variability by averaging data points across consecutive days or weeks. For example, fluctuations in daily performance will be reduced in graphical presentation of the information, if the average performance for two or three day blocks of time is plotted. As more data points are combined, the variability in graphical presentation is likely to decrease. More stable data points (based upon several days) provide a clearer basis for subsequent predictions.

Combining data into blocks and plotting averages in the above fashion only reduces the appearance of variability. It might be more useful to identify the sources that may account for variability, because such sources may provide important information about the client's problem and the manner in which it is recorded by observers. For example, performance may change drastically as a function of stimuli in the environment that systematically vary. Different staff, parents, or trainers may lead to different levels of performance because of the slightly different contingencies they employ (Redd & Birnbrauer, 1969). Alternatively, observers may invoke slightly different criteria for scoring behavior so that observer behavior, rather than client behavior, accounts for excessive variability. Identification of factors that may be systematically associated with high or low levels of performance may provide useful information for conducting treatment.

Behavior may be highly variable, even though no particular stimulus conditions or characteristics of assessment procedures can be identified as possible contributors. Large fluctuations in performance will still create possible difficulties for evaluating intervention effects. In such cases it may be useful to try to standardize conditions in the situation further so that a more consistent pattern of data emerges, or to develop the program in such a way that reductions in variability, if desirable, are trained directly.

Shifting Phases in the Design

In between-group research, details of the design usually are worked out prior to the study, and decisions that affect the basic design usually are not made during the study itself, barring special practical problems that emerge. In single-case designs, on the other hand, important decisions are made during the study itself and cannot be made in advance of seeing the data. The major decisions include how long a particular phase should be continued and when a new phase should begin. In general, phases are altered in such a way as to maximize the clarity of the demonstration.

The duration of a particular phase cannot be determined in advance of seeing the data, unless of course practical considerations (e.g., duration of hospitalization) rather than design requirements impose restraints. A given phase usually needs to be continued until clear predictions can be made about the anticipated level of future performance, if the same phase were continued. The presence of trends or excessive variability suggests that additional data might be needed to see whether the data stabilize. Occasionally investigators alter phases before a clear pattern emerges. In such cases only the most marked shifts in performance could be evaluated unambiguously.

Often data may appear to be stable, but a few data points may depart from the usual range a few days prior to the time the intervention may be tentatively scheduled to begin. When one or more days appear to depart from a previously stable rate, it may be important to continue baseline for an additional period. A few points that depart from the usual range of behavior may indicate the inception of a trend or random fluctuations. In either case it may be advisable to withhold the intervention. If an extreme data point emerges, a subsequent data point often will revert toward the mean (regression artifact). If the intervention effect is implemented immediately after an extreme data point, it may be unclear whether a shift in the opposite direction was due to intervention effects or to regression toward the mean. Of course, interpretation of any particular shift in performance is facilitated by observing the entire pattern of data within and across phases. When considering shifting phases, it is important to examine carefully the last few or several data points immediately prior to the point in time that the intervention will be implemented. The stability of the data immediately prior to changing phases may be especially important for inferring intervention effects.

As a general rule, no clear guidelines exist for specifying exactly when phases should be altered. General recommendations such as ensuring that the data are stable and do not show trends are of little value in the particular case when a decision has to be made about altering phases. Occasionally investigators have specified objective criteria in advance that indicate the data pattern that will be required before phases are altered (Scott, Peters, Gillespie, Blanchard, Edmunson, & Young, 1973; Wincze, Leitenberg, & Agras, 1972). For example, phases can be shifted when variability about the mean level of performance falls within a specific range for a period of five days, or when a given number of consecutive data points are not in the same direction above (or below) the mean. Specification of the conditions for altering phases is an excellent idea because it eliminates the subjectivity in deciding on any particular day whether treatment should be implemented or withdrawn. However, in practice it may be difficult to wait for the data to meet a particular pattern that might be disrupted by an occasional extreme data point. Conceivably rules for altering phases could be developed that specify that some number of data requirements are met rather than a too-stringent criterion that requires very protracted observations within a particular phase.

DATA EVALUATION

Data evaluation represents an extremely important topic for single-case experimental research. Single-case research invokes multiple criteria to evaluate the data that reflect concerns with both applied and experimental criteria. The gamut of criteria for data evaluation can be encompassed by discussing nonstatistical, statistical, and clinical or social criteria.

Nonstatistical Evaluation

Description. The main criterion for evaluating single-case data is based upon visual inspection. The underlying rationale is that single-case research should seek intervention effects that are especially potent (Baer, 1977). Visual inspection acts as a screening device in which only very dramatic intervention effects are clearly detected. Effects that are relatively weak are rejected as unimportant, even if these effects might be reliable according to other criteria such as statistical analyses.

The ability to apply visual inspection as a method of data evaluation depends heavily upon special characteristics of the data. Perhaps the single most important feature of single-case experimental designs is the continuous assessment of behavior over time. With extended observations, the investigator can see whether the data are stable without intervention, and whether performance then subsequently varies as intervention is implemented. In between-group outcome research, often assessment of performance is made on only two occasions (pre- and posttreatment). In such cases it is impossible to evaluate the pattern of performance over time independently of intervening treatment, which is the reason that comparisons are made between groups. In single-case research, intervention often is associated with abrupt changes in the pattern of data. The availability of multiple data points over time makes examination of the data through visual inspection less arbitrary than the method might appear at first glance.

It is difficult to specify the criteria underlying visual inspection that determine whether the effects are judged to be reliable. Indeed the objections to visual inspection are based in part on the difficulty in identifying the criteria so that they can be reliably invoked across experimenters. In the extreme cases in which intervention effects are especially clear, visual inspection presents no problem. For example, when performance of the client during baseline observation does not overlap with performance during the experimental phase, visual inspection is readily applied with little ambiguity. The data points during baseline may not approach the data points obtained during the intervention phase. When the effects of the intervention are not strong enough to obtain nonoverlapping data across separate phases, intervention effects might be evident by changes in trends over the different phases. For example, behavior may show an accelerating linear trend toward improvement during the intervention phase. The trend may be reversed as treatment is withdrawn and resume again when treatment is reinstated.

Actually the ease of evaluating single-case data with visual inspection is a function of several factors, including the magnitude of treatment effects, the presence or absence of trends in the data, the amount of variability within a given phase and across phases, and the duration of individual phases. For example, a smaller treatment effect can be detected through visual inspection, the more stable and less variable the data, and the longer the duration of the baseline phase. When the ideal data conditions are met, small treatment effects can be discerned through visual inspection. A clear instance of ideal data conditions for visual inspection might be evident when a program seeks to develop a type of behavior that was not previously present. The level of behavior prior to the program may be zero, for example, duration of exercise. This level on repeated observation occasions would be stable over time, show no trends, and no variability (mean and standard deviation $= 0$). Even a slight increase in exercise during an intervention phase would be easy to detect because of the pattern of data prior to treatment. Of course the ideal data conditions for visual inspection are not always met. But they do not have to be met to invoke this criterion. The main criteria are stable rates of data and the absence of trend during baseline phase. Such a baseline provides an excellent basis for predicting future performance and for judging whether performance during the intervention phase departs from what was predicted.

Considerations and Limitations. Visual inspection is based upon the view that single-case research should seek potent treatment effects. Only those effects that are obviously clear are considered to be important. Yet even though one may seek strong intervention effects, there are no guarantees that such effects will be found. It may be wise to consider the potential importance of those effects that do not seem obvious upon inspection. Many intervention techniques may produce only small changes in performance. Further refinements in the procedures may yield clinically important effects that are obvious. However, in the initial stages of treatment development, an investigator may wish to look for promising intervention techniques that produce reliable change. Visual inspection may not be very useful for initially identifying types of interventions worthy of further pursuit.

Statistical Evaluation

Description. The general rationale for using statistical analyses is quite familiar to researchers and hence need not be elaborated here. Discussion of statistical analyses in the context of single-case research is a matter of considerable controversy. Controversy exists over whether statistical tests should be used (Baer, 1977; Kazdin, 1976; Michael, 1974) and if they are used, which ones are appropriate (Hartmann, 1974; Kratochwill, 1978). Whether statistical analyses should be used is controversial because of the concern that statistical tests will "tease" out subtle treatment effects. Statistically reliable differences in the data may not reach dramatic levels of change. The fear is that using statistical criteria will lead researchers toward seeking statistically significant rather than clinically important effects.

As noted earlier, potent treatment effects may not always be found and indeed need not always be obtained to identify intervention strategies of applied importance. For example, intervention might be directed toward reducing energy consumption or reducing crime rate. A type of intervention that produces a reliable effect in either of these areas would be worth identifying even if the extent of the changes are not of the magnitude one would hope for.

The issue for single-case research is not whether statistical tests should be used, but rather what such tests might offer and when

they should be applied in addition to or as a substitute for visual inspection.[1] In many applications statistical evaluation may be especially useful. First, when the ideal design requirements for single-case research are not met, statistical analyses may be helpful in identifying reliable treatment effects. For example, when baseline data are not stable or reflect a trend in the anticipated direction of therapeutic change, visual inspection may be difficult to invoke. However, selected statistical analyses such as time-series analyses may be sensitive to different patterns of data that interfere with the application of visual inspection (Glass et al., 1975).

Second, statistical analyses may be especially useful when beginning in new areas of single-case research. In a new area of research, the investigator may examine several kinds of intervention, which are not well developed because the important parameters that maximize therapeutic change are unknown. Statistical tests may provide a way of detecting reliable treatment effects in cases in which visual inspection would have been insensitive to the differences across phases. Further work with the kinds of intervention that produce reliable effects may eventually yield the dramatic effects sought by advocates of visual inspection.

Considerations and Limitations. Several considerations dictate the utility of statistical tests for single-case research. The concern over drawing attention away from clinically important changes has been alluded to already. The concern would be evident, for example, in the case of a program that successfully reduced head banging in an autistic child from 100 to 50 instances per hour. Such changes, if evident for several days, might be statistically significant, but not at the level

---

[1]The present section elaborates the general method of statistical evaluation for single-case research and problems that arise. For details about specific statistical tests, other sources should be consulted (e.g., Glass et al., 1975; Kazdin, 1976, in press; Kratochwill, 1978).

that a clinically important change may have been achieved. Clinical rather than statistical significance would be essential. Of course, seeking statistically significant effects need not compete with also looking for effects that are important as well. However, in a great deal of clinical research using between-group designs, statistical analyses are used routinely and clinical importance of the findings is neglected.

An important consideration for single-case research pertains to the requirements that statistical analyses may place on the investigator. In applied work, it is often difficult to use single-case designs because they make special demands that can compete with clinical considerations. For example, most designs require a stable baseline prior to intervening. Yet the luxury of extensive assessment for severe clinical problems such as aggressive child behavior for purposes of obtaining a stable baseline does not exist. For specific designs, additional restrictions are evident. For example, in an ABAB design treatment may need to be withdrawn (second A phase) to demonstrate a causal relationship between the intervention and behavior change. Practical and ethical considerations militate against temporarily making the client's behavior worse to meet the design requirements. Similarly, in a multiple-baseline design, treatment is withheld, even if only temporarily, from some of the baselines, that is, behavior, clients, or situations. Yet in many clinical applications, intervention strategies must be implemented immediately in violation of the design requirements. From these few examples, it should be clear that trying to apply single-case designs can present difficulties.

Applying statistical tests to single-case research makes even greater demands on the investigator and treatment implementation. The demands that statistical tests make vary in part as a function of the specific tests that are used. However, for present purposes consider some of the demands that are relatively common among alternative tests.

To apply statistical tests, behavior usually has to be observed on several occasions within baseline and intervention phases. Extended baseline and treatment phases may be needed to obtain a sufficient number of occasions so that statistically significant differences can be detected. For most statistical tests that apply to single-case experimental designs, a larger number of occasions would be needed than if visual inspection were used to evaluate the data. For example, a return to baseline phase in an ABAB design might only last a few days and still serve its purpose for visual inspection. For statistical evaluation, a duration of only a few days usually would provide insufficient occasions to detect a statistically significant difference between phases. Hence, investigators might be required to implement phases that are longer than usual when contemplating the use of most statistical tests. If one of the longer phases is baseline, return to baseline, or withholding treatment, the demands of statistical analyses may be prohibitive for selected clinical applications.

An even greater demand than conducting protracted phases is made by selected statistical tests, for example, randomization tests. Some tests are based upon the notion that treatment is applied on random occasions. Thus the application of treatment to occasions (days), patients, clients, or behavior needs to be determined randomly (Edgington, 1980). For example, in a multiple-baseline design, the intervention might be applied to several different kinds of problem behavior of a client. Ordinarily the investigator might apply the intervention to behavior in a special order, say, according to the severity of the behavior. If the investigator intends to use a statistical test based upon randomization (such as Rn) (Revusky, 1967), the particular order of behaviors to which the intervention technique is applied must be determined randomly (see Kazdin, 1976). That is, when the intervention technique is to be implemented on the first occasion, the experimenter must decide on a random basis which baseline, behavior or client, receives the treatment. In each case, which baseline receives treatment is determined randomly. The random determination of the application of intervention techniques although required for statistical analyses, may alter the priorities of a particular clinical case.

In addition to specific demands that statistical tests may make for single-case research, one final consideration pertains to interpretation of the results of such tests. In most statistical tests that have been described for single-case research (Kazdin, 1976, in press; Kratochwill, 1978), a comparison is made between baseline and treatment (AB) phases. It is important to bear in mind that differences between such phases do not necessarily mean that the intervention was responsible for change. The logic of single-case experimental research, as outlined earlier, is based upon the *pattern* of data across several phases. At this point statistical comparisons need to take into account this overall pattern. If specific tests do not accomplish this, they may need to be supplemented with visual inspection.

Clinical Evaluation

Description.   A definite limitation of statistical evaluation is that it detracts from the question of the applied or clinical importance of behavior change. Visual inspection is not necessarily an improvement. Although visual inspection draws attention to the importance of achieving dramatic change, it does not provide guidelines for evaluating whether the magnitude of changes are important. Recently single-case research has begun to invoke criteria to address the clinical significance of behavior change. Clinical significance refers to the practical value of the effect of the intervention, that is, whether the change makes a "real" difference to the client (Risley, 1970).

Occasionally the clinical importance of the treatment changes are obvious. For example, to return to an earlier example, reduction of

head-banging in an autistic child from 100 to 50 instances per hour may be reliable but not clinically important. Without a virtual or complete elimination of behavior, the clinical value of the treatment can be challenged. Essentially, complete elimination probably would be needed to produce a clinically important change. Of course, in many cases the presence or absence of a certain kind of behavior is not necessarily the criterion for deciding whether an important change was achieved. Other criteria are necessary.

Recently Wolf (1978) has introduced the notion of *social validation,* which encompasses ways of evaluating whether intervention effects produce changes of clinical or applied importance. Although the methods apply to outcome research in general, their use has received special attention in single-case experimental designs. Social validation refers generally to consideration of social criteria for evaluating the *focus* of treatment, the *procedures* that are used, and the *effects* that they have. For present purposes, the features related to evaluating the effects of treatment are especially relevant.

Two methods for evaluating the clinical importance of treatment effects are referred to as *social comparison* and *subjective evaluation* (Kazdin, 1977a). The social comparison method refers to comparing the behavior of the client before and after treatment with the behavior of nondeviant peers. The question asked by this procedure is whether the client's behavior after treatment is distinguishable from the behavior of his or her peers. To answer this question, persons who resemble the client in subject and demographic variables need to be identified. These persons should *not* be identified as a clinical population but rather as individuals functioning normally. For many but certainly not all clinical problems, treatment can be evaluated by the extent to which it produces a change that brings clients to the performance levels of their nondeviant peers.

As an example, O'Brien and Azrin (1972) developed appropriate eating behavior of mentally retarded residents in a state hospital who seldom used utensils, constantly spilled food on themselves, stole food from others, and ate food previously spilled on the floor. Using prompts, verbal praise, and food reinforcement, these inappropriate acts were reduced dramatically. To address whether the changes were clinically important, the investigators compared the eating behavior of the retarded residents who received training with "normals." The normal sample consisted of a number of customers in a local restaurant who were watched by observers who recorded their eating behaviors. Interestingly, the level of the inappropriate mealtime behavior among the retarded prior to training was much higher than the level of the normal sample. However, after training, inappropriate behavior of the retarded fell slightly below the level of the normative sample. These results suggest that the magnitude of the changes achieved with training brought the residents to acceptable performance levels of people functioning in everyday life.

Several investigators have utilized the social comparison method to evaluate the clinical importance of change. For example, research has shown that conduct problem children differ from their nonproblem peers prior to treatment on a variety of disruptive and unruly behavior including aggressive acts, teasing, whining, and yelling. However, after treatment the disruptive behavior of these children has been brought into the range that appears to be normal and acceptable for their same age peer group (Kent & O'Leary, 1976; Patterson, 1974; Walker & Hops, 1976). Similarly, social behavior of withdrawn or highly aggressive children has been brought to the normative level of their peers (Matson, Kazdin, & Esveldt-Dawson, 1980; O'Connor, 1969). Treatments applied to a variety of adult and child populations have been evaluated using the social comparison method (see Kazdin, 1977a).

Another method of evaluating the importance of behavior change is subjective evaluation. The method refers to determining the

importance of the treatment change by assessing the opinions of individuals who are likely to have contact with the client. The question addressed by this method of evaluation is whether behavior changes are perceptably different among others with whom the client interacts. Persons who are in a special position through expertise or in relation to the client are asked to judge whether the changes in performance are important. Global evaluations are used to address this evaluation.

As an example, research with delinquents has occasionally used subjective evaluation to examine treatment effects. In one report, delinquent girls who resided in a home-style treatment facility were trained to engage in conversational skills such as answering questions and attending to others who were talking (Maloney et al., 1976). To evaluate the impact of training on overall conversation, persons with whom the delinquent girls might interact, such as probation officers, teachers, counselors, social workers, rated tapes of conversation. These judges rated posttreatment conversation as superior to pretraining conversation. Thus the behavior altered during treatment had implications for more general evaluations of overall conversation.

The subjective evaluation method has been used to evaluate treatment effects for a variety of target behavior and populations. For example, intervention strategies have led to changes in specific writing behavior among children that are related to judgments of student creativity (Van Houten, Morrison, Jarvis, & McDonald, 1974); improvements in specific public speaking behavior have been reflected in audience ratings of enthusiasm, sincerity, knowledge, and overall speaker performance (Fawcett & Miller, 1975); and training delinquent boys to interact differently in their conversations with police have been reflected in improvements on ratings of suspiciousness, cooperativeness, and politeness (Minkin et al., 1976). In the above studies, the global ratings of others were used to assess the impact of treatment. The ratings were used to assess whether changes of specific behavior had implications for more general characteristics of behavior according to others in contact with the client.

Considerations and Limitations. The use of normative data or global evaluations of client behavior represents an important step toward quantifying the extent to which the change produced in treatment is important. However, there are problems and limitations that need to be considered in the use of these procedures. For example, for the social comparison method, problems arise in identifying a normative group. To whom should mentally retarded persons, chronic psychiatric patients, or prisoners be compared in evaluating treatment and rehabilitation programs? Developing normative levels of performance might be an unrealistic ideal. Also it is unclear how to match subjects to select a normative sample. Perhaps the sample should be the same on subject and demographic variables such as age, gender, social class, education, and others. Yet the level of normative performance may depend upon the variables used to match normal and clinical populations.

For example, improvements in the verbal social behavior of a psychiatric patient closely approximated the behavior of other patients of similar education who were not verbally deficient (Stahl, Thomson, Leitenberg, & Hasazi, 1974). Yet the increase in verbal behavior was very discrepant from the level of intelligent normally functioning persons who were not patients. Thus the clinical impact of treatment would be evaluated quite differently depending upon the comparison group.

Even if a normative group can be identified, the range of behavior that would be defined as an acceptable level is difficult to specify. It is realtively simple to identify deviant behavior that departs markedly from the behavior of "normal" peers. But as behavior becomes slightly less deviant it is difficult to identify the point at which behavior

is within the normative range. A subjective judgment is needed to decide the point at which behavior is within the acceptable level. In any case, identifying a normative sample and the level of behavior that is regarded as acceptable illustrate some of the problems of applying the social comparison method.

Problems exist when applying the subjective evaluation method as well. The most salient issue is the problem of relying upon the opinions of others for determining whether treatment effects are important. Subjective evaluations of behavior are much more readily susceptible to biases on the part of the raters than are overt behavioral measures. Thus subjective evaluations must be treated very cautiously; it is possible that they will reflect change when overt behavior does not (Kazdin, 1973; Patterson, Cobb, & Ray, 1973; Schnelle, 1974). Also, the fact that persons who interact with the client claim there is a difference in behavior as a function of treatment does not necessarily mean that the amount of change is clinically significant. A small change in behavior may be reflected in the ratings, and the client's behavior may still depart considerably from the normative levels.

Although problems and potential limitations for determining the clinical or applied importance of behavior change exist, the methods point to a significant direction in clarifying the magnitude of intervention effects relative to the amount of change needed. For single-case experimental research, the social comparison and subject evaluation methods in many ways combine useful features of visual inspection and statistical evaluation methods mentioned earlier. As with visual inspection, the social comparison and subjective evaluation methods are concerned with identifying marked changes in behavior. As with statistical evaluation, these methods enable one to test in a quantifiable way whether treatment produced change sufficient to bring clients to the level of their peers or to improve in subjective ratings of others. Both social comparison and subjective evaluation methods represent an important addition to data evaluation for single-case research and indeed treatment outcome research in general.

PROBLEMS AND LIMITATIONS

Single-case experimental designs offer a number of advantages for treatment outcome research. Perhaps the most obvious advantage is that the methodology allows investigation of the individual client and experimental evaluation of treatment for that client. Traditionally, examination of the individual case has been restricted to anecdotal reports and case studies. The fact that only one individual is involved does not necessarily preclude careful evaluation of treatment. Despite the obvious advantages of single-case research designs, it is important to consider their limitations for treatment evaluation. Two limitations pertain to the types of questions that can be addressed and the generality of findings beyond the single case.

Range of Outcome Questions

Several alternative treatment evaluation strategies and therapy outcome questions can be delineated in clinical research (Kazdin, 1980b). The strategies and the questions they ask about treatment are enumerated in Table 14.1. As evident in the table, the strategies address questions about therapy outcome and the dimensions that can influence therapeutic change. Typically, these questions are addressed in between-group research by varying the treatment, and especially the control groups included in a particular study. In single-case research, the range of outcome questions that can be addressed is narrower than in between-group research.

The bulk of single-case experimental research fits into the treatment package strategy, in which a particular treatment package is compared to no treatment (baseline). For example, when treatment consists of, for example, a token economy, social skills training program, or intervention based upon positive practice, multifaceted treatments are

Table 14.1.   Treatment Evaluation Strategies and the Outcome Questions They Address

Treatment evaluation strategy	Outcome question addressed
1. Treatment package strategy	Does this treatment with all of its components lead to therapeutic change relative to no treatment?
2. Dismantling strategy	What aspects of the treatment package are necessary, sufficient, or facilitative for therapeutic change?
3. Parametric strategy	What variations of the treatment can be made to augment its effectiveness?
4. Constructive strategy	What procedures or techniques can be added to treatment to make it more effective?
5. Comparative strategy	Which treatment is more (or most) effective among a particular set of alternatives?
6. Client-variation strategy	What client characteristics interact with the effects of treatment? Or, for whom is a particular technique effective?

included as a package, and the goal is to assess whether treatment surpasses baseline performance. The basic question is whether treatment achieves change and does so reliably. Treatments evaluated in an ABAB or multiple-baseline design, for examples, usually illustrate the treatment package strategy.

The dismantling, parametric, and constructive strategies listed in Table 14.1 are similar in that they attempt to analyze aspects of treatment that contribute to therapeutic change. In its own way, each strategy examines what can be done to make treatment better. These strategies often are difficult to employ in single-case research because they involve comparisons of the full treatment package with other conditions such as the package minus selected ingredients (dismantling strategy), the package with variations of selected dimensions (parametic strategy), and the package with some additional procedure (constructive strategy). In single-case research comparisons are difficult to achieve between any two different kinds of intervention or variations of a particular intervention, because most of the designs depend upon implementing alternative experimental conditions at different points in time. For example, to compare the effects of token reinforcement with token reinforcement plus response cost (constructive strategy), these different kinds of intervention usually are implemented at different points in time as part of an ABAB design (with variations of the B or treatment phase). One of the conditions that is compared will need to come first and the other second. The different effects of the alternative conditions might be due to the specific procedures that are implemented or to the sequence effect, that is, the particular order in which the conditions appeared. The first (or second) condition may be more or less effective than the other or equally effective in part because of the position in which it appeared within the sequence. With a single case there is no unambiguous way to evaluate treatment because of the Treatment × Sequence confounding factor.

A seemingly viable solution to the problem would be to administer the two (or more) treatment conditions in a different order to different subjects. A minimum of two subjects would be needed, if two treatments were compared, so that each subject could receive the alternative treatments but in a different order. Presumably, if both subjects respond to the treatments in a consistent fashion, the effects of the sequence in which the treatments appeared can be ruled out as an influence.

Unfortunately, the above solution is not entirely satisfactory. Providing different subjects with a different order of conditions amounts to a between-group design rather than a single-case design. The possible interaction of treatment and sequence needs to be evaluated among *several* subjects to ensure that a particular treatment-sequence combination is not unique to, that is, does not interact with, a particular subject. Simply altering the sequence among a few subjects does not necessarily avoid the sequence problem unless there is a way in the final analyses to separate the effects of treatments, sequences, subjects, and their interactions.

The problem of evaluating variations of treatments as part of the dismantling, parametric, and constructive strategies extends to the comparative strategy as well. Even though the comparative strategy does not attempt to analyze alternative variations of a given treatment, it does of course examine the relative effectiveness of alternative treatments. In most single-case experimental designs, comparisons of different treatments are obfuscated by the sequence effects noted earlier. The simultaneous-treatment design attempts to provide an alternative in which two or more treatments or treatment variations can be compared in the same phase but under different stimulus conditions. While the design resolves the sequence problem elaborated above, it is possible that the results obtained are influenced by multiple-treatment interference, that is, the effects of introducing more than one treatment. For example, the effects of treatment 1 may be different when juxtaposed to treatment 2 than if these treatments were administered to entirely different subjects.

Overall, evaluating different intervention phases introduces ambiguity for in single-case experimental research. The possible influence of administering one treatment on all subsequent treatments exists for ABAB, multiple-baseline, and changing-criterion designs. Similarly, the possibility that juxtaposing two or more treatments influences the effects that either treatment exerts is a potential problem for the simultaneous-treatment design. This ambiguity has not deterred researchers from raising questions that fit into the dismantling, parametric, constructive, or comparative strategies. However, in such cases the conclusions are ambiguous because of the possible influence of factors discussed above.

The remaining strategy to appear in Table 14.1 is the client-variation strategy, which raises questions about the clients for whom treatment is suited. Specifically, the strategy addresses whether treatment is more or less effective as a function of particular client characteristics. The usual way that research approaches this question is through factorial designs in which subjects and treatment types are compared. The analyses examine whether the effectiveness of treatment interacts with the type of client, where clients are grouped according to such variables as age, diagnosis, socioeconomic status, severity of behavior, and so on. Single-case research obviously does not address the questions of the characteristics of the client that may interact with treatment effects. If a few subjects are studied and respond differently, the investigator cannot determine whether treatment was more or less effective as a function of particular characteristics of the subject.

In general, single-case research designs are highly suited to evaluating particular treatment packages and their effects on performance. Some of the more subtle questions of outcome research raise difficulties if examined with single-case designs. Single-case designs can address many of the important outcome questions, but in doing so raise ambiguities that are not evident in between-group research. In the case of client-variations as they relate to treatment, single-case designs are especially weak. Actually the questions posed by the client-variation strategy address the *generality* of the results among subjects. Generality of the results in single-case research is an important topic in its own right in evaluating this methodology and hence is treated separately below.

Generality of the Findings

Perhaps the major objection that arises in evaluating single-case research is that the results may not be generalizable to persons other than the client. This objection raises several important issues. To begin with, single-case experimental research grew out of an experimental philosophy that attempts to discover laws of individual performance (Kazdin, 1978b). There is a methodological heritage of examining variables that affect performance of individuals. Of course, interest in studying the individual reflects a larger concern with identifying generalizable findings that are not idiosyncratic. Hence the ultimate goal, even of single-case research, is to discover generalizable relationships.

The generality of findings from single-case research often is discussed in relation to between-group research. Because between-group research utilizes large numbers of subjects, the findings are often assumed to be more generalizable. As proponents of the single-case approach have noted, the use of large numbers of subjects in research does not by itself ensure generalizable findings (Sidman, 1960). In the vast majority of between-group investigations, results are evaluated on the basis of average *group* performance. The analyses do not shed light on the generality of treatment effects among individuals. Thus, if a group of 20 patients who received treatment show greater change than 20 patients who did not receive treatment, little information is available about the generality of the results. We do not know by this group analysis alone how many persons in the treatment group were affected in any important way. Ambiguity about the generality of findings from between-group research is not inherent in this research approach. However, investigators rarely look at the individual subject data as well as the group data to make inferences about the generality of effects among subjects within a given treatment condition. Certainly if the individual data were examined in between-group research, a great deal might be said about the generality of the findings.

Often the generality of the findings in between-group research is examined using the client-variation strategy, as outlined above. Performance of the individual is not examined. Rather, performance of classes of persons are examined to assess whether treatment(s) are differentially effective as a function of some subject variable. In this application, between-group research certainly can shed more light on the generality of the results than can single-case research. A factorial design examining Subject × Treatment interactions can provide information about the suitability of treatment for alternative subject populations.

Thus the generality of results from single-case research would seem to be a severe problem. Actually inherent features of the single-case approach may increase rather than decrease the generality of the findings. As noted earlier, investigators who use single-case designs have emphasized the need to seek intervention that produces dramatic changes in performance. Thus visual inspection rather than statistical significance is advocated. Interventions that produce dramatic effects are likely to be more generalizable across individuals than are effects that meet the relatively weaker criterion of statistical significance. Indeed, in any particular between-group investigation, the possibility remains that a statistically significant difference was obtained on the basis of "chance." The results may not generalize to other attempts to replicate the study, not to mention to other subjects. In single-case research, extended assessment across treatment and no-treatment phases, coupled with dramatic effects, reduces or may even rule out the possibility that the changes in performance could be attributed to chance.

Proponents of single-case research sometimes have suggested that the results may even be more generalizable than those obtained in between-group research because of the methodology and goals of these alternative approaches. The relative generality of findings from one approach over another may not be resolvable. However, it is important to note that generality is not necessarily a problem for single-case research. Findings obtained in single-case demonstrations appear to be highly generalizable because of the types of intervention that are commonly investigated. For example, various techniques based upon reinforcement have been effective across a large range of populations, settings, and target problems (e.g., Kazdin, 1978a).

The problem of single-case research is not that the results lack generality among subjects. Rather, the problem is that there are difficulties largely inherent in the methodology for assessing the dimensions that may dictate generality of the results. Within single-case research designs, there are no provisions for identifying client-treatment interactions. Focusing on one subject does not allow for the systematic comparison of different treatments among multiple subjects who differ in various characteristics, at least within a single experiment. Examining subject variables is more readily accomplished in between-group research.

UTILITY OF SINGLE-CASE RESEARCH FOR CLINICAL PSYCHOLOGY

Single-case research represents a methodological approach that has been utilized for both basic and applied research encompassing a number of disciplines. The approach has special utility for applied research in areas such as clinical psychology. Clinical psychology has a special commitment to the study of the individual. Indeed the field often is distinguished from other areas of psychology by its interest in understanding the individual (Allport, 1961; Korchin, 1976; Watson, 1951).

Much of clinical work is directed at the diagnosis, assessment, and treatment of the individual as seen in inpatient and outpatient work. Traditionally, investigation of the individual has been restricted to case studies, in which a person is studied in depth. Although the case study often provides fascinating analyses, the material usually is based upon anecdotal reports. In a case study, anecdotal reports about the improvements achieved in the client usually are subject to a large number of rival hypotheses. The absence of experimental control removes the case study from the realm of scientific knowledge. Case studies provide extremely important hypotheses for subsequent research, but the information itself usually is insufficient to provide empirically-based knowledge. Single-case research provides a means of combining the richness of clinical application with the requirements of scientific methodology. Clinical application need not be sacrificed by the methodology. Indeed application and research can act in concert in a way that has not been available in traditional research.

Scientific Study of Rare Phenomena

Many of the problems that are seen in clinical treatment are relatively rare. The relative paucity of cases means that a sufficient number of cases is rarely presented at the same time or in the same location to permit large-scale investigation. The opportunity to study the problem and to provide treatment must be made on an individual basis. Hence the only basis for information is the intensive study of the individual case. With rare clinical problems, even the traditional case study is very useful, for lack of alternative resources. For example, much of the information known about multiple personality as a clinical problem drives from intensive elaboration of clinical material (Thigpen & Cleckley, 1957).

Single-case experimental designs provide a unique opportunity to investigate rare phenomena and to provide scientifically-based information for subsequent applications. An excellent instance of single-case investigation of a relatively rare phenomena was provided by Barlow, Reynolds, and Agras (1973), who reported the treatment of a 17-year-old male who desired to be a female. The patient's behavior and attitudes reflected his transsexual interest, as evident in attraction to other males, a history of cross dressing, interest in traditionally feminine role behaviors such as knitting, crocheting, embroidering, sexual fantasies in which he imagined himself as a woman, effeminate mannerisms in sitting, standing, and walking, and so on. Extensive treatment based upon modeling, rehearsal, and feedback was used to alter a variety of effeminate mannerisms, speaking patterns, social skills, sexual fantasies, and sexual arousal. The effects of training were demonstrated in a combination of ABAB and multiple-baseline designs showing specifically that the intervention accounted for change. The report is unique in demonstrating the successful psychotherapeutic treatment of transsexuality. It is unlikely that this treatment could have been evaluated without the use of single-case experimentation, because of the difficulty of recruiting enough clients who would be interested in that treatment rather than in direct physical change through surgery. Yet the information provided is extremely valuable in demonstrating an effective treatment that may be of use with similar patients who might be interested in psychotherapy as a possible alternative to surgery.

Precursor to Large-Scale Application

Several advantages of single-case experimentation pertain to the manner in which treatment can be implemented and evaluated. For many problems that are seen in treatment, multiple procedures may need to be applied to produce the desired changes in the client. Single-case designs allow initial tests of whether treatment is likely to achieve the desired changes before it is applied widely or over a protracted period. There are several ways in which this gradual approach to therapeutic change can be valuable.

For clients with several problems or problems that encompass several situations, treatment can be implemented in a gradual fashion. At the beginning of treatment, the procedures can be applied to one behavior or to behavior in one situation. The modest initial focus provides information about the effectiveness of the procedure before it is applied widely. Baseline information may be obtained to encompass several areas of client functioning. However, treatment is first applied only to one area. If the intervention is successful, it can be extended to other problem areas. If it is not successful, or produces less than dramatic effects, changes can be made in an exploratory fashion until the desired changes are produced. Once an effective treatment has been identified, it can be applied more widely across the range of prob-

lem areas in need of treatment. This gradual approach is consistent with the clinical demands of treatment and also is based upon the rationale underlying the multiple-baseline designs, highlighted earlier.

In institutional settings, a multiple-baseline design approach has other advantages for implementing treatment. Typically, staff implement treatment to alter the behavior of individual patients or groups of patients. The multiple-baseline design permits staff to focus on one behavior initially and to extend the treatment to other kinds of behavior as initial successes are achieved. This approach has an obvious practical advantage of proceeding gradually, where staff are not likely to have the resources for larger scale multifaced treatments implemented all at once.

For the individual client, other single-case designs are well suited to the demands of treatment. Many problems seen in treatment represent new learning on the part of the client, and this learning is developed gradually. For example, developing social skills in withdrawn and reticent adults can proceed gradually by practicing and rehearsing specific skills and engaging in more of the behavior over time that approach the terminal goal. The approach of a changing-criterion design is suitable for many clinical problems, because the final behavior of interest is approached gradually as a function of the client's ability to meet the performance criteria. Hence treatment can proceed gradually and consider completely the individual client's rate of improvement.

Another practical feature of single-case designs pertains to their use in exploring new treatments. Hypotheses about effective treatments can be tested with the individual first before large-scale evaluation is undertaken in group research. Even if large numbers of clients are available for investigation, single-case research permits the investigator to develop treatment and to receive feedback about its success. When treatment is well developed in the individual case, larger treatment questions can be proposed and addressed in group investigations.

CONCLUSION

Single-case experimental methodology departs from the more familiar between-group approach in a variety of ways, including the manner in which assessment is conducted, the use of data to make decisions about aspects of the experimental design, and the methods of data evaluation. The methodology is more than the addition of a few designs to clinical psychology. Rather, single-case research reflects an approach toward treatment and its evaluation. Although the methodology naturally stresses experimental evaluation, many features of the approach and specific designs are quite suitable for clinical work.

Several features of the design permit consideration of the individual needs of the client. For example, treatment can be implemented on a gradual basis so that only certain behavior in certain situations is focused upon initially, as in one of the multiple-baseline designs. Also treatment goals can be approximated gradually by requiring the client only to perform approximations of the final goal, as in a changing-criterion design.

Occasionally some features of the designs may compete with clinical care, as epitomized by reversal phases in the ABAB design. However, rarely is only one design option available. Hence a design requirement that is undesirable for the client often can be circumvented with one of the many other options.

Single-case designs focus on the evaluation of treatment in the individual case. Treatment applications as practiced in ordinary clinical and hospital settings certainly warrant more frequent evaluation than they normally have received. Often little empirical justification exists for procedures that are used, and the accumulation of clinical experience over the years, as opposed to clinical evidence, is difficult to evaluate. Single-case designs offer a distinct option that allows the investigator-practitioner to further evaluate treatment progress for the individual client.

REFERENCES

Allport, G. W. (1961). *Pattern and growth in personality*. New York: Holt, Rinehart & Winston.

Baer, D. M. (1977). "Perhaps it would be better not to know everything." *Journal of Applied Behavior Analysis, 10,* 167–172.

Baer, D. M., Rowbury, T. G., & Goetz, E. M. (1976). Behavioral traps in the preschool: A proposal for research. *Minnesota Symposia on Child Psychology, 10,* 3–27.

Baer, D. M., Wolf, M. M., & Risley, T. R. (1968). Some current dimensions of applied behavior analysis. *Journal of Applied Behavior Analysis, 1,* 91–97.

Barlow, D. H., & Hayes, S. C. (1979). Alternating treatments design: One strategy for comparing the effects of two treatments in a single subject. *Journal of Applied Behavior Analysis, 12,* 199–210.

Barlow, D. H., Reynolds, J., & Agras, W. S. (1973). Gender identity change in a transsexual. *Archives of General Psychiatry, 29,* 569–576.

Bennett, P. S., & Maley, R. S. (1973). Modification of interactive behaviors in chronic mental patients. *Journal of Applied Behavior Analysis, 6,* 609–620.

Edgington, E. S. (1980). Random assignment and statistical tests for one-subject experimentation. *Behavioral Assessment, 2,* 19–28.

Fawcett, S. B., & Miller, L. K. (1975). Training public-speaking behavior: An experimental analysis and social validation. *Journal of Applied Behavior Analysis, 8,* 125–135.

Foxx, R. M., & Rubinoff, A. (1979). Behavioral treatment of caffeinism: Reducing excessive coffee drinking. *Journal of Applied Behavior Analysis, 12,* 335–344.

Glass, G. V., Willson, V. L., & Gottman, J. M. (1975). *Design and analysis of time-series experiments.* Boulder: Colorado Associated University Press.

Goetz, E. M., Holmberg, M. C., & LeBlanc, J. M. (1975). Differential reinforcement of other behavior and noncontingent reinforcement as control procedures during the modification of a preschooler's compliance. *Journal of Applied Behavior Analysis,* **8,** 77–82.

Hartmann, D. P. (1974). Forcing square pegs into round holes: Some comments on "An analysis-of-variance model for the intrasubject replication design." *Journal of Applied Behavior Analysis,* **7,** 635–638.

Hartmann, D. P., & Hall, R. V. (1976). The changing criterion design. *Journal of Applied Behavior Analysis,* **9,** 527–532.

Hayes, S. C., Brownell, K. D., & Barlow, D. H. (1978). The use of self-administered covert sensitization in the treatment of exhibitionism and sadism. *Behavior Therapy,* **9,** 283–289.

Hersen, M., & Barlow, D. H. (1976). *Single-case experimental designs: Strategies for studing behavior change.* New York: Pergamon Press.

Hersen, M., & Bellack, A. S. (1976). A multiple-baseline analysis of social-skills training in chronic schizophrenics. *Journal of Applied Behavior Analysis,* **9,** 239, 245.

Jones, R. R., Vaught, R. S., & Weinrott, M. (1977). Time-series analysis in operant research. *Journal of Applied Behavior Analysis,* **10,** 151–166.

Kazdin, A. E. (1973). Role of instructions and reinforcement in behavior change in token reinforcement programs. *Journal of Educational Psychology,* **64,** 63–71.

Kazdin, A. E. (1977a). Assessing the clinical or applied significance of behavior change through social validation. *Behavior Modification,* **1,** 427–452.

Kazdin, A. E. (1977b). The influence of behavior preceding a reinforced response on behavior change in the classroom. *Journal of Applied Behavior Analysis,* **10,** 299–310.

Kazdin, A. E. (1978a). The application of operant techniques in treatment, rehabilitation, and education. In S. L. Garfield & A. E. Bergin (Eds.), *Handbook of psychotherapy and behavior change* (2nd ed.). New York: Wiley.

Kazdin, A. E. (1978b). *History of behavior modification: Experimental foundations of contemporary research.* Baltimore: University Park Press.

Kazdin, A. E. (1978c). Methodology of applied behavior analysis. In A. C. Catania & T. A. Brigham (Eds.), *Handbook of applied behavior analysis: Social and instructional processes.* New York: Irvington.

Kazdin, A. E. (1979). Vicarious reinforcement and punishment in operant programs for children. *Child Behavior Therapy,* **1,** 13–36.

Kazdin, A. E. (1980a). *Behavior modification in applied settings* (2nd ed.). Homewood, Ill.: Dorsey.

Kazdin, A. E. (1980b). *Research design in clinical psychology.* New York: Harper & Row.

Kazdin, A. E. (in press) *Single-case research designs: Methods for clinical and applied research.* New York: Oxford University Press.

Kazdin, A. E., & Geesey, S. (1980). Enhancing classroom attentiveness by preselection of back-up reinforcers in a token economy. *Behavior Modification,* **4,** 98–114.

Kazdin, A. E. & Hartmann, D. P. (1978). The simultaneous-treatment design. *Behavior Therapy,* **9,** 912–922.

Kazdin, A. E., & Kopel, S. A. (1975). On resolving ambiguities of the multiple-baseline design: Problems and recommendations. *Behavior Therapy,* **6,** 601–608.

Kent, R. N., & O'Leary, K. D. (1976). A controlled evaluation of behavior modification with conduct problem children. *Journal of Consulting and Clinical Psychology,* **44,** 586–596.

Korchin, S. J. (1976). *Modern clinical psychology.* New York: Basic Books.

Kratochwill, T. R. (Ed.) (1978). *Single-subject research: Strategies for evaluating change.* New York: Academic Press.

Leitenberg, H. (1973). The use of single-case methodology in psychotherapy research. *Journal of Abnormal Psychology,* **82,** 87–101.

Lindsay, W. R., & Stoffelmayr, B. E. (1976). A comparison of the differential effects of three different baseline conditions within an ABAB experimental design. *Behaviour Research and Therapy,* **14,** 169–173.

Maloney, D. M., Harper, T. M., Braukmann, C. J., Fixsen, D. L., Phillips, E. L., & Wolf, M. M. (1976). Teaching conversation-related skills to predelinquent girls. *Journal of Applied Behavior Analysis,* **9,** 371.

Matson, J. L., Kazdin, A. E., & Esveldt-Dawson, K. (1980). Training interpersonal skills among mentally retarded and socially dysfunctional children. *Behaviour Research and Therapy,* **18,** 419–427.

Michael, J. (1974). Statistical inference for individual organism research: Mixed blessing or curse. *Journal of Applied Behavior Analysis,* **7,** 647–653.

Neisworth, J. T., & Moore, F. (1972). Operant treatment of asthmatic responding with the parent as therapist. *Behavior Therapy,* **3,** 95–99.

O'Brien, F., & Azrin, N. H. (1972). Developing proper mealtime behaviors of the institutionalized retarded. *Journal of Applied Behavior Analysis.* **5,** 389–399.

O'Connor, R. D. (1969). Modification of social withdrawal through symbolic modeling. *Journal of Applied Behavior Analysis, 2,* 15–22.

Patterson, G. R. (1974). Interventions for boys with conduct problems: Multiple settings, treatments, and criteria. *Journal of Consulting and Clinical Psychology, 42,* 471–481.

Patterson, G. R., Cobb, J. A., & Ray, R. S. (1973). A social engineering technology for retraining families of aggressive boys. In H. E. Adams & I. P. Unikel (Eds.), *Issues and trends in behavior therapy.* Springfield, Ill.: Charles C. Thomas.

Redd, W. H., & Birnbrauer, J. S. (1969). Adults as discriminative stimuli for different reinforcement contingencies with retarded children. *Journal of Experimental Child Psychology, 7,* 440–447.

Revusky, S. H. (1967). Some statistical treatments compatible with individual organism methodology. *Journal of the Experimental Analysis of Behavior, 10,* 319–330.

Risley, T. R. (1970). Behavior modification: An experimental-therapeutic endeavor. In L. A. Hamerlynck, P. O. Davidson, & L. E. Acker (Eds.), *Behavior modification and ideal mental health services.* Calgary, Alberta, Canada: University of Calgary Press.

Schnelle, J. F. (1974). A brief report on invalidity of parent evaluations of behavior change. *Journal of Applied Behavior Analysis, 7,* 341–343.

Scott, R. W., Peters, R. D., Gillespie, W. J., Blanchard, E. B., Edmunson, E. D. & Young, L. D. (1973). The use of shaping and reinforcement in the operant acceleration and deceleration of heart rate. *Behaviour Research and Therapy, 11,* 179–185.

Sidman, M. (1960). *Tactics of scientific research.* New York: Basic Books.

Stahl, J. R., Thomson, L. E., Leitenberg, H., & Hasazi, J. E. (1974). Establishment of praise as a conditioned reinforcer in socially unresponsive psychiatric patients. *Journal of Abnormal Psychology, 83,* 488–496.

Tigpen, C. H., & Cleckley, H. M. (1957). *Three faces of Eve.* New York: McGraw-Hill.

Thomson, N., Fraser, D., & McDougall, A. (1974). The reinstatement of speech in near-mute chronic schizophrenics by instructions, imitative prompts, and reinforcement. *Journal of Behavior Therapy and Experimental Psychiatry, 5,* 77–80.

Van Houten, R., Morrison, E., Jarvis, R., & McDonald, M. (1974). The effects of explicit timing and feedback on compositional response rate in elementary school children. *Journal of Applied Behavior Analysis, 7,* 547–555.

Wahler, R. G. (1975). Some structural aspects of deviant child behavior. *Journal of Applied Behavior Analysis, 8,* 27–42.

Walker, H., & Hops, H. (1976). Use of normative peer data as a standard for evaluating classroom treatment effects. *Journal of Applied Behavior Analysis, 9,* 159–168.

Watson, R. I. (1951). *The clinical method in psychology.* New York: Harper.

Wincze, J. P., Leitenberg, H., & Agras, W. S. (1972). The effects of token reinforcement and feedback on the delusional verbal behavior of chronic paranoid schizophrenics. *Journal of Applied Behavior Analysis, 5,* 247–262.

Wolf, M. M. (1978). Social validity: The case for subjective measurement or how applied behavior analysis is finding its heart. *Journal of Applied Behavior Analysis, 11,* 203–214.

CHAPTER 15

Individualized Measures of Psychotherapy Outcome

JIM MINTZ AND DONALD J. KIESLER

Cries of "Accountability!" from the public sector are increasingly reaching the ears of mental health practitioners and agencies. Psychiatrists, psychologists, social workers, rehabilitation counselors, psychiatric nurses, occupational therapists, and others are feeling increasing pressures from state legislatures and the U.S. Congress to demonstrate the effectiveness and cost efficiency of the mental health services they provide.

This challenge has pumped new blood into the science of mental health. Realizing that measurement problems are formidable, mental health scientists and practitioners are directing considerable efforts toward producing the data required by this accountability. These efforts in turn have focused on measurement procedures that might be economically and routinely applied in mental health settings for program evaluation activities.

In 1975, NIMH published an important contribution to researchers studying psychotherapy outcome, *Psychotherapy change*

This chapter is based on reports prepared for the Psychotherapy and Behavioral Intervention Section, Clinical Research Branch, Division of Extramural Research Programs, National Institute of Mental Health, by Dr. Mintz (under Contract No. PLDO5668–77) and Dr. Keisler (under Contract No. PLDO4317–77). The authors thank Dr. Irene Elkin Waskow of the NIMH for her role in initiating those reports. We also thank Ms. Rosa Surrence, Clinical Research Support Section, Brentwood VA Medical Center, Los Angeles, CA, for her careful work in editing and preparing the manuscript.

measures (Waskow & Parloff, 1975), the report of the Clinical Research Branch Outcome Measures Project. A primary goal of the report was to encourage the use of comparable criterion measures in diverse psychotherapy research projects. To this end, a "core battery" of outcome measures was recommended, culled from reviews by a distinguished group of consultants.

Included in the core battery were measures of "target complaints" to be completed by both patient and therapist. In addition, some measurement of therapeutic goals was described as crucial, though no explicit method for this was recommended. Target complaints and goal attainment scaling are sometimes referred to as "individualized" or "tailored" criteria, because their content differs from patient to patient.

The importance of such measures to a valid assessment of psychotherapy outcome seems so obvious on the basis of their face validity that one might think their place in an outcome battery would be assured. However, significant methodological difficulties exist in their application. Many of these are described by Waskow (1975). How are these problems to be elicited? How should they be scored, and by whom? How should various problems be combined within patients, and is it appropriate to compare patients on different kinds of problems? What about symptom substitution? Who should set goals, and when? What about changing goals and redefinitions of problems during therapy? Should change be measured by computing difference scores between pre- and posttreatment assessments of severity, or by rating improvement at the end of treatment? The methodological problems seemed serious enough that one of NIMH's consultants on the Outcome Measures Project recommended against inclusion of target complaints in the core battery (Imber, 1975).

The purpose of this chapter is to pull together the evidence regarding the strengths and weaknesses of two "individualized" or "tailored" measures of therapeutic outcome: (1) the Target Complaints procedure developed by Jerome Frank and his colleagues at Phipps Clinic in Baltimore, and (2) Goal Attainment Scaling, developed by Thomas Kiresuk and Robert Sherman at the Program Evaluation Resource Center in Minneapolis.

These have come to be labeled "individualized measures" of psychotherapy outcome (Waskow & Parloff, 1974) because of their extreme flexibility and the idiosyncratic content they encompass. These features permit their application to the entire range of clients or patients in the mental health field, a fascinating advantage that more traditional standardized and restricted measures of psychopathology do not provide.

A BRIEF HISTORY OF TAILORED OUTCOME CRITERIA

Pascal (1959) was an early advocate of behaviorism in the assessment of psychotherapy outcome. "Only an operationally defined set of behaviors which stand in functional relationship to independent variables can satisfy us if we are to stay with the methodology of the science of psychology" (Pascal, 1959, p. 23). Pascal and Zax (1956) defined individualized behavioral outcome criteria for 30 hospitalized patients on the basis of clinical records. The study was not controlled, and there was no way to assess the base rate probability for improvement on the kind of criteria they used. Nevertheless, this may have

been the first attempt to use individualized behavioral criteria for psychotherapy criteria.

Interest in tailoring criteria increased in the 1960s. Kiesler (1966) provided a powerful attack on what he called the myth of uniformity, and emphasized the need to consider the diversity of patients, therapists, and treatments. Rickard (1965) may have been the first to use the term "tailored" to refer to criteria chosen on a case-by-case basis. Like Pascal and Zax, he advocated choosing specific kinds of behavior, indicating that such behavior could be assessed reliably. Interestingly, Rickard suggested that a "board of judges, not necessarily psychologists," might be most appropriate to select the relevant target behavior. To a great degree, Goal Attainment Scaling is an implementation of Rickard's suggestions.

Target complaints were first used to assess psychotherapy outcome by the research group at the Phipps Clinic (Hoehn-Saric et al., 1964). Two years later, the same group published a methodological report on target complaints (Battle et al., 1966). Kiresuk and Sherman (1968) introduced Goal Attainment Scaling in 1968. By 1973 Kiresuk reported widespread applications of Goal Attainment scaling.

The rationale given by Kiresuk and Sherman (1968) for Goal Attainment Scaling is a good argument for the tailored criterion concept.

There has been a tendency to use a fixed battery of evaluation measures regardless of the individual patient characteristics or problems. . . . The use of the same psychometric or rating device for all patients inevitably led to evaluating some patients on variables that were irrelevant to their particular dilemma or circumstances. The clinicians justifiably objected. To rate all patients with regard to their anxiety level, sexual problems and thought disorder, whether or not these variables had to do with the patient's reason for coming to the clinic, appears to be unreasonable and wasteful. (Kiresuk & Sherman, 1968, p. 444)

The thrust of "individualized" measures of therapy outcome thus contrasts dramatically with the psychometric tradition of psychological testing. Instead of using universal measures of improvement, or measures designed to reflect change for groups of patients, the individualized measure attempts to assess change or improvement in terms of idiographic, idiosyncratic, and relatively unique behavioral dimensions "tailored" for the individual psychotherapy client or patient. Shlien (1966), in another context, articulates the basic argument of this individualized assessment emphasis:

All attempts to compare patients with one another in terms of any single criterion are fallacious and mainly for the convenience of the researcher. As a result, we actually discount to some extent the value of the outcome for each individual because we insist that the outcome be displayed through a measure which is somewhat foreign to any individual. Since it has to be phrased in terms common to all—the problem is how to translate each individual's change into a common demoninator for comparison's sake without losing those personal meanings. (Shlien, 1966, p. 128)

The two individualized measures reviewed below are geared to presenting complaints, problems, or treatment goals of the individual client or patient. Since they are tailored to the unique treatment situation of each patient, they are purported to be of much greater relevance and validity as outcome or program evaluation indexes, in contrast to "across the board" or standardized group measures tapping dimensions that may or may not be relevant to a particular patient. Respondents for these measures can be patients, therapists, various or combined treatment staff, family or other persons significant to the patient, or external observers, or any combination of the above. The measures thus provide considerable flexibility for recording different perspectives regarding the patient's problems or improvement. The measures also have the flexibility of being applicable at the initiation of treatment, at various stages throughout treatment, at termination, and at various stages of follow-up. They thereby permit the repeated measurement necessary for valid

assessment of treatment process and outcome. Finally, these measurement formats can be used to facilitate training and supervision as well as conceptualization of the treatment process, and in some instances can be modified as adjunct treatment methods themselves.

TARGET COMPLAINTS (TCs)

We implicitly trust the wisdom of the mental patient when he or she asserts that he or she has problems. As Tasto (1977) observes:

It is understandable historically how verbal reports came to be looked on as something less than the best predictor of other human behavior. Yet in the realm of clinical practice, the operational criteria for the existence of problems are self-reported verbalizations. If a patient says there is a problem, then there is a problem. And conversely, when the patient claims there is no problem, then there is no problem. Therapeutic intervention is considered to be progressing to the extent that the patient (and others who may also be involved) report that things are better and, conversely, therapeutic intervention may be considered to be of no value or even harmful as a result of the patient's (and sometimes others') report. With the exception of behaviors that are illegal and consequently defined as problems independently of the patient's view, it is the patient's complaint of anxiety, depression, insomnia, or the like that defines whether a problem exists for clinical purposes. (Tasto, 1977, p. 154)

It was out of a similar rationale and perspective that Frank and his colleagues developed the Target Complaint assessment device, "using each patient's spontaneously expressed presenting complaints (target complaints) as criteria for evaluating response to psychotherapy" (Battle et al., 1966, p. 184).

Theoretical Basis

The rationale was stated as follows:

The target-complaint concept is similar to the treatment criteria in other areas of medicine. The patient comes to a physician with a series of complaints or symptoms; the alleviation of these complaints is the criterion of the efficacy of the treatment. . . . In the absence of adequate knowledge of the causes of psychiatric complaints, we assume that psychotherapy has removed the causes if the complaints are permanently relieved, and no new ones are substituted for them. . . . Psychotherapy, more than other types of treatment, tends to be limited to dealing with those problems which the patient himself conceptualizes and discusses. . . . The initial complaints, when alleviated, may offer evidence to the patient that he has indeed made the right decision to come for help. . . . The initial complaints may shift in focus and scope, or disappear altogether and be replaced by others which may go through the same process. To the extent that psychotherapy patients evaluate the effectiveness of treatment by the degree of alleviation of distress associated with their main problems, a systematic program of psychotherapy research based on such criteria is feasible. (Battle et al., 1966, p. 185)

Setting Up a Target Complaints Scale

The original method of eliciting target complaints (Battle et al., 1966) stayed close to clinical practice. "What problems or difficulties do you have that you would like our help with?" This was followed up with requests for two more problems in a completely open-ended manner. "Anything else? . . . Anything Else?" The problems were recorded as given, although complaints that did not seem to the interviewer to be valid therapeutic issues were responded to by asking, "But which of the problems or complaints would you like to have help with in treatment?" If the patient persisted with the same complaint after this probe, it would be accepted as given.

The authors learned that the procedure needed some standardization so that patients' reports of TCs could be defined with more "clarity, specificity, and relevance" (Battle et al., 1966, p. 188). This took the form of a separate "target complaints" interview conducted by an interviewer trained to probe for clarification and specificity of the patient's

complaints, but careful not to suggest or lead the patient to mention problems not spontaneously expressed. Further, the interviewer insisted that patients report complaints "which the patient wanted to have changed in treatment" in contrast to irrelevant changes (e.g., "I don't have enough money to buy a new house," or "I would like to have my nose changed"). Also it was necessary for the interviewer to help the patient to group under one complaint area highly interrelated symptoms or complaint; For example, if a patient complained of headaches, dizziness, and butterflies in his stomach any time he had an argument with his wife, all three of these physical symptoms were grouped together into one complaint.

Battle et al. (1966) noted that separate complaints elicited often seemed to be parts of a common condition, and thus were difficult to rate separately. A similar conclusion was reached by Candy et al. (1972), and although Bloch et al. (1977) asked judges not to group complaints, they also noted that they often could reasonably have been grouped on the basis of clinical coherence.

As Bloch et al. (1977) noted, the clinical validity of complex complaints may seem higher, but they may prove difficult to explore psychometrically. Consider this presenting picture, reported by Battle et al. (1966), as an example of a complex target complaint. A patient "complained that she had poor appetite, lost weight, was constipated, had pains in the stomach but only at home because she had no company, no understanding from her children and lacked friends" (Battle et al., 1966, p.190). There are still no established guidelines or procedures for determining how many discrete complaints this represents. The question of whether the diverse complaints reported by each patient should be viewed as distinct entities or as several aspects of some common process or underlying condition is a basic theoretical problem each researcher must resolve.

Most subsequent studies using target complaints have not specified the manner of eliciting complaints. It is hard to see why minor variations in method would be very significant, as long as the basic nondirective character of the original approach is preserved. Increased standardization would undoubtedly be encouraged by the development of structured target complaint interviews. In this regard it is hardly surprising that the ubiquitous computer has found a place in the methodology of eliciting, scoring, and summarizing target complaints (Klein et al., 1975; Griest et al., 1973). Griest reports on a computerized interview designed for interactive use. The patient works at a computer terminal, giving his or her complaints directly to the computer. The interview elicits target complaints in an open-ended manner, and includes the Hopkins Symptom Checklist. Data are summarized and stored for future reference.

The TC method has been used most frequently in studies of adult outpatients, and it has apparently not been used with psychotic patients. Several studies (Holmes & Urie, 1975; Kent & O'Leary, 1976; Frey et al., 1975) have used some version of TC approach in studies of children. When the patients are adults, they are almost always the ones who define the target complaints; occasionally therapists or independent clinical judges have been used in addition to define complaints from their perspectives (Bloch et al., 1976; Candy et al., 1972; Luborsky et al., 1978). On the other hand, when the patients are children, TCs have been defined by adults: teachers (Kent & O'Leary, 1976), therapists (Holmes & Urie, 1975), or parents (Frey et al., 1976).

There is obviously no set limit on the number of complaints per patient, although the structure of the interview described by Battle et al. (1966) clearly tends to elicit three. Many studies have not reported this bit of information. Bloch et al. (1977) asked for three TCs from therapists, but reported that patients gave an average of 4.6, and that clinical judges, who were encouraged to be

specific and not to group complaints together, averaged 7.3 per patient. In the Penn Psychotherapy Project (Luborsky et al., 1980), the average number of TCs given by patients at the initial assessment was 2.8, which compares with the values of 2.2 and 2.8 given in the original studies by Battle et al. (1966). In some studies (e.g., Sloane et al., 1976) the number of complaints per patient has been explicitly set at three. This standardization solves some psychometric problems at the price of compromising the sensitivity to the individual that is a major strength of the method.

Scoring Target Complaints

It is standard practice to obtain ratings of severity of discomfort for each target complaint at the time they are elicited and again at the end of treatment. Improvement may be indexed in terms of the amount of change in severity, whether by a simple difference score or a more complex partialed or residual gain score. Another approach is to have the degree of improvement itself rated; even in this case, it is possible to use the initial severity ratings as covariates. Some researchers have advocated the use of severity ratings at the end of treatment as the most appropriate measures of treatment outcome. The relative merits of these strategies are discussed by Mintz, Luborsky, and Christoph (1979). Candy and his associates (Candy et al., 1972) had ratings made of degree of discomfort caused by the complaints, as well as the degree of unwanted behavior, attempting to capture both the intrapsychic and behavioral dimensions of the complaints. That distinction was seen as basic and essential by Strupp (1976).

For the severity ratings, Battle and her coworkers tried both a simple 4½ inch vertical line, anchored at the ends, and a 13-box scale with five anchors. They settled on the box scale, citing better reliability and patient preference for that format (Figure 15.1). Improvement ratings are typically made on a

Name *A. Client* Date: *9/14/79*

Problem: *Relating to people without anxiety*	Problem: *Dating*	Problem: *Unable to concentrate—want to go back to school.*
In general, how much does this problem or complaint bother you?	In general, how much does this problem or complaint bother you?	In general, how much does this problem or complaint bother you?
couldn't be worse	couldn't be worse	couldn't be worse
	x	
very much	very much	very much
x		
pretty much	pretty much	pretty much
		x
a little	a little	a little
not at all	not at all	not at all
Check the box which best describes the amount of disturbance felt because of this problem.	Check the box which best describes the amount of disturbance felt because of this problem.	Check the box which best describes the amount of disturbance felt because of this problem.

Figure 15.1. Sample target complaints form.

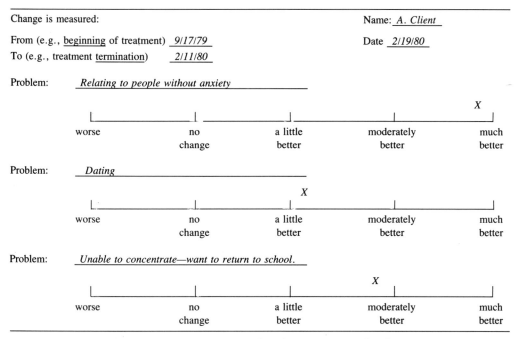

Change is measured: Name: *A. Client*

From (e.g., beginning of treatment) *9/17/79*   Date *2/19/80*
To (e.g., treatment termination)   *2/11/80*

Problem: *Relating to people without anxiety*

|_____|_____|_____|_____|
worse   no   a little   moderately   much
                change   better   better   better

Problem: *Dating*

|_____|_____|_____|_____|
worse   no   a little   moderately   much
                change   better   better   better

Problem: *Unable to concentrate—want to return to school.*

|_____|_____|_____|_____|
worse   no   a little   moderately   much
                change   better   better   better

Figure 15.2.   Target complaints improvement rating form.

5-point rating scale (Figure 15.2). However, this simple matter of standardizing the number of points on the rating scales used has not been done, and it is often difficult to compare results in different studies. For example, although Strupp and Bloxom (1973) and Piper, Debbane, & Garant (1977) both studied group therapy outcome at three months with a target complaint improvement measure, the results are obviously on a different scale, and thus one cannot compare them.

Whether pre–post treatment difference scores based on severity ratings or post-therapy ratings of degree of improvement are obtained, most researchers average the ratings obtained for all complaints. For example, Sloane et al. (1975) present some results for the separate complaints, but most of their analyses are based on averaged data across the three problems. Holmes and Urie (1975) appear to have summed rather than averaged severity ratings. When the number of problems per patient is not held constant, this procedure makes the resulting score highly correlated with the total number of complaints.

A word should be said about the difficulties involved in combining ratings from different problems. Consider two subjects, both of whom are asked to name their main complaint and rate its severity. Both do so. Assume that both name the same problem and that both give identical severity ratings. Now we ask for a second problem, and again both give identical content as well as identical ratings. Thus far, our hypothetical patients are identical, from the point of view of presenting complaints. When we ask for a third problem, however, a difference appears. Patient A cites a third problem, less severe than the first two. Patient B cannot think of a third problem. Which of these patients, in sum, has "more" complaint severity?

Intuitively, it does not seem correct that Patient A, who not only has problems 1 and 2 just as Patient B does, but in addition has Problem 3 to worry about, should wind up with a less severe rating, but the process of averaging ratings will do just that. On the other hand, a sum will yield a higher score for Patient A, but is likely to yield an even *higher* score for obsessional Patient C, who lists seven relatively mild problems and only one severe one.

Of course standardization of the number of problems per patient would eliminate this methodological problem, but at the price of imposing an artificial constraint on the patient. After all, one of the most attractive features of the method is its face validity. One is reminded of the Holtzman Inkblots (Holtzman et al., 1961), which impose a "one response per card" rule, in contrast to the freedom of the Rorschach technique. While psychometrics may have gained, the result has been a great loss in clinical appeal.

There is another issue to be considered with regard to the implications of summing or averaging severity scores to yield an index of overall severity. At the initial point, most patients may be expected to have at least one relatively severe problem. Thus variation on the main initial problem is likely to be small. In a sense, the severity rating on that problem is almost like a mathematical constant that is part of each patient's total score.

On the other hand, the second and third problems are more likely to vary in severity. Some patients will have only one severe problem, and then will report relatively mild ones. Others may have several severe problems.

The implication of this is that a total score, at least for initial severity, is likely to be more highly related to the severity of the secondary problems than to the severity of the primary problem. Data from the Penn Psychotherapy Project (e.g., Luborsky et al., 1980) confirm this. For a sample of 25 patients who gave three initial complaints, the first problem severity correlated .57 with the sum (or average) initial severity ratings, but the third problem correlated .82 with the same total score.

In almost all studies using the TC methodology, the ratings of severity or improve-

ment have been made by the individual who initially defined the problems. As noted above, this generally means the patient in the case of adult patients, or some collateral adult with child patients. In some cases additional ratings on these problems are also obtained from others. For example, Frey et al. (1976) had parents of the children being treated define and rate the problems, and had them rated by therapists also. Candy et al. (1972) attempted practically all combinations, but reported some difficulties with this. Patients were not asked to rate complaints identified by the clinical team if it was felt this might be disturbing to them, for example, if the team identified a problem such as "latent homosexuality." Also they reported that therapists were often unable to rate problems defined by patients because they conceptualized them in vastly different terms, something noted by Bloch et al. as well (1976). They reported that characterological problems were rarely reported by patients, for example, passive-dependency, while such problems were usually listed by judges. However, this was probably because they asked judges to list at least one such problem per patient.

Severity Ratings Versus Improvement Ratings

Waskow (1975) recommends obtaining pre–posttreatment severity ratings on target complaints, referring to Battle et al's. (1966) original methodological studies. However, most studies using target complaints to assess treatment outcome have used improvement ratings, including the original study by the Phipps group (Hoehn-Saric et al., 1966).

Does it matter? Perhaps so, although the relatively small number of studies in each area and the frequent confounding of factors suggests caution in interpretation of these results. Mintz (1977) reviewed 17 treatment outcome studies that used a TC measure. Of the 13 studies that used improvement ratings, all but one (Piper et al., 1976) found some significant results with the target complaints measure. However, only one of the four studies based on changes in severity scores was significant (Sloane et al., 1975). Of course the reliability problems of the brief target complaints measure are likely to be compounded by the use of a difference score, making it more difficult to obtain significant results unless effects are very large.

Sooner or later, perhaps researchers will begin to take seriously the fundamental difference that exists between status measures, difference scores, and ratings of change or improvement (Mintz et al., 1979). The decision to measure outcome using a pre–post measurement design or a posttreatment rating of improvement is not a trivial one; it is likely to have profound implications for the results obtained.

We must begin to consider the difference between how much one *has changed,* and how much one *thinks one has improved.* The evaluative connotations of the latter are quite crucial. Most but not all applications of the target complaints method have used improvement ratings. Goal Attainment Scales, as will be seen, are usually posttreatment status measures. We have begun to get some understanding about the relationship between change and the evaluation of that change (Mintz, 1972: Mintz et al., 1979). Hopefully, this will be the subject of increased attention in the future.

Reliability

Reliability of the target complaints method has not been studied a great deal. Battle et al. (1966) reported a series of relevant studies. The design was to elicit target complaints and then have the patient undergo a detailed psychiatric assessment interview. Following this, the target complaints were elicited and rated again. In one study the same interviewer saw the patient for both target complaint sessions; in another, the two target complaint sessions were done by different interviewers.

Battle et al. reported "reliable results," by which they appear to mean that the average severity ratings did not change much after the assessment interview. However, the lack of mean change does not necessarily imply a high degree of correlation. A correlation of .68 was reported between rankings of problems before and after the assessment interview. This correlation appears to be based on the ranks assigned to each problem by each patient. It indexes the degree to which patients continued to place their TCs in the same order of importance to them after the interview. This is quite different from determining the stability of overall problem severity, which is, after all, the score generally used. The correlation between the total pre- and posttreatment severity scores for each patient, the more usual reliability coefficient, was not reported.

In a study of content changes, Battle et al. reported identical content in 12 of 20 cases before and after the assessment interview. They state that in four of 20 cases, three or more judges agreed that the content of target complaints given after the interview was different in "some important part" from the preinterview content. It is a matter of judgment whether that much change in TC content after one interview is an acceptable degree of stability. Battle et al. thought so. They concluded that "target complaints, when properly elicited, can be obtained reliably from the patient, and in the majority of patients they do not change in their main content nor in their severity rating throughout an intensive psychiatric evaluation interview" (p. 191), whether elicited by the same or a different interviewer.

Bloch et al. (1977) did a detailed study of the reliability of ratings of severity and improvement on target complaints as defined and rated by clinical judges. They also seem to have computed statistics based on within-patient rankings. The statistic used was Kendall's coefficient of concordance. Translating the values reported into average correlation coefficients (Hays, 1973) yields median rho values of only .28 for severity ratings, and .38 for improvement ratings.

The fact that patients and judges in these studies could not reliably rank problems within cases does not preclude the possibility of highly reliable differences between patients in overall levels. In fact, if there is a strong common factor in the various complaint ratings of any individual patient, it is likely that differences among individual complaints will be largely due to unreliability, and the idea of ranking them would make very little sense at all. Of course the results presented might reflect unreliability too. In the absence of intraclass correlations, we cannot really know how to evaluate these findings.

Bierenbaum et al. (1976) reported a correlation coefficient of .79 for ratings of 21 target complaints from eight patients, apparently between a clinical psychologist's ratings and the patients' own ratings. Frey et al. (1976) reported a highly significant correlation ($r = .73$) between parents' ratings of target complaint improvement at termination and a one-month follow-up, indicating considerable test-retest stability.

In the Penn Psychotherapy Project (unpublished data), pretreatment severity ratings of the first and second listed problems were not significantly correlated for patients ($r = .20$) or therapists ($r = .21$). Change ratings obtained at the end of treatment did correlate significantly, indicating some common factor of improvement did exist. The correlation was higher for the therapists ($r = .59$) than for the patients ($r = .47$), but both were significant. Thus the internal consistency reliability of a pretreatment severity score would be low, while that of summed improvement ratings would be more acceptable.

Reliable differentiation among subjects would undoubtedly be increased if more than one item rating per complaint were used. It is not difficult to think of multi-item formats, although it is true that these make the method more cumbersome. Candy et al. (1972) had

distress and unwanted behavior rated for each complaint. One might go further than that. How severe is your problem? How much would you like to be rid of it? How many people out of 100 would you say have a more severe problem? How much of the day does this bother you? Note that all of these items could be used with almost any target complaint.

Validity

Concurrent validity studies involve correlating the target complaints measure with other measures of treatment outcome. There have been very few such correlations reported, although many researchers have had the data to calculate them. What data do exist suggest that improvement ratings on target complaints tap a broad improvement factor.

Hoehn-Saric et al. (1964) reported a correlation of .61 between patient ratings of improvement on target complaints and a therapist global improvement rating. They also reported significant but lower correlations with a measure of desirable therapy behavior derived from tapes of treatment and with length of treatment. Shorer (1970) reported a correlation of .71 between target complaints and a global improvement rating for treated patients, and of .78 for untreated patients. He does not indicate who made these ratings. Mintz, Luborsky, and Christoph (1979) indicate that patient's improvement ratings on target complaints load on a general improvement factor defined by a number of patient and therapist ratings of change or benefits from therapy.

Battle et al. (1966) also indicate that target complaints measures "correlated" significantly with global ratings by patient and therapist, as well as with the Social Ineffectiveness and Discomfort Scales used at the Phipps Clinic. However, no correlation coefficients are presented. From the description of results, it appears that the authors may have examined the patterns of outcome for these various measures, and interpreted as "correlated" measures that demonstrated similar patterns. This does not necessarily imply a high degree of correlation between measures.

Two studies of treatment of children obtained concurrent validity coefficients between therapists and parents of the patients. Holmes and Urie (1975) reported a correlation of .66 between target problem severity change scores of therapists and parents. They consider this an important validation of the target complaints method, since global measures of change made by parents and therapists were uncorrelated. However, the correlation they obtained was probably an artifact due to their method of scoring, one that researchers should be aware of in working with target complaints.

Their measure of target problems was a *sum* of items on a checklist checked off by the therapist as target areas of therapy. Since the total score used was a sum, it was highly correlated with the number of items checked. The therapist's definition of which were the target items was used to define both therapist and parent scores. Therefore, the high correlation may well have been produced simply because the number of items summed for the therapist and parent total scores was the same, determined by the therapist. To check this out, a similar computational method was applied to two sets of random numbers, letting the number of "target problems" vary randomly from one to nine, and taking "severity scores" for each from the random number table. When "therapist" and "parent" random ratings were correlated, the resulting correlation for a sample of ten "cases" was even higher than that reported by Holmes and Urie. This interpretation of their results is consistent with the findings of Frey et al. (1976). They found the correlation between parent and therapist ratings at termination was only .04, indicating no concurrent validity between parents of children in treatment and therapists.

Are Target Complaints Measures Sensitive?

Three studies (Hesbacher et al., 1968; Dasberg et al., 1974; Dasberg, 1975) obtained significant results favoring tranquilizing drugs over placebos with a target complaints improvement rating. Dasberg et al. (1974) reported significant correlations (roughly .50) between diazepam blood level indexes and target complaint improvement ratings; however, this was not replicated in a second study (Dasberg, 1975) with the same population and drug.

Studies have shown a significant advantage for "psychotherapy" (Shorer, 1970), psychotherapy and behavior therapy (Sloane et al., 1975), and behavior therapy with conduct problem children (Kent & O'Leary, 1976) over a no-treatment control on target complaint measures. Changes in target symptoms in the Penn Psychotherapy Project (Mintz, Luborsky, & Christoph, 1979) were enormous in statistical terms. They were far larger than the relative changes on global multi-item measures. For example, the patient's first target complaint, on the average, went from a mean of 3.2 to a mean of 7.4 on an 11-point scale, a change of over two standard deviations!

Several studies have compared the results for patients given a role induction for therapy with those not given it. The first use of the target complaint measure was in a study of a role induction procedure (Hoehn-Saric et al., 1964). That study reported significant positive effects of role induction on a target complaints improvement rating, but found nonsignificant results on a more general symptom scale.

Why was the target symptom measure better? The authors comment (Hoehn-Saric et al., 1964): "The Discomfort Scale lists many symptoms but does not necessarily include the target symptoms. Therefore specific change may not be reflected or may be obscured in the multitude of items." (p. 279).

That finding has been replicated and extended to the use of a film with group therapy patients (Strupp & Bloxom, 1973).

On the other hand, two studies that used pre–post difference scores in severity of target complaints did not obtain significant effects of a role induction procedure with adult outpatients (Sloane et al., 1970) and children (Holmes & Urie, 1975). Thus the results might be interpreted as indicating that role induction does not affect the degree of actual change in target complaint severity, but does affect the degree of perceived improvements. This is a good argument for including both kinds of ratings—improvement and severity—in the same study. In fact, it is possible that the failure of the multi-item Discomfort Scale noted by Hoehn-Saric et al. (1964) was due to the fact that it is a severity scale on which change is measured by calculating pre–post difference scores and not to its "irrelevant" symptom content.

The applicability of the TC methodology to the evaluation of group therapy has been challenged. Piper et al. (1976) found significant results for a multi-item measure of interpersonal functioning, but nonsignificant differences between group therapy and waiting list patients on target complaints improvement ratings, even when they considered only interpersonal target complaints. They felt the method is too specific for group therapy assessment, and suggested that group therapy may not be directed at patients' initially defined individual goals.

Indeed, the new member must often abandon pursuit of individual goals, especially those concerning his own psychiatric problems. . . . Deferment of focus on presenting problems may extend beyond the first three months (p. 1031).

Is the Content of Target Complaints Used?

Few researchers have shown interest in the content of specific complaints, although several authors have presented more or less or-ganized breakdowns of content for descriptive purposes (e.g., Battle et al., 1966; Bloch et al., 1976). Garwick and Lampman's (1972) system for defining complaints was developed in the context of goal scaling, but is relevant to target complaints also. Generally the target complaints measures are simply used as a composite along with other outcome measures. Sloan et al. (1975) present graphs depicting change on target complaints in different content categories. They suggest that effects of different types of therapy were not specific, but do not analyze the data statistically. They present a classification system for complaints, which has three axes or dimensions. Attempts to use it on unpublished data from the Penn Psychotherapy Project suggested that it is difficult to apply.

Johnson (1976) compared a sample of feminist patients with female psychotherapy patients from the Penn Psychotherapy Project on target complaint content and reported that the feminist women were less likely to have affective complaints. Hesbacher et al. (1968) categorized patients as either somatic or psychological dominant on the basis of their target complaints. They found that this classification was very useful in analyses of response to several tranquilizers. Although the idea of using the content of complaints as a basis for classification or for examination of differential treatment effects is a natural one, it has not been done very much.

Changes in Target Complaints During Treatment

Battle et al. (1966) described the process of psychotherapy as one of: "Constant definition, redefinition, and clarification . . . The initial complaints may shift in focus and scope, or disappear altogether and be replaced by others which may go through the same process." (p. 185).

Of course, the target complaint method, as they outline it, is based on pretreatment problem definitions, and therefore, it is not well suited to evaluating these changes. Although it could be extended in that direction, this has not been done systematically.

Where Is the Target Complaint Approach Most Useful?

As we have seen, target complaints have been used to study a wide variety of treatment modalities: drugs (e.g., Dasberg, 1975; Hesbacher et al., 1968), dynamic and behavior therapies (Sloane et al., 1975), group therapy (Frey et al., 1976), emotive therapy (Birenbaum et al., 1976), role induction procedures (Hoehn-Saric et al., 1964), and that vague entity Battle et al. (1956) refer to as "outpatient psychotherapy." The TC method is obviously flexible enough to permit its use in evaluation of virtually any modality. We suggest, however, that the method has particular utility in three situations.

The first of these is the individual behaviorally oriented case study, in which the TC approach is ideally suited to provide objective data regarding changes in specific individually identified symptoms. The second is the large controlled study of psychotherapy outcome conducted with a *heterogeneous* patient population presenting a variety of initial problems. While it seems that this kind of research strategy is relatively unpopular today (see Mintz, 1977, p.50), it was the strategy of one of the most influential recent outcome studies (Sloane et al., 1975). The final situation in which we suggest the TC approach may have special merit is in program evaluation studies aimed at summarizing the effectiveness of existing programs providing diverse services to heterogeneous client populations. An example of each of these kinds of applications is given below to demonstrate the potential utility of this measurement format.

An Individual Behavioral Case Study.
Liberman & Smith (1972) used TC as their basic dependent variable measure in an empirical single-case study of systematic de-

sensitization for a patient with multiple phobias. They used the 12-point box scale with each fear written at the top of the scale. The patient rated the TC scales for severity at least every 10 days over the course of therapy and at follow-up periods. Reliability checks on the patient's ratings were made during the baseline period; two separate administrations of the scale during the same day indicated complete stability of the ratings. After baseline was established, desensitization was applied at different times to each of four phobias in succession. Results showed that while desensitization was being targeted to each specific fear, the other fears continued to be a source of anxiety as reported by the patient. However, as each fear was in turn subjected to desensitization, there was a systematic reduction of TC distress.

A Controlled Randomized Study of a Heterogeneous Population.
Sloane et al. (1975) used the TC procedure as their major dependent variable in a large-scale psychotherapy outcome study. Ninety-four moderately severe psychoneurotic and personality disorder patients who applied for psychotherapy at a university outpatient clinic were randomly assigned to one of three experienced psychoanalytically oriented therapists, one of three experienced behavior therapists, or a waiting-list control group. The therapy patients were treated for a four-month period. During the first assessment interview the patient and psychiatric assessor (one of three) together identified the patients' leading three problems. The patient estimated when each target symptom first appeared, when he last experienced it, its average frequency and duration, and when he last felt at ease in that situation. After the TCs had been identified in this assessment interview, both patient and assessor independently rated their severity. At termination (four months later), and at a one-year follow-up, the *assessor* rated the severity of each TC on a 5-point scale (0 = absent, 1 = doubtful or trivial, 2 = mild, 3 = moderate, 4 = severe) "without re-

freshing his memory as to the initial severity." Improvement on the assessor's severity ratings was defined as the difference between the initial and posttreatment severity ratings of the symptoms. In addition, the patient and assessor also made, at termination and follow-up, a rating of the "amount of change" in each symptom since the original rating on a separate 13-point scale (ranging from "very much worse" or 0, through "no change" or 6, to "completely recovered" or 12).

Analysis of these target symptom ratings showed that "patients treated by behavior therapy and by psychotherapy improved equally in all three of their TCs after 4 months treatment, and significantly more than the waiting-list patients did" (p. 88). Both actively treated groups decreased an average of 1½ scale points in contrast to ½-scale point for the waiting-list controls. In other words, the therapy patients' TCs, all rated between "moderately severe" and "severe" at initial assessment, at termination were rated between the "mild" and "trivial" points on the 5-point scale.

A Program Evaluation Study. Rosen and Zytowski (1977) used the TC format in a study of 460 clients who completed counseling at a university student counseling service. At the first interview each client was asked to write down in his or her own words the problem(s) for which help was being sought, and to rate the severity of each problem. At termination the problem statement was transferred to a follow-up questionnaire that was mailed to each client, who was asked to rate the amount of relief he or she had experienced for each complaint (on a scale from -9 to +9) as a result of counseling. Of the 263 (57%) clients who returned the follow-up questionnaire, the mean index of relief reported was a +2.34 with a SD of 2.59. That is, half the former clients reported positive relief at a +2 or higher, and 77% reported positive relief for their TCs. In contrast, 23% reported no change or deterioration effects. Neither sex of client nor

experience of therapist related to TC improvement, but the more interviews the client had, the more relief in TCs he or she reported. The authors conclude, regarding the TC procedure, that "the individualized nature of the instrument makes it possible to plot outcome variables against several counselor variables, client variables, and problem types, limited only by the evaluator's ability to classify each of these variables" (p. 439).

Target Complaints: Recommendations to Researchers

Although much method development remains to be done, many researchers may wish to use the target complaints methodology now. For them, these comments are offered.

1. Interpretive problems will probably be somewhat more difficult if patients give differing numbers of complaints. It is recommended that all patients give the same number of "main complaints," a method that has been used successfully in many studies reviewed above (e.g., Sloane et al., 1975). Ratings should be made of improvement on each problem at the end of treatment as well as obtaining pre- and posttreatment severity ratings. The interrelationships among these indexes should be examined. When appropriate, covariance analysis may be utilized for either severity or improvement measures.

2. Classification of patients in terms of presenting complaints may be fruitful in analyses. Researchers should at least examine the possibility that differential treatment effects exist as a function of problem category.

3. If sums or averages are computed for overall indexes, statistics regarding intercorrelations among the components should be presented in order that infor-

mation will begin to accumulate regarding the internal consistency reliability of such composites.

4. Problems should probably be defined as discretely as possible. This is admittedly a matter of judgment. Should "crying," poor appetite," and "don't care about the "future" be listed as three complaints or as "depression"? Probably using a single term implying several kinds of component behavior would be better when there is a firm basis for thinking that the components are rather highly correlated, but it is best to err in the direction of specificity, even though this may make it difficult to obtain reliable rankings of problems within patients. If problems turn out to be highly correlated, they can be summed later. In fact, since averaging is usually done anyway, defining of many separate instances of one condition, as in the example of depression above, is tantamount to developing a small test or scale.

5. Changes in problem definition seem to be significant for outcome. If the method of obtaining posttreatment information is too tied to the initial problem list, much useful data may be lost. It is recommended that patients be asked at the end of treatment to define their main complaints again. Only after rating these for severity and improvement should ratings be obtained on the initial list. The important thing about symptom substitution from the point of view of focal measures is that this will not be revealed on such measures should it occur. This is another reason to inquire about symptoms at the end of treatment in an open-ended manner, asking not only for a definition of initial problems but also for any new problems that appeared during treatment.

6. When problems are defined by someone other than the patient, which at least has

face validity, some check on the validity of the resulting list should be made if possible.

7. For valid assessment of TCs it seems crucial that some form of standardized assessment interview be employed before therapy and at subsequent rating periods. Patients need assistance in translating their spontaneous original complaints into more precise, specific, and operational descriptions. Also some assistance is necessary for grouping highly redundant symptoms or complaints, and some judgment is necessary for eliminating complaints for which psychotherapy is irrelevant. Further, in doing all this, the interviewer has to be careful not to suggest or lead the patient to mention problems not spontaneously expressed. To underscore this necessity, Strupp (personal communication) reports that a major problem he found in attempting to use TC in a large-scale research project was "insufficient specificity of the targets. Often they were of the order: 'I want to feel better about myself,' 'get along better with people,' etc."

The key to this issue is what is referred to in the behavior therapy literature as "behavioral pinpointing." For clear communication and reliable evaluation, presenting complaints need to be translated, whenever possible, into operational definitions hooked to concrete, and overtly observable behavior. Sloane et al. (1975) were very careful in this regard to have the patient estimate "when each target symptom first appeared, when he first experienced it, its average frequency and duration, and when he last felt at ease in that situation" (p. 53). We will run into this identical theme with goal attainment scaling. Until a TC manual or similar standardized interviewer instructions are forthcoming, the interviewer instructions of Sloane et al. might be used as a guide.

It is also feasible to develop a brief instructional manual, with examples of "dos" and "don'ts," that might guide self-administration of the TC format to patients themselves. If instructions are detailed and clear enough, it may be possible for patients to fill in the TC format entirely by themselves. It would be important, however, to assess empirically the comparability of self-administered procedure to the interviewer procedure. If self-administration could be validly accomplished, the general applicability of the TC procedure would be enhanced markedly.

8. Although rate-rerate reliabilities found to date have been satisfactory to good, future studies should routinely assess stability-reliability, as well as interjudge reliability when multiple raters are used. Few studies have systematically looked at the intercorrelation of TCs with other independent outcome measures. Future studies should attack this construct validity problem by including whenever possible at least one independent measure and preferably multiple outcome criteria.

9. Along similar lines, the practice of obtaining TC ratings from both independent research assessors and from patients should be continued. Likewise, the therapist as well as various persons significant in the patient's life should not be ignored. The more rating perspectives used in a given study, the more validly results can be interpreted. The general psychotherapy literature suggests that very interesting agreements and disagreements emerge when patient, therapist, and external observers rate identical therapy events, including presenting complaints (Balch & Miller, 1974; Denner & Halprin, 1974; Feiffel & Eels, 1963; Klonoff & Cox, 1975; Mintz et al., 1973; Mintz et al., 1979; Rogers et al., 1967; Sloane et al., 1975; Strupp,

Fox, & Lessor, 1969). Further, some evidence suggests that congruence between patient and therapist ratings, assessments, or expectations may be an essential ingredient with respect to both continuation in treatment (Borghi, 1968; Heine & Trosman, 1960) and to successful outcome (Rogers et al., 1967).

Target Complaints: Conclusions

In conclusion, empirical evidence supports continued development and applications of the TC procedure in both scientific and program evaluation studies of psychotherapy and mental health intervention. Ratings of improvement on target complaints have been shown to be effective outcome measures in diverse therapy studies. The advantages of the method are considerable. It has substantial face validity from both scientific and program evaluation or consumer viewpoints. As Udell and Hornstra (1976) note:

Taken at face value, without interpretation or inference, presenting problems provide a unique body of information. As such, they constitute one of the few variables that stand at the interfaces of demographic, psychosocial and clinical data and can thus provide a fruitful, empirically grounded research tool. (p. 437)

Luborsky et al. (1971) state the point more soberly: "Although both the therapist and the patient may be biased judges, their estimates have some face validity and should be used along with the estimates of outside judges" (p. 158).

This face validity results primarily from TCs being a spontaneous report from the patient in his or her own words, recorded with a minimum of interpretation by the therapist or assessor. The procedure thus gives priority to the patient's report of the symptoms of which the patient is most aware and for which he or she is seeking treatment. The time demands and personnel costs for obtaining the TC measure are minimal. Only brief assessment interviews are required at each point of measurement, and they likely can be conducted by trained paraprofessionals. If the procedure can be standardized for self-administration, economy would be further enhanced.

A major advantage the TC format offers is its flexibility for evaluating groups of patients while still retaining content idiosyncratic to each patient, an advantage offered by all "individualized measures" of therapy outcome. To the extent that the changes in therapy are highly specific to indivudual patients, we should not expect all patients to improve on every dependent variable. A more respectful approach would determine whether each patient achieves remission of his or her TCs. As Fiske et al. (1970) state:

Increasing concern is being expressed in the literature about the appropriateness of assessing outcome in the same way for all patients. The patient typically comes in with one major complaint for which he seeks relief. Similarly, the therapist may develop particular outcome goals for each patient. Should not outcome be defined to be congruent with such individual aims? The methodology for studies with this orientation needs further development. (p. 729)

The TC procedure clearly permits investigators to avoid the outcome "uniformity myth" (Kiesler, 1966, 1971). By continual systematic attempts to apply differential treatment strategies to identical complaints or clusters of complaints, psychotherapy researchers can begin to fill in the Grid Model (Kiesler, 1971; see also Kendall & Norton-Ford, this volume), and begin to answer the crucial psychotherapy research question: which treatments by which therapists are more effective for which problems for which patients (Kiesler, 1966; Paul, 1967)?

Having described the strengths of the method, it must be noted that most of the basic methodological questions raised by Waskow (1975) and Imber (1975) have unfortunately not been systematically explored. It is not clear, for example, that the uniqueness of TCs is actually important at all. It may be that their demonstrated effectiveness in measuring therapy outcome is due to the fact that they tap a global improvement factor. Detailed concurrent validity data are lacking.

There has been a tendency to interpret differences between TC results and those obtained using broader symptom inventories such as the Hopkins Symptom Checklist (HSCL) as indicating that the latter measures include "irrelevant" items. However, measures like the HSCL are usually used as status measures, while TCs have usually been used as rated improvement measures. The lack of agreement between target complaint measures and HSCL results may not be due to the presence of irrelevant items on the HSCL. It may well have more to do with the difference between adjustment status and ratings of improvement. Data from the Penn Psychotherapy Project (Mintz et al., 1979) indicated that adjustment status and rated improvement are highly correlated (about .60) but clearly distinct factors.

Whether target complaints tap a particularly important and unique dimension of outcome or are essentially a very short scale of overall improvement is something to be learned by better measurement of target complaints, coupled with study of their relationships with other more general improvement ratings and with pre- and posttreatment assessments of adjustment status in specific and more general areas. The "better measurement" might well begin with multi-item measures of the target complaints, whether by use of standardized tests (see Bergin, 1971) or development of new formats for scoring individual complaints.

Content of the complaints has not been used enough by researchers. Practically all of the studies reviewed simply included the target complaints measure as one more criterion, with no special attention to its unique qualities. There has been practically no interest in using target complaints as a basis for breaking samples into subgroups for analyses. Hesbacher et al.'s (1968) observation that target complaints might serve a dual function as an outcome measure and a classification variable has gone largely unheeded to date.

Short-term stability of target complaints has not been determined, and the meaning of rapid changes in complaint severity has not been clarified in any detailed manner. No generally accepted content coding system exists, and methods of sorting out discrete complaints from complex presenting symptom pictures need to be developed. The impact of different methods of eliciting problems and recording them, or demographic variables, the nature and importance of shifts in problems, issues of symptom substitution, and many other questions remain to be studied in the future.

Finally, we must ask how central patient-defined target complaints are in typical therapy interactions. Consider this comment by Strupp (1976):

In a long-term study currently in progress at Vanderbilt University, male college students are being treated for anxiety, depression and shyness by relatively short-term psychotherapy. As part of the assessment interview preceding assignment to therapy, the patient, in conjunction with the clinician interviewer, formulates two to three targets, which assumedly become the focus of the subsequent therapy and which are made available to the therapist. Furthermore, changes in the target complaints are hypothesized to be critical indicators of therapeutic change. While our therapists, highly experienced practitioners, are not specifically instructed to gear their treatment efforts to the targets, it is clear to them that the targets are important foci. Nonetheless, it appears that none of the therapists view the targets as central to their therapeutic effort—in fact, they accord them little explicit recognition. (p. 15)

GOAL ATTAINMENT SCALING

Kiresuk and Sherman (1968) sought a measuring device that avoided both the relative inflexibility of standardized measures and the diffuseness of unstructured observation, yet one that would allow individualized problem definition, use each client as his or her own control in the definition of "success," and allow interpretable comparison of diverse treatment modalities (Kiresuk, 1973). After reviewing existing evalation strategies, they concluded that none sufficiently met these criteria. Goal Attainment Scaling, developed to accomplish these aims, was designed to measure service results for individual clients and was founded on the belief "that there are no adequate universal definitions of ultimate human service goals, but rather that service needs are best defined according to the unique problems of each client at a given time" (Kiresuk & Lund, 1977b).

Since Kiresuk and Sherman's (1968) seminal publication on Goal Attainment Scaling (GAS), over 150 organizations and individuals have adopted the technique as an evaluation device (Kiresuk & Lund, 1977a). In addition to the extensive applications of Kiresuk and his colleagues at the Program Evaluation Resource Center (previously Program Evaluation Project) in Minneapolis, GAS or closely related techniques have been applied in community mental health center programs throughout the country (Austin et al., 1976; Bolin & Kivens, 1974; Cline et al., 1973; Fiester & Fort, 1976; Kaplan & Smith, 1974, 1977; Kivens & Volin, 1976; Liberman & Bryan, 1977; Lombillo, Kiresuk, & Sherman, 1973; Rinn, Tapp, & Petrella, 1973; Rinn & Vernon, 1975; Turner, 1972; Wilson, 1974; Wilson & Mumpower, 1975); in crisis intervention (Beck et al., 1975; Speer & Cohen, 1975); in day treatment programs (Austin et al., 1976; Lefkowitz, 1974); in community after-care settings (Brown, 1973; Houts & Scott, 1975; Lynbaugh, 1974); in drug treatment programs (Hall & Mathison, 1975; Putnam et al., 1973; Westman, 1974); in alcoholism treatment (Kaplan & Smith, 1974); in mental hospitals (Meldman et al., 1975); in university medical school settings (Cline et al., 1973); in a county social service agency (Ames, 1975); in mental health services for children (Ricks et al., 1973; Ricks & Weinstein, 1976; Houts & Scott, 1973; Rosenthal & Levine, 1971; Wallin, 1974a, 1974b; Wallin & Koch, 1977); for adolescent mental health populations (Benedict, 1974; Gianturco & Ramm, 1974; Stoudenmire & Comola, 1973); for juvenile and adult probation services (Petersen, 1975); for neurologically impaired patients (Goodyear & Bitter, 1974); for the mentally retarded (Moriarty, 1974); and in rehabilitation (Goodyear & Bitter, 1974).

GAS has also been used to evaluate group counseling (Bush, 1972), T-groups (Mehaffey, 1972), family therapy (Santa-Barbara et al., 1974), behavior therapy approaches (Austin et al., 1976; Liberman & Bryan, 1977; Rinn et al., 1973; Rinn & Vernon, 1975; Rinn et al., 1975; Steinbook et al., 1977; Turner, 1972; Werry & Wollersheim, 1967); for empirical single case studies (Dowd & Kelley, 1975; Youell & McCullough, 1975); individualized instruction in educational settings (McGaghic & Menges, 1975; McGaghie et al., 1976); staff development programs (Benedict, 1975); training conferences (Canfield & Kliewer, 1977); and child-management classes (Rinn, Vernon, & Wise, 1975). Other applications include Bensing and Dekker (1973); Hart & Lange (1972); Levinson (1973), Mason (1975), Schmidt (1974), and Veer (1974).

Between 1969 and 1973, Kiresuk and his colleagues received NIMH support for development and dissemination of GAS as both an evaluation tool and clinical aid. This support launched a controlled study of psychotherapy at the Hennepin County Mental Health Service in Minneapolis, as well as multiple other projects. Since 1969, Kiresuk's Center has sponsored two national conferences on GAS (Garwick & Brintnall, 1976; Kiresuk, 1971), cosponsored with NIMH a national periodical (Evaluation), as well as launched its own journal (Goal Attainment Review) and its own newsletter (earlier P.E.P. Newsletter, recently P.E.R.C. Newsletter). In addition, the Cen-

ter provides direct consultation services and disseminates instructional materials such as the following: Programmed Instruction in GAS (Garwick, 1976a) in which users work through 121 questions on constructing and scoring the GAS Guide and recording change scores; Tables on Calculating GAS scores (Garwick & Brintnall, 1973); Guide to Goals: Format I (Garwick, 1972), a step-by-step procedure for the independent construction by clients of the GAS Guide; Guide to Goals: Format II (Garwick, 1976b), an aid to parents, staff, or other involved persons in developing a GAS Guide for children or adolescents; and a Dictionary of GAS (Garwick & Lampman, 1973), a compilation of numerous examples of GAS Guides. The Center also provides a Content Analysis Service for researchers throughout the country who employ GAS Guides. GAS Training Manuals are available for specific treatment programs: methadone maintenance (Putnam et al., 1973) and mental health services for children (Rickles et al., 1973).

Kiresuk's Center also distributes two major bibliographies on GAS: Garwick, McCree, and Brintnall (1976), which lists over 200 mostly unpublished reports, and Wallin (1974b), an annotated bibliography on use of GAS in youth-oriented facilities. Summary articles, mostly book chapters, are now appearing (Kiresuk, 1975, 1976; Kiresuk & Garwick, 1975; Kiresuk & Lund, 1975–1976; 1977a, 1977b, 1977c). Unequivocal evidence that GAS has arrived is the appearance of its first major critique (Seaberg & Gillespie, 1977) as well as a rejoinder (Kiresuk & Sherman, 1977).

By 1973, Kiresuk (1973) stated that the method of GAS had been successfully implemented at a community mental health center in Minnesota, and that there were "well over 70 users and former users of GAS" and "about 1600 contacts" regarding the method nationwide, with various other locations "conducting formal and informal studies." No citations were given to indicate where these were located.

There can be little doubt, however, that his appraisal of the popularity of GAS was substantially correct. Hargreaves et al. (1977) refer to GAS as the "most popular" individual goal scaling approach. But although they state that GAS has been presented as a measure sensitive to subtle individual change, "to our knowledge this remains to be demonstrated" (p. 244).

Although there are still relatively few studies using GAS as an outcome measure, there is no shortage of GAS literature. Most of the papers to be found are not psychotherapy studies. They simply state that GAS has been implemented in some facility. These papers are usually extremely favorable to GAS, and at times describe research projects that are "in progress," and promise results to come. Typically, we are told GAS is beneficial to staff, patients, and administrators, and is quick and easy (e.g., Davis, 1973). A large percentage of these papers are either unpublished or in GAS publications.

The overall impression one gets from reading these papers is that an exciting new methodology will shortly be bearing research fruit. However, goal attainment literature references are frequently *not* to published studies. Such material has in general not been through the critical review process given to published studies, and it deserves careful scrutiny. A point in a paper "documented" with a string of GAS references may not include any research studies at all in the list.

Theoretical Basis

Goal Attainment Scaling was intended primarily as a methodological aid to the assessor. In the best psychometric tradition, the goals were thought of simply as a sample of items from a large domain of results for the patient. Consider this quotation from Kiresuk and Sherman (1968).

During the initial period of use of this procedure, it is recommended that two independently operating goal selectors or committees select goals and

scale points for the same patients. . . . It is our expectation that favorable or unfavorable therapy outcome is a general phenomenon. One goal selector may perceive a patient's problems in terms of intrapsychic symptoms and psychodynamics, while another may see them in terms of his relationship to others. The first goal selector might specify anxiety level, psychiatric symptoms, transference and other psychodynamic insights as outcome events, while the other goal selector might choose reports of social interactions, management of social interaction or alterations in the way the patient understands his group membership and participation. It is our belief that success or failure with the one set of goals would imply a comparable success or failure in the other set. (p. 451)

Basically GAS is a methodology for developing personalized, multivariable, scaled descriptions that can be used for either therapy objective-setting or outcome measurement purposes. "The method is addressed to one central question: how can one meet the requirements of program evaluation, a peculiar mixture of management and science and, at the same time, provide for the unique characteristics of the treatment process and aspirations of individual clients (Kiresuk, 1977, p. 355)?"

Setting Up a Goal Attainment Scale

The core of Goal Attainment Scaling is a Goal Attainment Follow-up Guide (GAS Guide) such as the one illustrated in Figure 15.3 (reproduced from Kiresuk & Lund, 1977a). The GAS Guide looks like a grid with vertical lines separating different goals, and horizontal lines indicating treatment success with goals listed on discrete 5 point scales from least to most favorable outcomes. Each vertical column is called a "scale" (GAS Scale). When the GAS Guide is completed, each GAS Scale represents a separate client goal area. The five levels of each scale are defined by concrete behavior arranged along a hierarchy of possible results, ranging from the "Most Unfavorable Treatment Out-

Check whether or not the scale has been mutually negotiated between patient and CIC interviewer.

SCALE HEADINGS AND SCALE WEIGHTS

SCALE ATTAINMENT LEVELS	SCALE 1: Education Yes_ No X (w₁=20)	SCALE 2: Suicide Yes_ No_ (w₂=30)	SCALE 3: Manipulation Yes_ No X (w₃=25)	SCALE 4: Drug Abuse Yes X No_ (w₄=30)	SCALE 5: Dependency on CIC Yes X No_ (w₅=10)
a. most unfavorable treatment outcome thought likely (-2)	Patient has made no attempt to enroll in high school. ✓	Patient has committed suicide.	Patient makes rounds of community service agencies demanding medication, and refuses other forms of treatment. ✓	Patient reports addiction to "hard narcotics" (heroin, morphine).	Patient has contacted CIC by telephone or in person at least seven times since his first visit.
b. less than expected success with treatment (-1)	Patient is enrolled in high school, but at time of follow-up has dropped out.	Patient has acted on at least one suicidal impulse since her first contact with the CIC, but has not succeeded. ✓	Patient no longer visits CIC with demands for medication but continues with other community agencies and still refuses other forms of treatment. ✓	Patient has used "hard narcotics," but is not addicted, and/or uses hallucinogens (LSD, Pot) more than four times a month. ✓	Patient has contacted CIC 5-6 times since intake. ✓
c. expected level of treatment success (0)	Patient has enrolled, and is in school at follow-up, but is attending class sporadically (misses an average of more than a third of her classes during a week).	Patient reports she has had at least four suicidal impulses since her first contact with the CIC but has not acted on any of them.	Patient no longer attempts to manipulate for drugs at community service agencies, but will not accept another form of treatment.	Patient has not used "hard narcotics" during follow-up period, and uses hallucinogens between 1-4 times a month. *	Patient has contacted CIC 3-4 times since intake.
d. more than expected success with treatment (+1)	Patient has enrolled, is in school at follow-up, and is attending classes consistently, but has no vocational goals. *	*	Patient accepts non-medication treatment at some community agency. *	Patient uses hallucinogens less than once a month.	
e. best anticipated success with treatment (+2)	Patient has enrolled, is in school at follow-up, is attending classes consistently, and has some vocational goal.	Patient reports she has had no suicidal impulses since her first contact with the CIC.	Patient accepts non-medication treatment, and by own report shows signs of improvement.	At time of follow-up, patient is not using any illegal drugs.	Patient has not contacted CIC since intake. *

Figure 15.3. Good attainment follow-up guide.

511

come Thought Likely" to the "Most Favorable Outcome Thought Likely," with the "Expected Level of Success" at the middle level. Attainment levels are specified in concrete, objective, observable, operational terms.

Use of the GAS Guide involves the following steps (after Kiresuk & Lund, 1977b).

1. *Goal area selection.* The first step in constructing a GAS Scale involves selecting scale headings that identify high priority goal areas—specifying areas where undesirable kinds of behavior should be minimized, or where favorable kinds of behavior should be increased. Once a goal is selected, it is recorded in the title section above the scale. Usually three to five goal areas (scales) are identified.

2. *Weighting.* This second step is optional, but if used, involves the assignment of a numerical weight to each goal area or scale (usually 1 to 9 is adequate), with the weights reflecting the relative importance of the goal areas. The higher the number designated, the greater the importance of the particular scale. Weighting is a subjective judgment by the person(s) constructing the GAS Guide.

3. *Follow-up time selection.* The third step entails specifying the target time on which the scale will be scored. The degree of "expected" attainment specified at the middle level of each scale should be based on the target time on which the goal is to be scored after treatment intervention. The follow-up date may be the same for all goals (e.g., when a group of clients or programs are to be compared), or it may be adjusted to fit the unique characteristics of each goal scale.

4. *Statement of "Expected Outcome."* This step involves stating the outcome that is expected in each goal scale area, the

most probable result *if the client receives effective treatment,* taking into account the time of the follow-up and the type and amounts of service that are to be delivered. This middle level is the Guide constructor's judgment of the most probable level of attainment and must be stated in terms operational enough that two independent observers could agree on whether it has been attained (e.g., "employed full-time for the past month," "able to sleep eight uninterrupted hours each night," etc.)—in other words, concrete behavior that can be directly observed or reported. This can include psychological test results or rating scale scores. The "expected outcome" should be a realistic, pragmatic estimate, recording whatever outcome is really most likely to occur, the best prediction of "what will happen" as the result of treatment.

5. *Completion of the other scale levels.* Using the "expected outcome" as a benchmark, the constructor next fills in the four remaining outcome levels on each scale. The two adjacent cells represent less likely results, while the two extreme cells represent unlikely but still plausible results. A completed scale should contain five mutually exclusive levels (cells) representing an exhaustive and internally consistent continuum of all possible results in relation to a particular goal area. In practice it is often adequate to define the expected outcome and at least one of the levels above and one below the expected outcome. The Guide constructor then rates, by putting a checkmark usually at −1 and sometimes at −2, the level of the client's functioning at the time the Guide is constructed (pretreatment).

6. *Follow-up rating of outcome.* At the time of follow-up targeted for a given scale, an interviewer or observer determines which outcome level (−2 to

+2) best describes the client's functioning at follow-up, and puts an X or asterisk in the appropriate cell (at the rated level). Each scale may be scored at only one level, indicating that the client's attainment was at least at that level but not up to the next level.

7. *Calculating the GAS score.* Once goal attainment has been rated on each GAS Scale, at termination of treatment or at regular time-periods over the course of treatment, the Goal Attainment Score (GAS Score) is calculated. The GAS Score is an average of the outcome scores for the various GAS Scales that has been adjusted for the relative weights, if any, assigned to the goals, the varying number of goals, and the typical intercorrelation among the GAS Scales. It represents a global index of the degree to which outcome expectations have been realized. The Kiresuk and Sherman (1968) formula yields a score of 50 if scale results are at the "expected" level on the average, and this GAS Score has a standard deviation of about 10. Tables are available (Garwick & Brintnall, 1973) that have translated the formula GAS Score for GAS Guides with up to five scales and with weights of from 1 to 5.

The resulting scores are referred to as "T-scores," because, if certain assumptions hold true, they are expected to have a mean of 50 and a standard deviation of 10. Kiresuk and Sherman (1968) indicate that this formula creates a "standardized" measure, so that each subject receives equal weight in analyses. The truth of this assertion depends on several assumptions.

1. Outcome scores do not correlate with the weight given the goal.
2. Outcome scores average zero, or "expected level."

3. Outcome scores, unweighted, have a standard deviation of one.
4. Intercorrelations among scales are all equal.
5. The value of this correlation used in the computation is correct.

Since the average correlation among scales is not known, Kiresuk and Sherman suggest using an arbitrary value of .30, which is probably not too far off in most cases, and thus leads to small errors. Of course intraclass correlations could be computed by each researcher and used in the formula if desired. In any event, users are cautioned against overinterpretation of deviations of obtained standard deviations from the "expected value" of 10 using the formula.

Several authors (e.g., Romney, 1976; Kaplan & Smith, 1977) suggest that the complex GAS formula is unnecessary. It is based on several assumptions that are probably not usually true, but it appears that failure of these assumptions is probably not very important. In general, simpler formulas may be just as good, and less prone to misinterpretation as representing some kind of "standardized" value. Kaplan and Smith report a correlation of .99 between a weighted average and the "standardized T-scores."

Who Constructs the GAS Guide?

In the original application of GAS (Kiresuk, 1972, 1974, 1977), GAS Guides were constructed by separate intake workers, rather than by therapists. Further, neither clients nor therapists were permitted to see the GAS Guides, once constructed. Subsequent applications have deviated considerably from this procedure.

GAS guides have been constructed by the following persons or sets of persons: (1) therapist alone; (2) client alone using Garwick's (1973) Guide to Goals: Format I (Bolin & Kivens, 1975; Burns, 1974); (3) staffing conference, therapeutic team, or clinical staff

(Cline et al., 1973; Gianturco & Ramm, 1974; Ramney, 1976); (4) independent staff or researchers (e.g., Goodyear & Bitter, 1974; Kaplan & Smith, 1974, 1977; Liberman & Bryan, 1977; Whittington, 1975; Wilson, 1974); or by patient-therapist negotiation, also referred to as Contract Fulfillment Analysis (Lombillo et al., 1973; Moriarty, 1974; Rinn & Vernon, 1975).

Kiresuk and Lund (1977a) note that "in most clinical uses of GAS, the follow-up guide content is derived through a negotiation between the client and a mental health worker." Lombillo et al. (1973) list as benefits of a mutually negotiated GAS contract that it: (1) provides the therapist with a conceptual basis on which to organize his or her therapeutic efforts; (2) provides the patient with a structural framework for mobilizing his or her available problem-solving mechanisms and resources; (3) enables the patient and staff to set realistic expectations of clinic intervention in the patient's life situations; and (4) provides valuable administrative information about the problems clinic staff are handling.

Several studies suggest that clients taking part in setting treatment goals are more satisfied, more successful in reaching goals, and more adjusted according to various personality measures (Garwick, 1974; Jones & Barwick, 1973; La Ferriere et al., 1975; Smith, 1976; and Willer, 1975).

Stelmachers et al. (1972), however, found some real difficulties with client-therapist negotiation of treatment goals in a crisis intervention setting. "Often a reasonable contract cannot be negotiated between the therapist and the client because many CIC clients are by the very nature of their crisis confused, uncooperative, violent, or they have goals very different from or even contrary to those of the CIC staff."

Another series of studies shows important differences in the kind of goals set by clients, family members, or therapists. A general finding tends to be that clients tend to choose goals involving changes in their social or physical environment (so-called extrapsychic goals), whereas therapists pick goals that focus on changes in the client's personality or psychological environmment (intrapsychic goals)—Ellsworth et al. (1968), Garwick and Lampman (1972), McPartland and Richart (1966), Polak (1970), Shepperson, Mauger and Zinober (1975), Swanson (1971), Thompson and Zimmerman (1969), Wallin (1974), Wallin and Koch (1977), and Wilson (1972).

The upshot of these findings seems to be that it clearly makes a difference who constructs the GAS Guide. Patients, family members and significant persons, or therapists have distinctly different perspectives with separate emphases regarding treatment goals or objectives. It seems likely that valid applications of GAS need to tap *all* three distinct sources in GAS Guide construction, either: (1) by interviews with all three participants (patients, significant persons, and therapists) together or separately; (2) by contract negotiation between therapist and staff, patient, and significant persons; or (3) by separate and independent GAS Guide construction by patient, therapist and staff, and significant persons. Further, available evidence suggests that patients' participation in goal selection or knowledge of treatment goals facilitates positive treatment outcome.

Number of GAS Scales Constructed

Kiresuk and Lund (1977b) suggest that usually three to five goal scales are identified and constructed. Studies with GAS generally show that the average number of GAS scales used per patient range between one and five, with three to five being the most frequently used average number of scales. For example, Bolin and Kivens (1975), Houts and Scott (1975), and Stelmachers et al. (1972) report average numbers of scales per patient between 1 and 1.9; Houts and Scott (1975), Kaplan and Smith (1977), Liberman and Bryan (1977), and Peterson (1975) between

2.0 and 2.9; Austin et al. (1976), Garwick (1976), Garwick and Lampman (1972), Lefkovitz (1974), and Jones and Garwick (1976) between 4.0 and 5.0.

Computer modifications and applications of GAS tend to report much higher numbers of goals per patient, averaging 10 or more (Gianturco & Ramm, 1974; Wilson & Mumpower, 1975). In the computerized version of GAS described by Wilson and Mumpower (1975), goals are selected from a list of 703 provided. Relatives or close friends of patients selected more than 15 goals per patient, on the average. Obviously, providing goal lists for patients is a significant alteration of method with very significant consequences.

Garwick (1974) found that as the number of GAS scales increased, the mean scale scores, the mean total GAS score, and the correlation between the two all decreased, but not significantly. The observed decrease in the overall GAS score was relatively minor; and even though the sample size was generous ($n = 644$), the scores of guides composed of different numbers of GAS scales were not statistically different.

In their critique, Seaberg and Gillespie (1977) caution that:

Although the (GAS) procedure allows for the statement of as many problems as necessary, in practice there appear to be usually no more than five. There is a high degree of subjectivity at this stage of the procedure. Clear-cut criteria for determining which problems should be the focus of evaluation are absent. (pp. 6–7)

On the other hand, it doesn't seem clear at all what the alternative might be for this kind of individualized measure.

GAS Summary Scores

It is possible to derive two distinct summary scores from GAS guides (Kiresuk & Lund, 1877b): the GAS "score," and the GAS "change score." Both indexes average across the individual GAS Scales to get a total, summary score.

The GAS "score" uses only the follow-up GAS Guide to obtain a summary score. Hence it reflects only the patient's level of functioning at the follow-up period. It "gauges outcomes against the expectations of the person who constructed the goal scales" (Kiresuk & Lund, 1977b). Most studies employing the GAS score have reported means very close to 50, indicating that the samples of patients, on the average, usually attained their "expected" levels.

The GAS "change score" is calculated by subtracting the summary GAS score at intake from the summary GAS score at posttreatment follow-up. This change score "includes the scale constructor's expectations only as they are represented in the definitions of the intervals between the five score levels" (Kiresuk & Lund, 1977b). A negative score indicates retrogression or deterioration, a score near zero indicates little or no change, and a positive score indicates improvement or progress. In most applications, the average change score has been about $+15$ points (a 10-point change indicates movement of about one full GAS level).

Hence the GAS change score is a measure of "change in problem level" as the result of treatment, while the GAS score is an index of "attainment of therapeutic goals." The two scores have usually been found to be highly intercorrelated. "In general, however, we do not recommend use of the Change Score" (Kiresuk & Lund, 1977b).

Seaberg and Gillespie (1977) criticize the allocation of differential weightings to the scales on the GAS Guide.

The major problem here is that the criteria for judging importance are not specified. Differential importance could be ascribed to problem areas according to a variety of criteria. For example, "importance" might be (a) the estimated difficulty for a particular client to resolve the problem, (b) the correspondence between the problem and available therapies, (c) social desirability based on the clinician's values or community norms, (d) acknowledged importance to the client, (e) the length of time that a problem has persisted, (f) importance to the client's relatives or significant others in the client's environment, and so on. It is unlikely that the use of different criteria would result in the same rank order of importance for a given set of problems. It can be surmised, moreover, that different selection sources, and perhaps the same selection sources at different points in time, use various combinations of these criteria. (p. 7)

Inasmuch as the GAS authors now consider use of weightings as optional, we agree with Seaberg and Gillespie that use of differential weightings for separate goals in computing GAS scores or GAS change scores should be discontinued: "As noted by Nunnally (1967), weighted and unweighted summative scores usually correlate very highly. A classic study by Likert (1932) produced a correlation of .99 in comparing weighted and unweighted scale scores" (p. 7).

In a similar vein, it seems that GAS researchers might very profitably consider analyzing individual GAS Scale scores and change scores separately, in addition to combining the scale scores into the overall GAS score and change score. Mintz's (1972) study with target complaints found that one should be cautious about using an overall, average index to summarize various target symptoms. Mauger and Stolberg (1974) report that intercorrelations between the scores on individual scales on GAS Guides and the overall GAS score have ranged in various studies between .25 and .65. Because of this, they note, one should not be surprised if scores on separate outcome measures correlate poorly with the overall GAS score. The upshot seems to be that whenever one uses a derived score, such as the overall GAS score and GAS change score, one must also study carefully how the individual components contribute to the overall derived score as well as function independently on their own. In the case of GAS, this would definitely indicate analyzing the individual GAS scales separately, as well as averaged into the overall GAS score and change score.

Reliability

Kiresuk (1973) reported informally that the correlation between outcome scores on two follow-up guides constructed independently was "approximately .70," using a "total of 170 cases." No methods of study are presented. He reported "substantial content agreement" between these two sets of guides, indicating a correlation of .88. It is not clear what was correlated. Finally, he stated that the correlation between follow-up workers independently scoring the same follow-up guides with about one month between scorings is "also approximately .70." More detailed reports of these studies indicating the methods and samples were not found in the search of published literature.

Wallin and Koch (1977) studied content of goals selected by staff, researchers and parents. They reported that the content of goal guides developed by these three groups were quite different. The study is marred by the fact that the parent sample was a self-selected subset of the total group. Parent guides were compared with the total group, rather than with guides set up for their own children. It seems unlikely, however, that this accounts for the results. Perhaps parent, staff, and researcher represent sufficiently distinct viewpoints that the lack of agreement should be considered evidence for poor concurrent validity rather than poor reliability (Fiske, 1975).

However, Kiresuk and Sherman (1968) originally implied that goal guides set up by different individuals should be like alternate forms of a test. Wallin and Koch (1977) report poorer results for goals set by parents than for those set by staff or researchers. They note that it is difficult to tell whether this is a flaw in the guides of parents, or an accurate reflection of the fact that therapists did not work in directions meaningful to them.

In another study bearing on this, Kaplan and Smith (1977) reported an intraclass correlation of .71 for outcome ratings based on different goal scales set up by comparable goal selectors on the basis of comparable information. They had researchers set up goal guides after reading case materials. Based on these results, Kaplan and Smith suggest that more than one goal selector should be used.

Correlations among outcome ratings made by independent raters for the same scales have been reported to be good. Kaplan and Smith reported in intraclass correlation of .87. Austin et al. (1976) appear to have computed rank order correlations of outcome within patients, much as Battle et al. (1966) did with target complaints, to assess whether raters agree as to which problems within each case improve most and least. They report a median correlation of .93 at one clinic and .95 at another, very different from the results reported earlier for target complaints. This is either a function of greater variability within patients, due to the fact that behavioral goals are specified by a committee, or greater reliability of such goals. Goodyear and Bitter (1974) report very high correlations among 13 of 15 follow-up raters, but low and nonsignificant results for two raters from "different occupational backgrounds." They suggest that more than one follow-up rater is desirable.

McGaghie and Menges (1975) report correlations among scales rated by subjects themselves. Summing outcome scales obtained at termination and at eight-week follow-up into a global index yielded a reliability estimate of .77. The data actually indicate a very high correlation between ratings of behavioral and emotional improvement at termination ($r = .75$) and at follow-up ($r = .86$). Since both scales related to the same problem area, it is expected that there would be a strong common improvement factor. However, short-term stability was lower. The termination and eight-week ratings for behavioral improvement correlated only .45, while for emotional improvement the value was .60.

Grygelko et al. (1973) studied 44 cases, having two GAS guides constructed for the same client by two different clinicians (intake interviewer vs. therapist). There was a mean delay of about one month between the separate interviews. The authors' content analyzed the GAS Scales using Garwick's "isolated concerns method" and also divided the content units into 20 predefined content categories. Results showed that: (1) using the percentage of GAS Guides incorporating each type of content category for both interviewers revealed highly consistent frequencies of use of the 20 content categories for the client sample as a whole; whereas (2) calculations as to whether the two interviewers agreed on application of a given category to any particular client showed at best only moderate consistency; the stability varied dramatically (This ranged from $-.06$ to $+.64$) among the various content categories.

Content Validity of GAS

Content validity cannot be expressed as a single correlation coefficient. Content validity is the relative adequacy of a sample of behavior taken through the use of a measuring device. A test with good content validity will sample all relevant aspects of the domain of behavior that is to be assessed.

The main argument originally advanced for the validity of the Goal Attainment score is that of content validity, as originally put forth by Sherman (1974):

If an objective criterion for the desired measure can be obtained, the test score may be compared to the criterion, and the approach to the questions of validity is direct. But for the Goal Attainment score, as well as for many psychological tests, fixed criteria are not available, and other methods of assessing validity must be used. For the Goal Attainment score the most reasonable argument currently available is based upon the notion of content validity . . . Conceive a universe of all possible pairs of mental health professionals, one of which is the intake clinician . . . and the other mental health professional is a follow-up interviewer . . . If therapy outcome was then evaluated by a randomly chosen pair of professionals from this universe, the content validity argument applies. That is, a score so generated would be as valid as it is reliable if taken as a measure of the conceptual score that would result if all possible pairs of intake interviewers/follow-up interviews could be applied to a client, and the resulting scores averaged . . . As a definition of what is meant by mental health professionals when they speak of measuring "mental health therapy success," this conceptual score is at least as good as anything else that has been proposed. Such a score is, in a sense, the pooled common judgement of "all" mental health professionals.

Garwick and Lampman (1972) studied a random sample of 115 scales selected from the first 332 GAS guides at a county mental health service. Using Garwick's "isolated concerns" content analysis procedure, they found that 10 categories of goals handled 90.4% of the 1154 scales, and that the content of GAS Guides reflected the types of problems one would expect to find in individuals coming to a community mental health center for therapy. Lund (1972) determined the content of 50 GAS Guides randomly selected at a crisis intervention center, and compared it with the problems identified by the client on initial contact. The content of the GAS Guides was identical with the presenting problem list in more than 50% of the cases. This figure looks even better when it is noted that not all problems of these clients could be scaled because some were inappropriate for a psychiatric emergency service (e.g., "My electricity has been turned off.").

Validity of "Expected" Level of Attainment

A closely related question has to do with the validity of the "expected level of treatment success" identified by the GAS Guide constructor. Obviously biases of all sorts can influence how this expected level is defined on the GAS Guide. As Seaberg and Gillespie (1977) observe:

The criteria for setting referents are less than definitive. [The procedure] involves a high degree of subjectivity and leaves open the possibility of considerable variation caused strictly by the level of abstraction in which they are stated. . . . [Further] a bias toward stating goals that are too easily attainable could pervade this procedure regardless of who sets them (p. 7).

As Kiresuk and Lund (1977a) note, "A frequent answer to this concern has been implementation of a procedure for review or audit of the follow-up guides by individuals other than the original constructor(s) including research technicians, therapists, other staff, or consumer representatives."

Bolin and Kivens (1975), for example, conducted a peer review of treatment goals for an adult outpatient unit of a community mental health center.

All cases included in the evaluation sample are reviewed by a professional staff member other than the intake clinician to establish the clinical relevancy of the treatment goals; the intake summary and supporting materials comprise the clinical data base available to the peer reviewer. The peer reviewer also assesses the realism of the scale levels, given the presenting problems, level of functioning, prescribed treatment plan, and follow-up data, and critiques the formal characteristics of the scale governing "follow-upability."

Audette (1973) developed the "Goal Attainment Follow-up Guide Assessment Form," an attempt to determine whether the follow-up interviewer judged the GAS scales to be relevant or realistic for the client. The Guide Assessment form is scored at the end of the follow-up interview, after the GAS Guide has been scored, and consists of three questions: Are the scales relevant? (Yes–No); Are the scale levels realistic? (optimistic, right on, pessimistic); Would you have added any scales to this guide? (Yes–No, which ones?). Use of the assessment form showed that: (1) of a sample of 102 GAS Guides containing 320 GAS Scales, 93.01% were deemed "relevant" by the follow-up interviewer; (2) for 39 of the 102 guides the follow-up interviewer recommended additional scale headings; and

(3) 9.7% of GAS Scales were deemed "optimistic," 70.2% "right on," and 16.4% "pessimistic." Hence for this sample, the GAS Scales were judged relevant in more than 90% of the cases, and a majority of the scales were realistically tailored to evaluate the client's goal-attainment progress during the follow-up period.

Austin et al. (1976) controlled for possible systematic differences in construction of "expected" outcome levels for the two day-care centers contrasted in their study by using GAS Guide "therapeutic optimism ratings." To obtain these ratings, a panel of nine independent and "blind" clinical psychologists was asked to rate the degree of therapeutic optimism for each GAS Scale constructed, that is, to assess the degree of "reasonableness" of the "expected" outcome level set. For the task, each GAS Guide was accompanied by a brief clinical description of each patient (age, sex, diagnosis, educational level, source of income, and previous treatment). From this information each judge rated each GAS intake scale on a 5-point scale (1 = very pessimistic expectations for treatment, 3 = about the right degree of optimism, 5 = very high therapeutic optimism). Each scale was rated from 1 to 5, and a mean reasonableness value was obtained for the GAS Scales for each patient, with two judges rating each GAS Guide. These "therapeutic optimism" means were then summed for each of the day treatment centers. The results showed: (1) good interjudge reliability of these ratings (agreed within 0.5 scale points for 80% of the patients rated); and (2) there were no significant differences in the therapeutic optimism scores for the two centers (3.05 vs. 2.98, both at "about the right degree of optimism").

Carlson (1964) had an external observer rate the degree of reasonableness (Are the goals scaled reasonably? Not too optimistically or pessimistically?) on a 4-point scale (1 = yes, mostly; 2 = partly; 3 = not for the most part; 4 = not at all). His resulting mean reasonableness rating was 1.8, indicating that "in the judgement of a viewer not

connected with the program, the scales were reasonably scaled, that is, not too optimistically scaled."

Kaplan and Smith (1977) attempted to approach this validity issue indirectly. "It was assumed if the GAS was valid, difficult (seriously disturbed) patients should have the same chance of attaining their goals as less disturbed patients." Defining success as overall GAS scores of zero or higher, they found that their schizophrenics had 43% success, while their less disturbed patients had 76% success. They conclude that "certainly the two groups did not have an equal chance of success, as should have been the case had the expected outcomes been defined accurately" (p. 191).

Because of the nature of the scale points of a Goal Attainment Scale, what one is measuring is the degree to which expectations of the goal selector have been reached. For example, if a patient is rated at "less than expected outcome," this might mean a failure to improve, or might mean a failure to improve *enough*. Two papers reported "less than expected" levels of outcome for the average patient (Cline et al., 1973; Wallin & Koch, 1977), and both noted the problems this created in interpretation. The results themselves do not indicate whether treatment had been ineffective, or whether the goals had been inappropriate, either in terms of goal area, or in degree of optimism reflected in the definition of scale anchors.

This result implies either that treatment had been relatively ineffective, or that the goal attainment scales had been overly optimistic in assigning the expected level of treatment success. Review of the goal-attainment scales from this sample showed that over-optimism about results was the more influential cause here and, in turn, suggested the need for greater emphasis on training, diagnosis, course of illness, and expectancy for treatment (Cline et al., 1973, p. 107).

It is important to keep in mind that this duality of measurement—actual behavioral change versus expectation—is part and parcel of the GAS method. Kiresuk and Sherman (1968) were aware at the outset of the possibility that goals might be set inappropriately. They recommended a policy of random assignment of cases to therapists, so that goal selectors could not deliberately or unconsciously bias goals to favor one or another therapist or method. They also suggested that periodic program review of goals and the degree of goal attainment of series of patients would tend to have a self-correcting influence on the process of setting goals and specifying results. As useful as these suggestions may be for program evaluation implementations of GAS, such reviews would probably not be helpful in research, since changing standards of scaling in midstudy would compound interpretive difficulties.

Concurrent Validity

Content validity and face validity provide necessary but not sufficient evidence of the actual utility of an assessment method. It must be demonstrated that conclusions reached using the new assessment method show at least some agreement with conclusions reached using established methods which purport to measure the same behaviors. The concurrent validity of GAS could be evaluated by using GAS along with some other measure of achieving therapeutic goals on the same client sample. The results of both measures of reaching goals would be correlated to yield a validity coefficient. (Mauger & Strolberg, 1974, p. 14)

However, since GAS is a change measure, it is not likely that GAS scores would correlate highly or significantly with many standardized psychometric devices. As Kiresuk and Sherman (1977) argue:

Since GAS attempts to calibrate scale levels according to a client's potential to benefit from treatment, it is to be expected that it will correlate weakly with standardized outcome measures. Goal Attainment scores would be of little use if they correlated perfectly with, for example, a change score in the MMPI. (p. 9)

Low to moderate positive intercorrelations would be expected between GAS and such instruments as the Brief Psychiatric Rating Scale, the Self Rating Symptoms Scale, and the MMPI (Kiresuk & Lund, 1977b); with scales measuring degree of psychological adjustment (Mauger & Stolberg, 1974); and with most diagnostic, demographic, and treatment process measures (Garwick, 1975a).

So far GAS has not been used in a large number of multiple-criteria treatment studies. Stelmachers, Lund, & Meade (1972) found that a client satisfaction survey included as part of their follow-up with a sample of crisis intervention clients provided results that were supportive of their GAS findings. The mean GAS Score obtained was 51.69 indicating attainment of "expected" treatment success. The Client Satisfaction survey revealed likewise that 79% of the crisis clients were either "very satisfied" or "satisfied" with the services they received.

Mauger and Stolberg (1974) using 28 patients who had both GAS Guides and follow-up MMPI scores, examined the relationship between outcome as measured by the trait-oriented MMPI and by GAS. GAS scores and GAS change scores were correlated with pre- and posttherapy MMPI scores, as well as MMPI change scores. The results showed that both the MMPI data and the GAS data indicated that therapeutic changes occurred during treatment. All MMPI changes were in the direction of increased psychological health. The average GAS score was also highly positive, with about 84% of the patients showing some positive change. They found small negative intercorrelations among GAS indexes and post-MMPI scores, indicating that clients who are better adjusted at follow-up as measured by the MMPI tend to have achieved slightly more of the goals set for them in therapy. Mauger & Stolberg conclude that their findings offer support for the construct validity of GAS.

Liberman and Bryan (1977) report a follow-up study on the same day-care center populations studied by Austin et al. (1976), which provided evidence that GAS changes are associated with changes on independently derived behavioral measures. Fifteen randomly chosen patients served as their own controls in time series, experimental analyses of their treatment. Repeated measures were taken for up to eight months on target behavior such as rational versus delusional speech, social interaction, prevocational tasks, and phobias. Twelve of the patients showed marked improvement of 50% or more from the baseline periods as a result of the behavioral program, which was consistent with the positive outcome reported for these patients on GAS scores.

Santa-Barbara et al. (1974), reporting preliminary results of a family therapy outcome studying using GAS, found that "client satisfaction"is correlated with "recidivism," but GAS did not seem to be related to either recidivism or satisfaction. They found further that different outcome measures are influenced by totally different types of variables; for example, therapist variables are related to client satisfaction, whereas client variables are related to more objective measures of change such as GAS in the families. They conclude that these results

Indicate once again the necessity for the utilization of multifaceted outcome measures in the study of complex phenomena such as psychotherapy. . . Not all outcome measures are related . . . In spite of the complexity involved when using several outcome measures, such an approach seems necessary in order to understand the impact of therapy on the client and thereby gain some control over those factors which are influential. (p. 11)

Willer and Miller (1976b) report significant correlations between client and therapist GAS ratings ($r = .47$), but the value was not high. Client-rated goal attainment scores correlated with client ratings of satisfaction with treatment ($r = .49$) and goal specific adjustment ($r = .31$). Client GAS socres also correlated with length of stay in treatment ($r = .28$). Therapist GAS ratings did not correlate with any of these, and neither

client nor therapist GAS scores correlated with community adjustment or return to the hospital.

These results suggest that goal attainment, as it was measured in the present study, had inadequate concurrent and predictive validity. . . . It is suggested that GAS can only remain a viable tool for evaluation . . . if it is used conjointly with other more traditional measures of treatment outcome. (Willer & Miller, 1976, p. 1198).

Weinstein and Ricks (1978) report a significant relationship between GAS outcome and teacher rated improvement for one three-month period, but not for a second three-month period. GAS and parent improvement ratings did not correlate significantly. Nor did GAS improvement on the one selected goal relate to overall improvement on other goals that were not scaled, but which were rated for improvement.

On the whole, the results indicate weaker support for the influence of GAS on either case planning or upon treatment outcome than the widespread adoption of the GAS approach might suggest. . . . the results are consistent with findings by other GAS researchers that GAS is less than an adequate outcome measure for an adult psychiatric or family therapy population. Perhaps, as others have concluded, the clearest impact of GAS is that it helps focus and perhaps promotes positive perceptions of treatment goal progress on the part of clinicians and significant others. . . . the present results raise the question of whether such expenditures are worthwhile in relation to the benefits received. (Weinstein & Ricks, 1977, p. 8)

Are Goal Attainment Scales Sensitive to Change?

Besides the content and concurrent validity data presented above, the most important construct validity evidence for GAS concerns its ability to detect the effects of treatment, or to detect meaningful differences between treatments. As Kiresuk & Lund (1977b) state: "The criterion of sensitivity to differential treatment effects will ultimately determine whether GAS will have a permanent place in research and program evaluation methodology."

If we assume that goal selectors set goals that are different from the patient's current status, which seems most reasonable, then there is ample evidence from experimental studies and program evaluation reports that GAS reflects change, since most reports show average results to be around 50 or higher, indicating that "expected levels" of outcomes are usually reached. Of course, this tells little about the kinds of changes. The two studies that actually looked at difference scores both indicated substantial change in overall level over time (Goodyear & Bitter, 1974; Austin et al., 1976). The sensitivity of the GAS measure is not clear, however. There are few published outcome studies using the method, and it is premature to come to a conclusion.

Content Analyses of Treatment Goals

Garwick and Lampman (1972), using the procedure of "isolated concerns," did a content analysis of a sample of GAS Guides taken from the Four Mode Study (Kiresuk, 1972, 1974, 1977). They found that environmental problems were of most importance to community mental health clients, and that 90.4% of the goals could be classified into one of 10 categories: family and marital (10.4%), work-related (18.1%), education-related (3.0%), treatment-related (8.1%), sexuality-related (6.3%), suicide-related (4.4%), physical complaint (1.5%), anxiety and depression (11.1%), relationship-related (17.4%), and self-definition related (10.4%).

Apart from such descriptions of samples, however, goal content is rarely used in data analyses. Kaplan and Smith (1977) studied content for validity purposes, reporting that content and outcome were unrelated. Garwick and Lampman's (1972) content coding system was used by Wallin and Koch (1977), who reported a high reliability in applying

the system. As noted earlier, Wallin and Koch found content differences among guides prepared by parents, staff, and researcher, raising validity questions. However, no use of content of GAS in analysis of outcome by classifying subjects or examining subgroups was found.

Changes in Goals During Treatment

Goal Attainment Scaling does not make provisions for redefining goals during or after treatment, or for assigning new weights to individual goal areas as priorities change. This kind of operation is quite feasible with the method, but it has not been done in published studies. Of course it would introduce many issues of bias into the method. As with target complaints, the method is not sensitive to the appearance of new problems or redefinition of priorities.

Does GAS Improve Clinical Functioning?

A number of studies suggest that implementation of GAS or another goal-focused approach to assessment may have a positive therapeutic effect. Smith (1976) contributed the best of this group of studies. He found that adolescents in counseling for adjustment problems whose counselors made GAS in the first two interviews and focused repeatedly on them during counseling improved more than adolescents counseled without GAS over a one-month treatment course. A variety of outcome measures was used, including a goal-related improved measure.

Steinbrook et al. (1977) introduced GAS on an inpatient unit, and observed improved staff behavior in terms of rewarding appropriate behavior. However, nurses' observations of the patients indicated nonsignificant changes in patient behavior with the introduction of GAS. This curious result makes one wonder what the definition of "improved" staff behavior really means.

Tracey (1977) reported that the use of a

behavioral analysis report method of intake, stressing goal planning and adaptive behavior and resources of the patient, led to a greater likelihood of patients at a community mental health center following through with initial treatment contact, and decreased attrition once treatment began. Of course this method includes many ingredients in addition to goal planning, and is not really an implementation of Goal Attainment Scaling, but the results are consistent with GAS findings.

Willer and Miller (1976) studied the impact of client participation in goal setting on outcome for a sample of hospitalized patients ($N = 72$). They reported that degree of involvement of the client in goal setting was correlated with several outcome measures, namely client satisfaction, therapist and client ratings of goal attainment, and length of treatment. One artifact in the last result was that patients who left the hospital very quickly could not have participated in the process because of scheduling problems. Also the degree of client involvement in goal setting was based on self-report rather than random assignment. Participation in goal setting may have been due to inherent factors in the patient, which were responsible for the outcome differences. Or patients with poor results may have been unwilling to admit responsibility for the goal setting. In short, these results are not solid.

Weinstein and Ricks (1977) studied the impact of training in goal scaling on case planning and outcome in a children's outpatient facility. GAS training did not affect case planning skills as measured. Although statistical analyses of the outcome data were inappropriate to the hypotheses, inspection of the data suggests that goal scaling training may have had a positive impact as measured by teacher's ratings, but not as measured by parents' ratings.

Interestingly enough, Kiresuk and Sherman (1968) originally wrote negatively about the idea of focusing therapy on specific goal areas. For that reason they advised having goals set independently from the treatment process, and kept from the therapist, in order to "minimize the possibility that the therapist would focus only on the particular goals chosen, tending to spend less effort on the more general therapeutic improvement" (p. 451).

Strengths and Advantages of GAS

Many advantages for GAS are reported in the literature. The patient is measured on dimensions believed to be relevant and important to him or her, since goals are tailored to individual clients. As McGaghie et al. (1976) observe:

Goal attainment scaling and the standardized outcome scores it produces offer advantages over both the use of case studies and the use of standardized instruments. The method preserves the uniqueness of individual goals and yields a generalizable criterion score for comparative or correlational research subsequent to consolidation of individual scales. (p. 181)

Stoudenmire and Comola (1973), applying GAS in a therapeutic camp for adolescents, observe that GAS "is superior to the sole use of tests or rating scales because group tests frequently do not reveal the true attainment of individual campers. Some persons have needs that are not readily measured by standardized group tests" (p. 574). And Smith (1975) cogently notes that "psychometric instruments provide substantial opportunity for failing to measure what one intended and for averaging out meaningful changes occurring in opposite directions in different individuals" (p. 599).

GAS generates a meaningful numerical indicator of goal attainment that allows direct comparison of diverse treatment modalities (Bonstedt, 1973; Davis, 1973; Ellis & Wilson, 1973; Fiester & Fort, 1976; Kiresuk & Lund, 1977a). As Bonstedt (1973) notes:

With the ever increasing profusion of different approaches, orientations, and terminologies in psychiatry there is an increasing need for some common yardstick of comparison or evaluation that can be applied to these approaches as they work on different patients . . . . goal-based evaluative schemes have the advantage of being able to compare highly individualized, often widely different, treatment schemes by a common denominator: that is, what has happened to the patient with respect to his particular goals as the result of therapeutic intervention. (Ellis & Wilson, 1973, pp. 5–7)

Setting of specific goals may focus client, staff, and significant other persons on a target and energize movement toward it (Davis, 1973; Ellis & Wilson, 1973; Hargreaves et al., 1977). As Ellis and Wilson (1973) state:

Goal orientation forces the user to become more concerned with the course and end of treatment than with descriptions of symptoms, problems, and diagnostic labels. Prior specification of goals not only facilitates the assessment of progress by describing it as movement with respect to a fixed point—the goal—but also encourages precision in describing the problem and selecting appropriate methods for reaching the goal efficiently. (p. 6)

GAS provides individualized criteria of client progress as useful feedback to the clinic staff regarding the effectiveness of their endeavors, which in turn tends to increase staff incentive (Davis, 1973; Austin et al., 1976). In this regard Steinbook et al. (1977) studied the effects of introducing GAS in a hospital unit on accurate and effective staff use of social reinforcement treatment. They found that the general availability of individual GAS Guides to staff and patients led to significant change in staff reinforcement response to "appropriate" patient behavior. Specifically, the incidence of staff rewards for appropriate behavior increased, and the amount of appropriate behavior ignored by staff decreased. They conclude that "the goal-attainment scales seemed to serve as instructional guides for the delivery of social reinforcement."

According to Austin et al. (1976), GAS is an aid to clinicians in organizing and recording the process of therapy, and is useful to supervisors and program managers in determining the strengths and weaknesses of clinicians as matched with patients.

Moriarty (1974) emphasizes that the simple, concrete terms used in GAS "permit workers in several fields to comprehend aims and purposes. This encourages interdisciplinary cooperation" (p. 31).

GAS offers considerable advantages for use in program evaluation of mental health agencies as well as in peer review or other auditing procedures. Kiresuk (1977) notes that objectively determinable results specified in advance permit easy audit of both goal setting and attainment. And Erickson (1975) emphasizes: "It is not unlikely that the future will see hospitals called upon to demonstrate their ability to achieve goals in terms of demonstrated levels of symptom removal and of psychosocial functioning as a precondition of discharge" (p. 533).

The final and most crucial advantage, in terms of development of psychotherapy as a scientific endeavor, results from the GAS requirement that scale levels be defined in specific, observable, operational terms. Bonstedt (1973), as a result of his experience with GAS, reports that a strong positive asset of concrete goal setting for patients

was the quick effective understanding among the staff about exactly what was being attempted with each particular patient. When goals were set with such concrete references as "distance from home," "duration of time spent with or without a particular visible behavior," or ability to initiate and/or conduct a specified visible behavior with a specified number of particular persons, there was not much room left for either misunderstanding by some persons on a team of what was meant, or for a protracted debate at the time of the review as to whether and to what extent progress had been achieved (quite unlike past situations when the staff would try to agree, for instance, about whether "a person's super-ego was flexible enough," or the "ego-boundaries were firm enough"). (p. 4)

Kendall (1975) also underlines the importance of precise, operational definitions in psychiatry. He points out that "common technical terms like anxiety, delusion, thought disorder and so on may be used in quite different ways by different psychiatrists without their being aware that this is so" (p. 145). He goes on to state that "in general, all definitions which remain heavily dependent on inference . . . are likely to prove inadequate as there is abundant evidence that inferential judgements are consistently less reliable than those based on directly observable criteria" (p. 149). Finally, Kiresuk & Sherman (1968) describe all goal statements not expressed in observable, concrete terms as "basically platitudes or statements of good intentions" (p. 445).

Weaknesses and Disadvantages of GAS

The literature offers considerably fewer complaints and cautions regarding the GAS procedure. Perhaps the most frequently noted difficulty is the expense and effort of initiating and continuing its application in mental health agencies. Kaplan and Smith (1977), for example, reported that GAS proved quite expensive, requiring four to six work hours per patient to construct the individualized scales, a time estimate far exceeding that reported as usual by Kiresuk and colleagues. "It appears to be a low cost-benefit performance for outcome evaluation . . . our experience would suggest the use of a less complex and costly approach" (p. 192).

Hargreaves, Atkinson, & Odberg (1977) add:

In spite of . . . advantages it represents a major investment in staff orientation and continuing training to install Goal Attainment Scaling as a routine procedure . . . Several centers that use an individual goal attainment method report enthusiasm about its value as a routine part of a clinical program. However . . . it requires a level of enthusiastic support from treatment staff that will usually not be possible to enlist under such circumstances. (p. 236)

And Kivens and Bolin (1976) report, regarding a child inpatient unit of a community mental health center, that "although both GAS and needs assessment provided helpful information to the center . . . the benefits of their continued use did not outweigh the costs, and neither technique was adopted as a standard operating procedure in any program in the center."

Some clinicians seem to object strongly to the goal setting process itself, including translating these goals into objective results. Further, they may resist specifying goals because they fear "trivializing" the client's problems or fear that the changes may be irrelevant to the client's total adjustment (Cline et al., 1973).

Another caution heard is that the GAS procedure does not automatically guarantee appropriate description of goal expectancy levels, and the measure depends heavily upon the skill of the GAS Guide constructor (Cline et al., 1973). This clearly is a legitimate caution. As we have seen, steps have been taken to counteract this problem, including use of multiple informants for GAS Guide construction, reliability checks on the content of GAS Guides independently constructed, and use of external auditors to check on the relevance, reasonableness, or optimism level of "expected" GAS Scale levels.

Seaberg and Gillespie (1977) complain, with some justification, that GAS has thus far been primarily an inbred product of the Minneapolis group, and that "reports on the results of GAS from outside the . . . project are limited" (p. 4).

The basic notion of GAS, that a composite T-score of 50 indicates "reaching expected level" is true only in a complex sense. As with any measure that depends on summing or averaging, the average is only appropriate when the component values are distributed around that average with relatively little spread. With the unequal weighting of goals, the number of different possible interpretations for any particular T-score becomes enormous. From the point of view of assessing treatment efficacy, this may be acceptable, but the resulting situation is hardly likely to increase our understanding of specific behavioral influence processes.

GAS: Recommendations to Researchers

Construction of adequate GAS Guides requires some prior training experience. Potential users may avail themselves of the many training materials available from Kiresuk's Center before embarking on GAS studies. If patients are to construct their own Guides independently, they may find Garwick's (1972) Guide to Goals: Format I useful.

For research applications, whenever possible, GAS Guide construction and GAS Scale ratings should be based on information from the "tri-informants" in the situation: namely, patient, therapist, and significant persons. This can be accomplished either by interviews with all three informants between therapist/staff, patient, and significant persons, or by separate and independent Guide construction by patient, therapist/staff, and significant persons.

For research purposes, no less than three and not more than five GAS Scales should be incorporated in a GAS Guide. Study applications have found that these numbers are indeed practicable, and numerical standardization would assist considerably both in interpretation of results as well as in unraveling some of the statistical issues potentially imbedded in the GAS score and change score.

For research applications, researchers should *not* differentially weight the three to five scales on a GAS Guide. Weighting can compound statistical and interpretive problems, and unweighted scores have been shown to work as well anyway.

Researchers should include both the GAS score and the GAS change score in their data analyses and results. Over time, this will help considerably, both in comparing results and

in unraveling the similarities and differences of these two scores. Further, they should seriously consider the various possibilities of analyzing scores from individual GAS Scales separately. This would clarify whether different results emerge for individual versus aggregate scale scores and chart empirically the range of intercorrelations among them.

Although interjudge reliability for GAS Scale attainment levels at both intake and follow-up points have been almost universally good to high, researchers should routinely incorporate reliability assessments in their designs and report on results. The sources of unreliability are more multiple for individualized measures such as GAS, and each new application needs to be defended.

Any research application of GAS should incorporate as part of its design some independent audit of the reasonableness (relevance, optimism level, difficulty level) of the "expected level of success" scale definitions for its sample of GAS Guides. This control is particularly crucial for comparative studies (experimental vs. controls; or treatment$_1$ vs. treatment$_2$). In this regard we note the audit procedure used by Austin et al. (1976).

There is still too little data about the relationship between GAS and other methods of measuring treatment outcome. We recommend inclusion of "conventional" outcome measures to researchers interested in using GAS. The NIMH "core battery" (Waskow & Parloff, 1975) seems a good reference here. Whenever possible, investigators should report the interrelationships among criterion measures.

While definition of goals in precise behavioral terms may not be appropriate in all cases, an attempt should be made in all cases to obtain data concerning the bases of outcome ratings.

As Hargreaves et al. (1977) point out, the specificity of GAS makes it possible to miss important areas of outcome because they were not included as a goal area. This problem is equally true for target complaints or any focal measure. The suggestion of Hargreaves et al. obvious: include both focal and general measures in a combined approach.

GAS: Conclusions

Although the presentation of the method by Kiresuk and Sherman (1968) was a reasonable and careful one, stressing the value of precise behavioral specification of outcome in areas meaningful to the individual, and sensitive to the problems of distortion by individual goals selectors, implementations of GAS have moved away from the original plan. It is most important in evaluating the GAS literature to maintain a sharp distinction between reports of implementations, generally presented with enormous enthusiasm, papers that simply extoll the many virtues and potential applications of GAS, and the actual body of scientific literature.

Several serious issues are inherent in the method. One is the confounding of behavior change and expectation of the goal selector. Even when only one goal is determined, the outcome is an uncertain combination of actual change in behavior and the standards in the mind and value system of the individual or committee who set up the scale. When more than one goal, with differing weights, are combined into an overall index, these problems are compounded. This issue has been brought up in those papers in which the average client did not reach expected levels of outcome. However, the issue is equally true when the level is reached.

This is not of course unique to GAS. When subjects make any improvement rating, they are assessing how closely their current status meets their expectations. It might be argued that GAS has the advantage of at least making those expectations explicit so that they may be examined in their own right. All that GAS does, it might be said, is force one to be clear as to what one means by "improvement."

In so doing, however, the method runs into a major difficulty. By requiring specification of behavior defining outcome in each goal area, the method may be reducing complex

phenomena to simplistic terms. Making operational complex clinical phenomena may simply be too difficult a task for the variety of goal selectors in the typical study.

The kinds of goals Kiresuk and Sherman originally suggested held out the promise of integrating this method within dynamic approaches to treatment. However, the specification of results for such goal areas as "transference" or "insight," terms used by Kiresuk and Sherman originally, has not been the way the method has actually been used. The published studies have not typically come from a mental health setting at all. Indeed the notion of workers at a mental health center attempting to put into objective terms goals such as "transference" or "other psychodynamic insights" seems quite unrealistic.

There is little doubt that Goal Attainment Scaling has achieved enormous popularity in program evaluation. It has been recommended and implemented in mental health clinics, inpatient and outpatient facilities, psychology departments, even in the evaluation of research projects. However, to date there has been relatively little yeild for controlled or comparative psychotherapy research from the method.

At this point GAS offers considerable promise as a psychotherapy outcome measure and mental health program evaluation tool. In addition, GAS may be a useful adjunct to the treatment process itself, and it has obvious appeal as a training and supervisory instrument.

The very diversity of GAS's applications has presented some obstacles to its systematic development as a research and evaluation measure. As Garwick (1975a) observes:

The flexibility and pragmatic simplicity of GAS (as opposed to the theoretical complexity of its scaling and psychometric properties) often lead new users to implement it with relative casualness, and only later to decide to try making definitive, rigid inferences from the resulting data . . . the mere use of GAS does not lead to easily interpretable results, and . . . the way in which GAS is applied, especially its design, is crucial to the utility of the finding. (p. 1)

Obviously we have a lot yet to learn about this individualized measure, and problems do exist. Garwick (in Brintnall & Garwick, 1976, p. 15) perhaps provides the most appropriate closing perspective:

From an evaluative viewpoint, GAS is thought by some clinicians to produce more meaningful results than standardized measures of outcome. Clearly GAS is a compromise between the need for systematic evaluation and the need for clinical integrity. As in all compromises, some aspects of GAS may not seem perfectly attuned to all audiences. Still, in the balance, the approach is a workable attempt to yield high utilities for both clinical and program evaluation needs. Few other methodologies even attempt such a compromise, and so GAS is particularly intriguing for further study.

REFERENCES

Ames, R. (1975). Staff performance evaluation with goal attainment scaling in county social service agency. *Program Evaluation Resource Center Newsletter, 6, 1–3.*

Audette, D. (1973). Interviewer's assessment of goal attainment follow-up guide relevancy. *P.E.P. Newsletter,* May-June.

Austin, N. K., Liberman, R. P., King, L. W., & DiRisi, W. J. (1976). Comparative evaluation of two day treatment programs: Goal Attainment Scaling in behavior therapy vs. milieu therapy. *Journal of Nervous and Mental Disease,* **163,** 253–262.

Auerbach, A., Luborsky, L., Johnson, M. (1972). Clinicians' predictions of outcome of psychotherapy: Trials of a prognostic index. *American Journal of Psychiatry,* **128**(7), 830.

Balch, P., & Miller, K. (1974). Social class and the community mental health center: Client and therapist perceptions of presenting problems and treatment expectations. *American Journal of Community Psychology,* **2,** 243–253.

Beck, S., Gale, M., Springer, K., & Spitz, L. (1975). An evaluative study of Cincinnati General Hospital Emergency Service. *Goal Attainment Review,* **2,** 97–108.

Benedict, W. (1974). Goal-setting in residential treatment for adolescents. *P.E.R.C. Newsletter,* September–October.

Benedict, W. (1975). Utilizing goal attainment scaling to evaluate a staff development program. *Goal Attainment Review,* **1.**

Bensing, J., & Dekker, M. (1973). Goal attainment scaling II: een methode tot evaluatie van psychotherapieen. *Maandblad Seestelijke Volksgezondjekd,* **28,** 342–356.

Bergin, A. (1971). The evaluation of therapeutic outcomes. In A. Bergin & S. Garfield (Eds.), *Handbook of psychotherapy and behavior change.* New York: Wiley, pp. 217–270.

Bolin, D., & Kivens, L. (1974). Evaluation in a community mental health center: Huntsville, Alabama. *Evaluation,* **2,** 26–35.

Bolin, D., & Kivens, L. (1975). Evaluation in a community mental health center: Hennepin County Mental Health Service. *Evaluation,* **2,** 60–63.

Bonstedt, T. (1973). Concrete goal-setting for patients in a day hospital. *Evaluation,* **1.**

Borghi, J. H. (1968). Premature termination of psychotherapy and patent-therapist expectations. *American Journal of Orthopsychiatry,* **22,** 460–473.

Brintnall, J., & Garwick, G. (Eds.) (1976). *Applications of goal attainment scaling.* Minneapolis: Program Evaluation Resource Center.

Brown, T. (1973). The evaluation of community oriented indirect mental health services with goal attainment scaling. In G. Garwick & C. Vanderpool (Eds.), *Goal attainment scaling workshop compendium.* Minneapolis: Program Evaluation Resource Center.

Burns, M. (1976). Goal attainment scaling in a day treatment program. In G. Garwick & J. Brintnall (Eds.), *Proceedings of the second goal attainment scaling conference.* Minneapolis: Program Evaluation Resource Center.

Bush, J. F. (1972). The effects of fixed and random principal data interaction on individual goal attainment in group counseling. Ph.D. dissertation, Indiana State University. (Univ. M-Films, No. 72-7528)

Canfield, M., & Kliewer, D. (1977). Conference evaluation manual. In W. A. Hargreaves, C. C. Attkisson, & J. E. Sorensen (Eds.), *Resource materials for community mental health program evaluation* (2nd ed.). Washington, D. C.: U.S. Government Printing Office (DHEW Pub. No. (ADM) 77–328).

Carlson, G. D. (1974). Communication skills training in a family practice residency program. *Goal Attainment Review,* **1,** 55–68.

Cline, D. W., Rouzer, D. L., & Bransford, D. (1973). Goal-attainment scaling as a method for evaluating mental health programs. *American Journal of Psychiatry,* **130,** 105–108.

Davis, H. R. (1973). Four ways to goal attainment. *Evaluation,* **1,** 1–28.

Denner, B., & Halprin, F (1974). Clients and therapists evaluate clinical services. *American Journal of Community Psychology,* **2,** 373–386.

Dowd, E. T., & Kelly, F. D. (1975). The use of goal attainment scaling in a single case study research. *Goal Attainment Review,* **2,** 11–21.

Ellis, R. H., & Wilson, N. C. Z. (1973). Evaluating treatment effectiveness using a goal-oriented automated progress note. *Evaluation,* **1,** 6–11.

Ellsworth, R. B., Foster, L., Childers, B., Arthur, G., & Kroekel, D. (1968). Hospital and community adjustments as perceived by psychiatric patients, their families, and staff. *Journal of Consulting and Clinical Psychology* (Monograph supplement), **41,** 5–13.

Erickson, R. C. (1975). Outcome studies in mental hospitals: A review. *Psychological Bulletin,* **82,** 519–540.

Feifel, H., & Eells, J. (1963). Patients and therapists assess the same psychotherapy. *Journal of Consulting Psychology,* **17,** 113–121.

Fiester, A., & Fort, D. (1976). Implementation of an automated goal attainment system at a comprehensive community mental health center. *Hospital and Community Psychiatry,* **27,** 625–626.

Fiske, D. W., Luborsky, L., Parloff, M. B., Hunt, H. F., Orne, M. T., Reiser, M. F., & Tuma, A.H . 1970). Planning research on the effectiveness of psychotherapy. *American Psychologist,* **25,** 727–737.

Fiske, D. (1975). A source of data is not a measuring instrument. *Journal of Abnormal Psychology,* **84**(1), 20–23.

Garwick, G. (1972). *Guide to goals: Format I.* Minneapolis: Program Evaluation Project.

Garwick, G. (1974a). *A construct validity overview of goal attainment scaling.* Minneapolis, Minn.: Program Evaluation Project.

Garwick, G. (1974b). Recent findings on the use of goal-setting in human services agencies: The implementation, flexibility and validity of goal attainment scaling. *Goal Attainment Review,* **1,** 1–4.

Garwick, G. (1975a). Defining and validating goal attainment scaling. *Goal Attainment Review,* **2,** 1–10.

Garwick, G. (1976a). *Programmed instruction in goal attainment scaling* (2nd ed.). Minneapolis: Program Evaluation Resource Center.

Garwick, G. (1976b). *Guide to goals: Format II.* Minneapolis: Program Evaluation Resource Center.

Garwick, G., & Brintnall, J. (1973). *Tables for calculating the goal attainment score.* Minneapolis; Program Evaluation Resource Center.

Garwick, G., & Lampman, S. (1972). Typical problems bringing patients to a community mental health center. *Community Mental Health Journal,* **8,** 271–280.

Garwick, G., & Lampman, S. (1973). *Dictionary of goal attainment scaling.* Minneapolis: Program Evaluation Resource Center.

Garwick, G., McCree, J., & Brintnall, J. (1976). *Bibliography on goal attainment scaling and associated methodologies.* Minneapolis: Program Evaluation Resource Center.

Gianturco, D. T., & Ramm, D. (1974). Computer aided patient evaluation: A goal oriented approach. In J. L. Crawford (Ed.), *Progress in mental health information systems.* Cambridge, Mass.: Ballinger.

Goodyear, D., & Bitter, J. (1974). Goal attainment scaling as a program evaluation measure in rehabilitation. *Journal of Applied Rehabilitation Counseling,* **5,** 19–26.

Griest, J., Klein, M., Van Cura, L. (1973). A computer interview for psychiatric patient target symptoms. *Archives of General Psychiatry,* **2**(2), 247–253.

Grygelko, M., Garwick, G., & Lampman, J. (1973). Findings of content analysis: 1. Patterns of use and 2. Reliability. *P.E.P. Newsletter,* September–October.

Hall, J. N., & Mathison, M. T. (1975). Adaptation of goal attainment scaling to an outpatient drug treatment program. *Goal Attainment Review,* **2,** 109–115.

Hargreaves, W. A., Attkisson, C. C., & Sorensen, J. E. (Eds.) (1977). *Resource materials for a community mental health program evaluation* (2nd ed.). Washington, D. C.: U. S. Government Printing Office (DHEW Publication No. (ADM) 77–328).

Hagreaves, W. A., Attkisson, C. C., & Ochberg, F. M. (1977). Outcome studies in mental health program evaluation. In W. A. Hargreaves, C. C. Attkisson, & J. E. Sorensen (Eds.), *Resource materials for community metal health program evaluation* (2nd ed.). Washington, D. C.: U. S. Government Printing Office (DHEW Publication No. (ADM) 77–328).

Hargreaves, W., McIntyre, M., Attkisson, C., Siegel, L. (1977). Outcome measurement instruments for use in community mental health program evaluation. In W. Hargreaves, C. Attkisson, & J. Sorensen, *Resource materials for community mental health program evaluation.* Washington, D. C.: U. S. Department HEW, U. S. Government Printing Office, 243-250, Chapter 22.

Hays, W. (1973). *Statistics for the social sciences.* Holt, Rinehart & Winston, New York.

Heine, R. W., & Trosman, H. (1960). Initial expectations of the doctor-patient interaction as a factor in continuance in psychotherapy. *Psychiatry,* **23,** 275–278.

Hesbacher, P., Rickels, K., Weise, C. (1968). Target symptoms: A promising improvement criterion in psychiatric drug research. *Archives of General Psychiatry,* **18,** 595–600.

Hoehn-Saric, R., Frank, J., Imber, S., Nash, E., Stone, A., & Battle, C. (1964). Systematic preparation of patients for psychotherapy - I. Effects on therapy behavior and outcome. *Journal of Psychiatric Research,* **2**(4), 267–281.

Holtzman, W. H., Thorpe, J. S., Sevortz, J. D., Herron, E. W. (1961). *Inkblot perception and personality.* Austin, Tex.: University of Texas Press.

Houts, P. S., & Scott, R. A. (1973). To evaluate the effectiveness of achievement motivation training for mental patients being rehabilitated to the community. Unpublished project final report, Pennsylvania State University College of Medicine, Hershey, Pa.

Houts, P. S., & Scott, R. A. (1975). Goal planning in mental health rehabilitation: An evaluation of the effectiveness of achievement motivation training for mental patients being rehabilitated to the community. *Goal Attainment Review,* **2,** 33–51.

Imber, S. (1975). Patient direct self-report techniques. In I. Waskow & M. Parloff (Eds.), *Psychotherapy Change Measures.* Washington, D. C.: U. S. Government Printing Office.

Johnson, M. (1976) An approach to feminist therapy. *Psychotherapy: Theory, Research and Practice,* **13**(1), 72–76.

Jones, S., & Garwick, G. (1973). Guide to goals study: Goal attainment scaling as therapy adjunct? *P.E.P. Newsletter,* July–August, **4,** 1–3.

Kaplan, J. M., & Smith, W. G. (1974). An evaluation program for a regional health center. In J. L. Crawford (Ed.), *Progress in mental health information systems.* Cambridge, Mass.: Ballinger.

Kaplan, J. M., & Smith, W. G. (1977). The use of attainment scaling in the evaluation of a regional mental health program. *Community Mental Health Journal,* **13,** 118–193.

Kendall, R. E. (1975). *The role of diagnosis in psychiatry.* London: Blackwell Scientific Publications.

Kent, R., O'Leary, K. (1976). A controlled evaluation of behavior modification with conduct problem children. *Journal of Consulting and Clinical Psychology,* **4**(4), 586–596.

Kiesler, D. (1966). Some myths of psychotherapy research and the search for a paradigm. *Psychological Bulletin,* **65**(2), 110–136.

Kiesler, D. (1971). Experimental designs in psychotherapy research. In A. E. Bergin & S. L. Garfield (Eds.), *Handbook of psychotherapy and behavior change.* New York: Wiley.

Kiesler, D. (1977). *Use of individualized measures in psychotherapy and mental health program evaluation research: A review of target complaints, problem oriented record, and goal attainment scales.* Report prepared for the Psychotherapy and Behavioral Intervention Section, Clinical Research Branch, Division of Extramural Research Programs, National Institute of Mental Health, contract No. PLD04317-77.

Kiresuk, T. J. (Ed.) (1971). *Program evaluation forum papers.* Minneapolis: Program Evaluation Project.

Kiresuk, T. (1972). Goal attainment scaling at a county health service. *Evaluation,* **1,** 43–481.

Kiresuk, T. J. (1974). *Program evaluation project report, 1969–1973.* (NIMH Grant #5, RO1 1678904 and Grant #1 Rls MH2561902). Minneapolis: Program Evaluation Project.

Kiresuk, T. J. (1975). Goal attainment scoring and quantification of values. In M. Guttentag, T. Kiresuk, M. Oglesby, & J. Cahn (Eds.). *The evaluation of training in mental health.* New York: Behavioral Publications.

Kiresuk, T. J. (1976). Goal attainment scaling at a county mental health service. In E. Warren, M. Markson, & D. F. Allen (Eds.), *Trends in mental health evaluation.* Lexington. Mass.: D. C. Heath.

Kiresuk, T. J. (1977). Goal attainment scaling at a county mental health service. In W. A. Hargreaves, C. C. Attkisson, & J. E. Sorensen (Eds.), *Resource materials for community mental health program evaluation* (2nd ed.). Washington, D. C.: U. S. Government Printing Office (DHEW Pub. No. (ADM) 77–328).

Kiresuk, T. J., & Garwick, G. (1975). Basic goal attainment scaling procedures. In B. E. Comptom & B. C. Galaway (Eds.), *Social work processes.* Homewood, Ill.: Dorsey.

Kiresuk, T., & Lund, S. (1976). Process and outcome measurement using goal attainment scaling. In G. Glass (Ed.), *Evaluation studies review annual,* Vol. 1. Beverly Hills: Sage Publications. Also in J. Zusman & C. Wurster (Eds.), *Program evaluation: Alcohol, drug abuse, and mental health services.* Lexington, Mass.: D. C. Heath. 1975.

Kiresuk, T. J., & Lund, S. H. (1977a). Goal attainment scaling: Research, evaluation and utilization. In H.

C. Schulberg & F. Baker (Eds.), *Program evaluation in the health fields,* Vol. 2. New York: Behavioral Publications.

Kiresuk, T. J., & Lund, S. H. (1977b). Goal attainment scaling. In C. C. Attkisson, W. Hargreaves, M. J. Horowitz (Eds.), *Evaluation of human service programs.* New York: Academic Press.

Kiresuk, T. J., & Lund, S. H. (1977c). Program evaluation and the management of human services organizations. In W. F. Anderson, B. J. Frieden & M. J. Murphy (Eds.), *Managing human services.* New York: International City Management Association.

Kiresuk, T. J., & Sherman, R. E. (1968). Goal attainment scaling: A general method for evaluating comprehensive community mental health programs. *Community Mental Health Journal,* **4,** 443–453.

Kiresuk, T. J., & Sherman, R. (1977). A reply to the critique of goal attainment scaling. *Social work Research and Abstracts,* **13,** 9–11.

Kivens, L., & Bolin, D. (1976). Evaluation in a community mental health center: Hillsborough CMHC, Tampa Florida, *Evaluation,* **3,** 98–105.

Klein, M., Griest, J., & VanCura, L. (1975). Computers and psychiatry. *Archives of General Psychiatry,* **32**(7), 837–843.

Klonoff, H., & Cox, B. (1975). A problem-oriented system approach to analysis of treatment outcome. *American Journal of Psychiatry,* **132,** 836–841.

Krumboltz, J. D. (1966). Behavioral goals for counseling. *Journal of Counseling Psychology,* **13,** 153–159.

La Ferriere, L., & Calsyn, R. (1975). Goal attainment scaling: An effective treatment technique in short term therapy. Lansing: Michigan State University, unpublished report.

Lefkovitz, P. M. (1974). Program evaluation in a day treatment center. *Goal Attainment Review,* **1,** 44–48.

Levinson, E. (1973). Goal Attainment. *American Psychological Association Newsletter,* **6,** 3.

Liberman, R. P., & Smith, V. (1972). A multiple baseline study of systematic desensitization in a patient with multiple phobias. *Behavior Therapy,* **3,** 597–603.

Liberman, R. P., & Bryan, E. III. (1977). Behavior therapy in a community mental health center. *American Journal of Psychiatry,* **134,** 401–406.

Likert, R. A. (1932). *A technique for the measurement of attitudes* (Archives of Psychology Report No. 140). New York: Colubmia University Press.

Lombillo, J., Kiresuk, T., & Sherman, R. (1973). Evaluating a community mental health program—contract fulfillment analysis. *Hospital and Community Psychiatry,* **24,** 760–762.

Luborsky, L., Chandler, J., Auerbach, A., Cohen, J., & Bachrach, H. (1971). Factors influencing the outcome of psychotherapy: A review of quantitative research. *Psychological Bulletin,* **75,** 145–185.

Luborsky, L., Mintz, J., Auerbach, A., Christoph, P., Bachrach, H., Todd, T., Johnson, M., Cohen M., O'Brien, C. (1980). Predicting the outcomes of psychotherapy. Results of the Penn Psychotherapy Project. *Archives of General Psychiatry,* **37**(4), 471–481.

Lund, S. H. (1972). Clinical evaluation of a crisis intervention center. Minneapolis: Program Evaluation Resource Center.

Lynbaugh, T. (1974). Community living: A developmental approach to the treatment of young-adults with major psychological disorders. Ph.D. dissertation, University of Minnesota (Univ. M-Films, No. 74–10538).

Mason, E. (1975). Client specific program evaluation. Madison, Wis., Division of Mental Hygiene.

Mauger, P. A., & Stolberg, (1974). A study of the construct validity of goal attainment scaling: The MMPI and goal attainment. *Goal Attainment Review,* **1,** 13–19.

McGaghie, W. C., & Menges, R. J. (1975). Assessing delf-directed learning. *Teaching of Psychology,* **2,** 56–59.

McGaghie, W. C., Menges, R. J., & Dobroski, B. J. (1976). Self-modification in a college course: Outcomes and correlates. *Journal of Counseling Psychology,* **23,** 178–182.

McPartland, T., & Rochart, R. (1966). Social and clinical outcome of psychiatric treatment. *Archives of General Psychiatry,* **14,** 179–184.

Mehaffey, T. D. (1972). The effects of a T-group experience on clients with measured high and low dependency needs. Ph.D. dissertation, Indiana State University (Univ. M-Films No. 72–31936).

Meldman, M. J, Johnson, E., & McLeod, D. (1975). A goal list and a treatment methods index in an automated record system. *Hospital and Community Psychiatry,* **26,** 365–370.

Mintz, J. (1972). What is success in psychotherapy? *Journal of Abnormal Psychology,* **80,** 11–19.

Mintz, J., Auerbach, A., Luborsky, L., & Johnson, M. (1973). Patient's therapist's and observers' view of psychotherapy: A "Rashomon" experience or a reasonable concensus. *British Journal of Medical Psychology,* **46,** 83–89.

Mintz, J. (1977). *Tailoring psychotherapy outcome measures to fit the individual case: A review.* Report prepared for the Psychotherapy and Behavioral

Intervention Section, Clinical Research Branch, Division of Extramural Research Programs, National Institute of Mental Health, contract No. PLDO5668–77.

Mintz, J., Luborsky, L., & Christoph, P. (1979). Measuring the outcomes of psychotherapy: Findings of the Penn Psychotherapy Project. *Journal of Consulting and Clinical Psychology, 47*(2), 319–334.

Moriarty, B. (1974). Successful goal planning with the mentally disabled. *Social and Rehabilitation Record,* **1,** 28–31.

Nunnally, J. C. (1967). *Psychometric theory.* New York: McGraw-Hill.

Pascal, F. (1959). *Behavioral change in the clinic: A systematic approach.* New York: Grune & Stratton.

Pascal, F., & Zax, M. (1956). Psychotherapeutics: Success or failure. *Journal of Consulting Psychology,* **20**(5), 325–331.

Paul, G. L. (1967). Strategy of outcome research in psychotherapy. *Journal of Consulting Psychology,* **31,** 104–118.

Petersen, N. (1975). Court services evaluation ends. *P.E.R.C. Newsletter,* March-April.

Piper, W. Debbane, E. Garant, J. (1977). An outcome study or group therapy. *Archives of General Psychiatry,* **34** (September), 1027–1032.

Polak, P. (1970). Patterns of discord: Goals of patients, therapists and community members. *Archives of General Psychiatry,* **23,** 277–283.

Putnam, D. G., Kiesler, D. J., Bent, R. J., & Steward, A. (1973). Goal Attainment scaling training manual. Drug Abuse Services Section, Georgia Department of Human Resources, unpublished manuscript.

Putnam, D. G., Kiesler, D. J., Bent, R. J., McCaslin, C., Steward, A., & Senn, R. (1973). *A model for program evaluation and development: Descriptive and experimental methodology for drug abuse services.* Atlanta: Georgia Mental Health Institute.

Rickard, H. (1965). Tailored criteria of change in psychotherapy. *Journal of General Psychology,* **72,** 63–68.

Ricks, F., Clarke, F. G., Dlugacz, D., Prato, D., Rothwell, P., Shaw, R. C., & Sowa, E. (1973). Manual of case evaluation from the Dellcrest Children's Centre. Dell Children's Centre, Downsview, Ontario M3J 2E5, unpublished manuscript.

Ricks, R., & Weinstein, M. (1976). The influence of goal attainment scaling on treatment outcome. Downsview, Ontario: Dellcrest Children's Centre, *Data and Research Topics,* **5.**

Rinn, R. C., Tapp, L., & Petrella, R. (1973). Behavior modification with outpatients in a community men-

tal health center. *Journal of Behavior Therapy and Experimental Psychiatry,* **4,** 243–247.

Rinn, R. C., & Vernon, J. C. (1975). Process of evaluation of outpatient treatment in a community mental health center. *Journal of Behavior Therapy and Experimental Psychiatry,* **6,** 5–11.

Rinn, R. C., Vernon, J. C., & Wise, M. J. (1975).Training parents of behaviorally disordered children in groups: A three year's program evaluation. *Behavior Therapy,* **6,** 378–387.

Rogers, C., Gendlin, G., Kiesler, D., & Truax, C. (1967). *The therapeutic relationship and its impact: A study of psychotherapy with schizophrenics.* Madison: University of Wisconsin Press.

Romney, D. (1976). Treatment progress by objectives: Kiresuk's and Sherman's approach simplified. *Community Mental Health Journal,* **12**(3), 286–290.

Rosen, D., & Zytowskik D. G. (1977). An individualized, problem-oriented self-report of change as a follow-up of a university counseling service. *Journal of Counseling Psychology,* **24,** 437–439.

Rosenthal, A. J., & Levine, S. V. (1971). Brief psychotherapy with children: Process of therapy. *American Journal of Psychiatry,* **128,** 141–146.

Santa-Barbara, J., Woodward, C. A., Levin, S., Goodman, J. T., Streiner, D. L., Muzzin, L., & Epstein, N. B. (1974). Variables related to outcome in family therapy: Some preliminary analysis. *Goal Attainment Review,* **1,** 5–12.

Schmidt, H. (1974). Goal attainment scaling III. *Maandblad Gestelijke Volksgezondheid,* **19,** 1391145.

Seaberg, J. R., & Gillespie, D. F. (1977). Goal attainment scaling: A critique. *Social Work Research and Abstracts,* **13,** 4–9.

Shepperson, V., Mauger, P. A., & Zinober, J. (1975). Differences in clients' and therapists' evaluations of goal content and success in psychotherapy. *Goal Attainment Review,* **2,** 149–156.

Sherman, R. (1974). The content validity argument for the validity of the goal attainment score. *Program Evaluation Resource Center Newsletter,* **5,** 5–6.

Shlien, J. M. (1966). Cross-theoretical criteria for the evaluation of psychotherapy. *American Journal of Psychiatry,* **20,** 125–134.

Shorer, C. (1970). Improvement with and without psychotherapy. *Diseases of the Nervous System,* **31**(11), 155–160.

Sloane, R. B., Cristol, A., Pepernik, M., & Staples, F. (1970). Role preparation and expectation of improvement in psychotherapy. *Journal of Nervous and Mental Disease,* **150**(1), 18–26.

Sloane, R. B., Staples, F., Cristol, A., Yorkston, N., & Whipple, K. (1975). *Psychotherapy vs. behavior therapy*. Cambridge, Mass.: Harvard University Press.

Smith, D. L. (1976). Goal attainment scaling as an adjunct to counseling. *Journal of Counseling Psychology*, **23**, 22–27.

Smith, P. B. (1975). Controlled studies of the outcome of sensitivity training. *Psychological Bulletin*, **82**, 597–622.

Speer, D. C., & Cohen, E. (1975). Goal attainment scaling in a crisis service: a feasibility study that needed to be done. *Goal Attaiment Review*, **2**, 79–93.

Steinbrook, R. M., Jacobson, A. F., Mosher, J. C., & Davies, D. L. (1977). The goal-attainment scale: An instructional guide for the delivery of social reinforcement. *Archives of General Psychiatry*, **34**, 923–926.

Stoudenmire, J., & Comolo, J. (1973). Evaluating Camp Clime-Up: A two-week therapeutic camp. *Exceptional Children*, **39**, 573–574.

Strupp, H., Fox, R., & Lesser, K. (1969). *Patients view their psychotherapy*. Baltimore: The Johns Hopkins Press.

Strupp, H., Bloxom, A. (1973). Preparing lower class patients for group psychotherapy. *Journal of Consulting and Clinical Psychology*, **41**(3), 373–384.

Strupp, H. (1976). Themes for psychotherapy research. In J. Claghorn (Ed.), *Successful psychotherapy*. New York: Brunner/Massel, pp. 3-23.

Swanson, R. N. (1971). Goal oriented treatment evaluation: A universal and individualized approach. Paper presented at Western Psychological Association, April.

Stelmachers, Z., Lund, S., & Meade, C. (1972). Hennepin County Crisis Intervention Center: Evaluation of its effectiveness. *Evaluation*, **1**, 61–65.

Tasto, D. L. (1977). Self-report schedules and inventories. In A. R. Ciminero, K. S. Calhoun, & H. E. Adams, *Handbook of behavioral assessment*. New York: Wiley. pp. 153–193.

Thompson, A., & Zimmerman, R. (1969). Goals of counseling: whose? when? *Journal of Counseling Psychology*, **16**, 121–125.

Tracy, J. (1977). Impact of intake procedures upon client attrition in a community mental health center. *Journal of Consulting and Clinical Psychology*, **45**(2), 192–195.

Udell, B., & Hornstra, R. K. (1976). Presenting problems and diagnosis. *Comprehensive Psychiatry*, **3**, 437–445.

van der Hart, O., & Lange, A. (1972). Goal attainment scaling: een methode tot evaluatie van psychotherapieen, *Maandblad Geestelijke Volksgezondheid*, **27**, 502–510.

van der Veer, J. (1974). Goal attainment scaling IX: doelenkontrakt also evalutie-methode. Maandblad Geestelijke Volksgezondheid, **19**, 469–480.

Wallin, P. W. (1974). The use of Goal Attainment Scaling as a method of evaluating an inpatient child psychiatry service. Ph.D. dissertation, University of Minnesota (Univ. M-Films No. 74–17302).

Wallin, P. (1974). Annotated bibliography on goal attainment scaling in youth-oriented facilities. Program Evaluation Report. Ph.D. dissertation, University of Minnesota.

Wallin, P., & Koch, M. (1977). The use of goal attainment scaling as a method of evaluating an inpatient child psychiatry service. *Journal of the American Academy of Child Psychiatry*, **16**, 439–445.

Waskow, I. (1975). Selection of a core battery. In I. Waskow & M. Parloff (Eds.), *Phychotherapy change measures*. Washington, D. C.: U. S. Government Printing Office, pp. 245–269.

Waskow, I., & Parloff, M. (1975). *Psychotherapy change measures*. Washington, D. C.: U. S. Government Printing Office.

Weed, L. (1968). Medical records that guide and teach. *New England Journal of Medicine*, **278**, 593–657.

Weinstein, M., Ricks, F. (1977). Goal attainment scaling: Planning and outcome. *Canadian Journal of Behavioral Science*, **9**(1), 1–11.

Werry, J. S., & Wollersheim, J. P. (1967). Behavior therapy with children. *Journal of the American Academy of Child Psychiatry*, **6**, 346–370.

Westman, W. (1974). A solid front: Unity, timing, goal-oriented counseling—break drug addiction cycle. *Journal of Rehabilitation*, May-June, 15–17.

Whittington, H. (1975). A case for private enterprise in mental health. *Administration in Mental Health*, Spring, 23–28.

Willer, B. (1975). The relationship of goal attainment scores and client involvement in goal setting to inpatient therapeutic outcome. *Goal Attainment Review*, **2**, 53–63.

Willer, B., & Miller, G., (1976a). Client involvement in goal setting and its relationship to therapeutic outcome. *Journal of Clinical Psychology*, **32**(3), 687–690.

Willer, B., & Miller, G. (1976b). On the validity of goal attainment scaling as an outcome measure in mental health. *American Journal of Public Health*, **66**(12), 1197–1198.

Wilson, N. (1972). The tri-informant goal oriented automated progress note. Paper presented at American Psychological Association Convention, September.

Wilson, N. C. (1973). The tri-informant goal-oriented progress note. *Journal of Community Psychology,* **1,** 302–306.

Wilson, N. C. (1974). An information system for clinical and administrative decision-making, research and evaluation. In J.L. Crawford (Ed.), *Progress in mental health information systems.* Cambridge, Mass.: Ballinger.

Wilson, N. C., & Mumpower, J. L. (1975). Automated evaluation of goal-attainment ratings. *Hospital and Community Psychiatry,* **26,** 163–164.

Youell, K. F., & McCullough, J. P. (1975). Behavioral treatment of mucous colitis. *Journal of Consulting and Clinical Psychology,* **43,** 740–745.

CHAPTER 16

Research Design and Methods in Community Psychology

JEAN ANN LINNEY AND N. DICKON REPPUCCI

In 1965 a group of discontented psychologists met to discuss new directions for psychology and community mental health (Bennett, Anderson, Cooper, Hassol, Klein, & Rosenblum, 1966). They suggested that psychologists must become more active participants in the general problems facing society, such as poverty and desegregation, because these problems directly and indirectly influence the mental health of the population. This conference has often been cited as the birth of community psychology (Zax & Specter, 1974), for the directions and activities suggested there have characterized the past 15 years of growth and development within the field. While its primary roots are in clinical psychology and community mental health, community psychology has emerged as a distinct approach to the study of human behavior, intervention, and change (Heller & Monahan, 1977; Iscoe, Spielberger, & Bloom, 1977; Rappaport, 1977; Sarason, 1974; Sarason, Levine, Goldenberg, Cherlin, & Bennett, 1966).

At the time of this writing, there are no reviews of research methods particular to community psychology. There have been a few review papers on the nature and quality of research within the field (e.g., Bloom, 1980; Cowen, 1973; Kelly, Snowden, & Munoz, 1979; Novaco & Monahan, 1980) and some papers discussing particular practical difficulties with research and evaluation in community settings (e.g., Cowen, 1978;

Cowen & Gesten, 1980; Kelly, Munoz, & Snowden, 1979). Certainly the literature on program evaluation and evaluation research has expanded exponentially, but this area overlaps with only one segment of the work in community psychology. Perhaps the single most comprehensive presentation of research methods applicable to community psychology is the recent volume on quasi-experimentation by Cook and Campbell (1979).

Community researchers have been guided by the quest for redefinition of research questions and by their interest in particular issues and problems, only to be restrained by the methodologies available. Consequently researchers have examined a wide range of disciplines from psychology to anthropology to biology for research models that might be useful. They have drawn appropriate research strategies from several of the social sciences to the extent that it is difficult to identify a set of research methods that are unique to community psychology. This chapter is intended to overview the strategies available for community research, and in so doing bring together in one place research methods suitable for descriptive and causal inference investigation of community-based issues. It is divided into three major sections. The first section overviews the major foci and defining characteristics of community psychology. The second is an introduction to commonly utilized research designs and developing models. The third summarizes

535

issues in assessment and measurement. Because of the breadth of coverage desired, depth of discussion is necessarily limited. The reader is encouraged to engage in more detailed analysis of any of the specific methods and approaches discussed before adopting them for research purposes.

THE "BUSINESS" OF COMMUNITY PSYCHOLOGY

Community psychology is primarily concerned with the study of social settings and their interface with individuals. The goal is to view individuals and settings in ecological context to improve our understanding and contribute to the resolution of social problems. Implied in these activities is a research focus on the social and physical environment, and the need for multilevel, multivariable research methodologies As a field within psychology, community psychology has grown from several disciplines and continues to draw from the methodologies of these disciplines in its process of development. Community psychology shares with clinical psychology the concern for individual well-being, but its focus is more on prevention than cure. Moreover, its target of intervention is not the individual but rather populations of people, and the organizations and systems that affect these populations (Goodstein & Sandler, 1979; Heller & Monahan, 1977). Its basic values encompass a respect for cultural relativity, a valuing of diversity in human behavior, a focus on the strengths rather than weaknesses of individuals, and the adoption of an ecological perspective (Rappaport, 1977). It draws from social and organizational psychology research on group process and organizational behavior. Many of the content issues of concern to community psychologists are equally of interest to sociologists, anthropologists, educational researchers, urban planners, architects, and political scientists; issues such as work and family life, community organization, school

reform, and unemployment. For many of these social issues, the bulk of research and theory has been developed outside of psychology. The community psychologist, however, is concerned with their impact not only on individuals but also at the multiple levels of society, that is, individuals, small groups such as family or peers, organizations, and community, as they affect individuals.

Historically psychology has dealt primarily with the identification and understanding of the principles of behavior governing the individual and group levels. As a result there are many theories of personality and individual behavior (Hall & Lindzey, 1978), and a developing understanding of group process and group change (Minuchin, 1974; Yalom, 1975). At the organizational level of analysis, much of industrial psychology focuses on individuals in the organizational context (Porter, Lawler, & Hackman, 1975), while a smaller number of organizational psychologists are considering the functioning of organizations as entities and hypothesizing their principles of operation (Katz & Kahn, 1978). The institutional, community, and societal levels of analysis are domains virtually untouched by psychological research. Concomitantly we have paid little notice to the interrelations, transactions, and interfaces between and among the several levels. Apart from the theoretical work by Watzlawick, Weakland, and Fisch (1974) on change among individuals and families, few researchers have systematically or empirically examined cross-level relationships. Nevertheless, the importance of these interlevel relations is widely acknowledged. Family systems therapists have written extensively on the impact of family (group) interactional patterns on individual behavior (Minuchin, 1974). Similarly, organizational change agents, such as those attempting school reform or change within a human service facility, are routinely limited by the constraints of institutional regulations (Reppucci, 1977; Reppucci & Saunders, 1974; Sarason, 1971). It is in change endeavors that these interlevel maintenance mechanisms are most directly felt. However, interlevel linkage provides important feedback for the maintenance and change of settings and the individuals served by these settings. Therefore, in the design and evaluation of intervention, both implementation and potential results may be largely determined by the strength of cross-level maintenance mechanisms.

A levels schema has further implications for the conceptualization of research issues and the identification of relevant variables and constructs for the community psychologist. Implicit in the schema is the knowledge that multiple levels determine or contribute to both the creation of any issue and its problem resolution. Therefore, it is important to examine any problem or social issue from each of the levels within the schema. For example, the high school dropout is again becoming a major concern to educators and employers. Although the high school dropout rate has declined in the United States for the past 80 years, there are many social and economic factors contributing to its identification as a contemporary social problem. These are in large part a result of the multiple effects and systemic repercussions generated by an increasing number of adolescents out of school, for example, increasing the labor force too rapidly, higher unemployment, and reduction in school enrollments leading to teacher unemployment. Considering the school dropout issue within the levels of analysis schema leads to consideration of substantially different intervention strategies and research variables. Adopting the learned helplessness paradigm, Reppucci and Allen (1980) have analyzed the school dropout phenomena on four levels. At the individual level they suggest that students who evidence learned helplessness may be more likely to drop out of school. From this analysis any intervention efforts might focus on alleviating learned helplessness and assessing those results by means of measures of individual locus of control and school attendance. Adopting a group perspective, they

hypothesize that the peer group or family may not be supportive of education, may draw the student into other activities that compete with school, or may define status in terms that are mutually exclusive of education. From this analysis intervention efforts should be directed at altering the norms and behavior of families and peer groups, and outcome measures would include assessments of group variables. At the organizational and community level the relevant variables and explanations would be directed at school and community processes. Ultimately intervention goals might be defined at each of these levels, for example, intervention that affects classroom process may have radiating effects (Kelly, 1971) at the small group and individual levels including increased school attendance, or change in group composition and activities. Effects may also radiate to the community in the form of employment pattern changes or alterations in juvenile crime statistics.

A primary task of future research and theory building in community psychology is defining the linkage between the psychology of individuals and the psychology of social settings and social events, in other words, giving substance to the concept of person-environment fit. Related to this basic concern are questions with implications for intervention and social change, such as: identification of the critical components of treatment settings (e.g., group homes, residential programs, crisis centers) that contribute to desired behavior change (Price & Blashfield, 1975); how to produce ecological change within an existing setting (Reppucci, 1973); and the creation and maintenance of settings (Sarason, 1972). The ultimate goal is the development of preventive intervention (Cowen, 1977; 1980; Kelly, 1968; Kessler & Albee, 1977) that will enhance the quality of life for entire populations (Iscoe, 1974; Sarason, 1974).

How do we go about accomplishing these objectives? While the research strategies, the research settings, and the issues being addressed by community researchers are widely varied, the activities can be clustered into three major categories: (1) intervention, planned change, and research involving systematic, experimental manipulation of variables; (2) evaluation and policy analysis; and (3) descriptive and relational research contributing to the construction of conceptual models, the development of theory, and a data base to inform social policy. Ideally these three activities are interrelated, in that research directed toward theoretical development should suggest points of intervention and allow for the prediction of intervention consequences, both intended and unintended. Intervention activities and their careful evaluation can be designed to provide data on relationships and operating mechanisms within interdependent systems. The precipitation of change through directed intervention offers evidence of the patterns of interrelations within the system, for example, changing one part of the homeostatic system should result in some change among those variables that are interconnected. Similarly, monitoring change at multiple levels among multiple variables should lead to a better understanding of the operational system. Many of the issues of concern to community researchers are typically not within the realm of experimental control (e.g., the impact of poverty on family life, the effects of racially segregated education, community control of schools, the effects of joint custody decisions) for a variety of practical, legal, political, and ethical reasons. In these areas community researchers need to rely on alternative methods for research, that is, quasi-experimental models and descriptive, naturalistic observation methods, naturally occurring changes or interventions such as legislation and policy changes, and naturally occurring contrast groups.

The methodological tools utilized in community research are diverse. The nature of the content and the ecological context necessitates consideration of multiple independent and dependent variables, which in turn often requires sizable samples and observations. While the practical problems of managing such large research projects are considerable, the statistical difficulties involved in the data analysis are of equal weight. Nevertheless, the process of research and many of the problems of community psychologists are shared in other fields. While the community researcher may have little occasion to employ the Solomon-four-group-design (Campbell & Stanley, 1966) or other more traditional laboratory research methods, the objective of the research process remains the identification of causal patterns and relationships utilizing hypothesis testing models. As such, similar rules of inference and consideration of data are applicable.

In the following section an overview of commonly adopted research designs is presented, including quasi-experimental methods, observational methods allowing for causal inference, and descriptive ecological models. Although it is beyond the scope of this chapter to discuss the statistical procedures accompanying these methods, the use of multivariate analyses (Harris, 1975; Tatsuoka, 1971; Timm, 1975) is often presupposed. The development of multivariate methods has provided researchers with the tools necessary to examine relationships among the multiple variables and levels of analysis conceptualized, and has facilitated the creation of more alternative ecological designs.

RESEARCH DESIGNS TO ASSESS CHANGE AND IDENTIFY CAUSAL RELATIONSHIPS

An implicit goal in the research process is the ability to manipulate, isolate, and test the functions of specific variables germane to theory development. However, when psychological research moved out of the laboratory setting and focused on naturally occurring events and the precipitation of phenomena in ecological context, the opportunity to manipulate and gain experimental control over variables of interest was seriously limited. Given the concern for causal inference and the limitations on control, a variety of research strategies has been proposed for investigation of community-based phenomena.

Experimental Social Innovation

Among the designs and methods suggested for community research, perhaps the most similar to traditional "laboratory" psychological research methods is Fairweather's model of Experimental Social Innovation (ESI) (Fairweather, 1967; Fairweather & Tornatsky, 1977). While others have suggested strategies for "getting around" the problems stemming from inadequate control, Fairweather has argued that researchers must engage in strategies to obtain the necessary control and cooperation from community groups and participants. Basing his model on the assumption that social scientists should become more actively involved in the solution of social problems, he argues that systematic study of a problem will generate innovative alternatives. Careful implementation of these innovations, in conjunction with scientific evaluation and research, will then indicate which of the innovations is most effective in alleviating the problem addressed. In essence, Fairweather's model of ESI is the scientific method applied outside of the confines of the laboratory walls. He proposes that "To have an effective scientific evaluation of two or more models, an experiment must be carried out" (Fairweather, 1972).

Fairweather outlines the process of ESI beginning with the definition and delineation of an important human problem. Once the problem area is delineated, the researcher should become expert in all areas of knowledge related to this problem. Drawing from Lewin's (1946) action research model, Fairweather proposes that knowledge be gathered from existing literature and discussions with

those affected by the problem. For example, if one is concerned about school failure, several groups of people should be consulted, including those children failing in school, teachers, school administrators, parents, and perhaps other students who are not performing poorly but who may be directly or indirectly affected by these students. From this information, strategies can be devised that may correct the problem. Typically two or more strategies will emerge from this process, "treatment as usual" and one or more innovations or kinds of interventions. A multiple group experimental design can be employed to examine systematically the effects of these manipulations (Mahoney, 1978).

Throughout the process of problem formulation and intervention design the researcher has the opportunity to gain entry into the multiple settings potentially affected and to establish credibility with the persons involved. The researcher's credibility and the sense of trust established are critical to the development of an experimental design in a naturalistic setting, including random assignment to intervention groups, multiple assessments, and comparison-control groups. To ensure the integrity of the experiment, Fairweather suggests that extensive written agreements be arranged among all groups involved regarding the conditions and maintenance of the experimental program. Any anticipated difficulties might specifically be dealt with prior to the program implementation, including personnel, resource needs, and time demands. While this process may be unrealistic in many cases and legalistic in most, experienced community researchers and evaluators know all too well the difficulties that arise from misperceptions and misunderstandings about what commitments were being made (Cowen, 1978). Many community-based research projects are seriously compromised because of an absence of clarity in expectations and mutual responsibilities.

The implementation and assessment of the intervention groups would follow this process of entry and definition. The variables to be assessed would be consistent with and dependent upon the content and goals of the programs, would include multiple measures and assessments over time, and would consider the measurement of effects and change at several levels of analysis.

From this brief overview, the similarities between the ESI model and more traditionally conceived research should be apparent. In essence, Fairweather suggests a process of systematically creating and comparatively evaluating alternative settings, and the component parts of each intervention. In Fairweather's own work with the Community Lodge model of psychiatric treatment (Fairweather, Sanders, Cressler, & Maynard, 1969), systematic attempts to replicate the program have resulted in the identification of several essential components contributing to the efficacy of the model, for example, autonomy of each member, open lines of communication within the system, ability to substitute roles within the system, and the presence of defined work norms (Fairweather, 1979).

As a model for making causal inferences, the ESI research strategy is similar in power to the pretest-posttest control group design controlling for threats to internal validity (Campbell & Stanley, 1966). While the research is conducted in naturalistic field settings, the programs (or experimental manipulations) are generated and managed by the research team and are therefore somewhat contrived. As such, the external validity and generalizability of the research findings remain to be established. Rappaport, Seidman, and Davidson (1979) have reported the findings of an adolescent diversion program utilizing the ESI model, and have discussed several unintended consequences and results when the program supervisors and the locus of decision making were transferred from the research staff to the juvenile justice system itself. These authors suggest that the very creation and operation of the program by agents external to the juvenile justice system may have been integral to its success.

Fairweather's proposal for research within the ESI model implies and is based on a redefinition of the researcher's role as an activist and change agent as well as evaluator and scientist. This is quite compatible with the intervention-action and social change values of community psychology. The model is most useful for change programs and the examination of differential results when the investigator has sufficient control of the situations to randomly determine the intervention groups. Many although not all intervention programs initiated by the researcher should be amenable to this model of investigation. Fairweather suggests that the process of experimental social innovation does not end when the data are analyzed, but that the researcher is responsible for the dissemination of the findings and the further implementation of successful intervention (Fairweather, Sanders, & Tornatzky, 1974). While few researchers have continued into this secondary implementation phase, several have adopted the pre–post multiple group designs advocated.

Nonequivalent Control Group Designs

In most field research not engineered by the researcher, random assignment is difficult, if not impossible. Therefore, the formation of randomly determined and experimentally comparable groups is either precluded or severely restricted. Much intervention includes participation of all "subjects." For example, classroom intervention often affects all children in the classrooms, leaving no option for random selection within classrooms. Similarly, examination of a desegregation program that involves an entire school district removes the option of a within district control. In other kinds of intervention, participants frequently are recruited by self-selection and volunteering, which may yield a critically small sample, again precluding the formation of a randomly determined control group. In these circumstances the community researchers can identify a "similar" group or community agency not involved in the experimental manipulation. Such a nonequivalent group can be treated as a control group for comparison and the generation of causal relationships.

The identification of a suitable control group is a critical aspect of the design. In many kinds of community research, particularly organizational and systemic intervention methods, control groups are not readily apparent. Community researchers concerned with the investigation of system-wide changes in policy or programs that may affect the bulk of the population are often forced to seek nonequivalent control groups in other communities. For example, a school district may desegregate, adopt a new set of curricular materials, or require staff to participate in organizational development workshops to enhance communication within the school setting. In this kind of district or system-wide intervention a control group within the system is unavailable. If the researcher has been actively involved in the school setting prior to the change, he or she might be instrumental in shaping the implementation process to approximate a "true" experimental design allowing for comparison groups within the district, or a cohort model of implementation in which the intervention is "phased in" to the system allowing a series of comparisons among those involved and those not. Each group can also serve as its own control. For example, Mulvey and Reppucci (in press) introduced a conflict resolution training program in a community police department using a simple cohort procedure. Half of the police officers were trained in the first two-week session of training, while the remainder served as a control group. Eight weeks later the second group was trained, and follow-up assessments were completed on all trained officers.

When the researcher does not have this degree of input in implementing the intervention method, or when the expected outcome and impact of the intervention method are far-reaching, the researcher may need to identify a similar social system or community as a nonequivalent control group. Delaney, Seidman, and Willis (1978) evaluated the impact of a crisis intervention service on hospital admission rates in a mental health center catchment area. The crisis intervention service was designed to serve the entire catchment area and was intended to reduce hospital psychiatric admissions for the area. The systemic nature of the intervention precluded identification of a control group per se within the district. The researchers identified a second catchment area similar in population, employment, and geographical characteristics as a comparison group. Likewise Maccoby and his colleagues (Maccoby & Alexander, 1979; Maccoby & Farquhar, 1975) used three roughly comparable communities to investigate the use of mass media in reducing heart disease risk. One community received health education through the mass media alone. A second town received education through mass media and, for a selected high risk group, intensive education. A third town served as a no intervention control.

In such research situations, great care needs to be taken in the identification of the nonequivalent control group. The use of a control group design is based on the assumption that similar processes are affecting both the experimental and control groups, and that differences between the groups following the manipulation can be attributed to the treatment. Cook and Campbell (1979) have discussed in detail the potential validity threats, including selection-maturation interaction and differential statistical regression, stemming from the selection of a control group that may not be composed of members from the same population as the experimental group. Therefore, the adequacy of the control group is crucial to both the study's internal validity and the ecological validity of the findings. In selecting a nonequivalent control group, the researcher should consider as many variables as possible including demographic, psychosocial, organizational, and community factors in determining the "equivalence" of the groups. Researchers typically match individuals in groups for socioeconomic factors, racial composition, sex, age, and any other variables thought to be relevant to the experimental manipulation. When the unit of analysis is other than the individual, such as a school or classroom, the comparison groups should be selected on the basis of a similar variety of variables, for example, student demographics, teacher characteristics, size of setting, curriculum methods, school attitudes, organizational patterns, and type of community.

The nonequivalent control group design is frequently adopted for community-based intervention and evaluation research. With pre- and postassessments, the design parallels the experimental pre–post control group design (Campbell & Stanley, 1966). To the extent that the groups included in the design are comparable, group differences can be causally related to the intervention or experimental manipulation.

Time Series Designs

The time series design in its simplest form is a sequence of observations on a dependent variable over some time period. The frequently seen charts of monthly unemployment rates or wholesale indicators are examples of time series. Examination of the line defined by these indicators over time shows directional change and trends, for example, we are familiar with interpreting time series graphs showing increasing gasoline prices and declining SAT scores during recent years. The observations in a time series can be based on the same persons or on different but similar units. For example, a graph of daily or weekly weights for each member of a dieting group (same persons throughout) would display the effects of dieting over time. When more concerned with systematic change over time than change in specific persons, assessments can be made of different persons. For example, to examine performance on the SAT over time, the scores of different individuals each year would be included. Similarly, analysis of the quality of life, average family income, or hospital ad-

missions over time would include different samples of individuals over the years of observation.

To examine change resulting from an intervention, either experimentally introduced or "naturally" occurring, the *interrupted time series design* can be used in which two time series are compared, one prior to the intervention and the other following the intervention. Delaney, Seidman, and Willis (1978) employed the interrupted time series design to examine the impact of a crisis intervention service on psychiatric hospital admissions. They compared state hospital admissions in the service region for two years prior to the introduction of the service with admission rates for two years following the service's beginning. The graph of hospitalization rates showed a substantial decrease in the number of admissions following the availability of the service. In this data both the slope and the level of the lines differed pre to post, indicating that the overall number and the rate of hospital admissions changed following the commencement of the crisis service.

The interrupted time series may indicate change corresponding to the onset of an intervention, but causal inference from a single time series is weak, at best. For example, the changes reported by Delaney et al. (1978) might have corresponded to the opening of a new factory in the service region providing jobs and income for residents, or might have been part of more long-term regional trends or seasonal fluctuations. Without the addition of a nonequivalent control group and a sufficiently long time series, these rival hypotheses cannot be eliminated. Paralleling the *interrupted time series with a nonequivalent control group* time series substantially improves the design. While the validity threats due to history and selection (Cook & Campbell, 1979) may never be completely eliminated in a quasi-experimental design, with a substantial number of observations, a sufficiently long time series and multiple valid measures, causal inferences may be drawn from this design.

Cook and Campbell (1979) present a variation of the behavioral A-B-A reversal design with the *interrupted time series with multiple replications* design. In this design a treatment is introduced, removed, and reintroduced multiple times according to a planned schedule. The design is powerful for inferring causal relationships and may be useful in controlled settings such as schools, hospitals, and prisons, in which the intervention is discrete and the effects of the intervention are expected to dissipate rapidly. The research of Neitzel and Dade (1973) reporting the effects of introducing an experimental "release-on-recognizance" (ROR) program in an adult court system approximates this design. The researchers compared pretrial release figures and court appearance violations prior to, during, and following the termination of the program. While the researchers had expected that the program would change the court's use of this option following termination, they reported that ROR rates returned to preprogram levels. Although not totally intended, this design is illustrative of the interrupted time series with multiple replications. The ROR intervention program proved to be discrete, and the return to "base line" levels of performance dramatically demonstrated the program's short-term positive effect, while at the same time demonstrating its inability to change routine organizational practices. Reintroducing the ROR program and again withdrawing researcher involvement would provide for additional replications of program impact and further increase the power of causal interpretations drawn from this design.

One measurement issue of time series designs inheres in the fact that they are frequently adopted for analysis of changes over which the researcher has little or no control, for example, legislation or change in the past. Consequently archival data of some sort must form the dependent measures. Researchers are well aware of the difficulties inherent in archival data including problems of reliability, changes in recording procedures, and data collection priorities (Cook & Campbell, 1979; Cowen, 1978; Selltiz, Wrightsman, & Cook, 1976). Perhaps more significant should be a concern for the appropriateness of the dependent variables abstracted from archival records. Research reports typically include some explanation of why the measures examined were chosen and the shortcomings inherent, apologizing for the questionable relevance and validity of the measures. Since research is only as good as the measures adopted, the measurement problems of time series using archival data can be substantial. In circumstances in which archival data is used, the researchers should be cautious in inferring causal relationships and make every effort to understand and report the data problems suspected. Long-term continuous involvement in a particular social system with concomitant data collection can result in the building of data sources for subsequent time series analysis. However, given an often lengthy time period desired and the nature of the issues investigated with time series designs, measurement problems appear unavoidable.

A second measurement issue of all time series designs concerns the length of the time series, the number of observations, and the interval between observations. The total length of time included and the intervals of observation should be sufficiently long so that routine or random fluctuations may be distinguished from the intervention impact. The interval of observation is best determined by the nature of the phenomena investigated and consideration of base rates for various observation intervals. For example, Delaney et al. (1978) chose to analyze *quarterly* hospital admission data, while Johnson, Jurick, Kreb, and Rose (1978) examined *daily* bicycle accident statistics on a college campus. Unfortunately, most researchers' choice of observation intervals is determined more by the form of available records and archival data than as a result of theoretical or empirical rationales.

The overall time length included in the

design has implications both statistically and in terms of the identification of change effects. Most authors (Cook & Campbell, 1979; Glass, Wilson, & Gottman, 1975) dealing with the statistical analysis of time series designs suggest about 50 observation points for an adequate analysis. This "rule of thumb" may also bear on the determination of interval when possible. In reality, 50 observation time series may be extremely difficult to achieve. In general the series should be as long as practically possible, since apart from statistical considerations there are additional concerns about the real significance and validity of the findings. For example, using a very short time series examining the impact of a desegregation plan, Linney and Seidman (1978) have suggested that substantially different results are observed by including only a few additional observations. In the interrupted time series analysis, change may be immediately obvious following the intervention, or actual changes may take a longer time to appear. Similarly, change may be observed, but in a longer series of follow-up observations it may dissipate. It is only with sufficiently long observation periods that these different patterns of change can be examined adequately. What constitutes a "sufficiently long period" should again be determined whenever possible by theoretical consideration and realistic predictions based on previous research.

When a time series includes only one dependent measure, the findings usually add little to the construction of nomological networks (Cronbach & Meehl, 1955) or to the understanding of ecological interrelationships existing within the larger system. Collection of time series data for additional nonequivalent dependent variables and other theoretically related variables allows for more systematic consideration of change. For example, in their study of change in psychiatric hospitalization rates, Delaney et al. (1978) might also have gathered time series data on arrests for disorderly behavior or

vagrancy, number of clients seen at the mental health center, or the number of psychotropic drug prescriptions filled during the time periods of concern. If the community is conceptualized as an open system with interrelating parts and a cycling of resources, then such data would have provided a more comprehensive picture of the ecological interconnections. If hospital admissions are decreased as a consequence of a crisis intervention project, then those people (clients) should be utilizing other resources in the community or occupying other roles within the system. They may be in jail instead of the hospital, receiving outpatient services, or being maintained in the community by drug treatment. These variables are based on the assumption that they maintain a deviant role of some sort. It may be also the case that crisis intervention precipitated or facilitated role relationship changes (Fairweather, 1972), and the persons are filling more productive roles in society, such as attending school, seeking or maintaining employment, or living independently.

Similar time series data could be gathered on these and other relevant variables. Adopting the ecological perspective and the multilevel organization analysis of community psychology requires that research become more focused toward identifying systematic patterns and interrelationships. The examination of multiple measures allows not only for the enhancement of the validity of the study, but also for the elementary identification of interrelationships and limited hypothesis testing.

A similar strategy of multiple related dependent variables has been proposed by Cook and Campbell (1979) to isolate potential internal validity threats in the time series design due to history, that is, "the possibility that forces other than the treatment under investigation came to influence the dependent variable". By comparing time series data for measures that should be affected by the intervention and related measures not expected to change with the intervention, the investigator can separate intervention effects from historical changes. For example, to evaluate the effectiveness of the British breathalyser crackdown of 1967, Ross, Campbell, and Glass (1970) examined change in the total number of traffic fatalities, traffic fatalities on weekend nights only, and traffic fatalities during the hours the pubs were closed. The breathalyser test was intended to reduce the incidence of drunken driving and in turn associated traffic fatalities. If the breathalyser was effective, a reduction in fatalities should be the most dramatic on the weekend nights and have only minimal impact on the other times of day. Other effects, such as weather, safer cars, and crackdown on speeding, would not be expected to differentially affect these measures.

The time series designs are particularly useful for intervention and evaluation research among community psychologists. The designs allow for the determination of significant changes and for some causal inference, assuming the adequacy of the comparison group, the length of the time series, and the dependent measures. With multiple measures and multiple observations, reasonable reliability and construct validity among the variables can be established, and ecological systemic hypotheses may be examined. Typically, the phenomena of interest in community research are expected to show long-term, nonimmediate, or fluctuating effects, for example, the impact of birth control programs on adolescent pregnancy rates, or attitude changes stemming from public education efforts. Prevention programs, a primary focal issue within community psychology, may only be examined adequately after relatively long time periods. For example, an elementary school program designed to prevent adult psychiatric disorder can only be evaluated by assessments into adulthood. Cowen, Pederson, Babigan, Izzo, and Trost (1973) have reported an 18-year follow-up of the validity of their selection procedures for a school-based prevention program. While the design they employed was not an extended time series, the inclusion of fixed interval time series observations could have provided a more adequate evaluation of the preventive effects of this program and a clearer understanding of the pattern of change over time.

Practically speaking, there are an infinite number of obstacles to completing large scale, long-term time series designs, not the least of which are the geographical mobility rates of the participants and the expense involved in data collection. The point to be considered, however, is the importance of the time series design as a model for research. If more researchers were to adopt this approach, new sources of data or alternative strategies for data collection may become apparent. The Cowen et al. (1973) study is a good example of how an eye toward long-term examination may indicate sources of archival data. These investigators searched the county psychiatric records for the names of children who 18 years earlier had been identified as high risk for academic and behavioral difficulties. While there were many flaws in this particular data source, and causal inferences may be made only with extreme caution, the findings shed light on important variables such as early peer relationships and peer expectations, and generated further hypotheses for research. Given the concern for preventive intervention among community researchers (Price, Ketterer, Bader, & Monahan, 1980), the lack of long-term (or short-term for that matter) systematic follow-up is striking. Future research, particularly in the field of prevention, can be significantly strengthened by a longer time perspective, inclusion of a larger number of potentially relevant variables, and increased use of time series designs to examine both experimenter-induced and naturally occurring changes resulting from social, political, or economic factors outside the control of investigators.

Making Causal Inference from Passive Observation

Oftentimes the phenomena of interest to community researchers are not amenable to manipulation, nor are there appropriately discrete and identifiable "changes" that allow for interrupted time series analysis. For example, researchers have long been interested in the causal relationships between demographic factors and school performance, between individual aggression and viewing television violence, and between integrated classrooms and race relations. Three related strategies are presented here to deal with these and similar research issues: (1) cross lagged panel designs; (2) path analysis for causal modeling; and (3) epidemiological models. Being primarily correlational in nature, these strategies require large samples and relatively strong relationships among the variables for the identification of causal patterns that are determined by comparison of the relative magnitudes of the intercorrelations. The results can be used to generate hypotheses for further research and provide a means of examining nonmanipulable phenomena. However, it should be noted that definitions of significance for these relationships are less clear than those for hypothesis testing models. Moreover, sufficient controversy remains regarding the necessary and sufficient conditions for use of each strategy, that the reader is cautioned to pursue in more detail the statistical assumptions and requirements for each.

Cross Lagged Panel Designs.

Panel designs are employed to infer causal directionality among co-occurring measures or constructs assessed simultaneously at two or more times for a number of persons or other units. By examining and comparing the intercorrelations of the two measures at two time points, it is possible to determine causal relationships and test for "spuriousness," that is, that the dependent measures share a causal relation and do not covary as a consequence

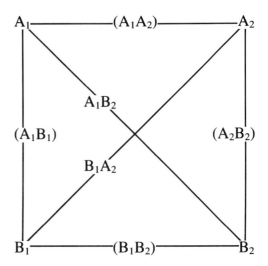

Figure 16-1. Model of cross lagged panel design and background correlations with two measures (A and B) and two assessment times (1 and 2).

of a third "spurious" variable (Kenny, 1975). Causal inferences are made in the context of the underlying relational conditions among the measures over time (Figure 16-1). First, the correlation between the two measures within each time period should be similiar across the assessment times included in the design ($A_1 B_1$ and $A_2 B_2$). This "stationarity" between measures indicates that the structural equation, or relationship between the variables, remains the same. Second, temporal stability or test retest reliability of each measure needs to be established. Ideally the reliability coefficients of each measure should be similar ($A_1 A_2$ and $B_1 B_2$). When these conditions are met, causal inferences can be drawn from differences in the cross lagged correlations ($A_1 B_2$ and $B_1 A_2$). The interpretation of the intercorrelation matrix reflects the assumption that a compilation or cumulative effect is indicative of causality. If both measures are reliable and the structural relation between them remains similar at each time point, then if A is a stronger cause of B, over time the correlation between A_1 and B_2 will be larger than B_1 and A_2 by virtue of this "storage process" (Cook & Campbell, 1979).

The stationarity and stability assumptions are basic to the cross lagged panel design logic. Several computational corrections have been offered to adjust the cross lagged correlations if the autocorrelations (reliability) or synchronous correlations (stationarity) are not adequate (Crano, Kenny, & Campbell, 1972). The Z transformation suggested by Peters and Van Voorhis (1940) can be used to test the significance of the differences between the cross lagged correlations. These "computational" corrections provide a procedure for statistical adjustments. However, reasonable ambiguity remains as to what magnitude of similarity or difference in correlations constitutes adherence to the assumptions.

The cross lagged panel design has been employed to examine a variety of hypothesized causal relationships including aggression and viewing television violence (Eron, Heusmann, Lefkowitz, & Walder, 1972), specific academic skills and achievement (Crano, Kenny, & Campbell, 1972), causal patterns among 15 cognitive skills (Atkin, Bray, Davison, Herzberger, Humphreys, & Selzer, 1977), air pollution and mortality (Lave & Sesken, 1977), and classroom racial composition and classroom behavior (Linney, 1978). This design is potentially useful for community psychologists to examine causal relationships among nonmanipulable organizational and societal level variables, for example, economic factors and psychiatric symptoms, school size and school achievement, or stress and family violence. The design can be expanded to include more than two assessment times and two variables, although adherence to the statistical assumptions becomes more difficult as the variables and assessments increase.

Path Analysis for Causal Modeling.
The ecological and systemic perspectives of community psychology indicate the need for research models allowing for multiplicative

causal relationships, and strategies for describing the interrelationship among an array of variables. While the time series, nonequivalent control group, and cross lagged panel designs may (and should) include multiple measures, the designs do not directly test for multiple causal relationships or contribute to the development of multivariable, ecological models of interrelationships. Causal modeling with path analysis techniques provides one approach for this kind of description and theory development. These techniques have gained increasing prominence in sociology, economics, and political science, and are appearing more and more frequently in the psychological research literature.

While the specifics of path analysis are quite complex and will not be presented here, in the most simple form the techniques are intended for the mapping of interrelationships among a set of variables theoretically and empirically determined to covary. The resulting model and the process of development are similar in form and process to the construction of "nomological nets" described by Cronbach and Meehl (1955) for establishing construct validity. As Cook and Campbell (1979) explain:

Starting from one's theoretical, empirical, and commonsense knowledge of a problem, one maps all of the latent variables one believes to be present and the probable causal links among them, indicating which paths are positive and which negative. One adds in the measured variables already available and those that might be obtained. . . . By adding in estimated path coefficients, one can derive predictions about the size and direction of the correlation coefficients that one would expect between measured variables. (pp. 307–308)

Like cross lagged panel analysis, large sample sets are required, since correlation is the primary statistic of path analysis. Similarly, the attribution of causal direction is rooted in examination of the pattern and relative magnitudes of a set of intercorrelations. While there are several specific techniques and "significance tests" available for systematically developing path models, identifying restrictive conditions and the causal ordering of variables, and dealing with method variance and the influence of unobserved variables (Duncan, 1975; Goldberger & Duncan, 1973; Jöreskog, 1970, 1974; Jöreskog & Sorhom, 1978), Cook and Campbell (1979), among others, warn that the technique should not be used in the absence of a theoretical model. Duncan (1975) asserts that "It is the gravest kind of fallacy to suppose that, from a number of competing models involving different causal orderings, one can select the true model by finding the one that comes closest to satisfying a particular test of overidentifying restrictions" (p. 50). Because of the sequential process of developing path models, and the multiple causal arrangements of variables possible, path analysis and causal modeling techniques may be most useful and most applicable for mapping and clarifying theoretical relationships among a set of variables, modifying the theoretical model, and generating hypotheses that might be tested with more experimental research methods.

In the psychological research literature, path analytic techniques have most commonly been employed for analysis of a set of individual level variables. For example, Maruyama and McGarvey (1980) examined the causal relationships among achievement, peer acceptance, adjustment, and family variables of elementary school children. For the community psychologist path analysis can be useful in developing ecological models to describe social-clinical phenomena. With large enough sample sizes and sufficient variance in the measures, the techniques may be utilized to develop models linking measures from several levels, including the individual, family, and organizational. For example, we may examine school performance including individual variables like aptitudes, interests, and achievement with organizational variables assessing schools, for example, classroom social climate (Moos, 1978), and the process of interaction occur-

ring in the classroom. Rutter, Maughan, Mortimore, and Ouston (1979) have examined these variables in the London public schools and utilized some forms of path analysis with log-linear modeling to determine causal relationships. They find significant causal relationships between a child's standardized achievement scores and the child's measured ability, family occupational status, and a composite of school process measures.

The major difficulty in utilizing this technique to link multiple levels of analysis stems from the restricted variance in the higher order level variables, for example, while individuals may fall along the full range of any particular measure, each organization has only one measurement for each variable, which applies equally to each individual within the organization. Hence in a school system there may be 1000 students and 10 schools. For the school variables, then, the sample size is actually only 10, and each of the measurements of those variables is repeated many times within the analyses. Thus restricted variance will seriously attenuate the correlations and potentially mask relationships.

Despite these measurement and statistical difficulties, the causal modeling designs have important heuristic and paradigmatic value for the development of multivariable, ecological models in community psychology. Researchers should be keenly aware of both the potential and the limitations of these techniques for theoretical development in the field.

Epidemiology. Research in community psychology may be directed at any one of several levels of organization and the relationships between them. As the field has grown and become more cognizant of the impact of social and community variables on various forms of behavioral adaptation, researchers have sought designs that might allow for description and analysis of these community variables. Epidemiology, "the study of the distribution and determinants of disease prevalence" (Bloom, 1977) in a community, offers a strategy potentially useful for description of community behavior patterns. Epidemiological research is primarily the bailiwick of sociologists, demographers, geographers, and public health specialists. Their work has been instrumental in the study of psychopathology and socioeconomic factors (Catalano, 1979; Faris & Dunham, 1939; Hollingshead & Redlich, 1958). Similarly, the model has been employed by community psychologists in the study of psychological disorder, social status, and stress (Dohrenwend & Dohrenwend, 1969).

Simply stated, epidemiology is concerned with counting cases of disease or disorder and determining the incidence and prevalence of the problems under study. By geographically displaying the cases identified and considering other factors that are similarly distributed, causal hypotheses may be generated linking the disorder with these other variables, for example, social conditions. While epidemiological analysis is frequently cited in conjunction with disease prevention in public health, the utility of the approach for prevention in mental health and other social service systems is less clearcut. Given the relativity and ambiguity in definitions of mental health and adjustment, the specification of what constitutes a case to be counted is often debatable, and thus the delineation of causal factors may be equally problematic. Heller and Monahan (1977) have suggested that the inherent disease focus of the method is a serious limitation to its use for community researchers in general. The strategy is most applicable to the study of relatively clearly defined categories of behavior, for example, school dropout, or specific handicapping condition, and rests on the assumption of the reliability of identification and reporting mechanisms.

The methodology can be useful as a measurement strategy and assessment technique for community based research. Incidence and prevalence statistics may be included as dependent variables, or utilized as descriptive assessments for the selection of nonequivalent control communities. Lewis (1977, 1978) has suggested the use of "nearest neighbor analysis" as an epidemiological technique for analyzing the spatial distribution of cases throughout the community in addition to consideration of overall incidence and prevalence rates. The method he describes allows for calculation of a spatial distribution statistic, indicating the degree to which the population of interest is clustered, randomly distributed, or widely dispersed throughout a community. Lewis (1978) has reported the use of this analysis for the distribution of both mental disorder and mental health facilities in a large community. Spatial distribution of particular behavior patterns may be a measure of other underlying social organizational variables in a community, and as such can be an important consideration in determining the "equivalence" of communities. Similarly, this index may be a relevant outcome measure at the community level, useful for assessing the impact of intervention and prevention programs.

Epidemiological research strategies consist primarily of determining the incidence and prevalence of a disease or specific behavioral phenomena. By identifying cases and patterns of incidence, the particular clustering of these cases may indicate covariations with other factors generating causal hypotheses. Within the epidemiological model competing hypotheses regarding causal relationships can be examined by utilizing the techniques in the consideration of naturally occurring changes and contrast groups. Together with cross lagged panel designs and path analyses these correlational models provide useful strategies for systematically studying nonmanipulable phenomena of interest to community researchers.

Research Methods in Ecological Context

Used in conjunction with a strategy of multivariable assessment and multivariate analysis, the designs overviewed in this chapter provide a set of tools for the researcher studying community systems and interventions.

The quasi-experimental designs such as time series and nonequivalent control group designs enable the researcher to draw causal inferences and assess change over time. Application of multivariate statistical techniques and path analysis designs make possible the delineation of multiple, ecological interrelationships among the variables within a working system. Given the "business" of community psychology as described earlier, one essential task remains for the researcher: the study of ecological relationships and interdependencies existing *between* and *among* social groups, organizations, and environments. Implicit in the levels of analysis conceptualization is the assumption that each level of organization has a unique set of operating "rules" (Heller & Monahan, 1977; Rappaport, 1977; Reiff, 1971), and as such the assessment of change as it radiates throughout the multiple levels of an ecological system requires a strategy of studying how changes in one level are "translated" at other levels. Description of these cross-level interdependencies and between-level linkage mechanisms, for example, person–environment transactions, requires a paradigm or conceptual schema for studying cross-level interactions and synapses. While the importance of such an integrative paradigm is widely recognized (Bronfenbrenner, 1979; Bruhn, 1974) in the social sciences, the technical and operational implications of such a model are not yet clearly diagrammed.

Applying the notion of ecology from the biological sciences, Kelly (1966; 1969) has proposed a model of Social Ecology as a research paradigm for studying human systems. Although the model does not define a particular measurement technology or set of unique research designs, the underlying conceptualization of operating social systems implies both specific research questions and the definition of appropriate units of analysis. Unlike other research designs described in this chapter, the Social Ecology paradigm posits a specific theoretical model of social systems and their functioning. As such, it is

as much a theory as it is a research methodology.

Mills and Kelly (1972) suggest that

The ecological perspective provides an approach to dealing with social systems that focuses on interrelationships among the members of significant social groups, and provides long term predictions for the effects of social change on a particular system by noting the manner in which these relationships change in the light of functions introduced as a result of interventions or alterations in environmental parameters. (pp. 157–158)

The "ecological principles" defined by Kelly and his colleagues (Kelly, 1979; Mills & Kelly, 1972; Trickett, Kelly, & Todd, 1972) offer a set of guidelines for studying social systems both in terms of person-environment transactions, and the link among the several organizational levels of analysis comprising and contributing to the system. The model is particularly useful for community researchers as a tool for examining relationships within any given level of analysis, allowing comparisons across diverse settings, and making inferential hypotheses about interlevel relationships, for example, organizational and community levels.

Based on research in biological and human ecosystems, four "ecological principles" have been defined that apply to all "living" systems: interdependence, cycling of resources, adaptation, and succession. Briefly, the principle of interdependence implies an interlocking system of components, that is, every part of any system is interrelated with other components of the system, and, as such, change in one place will have effects elsewhere in the system. If interdependence is assumed in human systems, then the research strategy of isolating and manipulating variables is relevant only to the extent that the dependent variables included represent an array of assessments of interrelated components, and the manipulations clarify or identify the nature of the interdependencies. The need for multiple measures of theoretically related constructs already stated further reflects this interdependence assumption. An a priori social ecological analysis can provide a guide in the selection of these dependent variables.

The second ecological principle states that any social system has a mechanism or set of mechanisms for cycling resources throughout the various components of the system. From a theoretical perspective, this principle suggests that the mechanisms governing the distribution and cycling of resources may be critical both for bringing about change and maintaining equilibrium in the system. Identifying resources and the pattern of resource cycling may be important in determining power, decision making, and role relationships within the system. For community-based interventions directed toward the development or redistribution of resources, change may be successful to the extent that the existing resource cycling system is compatible with or changed by the intervention. The principle of resource cycling suggests alternative "units of analysis" focusing on links among the various components of the ecosystem, for example, the rate of exchange, the pattern of resource distribution throughout the system (i.e., Lewis's "nearest neighbor analysis" described above), the temporal unit of cycling, or status enhancing resources exchanged among the ecosystem components.

The principle of adaptation is reflected in the notion that each environment requires a set of adaptive skills, and that specific behavior may be adaptive in one setting while maladaptive or inappropriate in another setting. In any social system, person-environment fit may be examined in the context of the principle of adaptation, that is, to what extent are the adaptative skills demanded by a setting consistent with the adaptive skills of the persons expected to function in the setting?

In any social setting, a continuous process of adaptation between both persons influencing environments and vice versa maintains a dynamic equilibrium and controls change over time. The principle of succession emphasizes this process of continual change over time. For the community researcher, succession implies that both the mechanisms of stability and change need be examined in the ecological study of behavior and in the design and implementation of intervention. The principle of succession is particularly relevant to the community researcher in highlighting the importance of a time perspective, the need for longitudinal research, and consideration of historical developments (Reppucci & Saunders, 1977; Sarason, 1972). The researcher should be alerted to the assessment and definition of systemic change already ongoing in the system.

Mills and Kelly (1972) have applied the Social Ecology model to analysis of cultural adaptation and change in three Mexican villages. Their analysis and application of the four ecological principles highlight the research implications of adopting this model. For example, application of these principles to the study of economic systems, political structures, religious systems, or education not only outline a multifaceted assessment strategy but also provide a set of metadimensions with which to link the several social systems and make comparisons cross-situationally and cross-culturally. Trickett, Kelly, and Todd (1972) have examined the public high school setting within the Social Ecology framework, and they discuss mechanisms linking processes at the individual, group, and organizational levels of analysis. For example, the mechanisms mediating component interdependencies may also determine what individual behavior is considered competent and adaptive, as well as the organizational rules and policies and the social atmosphere or climate of the setting. For example, one component mediating mechanism might be channels for help giving among individual students, students and faculty, maintenance staff and academic staff, administration and faculty, and so on. Particular organizational factors such as turnover rates or physical size should have predictable effects on help-giving mechanisms and on the nature, complexity, and strength of interdependencies within the system. Extending the implications of these relationships, Trickett, Kelly, and Todd (1972) predicted that in a frequently changing organization with high turnover, help giving would be directed toward survival in the setting, while help-giving mechanisms in low turnover schools would be directed toward maintenance of status positions. Different individual competencies and organization procedures would be adaptative in each setting. Continuing research (Edwards & Kelly, 1980; Kelly, 1979) has offered support for some of these predictions and further clarification of the relationships between coping and adaptation.

The Social Ecology paradigm described by Kelly and his colleagues is one model potentially useful for developing assessments of cross-level and transactional relationships. Other researchers have proposed theoretical constructs linking two or more levels of analysis in ways that parallel and expand this set of ecological principles. Barker's ecological psychology (Barker, 1968; Barker & Gump, 1964; Barker & Schoggen, 1973) and theory of "overmanning" and "undermanning" in behavior settings is similarly rooted in the notion of resource exchange and system adaptation linking individual level psychological phenomena with physical, structural aspects of the system. Watzalawick, Weakland, and Fisch (1974) have adapted the mathematical Theory of Groups and the Theory of Logical Types to explain system maintenance and change, suggesting that a distinction be made between variables describing the members of a group and the characteristics defining the class or group of members. Like the Social Ecology model, their formulation of systems highlights the interrelationships among members within a class, and the nature of the "rules" defining between-group relationships. While their analysis examines only two levels, the prin-

ciples they describe can be useful in the design of intervention and evaluation (Linney, 1978; Seidman, 1978; Rappaport, 1977). In a similar view, Bronfenbrenner (1977; 1979) has proposed a set of interlocking levels, that is, the microsystem, mesosystem, exosystem, and macrosystem, to be considered part of the "ecology of development." Like other ecologically oriented researchers, he proposes multiple cross-level effects that have an impact on the developing organism.

The methodological techniques and developing theoretical conceptions of network analysis and the study of social networks and support systems parallel the Social Ecological principles of interdependence and resource exchange (Mitchell, 1969; Sarason, Cohen, Lorentz, Carrol, & Maton, 1976; Stack, 1974). Psychologists have recently begun to identify the ways in which interfamilial, neighborhood, and community social support systems contribute to the prevention of socially unacceptable behavior such as child abuse (Garbarino, 1976; 1977) and the ways in which networks can be instrumental in buffering individuals through times of severe stress (Caplan & Killilea, 1974; Gottlieb & Todd, 1979; Tolsdorf, 1976). Interpersonal networks seem to be significant determinants of the utilization of helping services in a community (McKinley, 1973) and can be an important medium for precipitating behavioral change (Collins & Pancoast, 1976; Rueveni, 1979). While this area of research is in its infancy regarding issues of interest to community psychologists, the focus of research is the understanding of person–person interdependencies and patterns of resource exchange. Here also the rate of exchange and the nature of resource exchange are proposed as constructs defining interrelationships within the network. Thus they can provide a tool for quantification and comparison of person–person interactions.

Ecological formulations for theory and research, while neither new nor faddish, are acquiring increasing prominence (Catalano, 1979). The principles and underlying assumptions of ecological paradigms are quite consistent with the expressed values of community psychology and the research needs of the field. However, there are as yet few systematic research projects and types of intervention rooted in such a multilevel ecological paradigm. This may be due in part to the massive scope of such projects, and the extensive longitudinal perspective necessary. From a design point of view, any of the quasi-experimental and correlational designs may be appropriate within the context of the ecological research paradigm. While there is a need for further development in statistical procedures, perhaps the most pressing implications of the ecological orientation are for assessment and measurement strategies. As researchers become more facile with the assumptions and application of ecological and systems conceptions, more specificity in the technical research implications should follow.

MEASUREMENT AND ASSESSMENT

Measurement and assessment strategies are critically important in conducting research in any area. In fact, the utility of the research is largely dependent on the psychometric adequacy of the assessment techniques employed. If the researcher adopts poorly developed or psychometrically inadequate measurement instruments, the contribution of the research to the larger body of knowledge and theoretical development is tenuous at best. Mischel (1969) has suggested that the lack of replication and contradiction in so much of the research literature may be a function of unreliable and inadequately validated measurement techniques. For community researchers the problems and importance of assessment are equally salient. Given the primary foci of community research, measures of individual, organizational, and community constructs are of concern, as well as assessments of a transactional and interactional nature to assess between

component and cross-level relationships. In this section several general assessment strategies and specific measurement techniques useful to the community researcher are discussed.

Individual Level Assessment

Psychology has concerned itself with the study of individuals for over a century. During that time, scores of measures of individual functioning have been developed (Buros, 1972). From among the available measures community researchers often include those consistent with the underlying values and specific needs of community based research. Consistent with the valuing of diversity and cultural relativity, measures of individual-level variables that assess competencies, skills, and strengths are most desirable (Heller & Monahan, 1977; Kent & Rolf, 1979; Moos, 1976; Rappaport, 1977; Rappaport, Davidson, Mitchell, & Wilson, 1975). Instruments assessing only deficits or weaknesses to the exclusion of adaptative skills and competencies have little utility for the community researcher studying ecological relationships, coping, and adaptation. Specific assessment strategies reflecting strengths and coping adaptation include, for example, Tyler's (1978) Behavioral Attributes of Psychosocial Competence Scale, a self-report measure in which respondents indicate coping styles. Effective problem solving is reflected in the choice of active, planned strategies, selection of realistic goals, and evidence of learning from both success and failure experiences. Edwards and Kelly (1980) employed a multifaceted assessment procedure for individual satisfaction and competence emphasizing "positive aspects of adolescent development" in a longitudinal study of coping and adaptation in differing environmental contexts. Their battery included measures of self-esteem, participation in school activities, student initiative, and sense of involvement. Researchers examining personal support systems and networks also reflect the competence and strengths orientation including assessments of help giving and help seeking (Hirsch, 1980; Gottlieb & Todd, 1979). Likewise, measures of life stress may include positive accomplishments and life change such as job promotions, and personal honors as well as loss and undesirable change, such as death of a spouse or unemployment (Dohrenwend & Dohrenwend, 1974).

Researchers should be keenly aware of the degree to which a measure may be culture bound (Samuda, 1975). While intelligence tests and standardized achievement tests, most notably, have been identified as culturally biased (Kamin, 1974; Labov, 1975; Williams, 1971), measures of classroom behavior, problem solving, personality, or definitions of competence may be equally subject to these problems. For example, Berck, Seidman, and Rappaport (1978) have suggested that measures of problem solving skills, while ostensibly measuring coping skill and competence, may inherently reflect cultural bias in scoring procedures that, for example, devalue aggressive strategies for goal accomplishments. In choosing a measure or developing an instrument, careful attention should be given to the underlying assumptions of behavior reflected in the items and the influence of evaluative judgments stemming from those assumptions (Rappaport, 1977).

Organizational and Community Level Assessment

With its ecological assumptions and attention to person-environment fit, community psychologists have a need for assessments of ecological variables at the organizational and community level. Concern for situational or environmental impact on behavior is not unique to community researchers, as personality researchers have long debated the role of the situation in determining behavior (Bem & Allen, 1974; Mischel, 1973; Bowers, 1973; Kahle, 1979). For the community researcher the environment or situation to be assessed is a multidimensional set of constructs (Rutter, Maughan, Mortimore, & Ouston, 1979). Three essentially different strategies or definitions of the "environment" have been utilized in community research: (1) observation and quantification of features of the physical environment as they relate to behavior; (2) measurement of the perception of the participants in a setting; and (3) social indicator data and other measures of systemic operations. The latter two have been applied to both the organizational and community levels.

The Environment as Observed Features. Among environmental psychologists the physical and structural features of the setting are typically considered to be the environmental context potentially important in determining or influencing human behavior. With this definition of the setting, research has been conducted on many environmental issues, for example, the relationship between social behavior and architectural design; use of space and furniture arrangement; crowding, noise pollution, and stress; and crime and the lighting and physical design of buildings (Altman, 1975; Proshansky, Ittelson, & Rivlin, 1970; Stokols, 1978). With this largely physical definition of the environment, assessments can usually be made reliably and with little or no intrusion into the setting. The research results suggest that these features of the environment may influence the limits of behavior and thus be useful in predicting gross categories of behavior for groups of people.

Roger Barker (1965, 1968) has proposed a system of environmental assessment he calls Ecological Psychology. Similarly focusing on the observable physical environment, he postulates the "behavior setting" as the basic unit of analysis for the environment. In defining the behavior setting, Barker has intertwined the physical setting and aspects of behavior, that is, a behavior setting is a unit with time and space boundaries and a "standing pattern of behavior." With this definition, a basketball game might be a behavior setting having time and space boundaries and an expected or standing pattern of participant behavior. Barker hypothesizes that a synomorphic relationship exists between the physical conditions and the behavior patterns, so that certain kinds of behavior are unlikely to occur in particular settings, for example, people don't dance or party in church. When the synomorphy is inadequate, standing patterns will be less clear (e.g., church services in the school gymnasium), or the behavior might be seen as inappropriate (e.g., praying in the grocery store). Using the analogy of the spectator trying to understand a baseball game by watching only the player on first base, Barker asserts that one cannot understand patterns of behavior by examining individuals alone. Similarly, one would learn little about the game by observing the playing field alone. Instead he argues that the persons in the setting are largely interchangeable, and the behavior settings and associated synomorphs determine the behavior of participants.

After intensive observation in 13 high schools with population sizes varying from 35 to 2287 pupils, Barker and Gump (1964) have demonstrated several relationships between student satisfaction and sense of self-involvement, and the number of behavior settings, the diversity in settings available, and the roles played by participants in the schools. For example, more students in small schools take part in more activities and expressed a greater sense of involvement than students in the large schools. Wicker (1969) has replicated the positive relationship between sense of involvement and the small size of the organization in an analysis of the memberships of over 100 churches.

The basic assessment tool within Barker's ecological psychology is the behavior setting survey. The researcher first identifies all of the behavior settings in the system or community of interest, judging each against the defining features of time-space boundaries

and synomorphy. Each behavior setting is then described quantitatively or qualitatively on a set of dimensions including duration, number of participants, primary behavioral functions occurring in the setting, pressure for participation, and participatory roles. As used by Barker and his colleagues, the assessment technique is quite extensive and time consuming. For example, at their Midwest Psychological Research Station, Barker and his staff spent over 10 years studying a single community. However, Price and Blashfield (1975) report that the 455 behavior settings identified by Barker in the midwestern community can be factor analyzed into 12 distinct clusters or types. Wicker (1979) further suggests that the procedures may be streamlined by assessing a sample of the settings that occur in an organization or community. Overall, the procedures offer a strategy useful for description of various systems by either considering individual behavior settings or the sum of behavior settings comprising a social system or community. Although the techniques have been used primarily for description, they seem to be potentially sensitive to change, and offer a linking strategy between individual psychological processes and organizational-environmental features of the setting.

A third strategy within the general mode of observational assessment has been the development of environmental inventories to assess social settings. The HOME, Home Observation for Measurement of the Environment (Bradley & Caldwell, 1977), is an example of this measurement procedure. It consists of 45 Yes-No items answered by an observer following an in-home interview. The items assess the presence of physical objects such as toys and the occurrence of parental activities thought to be important to development, for example, Does the mother praise the child in the presence of the interviewer? Does the child get out of the house at least four times a week? For these kinds of assessment inventories the environment is defined in terms of observable physical features and patterns of interaction, which may be observed or elicited by an interviewer during the assessment.

The Environment as Perception of Social Climate.

A second major approach to the assessment of environments is based on the perception of the participants in the setting. Rudolf Moos and his associates (Insel & Moos, 1974; Moos, 1973; 1979) have developed the notion of the environment as the perceived psychosocial climate. Drawing from Murray's (1938) construct of beta press (i.e., the participants' consensual perception of environmental demands), Moos hypothesizes that environments have "personalities," which, like those of people, are conducive to differing styles of interaction and behavior. He states:

Personality tests assess personality traits or needs and provide information about the characteristic ways in which people behave. Social environments can be similarly portrayed with a great deal of accuracy and detail. Some people are more supportive than others. Likewise, some social environments are more supportive than others. Some people feel a strong need to control others. Similarly, some social environments are extremely rigid, autocratic and controlling. (Moos, 1975)

Moos has conceptualized three primary dimensions comprising social climate: (1) relationship components including supportiveness, involvement, and cohesion in the environment; (2) personal development dimensions including autonomy and self-enhancement; and (3) system maintenance and system change dimensions including order, clarity, and control in the setting. Various environments can be characterized and differentiated on these three dimensions. Moos further proposed that behavioral results in specific environments will be related to these dimensions, and across environments those results will be similar or different to the extent that the social climate of the settings is similar or different.

Moos has constructed a set of Social Climate Scales (Moos, 1974a) based on these assumptions, to assess treatment environments (Moos & Houts, 1968; Moos, 1974), correctional settings such as prison (Moos, 1975), and educational settings (Moos, 1979a; Trickett & Moos, 1974), as well as community work settings (Moos, 1975) and family environments (Moos, 1974). Each Social Climate Scale is composed of a set of True-False statements forming subscales to assess components of the relationship, personal development, and system maintenance dimensions. Typically, both the members or participants in the setting, for example, prisoners, and the staff or administrators of the setting complete the measure. The final description of the environment is recorded as the sum or mean response to the items of each dimension.

The Social Climate Scales are one of the most commonly used environmental assessment techniques. Moos (1974) has indicated that the measures of social climate are internally consistent and only moderately related to other organizational features such as size and characteristics of the members. Other researchers, however, have suggested that the measure is more an assessment of the persons in the setting than the environment (Alden, 1978), and that the three-dimensional schema may not be validated with other samples (Kohn, Jeger, & Koretzky, 1979; Wilkinson, 1973). These psychometric issues notwithstanding, research with the Social Climate Scales has supported the supposition that different environments have different behavioral outcomes (Insel & Moos, 1974; Moos, 1975; Moos, Petty, & Shelton, 1973; Moos & VanDort, 1979; Trickett & Moos, 1974).

Social Indicators and Organizational Processes.

Communities and social systems are frequently described in terms of population, growth rates, mobility or citizen income. These descriptors fall in the broad category known as social indicators (Heller & Monahan, 1977). Measures like these, considered individually or in aggregate, can be useful to the community researcher as assessments of community resources and community changes. Social indicators are most commonly employed in the field of economics as assessments of the impact of various economic policies and market changes. We are accustomed to hearing periodic reports of unemployment rates, housing starts, and mortgage rates. In time series form these indicators provide descriptive information on systemic functioning and provide feedback regarding change that is not tied directly to individual behavior, but has obvious implications for individual persons. As such, the use of social indicators may provide an assessment device useful for linking societal or community level analyses and individual or small group functioning (Catalano & Dooley, 1977; Dooley & Catalano, 1979). Indicators including rates of crime, delinquency, divorce, alcoholism, and psychiatric hospital admissions may be indexes of conflict, disruption, or stress in a community. Civic activities, city council meeting attendance, and neighborhood association membership may be measures of community involvement and the "sense of community" in a locality.

Social indicator data are available to the researcher from public records and are typically compiled by local government agencies. While unobtrusive and accessible, there are a variety of potential problems with the reliability of the data and the coding unit utilized, for example, changes in recording policies or definitional categories. Further research examining intercorrelations among a variety of social indicators is necessary to establish the construct validity of these measures and the relationships between these community level variables and individual behavior.

A second approach to the assessment of organizational variables comes from industrial and organizational psychologists, who offer several dimensional constructs to characterize settings, for example, power and authority, decision making, incentives, and determinants of role status. While most of the research utilizing these constructs has been directed toward business and industrial settings (Porter, Hackman, & Lawler, 1975), the conceptions of open systems, the strategies for precipitating organizational change, and the methods of assessment used have implications for community assessment as well. Reppucci, Dean, and Saunders (1975) and Sarata (1977) have employed measures of job design (Hackman & Lawler, 1971) and job satisfaction (Smith, Kandall, & Hahn, 1969) to evaluate change in human service organizations.

Katz and Kahn (1978) have described the dynamics of organizations and organization–environment relationships delineating five organizational subsystems or structures (production, maintenance, boundary, adaptive, and managerial) that together describe the dynamic functioning of an organization. Production structures are oriented toward task requirements and defining technical proficiency. Maintenance structures ensure stability and predictability in the organization, while adaptive structures plan for the organization's adjustment to changing internal or external conditions. Boundary structures are responsible for the procurement and flow of goods and resources from outside the organization into it, and vice versa. These mechanisms control exchange at the interface of the organization and other social systems. Managerial structures cut across these four systems and function to coordinate internal subsystems, resolve conflict, and coordinate external requirements with organizational needs. Paralleling the ecological principles introduced by Kelly (1966, 1969), these organizational processes and structures provide measures for organizational level analysis. Applying these constructs to the school setting, for example, production systems might include minimum requirements, competency testing, or grading criteria. Class meeting schedules and attendance requirements serve to ensure stability and predictability in the workday, while admissions requirements and selection procedures control resource input into the setting. Adaptive and managerial processes are potential constructs for the study of cross-level interface and system-system transactions. While these organizational dimensions at present have primarily heuristic value, further application to human service systems and development of more systematic assessment procedures is desirable.

Assessment Needs and Promising Directions

Currently there are several assessment options for measuring individual, organizational, and community variables. However, adopting a dynamic, ecological model and systemic focus has important implications for assessment and raises new problems for the community researcher. As Katz and Kahn (1978) have pointed out, "Social systems have structure, but it is a structure of events rather than physical parts, a structure therefore inseparable from the functioning of the system" (pp. 67–68). Consequently, assessment techniques of the constructs hypothesized by community researchers need to be capable of measuring functional relationships, and the mechanisms of homeostasis, adaptation, and change. As personality research has been criticized for assessments based on static, trait notions of behavior, community research may be similarly restricted by overreliance on measurements unable to assess and portray the dynamic processes maintaining equilibrium in systems.

Several conceptualizations of the environment have been proposed, yet the psychometric properties and associated nomological networks remain largely undetermined. Careful attention needs to be directed toward the specification of these organizational and community constructs and convergence among the several available measures. The recent work of Moos and Lemke (1979) with the Multiphasic Environmental Assessment Procedure includes assessments of physical characteristics, social climate perceptions, and organizational policy in the nursing home setting and represents a multimethod approach to organizational measurement. As with measures of individual behavior, measures of the environment should be similarly evaluated as to the degree of cultural bias or culture-boundness, and the nature of underlying assumptions regarding the salient features of the setting assessed.

Amidst these models of environment, the salient issue of concern for community researchers remains the determination of how environmental settings interface with and transact individual behavior. The notion of person-environment fit as a construct involving cross-level interface has been addressed largely in terms of adaptation, that is, if the individual is succeeding or adapting in the setting, a "good fit" is assumed. As a conceptual unit, the construct of person-environment match is rich, implying a dynamic equilibrium between two changing systems, the individual and the environment. However, neither the conceptual and theoretical implications nor the assessment strategies relevant to this notion have been sufficiently developed. The growing body of research on the dynamics of personal networks and resource exchange offers promising directions for assessing unit-to-unit interchange that could be similarly applied to other components. Similarly, applications of Markov chain analyses (Hertel, 1972) and methods for analysis of sequence and social interaction (Cairns, 1979) may lead to more dynamic units of analysis allowing for assessment of two or more mutually changing components.

PRACTICAL CONCERNS IN THE CONDUCT OF RESEARCH IN THE COMMUNITY

There are innumerable practical difficulties in conducting research in the community, not the least of which is acquiring the access necessary to evaluate the criterion variables of interest. These problems are often of a political and economic nature, and can present insurmountable difficulties for the researcher (Reppucci, 1977; Reppucci & Sarason, 1979). Moreover, ethical concerns may arise and must be given serious attention (Monahan, 1980; Reppucci & Clingempeel, 1978). Munoz, Snowden, and Kelly (1979) have identified a range of variables and influences affecting the process and outcome of community-based research, including factors presumably outside of the research realm such as the availability of funding, community openness, and the stability of the community settings. The list of variables affecting projects and the problems encountered by the researcher may be endless (Cowen, 1978). With each new project unique difficulties are likely to arise, and the community researcher must learn to be both resourceful and to have a tolerance for ambiguity and frustration.

Many methodological difficulties are related to problems in more traditional nonfield research, and represent serious threats to the internal and external validity of the research project. For example, Campbell and Stanley (1966) identify bias related to differential selection of respondents as a threat to the internal validity of a study. In many (if not most) community research projects the persons included in the study have been self-selected or selected by a "gatekeeper" of the service system. The process of self-selection, then, may result in a "healthier" population, as in one study of life satisfaction and sense of role competence among divorced single women (Kazak, 1979), in which respondents were recruited in a variety of ways but essentially volunteered to participate. Respondents' comments following participation included remarks like "I wouldn't have done this for you a year ago, I was in bad shape, but I've really pulled things together now." Selection by gatekeepers and agents of service delivery systems may similarly bias the sample included, although in the opposite direction. In a recent intervention (Rosenberg, Reppucci, & Linney, in press) designed

to examine the impact of parenting groups on the skills of "high-risk" parents, participants were referred by local social service personnel. Being a new and time-limited demonstration program, the referrals received seemed to represent that group of clients for whom no other services were appropriate, the group who seemed to have fallen through the cracks, or the group who had already participated in other available services but were still seen to be in need of help. As a result, the final parenting groups were composed of an extremely varied population, but one that in some ways bordered on what might be called "hard core." Selection biases like these may substantially alter the representativeness of the sample included, potentially threatening the internal validity of the research (i.e., regression to the mean) and the generalizability of the findings.

The internal validity of a community-based quasi-experiment may be unavoidably threatened by experimental mortality, that is, differential loss of respondents from the comparison groups (Campbell & Stanley, 1966). In work with high-risk populations, there is typically increased mobility and a greater incidence of life stressing events that may seriously jeopardize the integrity of the research and the participation of the respondents. For example, in a school-based secondary-prevention program (Seidman, Rappaport, Davidson, & Linney, in preparation) while care was taken to randomly assign children to the intervention and comparison groups, when postassessments were conducted, it became apparent that almost every child in the "treatment-as-usual" comparison group had left the school district. In this instance, despite the careful concern for an adequate research design and random assignment, the researchers were left with no comparison group and had to resort to the selection of a matched control group. In intervention projects with the elderly, the problems of experimental mortality are blatantly apparent in that one must be prepared for the reality that participants may die during the course of the intervention and research periods.

Multiple treatment interference, a threat to external validity cited by Campbell and Stanley (1966), is a particular concern to community-based research. The difficulty arises when one is attempting to determine the effects of a particular treatment or intervention, and additional "treatments" are occurring simultaneously. As Cowen (1978) describes:

A behavior modification program for hospital patients may take place alongside of drug-therapy and patient ward-governance programs. A school mental health intervention may co-occur with Glasser circle and Distar programs (Cowen et al., 1974). The intermixing of such programs not only makes it difficult to evaluate their separate contributions but also often means that an ostensibly pure experimental program is in fact that program *plus* (emphasis added) several overlapping services or programs in one setting, compared to another (so-called control) setting, which happens not to have that particular program but does have three or four other programs addressed to similar behaviors in comparable target subjects. (p. 803)

While many of these "fatal flaws" in experimental integrity are not unique to community research, they are particularly common and, some have argued, inherent in the process (Cowen, 1978). Unlike laboratory-based research, in which the experimenter seeks to eliminate all threats to validity and may rerun the study if the design validity is threatened, community researchers are more likely to try to anticipate and systematically record these events. The community researcher rarely has the decision-making power and control necessary to eliminate these factors (Reppucci & Saunders, 1974). In fact, given the concern for researching phenomena in ecological context and identifying and describing naturally occurring transactions, these "threats" to validity, while presenting difficulties in causal inference, add richness to the data and can be considered as case study experiments within the larger experiment.

With the overview of community research presented here, even the most naive and inexperienced researcher can envision the difficulties of research in the community. The conditions of entry and means of access to the setting, the time and resources necessary, the constraints of the real world, ethical considerations, and changing social and political conditions influence the research process in ways frequently not anticipated. Nevertheless, the issues outlined by this developing area necessitate that research be done in these field settings. As Rappaport (1977) has said:

What we now must recognize is that the traditional ideal of applying laboratory verified hypotheses to field settings is unrealistic as a means of developing community psychology. Rather than only transferring the results of laboratory studies to the natural environment, we will need to both generate and test hypotheses in the very settings we wish to change. (p. 156)

To facilitate the process of completing this type of research, several have suggested a redefinition of the role of the researcher away from the "ivory tower academic" toward a mutual collaborator with both service providers and recipients in the social and community systems of concern (Fairweather, 1972; Kelly, 1970; Rappaport, 1977). Certainly such a collaboration, originally suggested by Kurt Lewin under the rubric "action research," would aid in data collection, although it would also significantly increase the time frame of most projects. However, more importantly, active cooperation might demystify the research process for potential "subjects" and provide invaluable ethnographic data for the researcher to understand better the mechanisms operative in the setting. Too often the researchers and participants become antagonists and the potential for future research, or even continuing research to completion, disappears as the researcher attempts to adhere rigidly to the demands of experimental design, and participants are increasingly disrupted by these demands. Flexibility, feedback, and willingness to participate actively in a setting will often alleviate several of these difficulties (Suchman, 1976).

With the pressures for rapid research productivity among academic psychologists and the practical difficulties of conducting community research, too much research in the field has been guided by what is available and allowable, rather than conceptual foundations or theoretical models. Cowen (1978) has discussed this problem in the selection of dependent measures in program evaluation studies. Similarly, Novaco and Monahan's (1980) review of research in the field implies a need for more serious concern with theoretical development and programmatic research.

As community psychology has emerged as a distinct area of inquiry with a set of guiding values and content domains, researchers have applied a wide array of research strategies to study the issues of concern. With the data collected and research reported thus far, it is clear that research in the community is possible and potentially useful for planning and policy decisions at the local and national levels (Fairweather & Tornatzky, 1977; Monahan, 1977). Hence the importance of well-designed, conceptually grounded research in the community can not be overstated.

REFERENCES

Alden, L. (1978). Factor analysis of Ward Atmosphere Scale. *Journal of Consulting and Clinical Psychology, 46,* 175–176.

Altman, I. (1975). *The Environment and social behavior: Privacy, personal space, territory, crowding.* Monterey, Calif.: Brooks-Cole.

Atkin, R., Bray, R., Davison, M., Herzberger, S., Humphreys, L. G., & Selzer, U. (1977). Cross lagged panel analysis of sixteen cognitive measures at four grade levels. *Child Development, 48,* 944–952.

Barker, R. G. (1965). Explorations in ecological psychology. *American Psychologist, 20,* 1–14.

Barker, R. (1968). *Ecological psychology.* Stanford, Calif.: Stanford University Press.

Barker, R. G., & Gump, P. V. (Eds.) (1964). *Big school, small school: High school size and student behavior.* Stanford, Calif.: Stanford University Press.

Barker, R. G., & Schoggen, P. (1973). *Qualities of community life: Methods of measuring environment and behavior applied to an American and an English Town.* San Francisco: Jossey-Bass.

Bem, D., & Allen, A. (1974). On predicting some of the people some of the time: The search for cross-situational consistencies in behavior. *Psychological Review, 81,* 506–520.

Bennett, C. C., Anderson, L. S., Cooper, S., Hassol, L., Klein, D. C., & Rosenblum, G. (Eds.) (1966). *Community psychology: A report of the Boston conference on the education of psychologists for community mental health.* Boston: Boston University Press.

Berck, P., Seidman, E., & Rappaport, J. (1978). *Preparing elementary school children for junior high: An interpersonal problem solving intervention.* Unpublished manuscript. Indiana University, Purdue University at Indianapolis.

Bloom, B. L. (1977) *Community mental health: A general introduction.* Monterey, Calif.: Brooks-Cole.

Bloom, B. L. (1980). Social and community interventions. *Annual Review of Psychology, 31,* 111–142.

Bowers, K. S. (1973). Situationism in psychology: An analysis and a critique. *Psychological Review, 80,* 307–336.

Bradley, R., & Caldwell, B. (1977). Home Observation for Measurement of the Environment: A validation study for screening efficiency. *American Journal of Mental Deficiency, 81,* 417–420.

Bronfenbrenner, U. (1977). Toward an experimental ecology of human development. *American Psychologist, 32,* 513–531.

Bronfenbrenner, U. (1979). *The ecology of human development: Experiments by nature and design.* Cambridge, Mass.: Harvard University Press.

Bruhn, J. (1974). Human ecology: A unifying science? *Human Ecology, 2,* 105–125.

Buros, O. K. (1972). *The seventh mental measurements yearbook.* Highland Park, N. J.: Gryphon Press.

Cairns, R. B. (Ed.) (1979). *The analysis of social interactions.* Hillsdale, N. J.: Lawrence Erlbaum Associates.

Campbell, D. T., & Stanley, J. C. (1966). *Experimental and quasi-experimental design for research.* Chicago: Rand McNally.

Caplan, G., & Killelea, M. (Eds.) (1974). *Support systems and mutual help: Multidisciplinary explorations.* New York: Grune & Stratton.

Catalano, R. (1979). *Health, behavior and the community: An ecological perspective.* New York: Pergamon Press.

Catalano, R., & Dooley, D. (1977). Economic predictors of depressed mood and stressful life events. *Journal of Health and Social Behavior,* **18,** 292–307.

Collins, A., & Pancoast, D. (1976). *Natural helping networks.* Washington, D. C.: National Association of Social Workers.

Cook, D., & Campbell, D. T. (1979). *Quasi-experimentation: Design and analysis issues in field settings.* Chicago: Rand McNally.

Cowen, E. L. (1973). Social and community interventions. *Annual Review of Psychology,* **24,** 423–472.

Cowen, E. L. (1977). Baby steps toward primary prevention. *American Journal of Community Psychology,* **5,** 217–227.

Cowen, E. L. (1978). Some problems in community program evaluation research. *Journal of Consulting and Clinical Psychology,* **46,** 792–805.

Cowen, E. L. (1980). The wooing of primary prevention. *American Journal of Community Psychology,* **8,** 258–284.

Cowen, E. L., & Gesten, E. L. (1980). Evaluating community programs: Tough and tender perspectives. In M. S. Gibbs, J. R. Lachenmeyer, & J. Sigal (Eds.), *Community psychology: Theoretical and empirical approaches.* New York: Gardner Press.

Cowen, E. L., Pederson, A., Babigan, H., Izzo, L. D., & Trost, M. A. (1973). Long term follow-up of early detected vulnerable children. *Journal of Consulting and Clinical Psychology,* **41,** 438–446.

Crano, W. D., Kenny, D. A., & Campbell, D. T. (1972). Does intelligence cause achievement?: A cross lagged panel analysis. *Journal of Educational Psychology,* **63,** 258–275.

Cronbach, L. J., & Meehl, P. E. (1955). Construct validity in psychological tests. *Psychological Bulletin,* **52,** 281–302.

Delaney, J. A., Seidman, E., & Willis, G. (1978). Crisis intervention and the prevention of institutionalization: An interrupted time series analysis. *American Journal of Community Psychology,* **6,** 33–45.

Dohrenwend, B., & Dohrenwend, B. (1969). *Social status and psychological disorder.* New York: Wiley.

Dohrenwend, B. S., & Dohrenwend, B. P. (1974). *Stressful life events: Their nature and effects.* New York: Wiley.

Dooley, D., & Catalano, R. (1979). Economic, life and disorder changes: Time series analyses. *American Journal of Community Psychology,* **1,** 381–396.

Duncan, O. D. (1975). *Introduction to structural equation models.* New York: Academic Press.

Edwards, D. W., & Kelly, J. G. (1980). Coping and adaptation: A longitudinal study. *American Journal of Community Psychology,* **8,** 203–216.

Eron, L. D., Huesmann, L. R., Lefkowitz, M. M., & Walder, L. O. (1972). Does television violence cause aggression? *American Psychologist,* **27,** 253–263.

Fairweather, G. (1967). *Methods for experimental social innovation.* New York: Wiley.

Fairweather, G. W. (1972). *Social change: The challenge to survival.* Morristown, N. J.: General Learning Press.

Fairweather, G. W. (1979). Experimental development and dissemination of an alternative to psychiatric hospitalization: Scientific methods for social change. In R. F. Munoz, L. R. Snowden, & J. G. Kelly (Eds.). *Social and psychological research in community settings.* San Francisco: Jossey-Bass, pp. 305–342.

Fairweather, G. W., Sanders, D. H., Cressler, D. L., & Maynard, H. (1969). *Community life for the mentally ill: An alternative to institutional care.* Chicago: Aldine.

Fairweather, G., Sanders, D., & Tornatsky, L. (1974). *Creating change in mental health organizations.* New York: Pergamon Press.

Fairweather, G. W., & Tornatsky, L. (1977). *Experimental methods for social policy research.* Elmsford, N. Y.: Pergamon Press.

Faris, R. E., & Dunham, H. W. (1939). *Mental disorders in urban areas: An ecological study of schizophrenia and other psychoses.* Chicago: University of Chicago Press.

Garbarino, J. (1976). A preliminary study of some ecological correlates of child abuse. The impact of socio-economic stress on mothers. *Child Development,* **47,** 178–185.

Garbarino, J. (1977). The price of privacy in the social dynamics of child abuse. *Child Welfare,* **56,** 565–575.

Glass, G. V., Wilson, V. L., & Gottman, J. M. (1975). *Design and analysis of time-series experiments.* Boulder: Colorado Associated University Press.

Goldberger, A. S., & Duncan, O. D. (1973). *Structural equation models in the social sciences.* New York: Seminar Press.

Goodstein, L.D., & Sandler, S. (1978). Using psychology to promote human welfare: A conceptual analysis of the role of community psychology. *American Psychologist,* **33,** 882–892.

Gottlieb, B. H., & Todd, D.M. (1979). Characterizing and promoting social support in natural settings.

In R. F. Munoz, L. R. Snowden, & J. G. Kelly (Eds.) *Social and psychological research in community settings.* San Franciso: Jossey-Bass.

Hackman, J. R., & Lawler, E. E. (1971). Employee reactions to job characteristics. *Journal of Applied Psychology, 55,* 259–286.

Hall, C. S., & Lindzey, G. (1978). *Theories of personality* (3rd ed.). New York: Wiley.

Harris, R. J. (1975). *A primer of multivariate statistics.* New York: Academic Press.

Heller, K., & Monahan, J. (1977). *Psychology and community change.* Homewood, Ill.: Dorsey Press.

Hertel, R. K. (1972). Application of stochastic process analysis to the study of psychotherapeutic processes. *Psychological Bulletin, 77,* 421–430.

Hirsch, B. J. (1979). Psychological dimensions of social networks: A multimethod analysis. *American Journal of Community Psychology, 7,* 263–277.

Hollingshead, B. B., & Redlich, F. C. (1958). *Social class and mental illness: A community study.* New York: Wiley.

Insel, P. M., & Moos, R. H. (1974). Psychological environments: Expanding the scope of human ecology. *American Psychologist, 29,* 179–188.

Iscoe, I. (1974). Community psychology and the competent community. *American Psychologist, 29,* 607–613.

Iscoe, I., Bloom, B., & Speilberger, C. (Eds.) (1977). *Community psychology in transition.* Washington, D. C.: Hemisphere.

Ittleson, W. H., Proshansky, H. M., & Rivlin, L. G. (1972). Bedroom size and social interaction of the psychiatric ward. In J. F. Wohlwill & D. H. Carson (Eds.), *Environment and the social sciences: Perspectives and applications.* Washington, D. C.: American Psychological Association.

Johnson, M. S., Jurick, N. C., Kreb, A. R., & Rose, T. L. (1978). The wheels of misfortune: A time series analysis of bicycle accidents on a college campus. *Evaluation Quarterly, 2,* 608–619.

Jöreskog, K. G. (1974). Analyzing psychological data by structural analysis of covariance matrices. In R. C. Atkinson, D. H. Krantz, & P. D. Suppes (Eds.), *Contemporary Developments in Mathematical Psychology,* Vol. 2. San Francisco: W. H. Freeman.

Jöreskog, K. G. (1970). A general model for analysis of covariance structures. *Biometrika, 57,* 239–251.

Jöreskog, K. G., & Sorhom, D. (1978). *LISREL IV: Analysis of linear structural relationships by the method of maximum likelihood: User's guide.* Chicago: International Educational Services.

Kahle, L. R. (1979). *New directions for methodology of behavioral science: Methods for studying person-situation interactions.* San Francisco: Jossey-Bass.

Kamin, L. G. (1974). *The science and politics of I.Q.* Potomac, Md.: Erlbaum Associates.

Katz, D., & Kahn, R. (1978). *The social psychology of organizations* (2nd ed.). New York: Wiley.

Kazak, A. (1979). *Life satisfaction and role-specific perceived competence in single parent divorced women.* Unpublished Master's Thesis, University of Virginia.

Kelly, J. G. (1966). Ecological constraints on mental health services. *American Psychologist, 21,* 535–539.

Kelly, J. G. (1968). Toward an ecological conception of preventive interventions. In J. Carter (Ed.), *Research contributions from psychology to community mental health.* New York: Behavioral Publications.

Kelly, J. G. (1969). Naturalistic observations in contrasting social environments. In E. P. Willems & H. L. Raush (Eds.), *Naturalistic viewpoints in psychological research.* New York: Holt, Rinehart & Winston.

Kelly, J. G. (1970). Antidotes for arrogance: Training for community psychology, *American Psychologist, 25,* 524–531.

Kelly, J. G. (1971). The quest for valid preventive interventions. In C. D. Spielberger (Ed.), *Current topics in clinical and community psychology,* Vol. 2. New York: Academic Press.

Kelly, J. G., Munoz, R. C., & Snowden, L. R. (1979). Characteristics of community research projects and the implementation process. In R. F. Munoz, L. R. Snowden, & J. G. Kelly (Eds.), *Social and psychological research in community settings.* San Francisco, Jossey-Bass.

Kelly, J., Snowden, L., & Munoz, R. (1977). Social and community interventions. *Annual Review of Psychology, 28,* 323–361.

Kenny, D. A. (1975). Cross lagged panel correlations: A test for spuriousness. *Psychological Bulletin, 82,* 887–903.

Kent, M. W., & Rolf, J. E. (Eds.) (1979). *Primary prevention of psychopathology,* Vol. 3. *Social competence in children.* Hanover, N. H.: University Press of New England.

Kessler, M., & Albee, G. (1977). An overview of literature of primary prevention. In G. Albee & J. Joffe (Eds.) *Primary prevention pf psychopathology: The issues,* Vol. 1. Hanover, N. H.: University Press.

Kohn, M., Jeger, A. M., & Koretzky, M. B. (1979). Social ecological assessment of environments: Toward a two-factor model. *American Journal of Community Psychology, 7,* 481–495.

Labov, W. (1975). Academic ignorance and Black intelligence. In M. Maehr & Stallings (Eds.), *Culture, child and school: Sociocultural influences on learning.* Monterey, Calif.: Brooks-Cole.

Lave, L. B., & Sesken, E. P. (1977) *Air pollution and human health.* Baltimore: Johns Hopkins University Press.

Lewin, K. (1946). Action research and minority problems. *Journal of Social Issues, 2,* 34–46.

Lewis, M. S. (1977). Trend surface analysis of community variables. *Psychological Bulletin, 84,* 940–949.

Lewis, M. S. (1978). Nearest neighbor analysis of epidemiological and community variables. *Psychological Bulletin, 85,* 1302–1308.

Linney, J. A. (1978). *A multivariable, multilevel analysis of a midwestern city's court-ordered desegregation.* Unpublished Ph.D. dissertation, University of Illinois, Urbana.

Linney, J. A., & Seidman, E. (1978). *Court-ordered desegregation: Shuffling the deck or playing a different game.* Paper presented at the annual meeting of the American Psychological Association, Toronto.

Maccoby, N., & Alexander, J. (1979) Reducing heart disease risk using the mass media. In R. F. Munoz, L. R. Snowden, & J. G. Kelly (Eds.), *Social and psychological research in community settings.* San Francisco: Jossey-Bass.

Maccoby, N., & Farquhar, J. W. (1975). Communication for health: Unselling heart disease. *Journal of Communication, 25,* 114–126.

Mahoney, M. (1978). Experimental methods and outcome evaluation. *Journal of Consulting and Clinical Psychology, 46,* 660–672.

Maruyama, G., & McGarvey, W. (1980). Evaluating causal models: An application of maximum-likelihood analysis of structural equations. *Psychological Bulletin, 87,* 502–512.

McKinlay, J. B. (1973). Social networks, lay consultation, and help seeking behavior. *Social Forces, 51*(3), 275–292.

Mills, R. C., & Kelly, J. G. (1972). Cultural and social adaptations to change: A case example and critique. In S. Golann & C. Eisdorfer (Eds.), *Handbook of community mental health.* New York: Appleton-Century-Crofts.

Minuchin, S. (1974). *Families and family therapy.* Cambridge, Mass.: Harvard University Press.

Mischel, W. (1969). Continuity and change in personality. *American Psychologist, 24,* 1012–1018.

Mischel, W. (1973). Toward a cognitive social learning reconceptualization of personality. *Psychological Review, 80,* 252–283.

Mitchell, J. C. (Ed.) (1969). *Social networks in urban situations.* New York: Humanities Press.

Monahan, J. (1977). Community psychology and public policy: The promise and the pitfalls. In B. D. Sales (Ed.), *Psychology in the legal process.* New York: Halsted.

Monahan, J. (Ed.) (1980). *Who is the client? The ethics of psychological intervention in the criminal justice system.* Washington, D. C.: American Psychological Association.

Moos, R. H. (1973). Conceptualizations of human environments. *American Psychologist, 28,* 652–665.

Moos, R. H. (1974). *Evaluating treatment environments: A social ecological approach.* New York: Wiley.

Moos, R. H. (1974a) *The social climate scales: An overview.* Palo Alto, Calif.: Consulting Psychologists Press.

Moos, R. H. (1975). *Evaluating correctional and community settings.* New York: Wiley-Interscience.

Moos, R. H. (Ed.) (1976). *Human adaptation: Coping with life crises.* Lexington, Mass.: D. C. Heath.

Moos, R. H. (1979). Improving social settings by social climate measurement and feedback. In R. F. Munoz, L. R. Snowden, & J. G. Kelly (Eds.), *Social and psychological research in community settings.* San Francisco: Jossey-Bass.

Moos, R. H. (1976a). *Evaluating educational environments.* San Francisco: Jossey-Bass.

Moos, R. H., & Houts, P. S. (1968). Assessment of the social atmosphere of psychiatric wards. *Journal of Abnormal Psychology, 73,* 595–604.

Moos, R. H., & Lemke, S. (1979). *Multiphasic environmental assessment procedure.* Palo Alto, Calif.: Social Ecology Laboratory.

Moos, R. H., Petty, C., & Shelton, R. (1973) Perceived ward climate and treatment outcome. *Journal of Abnormal Psychology, 82,* 291–298.

Moos, R. H., & VanDort B. (1979). Student physical symptoms and the social climate of college living groups. *American Journal of Community Psychology, 1,* 31–43.

Mulvey, E. P., & Reppucci, N. D. (in press). Police crisis intervention training: An empirical investigation. *American Journal of Community Psychology.*

Murray, H. A. (1938). *Explorations in personality.* New York: Oxford University Press.

Neitzel, M. T., & Dade, J. T. (1973). Bail reform as an example of a community psychology intervention in the criminal justice system. *American Journal of Community Psychology, 1,* 238–247.

Novaco, R. W., & Monahan, J. (1980). Research in community psychology: An analysis of work published in the first six years of the American Journal of Community Psychology. *American Journal of Community Psychology,* **8,** 131–146.

Peters, C. C., & Van Voorhis, W. R. (1940), *Statistical procedures and the mathematical bases.* New York: McGraw-Hill.

Porter, L., Lawler, E., & Hackman, R. (1975). *Behavior in organizations.* New York: McGraw-Hill.

Price, R. H., & Blashfield, R. K. (1975). Explorations in the taxonomy of behavior settings: Analysis of dimensions and classifications of settings. *American Journal of Community Psychology,* **3,** 335–351.

Price, R. H., Ketter, R. F., Bader, B. C., & Monahan, J. (Eds.) (1980). *Prevention in mental health: Research, policy and practice.* Beverly Hills, Calif.: Sage.

Proshansky, H. M., Ittelson, W. H., & Rivlin, L. G. (1970) *Environmental psychology: Man and his phsycial setting.* New York: Holt, Rinehart & Winston.

Rappaport, J. (1977). *Community psychology: Values, research and action.* New York: Holt, Rinehart & Winston.

Rappaport, J., Seidman, E., & Davidson, W. S. (1979). Demonstration research and manifest versus true adoption: The natural history of a research project to divert adolescents from the legal system. In R. F. Munoz, L. R. Snowden, & J. G. Kelly (Eds.), *Social and psychological research in community settings.* San Francisco: Jossey-Bass.

Reiff, R. R. (1971). From Swampscott to swamp. *Division of Community Psychology Newsletter,* **7,** 1–3.

Reppucci, N. D. (1973). The social psychology of institutional change: General principles for intervention. *American Journal of Community Psychology,* **1,** 330–341.

Reppucci, N. D. Implementation issues for the behavior modifier as institutional change agent. *Behavioral Therapy,* 1977, **8,** 594–605.

Reppucci, N. D., & Allen, J. (1980). *Reconceptualizing the School Drop-Out Problem.* Paper presented at the Southeastern Psychological Association Annual Meeting, Washington, D. C.

Reppucci, N. D., & Clingempeel, W. G. (1978). Methodological issues in research with correctional populations. *Journal of Consulting and Clinical Psychology,* **46,** 727-746.

Reppucci, N. D., Dean, C. W., & Saunders, J. T. (1975). Job design variables as change measures in a correctional facility. *American Journal of Community Psychology,* **3,** 315–325.

Reppucci, N. D., & Sarason, S. B. (1979). Public policy and human service organizations. *American Journal of Community Psychology,* **7,** 521–542.

Reppucci, N. D., & Saunders, J. T. (1974). Social psychology of behavior modification: Problems of implementation in natural settings. *American Psychologist,* **29,** 649–660.

Reppucci, N. D., & Saunders, J. T. (1977). History, action and change. *American Journal of Community Psychology,* **5,** 399–412.

Rosenberg, M., Reppucci, N. D., & Linney, J. A. (in press). Implementing human service programs: Issues in need of consideration. *Analysis and Intervention in Developmental Disorders.*

Ross, H. L., Campbell, D. T., & Glass, G. V. (1970). Determining the social effects of a legal reform: The British "breathalyser" crackdown of 1967. *American Behavioral Scientist,* **13,** 493–509.

Rueveni, U. (1979). *Networking families in crisis.* New York: Human Sciences Press.

Rutter, M., Maughan, B., Mortimore, P., & Ouston, J. (1979). *Fifteen thousand hours: Secondary schools and their effects on children.* Cambridge, Mass.: Harvard University Press.

Samuda, R. J. (1975). *Psychological testing of American minorities.* New York: Harper & Row.

Sarason, S. B. (1971). *The culture of the school and the problem of change.* Boston: Allyn & Bacon.

Sarason, S. (1972) *The creation of settings and the future societies.* San Francisco: Jossey-Bass.

Sarason, S. B. (1974). *The psychological sense of community: Prospects for a community psychology.* San Francisco: Jossey-Bass.

Sarason, S. B., Carroll, C., Maton, K., Cohen, S., & Lorentz, F. (1977). *Human services and resource networks.* San Francisco: Jossey-Bass.

Sarason, S. B., Levin, M., Goldenberg, I., Cherlin, D. L., & Bennett, E. (1966). *Psychology in community settings.* New York: Wiley.

Sarata, B. (1977). Job design and staff satisfaction in human service settings. *American Journal of Community Psychology,* **5,** 229–236.

Seidman, E. (1978) Justice, values, and social science: Unexamined premises. In R. Simon (Ed.), *Research on Law and Sociology,* Vol. 1. Greenwich, Conn.: JAI Press.

Seidman, E., Rappaport, J., Davidson, W. S., & Linney, J. A. (in preparation). *Changing human service systems: Interventions with children, adults, and the elderly.*

Selltiz, C., Wrightsman, L. S., & Cook, S. W. (1976). *Research methods in social relations* (3rd ed.). New York: Holt, Rinehart & Winston.

Smith, P., Kandall, L., & Hulin, C. (1969) *The measurement of satisfaction in work and retirement*. Chicago: Rand-McNally.

Stack, C. (1974). *All our kin: Strategies for survival in a black community*. New York: Harper & Row.

Stokols, D. (1978). Environmental psychology. *Annual Review of Psychology, 29*, 253–296.

Suchman, E. A. (1976). *Evaluative research: Principles and practice in public service and social action programs*. New York: Russell Sage.

Tatsuoka, M. M. (1971). *Multivariate analysis: Techniques for educational and psychological research*. New York: Wiley.

Timm, N. H. (1975). *Multivariate analysis with applications in education and psychology*. Monterey, Calif.: Brooks-Cole.

Tolsdorf, C. (1976). Social networks, support, and coping: An exploratory study. *Family Process, 15*, 407–417.

Trickett, E., Kelly, J. G., & Todd, D. (1972). The social environment of the high school: Guidelines for individual change and organizational development. In S. Golann & C. Eisdorfer (Eds.), *Handbook of community mental health*. New York: Appleton-Century-Crofts.

Trickett, E. J., & Moos, R. H. (1974). Personal correlates of contrasting environments: Student satisfactions in high school classrooms. *American Journal of Community Psychology, 2*, 1–11.

Tyler, F. B. (1978). Individual psychosocial competence: A personality configuration. *Education and Psychological Measurement, 38*, 309–323.

Watzlawick, P., Weakland, J. H., & Fisch, R. (1974). *Change: Principles of problem formation and problem resolution*. New York: Norton.

Wicker, A. W. (1969). Size of church membership and members' support of church behavior settings. *Journal of Personality and Social Psychology, 13*, 278–288.

Wicker, A. W. (1979). *An introduction to ecological psychology*. Monterey, Calif.: Brooks-Cole.

Wilkinson, L. (1973). An assessment of the dimensionality of Moos' social climate scale. *American Journal of Community Psychology, 1*, 342–350.

Williams, R. L. (1971). Abuses and misuses in testing black children. *The Counseling Psychologist, 2*, 62–73.

Yalom, I. (1975). *The theory and practice of group psychotherapy*. New York: Basic Books.

Zax, M., & Specter, G. A., (1974). *An introduction to community psychology*. New York: Wiley.

PART FIVE

Areas of Clinical Research

Special Populations

CHAPTER 17

Research Methods in
Developmental Psychopathology

THOMAS M. ACHENBACH, Ph.D.

This chapter will deal primarily with research on psychopathology occurring from infancy through adolescence. The term *developmental psychopathology* stresses the importance of viewing psychopathology in relation to developmental changes during this period. Developmental changes are important in later life as well, but most adults reach stable plateaus in physical, cognitive, social, and educational growth. Children and adolescents, by contrast, continually experience marked changes in these spheres. Their behavior, normal as well as abnormal, therefore needs to be viewed in the context of change and expectations of change.

A developmental perspective is necessary not only in seeking the origins of psychopathology but also in judging what is pathological. Much behavior that is normal at one age, for example, is considered pathological if it persists to later ages, whereas other behavior is considered pathological if it emerges too early. Though obvious, this is often ignored by adult-oriented conceptions of psychopathology. Other differences between the study of psychopathology in children and adults also need special emphasis. For convenience, I will use "children" to denote the entire age range from infancy through adolescence, but the specific contrasts with adults will vary with the developmental level of the child.

DIFFERENCES BETWEEN THE STUDY OF PSYCHOPATHOLOGY IN CHILDREN AND ADULTS

Some of the differences are intrinsic to the contrasting developmental levels of children and adults. Other differences stem from the contrasting ecological contexts in which children and adults are judged. Still others reflect the differing histories of the study of psychopathology in children and adults. After highlighting these differences, I will consider developmental research strategies, definitions of developmental variables, and needed advances in child clinical research.

Intrinsic Developmental Differences

The changes occurring from birth to maturity are far more dramatic than at any other period of the life cycle. Beginning as a totally dependent organism, the child, if all goes well, makes an amazing series of advances in appearance and competence. Individual differences, though important, are dwarfed by massive age differences: Compare almost any six-month-old, three-year-old, seven-year-old, and 14-year-old on almost any dimension, for example. Although more subtle than overt physical changes, transformations of cognitive and social-emotional functioning are equally important, as are the effects of cumulative experience.

To understand psychopathology in children, we need to know their attained levels of development and how these fit into a sequence of developmental tasks and achievements. The sequence is governed jointly by biological and environmental factors. Although physical development follows a fairly uniform sequence, its rate and many aspects of bodily functioning reflect individual variations in genetic, nutritional, and other influences.

Like physical growth, the general sequence of cognitive growth also shows considerable uniformity. Social development may likewise follow an ordered developmental sequence, but this has not been as well mapped as physical and cognitive development. One promising approach has been to apply cognitive theory and methods to the study of children's grasp of social phenomena, under the banner of *social cognition* (Flavell & Ross, 1981). Emotional functioning is still harder to conceptualize in terms of an ordered sequence, although it is clear that progressive differentiation of emotions depends on physical, cognitive, and social growth.

Somewhat easier to view in developmental terms is the educational progress typifying children in a particular culture; despite wide variations in customs, every culture inculcates skills and mores in its young. The procedures for doing so and the standards for achievement are generally geared to the child's age. Success in meeting these standards depends jointly on the child's abilities and the appropriateness of the educational regimen. Mismatches between the child and the regimen may be responsible for psychopathology that might not otherwise occur.

The intrinsic developmental differences between children and adults are relevant to the study of child psychopathology in many ways. First, *developmental level* must be considered in assessing specific behavior;

certain troublesome behavior may in fact be quite typical of a particular developmental period, for example. Second, *unevenness* in attainment on different dimensions, such as more advanced physical than cognitive development, can lead to inappropriate expectations for a child. Third, *transitions* from one level to another may spawn adaptive problems that are merely by-products of progress rather than intrinsically pathological. The two-year-old's newfound power to form mental images may be frightening until the child is able to discriminate real from imagined dangers, for example. Fourth, *lacking adult notions* of mental disorders and patienthood, children seldom contribute spontaneously to the assessment and treatment processes so central to prevailing approaches to psychopathology.

Ecological Differences

Beside intrinsic developmental differences, their contrasting social ecologies require different approaches to the study of psychopathology in children and adults. An especially critical difference is the greater dependence of children on their families; children's behavior usually mirrors stresses and strengths in the family system, as well as the idiosyncratic models and customs of the family subculture. It is also essential to recognize the family's pivotal role as a source of data on children's behavior and as a constraint on behavioral change; unlike adults, children do not initiate mental health contacts and are not free to alter their life circumstances. Instead referral, assessment, and change depend heavily on the child's family. Children's dependent status also means that their achievements and failures reflect the opportunities, supports, and obstacles provided by their families more than is generally true for adults.

In addition to the critical role of their families, children's social ecology is distinguished by pervasive age grading of opportunities and expectations. Schools are the most obvious source of age grading, but toys, activities, and the attitudes of other children and adults are keyed to assumptions about what is appropriate at each age. This offers clearer behavioral guidelines than prevail for adults, but should not imply that nonnormative behavior is necessarily pathological.

Useful as they are for assessing children's developmental progress, behavioral norms should not be the only criteria. Temporary deviations from norms may be far less important than the long-term adaptive significance of particular behavior. Likewise, behavior typical of a child's subculture may sometimes be more ominous for long-term adaptation than certain atypical behavior. Until we have better longitudinal data on relations between specific child behaviors and long-term outcomes, these distinctions will be hard to make. Yet the impact of particular behaviors on children's developmental progress is crucial in assessing their pathological significance. Whereas adult treatment may aim to alleviate impediments to functioning or to restore a previously attained level of functioning, child treatment must promote continued adaptive development. Furthermore, a child's *lack* of competence may be more ominous than the *presence* of behavior that vexes adults without actually hindering the child's adaptive progress.

Other ecological differences stem from the mental health systems for children and adults: Psychopathology in children typically comes to professional attention only after adults—especially parents or teachers—decide that a child needs help. Children themselves rarely instigate referral; they seldom have much grasp of its implications and often resist it. Given the nature of the referral process, there is usually a long accumulation of behavior troubling to adults before anything is done. This behavior often involves failure to progress according to normative expectations rather than explicitly pathognomonic symptoms like those for which adults are re-

ferred. When something is finally done, mental health referral is often one of many options that depend as much on the whims of the relevant adults and on the available resources as on the child's needs.

Following referral, intervention options also reflect the ecological differences between the child and adult mental health systems. Even when the child is the identified patient, parents and other adults are often the paying clients to whom mental health workers are beholden, and contacts are sustained only if the key adults assent. Because the adult client may contribute to the child's problems, modifying the adult's behavior without jeopardizing the contact raises conflicts of interest. Not only does this interfere with helping individual children, but the difficulty of changing the relevant adults makes it hard to test causal relations between their behavior and children's problems.

Scientific Differences

Partly as a result of developmental and ecological differences between the target groups, the study of psychopathology in children has followed a very different path from the study of psychopathology in adults. Until the twentieth century, there was little recognition of psychopathology in children, other than the most obvious forms of mental retardation (Achenbach, 1982). Despite twentieth-century beliefs in the childhood roots of adult disorders and in the prophylactic power of early intervention, there has been far less research on disturbed children than disturbed adults. Instead, models for child treatment have been derived largely from adult treatment, whereas research on child behavior has been pursued mainly by developmental and educational psychologists concerned with normal functioning. As a result, our picture of disturbed children has been formed by downward extrapolations of adult clinical concepts, intersecting occasionally with lateral extrapolations of developmental concepts, but insufficient programmatic research on child psychopathology per se.

Nosological Differences

The first edition of Kraepelin's (1883) nosology, on which modern psychiatry is based, contained no childhood disorders. Seventy years later, the official American nosology, the first edition of the American Psychiatric Association's (1952) *Diagnostic and statistical manual* (DSM-I), offered only two: *childhood schizophrenia* and *adjustment reaction of childhood*. Eighty-five years after Kraepelin, DSM–II (American Psychiatric Association, 1968) added several behavior disorders of childhood. However, with the possible exception of the *hyperkinetic reaction,* these have not achieved the status of adult categories such as schizophrenia and manic-depressive disorders as foci of research, theory, training, and treatment.

DSM–III Syndromes. DSM–III (American Psychiatric Association, 1980) bases its major adult syndromes on research criteria, but there is little research basis for its childhood syndromes. Instead, they stem mainly from the DSM Task Force's negotiated consensus. Although DSM–III has added childhood syndromes, it remains to be seen whether distinctions between such syndromes as undersocialized aggressive and undersocialized nonaggressive conduct disorder, or attention deficit disorder with hyperactivity and attention deficit disorder without hyperactivity, reflect genuine differences among children. Initial studies indicate that DSM–III child diagnoses may be even less reliable than DSM–II diagnoses (Cantwell, Russell, Mattison, & Will, 1979; Mattison, Cantwell, Russell, & Will, 1979; Mezzich & Mezzich, 1979).

Multiaxial Aspects of DSM-III. Broadening the DSM by adding four axes to the syndromal nosology also has a weaker basis for children than adults. Indeed, with the

exception of the separate axis for coding organic diseases, the multiaxial system contains some curious contradictions (Rutter & Shaffer, 1980). Mental retardation, for example, is included on the same axis as syndromes of emotional and behavioral disorders. Even though multiple entries from a single axis are allowed, the child's level of intellectual functioning is an important facet of adaptation quite different from the behavioral and emotional disorders chiefly comprising Axis I.

Mental retardation implies a slower *rate* of intellectual development than is typical for one's age mates. It is assessed in relation to a distribution of abilities ranging from far below average for one's age, to average and superior levels. Because everyone can be located at some point on this dimension, regardless of other Axis I disorders, this facet of adaptation is important to recognize independently of specific disorders.

As Rutter and Shaffer (1980) have noted, it is not only illogical to imply that retardation represents the same level of discourse as other Axis I disorders, but when retardation is used as an Axis I diagnosis, it tends to be at the expense of other Axis I diagnoses. Thus, although clinicians may agree that a child is retarded, some seem to regard this as a complete diagnosis, whereas others add more Axis I diagnoses (Cantwell et al., 1979).

Furthermore, the current ideology of normalization for the retarded holds that each child should be helped to develop as normally as possible in as many areas as possible (Menolascino, 1977). Like the dimensional concept of ability, this implies that retardation should not be regarded as a categorical disorder equivalent to medical diseases or their Axis I counterparts. Instead, a child whose cognitive development is so slow as to require special help may or may not also have a psychiatric disorder; but merely being slow to develop is not equivalent to having a psychiatric disorder. The same can be said of developmental disorders coded on Axis

II, such as *developmental reading disorder, developmental arithmetic disorder,* and *developmental articulation disorder.*

Categorical versus Dimensional Approaches. The contrast between the concept of retardation as a band of gradations on a continuous dimension and the other Axis I categories illustrates a general dilemma for the study of psychopathology: Are categorical or dimensional approaches more appropriate for conceptualizing emotional and behavioral problems? Despite its additional axes for coding supplementary information, DSM–III is essentially a categorical system requiring choices among types of disorders. The research diagnostic criteria (RDC) underpinning diagnosis of the major adult disorders have enabled well-trained diagnosticians to make such choices for at least the more florid disorders in at least some disturbed adults (Spitzer, Endicott, & Robins, 1978). However, extrapolation of this approach to unvalidated children's disorders in DSM-III has not yielded good reliability (Cantwell et al., 1979; Mattison et al., 1979; Mezzich & Mezzich, 1979).

A different approach is to view problem behavior in terms of dimensions or degrees, just as intellectual ability is viewed. This approach is exemplified by multivariate efforts to formulate rating scales for children's disorders (Achenbach & Edelbrock, 1978). It is not inherently inconsistent with the DSM's categorical approach, as most of the DSM categories imply quantitative-dimensional criteria: The diagnosis of attention deficit disorder with hyperactivity, for example, requires the presence of at least two out of a list of five symptoms of hyperactivity, three out of a list of five symptoms of inattention, and three out of a list of six symptoms of impulsivity. Quantitative-dimensional judgments are also implicit in assessing specific symptoms from these lists, such as excessive running or climbing, difficulty staying seated, often doesn't seem to listen, and often acts before thinking. The

diagnostician must decide whether the child's behavior meets the quantitative criteria implied by the terms "excessive," "often," and "difficulty." However, the categorical nature of the ultimate diagnoses masks their dimensional origins.

Considering the lack of validated taxa, it may be premature to give categorical diagnosis priority over the descriptive dimensions that underlie them and that more directly reflect children's actual behavior. Furthermore, the developmental and ecological differences between adults and children may make categorical diagnosis of children's disorders inappropriate anyway. The quest for an effective taxonomy is one of the most pivotal themes in the study of child psychopathology, and one we will encounter again.

INFERRING DEVELOPMENTAL CHANGE

The study of psychopathology in children shares many of the aims and problems of developmental psychology. Most central is the assessment of stability and change in individuals as they age. The salient research problems can be grouped under several headings. One concerns strateigies for inferring developmental changes in particular variables. A second concerns the operational definition of variables amenable to study over developmentally significant periods. A third, especially crucial for research on psychopathology, concerns interactions between development and intervening events, such as traumas and treatments. And a fourth concerns comparisons of the developmental course of different groups, such as those having different risks for a particular disorder.

Developmental Research Strategies

Many behavioral changes are studied with no reference to "development." Consider, for example, learning, cognitive, or social psychological studies of the effects of variations

in Stimulus X on Response Y in college sophomores. The subjects are assumed to typify
a stable psychological system that can be
understood by observing short-term responses to external stimuli. The addition of
an ill-defined notion like "development"
seems wholly superfluous in such research.

Yet if we compare college sophomores
with third-graders and preschoolers, any effect of Stimulus X on Response Y would be
dwarfed by the enormous age differences in
response to the entire experimental situation,
not to mention Stimulus X. Researchers who
rely on college student subjects might explain
away the age differences in terms of their
own theoretical models. Learning theorists,
for example, might argue that the subjects'
different learning histories account for differences in their responses, whereas cognitive theorists could invoke changes in information-processing capacities, and social
psychologists could credit socialization histories. While all three might be partly correct, each would capture but a small facet of
changes far more massive than those ordinarily studied within their paradigms. These
greater changes, so obvious as children grow
up, are the primary subject matter of developmental psychology.

Although no single definition of development is likely to serve all purposes, the
concept of development is heuristically valuable in much the same way as the concept
of "learning." Used in this way, development
refers to changes in structure and functioning, occurring over periods ranging from
months to years in an ordered sequence that
is similar for most members of a species.
Most developmental changes are somehow
related to organic maturation, but to identify
developmental sequences, we do not need to
know their specific determinants. Verifying
causation is often an ultimate goal, but developmental sequences must be *described*
before causal hypotheses can be tested.

"Real-Time" Longitudinal Studies. The
most obvious approach to describing developmental change is by studying the same

subjects as they age, that is studying them
longitudinally. Research in which investigators actually wait for the aging to occur in
order to make successive assessments is
known as *real-time longitudinal research*
(Robins, 1979). In hope of gleaning a total
picture of development, several ambitious
real-time longitudinal studies were launched
in the 1920s (e. g., Bayley, 1970; Kagan
& Moss, 1962). Their findings on people
followed from infancy through adulthood
have served as landmarks of developmental
research. However, the need for such lengthy
commitments of resources, researchers, and
subjects limits the feasibility of long-term
longitudinal studies, especially for low base-
rate phenomena such as specific syndromes
of psychopathology. As we shall see later,
the ability of longitudinal studies to reveal
developmental change is not as great as once
hoped either, although "high risk" longitudinal research on groups selected for elevated
risks of particular disorders may produce data
not otherwise obtainable.

Follow-Up Studies. Various shortcuts are
used to link data obtained on the same subjects at different ages without the long waits
needed for real-time longitudinal studies.
Follow-up studies, also known as "catch-up"
studies (Robins, 1979), start with preexisting
records made at one age and then assess the
subjects at a later point in their lives. Child
guidance clinic records, for example, have
been used to identify people referred for behavior problems in childhood; these people
have then been followed up in adulthood to
ascertain outcomes (e. g., Robins, 1974).

If (1) all biases affecting the initial pool
of records are known; (2) the records provide
uniform data on variables important to the
research; (3) all subjects are assessed at follow-up; and (4) their histories from the initial
records to follow-up are well documented,
then a follow-up study might approximate
the yield of a good real-time longitudinal
study. These conditions are seldom met,
however. The best chance for obtaining initial records on unbiased samples, or samples

whose biases can be pinpointed, is when the records have been uniformly kept for entire populations. Few such records exist in the United States. It is seldom possible to get follow-up data on an entire sample either, and the intervening histories and causes of attrition are usually harder to document than for subjects followed in real time.

Follow-Back Studies. Follow-back studies are the reverse of follow-up studies. They start with cases known to have particular outcomes and then seek data on their earlier characteristics. The best way to obtain valid follow-back data is by locating preexisting records on the index cases, instead of having informants recall information about them. Recall is not only of dubious accuracy but also biased by knowledge of the current status of the index cases. If an informant knows the index case is psychotic, for example, the informant is more likely to show a *pathological bias* in recalling characteristics consistent with the current pathology.

Even where preexisting records are used, follow-back studies are vulnerable to biases in the initial and follow-back data, as well as in documenting the intervening histories. Unless all people with a particular outcome have equal chances of being identified, the ones actually found may be atypical. For example, schizophrenics having the worst outcomes may by easiest to find, because they are clinically diagnosed and hospitalized. By contrast, normal people having the best outcomes may be especially easy to find, because they are reputable citizens. Schizophrenics and normal people who have intermediate results may be harder to identify than other groups because they do not stand out. As a result, follow-back comparisons between identified schizophrenics and normals may be misleading because they compare the worst segment of one diagnostic group with the best segment of another group.

In tracing the early records of index cases, biases may also affect the completeness of the records and their preservation. School records, for example, may be least adequate

for index cases whose families moved often; the moves may, in turn, be related to adult outcomes. New regulations on the privacy of records and routine destruction of school, clinic, and juvenile court records also undermine the follow-up and follow-back strategies.

Cross-Sectional Studies. Where the goal is to identify age differences or age norms for particular variables rather than to trace the course of individual differences, cross-sectional studies are widely used. Because they are relatively inexpensive, these are by far the most common developmental studies. They are probably the only feasible way to obtain large-scale normative data typifying different age groups at a particular moment in history. However, cross-sectional data seldom permit inferences about developmental change. This is because obtained differences among subjects who differ in developmental level can arise from so many possible sources other than their developmental differences.

Some of the clearest errors in drawing longitudinal inferences from cross-sectional data have arisen in comparisons of the IQ test performance of different age groups. In standardizing the WAIS, for example, Wechsler (1955) found better performance by younger adults than older adults. Similarly, Kennedy, VanDeRiet, and White (1965) found higher Binet IQs in young black elementary school children than in their older schoolmates. Both findings implied that ability declined with age. Yet later longitudinal studies failed to show declining ability (Kangas & Bradway, 1971; Kennedy, 1969). Why?

The performance differences between age groups in the cross-sectional studies were due to differences in the *cohorts* used to represent each age group. Even though Wechsler's subjects were chosen to be representative of their cohorts, the older cohorts were generally less educated than the younger cohorts; this difference in education level, rather than a *decline* of ability, caused the negative correlation between age and performance evident in the cross-sectional data. In the Kennedy et al. (1963) study, cohort differences arose because all the subjects were drawn from elementary schools. As a result, the youngest cohorts included larger proportions of children who began school early because of exceptional ability; the oldest cohorts, by contrast, included children retained in elementary school because of poor performance. When Kennedy (1969) retested the same children five years later, he found no significant decline in IQ.

Many more subtle biases can also arise in cross-sectional comparisons, even if entire populations are compared. Declining birth rates, for example, mean that the average birth rank of today's 16-year-olds differs from that of today's six-year-olds. Differences between six- and 16-year-olds could thus reflect experiential differences related to birth order rather than age differences per se. It would therefore be risky to predict that, when they reach 16, today's six-year-olds will be acting like today's 16-year-olds. Such problems are not unique to cross-sectional studies, however, as we shall see in the next section.

Life-Span Analyses

In response to the problems of inferring developmental changes from the traditional cross-sectional and longitudinal designs (listed in Table 17.1), life-span developmental psychologists have advocated separating three major sources of variance (e. g., Schaie, 1965). These are (1) variance associated with the subjects' *age at assessment;*

(2) variance associated with the subjects' *cohort;* and (3) variance associated with the *time of assessment.*

Identifying variance associated with age, and other indexes of developmental level, is of course a primary aim of developmental research. Yet, as we saw from the erroneous conclusions about age declines in IQ test performance, cohort differences can be misinterpreted as age differences. Furthermore, culture-historical changes occurring over a particular period can affect people who happen to be of different ages (and cohorts). As an example, Nesselroade and Baltes (1974) found that cultural changes from the beginning to the end of a longitudinal study accounted for more variance than age changes in the personalities of four cohorts of adolescents. When cross-sectional or longitudinal studies show differences between subjects of different ages, it may not be clear whether the differences are associated with age per se, cohort differences, cultural-historical changes, or some combination of all three.

To highlight the three sources of variance, life-span developmentalists have proposed combining longitudinal and cross-sectional strategies into the hybrid *sequential* designs described next.

The Longitudinal Sequential Design. As shown in Table 17.2a, this design follows several cohorts simultaneously in a longitudinal study. Studying several cohorts over the same longitudinal period makes it possible to do cross-sectional comparisons between them at any point in the study, as well as longitudinal comparisons of the develop-

Table 17.1. Traditional Development Designs

Design	Index sample	Target data
Real-time longitudinal	Young subjects	Continuous data on index sample
Follow-up	Records on young subjects	Outcome data on index sample
Follow-back	Outcome data on old subjects	Earlier records on index sample
Cross-sectional	Subjects from different age cohorts	Comparable data on subjects of different ages

Table 17.2.   Life-Span Developmental Designs[a] (adapted from Achenbach, 1978a)

```
1975                    | 1985    1986    1987 |
1976            | 1985    1986    1987 |
1977   | 1985    1986    1987 |

         8       9      10      11      12
```
Age studied

(a) Longitudinal sequential design in which three two-year longitudinal studies are performed simultaneously on samples from three birth cohorts.

```
1975                    | 1985 | 1986 | 1987 |
1976            | 1985 | 1986 | 1987 |
1977   | 1985 | 1986 | 1987 |

         8       9      10      11      12
```
Age studied

(b) Cross-sectional sequential design in which three samples are drawn from each of three cohorts on three occasions from 1985 through 1987.

```
1975   | 1985 | 1986 | 1987 |
1976   | 1986 | 1987 | 1988 |
1977   | 1987 | 1988 | 1989 |

         8       9      10
```
Age studied

(c) Time-lag sequential design in which three samples from each of three cohorts are compared on three occasions from 1985 to 1987, 1986 to 1988, and 1987 to 1989, respectively.

KEY

[a] ☐ indicates cohort.

☐ indicates separate samples within cohort.

mental course followed by each cohort. We can thus determine whether changes occurring over time in one cohort likewise occur in the other cohorts regardless of age, or whether the changes occur only at particular ages. The longitudinal sequential design also enables us to do time-lag comparisons. These are comparisons between members of different cohorts as they reach a particular age in different years. As shown in Table 17.2a, for example, children born in 1975, 1976, and 1977 can be compared when they reach age 10 in 1985, 1986, and 1987, respectively, to determine whether there are secular changes in 10-year-olds' behavior over those three years.

Longitudinal sequential designs also enable us to obtain longitudinal data over shorter intervals than would be required by real-time longitudinal studies of the same age span. In Table 17.2a, for example the overlap of three cohorts may make it possible to draw conclusions about development from ages eight through 12 in only three years.

The Cross-Sectional Sequential Design. This design draws cross-sectional samples from several birth cohorts at successive points in time. As Table 17.2b shows, it is similar to the longitudinal sequential design, except that we assess *different* samples from each cohort on each occasion, instead of repeatedly assessing the same samples. Because we draw new samples for each assessment, this design is not vulnerable to the biasing effects of initial selection for expected long-term availability, attrition, or repeated testing. However, it has the disadvantage of precluding longitudinal study of changes in the same subjects, and it risks confounding sample differences with the age and cohort effects of interest.

The Time-Lag Sequential Design. As shown in Table 17.2c, this design compares different samples from each of several cohorts as they reach particular target ages in different years. Although the other sequential designs can also yield time-lag comparisons for one or more ages as a by-product of their other aims, the primary aim of the time-lag sequential design is to detect secular trends in the behavior of subjects at a particular age.

Limitations of Life-Span Approaches

Life-span developmentalists have sought to pinpoint sources of variance often confounded in developmental studies. Their sequential designs are intended as ideal models for disentangling variance associated with age (and other developmental indexes) from variance associated with cohort and time of assessment. Unhappily, the need for many interlocking observations on different birth cohorts over developmentally significant intervals limits the practicality of such designs. The limitations are especially severe for the study of psychopathology, in which the number of available subjects having particular disorders is often small, and many other important variables such as gender, race, intelligence, family background, and treatment status must be controlled.

Another limitation of the sequential designs is that they cannot fully separate the three major sources of variances. At most, only two of the three variables of age, cohort, and time of assessment can be separated. The

choice of a birth cohort and age of assessment, for example, automatically determines the time of assessment, because a particular cohort reaches a particular age at only one point in time. Likewise, the choice of a birth cohort and time of assessment automatically determines the age of assessment. And the year and age of assessment determine the cohort to be assessed.

The impossibility of varying age, cohort, and time of assessment independently of each other means that variance due to one can be inextricably confounded with variance due to at least one other. Critics have shown that the sequential designs and their practical applications do not really fulfill the claims of life-span researchers (Adam, 1978; Horn & Donaldson, 1976, 1977). Furthermore, the biases in carefully executed traditional designs may be no worse in practice than the biases of life-span designs (Botwinick & Siegler, 1980; McCall, 1977). Nevertheless, the sequential designs offer helpful strategies for triangulating developmental research questions. Even if they cannot totally solve the problems of confounded variance, they spotlight more sources of variance than traditional longitudinal and cross-sectional designs. Giving cohort and time-of-assessment effects as much recognition as age effects may be especially helpful in the developmental study of psychopathology, where secular trends in disorders are often of great interest.

Recent alarm about hyperactivity, for example, has raised questions of whether it is essentially a normal developmental phenomenon no longer tolerated by our society or an illness spread by food additives and other pollutants (Achenbach, 1982, Chapter 11). Are there really age changes, secular changes, or both in children's activity levels? Longitudinal sequential comparisons of several cohorts as they traverse early and middle childhood would help to elucidate age, cohort, and time-of-assessment effects, subject to further testing through studies converging on specific etiological hypotheses.

Developmental versus Trait Variance

An inferential problem not directly addressed by life-span designs concerns the separation of developmental variance from trait variance. With respect to hyperactivity, for example, developmental variance reflects changes in activity level in the same individuals as they age; trait variance, by contrast, reflects individual differences in activity level that persist over developmentally significant periods. Both sources of variance may affect a particular behavior.

As an illustration, consider the attentional deficits that are now regarded as the hallmark of hyperactivity: Survey data on normal children show that eight- and nine-year-old boys are the group most often reported to have attentional problems (Achenbach & Edelbrock, 1981). Since most children diagnosed hyperactive are also boys of this age, it is important to distinguish among the following possibilities: (1) if boys' attentional problems normally rise to a peak at ages eight and nine, perhaps some boys' peak is high enough or their environments are intolerant enough to get them labeled as hyperactive; (2) perhaps attentional ability is a stable trait, and boys lacking this ability are identified as hyperactive when school standards rise to a point they cannot meet, typically at the age of eight or nine; (3) perhaps (1) and (2) are both relevant, in that developmental change, poor attentional ability, and rising standards all help to maximize the probability that a particular boy will be called hyperactive at the age of eight or nine.

Developmental research has emphasized developmental variance, whereas research on psychopathology has emphasized trait variance, whether conceived in terms of categorical or dimensional constructs. However, the search for persisting individual differences is complicated in several ways by the effect of developmental differences on almost all measures of child behavior. First, when children are repeatedly assessed over developmentally significant periods, they are likely to show developmental changes even if they also retain a stable rank order within their cohort. Second, unless all members of a sample are at the same developmental level, individual differences in a trait may reflect developmental differences as well as trait differences. Third, when significant covariation is found among measures that change over the course of development, this covariation may reflect the variance the measures share with development, rather than stable individual differences in an independent trait. Analyses of developmentally heterogeneous samples, for example, can yield significant relations among measures merely because certain scores on each measure occur only in subjects of a particular age. Likewise, factor analyses of developmentally heterogeneous samples can yield age factors that may be mistaken for trait factors.

Separating Developmental from Trait Variance. Returning now to the example of attentional problems, these are often measured in terms of a traitlike dimension extending from careless, impulsive responding at one extreme to careful, reflective responding at the other extreme. However, measures of this trait also correlate with developmental indexes such as chronological age (CA) and mental age (MA). When children differ in their impulsivity scores, does this indicate trait differences, developmental differences, or both? (Note that the methodological issue is the same, whether the variable in question is called impulsivity, attention deficit, self-control, ego control, or X.)

To separate trait variance from cognitive developmental variance, Achenbach and Weisz (1975) administered the Stanford-Binet and a test of impulsivity to preschoolers on two occasions, six months apart. They found a significant correlation between Time 1 and Time 2 impulsivity scores, suggesting that the test reflected stable trait variance. Yet regression of Time 2 scores on both MA and Time 1 scores showed that considerably more of the variance in Time 2 scores could be accounted for by MA than by Time 1 impulsivity. A significant correlation was also found between impulsivity and hypothesis usage, which is assumed to be a central facet of the impulsivity-reflectivity dimension (Kagan & Kogan, 1970). However, partialling out MA reduced this correlation to nonsignificance.

Cognitive development may thus account for much of the variance that has been interpreted in terms of a trait of impulsivity. Measures of self-concept, moral development, and field independence have likewise been found to share considerable variance with general cognitive development in children (Katz & Zigler, 1967; Taylor & Achenbach, 1975; Weisz, O'Neill, & O'Neill, 1975). Although assessment of persisting individual differences is an important aim of research on psychopathology, it is equally important to show that these differences represent reliable variance other than that already explained by general developmental indexes. Otherwise, we risk mistaking developmental for trait variance and a proliferation of "traits" more parsimoniously understood in terms of development.

DEFINING DEVELOPMENTAL VARIABLES

Until now, we have discussed developmental change without much attention to *what* changes. Developmental research aims not only to assess change but also to identify variables amenable to study over developmentally significant periods. Other than physical parameters such as height and weight, few variables can be operationally defined in a uniform fashion over lengthy periods of development.

Cognitive Variables

To date, the closest psychological approximation to variables like height and weight is probably the IQ. But even the seeming

simplicity of IQ masks complexities that distinguish developmental research from other kinds: Compare, for example, the Binet items administered at ages four and 14. About the only thing common to these levels is vocabulary, and even this involves not only different words but different methods of assessing word knowledge. The Wechsler tests are organized around subtests extending over several ages, but the content and scoring standards change markedly within the subtests. Despite greater ease of administration and profile analysis, the Wechsler approach has not proved more valid than the potpourri MA approach of the Binet (Kaufman, 1973).

Beside age changes in content and scoring, the IQ obviously differs from linear variables in assigning each individual a score *relative* to a normative sample of age mates, rather than directly designating a *quantity* of the variable in question. Although no known linear variable underlies IQ, individuals retain fairly stable rankings relative to their age mates, and their scores significantly predict academic performance (Achenbach, 1982, Chapter 8). Something important must therefore underlie the IQ. What is it about the hodgepodge of IQ test items that hangs together across years of development?

Piagetian research on cognitive development points to major structural changes at around the ages of two, seven, and 11 (Piaget, 1970). Most IQ tests are not explicitly designed to detect theoretically important changes of this sort. Yet MA scores on IQ tests correlate well with measures of the transitions hypothesized by Piaget (Achenbach, 1969, 1970, 1973). Could these correlations merely reflect components of environmental programming common to children of a particular CA?

Probably not, because the Piagetian measures also correlate well with MA in retarded adults whose CAs are far above their MA, and in high IQ children whose CAs are below their MAs. Although we still lack detailed maps of cognitive development, it seems clear that IQ test items, originally selected mainly for their relations to age and school performance, indirectly index underlying structural changes. Furthermore, the stability of IQ suggests enduring individual differences in the rate at which these changes occur. Despite our ignorance of the exact determinants of cognitive development, convergence among diverse empirically and theoretically derived measures thus suggests guidelines for the definition of other developmental variables.

Noncognitive Variables

Except for mental retardation and learning disabilities, cognitive variables are typically of less concern to clinicians than noncognitive variables. Yet far less has been done to operationalize and validate noncognitive measures that can be used at different developmental levels, show how a child compares with normal age mates, and provide comparisons across developmental periods. In longitudinal studies, a dominant approach has been to form composite variables for each age level by aggregating diverse personality data for that age via *Q*-sorts (Block & Block, 1980) or factor analysis (Waldrop & Halverson, 1975). Developmental analyses have then been made by computing correlations between the composite variables derived for one age and those derived for another. Although this is a useful heuristic strategy, the obtained relationships have generally been weak, have been restricted to normal samples, and have not been linked to clinical disorders. As a result, this approach has not yet yielded measures capable of guiding programmatic child clinical research.

The task of operationally defining noncognitive variables for the study of child psychopathology differs somewhat from the task faced by the early IQ test builders, but a comparison may be instructive. An advantage enjoyed by the test builders was their clear target criterion—school performance—against which to validate their measures. (The fact that IQ tests soon proved more re-

liable than the teacher ratings used as validating criteria illustrates the potential power of psychometric bootstrapping.) A second advantage was the focus on behavior assessable by an examiner in terms of right and wrong responses to structured tasks. A third advantage was that the *quantity* of correct responses and the *quality* of solutions to problems typically increased with age. Yet these features emerged only after considerable trial-and-error tinkering with other approaches to intelligence testing. They became explicit only when efforts to diagnose intelligence as a static faculty gave way to Binet and Simon's (1905) normative-developmental approach.

The developmental aspect of IQ tests inheres mainly in their age grading of items, scoring, and norming. They were not designed to reveal developmental differences in structure or process; nor have more theoretically based efforts yet produced standardized instruments for doing so. Nevertheless, a normative-developmental approach may be as useful for noncognitive variables as it has been for IQ tests.

Like the quest for a measurement framework in the early history of cognitive research, the quest for a taxonomy of behavior disorders has preoccupied child clinical researchers. Following sporadic earlier efforts, the 1960s and 1970s brought a surge of multivariate research aimed at creating empirically based taxonomies. Despite great diversity of methods, subject samples, instruments, and raters, these efforts have shown considerable convergence on a few broad band syndromes and more numerous narrow band syndromes (Achenbach & Edelbrock, 1978). However, most of these efforts have stopped short of translating multivariate groupings of items into procedures for discriminating among individual children. Their failure to separate age groups also masks developmental differences in the prevalence and patterning of behavior problems. Furthermore, a lack of validating criteria and normative data precludes judgments about the clinical significance of most of the multivariate findings. In short, multivariate efforts to objectify the taxonomy of childhood behavior disorders shows flaws reminiscent of pre-Binet efforts to objectify the assessment of intelligence.

Empirically Defining Behavior Disorders: An Example

Using a normative-developmental approach, we have sought to translate multivariate findings into practical tools for assessing behavior disorders. We started with a checklist of behavior problems derived from surveys of psychiatric case histories and the literature on child psychopathology. To take account of social competencies that may be as important as behavior problems, we also tried various approaches to assessing children's positive adaptive behavior. Because parents' perceptions are crucial in the evaluation of most disturbed children, they were chosen as key informants, although we have also obtained parallel data from clinicians, teachers, trained observers, and children themselves. Our basic data collection instrument, the Child Behavior Checklist (CBCL), was refined through a series of pilot editions tested with parents of disturbed children as respondents (See Achenbach, 1978b, 1979, for details). The CBCL includes 20 social competence and 118 behavior problem items designed to be reported by parents in a structured format requiring a minimum of inference.

To obtain clinical data, we enlisted the aid of 30 outpatient mental health settings. Parents of children referred to these settings filled out the CBCL at intake. We then used these data to construct social competence and behavior problem scales. The competence items were grouped into three scales reflecting school performance and participation in activities and social relations. Scoring procedures were based on the distributions of responses we found in our clinical samples.

Multivariate Description of Behavior Disorders. We used principal components analyses to identify syndromes of behavior problems reported by parents. In order to reflect age and sex variations in the prevalence and patterning of behaviors, we analyzed each sex separately at ages 4–5, 6–11, and 12–16, using data on over 2000 disturbed children. The age intervals were chosen for their correspondence to important milestones in cognitive, educational, social, and biological development.

Several rotations of each principal components solution were performed to identify factors that were especially robust. From the various rotations for a particular age-sex group, one was chosen as the best representation of factors that remained intact throughout the various rotations. Factors having at least six items loading $\geq$ .30 were retained as the basis for the behavior problem scales for that age-sex group. Each scale consists of the items loading highest on one of the factors. For convenience, each scale has been given a descriptive title (shown in Table 17.3), but these titles do not necessarily imply discrete nosological categories. Instead a child's standing on a particular scale is operationally defined as the sum of his or her scores on the behavior problems comprising that scale.

Some of the scales resemble DSM nosological categories. But the lack of empirical validation for the DSM child categories means that the DSM should not necessarily be viewed as a validating criterion for the empirically derived scales. As argued in more detail elsewhere (Achenbach, 1980a, 1980b), the DSM and empirical approaches are different facets of a common quest for taxonomic order in child psychopathology; using them in tandem to evolve a better overall approach may make more sense than setting one up as the arbiter of the other.

Preserving a Comprehensive Picture. The lack of well-validated nosological constructs for children's behavior disorders argues against prematurely narrowing our picture of such disorders into focalized, forced-choice categories. To preserve a comprehensive picture of the behavior problems reported on the Child Behavior Checklist, we therefore assembled the behavior problem and social competence scales into a profile format, called the Child Behavior Profile. The Profile shows a child's scores on every item of every scale, as well as providing a graphic display of each scale score relative to all others. The raw scores for each scale are transformed into normalized *T* scores derived from CBCL data on 1300 normal (nonreferred) children. The scales themselves were derived on clinical samples in order to reflect syndromes occurring among disturbed children, but the nonclinical norms make it possible to compare

a child with normal children of the same age and sex.

Hierarchical Aspects. Because different taxonomic levels may be needed for different purposes, we have done second-order factor analyses of the behavior problem scales of each edition of the Profile. For each edition, we found two broad band groupings of behavior problems resembling those designated as Inhibited versus Aggressive and Personality Disorder versus Conduct Disorder in other multivariate studies (Miller, 1967; Quay, 1979). We have labeled these broad band syndromes *Internalizing* and *Externalizing*.

In Table 17.3, the narrow band scales forming these broad band syndromes on each

Table 17.3. Behavior Problem Scales of the Child Behavior Profile

Group	Internalizing scales[a]	Mixed scales	Externalizing scales[a]
Boys aged 4–5	1. Social withdrawal 2. Somatic complaints 3. Immature 4. Depressed	1. Sex problems	1. Delinquent 2. Aggressive 3. Schizoid
Boys aged 6–11	1. Schizoid 2. Depressed 3. Uncommunicative 4. Obsessive compulsive 5. Somatic complaints	1. Social withdrawal	1. Delinquent 2. Aggressive 3. Hyperactive
Boys ages 12–16	1. Somatic complaints 2. Schizoid 3. Uncommunicative 4. Immature 5. Obsessive compulsive	1. Hostile withdrawal	1. Hyperactive 2. Aggressive 3. Delinquent
Girls aged 4–5	1. Depressed 2. Somatic complaints 3. Schizoid 4. Social withdrawal	1. Sex problems	1. Obese 2. Aggressive 3. Hyperactive
Girls aged 6–11	1. Depressed 2. Social withdrawal 3. Somatic complaints 4. Schizoid obsessive		1. Cruel 2. Aggressive 3. Delinquent 4. Sex problems 5. Hyperactive
Girls aged 12–16	1. Anxious obsessive 2. Somatic complaints 3. Schizoid 4. Depressed withdrawal	1. Immature hyperactive	1. Cruel 2. Aggressive 3. Delinquent

[a]Scales are listed in descending order of their loadings on the second-order Internalizing and Externalizing factors. Because the scales were derived separately and subjected to separate second-order analyses for each age/sex, the composition of the scales and their second-order locations vary among the age/sex groups.

edition of the Profile are listed under the Internalizing and Externalizing headings. Scales not clearly aligned with one second-order factor more than the other are listed under the Mixed heading. The Profile provides T scores for Internalizing and Externalizing, as well as for total behavior problem and social competence scores. In addition, we have reported prevalence data on every behavior problem and competence item for demographically matched disturbed and normal children aged four to 16 (Achenbach & Edelbrock, 1981). Using hierarchical cluster analysis, we have also constructed a multilevel typology of profiles for disturbed children and have assessed differential correlates of the profile types (Edelbrock & Achenbach, 1980).

It is thus possible to use data collected with the CBCL at several levels of analysis: individual items; narrow band behavior problem and competence scales; broad band groupings of behavior problems; total scores; and profile types. Good interrater and test-retest reliabilities have been found for all levels of analysis. Hand-scored and computerized versions of the Profile make it readily usable in clinical and research contexts alike. It can also be used to assess changes in behavior over time or as a function of interventions. Despite this array of possibilities, however, the Child Behavior Profile is viewed as but an early step in a long-term bootstrapping sequence. As such, it is subject to revision or replacement as better ways of defining children's behavior disorders evolve. Until we know what variables and what levels of analysis are the most productive, we will continue to need provisional systems of this sort. The more they foster multilevel and multidimensional analysis, the more valuable they are likely to be.

Validating Behavioral Taxa

Factor-analytically derived behavioral syndromes and cluster-analytically derived profile types can be viewed as taxonomic constructs. (For a detailed appraisal in terms of *taxometrics,* see Achenbach, 1981.) As constructs, they need validation. One type of validity is the power to discriminate between normal and disturbed children. We have found that clinically referred children in fact score significantly higher on all our behavior problem scales and lower on all our social competence scales than demographically matched nonreferred children. (Achenbach, 1978b; Achenbach & Edelbrock, 1979).

Another type of validity would be the demonstration of a different etiology for each behavioral taxon. However, there are as yet few testable hypotheses as to the specific etiologies of children's behavior disorders. Furthermore, efforts to isolate a focalized behavior disorder have often been frustrated as the disorder seemed to fade into a web of interconnections with other behaviors. This has been painfully evident in research on hyperactivity and learning disorders; it also seems evident in the quest for childhood depression (Achenbach, 1982, Chapter 11).

Grouping children according to their similarities on a few critical symptoms may ignore their equally important differences in other areas. Although highly focalized behavior disorders and specific etiologies may yet be verified, it seems likely that most behavior disorders of childhood will not fit neatly into narrow nosological categories, each with its own specific cause and cure. Instead most disorders are probably shaped by complex combinations of constitutional and environmental factors. An improved taxonomy may aid the search for causes, but it is unrealistic to expect many behavioral taxa to be validated by discovery of specific etiologies in the near future.

Because the exact determinants of developmental variables are usually hard to prove, they must be evaluated largely in terms of construct validity. Construct validity is adduced via convergent and discriminant agreement among diverse measures of the same construct and via sensitivity to expected stability and change in the construct. For developmental variables, most important relations among measures, as well as the most important aspects of stability and change, are those occurring over developmental periods ranging from months to years. Prior to adulthood, IQ tests are evaluated in terms of their prediction of achievement and are calibrated according to cognitive advances that are normed in intervals of months, for example. The construct validity of more theoretically based cognitive developmental measures, such as Piagetian tasks, can be evaluated in terms of the *order* in which they are mastered by children as they age.

In validating multivariate behavioral taxa, however, we lack ready-made criteria like academic performance, normative age progressions, and theoretical orderings. Yet we can determine whether the taxa are differentially related to other important variables, concurrently as well as over significant developmental periods. Concurrent correlations with specific competencies, cognitive level, family dynamics, organic functioning, and demographic variables, for example, can suggest more comprehensive diagnostic formulations than offered by a descriptive taxonomy alone. Cross-sectional comparisons of the composition and distribution of behavioral taxa at different ages can suggest developmental hypotheses and age differences in service needs. Longitudinal research, preferably using life-span approaches, can show whether different taxa have different antecedents and outcomes. Such differences help to suggest causal hypotheses, predict the typical course of particular disorders, and link childhood disorders with adult disorders.

If multivariate behavioral taxa are found to predict different outcomes, this would enable us to focus research efforts on helping those having the worst outcomes. The content of the taxa, their distributions and hierarchical relations, antecedents, and concurrent correlations with other variables should be rich sources of hypotheses about why certain ones have especially poor outcomes. Empirically derived taxonomies can thus provide nodes around which to integrate services, research, and theory. However, tests of causal hypotheses and better matching of treatment to the needs of children at risk for poor outcomes will require experimental-developmental approaches, to which we now turn.

EXPERIMENTAL-DEVELOPMENTAL RESEARCH

With adjustments for the developmental level of the subjects, many standard tools of behavioral research can be applied to the study of child psychopathology (Achenbach, 1978a). Experimental designs, for example, have been widely used to study drug and behavior therapies for children. The specificity of these treatments and their target symptoms, as well as their amenability to tight control, makes them especially good candidates for experimental research. The result has been a succession of increasingly sophisticated placebo-controlled, double-blind, cross-over, reversal, single-subject, and multiple-baseline studies. These have helped objectify our knowledge of psychopathology. They have also supported the efficacy of certain drug and behavior therapies. However, they have not fully incorporated developmental perspectives.

The experimental studies have typically assessed outcomes over relatively brief periods. When children are followed up over developmentally more significant periods, the apparent efficacy of drug and behavior therapies fades (Mash & Dalby, 1979; Weiss & Hechtman, 1979). Furthermore, when problems other than the target symptoms were assessed, little benefit was found over even the short span of the experimental studies. Although it is assumed that alleviating the target symptoms will enhance social and educational development, this has not happened (Achenbach, 1982, Chapter 11). The very different dose-response curves for the effects of stimulant drugs on hyperactivity, cognitive functioning, and physiological parameters, for example, indicate that treatments effective for the target symptoms may in fact interfere with other aspects of adaptation (Sprague & Sleator, 1977).

Experimental treatment studies have also failed to examine treatment-client interactions: Most have been designed to answer the question "Does Treatment X work?" without answering the more important question of "What treatment works best for whom?" When children are selected because they have certain target symptoms, and Treatment X is found to alleviate the symptoms more than a placebo, we still do not know whether X is the treatment of choice for most children with those symptoms. In fact, in the rare studies reporting even post hoc analyses of treatment–client interactions, child characteristics such as age and SES were found to account for more variance than the main effects of treatment type (Love & Kaswan, 1974; Miller, Barrett, Hampe, & Noble, 1972).

To benefit children, experimental treatment research thus needs to be broadened in several ways: (1) to assess outcomes over developmentally significant periods; (2) to assess aspects of functioning other than a few target smptoms; and (3) to identify interactions between child and treatment characteristics that will tell us what works best for whom.

Just as experimental research needs a developmental facet, the impossibility of fully separating age, cohort, and time-of-assessment variance in nonexperimental developmental designs argues for adding an experimental facet to developmental studies. Once nonexperimental developmental studies have uncovered putative predictors of outcome, we must compare the effects of different treatment modalities for high-risk children using type-of-treatment by type-of-child designs, with adequate follow-up periods.

In order to combine experimental and developmental strategies, the target symptoms favored for experimental research can be viewed as components of higher-order taxa subsuming more aspects of functioning and capable of spanning significant developmental periods. The behavior profile types described earlier exemplify higher-order taxa of this sort. Thus, experimental-developmental research can start with follow-ups comparing outcomes for children grouped according to profile type in order to determine which type typically have the worst outcomes. Thereafter, candidate treatments that are hypothesized to offer the best hopes for the poor-outcome types could be selected. Where it is possible to study more than one treatment and more than one type of subject (for example, children differing in profile pattern or age or SES), we can compare treatments in a factorial design using the different client types to determine what works best for whom (see also Kendall & Norton-Ford, this volume). Even where only one treatment is of interest, we need to experimentally compare its effects, using cross-over, reversal, or group-comparison designs, on children who are grouped according to potentially relevant variables such as profile pattern, age, and SES. We can thus document variations in treatment effects more clearly than in designs that treat children manifesting target symptoms as a homogeneous group.

RELATIONS BETWEEN RESEARCH AND SERVICE NEEDS

Behavioral approaches emphasize specific behavior problems and treatment goals. Yet in many child clinical settings, behavioral terminology and paraphernalia are indiscriminately mixed with more traditional clinical practices (Buckholdt & Gubrium, 1979). Although both may have something to contribute, neither provides comprehensive guidelines for assessment, treatment, and evaluation of outcome in a developmental context. Instead, there is a tendency to vacillate between molecular behavior and more molar intrapsychic concepts without explicitly blending the two. Although the intrapsychic concepts are not easy to define operationally, they nevertheless reflect a need to view individual children as more than the sum of their problem behavior. Higher order constructs are needed both to integrate diverse behavior into a comprehensive picture of functioning at a particular point in a child's life and to provide a basis for planning and reassessment over time. Child clinical services could thus benefit from taxonomic nodes like those needed for the integration of experimental and developmental research.

Use of a common assessment framework by clinicians and researchers would encourage more cross-fertilization than we have yet seen. Instead of a research literature based on esoteric measures foreign to clinical practice and clinical practice unaided by research findings, we could gear research more closely to clinical needs and more directly test research findings in practice. Both research and practice would profit from a common framework for assessing behavior disorders, provisional though it may be.

SUMMARY

The term "developmental psychopathology" stresses the importance of a developmental perspective for the study of psychopathology. Developmental, ecological, scientific, and nosological differences all distinguish research on child disorders from research on adult disorders. The official psychiatric nosology also has a much weaker empirical base for child than adult disorders. Considering the lack of validated nosological taxa, it may be premature to impose categorical diagnoses on children's behavior problems.

Like developmental psychology, the study of psychopathology in children is concerned with inferences about developmental change. Such changes are often studied using *real-time longitudinal, follow-up, follow-back,* and *cross-sectional* designs. However, life-span developmental psychologists have shown that these designs may confound variance in age, cohort, and time of assessment. To separate these sources of variance, they have proposed combining longitudinal and cross-sectional strategies in *longitudinal sequential, cross-sectional sequential,* and *time-lag sequential* designs. Although sequential designs cannot fully disentangle all three sources of variance, they do permit more comprehensive analyses than the nonsequential designs. Beside the sources of variance highlighted by life-span analyses, developmental research must also distinguish between *developmental variance* and *trait variance.* This is especially true in research on individual differences that persist over significant developmental periods.

Another problem common to the study of normal and abnormal development is the definition of variables that can be assessed over significant developmental periods. The current quest for a measurement framework for children's behavior disorders resembles the quest for a cognitive measurement framework early in this century. The *normative-developmental* approach used in cognitive measurement can be applied to noncognitive variables as well. This has been done in formulating multivariate taxa of children's behavioral problems. Such taxa offer organizing structures for the study of child psychopathology at multiple levels of analysis. However, these taxa need to be tested through experimental-developmental research and applications to clinical services.

REFERENCES

Achenbach, T. M. (1969). Conservation of illusion-distorted identity: Its relation to CA and MA in normals and retardates. *Child Development,* **40,** 663–679.

Achenbach, T. M. (1970). The Children's Associative Responding Test: A possible alternative to group IQ tests. *Journal of Educational Psychology,* **61,** 340–348.

Achenbach, T. M. (1973). Surprise and memory as indices of concrete operational development. *Psychological Reports,* **33,** 47–57.

Achenbach, T. M (1978a). *Research in developmental psychology: Concepts, strategies, methods.* New York: Free Press.

Achenbach, T. M. (1978b). The Child Behavior Profile: I. Boys aged 6–11. *Journal of Consulting and Clinical Psychology,* **46,** 478–488.

Achenbach, T. M. (1979). The Child Behavior Profile: An empirically-based system for assessing children's behavioral problems and competencies. *International Journal of Mental Health,* **7,** 24–42.

Achenbach, T. M. (1980a). DSM–III in light of empirical research on the classification of child psychopathology. *Journal of the American Academy of Child Psychiatry,* **19,** 395–412.

Achenbach, T. M. (1980b). What is child psychiatric epidemiology the epidemiology of? In F. Earls (Ed.), *Psychosocial epidemiologic studies of children.* New York: Neale Watson Academic Publishers.

Achenbach, T. M. (1981). The role of taxonomy in developmental psychopathology. In M. E. Lamb and A. L. Brown (Eds), *Advances in developmental psychology,* Vol. 1. Hillsdale, N. J.: Erlbaum.

Achenbach, T. M. (1982). *Developmental psychopathology* (2nd ed.). New York: Wiley.

Achenbach, T. M., & Edelbrock, C. S. (1978). The classification of child psychopathology: A review and analysis of empirical efforts. *Psychological Bulletin,* **85,** 1275–1301.

Achenbach, T. M., & Edelbrock, C. S. (1979). The Child Behavior Profile: II Boys aged 12–16 and girls aged 6–11 and 12–16. *Journal of Consulting and Clinical Psychology,* **47,** 223–233.

Achenbach, T. M., & Edelbrock, C. S. (1981). Behavioral problems and competencies reported by parents of normal and disturbed children aged 4 through 16. *Monographs of the Society for Research in Child Development,* **46,** Serial No. 188.

Achenbach, T. M., & Weisz, J. R. (1975). Impulsivity-reflectivity and cognitive development in preschoolers: A longitudinal analysis of developmental and trait variance. *Developmental Psychology,* **11,** 413–414.

Adam, J. (1978). Sequential strategies and the separation of age, cohort, and time-of-measurement contributions to developmental data. *Psychological Bulletin,* **85,** 1309–1316.

American Psychiatric Association (1952). *Diagnostic and statistical manual of mental disorders* (1st ed.). (2nd. ed., 1968, 3rd ed., 1980). Washington, D.C.: A.P.A.

Bayley, N. (1970). Development of mental abilities. In P. E. Mussen (Ed.), *Carmichael's manual of child psychology.* New York: Wiley.

Binet, A., & Simon, T. (1905). New methods for the diagnosis of the intellectual level of subnormals. *L'anneé psychologique.* Translated and reprinted in A. Binet and T. Simon, *The development of intelligence in children.* Baltimore: Williams & Wilkins, 1916.

Block, J. H., & Block, J. (1978). The role of ego-control and ego-resiliency in the organization of behavior. In W. A. Collins (Ed), *Minnesota symposia on child psychology,* Vol. 13. Hillsdale, N. J.: Erlbaum.

Botwinick, J., & Siegler, I. C. (1980). Intellectual ability amont the elderly: Simultaneous cross-sectional and longitudinal comparisons. *Developmental Psychology,* **16,** 49–53.

Buckholdt, D. R., & Gubrium, J. F. (1979). *Caretakers: Treating emotionally disturbed children.* Beverly Hills, Calif.: Sage.

Cantwell, D. P., Russell, A. T., Mattison, R., & Will, L. (1979). A comparison of DSM–II and DSM–III in the diagnosis of childhood psyciatric disorders. *Archives of General Psychiatry,* **36,** 1208–1213.

Edelbrock, C., & Achenbach, T. M. (1980). A typology of Child Behavior Profile patterns: Distribution and correlates for disturbed children aged 6–16. *Journal of Abnormal Child Psychology,* **8,** 441–470.

Flavell, J. H., & Ross, L. (1981). *Social cognitive development.* New York: Cambridge University Press.

Horn, J. L., & Donaldson, G. (1976). On the myth of intellectual decline in adulthood. *American Psychologist,* **31,** 701–719.

Horn, J. L., & Donaldson, G. (1977). Faith is not enough: A response to the Baltes-Schaie claim that intelligence does not wane. *American Psychologist,* **32,** 369–373.

Kagan, J., & Kogan, N. (1970). Individuality and cognitive performance. In P. H. Mussen (Ed.). *Carmichael's manual of child psychology.* New York: Wiley.

Kagan, J., & Moss, H. A. (1962). *Birth to maturity.* New York: Wiley.

Kangas, J., & Bradway, K. (1971). Intelligence at middle age: A thirty-eight year follow-up. *Developmental Psychology,* **5,** 333–337.

Katz, P., & Zigler, E. (1967). Self-image disparity: A developmental approach. *Journal of Personality and Social Psychology,* **5,** 186–195.

Kaufman, A. S. (1973). Comparison of the WPPSI, Stanford-Binet, and McCarthy Scales as predictors of first grade achievement. *Perceptual and Motor Skills,* **36,** 67–73.

Kennedy, W. A. (1969). A follow-up normative study of Negro intelligence and achievement. *Monographs of the Society for Research in Child Development,* **34,** Serial No. 126.

Kennedy, W. A., VanDeRiet, V., & White, J. C. (1963). A normative sample of intelligence and achievement of Negro elementary school children in the southeastern United States. *Monographs of the Society for Research in Child Development,* **28,** Serial No. 90.

Kraepelin, E. (1883). *Compendium der psychiatrie.* Leipzig: Abel.

Love, L. R., & Kaswan, J. W. (1974). *Troubled children: Their families, schools, and treatments.* New York: Wiley.

Mash, E. J., & Dalby, J. T. (1979). Behavioral interventions for hyperactivity. In R. L. Trites (Ed.), *Hyperactivity in children. Etiology, measurement, and treatment implications.* Baltimore: University Park Press.

Mattison, R., Cantwell, D. P., Russell, A. T., & Will, L. (1979). A comparison of DSM–II and DSM-III in the diagnosis of childhood psychiatric disorders. *Archives of General Psychiatry,* **36,** 1217–1222.

McCall, R. B. (1977). Challenges to a science of developmental psychology. *Child Development,* **48,** 333–344.

Menolascino, F. J. (1977). *Challenges in mental retardation: Progressive ideology and services.* New York: Human Services Press.

Mezzich, A. C., & Mezzich, J. E. (1979). Reliability of DSM–III vs. DSM–II in child psychiatry. Presented at the American Psychiatric Association, Chicago.

Miller, L. C. (1967). Louisville Behavior Check List for males, 6–12 years of age. *Psychological Reports,* **21,** 885–896.

Miller, L. C., Barrett, C. L., Hampe, E., & Noble, H. (1972). Comparison of reciprocal inhibition, psychotherapy, and waiting list control for phobic children. *Journal of Abnormal Psychology,* **79,** 269–279.

Nesselroade, J. R., & Baltes, P. B. (1974). Adolescent personality development and historical change: 1970–1972. *Monographs of the Society for Research in Child Development,* **39,** Serial No. 154.

Piaget, J. (1970). Piaget's theory. In P. E. Mussen (Ed.), *Carmichael's manual of child psychology,* New York: Wiley.

Quay, H. C. (1979). Classification. In H. C. Quay & J. S. Werry (Eds.), *Psychopathological disorders of childhood* (2nd ed.). New York: Wiley.

Robins, L. N. (1974). *Deviant children grown up.* Huntington, N. Y.: Krieger, 1974.

Robins, L. N. (1979). Longitudinal methods in the study of normal and pathological development. In K. P. Kisker, J. E. Meyer, C. Müller, & E. Strömgren (Eds.), *Psychiatrie der Gegenwart,* Band I. Heidelberg: Springer.

Rutter, M., & Shaffer, D. (1980). DSM–III—A step forward or back in terms of the classification of child psychiatric disorders. *Journal of the American Academy of Child Psychiatry,* **19,** 371–394.

Schaie, K. W. (1965). A general model for the study of developmental problems. *Psychological Bulletin,* **64,** 92–107.

Spitzer, R. L., Endicott, J., & Robins, E. (1978). Research diagnostic criteria: Rationale and reliability. *Archives of General Psychiatry,* **35,** 773–782.

Sprague, R. L., & Sleator, E. K. (1977). Methylphenidate in hyperkinetic children: Differences in dose effects on learning and social behavior. *Science,* **198,** 1274–1276.

Taylor, J., & Achenbach, T. M. (1975). Moral and cognitive development in normal and retarded children. *American Journal of Mental Deficiency,* **80,** 43–50.

Waldrop, M. F., & Halverson, C. F. (1975). Intensive and extensive peer behavior: Longitudinal and cross-sectional analyses. *Child Development,* **46,** 19–26.

Wechsler, D. (1955). *Manual for the Wechsler Adult Intelligence Scale.* New York: Psychological Corporation.

Weiss, G., & Hechtman, L. (1979). The hyperactive child syndrome. *Science,* **205,** 1348–1354.

Weisz, J. R., O'Neill, P., & O'Neill, P. C. (1975). Field dependence-independence on the Children's Embedded Figures Test: Cognitive style or cognitive level? *Developmental Psychology,* **11,** 539–540.

CHAPTER 18

Research Methods in Contemporary Medical Psychology

LAURENCE A. BRADLEY AND CHARLES K. PROKOP

DEFINITION OF MEDICAL PSYCHOLOGY

The terms "medical psychology" and "behavioral medicine" have appeared with increasing frequency in the social science and biomedical literature during the past four years.[1] There appears to be a growing consensus that medical psychology is a specialty area within behavioral medicine (Masur, 1979; Pomerleau & Brady, 1979). There is, however, disagreement concerning the appropriate scope and definition of medical psychology (Bradley & Prokop, 1981). We agree with Masur (1979) that the problem areas addressed by medical psychology are identical to those addressed by the larger field of behavioral medicine as defined by the Academy of Behavioral Medicine Research. Thus medical psychology represents one of many disciplines "concerned with the development and integration of behavioral and biomedical science knowledge and techniques relevant to health and illness and the

application of this knowledge and these techniques to prevention, diagnosis, treatment, and rehabilitation" (Schwartz & Weiss, 1978, p. 250).

Medical psychology also provides three relatively unique contributions to behavioral medicine (Bradley & Prokop, 1981). These consist of: (1) assessment approaches rarely taught outside of psychology training programs, for example, assessment of brain-behavior relationships and functional analysis of behavior; (2) certain approaches to treatment and rehabilitation, for example, cognitive retraining approaches to rehabilitation of central nervous system dysfunction; and (3) methods for the empirical evaluation of assessment, preventive, and treatment strategies. The empirical research of medical psychologists is particularly noteworthy, because sophisticated evaluations of assessment techniques as well as preventive and treatment interventions may provide for important advances in the quality of medical care and health maintenance (Bradley & Prokop, 1981).

Gentry and Matarazzo (1981) recently pointed out that medical psychology may prove to be a dominant force in the development of behavioral medicine, since psychologists are licensed health professionals who may directly intervene in health and illness behavior and comprise the largest group of nonphysician behavioral scientists within medical schools. However, it should be stressed that until recently the research efforts

---

[1]Although Birk (1973) introduced the term "behavioral medicine" in the context of defining biofeedback as a learning theory based approach to the treatment of physiological disorders, the Yale Conference on Behavioral Medicine (Schwartz & Weiss, 1977a) is generally given credit for recognizing behavioral medicine as a medical discipline (Holden, 1980).

We wish to thank Joseph D. Matarazzo and Dennis C. Turk for their helpful comments concerning an earlier version of this chapter.

of medical psychologists frequently have been unduly influenced by the concepts of *psychosomatic medicine*. That is, medical psychology research often has focused upon the etiology and pathogenesis of physical disease (Schwartz & Weiss, 1977b) rather than evaluations of assessment, preventive, and treatment methods for medical disorders. For example, the medical psychology literature on chronic back pain that appeared in the early 1970s contained many studies regarding personality attributes that may be related to the chronic pain experience (Bradley, Prokop, Gentry, Van der Heide, & Prieto, 1981). Although these studies did identify some consistent effects of chronic pain upon cognition, affect, and behavior, they also tended to foster an "illusion of homogeneity" (Fordyce, 1976, p. 141) regarding chronic pain patients. This illusion of homogeneity has been reflected in the tendency of many investigators to examine the effects of inpatient treatment programs offering numerous therapies (e.g., contingency management, biofeedback) upon the behavior of patients with pain of various etiologies (Turk & Genest, 1979; Ziesat, 1981). Such studies have not permitted the identification of particular treatment strategies that have optimal therapeutic effects upon individuals with pain problems of identical etiologies. Indeed only within the recent past have investigators sought to delineate the characteristics of relatively small, homogeneous subgroups of chronic pain patients that may show differential response to various treatments (e.g., Bradley, Prokop, Margolis, & Gentry, 1978; Prokop, Bradley, Margolis, & Gentry, 1980) and to develop intervention techniques that take into account individual differences in coping strategies and related cognitions (Genest & Turk, 1979; Turk & Follick, 1979; Turk, Sobel, Follick, & Youkilis, 1980).

The influence of psychosomatic medicine concepts upon medical psychology research may be attributed in part to the reluctance of medical psychologists to engage in collaborative research with medical specialists other than psychiatrists. A recent survey indicated that 80% of medical school psychologists perform their research either alone or with another psychologist or a pschiatrist (Nathan, Lubin, Matarazzo, & Persely, 1979). As stated by Gentry and Matarazzo (1981), it is essential for medical psychologists to become more closely allied with their medical colleagues in areas other than psychiatry if their research findings are to be acknowledged as valuable by the biomedical community. We are hopeful that the interdisciplinary composition of the Academy of Behavioral Medicine Research, the Society of Behavioral Medicine, and the editorial board of the *Journal of Behavioral Medicine* will encourage psychologists and physicians to engage in more collaborative research and to educate one another regarding the terminologies and concepts of their respective disciplines.

This chapter presents a representative review of the medical psychology literature published within the past several years. The review will examine the major research procedures currently used by medical psychologists, including: (1) psychometric investigations of paper-and-pencil assessment instruments as well as behavioral, physiological, and cognitive assessment techniques; (2) single-subject (or small N) and group treatment outcome research; (3) the use of nonclinical populations in the development of laboratory-based assessment and treatment techniques that can be tested with clinical populations in the medical setting; and (4) evaluations of health promotion or disease prevention programs. In the following section examples will be given of recent clinical assessment research concerning the instruments used in medical psychology. Research involving outcome studies, laboratory-developed assessment and treatment interventions, and disease prevention programs will be dealt with in the section on major areas of medical psychology research. Methodological difficulties associated with the major research areas will be examined in the context of this discussion. Finally, we will discuss the appropriate education of medical psychologists.

OVERVIEW OF INSTRUMENTS USED IN MEDICAL PSYCHOLOGY

Currently there is a great deal of controversy within medical psychology and behavioral medicine regarding what instruments and methods are most appropriate for the assessment of medical patients. As previously noted, medical psychology has been unduly influenced in the past by the concepts of psychosomatic medicine. Given that the foundations of psychosomatic medicine lie within the fields of psychoanalysis and psychiatry, it should not be surprising that traditional projective and paper-and-pencil tests were commonly accepted by medical psychologists as appropriate assessment devices until the 1970s. Throughout the preceding decade, however, it was increasingly recognized that with certain types of medical patients, for example, persons with various forms of cancer and neuropathology, the use of traditional assessment strategies that focus primarily on individual variables might lead to a situation in which patients' attempts to cope with disease would be interpreted as indicative of psychopathology (Bradley, Prokop, & Clayman, 1981). This potential for confusing effect with cause in the assessment of medical patients may be attributed to the fact that little normative data have been produced by representative medical patient populations for most traditional assessment instruments, and that patients' behaviors are influenced by contextual factors such as the sequelae of their physical disorders (e.g., reduced cognitive abilities and self-sufficiency as shown by some chronically ill geriatric patients) and the environments within which they find themselves (home vs. institution; Bradley, Prokop, & Clayman, 1981).

The decade of the 1970s also was marked by the compilation of evidence that the use of traditional psychological tests to identify the personality traits associated with particular diseases or medical disorders had little likelihood of success. For example, several recent papers have documented the failure to identify specific personality types or traits associated with hypertension (Goldstein, 1981; Harrell, 1980), bronchial asthma (Alexander, 1981), cancer (Barofsky, 1981), and alcohol and other forms of substance abuse (Penk, Woodward, Robinowitz, & Parr, 1980; Schwartz & Graham, 1979; Sobell & Sobell, 1977).

As a result of the growing disillusionment with traditional assessment instruments and the early successes reported in the literature concerning the application of behavioral techniques to the treatment of medical disorders, behavioral assessment techniques were increasingly accepted among behavioral medicine and medical psychology specialists during the 1970s. As noted by Keefe (1979), many of these specialists rejected the use of traditional psychological tests, with the exceptions of the Wechsler intelligence scales, Halstead-Reitan neuropsychological test batteries, and a small number of personality inventories such as the MMPI. They often adopted questionnaires to help them determine the relationships between specific kinds of target behaviors associated with various medical disorders and the controlling stimuli that would precede or follow the behaviors. The unfortunate result, however, was that the traditional psychometric task of accumulating reliability and validity data for the new measures tended to be neglected (Keefe, 1979; Russo, Bird, & Masek, 1980).

The rejection of psychometric principles currently is being reexamined by medical psychology and behavioral medicine specialists as well as by other behaviorally oriented psychologists. There appears to be increasing recognition that, although psychometric investigations of assessment techniques in behavioral medicine and medical psychology pose some special difficulties, for example, reactivity effects associated with some self-observation procedures may reduce reliability of measurement, it is necessary for medical psychologists to provide data regarding the reliability and validity of their assessment methods (Keefe, 1979; Matarazzo, Carmody, & Jacobs, 1980; Matarazzo, Matarazzo, Wiens, Gallo, & Klonoff, 1976; Russo et al., 1980).

The following discussion first will review recent research regarding the construction of a questionnaire and a set of relatively bias-free rating scales for assessing patients' pain experience which reflects the reemergence of important psychometric issues in the assessment research of medical psychologists. Next we will examine recent trends and advances in the measurement of overt behavior and physiological responses. The discussion will conclude with a brief review of the recent advances made in the assessment of patient cognition.

Psychometric Issues in Assessment: The McGill Pain Questionnaire and Relatively Bias-Free Ratio Scales of Verbal Pain Descriptors

One of the most difficult tasks facing the medical psychologist is the measurement of clinical pain. Pain is a subjective, unpleasant experience that *may be* associated with actual or potential tissue damage and that is determined by physical sensations, affective reactions, and cognitions (Graham, Bond, Gerkovich, & Cook, 1980; IASP Subcommittee on Taxonomy, 1979). Despite the complexity of the pain experience, investigators usually have assessed clinical pain by asking individuals to rate the intensity of their pain along numerical, verbal, or visual analogue scales (Bradley, Prokop, Gentry, et al., 1981; Gracely, 1979). Apart from the fact that all of the measures of pain intensity noted above assess only one dimension of the pain experience, the use of these measures may be criticized on several grounds. First, when using numerical or verbal scales, one cannot

make the assumption that the differences between the scale categories, (e.g., mild vs. moderate and moderate vs. severe) are equal to one another (Gracely, 1979). Second, numerical and verbal scales suffer from a lack of sensitivity (Wolff, 1978); this is due to the fact that scale categories must be limited, since human sensory information processing is restricted to effective discrimination of approximately seven categories (Bradley, Prokop, Gentry, et al., 1981). Third, although the use of visual analogue scales eliminates the problem of the limited categories associated with numerical and verbal scales, there is conflicting evidence concerning the sensitivity of these scales (Gracely, 1979; Scott & Huskisson, 1976).

The McGill Pain Questionnaire (Melzack, 1975; MPQ) represents an attempt to develop a multidimensional measure of pain that is free from many of the difficulties associated with numerical, verbal, and visual analogue scales. Melzack and Torgerson (1971) used an interval scaling procedure to develop a pain intensity scale consisting of five verbal descriptors. These descriptors then were used as anchor words for subjects of various cultural, socioeconomic and educational backgrounds (i.e., university students, physicians, and medical patients) in a second scaling procedure that produced 16 verbal descriptor category scales. Melzack (1975) later expanded the 16 category scales to 20 in order to encompass descriptors that were necessary for patients to adequately describe their pain. Thirteen of the category scales are considered to be representative of the *sensory* (e.g., temporal, spatial) qualities of pain; the *affective* (e.g., tension, fear) dimension of pain is represented by six category scales; and the *evaluative* (i.e., overall subjective intensity) dimension is represented by one scale.

The tripartite structure of the MPQ allows the investigator to derive several types of pain measures. These measures are: (1) Present Pain Intensity (PPI), or a numerical rating along the interval scale used by Melzack and

Torgerson (1971) in the construction of the first 16 category scales; (2) Number of Words chosen (NWC) from among the 20 category scales; and (3) Pain Rating Index (PRI), which may be the sum of the rank values of the descriptors chosen from each of the three major pain dimensions or across all dimensions.

Data regarding the psychometric properties of the MPQ have not been produced as rapidly as have investigations that have used the MPQ as a measure of treatment efficacy (Graham et al., 1980). All of the early studies concerning the reliability (Melzack, 1975) and validity (Fox & Melzack, 1976; Melzack & Perry, 1975) of the instrument were performed by Melzack's research group. Recently, however, other investigators have begun to study the psychometric properties of the MPQ. For example, Graham et al. (1980) examined the reliability of the MPQ using a sample of cancer patients who were undergoing training in biofeedback and hypnosis for pain management. Eighteen patients were administered the MPQ four times at weekly intervals prior to treatment. Across the first two administrations, the consistency of category scale choices ranged from 35 to 90% with a mean of 75%. The mean consistency rating between the second and third administrations was 66% (range 40 to 90%), and that between the third and fourth administrations was 80.4% (range 60 to 95%). These consistency ratings were very similar to Melzack's (1975) mean consistency score of 70.3% across three administrations within one week. Thus individuals' choices of category scales appear to be adequately reliable across one-week time periods.

The validity of the MPQ has been assessed in two ways. First, various investigators (Fox & Melzack, 1976; Melzack & Perry, 1975) have examined changes in the descriptor choices made by patients following the administration of an analgesic treatment. For example, Fox and Melzack (1976) administered both transcutaneous electrical stimulation and acupuncture in a counterbalanced

fashion to 12 chronic low back pain patients. Although there was no difference in the efficacy of the two treatments, it was found that both acupuncture and electrical stimulation produced substantial reductions (more than 33% decreases) in the PPI and total PRI scores in a large number (50 to 75%) of the patients.[2] More recently Van Buren and Kleinknecht (1979) used the MPQ to assess changes in pain among oral surgery patients following tooth extraction procedures. It was found that patients showed significant reductions in their sensory and evaluative PRI and their PPI scores during the time period ranging from the evening of the surgery to two days following surgery. In summary, the preceding studies have provided preliminary evidence that the PPI and PRI measures of the MPQ are sensitive to changes in pain experiences following the administration of analgesic and algesic intervention. These studies, then, have provided some evidence of the content and construct validity of the MPQ.

The second approach used in investigations of the validity of the MPQ has involved factor analyses of subjects' responses. Evidence for the MPQ's construct validity may be provided if relatively independent factors composed of sensory, affective, and evaluative descriptors or category scales, respectively, are extracted. Two early investigations (Crockett, Prkachin, & Craig, 1977; Leavitt, Garron, Whisler, & Sheinkop, 1978) suggested that there were five and seven dimensions, respectively, underlying subjects' MPQ responses. However, these results must be viewed with caution due to the methodological deficiencies associated with both the Crockett et al. and Leavitt et al. studies (Bradley, Prokop, Gentry et al., 1981). Two relatively sophisticated investigations have provided strong evidence concerning the con-

[2]Melzack (1975) has recommended that change scores be used to assess pre- to posttreatment variations in persons' responses to the MPQ. However, both Prokop and Bradley (1981) and Graham et al. (1980) have suggested that the use of change scores is inappropriate.

struct validity of the MPQ. Reading (1979) factor analyzed the MPQ responses of 166 gynecology clinic patients with menstrual pain. Four factors were extracted; two were comprised of sensory category scales, one was comprised of affective scales, and one was defined by both affective and evaluative scales. A recent factor analysis of the MPQ responses of 198 patients with low back pain (Prieto, Hopson, Bradley, Byrne, Geisinger, Midax, & Marchisello, 1980) produced three factors that were composed solely of sensory, affective, and evaluative category scales, respectively. A fourth factor also was extracted, which was defined by both sensory and affective scales. The results of the Reading (1979) and Prieto et al. (1980) studies, therefore, provide strong support for Melzack and Torgerson's (1971) tripartite conceptualization of the MPQ's structure and for the continued use of the sensory, affective, and evaluative PRIs for scoring purposes. However, although these studies and those conducted by Fox and Melzack (1976), Melzack and Perry (1975), and Van Buren and Kleinknecht (1979) have produced encouraging evidence regarding the construct validity of the MPQ, they have not addressed the traditional questions concerning the concurrent and predictive validity of the instrument.

The present discussion has illustrated how contemporary medical psychologists have used psychophysical scaling and psychometric techniques in order to develop a paper-and-pencil measure of the multidimensional construct of pain. Although there is a great need for further investigation of the reliability and validity of the instrument, the MPQ does represent a major advance in the assessment of clinical pain. Nonetheless there remains a need for a verbal descriptor scale that would permit investigators to determine the factors common to both clinical and experimental pain. Unlike the MPQ, such a descriptor scale should be relatively insensitive to potential bias associated with range, distribution, and category end effects. Gracely,

McGrath, and Dubner (1978a; 1978b) have used magnitude estimation and cross-modality matching to develop relatively bias-free, verbal descriptor scales of sensory intensity and affect. Gracely and his colleagues have performed a series of investigations that have provided impressive evidence regarding the reliability, objectivity (Gracely et al., 1978a), and validity (Gracely et al., 1978b; Gracely, Dubner, & McGrath, 1979) of the two descriptor scales. They also have provided some preliminary evidence that the scales may permit valid evaluations of clinical as well as experimental pain. For example, Gracely, Dubner, McGrath, and Heft (1978) demonstrated that noxious stimulation—that is, application of ethyl chloride to the exposed dentin of a recently excavated cavity preparation—which resembled clinical pain could be scaled along sensory and affective dimensions as well as electrocutaneous stimulation of intact teeth. Gracely (1979) also showed that a small patient sample ($N = 4$) could scale the sensory intensity of chronic oral-facial pain as readily and reliably as the sensory intensity evoked by experimental noxious stimulation. Thus the Gracely, Dubner, et al. (1978) and Gracely (1979) investigations suggest that relatively bias-free ratio scales of the sensory and affective dimensions of pain may provide valid assessments of both experimental and clinical pain. It is necessary, however, to perform further investigations with large numbers of persons suffering clinical pain before the scales may be accepted as useful clinical instruments.

Assessment of Overt Behavior and Physiological Responses

One of the most important assessment methods in medical psychology is the measurement and recording of overt behavior. As previously noted in this chapter, medical psychologists in the 1970s began to adopt behavioral methods of assessment as evidence accumulated regarding the poor utility of the concept that certain personality types were associated with various medical disorders. However, the growing popularity of behavioral assessment methods during the preceding decade also must be attributed in part to the value of behavioral assessments in treatment planning and evaluation. Keefe (1979) has presented five principles of behavioral assessment that illustrate the value of behavioral assessment in medical psychology and behavioral medicine. First, presenting problems are defined in terms of observable and measurable behavior or responses; for example, a complaint of diffuse chronic pain may be defined in terms of daily medication intake and the number of hours each day spent sitting, standing, or reclining. Second, measurements of the behavior or response of interest are repeated over time. These repeated measurements allow for determination of the baseline occurrence of the behavior or responses of interest, which later may be compared to measurements of the same behavior or responses following treatment. In addition, repeated measurements allow for monitoring what stimuli reliably precede or follow the behavior or responses of interest, and thus may control them. Third, assessment data and instruments are used to plan and in some cases provide treatment. For example, assessment may reveal that attention from family members usually follows a patient's complaint of headache. Family members therefore may be instructed in methods of changing their behavior in order to eliminate the reinforcement of verbal pain behavior and to increase the reinforcement of well behavior. Fourth, treatment intervention is introduced in a systematic fashion so that its effectiveness may be evaluated. For example, Cairns and Pasino (1977) used a multiple baseline reversal design in order to determine the effects of verbal reinforcement and graphic feedback displays upon the activity levels (i.e., distances walked or ridden on a stationary exercycle) of chronic pain patients. It was demonstrated that, contrary to the common assumption that graphic feed-

back displays of activity levels are helpful to patients (Cairns, Thomas, Mooney, & Pace, 1976), verbal reinforcement was more closely associated with significant increases in patient activity levels than was graphic feedback. Fifth and finally, an evaluation must be made of the generalization of treatment effects. This entails measurement of the behavior or responses of interest in several settings, such as home and work environments as well as the clinic. A patient being treated for tension headaches therefore may be asked to monitor and record his or her headache activity and medication intake on a continuous or time sampling basis each day. Treatment would not be considered successful if the patient was able to maintain low frontal EMG levels in the treatment setting, but reported little or no change from baseline in daily headache activity or medication intake.

Behavioral Assessment Methods   There are four major methods of behavioral assessment used in medical psychology research (Keefe, 1979). These include (1) structured and unstructured interviews; (2) questionnaires and traditional psychological tests; (3) self-observation and direct observation; and (4) psychophysiological assessment.

Structured   and   Unstructured   Interviews.   Interviews may be used to: (1) help specify the presenting complaint of the patient; (2) develop the learning history associated with the presenting complaint; (3) educate the patient concerning possible treatment modalities; (4) reinforce the patient for various behaviors such as accurate self-observation of the presenting complaint or adherence to a therapeutic regimen; and (5) obtain a sample of a broad range of patient behaviors (Keefe, 1979).

In the medical setting, interviews also may aid in the identification of patient coping strategies and in patient classification. Most of the literature regarding the identification of coping strategies is associated with the study of chronic illness (e.g., Barofsky, 1981).[3] Turk and Follick (1979) have noted that all chronic illnesses produce harmful effects on multiple areas of functioning that vary over time; it is necessary, then, to identify, assess, and perhaps remediate the various coping strategies used by patients with chronic illnesses as they confront changing adjustment demands during the course of their illnesses. For example, ostomy patients must deal with challenges concerning the mechanical management of their appliance, adjustment of their vocational activities, social activities, marital-sexual relationships, and family roles, and their own emotional reactions (Turk et al., 1980).

Turk et al. have suggested that interviews as well as other measures such as questionnaires and behavioral observations may be used to assess the coping responses of individual patients or patient groups. They have proposed a sequential criterion analysis approach to the identification of coping strategies that consists of three stages. Initially problems requiring adaptive responses that the patient presently experiences or believes he or she will encounter are identified. Next, overt and covert adaptive responses within the patient's repertoire are sampled, and finally, the efficacy of these responses is evaluated. Turk and Follick (1979) have proposed that a sequential criterion analysis may serve as the first phase of a systematic research program concerning the development of successful coping strategies in patients with various chronic illnesses. However, empirical studies from this program have not appeared in the literature to date.

The use of interviews for the classification of patients is most closely associated with research concerning the Type A or coronary-prone behavior pattern (Chesney, Eagleston & Rosenman, 1981). The Type A pattern is characterized by intense ambition and competitive drive, a persistent sense of time urgency and preoccupation with occupational deadlines, and poorly modulated hostility (Friedman & Rosenman, 1959; Glass, 1977; Manuck & Garland, 1979). Persons who do not display the above-noted characteristics are designated as showing a Type B behavioral pattern. As noted by Chesney, Eagleston, and Rosenman (1981), a large number of independent studies have confirmed that Type A behavior places a person at risk for coronary heart disease (CHD).[4]

The Structured Interview (reprinted in Chesney et al., 1981; SI) is the major instrument used for the assessment of Type A behavior. The SI consists of 26 interviewer-administered, standardized questions and a set of challenging probes that are designed to elicit a maximum of Type A responses during the interviewer–interviewee verbal exchange. The administration of the SI requires approximately 10 to 15 minutes and is videotaped or audiotaped for evaluation by trained raters. Despite the excellent results of psychometric investigations of the interrater and test-retest reliabilities associated with the SI (Chesney et al., 1981) and the positive association often found between the Type A pattern and CHD, a number of issues have been raised that must be addressed in future research efforts. First, at least seven paper-and-pencil questionnaires and at least eight interview formats have been developed as alternative assessment methods to the standard SI. Chesney et al.'s (1981) recent review of these measures indicates that there is a great deal of conflicting data regarding the extent to which the alternative assessment

---

[3]Interviews are also used to assess the coping strategies of patients who are about to undergo stressful medical procedures. The reader may refer to "Preparation for Stressful Medical Procedures" for a discussion of research concerning psychological preparation of patients for these procedures.

[4]Dimsdale and his colleagues (Dimsdale, Hackett, Catanzano, & White, 1979; Dimsdale, Hackett, Hutter, & Block, 1980; Dimsdale, Hackett, Hutter, Block, Catanzano, & White, 1979) recently have completed a series of investigations that failed to show a significant relationship between the Type A pattern and coronary heart disease.

techniques correlate with the standard SI, with one another, and with the future onset CHD. This variability in the measurement of Type A behavior in turn poses important difficulties for research regarding three additional major issues in Type A research. These issues are: (1) what particular components of the Type A pattern are the best predictors of the incidence of CHD (Matthews, Glass, Rosenman, & Bortner, 1977); (2) what environmental circumstances reliably elicit Type A behavior and interact with what physiological mechanisms and individual difference variables to mediate the relationship between Type A behavior and CHD (see a series of studies by Dembroski, 1979; Dembroski, MacDougall, Shields, Petitto, & Lushene, 1978; Dembroski, MacDougall, & Shields, 1977; Dembroski, MacDougall, & Lushene, 1979; Glass, 1977; Manuck, Craft, & Gold, 1978; Manuck & Garland, 1979; Streufert, Streufert, Dembroski, & MacDougall, 1979); and (3) what particular cognitive, behavioral, emotional, and physiological responses should serve as the targets of modification in Type A intervention programs (Chesney et al., 1981; Roskies, 1979). MacDougall, Dembroski, and Musante (1979) recently have suggested that both the standard SI and the Jenkins Activity Survey (Jenkins, Rosenman, & Friedman, 1967) be used together in investigations concerning the Type A pattern, and that at present no other paper-and-pencil instruments should be substituted for these two measures. Until this or some other standardization of measurement of the Type A pattern is accepted by investigators, it is likely that conflicting data will be generated regarding the three important issues discussed above.

Questionnaires and Traditional Psychological Tests. It was noted previously in this chapter that, in the past, behaviorally oriented medical psychologists have tended to eschew the use of traditional psychological tests with the exceptions of the Wechsler intelligence scales, Halstead-Reitan neuro-psychological test batteries, and a few personality inventories such as the MMPI.[5] However, behaviorally oriented medical psychologists have begun to use the McGill Pain Questionnaire and various Type A scales for patient classification and evaluation of treatment outcome (e.g., Jenni & Wollersheim, 1979; Rybstein-Blinchik, 1979; Suinn & Bloom, 1978.) Other questionnaires used for the purposes noted above include the Rathus Assertiveness Scale (Rathus, 1973), Rotter I-E Scale (Rotter, 1966), Zung Depression Scale (Zung, 1965), and the State-Trait Anxiety Inventory (Spielberger, Gorsuch, & Lushene, 1970). The questionnaires (Keefe, 1979) used primarily for clinical assessment purposes by behaviorally oriented medical psychologists have included (1) general history questionnaires such as the Social Readjustment Rating Scale (Holmes & Rahe, 1967); (2) problem-oriented questionnaires such as the Short Portable Mental Status Questionnaire (Pfeiffer, 1975) and the Michigan Alcoholism Screening Test (Selzer, 1971); and (3) questionnaires designed to identify environmental stimuli that control various target behaviors, such as the University of North Carolina Pain Questionnaire (Duncan, Gregg, & Ghia, 1978). Behaviorally oriented medical psychologists sometimes have constructed their own questionnaires for the purposes of patient assessment and evaluation of treatment outcome. For example, Follick and his colleagues have constructed a brief questionnaire that assesses chronic pain patients' utilization of medical care resources (Follick, Zitter, Kulich, & Harris, 1979). The effectiveness of a behaviorally oriented treatment program (Follick et al., 1979) for a single outpatient was demonstrated in part by a decrease in yearly health care utilization costs from nearly $1200 (one year before treatment) to only $60 (one year after treatment).

[5]See Bellack and Hersen (1977), Gynther & Green (this volume), and Tasto (1977) for discussion of the psychometric difficulties associated with self-report measures of behavior.

In summary, it is apparent that a large number of questionnaires are being used for the purpose of behavioral assessment by medical psychologists. This phenomenon is not viewed positively by all medical psychologists (Russo et al., 1980). Keefe (1979) has warned that information derived from questionnaire responses should be viewed as "a limited piece of information that needs to be validated against data gathered through other methods of behavioral assessment" (p. 115). The extent to which even the behaviorally oriented medical psychologists follow procedures similar to that recommended by Keefe (1979) currently is unknown.

Self-Observation and Direct Observation. Self-observation and direct observation of behavior entail the recording of one or more discrete target behaviors—that is, overt acts, subjective experiences such as headaches, or physiological responses—either by patients or observers, respectively. In addition, many of the self-observation and direct observation procedures permit the recording of various environmental or internal stimuli such as cognitions that precede, accompany, or follow the target behavior(s) of interest and thus may control the behavior(s). Both self-observation and direct observation require, however, that the individuals chosen to perform the assessment be trained to accurately discriminate the target behavior(s) of interest. A detailed discussion of the necessity of carefully training individuals to accurately discriminate and record target behavior may be found in Ciminero, Nelson, and Lipinski (1977), Cone and Foster (this volume), and Kent and Foster (1977).

An excellent example of direct observation procedures are those used in Fordyce's (1976) inpatient operant pain treatment program. The kinds of target behavior are pain (e.g., grimaces) and well behaviors (e.g., performing sit-ups) that are quantified as movement cycles. A movement cycle is defined as beginning with the start of a particular behavior and ending when the patient is capable of repeating the behavior. Health professionals such as occupational therapists and nurses are trained to record the various target behaviors in terms of movement cycles during specified time periods.

Self-observation procedures also are used to assess pain patients' behavior in inpatient treatment programs. For example, Taylor, Zlutnick, Corley, and Flora (1980) describe a treatment program in which patients are required to record on an hourly basis the type and quantity of medication ingested as well as the number of minutes spent sitting, walking or standing, and reclining.

The examples of direct observation and self-observation described above entailed the recording of overt acts. Physiological responses also may be employed in conjunction with these methods. An example of the direct observation of physiological responses may be found in the use of measurements of carbon monoxide levels in expired breath and saliva thiocyanate levels to help increase the accuracy of smoking behavior evaluations (Evans, Rozelle, Mittelmark, Hansen, Bane, & Harris, 1978; Hurd, Johnson, Pechacek, Bast, Jacobs, & Luepker, 1980; Prue & Martin, 1980). These physiological measures also are increasingly being used to evaluate the outcome of smoking prevention and treatment interventions (Glasgow & Bernstein, 1981). For example, Pechacek, Luepker, and Pickens (1980) reported the use of saliva thiocyanate measurement to assess the effectiveness of a smoking prevention program administered to a junior high school student population.

Portable measurement devices may be used by patients to monitor various physiological responses. For example, Nirenberg and his colleagues (Nirenberg, Ersner-Hershfield, Sobell, & Sobell, 1981) noted that it may be particularly useful to train patients who wish to control their drinking behavior to measure their breath alcohol levels by means of portable breath testers (Sobell & Sobell, 1975). Similarly, Roskies (1979) described a project concerning the effectiveness of a stress management program for middle-aged, Type Λ corporate managers involving self-observation of systolic and diastolic blood pressures at specific intervals using an electronic device designed for home use.

It is obvious that subjective experiences, such as the onset of pain, may be assessed only by self-observation procedures. A large number of investigations concerning the efficacy of various behavioral treatments for headaches, for example, have required patients to monitor and record the frequency of headache on a daily basis or the intensity of headaches on a four-hour, two-hour, or hourly basis (Collins & Thompson, 1979). However, the large number of variations in self-monitoring procedures used with headache pain makes it difficult to compare studies of headache interventions with one another (Adams, Feuerstein, & Fowler, 1980; Thompson & Adams, 1979).

Two general issues should be addressed by investigators who use measures derived from direct observation or self-observation procedures.[6] The first issue is concerned with the reliability of the measurements. It is necessary to provide data regarding the reliability of assessment measures based on direct observation and self-observation procedures, if the results of investigations using these measures are to be accepted with confidence. Investigators who have examined the reliability of direct observations of behavior usually have employed multiple observers to record subjects' target behaviors and have presented various measures of the extent of agreement among observers. For example, Rybstein-Blinchik (1979) asked observers to record the display of six kinds of pain behavior by chronic pain patients during cognitive-behavioral group therapy sessions. A measure of average interrater reliability was derived by dividing the sum of agreements for all pain behaviors by the total number of

[6]Detailed discussions of these issues may be found in Cone and Foster (this volume) and Ciminero, Nelson, and Lipinski (1977).

observations. It recently has been recommended, however, that investigators assess the reliability of agreements among observers by means of the kappa coefficient (Cohen, 1960) or the phi coefficient in order to correct for the occurrence of chance agreements (Conger, 1980; Kent & Foster, 1977).

It also may be desirable to obtain estimates of the proportion of variance in subject behavior that may be attributed to raters as opposed to that which may be attributed to subjects. Mitchell (1979) has outlined the procedures, based upon generalizability theory (Cronbach, Gleser, Nanda, & Rajaratnam, 1972) and variance estimates derived from analysis of variance, that are required to obtain estimates of the determinants of subject behavior. This may allow for more precise conclusions regarding subject behavior than would be possible on the basis of agreement coefficients alone. These procedures also may be used in assessing the reliability of subject behavior in various settings, for example, situations that provide differential reinforcement for illness behavior.

The reliability of direct observations of physiological responses often has been assumed but not investigated (Russo et al., 1980). This is ill-advised given that the technicians who undertake the analysis of physiological variables may well show great disparities in proficiency and thus produce unreliable assessments. Cataldo and Russo (1979) have suggested that investigators may wish to monitor technician adherence to laboratory procedures in order to increase reliability. In addition, some investigators have attempted to assess the reliability of physiological data by comparing the data with some objective criterion. For example, Pechacek et al. (1980) have developed a digital smoking recorder that can measure successive puff intervals and interpuff intervals among ambulatory smokers over a 24-hour period with accuracy up to ± .25 seconds. The recorder currently is being used to provide a criterion against which to validate carbon monoxide, cotinine, and thiocyanate measures of smoking behavior.

Assessments of the reliability of self-observed physiological and behavioral data have been performed by comparing the self-observed data with data recorded by other individuals. For example, Roskies (1979) verified blood pressure levels recorded at home by Type A managers by having a nurse measure the managers' blood pressure levels with a mercury sphygmometer on the same day the self-observations took place. Similarly, Taylor et al. (1980) determined the reliability of chronic pain patients' self-observations of activity level and medication intake by comparing their data with nurses' observations of patient activity and records of medication administration.

The assessment of the reliability of self-observations of subjective experiences is quite difficult, since the self-observed data of interest often cannot be compared with objective criteria or with measurements of the same experiences by others. However, Collins and Thompson (1979) developed three unobtrusive measures of inaccurate recording of self-observed headache activity by college students. One procedure, for example, entailed the color coding of the forms on which headache activity was recorded, so that it could be determined whether subjects falsified the dates of their recordings, as by recording headache activity for time periods that had not yet occurred.

The second general issue that should be addressed by psychologists who rely on assessments based upon self-observation or direct observation is the validity of the assessment measures. Medical psychologists typically have been interested in the content validity of measures derived from self-observation and direct observation procedures. That is, they have been concerned with the question of whether or not their choice of measure may be considered a representative sample of the domain of target behaviors or responses of interest (Anastasi, 1976). The content validity of assessment measures used

in medical psychology usually has been examined by determining the agreement between assessments based upon different measurement procedures, or assessments derived from the same procedures used in different settings. An example of the former type of evaluation procedure was provided by Rybstein-Blinchik (1979). She compared the effects of three types of cognitive training strategies upon chronic pain patients' scores on the McGill Pain Questionnaire, direct observations of patients' pain behaviors, and nurses' covert observations of patient recidivism and disturbances in patients' sleeping, eating, and medication intake. It was found that the most effective cognitive strategy produced relatively greater positive changes on all measures except that based on nurses' covert observations. Rybstein-Blinchik questioned the validity of this measure, given its lack of agreement with the other assessment measures and the fact that the nurses who made the observations had not received adequate training in defining the criterion behaviors.

Evaluations of the validity of the same assessment measures used in different settings are uncommon. An example, however, of the examination of the correspondence of various physiological measures across settings is provided by Roskies (1979). In this ongoing investigation of the effectiveness of a Type A intervention project, both pre- and posttreatment measures of catecholamine levels and serum testosterone are provided by Type A individuals in the field situation and in a contrived laboratory situation. Thus it will be possible to determine if intervention-related changes in the physiological measures assessed in the field situation are consistent with changes in the same measures assessed in the laboratory.

Psychophysiological Assessment. This form of assessment, which is performed in a controlled laboratory environment, entails the observation of physiological responses as they relate to psychological variables (Kallman & Feuerstein, 1977). A detailed description of the use of psychophysiological assessment is provided by Katkin and Hastrup (this volume). However, while the use of the psychophysiology laboratory allows one to control the influence of extraneous variables upon the responses of interest, any inferences drawn on the basis of laboratory assessment must be validated by other sources of data. For example, Agras and Jacob (1979) have pointed out that investigations of blood pressure biofeedback for the treatment of hypertension often use systolic or diastolic pressure levels recorded before and during treatment sessions in order to evaluate treatment outcome. These physiological assessments are inadequate, since the crucial question from the patients' perspective is whether or not treatment reduces the risk of incurring cardiovascular disease by allowing patients to control their blood pressure levels in the natural environment. Therefore, the efficacy of blood pressure biofeedback for the treatment of hypertension must be evaluated in studies that include: (1) the assessment of patients' blood pressure levels in the environment and in the laboratory without feedback; and (2) long-term follow-up of the incidence of cardiovascular disease among patients who receive biofeedback training.

Assessment of Cognition

A form of assessment that recently has attracted a great deal of interest from medical psychologists is the assessment of patients' cognition. Interest in the evaluation of persons' thoughts is not a new development in psychology. However, Bandura's (1977) exposition regarding the role of changes in cognitive appraisals of self-efficacy in the mediation of behavioral change has led behaviorally oriented medical psychologists to attempt to develop reliable and valid cognitive assessment procedures (Genest &

Turk, 1981; Kendall & Hollon, 1981). These assessment procedures are essential to the further investigation of the role of cognition in the development of disorders as well as the coping process, and to the confirmation that treatment interventions designed to change cognitive activity and related behavior actually do alter the cognitions of interest (Kendall & Korgeski, 1979).

With the exception of Kendall's (Kendall, Williams, Pechacek, Graham, Shisslak, & Herzoff, 1979) recent work regarding the effectiveness of cognitive-behavioral and patient-education interventions for reducing patient distress during a cardiac catherization procedure (see Preparation for Stressful Medical Procedures, later in this chapter), the only systematic examination of the roles of cognitive activity in the assessment and treatment of medical disorders may be found in the experimental pain literature. Although there have been investigations of the effectiveness of cognitive-behavioral intervention for the treatment of chronic pain (e.g., Rybstein-Blinchik, 1979), most of the work regarding the relationship between cognition and pain experience performed to date has been produced in laboratory settings; the cognitive-behavioral treatment studies performed with chronic pain patients in clinical settings will be discussed later in the chapter.

The importance of cognitive activity in the experience of pain has been explicated in three recent laboratory studies (Leventhal, Brown, Shacham, & Engquist, 1979; Price, Barrell, & Gracely, 1980; Spanos, Radtke-Bodorik, Ferguson, & Jones, 1979). Although the experimental paradigms and the cognitive assessment methods differed across studies, each investigation demonstrated that cognitive activity that directs attention away from noxious stimulation may effectively reduce various aspects of the pain experience. A detailed discussion of these studies is beyond the scope of this chapter, but the results suggest that attempts to control the stress of noxious stimulation may be conceptualized as a series of procedures involving representation and encoding of the stimulation along sensory or affective dimensions, use of various coping strategies, and cognitive appraisals of the utility of these strategies (Leventhal et al., 1979). It should not be surprising, then, that Sanders (1979) recently recommended that it is necessary to assess chronic pain patients' cognitions as well as their overt behavior and physiological responses before implementing a treatment strategy. Genest and Turk (1979) have expanded upon Sanders' recommendation by pointing out that three major models for the treatment of chronic pain (Fordyce, 1976; Gottlieb, Strite, Koller, Madorsky, Hockersmith, Kleeman, & Wagner, 1977; Sternbach, 1974) all involve: (1) the assessment and alteration of patients' cognitions regarding their pain problems; (2) the development, acquisition, and rehearsal of new cognitive and behavioral skills for coping with pain that will enhance patients' expectations of personal efficacy with regard to pain control (Genest, 1978); and (3) techniques for the maintenance and generalization of positive therapeutic change. Indeed Genest and Turk (1979) have proposed a model for group therapy with chronic pain patients that, unlike the treatment models noted above, explicitly recognizes and uses these three aspects of treatment.

The assessment strategies advocated by Genest and Turk include: (1) self-observation of painful episodes followed by group discussion of covert (as well as overt) events that are associated with these episodes; (2) behavioral trials, such as the cold pressor task, during or following which patients may verbally report their cognitions; (3) patient comparisons of cognitions during clinical pain episodes and behavioral trials; and (4) imagery procedures during which patients imagine an episode of clinical pain and verbally report their pain-related thoughts, images, and behaviors as they relive the pain experience. All of the cognitive assessment procedures noted above may be considered as "think-aloud" approaches to cognitive as-

sessment (Genest & Turk, 1981) or procedures for assessing patients' "self-referent speech" (Kendall & Hollon, 1981). They do not, however, exhaust the range of cognitive assessment techniques available to investigators and clinicians. It remains for future research to determine what specific assessment procedures allow what types of chronic pain patients to most reliably produce pain-related cognitions that mediate patients' clinical pain experiences and may be modified in order to help improve patients' coping strategies and expectations of personal efficacy concerning their ability to control pain (Kendall & Korgeski, 1979).

Summary

As medical psychologists have dissociated themselves from the traditions of psychosomatic medicine, they have greatly expanded their armamentarium of assessment techniques. Medical psychologists currently tend to use a wide variety of behavioral and cognitive assessment procedures in order to identify specific target behavior and the controlling stimuli that are associated with various medical disorders. This behavior is assessed repeatedly across time in order to systematically evaluate the long-term effectiveness of treatment interventions. Some assessment procedures, however, have not been fully evaluated with respect to their reliability and validity (e.g, the McGill Pain Questionnaire). In addition, it is not known to what extent some types of patients would be willing to undergo the assessment procedures that have been proposed but not fully evaluated by medical psychologists. It is conceivable, for example, that a large number of chronic pain patients would refuse to expose themselves to noxious stimulation for the purpose of cognitive assessment (cf. Genest & Turk, 1979). Nonetheless, the medical psychology assessment literature recently has been characterized by increased concern for psychometric issues. It may be expected that as assessment techniques are refined and improved, it will be possible to develop more effective and reliable treatment interventions for medical disorders.

MAJOR AREAS OF MEDICAL PSYCHOLOGY RESEARCH

The following discussion of the primary areas of medical psychology research presents critical evaluations of the major kinds of treatment interventions currently used by medical psychologists. When appropriate, the discussion of each area will summarize the conclusions of reviewers of the treatment outcome literature published through 1978. The post-1978 outcome literature then will be carefully examined in order to determine those conclusions that require modification.

Chronic Pain

Medical psychologists have produced much research regarding the physiological mechanisms underlying the experience of acute and chronic pain as well as the assessment and treatment of chronic pain. Here we will confine ourselves to examining the literature regarding the treatment of chronic pain published since 1978. It should be noted that the neurophysiology of pain is discussed in Melzack and Dennis (1978), Melzack (1979), and Zimmermann (1979); both Sanders (1979) and Bradley, Prokop, Gentry, et al. (1981) have reviewed the assessment of chronic pain.

The Treatment of Chronic Pain. The three major techniques used by medical psychologists to treat chronic pain consist of various forms of EMG and EEG biofeedback training, inpatient contingency management, and cognitive-behavioral treatment (Genest & Turk, 1979; Ziesat, 1981). Some treatment programs use a multimodal format that includes one or more of the treatment approaches noted above as well as other inter-

ventions such as chemotherapy, vocational rehabilitation, sexual and marital counseling, and physical therapy (Follick, Zitter, & Kulich, in press; Gottlieb et al., 1977). Several recent reviews of the treatment outcome literature have concluded that the treatment interventions used by medical psychologists do seem to be effective for some patients (Sanders, 1979; Turk & Genest, 1979; Ziesat, 1981). These reviews have noted, however, that the majority of outcome studies suffer from: a lack of rigorous experimental controls and adequate follow-up assessment; a failure to identify the components of multimodal treatment programs that are crucial in effecting patient change; and insufficient attention to the covert experiences and activities of chronic pain patients (e.g., belief in their ability to control pain, adequacy of their coping strategies). Sanders (1979) summarized the "state of the art" by noting that the techniques currently found in the literature were at best only crude approximations of the treatment techniques needed to effectively deal with chronic pain. Since the preparation of the Sanders (1979), Turk and Genest (1979), and Ziesat (1981) reviews, some progress has been made in the validation of treatments for chronic pain. The following discussion will assess whether the results of the recent literature suggest that the conclusions of these three reviews should be altered.

The Use of Experimental Controls. Both Jeans (1979) and Rybstein-Blinchik (1979) recently have produced outcome studies that employed quite rigorous experimental controls. Jeans (1979), for example, used a double-blind, cross-over design to examine the effects of two types of brief, high intensity, transcutaneous electrical stimulation (TES) upon the responses of chronic pain patients to the McGill Pain Questionnaire. The two TES treatments, stimulation of points in the painful area and stimulation of distant trigger or acupuncture points, were contrasted with the control treatments of sham stimulation at the painful site and stimulation of distant, nonrelevant points. It was reported that, relative to the three other procedures, stimulation of points in the painful area produced significantly greater decreases on the Present Pain Intensity and Pain Rating indexes of the MPQ.

Rybstein-Blinchik (1979) compared the effects of three different cognitive treatments and a control procedure offered in a group format upon the pain behavior and MPQ responses of patients with pain of various etiologies. It was found that the "relevant" cognitive strategy, which involved the reinterpretation of noxious physical sensations using terms that were incompatible with pain, produced significantly greater decreases in patients' pain behaviors and MPQ Pain Rating Index scores than did the two other cognitive treatments and the control procedure. A major methodological advance associated with this investigation was the demonstration that patients' expectancies of change did not vary across the experimental conditions. Thus the effects associated with the relevant cognitive treatment were not artifacts of different beliefs among patients regarding the effectiveness of the treatments they received. A second major methodological advance associated with the Rybstein-Blinchik study was that both behavioral and subjective estimation procedures were used to assess outcome. Several authors recently have suggested that, since pain is a multidimensional phenomenon, investigators should use multiple objective and subjective measures of pain in treatment outcome studies (Bradley, Prokop, Gentry, et al., 1981; Frederiksen, Lynd, & Ross, 1978; Reading & Cox, 1979). Greater confidence may be placed in a treatment that is shown to effectively modify several dimensions of patients' pain experiences (e.g., behavior as well as subjective reports of pain) relative to a treatment that is demonstrated to alter only one dimension of pain.

Follow-Up Assessment and Identification of Active Treatment Components. Although the Jeans (1979) and Rybstein-Blinchik (1979) investigations were characterized by relatively sophisticated experimental designs, both suffered from inadequate follow-up data concerning the maintenance of therapeutic change. Long-term follow-up periods are essential, since they allow investigators to determine if the changes produced by patients are maintained in the natural environment such as home or job. This is a particularly crucial concern in the pain treatment literature, given the evidence that there is extensive communication regarding pain in patients' families (Swanson & Maruta, 1980) and that spouses tend to act as discriminative cues for patients' experiences of pain (Block, Kremer, & Gaylor, 1979).

Only four studies (Eriksson, Sjölund, & Nielzén, 1979; Roberts & Reinhardt, 1980; Swanson, Maruta, & Swenson, 1979; Taylor et al., 1980) have been published since 1978 that have included follow-up periods of sufficient length (six months or longer; see Long & Hagfors, 1975) to minimize the role of placebo factors in the mediation of patient change. Roberts and Reinhardt (1980) conducted a follow-up study on all patients evaluated for treatment in an inpatient contingency management program between 1969 and 1977. Thus the *postevaluation* follow-up period of patients ranged from one to eight years. Of the 124 patients evaluated for treatment, only 34 actually were treated; 56 were rejected, while 34 refused treatment. Twenty-six of the 34 treated patients participated in the follow-up study. The patients and their spouses completed the MMPI both at the initial evaluation and at the follow-up. In addition, the patients completed a questionnaire during the evaluation and follow-up procedures; however, the two questionnaires were not entirely comparable to one another. It was reported that 20 of the 26 treated patients met the criteria that defined successful outcome at follow-up. In addition, there were significant reductions between evaluation and follow-up in patients' self-reports of medication usage, hours spent each week lying down, and in patients' scores on the *Hs, D, Hy,* and ego strength scales of the MMPI. Patients' self-reports of hours spent each week standing and walking also showed significant increases between the evaluation and outcome periods. However, the Roberts and Reinhardt (1980) investigation suffered from the sole use of self-report data. As noted earlier, greater confidence may be placed in outcome data if those data are derived from several sources. Because self-report data are susceptible to demand characteristics and other distortions, the results of the Roberts and Reinhardt (1980) study must be viewed with caution.

Taylor et al. (1980) performed a six-month follow-up study on a brief treatment program for seven inpatients suffering from chronic abdominal or headache pain. The treatment intervention consisted of withdrawal from prescription drugs as well as brief training in relaxation techniques (1.5 hours) and brief, supportive therapy (approximately three hours). The outcome data consisted of self-reports concerning pain intensity, mood, activity level, and medication usage. It was found that five patients maintained significant reductions in their reports of pain intensity at the six-month follow-up. However, relative to the baseline period, only two patients maintained significant increases in their positive mood ratings, and only three patients showed increases in nonreclining activity time at the follow-up. Five patients reported taking some kind of analgesic or hypnosedative medication at follow-up; nonetheless, only three patients' reports concerning their medication usage were consistent with the results of urine tests taken at follow-up.

The Taylor et al. (1980) investigation represented an improvement relative to the Roberts and Reinhardt (1980) study, in that the same dependent measures were used during the baseline, posttreatment, and follow-up

periods. In addition, patients' self-reports were shown to be consistent with nurses' observations on 108 of 115 occasions (94%) during the course of their hospitalization. The necessity of validating patients' self-reports was illustrated by the failure of several of the patients to accurately report their drug usage at follow-up. In general, however, the Taylor et al. (1980) study represents a well-designed investigation of treatment outcome.

Swanson et al. (1979) followed 104 of 200 chronic pain patients for three months, and 75 of the same 200 patients for one year. The patients had been treated in an inpatient program providing "behavior modification, physical rehabilitation measures, medication management, education, group discussions, biofeedback-relaxation techniques, family member participation, and supportive psychological treatment" (p. 56). Patients responded to mailed questionnaires that assessed pain intensity, adherence to medication, additional treatment seeking, and employment status. Based on these self-report measures, Swanson et al. (1979) reported that 25% of the patients admitted to the program, or 65% of those who originally were rated by staff as successfully treated at discharge, maintained their treatment gains.

The Swanson et al. (1979) investigation suffered from two major methodological difficulties. First, all of the follow-up measures were based solely on self-report. In addition, all follow-up measures, with the exception of the subjective pain intensity rating, differed from the pretreatment measures. No systematic comparisons could be performed, therefore, of patients' functioning at pretreatment and follow-up. Furthermore, the patients' self-reports of medication adherence must be viewed with particular caution in view of the findings of Taylor et al. (1980) noted above. However, Swanson et al. (1979) did report some patient variables that may prove to be useful in the identification of patients who are most likely to benefit from a multimodal inpatient treatment program. These variables included pain intensity and duration, number of previous surgeries, medication intake, and time out of work. These variables require further study in several treatment settings, since Swanson et al. (1979) failed to present mean values for the success and failure groups on the variables. The study of several treatment settings may reveal that predictors of successful treatment vary across settings (Block, Kremer, & Gaylor, 1980).

Finally, Eriksson et al. (1979) reported a follow-up study of 123 Swedish patients with chronic pain of various etiologies who were treated with conventional transcutaneous nerve stimulation (high frequency stimulation; TNS) or acupuncture-like TNS (high intensity, low frequency stimulation). The patients were followed for two years or until they reported they no longer desired to continue the TNS treatment. All patients using TNS completed visual analogue scales concerning their current pain intensity relative to that experienced before treatment at three, 12, and 24 months following the start of treatment. At these times patients also completed questionnaires regarding changes in social activities after stimulation and past as well as current medication intake. It was found that 38 of 123 patients (31%) continued to use TNS at the two-year assessment. Seventy-nine percent of these 38 patients reported greater than 50% pain relief, while 21% reported less than 50% pain relief. In addition, one-year follow-up data were presented regarding patients' self-reports of analgesic intake and increases in social activity. Of the 36 patients who reported greater than 50% pain relief, 21 reported decreases ranging between 50 and 100% in analgesic intake, and 18 reported increased social activity. It was concluded that peripheral electrical stimulation represented a powerful intervention method for the treatment of chronic pain, particularly with persons suffering from neuralgia, dorsalgia, and centrally evoked pain.

The Eriksson et al. (1979) study represents the weakest follow-up investigation reported in the recent literature. In addition to the fact that the outcome data consisted solely of self-reports, all ratings and responses provided by the patients were made on a retrospective basis. Thus the major methodological flaws associated with the investigation render the results suggestive at best.

Of the follow-up studies discussed above, only the Taylor et al. (1980) investigation contained none of the traditional methodological flaws that would raise doubts concerning the validity of the reported results. However, it did suffer from the fact that it was impossible to determine if the long-term effects that were found were due to the detoxification procedure, relaxation training, supportive therapy, or some combination of the three treatments offered to patients. Thus neither the pre-1978 nor the post-1978 chronic pain treatment literature allows one to draw any firm conclusions concerning the generalization and maintenance of treatment gains produced by the kinds of therapeutic interventions typically used by medical psychologists. It also may be concluded that the single outcome study of a multifaceted intervention that included both rigorous controls and an adequate follow-up period (Taylor et al. 1980) failed to delineate which treatment components actually were responsible for patient change.

Patients' Covert Experiences and Activities. The post-1978 literature regarding pain treatment contains a large number of laboratory investigations of a multifaceted cognitive-behavioral intervention for the control of pain that has been termed stress inoculation training (Turk, 1978a). These studies represent an improvement relative to the pre-1978 pain treatment literature, in that they include systematic attempts to identify the active ingredient of the treatment package and devote a great deal of attention to persons' cognitive processes, that is, coping skill repertoires, self-statements regarding their ability to cope effectively, and so on.

In addition, the investigations concerning stress inoculation training provide an excellent example of the manner in which medical psychologists may develop treatment intervention techniques within a laboratory setting, which then may be further evaluated in a clinical context.

Meichenbaum and Cameron (1973) developed the original stress inoculation training package as an intervention for anxiety-based disorders such as phobias. Turk (1975, 1977) later adapted the procedure for pain management within a laboratory setting. Turk's modified procedure consisted of: (1) an *educational component* concerning the multidimensional nature of pain; (2) a *skills acquisition* phase in which subjects were taught various coping strategies such as relaxation exercises and attention diversion, which might help them to control various aspects of the pain experience; (3) *self-instructional training* or guided practice in the generation and use of adaptive self-statements during different phases of the pain experience; and (4) an *application* phase in which subjects role played the use and teaching of the techniques that they had learned.

Turk (1975; 1977) examined the efficacy of stress inoculation training in two similar investigations. Both studies demonstrated that stress inoculation training, relative to an attention placebo procedure, significantly enhanced male college students' tolerance of noxious stimulation. Turk (1978a; 1978b) attributed the relative efficacy of the stress inoculation paradigm to the fact that subjects who were exposed to the treatment package were treated as collaborators with the trainer; subjects were encouraged to develop their own lists of positive self-statements and to use those statements and the various coping strategies that were most helpful for them. As a result, it was hypothesized that subjects came to believe that they could produce the responses necessary to control their pain experiences (Turk, 1978b). Thus the active ingredient of stress inoculation training may be the participation of subjects in the generation of coping strategies and self-statements and the subsequent development of perceptions of enhanced self-efficacy.

A series of laboratory investigations has been conducted to determine the validity of Turk's hypothesis concerning the active ingredient of stress inoculation training. For example, Girodo and Wood (1979) demonstrated in a well-controlled study that self-instructional training alone produced no greater reductions in subjects' pain intensity ratings across trials of a cold pressor task than did no-treatment and placebo control procedures. However, the addition to self-instructional training of either an educational rationale or a hypnotic induction procedure designed to promote positive expectancies among subjects produced significantly greater reductions in pain intensity ratings than did self-instructional training alone. It was concluded that, similar to Turk's hypothesis, the belief that one can use self-statements to control pain, regardless of whether the belief is induced directly or by inference, is an important contribution to the positive effects of self-instructional training.

Worthington (1978) examined the independent effects of self-instructional training, choice of imagery coping strategies, and the quality (positive vs. neutral) of the imagery upon subjects' tolerance of cold pressor pain and their pain intensity ratings. It was found that allowing subjects their choice of imagery strategies produced significantly greater increases in tolerance and reductions in intensity ratings across trials of a cold pressor task than did providing subjects with predetermined imagery strategies. The results of the investigation therefore lent credence to Turk's hypothesis that allowing subjects to choose the coping strategies that are most effective for them enhances the effectiveness of the stress inoculation training procedure.

Hackett and Horan (1980; Horan, Hackett, Buchanan, Stone, & Demchik-Stone, 1977) have conducted two investigations concerning the active ingredients of stress inoculation training. Horan et al. (1977) examined the relative efficacy of a no-treatment control condition, educational and self-help instruction, coping skills and self-instruction training, and the full stress inoculation package upon changes across trials in subjects' discomfort ratings as well as tolerance and threshold for a cold pressor task. It was found that the stress inoculation training procedure produced significantly greater increases in subjects' tolerance and threshold for the cold pressor task than did the educational and self-help instruction. Furthermore, the coping skills and self-instruction training component independently produced significant decreases in subjects' discomfort ratings and significant increases in threshold and tolerance across task trials. It was concluded that, similar to the findings of Girodo and Wood (1979), an educational component appeared to be necessary in order to help individuals learn to better cope with pain. However, the coping skills component appeared to be the major active ingredient of stress inoculation training.

In another investigation, Hackett and Horan (1980) attempted to examine the separate contributions of the sensory discriminative (i.e., relaxation training), motivational affective (i.e., imagery and nonimagery coping strategies), and cognitive evaluative (i.e., self-instructional training) components of the coping skills training provided in the stress inoculation training package. It was found that the sensory discriminative component alone produced significant increases in subjects' tolerance across trials of a cold pressor task. In addition, the motivational affective component produced significantly greater increases in subjects' thresholds for pain than did a combination of the motivational affective and cognitive evaluative components. No effects were found for the cognitive evaluative training alone. Since there were no differences between treatment conditions regarding subjects' pretreatment perceptions of the efficacy of the training component provided to

them, it was concluded that relaxation skills may be the principal ingredient of the coping skills training offered in the stress inoculation package. This conclusion is not consistent with Turk's hypothesis regarding the importance of the development of individually tailored self-instructions and coping strategies as well as the development of increased perceptions of self-efficacy. However, postexperimental questioning revealed that 45% of the subjects who received the cognitive evaluative training component ignored the training during the second trial of the cold pressor task. It may have been that subjects' low acceptance of the cognitive evaluative training accounted for its relative ineffectiveness in helping subjects control their pain responses. Thus the Hackett and Horan (1980) investigation may not have represented a valid test of Turk's hypothesis regarding the active ingredients of stress inoculation training.

The studies reviewed above consistently have shown that stress inoculation training produces significant increases in subjects' tolerance of noxious stimulation relative to placebo control procedures (Turk, 1975, 1977; Horan et al., 1977). In addition, the investigations have provided data that generally are consistent with Turk's (1978a) hypothesis that the effects produced by the treatment package are mediated primarily by subjects' choice of coping strategies and self-statements that they consider most helpful to them (Worthington, 1978) and their subsequent perceptions of increased self-efficacy (Girodo & Wood, 1979).

Genest and Turk (1979) recently provided a model for behavioral group therapy with chronic pain patients that was based upon the stress inoculation package. Although this model has not yet been tested in the clinical situation, Turner, Heinrich, McCreary, and Dawson (1979) examined the effectiveness of a similar group therapy treatment upon patients' self-reports of pain intensity and physical and psychosocial dysfunction. Patients with chronic low back pain were randomly assigned to a cognitive-behavioral training condition, a progressive relaxation treatment condition, or a waiting list-attention (i.e., weekly telephone call with a therapist) control condition. Patients' self-reports of pain and dysfunction were provided in a questionnaire format before the first week of treatment, during the fifth week of treatment, and one month after the completion of treatment. It was found that after five weeks both treatment interventions produced significant decreases in patients' self-reports of pain intensity as well as physical and psychosocial dysfunction. There was no change in the waiting list patients' self-reports of dysfunction; however, their pain ratings showed a significant increase during the treatment period. At one-month follow-up, patients in both treatment conditions maintained their improved levels of physical and psychosocial functioning. The patients who received progressive training reported pain intensity levels that nearly were equal to those produced at pretreatment. Thus the patients who were provided with the cognitive-behavioral intervention showed significantly lower self-reports of pain intensity at follow-up than did patients who were given progressive relaxation training.

The Turner et al. (1979) investigation represents the first attempt to examine the efficacy of stress inoculation training for the control of clinical pain.[7] The results are particularly encouraging, since the cognitive-behavioral treatment was provided in five one-hour sessions and was maintained at a one-month follow-up. Nonetheless, the results must be regarded with caution, since only self-reports were used as outcome measures and there was no attempt to corroborate patients' reports with more objective data (Taylor et al., 1980). In addition, the use of only a one-month follow-up period and the failure to assess patient expectancies across the experimental conditions does not allow one to rule out the possibility that patient improvement was due to placebo factors or differential beliefs in the efficacy of the treatments offered to patients. No definitive statement may be made, then, concerning the clinical effectiveness of stress inoculation training. There is a need for a great deal of research concerning the clinical effectiveness of the stress inoculation package relative to that of other group-based interventions and credible placebo control treatments. These future studies must include multiple measures of patient outcome (e.g., self-observations, subjective estimations, behavioral recordings), and adequate follow-up periods (greater than six months). If these investigations do provide positive evidence regarding the effects of stress inoculation training, it will be necessary to conduct component analyses to determine the active ingredients of the clinical treatment package. Finally, it will be necessary to determine if there are specific etiological groups that respond in an optimal fashion, or conversely, tend to regress, when provided with stress inoculation training.

Conclusion. Investigators of treatments for chronic pain patients appear to have responded to a number of the criticisms found in reviews of the pre-1978 literature. Recent outcome studies have included relatively sophisticated placebo control conditions (Jeans, 1979), examination of subjects' expectancies regarding the efficacy of experimental and control treatments (Rybstein-

---

[7]The Rybstein-Blinchik (1979) investigation discussed earlier in this chapter examined the efficacy of various cognitive strategies that were provided to patients in a training context similar to that of stress inoculation. However, patients were limited to the use of only one cognitive strategy. In addition, Hartman and Ainsworth (1980) recently have provided preliminary data suggesting that stress inoculation training may be particularly effective if it is provided following EEG alpha biofeedback training. However, the methodology of the study was flawed by lack of an attention placebo control group, an inadequate baseline period, the use of only the MPQ as an outcome measure, and an inadequate follow-up period (four to six weeks following the end of treatment).

Blinchik, 1979), and multiple measures of outcome (Rybstein-Blinchik, 1979). In addition, a number of laboratory studies have been produced regarding the effectiveness of the stress inoculation training package (Turk, 1978), which places primary emphasis upon persons' generation of coping strategies and self-statements and perceptions of self-efficacy regarding their coping abilities. The generally positive results of these studies have encouraged investigators (e.g., Genest & Turk, 1979; Turner et al., 1979) to develop cognitive-behavioral treatments for use with chronic pain patients in group settings that require rigorous testing in the clinical situation. However, there are some deficiencies within the literature that have not been resolved. For example, most of the treatment outcome studies have suffered from follow-up assessments that have been inadequate in terms of length (Jeans, 1979; Rybstein-Blinchik, 1979; Turner et al., 1979) or measurement techniques (Eriksson et al., 1979; Roberts & Reinhardt, 1980; Swanson et al., 1979; Turner et al., 1979). The treatment outcome literature also has failed to provide analyses of the relative importance of the various components of the multimodal treatment programs (Gottlieb et al., 1977) that have been used with chronic pain patients. Finally, no investigations have been performed regarding the identification of treatment strategies that may have optimal effects upon specific subgroups of chronic pain patients which show unique, pain-related behaviors (Bradley, Prokop, Gentry, et al., 1978; Prokop et al., 1980).

In summary, the current "state of the art" concerning interventions for chronic pain is somewhat more sophisticated than that described by Sanders in 1979. Yet none of the treatments such as contingency management, stress inoculation training, or multimodal therapies typically used by medical psychologists, have been investigated in a systematic and methodologically rigorous fashion. Thus no definitive statements may be made regarding the clinical effectiveness of these treatment interventions. Nevertheless, further refinements of outcome research methodology and the future development of systematic outcome research programs in various pain treatment centers may lead to the identification of promising treatment strategies for specific subgroups of patients.

Stress-Related Disorders

There is currently some disagreement with regard to what disorders may be defined as stress-related. Blanchard and Ahles (1979), for example, define stress-related disorders as comprising the psychophysiological disorders identified by the American Psychiatric Association's *DSM–II: Diagnostic and statistical manual of mental disorders* (1968). In contrast, Stoyva (1979) limited his review of stress-related disorders to those disorders that involve a response to stress primarily characterized by muscular activity. Burish (1981) noted that responses to stress can involve three systems in addition to the somatic-motor system emphasized by Stoyva. These are the autonomic nervous system, self-report of negative affect, and self-report of negative cognitive activity. A response to stress may involve "multidimensional changes in any or all of the four response systems" (Burish, 1981, p. 396). Despite the disagreement regarding the definition of stress-related disorders, a large number of investigations have been produced regarding the effectiveness of various forms of relaxation training and biofeedback procedures upon numerous disorders labeled as stress-related. The proliferation of outcome studies probably is due primarily to the large body of basic research that has demonstrated that persons can learn to gain control of autonomic responses such as blood pressure, heart rate, peripheral vasomotor activity, and EMG activity (Shapiro & Surwit, 1979), and to the encouraging results of several case studies published in the early and mid-1970s concerning the effectiveness of biofeedback and relaxation training for the treatment of various stress-related disorders.

The present discussion focuses upon those disorders that previous reviewers generally have identified as stress-related and for which a substantial body of outcome literature has been produced since 1978. These disorders include tension and migraine headache, essential hypertension, and Raynaud's Disease.

Tension Headache. A great deal of literature has been produced regarding the efficacy of electromyographic or EMG feedback of frontal muscle activity for the treatment of tension headache. It generally has been assumed that the etiology of tension headaches is "the sustained contraction of the skeletal muscles of the head and neck" (Nuechterlein & Holroyd, 1980, p. 866). EMG biofeedback often has been regarded as the treatment of choice for tension headaches because it has been assumed that it reliably leads to reduced tension in the frontal area (Burish, 1981).

The reviewers of the pre-1978 tension headache treatment literature have agreed that EMG biofeedback does reduce frontal EMG levels and self-reports of tension headache activity; however, the reductions generally are no greater than those produced by various relaxation procedures (Beaty & Haynes, 1979; Blanchard & Ahles, 1979; Blanchard, Ahles, & Shaw, 1979; Burish, 1981; Jessup, Neufeld, & Merskey, 1979; Nuechterlein & Holroyd, 1980; Turk, Meichenbaum, & Berman, 1979). It may be that the major significance of the investigations examined by these reviewers is to be found not in the reported results but in the questions posed by the results. That is, several of the reviewers have agreed that there are several issues concerning the use of EMG biofeedback for the treatment of tension headache that should be examined in future research. First, it is necessary to determine what mechanisms account for the effectiveness of EMG biofeedback training in reducing headache

activity (Beaty & Haynes, 1979; Blanchard & Ahles, 1979; Blanchard et al., 1979; Jessup et al., 1979; Turk et al., 1979). Second, since biofeedback training is a palliative rather than a direct action intervention, that is, its emphasis is upon modification of a person's response to stress rather than upon altering the stressful situation itself, it is necessary to investigate whether attention to individuals' cognitive appraisals of and attempts to change stressful situations add to the efficacy of biofeedback training (Beaty & Haynes, 1979; Burish, 1981; Jessup et al., 1979; Turk et al., 1979). Finally, researchers should examine whether interpatient differences on one or more dimensions underlie differential response to EMG biofeedback treatment (Beaty & Haynes, 1979; Blanchard & Ahles, 1979; Blanchard et al., 1979; Burish, 1981; Jessup et al., 1979; Nuechterlein & Holroyd, 1980). The following discussion will critically examine the results of recent investigations that addressed the above-noted issues. In addition, three studies will be discussed that provided additional evidence regarding the effectiveness of EMG biofeedback training to relaxation training.

Mechanisms Responsible for the Effectiveness of EMG Biofeedback Training. Three recent investigations have attempted to determine what factors mediate the therapeutic effects of EMG biofeedback training. Borgeat, Hade, Larouche, and Bedwani (1980) failed to provide positive evidence regarding the role of the therapist–patient relationship in EMG biofeedback training. Holroyd and Andrasik, however, have performed two investigations that have produced meaningful results regarding the cognitive mechanisms that may mediate the effects of EMG biofeedback training. In the first investigation (Holroyd, Andrasik, & Noble, 1980), tension headache patients were assigned to either frontal EMG biofeedback training, a meditation "pseudo-therapy" that provided no means with which to learn relaxation or control of EMG activity, or to a self-observation control group. Assessments following the first treatment session and at the completion of treatment revealed that patients in the EMG biofeedback and pseudotherapy conditions rated their treatments as equally credible. The results indicated that only the patients who received EMG biofeedback training produced significant reductions in headache activity relative to the self-observation control patients following treatment and at one-month follow-up. Only the patients who received EMG biofeedback produced significant reductions in frontal EMG levels from pretreatment to posttreatment. However, reductions in EMG activity were not associated with changes in headache activity. It was concluded that the effectiveness of EMG biofeedback in the treatment of tension headache cannot be attributed solely to patients' expectancies regarding treatment efficacy or to attention from the therapist. Given the lack of relationship between reductions in EMG levels and headache activity, it was posited that the patients who received frontal EMG feedback may have learned to accurately monitor the onset of headache symptoms and produce various coping responses that were incompatible with continued exacerbation of headache symptoms.

Andrasik and Holroyd (1980) further examined the role of frontal EMG biofeedback in the treatment of tension headache by assigning patients to a self-observation control group or to one of three biofeedback conditions designed to produce either decreased, stable, or increased frontal EMG levels. Measures taken at the end of the first session and at a six-week follow-up revealed no differences between the three biofeedback conditions in patients' perceptions of treatment credibility. The results showed that the patients in each biofeedback condition learned to control their EMG levels in the appropriate manner. At follow-up, patients in all biofeedback conditions showed significant and equivalent improvement on six measures of headache activity relative to patients in the

control condition. In an effort to provide an explanation for the obtained results, the patients were asked to describe the strategies they learned to control their headaches as a result of their treatment. The majority of the responses indicated that patients used skills such as imagery, controlled breathing, self-statements, and refocusing of attention that are commonly taught in cognitive coping skills programs. Thus the investigation provided additional support for Holroyd et al.'s (1980) hypothesis that frontal EMG feedback may allow persons to accurately monitor the onset of headaches and produce coping responses that are incompatible with increases in headache activity. However, the participants in the two studies discussed above were college students. These students may differ from the larger population of headache sufferers with respect to their conceptualization and use of biofeedback training. It is necessary, then, to attempt to replicate the results of Holroyd et al. (1980) and Andrasik and Holroyd (1980) in other laboratories using different samples of headache sufferers.

The Addition of Stress Coping Skills to Biofeedback Training Programs. The results reported by Holroyd and Andrasik suggest that if EMG biofeedback training allows at least some persons to use cognitive coping skills to decrease headache activity, it may be worthwhile to formally provide training in stress management skills within the context of biofeedback treatment. This idea is consistent with the suggestions of Burish (1981), Beaty and Haynes (1979), Jessup et al. (1979), and Turk et al. (1979). Recently Steger and Harper (1980) assigned headache patients to either a home relaxation treatment condition or to a comprehensive treatment condition that included four EMG biofeedback training sessions and four sessions that combined biofeedback training with instruction in general stress coping strategies. Following six weeks of treatment, it was found that patients in both treatment conditions had produced significant reductions in frontal

EMG levels. However, only those persons who received the comprehensive treatment program produced significant reductions in self-reports of headache frequency and intensity as well as the frequency of severe headaches.

The Steger and Harper (1980) investigation did provide some supportive evidence regarding the value of building direct action strategies into biofeedback training programs. However, the two treatment conditions differed from one another in terms of the amount of therapist contact provided to the headache sufferers. In addition, there was no assessment of the expectancies generated by the two treatments. Thus the difference in the effectiveness of the treatment conditions may have been due to variations in patient expectancies or therapist contact. Finally, the design of the investigation precluded an assessment of whether or not instruction in stress coping strategies provided benefits additional to those associated with biofeedback training. The questions raised concerning the value of providing tension headache patients with training in stress coping techniques must be answered in the future by well-controlled research investigations.

Comparisons of Frontal EMG Biofeedback Training with Relaxation Training. Despite the general consensus that relaxation training produces reductions in headache activity equivalent to those produced by biofeedback training, three recent investigations have provided additional comparisons of the two treatments. Schlutter, Golden, and Blume (1980) assigned patients either to hypnosis, frontal EMG biofeedback training, or a multitreatment condition that included EMG biofeedback and progressive relaxation training. It was found that all treatments produced equivalent and significant reductions in self-reports of headache activity from pretreatment through a 10 to 14 week follow-up period.

Gray, Lyle, McGuire, and Peck (1980) examined the relative effectiveness of accurate versus false EMG feedback as well as the relative effectiveness of accurate EMG feedback versus relaxation training.[8] Patients with tension headaches or mixed muscle tension and migraine headaches were assigned to one of the three treatment conditions. However, persons in both the accurate and false biofeedback conditions received brief instruction in relaxation techniques. It was found that all treatment groups showed a nonsignificant tendency to decrease EMG levels between the pretreatment and posttreatment periods. It also was found that relaxation training produced significantly greater decreases in headache frequency and intensity at posttreatment relative to the other interventions. At a one- to six-month follow-up, differences between the treatment groups in headache frequency and intensity disappeared, although the relaxation training group reported significantly shorter durations of headache intensity than both of the biofeedback groups.

Finally, Stephenson, Cole, and Spann (1979) compared the therapeutic effectiveness of frontal EMG biofeedback, relaxation training, and a combined biofeedback and relaxation training treatment. The tension headache patients showed equivalent and significant reductions in frontal EMG levels, self-reports of headache frequency, intensity, and duration, and self-reports of medication intake from pretreatment to a two-week follow-up.

In summary, all of the studies discussed above showed that on nearly all measures of therapeutic effectiveness, relaxation training appears to be equally effective as EMG biofeedback training. Although the Gray et al. (1980) investigation confounded relaxation training with the biofeedback interventions, it may be concluded that there currently ex-

---

[8]Several authors recently have pointed out the methodological difficulties associated with false feedback procedures (Burish, 1981; Gatchel, 1979; Katkin & Goldband, 1979).

ists no rationale for providing headache sufferers with EMG biofeedback rather than less expensive instruction in relaxation training. However, it may be that certain patient characteristics are related to differential responses to EMG biofeedback and relaxation training.

Individual Differences that May Mediate Response to Treatment. It was noted previously that several reviewers have suggested that some individual difference variables may be related to patients' responses to EMG biofeedback training. If this were true, it might be possible to investigate the question "what types of patients respond best to what types of treatment for tension headache?" (Beaty & Haynes, 1979; Blanchard & Ahles, 1979; Blanchard et al., 1979; Burish, 1981; Jessup et al., 1979; Nuechterlein & Holroyd, 1980). Unfortunately, the small sample sizes used in the studies reviewed above (N = 20 to 48) precluded examination of the relationships between patient characteristics and outcome within each treatment condition. Three studies, however, examined the relationship between various attributes of patients at pretreatment and therapeutic outcome across treatment conditions (Andrasik & Holroyd, 1980; Schlutter et al., 1980; Stephenson et al., 1979). The patient attributes chosen for assessment varied widely across investigators. Nonetheless, a negative and significant correlation was reported between patient age and reduction in headache activity between posttreatment and follow-up (Schlutter et al., 1980). Positive and significant correlations also were found between reductions in headache activity between pretreatment and follow-up and patients' scores on a measure of Type A behavior (Stephenson et al., 1979) and patients' rejection of the self-descriptor "easy-going" (Schlutter et al., 1980). In summary, there may be some general relationship between patient response to some tension headache treatments and (a) patient age and (b) patient endorsement of a hard-driving lifestyle. These possible relationships should be examined in future research.

Summary. The literature produced since 1978 does not provide a firm basis for altering the conclusions of previous reviewers that EMG biofeedback training produces reductions in patient EMG levels and self-reports of tension headache activity, and generally is no more effective than various relaxation procedures. There is some evidence, however, to suggest that the therapeutic effects of EMG biofeedback training might be enhanced if biofeedback treatment packages included training in direct action coping strategies such as stress management (Andrasik & Holroyd, 1980; Holroyd et al., 1980; Steger & Harper, 1980). Other evidence suggests that chronological age and the adoption of a hard-driving lifestyle might be related to patient improvement. Future research must determine if training in direct coping strategies adds significant therapeutic effectiveness to biofeedback or relaxation training regimens and whether there are patient attributes that are related to different response to various treatments.

Migraine Headaches. Migraine headaches generally are characterized by recurrent episodes of head pain that initially are unilateral but later become more generalized; the pain often is described as "throbbing" and may be accompanied by nausea, vomiting, dizziness, and photophobia (Adams et al., 1980; Blanchard & Ahles, 1979; Blanchard et al., 1979; Holmes, 1981). In addition, migraine headaches may be subdivided into common, cluster, and classic forms. The majority of investigations regarding the effectiveness of various treatments for migraine headaches have used subjects with classic or common migraine headaches (Blanchard et al., 1979).

Investigators have examined the effectiveness of two biofeedback interventions with migraine headache patients. The effectiveness of finger temperature biofeedback has been studied because it generally has been assumed that increases in peripheral blood flow lead to heightened relaxation, and produce decrements in blood flow to the extra-cranial vasculature and reports of pain (cf. Holmes, 1981). A small number of investigations have assessed the therapeutic effects of cephalic vasomotor response (CVMR) feedback because it has been assumed that this method, which is designed to produce reductions in pulse amplitude in the temporal artery, provides a more direct means of reducing extracranial pressure than does finger temperature feedback training.

Six major reviews of the treatment literature have appeared within the past two years (Adams et al., 1980; Blanchard & Ahles, 1979; Blanchard et al., 1979; Holmes, 1981; Jessup et al., 1979; Turk et al., 1979). These reviews have reached similar conclusions regarding the migraine headache literature. These conclusions are: (1) there is no evidence that changes in finger temperature are related to changes in cerebral blood flow; (2) the small number of controlled investigations in the literature provide minimal evidence that finger temperature feedback produces reductions in migraine activity beyond those that may be attributed to placebo effects; (3) finger temperature feedback training appears to be no more effective than relaxation training; and (4) there currently are too few controlled investigations involving CVMR feedback training to draw conclusions about its effectiveness as a treatment intervention. The following discussion will determine if the results of recent empirical studies require modification of the above-noted conclusions.

The Relationship Between Changes in Finger Temperature and Changes in Cerebral Blood Flow. Only one recent investigation has examined the relationship between changes in finger temperature and cerebral blood flow (Mathew, Largen, Dobbins, Meyer, Sakai, & Claghorn, 1980). These investigators trained common and classic migraine patients to either increase or decrease finger temperature. Seven correlations between skin temperature and blood flow in

various cerebral regions were calculated. Only the relationship between skin temperature and right parietal blood flow reached significance. Examination of the changes in blood flow in various cerebral regions within the finger warming and cooling conditions showed mixed results. This investigation and a similar study using normal subjects (Largen, Mathew, Dobbins, Meyer, & Claghorn, 1978) strongly suggest that changes in finger temperature are not reliably related to changes in cerebral blood flow, and raise serious questions concerning the theoretical rationale of providing migraine sufferers with finger temperature feedback training.[9]

The Specific Effects of Finger Temperature Feedback. Two recent investigations have attempted to determine if finger temperature feedback produces reductions in migraine activity beyond those that may be attributed to placebo factors. Lake, Rainey, and Papsdorf (1979) assigned classic migraine patients to either a frontal EMG feedback, finger temperature feedback, finger temperature feedback plus rational emotive therapy (RET), or a self-observation control condition. It was found that patients in all groups produced significant and equivalent decreases in headache activity from pretreatment to a three-month follow-up. The results of this study suggest that finger temperature feedback training alone and in combination with RET has no greater therapeutic effect than that associated with self-observation. However, patients in the finger temperature feedback conditions demonstrated appropriate control of finger temperature only in approximately one-third of the feedback sessions. Thus the lack of between-group differences may be attributed to the failure

---

[9]The reader also should examine a recent study by McArthur and Cohen (1980), which demonstrated that persons experience significant increases in frontal EMG levels and decreases in finger pulse amplitude during migraine episodes, but show no changes in head or finger temperature or heart rate.

of the biofeedback patients to learn to control their finger temperatures.

Kewman and Roberts (1979) trained migraine patients to increase or decrease their finger temperatures in a double-blind experiment. The self-reports of headache activity of these patients as well as those of patients assigned to a self-observation control group were examined at pretreatment and at a six-week follow-up. It was found that patients who learned to reliably increase finger temperature showed significant improvement; however, their improvement was no greater than that of patients who learned to decrease finger temperature, failed to meet their learning criterion, or served in the control group. The results of this investigation and that of Lake et al. (1979) strongly suggest that the therapeutic effects of finger temperature biofeedback are no greater than those that may be attributed to placebogenic factors within the treatment situation (Holmes, 1981).[10]

The Relative Effectiveness of Finger Temperature Feedback and Relaxation Training.   Only one recent investigation has compared the effects of finger temperature biofeedback with those associated with relaxation training. This investigation (Silver, Blanchard, Williamson, Theobald, & Brown, 1979) actually represented a one-year follow-up of a study reported by Blanchard, Theobald, Williamson, Silver, and Brown (1978). The original study included a three-month follow-up that showed no significant differences on any of five indexes of improvement between migraine patients assigned to a progressive relaxation training or a finger temperature feedback and autogenic training condition. In the follow-up investi-

gation, 18 of the original 26 patients self-monitored their headache activity and medication intake. The same five indexes of improvement used in the original study were employed in the one-year follow-up. It was found that patients in both treatment groups had maintained their therapeutic gains; however, patients who received relaxation training showed significantly less medication intake one year following treatment than did those who received biofeedback and autogenic training.[11] Given the lack of additional prospective research, there is no reason to alter the previous reviewers' conclusions that the therapeutic effects of relaxation training and finger temperature feedback training are equivalent.

The Efficacy of CVMR Feedback Training.   Two recent investigations have examined the efficacy of CVMR feedback training. In the first study (Quintanar, Cacioppo, Monyak, Alvarez, & Snyder, 1980), migraine patients were assigned either to CVMR training, a control condition with feedback yoked to the CVMR group, paced respiration training, or a no-treatment control group. It was noted that patients provided with CVMR feedback did learn to suppress cranial vasodilation during training and showed the greatest decrease in headache intensity during a follow-up period of unspecified length. However, due to the absence of statistical analyses in this brief report, it is impossible to make any judgment concerning the efficacy of CVMR feedback training.

Bild and Adams (1980) assigned classic and common migraine patients to either CVMR feedback training, frontal EMG training, or a self-observation control group. Pa-

---

[10]Drury, DeRisi, and Liberman (1979) recently showed that four migraine patients who were successfully trained to increase finger temperature showed significant decreases in headache intensity ratings. However, the design of the investigation precluded the attribution of the therapeutic effects to the learned control of finger temperature rather than to patient expectancies or other nonspecific factors.

[11]Two recent studies that involved analysis of retrospective questionnaire data also suggest that migraine patients treated with finger temperature feedback training (Sargent, Solbach, & Coyne, 1980) or a combination of skin temperature feedback with autogenic training, relaxation training, or EMG feedback training (Diamond, Medina, Diamond-Falk, & DeVeno, 1979) generally are able to maintain their therapeutic gains.

tients in both treatment groups learned the appropriate response. It was found that, at six weeks following treatment, the CVMR feedback group showed significant reductions in headache frequency relative to the EMG feedback and control groups. In addition, the CVMR feedback group reported greater reductions in medication intake relative to the two other groups. At a three-month follow-up, however, both the CVMR and EMG feedback groups showed equivalent and significant reductions from pretreatment levels in headache frequency and duration. The results of this investigation suggest that CVMR feedback may effectively reduce migraine activity; however, the therapeutic effect of CVMR feedback may only be marginally greater than that associated with the specific frontal relaxation response. Thus neither this study nor any previously published report has provided strong evidence that there are specific as well as nonspecific therapeutic effects associated with CVMR training.

Summary.   Unlike the majority of the research investigations published prior to 1978, most of the recent investigations concerning the efficacy of various treatments for migraine headaches have consisted of controlled outcome studies. Nonetheless, there is no robust evidence within the recent literature that suggests the conclusions of the previous reviewers should be altered. That is, it appears that the therapeutic effects associated with both finger temperature biofeedback and CVMR feedback training are due primarily to nonspecific factors within the treatment situation rather than to specific physiological mechanisms. It would be useful, however, to examine the efficacy of finger temperature feedback and CVMR feedback training relative to a credible placebo control treatment and a no-treatment control condition. It also would be useful for investigators in the migraine headache area to begin to examine two questions that recently have been posed by tension headache re-

searchers. These are: (1) what skills do patients learn to use for headache control as a function of biofeedback training (Andrasik & Holroyd, 1980); and (2) are individual difference variables related to differential treatment response?

Raynaud's Disease.   Raynaud's Disease is a disorder characterized by the constriction of the small blood vessels in the hands, feet, and occasionally the face. As a result of the decreased blood flow, the patient experiences decreases in skin temperature in the afflicted areas; in extreme cases, the lack of blood flow may lead to gangrene. The etiology of Raynaud's Disease is unknown, but it generally is accepted that both environmental and emotional factors may precipitate episodes of the disorder. Given that laboratory investigations have demonstrated that normal subjects can learn to control peripheral vasomotor activity (Shapiro & Surwit, 1979), a number of case studies and one controlled investigation were conducted between 1972 and 1978 regarding the efficacy of finger temperature and other forms of biofeedback as treatments for Raynaud's Disease. Two major reviews of the literature (Holmes, 1981; Sappington, Fiorito, & Brehony, 1979) have concluded that the research published prior to 1979 provided no evidence to support the use of finger temperature feedback training as the treatment of choice for Raynaud's Disease. The following discussion will examine the outcome literature published during the past two years to determine if this conclusion should be altered.

The Efficacy of Finger Temperature Biofeedback.   The first well-controlled group outcome study concerning the use of finger temperature feedback training for Raynaud's Disease was published by Surwit, Pilon, and Fenton (1978). These investigators demonstrated that finger temperature feedback training provided no additional clinical benefit to autogenic training regardless of whether the training was conducted in a laboratory or the home situation. In addition, an examination of patients' scores on the Psychological Screening Inventory (PSI) revealed that patient age and PSI Alienation scores were significantly associated with improvement on laboratory cold stress tests in a positive and negative fashion, respectively (Surwit, Bradner, Fenton, & Pilon, 1979).

Keefe, Surwit, and Pilon (1979) performed a one-year follow-up study of 19 of the 30 patients treated in the Surwit et al. (1978) investigation. The patients' self-reports of the frequency of vasospastic episodes at follow-up were approximately equal to those reported four weeks following the completion of training. However, patients were unable to maintain control of finger temperature during a cold stress challenge. Indeed their finger temperature readings during the challenge were identical to those found prior to the beginning of treatment. The failure to maintain control of finger temperature was attributed to patients' discontinuation of practice of the skills they learned during training.

Keefe, Surwit, and Pilon (1980) attempted to determine whether: (1) more sophisticated home monitoring equipment than that used in the Surwit et al. (1978) study would enhance the clinical effectiveness of finger temperature feedback training; and (2) the therapeutic effects of autogenic training were greater than those that could be obtained by means of progressive relaxation. Female patients were assigned to either an autogenic training, progressive relaxation, or a combined autogenic and skin temperature feedback condition. In addition, patients were instructed to practice what they learned twice a day at home. It was found that across all treatment groups, patients showed improved control of finger temperature during cold stress challenges repeated throughout the course of training; their control of skin temperature at the fifth week of training was significantly better than that at pretreatment. Analysis of self-report data revealed that patients who received autogenic training or pro-

gressive relaxation showed significantly greater reductions in vasospastic attacks than did patients who received both autogenic and biofeedback training at posttreatment and at a four-week follow-up. However, given that the latter treatment group reported far fewer vasospastic attacks during the pretreatment period than did the autogenic and relaxation training groups ($p < .06$), the between-group differences found at posttreatment and follow-up were probably artifactual in nature. Keefe et al. (1980) therefore concluded that their series of investigations demonstrated that relatively simple and economical relaxation techniques alone could be used to effectively treat Raynaud's Disease.

Two investigators who were not associated with the Surwit and Keefe research group have examined the clinical efficacy of finger temperature feedback training with Raynaud's Disease. Jacobson, Manschreck, and Silverberg (1979) examined the self-reports of patients who received either relaxation training or finger temperature feedback and relaxation training. It was found that, consistent with the reports of Surwit and Keefe, patients' global ratings of improvement at one-month follow-up revealed no differences between the treatment groups.

Guglielmi and Roberts (1980) performed a double-blind study of the relative efficacy of finger temperature feedback training, EMG-assisted relaxation, and self-observation. The results showed that, across treatment conditions, patients produced a marked reduction in symptoms from pretreatment to posttreatment. There were no significant between-group differences in symptomatology.

Summary. Recent investigations performed in several laboratories have failed to demonstrate that finger temperature feedback training is more effective than various relaxation techniques in reducing the vasospastic episodes associated with Raynaud's Disease. However, the specific physiological mechanisms that mediate patient improvement as a function of relaxation training remain unknown. Both Surwit et al. (1978) and Keefe et al. (1980) examined patient heart rate during cold stress challenges to determine if central sympathetic activity might be involved in patients' response to treatment. The results of these comparisons were inconsistent with one another. It also is unclear whether there might be individual differences on various dimensions that are related to differential patient response to various treatment modalities. In summary, the current research suggests that there is no reason to consider finger temperature feedback training as a more effective treatment than autogenic or simple relaxation training. The literature also indicates that it is necessary to further investigate the efficacy of autogenic and relaxation training relative to control procedures in order to determine what factors mediate patient improvement as a function of treatment.

Essential Hypertension. Essential hypertension is defined as sustained elevated blood pressure of unknown etiology. As noted by Coates, Perry, Killen, and Slinkard (1981), elevated blood pressure is a major risk factor for cardiovascular disease and its associated threats to life. There is a positive association between blood pressure level and response to pharmacotherapy; nonetheless, it generally is accepted that behavioral intervention shows promise as an adjunctive treatment with or an alternative to pharmacotherapy for persons who show borderline or mild elevations in blood pressure, or who show relatively high blood pressure elevations and do not respond well to medication (Agras & Jacob, 1979; Herd, 1981). Three major reviews of the literature regarding the use of blood pressure biofeedback training for the treatment of hypertension (Blanchard & Ahles, 1979; Holmes, 1981; Shapiro, Schwartz, Ferguson, Redmond, & Weiss, 1977) concluded that there was no evidence to suggest that blood pressure biofeedback may be used as an effective treatment for essential hypertension. Blanchard and Ahles (1979) pointed out, however, that the evidence did suggest that regular practice of some form of relaxation is beneficial to a large number of hypertensive persons.

Only two outcome studies have appeared since the publication of the Blanchard and Ahles (1979) and Holmes (1981) reviews. The first study (Sedlacek, Cohen, & Boxhill, 1979) did not directly address either of the two conclusions noted above. The investigators assigned patients to either an EMG and thermal biofeedback condition, a relaxation training condition, or a no-treatment control group. Patients in both treatment groups also were given "home exercises to be practiced daily for a total of 30 minutes" (p. 259). It was found that at a four-month follow-up, only the biofeedback group showed significant and nearly significant ($p < .06$) reductions from pretreatment levels in diastolic and systolic blood pressure, respectively. The results of this study were, given the nature of the biofeedback treatments, quite unexpected and inconsistent with those generated by the majority of previous investigations (Blanchard & Ahles, 1979; Holmes, 1981). However, in line with Blanchard and Ahles' (1979) emphasis upon the regular practice of some relaxation technique, it may have been that patients in the biofeedback group practiced their home exercises more faithfully than did patients in the relaxation group. There are no data, however, to support this speculation.

In a well-controlled investigation, Blanchard, Miller, Abel, Haynes, and Wicker (1979) compared the effectiveness of blood pressure biofeedback, frontal EMG feedback, and relaxation training. Patients in all groups were instructed to practice what they had learned in the laboratory at home. The investigation is particularly notable in that it attempted to assess the short-term generalization of treatment effects by means of pre- and posttreatment measurements of patients' blood pressure levels while sitting, standing, and reclining in a physician's office. With regard to laboratory measurements of systolic blood pressure, there were no differences between the treatment groups at the end of a four-month follow-up period. There was a significant difference, nonetheless, between the pre- and posttreatment measures of systolic blood pressure assessed by physicians for the relaxation-trained patients in both the sitting and standing positions. With regard to laboratory measures of diastolic blood pressure, it was found that at the end of follow-up, patients who received blood pressure biofeedback showed significantly lower blood pressure levels than did patients who received EMG biofeedback. However, there was a significant between-group difference in pretreatment diastolic blood pressure with the EMG treatment group showing the highest levels. The difference at follow-up, therefore, may have been an artifact of pretreatment levels. Analysis of physicians' assessments of diastolic blood pressure showed a significant pre- to posttreatment decrease in the relaxation-trained patients' blood pressure levels in the sitting position. It was concluded that EMG biofeedback clearly showed no clinical usefulness and that neither the blood pressure biofeedback nor the relaxation training showed any long-lasting, generalized effects on blood pressure levels.

Summary.   The results of both the Sedlacek et al. (1979) and Blanchard et al. (1979) investigations were difficult to interpret due to the confounding of home practice exercises with various treatments and, in the case of the latter study, a between-group difference in pretreatment diastolic blood pressure levels. As a result, it must be concluded that there currently exists no strong evidence to support the use of blood pressure biofeedback as a treatment for essential hypertension.

With respect to future research, efforts should be made to determine if specific patient attributes are related to differential response to relaxation training and blood pressure biofeedback treatments. In addition, given Blanchard and Ahles' (1979) assertion that home practice of relaxation may be critical for patient improvement, investigators should either systematically compare the effectiveness of various laboratory-based interventions that either do or do not include a home practice component, or attempt to ensure that all treatment groups comply equally well with instructions to engage in home practice.

Conclusion.   Most of the investigations reviewed in this discussion were controlled, group outcome studies in which various behavioral treatments were compared with one another or with control treatments such as "false" biofeedback and self-observation. Although some of the investigations suffered from methodological difficulties that hindered data interpretation, the majority of these studies represented an advance over the large number of case studies and uncontrolled clinical trials that were reported in the early and mid-1970s. Nonetheless, current investigations of treatment for stress-related disorders must be characterized as "Phase I" or "Phase II" trials (Schwartz, Shapiro, Redmond, Ferguson, Ragland, & Weiss, 1979). That is, the results of these investigations allow some estimates to be made of the costs and benefits associated with the various treatment strategies. Unfortunately, they provide no information regarding the short- or long-term effects of the treatment strategies upon large numbers of patients in a variety of settings. It is possible, however, to draw some preliminary conclusions regarding the treatment of stress-related disorders.

The first conclusion suggested by the evidence is that there currently exists no justification for providing relatively costly and time consuming biofeedback training regimens rather than autogenic or simple relaxation training to persons suffering from tension or migraine headaches, Raynaud's Disease, or essential hypertension. Indeed Russo et al. (1980) have termed relaxation training the "behavioral medicine aspirin" (p. 7).

The second conclusion that can be derived from the treatment literature is that it is not yet known what physiological mechanisms mediate the demonstrated therapeutic effects of relaxation training and some of the biofeedback training regimens (Russo et al., 1980). There have been a number of demonstrations that some of the theoretical rationales for the application of behavioral intervention techniques to certain stress-related disorders are not valid. For example, it has been demonstrated that reductions in frontal EMG levels do not necessarily correlate with changes in tension headache activity, and that finger temperature warming is not highly associated with changes in cerebral blood flow. It may have been, however, that the rationales posited by medical psychologists were overly simplified. For example, Schwartz et al. (1979) have noted that there are four levels of subsystems—that is, patterns of neural activity, peripheral neural-humoral activity, organ behavior, and hemodynamic components—that interact with one another in order to regulate blood pressure. Thus numerous sources of internal and external stimulation may affect one or more levels of subsystems and through a complicated series of subsystem interactions produce blood pressure disregulation. Similarly, the overt symptoms associated with other stress-related disorders may be considered as the end products of various dysfunctional interactions among various levels of physiological subsystems including the brain. The successful application of a behavioral intervention with a stress-related disorder therefore must involve the alteration of complicated interactions among several levels of physiological subsystems. The delineation of these physiological subsystems, their interactions with one another, and the manner in which the interactions may be modified by behavioral intervention, poses an important challenge to medical psychologists and other behavioral medicine specialists.

The final conclusion that may be derived from the outcome literature is that inadequate attention has been paid to the question of whether individual differences on various dimensions are related to differential response to various treatments for specific stress-related disorders. The preceding discussion suggested that there may be numerous etiologies associated with hypertension and other stress-related disorders. It may well be, therefore, that different behavioral treatments will produce, perhaps in combination with specific biomedical, cognitively oriented, or direct-action interventions, optimal patient responses as a function of specific etiologies. As more is learned regarding the various etiologies of the stress-related disorders, it will become increasingly likely that specific, optimal treatments for individual patients will be developed.

In summary, the outcome research regarding stress-related disorders produced during the past two years has been characterized by greater methodological sophistication than that associated with previous investigations. However, medical psychologists may have to develop much more complex conceptualizations of the etiologies of stress-related disorders than they currently maintain if there is to be significant progress in the development of effective treatments and the understanding of the physiological processes that mediate patient response to these treatments.

Coronary Heart Disease

Research on coronary heart disease (CHD) has focused upon two primary issues. The first has been the identification and modification of individual factors presumably involved in the development of CHD (e.g., cigarette smoking, obesity, hypertension), while the second has involved the study of a complex pattern of coronary prone behaviors, typically conceptualized as the Type A behavior pattern (see "Structured and Unstructured Interviews" above). The following discussion will critically examine recent research regarding community-based interventions directed toward altering the major risk factors for CHD and issues in the study of the Type A behavior pattern and its modification.

Risk Factors and Their Alteration. A detailed review of the major and minor risk factors for CHD has been presented by Herd (1981). Although some of these factors, such as diabetes mellitus, require medical or surgical intervention, particularly in their acute phases, psychological and behavioral intervention may play an important role in the management of patients following medical-surgical treatment as well as in efforts to prevent the development of CHD.

Herd (1981) has pointed out that the evaluation of preventive and treatment intervention for CHD risk factors has been hindered by the long time periods required for observing the effects of the intervention upon the life span and vocational endeavors of individuals. Indeed the majority of the medical psychology literature concerning CHD risk factors has consisted of short-term evaluations of interventions designed to alter or control single factors such as obesity (see a review by Stuart, Mitchell, & Jensen, 1981), smoking behavior (see reviews by Glasgow & Bernstein, 1981; Leventhal & Cleary, 1980), and essential hypertension (see "Stress-Related Disorders" above) among adults. Some attention also has been directed toward the prevention of factors such as cigarette smoking and obesity among children and adolescents (see a review by Coates et al., 1981). Despite the methodological weaknesses associated with much of the literature, several kinds of behavioral intervention have been shown to effectively alter CHD risk factors among adults for short periods of time; the use of behavioral intervention with children and adolescents has not yet been shown to be highly efficacious. However, recent evidence suggests that CHD risk factors tend to cluster together, particularly at high levels, and act synergistically rather than additively in increasing the chances of CHD occurrence (Criqui, Barrett-Connor, Holdbrook, Austin,

& Turner, 1980). This evidence, in addition to recent theoretical and empirical work regarding the reciprocal interaction model of behavior change (Bandura, 1978; Coates & Thoresen, 1980), has led to considerable attention being directed toward attempts to develop and evaluate community-based, multiple CHD risk factor reduction programs.

The North Karelia Project. The North Karelia Project represents a cooperative effort between a Finnish community, the Finnish government and behavioral and medical scientists to educate and modify the behavior of a subset of Finland's population, which was discovered to have an extremely high incidence of atherosclerotic disease. A report on the portion of the project concerning smoking reduction recently has been published (McAlister, Puska, Koskela, Pallonen, & Maccoby, 1980). A seven-session, smoking cessation course was broadcast over Finnish television during February and March of 1978. Also, special community organization efforts, for example, the formation of self-help groups by local health centers, were conducted in the province of North Karelia. National surveys conducted both prior to and following the broadcast of the series revealed significant reductions in the number of women who reported smoking 20 or more cigarettes per day, and men who reported themselves to be "moderate smokers." Although no positive evidence was reported regarding the effects of the community organization efforts in North Karelia, it was concluded on the basis of the data that approximately "1% of the smokers in Finland achieved at least 6 months of cessation" (McAlister et al., 1980, p. 378) due in part to the televised smoking course and related publicity. Given the small cost of producing the smoking course, the intervention program was described as "unusually cost effective" (p. 378).

The major methodological difficulties associated with the North Karelia report were its reliance upon self-report measures of smoking that were susceptible to distortion, and the use of only a one-month follow-up period between the end of the smoking course and the second national survey. The latter is particularly important, since it is not currently possible to determine if the significant effects that were reported were maintained after the publicity regarding the smoking cessation program had diminished. The televised course was repeated approximately nine months following the second national survey, and three months later a third survey was completed. Although the surveys suggest that nearly 2% of Finland's smokers "have achieved between 3 months and 1 year of abstinence" (p. 379), the rebroadcasts of the smoking cessation course preclude any conclusions regarding maintenance of change.[12]

A recent description of the comprehensive North Karelia Risk Factor Reduction Program (Puska, Tuomilehto, Salonen, Neittaanmäki, Maki, Virtamo, Nissinen, Koskela, & Takalo, 1979) suggested that smoking was the risk factor that was least affected by the community-based program. The program interventions consisted of: (1) information provision by mass media as well as public educational meetings; (2) reorganization of existing health care services and creation of new services; (3) training of community leaders, teachers, and program workers; and (4) promotion of sales of health articles and low-fat dairy and meat products as well as enforcement of smoking restrictions. Two independent samples of adults in North Karelia and two adult samples in a control county (Kuopio) were assessed by means of questionnaires and physical ex-

aminations prior to initiation of the program in 1972 and in 1977, respectively. The effect of the program was evaluated by measuring the net reduction of three risk factors (smoking, serum cholesterol concentration, and raised blood pressure level) and a multiple logistic function of risk factors in North Karelia (the reduction in North Karelia minus the reduction in the control area). Only minimal net reductions in North Karelia were found as a function of the program with regard to the self-reported prevalence of smoking and amount of daily smoking. However, significant net reductions were found among the males with regard to serum cholesterol concentration, systolic and diastolic blood pressure level, prevalence of hypertension, and CHD risk scores estimated from the multiple logistic function. Similar net reductions were reported for the females on all of the variables noted above with the exception of serum cholesterol concentration. It was concluded that the community-based program effectively lowered the CHD risk among the male and female populations of North Karelia.

Although the results of the North Karelia project are encouraging, the Puska et al. (1979) study may be criticized for its use of independent samples at the initial and posttest periods and its failure to note that the mean reductions in the various risk factors within the North Karelia population generally were quite small (for example, mean systolic blood pressure for the 1972 and 1977 male samples were 147.3 and 143.9, respectively). In addition, the report did not provide information regarding the length of time during which the program components were instituted. That is, it is possible that some or all components of the program were still being carried out at the time the posttest was conducted. The conclusion that the observed risk factor changes within the North Karelia population may "be called permanent" (Puska et al., 1979, p. 13) may not be accepted. Furthermore, there are no current data regarding the relationship between risk factor changes in

---

[12]Best (1980) described the effects of a smoking cessation series televised in Bellingham, Washington. Follow-up data suggested that approximately 50% of viewers who had abstained from smoking at the end of the series had relapsed within the following six months. These data may have underestimated the degree of relapse to some extent due to a high rate of attrition during the follow-up period.

North Karelia and morbidity and mortality due to CHD. Finally, it is important to note that North Karelia is characterized by low socioeconomic standing, few medical resources, and high unemployment (Puska et al., 1979). It is uncertain, then, whether the risk factor reductions achieved in North Karelia may be replicated in more urban areas either in Finland or in other countries.

The Stanford Three Community Study. This investigation represents one project sponsored by the Stanford Heart Disease Prevention Program (see Coates et al., 1981, for descriptions of other projects sponsored by the SHDPP). The Three Community Study (Meyer, Nash, McAlister, Maccoby, & Farquhar, 1980) involved the screening of persons in three small California communities regarding their risk for cardiovascular disease. Those persons who were at higher than average risk were studied for a three-year period. High-risk individuals in one community were exposed to a media campaign that emphasized knowledge of risk factors and skills to change these factors. One-third of the high risk persons in a second community were exposed to the same media campaign as that described above, while two-thirds of the high-risk population in the community were both exposed to the media campaign and invited to participate in various aspects of a face-to-face instruction intervention based on social learning theory and behavioral techniques such as self-observation of target behavior and guided practice of alternate behavior. High-risk individuals in a third community served as a no-treatment control group. The media campaigns were conducted intensively during the first two years of the study and were continued at a reduced level during the final year. The face-to-face instruction procedures were conducted during a 2½-month period during the first study year; maintenance activities were provided during the second year and were faded out during the third year of the study. Physiological and self-report data were col-

lected at baseline and at three annual assessment periods; the physiological measures served in part as indexes of the validity of self-report data, for example, plasma cholesterol and thiocyanate levels for self-reported dietary and smoking changes, respectively.

The results indicated that, with regard to risk factor reduction measured by a multiple logistic function of risk factors, persons exposed to the media campaign and intensive instruction showed a significantly greater decrease after one year than did persons in the community that received solely the media campaign and persons who received no treatment. The globally measured risk factor reduction achieved by the media campaign-intensive instruction individuals was maintained across the remaining two years of the study. Persons who were exposed only to the media campaign were generally superior in risk factor reduction to those who received no treatment, although the effects of the media campaign were not fully maintained as the campaign was reduced during the third study year. The risk factor reductions that were found as a function of the various treatments appeared to be due primarily to reductions in smoking behavior. Furthermore, an analysis of the baseline data of those persons who dropped out of the study suggested that individuals who failed to complete the program initially were at a greater risk for CHD than those who were followed for three years. It was concluded that the media campaign plus intensive instruction had a greater impact on CHD risk factor reduction than did the media campaign alone, although the media "have the power to influence the risk of coronary heart disease and some related behavior" (Meyer et al., 1980, p. 141).

This ambitious study has been criticized on several grounds. Kasl (1980) suggested that it would have been useful to examine the relationships among the various changes in the self-report and physiological measures, and the characteristics of those individuals who did change on various dimensions as opposed to those who did not. Kasl also criticized the use of an overall risk factor score on the grounds that it tended to obscure the sources of changes in the individual risk factors and may not have reflected changes in behavior, such as diet, that have benefits that are not immediately apparent. Finally, Kasl warned that the conclusions drawn on the basis of a study of three relatively small communities may not be applicable to other areas such as large urban districts.

Leventhal, Safer, Cleary, and Gutmann (1980) also have raised serious questions regarding the results of the Three Community Study. They argued that the investigation suffered from: (1) undue emphasis upon individual change relative to change among community institutions; (2) inadequate consideration of large dropout rates among high risk individuals, baseline differences in systolic blood pressure between persons in the control and media-only conditions, and a lack of a face-to-face intervention-only control condition; (3) the use of a large number of *t*-test comparisons and differential use of one- and two-tailed tests of significance; and (4) different knowledge among individuals in the various treatment conditions concerning their high risk status.[13] Leventhal et al. (1980) further criticized the study on the grounds that it neither articulated a theory regarding the relationship between media-based interventions and life style change nor did it demonstrate that the media campaigns produced significant lifestyle changes among the participants.

The SHDPP investigators (Meyer, Maccoby, & Farquhar, 1980) have responded to

several of the criticisms provided by Kasl (1980) and Leventhal et al. (1980) and, furthermore, they have incorporated a number of the criticisms in an ongoing, community-based intervention program involving five cities. The five-city project also will assess morbidity and mortality, results that were not evaluated in the North Karelia and Three Community Studies. Until long-term assessments of these variables are conducted in community-based intervention programs, it will be impossible to determine if the relatively modest intervention effects reported by the North Karelia and SHDPP investigators may result in improvement in the health status of entire communities.

The Coronary Prone Behavior Pattern. The Type A behavior pattern, "primarily characterized by intense ambition, competitive 'drive,' constant preoccupation with occupational 'deadlines,' and a sense of time urgency" (Friedman & Rosenman, 1959, p. 1295), has been identified as a CHD risk factor (Chesney et al., 1981; Herd, 1981). However, as noted in "Structured and Unstructured Interviews" above, controversy exists as to what elements of Type A behavior best predict CHD, what physiological, individual difference, and environmental variables mediate the relationship between the Type A pattern and CHD, and what effects Type A modification programs have upon behavioral, cognitive, emotional, and physiological variables as well as the probability of CHD development. The following discussion reviews recent literature in these areas and provides suggestions for future research.

Type A Behavioral Elements and CHD. Chesney et al. (1981) have noted that a number of longitudinal field, autopsy, and angiographic studies have established a relationship between Type A behavior (as measured by various instruments described in "Structured and Unstructured Interviews" above) and CHD that is independent of the

[13]We share the concerns of Leventhal et al. (1980) regarding the large number of comparisons and the failure to control for baseline differences in systolic blood pressure levels between treatment conditions. It would have been helpful if outcome had been evaluated by means of analysis of residualized scores (Cronbach & Furby, 1970) rather than change scores. Such an analysis would have controlled for initial between-group differences on the outcome measures.

influences of other CHD risk factors. However, since the preparation of their review, several studies published by Dimsdale and his colleagues have failed to find significant relationships between Type A behavior, assessed by both the Structured Interview and the Jenkins Activity Survey, and coronary vessel disease, angina symptoms, and history of myocardial infarction (Dimsdale, Hackett, Catanzano, et al., 1979; Dimsdale, Hackett, Hutter, et al., 1979; 1980). Given these conflicting findings and the need to determine what elements of the Type A pattern should serve as intervention targets (Chesney et al., 1981; Roskies, 1980), some effort has been directed toward identifying the particular elements of Type A behavior that best predict CHD development.

Matthews, Glass, Rosenman, and Bortner (1977) factor analyzed global ratings as well as ratings of the interview responses and speech stylistics of 186 males who initially were studied by Friedman and Rosenman (1959). The analysis revealed that scores derived for two factors labeled "competitive drive" and "impatience" were significantly associated with CHD development. However, only four (particularly rated potential for hostility) of the eight items that loaded on the factors were found to discriminate between men who did and did not develop CHD.

It is interesting to note that the "competitive drive" and "impatience" factors found by Matthews et al. on the basis of interview ratings are quite similar to two ("hard driving competitiveness" and "speed and impatience") of the three factors that have been extracted from the Jenkins Activity Survey (Zyzanski & Jenkins, 1970) of Type A behavior. However, the results reported by Matthews et al. (1977) must be considered cautiously, because the ratings were made only by one observer and no attempt was made to cross-validate the derived factors. A multidimensional analysis of the Type A pattern is currently being conducted at the Stanford Research Institute (Tasto, Chesney,

& Chadwick, 1978) in order to identify behavioral measures that may serve as specific targets for modification interventions. Nonetheless, little empirical data exist concerning the specific individual elements of the Type A pattern that are most highly related to the development of CHD.

Mediators of the Type A Pattern-CHD Relationships. A number of investigators have sought to delineate the interactions among various environmental, individual difference, and physiological variables that might mediate the relationship between Type A behavior and CHD. One advantage of this approach is that it may ultimately be possible to attempt to modify specific maladaptive responses of some Type A persons to particular environmental conditions rather than attempt to modify particular elements of the Type A pattern that persons at risk for CHD might view as adaptive or necessary for vocational success (Roskies, 1980).

The environmental variables used by most investigators have been various physical and psychological stressors. It has been consistently shown, however, that psychological stressors, particularly those that threaten self-esteem, most reliably evoke behavioral differences between Type A and Type B individuals (Dembroski, 1979; Dembroski, MacDougall, Herd, & Shields, 1979; Manuck, Craft, & Gold, 1978).

The physiological variables examined by most investigators have been measures of sympathetic nervous system activity such as systolic and diastolic blood pressure levels and heart rate. Underlying this choice of physiological variables has been the hypothesis that the greater degree of atherosclerosis found in Type A as compared to Type B individuals may be related to more numerous and intense episodes of sympathetic arousal and heightened endocrine activity among Type A persons (Roskies, 1979; Williams, 1978).

The individual difference variables that have been examined in relation to psychological stress and sympathetic nervous system activity have varied greatly among investigators. For example, Dembroski et al. (1979) examined the cardiovascular responses of Type A and B individuals who were administered various tasks under either high or low challenge instructions. The results showed that Type A individuals displayed significantly higher systolic blood pressure levels than did Type B individuals while performing a reaction time test under both high and low challenge conditions. However, despite the fact that high challenge instructions actually enhanced this difference in blood pressure levels, there were no differences in the mood state ratings produced by Type A and Type B persons. It also was found that, among Type A individuals, those identified as high in hostility and competition showed equivalent levels of cardiovascular arousal in both high and low challenge conditions, while those who were low on the dimension showed marked arousal only in the high challenge condition. These results provided additional evidence for the important role hostile or competitive behavior may play in the development of CHD and suggested that risk for CHD may vary among Type A persons as a function of their tendency to display hostile-competitive behavior.

Other investigators have focused upon the tendency of some Type A individuals to fail to report physical symptoms following strenuous task effort (Carver, Coleman, & Glass, 1976). Weidner and Matthews (1978) exposed Type A and Type B college students to either predictable, unpredictable, or no noise while they performed a series of arithmetic problems. It was found that across all noise conditions, Type A persons who expected to continue working on their problems when dependent measures were assessed produced lower reports of physical symptoms (e.g., racing heart, upset stomach) and less fatigue than did Type A persons who did not expect to continue the problem solving task. Type B students showed no difference in symptom reports or fatigue as a function of

expectations. It was suggested that the tendency of Type A individuals to fail to report physical symptoms and fatigue until the perceived end of a task might help to explain their increased CHD risk, in that "their lack of symptom reporting may not allow them to use body symptoms as a cue to alter behavior or to seek early intervention treatment" (p. 1220).

Additional support for the above-noted conclusion was provided by Matthews and Brunson (1979). These investigators performed a series of studies that indicated that Type A individuals tend to suppress their attention to peripheral tasks or irrelevant peripheral events that might distract them from a task they perceive as salient. It was suggested that if prodromal physical symptoms are perceived by these persons as irrelevant peripheral events, delay in attending to symptoms actually may increase CHD risk. It was further noted that the attentional style of Type A persons might also be directly involved in the development of CHD, since there is some evidence that persons who are continually hyperalert may subject their cardiovascular symptoms to great physical loads with little respite and thus eventually suffer heart disease (Williams, 1975).

Pittner and Houston (1980) recently examined the role that various cognitive coping strategies may play in Type A persons' failure to attend to "irrelevant" events during task performance. The pulse and heart rates and systolic and diastolic blood pressure levels of Type A and Type B individuals were assessed during digit recall task performance under either threat of shock, threat to self-esteem, or low threat conditions. Following the completion of the task, the participants were presented a list of 11 statements indicative of different coping strategies and were asked to choose and rank those statements that best described their thoughts after the various threat conditions had been introduced. It was found that when self-esteem was threatened, Type A individuals showed significantly higher systolic and diastolic blood pressure levels than Type B individuals; there were no differences between Type A and Type B persons in the threat to self-esteem condition with regard to self-reported anxiety, depression, and hostility. Analysis of the coping strategy choices revealed that when self-esteem was threatened, Type A individuals used denial to a significantly greater extent than did Type B individuals, and Type A persons' use of denial contributed to their reporting less affective distress relative to psychophysiological arousal levels than did Type B persons. Similar to the conclusions of Matthews and Brunson (1979), Pittner and Houston (1980) suggested that Type A persons' conscious efforts to direct their attention away from aversive internal events might lead them to delay seeking medical treatment following the experience of prodromal symptoms and to endure prolonged or frequent periods of stress that might adversely affect their cardiovascular systems.

The evidence reviewed above must be viewed as preliminary. However, it does suggest that two specific, maladaptive response patterns shown to various degrees by Type A individuals might be considered as possible intervention targets. First, the tendency of highly competitive or hostile Type A persons to show cardiovascular arousal across environmental conditions that vary in terms of threat to their self-esteem may be particularly maladaptive (Dembroski et al., 1979). If this relationship between hostility-competitiveness, environmental conditions, and physiological arousal is replicated in future research, it may be valuable to attempt to train highly hostile Type A persons to discriminate between situations that are and are not truly threatening, and to modify their behavioral and cardiovascular responses to threatening situations.

The second maladaptive response pattern that should receive further attention is the tendency of Type A individuals to direct their attention away from events perceived as irrelevant. It might be useful to train Type A

persons who consistently deny negative affect or arousal when self-esteem is threatened to discriminate between truly irrelevant events such as background noise and internal phenomena that indicate high cardiovascular arousal. It might also be useful to teach these persons different coping strategies for irrelevant and relevant events, for example, denial might be the acceptable strategy for auditory stimulation, but controlled breathing might be the acceptable strategy for flushed face and racing heart.

However, several methodological problems must be resolved in future research before the above-noted suggestions are implemented. First, as discussed earlier in this chapter, the studies reviewed in the preceding discussion varied with regard to the instruments used to assess the Type A pattern. Thus no conclusions may be drawn regarding the maladaptive response patterns found among Type A persons that may serve as intervention targets until a consensus is reached as to the best means of measuring the Type A pattern. Second, the vast majority of investigations regarding the Type A pattern have used white middle-class males as subjects. It is necessary to determine to what extent the findings produced thus far regarding the Type A pattern may generalize to females both in and out of the work force and male and female individuals of various cultural groups (Cohen, Matthews, & Waldron, 1978). Finally, there is no evidence that shows a direct relationship between maladaptive response patterns such as denial of cardiovascular arousal and development of CHD or incidence of CHD events (Williams, 1978). Until such evidence is provided, investigators must remain aware that the choice of various maladaptive response patterns as intervention targets must be based on circumstantial evidence.

Modification of the Type A Behavior Pattern. Due to the above-noted difficulties in identifying specific elements of the Type A pattern or specific maladaptive responses to environmental conditions that might serve as adequate intervention targets, only a small number of attempts have been made to systematically evaluate Type A intervention strategies. Chesney et al. (1981) have reviewed the intervention literature, which consists of one study of a relatively global strategy (Rosenman & Friedman, 1977) and four studies of strategies involving the teaching of adaptive stress management responses (Jenni & Wollersheim, 1979; Roskies, Spevack, Surkis, Cohen, & Gilman, 1978; Roskies, Kearney, Spevack, Surkis, Cohen, & Gilman, 1979; Suinn & Bloom, 1978). The Rosenman and Friedman investigation (1977) thus far has provided only anecdotal evidence, although a large-scale, controlled investigation of the effectiveness of this treatment strategy is currently ongoing. The results of the four studies regarding the efficacy of teaching adaptive stress management responses have been encouraging. However, the results of the studies must be viewed with great caution since all of the studies have lacked appropriate control groups (either attention placebo or no-treatment groups), have varied from one another with regard to outcome measurement, and have failed to report extended follow-up data regarding morbidity and mortality (Chesney et al., 1981).

Since the preparation of the Chesney et al. review (1981), one additional study (Rahe, Ward, & Haynes, 1979) has appeared regarding the effectiveness of brief group therapy with myocardial infarction patients. Although a three-to-four year follow-up assessment produced encouraging results, with particular regard to mortality rates between treated and control patients, the data must be considered as tentative due to the lack of a credible attention placebo treatment, failure to assess Type A behavior prior to or following treatment, and reliance primarily upon self-report and interview data.

In summary, the conclusions originally provided by Chesney et al. (1981) regarding the absence of evidence for the efficacy of Type A intervention programs must remain unaltered. That is, no firm evaluative statements may be made on the basis of the current literature. However, the maladaptive elements of the Type A pattern may be subject to alteration. Future research must determine, then, if alteration of Type A behavior actually will lead to improved survival over long follow-up periods.[14]

Conclusion.   Current research concerning the modification of CHD risk factors and the Type A behavior pattern must be considered as only the first steps toward the systematic use of cognitive and behavioral intervention strategies for the promotion of health. The few studies of community-based intervention strategies have suffered from important methodological and conceptual shortcomings such as over-reliance on self-report data and lack of follow-up data on morbidity and mortality rates. However, the attempts of the SHDPP investigators to incorporate the criticisms of others in their research efforts is encouraging. Investigations concerning the Type A pattern also suffer from methodological and measurement (e.g., proliferation of Type A scales) problems. It is unclear to what extent conclusions drawn from studies regarding the variables that mediate the Type A-CHD risk relationship may generalize to populations such as females and nonwhite males. The difficulties associated with basic research concerning the Type A pattern have been reflected in the conflicting methodologies and measurement techniques employed in the clinical intervention studies. Nonetheless, there is some consistency in the results of the intervention studies that suggests that attempts to modify maladaptive aspects of the Type A pattern will prove to be successful. However, long-

---

[14]Both Chesney et al. (1981) and Roskies (1980) have provided excellent reviews of the methodological difficulties associated with designing a Type A intervention program.

term follow-up evaluations of interventions that include assessment of mortality and morbidity data will be necessary.

Other Areas of Research

The following discussion critically examines the literature in three relatively new areas: cancer, preparation for stressful medical procedures, and compliance with medical regimens.

Cancer.   Research regarding the various forms of cancer falls within two major categories. The first is comprised of investigations regarding psychological factors that may influence the onset or clinical course of cancer, while the second category consists of studies concerning the effectiveness of intervention designed to help cancer victims to better cope with their disease or its treatment. The first area of research reflects the psychosomatic medicine tradition and is based upon the assumption that psychological factors may influence the pathophysiology of cancer; the second area is associated with the view that psychological issues are relevant to the process of coping with chronic disease.

Psychological Factors Related to Pathophysiology.   There currently exists some controversy as to whether or not the development of cancer may be associated with a variety of psychological mechanisms and environmental events, including loneliness following the loss of a loved object (Horne & Picard, 1979; LeShan, 1969), inhibited emotional expression (Kissen, 1963), and the suppression of anger (Greer, 1979). Recently it has been suggested that the development of cancer may be related to an interaction between stressful life events and an individual's cognitive style or personality; in some persons this interaction leads to a sense of hopelessness and suppression of the immune system, which in turn results in a predisposition to cancer (Simonton, Matthews-Simonton, & Creighton, 1978).

Research regarding the relationships between psychological events and cancer has been plagued by a variety of methodological difficulties. Watson and Schuld (1977) noted that investigations frequently have not included appropriate control groups against which to compare the behavior or test responses of cancer patients. In addition, investigations typically have examined the retrospective responses of patients who already had been diagnosed as suffering from cancer; thus it has been unclear whether the reported findings have reflected premorbid traits or reactions to the disease (Greer, 1979). Finally, Barofsky (1981) raised serious questions regarding the validity of the administration of standardized psychological tests to cancer patients without consideration of the differences between these patients and the instruments' standardization samples. In the most comprehensive review of the literature to date, Fox (1978) concluded that the methodological flaws noted above and numerous others preclude drawing any conclusions regarding the possible etiologic role of psychological factors in the development of cancer.

Two studies recently have been performed that have been free of many of the methodological weaknesses found in the literature. Watson and Schuld (1977) compared the premorbid MMPI profiles and diagnoses of psychiatric patients with malignant neoplasms, benign growths, or no evidence of cancer and found no differences between the patient groups. The authors suggested that previous studies supporting a psychogenic component to cancer actually may have assessed the impact of the disease on personality or attempts to cope with the disease rather than the premorbid characteristics of the patients. However, Watson and Schuld noted that their results did not rule out the hypothesis that cancer might be an immediate reaction to stress, as the MMPI was administered to the cancer sample at least two years prior to the diagnosis of cancer.[15]

Dattore, Shontz, and Coyne (1980) used multiple discriminant analysis to compare the premorbid MMPI profiles of a cancer patient sample with those of cancer-free medical and psychiatric patients. It was reported that cancer patients showed greater repressive tendencies, fewer self-reported symptoms of depression, and less denial of hysteria than cancer-free patients. The use of a primarily nonpsychiatric population represented a methodological improvement relative to the Watson and Schuld (1977) investigation (see Thomas, Duszynski, & Shaffer, 1979, for further discussion of the choice of control groups). However, Dattore et al. (1980) pointed out that although the patient groups were significantly different from one another, the degree of between-group separation was such that many errors would have been made if cancer proneness in individuals had been assessed by means of the discriminant function. Furthermore, cross-validation of the reported findings are necessary before confidence may be placed in them (Prokop & Bradley, 1981). In summary, despite the methodological improvements associated with this study and that of Watson and Schuld (1977), there is little evidence to suggest that personality attributes or other psychological factors are related to the onset of cancer.

---

[15]Kellerman (1978) argued that the use of a purely psychiatric sample and an overrepresentation of alcoholics in the malignancy group prevented the Watson and Schuld (1977) investigation from being considered a fair test of the cancer-prone personality hypothesis. However, Watson and Schuld (1978) pointed out that since the diagnoses and MMPI profiles of psychiatric patients should have been more heterogeneous than those of the normal population, the chances of finding between-group differences should have been increased rather than decreased. They further demonstrated that when the alcoholics were deleted from the patient sample, significant between-group differences still were absent.

Coping with Cancer and its Treatment. With the recent interest in psychological factors as possible etiologic agents in cancer, attention has been increasingly directed toward investigating patients' adaptation to the emotional distress associated with cancer and its treatment (Surawicz, Brightwell, Weitzel, & Othmer, 1976). Wellisch (1981) has provided a review of psychological interventions employed with cancer patients, their families, and treatment staff. He has concluded that since most of the research has been descriptive in nature, there is a great need in the intervention literature for investigations with rigorous experimental controls and follow-up measures. Meyerowitz (1980) has reviewed the literature on both premorbid and postmastectomy individual and environmental variables that influence the psychological impact of breast cancer. In addition to providing conclusions quite similar to those of Wellisch (1981), she has stressed the need for greater interest in the quality of patients' lives subsequent to the diagnosis of breast cancer, particularly in view of the increase in patients' life spans following diagnosis as medical treatment has become more effective.

Sobel and Worden (1979) examined the MMPI profiles of newly diagnosed cancer patients judged as experiencing high emotional distress with those rated as experiencing relatively little distress. Although the MMPI profiles were found to significantly discriminate between the high and low distressed groups, the degree of discrimination was not as great as the authors had expected. It was concluded that since cancer patients seemingly attempt to cope with their illnesses in many idiosyncratic ways, it is necessary for psychologists to engage in task analyses of the different coping patterns among cancer patients using procedures such as the sequential criterion analysis (Turk et al., 1980) discussed in "Structured and Unstructured Interviews" above. Furthermore, Turk and Follick (1979) have suggested that the stress inoculation approach (Meichenbaum & Cameron, 1973; see "Chronic Pain" above) should be investigated as a device for modifying maladaptive coping patterns in patients with chronic illnesses such as cancer.

Despite the increased interest shown by medical psychologists in the coping skills of cancer patients, no empirical evaluations of interventions designed to facilitate coping have appeared in the literature to date.[16] Several case studies, however, have shown that behavior therapy techniques may be used to treat some undesirable side effects of cancer treatment such as anorexia (Cairns & Altman, 1979), nausea and vomiting (Burish & Lyles, 1979), and excessive coughing and regurgitation of saliva (Redd, 1980). These case studies have shown that some psychologists may successfully use their skills with some patients who develop maladaptive behavioral responses as they undergo cancer treatment. The further development and rigorous evaluation of psychological procedures designed to help patients acquire and effectively use adaptive coping skills must be considered as an important challenge to medical psychologists, particularly in light of recent suggestions that psychological adjustment may influence survival intervals following the diagnosis of cancer (Achterberg, Matthews-Simonton, & Simonton, 1977).

Preparation for Stressful Medical Procedures.   A variety of psychological techniques have been employed in attempts to prepare individuals for exposure to stressful medical procedures. Kendall and Watson (1981) reviewed the empirical literature concerning the effectiveness of numerous interventions grouped within the categories of psychological support, information provision, skills training, hypnosis, relaxation

training, filmed modeling, and cognitive-behavioral approaches. It was concluded that all of the general approaches noted above have been shown to benefit patient adjustment to some stressful procedures. However, different treatments appear to have optimal effects on different measures of patient response. For example, skills training (e.g., instruction in proper turning in bed, coughing) seems to be most effective in speeding patient recovery, reducing distress related to pain, and helping patients to return to a normal routine, but it does not appear to reduce patient anxiety and personal distress. Kendall and Watson (1981) noted that future research concerning preparation for stressful medical procedures should examine treatments that are designed to effect specific desired results and incorporate three types of dependent measures—patients' emotional responses, observers' ratings of adjustment, and hospital stay variables.

Kendall and Watson (1981) also emphasized that individual differences among patients must be carefully considered by investigators of preparations for stressful medical procedures. The importance of individual differences was made clear in a recent study by Katz, Kellerman, and Siegel (1980). The anxiety responses of children suffering from cancer and undergoing bone marrow aspiration were assessed by observers trained in the use of a behavior checklist designed specifically for aspiration procedures. It was found that anxiety responses differed both quantitatively and qualitatively as a function of age and sex. That is, younger children showed less muscle tension and more anxious behavior than did older children, while females displayed more anxiety and comfort-seeking behavior than did males. Such differences might have powerful implications for the type of intervention best suited to aid with a particular individual's adjustment to a stressful procedure. For example, on the basis of the Katz et al. (1980) investigation, it might be hypothesized that older children would better respond to an

---

[16]Gordon and his colleagues (1980) reported the outcome of a psychosocial intervention for adult cancer patients following the preparation of this chapter.

intervention that included deep muscle relaxation training than would younger children.

Patients' levels of experience with the medical procedure for which they receive a psychological preparation represents an individual difference variable that may play an important role in the intervention's effectiveness. Klorman, Hilpert, Michael, LaGana, and Sveen (1980) exposed pedontic patients to mastery or coping models on videotape and reported that both of these types of models reduced the disruptive behavior of patients during treatment relative to unprepared control patients undergoing the same dental treatment. Examination of individual subjects' data revealed that the between-group difference was due primarily to the decrease in disruptive behavior among patients without prior exposure to the dental treatment who received psychological preparation.

The Katz et al. (1980) and Klorman et al. (1980) investigations also demonstrated the advantage of using a rating form with operational definitions of specific behavior as a dependent measure rather than more global, clinical impression data. Katz et al. noted that some clinicians have reported an impression that children tend to habituate to bone marrow aspiration procedures and that nurses' global ratings of children's anxiety tend to decrease with repeated procedures. However, Katz et al. found that, consistent with the children's self-report, behavioral ratings by the trained observers showed no decrease across repetitions of the aspiration procedures. Similarly, Klorman et al. assessed patient disruptiveness both by observers' recordings on a behavioral checklist and dentists' global observations. The effectiveness of the filmed modeling procedures in reducing disruptive behavior was apparent only in the analysis of the behavioral checklist data.

A final conclusion drawn by Kendall and Watson (1981) regarding the literature on preparations for stressful medical procedures

was that stress inoculation training (Meichenbaum & Cameron, 1973) might be a particularly promising method of patient preparation. Stress inoculation training and similar cognitive-behavioral interventions (Kendall & Hollon, 1979), particularly in conjunction with other approaches such as relaxation training, may be especially effective as they allow individuals to strengthen and thus better utilize their own preferred coping strategies rather than requiring all individuals to learn the same coping procedure as defined by the investigator or clinician (see Kendall, in press).

Kendall, Williams, Pechacek, Graham, Shisslak, and Herzoff (1979) compared the effects of a cognitive-behavioral intervention similar to stress-inoculation training, an educational approach, an attention placebo treatment, and normal hospital routine on male patients' adjustment to a cardiac catheterization procedure. Both experimental treatment procedures produced significantly lower self-reports of anxiety (as measured by a short form of the State-Trait Anxiety Inventory; Spielberger, Gorsuch, & Lushene, 1970) following the catheterization procedure than did the two control conditions. During the catheterization procedure, both physicians and technicians rated the cognitive-behavioral treatment group as displaying significantly better adjustment than the education group, and both treatment groups as showing significantly better adjustment than the controls. Patients noted their positive and negative self-statements (i.e., cognitions during the procedure) on a specially constructed checklist following catheterization. It was found that negative self-statements were significantly and negatively associated with the adjustment ratings; positive self-statements were not significantly correlated with adjustment.

The Kendall et al. (1979) investigation provided two methodological advances relative to previous studies regarding psychological preparation. First, in addition to the use of multiple observers' ratings of patient behavior, the Kendall et al. study included a short self-report form of anxiety that was both unobtrusive and nonreactive. Short self-report forms are particularly useful measures in studies of stress and coping in which lengthy self-assessments may be quite bothersome to patients. The assessment of patients' cognitions represented the second methodological advance associated with the Kendall et al. (1979) study. Although the correlations between patients' self-statements and observers' ratings of adjustment did not conclusively demonstrate that the effects of the cognitive-behavioral procedure were mediated by patients' cognitions, the Kendall et al. (1979) investigation represents one of the few attempts to examine the role of cognition in the coping process (Kendall & Korgeski, 1979).

In summary, the study of psychological preparations for stressful medical procedures represents one of the most promising areas of medical psychology research examined in this chapter. The major conclusions that can be drawn from the literature are that: (1) a large number of psychological preparations are effective with various stressful procedures; (2) there are individual differences among patients that are related to response to various treatments; (3) there are differences among preparations with regard to the aspects of patient functioning that show optimal response; and (4) cognitive-behavioral techniques, such as stress inoculation training, may prove to be a particularly valuable means of psychological preparation. It is necessary, however, for future investigators to produce well designed and rigorously controlled studies that will assess "what type of treatment, presented how, when, and by whom, will produce what effects for what types of patients" (Kendall & Watson, 1981, p. 217).

Compliance with Medical Regimens. The problem of fostering patient compliance with prescribed treatment regimens is quite important, because noncompliance probably compromises the potential benefits of any treatment protocol, and may well lead to misinterpretations of treatment outcome investigations, that is, when compliance rates vary across treatments. Noncompliance issues are especially likely to occur in treatment programs, such as those found throughout the medical psychology literature, that require extensive alterations in patients' lifestyles such as smoking cessation, weight reduction, and modification of Type A behavior (Masur, 1981). Nonetheless, there currently is little understanding of the phenomenon of noncompliance, and relatively few investigations regarding compliance enhancement techniques in the medical psychology literature are derived from a testable theoretical model (Masur, 1981).

One general review (Masur, 1981) and two reviews of compliance regarding patients with specific diseases (Watts, 1980; Windsor, Green, & Roseman, 1980) recently have been published. These reviews identified several factors that have been shown to influence patient compliance including demographic variables (Masur, 1981), complexity, cost, duration, and side effects of treatment (Masur, 1981; Watts, 1980; Windsor et al. 1980), and psychosocial factors such as the patient-service provider interaction and factors in the patient's environment that tend to precede and follow health-related behavior (Masur, 1981).

Brody (1980) recently presented evidence that supports the notion that numerous variables affect patient compliance. He used discriminant function analysis to demonstrate that a combination of treatment (number of medications and ancillary interventions), psychosocial (satisfaction with physician), and demographic (living alone vs. with others) factors could correctly classify 70% of a sample of patients with respect to accuracy of immediate recall of discussions with their physicians. However, the variables that affect compliance may vary as the patient undergoes treatment or as the patient's disease progresses through various stages. For example, O'Brien (1980) demonstrated that the treatment team's and the family's expectations regarding patient compliance increase and decrease, respectively, in affecting compliance as hemodialysis treatment proceeds.

Given the evidence noted above, it appears essential to develop some theoretical model with which to develop and test hypotheses regarding the factors affecting patient compliance with specific treatments at particular stages of various diseases as well as techniques for enhancing compliance. Masur (1981) has suggested that it would be valuable to use a modified version of the Becker and Maiman (1975) Health Belief Model (HBM) for deriving and testing hypotheses. The model specifies that several factors interact with one another to produce compliant or noncompliant behavior. These are: (1) "readiness" factors such as general health motivations, perceived value of the threat of illness, and the perceived probability that compliance will reduce the threat of illness; (2) "modifying and enabling" factors such as the demographic, treatment, and psychosocial variables noted above; and (3) "cues to action" such as internal stimuli (e.g., feelings of physical discomfort) and external cues (e.g., postcard reminders of physician appointments, programmed medication dispensers). Furthermore, the probability that the behavior of interest will occur in the future is dependent upon the direct and indirect consequences of performing the behavior.

In summary, the degree to which patients comply with the treatment regimens offered by medical psychologists will affect the empirical evaluations of those regimens. Although there is considerable documentation that numerous variables are related to patient compliance, there currently exists no widely accepted theoretical framework within the medical psychology literature that may be used to develop and test hypotheses concerning compliance. The use of a model, such as Masur's revision of the HBM, would allow for attempts to identify patients at risk for noncompliance on the basis of readiness

factors, modifying and enabling factors, and some internal cues to action. If high-risk patients could be identified, it then would be possible to develop and evaluate various kinds of intervention for reducing the risk of noncompliance that were directed toward specific patient cognition and behavior as well as psychosocial and treatment factors.

Conclusions. All three of the research areas reviewed above have just begun to serve as targets of systematic investigations by medical psychologists. Some of these areas, that is, influence of psychological factors upon cancer onset and compliance with medical regimens, are associated with an established body of literature plagued by methodological or theoretical weaknesses. Regardless of the quality of the past literature, all three of the areas reviewed above require continued programmatic research efforts with greater specificity in the hypotheses that are tested and in the measurement procedures. For example, it appears necessary for researchers interested in cancer to clearly delineate the characteristics of the control samples against which they compare the premorbid attributes of specific cancer patient groups. Researchers also must specify the particular coping strategies of various cancer patients that require intervention, and devise intervention techniques that may be tailored to suit the special coping needs of the individual, for example, stress inoculation training. Similarly, investigators interested in fostering improved coping among persons undergoing stressful medical procedures must obtain measures of the precise kinds of behavior that are presumed to reflect either adequate or inadequate patient coping as well as unobtrusive and nonreactive assessments of patients' emotional responses. Furthermore, those investigators who wish to investigate the efficacy of cognitive-behavioral interventions should assess patients' cognitions in order to determine the role of cognition in the coping process and whether or not the effects of the interventions actually are mediated by changes in patients' cognitions. With regard to patient compliance, it is necessary for investigators to adopt a theoretical model from which hypotheses may be derived that incorporates the premises that numerous factors interact with one another to produce and maintain compliant or noncompliant behavior, and that the relationships among these factors change as a disease or treatment regimen progresses. Future studies concerning cancer, preparations for stressful medical procedures, and compliance with medical regimens may prove to be quite beneficial if investigators adopt the suggestions outlined above.

FUTURE CONCERNS

Medical psychology research has provided some important contributions to the assessment, prevention, and treatment of a wide variety of health-related problems. However, if the contributions of medical psychology to the larger field of behavioral medicine are to be both maximal and valued by the biomedical community, several issues must be addressed in future training and research efforts. The following discussion will examine three major issues: the appropriate education of medical psychologists; increased emphasis upon preventive intervention; and realistic presentations of the efficacy of medical psychology's contributions to behavioral medicine.

Education of Medical Psychologists

Medical psychology, as we define it, is a relatively young specialty area. Consequently, most persons who currently identify themselves as medical psychologists received their training in traditional doctoral programs in psychology. Gentry and Matarazzo (1981), however, have noted that more focused training in medical psychology and behavioral medicine is being made available to students enrolled in graduate psychology programs (see Matarazzo, 1980, for a list of doctoral and postdoctoral programs related to behavioral medicine and medical psychology). We suggest that graduate programs with medical psychology specialty tracks provide training in areas such as physiology, anatomy, and behavioral pharmacology as well as extensive practicum experiences in hospital and rehabilitation settings. Such didactic and applied offerings as those noted above would, in addition to providing students with requisite skills for work in medical settings, lead to the development of more sophisticated research questions regarding the role of behavioral factors in health-related problems, for example, how may behavioral intervention affect the interacting physiological subsystems that regulate blood pressure. Unless medical psychologists and their students ask research questions that are meaningful to the biomedical community, they will be unable to effectively contribute to multidisciplinary research efforts and will be discredited by their biomedical colleagues.

Preventive Efforts

Matarazzo (1980) recently has called for increased emphasis upon the promotion of health among behavioral medicine and medical psychology specialists. Indeed he has suggested the replacement of the term *medical psychology* with *health psychology* and the formation of a specialty area of *behavioral health* within the discipline of behavioral medicine. Although we disagree with the introduction of new terms that only may increase the existing confusion regarding the role of psychology in behavioral medicine (Bradley & Prokop, 1981), medical psychologists need to devote greater efforts to the development of disease prevention programs such as the Stanford Heart Disease Prevention Program. Research, training, and service endeavors in prevention should be far more cost effective than work in the treatment of disease and rehabilitation (Matarazzo, 1980, 1981). It also would be desirable for medical psychologists who are involved in treatment and rehabilitation efforts to emphasize the prevention of long-term, disease-related disability. An emphasis on the prevention of disability is evident in the research reviewed in this chapter concerning the treatment of chronic pain and essential hypertension, coping with the effects of cancer and its treatment, patient compliance, and psychological preparations for stressful medical procedures. The inclusion of the compliance and psychological preparation literature within the area of disability prevention may seem unusual. However, patients may be less likely to needlessly suffer debilitating effects of disease if they adhere to their treatment regimens, and they may be more willing to undergo some diagnostic and treatment procedures if they are able to effectively deal with the stress of those procedures. Research on the prevention of disease and long-term disability also might lead to an increased acceptance by individuals of their personal responsibility for their own health by increasing their awareness of the role of behavioral factors in the maintenance of health, and their active participation in the treatment process when their health is threatened.

The Evaluation and Presentation of Medical Psychology

The field of medical psychology is attracting increasing attention from health care professionals, governmental funding agencies, and the media (Bradley, Prokop, & Clayman, 1981; Matarazzo, 1980). Associated with this attention is the risk that medical psychology may oversell its contributions to behavioral medicine. A review of the material presented in this chapter reveals that much of the medical psychology literature suffers from theoretical (e.g., patient compliance, stress-related disorders) and methodological (e.g., chronic pain, Type A behavior pattern) weaknesses that preclude any conclusions regarding the effectiveness of various intervention techniques. Even the literature that

is associated with relatively sophisticated methodologies, such as treatment of tension and migraine headaches, generally has failed to provide evidence that positive intervention effects may be maintained for more than a few months. Thus, in order to retain credibility with the public and their fellow professionals, medical psychologists must present dispassionate evaluations of their work in both the professional literature and media presentations. The promising reports that are available, however, should encourage medical psychologists to actively seek funds from governmental and private sources to develop improved assessment, preventive, and treatment techniques for health-related problems.

CONCLUSIONS

The research problems currently addressed by medical psychologists are consistent with those associated with the larger field of behavioral medicine. In general, current medical psychology research efforts reflect greater methodological sophistication than research investigations conducted in the 1960s and early 1970s. Nonetheless, there remains a great need for medical psychologists to: demonstrate the reliability and validity of many of their assessment techniques; increase their use of appropriate experimental control procedures, including the use of credible attention placebo controls, and multiple, specific outcome measures; provide evaluations of the long-term effects of their preventive and treatment intervention techniques; acknowledge the complex etiologies of many health problems, such as stress-related disorders; and devote greater attention to the prevention of disease and disease-related disability.

Despite the need for the theoretical and methodological advances outlined above, we are encouraged by the preliminary but growing interest in tailoring specific intervention techniques for individuals or patient subgroups reflected in the literature concerning chronic pain, the Type A behavior pattern, cancer treatment, and psychological preparations for stressful medical procedures. In these areas there also is increasing emphasis on the cognitive activities of patients. It may be that, as medical psychologists continue to expose themselves to the idiosyncratic covert experiences of various persons, they will show greater appreciation of the need to develop optimal treatment approaches for individual patients or patient subgroups. We are hopeful that the trend toward cognitive assessment and the tailoring of specific, optimal intervention techniques will continue.

REFERENCES

Achterberg, J., Matthews-Simonton, S., & Simonton, O. C. (1977). Psychology of the exceptional cancer patient: A description of patients who outlive predicted life expectancies. *Psychotherapy: Theory, Research and Practice.* **14,** 416–422.

Adams, H. E., Feuerstein, M., & Fowler, J. L. (1980). Migraine headache: Review of parameters, etiology, and intervention. *Psychological Bulletin,* **87,** 217–237.

Agras, S., & Jacob, R. (1979). Hypertension. In O. F. Pomerleau & J. P. Brady (Eds.), *Behavioral medicine: Theory and practice.* Baltimore: Williams & Wilkins.

Alexander, A. B. (1981). Behavioral approaches in the treatment of bronchial asthma. In C. K. Prokop & L. A. Bradley (Eds.), *Medical psychology: Contributions to behavioral medicine.* New York: Academic Press.

American Psychiatric Association (1968). *DSM-II: Diagnostic and statistical manual of mental disorders.* Washington, D. C.: American Psychiatric Association.

Anastasi, A. (1976). *Psychological testing* (4th ed.). New York: MacMillan.

Andrasik, F., & Holroyd, K. A. (1980). A test of specific and nonspecific effects in the biofeedback treatment of tension headache. *Journal of Consulting and Clinical Psychology,* **48,** 575–586.

Bandura, A. (1977). Self-efficacy: Toward a unifying theory of behavioral change. *Psychological Review,* **84,** 191–215.

Bandura, A. (1978). The self-esteem system in reciprocal determinism. *American Psychologist,* **33,** 344–358.

Barofsky, I. (1981). Issues and approaches to the psychosocial assessment of the cancer patient. In C. K. Prokop & L. A. Bradley (Eds.), *Medical psychology: Contributions to behavioral medicine.* New York: Academic Press.

Beaty, E. T., & Haynes, S. N. (1980). Behavioral intervention with muscle-contraction headache: A review. *Psychosomatic Medicine,* **41,** 165–180.

Becker, M. H., & Maiman, L. A. (1975). Sociobehavioral determinants of compliance with health and medical care recommendations. *Medical Care,* **13,** 10–24.

Bellack, A. S., & Hersen, M. (1977). Self-report inventories in behavioral assessment. In J. D. Cone & R. P. Hawkins (Eds.), *Behavioral assessment: New directions in clinical psychology.* New York: Brunner/Mazel.

Best, J. A. (1980). Mass media, self-management, and smoking modification. In P. O. Davidson & S. M. Davidson (Eds.), *Behavioral medicine: Changing health lifestyles.* New York: Brunner/Mazel.

Bild, R., & Adams, H. E. (1980). Modification of migraine headaches by cephalic blood volume, pulse, and EMG biofeedback. *Journal of Consulting and Clinical Psychology,* **48,** 51–57.

Birk, L. (Ed.) (1973). *Biofeedback: Behavioral medicine.* New York: Grune & Stratton.

Blanchard, E. B., & Ahles, T. A. (1979). Behavioral treatment of psychophysical disorders. *Behavior Modification,* **3,** 518–549.

Blanchard, E. B., Ahles, T. A., & Shaw, E. R. (1979). Behavioral treatment of headaches. In M. Hersen, R. M. Eisler, & P. M. Miller (Eds.), *Progress in behavior modification,* Vol. 8. New York: Academic Press.

Blanchard, E. B., Miller, S. T., Abel, G. G., Haynes, M. R., & Wicker, R. (1979). Evaluation of biofeedback in the treatment of borderline essential hypertension. *Journal of Applied Behavior Analysis,* **12,** 99–109.

Blanchard, E. B., Theobald, D. E., Williamson, D. A., Silver, B. V., & Brown, D. A. (1978). Temperature biofeedback in the treatment of migraine headaches: A controlled evaluation. *Archives of General Psychiatry,* **35,** 581–588.

Block, A. R., Kremer, E. F., & Gaylor, M. (1979). Behavioral treatment of chronic pain: The spouse as a discriminative cue for pain behavior. Paper presented at the meeting of the Society of Behavioral Medicine, San Francisco, December.

Block, A. R., Kremer, E., & Gaylor, M. (1980). Behavioral treatment of chronic pain: Variables affecting treatment efficacy. *Pain,* **8,** 367–375.

Borgeat, F., Hade, B., Larouche, L. M., & Bedwani, C. N. (1980). Effect of therapist's active presence on EMG biofeedback training of headache patients. *Biofeedback and Self-Regulation, 5,* 275–282.

Bradley, L. A., & Prokop, C. K. (1981). The relationship between medical psychology and behavioral medicine. In C. K. Prokop & L. A. Bradley (Eds.), *Medical psychology: Contributions to behavioral medicine.* New York: Academic Press.

Bradley, L. A., Prokop, C. K., & Clayman, D. A. (1981). Medical psychology and behavioral medicine: Summary and future concerns. In C. K. Prokop & L. A. Bradley (Eds.), *Medical psychology: Contributions to behavioral medicine.* New York: Academic Press.

Bradley, L. A., Prokop, C. K., Gentry, W. D., Van der Heide, L. H., & Prieto, E. J. (1981). Assessment of chronic pain. In C. K. Prokop & L. A. Bradley (Eds.), *Medical psychology: Contributions to behavioral medicine.* New York: Academic Press.

Bradley, L. A., Prokop, C. K., Margolis, R., & Gentry, W. D. (1978). Multivariate analyses of the MMPI profiles of low back pain patients. *Journal of Behavioral Medicine, 1,* 253–272.

Brody, D. S. (1980). An analysis of patient recall of their therapeutic regimens. *Journal of Chronic Diseases, 33,* 57–63.

Burish, T. G. (1981). EMG biofeedback in the treatment of stress-related disorders. In C. K. Prokop & L. A. Bradley (Eds.), *Medical psychology: Contributions to behavioral medicine.* New York: Academic Press.

Burish, T. G., & Lyles, J. N. (1979). Effectiveness of relaxation training in reducing the aversiveness of chemotherapy in the treatment of cancer. *Journal of Behavior Therapy and Experimental Psychiatry, 10,* 357–361.

Cairns, G. F., & Altman, K. (1979). Behavioral treatment of cancer-related anorexia. *Journal of Behavior Therapy and Experimental Psychiatry, 10,* 353–356.

Cairns, D., & Pasino, J. A. (1977). Comparison of verbal reinforcement and feedback in the operant treatment of disability due to chronic low back pain. *Behavior Therapy, 8,* 621–630.

Cairns, D., Thomas, L., Mooney, V., & Pace, J. B. (1976). A comprehensive treatment approach to chronic low back pain. *Pain, 2,* 301–308.

Calhoun, K. S., & Adams, H. E. (Eds.) (1977). *Handbook of behavioral assessment.* New York: Wiley.

Carver, C. S., Coleman, A. E., & Glass, D. C. (1976). The coronary-prone behavior pattern and suppression of fatigue on a treadmill test. *Journal of Personality and Social Psychology, 33,* 460–466.

Cataldo, M. F., & Russo, D. C. (1979). Developmentally disabled in the community: Behavioral/ medical considerations. In L. A. Hamerlynck (Ed.), *Behavioral systems for the developmentally disabled,* Vol. 2. *Institutional, clinic, and community environments.* New York: Brunner/Mazel.

Chesney, M. A., Eagleston, J. R., & Rosenman, R. H. (1981). Type A behavior: Assessment and intervention. In C. K. Prokop & L. A. Bradley (Eds.), *Medical psychology: Contributions to behavioral medicine.* New York: Academic Press.

Ciminero, A. R., Nelson, R. O., & Lipinsky, D. P. (1977). Self-monitoring procedures. In A. R. Ciminero, K. S. Calhoun, & H. E. Adams (Eds.), *Handbook of behavioral assessment.* New York: Wiley.

Coates, T. J., Perry, C., Killen, J., & Slinkard, L. A. (1981). Primary prevention of cardiovascular disease in children and adolescents. In C. K. Prokop & L. A. Bradley (Eds.), *Medical psychology: Contributions to behavioral medicine.* New York: Academic Press.

Coates, T. J., & Thoresen, C. E. (1980). Obesity in children and adolescents: The problem belongs to everyone. In J. M. Ferguson & C. B. Taylor (Eds.), *A comprehensive handbook of behavioral medicine.* Jamaica, N. Y.: Spectrum.

Cohen, J. A. (1960). A coefficient of agreement for nominal scales. *Educational and Psychological Measurement, 20,* 37–46.

Cohen, J. B., Matthews, K. A., & Waldron, I. (1977). Section summary: Coronary-prone behavior: Developmental and cultural considerations. In T. Dembroski, S. M. Weiss, J. L. Shields, S. G. Haynes, & M. Feinleib (Eds.), *Proceedings of the Forum on Coronary-Prone Behavior.* Washington, D. C.: DHEW No. (NIH)78–1451.

Collins, F. L., & Thompson, J. K. (1979). Reliability and standardization in the assessment of self-reported headache pain. *Journal of Behavioral Assessment, 1,* 73–86.

Conger, A. J. (1980). Integration and generalization of kappas for multiple raters. *Psychological Bulletin, 88,* 322–328.

Criqui, M. H., Barrett-Conner, E., Holdbrook, M. J., Austin, M., & Turner, J. D. (1980). Clustering of cardiovascular disease risk factors. *Preventive Medicine, 9,* 525–533.

Crockett, D. J., Prkachin, K. M., & Craig, K. D. (1977). Factors of the language of pain in patient and volunteer groups. *Pain, 4,* 175–183.

Cronbach, L. J., & Furby, L. (1970). How we should measure change—or should we? *Psychological Bulletin, 74,* 68–80.

Cronbach, L. J., Gleser, G. C., Nanda, H., & Rajaratnam, N. (1972). *The dependability of behavioral measurements: Theory of generalizability for scores and profiles.* New York: Wiley.

Dattore, P. J., Shontz, F. C., & Coyne, L. (1980). Premorbid personality differentiation of cancer and noncancer groups: A test of the hypothesis of cancer proneness. *Journal of Consulting and Clinical Psychology*, **48**, 388–394.

Dembroski, T. M. (1979). Cardiovascular reactivity in Type A coronary-prone subjects. In D. J. Oborne, M. M. Gruneberg, & J. R. Eiser (Eds.), *Research in psychology and medicine*, Vol. 1. London: Academic Press.

Dembroski, T. M., MacDougall, J. M., Herd, J. A., & Shields, J. L. (1979). Effects of level of challenge on pressor and heart rate responses in Type A and B subjects. *Journal of Applied Social Psychology*, **9**, 208–228.

Dembroski, T. M., MacDougall, J. M., & Lushene, R. (1979). Interpersonal interaction and cardiovascular response in Type A subjects and coronary patients. *Journal of Human Stress*, **5**, 28–36.

Dembroski, T. M., MacDougall, J. M., & Shields, J. L. (1977). Physiologic reactions to social challenge in persons evidencing the Type A coronary-prone behavior pattern. *Journal of Human Stress*, **3**, 2–9.

Dembroski, T. M., MacDougall, J. M., Shields, J. L., Petitto, J., & Lushene, R. (1978). Components of the Type A coronary-prone behavior pattern and cardiovascular responses to psychomotor performance challenge. *Journal of Behavioral Medicine*, **1**, 159–176.

Diamond, S., Medina, J., Diamond-Falk, J., & De-Veno, T. (1979). The value of biofeedback in the treatment of chronic headache: A five-year retrospective study. *Headache*, **19**, 90–96.

Dimsdale, J. E., Hackett, T. P., Catanzano, D. M., & White, P. J. (1979). The relationship between diverse measures of Type A personality and coronary angiographic findings. *Journal of Psychosomatic Research*, **23**, 289–293.

Dimsdale, J. E., Hackett, T. P., Hutter, A. M., & Block, P. C. (1980). The risk of Type A mediated coronary artery disease in different populations. *Psychosomatic Medicine*, **42**, 55–62.

Dimsdale, J. E., Hackett, T. P., Hutter, A. M., Block, P. C., Catanzano, D. M., & White, P. J. (1979). Type A behavior and angiographic findings. *Journal of Psychosomatic Research*, **23**, 273–276.

Duncan, G. H., Gregg, J. M., & Ghia, J. N. (1978). The pain profile: A computerized system for assessment of chronic pain. *Pain*, **5**, 275–284.

Drury, R. L., DeRisi, W. J., & Liberman, R. P. (1979). Temperature biofeedback treatment for migraine headache: A controlled multiple baseline study. *Headache*, **19**, 278–284.

Erikson, M. B. E., Sjölund, B. H., & Nielzén, S. (1979). Long-term results of peripheral condition-ing stimulation as an analgesic measure in chronic pain. *Pain*, **6**, 335–347.

Evans, R. I., Rozelle, R. M., Mittelmark, M. B., Hansen, W. B., Bane, A. L., & Harris, J. (1978). Deterring the onset of smoking in children: Knowledge of immediate physiological effects and coping with peer pressure, media pressure, and parent modeling. *Journal of Applied Social Psychology*, **8**, 126–135.

Follick, M. J., Zitter, R. E., Kulich, R. J., & Harris, R. (1979). An outpatient-based behaviorally oriented, multidisciplinary approach to the management of chronic pain. Paper presented at the meeting of the Association for Advancement of Behavior Therapy, San Francisco, December.

Follick, M. J., Zitter, R. E., & Kulich, R. J. (in press). Outpatient management of chronic pain. In T. J. Coates (Ed.), *Behavioral medicine: A practical handbook*. Champaign, Ill.: Research Press.

Fordyce, W. E. (1976). *Behavioral methods for chronic pain and illness*. St. Louis: C. V. Mosby.

Fox, B. H. (1978). Premorbid psychological factors as related to cancer incidence. *Journal of Behavioral Medicine*, **1**, 45–133.

Fox, E. J., & Melzack, R. (1976). Transcutaneous electrical stimulation and acupuncture: Comparison of treatment for low back pain. *Pain*, **2**, 141–148.

Frederiksen, L. W., Lynd, R. S., & Ross, J. (1978). Methodology in the measurement of pain. *Behavior Therapy*, **9**, 486–488.

Friedman, M., & Rosenman, R. H. (1959). Association of specific overt behavior pattern with blood and cardiovascular findings: Blood cholesterol level, blood clotting time, incidence of arcus senilis, and clinical coronary artery disease. *Journal of the American Medical Association*, **169**, 1286–1296.

Gatchel, R. J. (1979). Biofeedback and the modification of stress-related disorders: The impact of placebo factors. In D. J. Oborne, M. M. Gruneberg, & J. R. Eiser (Eds.), *Research in psychology and medicine*, Vol. 1. London: Academic Press.

Genest, M. (1978). A cognitive-behavioral bibliotherapy to ameliorate pain. Paper presented at the meeting of the American Psychological Association, Toronto, August.

Genest, M., & Turk, D. C. (1979). A proposed model for behavioral group therapy with pain patients. In D. Upper & S. M. Ross (Eds.), *Behavioral group therapy: An annual review*. Champaign, Ill.: Research Press.

Genest, M., & Turk, D. C. (1981). Think-aloud approaches to cognitive assessment. In T. Merluzzi, C. Glass, & M. Genest (Eds.), *Cognitive assessment*. New York: Guilford Press.

Gentry, W. D., & Matarazzo, J. D. (1981). Medical psychology: Three decades of growth and development. In C. K. Prokop & L. A. Bradley (Eds.), *Medical psychology: Contributions to behavioral medicine.* New York: Academic Press.

Girodo, M., & Wood, D. (1979). Talking yourself out of pain: The importance of believing that you can. *Cognitive Therapy and Research,* **3,** 23–33.

Glasgow, R. E., & Bernstein, D. A. (1981). Behavioral treatment of smoking behavior. In C. K. Prokop & L. A. Bradley (Eds.), *Medical psychology: Contributions to behavioral medicine.* New York: Academic Press.

Glass, D. C. (1977). *Behavior patterns, stress, and coronary disease.* Hillsdale, N. J.: Lawrence Erlbaum.

Goldstein, I. B. (1981). Assessment of hypertension. In C. K. Prokop & L. A. Bradley (Eds.), *Medical Psychology: Contributions to behavioral medicine.* New York: Academic Press.

Gordon, W. A., Freidenbergs, I., Dillen, L., Hibbard, M., Wolf, C., Levine, L., Lipkins, R., Ezrachi, O., & Lucido, D. (1980). Efficacy of psychosocial intervention with cancer patients. *Journal of Consulting and Clinical Psychology,* **48,** 743–759.

Gottlieb, H., Strite, L. C., Koller, R., Madorsky, A., Hockersmith, V., Kleeman, M., & Wagner, J. (1977). Comprehensive rehabilitation of patients having chronic low back pain. *Archives of Physical Medicine and Rehabilitation,* **58,** 101–108.

Gracely, R. H. (1979). Psychophysical assessment of human pain. In J. J. Bonica, J. C. Liebeskind, & D. Albe-Fessard (Eds.), *Advances in pain research and therapy,* Vol. 3. New York: Raven Press.

Gracely, R. H., Dubner, R., & McGrath, P. (1979). Narcotic analgesia: Fentanyl reduces the intensity but not the unpleasantness of painful tooth pulp sensations. *Science,* **203,** 1261–1263.

Gracely, R. H., Dubner, R., McGrath, P., & Heft, M. (1978). New methods for pain measurement and their application to pain control. *International Dental Journal,* **28,** 52–65.

Gracely, R. H., McGrath, P., & Dubner, R. (1978a). Ratio scales of sensory and affective pain descriptions. *Pain,* **5,** 5–18.

Gracely, R. H., McGrath, P., & Dubner, R. (1978b). Validity and sensitivity of ratio scales of sensory and affective verbal pain descriptors: Manipulation of affect by Diazepam. *Pain,* **5,** 19–29.

Graham, C., Bond, S. S., Gerkovich, M. M., & Cook, M. R. (1980). Use of the McGill Pain Questionnaire in the assessment of cancer pain: Replicability and consistency. *Pain,* **8,** 377–387.

Gray, C. L., Lyle, R. C., McGuire, R. J., & Peck, D. F. (1980). Electrode placement, EMG feedback, and relaxation for tension headaches. *Behaviour Research and Therapy,* **18,** 19–23.

Greer, L. S. (1979). Psychological enquiry: A contribution to cancer research. *Psychological Medicine,* **9,** 81–89.

Guglielmi, R. S., & Roberts, A. H. (1980). A double-blind study of the effectiveness of skin temperature self-regulation as a treatment for Raynaud's disease. *Psychophysiology,* **17,** 299. (Abstract)

Hackett, G., & Horan, J. J. (1980). Stress inoculation for pain: What's really going on? *Journal of Counseling Psychology,* **27,** 107–116.

Harrell, J. P. (1980). Psychological factors and hypertension: A status report. *Psychological Bulletin,* **87,** 482–501.

Hartman, L. M., & Ainsworth, K. D. (1980). Self-regulation of chronic pain. *Canadian Journal of Psychiatry,* **25,** 38–43.

Herd, J. A. (1981). Treatment of cardiovascular disorders. In C. K. Prokop & L. A. Bradley (Eds.), *Medical psychology: Contributions to behavioral medicine.* New York: Academic Press.

Holden, C. (1980). Behavioral medicine: An emergent field. *Science,* **209,** 479–481.

Holmes, D. S. (1981). The use of biofeedback for treating patients with migraine headaches, Raynaud's disease, and hypertension: A critical evaluation. In C. K. Prokop & L. A. Bradley (Eds.), *Medical psychology: Contributions to behavioral medicine.* New York: Academic Press.

Holmes, T. H., & Rahe, R. H. (1967). The social readjustment rating scale. *Journal of Psychosomatic Research,* **11,** 213–218.

Holroyd, K. A., Andrasik, F., & Noble, J. (1980). A comparison of EMG biofeedback and a credible pseudotherapy in treating tension headaches. *Journal of Behavioral Medicine,* **3,** 29–39.

Horan, J. J., Hackett, G., Buchanan, J. D., Stone, C. I., & Demchik-Stone, D. (1977). Coping with pain: A component analysis of stress inoculation. *Cognitive Therapy and Research,* **1,** 211–221.

Horne, R. L., & Picard, R. S. (1979). Psychosocial risk factors for lung cancer. *Psychosomatic Medicine,* **41,** 503–514.

Hurd, P. D., Johnson, C. A., Pechacek, T., Bast, L. P., Jacobs, D. R., & Luepker, R. V. (1980). Prevention of cigarette smoking in seventh grade students. *Journal of Behavioral Medicine,* **3,** 15–28.

IASP Subcommittee on Taxonomy. (1979). Pain terms: A list with definitions and notes on usage. *Pain,* **6,** 249–252.

Jacobson, A. M., Manschreck, T. C., & Silverberg, E. (1979). Behavioral treatment for Raynaud's disease: A comparative study with long-term follow-up. *American Journal of Psychiatry,* **136,** 844–846.

Jeans, M. E. (1979). Relief of chronic pain by brief, intense transcutaneous electrical stimulation: A double-blind study. In J. J. Bonica, J. C. Liebeskind, & D. Albe-Fessard (Eds.), *Advances in pain research and therapy,* Vol. 3. New York: Raven Press.

Jenkins, C. D., Rosenman, R. H., & Friedman, M. (1967). Development of an objective psychological test for the determination of the coronary-prone behavior pattern in employed men. *Journal of Chronic Diseases,* **20,** 371–379.

Jenni, M. A., & Wollersheim, J. P. (1979). Cognitive therapy, stress management training, and the Type A behavior pattern. *Cognitive Therapy and Research,* **3,** 61–73.

Jessup, B. A., Neufeld, R. W. J., & Merskey, H. (1979). Biofeedback therapy for headache and other pain: An evaluative review. *Pain,* **7,** 225–270.

Kasl, S. V. (1980). Cardiovascular risk reduction in a community setting: Some comments. *Journal of Consulting and Clinical Psychology,* **48,** 143–149.

Katkin, E. S., & Goldband, S. (1979). The placebo effect and biofeedback. In R. J. Gatchel & K. D. Price (Eds.), *Clinical applications of biofeedback: Appraisal and Status.* New York: Pergamon Press.

Katz, E. R., Kellerman, J., & Siegel, S. E. (1980). Behavioral distress in children with cancer undergoing medical procedures: Developmental considerations. *Journal of Consulting and Clinical Psychology,* **48,** 356–365.

Keefe, F. J. (1979). Assessment strategies in behavioral medicine. In J. R. McNamara (Ed.), *Behavioral approaches to medicine.* New York: Plenum.

Keefe, F. J., Surwit, R. S., & Pilon, R. N. (1979). A one-year follow-up of Raynaud's patients treated with behavioral therapy techniques. *Journal of Behavioral Medicine,* **2,** 385–391.

Keefe, F. J., Surwit, R. S., & Pilon, R. N. (1980). Biofeedback, autogenic training, and progressive relaxation in the treatment of Raynaud's disease: A comparative study. *Journal of Applied Behavior Analysis,* **13,** 3–11.

Kellerman, J. (1978). A note on psychosomatic factors in the etiology of neoplasms. *Journal of Consulting and Clinical Psychology,* **46,** 1522–1523.

Kendall, P. C. (in press). Stressful medical procedures: Cognitive-behavioral strategies for stress management and prevention. In D. Meichenbaum and M. Jaremko (Eds.), *Stress prevention and management: A cognitive-behavioral approach.* New York: Plenum.

Kendall, P. C., & Hollon, S. D. (1979). *Cognitive-behavioral interventions: Theory, research, and procedures.* New York: Academic Press.

Kendall, P. C., & Hollon, S. D. (1981). Assessing self-referent speech: Methods in the measurement of self-statements. In P. C. Kendall & S. D. Hollon (Eds.), *Assessment strategies for cognitive-behavioral interventions.* New York: Academic Press.

Kendall, P. C., & Korgeski, G. P. (1979). Assessment and cognitive-behavioral interventions. *Cognitive Therapy and Research,* **3,** 1–21.

Kendall, P. C., & Watson, D. (1981). Psychological preparation for stressful medical procedures. In C. K. Prokop & L. A. Bradley (Eds.), *Medical Psychology: Contributions to behavioral medicine.* New York: Academic Press.

Kendall, P. C., Williams, L., Pechacek, T. F., Graham, L. G., Shisslak, C. S., & Herzoff, N. (1979). Cognitive-behavioral and patient education interventions in cardiac catheterization procedures: The Palo Alto medical psychology project. *Journal of Consulting and Clinical Psychology,* **47,** 49–58.

Kent, R. N., & Foster, S. L. (1977). Direct observational procedures: Methodological issues in naturalistic settings. In A. R. Ciminero, K. S. Calhoun, & H. E. Adams (Eds.), *Handbook of behavioral assessment.* New York: Wiley.

Kewman, D. G., & Roberts, A. H. (1979). Skin temperature biofeedback and migraine headaches: A double-blind study. *Biofeedback and Self-Regulation,* **4,** 257. (Abstract)

Kissen, D. M. (1963). Personality characteristics in males conducive to lung cancer. *British Journal of Medical Psychology,* **35,** 27–36.

Klorman, R., Hilpert, P. L., Michael, R., LaGana, C., & Sveen, O. B. (1980). Effects of coping and mastery modeling on experienced and inexperienced pedodontic patient's disruptiveness. *Behavior Therapy,* **11,** 156–168.

Lake, A., Rainey, J., & Papsdorf, J. D. (1979). Biofeedback and rational-emotive therapy in the management of migraine headaches. *Journal of Applied Behavior Analysis,* **12,** 127–140.

Largen, J. W., Mathew, R. J., Dobbins, K., Meyer, J. S., & Claghorn, J. L. (1978). Skin temperature self-regulation and non-invasive regional cerebral blood flow. *Headache,* **18,** 203–210.

Leavitt, F., Garron, D. C., Whisler, W., & Sheinkop, M. B. (1978). Affective and sensory dimensions of back pain. *Pain,* **4,** 273–281.

LeShan, L. L. (1959). Psychological states as factors in the development of malignant disease: A critical review. *Journal of the National Cancer Institute,* **22,** 1–18.

Leventhal, H., Brown, D., Shacham, S., & Engquist, G. (1979). Effects of preparatory information about sensations, threat of pain, and attention on cold pressor distress. *Journal of Personality and Social Psychology, 37,* 688–714.

Leventhal, H., & Cleary, P. D. (1980). The smoking problem: A review of the research and theory in behavioral risk modification. *Psychological Bulletin, 88,* 370–405.

Leventhal, H., Safer, M. A., Cleary, P. D., & Gutmann, M. (1980). Cardiovascular risk modification by community-based programs for life-style change: Comments on the Stanford study. *Journal of Consulting and Clinical Psychology, 48,* 150–158.

Long, D. M., & Hagfors, N. (1975). Electrical stimulation in the nervous system: The current status of electrical stimulation of the nervous system for relief of pain. *Pain, 1,* 109–114.

MacDougall, J. M., Dembroski, T. M., & Musante, L. (1979). The structured interview and questionnaire methods of assessing coronary-prone behavior in male and female college students. *Journal of Behavioral Medicine, 2,* 71–83.

Manuck, S. B., Craft, S., & Gold, K. J. (1978). Coronary-prone behavior pattern and cardiovascular response. *Psychophysiology, 15,* 403–411.

Manuck, S. B., & Garland, F. N. (1979). Coronary-prone behavior pattern, task incentive, and cardiovascular response. *Psychophysiology, 16,* 136–142.

Masur, F. T. (1979). An update on medical psychology and behavioral medicine. *Professional Psychology, 10,* 259–264.

Masur, F. T. (1981). Adherence to health care regimens. In C. K. Prokop & L. A. Bradley (Eds.), *Medical psychology: Contributions to behavioral medicine.* New York: Academic Press.

Matarazzo, J. D. (1980). Behavioral health and behavioral medicine: Frontiers for a new health psychology. *American Psychologist, 35,* 807–817.

Matarazzo, J. D. (1981). Behavioral health: A responsibility of and opportunity for academic, scientific, and professional psychology. Manuscript submitted for publication.

Matarazzo, J. D., Carmody, T. P., & Jacobs, L. D. (1980). Test-retest reliability and stability of the WAIS: A literature review with implications for clinical practice. *Journal of Clinical Neuropsychology, 2,* 89–105.

Matarazzo, J. D., Matarazzo, R. G., Wiens, A. N., Gallo, A. E., & Klonoff, H. (1976). Retest reliability of the Halstead Impairment Index in a normal, a schizophrenic, and two samples of organic patients. *Journal of Clinical Psychology, 32,* 338–349.

Mathew, R. J., Largen, J. W., Dobbins, K., Meyer, J. S., Sakai, F., & Claghorn, J. L. (1980). Bio-

feedback control of skin temperature and cerebral blood flow in migraine. *Headache, 20,* 19–28.

Matthews, K. A., & Brunson, B. I. (1979). Allocation of attention and the Type A coronary-prone behavior pattern. *Journal of Personality and Social Psychology, 37,* 2081–2090.

Matthews, K., Glass, D. C., Rosenman, R. H., & Bortner, R. (1977). Competitive drive, pattern A, and coronary heart disease: A further analysis of some data from the Western Collaborative Group Study. *Journal of Chronic Diseases, 30,* 489–498.

McAlister, A., Puska, P., Koskela, K., Pallonen, U., & Maccoby, N. (1980). Mass communication and community organization for public health education. *American Psychologist, 35,* 375–379.

McArthur, D. L., & Cohen, M. J. (1980). Measures of forehead and finger temperature, frontalis EMG, heart rate and finger pulse amplitude during and between migraine headaches. *Headache, 20,* 134–136.

Meichenbaum, D., & Cameron, R. (1973). Stress inoculation: A skills training approach to anxiety management. Unpublished manuscript, University of Waterloo.

Melzack, R. (1975). The McGill Pain Questionnaire: Major properties and scoring methods. *Pain, 1,* 277–299.

Melzack, R. (1979). Current concepts of pain. In D. J. Oborne, M. M. Gruneberg, & J. R. Eiser (Eds.), *Research in psychology and medicine,* Vol. 1. London: Academic Press.

Melzack, R., & Dennis, S. G. (1978). Neurophysiological foundations of pain. In R. A. Sternback (Ed.), *The psychology of pain.* New York: Raven Press.

Melzack, R., & Perry, C. (1975). Self-regulation of pain: The use of alpha-feedback and hypnotic training for the control of chronic pain. *Experimental Neurology, 46,* 452–469.

Melzack, R., & Torgerson, W. S. (1971). On the language of pain. *Anesthesiology, 34,* 50–59.

Meyer, A. J., Maccoby, N., & Farquhar, J. W. (1980). Reply to Kasl and Leventhal et al. *Journal of Consulting and Clinical Psychology, 48,* 159–163.

Meyer, A. J., Nash, J. D., McAlister, A. L., Maccoby, N., & Farquhar, J. W. (1980). Skills training in a cardiovascular health education campaign. *Journal of Consulting and Clinical Psychology, 48,* 129–142.

Meyerowitz, B. E. (1980). Psychosocial correlates of breast cancer and its treatment. *Psychological Bulletin, 87,* 108–131.

Mitchell, S. K. (1979) Interobserver agreement, reliability, and generalizability of data collected in observational studies. *Psychological Bulletin,* **86,** 376–390.

Nathan, R. G., Lubin, B., Matarazzo, J. D., & Persely, G. W. (1979). Psychologists in schools of medicine: 1955, 1964, and 1977. *American Psychologist,* **34,** 622–627.

Nirenberg, T., Ersner-Hershfield, S., Sobell, L. C., & Sobell, M. B. (1981). Behavioral treatment of alcohol problems. In C. K. Prokop & L. A. Bradley (Eds.), *Medical psychology: Contributions to behavioral medicine.* New York: Academic Press.

Neuchterlein, K. H., & Holroyd, J. C. (1980). Biofeedback in the treatment of tension headache. *Archives of General Psychiatry,* **37,** 866–873.

O'Brien, M. I. (1980). Hemodialysis regimen compliance and social environment: A panel analysis. *Nursing Research,* **29,** 250–255.

Pechacek, T., Luepker, R. V., & Pickens, R. C. (1980). Advances in the measurement of smoking behavior. Paper presented at the meeting of the Society of Behavioral Medicine, New York, November.

Penk, W. E., Woodward, W. A., Robinowitz, R., & Parr, W. C. (1980). An MMPI comparison of polydrug and heroin abusers. *Journal of Abnormal Psychology,* **89,** 299–302.

Pfeiffer, E. (1975). A short portable mental status questionnaire for the assessment of organic brain defect in elderly patients. *Journal of the American Geriatric Society,* **23,** 433–441.

Pittner, M. S., & Houston, B. K. (1980). Response to stress, cognitive coping strategies, and the Type A behavior pattern. *Journal of Personality and Social Psychology,* **39,** 147–151.

Pomerleau, O. F., & Brady, J. P. (1979). Introduction: The scope and promise of behavioral medicine. In O. F. Pomerleau & J. P. Brady (Eds.), *Behavioral medicine: Theory and practice.* Baltimore: Williams & Wilkins.

Price, D. D., Barrell, J. J., & Gracely, R. H. (1980). A psychophysical analysis of experiential factors that selectively influence the affective dimension of pain. *Pain,* **8,** 137–149.

Prieto, E. J., Hopson, L., Bradley, L. A., Byrne, M., Geisinger, K. F., Midax, D., & Marchisello, P. J. (1980). The language of low back pain: Factor structure of the McGill Pain Questionnaire. *Pain,* **8,** 11–19.

Prokop, C. K., & Bradley, L. A. (1981). Methodological issues in medical psychology research. In C. K. Prokop & L. A. Bradley (Eds.), *Medical psychology: Contributions to behavioral medicine.* New York: Academic Press.

Prokop, C. K., Bradley, L. A., Margolis, R., & Gentry, W. D. (1980). Multivariate analyses of the MMPI profiles of multiple pain patients. *Journal of Personality Assessment,* **44,** 246–252.

Prue, D. M., Martin, J. E., & Hume, A. S. (1980). A critical evaluation of thiocyanate as a biochemical index of smoking exposure. *Behavior Therapy,* **11,** 368–379.

Puska, P., Tuomíehto, J., Salonen, J., Neittaanmäki, L., Maki, J., Virtamo, J., Nissinen, A., Koskela, K., & Takalo, T. (1979). Changes in coronary risk factors during comprehensive five-year community programme to control cardiovascular diseases (North Karelia project). *British Medical Journal,* **2,** 1173–1178.

Quintanar, L. R., Cacioppo, J. T., Monyak, N., Alvarez, L., & Snyder, C. (1980). The effects of cranial vasconstriction and paced respiration on migraine. *Psychophysiology,* **17,** 284. (Abstract)

Rahe, R. H., Ward, H. W., & Hayes, V. (1979). Brief group therapy in myocardial infarction rehabilitation: Three-to-four-year follow-up of a controlled trial. *Psychosomatic Medicine,* **41,** 229–242.

Rathus, S. A. (1973). A 30-item schedule for assessing assertive behavior. *Behavior Therapy,* **4,** 398–406.

Reading, A. E. (1979). The internal structure of the McGill Pain Questionnaire in dysmenorrhea patients. *Pain,* **7,** 353–358.

Reading, A. E., & Cox, D. W. (1979). The measurement of pain. In D. J. Oborne, M. M. Gruneberg, & J. R. Eiser (Eds.), *Research in psychology and medicine,* Vol. 1. London: Academic Press.

Redd, W. H. (1980). Stimulus control and extinction of psychosomatic symptoms in cancer patients in protective isolation. *Journal of Consulting and Clinical Psychology,* **48,** 448–455.

Roberts, A. H., & Reinhardt, L. (1980). The behavioral management of chronic pain: Long-term follow-up with comparison groups. *Pain,* **8,** 151–162.

Rosenman, R. H., & Friedman, M. (1977). Modifying Type A behavior pattern. *Journal of Psychosomatic Research,* **21,** 323–331.

Roskies, E. (1979). Evaluating improvement in the coronary-prone (Type A) behavior pattern. In D. J. Oborne, M. M. Gruneberg, & J. R. Eiser (Eds.), *Research in psychology and medicine,* Vol. 1. London: Academic Press.

Roskies, E. (1980). Considerations in developing a treatment program for the coronary-prone (Type A) behavior pattern. In P. O. Davidson & S. M. Davidson (Eds.), *Behavioral medicine: Changing health lifestyles.* New York: Brunner/Mazel.

Roskies, E., Kearney, H., Spevack, M., Surkis, A., Cohen, C., & Gilman, S. (1979). Generalizability and durability of treatment effects in an intervention program for coronary-prone (Type A) managers. *Journal of Behavioral Medicine,* **2,** 195–207.

Roskies, E., Spevack, M., Surkis, A., Cohen, C., & Gilman, S. (1978). Changing the coronary-prone (Type A) behavior pattern in a nonclinical population. *Journal of Behavioral Medicine*, **1**, 201–216.

Rotter, J. B. (1966). Generalized expectancies for internal versus external control of reinforcement. *Psychological Monographs*, **80**, Whole No. 609.

Russo, D. C., Bird, P. L., & Masek, B. J. (1980). Assessment issues in behavioral medicine. *Behavioral Assessment*, **2**, 1–18.

Rybstein-Blinchik, E. (1979). Effects of different cognitive strategies on chronic pain experience. *Journal of Behavioral Medicine*, **2**, 93–101.

Sanders, S. H. (1979). Behavioral assessment and treatment of clinical pain: Appraisal of current status. In M. Hersen, R. M. Eisler, & P. M. Miller (Eds.), *Progress in behavior modification*, Vol. 8. New York: Academic Press.

Sappington, J. T., Fiorito, E. M., & Brehony, K. A. (1979). Biofeedback as therapy in Raynaud's disease. *Biofeedback and Self-Regulation*, **4**, 155–169.

Sargent, J. D., Solbach, P., & Coyne, L. (1980). Evaluation of a 5-day non-drug training program for headache at the Menninger Foundation. *Headache*, **20**, 32–41.

Schlutter, L. C., Golden, C. J., & Blume, H. G. (1980). A comparison of treatments for prefrontal muscle contraction headache. *British Journal of Medical Psychology*, **53**, 47–52.

Schwartz, G. E., Shapiro, A. P., Redmond, D. P., Ferguson, D. C. E., Ragland, D. R., & Weiss, S. M. (1979). Behavioral medicine approaches to hypertension: An integrative analysis of theory and research. *Journal of Behavioral Medicine*, **2**, 311–363.

Schwartz, G. E., & Weiss, S. M. (Eds.) (1977a). *Proceedings of the Yale Conference on Behavioral Medicine* (DHEW Publication No. NIH 78–1424). Washington, D. C.: U. S. Government Printing Office.

Schwartz, G. E., & Weiss, S. M. (1977b). What is behavioral medicine? *Psychosomatic Medicine*, **39**, 377–381.

Schwartz, G. E., & Weiss, S. M. (1978). Behavioral medicine revisited: An amended definition. *Journal of Behavioral Medicine*, **1**, 249–251.

Schwartz, M. F., & Graham, J. R. (1979). Construct validity of the MacAndrew Alcoholism Scale. *Journal of Consulting and Clinical Psychology*, **47**, 1090–1095.

Scott, P. J., & Huskisson, E. C. (1976). Graphic representation of pain. *Pain*, **2**, 175–184.

Sedlacek, K., Cohen, J., & Boxhill, C. (1979). Comparison between biofeedback and relaxation response in the treatment of hypertension. *Biofeedback and Self-Regulation*, **4**, 259–260. (Abstract)

Selzer, M. L. (1971). The Michigan Alcoholism Screening Test: The quest for a new diagnostic instrument. *American Journal of Psychiatry*, **127**, 1653–1658.

Shapiro, A. P., Schwartz, G. E., Ferguson, D. C. E., Redmond, D. P., & Weiss, S. M. (1977). Behavioral methods in the treatment of hypertension. *Annals of Internal Medicine*, **86**, 626–636.

Shapiro, D., & Surwit, R. S. (1979). Biofeedback. In O. F. Pomerleau & J. P. Brady (Eds.), *Behavioral medicine: Theory and practice*. Baltimore: Williams & Wilkins.

Silver, B. V., Blanchard, E. B., Williamson, D. A., Theobald, D. E., & Brown, D. A. (1979). Temperature biofeedback and relaxation training in the treatment of migraine headaches. *Biofeedback and Self-Regulation*, **4**, 359–366.

Simonton, O. C., Matthews-Simonton, S., & Creighton, J. (1978). *Getting well again*. Los Angeles: Tarcher.

Sobel, H. J., & Worden, J. W. (1979). The MMPI as a predictor of psychosocial adaptation to cancer. *Journal of Consulting and Clinical Psychology*, **47**, 716–724.

Sobell, L. C., & Sobell, M. B. (1977). Alcohol problems. In R. B. Williams, Jr. & W. D. Gentry (Eds.), *Behavioral approaches to medical treatment*. Cambridge, Mass.: Ballinger.

Sobell, M. B., & Sobell, L. C. (1975). A brief technical report on the Mobat: An inexpensive portable test for determining blood alcohol concentration. *Journal of Applied Behavior Analysis*, **8**, 117–120.

Spanos, N. P., Radtke-Bodorik, L., Ferguson, J. D., & Jones, B. (1979). The effects of hypnotic susceptibility, suggestions for analgesia, and the utilization of cognitive strategies on the reduction of pain. *Journal of Abnormal Psychology*, **88**, 282–292.

Spielberger, C. D., Gorsuch, R. L., & Lushene, R. E. (1970). *Manual for the State-Trait Anxiety Inventory*. Palo Alto, Calif.: Counseling Psychologist Press.

Steger, J. C., & Harper, R. G. (1980). Comprehensive biofeedback versus self-monitored relaxation in the treatment of tension headache. *Headache*, **20**, 137–142.

Stephenson, N. L., Cole, M. A., & Spann, R. (1979). Response of tension headache sufferers to relaxation and biofeedback training as a function of personality characteristics. *Biofeedback and Self-Regulation*, **4**, 250. (Abstract)

Sternbach, R. A. (1974). *Pain patients: Traits and treatment*. New York: Academic Press.

Stoyva, J. M. (1979). Musculoskeletal and stress-related disorders. In O. F. Pomerleau & J. P. Brady (Eds.), *Behavioral medicine: Theory and practice*. Baltimore: Williams & Wilkins.

Streufert, S., Streufert, S. C., Dembroski, T. M., & MacDougall, J. M. (1979). Complexity, coronary prone behavior and physiological response. In D. J. Oborne, M. M. Gruneberg, & J. R. Eiser (Eds.), *Research in psychology and medicine*, Vol. 1. London: Academic Press.

Stuart, R. B., Mitchell, C., & Jensen, J. A. (1981). Therapeutic options in the management of obesity. In C. K. Prokop & L. A. Bradley (Eds.), *Medical psychology: Contributions to behavioral medicine*. New York: Academic Press.

Suinn, R. M., & Bloom, L. J. (1978). Anxiety management training for pattern A behavior. *Journal of Behavioral Medicine*, **1**, 25–37.

Surawicz, F. G., Brightwell, D. R., Weitzel, W. D., & Othmer, E. (1976). Cancer, emotions, and mental illness: The present state of understanding. *Journal of the American Psychiatric Association*, **133**, 1306–1309.

Surwit, R. S., Bradner, M. N., Fenton, C. H., & Pilon, R. N. (1979). Individual differences in response to the behavioral treatment of Raynaud's disease. *Journal of Consulting and Clinical Psychology*, **47**, 363–367.

Surwit, R. S., Pilon, R. N., & Fenton, C. H. (1978). Behavioral treatment of Raynaud's disease. *Journal of Behavioral Medicine*, **1**, 323–335.

Swanson, D. W., & Maruta, T. (1980). The family's viewpoint of chronic pain. *Pain*, **8**, 163–166.

Swanson, D. W., Maruta, T., & Swenson, W. M. (1979). Results of behavior modification in the treatment of chronic pain. *Psychosomatic Medicine*, **41**, 55–61.

Tasto, D. L. (1977). Self-report schedules and inventories. In A. R. Ciminero, K. S. Calhoun, & H. E. Adams (Eds.), *Handbook of behavioral assessment*. New York: Wiley.

Tasto, D. T., Chesney, M., & Chadwick, J. (1977). Multidimensional analysis of Type A/B behavior. In T. Dembroski, S. M. Weiss, J. L. Shields, S. G. Haynes, & M. Feinleib (Eds.), *Proceedings of the Forum on Coronary-Prone Behavior*. Washington, D. C.: DHEW Publication No. (NIH)78-1451.

Taylor, C. B., Zlutnick, S. I., Corley, M. J., & Flora, J. (1980). The effects of detoxification, relaxation, and brief supportive therapy on chronic pain. *Pain*, **8**, 319–329.

Thomas, C. B., Duszynski, K. R., & Shaffer, J. W. (1979). Family attitudes reported in youth as potential predictors of cancer. *Psychosomatic Medicine*, **41**, 287–302.

Thompson, J. K., & Adams, H. E. (1979). A comparison of two self-monitoring procedures in self-reported headache pain assessment. Paper presented at the meeting of the Association for Advancement of Behavior Therapy, San Francisco, December.

Turk, D. C. (1975). Cognitive control of pain: A skills training approach. Unpublished master's thesis, University of Waterloo.

Turk, D. C. (1977). A coping skills-training approach for the control of experimentally-produced pain. Ph.D. dissertation, University of Waterloo.

Turk, D. C. (1978a). Cognitive behavioral techniques in the management of pain. In J. P. Foreyt & D. P. Rathjen (Eds.), *Cognitive behavior therapy*. New York: Plenum.

Turk, D. C. (1978b). The application of cognitive and behavioral skills for pain regulation. Paper presented at the meeting of the American Psychological Association, Toronto, August.

Turk, D. C., & Follick, M. J. (1979). Coping with chronic illness: A proposal for a preventative model of intervention. Paper presented at the meeting of the American Psychological Association, New York, August.

Turk, D. C., & Genest, M. (1979). Regulation of pain: The application of cognitive and behavioral techniques for prevention and remediation. In P. C. Kendall & S. D. Hollon (Eds.), *Cognitive-behavioral interventions: Theory, research, and procedures*. New York: Academic Press.

Turk, D. C., Meichenbaum, D. H., & Berman, W. H. (1979). Application of biofeedback for the regulation of pain: A critical review. *Psychological Bulletin*, **86**, 1322–1338.

Turk, D. C., Sobel, H. J., Follick, M. J., & Youkilis, H. D. (1980). A sequential criterion analysis for assessing coping with chronic illness. *Journal of Human Stress*, **6**, 35–40.

Turner, J., Heinrich, R., McCreary, C., & Dawson, E. (1979). Evaluation of two behavioral interventions for chronic low back pain. Paper presented at the meeting of the American Pain Society, San Diego, September.

Van Buren, J., & Kleinknecht, R. A. (1979). An evaluation of the McGill Pain Questionnaire for use in dental pain assessment. *Pain*, **6**, 23–33.

Watts, F. N. (1980). Behavioural aspects of the management of diabetes mellitus: Education, self-care, and metabolic control. *Behaviour Research and Therapy*, **18**, 171–180.

Watson, C. G., & Schuld, D. (1977). Psychosomatic factors in the etiology of neoplasms. *Journal of Consulting and Clinical Psychology,* **45,** 455–461.

Watson, C. G., & Schuld, D. (1978). Psychosomatic etiological factors in neoplasms: A response to Kellerman. *Journal of Consulting and Clinical Psychology,* **46,** 1524–1525.

Weidner, G., & Matthews, K. A. (1978). Reported physical symptoms elicited by unpredictable events and the Type A coronary-prone behavior pattern. *Journal of Personality and Social Psychology,* **36,** 1213–1220.

Wellisch, D. K. (1981). Intervention with the cancer patient. In C. K. Prokop & L. A. Bradley (Eds.), *Medical psychology: Contributions to behavioral medicine.* New York: Academic Press.

Williams, R. B. (1975). Physiological mechanisms underlying the association between psychosocial factors and coronary disease. In W. D. Gentry & R. B. Williams, Jr. (Eds.), *Psychological aspects of myocardial infarction and coronary care.* St. Louis: C. V. Mosby.

Williams, R. B. (1977). Psychophysiological differences between Type A and Type B individuals that may lead to coronary heart disease. In T. M. Dembroski, S. M. Weiss, J. C. Shields, S. G. Haynes, & M. Feinleib (Eds.), *Proceedings of the Forum on Coronary-Prone Behavior.* Washington, D. C.: DHEW Publication No. (NIH)78-1451.

Windsor, R. A., Green, L. W., & Roseman, J. M. (1980). Health promotion and maintenance for patients with chronic obstructive pulmonary disease: A review. *Journal of Chronic Diseases,* **33,** 5–12.

Wolff, B. B. (1978). Behavioral measurement of human pain. In R. A. Sternbach (Ed.), *The psychology of pain.* New York: Raven Press.

Worthington, E. L. (1978). The effects of imagery content, choice of imagery content, and self-verbalization on the self-control of pain. *Cognitive Therapy and Research,* **2,** 225–240.

Ziesat, H. A., Jr. (1981). Behavioral approaches to the treatment of chronic pain. In C. K. Prokop & L. A. Bradley (Eds.), *Medical psychology: Contributions to behavioral medicine.* New York: Academic Press.

Zimmermann, M. (1979). Peripheral and central nervous mechanisms of nociception, pain, and pain therapy: Facts and hypotheses. In J. J. Bonica, J. C. Liebeskind, & D. G. Albe-Fessard (Eds.), *Advances in pain research and therapy,* Vol. 3. New York: Raven Press.

Zung, W. W. K. (1965). A self-rating depression scale. *Archives of General Psychiatry,* **12,** 63–70.

Zyzanski, J. J., & Jenkins, C. D. (1970). Basic dimensions within the coronary-prone behavior pattern. *Journal of Chronic Diseases,* **22,** 781–795.

CHAPTER 19

A Multidimensional Perspective
on Clinical Neuropsychology Research

SUSAN B. FILSKOV AND EILEEN LOCKLEAR

Clinical neuropsychology is a relatively new and increasingly significant field of study. In 1979 the American Psychological Association created a special division for members interested in clinical neuropsychology, signaling the growing interest in the applied study of brain–behavior relationships. A variety of new journals, books, and reviews in this specialty has been appearing recently.

Clinical neuropsychology had its beginnings in many different disciplines, including experimental psychology, neurology, neurophysiology, and of course clinical psychology. Thus it is truly an interdisciplinary science, diverse in methodology and theoretical models. Because of this diversity, special research problems arise. Depending on the researchers' backgrounds, decisions are made regarding what is suitable for investigation, how it is to be studied, and with what subject samples. These decisions necessarily limit the scope of a project. No one study can encompass every relevant variable within its design; however, conclusions from any study are limited by important variables that are ignored or not controlled.

In order to present important issues in neuropsychological research, we have identified three basic dimensions. Consideration of these dimensions aids in the design of studies and in the interpretation of neuropsychological data (Figure 19.1). This model represents an adaptation of a "white box" conception of human behavior (Filskov, Grimm,

& Lewis, 1981). In direct contrast to the popular black box model in psychology, this model emphasizes that understanding what goes on "inside the head" is necessary, although not sufficient, for understanding the behavior of the individual.

The three dimensions include: subject variables, measurement issues, and time parameters. This three-dimensional perspective delineates resultant interactions of variables within the model. Some of the areas of research have been heavily investigated; for example, psychometric studies involving single examination of normal, impaired, or psychiatric patients, while other areas are just beginning to be investigated, such as "neurometric" techniques with special populations and longitudinal designs. Space constraints prevent extensive discussion of each of these issues. Therefore review articles will be mentioned where applicable.

THE SUBJECT DIMENSION

The identification and careful selection of subject groups is one of the most crucial steps in a neuropsychological study, since criterion groups used can greatly influence the type of results obtained. If these groups are not carefully sampled, the internal validity of a study is threatened, rendering its results uninterpretable (Campbell & Stanley, 1963). Furthermore, the type of subjects employed

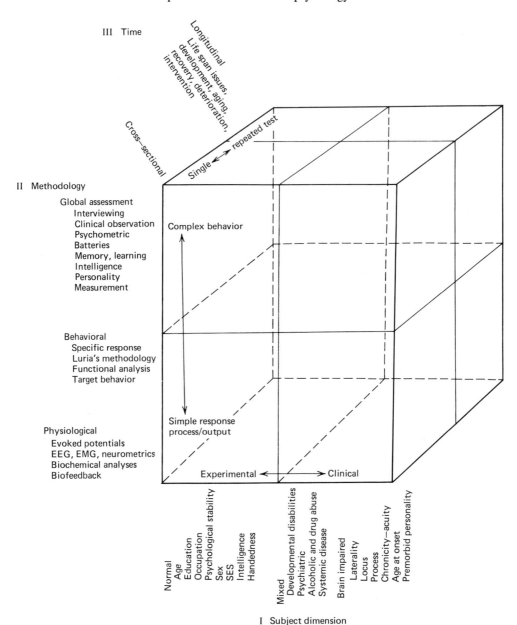

Figure 19.1. The three-dimensional model of research issues. Adapted from Filskov, Grimm, & Lewis, 1981.

limits a study's external validity, since the results can only be generalized to the subject population being sampled. Finally, the valid use and interpretation of neuropsychological tests in research requires considering a number of subject characteristics. We shall now discuss several of the most critical subject variables that must be considered, beyond the simplistic dichotomy of "normal" versus "impaired."

Normal Subject Groups

Age. One of the most important subject characteristics, for both normal and impaired subjects, is age. The fact that age is related to neuropsychological test performance has been demonstrated by a wide variety of studies (Aftanas & Royce, 1969; Reed & Reitan, 1963 a and b; Reitan, 1955; Vega & Parsons, 1967). This finding has important implications for neuropsychological research, since attempts to compare subjects on other variables can be confounded by age differences between subject groups. For example, a study comparing test scores of schizophrenic and brain-damaged subjects is difficult to interpret if the schizophrenic group is younger on the average than the brain-damaged group. Thus it has become common practice to select research subjects so that the groups are equivalent for average age. Even more rigorous practices include individual matching of subjects for age across experimental groups, and adjusting dependent variable scores for age effects by analysis of covariance.

The effect of age is also important to consider when using neuropsychological test scores for clinical or research purposes. Vega and Parsons (1967) showed that hit rates for separating normal from impaired subjects are related to the subject's age, when standard cutoff scores are used. False negatives, or misclassified impaired subjects, tended to be younger than correctly classified impaired subjects; while false positives, or misclassified normals, were older than correctly classified normals. Anthony, Heaton, and Lehman (1980) report that the error patterns associated with two empirical indexes for the identification of brain damage also are associated with age, as well as education and intelligence.

In actual practice, neuropsychologists do not strictly adhere to statistical cutoff scores, but instead evaluate obtained scores relative to a patient's age, education, occupation, and other relevant variables. A more objective method for evaluating test results relative to a subject's age is to use age-corrected scores when they are available, especially when the Wechsler Adult Intelligence Scale is employed. Vogt and Heaton (1977) showed that using age-corrected scale scores in WAIS pattern indexes can increase successful identification of subjects as normal versus impaired.

Kiernan and Matthews (1976) report that false positive error rates, that is, misclassifying normal older subjects as impaired, can also be improved by the use of *T*–score averaging of Halstead-Reitan Battery scores in place of reliance on the Impairment Index. They derived normative data for two age classifications: less than 35, and 35 or above. Using a mean *T*-score, averaged across all seven HRB subtests, and a cutting score of one standard deviation unit below the mean to identify impaired subjects, they only misclassified 5% of the older normal persons, whereas the Impairment Index, based on standard cutoff scores that do not take age into consideration, misclassified 30% of the older normal persons. With impaired subjects, the two techniques achieved equal accuracy of prediction.

It is unfortunate that, despite the considerable evidence that subject age is significantly related to neuropsychological test performance, researchers working with test batteries such as the Halstead-Reitan have never gathered together a set of systematic, generalized age norms and made them available in one accessible place such as a test manual. If such age norms were available, research data could become more consistent and comparable across studies, and diagnostic accuracy of tests in clinical use might be improved.

The correction strategies described above deal with age as a confounding factor, the effects of which must be minimized through adequate controls. A second strategy for approaching the age problem has been taken by some researchers: to directly examine the relationship of age to neuropsychological test performance, in order to determine which tests are most sensitive to differences in age, and to investigate whether the effects of aging are comparable to a process of organic deterioration (Aftanas & Royce, 1969; Fitzhugh, Fitzhugh, & Reitan, 1964; Goldstein & Shelly, 1975; Overall, Hoffman, & Levin, 1978; Reed & Reitan, 1963 a and b).

Generally these studies have found that the tests most sensitive to age effects are those involving complex sensory discriminations, motor speed, and certain memory abilities (Botwinick, 1981). These specific age-related changes do not appear to be comparable to the effects of chronic, diffuse brain damage, which results in more generalized deficits on a variety of tasks (Overall & Gorham, 1972; Overall et al., 1978).

It is interesting to note the methodological progression evident in investigations of age effects. The earliest studies employed simple correlations between age and test scores (Reitan, 1955), rank order correlations (Reed and Reitan, 1963 b) or *t*-tests between test scores of "younger" and "older" subjects (Reed & Reitan, 1963a). Advances in multivariate statistical techniques have made sounder, more powerful approaches available, such as Overall and Gorham's (1972) discriminant function analysis to determine the best weighted combination of WAIS subtests to discriminate four different age groups.

Another multivariate technique applied to aging studies is factor analysis. Goldstein and Shelly (1975) combined two procedures by factor-analyzing 26 neuropsychological tests, and then utilizing the resulting factors in a discriminant function analysis. Although susceptible to abuses and misinterpretations, as discussed in our section on statistics, these sophisticated techniques are excellent for multivariate problems such as the identification of differential deficit patterns associated with normal aging and chronic brain damage.

Education. Education, IQ, and occupation form a cluster of variables with sig-

nificant impact on neuropsychological data. Educational level of a subject has repeatedly been found to be significantly related to neuropsychological test performance (Granick & Friedman, 1967; Vega & Parsons, 1967). Significant correlations between years of education and test scores are typically found with normal subjects. With impaired subjects, the correlations tend to be lower, and reach significance less frequently (Prigatano & Parsons, 1976).

Finlayson, Johnson, and Reitan (1977) compared two widely used neuropsychological measures, the Wechsler-Bellevue Scales and the Halstead-Reitan Battery, for their relative sensitivity to educational level in normal and impaired subjects by means of an analysis of variance. They discovered that the Wechsler-Bellevue test is more susceptible than the Halstead-Reitan to the effects of education, especially with normal subjects. With brain-damaged subjects, educational level had a significant influence only on WAIS verbal scales. Since the Halstead-Reitan was less affected by education than the WAIS, it thus may be less susceptible to the confounding effects of educational differences across subjects.

WAIS scores are poor indicators of brain damage for a variety of reasons (Reitan, 1959), including their sensitivity to educational attainment. To increase the predictive accuracy of WAIS IQs in discriminating normal and impaired subjects, Leli and Filskov (1979) used an empirical/actuarial approach. They adjusted WAIS IQs for education by assigning a rating of 1 to 3 to each subject, indicating whether the obtained IQ was equivalent to, higher, or lower than that expected based on the subject's education level. They also employed a rating of how much the obtained WAIS deviated from that expected for the subject's occupational group. When entered into a discriminant function analysis, these indexes achieved better accuracy at separating normal and impaired subjects than the actual IQ scores themselves.

Again the implication for the planning of research projects is that subject groups be composed of equivalent mean educational levels, or that some adjustment of test scores be carried out to minimize educational differences.

Occupation. Parsons and Prigatano (1978) note that a subject's occupation can lead to spurious neuropsychological data if specific skills have been overlearned on the job. In other words, neuropsychologic functioning may be obscured by such habitual, overlearned skills demonstrated by a patient. Thus it is desirable for researchers to include an adequate range of occupations in their subject sample, and to report subjects' occupations in research publications.

Since it is a reflection of the subject's prior levels of functioning, occupation can also serve a useful rather than confounding role in research, if it is employed as a standard against which obtained test scores are evaluated. The previously described study by Leli and Filskov (1979) demonstrated the increase in predictive accuracy that can be achieved using such a strategy.

Intelligence. Another potentially confounding influence on research data is a subject's general intellectual level. Studies that employ IQ tests such as the WAIS are particularly susceptible to this problem. For example, an obtained WAIS Full Scale IQ of 80 could reflect low intellectual abilities in an unimpaired person, brain impairment in a person of average premorbid intellectual capacities, or spuriously low score caused by current emotional factors.

In a study of the accuracy of the WAIS Discrepancy Index as a predictor of brain impairment, Todd, Coolidge, and Satz (1977) found that its accuracy varies as a function of IQ level, with subjects having Full Scale IQs over 110 showing the greatest discrepancy scores. As Smith (1962) notes, when using tests of "intelligence" such as the WAIS, it is difficult to separate the effects of brain damage from the effects of mental functions the tests were designed to measure. Other than the WAIS, certain neuropsy-

chological test results can be confounded by intellectual level. The Category Test, which is the single best predictor of brain impairment on the Halstead-Reitan Battery, appears to also be the most sensitive test in the battery to effects of intelligence. A correlation of $-.87$ between WAIS Full Scale IQ and Category Test errors was obtained with normal subjects by Shore, Shore, and Pihl (1971). Thus, since high Category error scores can reflect low intelligence in a normal subject *or* the presence of brain impairment, this test should be interpreted relative to what is expected based on other indications of the subject's intellectual level. Logue and Allen (1971) devised an objective strategy for evaluating Category Scores relative to intelligence through the use of a predictor table that provides expected Category scores for given WAIS IQs. If the obtained Category errors are higher than would be predicted for an unimpaired subject, a more accurate conclusion may be possible as to the presence of brain impairment. Unfortunately, this strategy assumes that the WAIS Full Scale IQ is not affected by the presence of brain damage and can be used as a predictor of premorbid intelligence. This assumption is unwarranted, since WAIS scores can be very sensitive to brain impairment, especially if they are adjusted for educational level and age.

Another strategy that involves the assumption that WAIS IQ are not sensitive to the effects of brain damage involves matching groups of subjects on their present IQ and then comparing them on other neuropsychological variables. As Heaton, Baade, and Johnson (1978) point out, this technique is quite inappropriate, since matching subjects on the basis of one somewhat sensitive neuropsychological instrument such as the WAIS, and then comparing them on a second more sensitive test, provides a spuriously low estimate of the sensitivity of the second test.

Rather than using intelligence level as a nuisance variable that must be controlled for, intelligence test scores can be employed as impairment indicators through the replacement of actual IQ scores by clinical rating scales, such as those used by Leli and Filskov (1979). Judges assigned numerical ratings representing their estimate of the extent to which obtained IQ scores deviated from that expected relative to educational and occupational attainments. These numbers are more comparable across experimental groups than unadjusted IQ scores.

Rather than use clinical ratings, Wilson et al. (1978) devised an objective strategy for predicting premorbid IQ from a subject's education and race. This predicted IQ could be objectively compared to obtained IQ scores, with the difference employed as a variable for comparison across subjects.

Socioeconomic Status. The general variable of socioeconomic status can be quite important, especially in research with children, since many factors associated with lower socioeconomic levels can be related to impaired neurological status (e.g., Amante et al., 1977). Such factors include inadequate prenatal and postnatal medical care, poor nutrition, and lack of environmental stimulation in infancy. Parsons and Prigatano (1978) suggest that neuropsychological studies of children report the family socioeconomic background so that this variable can be considered in interpretation of the results (e.g., Dunleavy & Baade, 1980).

Handedness and Dominance. It is essential to determine the handedness of subjects, since this variable can greatly influence test performance, and may be related to such factors as hemispheric lateralization for speech and language functions (Berent, 1981; Hardyck & Petrinovich, 1977; Kinsbourne, 1981). Right-handedness appears to be more reliably assessed than left-handedness (Satz, Achenbach, & Fennell, 1967), and right-handers also appear to have more clearly lateralized language functions (Satz, 1977). For this reason many studies have only included right-handers in their samples.

When comparing groups on tasks that

might be affected by handedness, researchers should be careful to use test scores from the subjects' preferred side. If left-handed subjects are included, examine results separately for left- and right-handed persons.

There has been much study recently of hemispheric specialization as defined by such behavioral measures as lateral eye movements (Galin & Ornstein, 1974; Schwartz, Davidson, & Meier, 1975) and dichotic listening (Kimura, 1967; Satz, 1977). Just as the myth of left-handers being right-hemisphere dominant for language has hopefully been laid to rest (see above), the idea that these behavioral measures can establish specialized dominance is equally fallacious (Satz, 1977). These measures are fascinating from a theoretical perspective, but do not have applied value to hemispheric dominance. Satz (1977) makes this point very effectively in a recent article, and the reader is referred to it for further discussion of this complex issue.

Sex. Sex differences in verbal and spatial abilities are a common finding, with males generally better at spatial tasks and females at verbal ones (see McGee, 1979, for a review of the literature). Evidence also suggests that males show greater hemispheric lateralization for verbal and spatial tasks (to the left and right hemispheres, respectively) than females (McGee, 1979). Females appear to have bilateral representation of these abilities.

Much of this evidence stems from neuropsychological studies, which have revealed that males tend to show a greater decline in verbal abilities than females following left hemisphere damage (McGlone, 1977), and a greater decline in spatial abilities following right hemisphere damage (Lansdell, 1968; McGlone & Kertesz, 1973).

Furthermore, it appears that females may rely on their verbal abilities in spatial tasks more than men do, since females with left hemisphere damage showed a high correlation (.626) between their scores on the Block

Design test and an Aphasia battery (McGlone & Kertesz, 1973).

Motor skills also tend to differ between the sexes, with females showing poorer tapping speed and grip strength than males (King, Hannay, Masek, & Burns, 1978; Kupke, Lewis, & Rennick, 1979). Kupke et al., also found that anxiety had a more detrimental effect on females' motor performance than it did for males.

Differential abilities between the sexes and differential deficit patterns associated with brain damage in males and females indicate that the proportion of male and female subjects should be equivalent across experimental groups. Before combining the data from males and females for further analysis, statistical tests should be done to determine if there are sex differences on the variable in question. If so, separate data analyses should be considered. Furthermore, studies that only use subjects of one sex, such as the many employing male Veterans Administration patients exclusively, should include a notation that the results can only be generalized to the sex involved. Also interpretation of neuropsychological test scores should involve the use of separate norms for the sexes whenever these are available, such as those provided for the Finger Tapping Test (Russell, Neuringer, & Goldstein, 1970).

Psychological Factors. When designating subjects as "normal" for a research study, various psychological factors should be considered. Subjects experiencing emotional problems may be depressed or anxious, which can interfere with their test performances (Kupke et al., 1979). Furthermore, persons experiencing psychological problems often are using psychotropic medications, which also influence neuropsychological abilities (as discussed more fully in a later section of the chapter). If test data are being used from subjects who have histories of drug or alcohol abuse, actual organic deficits may be present (Grant, Mohns, Miller, & Reitan, 1976; Overall et al., 1978; Parsons

& Farr, 1981; Williams, Ray, & Overall, 1973). A sound research project will carefully screen normal subjects for these factors.

Medical Controls. A typical procedure used to eliminate any confounding effects of hospitalization per se is the use of patients hospitalized for conditions other than brain damage as nonimpaired control groups. Such groups should be as carefully screened as possible to eliminate any patients with systemic diseases and brain-impairing medical conditions such as kidney, metabolic or vascular diseases, or a history of epileptic seizures or head trauma.

Developmental Disabilities. A variety of children's disorders appears to be related to neurological functioning, and will significantly influence neuropsychological data. Such disorders include learning disabilities, hyperactivity, and epileptic seizures (Reitan & Davison, 1974). Children who are identified as normal controls should be carefully screened for any history of such conditions.

Summary. The previous description of relevant subject characteristics to consider in research plans reveals the great difficulty inherent in identifying "normal" subjects. Various suggestions have been made to deal with these problems, including the use of standardized test scores for age, education, and sex when these are available. A final important step is the inclusion in research articles of demographic subject characteristics that are as complete as possible, to aid in the interpretation of obtained results and to facilitate future replication.

Psychiatric Patients

One of the most frequently employed criterion groups in neuropsychological research has been patients suffering from functional psychiatric disturbances. Much attention has been directed toward the question of whether neuropsychological tests can be used to differentiate brain-impaired from psychiatric patients. The great interest in this question is due in part to the frequency with which this question of differential diagnosis is encountered in applied settings. Unfortunately, despite its considerable relevance to theoretical and applied issues, research comparing impaired with psychiatric patients is subject to serious methodological problems.

In their review of 94 such studies, Heaton et al. (1978) describe methodological problems encountered in a majority of the research attempts. One of the major issues involves the assignment of a psychiatric diagnosis. Studies examined by Heaton et al. rarely indicated criteria used for assigning this diagnosis, what sort of clinician made the diagnosis, whether the initial or discharge diagnosis was used, and whether any neurological tests had been performed to confirm the absence of brain impairment. Since psychiatric diagnostic groupings tend to be relatively poorly defined, and considerable disagreement exists as to definitions of various disorders, it is crucial to employ explicit criteria in selecting psychiatric subject samples. As stated by Boll (1978), "No field can move ahead of its criterion" (p. 628), thus emphasizing the importance of standardized, replicable diagnostic criteria.

Recent developments in classification strategies include Spitzer et al.'s Research Diagnostic Criteria (Spitzer, Endicott, & Robins, 1978) and the latest revision of the Diagnostic and Statistical Manual of Mental Disorders (American Psychiatric Association, 1980). These diagnostic systems are aimed at increasing the reliability and replicability of psychiatric diagnoses by employing explicit, behaviorally defined inclusion and exclusion criteria for each type of disorder and by providing "Decision Trees" for making differential diagnoses. Unfortunately, the major criterion relied upon for differentiating "Organic Mental Disorders" from any other psychiatric condition is the presence of a known organic etiological factor by history, examination, or laboratory

testing. Thus one can encounter difficulty in dealing with those crucial discriminations where evidence of organic etiology may be questionable or totally absent. Furthermore, it is advisable to bear in mind the classic maxim, "Absence of evidence is not evidence of absence." Sole reliance on this system could result in incorrect assignment of a psychiatric diagnosis, especially to organic conditions in early stages, which are difficult to detect medically.

An example of rigorous screening procedures for the selection of schizophrenic subjects is provided by Chelune, Heaton, Lehman, and Robinson (1979). Their criteria involved the diagnosis of the treating psychiatrist, confirmation of this diagnosis by an independent psychologist and psychiatrist, and by a computer scoring of the Psychiatric Status Schedule, and ruling out of organic disease using neurological procedures.

Failure to rule out neurological disease is a serious problem in a majority of the studies that have compared subjects with a primary psychiatric diagnosis to those diagnosed as brain-impaired. There is growing evidence that a variety of psychiatric disorders is actually associated with organic disease (Reitan, 1976). For example, a group of 85 patients diagnosed as hysterics was followed up by Slater and Glithero (1965), who discovered that eight of these patients had died of physical illnesses that were likely present when the diagnosis of hysteria was made. Furthermore, 31 of the living 73 patients subsequently had received diagnoses of organic illness, either in conjunction with or in replacement of their original diagnosis of hysteria. Several supposed functional disorders have been shown to be related, whether primarily or secondarily, to brain impairment. For instance, depressive symptoms have been associated with biochemical dysfunctions (Aillon, 1971; Schildkraut, 1973) and also have been reported as a typical concomitant of brain impairment, especially when damage is lateralized in the left hemisphere

(Berent, 1981; Gainotti, 1972). Psychopathic patients show frequent EEG abnormalities, which have been attributed to cortical dysfunction or immaturity (Hare, 1970). Neuropsychological factors have been found to be associated with delinquent behavior in adolescents (Spellacy, 1977) and in recidivist aggressive criminals (Monroe et al., 1977).

The largest body of evidence for an organic basis to a psychiatric disorder is probably associated with schizophrenia (Reitan, 1976). This evidence includes pneumoencephalographic data (Haug, 1963), CAT scan evidence (Johnstone, Crow, Husband, & Kriel, 1976), EEG findings (Mirsky, 1969), and biochemical findings (Synder, 1976), all indicating neurological impairment associated with schizophrenia. Furthermore, neuropsychological test data reveal very similar performance for brain-impaired subjects and chronic schizophrenics (Heaton et al., 1978; Heaton & Crowley, 1981).

It is evident that we cannot assume that "brain damage" and "psychiatric" disturbances are discrete, homogeneous, nonoverlapping entities. As Boll (1978) indicated in his discussion of schizophrenia, attempting to psychometrically distinguish brain damage and psychiatric conditions involves unfounded assumptions that psychiatric disturbances are not neurological disorders, that psychiatric patients will not acquire brain damage, and that brain-damaged subjects do not develop psychiatric problems. Chelune et al. (1979) suggest that a more profitable orientation for future research is the investigation of how organic and psychiatric conditions interact to produce a given behavioral manifestation, and the implications that these interactions have for a patient's adaptive abilities. Crockett, Clark, and Klonoff (1981) recommend multifactor research investigations comparing chronic and acute disorders; right, left, and diffuse brain-damaged subjects; and psychiatric patients with reliable behaviorally defined diagnoses.

An additional problem revealed by Heaton et al.'s (1978) review of neuropsychological research with psychiatric groups was the typical failure of these studies to report the length of hospitalization or chronicity of illness, for both psychiatric and brain-impaired subjects. These variables can significantly influence neuropsychological test results, and should be dealt with through adequate research controls. Chelune et al. (1979) handled this problem by employing schizophrenic subjects who had received their neuropsychological evaluation within one month after hospitalization.

The effects of medication and other treatments such as electroconvulsive therapy (ECT) are critical features often overlooked in studies of psychiatric patients. Heaton and Crowley (1981) emphasize that treatment influences, such as short- and long-term drug effects and a history of ECT, should be taken into account when deciding when to administer neuropsychological tests to a psychiatric patient and how to interpret the results.

The effects of such somatic treatments can range from an enhancement of test performance to a neutral effect to an impairment of performance. A variety of parameters are relevant to treatment effects and should be considered by researchers. These parameters include type of drug, dosage (of medication or electrical voltage), interval from onset of treatment and most recent treatment to time of testing, tolerance reactions, drug interactions, diagnostic group, since drug responses can vary across diagnostic groups, and for ECT, number of previous courses of treatment and number of treatments received per course.

In planning and evaluating research dealing with psychiatric and impaired subjects, it is important to consider base rates. Since the proportion of impaired subjects included in research groups typically exceeds the base rate for organicity in psychiatric settings, obtained hit rates from the studies in question may actually overestimate success rates for using neuropsychological tests to identify impaired patients in psychiatric settings. The selection of a test cutoff score in research aimed at diagnostic prediction should take into account base rates, and also the relative costs of false positive versus false negative errors. Because it is less desirable to diagnose an impaired subject as psychiatric than to make the reverse error (Satz et al., 1970), it may be best to accept a larger false positive error rate in order to minimize false negatives. Heaton et al. (1978) suggest that research publications in this area would be even more helpful in deciding issues if they included false positive and false negative rates, as well as the cutoff scores used. Several recent studies have started to report these important data (Anthony, et al., 1980; Leli & Filskov, 1979).

Malingerers

A special subject issue that falls into that gray area between normal and brain-impaired classifications is the malingering patient. When a person is being tested for workman's compensation or civil litigation purposes, tendencies to exaggerate deficits may influence test data. Heaton, Smith, Lehman, and Vogt (1978) showed that 10 neuropsychologists making blind diagnostic decisions were only able to distinguish true head trauma cases from malingering volunteers at chance levels (50 to 68% accuracy). More accurate prediction was achieved through a stepwise discriminant function analysis, which, if subjected to cross-validation, could prove to be a useful technique to employ to detect patients who are suspected of malingering. The function indicated that the pattern of deficits associated with malingering included motor and sensory deficits but relatively good cognitive ability (i.e., Category Test, Tactual Performance Test, and Trails B). A personality measure, the MMPI, was equally successful at identifying malingering subjects. As noted, further research needs to be done on this issue, including the cross-validation of the functions obtained here. It is evident that both personality test data and

neuropsychological test data can be used in conjunction for the identification of response patterns of malingering patients.

Impaired Patients

There has been a great deal of discussion concerning the many significant issues involved in employing a brain-damaged patient group in a research study (Boll, 1978; Chapman & Wolff, 1959; Parsons & Prigatano, 1978; Smith, 1975, 1980); therefore, we will cover these points briefly and refer the reader to listed references for more extensive coverage.

One of the initial considerations in planning a study should be the use of firmly established, specific diagnostic criteria for identifying a subject as impaired (Chelune et al., 1979). An important diagnostic issue frequently overlooked is that a neuropsychological test should NOT be used as part of the diagnostic criteria if the test itself is a subject of the investigation (for example, Russell et al., 1970).

Essential subject variables to be considered when studying impaired patients include age of onset of impairment (Boll, 1974; Reitan, 1976; Smith, 1981), laterality of damage, localization, acuteness versus chronicity (Fitzhugh et al., 1961; Reitan, 1964), type of pathological process or event, whether the process is resolving or evolving, presence of compensating mechanisms, and length of time since onset (Smith, 1975, 1981). Smith (1981) theorizes that integrity of the forebrain commissures is a typically neglected critical variable that can determine the development of compensatory language mechanisms; therefore, studies of language dysfunctions may continue to provide contradictory findings until this variable is taken into account. Another potentially confounding factor is the presence of aphasia. It is important to distinguish inability to comprehend instructions and questions, or inability to communicate a response, from actual impairment on the task involved (Parsons & Prigatano, 1978).

Emotional reactions to brain impairment can also influence a subject's response patterns (Parsons & Prigatano, 1978) since, for example, a depressed patient may do poorly on a task because of low motivation and energy, rather than an inability to perform. In short, precise diagnostic procedures, careful screening of impaired subjects, and detailed reporting of diagnostic information should be standard practice in any neuropsychological investigation.

Even then, high variability exists among subjects who are specifically selected on the basis of a diagnostic category, lesion site, or particular behavioral deficit (Crockett et al., 1981). Such individual differences, which can be significant for study in their own right, are obscured by group treatment of data. For this reason, the case study approach is recommended for careful documentation of recovery, decline, or response to treatment manipulations. Smith (1975, 1981) provides examples of his use of this strategy for illustration of different principles of human brain function.

Summary of the Subject Dimension

As noted in the beginning of this section, selecting a subject group is one of the most crucial steps in carrying out a research project. It has been recommended that experimenters employ clearly specified selection and diagnostic criteria, representative sampling of the population to which results will be generalized, and adequate controls for factors such as age, education, medication, length of illness, and so on.

Relevant subject information should be included in all research reports to aid in interpretation of results. Furthermore, it is desirable to report when a study employs data that have been analyzed in previous publications. Clearly delineated subject groups can be difficult to gather, and therefore it is often feasible to use accumulated data for purposes other than those originally intended. However, readers should be informed of this fact

so that it is clear that results are being extended with the original subject sample.

A final recommendation is that more effort be directed toward expansion of psychometric normative data to include a greater number of subject variables, especially age. Bak and Greene (1980) suggest the generation of norms for 10-year age intervals, with groupings according to education level. Such normative data should be obtained using male and female subjects, with separate norms established when significant sex differences are noted.

METHOD OF MEASUREMENT DIMENSION

From an historical perspective, clinical neuropsychological studies have emphasized diagnosis. Assessment procedures have been primarily directed toward accurate classification of impairment, lateralization, and localization of brain damage. Thus psychometric testing has become a primary focus, and the validity of the various test batteries has been well established (Filskov & Goldstein, 1974; Godden, Hammeke, & Purisch, 1978; Lewis et al., 1979; Satz et al., 1970). Now, new directions are occurring in the development of rehabilitation strategies, where the psychometric approach cannot provide a total answer for the evaluation of the proper course of treatment, success of intervention, or adjustment of the individual patient. Global evaluations (e.g., interviewing, activities of daily living), behavioral types of measurement (Goldstein, 1979), and neurophysiological measures such as evoked potential, EEG, and so on, are now being added to the psychometric data base for more comprehensive information (refer to Figure 19.1).

An extensive review of all problems of measurement in clinical neuropsychology is beyond the scope of this chapter. The reader is referred to several sources dealing with more traditional psychometric measures such as the WAIS and the copying tests (Filskov

& Leli, 1980; Lezak, 1976), the extensively used Halstead-Reitan Neuropsychological Battery (Boll, 1980; Reitan, 1974), and the more recently developed Luria-Nebraska Battery (Golden, 1981). Selection of a method of measurement is a crucial step in planning research. Employing a standardized test is not in itself sufficient to ensure valid and reliable assessment. A psychometrician's level of skill and training have a tremendous impact on the test results obtained from brain-impaired patients who represent special testing problems. Heaton and Heaton (1981) give an excellent review of the skills necessary to motivate performance within the limits of standardization.

Global Measures

Within rehabilitation settings, global measures of adaptive functioning are frequently obtained as part of an extensive evaluation (Diller & Gordon, 1981). Standard procedures such as interviews, evaluation of the patient's environment, and activities of daily living schedules provide necessary information for intervention. Certainly level of motivation and social behavior are vital to the rehabilitation process of brain impaired patients, but have not received much attention psychometrically. There have been some efforts to quantify these global behaviors, for example, Pfeiffer's Multidimensional Functional Assessment (1975). A patient's improvement on neuropsychological measures does not necessarily give indication of improved adaptive behavior. The most important aspect of competence in the final analysis is the ability to perform the complex acts necessary for living.

Psychometrics.   For the purpose of this chapter, "psychometric" tests are those measures that are given in a standardized manner, have normative information available for certain groups, and have established reliability and validity. Quantitative scores are derived describing a subject's performance relative

to a group, for example, standard score, percentile, and grade level. Not surprisingly, much of the psychometric research has been used to extend normative data to a wider range of subject characteristics, validate neuropsychological batteries with certain patient groups, or infer deficits from test scores. This process is in direct contrast to experimental paradigms, where researchers seek significant differences between groups of selected brain-damaged patients. Such work is certainly of theoretical importance, but is lacking in standardization or normative data and cannot be clinically applied to the individual case.

Most traditional psychometric measures tend to look at constructs such as intelligence, memory, or personality, which may or may not be applicable to issues of brain impairment. They often were not constructed for the particular purpose for which they are currently being applied, or designed, with current knowledge about brain-behavior principles. Poor performance on these tests obviously can be caused by a variety of factors with different organic or emotional bases (Barnes & Lucas, 1974; Parsons & Prigatano, 1978).

In direct contrast, neuropsychological test batteries were expressly designed for the prediction of brain impairment and description of brain deficits. However, sole use of quantified scores, a statistical cutoff point on the Halstead Impairment Index, provides little useful information. Essential interpretations are inferential ones where intra- and interindividual differences in test performance are clinically inspected. Level of performance (Chelune et al., 1979), pattern analysis (DeWolfe, Barrell, Becker, & Spaner, 1971), side of body comparison, and a pathognomonic sign approach are some of the inferential methods that have been used and described elsewhere (Boll, 1978; Reitan, 1974). The newer Luria battery also uses a qualitative approach in addition to quantitative information (Golden, 1981; Lewis et al., 1979). Other research groups deal primarily with the qualitative characteristics of performance, how the patient executes a task, rather than raw or standard test scores (Kaplan, 1980).

A combined clinical/actuarial approach, in which quantitative test scores are interpreted by experienced clinicians, provides additive information leading to successful test interpretation (Filskov & Goldstein, 1974; Goldstein, Kleinknecht, & Deysach, 1975). In a study by Selz and Reitan (1979), the four clinical inferential methods discussed above were used to develop 37 classification rules for use with learning-disabled and brain-damaged children. A scoring system was derived, and cutoff scores were selected empirically, resulting in an actuarial formula that achieved 73.3% correct classification overall. Thus a clinical decision-making process was transformed into a successful, empirically based classification formula.

Hopefully, the era of single broadband tests for "organicity" is over. Impaired patients have proved to be too heterogeneous for a five-minute diagnostic screening procedure. A better approach is use of test batteries to determine deficits present, and the direct implications these have for the ability to learn, daily functioning, or rehabilitation.

Since there are so many problems associated with traditional tests, an important question is: Should we attempt to improve existing tests or throw them out and come up with new ones? If traditional tests continue in use, modifications need to be made in such areas as memory (Erickson & Scott, 1977), where the Wechsler Memory Scale, even with its recent revisions (Russell et al., 1975) is not adequate to analyze all aspects of memory. Psychometric methods are certainly better than nonstandardized examinations and have proven their effectiveness in diagnosis, but they reflect end products rather than direct brain processes. They are especially good at description of deficits, but represent only one level of assessment. Other aspects of assessment may have more utility

for monitoring recovery and response to treatment.

Behavioral Assessment. We are going to use this term broadly to include procedures that focus on the response per se rather than its comparison with a mean performance level, that is, the psychometric approach. The response can be one that is elicited by stereotyped conditions or more naturally occurring environmental situations.

Luria (1965, 1973) in particular presented an individualized method of determining deficits by taking complex behavior and breaking it down into different response components in a sensory system. For example, a patient may not be able to respond to a visual stimulus. This inability may occur for a variety of reasons including memory, visual recognition, or language articulation problems. Through Luria's systems analysis, the deficit could be clearly delineated with direct implications for treatment intervention. Golden's standardized adaptation of Luria's work has been reported to have high validity (Golden et al., 1978), yet sole reliance on the psychometric aspects of this battery may result in a loss of the richness of Luria's original methodology. Indeed Golden (1981) addresses the necessity of additional qualitative interpretation for the Luria-Nebraska Battery.

Beyond the issue of level of measurement, recent research on the Luria-Nebraska reported by Golden and his colleagues raises a number of methodological questions discussed elsewhere in this chapter. Adams (1980) criticizes this collection of research for its poor handling of subject variables such as diagnostic criteria, medication, chronicity, and statistical weaknesses such as overuse of *t*-tests and improper use of multivariate statistics. A rebuttal to many of these criticisms is presented by Golden (1980).

Goldstein (1979), in his article "Methodological and theoretical issues in neuropsychological assessment," states that individual assessment is becoming "psychometrized."

However, he feels that there is value in continuing emphasis on psychometrics rather than more global behavioral measures, because traditional neuropsychological tests, which assess primarily cognitive, perceptual, and motor abilities, provide a vital core of information for understanding more complex behavioral deficits. After obtaining basic deficit information, a more molar behavioral analysis can be successfully carried out. The behavioral assessment approach appears to be particularly applicable to rehabilitation programs after more classical psychometric evaluation has been conducted (Goldstein, 1979). At the point where strengths and deficits have been established, target behavior can then be identified for relearning using multiple baseline designs (Diller, 1976; Diller & Gordon, 1981; Golden, 1978; Hersen & Barlow, 1976).

Physiological Measures. At the most molecular level, methods are being improved that look at direct processes and outputs of the brain. Sophisticated EEG techniques and examination of evoked potentials (EPS) can yield insights into the structural integrity of the brain as well as functions concerned with reception, encoding, and processing. In a new system in this area, called "neurometrics," critical features of computer-amplified electrophysiological data are analyzed into resulting profiles of brain functions (John, 1977; John et al., 1977; Thatcher & John, 1977).

Drawing upon developments in computer methods, multivariate statistical procedures, and mathematical "numerical taxonomy" techniques, neurometrics is an advanced research system applicable to a wide variety of issues. Potential applications include early identification of brain disease and developmental brain dysfunctions; quantification of drug effects; and even establishment of a relationship between differences in cerebral processes and cognitive styles (John, 1977). John and his co-workers have used the techniques to successfully differentiate such diverse subject groups as learning-disabled children or elderly persons with cognitive deterioration from matched controls. John (1977) emphasizes that not only was the neurometric system significantly more successful at identifying learning-disabled children than a set of traditional psychometric measures (one wonders how valid his criteria were) but also the neurometric data only takes minutes to collect as opposed to hours of psychological testing. It appears that specific neuropsychological test data were not collected on John's samples, calling into question some of his conclusions.

John et al. made the significant discovery in their experiments that subject groups previously treated in research studies as homogeneous entities (i.e., "learning disability") can actually be separated on the basis of physiological functioning into distinct subgroups (supporting Rourke's 1981 neuropsychological studies) with learning-disabled children, each of which may eventually be found to differ in etiology and optimal treatment program. It seems that such neurophysiological measures of brain functioning will prove to be valuable tools for research, diagnostic, and treatment applications. However, it would be naive to assume that such data could replace necessary direct behavioral information gathered from neuropsychological testing and academic measures of level of performance.

One of the most effective uses of neurophysiological measurement has been in its application to biofeedback. Although only in its beginning stages (much $N = 1$ research, poor experimental design), these techniques hold promise in many areas of neurological dysfunction. For instance, EEG feedback appears to be effective in the treatment of certain epileptic conditions (Sterman & Macdonald, 1978; Sterman, Macdonald, & Stone, 1974). Electromyographic (EMG) feedback has been used successfully in increasing neuromuscular control (Baker,

1979; Cleeland, 1973, 1981). This relatively new avenue of research holds promising prospects for clinical neuropsychologists.

In this review of measurement issues in clinical neuropsychology, we were disappointed to find relatively few studies that report findings based on different types of measures. Most research, including our own, has tended to focus exclusively on one method of evaluation, ignoring important findings from other methodologies. Multimodal measurement, which includes psychometric examination, is recommended for the most comprehensive evaluation, since no behavior is unidimensional. For example, Weiss and Hechtman (1979) identify seven areas of assessment in diagnosis and treatment of the "hyperactive syndrome." These areas include assessment of developmental history, behavior patterns, education, personality, family interactions, school environment, and neurological status. This assessment plan reflects the importance of attempting to understand the syndrome only in its complexity from social, psychological, and biological viewpoints. A multidimensional perspective with multiple baseline data points is necessary to explain the various manifestations, etiology, and course of any behavioral disorder, especially those with a neurological underpinning. Rather that isolated findings on a single dimension, data gathered from several methods of measurement will enhance understanding of brain-behavior phenomena.

THE TIME DIMENSION

The impact of time on the dynamics of both normal and neuropathological brain functioning has been discussed and documented by many researchers (Meier, 1974; Parsons & Prigatano, 1978; Smith, 1975, 1981). Changes associated with early development and normal aging are important areas of current research (Botwinick, 1978, 1981; Kins-

bourne, 1975, 1981; Klonoff & Low, 1974). Changes in the state of the brain associated with disease progression or recovery also reflect the importance of the temporal dimension (see Figure 19.1). Additionally, intervention strategies by definition are independent variables that can only be studied over the course of time.

A popular approach to the investigation of changes over time has been the cross-sectional design, for example, comparison of different age groups or of groups of patients varying posttraumatic intervals. The design has seen frequent use in studies of normal development and aging effects (Botwinick, 1981; Klonoff & Low, 1974). The major problem with this design is that cohort differences, such as cultural influences or educational level, can confound actual changes that occur. For example, early cross-sectional research with the WAIS revealed evidence of generalized decrements across all subtest measures with age (Matarazzo, 1972). It was only after more extensive longitudinal studies were carried out that these apparently global, age-related changes were reinterpreted as cohort differences in environmental opportunities. The more appropriate longitudinal studies have revealed differential change in intellectual abilities, with verbal skills showing little or no change, and perceptual-motor skills showing the most decrement (Schaie & Labouvie-Vief, 1974).

Other problems associated with cross-sectional designs are discussed by Smith (1975, 1981), who proposes that confusing evidence exists about deteriorating or improving patterns of brain impairment, because research to date has primarily consisted of single examinations of relatively heterogeneous groups of patients. He suggests that investigations of brain functioning should involve repeated testing with highly selected samples over an extensive time period. Problems arise with single examinations because there is much variability in the course of different diseases and within cases of the same disease. Patients can evidence "plateaus," remissions, or even extreme progression or improvement. These phenomena can best be dealt with by serial examinations of the same patients.

For instance, in an investigation of symptom progression in multiple sclerosis (MS) Ivnik (1978b) compared three groups of patients whose duration of the disease was one to five years, six to ten years, or greater than 10 years, and found few differences in neuropsychological functioning across these groups. However, this cross-sectional group design may have obscured changes because individuals vary in the rate at which the disease progresses. Therefore, he performed another investigation involving the retesting of the same patients, so that all subjects served as their own controls (Ivnik, 1978a). MS and non-MS neurological patients were matched on age at first testing, length of test-retest interval, sex, and years of formal education. By changing his procedure to this longitudinal design, he found significant deterioration over a one-year period within MS patients on tests requiring motor coordination, complex sensory discrimination, and cognitive tasks with a motor component. Higher-order cognitive functions were less adversely affected. This longitudinal design gives stronger evidence of the deficits suggested in between-group studies comparing MS patients to other neurologically impaired patients (Matthews, Cleeland, & Hopper, 1970) and to normal controls (Reitan, Reed, & Dyken, 1971).

Repeated-measures designs can be used with groups or with individual cases. The clinical case study approach involving extensive follow-up of single cases has been used to great value for both theoretical and applied purposes by a variety of researchers (Hebb & Renfield, 1940; Luria, 1972; Milner, Corkin, & Teuber, 1968; Scoville, 1968). Experimental designs have been developed to aid in the systematic study of single subjects (Hersen & Barlow, 1976). However, there are serious weaknesses and

pitfalls involved in the use of single cases in research, as discussed by Kazdin (1978). A particular problem in the study of brain-impaired individuals is that often the most theoretically relevant and extensively followed cases have little generalizability or practical utility. If they are planned and executed carefully, ongoing studies of individual cases can provide useful, in-depth knowledge about the effects of a range of variables on many brain functions. For examples of such studies see Smith (1981).

Although longitudinal designs involving repeated testing of the same individuals are useful for avoiding the confounding factors of cross-sectional studies, repeated-measures designs have special methodological problems associated with them (Cook & Campbell, 1979). Patients not experiencing problems may not return; lower SES groups may be unable to afford continued follow-up; patients with worsening conditions may be unable to participate. Particularly in brain-impaired groups, in which extremely low scores are expected, the statistical artifact of regression toward the mean may account for significant improvement in scores. Spontaneous recovery, maturation, and improved emotional adjustment may be factors that also confound results in studies of intervention strategies in which there is no experimental control. Practice effects may occur with repeated testing, since many tests do not have parallel forms. Changes in age necessitate changes in instrumentation (e.g., Stanford-Binet to WISC-R; WISC-R to WAIS). Even within the same instruments, it has been found that factor structures can change with age (Klonoff, 1971). Therefore, even when using the same test over time, you may not be tapping the same abilities. This problem can be further complicated when you must change test instruments as the subjects age.

In order to deal with the weaknesses of cross-sectional and longitudinal designs, various alternatives have been developed that basically combine both types of approaches. Examples of such alternatives are provided by Schaie (1965); for example, cross-sequential or time lag comparisons. These designs have been used in developmental research and have applicability to some of the significant issues in clinical neuropsychology.

In summary, designs that deal with the temporal dimension have been identified as important directions for future research. Follow-up over a long period is necessary to illustrate patterns of cerebral recovery, reorganization, or deterioration. It is important to assess an adequate range of higher cortical abilities and functions. Evaluations should be scheduled at standard times to accumulate baseline data. Three-month, six-month and one-year follow-up times appear to be accepted practice (Meier, 1974; Smith, 1981), so that results can be comparable across research groups. Meier (1974) reports initiating behavioral evaluations even earlier, that is, 30, 60, and 180 days after symptom onset, in order to determine the pattern and extent of immediate recovery as related to eventual outcome. Finally, many of these problems associated with time and repeated testing are not remediable, such as regression toward the mean or practice effects. However, the researcher should be cognizant of these factors when interpreting results, and address them statistically when possible.

STATISTICAL ISSUES

Multivariate Techniques

Multivariate statistics have been increasingly used in psychological research in the past decade. Studies of brain–behavior relationships, which require consideration of a number of subject and method variables simultaneously, are a prime area of investigation with procedures such as multiple regression analysis, factor analysis, and multivariate analysis of variance. Also classification techniques such as discriminant function analysis

are very important for the problem of discriminating between impaired and normal subjects, or among different types of brain-impaired patients. Unfortunately, multivariate statistical techniques are subject to a number of abuses, and many neuropsychological investigations have suffered from these abuses.

A critical factor in multivariate research is the use of a sufficiently large subject sample. Because these techniques capitalize on error to achieve maximum predictability, large samples are needed to avoid obtaining spurious results. This safeguard is especially important when large numbers of predictor variables are employed. In their excellent critique of neuropsychological investigations using linear discriminant function analysis, Fletcher, Rice, and Roy (1978) demonstrate how successful classification rates can be inappropriately inflated by a small sample size and large numbers of predictors. They suggest that the current value of neuropsychological tests for separating subject groups may be overestimated, since few of the relevant studies have used an adequate number of subjects (e.g., Goldstein & Halperin, 1977; Goldstein & Shelley, 1973). Examples of investigations making this critical error continue to appear in the literature (Golden et al., 1978; Purisch, Golden, & Hammeke, 1978). Studies that exemplify appropriate, well-planned uses of multivariate statistics are provided by Overall and Gorham (1972), Overall et al. (1978), and Fletcher et al. (1978).

A crucial but often omitted safeguard in multivariate studies is the cross-validation of regression equations or discriminant functions on different subject samples from that with which they were derived. Since predictive ability is inflated typically with the derivation sample, cross-validation provides a more accurate picture of predictive accuracy (see, e.g., Leli & Filskov, 1979). Procedures are also available for the *estimation* of shrinkage that will occur, which are useful when immediate cross-validation is not possible (see Fletcher et al., 1978, or Kerlinger & Pedhazur, 1973).

Interpretation of results obtained with multivariate approaches frequently is distorted by basic misconceptions. Multivariate techniques are descriptive rather than inferential tools, and should only be used with great caution for purposes of making inferences, for example, about differences between subject groups or about the relative importance of predictor variables. Stepwise procedures for including predictor variables into a function are particularly unreliable and can be very misleading. More valid approaches for making inferences about relative contributions of predictor variables include use of the canonical correlation and standardized discriminant weights (Fletcher et al., 1978).

An important limitation to be borne in mind about predictive techniques such as multiple regression analysis or discriminant function analysis is that their practical utility for discriminating groups is balanced by their weakness in clinical applicability. Since most test scores are multiply determined, subjects can perform poorly for different reasons, achieving different patterns of test scores but still receiving identical final scores and the same group classification using a multivariate predictive equation. Furthermore, it can often be the case that significant differences between large groups on a set of variables does not necessarily indicate significant discriminative power with individual subjects. Finally, conclusions and generalizations are limited by populations that are sampled and variables that are uncontrolled.

It should be emphasized in conclusion that many of the complex problems involved in neuropsychological investigations necessitate the use of multiple independent and dependent variables. Such problems in turn necessitate the use of multivariate data analysis techniques. Studies that continue to rely on literally hundreds of t-tests, simple correlations (Watson, Davis, & McDermott, 1976) or chi-square tests (Watson & Plemel, 1978) are no longer justifiable. Researchers

must be adequately trained in the use of multivariate statistics so as to be aware of their appropriate applications and potential misuses.

Factor Analysis

Factor analysis has become a very popular multivariate tool and is being applied to neuropsychological test batteries with increasing frequency (Aftanas & Royce, 1969; Barnes & Lucas, 1974; Lansdell, 1971; Lansdell & Donnelly, 1977; Royce, Yendall, & Bock, 1976). Appropriate use of this technique can provide valuable information about issues such as the factor structure of neuropsychological tests, and how factor structures differ in normal and impaired subjects or across different age groups. Also the use of factor scores can result in increased predictive ability over unfactored test scores. For example, Lansdell and Smith (1975) factor-analyzed the WAIS to eliminate the influence of verbal ability on Performance test scores, and found greater differences between left- and right-hemisphere damaged patients when scores on the nonverbal visual-motor factor were used to compare groups, in place of the Performance IQ.

Although quite valuable, factor analytic studies require an experimenter to make a large number of decisions, and each of these decision points can be associated with unfounded assumptions or incorrect procedures. Comrey (1978) provides an excellent discussion of the varied problems encountered when carrying out a factor analysis. These issues include the type of subjects used (normal, impaired, or both), number of subjects, selection of test variables, choice of an acceptable factor-loading criterion for associating tests with factors, choice of a factor extraction procedure, deciding how many factors to rotate, whether to use orthogonal or oblique rotation, and so on. Again cross-validation of results is a critical, often overlooked step.

One subjective step in the process, which

is rather unique to factor analysis, involves the selection of verbal labels to identify the content of obtained factors. This choice of labels is often arbitrary and can be quite misleading. For example, one might question whether it is truly appropriate to call a factor "visuomotor" when two of the four tests loading highly on the factor are the Category Test and the WAIS Picture Arrangement Test (Lansdell & Donnelly, 1977). This problem can be mitigated if a researcher provides detailed data in publications, including correlation matrices and factor matrices obtained, so that readers have adequate information to evaluate the conclusions made.

As so aptly stated by Comrey (1978), "The moral of the story, therefore, is to plan ahead" when using multivariate techniques. Assumptions and limitations of the statistical approach to be used should influence an investigation from its earliest planning stages on. Important decisions are made at every step of an investigation, and these decisions should be made in light of research goals, the type of design being used, subjects to which results will be generalized and the type of data analysis planned.

CONCLUSIONS

We have reviewed some of the methodological problems that are often unavoidable in neuropsychological research. The interaction of these design problems—subject variables, measurement, and time parameters—complicate any experimental or quasi-experimental study of brain-behavior relationships in clinical neuropsychology. Unlike a pure experimental model, in the typical neuropsychological investigation, many independent variables are uncontrollable, such as type, magnitude and site of lesion, behavioral effects, and patient characteristics, thereby increasing error variance. Recognition of methodological issues can certainly lead to more careful planning of one's research, including collection of comprehensive subject data,

multidimensional measurement, follow-up testing, and consideration of statistical problems. Studies that deal with the issues raised in this chapter, incorporating both research utility and sound design, can greatly add to our present knowledge in clinical neuropsychology.

REFERENCES

Adams, K. (1980). In search of Luria's battery: A false start. *Journal of Consulting and Clinical Psychology,* **48,** 511–516.

Aftanas, M., & Royce, J. (1969). A factor analysis of brain damage tests administered to normal subjects with factor score comparisons across ages. *Multivariate Behavioral Research,* **4,** 459–474.

Aillon, G. (1971). Biochemistry of depression: A review. *Behavioral Neuropsychiatry,* **3,** 2–19.

Amante, D., Van Houten, V., Grieve, J., Bader, C., & Margules, P. (1977). Neuropsychological deficit, ethnicity, and socioeconomic status. *Journal of Consulting and Clinical Psychology,* **45,** 524–535.

American Psychiatric Association (1980). *Diagnostic and statistical manual of mental disorders* (3rd ed.). Washington, D.C.: A.P.A.

Anthony, W., Heaton, R., & Lehman, R. (1980). An attempt to cross-validate two actuarial systems for neuropsychological test interpretation. *Journal of Consulting and Clinical Psychology,* **48,** 317–326.

Bak, J., & Greene, R. (1980). Aging and neuropsychological functioning. *Journal of Consulting and Clinical Psychology,* **48,** 395–399.

Baker, J. P. (1979). Biofeedback in specific muscle retraining. In J. V. Basmajian (Ed.), *Biofeedback: Principles and practices for clinicians.* Baltimore: Williams & Wilkins.

Barnes, G., & Lucas, G. (1974). Cerebral dysfunctions vs. psychogenesis in Halstead-Reitan tests. *Journal of Nervous and Mental Disease,* **158,** 50–60.

Berent, S. (1981). Lateralization of brain function. In S. F. Filskov & J. Boll (Eds.), *Handbook of clinical neuropsychology.* New York: Wiley.

Boll, J. (1974). Behavioral correlates of cerebral damage in children aged 9 through 14. In R. Reitan & L. Davison (Eds.), *Clinical neuropsychology: Current status and applications.* Washington, D.C.: V. H. Winston.

Boll, J. (1978). Diagnosing brain impairment. In B. Wolman (Ed.), *Clinical diagnosis of mental disorders: A handbook.* New York: Plenum Press.

Boll, J. (1981). The Halstead-Reitan neuropsychological battery. In S. B. Filskov & T. J. Boll (Eds.), *Handbook of clinical neuropsychology*. New York: Wiley.

Boll, J. (1977). A rationale for neuropsychological evaluation, *Professional Psychology, 8,* 64–71.

Botwinick, J. (1978). *Aging and behavior* (2nd ed.). New York: Springer Publishing.

Botwinick, J. (1981). *Neuropsychology of aging*. In S. Filskov and J. Boll (Eds.), *Handbook of clinical neuropsychology*. New York: Wiley.

Botwinick, J., & Sotrandt, M. (1974). *Memory, related functions and age.* Springfield, Ill.: Charles C. Thomas.

Campbell, D., & Stanley, J. (1963). *Experimental and quasi-experimental designs for research.* Chicago: McNally Publishing.

Chapman, L., & Wolff, H. (1959). The cerebral hemispheres and the highest integrative functions of man. *Archives of Neurology, 1,* 19–35.

Chelune, G., Heaton, R., Lehman, R., & Robinson, A. (1979). Level versus pattern of neuropsychological performance among schizophrenic and diffusely brain-damaged patients. *Journal of Consulting and Clinical Psychology, 47,* 155–163.

Cleeland, C. S. (1973). Behavioral techniques in the modification of spasmodic torticollis. *Neurology, 23,* 1241.

Cleeland, C. S. (1979). Biofeedback and other behavioral techniques in the treatment of disorders of voluntary movement. In J. V. Basmajian (Ed.), *Biofeedback principles and practices for clinicians.* Baltimore: Williams & Wilkins.

Cleeland, C. S. (1981). Biofeedback as a clinical tool: Its use with the neurologically impaired patient. In S. B. Filskov & T. J. Boll (Eds.), *Handbook of clinical neuropsychology*. New York: Wiley.

Comrey, A. (1978). Common methodological problems in factor analysis. *Journal of Consulting and Clinical Psychology, 46,* 648–659.

Cook, J., & Campbell, D. (1979). *Quasi-experimentation: Design and analysis issues for field sittings.* Chicago: Rand McNally.

Crane, G. (1968). Tardive dyskinesia in patients treated with major neuroleptics: A review of the literature. *American Journal of Psychiatry, 124,* 40–48.

Crockett, D., Clark, C., & Klonoff, H. (1981). Introduction: An overview of neuropsychology. In S. Filskov & T. J. Boll (Eds.), *Handbook of clinical neuropsychology*. New York: Wiley.

DeWolfe, A., Barrell, R., Becker, B., & Spaner, F. (1971). Intellectual deficit in chronic schizophrenia and brain damage. *Journal of Consulting and Clinical Psychology, 36,* 197–204.

Diller, L. A. (1976). A model of cognitive retraining in rehabilitation. *The Clinical Psychologist, 29,* 13–15.

Diller, L. A., & Gordon, W. A. (1981). Rehabilitation and clinical neuropsychology. In S. B. Filskov & T. J. Boll (Eds.), *Handbook of clinical neuropsychology*. New York: Wiley.

Dunleavy, R., & Baade, L. (1980). Neuropsychological correlates of severe asthma in children 9–14 years old. *Journal of Consulting and Clinical Psychology, 48,* 214–219.

Erickson, R., & Scott, M. (1977). Clinical memory testing: A review. *Psychological Bulletin, 84,* 1130–1149.

Filskov, S. B., & Goldstein, S. G. (1974). Diagnostic validity of the Halstead-Reitan neuropsychological battery. *Journal of Consulting and Clinical Psychology, 42*(3), 382–388.

Filskov, S. B., Grimm, B. H., & Lewis, J. A. (1981). Brain-behavior relationships. In S. B. Filskov & T. J. Boll (Eds.), *Handbook of clinical neuropsychology*. New York: Wiley.

Filskov, S. B., & Leli, R. A. (1981). Assessment of the individual in neuropsychological practice. In S. B. Filskov & T. J. Boll (Eds.), *Handbook of clinical neuropsychology*. New York: Wiley.

Finlayson, M., Johnson, K., & Reitan, R. (1977). Relationship of education to neuropsychological measures in brain-damaged and non-brain-damaged adults. *Journal of Consulting and Clinical Psychology, 45,* 536–542.

Fitzhugh, K., Fitzhugh, L., & Reitan, R. (1961). Psychological deficits in relation to acuteness of brain dysfunction. *Journal of Consulting and Clinical Psychology, 25,* 61–66.

Fitzhugh, K., Fitzhugh, L., & Reitan, R. (1964). Influence of age upon measures of problem solving and experiential background in subjects with longstanding cerebral dysfunction. *Journal of Gerontology, 19,* 132–134.

Fletcher, J., Rice, W., & Roy, R. (1978). Linear discriminant function analysis in neuropsychological research: Some uses and abuses. *Cortex, 14,* 564–577.

Gainotti, G. (1972). Emotional behavior and hemispheric side of lesion. *Cortex, 8,* 41–55.

Galin, D., & Ornstein, R. (1974). Individual differences in cognitive styles: I. Reflective eye movements. *Neuropsychologia, 12,* 357–376.

Golden, C. J. (1978). *Diagnosis and rehabilitation in clinical neuropsychology.* Springfield, Ill.: Charles C Thomas.

Golden, C. J. (1980). In reply to Adams' "In search of Luria's battery: A false start." *Journal of Consulting and Clinical Psychology, 48,* 517–521.

Golden, C. J. (1981). A standardized version of Luria's neuropsychological tests: A quantitative and qualitative approach to neuropsychological evaluation. In S. B. Filskov & T. J. Boll (Eds.), *Handbook of clinical neuropsychology*. New York: Wiley.

Golden, C., Hammeke, J., & Purisch, A. (1978). Diagnostic validity of a standardized neuropsychological battery derived from Luria's neuropsychological tests. *Journal of Consulting and Clinical Psychology*, **46,** 1258–1265.

Goldstein, G. (1979). Methodological and theoretical issues in neuropsychological assessment. *Journal of Behavioral Assessment*, **1,** 23–41.

Goldstein, G., & Halperin, K. (1977). Neuropsychological differences among subtypes of schizophrenia. *Journal of Abnormal Psychology*, **86,** 34–40.

Goldstein, G., & Shelly, C. (1975). Similarities and differences between psychological deficit in aging and brain damage. *Journal of Gerontology*, **30,** 448–455.

Goldstein, S., Deysach, R., & Kleinknecht, R. (1973). Effect of experience and the amount of information on identification of cerebral impairment. *Journal of Consulting and Clinical Psychology*, **41,** 30–34.

Granick, S., & Friedman, A. (1967). The effect of education on the decline of psychometric test performance with age. *Journal of Gerontology*, **31,** 191–195.

Grant, J., Mohns, L., Miller, M., & Reitan, R. (1976). A neuropsychological study of polydrug users. *Archives of General Psychiatry*, **33,** 973–978.

Hardyck, C., & Petrinovich, L. (1977). Left-handedness. *Psychological Bulletin*, **84,** 385–404.

Hare, R. (1970). *Psychopathy*. New York: Wiley.

Haug, J. (1963). *Pneumoencephalographic studies in mental disease*. Norway: Scandinavian University Books.

Heaton, R., Baade, L., & Johnson, K. (1978). Neuropsychological test results associated with psychiatric disorders in adults. *Psychological Bulletin*, **85,** 141–162.

Heaton, R., & Crowley, J. (1981). Effects of psychiatric disorders and their somatic treatments. In S. B. Filskov & T. J. Boll (Eds.), *Handbook of clinical neuropsychology*. New York: Wiley.

Heaton, R., Smith, H., Lehman, R., & Vogt, A. (1978). Prospects for faking believable deficits on neuropsychological testing. *Journal of Consulting and Clinical Psychology*, **46,** 892–900.

Heaton, S. K., & Heaton, R. R. (1981). Testing the impaired patient. In S. B. Filskov & T. J. Boll (Eds.), *Handbook of clinical neuropsychology*. New York: Wiley.

Hebb, D., & Renfield, W. (1940). Human behavior after extensive bilateral removals from the frontal lobes. *Archives of Neurology and Psychiatry*, **44,** 421–438.

Hersen, M., & Barlow, D. (1976). *Single-case experimental designs: Strategies for studying behavior change*. New York: Pergamon Press.

Ivnik, R. (1978a). Neuropsychological stability in multiple sclerosis. *Journal of Consulting and Clinical Psychology*, **46,** 913–923.

Ivnik, R. (1978b). Neuropsychological stability in multiple function of the duration of M.S.-related symptomatology. *Journal of Clinical Psychiatry*, **39,** 304–307, 311–312.

John, E. (1977). *Neurometrics: Clinical applications of quantitative electrophysiology*. New York: Halsted Press.

John, E. R., Karmel, B. L., Corning, W. C., Easton, P., Brown, R., Ahn, H., John, M., Harmony, T., Prichep, L., Toro, A., Gerson, I., Bartlett, F., Thatcher, R., Kaye, H., Valdex, P., & Schwartz, E. (1977). Neurometrics. *Science*, **196,** 1393–1410.

Johnstone, E., Crow, J., Husband, J., & Kriel, L. (1976). Cerebral ventricular size and cognitive impairment in chronic schizophrenia. *Lancet*, **2,** 924–926.

Kazdin, A. (1978). Methodological and interpretive problems of single-case experimental designs. *Journal of Consulting and Clinical Psychology*, **46,** 629–642.

Kerlinger, F., & Pedhazur, (1973). *Multiple regression in behavioral research*. New York: Holt, Rinehart & Winston.

Kiernan, R., & Matthews, C. (1976). Impairment index versus T-score averaging in neuropsychological assessment. *Journal of Consulting and Clinical Psychology*, **44,** 951–957.

Kimura, D. (1967). Functional symmetry of the brain in dichotic listening. *Cortex*, **3,** 163–178.

King, D., Hannay, H., Masek, B., & Burns, J. (1978). Effects of anxiety and sex on neuropsychological tests. *Journal of Consulting and Clinical Psychology*, **46,** 375–376.

Kinsbourne, M. (1975). The ontogeny of cerebral dominance. *Annals of the New York Academy of Science*, **273,** 244–250.

Kinsbourne, M. (1981). The development of cerebral dominance. In S. B. Filskov & T. J. Boll (Eds.), *Handbook of clinical neuropsychology*. New York: Wiley.

Klonoff, H. (1971). Factor analysis of a neuropsychological battery for children aged 9 to 15. *Perceptual and motor skills*, **32,** 603–616.

Klonoff, H., & Law, M. (1974). Disordered brain function in young children and early adolescents: Neuropsychological and electroencephalic correlates.

In R. Reitan and L. Davison (Eds.), *Clinical neuropsychology: Current status and applications.* Washington, D. C.: V. F. Winston, pp. 121–178.

Kupke, J., Lewis, R., & Rennick, P. (1979). Sex differences in the neuropsychological functioning of epileptics. *Journal of Consulting and Clinical Psychology, 47,* 1128–1130.

Lansdell, H. (1968). The use of factor scores from the Wechsler-Bellevue scale of intelligence in assessing patients with temporal lobe removals. *Cortex, 4,* 257–268.

Lansdell, H. (1971). A general intellectual factor affected by temporal lobe dysfunction. *Journal of Clinical Psychology, 27,* 182–184.

Lansdell, H., & Donnelly, E. (1977). Factor analysis of the Wechsler adult intelligence scale subtests and the Halstead-Reitan category and tapping tests. *Journal of Consulting and Clinical Psychology, 45,* 412–416.

Lansdell, H., & Smith, F. (1975). Asymmetrical cerebral function for two WAIS factors and their recovery after brain injury. *Journal of Consulting and Clinical Psychology, 43,* 923.

Leli, D., & Filskov, S. B. (1979). Relationship of intelligence to education and occupation as signs of intellectual deterioration. *Journal of Consulting and Clinical Psychology, 47,* 702–707.

Lewis, G., Golden, C., Moses, J., Osmon, D., Purisch, A., & Hammeke, J. (1979). Localization of cerebral dysfunction with a standardized version of Luria's neuropsychological battery. *Journal of Consulting and Clinical Psychology, 47,* 1003–1019.

Lezak, M. D. (1976). *Neuropsychological assessment.* New York: Oxford University Press.

Logue, P., & Allen, K. (1971). WAIS-predicted category test scores with the Halstead neuropsychological battery. *Perceptual and Motor Skills, 33,* 1095–1096.

Luria, A. R. (1965). *Higher cortical functions in man.* New York: Basic Books.

Luria, A. R. (1973). *The working brain.* New York: Basic Books.

Luria, A. R. (1972). *The man with a shattered world.* New York: Basic Books.

Matarazzo, J. (1972). *Wechsler's measurement and appraisal of adult intelligence.* New York: Oxford University Press.

Matthews, C., Cleeland, C., & Hopper, C. (1971). Neuropsychological patterns in multiple sclerosis. *Diseases of the Nervous System, 31,* 161–170.

McGee, M. (1979). Human spatial abilities: Psychometric studies and environmental, genetic, hormonal and neurological influences. *Psychological Bulletin, 86,* 889–918.

McGlone, J. (1977). Sex differences in the cerebral organization of verbal functions in patients with unilateral brain lesions. *Brain, 100,* 775–793.

McGlone, J., & Kertesz, A. (1973). Sex differences in cerebral processing of visuospatial tasks. *Cortex, 9,* 313–320.

Meier, M. J. (1974). Some challenges for clinical neuropsychology. In R. M. Reitan & L. A. Davison (Eds.), *Clinical neuropsychology: Current status and applications.* Washington, D. C.: V. H. Winston.

Milner, B., Corkin, S., & Teuber, H. (1968). Further analysis of the hippocampal amnesic syndrome: 14-year follow-up study on H. M. *Neuropsychologia, 6,* 215–234.

Mirsky, A. (1969). Neuropsychological bases of schizophrenia. In P. Mussen and M. Rosenzweig. *Annual review of psychology,* Vol. 20. Palo Alto: Annual Reviews, Inc.

Monroe, R., Hulfish, B., Bolis, G., Lion, J., Rubin, J., McDonald, M., & Barcik, J. (1977). Neurologic findings in recidivist aggressors. In C. Shogass, A. Gershon, & A. Friedhoff. *Psychopathology and brain dysfunction.* New York: Raven Press.

Overall, J., & Gorham, D. (1972). Organicity versus old age in objective and projective test performance. *Journal of Consulting and Clinical Psychology, 39,* 98–105.

Overall, J., Hoffman, N., & Levin, H. (1978). Effects of aging, organicity, alcoholism, and functional psychopathology on WAIS subtest profiles. *Journal of Consulting and Clinical Psychology, 46,* 1315–1322.

Parsons, O., & Farr, A. (1981). The neuropsychology of alcohol and drug abuse. In S. B. Filskov & T. J. Boll (Eds.), *Handbook of clinical neuropsychology.* New York: Wiley.

Parsons, O., & Prigatano, G. (1978). Methodological considerations in clinical neuropsychological research. *Journal of Consulting and Clinical Psychology, 46,* 608–619.

Pfeiffer, E. (1975). *Functional assessment: The OARS multidimensional questionnaire.* Durham, N. C.: Duke University Center for the Study of Aging and Human Development.

Prigatano, G., & Parsons, O. (1976). Relationship of age and education to Halstead test performance in different patient populations. *Journal of Consulting and Clinical Psychology, 44,* 527–533.

Purisch, A., Golden, C., & Hammeke, J. (1978). Discrimination of schizophrenic and brain-injured patients by a standardized version of Luria's neuropsychological tests. *Journal of Consulting and Clinical Psychology, 46,* 1266–1273.

Reed, H., & Reitan, R. (1963a) A comparison of the effects of the normal aging process with the effects of organic brain-damage on adaptive abilities. *Journal of Gerontology, 18,* 177–179.

Reed, H., & Reitan, R. (1963b). Changes in psychological test performance associated with the normal aging process. *Journal of Gerontology, 18,* 271–274.

Reitan, R. (1959). The comparative effects of brain damage on the Halstead impairment index and the Wechsler-Bellevue scale. *Journal of Clinical Psychology, 15,* 281–285.

Reitan, R. (1955). The distribution according to age of a psychologic measure dependent upon organic brain functions. *Journal of Gerontology, 10,* 338–340.

Reitan, R. (1974). Methodological problems in clinical neuropsychology. In R. M. Reitan & L. A. Davison (Eds.), *Clinical neuropsychology: Current status and applications.* Washington, D. C.: V. H. Winston.

Reitan, R. (1976). Neurological and physiological basis of psychopathology. In M. Rosenzweig & L. Porter (Eds.), *Annual review of psychology,* Vol. 27. Palo Alto, Calif.: Annual Reviews, Inc.

Reitan, R. (1964). Psychological deficits resulting from cerebral lesions in man. In J. Warren & K. Akert (Eds.), *The frontal granular cortex and behavior.* New York: McGraw-Hill.

Reitan, R., & Davison, L. (Eds.) (1974). *Clinical neuropsychology: Current status and applications.* Washington, D. C.: V. H. Winston.

Reitan, R., Reed, J., & Dyken, M. (1971). Cognitive psychomotor, and motor correlates of multiple sclerosis. *Journal of Nervous and Mental Disease, 153,* 218–224.

Royce, J., Yendall, L., & Bock, C. (1976). Factor analytic studies of human brain damage: I. First and second order factors and their brain correlates. *Multivariate Behavioral Research, 11,* 381–418.

Russell, E., Neuringer, C., & Goldstein, G. (1970). *Assessment of brain damage: A neuropsychological key approach.* New York: Wiley-Interscience.

Satz, P. (1977). Laterality tests and inferential problems. *Cortex, 13*(2), 208–212.

Satz, P. (1979). A test of some models of hemispheric speech organization in the left- and right-handed. *Science, 203,* 1131–1133.

Satz, P., Achenbach, K., & Fennell, E. (1967). Correlations between manual laterality and predicted speech laterality in a normal population. *Neuropsychologia, 5,* 295–310.

Satz, P., Fennell, E., & Reilly, C. (1970). Predictive validity of six neurodiagnostic tests. *Journal of Consulting and Clinical Psychology, 34,* 375–381.

Schaie, K. (1965). A general model for the study of developmental problems. *Psychological Bulletin, 64,* 92–107.

Schaie, K., & Labouvie-Vief, G. (1974). Generational versus ontogenetic components of change in adult cognitive behavior: A fourteen-year cross-sequential study. *Developmental Psychology, 10,* 305–320.

Schildkraut, J. (1973). Norepinephrine metabolism in the pathophysiology and classification of depressive and manic disorders. In J. Cole, A. Freedman, & A. Friedhoff, *Psychopathology and psychopharmacology.* Baltimore: Johns Hopkins University Press.

Schwartz, C., Davidson, R., & Meier, F. (1975). Right hemispheric lateralization for emotion: Interactions with cognition. *Science, 190,* 286–288.

Scoville, W. (1968). Amnesia after bilateral mesial temporal lobe excision: Introduction to case H. M. *Neuropsychologia, 6,* 211–213.

Selz, M., & Reitan, R. (1979). Rules for neuropsychological diagnosis: Classification of brain function in older children. *Journal of Consulting and Clinical Psychology, 47,* 258–264.

Shore, C., Shore, H., & Pihl, R. (1971). Correlations between performance on the category test and the Wechsler adult intelligence scale. *Perceptual and Motor Skills, 32,* 70.

Slater, E., & Glithero, E. (1965). A follow-up of patients diagnosed as suffering from "hysteria." *Journal of Psychosomatic Research, 9,* 9–13.

Smith, A. (1962). Ambiguities in concepts and studies of "brain damage" and organicity. *Journal of Nervous and Mental Disease, 135,* 311–326.

Smith, A. (1975). Neuropsychological testing in neurological disorders. *Advances in Neurology, 7,* 49–110.

Smith, A. (1981). Principles underlying human brain functions reflected in neuropsychological sequellae of different neuropathological processes. In S. B. Filskov & T. J. Boll (Eds.), *Handbook of clinical neuropsychology.* New York: Wiley.

Snyder, S. H. (1976). The dopamine hypothesis of schizophrenia: Focus on the dopamine receptor. *American Journal of Psychiatry, 133,* 197–202.

Spellacy, F. (1977). Neuropsychological differences between violent and non-violent adolescents. *Journal of Clinical Psychology, 33,* 966–969.

Spitzer, R., Endicott, J., & Robins, E. (1978). Research diagnostic criteria: Rationale and reliability. *Archives of General Psychiatry, 35,* 773–782.

Sterman, M. B., & Macdonald, L. R. (1978). Effects of central cortical EEG feedback on incidence of poorly controlled seizures. *Epilepsia, 19,* 207.

Sterman, M. B., Macdonald, L. R., & Stone, R. K.

(1974). Biofeedback training of the sensorimotor EEG rhythm in man: Effects on epilepsy. *Epilepsia, 15,* 395.

Thatcher, R., & John, E. (1977). *Foundations of cognitive processes.* New York: Halsted Press.

Todd, J., Coolidge, F., & Satz, P. (1977). The Wechsler adult intelligence scale discrepancy Index: A neuropsychological evaluation. *Journal of Consulting and Clinical Psychology, 45,* 450–454.

Vega, A., & Parsons, O. (1967). Cross-validation of the Halstead-Reitan tests for brain damage. *Journal of Consulting Psychology, 31,* 619–625.

Vogt, A., & Heaton, R. (1977). Comparison of Wechsler adult intelligence scale indices of brain dysfunction. *Perceptual and Motor Skills, 45,* 607–615.

Watson, C., Davis, W., & McDermott, M. (1976). MMPI-WAIS Relationships in organic and schiz-

ophrenic patients. *Journal of Clinical Psychology, 32,* 539–540.

Watson, C., & Plemel, G. (1978). An MMPI scale to separate brain-damaged from functional psychiatric patients in neuropsychiatric settings. *Journal of Consulting and Clinical Psychology, 46,* 1127–1132.

Williams, J., Roy, C., & Averall, J. (1973). Mental aging and organicity in an alcoholic population. *Journal of Consulting and Clinical Psychology, 41,* 392–396.

Wilson, R., Rosenbaum, G., Brown, C., Rourke, D., Whitman, D., & Grisell, J. (1978). An index of premorbid intelligence. *Journal of Consulting and Clinical Psychology, 46,* 1554–1555.

Weiss, G., & Hechtman, L. (1979). The hyperactive child syndrome. *Science, 205,* 1348–1354.

PART SIX
Afterword

CHAPTER 20

Research in Clinical Psychology: Serving the Future Hour

NORMAN GARMEZY

Predicting the future course of any discipline is a cavalier venture, in which the act of forecasting tends to be marked more by hubris than wisdom. To attempt to do so in the field of mental health seems particularly unwise, for here scientific advance is disproportionately small relative to the magnitude of society's problems that experts are called upon to solve. Thus I must bypass the editorial charge to reflect on the future, and will focus initially on some aspects of the contemporary scene that point to the growing importance of various research areas to which clinical psychologists contribute. In the course of doing so, I will comment on two geopolitical problems that may have to be dealt with in the future, because of their long-term consequences for our research enterprise.

It is an honor to be paired with David Shakow, the devoted father of contemporary clinical psychology, whose final publication appears herein. Here the pairing takes the form of a set of perspective-laden bookends that enclose the chapters of this Handbook. Shakow's opening chapter offers a view of clinical psychology's research past; this closing chapter, in part, provides a perspective on the future. The chapters that are framed by our two presentations offer telling evidence of clinical psychology's productive present. Produced by a multigenerational set of authors (several older, but many more younger), these chapters lead me to a question: Within the context of the current volume, what do the following individuals have in common? (The list is merely representative, not inclusive.) Jeanne Block, Al Bandura, Wanda Bronson, Paul Mussen, Seymour Sarason, Gordon Paul, Charles Spielberger, Jack Block, Walter Mischel, Seymour Epstein, Richard Lazarus, John Flavell, Philip Holzman, Ed Zigler, Wayne Holtzman, Steven Matthysse, Brendan Maher, David Elkind, Allan Mirsky, Paul E. Meehl, Irving Gottesman, Oscar Parsons, David Lykken, Hans Strupp, Lewis Goldberg, Douglas Jackson, Jerry Wiggins, Carroll Izard and Harrison Gough.

One answer is obvious: *They are all prime research talents in psychology.* Another answer is less obvious, but more interesting: *All received their doctorates, specializing in clinical psychology.*

Consider the diversity represented by their major contributions to a variety of psychology's special fields: developmental psychology, Piagetian theory, personality theory, behavior therapy, behavior genetics, community psychology, learning, cognitive psychology, psychodiagnosis, psychophysiology, psychopathology, neuropsychology, biochemistry, theoretical genetics, psychopharmacology, neuroanatomy, psychometrics, and several others.

Examine their specific research contributions and witness the vigor and breadth of concept, method and content reflected in their work: Q-sort methodology, the longitudinal study of lives, ego resilience in children, social learning theory and research, aggression, television and children's behavior, prosocial behavior, public policy affecting children, parent–child relations, thought disorder in schizophrenia, aftercare of chronic schizophrenic patients, token economies, social cognition, brain–behavior relationships, adoptee and twin study methodology, clinical and actuarial prediction, trait and situational contributions to behavior, eye tracking in schizophrenia and the affective disorders, children at risk, research on neurotransmitters, information processing and memory storage in mental disorders, genetics of schizophrenia and the affective disorders, cognitive style, stress and coping, alcoholism, psychotherapy, anxiety and its emotional correlates, and so on.

In similar fashion I could have constructed multiple lists of equally prestigious researchers, or a companion list of productive nationally recognized contributors to the *practice* of clinical psychology, some of whom would be clones of the list above. These individuals were also reared in those very same graduate clinical psychology training programs, replicates of which are viewed by some as benighted because of their old-fashioned twin focus on training graduate clinical psychology students for both *science* and *professional practice*.

THE UNIQUE NATURE OF CLINICAL PSYCHOLOGY TRAINING

The current list of Handbook authors makes it evident that the dual achievements of previous generations of clinical psychologists are being repeated by a new, but equally productive, cast of scholars in clinical psychology, who also find no discomfort at being cast in the dual roles of scientist and clinician. This basic reaffirmation is evident in Kendall and Norton-Ford's (this volume) introduction to their chapter on therapy out-

come research. "Clinical psychologists," they write, "are scientists who evaluate their theories with rigor and practitioners who utilize a research-based understanding of human behavior and social contexts to aid people in resolving psychological dysfunctions and enhancing their lives."

Such attitudes and abilities are hallmarks of the training of clinical psychologists, whose graduate programs emphasize the co-development of a scientist-practitioner orientation in the same person. A recent survey extending over a five-year span (1975 to 1980), conducted by the Psychology Education Branch of NIMH's Division of Manpower and Training Programs, reveals that these programs continue to provide clinical psychologists for both research and service to the general public. The survey, conducted by Dr. Stanley Schneider, Branch Chief, was directed toward more than 3000 psychology graduates from 105 clinical training programs who have received training grant support from NIMH. Survey results indicate that:

1. Two-thirds of the recent graduates are now working in organized service settings, primarily community health centers, hospitals, schools, state and federal government agencies, penal and correctional institutions, and industry.

2. A little less than 25% have moved into academic and research positions.

3. Only 4.5% of the graduates have entered private practice.

4. Work with children and families absorb the efforts of some 30% of the recent graduates.

5. Eighteen percent serve small towns and rural areas, regions of national neglect that clinical psychologists are at least partially attempting to meet (ADAMHA News, January 9, 1981).

Our sense of responsibility to national needs seems to be clearly evident in the human services arena. The same apparently is true on the research side. In a statement presented to a National Research Council Committee studying the nation's needs for biomedical and behavioral research personnel, Carson (1980) summed up our responsive history as researchers:

This history of clinical psychology, while a very short one as disciplines go, is in this respect a very proud one. The effective founders, many of whom are still alive, have every right to rejoice in the unprecedented success of their brainchild, the essence of which is the so-called scientist-practitioner. While not every graduate of such training programs has become a notable researcher—or even a researcher at all—a very substantial portion of them, including those in direct service jobs, continue active research programs and publish their results, as indicated in a recent survey by Bornstein and Wollersheim (1978). In another recent survey of authors of articles published between 1972 and 1976 in the *Journal of Consulting and Clinical Psychology. . .* , Kendall and Ford (1979) reported that 72% of these authors characterized their advanced training as having been of this type, [while] another 13% indicated "experimental psychopathology," a related curriculum, as having been the focus of their graduate work . . . Not surprisingly, the graduates of more professionally oriented programs were minimally represented in this somewhat elite authorship sample.

The dominant motives for doing research, according to the latter survey of 333 persons, were the social importance of the problem, and the impetus provided researchers by a search to answer an "applied-clinical question." Theory testing, by comparison, played a significant role in studying the problem for one-third of the respondents. The authors note:

It is not true that clinical research is . . . being conducted by psychologists who have little commitment to clinical practice. Rather, published clinical research comes from persons trained as scientist-practitioners and far less frequently from persons trained exclusively as researchers, ther-

apists, or assessors . . . The present finding suggest that quality clinical researchers are the product of training that sought to integrate research and practice components (Kendall & Ford, 1979; p. 104).

Since concerns have been expressed, both implicitly and explicitly, about psychology's failure to engage in socially relevant research (Smith, 1973; Miller, 1969; Bronfenbrenner, 1977; Campbell, 1969), it is important to note that the "fundamental motivation" expressed by the researchers was the social relevance of their studies. Whatever the success of the achievement, (and assuming self-deception to be minimal) the basic motivations of the researcher appear to be in the direction of social responsibility and not in the achievement of more material incentives such as consultantships, educational goals, or the reasonable desire to publish rather than to perish.

There are contrasting views, however, regarding the research side of the clinical psychologist's activities. One survey, unbiased by those who publish successfully (i.e., the Kendall-Ford sample), provides a different picture of current research activity. Garfield and Kurtz (1976) in their survey of 855 Members and Fellows of APA's Division of Clinical Psychology, reported that 58.7% of their respondents perceived themselves primarily in the role of clinical practitioner, while 25% saw their primary role as that of academician (20%) or researcher (4.7%). Almost three-quarters of the sample expressed satisfaction with their careers and with their graduate training in university-based clinical psychology programs, despite the marked differences that existed within the group in terms of their theoretical orientations and ideological allegiance, whether it be behavioral, intuitive-objective, psychoanalytic-psychodynamic, and so on.

In sum, clinical psychologists are a heterogeneous lot. If there is a cutting variable, it resides in a behavioral-nonbehavioral orientation; the former tend to engage more in research-related activity, the latter more typically in clinical functions. But these are markedly overlapping groups, leading Bornstein and Wollersheim (1978), conductors of one of the surveys, to conclude that "psychologists of both persuasions seem to maintain a fair amount of both scientist and practitioner" (p. 662).

There are, however, portents of the future in some of these data. Since this is a disquisition on the 1980s rather than the 1970s, I wish to begin crystal-ball gazing with a discussion of two geopolitical realities that are likely to influence the future of clinical psychological research. One is external to our discipline, the biological revolution in psychiatry; the other is an internal matter, the rapid proliferation of the professional schools of clinical psychology.

BIOLOGICAL PSYCHIATRY AND CLINICAL PSYCHOLOGICAL RESEARCH

The advent of chlorpromazine in the mid-1950s wrought a revolution in psychiatric treatment. Over the past 25 years that event has been furthered by the expansion of knowledge in pharmacology, biochemistry, molecular chemistry of genetics, human cytogenetics, neurophysiology, and the neurosciences that is without parallel for any comparable time span in the history of these sciences. Technological developments accompanying these advances have provided research tools that permit psychiatric applications of the basic research findings drawn from these fields. The net effect has been a biological revolution in psychiatry that has had wide ramifications for the treatment of severe mental disorders.

This surge of biological advances in psychiatry has been a source of enormous encouragement to that discipline, and will in time provide a transition point for the capture of young medical talent into psychiatry stimulated by the possibility of major break-throughs in understanding basic biological processes implicated in schizophrenia and severe mood disorders. This is the impetus behind a phrase now grown commonplace: "Psychiatry is turning back to medicine." However stereotypical the phrasing, it is not one to be scoffed at. A century of psychiatry's yearning for inclusion in the corpus of medicine appears more tenable now than ever before, although the major data base for the revolution still lies in drug effectiveness with the major psychoses, an effectiveness that remains, despite the erosion of successive hypotheses related to neurotransmitters and their presumed relationship to the processing of specific excitatory and inhibitory informational messages. The fact that therapeutic drugs appear to exert their effects by facilitating or inhibiting the effects of these chemical messengers is a finding of momentous significance, but one far from proving the etiological specificity of schizophrenia, to cite one example. Our knowledge of the many neurotransmitters and neuromodulators in the brain is still fragmentary. But a road appears to have been opened for reaching a rational biochemical basis for drug treatment. Unfortunately, some very disturbing physical realities impinge upon such treatments. Long-term high dosage treatments with antipsychotic medication has often produced irreversible neurological syndromes. What are side effects for the psychiatrist are main effects for the patient. In the case of other drugs, data on long-term effects on the person are not yet available. At a more basic level, the ascription of causation, there remains a very distant and difficult step from intervention to etiology, a reality too frequently ignored by therapeutic advocates of all persuasions, whether biological or behavioral.

Despite these limitations one cannot gainsay the extraordinary sense of achievement and hope conveyed to psychiatry and to many patients by these biological advances. But psychologists have often reacted with a curious ambivalence to these important discoveries. New discoveries are looked upon with a skepticism that is not born of healthy doubts alone, while failures to sustain the first generation of biochemical hypotheses are greeted with almost an adversarial pleasure. At the more extreme end of the spectrum there are biophobes in our discipline who totally deny not only genetic advances in schizophrenia and the affective disorders but the very existence of mental disorder itself. Their denial takes form in the resolute search for methodological and research design weaknesses in the biogenetic studies that might undo the recent findings and negate their potential significance. Would that equally diligent appraisals were made by these critics of the shortcomings in our own behavioral research in psychopathology!

This unseemly behavior by our colleagues can be more than equaled by the posturings of some psychiatrists. Behavioral advances in psychopathology are often contested in a fashion comparable to the denial of biological significance by some psychologists. How else can one explain the marked neglect by psychiatry of the brilliant program of research comparing the efficacy of behavioral and psychosocial treatments versus drug therapy with chronic state hospital patients conducted by Gordon Paul and his colleagues (Paul & Lentz, 1977)? An extraordinary program of research that shows the comparative disadvantages of drug treatment has brought forth from psychiatry the most nonbenign neglect it has been my displeasure to witness over the past 30 years.

The nadir for me in this disputatious exchange between disciplines—whose adherents should know better—took place this year with total unexpectedness in the very first session of my first-year Minnesota seminar, An Introduction To Research In Psychopathology. The seminar is intended solely for newly admitted clinical psychology graduate students, and the first session is given over to provocative question-answer exchanges ("Tell me what you consider to be an important problem that demands solution in the field of psychopathology?" "Do you think it is possible that 10 years hence you will be technologically obsolescent?"). Sitting in the classroom was a young man with impeccable credentials: a fine mind, highly motivated, and surprisingly knowledgeable about psychopathology. He had come to Minnesota because of the clinical psychology program's emphasis on the old-fashioned virtues that gladden the hearts of research-minded psychopathologists: active research involvement of students and faculty, a positive view of psychiatric classification, an emphasis on assessment, behavior genetics, experimental psychopathology, psychophysiology, and behavioral intervention. He had served as a research assistant in a department of psychiatry that was strongly biologically minded and highly productive in research. (Here were the roots of his sophistication.) His graduate application bore the evidence of a number of multiple coauthored papers written in collaboration with several of that department's major psychiatric researchers.

My question to him was a simple one, and his response caught me by surprise. "What do you want to be doing 10 years from now?" His reply to my question was framed by an interview he had had with his famed department chairman as he prepared to leave for graduate school. Our student had talked with his mentor about career directions, indicating that he hoped to be able to continue to do research in a department of psychiatry in a medical school after receiving his doctorate. In response to this stated aspiration the chairman had replied that psychiatry departments in the future would not be hiring psychologists, because the advances in biological psychiatry would make their presence unnecessary. Therefore, the student indicated he wasn't certain where he might be a decade hence.

I do not want to overestimate the power of $N = 1$ in this incident (although I do have other incidents I could put into the hopper). But after a semester of watching this young student in action and observing his major talents for research and scholarship, and his substantial level of motivation and aspiration, I am bemused by the counsel provided by this major figure of American psychiatry. I am aware that all revolutions, including biological ones, create in some of its revolutionists an unyielding adherency. I remain hopeful that wiser heads will prevail, and psychiatry's revolution will traverse its peaceful course toward science. But if the leaders of psychiatry share the view of our anonymous chairman (and I doubt that they do), then the science of psychopathology is indeed in trouble. For psychiatry can by its actions close off opportunities for psychologists to remain partners in the study of psychopathology. Such exclusions would remove from psychopathology the necessary sophistication in the behavioral domain that is prerequisite for understanding the complexity of mental disorder. Yearning and pining for that long-sought closeness to medicine does not require psychiatry to dissolve its ties to the knowledge base provided by behavioral scientists. It would be ironic were this to transpire in psychiatry at the very moment that other medical specialties, long comfortably ensconced in medicine's domain, are beginning to realize that psyches have power to modify somas. This reality is behind the growth of behavioral medicine so excitingly and critically reported by Bradley and Prokop (this volume) in their chapter on research methods in medical psychology. This reality also lay behind my reassuring reply to the graduate student that it was unlikely to happen; that wiser heads would prevail; and that even if the chairman's psychophobia was to prove contagious and transmittable to other departments of psychiatry, there would be other departments in medical schools that would use his talents since there was another revolution taking place called behavioral medicine.

I am not considering a literal barrier to employment in psychiatry departments as a likely event. Rather, I am thinking of an attitudinal bent that asserts there is a dominance hierarchy in the sciences that contribute to mental health, and behavioral researchers by fiat are to be accorded low status in that hierarchy. Talented young psychologists, having experienced the intellectual freedom that marks major graduate departments of psychology, are unlikely to accept an atmosphere for research if it is marked by pretensions to superiority not rooted in a primacy usually given to the quality of intellectual appraisal and the search for scientific truth that marks good science. But were this to happen, there would be an erosion of psychological talent in psychopathology, and that should concern future faculties and the students they will train.

Psychologists also have a duty to perform. Too long have psychologists boasted of *their* research traditions and scoffed at psychiatry's efforts to be scientific. Our smugness is bound to be shattered in the very near future as psychiatry's young research talents come to the fore. We too will have to inform our students in our classrooms of the scientific challenge in which status is best monitored by achievement and not by merely being critical of the work of others. There are pretentious members of both disciplines who profess to operatic stardom without ever having sung an aria.

A second tendency in clinical psychology is to eschew a serious effort to study significant problems in psychopathology in favor of weak experimental analogues. The richness of psychopathological processes is not readily transferred to the laboratory, and a clinical psychologist's research responsibility typically resides with the truly disordered and not with the pseudo-disordered (e.g., the predilection for some to study the ubiquitous college sophomore enrolled in the introductory psychology course).

My colleague, Auke Tellegen, makes a point about this last statement with which I do agree. Tellegen points to the work of Depue and his colleagues (Depue, 1979; Depue and Evans, in press; Depue et al., in press) and Chapman and his collaborators

(1980; in press) to indicate that it is not pseudo-psychopathological research to study cyclothymes, schizoids, and schizotypes, who likely share certain dispositional attributes with more severely disturbed people, but are sufficiently competent and functional to remain out of mental hospitals. Not only do I agree with Tellegen, but I recognize that studies involving such persons constitute the important area of risk research. There is virtue in systematically studying persons who are at risk or those who fall between the normal and the disordered ends of the spectrum of adaptation. Such persons can help to answer a critical issue in research into normal and psychopathological functioning: "Is there continuity or discontinuity between the ordered and the disordered?" Persons at risk can provide information about relevant antecedents to psychopathology as well as possible predispositional elements involved in various mental disorders.

Reconciliation needs to be made between the two disciplines in the joint effort to create a science of psychopathology. I take my sermon for the day from a supplement to the Task Force Panel Report on Mental Health Research that was submitted to the President's Commission on Mental Health (Research Opportunities and Options, 1978). In the closing paragraph of a section on basic processes research, the panel report reads as follows:

The overriding message is clear. We will only understand, treat and prevent the development of abnormal psychological processes when we know and understand normal basic psychological and biological processes. We must understand them at their juncture. This same message has come over and over again from the physical sciences and from molecular biology. We can only control, manipulate, alter, and improve when we understand the normal state of affairs. We put a man on the moon because we understood enough about the physical universe. We can recombine chromosomes in bacteria to make them manufacture rare hormones only because we understand enough about the molecular bases of normal ge-

netics and the biochemistry of gene action. The same is true in mental health. We must come to understand normal basic psychological processes and their neurobiological substrate. With that understanding will come the effective methods of prevention, treatment, and cure of mental illness. Mental illness, in the last analysis reflects basic psychological and biological processes gone wrong. (p. 1675)

THE PROFESSIONAL SCHOOL MOVEMENT AND CLINICAL PSYCHOLOGICAL RESEARCH

The expansion of the professional schools-of-clinical-psychology-movement has been nothing short of phenomenal. From its slow beginnings in the 1960s, there has been a rapid proliferation of new institutions in the 1970s, several of which are university based, while most of the others remain freestanding institutions.

The brief discussion that follows of the relationship that I perceive to exist between that movement and the future of research in clinical psychology can not be viewed as an objective statement of the status of the professional schools, their origins, curricula, faculty, and students. I am not qualified to do that, because I lack knowledge about individual schools and their training programs. I am, however, aware of the heavy emphasis placed on clinical practice in these graduate programs. Indeed dissatisfaction with the traditional scientist-practitioner model was one argument used for establishing the new schools. I am partially aware of the research demands of some of the new schools, having reviewed years of the International Dissertation Abstracts for an entirely different purpose. In the course of my search I have read many abstracts of doctoral dissertations written by graduates of some of the older professional school programs. If I find shortcomings in these studies, that is not a wholly unique experience when cast against the background of other studies conducted by students in more traditional programs. But the output of the professional schools does seem to be of poorer quality to me; and they do not seem to reflect significant probings into clinical phenomena. One would hope that professional school faculty would require that the dissertations of their graduate students would meet the criterion of a major contribution to knowledge in the practice of clinical psychology.

Many different views have been expressed about the professional school movement. Some perceive it as a needed step, seeing the difficulty of trying to embody in the same person the requisite talents of both scientist and professional (Albee & Loeffler, 1971). Others have argued that the state of our basic knowledge supports a view of clinical psychology as a profession capable of serving a clientele that needs the knowledge possessed by clinical psychologists trained in professional schools (Peterson, 1976). Still others attack the "traditionalism" of university departments of psychology (Rogers, 1973). In an article, "Some New Challenges," Rogers labels psychology as a "pseudo-science," adding that in graduate departments that frown on creativity, the doctoral dissertation is a "safe mediocrity." Rogers is an influential figure, and quotes from his article capture the intensity of his opposition to the university-based training programs in clinical psychology. The quotes also provide some understanding of the congruence of his points of attack and the philosophy that students espoused in the 1960s and early 1970s.

The Ph.D. thesis has, in most universities, become a travesty of its true purpose. . . .

Another great challenge of our times to the psychologist is to develop an approach which is focused on constructing the new, not repairing the old; which is designing a society in which problems will be less frequent, rather than putting poultices on those who have been crippled by social factors. . . .

Will the school psychologist be content with the attempt to diagnose and remedy the individual ills created by an obsolete school system with an irrelevant curriculum, or will he insist on having a part in designing an opportunity for learning in which the students' curiosity can be unleashed and in which the joy of learning replaces the assigned tasks of the prisons we now know as schools? . . .

As clinicians we have seen our task in such degrading ways that I do not know whether we can lift our view enough to see the function we might be serving. . . .

The . . . challenge I wish to raise, especially for clinical and social psychologists, is the radical possibility of sweeping away our procedures for professionalization. There are as many *certified* charlatans and exploiters of people as there are uncertified. . . .

Only the younger generation, I believe, can help us to see the awful dehumanization we have bred in our educational system by separating thoughts, which are to be approved, from feelings, which are somehow seen as animal in origin. Perhaps the young can make us whole again.

It is not difficult to see how these views of one of psychology's leading figures and a seer of the new humanism fitted so the mood on American campuses in the 1960s and 1970s. Their ring of stereotypy as we move into the 1980s is a cue to the changing scene. But in the 1960s, as others, less talented and less contributory than Rogers, took up his cry, the consequences for the research enterprise in clinical psychology was incalculable.

Whereas previously attacks on clinical programs had focused on shortcomings on the clinical practice side, now the more vulnerable corpus of clinical psychology—from the standpoint of its identity with general psychology—also became the target of criticism. In opposition to Rogers' position I urge a reading of Hans Strupp's (1976) Presidential Address to APA's Division of Clinical Psychology. I cannot substitute my words for Strupp's. That would only produce an inferior paraphrasing of his insightful statement of the problems generated by those who, heeding Rogers' words, called for an all-out attack on the structure and content of graduate training in clinical psychology.

What we are being asked by the irrationalists to do, on the basis of admitted deficiencies, one-sided emphases, and miscarriages in academic programs, is to abandon clinical psychology as a science. Having misidentified reason and rationality as a counterproductive and nefarious force in doctoral programs in clinical psychology, . . . the irrationalists advocate the model of the encounter group and human potential development as the royal road to salvation. Surely, no one can seriously oppose the ideal of the therapist as a fully functioning person; however . . . the field has staunchly maintained for a generation that there is more to clinical psychology than the delivery of clinical services or the facilitation of growth. The issue, unfortunately, has been confounded by the undeniable and growing need for well-trained individuals who are interested in turning their attention to the solution of pressing social problems, a goal that hardly needs defense. However, what is being sold short in the process is the basic science component of our field—the patient nurturance of an inquiring and critical attitude in our students, the kindling of intellectual curiosity, the furtherance of investigative skills—all of which have on more than rare occasions been inspired by creative scientists and researchers, many of whom in fact hold respected positions in our universities and make their contributions to what is loosely called "clinical training." Although many candidates for graduate degrees in clinical psychology have a strong, though often poorly formulated desire to receive training for the helping role, they are vague about their career objectives and they have particularly fuzzy ideas about the meaning of research in clinical psychology as well as the gratifications that can accrue to the individual who requires both sensitive understanding of clinical phenomena and the desire to advance knowledge by sophisticated methods of inquiry. Instead, research training is frequently impugned as stifling the students' ingenuity and creativity. (p. 565)

Other trainers in graduate clinical psychology programs also sensed the exaggeration in Rogers' content and tone, and perhaps this contained the magnitude of the programmatic change that was affected. (However, one positive change was the expansion of clinical programs to incorporate community activities as part of practicum and field work experiences.) But a larger effect was provided by the emerging leadership of many of the professional schools. The research role of the professional school candidate was either given a markedly reduced status or was eliminated entirely. Some professional schools made an effort to maintain the research component to the extent that good consumerism of the published research output was made one goal of training.

Perhaps there is no need for a concern about the issue as long as a nucleus of university-based programs continues to adhere to a training philosophy of the scientist-practitioner model. But there is one potential effect that implicates an extension of Gresham's Law. R. H. Ashworth, (1980) Commissioner of the Texas College and University System, recently spoke to this problem in a broader context:

In the marketplace, says Gresham's law of economics, bad money drives out the good. In higher education it appears at times as though the bad degrees drive out the good ones. How can quality education survive when standards are set lower and lower to attract students, many of whom seem to care next to nothing for the quality of the degree, and whose employers do not care, either? (p. 64)

In citing the above I do not imply that all professional schools are inadequate and set low standards, while asserting that traditional university programs are invariably good. Indeed I am of the view that individual differences within groupings prevail, and that it is necessary to protect good departments and good professional schools by a banding together of quality programs and a joint willingness to police our field. Without it clinical psychology's reputation as a contributing discipline to the mental health field will be eroded with severe employment consequences for the graduates of good programs (Gresham's Law, you see) who have trained under the university and professional school models.

Nor do I suggest that the students in better professional schools are untalented. That many of them are able, talented candidates seems a reasonable supposition given the current difficulty all students have of being admitted to clinical psychology graduate programs. On the basis of a survey of 77 APA-approved training programs in clinical psychology, Nyman (1973) reports that "clinical psychology turns away from its doors close to 80% of the candidate population" (p. 934). Many of these rejected candidates have the abilities needed for superior graduate school performance and are just as likely to be applicants to graduate professional schools of clinical psychology as to traditional university-based programs.

To sum up, I see two political factors at work with possible consequences in the 1980s for research training and activity in clinical psychology: (1) The biological revolution in psychiatry could conceivably narrow the placement of psychologists in medical settings where research on the origins, course, and treatment of the severe mental disorders is a central institutional mission. If that revolution brings in its wake a denigration of the behavioral contributions to all three areas of research and practice, then psychologists are more likely to seek employment in more probehavioral settings. The expansion of behavioral medicine (or "health psychology") into medical specialties that have not previously made wide use of psychologists' talents and skills is a strong compensatory factor, but it is not a substitute for research in behavior pathology. (2) An internal problem is posed by the growth of professional schools of clinical psychology, whose faculties often perceive research training as an unnecessary component of a clinical psychologist's training. The growing number of graduates of these schools, which in the future will surpass those of university-based

programs, can change the perception of clinical psychology as a research-oriented discipline and serve further to contain or reduce the allegiance of clinical psychologists to research activities.

A union of strong training programs under both the university-based and professional school models is suggested as a possible solution for maintaining standards in training students as research consumers or research investigators.

ON THE SIDE OF CONTENT IN FUTURE RESEARCH IN CLINICAL PSYCHOLOGY

The multiple content chapters of this volume suggest many of the important areas of research that will see extended investigation during the decades ahead. The content selections of the editors and the detailed analyses of their current research standing as reflected in the authors' reports portray not only a contemporary vitality but a future significance as well. Obviously there are some chapters that are closer to my heart, but this is determined primarily by a congruence of interests rather than by a hierarchy of presumed importance.

Erasmus Hoch (this volume) has provided his predictions of future trends: sleep and dreaming; altered states of consciousness; nonverbal communication; pupillometrics; hypnosis; simulation research using field and laboratory methods and computer paradigms; biofeedback; cerebral lateralization; and clinical technology (including computerized assessments).

There is no overlap between Dr. Hoch's listing and mine, which reflects a very simple fact: there is a tremendous diversity among clinical psychologists in the research areas they hold near and dear.

My list is a compound of eclecticism and past and present research participation. I emphasize the contents of child clinical psychology because, like child psychiatry, it is, by comparison with its adult counterpart, relatively underdeveloped despite its obvious importance for providing us with a developmental perspective on the adult psychopathologies.

On the side of method, I believe that our future interests are well served by a broadened use of a range of research methods that extend from Kazdin's concern with single-subject experimental designs to the significance of complex naturalistic observational methods espoused by Cone and Foster. My growing concern with developmental models in psychopathology also leads me to agree with Achenbach that we must pay greater attention to follow-up, cross-sectional, longitudinal, and longitudinal-sequential designs as means of extending our knowledge of what we can call "life span developmental psychopathology." Clinical psychologists and developmental psychopathologists have paid minimal attention to the life-span methodologies espoused by the emerging cadre of life-span developmentalists (Nesselroade & Reese, 1973). The method of retrospective reconstruction is too fraught with error to provide us with any degree of comfort in emulating use of the central method of psychiatry for historical case reconstruction.

As to specific areas of research, here are my "Best Ten" selections as future research priorities in child clinical psychology and developmental psychopathology. There is no effort here to order them by presumed importance.

1. There is need for more extensive comparative studies of cognitive, social, and emotional development in three groups of children: normal children, children at risk for specific disorders (such as antisocial behavior, schizophrenia, affective disorders, developmental disabilities), and children who are manifestly disturbed. Although such studies pose major logistical problems, they would provide information about significant similarities and differences that exist in three critical domains of functioning for children who differ in risk potential.

2. To enhance our understanding of organic factors in relation to behavioral adaptation, we need to have more basic and applied research on conditions implicating brain dysfunction and its sequelae. Such studies should include variables that will allow a study of the interaction of organic factors with familial factors that tend to exacerbate or mitigate dysfunctional behaviors (Eisenberg & Earls, 1975; Rutter et al., 1970; Werner et al., 1971).

3. Systematic studies of attachment behavior and cognitive and social-emotional development in stressed families is a critical area of research that has scarcely received the attention it deserves. Included among the high-risk families are those headed by adolescent unmarried mothers, families undergoing divorce or separation, others caught up in the poverty cycle, families marked by battered children or battered wives, parents and offspring with a history of markedly antisocial behavior, families that have undergone recent dislocation and immigration, and so on.

4. We have need for broad-gauged studies of children exposed to various forms of stressors and their patterns of adaptive and maladaptive behavior in coping with stressful events. In this area, cross-sectional and short-term longitudinal studies of children who maintain competence in the presence of stress are particularly in short supply. Vulnerable and "invulnerable" cohorts might include children of poverty, physically handicapped children, mentally retarded children, children exposed to parental loss, offspring of emotionally and psychiatrically disordered parents, children suffering from

physical (including potentially terminal) illnesses, children living in high-delinquency areas, children of migrant, dislocated and immigrant families, and so on.

5. The creation of appropriate models and methods for studying coping mechanisms in children has been an area of major neglect. This literature is primarily a descriptive one replete with case studies. Systematic research is virtually nonexistent, although the future for research in this area remains a promising one.

6. Community and epidemiological studies of the incidence and prevalence of children's behavior disorders and developmental disabilities are more in evidence in Great Britain than in the United States. There is evidence, however, of a growing interest in epidemiological research at the National Institute of Mental Health which could rectify this shortcoming.

7. Studies of the environmental and organic antecedents of learning disabilities, attentional disturbances, distraction and overactivity in children are needed. Behavioral patterns are particularly important, since these deficiencies, if untreated, can exacerbate children's incompetencies and lead to future restrictions of opportunities.

8. The problem of the classification of childhood disorders will be with us for a considerable period of time. Its revision in DSM III by (as Achenbach terms it) "negotiated consensus" left this area one of the weakest segments of the revised *Diagnostic and statistical manual*. An improved classification of children's behavior by psychologists has been suggested to the American Psychological Association, and appears to be a viable, circumscribed proposition. The Board of Directors of APA has established a Task Force chaired by Achenbach with members C. Keith Conners and Herbert C. Quay (Achenbach, 1980). The Committee has now forwarded its report and a set of recommendations to the Board of Directors. The report proposes that a set of projects be undertaken aimed at creating and standardizing an instrument to be used in assessing both children's behavior disorders and competencies, in the hope that it will lead to a "standard tool for clinical, research, training, administrative, and epidemiological purposes."

9. Such a classification instrument possessing demonstrable reliability and validity would permit investigators to conduct studies of treatment effects in children characterized by more homogenous target behaviors. Only when such an instrument is available can we begin to search out the answer to the complex question raised by Kendall and Norton-Ford in their review of therapy outcome research. "What therapy, conducted by what therapist with what clients, produces what effects?"

We have had few systematic studies evaluating various forms of therapy with different types of disturbed children. Historically, this neglect is a function of the powerful role played for decades by psychoanalysis in the treatment of disturbed children. New behavioral and pharmacological techniques have now begun to compete significantly with the older psychoanalytically oriented therapy, but, as noted in this volume, the research designs that have been used reveal many shortcomings.

Very carefully designed studies are essential in drug therapy, since the potential consequences stemming from such usage are very serious unless there are systematic long-term investigations of the potential negative as well as possible positive effects.

10. Systematic studies of disturbed emotional states of children including phobias, anxiety, and particularly depression are now coming into prominence. The antecedents and consequences of such states as well as techniques for ameliorating them and sustaining such changes outside the treatment room are particularly significant areas for research. Such studies must take into account the developmental stages of the treated children.

If I could add an eleventh area that moves beyond childhood, I would select behavioral medicine. Bradley and Prokop have provided in this volume a splendid review of new developments that indicate the ways in which clinical psychologists and other psychological specialists are infusing modes of investigation and treatment and psychological thinking into medical areas in which hitherto these have been conspicuously absent. In time such contributions may equal or even transcend our research efforts in psychopathology. I believe that affiliations with psychiatry will remain intact, but it must not be our sole alliance. Medical specialists have realized in the past that psychological factors have played an important role in disease, but their views about these factors and their measurement and meaning have been somewhat restricted, often to the narrower formulations of traditional psychiatric thinking. These new opportunities for expansion into health psychology may be one of the most productive and exciting new developments open to clinical psychology in the decade ahead.

There are many other research areas to which clinical psychologists will make contributions in the decade ahead. My presentation of 11 areas of needed research activity can be matched by other sets of 11 Best by

other colleagues. Perhaps this is the best tribute of all, that graduate programs with fundamentally similar training philosophies and contents can produce the range of clinical and experimental investigators that mark the field of clinical psychology today. There is every reason to assume that the future will see an extension of our research output into new and exciting areas. It inheres in the growing power of clinical psychology's research contributions.

Enough, if something from our hands have
  power
To live, and act, and serve the future hour.
William Wordsworth

REFERENCES

Achenbach, T. M., Conners, C. K., Quay, H. C. (1980). *Report of The Task Force on Descriptive Classification of Children's Behavior*. Washington, D. C.: American Psychological Association, September (unpublished document).

Albee, G. W., & Loeffler, E. (1971). Role conflicts in psychology and their implications for a reevaluation of training models. *The Canadian Psychologist*, **12,** 465–481.

Ashworth, K. H. (1980). Gresham's Law in the marketplace of ideas: Are bad degrees driving out the good? *The Chronicle of Higher Education*, October 6.

Bronfenbrenner, U. (1977). Toward an experimental ecology of human development. *American Psychologist*, **32,** 513–531.

Bornstein, P. H., & Wollersheim, J. P. (1978). Scientist-practitioner activities among psychologists of behavioral and nonbehavioral orientations. *Professional Psychology*, **9,** 659–664.

Campbell, D. T. (1969). Reforms as experiments. *American Psychologist*, **24,** 409–429.

Carson, R. C. (1980). Statement to the Committee on a Study of National Needs for Biomedical and Behavioral Research Personnel, Commission on Human Resources, National Research Council. Washington, D. C., June.

Chapman, L. J., & Chapman, J. P. (1980). Scales for rating psychotic and psychoticlike experiences as continua. *Schizophrenia Bulletin*, **6,** 476–489.

Chapman, L. J., Edell, W. S., & Chapman, (1980) J. P. Physical anhedonia, perceptual aberration, and psychosis proneness. *Schizophrenia Bulletin*, **6,** 639–653.

Depue, R. A. (1979). *The psychobiology of depressive disorders: Implications for the effects of stress.* New York: Academic Press.

Depue, R. A., et al. (in press). Persons at risk for bipolar depressive disorders. *Monograph Supplement, Journal of Abnormal Psychology.*

Depue, R. A., & Evans, R. (in press). The psychobiology of depressive disorders: From pathophysiology to predisposition. In B. A. Maher (Ed.), *Progress in Experimental Personality Research,* Vol. 10. New York: Academic Press.

Eisenberg, E., & Earls, F. J. (1975). Poverty, social depreciation, and child development. In D. A. Hamburg (Ed.), *American Handbook of Psychiatry,* Vol. 6. New York: Basic Books, pp. 275–291.

Garfield, S. L., & Kurtz, R. (1976). Clinical psychologists in the 1970's. *American Psychologist,* **31,** 1–9.

Kendall, P. C., & Ford, J. D. (1979). Reasons for clinical research: Characteristics of contributors and their contributions to the Journal of Consulting and Clinical Psychology. *Journal of Consulting and Clinical Psychology,* **47,** 99–105.

Miller, G. A. (1969). Psychology as a means of promoting human welfare. *American Psychologist,* **24,** 1063–1075.

Nesselroade, J. R., & Reese, H. W. (Eds.) (1973). *Life span developmental psychology: Methodological issues.* New York: Academic Press.

Nyman, L. (1973). Some odds on getting into Ph.D. programs in clinical and counseling programs. *American Psychologist,* **28,** 934–935.

Paul, G. L., & Lentz, R. J. (1977). *Psychosocial treatment of chronic mental patients: Milieu vs. social-learning programs.* Cambridge, Mass.: Harvard University Press.

Peterson, D. R. (1976). Is psychology a profession? *American Psychologist,* **31,** 572–581.

Research Opportunities and Options (1978). In Supplement: Overview of Mental Health Research. *Task Panel Reports Submitted to The President's Commission on Mental Health.* Appendix Vol. 4, Washington, D. C.: U. S. Government Printing Office.

Rogers, C. R. (1973). Some new challenges. *American Psychologist,* **28,** 379–387.

Rutter, M., Tizard, J., & Whitmore, K. (1971). *Education, health and behavior.* London: Longmans, Green.

Smith, M. B. (1973). Is psychology relevant to new priorities. *American Psychologist,* **28,** 463–471.

Strupp, H. H. (1976). Clinical psychology, irrationalism, and the erosion of excellence. *American Psychologist,* **31,** 561–571.

Werner, E. E., Bierman, J. E., & French, F. F. (1971). *The children of Kauai.* Honolulu: University of Hawaii Press.

Author Index

Full references appear at the end of each chapter.

Subject Index

Coping strategies, 209, 597, 603–604, 609–610,
  614–626, 635–636
  and biofeedback, 614–615
  and imagery, 609
Coronary heart disease, 598, 623–632
  coronary prone behavior pattern (Type A),
    627–632
  North Karelia Project, 624–626
  risk factors, 624
  Stanford Three Community Study, 626–627
Correlational approach, 6–7, 121, 223, 369,
  434–435, 446
Cortical evoked response, 391
Cost-effectiveness, 381
Counterbalancing, 236
Counterdemand expectancy, 444
Criterion, accepted, 129, 141
Criterion reference testing, 359
Criterion selection, 361
Cross-cultural research, 273–308
  abnormal behavior, 299
  cost of, 301
  importance of indigenous collaboration, 283, 284
  methods of, 287–301
  outline of (table), 289–300
  problems of equivalence in, 282–283
  role of theory in, 282
  sponsorship in, 301
  strategies of, 274
  value of, 274–275
Cross-lagged panel design, 546
Cross-sectional consistency, 358
Cross-sectional research designs, 374, 665
Cross-sectional studies, 575, 576, 577–578, 587, 666
Cross-sequential analysis, 374, 667
Cross-validation, 377
  double, 380
  partial, 378
Cuddle factor, 105
Cultunit, 276
Cultural bias, 554, 558
Cultural description, 289
Cultural diffusion, 276
Culture-bound measure, 554
Culture-specific disorders, 277, 278
Cumulative recorder, 106

Data analyses:
  single-case designs, 475–482
  statistical, 477
  visual inspection, 475
  see also Analysis of data
Debriefing, 73
Deception, 71–75
  alternatives to, 73–75
  arguments against, 71–72
  arguments for, 71
  debriefing, 73

Decision trees, 658
Defense mechanisms, 119
Deficit, social, 267
Delinquency, 658
Demand:
  characteristics, 607
  effects, 243–244
Demographics, 291, 369
Dependent personality disorder, 213
Dependent variables, 224, 447
Depression, 24–25, 256, 265, 267, 277
  attribution theory, 24–25
  learned helplessness, 24
  and target complaints, 505
Deprivation, level of, 107
Desensitization, 405
Despair, 257
Deterioration effect, 29, 432
Developmental articulation disorder, 573
Developmental disabilities, 652, 657
Developmental disorder, 572
Developmental level, 570
Developmental psychopathology,
  research methods in, 569–589
Developmental variance vs. trait variance, 579
Diagnosis, 34–36, 305–307, 374, 377–378, 658
  context-dependent, 36
  cross-cultural issues, 298–299
  error, 135
  mislabelling, 36
  of personality, 189
  psychiatric, 202, 213
  reliability, 35
Diagnostic and Statistical Manual (DSM), 612. *See
  also* DSMII; DSM III
Dichotic listening, 656
Differential Personality Inventory (DPI), 363
Directional fractionation, 400
Direct observation, *see* Observational assessment
Disattentional processes, 20
Discomfort Scale, 501–502
Discovery, notion of, 366
Discrepancy scores, 189
Discriminant function analysis, 141, 379
  in neuropsychology, 654, 667
Discriminant validity, 189, 372
Discrimination, 256
Disease:
  explicit definition, 132–133
  silent disease, 135
Dismantling strategies, 432, 443, 482–483
Documentary studies, 290–291
Dominance, 184, 209, 274, 379
Dose-response, 253
Double blind, 242, 251
Dreaming, 39, 367
Dropout, school, 537
Drug abuse, 657

Drug effects, and single-case experimental designs, 471
DSM II, 203, 206, 207
DSM III, 211, 212, 277, 298, 572
Dyadic transactions, 200, 215

Ecological context, 536, 539, 549, 569
Ecological model, 558
Ecological principles, 557
EDA, *see* Electrodermal activity
Education, 653, 654, 655
Edwards Personal Preference Scale, 357, 370
EEG, *see* Electroencephalogram
"Effect size," 454
Ego strength, 607
Ego-threat, 33–34
Eighth Mental Measurements Yearbook, 360
EKG, *see* Electrocardiogram
Electrical stimulation, 114, 387
Electrocardiogram, 390, 399, 400, 402, 404, 652
Electrocardiography, in schizophrenia, 408–409
Electroconvulsive therapy, 113, 659
Electroculogram (EOG), 409
Electrode placement configuration, 392
Electrodermal activity (EDA), 389, 395, 396, 397
  in psychopathy, 410
  responsibility, 396
  in schizophrenia, 407–408
Electrodes, in EEG, 390
Electroencephalogram, 389, 390, 391, 392, 393, 652, 658, 661, 664
  in psychopathy, 409–410
  in schizophrenia, 408–409
Electromyogram (EMG), 389, 393, 394, 398
  technical considerations in, 394–395
Electroshock, *see* Electroconvulsive therapy
EMG, *see* Electromyogram
Emic-etic distinction, 280–281
Emotions, 31–33
  cognitive determinants, 32
  physiological determinants, 32
  positive/negative, 32
Empirical-clinical principle, 430–431
Empirical keying, 358
Empirical trials of taxometric methods:
  biological sex taxonomy, 154–156
  cluster methods, 153–154
  consistency hurdles method, 160–161
  MAXCOV-HITMAX method, 166
  normal method, 169–171
Encounter groups, 446
Endocrine glands, 388
Environmental psychology, 40
Epidemiology, 548
  model, 546
  research, 291
Epilepsy, 113, 651
Epinephrine, 31–32

Equivalence, 541, 547
  problems of, 282
ERP, *see* event related potential
Essential hypertension, 621–623
  blood pressure biofeedback, 621–622
Estimation of shrinkage, 667
Ethics, 59–94, 251–252
  clinical issues, 85–88
  codes, 61–62
  confidentiality, 75–81
  deception, 71–75
  decision making, 62–66
  ethical principle, 80–81
  harms and benefits, 80–81
  informed consent, 66–71
  regulations, 61–62
  review boards, 61–62
  social costs, 89–91
  in treatment research, 85–88
Ethnography, 289
Etiology, 131, 246
Event recording, 320–321
  compared to interval recording, 322
Event related potential, 391
Evoked potential, 38, 391, 652, 661, 664
Exclusion test, 134, 153
Expectancies, 228, 243, 442, 444, 514, 519, 604, 606, 611, 614
  counterdemand, 444
  manipulations in treatment research, 444
  neutral, 444
  and treatment outcome, 442
Experience:
  cross-cultural, 273
  interpersonal, 190
Experiential World Inventory, 363
Experimental contributions, to clinical psychology, 13–57
  paradigms, 18–26
  prototypes, 15–18
Experimental methods, 102, 369
  quasi-experimental, 223–224
  research designs, 232–233
  in research in psychopathology, 223–248
  and therapy outcome, 434–435
  true, 223–224
Experimental neurosis, 256
Experimental social innovation, 539, 540
Externalizing behavior, 583, 584
External validity, 224, 240, 437, 440, 560
  examples, 440
Extinction, 106
Extreme group approach, 369
Eye movements, 409, 656

Facets, 209
  analysis, 185
  design, 214

available systems, 314
family interaction coding system, 331
interactional systems, 318–319
sequential systems, 319
types of, 319–322
"Observer drift," 335
expectations of, 334
feedback from experimenters, 335
instrument decay, 325
interobserver reliability, 325–327
participant/nonparticipant, 332
prior experience, 333
recalibration checks, 325, 331
training, 328, 333
see also Observational assessment
Obvious items, 376
Occupation, 655
Open concepts, 133, 134, 137
clinical taxa as, 136–138
gene, 137–138
taxometric formalism, 138
three kinds of, 136–137
see also Concepts, defined by networks
Operational definition, 136
Optimism, 274
Organic deterioration, 654
Organicity, 663
Organic mental disorder, 658
Outcome, evaluation of, 200
at community level, 549
see also Therapy outcome

Pain, 592
assessment of, 594–596
McGill Pain Questionnaire, 594–596, 599, 602, 605–606
qualities of, 594
treatment of, 605–612
Paradox, 444
Paranoid personality disorder, 192, 212
Parapsychological phenomena, 40
Parasympathetic division, 388
Paresis, 142–143
Parsimony, 259
Participant observers, 6, 332
Passive-aggressive personality disorder, 212
Passive observation, 546
Passivity, 274
Path analysis, 546, 548
Pathognomic signs, 133
two-way pathognomicity, 134
Pathological bias, 575
Pathologic symptom disorder, 209
Pattern analysis, 662
Patterning, in psychophysiological research, 414–415
Peripheral nervous system, 388
Personal Data Sheet, 357

Personality, 652, 662
cross-cultural assessment, 297–298
disorder, 192. See also specific disorders
five principles basic to understanding, 5
inventories, 357
pattern, 209
process, 274
theory of, 214
Personality assessment, cross-cultural uses, 298–299. See also Assessment; Self-report
Personality Research Form (PRF), 370
Person perception, 202, 203
Pfiffer's Multidimensional Functional Assessment, 662
Pharmacological therapy, 253
Pharmacology, 680
Physiological responses:
assessment in medical psychology, 597–603
see also Psychophysiological research
Physiologist, 104
Piagetian research, 580
Picture Arrangement Test, 669
Placebo, 45, 228, 242. See also Attention-placebo
Planned change, 538
Plethysmograph, 403
Policy analysis, 538
Polygraph, 389–390, 399
electronics of, 397
Popularity, 365
Populations, multiethnic, 273
Positive findings, 376
Potentiation, 266
Power dimension, 193, 195
Power tables, 370
Practicality, 258–260
Prediction, 26–27
clinical vs. statistical, 26
and decision, 26–27
Predictive validity, 129
Preparation, for research, 3–8
for stressful medical procedures, 634–636
Prepared mind, 96
Preparedness, 109
Private dimensions, 361
Prevention, 253, 536, 624–626, 638–639
secondary, 559
Process of therapy, 433
Professional schools, 683
Profile, prototypic, 213
Profile types, 193
Program evaluation, 535
Projective techniques, in cross-cultural research, 278, 297–298
Promethazine, 115
Proprarolol, 115, 116
Prospective study, 246
Prototypes, within person categories, 202, 203
Proxemics, 40